P9-DHQ-438

lgbt

encyclopedia of lesbian, gay, bisexual, and transgender history in america

editorial board

lgbt

encyclopedia of lesbian, gay, bisexual, and transgender history in america

MARC STEIN
editor in chief

2

H.D. to Queer Theory

CHARLES SCRIBNER'S SONS®

New York • Detroit • San Diego • San Francisco • Cleveland • New Haven, Conn. • Waterville, Maine • London • Munich

Encyclopedia of Lesbian, Gay, Bisexual, and Transgender History in America

Marc Stein, *Editor in Chief*

For more information, contact
Charles Scribner's Sons
An imprint of The Gale Group
300 Park Avenue South
New York, NY 10010

LIBRARY OF CONGRESS CATALOGING-IN-PUBLICATION DATA

Encyclopedia of lesbian, gay, bisexual, and transgender history in America / Marc Stein, editor in chief.
p. cm.
Includes bibliographical references and index.
ISBN 0-684-31261-1 (hardcover set: alk. paper) — ISBN 0-684-31262-X (v. 1) — ISBN 0-684-31263-8 (v. 2) — ISBN 0-684-31264-6 (v. 3)
1. Homosexuality—United States—History—Encyclopedias. 2. Gays—United States—History—Encyclopedias. 3. Bisexuals—United States—History—Encyclopedias. 4. Transsexuals—United States—History—Encyclopedias. I. Stein, Marc. II. Title.
HQ76.3.U5E53 2003
306.76'6'097303—dc22
##########

This title is also available as an e-book.
ISBN 0-684-31427-4 (set)
Contact your Gale sales representative for ordering information

Printed in United States of America
10 9 8 7 6 5 4 3 2 1

lgbt

encyclopedia
of
lesbian, gay,
bisexual, and
transgender
history
in america

H

H. D. (b. 10 September 1886; d. 27 September 1961), writer.

H. D. was born Hilda Doolittle in Pennsylvania in 1886. She dropped out of Bryn Mawr College, where another poet, Marianne Moore, was a fellow student, and was briefly engaged to Ezra Pound before leaving for Europe in the élan of a first lesbian affair with Frances Gregg in 1911. Choosing exile in London as a condition for her own marginal modernism, she emerged as the exemplary imagist poet, first published in *Poetry* (Chicago) in 1913 under the gender-free initials "H. D."

The much-anthologized "Oread" displays the dynamic minimalism of this early phase in six lines of free verse. Less well known are woman-centered longer poems such as "Eurydice," which anticipate the mythic revisionism of such later poets as Adrienne Rich. These prepared H. D. for the great work of her maturity: the visionary *Trilogy* of World War II, written in London under bombardment, and the revisionary *Helen in Egypt*, written in Switzerland and published just before her death in 1961. Both are peace poems, challenging Homeric epic and European history with a prophetic voice that places them beside T. S. Eliot's *Four Quartets* and Pound's *Cantos.*

H. D. lived in the vortex of world wars, and also that of conflicted sexualities. Her relationships with two British writers illustrate this. Married to fellow poet Richard Aldington in 1913, she met the novelist Bryher (Annie Winifred Ellerman) in 1918, and they became lifelong companion-lovers, despite Bryher's two "white" marriages (from the French *mariages blanc,* or marriages without sexual relations) and lesbian affairs on both sides. The second of Bryher's marriages, to the Scottish cinéaste Kenneth Macpherson (who was then H. D.'s lover), connected them with gay men on both sides of the Atlantic, but their enduring connections were with lesbians such as Amy Lowell and May Sarton in New England, and Sylvia Beach and Gertrude Stein in Paris. H. D.'s poems to Bryher register a complex commitment: "I Said" and "We Two" defend their solidarity in the face of an uncomprehending world; "Halcyon" and "Hyacinth" elaborate the Sapphic landscape of their shared imagination; "To Bryher" (from the novel *Palimpsest)* celebrates the steadfastness of this flawed but undaunted patron.

Two presences from the literary past are felt in H. D.'s writings. One is the late nineteenth-century British aesthete Oscar Wilde; the other is the great lyric poet of antiquity, Sappho of Lesbos. Both connect her with homosexual cultures over two and a half millennia, and separate her from the homophobia and misogyny of her closest male contemporaries among expatriate American modernists in the early twentieth century.

H. D. identified with Wilde as a decadent committed to the artistic "personality," in contrast to the "impersonality" upon which Eliot and Pound insisted. Like Wilde, she believed that art opens the mind to intensities of feeling, and so placed aesthetic experience on a par with erotic experience. The poetic effect of this is felt in the Wildean ecstasy of "At Baia": "Lover to lover, no kiss, / no touch, but forever and ever this" (*Collected Poems: 1912–1944,* p. 128).

In a more austere mode, "Fragment Thirty-six" uses a verse from Sappho to dramatize the artist's dilemma:

I know not what to do,
my mind is reft:
is song's gift best?
is love's gift loveliest? (p. 165)

This is one of a number of poems by H. D. that blow the embers of her Sapphic inheritance into living flame. Sappho was a vital female antecedent for H. D.; fragments from the earlier poet's surviving verse glow at the heart of H. D.'s poetry and prose. The *Collected Poems* opens with the "acrid fragrance" of "Sea Rose" (p. 5), and later lyrics such as "Eros" ring the changes on Sappho's celebrated description of love as "bittersweet." While H. D.'s "Notes on Thought and Vision" for Havelock Ellis honors an intellectual tradition among male homosexuals extending from Socrates to Leonardo da Vinci, her essay "The Wise Sappho" pays homage to a woman who loved women and whose poems to them were neither romantic nor sentimental but "magnetic, vibrant," energizing lives and writings beyond her own.

Sigmund Freud, who analyzed H. D. in the 1930s, declared her "the perfect bi-," and later critics such as Claire Buck and Rachel DuPlessis have located the tensions in her work on a bisexual borderline. Susan Friedman has shown how vividly the novels *Asphodel, Her,* and *Paint It Today* resist the plot of heterosexual romance, and in her introduction to the last of these, Cassandra Laity characterizes *Paint It Today* as "a modern homoerotic novel of passage" (p. xviii). The fault line between H. D.'s established reputation as a poet and this posthumously published fiction reminds us that she was a contemporary of both Radclyffe Hall and Virginia Woolf, and has far-reaching implications for our understanding of modernism.

Bibliography

Bryher. *The Heart to Artemis: A Writer's Memoirs.* New York: Harcourt Brace, 1962.

Buck, Claire. *H. D. and Freud: Bisexuality and a Feminine Discourse.* New York: St. Martin's, 1991.

Collecott, Diana. *H. D. and Sapphic Modernism: 1910–1950.* New York: Cambridge University Press, 1999.

DuPlessis, Rachel Blau. *H. D.: The Career of That Struggle.* Brighton, England: Harvester Press, 1986.

Friedman, Susan Stanford. *Penelope's Web: Gender, Modernity, H. D.'s Fiction.* New York: Cambridge University Press, 1990.

Friedman, Susan Stanford, and Rachel Blau DuPlessis, eds. *Signets: Reading H. D.* Madison: University of Wisconsin Press, 1990.

Guest, Barbara. *Herself Defined: The Poet H. D. and Her World.* Garden City, N.Y.: Doubleday, 1984.

Laity, Cassandra. "Lesbian Romanticism." Introduction to H. D., *Paint It Today.* New York: New York University Press, 1992.

Diana Collecott

HALL, Murray H. (b. c. 1831; d. 19 January 1901), political official.

Reliably accurate information about Murray Hall is scarce, as most existing accounts of his life are based on unreliable newspaper reports published after his death, when the discovery that he was female generated sensational publicity. Probably born Mary Anderson in Govan, Scotland, then orphaned and employed as a man in Edinburgh, Hall surfaced in New York during the mid-1870s. Accompanied by a woman identified as his wife, he opened an employment bureau. After complaining that he flirted with too many other women, his wife disappeared three years later. By the mid-1880s Hall and his second wife Cecilia Hall had informally adopted a daughter Imelda, known as Minnie. During this period Hall became a bail bondsman and found a niche with the Tammany Hall Democratic Party machine in New York City. He associated with a wide circle of the city's political figures and developed a reputation for cigar chomping, poker playing, and being "sweet on women" (Katz, p. 235). His second wife, who also reportedly complained about his attentions to other women, died a few years before Hall's own death in 1901. Upon his death, his physician, Dr. William C. Gallagher, revealed to a surprised public that Hall had, in fact, been born a female.

The revelation that Hall was "really" a woman generated scandalous headlines and many newspaper accounts of the stunned surprise of his associates. The *New York Times* report of 19 January 1901 proclaimed that "Murray Hall Fooled Many Shrewd Men" and detailed the reactions of many, including state senator Bernard F. Martin who declared, "I wouldn't believe it if Dr. Gallagher, whom I know to be a man of undoubted veracity, hadn't said so"; and Martin's aid, Joseph Young, who said, "A woman? Why, he'd line up to the bar and take his whiskey like any veteran, and didn't make faces over it, either. If he was a woman he ought to have been born a man, for he lived and looked like one" (Katz, p. 234).

The story of Hall reappeared in the press following the inquest into his death on 28 January and when his will was filed on 19 March. His daughter Imelda, then twenty-two, testified at the inquest that she had not suspected her father was a woman. When the coroner corrected her reference to Hall as "he" with "Wouldn't you better say she?" Imelda reportedly replied, "No, I will never say she" (Katz, p. 237).

Hall's birth as a female and adult life as a man were recounted by Jonathan Ned Katz in 1976 in *Gay American History*. Katz included documents concerning Hall's life and death in a section of his book titled "Passing Women" that emphasized the probable lesbianism of born females who lived and worked as men and married women. Since 1976 political activists, historians, and commentators have debated possible interpretations of Hall's life. Might *she* best be understood as a woman who passed as a man in order to make a decent living in a world where orphaned young women, and single women generally, had great difficulty living independently? Or might *she* be considered a lesbian, who lived as a man in order to flirt with and marry women without persecution? Or might *he* be included in a history of female-to-male transgenderism? Was Hall's masculinity a "disguise" employed by a woman, or the deeper "truth" of Hall's lived gender identity? Can Hall's life be viewed as an implicitly feminist critique of the male-dominated world of politics, or as an antifeminist rejection of women's efforts to be included in political life as *women*? Or, are none of these interpretations persuasive? Whatever the interpretation offered, there can be no dispute that Hall carefully hid his female body, even as he died of breast cancer over a period of approximately six years, and that he lived persuasively as a philandering married man in the world of homosocial urban politics.

Bibliography

Ellis, Havelock. *Studies in the Psychology of Sex.* Philadelphia: F.A. Davis, 1901.

Katz, Jonathan Ned. *Gay American History: Lesbians and Gay Men in the U.S.A.* New York: Thomas Y. Crowell, 1976.

Meyerowitz, Joanne. *How Sex Changed: A History of Transsexuality in the United States.* Cambridge, Mass.: Harvard University Press, 2002.

West, Marian. "Women Who Have Passed as Men." *Munzey's Magazine* 25 (1901).

Elizabeth A. Duggan

See also DEMOCRATIC PARTY; MARRIAGE CEREMONIES AND WEDDINGS; TRANSSEXUALS, TRANSVESTITES, TRANSGENDER PEOPLE, AND CROSS-DRESSERS.

HALL, Thomasine/Thomas (b. 1603; d. ?), colonist.

Thomasine/Thomas Hall was raised as a girl in Newcastle-upon-Tyne and London, England, served in the English army during its 1627 campaign against the French on the Isle of Rhe, and then migrated to Virginia, where Hall's claims to be both woman and man brought her/him to the attention of the colony's General Court. In 1629 Hall's neighbors in Warrosquoyacke, Virginia, began a series of searches of Hall's body. It is not clear what sparked their inquiry. It might have been rumors that Hall had been engaged in sexual activity with a servant maid or the more unusual report that s/he was both a woman and a man.

Hall suffered through two examinations at the hands of Warrosquoyacke's married women, who concluded on the basis of a "peece of flesh" protruding from Hall's lower belly that s/he was a man. Their tenacious insistence that s/he was a man eventually convinced the plantation commander, who had initially ignored their findings. Upon donning men's clothes, Hall became fair game for the men of Warrosquoyacke, who conducted their own impromptu examination and concurred that s/he was indeed a man. The matter did not rest there, however, as the locals sent the case to the General Court at Jamestown.

Justices in that court declined to initiate their own physical investigation, preferring to elicit from Hall a narrative of her/his gender history. Hall told a tale of early female identity, rooted in female dress, needlework, long hair, and the name "Thomasine." S/he did not divulge any dramatic anatomical event like the delayed descent of testicles that might have motivated her/his decision to become a man, but instead linked it to her/his brother's entry into the English army. S/he marked this shift in gender performance with a change of clothes and the richly symbolic gesture of cutting her/his hair. Upon leaving the army, Hall briefly changed back into women's clothes to earn money doing needlework in Plymouth, England, before shipping out to Virginia as a man. Once in the colony, s/he mainly wore men's clothes with the exception of an excursion in women's dress to "gett a bit for my Catt," a mysterious reference that could reflect an effort to satisfy either economic or sexual needs. The justices responded to Hall's narrative punitively out of a desire to stabilize her/his performed identity, but elected not to choose one gender identity as primary. Rather, they declared Hall to be both woman and man and ordered Hall to don a female headdress, apron, and cross-cloth over her/his male attire. Everyone would thus immediately recognize Hall's gender ambiguity; no one would be able to engage in sexual relations with Hall without fear of committing a same-sex offense.

Hall's gender changes and the response to them reveal a great deal about the meaning of gender for early Anglo Virginians. Same-sex sexual activity was not unknown in early Virginia, yet most of Hall's neighbors seem to have believed that an expressed gender identity reflected anatomical sex and coincided with certain heterosexual sexual behaviors. Hall's alleged sexual past—that s/he had "layn" with a woman named Great Besse—meant to Hall's neighbors that s/he must be anatomically male. Thus, s/he transgressed if s/he dressed as a woman. Despite popular European traditions that warned young girls of the perils of strenuous activity—the heat generated might make testicles descend—and Galenic medical theories that understood the female body to be an imperfect version of the male body rather than a separate entity altogether, Hall's neighbors adhered to a popular view of gender as rooted in anatomical difference and performed through clothing, labor, and sexual history.

Hall's case also reminds us that, while most early modern people exercised only limited choices over how they expressed their gender identities and, indeed, many might have thought of these identities as frighteningly unstable and porous, a few notable individuals made dramatic choices. Most Atlantic world stories of people cross-dressing (dressing in clothes customary for the opposite sex for the purpose of passing as a member of that sex) involved women passing as men to take advantage of military opportunities that would otherwise not be available to them, or of aristocratic men dressing as women. Hall's story bears some resemblance to the female pattern, although her/his motives were somewhat different. Hall's account of her/his own life suggests that a primary identity as female had taken hold during the years s/he had been raised, dressed, and trained as a girl. Hall's male identity, in contrast, while possibly sparked by a desire to accompany her/his brother or by the unexpected descent of testicles, seems to have been overlaid on top of this one. S/he seemed to feel that both identities were rightfully hers/his based on the claim to be anatomically both male and female and on the experience of meeting both sets of gender expectations. In contrast to the General Court's order that s/he wear both male and female attire, s/he had carefully chosen to perform her/his identities sequentially, conforming to rather than challenging normative behaviors for each gender.

Bibliography

Brown, Kathleen. "'Changed . . . into the Fashion of Man': The Politics of Sexual Difference in a Seventeenth-Century Anglo-American Settlement." *Journal of the History of Sexuality* 6 (1995): 171–193.

Katz, Jonathan Ned. *Gay/Lesbian Almanac: A New Documentary.* New York: Harper and Row, 1983.

Norton, Mary Beth. *Founding Mothers and Fathers: Gendered Power and the Forming of American Society.* New York: Knopf, 1996.

Vaughan, Alden. "The Sad Case of Thomas(ine) Hall." *Virginia Magazine of History and Biography* 86 (1978): 146–148.

Kathleen M. Brown

See also COLONIAL AMERICA; INTERSEXUALS AND INTERSEXED PEOPLE; TRANSSEXUALS, TRANSVESTITES, TRANSGENDER PEOPLE, AND CROSS-DRESSERS.

HAMMOND, James Henry **(b. 15 November 1807; d. 13 November 1864), planter, politician.**

Born into a middle-class family in the South Carolina upcountry, James Henry Hammond fulfilled many of the expectations of his demanding, financially unsuccessful father. The eldest of eight children, Hammond in 1823 entered South Carolina College in Columbia, a training ground for the state's elite political leadership. He perfected his debating skills as a member of the college's Euphradian Society, serving as valedictory orator for his graduation in 1825. In addition to his scholarly achievements as a young man, Hammond may have had a very active sex life. In an 1826 letter to Hammond, classmate Thomas Jefferson Withers reminisced about feeling the "exquisite touches" of Hammond's "long fleshen pole," and he celebrated Hammond's "furious lunges" at bedfellows. In another 1826 letter, Withers portrayed Hammond "braying, like an ass, at every she-male you can discover" (Duberman, pp. 87–88). Though inconclusive as to whether Hammond had homosexual encounters with Withers or other men, the playful tone of the letters suggests that Withers, Hammond, and their larger social circle had carefree attitudes about male same-sex desire.

In 1828 Hammond opened a law practice in Columbia, and he soon became an articulate spokesman for South Carolina's states' rights, antifederal tariff nullification movement. From 1830 to 1831 he also edited the *Southern Times*, a nullification newspaper. The political establishment in South Carolina in the late 1820s and early 1830s favored a one-party system dominated by wealthy elites, limited suffrage, a hierarchical social order, and a plantation economy that distinguished it from the democratic, urban, industrial North. By his mid-twenties Hammond was known as an effective advocate for the political establishment, warning of the excesses of Jacksonian democracy. He joined the ranks of the South Carolina aristocracy with his marriage to Catherine Fitzsimons in 1831, acquiring an estate with nearly eleven thousand acres and 147 slaves.

At Silver Bluff, a small South Carolina community across the Savannah River from Augusta, Georgia, Hammond tried to dominate his newly acquired slaves by regulating their religion, marriages, child rearing, and work routines. He aimed to be the quintessential patriarch, controlling the lives of his wife, children, siblings, slaves, and overseers. His notoriety as a nullifier and defender of the status quo helped him win a U.S. congressional seat in 1834. Though he only served one term, he gained national fame by moving that the U.S. House of Representatives refuse any acknowledgment of petitions regarding slavery. Insisting that Congress lacked constitutional authority to act on slavery, Hammond solidified his reputation as a strict constructionist of the U.S. Constitution. He also served as South Carolina's governor from 1842 to 1844, using his tenure to promote his proslavery views.

According to Hammond, slavery served as the foundation for republican societies. He argued that black slaves in the South labored under more favorable conditions than did free laborers in Europe or the North. His belief in black inferiority did not prevent him from having sexual liaisons with two slave women: Sally Johnson and her daughter Louisa Johnson. He apparently fathered a child with both Sally and Louisa, adding two illegitimate children to the eight legitimate children he fathered with his wife, Catherine.

Though Hammond also served as a U.S. senator from 1857 to 1860, rumors of sexual improprieties with a teenage niece may have hampered his two previous attempts at winning a Senate seat. In the fall of 1843, the nineteen-year-old daughter of Hammond's brother-in-law, Wade Hampton II, told her father that Hammond had attempted to seduce her the previous spring. Hampton used this information to blackmail Hammond, contributing to his Senate defeats in 1846 and 1850. Rumors about the Hampton affair dogged Hammond throughout the 1840s and early 1850s and led to the Hammonds' social ostracism among many elite South Carolinians.

However, Hammond revived his political career in the early 1850s. In the summer of 1850, he served as one of four South Carolina delegates at the first Nashville Convention, a pan-southern convention organized to discuss southern positions on Henry Clay's compromise bill on territorial questions. By the time of his 1857 election to replace A. P. Butler in the U.S. Senate, Hammond had gained a reputation as a cautious statesman. He continued to defend the South's slave system and to deny that the U.S. Congress had any power to regulate slavery, but he also believed that the South had a stronger position inside the Union than outside of it. Consequently, his moderation in the 1850s reduced his later influence in Confederate South Carolina. From the beginning of the American Civil War in April 1861 until his death in the fall of 1864, Hammond criticized Confederate policies that allowed officials to confiscate his food supplies and impress his slaves into labor. Hammond died at Redcliffe, the neoclassical mansion he built in 1858.

Bibliography

Duberman, Martin. " 'Writhing Bedfellows' in Antebellum South Carolina: Historical Interpretation and the Politics of Evidence." *Journal of Homosexuality* 6, nos. 1–2 (Fall–Winter 1980–1981): 85–101.

Faust, Drew Gilpin. *James Henry Hammond and the Old South: A Design for Mastery.* Baton Rouge: Louisiana State University Press, 1982.

Hammond, James Henry. *Gov. Hammond's Letters on Southern Slavery: Addressed to Thomas Clarkson, the English Abolitionist.* Charleston, S.C.: Walker and Burke, 1845.

Kolchin, Peter. *American Slavery, 1619–1877.* New York: Hill and Wang, 1993.

Will C. Holmes

See also POLITICAL SCANDALS.

HAMPTON, Mabel **(b. 2 May 1902; d. 26 October 1989), entertainer, domestic worker, activist.**

In 1984 Mabel Hampton addressed the rain-soaked crowd at New York's annual gay pride rally with these words: "I, Mabel Hampton, have been a lesbian all my life, for eighty-two years, and I am proud of myself and my people. I would like all my people to be free in this country and all over the world, my gay people and my black people" (Nestle, p. 48). Orphaned at birth in Winston-Salem, North Carolina, at age seven, Hampton was taken to live with her uncle and aunt in Greenwich Village after the sudden death of her beloved grandmother. Though she was to spend the rest of her life in New Jersey and New York City, Hampton never forgot the colors of those early southern days:

> We had a backyard; I can see it right now, that backyard. It had red roses, white roses, roses that went upside the house. On Saturdays we go out hunting blackberries, strawberries, peaches. My girlfriends lived on each side of the street: Anna Lou Thomas, Hattie Harris, Lucille Crump. Oh-OOh-O Anna Lou Thomas, she was good lookin, she was a good lookin girl. (Nestle, p. 31)

As a seven-year-old, Hampton danced in the streets for the pennies thrown from Village windows. After mistreatment by her uncle, Hampton ran away to Hoboken, New Jersey, where she was taken in by the Whites, an African American family.

At the beginning of the 1920s, Hampton left her job as a domestic worker and joined an all-women's dance group performing in Coney Island. Appearing in all-black reviews at Harlem's Garden Of Joy and the Lafayette Theater in Harlem, she enjoyed herself at several of the pansexual parties thrown by A'lelia Walker, the famous flapper daughter of Madame Walker. Swept up by the free-swinging cultural life of the Harlem Renaissance, Hampton socialized with Gladys Bentley, Moms Mabely, Alberta Hunter, and the Waters, as she called Ethel Waters and her girlfriend.

After being falsely arrested on charges of prostitution during an all-women's party in Harlem, Hampton spent thirteen months in the Bedford Hills Prison for Women, where she found tenderness in the arms of other women. In 1927 Hampton was in the audience for a performance of the lesbian-themed play, *The Captive* (soon to be closed by the anti-vice police), and met Helen Menken, the leading lady who asked her, "Why did you like the show?" The twenty-five-year-old Miss Hampton replied, "Because it seems a part of my life and what I am and hope to be" (Nestle, p. 37).

In 1932 Hampton met Lillian Foster, the woman who would be her wife until Foster's death in 1978. They made their home in the Bronx, Foster working as a presser and Hampton as a domestic worker and matron at Jacobi Hospital. Hampton was an air raid warden during the war, heard Paul Robeson's concert at Carnegie Hall in 1940, followed the careers of Josephine Baker and Christine Jorgensen, and attended performances of the National Negro Opera Company. In her beloved study, Hampton organized her growing library of books on African American culture, LGBT culture, and mysticism, becoming a lifelong member of The Order of the Eastern Star and the Rosicrucians. For the next twenty years, the Bronx home of the two women was a gathering place for a community of Bronx lesbian women who held house parties, organized all-lesbian boat trips up the Hudson River, and attended Harlem's yearly drag balls, huge events that attracted hundreds of people.

In the 1960s Hampton, still working in the hospital, supported the civil rights movement and became involved in the early LGB rights movement. Lillian Foster died in 1978 and Hampton spent more time at the Upper West Side home of the Lesbian Herstory Archives, where she held court every Thursday night for adoring visitors from all over the world, answering questions about her life with her anthem, "What do you mean, when did I come out? I was never in!" (Nestle, p. 27). She appeared in the films *Silent Pioneers* (1984) and *Before Stonewall* (1985); gave interviews; became friends with Ann Allen Schockley, Jewelle Gomez, and Audre Lorde; and attended lesbian music festivals. She marched in the first March on Washington for Lesbian and Gay Rights on 14 October 1979 and participated throughout the 1980s in the yearly New York lesbian and gay pride marches. When she could no longer walk the distance, she took great pleasure in riding with the SAGE (Senior Action in a Gay Environment) contingent. Hampton died of a stroke on 26 October 1989. To the obituary written by her friends, the *New York Times* added the misleading ending line: she leaves no survivors.

Through her generosity in sharing her stories, Hampton changed the American historical record. In her many oral history tapes and video interviews, she brought alive the twentieth-century realities of a working-class, African American lesbian woman who stood her ground.

Bibliography

Hampton, Mabel. Special Collection. Lesbian Herstory Archives, Brooklyn, New York.

Hampton, Mabel. "I Didn't Go Back There Anymore: Mabel Hampton Talks about the South." *Feminary* 10 (1979): 7–17.

Nestle, Joan. "I Lift My Eyes to the Hill: The Life of Mabel Hampton As Told by a White Woman." In *A Fragile Union: New and Selected Writings.* San Francisco: Cleis Press, 1998.

Joan Nestle

See also LESBIAN HERSTORY ARCHIVES.

HANSBERRY, Lorraine (b. 19 May 1930; d. 12 January 1965), writer, activist.

Lorraine Hansberry was the youngest of four children born to Carl A. Hansberry and Nanny Perry Hansberry on Chicago's South Side. Hansberry's formative years were spent in the social and political milieu of the black middle class: a comfortable material existence coupled with a real commitment to continued political agitation for productive change in the racial climate of the United States. In 1938 her family challenged Chicago's discriminatory real estate practices in a test case for integrated housing, a case that ultimately culminated in a victorious 1940 U.S. Supreme Court decision (*Hansberry v. Lee*).

Hansberry's uncle, Leo Hansberry, was also a strong influence on her ideological beliefs. He had a distinguished career as a professor of African history at Howard University and is often credited with helping to shape Hansberry's Pan-African and global perspectives on the black liberation movement.

As a youth, Hansberry came into regular contact with celebrated artists and activists such as Paul Robeson, Walter White, and Duke Ellington, and as an adult, with literary and political luminaries such as James Baldwin, Richard Wright, and Langston Hughes. From her childhood, when her family became a national test case for integration, to the time she wrote her award winning play *A Raisin in the Sun* (1959) that addressed this American dilemma, Hansberry was an integral part of the social fabric of black activism.

As a student at the University of Wisconsin, Hansberry frequented the theater, where she sat in on a rehearsal of Sean O'Casey's *Juno and the Paycock,* which she later claimed was the initial inspiration behind her ambition to become a playwright. In 1950 Hansberry left college and relocated to New York City, where she worked as a reporter for Robeson's radical black newspaper *Freedom.* Hansberry wrote reviews and essays, and became a respected associate editor of the newspaper during her three year tenure there; she also assumed an active role in civil rights agitation during this period.

Lorraine Hansberry. The playwright is primarily remembered for her landmark 1959 play, *A Raisin in the Sun,* about integration, racism, and African American yearnings. **[Bettmann/corbis]**

Hansberry resigned from the paper in 1953 when she married Robert Nemiroff; that same year she also began to devote her energies to playwrighting. She maintained a lasting intellectual and artistic relationship with Nemiroff despite their subsequent divorce, during which Hansberry came out as a lesbian. Nemiroff was later criticized for his editing of her writings on these subjects after her death.

For Hansberry, *A Raisin in the Sun* offered her the opportunity to translate for the dramatic stage the passionate struggle of black communities globally, one with which post–World War II America now grappled: racial discrimination. *A Raisin in the Sun* depicts the Youngers, an African American family residing on the South Side of Chicago in the 1950s at a transitional moment in their lives: the senior Mrs. Younger is about to receive a check for ten thousand dollars from the deceased Mr. Younger's insurance policy. Much of the dramatic development of the characters revolves around the question of how best to spend this money; each member of the family nurtures a certain dream of success. Ultimately a good portion of the monies is used to purchase a house in a neighborhood in which the white residents practice a new urban northern form of racism, one that exhibits a covert professional manner: a neighborhood improvement society attempts to buy out the Youngers before they move into the neighborhood. Crafted upon aesthetics of naturalism theatre, a form of realism, Hansberry's play foregrounds the historical realities of southern migration, generational conflicts, and the development of black individuality within the collective family. Her play is an impactful theatrical exploration of a black family's response to historical change, gender roles, and the economic oppression of segregation. The play became an immediate success, making Hansberry the youngest playwright and the first black ever to win the New York Drama Critics Circle award for Best Play of the Year. She was also the first black woman to have a play produced on Broadway and then later purchased for its movie rights, in this instance by Columbia Pictures. Hansberry's instant celebrity status led to the birth of drama movements such as the revolutionary black theater enclave of the1960s and enabled her to lend her writing talents to civil rights organizations.

At the time of Hansberry's death in 1965, her play *The Sign in Sidney Brustein's Window* was having a not-so-successful run; she was also putting the finishing touches on an unpublished play, *The Arrival of Mr. Todog,* a satire of Samuel Beckett, and had begun work on a drama based on the life of Mary Wollstonecraft, an eighteenth-century feminist.

Hansberry's contribution to lesbian culture may be linked to her role in the black civil rights movement and the road it paved for the women's liberation movement of the 1960s. Additionally, Hansberry wrote unpublished essays and letters in which she began to detail her vision of lesbian and radical feminism. Among her known writings on these topics were several letters published in the *Ladder,* a predominately white mid-twentieth-century lesbian publication, in which she made incisive observations about the intersections of homophobia and misogyny, and the economic and psychic pressure on lesbians to marry. As Hansberry committed her ideas on gender and sexuality to paper and public view, she terminated her marriage and asserted her own lesbianism. Unfortunately, Hansberry's life was cut tragically short when she died of cancer at the age of thirty-four.

Bibliography

Cheney, Anne. *Lorraine Hansberry.* Boston: Twayne, 1984.

Nemiroff, Robert. *To Be Young, Gifted, and Black: Lorraine Hansberry in Her Own Words.* Adapted by Robert Nemiroff. With original drawings and art by Lorraine Hansberry. Introduction by James Baldwin. Englewood Cliffs, N.J.: Prentice-Hall, 1969.

Sinfield, Alan. *Out on Stage: Lesbian and Gay Theatre in the Twentieth Century.* New Haven, Conn.: Yale University Press, 1999.

Laura A. Harris

See also THEATER AND PERFORMANCE.

HARING, Keith (b. 4 May 1958; d. 16 February 1990), artist, writer, activist.

Keith Haring was one of a number of U.S. artists who achieved rock-star levels of international celebrity in the 1980s. Haring's post-Pop brand of postmodern primitivism exploded across the art world and popular culture more generally, and he became the unofficial iconographer of the gay liberation and AIDS activist movements in Europe and the United States. Living as a gay artist with (and eventually dying from) AIDS attuned Haring to the perverse intersections of indifferent government and inadequate health care systems, the rise of neoconservative politics and fundamentalist religion, globalizing media conglomerates, and the 1980s cult of fame and celebrity. Haring engaged all of these issues in an art that was deceptively simple and sexually playful, bridging ancient and modern as well as popular and elite traditions. His signature was the absurdly naïve, primary-colored crawling baby, barking dog, or jumping man graphically limned with thick lines and drawn from such diverse sources as comic book art, hip-hop music, urban graffiti, South American street dance, and ancient petroglyphs.

Born in Reading, Pennsylvania, Haring attended art school in Pittsburgh in the late 1970s before moving to New York City to study at the School of Visual Arts. By 1980 he was curating other artists' shows and exhibiting his work in small galleries. In 1981 he began drawing with chalk on black paper in space allotted to large-format poster advertising in New York City's subway stations. His early social circle included so-called bad boy artists Kenny Scharf and Jean-Michel Basquiat, the latter of whom produced similar graffiti-inspired imagery in nontraditional urban spaces. Haring's first major gallery show was in 1982 at Tony Shafrazi Gallery and that year he participated in Documenta 7, the prestigious German showcase of contemporary art. In 1983 Haring exhibited at the equally prestigious Whitney Museum Biennial, and he went on to fulfill numerous international mural commissions. Along the way he appeared on MTV, associated with pop stars, socialites, and famous artists, and was profiled in both art and general readership magazines. He died of complications related to AIDS in New York City in 1990.

Visually recalling the style of Andy Warhol and other British and U.S. Pop artists of the 1960s and later, Haring similarly crossed between high and low arenas, exploiting the mass-media saturated, consumer-oriented cultures that reigned in global metropolitan centers in the late twentieth century. Although Haring produced artworks in traditional formats of painting and sculpture shown in the conventional art institutions of the gallery and museum, his imagery appeared in every imaginable format and medium: blimps, posters, videos, Swatch watches, the bodies of dancer Bill T. Jones and singer-actress Grace Jones, subway walls, Absolut Vodka advertisements, lampposts, leather jackets, set designs, buses, T-shirts, and album covers. In 1986 Haring further blurred art and commerce by opening the Pop Shop, a SoHo outlet for Haring-designed, mass-produced T-shirts, inflatable animals, posters, and other sorts of giddy consumer items. He was famous for handing out drawings like tips at restaurants and hotels. In his journals he wrote, "Usually the people who are the most generous are people who have the least to give. I learned this first-hand as a newspaper carrier when I was 12 years old. The biggest tips came from the poorest people. I was surprised by this, but I learned it as a lesson" (Haring, p. xiii).

Keith Haring. The commercially savvy 1980s post-Pop artist, celebrity, and activist sits in front of his *Crack is Wack* mural. **[Owen Franken/corbis and the estate of Keith Haring]**

Haring was one of a number of 1980s gay male activist-artists who used visual imagery to critique the overwhelming power of the anonymous city and the manifest inhumanity of intractable corporate and governmental bureaucracies. With a satirical wit and bright colors, his art aimed to shock and cajole the complacent into an awareness of their physical world and the people who inhabited it. Continuing a long artistic tradition of collage and appropriation, Haring cut up and rearranged words from *New York Post* headlines, then pasted them as posters around New York City. One example was "Ronald Reagan Accused of TV Star Sex Death: Killed & Ate Lover."

His good-natured yet biting style of graphic agitprop (agitational propaganda) would be taken up in the late 1980s and early 1990s by AIDS activist groups like ACT UP (AIDS Coalition to Unleash Power), Gran Fury, and Queer Nation. His imagery became inseparable from the "queer" moment from the mid-1980s to early 1990s, visible on confrontational posters, bumper stickers, bus billboards, and buttons. The best known are probably his Safe Sex images and his 1989 "speak no evil, hear no evil, see no evil" figures with the now-famous slogan "Ignorance=Fear, Silence=Death, Fight AIDS, Act Up," which became an international slogan of AIDS activist movements.

Bibliography

Blinderman, Barry. *Keith Haring: Future Primeval.* Normal: University Galleries, Illinois State University, 1990. Exhibition catalog.

Celant, Germano, ed. *Keith Haring.* Munich: Prestel, 1992. Exhibition catalog.

Gruen, John. *Keith Haring: The Authorized Biography.* New York: Prentice Hall, 1991.

Haring, Keith. *Keith Haring Journals.* New York: Viking, 1996.

Sussman, Elisabeth. *Keith Haring.* New York: Whitney Museum of American Art, 1997. Exhibition catalog.

Michael J. Murphy

See also AIDS AND PEOPLE WITH AIDS; AIDS COALITION TO UNLEASH POWER (ACT UP); QUEER NATION; VISUAL ART.

HARLEM RENAISSANCE

The Harlem Renaissance acquired its name in reference to the urban neighborhood of Harlem, New York, where during the 1920s an unprecedented moment of black literary, intellectual, cultural, and artistic production occurred. That moment arose out of a set of overlapping historical and social forces, primarily the tremendous northern urban migration of blacks fleeing the South's broken Reconstruction promises and responding to national labor demands before, during, and after World War I. The Harlem Renaissance period (roughly from 1920 to 1935) witnessed a torrent of political essays, poems, novels, biographies, histories, paintings, sculptures, plays, musicals, dances, and blues and jazz compositions and performances, areas of black American cultural production that had the greatest influence on twentieth-century American popular culture and style. Indeed, this influence extended beyond the United States as the black American renaissance was linked to an international African diaspora. For example the birth of the Negritude movement in late 1920s Paris was heavily influenced by black American expatriates and the enthusiastic example of black American artists, who reinvented Western traditions of form and content and included racial protest as a formal aesthetic. In Senegal, Léopold

Apollo Theater. The centerpiece of popular culture for African Americans in Harlem for decades after its opening on 125th Street in the mid-1930s. **[AP/Wide World Photos]**

Sédar Senghor embraced the term Negritude and later refined its interpretation. Senghor's concept of the term served to reverse the system of ideologies set in place by colonial rule. In the United States and the Caribbean Marcus Garvey's "Back to Africa" movement and Universal Negro Improvement Association formed in New York during the Harlem Renaissance in turn influenced both the Rastafarian movement in Jamaica and the Nation of Islam movement in the U.S.

Traditional canonical interpretations of the Renaissance often emphasize the internationally well-received black intellectual and literary luminaries, high-profile public figures who fore-grounded questions of racism and poverty in a consistently uplifting manner. Intellectual, sociologist, philosopher, and activist W. E. B. Dubois was the editor of *Crisis*, the journal of the National Association for the Advancement of Colored People, which he had helped found. Sociologist Charles Johnson was one of the originators of the idea of artistic production as a cultural arena in which African Americans could claim equal rights. Poets Countee Cullen and Langston Hughes were responsible for demonstrating the capacity of blacks to compose in sonnet form and to originate new American poetry forms out of the blues. Sculptural artists Roland Barthes and Augusta Savage used African aesthetics to international acclaim. Civil rights activist James Weldon Johnson was also a poet, novelist, and Broadway composer. Anthropologist and folklorist Zora Neale Hurston, who wrote novels, essays, and plays and was a "New Woman" model, illuminated the power of rural southern black culture. Writers Alice Dunbar-Nelson and Angelina W. Grimké addressed issues that affected African American women of their time. These were just a few of the canonically recognized Renaissance artists who contributed to the project of "racial uplift," the primary goal of Renaissance originators and forefathers DuBois and Johnson.

The Queer Renaissance

The Harlem Renaissance was also a period that witnessed the presence, survival, and growth of a thriving black queer community in urban America. While history demonstrates the yearning of African Americans to find financial and physical security in the promised land of the North when it was brutally denied to them in the South, a less emphasized historical narrative suggests that escape to urban anonymity and a diverse milieu also motivated black queers. For example, infamous blues singer Gladys Bentley escaped to Harlem as a teenage runaway when her family placed too much scrutiny on her masculine desires and traits. There was also the eloquent youthful poet Mae Cowdery who won various Crisis poetry competitions and produced verse suggestive of queer lesbian desire; she engaged in her own version of gender-bending when she appeared in a 1927 Crisis photo sporting slicked back hair, a bow tie, and a tailored man's suit. However, despite the relative tolerance of homosexuality in black communities of the North, African Americans had the same difficulties as their white counterparts: Mable Hampton, a newcomer to Harlem from North Carolina, was arrested on prostitution charges in 1920 and the career of Augustus Granvill Dill, business editor of the *Crisis* and protégé of W. E. B. Du Bois, was destroyed when he was arrested for soliciting sex in a public restroom. Despite these difficulties LGBT African Americans were able to forge a thriving community.

The success of the Harlem Renaissance as a cultural movement seeking civil rights for black Americans and challenging white supremacy was predicated upon the coming together of a collection of unlikely, queer social acquaintances: a homoerotic camaraderie of elite black

Nella Larsen. The first African American woman (second from left) to receive a Guggenheim Fellowship, this member of the Harlem Renaissance is remembered for her two published novels, *Quicksand* (1928) and *Passing* (1929). [corbis]

male intellectuals and writers; an elite cadre of white male and female intellectuals, writers, and philanthropists; a black female artistic and intellectual network that resisted traditional gender roles; and a small but flamboyant group of black and white artists, socialites, performers, and heiresses whose public personas, genders, and sexualities were always under scrutiny in gossip columns or other forms of social observation.

One highly visible example of this unprecedented type of alliance can be found in the otherwise socially impossible friendship that the Harlem Renaissance produced between Carl Van Vechten, the sophisticated gay white heir and music critic, and Gladys Bentley, the transgendered, dispossessed lesbian blues performer. Their friendship, which arose out of social mixing across class and race boundaries in a modern urban milieu, was founded on the recognition of queer camaraderie. Van Vechten's power of generous, self-gratifying white male patronage and Bentley's charismatic cross-dressing blues persona contributed to a friendship that highlights the social dynamics of the Harlem Renaissance. In this remarkable, brief, yet spectacular eruption of black cosmopolitan urbanity, the coming together in a mutually productive and pleasurable relationship of such previously apparently unrelated figures as Van Vechten and Bentley exemplifies some of the central dynamics of the queer Harlem Renaissance.

From Richard Bruce Nugent, who was renowned in Renaissance circles for his flaming manner and bohemian attire and who published what may be the first openly gay black male piece of short fiction in the twentieth century, *Smoke, Lilies, and Jade* (1925), to millionaire heiress A'Lelia Walker, who showered what may be characterized as "fag-hag" affections on black male social circles through extravagant parties and literary salon fundraisers, the Harlem Renaissance was profoundly queer.

Private parties and gatherings such as Walker's became the best place for LGBT Harlem to socialize. "Rent parties," invented in the South and held to raise rent money, were the most common type of party. Alexander Gumby, a postal clerk, held popular literary gatherings at his studio on Fifth Avenue and 131st street. Another form of social gathering was the "buffet flat" which also originated in the South. This was usually a place where one could go after hours for drink and possibly a place to sleep.

Beyond the black queer spectacles found between the lines of fictional texts and gossip columns, there is a list of Harlem Renaissance artists whose sexual identities have been the subject of much speculation and debate. On the list are Alain Locke, the first black Rhodes scholar and in many respects the leader of the Renaissance; blues poet Langston Hughes; English sonnet poet Countee Cullen and his longtime lover Harold Jackman; novelist and provocateur Wallace Thurman; West Indian novelist and Marxist Claude McKay; prolific poet Georgia Douglas Johnson; and poet and playwright Angelina Grimké.

The Harlem Renaissance, understood as both a civil rights movement and a movement of black urban modernity imbued with expressions of sexual difference, offers an historical opportunity to recognize the queer lives of black artists and intellectuals and to draw out the theoretical implications that this cultural moment offers black queer studies as it contributes further insights into North American histories of race and sexuality.

In discussing queer sexuality in the Renaissance, a useful rubric is that of invisibility, recognizing a private Harlem black queer space that existed beyond Harlem's public representations. This can be seen in novels containing representations of ambivalent sexual alterity, in cultural insider narratives of queerness, and in the performances of Gladys Bentley, who like her famous counterparts Ma Rainey and Bessie Smith was a pioneer in the rise of the black female blues singer during the 1920s. However, unlike Rainey and Smith, Bentley built her career as a notorious Harlem performer, a well-known queer "secret" of the in-crowd of Harlemites and white patrons such as Van Vechten who attended her show. Bentley's success as a blues singer was linked with her overtly classed public lesbian persona—one that proudly displayed the "bull dagger" image. Eric Garber writes that this image was "the one identifiable black lesbian stereotype of this period: the tough-talking, masculine acting, cross-dressing, and sexually worldly 'bulldagger.'" (Garber p. 58). Bentley's blues artistry entailed a gender performance that was strongly connected to the active LGBT subculture of the Harlem Renaissance period and to a black working-class social milieu.

As an example of this type of theoretical thrust, Bentley's "open secret" importantly served to both transgress and produce the racial and sexual identity dictates of the Renaissance, namely that of black middle-class heterosexuality. Public heteronormative space was defined in opposition to the open secret of queer private space in public. In the case of Bentley's persona and Harlem's image, what made the space and its subjects nominally "straight" and "middle-class" was its opposition to a circulating public narrative, the "open secret," of black queerness and working-class identity. Garber notes that while Bessie Smith sang about "mannish acting women," and Ma Rainey enjoyed "wearing a collar and a tie" in "Prove It On Me Blues," Bentley made the black bulldagger role that Lucille Bogan sang about in her 1935 "B.D. Women Blues" the center of her performance. Bentley performed in tuxedos and top hats, sang to women in the audience, exulted in being the object of sexually suggestive queer gossip, and married her female lover in a highly publicized wedding. So compelling was Bentley's gender performance that decades later artist Romare Bearden mistook her for a cross-dressing male when he identified her as a male-to-female impersonator called Gladys Bentley who sang at the Clam House. This exemplifies the queer readings and misreadings that have been generated by the Harlem Renaissance.

Bibliography

Bernard, Emily, ed. *Remember Me to Harlem, The Letters of Langston Hughes and Carl Van Vechten.* New York: Vintage Books, Random House, Inc., 2002.

Carby, Hazel. *Reconstructing Womanhood: The Emergence of the Afro-American Woman Novelist.* New York: Oxford University Press, 1987.

Chauncey, George. *Gay New York: Gender, Urban Culture, and the Making of the Gay Male World, 1890-1940.* New York: Basic Books, 1994.

Constantine-Simms, Delroy, ed. *The Greatest Taboo: Homosexuality in Black Communities,* Volume 1. Los Angeles: Alyson Books, 2001.

Davis, Angela Y. *Blues Legacies and Black Feminism.* New York: Vintage Books, 1999.

DuCille, Ann. *The Coupling Convention: Sex, Text and Tradition in Black Women's Fiction.* New York: Oxford University Press, 1993.

Garber, Eric. "Gladys Bentley: The Bulldagger Who Sang the Blues," *Outlook 1* (Spring 1988): 52-61.

———. "A Spectacle in Color: The Lesbian and Gay Subculture of Jazz Age Harlem." In *Hidden from History: Reclaiming the Gay and Lesbian Past.* Edited by Martin Duberman, Martha Vicinus, and George Chauncey Jr. New York: Meridian, 1989.

Hull, Gloria T. *Color, Sex, and Poetry: Three Women Writers of the Harlem Renaissance.* Bloomington: Indiana University Press, 1987.

McDowell, Deborah E. "Introduction." *Quicksand and Passing.* New Brunswick, N.J.: Rutgers University Press, 1986.

Watson, Steven. *The Harlem Renaissance: Hub of African-American Culture, 1920-1930.* New York: Pantheon Books, 1995.

Laura A. Harris

See also BAKER, JOSEPHINE; BENTLEY, GLADYS; BISEXUALITY, BISEXUALS, AND BISEXUAL MOVEMENTS; DUNBAR-NELSON, ALICE; COUNTEE, CULLEN; GRIMKÉ, ANGELINA WELD; HUGHES, LANGSTON; LITERATURE; LOCKE, ALAIN; MCKAY, CLAUDE; NUGENT, RICHARD BRUCE; NILES, BLAIR; THURMAN, WALLACE; VAN VECHTEN, CARL; WALKER, A'LELIA.

HART, Alan L. (b. 4 October 1890; d. 1 July 1962), physician, novelist.

Alan Lucill Hart, public health physician and man of letters, inspired scores of transgender activists with his story of courage and adaptation in the face of adversity. Public attention was first brought to Hart's extraordinary life with the 1976 publication of Jonathan Ned Katz's *Gay American History.* Katz reprinted Hart's autobiographical account, which had first been published in 1920 by Hart's psychiatrist and professor, Dr. Joshua Allen Gilbert, as a case study of female sexual inversion. In his second book, published in 1983, Katz revealed the later identity of Lucille Hart as Dr. Alan L. Hart, a successful physician, author of four novels, and married man. Years before Christine Jorgensen, Hart had used modern medical surgery to assist in his own gender transformation. Forced to hide this transformation during his own lifetime, Hart was retrospectively validated during the 1990s through a reinterpretation that shifted his identity from lesbian lover to transgender hero.

Hart was born Lucille Alberta Hart in Halls Summit, Kansas, the daughter of Alan L. Hart and Edna Bamford. In 1891 Hart's father, a successful merchant in Halls Summit, died in a typhoid fever epidemic, forcing Hart's mother to return to her native Oregon to raise her child. Mrs. Hart remarried, and the young Lucille spent the remainder of her childhood and teenage years in Albany, Oregon.

While a student at Albany College, Hart carried on a number of love affairs with women; delighted in all masculine pursuits, including driving automobiles; and was an accomplished debater and writer for the school newspaper and yearbook. Hart attended Stanford University, and in 1917 graduated top in his class from the University of Oregon Medical College. The university yearbook is the first public document that reveals Hart's use of the male persona "Alan Lucill Hart." Around the summer of 1917, Hart underwent a hysterectomy and began a final transformation to manhood. A professor of Hart's later wrote, "she entered a hospital at Berkeley, submitted to certain operational procedures, and emerged, an authentic male being" (Gilbert, p. 317). Upon returning to Albany, Hart paid a visit to the editor of the *Albany Democrat-Herald* and "announced that he was no longer [Lucille] but Allan [sic], and was to be addressed and referred to with the proper designative 'Mr' " (William G. Thatcher, "Oregon Authors I Have Known," 1953, p. 36).

In February 1918 Dr. Hart eloped with a Portland schoolteacher, Inez Stark, to Martinez, California, where

Alan Hart. A portrait of the public health physician, novelist, and transgender pioneer (born Lucille Alberta Hart), taken in Billings, Montana, c. 1921. **[Wyoming State Museum]**

he obtained a marriage license using a fictitious name. The couple moved to the tiny fishing village of Gardiner on the Oregon coast, where Hart intended to take over another man's medical practice. Their residence was short-lived. While newspaper accounts indicate that Hart left due to influenza, there is ample evidence to suggest that he had been recognized by a former medical college acquaintance from Portland, and as Gilbert noted in his article, "the hounding process began, which our modern social organization can carry on to such perfection and refinement against her own members" (p. 317).

Hart obtained a legal divorce from his wife in 1925 after she deserted him, and a few months later on 15 May 1925 married Edna "Ruddy" Ruddick at the Episcopalian Church of the Transfiguration in New York City.

Over the next twenty years Hart lived in twelve locations across the United States from Huntley, Montana, where he engaged in a general medical practice, to Albuquerque, New Mexico, where he found work in a tuberculosis sanitarium. In 1928 he obtained a master's degree in radiology from the University of Pennsylvania, and in 1948 he received a master's of public health degree from Yale University. In the 1930s Hart spoke frequently to community groups across Idaho, and helped coordinate that state's antituberculosis campaign.

Hart's literary career began with the submission of a manuscript based on his experiences as a doctor in Gardiner. W. W. Norton was impressed with the story and published Hart's first novel, *Dr. Mallory,* in 1935 to some critical acclaim. Hart's second novel, *The Undaunted* (1936), was the story of a physician working in a research institute to find a cure for pernicious anemia. In the second book, Hart presents a homosexual character as a sympathetic figure—Sandy Farquhar is a radiologist trying to get by in a world that treats him as an outcast. Two more novels and a layman's book about x-rays followed.

During the 1930s and 1940s, Hart promoted his books with speaking engagements at literary clubs and bookstores, and in 1935 he made a radio appearance in Portland, Oregon. While such activities brought Hart public acclaim for his achievements, they also meant risking exposure of his gender transformation. Nonetheless, he largely kept his secret during his lifetime, though his transformation from Lucille to Alan was undoubtedly known to some friends and relatives. It was common gossip in Hart's hometown of Albany, Oregon.

Hart and his second wife settled in Hartford, Connecticut, in 1945 and joined the Unitarian church. Hart served as director of the State Health Department Office of Tuberculosis Control until his death at age seventy-one on 1 July 1962. His remains were cremated and the ashes spread in Olympic National Forest in Washington state.

Bibliography

Bates, Tom. "Decades ago, an Oregon Doctor Tried to Redefine Gender." *The Oregonian,* 14 July 1996, Section B, pp. 1–5.

Gilbert, J. Allen. "Homosexuality and Its Treatment." *Journal of Nervous and Mental Diseases* 52, no. 4 (October 1920).

Katz, Jonathan Ned. *Gay American History: Lesbians and Gay Men in the U.S.A.* New York: Crowell, 1976.

———. *Gay/Lesbian Almanac: A New Documentary.* New York: Harper, 1983.

Powers, Alfred. *History of Oregon Literature.* Portland, Ore.: Metropolitan Press, 1935.

Tom Cook

See also TRANSSEXUALS, TRANSVESTITES, TRANSGENDERED PEOPLE, AND CROSS-DRESSERS.

HART, Lorenz Milton (b. 2 May 1895; d. 22 November 1943), lyricist.

Lorenz Milton Hart was born in New York City to an upper-middle-class, German-Jewish family. He spent his childhood and most of his adulthood living with his family in a large brownstone house on the Upper West Side of Manhattan. His love for theater began at summer camp in the Catskills. Hart studied journalism at Columbia University, but his real passion was for amateur theatrical groups. Hart wrote, performed, and directed for Columbia's Player's Club. Ironically, one of his fellow thespians at Columbia was Oscar Hammerstein II, who would replace him as Richard Rodgers's collaborator. After leaving Columbia, Hart worked for the Shubert organization as a translator of German plays and operettas. Early in 1919 he met Rodgers, a prodigious high school senior. Their first composer–lyricist collaboration, "Any Old Place with You," was performed as part of a Lew Fields revue, *A Lonely Romeo,* in August 1919, launching a brilliant, complicated partnership that lasted over two decades.

While Rodgers went on, after Hart's death, to work with Hammerstein and, later, a number of other lyricists, Hart worked exclusively with Rodgers. The two men quickly moved from writing songs and scores for amateur shows to writing for sophisticated Broadway revues, then to writing the scores for some of the classic musicals of the 1920s and 1930s. The team spent the 1920s writing for Broadway, but with the advent of sound film, Hollywood producers were eager to attract hit composers. Unfortunately, the team was assigned to some forgettable musical projects that did not inspire their best work. Rodgers and Hart then returned to Broadway in the mid-1930s and created a string of hit musicals including *On Your Toes* (1936), *Babes in Arms* (1937), *The Boys from Syracuse* (1938), and *Pal Joey* (1940), filled with songs that would become standards.

Hart's best lyrics, easily separated from the context of the shows for which they were written, are the most confessional of any major Broadway bard. They reveal a man who hated his own appearance and ached at his separation from the conventional heterosexual romance that lies at the heart of popular song. His best lyrics are cries of unrequited desire and love. Hart was under five feet tall with an disproportionately large, prematurely balding head. Again and again, his lyrics describe people whose looks are "unphotographable." He was hardly the only homosexual in the theater during his career—his most celebrated lyricist peers, Cole Porter and Noel Coward, were also gay, as were many performers, directors, designers, and choreographers—yet Hart could neither deny

Lorenz Hart. The variously witty, sardonic, yearning, and wistful lyrics of Broadway composer Richard Rodgers's first songwriting partner both marked and masked the conflicted and profoundly unhappy personality of this undersized man, a giant of the American musical theater for two decades. **[John Springer Collection/corbis]**

nor accept his homosexuality. On the one hand, his most constant companion, Milton "Doc" Bender, was also his procurer; on the other, young men who had sex with Hart attested to his self-loathing about his homosexuality. Hart's negative self-image was complicated by his professional relationship with the extremely straight, disciplined, uptight Rodgers, whom he called "the Principal." Hart was anything but disciplined, often disappearing for days at a time and turning in his contributions at the last minute. Fortunately, he could write his brilliant lyrics quickly and with little need for revision. If anything, his work came too easily for him. No doubt Hart's self-hatred and complex relationship with his partner exacerbated the alcoholism that would finally destroy his career and lead to his death at the age of forty-eight.

In the Golden Age of Broadway song, lyrics were expected to be virtuosic displays of wit and poetic invention. Hart's lyrics are filled with surprising rhymes and clever, ironic figures of speech. He was more versatile than Cole Porter, more literate than Irving Berlin. Part of the complexity of Hart's lyrics is the pleasant but acerbic aftertaste: his best lyrics for both ballads and patter songs focus either on love as a fantasy never quite fulfilled or on love that is unhappy, but better than nothing. Real love, for Hart, is often painful, and most love is unrequited. As playwright Jerome Lawrence once observed, Hart "is the poet laureate of masochism." It is appropriate that Rodgers and Hart's masterpiece is the very cynical *Pal Joey,* the saga of an affair between a "half pint" hustler and a world-wise society woman who has no illusions about what Joey can and cannot provide.

By the early 1940s, Hart's drinking and disappearances were seriously threatening the most successful songwriting team of the period. Their last collaboration, *By Jupiter* (1942), had to be written in Doctor's Hospital in New York while Hart was drying out. Hart had no interest in writing lyrics for what would turn out to be *Oklahoma!* (1943), so Rodgers, with Hart's blessing, collaborated with Hammerstein. Some think that the enormous success of this legendary Rodgers and Hammerstein collaboration was the final blow in Hart's downfall. After *Oklahoma!* Rodgers collaborated one final time with Hart on an extensive revision of Mark Twain's *A Connecticut Yankee in King Arthur's Court* (1889). Though Hart was unusually sober and disciplined during the composition, perhaps trying to prove to "the Principal" that he still could be a collaborator, he arrived at the opening so drunk that he had to be escorted from the theater. He died of pneumonia on 22 November 1943.

Bibliography

Clum, John M. *Something for the Boys: Musical Theater and Gay Culture.* New York: St. Martin's Press, 1999.

Hart, Dorothy. *Thou Swell, Thou Witty: The Life and Lyrics of Lorenz Hart.* New York: Harper and Row, 1976.

Hart, Dorothy, and Robert Kimball, eds. *The Complete Lyrics of Lorenz Hart.* New York: Da Capo, 1995.

Marx, Samuel, and Jan Clayton. *Rodgers and Hart: Bewitched, Bothered, and Bedeviled, An Anecdotal Account.* New York: Putnam, 1976.

Nolan, Frederick. *Lorenz Hart: A Poet on Broadway.* New York: Oxford University Press, 1994.

John M. Clum

See also MUSIC: BROADWAY AND MUSICAL THEATER.

HART, Pearl **(b. 7 April 1890; d. 22 March 1975), attorney, activist, civic leader.**

Pearl Hart was born in Traverse City, Michigan, as Pearl Minnie Harchovsky, the fifth daughter in a family of Russian Jewish immigrants. Her father moved the family to Chicago before Hart began school. Nurtured in a large, loving family, she had a personality that fused the compassionate outlook of her mother, a social worker, with the wisdom and intellect of her father, an orthodox rabbi.

Hart graduated in 1914 from the John Marshall Law School in Chicago and became one of the first female attorneys in that city to practice criminal law. Her legal career focused on the needs of women, children, and immigrants. Only in the twilight of her life did Hart turn her attention to nurturing the growth of the LGBT community in Chicago.

Underlying all of Hart's legal and social activism was a commitment to the civil liberties of the individual citizen. At various points in her career, she confronted police abuses of power. In the 1930s, for example, she tackled the problem of women arrested for prostitution on the flimsiest of pretenses. In the 1950s Hart turned her legal skills to fighting the attempts of the federal government to deport naturalized immigrants accused of subversive activities. She appealed the case of *U.S. v. Witkovich* to the U.S. Supreme Court, and, in 1957, the Court decided in her favor. In the 1960s she was one of the few attorneys in Chicago who defended gay men. Throughout her career, she was devoted to what is the most vulnerable group in any society—children. She was recognized as a national expert on the juvenile justice system and its reform.

Hart's activist record is reflected in the numerous organizations she helped establish and to which she belonged. She was a founding member of the National Lawyers Guild, the American Committee for the Protection of the Foreign Born, the Chicago Committee to Defend the Bill of Rights, and Mattachine Midwest. She served in various leadership positions in these and many other groups.

As a natural outgrowth of her commitment to social change, Hart was also drawn to politics. Registered as an Independent or Progressive Party candidate, she ran for judgeships in 1928, 1932, 1947, and 1948, and for a seat as a Chicago alderman in 1947 and 1951. She lost all six elections. Her failures to gain political office were balanced by her success as a teacher. Hart taught criminal law at her alma mater, John Marshall, from 1946 until 1971.

Hart was widely respected for her role as a mentor to women law students and lawyers. She was a popular public speaker, addressing groups that ran the gamut from national conventions to neighborhood organizations. She devoted countless pro bono hours of legal work to the causes she believed in and to indigent clients. Despite the seriousness of the goals to which she dedicated her life, Hart was fond of telling jokes and of collecting new ones. Her physical stature was striking. She was close to six feet tall and weighed around 200 pounds.

Hart remained a closeted lesbian throughout her life. In the 1920s Hart began a relationship with J. Blossom Churan, a stage actress. In the 1940s Churan had an affair with a physician, Bertha Isaacs. Hart proposed that all three live together, which they did until Churan's death in 1973. In 1963 Hart began a relationship with poet and author Valerie Taylor, which lasted until Hart's death in 1975.

Hart first became publicly identified with the LGBT community in Chicago when she addressed attendees at the initial organizing meeting of Mattachine Midwest on 27 July 1965. Hart cofounded the group along with two men, Bob Basker and Ira Jones.

Hart's efforts on behalf of the Chicago LGBT community were twofold. First, she defended gay men nabbed in bar raids, those accused of soliciting sex in public places, and those entrapped to do so. Second, she served as Mattachine Midwest's legal counsel from its inception until her death. Hart defended her clients without engaging in the bribery and other forms of corruption so common in the disposition of such cases. Her immaculate reputation earned her the affectionate title "Guardian Angel of Chicago's Gay Community."

Lesbians active in the Daughters of Bilitis also knew of Hart's reputation. Del Martin, editor of the *Ladder,* solicited her opinion on the repeal of Illinois's sodomy laws for an article in the March 1962 issue of the magazine.

Hart died on 22 March 1975 of pancreatic cancer complicated by heart disease. She practiced law for sixty-one years with compassion, integrity, and an unwavering commitment to social justice, in the finest tradition of the U.S. Left. She was posthumously inducted into the Chicago Gay and Lesbian Hall of Fame in 1992 and awarded a Chicago Tribute Marker of Distinction in 2002.

Bibliography

Bradford, Jim. "Pearl Hart Is Remembered on the Anniversary of Her Passing." *Chicago GayLife,* 15 March 1976, pp. 1, 6.

Gatland, Laura. "Guardian of Justice." *John Marshall Comment* (winter 1998): 20–24.

Ginger, Ann Fagan. *The National Lawyers Guild: From Roosevelt through Reagan.* Philadelphia: Temple University Press, 1987.

———. *Carol Weiss King: Human Rights Lawyer, 1895–1952.* Niwot: University Press of Colorado, 1993.

Hart, Pearl. Papers. Chicago Historical Society, Chicago, Illinois.

Martin, Del. "New Illinois Penal Code—What Does It Mean?" *Ladder,* March 1962, pp. 14–15.

Sendziak, Karen C. "Pearl M. Hart." In *Before Stonewall: Activists for Gay and Lesbian Rights in Historical Context.* Edited by Vern L. Bullough. New York: Haworth, 2002.

Karen C. Sendziak

HARTLEY, Marsden (b. 4 January 1877; d. 2 September 1943), artist, writer.

Edmund Hartley was born in Lewiston, Maine, to English immigrant working-class parents. After his mother's death when he was eight, he lived with an older sister nearby until rejoining his remarried father in 1893 in Cleveland, Ohio. There he began taking art classes, entered the Cleveland School of Art in 1898, and soon after received an annual stipend to study for five years in New York. After spending a year at the Chase School, Hartley transferred to the National Academy of Design, where he garnered several awards. At this time, he began spending summers in Maine and worked for two years as an extra in a New York theater company. Aside from his artistic studies, Hartley had no formal education beyond the age of sixteen, but he developed wide-ranging literary and intellectual interests, including a lifelong study of spiritual philosophy and mysticism.

Hartley's earliest known painting (ca. 1905) is, revealingly, a depiction of Walt Whitman's house in Camden, New Jersey; at the time, he knew several members of Whitman's circle. In 1906, Hartley moved back to Lewiston, adding his stepmother's maiden name, Marsden, to his own, then dropping Edmund entirely two years later. Moving to North Lovell, Maine, he painted a number of mountain landscapes in an impressionist style. In 1909, he was introduced to the famed New York art dealer and photographer Alfred Stieglitz, who quickly gave Hartley his first solo exhibition at his 291 Gallery and was to exhibit his works until 1937. Moving to New York, he also met the eccentric landscape painter Albert Pinkham Ryder, painting several landscapes in a similar dark style. Circulating within a wide circle of artists, writers, and patrons, Hartley imbibed much of the newest European and American art at Stieglitz's gallery and elsewhere, being particularly influenced by Pablo Picasso and Paul Cézanne.

Hartley made his first trip to Europe in 1912–1913, staying in Paris (where he was befriended by Gertrude Stein), Berlin, and Munich. He was strongly affected by his sojourn in Germany, forming important artistic ties to Wassily Kandinsky, among others, and being seduced by the relative openness of gay life in prewar Berlin, in addition to admiring the manifest military culture and pageantry. After a brief trip to New York, Hartley returned to Berlin and stayed until late 1915, a crucial period for his painting. He developed a boldly colored abstract style, most notably exhibited in the German military paintings of 1913–1914, in large part a memorial to an apparent lover, Karl von Freyburg, a young officer who was killed in October 1914. Although receiving lukewarm notice when exhibited by Stieglitz in 1916 (partly because of anti-German feeling), these works are now commonly accepted as important early exponents of American modernism. Through knowledge of Hartley's life, their encoded gay symbolism has also now been successfully elucidated.

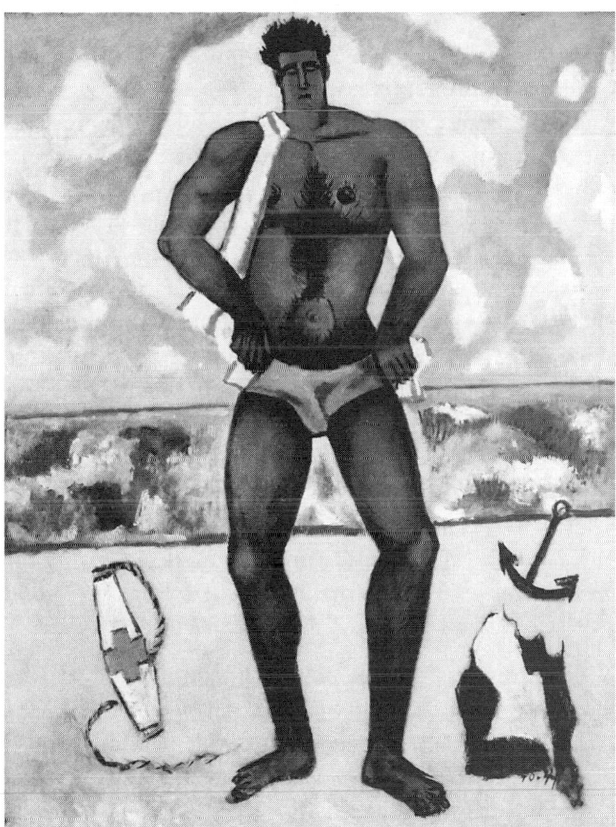

Canuck Yankee Lumberjack at Old Orchard Beach, Maine, 1940–41. A late work by the Maine-based but peripatetic artist, best known for his landscapes and supermasculine figure paintings. [Hirshhorn Museum and Sculpture Garden, Smithsonian Institution, Washington, D.C.]

Realizing that his advanced style did not suit the time, Hartley spent the next twenty years restlessly searching for a place and a distinctive personal vision. Never staying longer than a few months in any lodging, he sojourned, sometimes repeatedly, in Provincetown, Massachusetts (where he shared a house with the painter Charles Demuth), Bermuda, Maine, New Mexico, California, Paris, Berlin, Italy, Provence, New Hampshire, Mexico, and Bavaria. Often vacillating in his work between more literal objectivity and subjective symbolism, Hartley gradually developed a pared-down style that at once reflected the cultural taste for a more "American" representation and yet was true to his own spiritual energy. He continued to alternate periods of rural isolation with active participation in artistic and literary circles in the United States and Europe; his own poems and essays were being published in prestigious journals such as *Camera Work, Dial,* and *Poetry.* He won a Guggenheim fellowship in 1931 and spent it working in Mexico. After a last European stay in 1933, Hartley returned to New York and a period of severe financial hardship during the Great Depression before finally settling for good in New England.

Hartley was considerably reenergized by his experiences living with a fishing family in 1935–1936 on the coast of Nova Scotia, reworking earlier painting motifs, exploring the harsh environment, and enjoying the idealized comfort of a domestic life. He became particularly attached to the young son of the family, Aldy Mason, whose drowning in September 1936 deeply affected him. Excepting brief stays in New York, he spent the rest of his life in Maine. In addition to painting powerful depictions of the rocky coast and Mount Katahdin, Hartley devoted himself significantly to figure painting, including archaic depictions of the Mason family in *Fishermen's Last Supper* and the homoerotic *Christ Held by Half-Naked Men* of 1940–1941; homages to Abraham Lincoln and Albert Pinkham Ryder; and portrayals of handsome local lobstermen, boxers, and swimmers. Such supermasculine figures as *Madawaska–Acadian Light-Heavy* (1940) almost flagrantly represent Hartley's desires, yet ironically during wartime also were able to symbolize for the public an unthreatening ideal of manhood, indeed winning for him a 1942 purchase prize from the Metropolitan Museum of Art exhibition "Artists for Victory." It was only in the last two years of his life that Hartley began to receive wide recognition again and to achieve more significant sales of his work. He died in Ellsworth, Maine, in 1943.

Hartley always maintained a delicate balance between openness and discretion in his life and art. Somewhat of a dandy in appearance and sophisticated tastes, he remained coy about his personal affairs, apparently including at least one heterosexual liaison. Freely participating in gay society from 1913 Berlin to 1942 New York (where he was photographed by George Platt Lynes), he also retained to the end of his life such telling souvenirs as a signed photograph of Whitman, along with a private stock of nude photographs and physique magazines. Barbara Haskell's catalog for the 1980 Whitney Museum retrospective was the first mainstream recognition of Hartley's homosexuality, followed by more in-depth explorations by Townsend Ludington, Jonathan Weinberg, and others.

Bibliography

Hartley, Marsden. *Somehow a Past: The Autobiography of Marsden Hartley.* Edited by Susan Elizabeth Ryan. Cambridge, Mass.: MIT Press, 1997.

Haskell, Barbara. *Marsden Hartley.* New York: Whitney Museum of American Art, 1980.

Kornhauser, Elizabeth Mankin, ed. *Marsden Hartley.* Hartford, Conn.: Wadsworth Atheneum Museum of Art, 2002.

Ludington, Townsend. *Marsden Hartley: The Biography of an American Artist.* Rev. ed. Ithaca, N.Y.: Cornell University Press, 1998.

Weinberg, Jonathan. *Speaking for Vice: Homosexuality in the Art of Charles Demuth, Marsden Hartley, and the First American Avant-Garde.* New Haven, Conn.: Yale University Press, 1993.

David P. Becker

See also DEMUTH, CHARLES; LYNES, GEORGE PLATT; STEIN, GERTRUDE, AND ALICE B. TOKLAS; VISUAL ART; WHITMAN, WALT.

HATE CRIMES LAW AND POLICY

In December 2002 the *Philadelphia Inquirer* ran a front-page headline announcing "How Pa. Heartland Went for Gay Rights. The Hate Crime Law Extends Even to the Transgendered. Observers Are Stunned." The story reported that "a remarkable thing has happened in Pennsylvania. The state legislature passed an amendment to the hate crimes law that made Pennsylvania only the fifth state in the union to protect not only gays, lesbians, and bisexuals, but also those who are transgendered." The writers explained that this landmark decision signaled that gay rights were possible even "in a state renowned for its heartland conservatism" and that such a shift was attributable to a successful lobbying campaign that spanned nine years (Harris and Worden, p. A1). Situating this legal policy in historical context, however, requires understanding the long history of violence against LGBT people, as well as acknowledging policy reforms beginning in the 1970s designed to curb such violence and protect those who are targeted because of their sexual identity, behavior, and desire.

A History of Violence against LGBT People

Violence against LGBT people is not new, nor is it anomalous; it has been documented for as long as the lives of LGBT people have been documented. In a 1980 volume, John Boswell discusses the scholarly evidence for violence against gay men and lesbians in western Europe from the beginning of the Christian era to the fourteenth century. In *Gay American History* (1976), which covers the four-hundred-year period from 1566 to 1966, Jonathan Katz describes a history of violence directed against LGBT individuals because of their dress, sexual orientation, sexual identity, or sexual behavior. Historically, such violence included castration, beatings, imprisonment, burning, choking, electrical shocks, and execution. Katz documents many historical moments in which the official government sanction for sodomy or other homosexual acts or behaviors was death by hanging, drowning, or some other means. These actions were accepted as legitimate state policy and necessary responses to homosexuality or gender-inappropriate behavior.

In the latter part of the twentieth century, the National Gay and Lesbian Task Force (NGLTF) began documenting literally thousands of incidents of violence against sexual minorities in the United States. Collecting reported incidents of violence, as well as many that have gone unreported, the NGLTF has focused on an array of manifestations of violence against LGBT people (including the particular targeting of LGBT people who are AIDS-positive or suspected of having AIDS): homicide, AIDS-related incidents, harassment and assault, conspiracy, attacks on LGBT establishments, police abuse and negligence, violence on college campuses, violence by family members, violence in jails and prisons, and, most frequently, anti-LGBT defamation. Documented cases of anti-LGBT violence throughout history provide evidence for the claim made by Virginia Apuzzo, former executive director of the NGLTF, that "to be gay or lesbian is to live in the shadow of violence" (cited in Comstock, p. 54). It is easy to extend this well-founded claim to bisexual and transgender people.

Despite many calls for the government to monitor and respond to bias-motivated violence in the United States, including violence against sexual minorities, it was not until the late 1980s that the federal government heeded the demands of many civil rights groups and community organizations and began to study the nature of bias-motivated violence against minorities. In one of the first government-sponsored efforts to assess the scope of violence directed toward minorities in the United States, the U.S. Justice Department commissioned a report on bias-motivated violence in 1987. This report found that "the most frequent victims of hate violence today are Blacks, Hispanics, Southeast Asians, Jews, and gays and lesbians. Homosexuals are probably the most frequent victims" (cited in Vaid, p. 11).

Shortly after the release of this pathbreaking report, the Federal Bureau of Investigation began to collect data on crimes committed because of bias toward homosexuals, as part of its larger effort to track bias-related crime in general in the United States. Beginning in the early 1990s, the Uniform Crime Report (UCR) included annual data on violence against people because of their sexual orientation. Despite the underreported and selectively reported nature of anti-LGBT violence, the data reveal three important trends in *reported* violence against sexual minorities. First, bias-motivated violence directed toward both gay men and lesbians has increased. Second, violence based on sexual orientation is the second most frequently reported type of hate crime in the United States, with race-based violence being the most frequently reported type of bias crime in the United States. And third, officially reported violence directed toward gay men is more common than violence directed toward lesbians. Official data from state and city agencies generally confirm the patterns revealed by the UCR data.

In addition to government reports, various non–government sponsored studies reveal the contours of crimes against gay men and lesbians. Notably, state-sponsored reports of violence based on sexual orientation or sexuality rarely focus on violence against transgender people. However, the National Coalition of Anti-Violence Programs (NCAVP), a coalition of LGBT-sponsored anti-violence organizations, is an exception. The NCAVP annually releases a report titled "Anti-Lesbian, Gay, Bisexual, and Transgender Violence," which summarizes known incidents of violence against LGBT individuals in cities, states, and/or regions across the United States.

Changing Legal and Extralegal Responses to Violence against Sexual Minorities

The 1980s and 1990s saw the emergence of an array of legal and extralegal responses designed to bring attention to and curb such violence against sexual minorities. In the process, "gay bashing" and other forms of violence against sexual minorities has, for the first time in history, been deemed a national social problem and, in many jurisdictions, a bona fide hate crime. This has occurred primarily as a result of sustained community activism and attendant legal reform.

In the latter part of the twentieth century a plethora of community-based activist groups defined anti–gay and lesbian violence as a social problem in need of remedy.

FIGURE 1

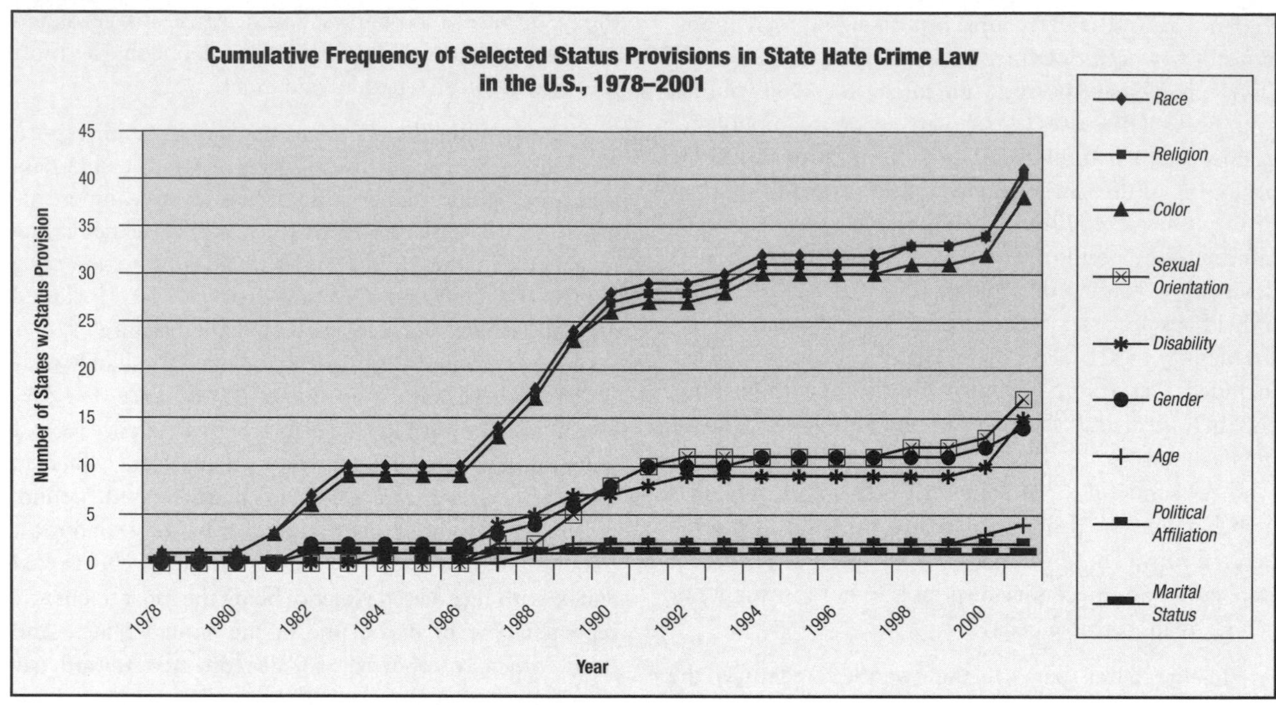

Most notably, in the 1980s and the 1990s gay- and lesbian-sponsored antiviolence projects emerged and proliferated. These organizations document and publicize the incidence and prevalence of anti–gay and lesbian violence, establish crisis intervention and victim assistance programs, sponsor public education campaigns, and undertake surveillance efforts in the form of street patrols. Combined, these activities comprise an "unprecedented level of organizing against violence" (National Gay and Lesbian Task Force, p. 22) that has ensured that anti–gay and lesbian violence has "finally taken its place among such societal concerns as violence against women, children and ethnic and racial groups" (Comstock, p. 1). By the late 1990s violence against transgender people had also begun to receive national attention.

The success of LGBT community activism was evident by the end of the twentieth century in the number of jurisdictions across the United States that had passed laws to enhance the penalty for crimes that manifest evidence of prejudice based on sexual orientation, presumably to deter gay bashing and to punish perpetrators of violence who target sexual minorities.

Although the idea of including sexual orientation as a provision in hate crime policy was introduced early on in the process of making hate crime policy, such protection did not find a secure home in hate crime law until about halfway through a larger process of legal reform designed to curb bias-motivated violence. Moreover, even when including sexual orientation as a provision in hate crime law gained legitimacy, it nonetheless remained a less-accepted provision in hate crime policy than those identified as core provisions—such as race, religion, and ethnicity.

Following the lead of the states, in the 1990s the federal government passed two laws that recognized violence against sexual minorities in general and gays and lesbians in particular as an important social problem in need of public resources and legal redress. First, on 23 April 1990 President George H. W. Bush signed into law the *Hate Crime Statistics Act of 1990* (HCSA), which required the U.S. attorney general to collect data on "crimes that manifest evidence of prejudice based on race, religion, disability, sexual orientation, or ethnicity, including where appropriate the crimes of murder, non-negligent manslaughter; forcible rape; aggravated assault, simple assault, intimidation; arson; and destruction, damage, or vandalism of property (U.S. Code, vol. 28, sec. 534 [2000]). As a data collection law, the HCSA merely requires the attorney general to gather and make available to the public information on bias-motivated crime. The goal was that this empirical data would then serve as a tool for developing more effective policy: defining and counting bias-motivated crimes would enable public policymakers to identify trends, fashion effective responses, design prevention strategies, and develop sensitivity to the particular needs of victims of hate crime, including LGBT people.

The second law to deal with hate crime at the federal level was passed as part of the *Violent Crime Control and Law Enforcement Act of 1994,* U.S. Public Law 103-322 (103d Congress, 2d session, 24 January 1994). Section 280003 of Public Law 103-322, which became known as the Hate Crimes Sentencing Enhancement Act (HCSEA), identified eight predicate crimes—murder; non-negligent manslaughter; forcible rape; aggravated assault; simple assault; intimidation; arson; and destruction, damage, or vandalism of property—for which judges are allowed to enhance penalties of "not less than three offense levels for offenses that finder of fact at trial determines beyond a reasonable doubt are hate crimes." For the purposes of this law, "hate crime" is defined as criminal conduct wherein "the defendant intentionally selected any victim or property as the object of the offense because of the actual or perceived race, color, religion, national origin, ethnicity, gender, disability, or sexual orientation of any person." Although broad in form, this law only covers hate crimes that take place on federal lands and properties.

Despite the fact that both of these federal efforts are limited—the HCSA does not mandate punishment for offenders and the HCSEA only covers a limited set of circumstances in which violence occurs—the inclusion of "sexual orientation" in these federal policies proved controversial. In the case of the HCSA, for example, passage of the law was delayed for years as conservative legislators questioned the appropriateness of including "sexual orientation" in the law.

Ultimately, however, state and federal laws in combination essentially created a new category of criminal conduct: anti–gay and lesbian violence, a category of crime that has since been expanded to include violence against transgender people. Federal and state policy has brought newfound attention to the age-old problem of violence against sexual minorities and, in the process, redefined it as a social problem. The consequence of legal reform being brought to bear on the problem of gay bashing in the United States is perhaps best revealed in a 1988 case involving the beating death of an Asian American gay man. In the process of adjudicating this case, a Broward County, Florida, circuit judge jokingly asked the prosecuting attorney, "That's a crime now, to beat up a homosexual?" The prosecutor answered, "Yes sir. And it's a crime to kill them." The judge replied, "Times really have changed" (Stryker).

As the twenty-first century begins, even public officials and religious officials who oppose homosexuality as an identity, behavior, or lifestyle have begun to speak out in defense of homosexuals as undeserving targets of discriminatory violence. For example, in June 2000 U.S. Senator Gordon Smith of Oregon encouraged his fellow Republicans to favor federal legislation protecting homosexuals from violence, "I think many [religious conservatives] in the Senate are reflexively inclined to vote no. I understand that because I shared those feelings for a long, long, time. You don't have to agree with everything the gay community is asking. I don't, but we ought to agree on protecting them and all Americans" (Rubin, p. A14).

Policy-mandated promises of protection and legal redress have begun to take form in the United States. For example, nearly six years after two lesbians were bound and gagged and had their throats slit while camping and hiking in the Shenandoah National Park, U.S. Attorney General John D. Ashcroft held an historic nationally televised press conference on 11 April 2001 to announce that the U.S. Justice Department was invoking the federal hate crimes statute for the first time to charge the alleged murderer with hate crime. In announcing the indictment, Ashcroft spoke at length about his meeting with the parents of the victims and about the lives and characters of the young women: two midwesterners who migrated to New England, met and became lovers, and shared the love of science and the outdoors. Justifying the invocation of federal hate crime law, which carries with it enhanced penalties, Ashcroft announced that, according to federal prosecutors, Darrell David Rice, a computer programmer from Columbia, Maryland, was, by his own account, a man who hated lesbians and enjoyed intimidating and assaulting women. Sometime after being arrested, Rice told law enforcement officials that he intentionally selected women to assault because they are more vulnerable than men and that the victims in this case deserved to die because he believed they were homosexuals. Ashcroft declared "criminal acts of hate run counter to what is best in America, our belief in equality and freedom. The Department of Justice will aggressively investigate, prosecute, and punish criminal acts of violence and vigilantism motivated by hate and intolerance." Moreover, he said, "we will pursue, prosecute, and punish those who attack law-abiding Americans out of hatred for who they are" and "hatred is the enemy of justice, regardless of its source" (U.S. Department of Justice). It is nothing short of historic that the U.S. attorney general, a Republican appointee at the highest level of government, called the murder of Julianne Marie Williams and Laura Winans a hate crime in a nationally televised press conference and mandated that it be prosecuted as such by the state.

Bibliography

Boswell, John. *Christianity, Social Tolerance, and Homosexuality.* Chicago: University of Chicago Press, 1980.

Comstock, Gary. *Violence against Lesbians and Gay Men.* New York: Columbia University Press, 1991.

Harris, Linda K., and Amy Worden. "How Pa. Heartland Went for Gay Rights: The Hate Crimes Law Extends Even to the Transgendered. Observers are Stunned." *Philadelphia Inquirer,* 15 December 2002, p. A1.

Herek, Gregory, and Kevin T. Berrill. *Hate Crimes: Confronting Violence against Lesbians and Gay Men.* Newbury Park, Calif.: Sage, 1992.

Jenness, Valerie. "Managing Differences and Making Legislation: Social Movements and the Racialization, Sexualization, and Gendering of Federal Hate Crime Law in the U.S., 1985–1998." *Social Problems* 46, no. 4 (1999): 548–571.

Jenness, Valerie, and Kendal Broad. *Hate Crimes: New Social Movements and the Politics of Violence.* New York: Aldine de Gruyter, 1997.

Jenness, Valerie, and Ryken Grattet. *Making Hate a Crime: From Social Movement to Law Enforcement Practice.* New York: Russell Sage, 2001.

Katz, Jonathan. *Gay American History: Lesbians and Gay Men in the U.S.A.* New York: Crowell, 1976.

National Coalition of Anti-Violence Programs. *Anti–Lesbian, Gay, Bisexual, and Transgender Violence in 1998.* New York: New York City Gay and Lesbian Anti-Violence Project, 1999.

National Gay and Lesbian Task Force (U.S.) Policy Institute. *Anti-Gay/Lesbian Violence, Victimization, and Defamation in 1990.* Washington, D.C.: NGLTF Policy Institute, 1991.

Rubin, Alissa J. "Public More Accepting of Gays, Poll Finds." *Los Angeles Times,* 18 June 2000, p. A14.

Stryker, Jeff. "Asking for it." Appeared 23 October 1998. Available from www.salon.com.

U.S. Department of Justice. "Attorney General Transcript: News Conference with USA John Brownlee: Indictment of Darrell David Rice: April 10, 2002: DOJ Conference Center." Available from http://www.usdoj.gov/ag/ at "Speeches 2002."

Vaid, Urvashi. 1995. *Virtual Equality: The Mainstreaming of Gay & Lesbian Liberation.* New York: Anchor Books.

Valerie Jenness

See also ANTI-DISCRIMINATION LAW AND POLICY; CRIME AND CRIMINALIZATION; DISCRIMINATION; FEDERAL LAW AND POLICY; RAPE, SEXUAL ASSAULT, AND SEXUAL HARASSMENT LAW AND POLICY; SEXUAL ABUSE, EXPLOITATION, HARASSMENT, AND RAPE; VIOLENCE.

HAY, Harry **(b. 7 April 1912; d. 24 October 2002), activist.**

Harry Hay was born in the coastal resort town of Worthing, England. He was given the name Henry Jr. by his father, a wealthy mining engineer and real estate investor, and his mother, Margaret Neall, daughter of an elite military family who spent much of her early life in Johannesburg, South Africa. Like his father, he went by the name Harry. The oldest of three children, Harry moved with his family in 1914 to Chile, where his father had taken a job managing a copper mine in the Andes Mountains. After two years, the Hays relocated to southern California, first in Orange County, and three years later settling permanently in Los Angeles.

Hay graduated in 1929 from Los Angeles High School at the age of seventeen. He excelled in his classes and developed a lifelong love of the outdoors and of Native American culture. At fourteen, he had his first homosexual relationship with a merchant seaman he met on a steamer from San Francisco to Los Angeles. For years, Hay had been conscious of his desires for men, and now he kept his identity a tightly guarded secret from his father (who already suspected that his son was overly effeminate) and the rest of his family and friends. He enrolled at Stanford University in 1930. During college, he made frequent trips to nearby San Francisco and explored the homosexual underground of nightclubs and speakeasies, enchanted by the close-knit networks of men "like him" and the thrill of sexual adventure. By his third year at Stanford, the burden of hiding his homosexuality had become too much to bear, and Hay began telling friends, acquaintances, and anyone who would listen that he loved men. University officials responded by rescinding his scholarship. Unable to afford tuition, Hay dropped out with the intention of returning, but never did.

Having taken several drama electives during college and performed in numerous plays, Hay returned to Los Angeles in the fall of 1932 and immersed himself in the local theater scene. He met and had a romantic relationship with the leftist actor Will Geer (best known as Grandpa on the 1970s television series *The Waltons*). Geer introduced Hay to the Communist Party, beginning Hay's decades-long involvement. Hay quickly established himself as a fiercely loyal and devoted party member, attending meetings and demonstrations, and studying and teaching Marxist theory. Nevertheless, communism offered little room for the open expression of homosexuality and, once again, Hay was forced to keep secret his sexual activity (of which there was a great deal, according to his biography). Valuing his political commitments over personal ones, Hay even experimented with heterosexuality, marrying fellow Communist Party member Anita Platky in 1938. The couple adopted two daughters, Hannah (1943) and Kate (1945), and Hay attempted to live the dream of heterosexual domestic bliss—albeit one in which he frequented nearby Echo Park for sex with other men.

Hay chafed, however, at having to live a lie at home and in the Communist Party. He wrote several position papers in the late 1940s contending that homosexuals should be recognized as a minority group deserving acceptance and freedom from legal persecution; during this period he also fell in love with a man, designer Rudi Gernreich. In the summer of 1950 he started a relationship with Gernreich, and the two of them, along with friends Robert Hull, Charles Rowland, and Dale Jennings, organized weekly meetings to talk about their experiences as gay men. By 1951 word of the group had spread, and increasing numbers of gay men and a few lesbians began attending the meetings and forming new chapters. The Mattachine Society became more than a means of consciousness raising or a place to find comfort in a hostile culture (although it was both). Members sought to change legal, medical, and popular misconceptions and stereotypes about homosexuality; they strategized about ways to counter decades of vilification as well as current notions—put forward by U.S. Senator Joseph McCarthy, the House Committee on Un-American Activities (HUAC), and the armed forces—that LGBT people were not merely sick or criminal, but that they threatened the morale and safety of a nation locked in a cold war against communism.

Hay's rapturous involvement with and leadership in the Mattachine Society quickly propelled him to confess the truth to his wife of thirteen years. In September 1951 the couple divorced. That year he also made the heartrending decision to leave the Communist Party, for fear of bringing greater scrutiny and reprisals to an already besieged organization. Only two years later, Hay was forced out of the Mattachine Society after the proliferation of chapters across California led to infighting, shifting alliances, and changing goals (not to mention the rise of anticommunism within the organization). In 1955 Hay was called to testify before HUAC, which further alienated him from his homosexual activist counterparts. He sought refuge in a largely unfulfilling eleven-year relationship with a young Danish designer, Jorn Kamgren.

Hay's spirit of intellectual, spiritual, and political engagement was rekindled in the mid-1960s, when he fell in love with John Burnside, a UCLA-educated engineer and scientist who remained with Hay until his death. Together, they participated in post–Stonewall Riots activism by helping to found the Southern California Gay Liberation Front in 1969. The following year they moved to San Juan Pueblo in northern New Mexico, where they lived for more than a decade and forged bonds with many disparate LGBT student and political groups as well as individuals. Inspired in part by his years of immersion in Native American life and in part by his alienation from a gay culture that he saw as increasingly consumerist and superficial, in 1979 Hay and several of his friends began a loosely organized movement known as the Radical Faeries. For the next twenty-five years, the Faeries celebrated spirituality, ecology, and the uniqueness of male sexuality, at their own separate retreats as well as in gay pride marches and political demonstrations.

Harry Hay. The longtime activist, a member of the Communist Party for two decades, cofounded the Mattachine Society in 1951, the Southern California Gay Liberation Front in 1969, and the Radical Faeries in 1979. **[Daniel Nicoletta]**

Both the Mattachine Society and Radical Faeries operated on a central tenet of Harry Hay's: that homosexuality was inherently different from heterosexuality, and that homosexuals had a distinctive set of values and practices that deserved to be recognized, cherished, and celebrated. His ideas and his leadership influenced two generations of activists, and Hay became enshrined as an icon in the history and lore of the movement for LGBT equality.

Bibliography

D'Emilio, John. *Sexual Politics, Sexual Communities: The Making of a Homosexual Minority in the United States, 1940–1970.* Chicago: University of Chicago Press, 1983.

Roscoe, Will. *Radically Gay: Gay Liberation in the Words of Its Founder.* Boston: Beacon Press, 1996.

Timmons, Stuart. *The Trouble with Harry Hay: Founder of the Modern Gay Movement.* Boston: Alyson, 1990.

Stacy L. Braukman

See also ANARCHISM, COMMUNISM, AND SOCIALISM; HOMOPHILE MOVEMENT; MATTACHINE SOCIETY; POOR PEOPLE'S MOVEMENTS; RADICAL FAERIES.

HEALTH AND HEALTH CARE LAW AND POLICY

Health and health care laws and policies affecting U.S. LGBT people exist at multiple levels—local, state, federal, and international—and influence both public and private sectors. The health care system in the United States contains a mixture of private and public elements. Most Americans obtain health insurance through their private employers and most obtain health care through private providers. The state, however, regulates the private health care system, funds health care for particular groups (public sector employees, the elderly, the poor, members of the military, veterans, etc.), owns facilities such as public and veterans' hospitals, sponsors health-related research and development, coordinates health education programs, and maintains a variety of public health programs (including programs dealing with sexually-transmitted diseases). Health laws and policies guide agencies and associations in the organization and financing of services and resources relevant to the general population and to particular groups. While this is the allocative function of health laws and policies, the dogmatic function can be used to control and eradicate not only defined behavior but also the existence of specific groups.

Before 1967

Beginning in the late nineteenth century, homosexuality and transgenderism were conceptualized as illnesses (and specifically as mental illnesses) in the United States. This view, in combination with views of homosexuality and transgenderism as sinful and criminal, was the basis for a variety of health and health care laws and policies that damaged and discriminated against LGBT people. U.S. health law and policy was heterosexist and gender-normative in multiple ways. Rights, privileges, and benefits such as hospital visitation rights, rights to make medical decisions for incapacitated partners, health insurance benefits, and reproductive services, for example, were commonly granted to heterosexually married couples and denied to same-sex couples. Various laws, including statutes providing for the institutionalization of the mentally ill, indeterminate sentencing for sexual psychopaths, and the exclusion and deportation of immigrants with psychopathic personalities, used health-related justifications for discriminating against LGBT people. Moreover, many laws and policies permitted (and sometimes even required) the health care system to engage in violent, cruel, and sadistic practices (including castration, electroshock aversion therapy, and denial of sex-reassignment surgery) against LGBT people. Though countless LGBT Americans received adequate health care, they had good reason to fear and distrust health-related laws and policies in the United States.

Continuity and Change

In September 1967, the Director of the National Institute of Mental Health (NIMH), Dr. Stanley Yolles, appointed a Task Force on Homosexuality. The task force's final report, released in 1969, consisted of recommendations from the NIMH as well as seven background papers by "experts," including Evelyn Hooker, John Money, Judd Marmor, and Jerome Frank. Despite the content of the papers and their recommendations for the establishment of a Center for the Study of Sexual Behavior, much of the language in the report was quite contemptuous. For example, the report authors endorsed the goal of preventing homosexuality from developing within children and adolescents. As to treatment, the task force report condoned imprisonment and called for rehabilitative measures.

In 1969 the Stonewall Riots in New York City marked the beginning of a new wave of LGBT activism, which had major effects on conceptions of homosexuality and transgenderism as illnesses. In 1970 in San Francisco, LGBT activists protested and disrupted the meeting of the American Psychiatric Association (APA), contesting the labeling of homosexuality as a mental disorder in the Diagnostic and Statistical Manual (DSM) used by psychiatrists. At the next APA annual meeting in 1971 in Washington, D.C., a panel of gay men and lesbians was organized, but protests continued. At the 1972 APA convention in Dallas, Texas, organizers offered another panel addressing LGB issues. This panel included psychiatrist John Fryer, who wore a disguise for fear of losing his medical license. In 1973, the APA officially removed homosexuality from the DSM after researchers failed to demonstrate a link between same-sex behaviors and mental illness.

In the same year that homosexuality was removed from the DSM, however, a new diagnosis, gender dysphoria disorder, was constructed and officially added. This term was dropped from the DSM in 1987 because in the

U.S. almost all homosexuals first go through a phase in which homosexuality is distonic. The APA decision had major ramifications on LGBT health law and policy in the United States, although many statutes (e.g., immigration statutes) continued to rely on now-discredited links between homosexuality and mental illness, and LGBT people continued to be excluded from health-related policies restricted to married partners.

In the 1960s, 1970s, and 1980s, various national groups emerged that assisted in developing health policies and influencing legislation affecting LGBT people. These included the Sexuality Information and Education Council of the United States (1964); the Lesbian, Gay, Bisexual, and Transgender Caucus of Public Health Workers (1975); the National Association of Lesbian and Gay Addiction Professionals (1979); and the American Association of Physicians for Human Rights (1981), which changed its name to the Gay and Lesbian Medical Association in 1994. Various political and legal reform organizations, including the Human Rights Campaign Fund, Lambda Legal Defense, and the National Gay and Lesbian Task Force also lobbied policymakers on health issues affecting LGBT populations.

In 1979, the federal government began the *Healthy People* initiative, focusing on specific diseases and disorders that federal officials believed needed to be addressed and encouraging state and local communities to develop similar plans. The document is amended each decade. Not until *Healthy People 2010* did the U.S. Department of Health and Human Services officially identify LGB people as a subpopulation in the United States that experiences significant health disparities.

Marriage, Domestic Partnership, and Living Wills

Marriage, the legal union of two individuals, is a basic institution in American society. Although the state of Vermont has enacted a "civil unions" law for same-sex couples, no state currently permits same-sex marriage. Marriage not only symbolizes a couple's relationship, but also provides legal advantages—including health insurance coverage, hospital visitation rights, and medical decision-making powers—for partners. Without a legal mechanism to establish same-sex primary relationships, the ability to obtain health insurance for a partner can be restricted; the rights of a partner to visit an ill or dying spouse in the hospital can be denied; the right to make decisions for a medically incapacitated partner can fall on deaf ears; the power to determine long-term care needs for and maintain access to ill partners can be usurped by blood relatives; and the right to receive bereavement and caregiving leave can be restricted.

To address these and other problems, the term domestic partner was coined in San Francisco in the early 1980s. In various contexts, this designation gives LGBT partners legal standing comparable to marital partners. Over the last three decades, numerous private and public employers have adopted domestic partner benefits schemes, offering LGBT people some of the benefits of marriage. Domestic partners can receive various types of health-related benefits, including dependent life and disability insurance, pension benefits, adoption assistance and day-care, long-term care, bereavement and sick leave, and relocation expenses.

Another mechanism to deal with health-related discrimination is living wills. Living wills or advance directives provide written instructions for health care providers about individuals' preferences in the event that they are terminally ill or unable to respond for themselves. Since the law does not recognize same-sex couples, living wills are critical. In the absence of living wills, courts usually look to the closest biological family member to assist in making life-sustaining and other medical decisions. Such decisions have sometimes circumvented prior verbal communications among same-sex couples. Many legal advocates suggest that even with living wills LGBT individuals should notify in writing all health care providers of their medical directives and request that these instructions become part of all medical records. This additional step assists health care providers in becoming ombudspersons if biological family members attempt to negate living wills. In addition to arranging for living wills, many LGBT people now arrange for a durable power of attorney for health care or a surrogate medical decision-maker. This individual, whether a domestic partner, friend, or a biological family member, makes medical decisions on the patient's behalf when the individual is incapacitated. The durable power of attorney for health care, however, does not grant authority to withhold or withdraw treatment without a living will.

LGBT people have thus found various ways to promote equality in health care rights.

AIDS

Laws and policies related to the AIDS epidemic have affected LGBT people in significant ways in the last two decades. During the 1980s, for example, the U.S. Congress and the Reagan administration passed appropriation riders to AIDS funding bills that forbade funding for AIDS education programs that promoted or encouraged homosexuality. In 2003, the Bush administration is still promoting regulations that limit the ability for AIDS service organizations to promote health in general and LGBT health in particular. For example, information on sexual health was removed from government Web sites in an effort to promote abstinence as recently as 2003. The administration requires organizations to develop community review committees to review and tone down AIDS information that may be objectionable to conservative community leaders.

Congressional and administration conservatives have implemented internal policies to reject research and grant proposals based on key words related to sexual and gender minorities. Despite the sanctioned *Healthy People 2010 Companion Document on LGBT Health* that clearly documents the need for research and data collection related to LGBT health outcomes, little is being done by government agencies. There is a fear among conservatives that the outcomes of research will ultimately drive policy and create equality for LGBT people.

Government laws and policies have also permitted and sometimes sanctioned AIDS-based discrimination against LGBT people. Because of the AIDS epidemic's disproportionate impact on gay men, for example, some insurance underwriters categorize gay men as high-risk, thereby justifying increased insurance rates or rejection of coverage for men known to be gay, men working for LGBT organizations, unmarried men who live in particular geographic areas, and men who work in stereotypically gay professions. Current laws permit insurance carriers to require testing for HIV prior to issuing coverage. Profiling gay men as high-risk candidates for AIDS not only promotes prejudices and discrimination within this already marginalized community, but also ignores the changing demography of the epidemic.

AIDS-based discrimination continues to be a problem in the United States. With the passage of the Americans with Disabilities Act in 1990, many thought AIDS discrimination would end. However, conservative decisions by lower courts have lessened the applicability of the legislation to people living with AIDS. Lower court decisions still permit employment discrimination for people living with HIV and AIDS. In 1998, the Supreme Court ruled in a somewhat more inclusive manner by allowing employers to limit hiring individuals based on medical conditions. As of 2003, there were court cases being heard or that were pending related to providing HIV care and testing in prisons, discriminating in disability insurance, exposing others to HIV infection, evicting homeless men with HIV from shelters, disallowing men with HIV from becoming police officers, and limiting adoption to non-HIV individuals.

The Future

In response to the health concerns of LGBT populations, the Health and Resources Services Administration of the federal government provided federal funding in 2000 to the Gay and Lesbian Medical Association and Columbia University's Center for LGBT Health to coauthor a white paper titled *Lesbian, Gay, Bisexual, and Transgender Health: Findings and Concerns.* This paper and *Healthy People 2010* formed the foundation for the *Healthy People 2010 Companion Document for LGBT Health*, a momentous federally funded, community-written document that discusses issues, concerns, and recommendations for policy and research for LGBT populations. One critical byproduct of this effort was the formation of the National Coalition for LGBT Health, which advocates in the areas of health-care research, policy, and law.

Bibliography

Achtenberg, Roberta, ed. *Sexual Orientation and the Law.* New York: C. Bordman Co. 1991.

Bayer, Ronald. *Homosexuality and American Psychiatry: The Politics of Diagnosis.* Princeton, N.J.: Princeton University Press, 1987.

Cabaj, R. P., and T. S. Stein, eds. *Textbook of Homosexuality and Mental Health.* Washington, D.C.: American Psychiatric Press, Inc., 1996.

Cain, Patricia A. *Rainbow Rights.* Boulder, Colo.: Westview Press, 2000.

Editors of the Harvard Law Review. *Sexual Orientation and the Law.* Cambridge, Mass.: Harvard University Press, 1990.

Elisason, Michele J. *Who Cares? Institutional Barriers to Health Care for Lesbian, Gay, and Bisexual Persons.* New York: NLN Press, 1996.

Eskridge, William N., Jr. *GAYLAW: Challenging the Apartheid of the Closet.* Cambridge, Mass.: Harvard University Press, 1999.

———, and Nan D. Hunter. *Sexuality, Gender, and the Law.* Westbury, N.Y.: Foundation Press, 1997.

Gay and Lesbian Medical Association and LGBT Health Experts. *Healthy People 2010: Companion Document for Lesbian, Gay, Bisexual, and Transgender Health,* 2001.

Hunter, Nan D., Sherry E. Michaelson, and Thomas B. Stoddard, eds. *The Rights of Lesbians and Gay Men: The Basic ACLU Guide to a Person's Rights.* 3d ed. Carbondale: Southern Illinois University Press, 1992.

Livingood, J. M., ed. *Task Force on Homosexuality: Final Report and Background Papers, DHEW Pub. No. (HSM) 72-9119.* Rockville, MD: NIMH, 1972.

Meyerowitz, Joanne. *How Sex Changed: A History of Transsexuality in the United States.* Cambridge, Mass.: Harvard University Press, 2002.

U.S. Department of Health and Human Services. *Healthy People 2010.* 2d ed. With Understanding and Improving

Health and Objectives for Improving Health, 2 volumes, Washington, D.C.: Government Printing Office, 2000.

Rodger L. Beatty, Michael D. Shankle, Nancy J. Kennedy

See also AIDS AND PEOPLE WITH AIDS; ANTI-DISCRIMINATION LAW AND POLICY; DISCRIMINATION; EMPLOYMENT LAW AND POLICY; FAMILY LAW AND POLICY; FEDERAL LAW AND POLICY; HEALTH, HEALTH CARE, AND HEALTH CLINICS; IMMIGRATION, ASYLUM, AND DEPORTATION LAW AND POLICY; SEXUALLY-TRANSMITTED DISEASES; TRANSGENDER AND GENDER IMPERSONATION LAW AND POLICY.

HEALTH, HEALTH CARE, AND HEALTH CLINICS

LGBT communities are highly diverse in terms of sex, gender, age, race, ethnicity, religion, class, nationality, and citizenship, and all of these factors affect health and health care. Moreover, despite common concerns about health, these four communities also have different health needs and agendas.

LGBT persons have many of the same health needs and concerns that all other members of society have, but they also have additional needs. For example, while many youth experiment with alcohol or drugs and need education to prevent (or treat) addictions and related health problems, sexual minority youth tend to use drugs more frequently. If this is because being LGBT places these youth under extraordinary social pressures or encourages them to join social networks where drugs are more available and attractive to use, distinct types of health education are needed. To take another example, many menopausal women must decide about the risks and benefits of taking estrogen, but many male-to-female transgender women of any age worry about the risks of *not* taking estrogen. Successful LGBT health policy requires attention to these and many other distinctive aspects of LGBT health.

LGBT Health Issues

An increasing body of research suggests that health disparities exist between LGBT people and their non-LGBT counterparts. However, most of this evidence comes from small descriptive studies. More evidence needs to be gathered about the general health of transgender people, partially because that group is so internally diverse.

Two publications synthesize much of the existing literature and research on LGBT health. *LGBT Health: Findings and Concerns* and *Healthy People 2010: Companion Document for Lesbian, Gay, Bisexual, and Transgender (LGBT) Health* provide evidence of what is known and what is unknown. The former was written by members of the Center for Lesbian, Gay, Bisexual, and Transgender Health at Columbia University. Members of the Gay and Lesbian Medical Association, in collaboration with other LGBT individuals and organizations, developed the *Companion Document*. The group responsible for the *Companion Document* then evolved into the National Coalition for LGBT Health.

Healthy People 2010 proposes a national agenda for promoting the health of all people in the United States. Its goals are to increase the quality and quantity of healthy life and to eliminate health disparities between groups—specifically racial and ethnic majority and minority groups. The *Companion Document* demonstrates that sexual and gender minority groups must also be considered a priority.

Among their various health issues, lesbians report being most concerned about cancer and want greater access to cancer screening. Lesbians desire improved cancer screening in part because of their understanding that they may be at increased risk for breast cancer due to such factors as lack of pregnancy, obesity, and use of alcohol. Lesbians may also be at increased risk of developing cervical cancer, primarily because of the false belief, common among lesbians and health care providers alike, that lesbians do not need Pap smears. If lesbians are not screened regularly, the disease may be diagnosed later, with less likelihood of effective treatment.

Gay men have been at high risk for HIV and other sexually transmitted diseases, and the risk seems to be rising. Persons with HIV are also at greater risk for opportunistic infections, and gay men appear to be at higher risk for anal cancer.

Bisexual men and women have higher rates of sexually transmitted infections (STIs) than lesbians, gay men, or heterosexuals. This is probably because they have higher average numbers of sexual partners, but studies also suggest that bisexuals do not perceive themselves to be at higher risk for STIs.

Health care issues for transgender persons include obtaining hormones and surgeries. Female to male transsexuals may minimize their risk of developing cancers of the breast, cervix, or ovary if they have those organs removed, but there are also various risks associated with taking androgen hormones.

Many LGBT people share various mental health problems related to the stresses of living in a society in which heterosexism is the norm and discrimination and violence are all too common. Transgender persons often must be diagnosed as having Gender Identity Disorder to receive care, which, some have argued, may lead them to strategically feign symptoms in order to be considered eligible for surgery. LGBT people with serious mental illnesses may experience discrimination both from society in general and from within LGBT communities. There is now a growing LGBT mental health care consumer/survivor movement in the United States working to build acceptance and affirmation of LGBT people with psychiatric illnesses.

Although the evidence is conflicting, there is a common perception that lesbians and gay men are more likely to use alcohol and drugs and to smoke cigarettes than heterosexual people are. Evidence suggests that use is higher in younger people and decreases with age. Many LGBT people are also in recovery from addictions.

Intimate partner violence is also a problem among LGBT people. Rates appear to be similar to those for heterosexual or bisexual couples, but abused lesbians and gay men may be less likely to seek help than heterosexual women.

Members of all LGBT groups confront issues related to parenting. They may have children from former marriages or relationships or they may want to have children in their current life situations. Although issues related to the bearing of children differ among diverse LGBT groups, fostering and adoption issues may be similar. Both state regulations and individual health care providers can make parenting difficult for LGBT people. Lesbians may not have access to sperm banks, and same-sex partners may not be able to adopt children. Any non-heterosexual parents may rightly fear the loss of their children through custody battles.

Aging is also a significant health issue for LGBT people. Older LGBT people, for example, worry about being alone in an environment, such as a nursing home, that pays no attention to minority sexualities and genders.

Barriers to Health Care

What LGBT people have most in common in the area of health is the difficulty of accessing quality health care. Barriers to health care result from homophobia, transphobia, and heterosexism in society, the hostility and ignorance of health care providers, and the attitudes and behaviors of LGBT people themselves.

Perhaps the most common barrier to adequate health care for LGBT people is the assumption by health care providers that all people are heterosexual. For example, the assumption that a woman without a male partner is not sexually active can have dangerous consequences. Health care providers may also treat clients in a homophobic or transphobic manner, using harsh or rude language and behavior, avoiding LGBT clients, or manifesting hostility in interactions.

Another problem among health care providers is the lack of knowledge most have about providing care to LGBT people. This is because professional education for doctors, nurses, psychologists, and social workers has been extremely limited with respect to LGBT health. In addition, conventional medical science requires research or best evidence as the basis for care. Because there has been very little non-homophobic or transphobic research on LGBT health, providers do not have sufficient evidence and can thus feel inadequately prepared to deal with sexual and gender minority clients.

Barriers to quality health care originating within LGBT persons themselves relate primarily to fear. Many LGBT people are afraid to disclose their identity as LGBT to health care providers, because they expect negative and homophobic responses that will severely affect the kind of health care they receive.

Disclosure by LGBT people has been increasing, however, though there is evidence that men disclose more readily than women do. There are three types of disclosure: Planned, or active, disclosure is when an individual consciously decides, prior to a health care visit, to "come out" to the provider. This allows the person to plan for possible reactions from the provider. Passive disclosure is when a LGBT person assumes, on the basis of their health history or personal characteristics, that the provider knows she or he is a member of a sexual or gender minority. In this case the LGBT person does nothing to affirm or deny that presumed assumption. Finally, there is unplanned disclosure. In this case the individual either actively decides not to disclose or has not even considered the possibility, but something occurs during the health care interaction that causes the individual to believe that disclosure is necessary. Unplanned disclosure can cause a person to feel very unsafe.

Another major barrier to access for LGBT people is financial. Individuals may lack health care insurance or other health coverage because they are not covered under a partner's policy or they may be employed in jobs that do not provide coverage, or they may be unemployed.

Interactions between health care providers and LGBT people affect care-seeking behaviors. Negative expectations can result from an individual's bad experience and may cause a person to never seek health care again. Hearing that someone else has had a bad experience can also prevent an individual from seeking needed health care.

The AIDS crisis has both helped and hindered access to care for LGBT people. When health care providers could not avoid the large numbers of gay men who needed care or were dying, attitudes and knowledge did improve. However, with that came what has been called "AIDS stigma," in which health care providers assume that all gay men, and often lesbians too, are HIV-positive. Even as that attitude has modified, LGBT people often continue to be treated as groups always at risk.

Health Alternatives

One response to lack of access to and poor interactions with health care providers has been to seek care outside of the mainstream health care system. One source of alternative care is providers of what is known as complementary and alternative medicine (CAM). CAM providers, such as massage therapists, acupuncturists, herbalists, and naturopaths, are believed to be more holistic in their approaches and more open to diverse clients. Consequently, reportedly large numbers of sexual and gender minorities seek care from these kinds of providers.

But an even more important result of lack of access to care is the creation by LGBT people of their own health care clinics and support groups as a safe alternative to mainstream health care. Beginning in the 1970s, LGBT people, both health care providers and activists from outside the medical profession, opened clinics to meet needs that were not being met in the mainstream health care delivery system. In so doing, they put themselves at the center of care, rather than at the margins of mainstream health care systems.

LGBT health services or clinics opened in several major cities in the 1970s. One principal service they offered was confidential screening (with or without treatment) for STIs, especially for gay men. Howard Brown Health Center, in Chicago, began in 1971 with that mission, as did the Whitman-Walker Clinic in Washington, D.C., in 1978. These and other centers are thriving today as providers of care to persons with HIV/AIDS. The Fenway Community Health Center, in Boston, opened in 1971 as a grassroots neighborhood health clinic. It is now a model for providing comprehensive health services to LGBT people.

In the lesbian community, a whole network of lesbian (or women's) clinics and support groups developed in the 1970s. Lyon-Martin Women's Health Services, in San Francisco, opened in 1979 as a free-standing clinic, specifically to meet the needs of lesbians who were not accessing mainstream health care because of fears of discrimination. An all-volunteer, all-woman staff provided care. The clinic has expanded to provide a variety of primary care and other services for all women, but especially lesbians, women of color, poor women, and transgender women.

Following the onset of the HIV epidemic, the need for alternative clinics was even greater, since gay men were being diagnosed with HIV at incredibly high rates, and mainstream health care was very homophobic. Existing clinics expanded their services to include HIV treatment, and new clinics opened. In addition, the HIV epidemic motivated LGBT people to pioneer important sex education and safer sex programs and campaigns for sexual and gender minorities and others.

More recently, LGBT people have recognized the need to work together to improve their health and the delivery of health care. In 1996–1997 the Mary-Helen Mautner Project for Lesbians with Cancer in Washington, D.C., with funding from the Centers for Disease Control and Prevention, developed a curriculum for educating health care professionals about providing culturally competent care to lesbians. The curriculum is to be implemented nationwide. In Chicago, the first city in the United States to mandate cultural competency training for city health workers, the Lesbian Community Cancer Project collaborated with the Chicago Department of Public Health's Office of Lesbian and Gay Health to train staff at all Chicago Public Health Clinics.

Finally, in October 2000, the National Coalition of LGBT Health was founded to work for the improvement of LGBT health and health care. More than forty-five agencies and organizations have committed to working together. Their first national conference was held in August 2002 with more than 300 persons in attendance. At the dawn of a new millennium, the future appears promising.

Bibliography

Claes, Jacalyn A., and Wayne Moore. "Issues Confronting Lesbian and Gay Elders: The Challenge for Health and Human Services Providers." *Journal of Health and Human Services Administration* 23 (2000): 181–202.

Dean, Laura, et al. "Lesbian, Gay, Bisexual, and Transgender Health: Findings and Concerns." *Journal of the Gay and Lesbian Medical Association* 4 (2000): 101–151.

Eliason, Michele J., and Robert Schope. "Does 'Don't Ask Don't Tell' Apply to Health Care: Lesbian, Gay, and Bisexual People's Disclosure to Health Care Providers." *Journal of the Gay and Lesbian Medical Association* 5 (2001): 125–134.

Gay and Lesbian Medical Association. "Healthy People 2010: Companion Document for Lesbian, Gay, Bisexual, and Transgender (LGBT) Health." Available from http://www.lgbthealth.net.

Klitzman, Robert L., and Jason D. Greenberg. "Patterns of Communication between Gay and Lesbian Patients and Their Health Care Providers." *Journal of Homosexuality* 42 (2002): 65–75.

Meyer, Ilan H. "Why Lesbian, Gay, Bisexual, and Transgender Public Health?" *American Journal of Public Health* 91 (2001): 856–859.

Oriel, Kathleen A. "Medical Care of Transsexual Patients." *Journal of the Gay and Lesbian Medical Association* 4 (2000): 185–194.

Ponticelli, Christy M., ed. *Gateways to Improving Lesbian Health and Health Care: Opening Doors.* New York: Haworth, 1998.

Schilder, Arn J., et al. "'Being Dealt With as a Whole Person': Care Seeking and Adherence: The Benefits of Culturally Competent Care." *Social Science and Medicine* 52 (2001): 1643–1659.

Solarz, Andrea L., ed. *Lesbian Health: Current Assessment and Directions for the Future.* Washington, D.C.: National Academy Press, 1999.

Stevens, Patricia E., and Sarah Morgan. "Health of LGBT Youth." *Journal of Child and Family Nursing* 2 (1999): 237–249.

Linda A. Bernhard

See also AIDS AND PEOPLE WITH AIDS; AIDS SERVICE ORGANIZATIONS; ALCOHOL AND DRUGS; GYMS, FITNESS CLUBS, AND HEALTH CLUBS; HEALTH AND HEALTH CARE LAW AND POLICY; MEDICINE, MEDICALIZATION, AND THE MEDICAL MODEL; PSYCHOLOGY, PSYCHIATRY, PSYCHOANALYSIS, AND SEXOLOGY; PSYCHOTHERAPY, COUNSELING, AND RECOVERY PROGRAMS; SEXUALLY TRANSMITTED DISEASES.

HEAP, JANE. see ANDERSON, MARGARET, AND JANE HEAP.

HEMPHILL, Essex **(b. 16 April 1957; d. 4 November 1995), writer, performer, activist.**

Essex Hemphill was arguably the most talented and most critically successful black gay male poet to emerge after the Harlem Renaissance of the 1920s. Born in Chicago, Illinois, as the second of five children, he was raised in southeast Washington, D.C., where he began to write poetry at the age of fourteen. He briefly attended the University of Maryland at College Park but left before receiving a degree. During the late 1970s and early 1980s, Hemphill became a prominent member of the quickly developing community of black LGBT artists and intellectuals in Washington, D.C., a community that included filmmaker Michelle Parkeson, activists Gil Gerald and Louis Hughes, and musician Wayson Jones. Washington was also visited often by the likes of black lesbian critic Barbara Smith, writer and editor Joseph Beam, and poet Pat Parker. Indeed, "Chocolate City," as it was often called, was for a time the recognized center of black LGBT cultural and political activity in the United States, housing the now defunct National Coalition of Black Lesbian and Gays as well as several black lesbian and gay businesses and local civic organizations.

With Wayson Jones, Hemphill started to present his poetry at various venues in the city, eventually developing a style that built upon the aesthetics of the black arts movement of the 1960s and 1970s. Like that earlier generation of poets, Hemphill stressed the idea that poetry should be performed, even sang, in order to reach the masses of black and LGBT people. Hemphill's highly rhythmic, jazz-influenced poetry and performance soon captivated audiences in Washington and elsewhere. Many saw him as not only one of the very first writers to portray the reality of black and LGBT experience without apology but also one of the finest technicians of contemporary American poetry. As comfortable with black American vernacular traditions as with classical poetic forms, Hemphill was able to portray to his audiences—black, LGBT and otherwise—that the everyday reality of their lives was, in fact, the substance of which poetry is made.

Self-publishing his first two collections of poetry, *Earth Life* (1985) and *Conditions* (1986), Hemphill first came to national attention when his work appeared in the 1986 collection of black gay male writers *In the Life*, edited by Joseph Beam. That same year Hemphill received a poetry fellowship from the National Endowment for the Arts. He soon became something of a cult figure when in 1989 he was featured in two films by black gay directors, *Tongues Untied* by Marlon Riggs and *Looking for Langston* by Isaac Julien. Hemphill's star status among American poets continued to develop as he read and lectured at, among other places, Harvard University, Yale University, the University of Pennsylvania, the Massachusetts Institute of Technology, the University of California at Los Angeles, the City University of New York, the Folger Shakespeare Library, and the Whitney Museum, as well as a host of LGBT venues. Honoring the memory of Joseph Beam, who died in 1988, Hemphill moved to Philadelphia and continued the work that Beam had begun on a second collection of black gay male writers. When *Brother to Brother: New Writings by Black Gay Men* was published by Alyson Publications in 1991, Hemphill became the undisputed leader of an emergent black gay male arts community. The following year, Hemphill published his first work with a major press, *Ceremonies: Poetry and Prose*, for which he won the National Library Association's Gay, Lesbian and Bisexual New Writer's Award.

In this work Hemphill demonstrates with absolute clarity that the work of the intellectual is necessarily both aesthetic and political. He treats topics such as AIDS, racial stereotyping, homophobia in the black community, and the pleasures of sex with a precision and delicacy that is, at times, breathtaking. In 1993 his contributions to American arts and letters were further recognized when he became a visiting fellow at the Getty Center for the History of Art and Humanities in Santa Monica, California.

During the last years of his life, Hemphill continued to speak out with great courage and poise about racism, both inside and outside the LGBT community, and homophobia, both inside and outside the black American community. He also pointed out, however, the ways in which AIDS was ravaging both communities. Strangers and friends alike will remember the phrase that Hemphill repeated whenever he took his leave, "Take care of your blessings." Essex Hemphill died in November 1995 in Philadelphia from complications related to HIV. He was thirty-eight.

Bibliography

Hemphill, Essex. *Earth Life: Poems.* Washington, D.C.: Be Bop, 1985.

———. *Conditions: Poems.* Washington, D.C.: Be Bop, 1986.

———. *Ceremonies: Prose and Poetry.* 2d ed. San Francisco: Cleis Press, 2000.

Robert Reid-Pharr

See also BEAM, JOSEPH; LITERATURE; RIGGS, MARLON.

HENRY, George (b. 13 June 1889; d. 23 May 1964), psychiatrist.

George W. Henry was an American psychiatrist who specialized in the study and treatment of homosexuality. He grew up in Oswego, New York, and received his bachelor's degree from Wesleyan University in 1912 and his medical degree from Johns Hopkins University in 1916. Henry was on the psychiatric staff of New York Hospital from 1918 through 1954 and held a professorship of psychiatry at the Cornell Medical School from 1930 through 1957. Beginning in the 1930s, he also conducted a private practice in New York City and in 1942 his association with New York Hospital became part time.

Henry's first study of homosexuality was published in 1933; using a sample of psychiatric patients, it dealt with the constitutional etiology of homosexuality. The following year he was invited by the Committee for the Study of Sex Variants to become a member and direct a research project on homosexuality. Robert Latou Dickinson, a gynecologist and sex researcher, founded the interdisciplinary committee in 1935. Henry's former teacher at Johns Hopkins, Adolf Meyer, was one of the committee organizers. The impetus for creating a committee devoted to research on homosexuality stemmed from a study launched by Jan Gay, a lesbian activist-researcher who approached Dickinson so she could obtain the medical sponsorship she needed to publish her work. Gay, whose real name was Helen Reitman (daughter of medical reformer Ben L. Reitman), was a widely traveled writer and language translator who, in the 1920s, visited Magnus Hirschfeld's Institute for Sexual Science in Berlin. At the institute, she learned how to conduct a survey on sexuality, which inspired her to carry out an ambitious investigation based on interviewing three hundred lesbians in Berlin, Paris, London, and New York City. At Dickinson's suggestion, Gay agreed to focus her study on a new sample of lesbians in New York City as well as a sample of homosexual men from that city. It was this research project, known as the sex variants study, that Henry was invited to direct.

Gay was employed as Henry's research assistant and was responsible for recruiting the sex variants sample and obtaining personal and family histories. Henry then conducted in-depth interviews, which were actually based on Gay's original set of questions. Over two hundred women and men volunteered to be in the study. From this sample, Henry selected a subset of forty women and forty men to constitute the case studies in his 1941 two-volume *Sex Variants: A Study of Homosexual Patterns.* These individuals were selected, according to Henry, because they were especially informative in their interviews. Henry made no reference to Gay's original manuscript and role in conceiving and initiating the research project. Gay's activist legacy, however, lives through the voices of the research participants, which are preserved in the publication of the sex variants monograph. Each case study contains the participant's autobiographical account in his or her own words, followed up by Henry's psychiatric analysis. Despite Henry's conventional template of pathologizing homosexuality, the sex variants monograph reveals the self-determination of LGBT lives as experienced in the 1930s.

Henry's association with the sex variants committee also led to a collaborative relationship with Alfred A.

Gross, a gay defrocked Episcopalian priest. As a result of his church dismissal, Gross became a private patient of Henry's in 1937. At Henry's suggestion, Gross agreed to work as his research assistant. Initially sponsored by the sex variants committee, Henry and Gross engaged in a series of research studies on male homosexual sex offenders. Like Gay, Gross recruited and conducted preliminary interviews with the research participants. Gross, however, was more adept than Gay in ensuring that his work with Henry would be acknowledged. In several published articles in the late 1930s and early 1940s Gross received co-authorship.

During World War II, Henry, officially, and Gross, unofficially, played a major role in New York City in screening inductees for homosexuality in the wartime draft. Under Henry's authorization, Gross conducted the screening interviews and thus provided the basis for decisions that disqualified men for military service. Gross's interviews were also aimed at adding to the case history database of Henry's research. When Henry published his popular version of the sex variants monograph in 1955, titled *All the Sexes,* he incorporated the selective service cases as part of his analysis.

After the war, Henry was approached by a group of Quakers to work with them in organizing a social agency devoted to helping young men arrested on charges of homosexual behavior. In 1946 the Civil Readjustment Committee was established with Henry as chief psychiatrist and Gross as executive secretary. It was Gross who administered the day-to-day operations and conducted the necessary liaisons with the legal and social service system. In 1947 the Quakers withdrew their sponsorship and Gross took the initiative in organizing a new committee in the form of a nonprofit foundation, named the George W. Henry Foundation. Gross's role as the foundation's creator reflected the increasingly dominant position he played in his association with Henry. Henry provided the stamp of authority and the cloak of respectability needed for helping a stigmatized population. Gross continued to function as the executive he had been for the Quaker committee as well as the ghostwriter of many of Henry's official reports. The Henry Foundation generally operated as an effective safety net for young men in legal trouble during the postwar era. Henry continued as chief psychiatrist until his death in 1964. In 1972, with the arrival of the gay liberation movement and Gross's death, the Henry Foundation had outlived its paternalistic function and was dissolved.

Henry's official contribution to the study and treatment of homosexuality masks and distorts the pioneering work of lesbian activist Jan Gay and gay activist Alfred Gross. While Henry espoused the medical model of homosexuality, he should nevertheless be given credit for his consistent call for social tolerance and understanding with regard to homosexuality, a position in contrast with the intemperate and hostile attitudes toward homosexuals often expressed by his fellow psychiatrists.

Bibliography

Bayer, Ronald. *Homosexuality and American Psychiatry: The Politics of Diagnosis.* New York: Basic Books, 1981.

Minton, Henry L. *Departing from Deviance: A History of Homosexual Rights and Emancipatory Science in America.* Chicago: University of Chicago Press, 2002.

Rosario, Vernon A. *Homosexuality and Science: A Guide to the Debates.* Santa Barbara, California: ABC-CLIO, 2002.

Terry, Jennifer. *An American Obsession: Science, Medicine, and Homosexuality in Modern Society.* Chicago: University of Chicago Press, 1999.

Henry L. Minton

See also MEDICINE, MEDICALIZATION, AND THE MEDICAL MODEL; MILITARY LAW AND POLICY; PSYCHOLOGY, PSYCHIATRY, PSYCHOANALYSIS, AND SEXOLOGY.

HETEROSEXISM AND HOMOPHOBIA

Heterosexism is often defined as a prejudice or bias in favor of heterosexuality as the norm over and against homosexuality. Such intolerance is primarily understood in relation to gay and lesbian people. However, the term can also be used to describe attitudes against bisexual, transgender, and queer individuals. Some heterosexual people who do not model traditional standards of masculinity, femininity, and heterosexuality also experience the effects of heterosexism. As far as can be determined, the term heterosexism first appeared in a paper titled "Articulation of Bias" delivered to the National Council of Teachers of English in San Francisco in 1979 by the American linguist and English professor Julia Penelope (b. 1941). Penelope declared, "Heterosexism designates, in particular, those central social structures which proscribe heterosexuality as the only 'natural' sexual interest." (p. 1). In the same year *Ms.* magazine used the word heterosexist to designate and criticize analysis that assumes a heterosexual perspective (Jan., p. 4). In 1986, *Time* magazine used the term in relation to religious teachings: "Radical homosexual groups . . . place homosexuality and heterosexuality on equal footing and denounce the church's traditional teaching as 'heterosexist'" (Dec., p. 17).

Heterosexism includes informal and institutionalized sets of beliefs and practices that assume, favor, or even mandate heterosexuality. Heterosexuality is a modern sociopolitical institution that restricts the expression of sexuality to relationships between a man and woman and privileges monogamous, married couples with children. Monique Wittig claims in *The Straight Mind* that heterosexism is the enforcement of the heterosexual political regime. As such, heterosexism is evident within a number of domains, including families, the workplace, religion, politics, the media, schools, and of course, sexualities.

While the term heterosexism was coined fairly recently, the more familiar designation of homophobia was first used in 1920 in a reference that described feelings of fear in *Chambers's Journal* (June 5, p. 418). The term homophobia became more widely known after 1969 when *Time* magazine stated, "Such homophobia is based on understandable instincts among straight people, but it also involves innumerable misconceptions and oversimplifications." (Oct. 31, p. 61). George Weinberg referred to psychological aspects of homophobia in 1972 in *Society and the Healthy Homosexual*. As commonly used today, homophobia is extreme and irrational aversion, fear, or contempt of homosexuality and homosexuals. In a narrower sense, it can be defined as a phobia about homosexuality and homosexuals. Behaviors based on such feelings may be described as homophobic. Homophobic acts are sometimes interpreted as only fear based reactions to the unknown. However the intensity of the vio lence generated from homophobia suggests otherwise.

The related term, biphobia, refers to fear of bisexuals. Transphobia is the fear of transgender people. There are debates within the transgender community about the extent and effects of homophobia. Transgender people are frequent targets of violence, but it is often difficult to determine if attackers are provoked by what they assume to be a sexual abnormality or a gender violation. Considering the strong link between gender and sexuality, it is likely that any deviation from the heterosexual norm is perceived as a threat. Transphobia is exhibited within LGB communities, biphobia within LGT communities, and homophobia within trans and bi communities.

Both heterosexism and homophobia can be placed on a continuum of individual and social anti-LGBT feelings. Both terms suggest that heterosexuality is inherently normal and thus superior. However, heterosexism can sometimes be the result of careless or unthinking acts often based on ignorance whereas homophobia refers to intentional thoughts, acts, or strategies by particular individuals or institutions against LGBT people.

Expressions of Heterosexism and Homophobia

Heterosexism is evident in the automatic assumption that everyone is straight or heterosexual unless named as otherwise. Examples of heterosexism include the expectations that families should be based on the sexual union of a man and a woman and that all normal adults should marry a person of the opposite sex. Additional examples include forcing people to indicate that they are married or single on bureaucratic forms, assuming an absence of eroticism in single-sex environments or presuming that if a LGBT person of the same sex or gender shows friendliness, she or he is making a sexual advance. Heterosexism is also evident in reacting negatively to public displays of affection between men and between women, but accepting the same displays from heterosexual partners.

Examples of homophobia include verbal assaults, physical attacks, the removal of children from LGBT parents, and overt discrimination in housing, health care, employment, taxes, pensions, and immigration. In the United States homophobic acts or gay bashing in the form of intentional violence against gay men and lesbians is reflected in the 1978 assassination of San Francisco supervisor Harvey Milk and in the 1998 lynching of University of Wyoming student Matthew Shepard. Shepard's attackers savagely beat him, then tied him to a split-rail fence on a deserted road in Wyoming and left him to die. In 1987 the U.S. Department of Justice reported that homosexuals were the most frequent victims of hate violence. Studies also show that LGBT people of color are at an increased risk of attack as potential objects of both racist and homophobic violence.

Explanations for Heterosexism and Homophobia

Like racism and sexism, homophobia and heterosexism are complex social prejudices. Within current social, economic, and political systems, if sexuality is to be accepted at all, it must be located within a relationship between a man and a woman, and most preferably within a traditional marriage. From this perspective, sexualities of LGBT people seem inappropriate and offensive. The boundaries of culturally approved forms of sexuality are clearly challenged by homosexuality, adultery, prostitution, and pederasty. Homophobia and heterosexism are attempts to restrain and reform LGBT people and movements in support of a purely heterosexual lifestyle as reflected in the conventional nuclear family.

Scholars have explored many possible explanations for homophobia and heterosexism. Some argue that they are the products of the internal psychological repression of same-sex desire that all straight-identified people enact. In other words, homophobia and heterosexism are generated by straight people who respond negatively to their own same-sex desires. Others link heterosexism and homophobia to an antisexual culture that is particularly suspicious of forms of sexual expression oriented to pleasure rather than reproduction and linked with oral and anal erogenous zones (in addition to vaginal and phallic ones). Still others see homophobia and heterosexism as rooted in capitalist systems that benefit most from individuals who live and work within traditional heterosexual nuclear families. One of the more influential schools of thought is that homophobia and heterosexism are best explained with reference to the needs of straight men and patriarchal structures, which gain from anything that keeps women tied to men, keeps men linked with masculinity and women linked with femininity, and keeps homosocial relations between men free from the dynamics of homoeroticism.

Many recent theorists have emphasized the ways in which LGBT genders and sexualities challenge traditional categories of sex, gender, and sexuality. According to queer theorist Judith Butler in *Gender Trouble*, the diversity of genders and sexualities made known through LGBT people suggests that traditional boundaries of sex, gender, and sexuality may be more fluid and not as rigid as previously assumed. Homophobia and heterosexism police these boundaries to prevent the dominant order from breaking down.

Another recent emphasis in interpretations of homophobia and heterosexism emphasizes intersections of gender and sexuality with race, class, and colonization. As Patricia Hill Collins points out in *Black Feminist Thought* (p. 126–127), for example, black lesbians' work on homophobia investigates how heterosexism's impact on African American women remains embedded in larger social structures. Homophobia, then, is understood as one part of a historically specific matrix within simultaneous systems of domination related to race, class, gender, and sexuality. Heterosexism and homophobia are also embedded in colonization. Paula Gunn Allen claims in *The Sacred Hoop* (p. 198), for instance, that for Native Americans homophobia has steadily increased as a result of colonization by Europeans and Euro-Americans and the internalization of Christian capitalist values in place of traditional tribal ones.

Still others who have sought to understand the roots of homophobia and heterosexism emphasize the interests and ideas of particular professional and occupational groups, including religious, scientific, and legal/political elites. The religious stances of many mainline Christian denominations have been particularly influential in shaping perspectives on homosexuality. Homosexuality is one of the most divisive issues in churches today. According to some Christians, but not all, the Bible clearly indicates that homosexual acts are sinful, unnatural, and immoral. However, religious scholars such as Mark Jordan, J. Michael Clark, and Elizabeth Stuart call for a restructuring of Christian sexual ethics that counters traditional morality and literal Biblical interpretations in favor of a multifaceted approach. Analyses of Biblical passages are considered in relation to contemporary cultural interpretations of homosexuality. This requires the reassessment of heterosexist attitudes and overzealous religious reactions in response to LGBT people. Medical and scientific elites have also contributed greatly to homophobia and heterosexism. Until 1973 the American Psychiatric Association (APA) considered homosexuality to be a form of mental illness. Counseling and psychiatric services were offered to LGB people to overcome these disorders. Many people continue to hold to this belief. Some medical practitioners and clinicians offer treatments intended to cure lesbians and gays of their "affliction." Nevertheless, the official APA position has changed dramatically.

Internalized Homophobia

Living within a climate of discrimination and hostility is very difficult for LGB people. Many live in a continual state of fear of others learning of their sexuality. This fear and the heterosexist expectations that become ingrained and rooted within LGB people can produce feelings of "internalized homophobia." Internalized homophobia is a form of self-judgment, self-hate, and self-loathing that results from the absorption of attitudes of cultural oppression and prejudice against LGBT people. When the norms of society suggest that alternative sexualities are unacceptable, LGBT people must continually formulate their own sense of themselves in the face of this discrimination. This process involves a continual "coming out" process to the self while reconciling family, peer, and religious expectations alongside personal experiences.

According to J. Michael Clark in *Defying the Darkness*, the difficult task for LGBT people in responding to heterosexism and homophobia is in the daily battle with the demons of low self-esteem. Clark declares that LGBT people must learn to purge their bodies of internalized homophobia while reconstructing their lives as assertive, unapologetic, and self-affirming in relationship with each other (p. 50). Mary Hunt, a lesbian feminist theologian, suggests in *Fierce Tenderness* that culturally embedded homophobia affects same-sex friendships. For example, it prevents men from developing deeply intimate or physically affectionate friendships with each other; and it sometimes prevents the development of even the minimal amount of self-love necessary to enter into a true friendship. LGBT people often live with the effects of internalized homophobia while trying to claim their lives and relationships as whole.

Responses to Heterosexism and Homophobia

LGBT people challenge heterosexism and homophobia by lobbying for rights through the legalization of marriage and availability of health care and other benefits for partners and children. LGBT groups, individuals, and allies provide education within religious forums and public schools regarding the discrimination and violence still evident in society. For example, with the assistance of LGBT religious groups like those within the Welcoming movement, many churches are claiming open and affirming stances that welcome all people. Gay and straight alliance groups offer programs for teachers, counselors, and healthcare professionals, and curriculum that includes LGBT subjects is being developed for use in school classrooms. Heterosexism and homophobia will be overcome when the legal recognition already constitutionally guaranteed to all individuals in the U.S. is extended to LGBT people.

Bibliography

Allen, Paula Gunn. *The Sacred Hoop: Recovering the Feminine in American Indian Traditions.* Boston: Beacon Press, 1992.

Butler, Judith. *Gender Trouble: Feminism and the Subversion of Identity.* New York: Routledge, 1999.

Clark, J. Michael. *Defying the Darkness: Gay Theology in the Shadows.* Cleveland, Ohio: Pilgrim Press, 1997.

Collins, Patricia Hill. *Black Feminist Thought: Knowledge, Consciousness, and the Politics of Empowerment.* New York: Routledge, 2000.

Foucault, Michel. *The History of Sexuality,* Volume 1. New York: Vintage Books, 1980.

Hunt, Mary E. *Fierce Tenderness: A Feminist Theology of Friendship.* New York: Crossroad, 1991.

Mollenkott, Virginia R. *Omnigender: A Trans-Religious Approach.* Cleveland, Ohio: Pilgrim Press, 2001.

Penelope, Julia. "Articulation of Bias: Hoof and Mouth Disease." Paper presented at the annual meeting of the National Council of Teachers, San Francisco, California, November 22–24, 1979. Education Resources Information Center, 79998.

Rich, Adrienne. "Compulsory Heterosexuality and Lesbian Existence." *Signs: Journal of Women in Culture and Society* 5 (1980): 631–660.

Ruether, Rosemary Radford. "Homophobia, Heterosexism, and Pastoral Practice." In *Homosexuality in the Priesthood and the Religious Life.* Edited by Jeannine Gramick. New York: Crossroad, 1989.

Sedgwick, Eve Kosofsky. *Epistemology of the Closet.* Berkeley: University of California Press, 1994.

Wittig, Monique. *The Straight Mind and Other Essays.* Boston: Beacon Press, 1992.

Julie J. Kilmer

See also DISCRIMINATION; HOMOEROTICISM AND HOMOSOCIALITY; STEREOTYPES.

HETEROSEXUALITY. see HOMOSEXUALITY AND HETEROSEXUALITY.

HICKOCK, LORENA. see ROOSEVELT, ELEANOR, AND LORENA HICKOCK.

HIGHSMITH, Patricia (b. 19 January 1921; d. 4 February 1995), writer.

Born Mary Patricia Plangman in Fort Worth, Texas, she later took her stepfather's name, Highsmith. At age six Patricia Highsmith moved to New York City, where her maternal grandmother raised her. Highsmith showed an early talent for visual arts, including painting and sculpting, but writing was her strong suit, perhaps spurred by her learning to read before kindergarten. Her reading habits as a child tended toward the morbid: early favorites included a history of World War I with photographs from the trenches and a book of psychiatric case histories featuring serial murderers, pyromaniacs, and the like. Highsmith later commented that this book taught her that individuals might look outwardly "normal" while hiding sinister secrets. She penned short stories as a girl and continued to do so while majoring in English at Barnard College. After graduating in 1942, Highsmith supplied plot lines for a comic book publisher before turning her hand to full-time fiction writing.

Highsmith's debut as a fiction writer and initial claim to fame came with the 1950 publication of *Strangers on a Train.* The plot revolves around the "trading" of murders between Guy, an architect in a loveless marriage, and Bruno, a sociopathic homosexual with an abusive father. Once Bruno murders Guy's wife, he insists that Guy return the favor and kill his father. Ultimately, Guy does murder Bruno's father, highlighting a common theme in Highsmith's work, the presence of violence and amorality in all people, "regular guys" included.

Following the success of her first novel (and the purchasing of its rights by Alfred Hitchcock, who turned it into a film), Highsmith wrote *The Price of Salt.* The unabashed lesbian content scared off her publisher, and Highsmith published the book in 1952 under the pseu-

Patricia Highsmith. A suitably askew photograph of the decidedly unconventional writer, who was drawn to sociopathic murderers and other outsiders in her fiction (which also included a lesbian novel published under a pseudonym). **[Sophie Bassouls/corbis SYGMA]**

donym Claire Morgan. Highsmith's novel marked a dramatic shift in the consciousness of lesbian fiction. The conflict in the novel moves from being the protagonist's lesbianism to being the prejudices the world holds against the lesbian. Along with this, Morgan forms the lesbian identities of her protagonists against the typical conception of the lesbian as perverse, deviant, and abnormal. This shift in consciousness clearly had an impact on the novel's readers.

Highsmith is perhaps best known in the United States as the author of *The Talented Mr. Ripley* (1955) and other novels in a series that features the openly gay and sociopathic Tom Ripley. Ripley is a canny, amoral con artist who commits crimes high and low, from petty thefts to major felonies. In the opening book of the series, the father of Dickie Greenleaf, who wants Tom to go to Italy and convince Dickie to return home to take on the family business, hires Ripley. Ripley's sexual obsession with Dickie Greenleaf is conflated with his wanting to be Dickie Greenleaf. Once Ripley has murdered Dickie, he takes on his identity and life, for a time. When a mutual friend discovers the ruse, Ripley murders him as well, blames Dickie for the murder, and fakes Dickie's suicide. Ripley then forges Dickie's will, leaving everything to himself. The suspense in the series of novels is less about whom Ripley will murder than about how exactly he will succeed in evading justice for his crimes. Through this approach, Highsmith encouraged readers to become complicit with him: they want him to get away with murder. Readers are thus forced to take responsibility for Ripley's crimes.

Highsmith spent most of her life unpartnered and alone. In 1963 she moved permanently to Europe and she died in Switzerland in 1995. In addition to the French Grand Prix de Littérature Policière awarded in 1957, Highsmith was awarded the Silver Dagger by the British Crime Writers Association in 1964 and in 1979 received the Grand Master award from the Swedish Academy of Detection. In the United States, she received the O. Henry Memorial and Edgar Allen Poe Awards.

The writer Michael Bronski argues that while some critics might only see a bleak view of human nature in the works of Highsmith, this is too simplistic a characterization. Rather, Highsmith offers a persistent analysis of conventional mores, most often through homosexual characters whose outsider status places them in the position to offer such a critique.

> . . . between the pleasure of a kiss and of what a man and woman do in bed seems to me only a gradation. . . . I wonder do these men grade their pleasure in terms of whether their actions produce a child or not. . . . It is a question of pleasure after all, and what's the use of debating the pleasure of an ice cream cone versus a football game. . . . But their attitude was that I must be somehow demented or blind (plus a kind of regret, I thought, at the fact a fairly attractive woman is presumably unavailable to men). Someone brought "aesthetics" into the argument, I mean against me of course. I said did they really want to debate that—it brought the only laugh in the whole show. (Patricia Highsmith, writing as Claire Morgan. *The Price of Salt.* 1952. Tallahassee, Fla.: Naiad, 1984: 246.)

Bibliography

Bronski, Michael. "The Subversive Ms. Highsmith." *Gay and Lesbian Review Worldwide* 7, no. 2 (spring 2000): 13–16.

Chin, Paula. "Through a Mind, Darkly: Writing of Murder and Madness, Patricia Highsmith Heeds a Strange Muse." *People Weekly* 39, no. 1 (January 11, 1993): 93–95.

Russell, Sue. "The Talented Patricia Highsmith: Lesbian Class Avenger." *Lambda Book Report* 8, no. 9 (2000): 12–13.

Linnea A. Stenson

See also LITERATURE; PULP FICTION: LESBIAN.

HINDUS AND HINDUISM

Hinduism is one of the world's oldest living religions—the earliest extant Hindu text, the Rig Veda Samhita, was composed around 1500 BCE, and Varanasi, a Hindu center, is the world's oldest continuously inhabited city. Hindus constitute about a sixth of the world's population today. Most Hindus live in India, but there are now close to a million Hindus, both Indians and non-Indians, in the United States.

Americans have long been interested in Hinduism. Nineteenth-century transcendentalists Ralph Waldo Emerson and Henry David Thoreau appreciated texts such as the Bhagvadgita after they were translated into English in the late eighteenth century. In 1893, Swami Vivekananda (1863–1902), disciple of Sri Ramakrishna (1836–1886), was widely acclaimed when he spoke at the World Parliament of Religions in Chicago. This interest was later heightened by U.S. sympathy with the Gandhi-led movement for Indian independence, which foregrounded Hindu emphasis on nonviolence. In U.S. literature, interest in Hinduism often intersects with interest in same-sex bonding, among writers from Walt Whitman to Allen Ginsberg.

Mainstream Hindus tend to regard all beings, including humans, animals, and gods and goddesses, as manifestations of one universal Atman (Self/Spirit). Realizing the identity of individual selves with the universal Self leads to peace and liberation from the cycle of rebirth. Sensual desire and worldly attachments are not evil but do obstruct this realization. In mainstream Hindu philosophy, heterosexual desire is not viewed as superior to homosexual desire, since both result in egotistic attachments. Differences in gender, sexuality, caste, and class are thought to be the result of attachments in previous lives, not essential attributes of the self. Hindu texts posit desire as one of the four aims of life, which cannot be avoided but must be experienced and transcended. The fourth-century *Kamasutra* catalogs all types of desire, including same-sex desire, and gives a nonjudgmental account of male–male sexual relations.

In Hindu societies, same-sex relationships tend to coexist with heterosexual marriage and parenthood and are usually expressed in the form of visible romantic friendships or less visible liaisons. Although homosexual and transgender relationships have been represented in Hindu texts from several centuries before the Christian era up to the present, there is no record of anyone in India being executed for homosexuality. When Europeans arrived in India, they were shocked by the relatively unashamed prevalence of same-sex relations, and when the British established their Indian empire they made sodomy a criminal offense. Although many Indians (in India and elsewhere) internalized this new homophobia, it continued to be countered by older Hindu perspectives. Consequently, modern Hindus tend to experience social shame rather than religious guilt about their homosexuality.

Since the nineteenth century many European and U.S. homosexuals have travelled East in search of less homophobic cultures. Several also turned to Eastern religions and teachers. Novelist Christopher Isherwood (1904–1986) joined the Ramakrishna Mission, and with his guru, Swami Prabhavananda (1893–1976), translated into English several Hindu texts, including the *Bhagvadgita.* In *My Guru and His Disciple,* Isherwood recounts how Prabhavananda advised him to see his male lover as the young Lord Krishna (p. 25). When reading about the persecution of Oscar Wilde, Prabhavananda remarked, "Poor man. All lust is the same" (p. 254).

Along the same lines, philosopher Jiddu Krishnamurti (1895–1986), who traveled throughout the world discussing spiritual matters with seekers and set up a center in Ojai, California, said that homosexuality, which, like heterosexuality, has been a fact for thousands of years, is made into a problem only because of human beings' overemphasis on sex. Rather than heightening conflict by trying to suppress one's desire for a beautiful man, woman, or other object, he advised enjoying beauty without trying to possess or control it.

In the twentieth century, the spread of yoga and vegetarianism as health practices have helped popularize Hindu ideas and practices, also drawing more LGBT Americans to Hindu teachers. For example, many U.S. LGBT people are among the disciples of female guru Gurumayi Chidvilasananda (born 1955), successor to Swami Muktananda (1908–1982) as head of the Siddha Yoga tradition, which has centers all over the world, including several locations in the United States.

While most report a supportive environment, a few who have left the organization say the atmosphere was homophobic.

Indian Hindus living in the United States constitute a highly educated, successful group that maintains strong ties with India. Although influenced by modern forms of homophobia, they are also exposed to LGBT movements and literature developed in the West. There are now many Indian LGBT groups in the United States and India, most of whose members are Hindu in origin. There are prominent activists of Hindu origin, such as Urvashi Vaid, in U.S. LGBT movements.

Some modern right-wing Hindu groups, active both in India and the United States, express virulent opposition to homosexuality, inaccurately claiming that it was unknown to ancient Hindus and was introduced by West Asian Muslims or by Europeans. Influenced by this myth, many Hindus in the U.S. objected to Deepa Mehta's depiction of lesbianism in a Hindu family in her 1998 film *Fire.*

Trikone, the LGB South Asian magazine that was published in San Francisco since 1986, has included many essays on Hinduism and homosexuality. *Trikone's* 1996 special issue on this theme carried an interview (pp. 6–7) with Jim Gilman, a gay U.S. follower of Swami Chinmayananda (1916–1993). This interview reveals the range of attitudes to homosexuality among Hindus today. Chinmayananda was always accepting of his LGB followers, but some heterosexual followers expressed discomfort and asked him his opinion of homosexuality. His response was: "There are many branches on the tree of life. Full stop. Next question." After Chinmayananda's death, his successor removed Gilman, who had taken vows of celibacy, from his teaching position at Chinmaya Mission. The reason cited was Gilman's past as a sexually active gay man. Gilman continues to teach Vedanta philosophy independently to small groups.

Academic South Asian studies in the United States tends to ignore the presence of same-sex relationships in Hindu cultures, but a few U.S. scholars and publishers have contributed to making this presence visible. Since the late twentieth century, LGBT Indians in the United States have begun to produce literature, films, critical commentary, and memoirs that shed light on Hindu approaches to LGBT issues and that circulate both in India and the United States. Several Hindu same-sex weddings, some conducted by Hindu priests, have also taken place in the United States (and many more in India), some between Indians and some between Indians and non-Indians.

Bibliography

Isherwood, Christopher. *My Guru and His Disciple.* New York: Penguin, 1980.

Trikone 11, no. 3 (July 1996), special issue on Hinduism and Homosexuality.

Vanita, Ruth, ed. *Queering India: Same-Sex Love and Eroticism in Indian Culture and Society.* New York: Routledge, 2002.

Vanita, Ruth, and Kidwai, Saleem. *Same-Sex Love in India: Readings from Literature and History.* New York: Palgrave-St. Martin's, 2000.

Ruth Vanita

See also ASIAN AMERICANS; GINSBERG, ALLEN; CHURCHES, TEMPLES, AND RELIGIOUS GROUPS; ISHERWOOD, CHRISTOPHER; WHITMAN, WALT.

HISTORY

Systematic research on LGBT history was all but nonexistent before 1970. Like women and African Americans, LGBT people only asserted the significance of their historical experiences after they created a social movement. Historical research is inescapably political: which groups merit historians' attention is at least partly a function of the power those groups wield in the present. LGBT historical research has consistently reflected profound concern for the connections between scholarship and politics.

The earliest studies in LGBT history consisted of efforts to find LGBT persons in the past and write about them. But even some of the first forays into LGBT history, and the history of sexuality more generally, depended on and bespoke an astute suspicion that sexuality would prove as important a category of human identity for understanding the past as gender, race, or class. By demonstrating that the very notion of "sexuality" as a defining element of human identity (much less the specifics of sexual identity categories) varies enormously across time and space, historians have contributed crucially to the growing recognition that sexuality, in particular LGBT identities, has much more to do with power differentials than it does with nature or biology.

Or, as the vast majority of historians studying these issues would put it, sexuality is a social construction. Social constructionism refers to the belief that identity categories generally, especially sexual identity categories, reflect the influence of various social, cultural, and political factors—including economic organization, familial structure, religious and educational institutions, social movements, and especially in modern Western societies, the "expert" opinions of mental health professionals and medical researchers. The "social construction" position opposes the "essentialist" position, according to which sexuality is a natural, inherent quality that all humans have possessed in all places, at all times, whatever the variation in the expression of that quality.

Early Academic Scholarship

After considerable debate during the late 1980s and early 1990s, the constructionist position has come to dominate historical approaches to LGBT topics. This is so in part because the constructionist position depends heavily on historical evidence. Carroll Smith-Rosenberg provided an important part of the argument before the debate emerged, in her groundbreaking article "The Female World of Love and Ritual," which appeared as the first article in the first issue of the women's studies journal, *Signs,* in 1975. With her account of intense friendships among respectable, middle-class white women of the nineteenth century, Smith-Rosenberg demonstrated that assumptions about connections between emotional commitment and sexual activity that characterized the post–World War II period did not necessarily obtain in an earlier period. Literary scholar Lillian Faderman took a more essentialist position soon after, arguing in "The Morbidification of Love between Women" and elsewhere that intense female relationships in various guises have always existed. The impulse of psychologists and other authority figures of the late nineteenth and early twentieth centuries to represent such relationships as pathological reflected men's anxieties about changing gender norms in the period. Joining this discussion, Blanche Wiesen Cook wrote in 1979 about "The Historical Denial of Lesbianism," arguing that historians systematically refused to see evidence of sexual activity in prominent female couples and friendship networks of the same period. These articles all illustrate the important, complicated, and unpredictable relationships between gender and sexuality as historical topics.

Community-based Research

In 1976 Jonathan Ned Katz published *Gay American History,* a massive collection of documents from the beginning of European settlement in North America to the 1970s. Katz was not a professional historian, and given the conservatism of history as a discipline it is unlikely that anyone could have survived as a professional historian while producing *Gay American History* during the 1970s. The conflicted relationship between LGBT history and the de facto gatekeepers to the profession is an important factor to consider in understanding historians' coverage of LGBT persons in the past. Katz is only one historian covering LGBT topics whose contributions to the field have come more in spite of than thanks to the canons of the discipline.

Other prominent early examples of nonprofessional historians include Vern Bullough, who has produced fourteen major publications on LGBT history since 1973—as part of a total corpus of nearly one hunded publications dealing with various aspects of the history of nursing, medicine, and gender and sexuality—and who has long held academic appointments; and Allen Bérubé, who published the groundbreaking *Coming Out Under Fire: The History of Gay Men and Women in World War II* in 1990, but who does not hold a university appointment. Bérubé helped found the San Francisco Lesbian and Gay History Project in 1978. Joan Nestle, lesbian author and activist who founded the Lesbian Herstory Archives in New York City in 1973, taught writing at Queens College from 1966 to 1995, but does not have formal training as a historian.

The San Francisco Lesbian and Gay History Project, the Lesbian Herstory Archives, and other community-based LGBT collections also have tended to operate outside of the historical profession while proving crucial in the historical reconstruction of LGBT lives in the United States. The Gerber-Hart Library in Chicago is a freestanding institution dedicated to the preservation of queer history. The History Project in Boston published *Improper Bostonians: Lesbian and Gay History from the Puritans to Playland* in 1998. *Becoming Visible: An Illustrated History of Lesbian and Gay Life in Twentieth-Century America,* edited by Molly McGarry and Fred Wasserman (1998), is the outcome of a major 1994 exhibit on LGBT history at the New York Public Library. The GLBT Historical Society, based in San Francisco, has extensive archival collections and plans to build the world's first major museum dedicated to LGBT history and culture.

Lack of scholarly affiliation has not impaired the intellectual sophistication of the resulting work. Katz's *Gay American History* reflected the entire range of intellectual and political impulses behind LGBT history. By its very existence it amply demonstrated the continuous existence of LGBT persons in the American past, few of them famous beyond the fleeting notoriety they experienced during trials for sodomy or cross-dressing. At the same time, introducing the revised version of the book in 1992, Katz participated in the constructionist debate, arguing that terms appropriate to the late twentieth century, especially "homosexual," did not accurately capture understandings of same-sex desire and activity before the late nineteenth century.

The Field Grows

The first major collection to include academic work on LGBT history in the United States appeared in 1979, when the *Radical History Review* published a collection of articles on the history of sexuality that included Robert Padgug's piece on how to conceptualize the history of sexuality. He cited French philosopher Michel Foucault's *The History of Sexuality,* which first appeared in English in 1978, Smith-Rosenberg's article, and a 1968 article by British sociologist Mary McIntosh, "The Homosexual Role," which argued that the designation "homosexual" served to distinguish normality from deviance. Each of these works played a major role in the essentialist-constructionist debate. Although Foucault's work has since come to dominate scholarly inquiry into issues of sexuality, *The History of Sexuality* was at the time only one in an array of major sources, theoretical and empirical, in the field.

The entire issue of the *Radical History Review* from which Padgug's article came appeared in 1989 as *Passion and Power: Sexuality in History.* This volume illustrated the connection between LGBT history and the history of sexuality more generally, containing such major contributions as John D'Emilio's "The Homosexual Menace: The Politics of Sexuality in Cold War America," which demonstrated that more people lost federal jobs for suspicion of "homosexuality" than of communism during the second red scare; George Chauncey's "From Sexual Inversion to Homosexuality: The Changing Medical Conceptualization of Female 'Deviance,'" an important study showing significant variation in researchers' and clinicians' conceptions of same-sex sexuality in the late nineteenth and early twentieth centuries; and Elizabeth Kennedy and Madeline Davis's "The Reproduction of Butch-Fem Roles: A Social Constructionist Approach," which provided both conceptual discussion of the constructionist debate and a foretaste of their subsequent book, *Boots of Leather, Slippers of Gold: The History of a Lesbian Community* (1993), a unique and enormously valuable oral history of lesbians in Buffalo, New York. *Passion and Power* also contained explorations of non-LGBT sexualities, including important considerations of variation in sexual definition and experience along the axes of class and race.

Another important collection, *Historical Perspectives on Homosexuality,* appeared in 1981 as a reprint of a special issue of the *Journal of Homosexuality,* first published in 1980 (reprinted again in 1985 under the title, *The Gay Past: A Collection of Historical Essays).* It covered a wide range both chronologically and geographically, with the lead essay discussing European laws prohibiting lesbian sexual activity from 1270 to 1791. This range itself indicated the paucity of scholarship in the field: edited collections on specific topics in history rarely cover several centuries and all of Western Europe plus the United States.

Historical Perspectives on Homosexuality was also important for publishing "'Writhing Bedfellows,' 1826: Two Young Men from Antebellum South Carolina's Ruling Elite Share 'Extravagant Delight'," by Martin Bauml Duberman. Duberman, who established his career as a historian before coming out of the closet and writing about LGBT history, would go on to publish the only major historical work to date on the Stonewall riots of 1969, *Stonewall* (1993). He played a key role in the founding of the Center for Lesbian and Gay Studies (CLAGS) in 1986; CLAGS would find a permanent institutional home at the City University of New York's Graduate Center in 1991.

Another prominent scholar from this period, John Boswell, published *Christianity, Social Tolerance, and Homosexuality: Gay People in Western Europe from the Beginning of the Christian Era to the Fourteenth Century* in 1980. His title alone demonstrated his essentialist conviction that one may properly apply modern notions of sexual orientation across the entire sweep of Western history and presumably across all of human history. With this book and the subsequent *Same-Sex Unions in Premodern Europe,* Boswell attracted an unprecedented degree of attention from the general public for studies of medieval history by arguing that the modern assumption of long-standing hostility toward sexual minorities throughout the Christian era was false.

Boswell began *Christianity, Social Tolerance, and Homosexuality* with the observation that no historian can examine the past without bringing her or his present concerns and assumptions to the task. In disputing the constructionist thesis, he stated his conviction that to assert the absence of the categories "homosexual" or "gay person" in the past would be not only empirically false, but also damaging to the social movement for LGBT civil rights in the present. Certainly many activists exhorted LGBT people to participate in political activism in part by insisting on the immutability of sexual identity. They analogized to racial identity for purposes of conforming to American civil rights law and policy, convinced that the U.S. public was more likely to support LGBT rights if they saw LGBT people as "born that way."

Subsequent research, however, raised significant doubts about the thesis that a transhistorical conception of homosexual or gay identity was a necessary linchpin for political activism in the present. In 1983, D'Emilio published *Sexual Politics, Sexual Communities: The Making of a Homosexual Minority in the United States, 1945 to 1970*, arguably the single most important contribution to the field of LGBT American history as of 2004. D'Emilio's was the first study of the "homophile" movement—the precursor to the post–Stonewall riots (1969) LGBT civil rights movement—by a professional historian. Despite the manifest importance and quality of his work, D'Emilio struggled to establish his career, spending over a decade at a primarily undergraduate teaching institution before winning major research grants and a position at a research institution, the University of Illinois at Chicago.

D'Emilio's study of the United States in the first twenty-five years after World War II fell well within the scope of sexuality as defined in constructionist terms. The subtitle of the book, *The Making of a Homosexual Minority*, revealed the claim that homophile activists in the late 1950s and 1960s had deliberately cultivated in LGBT persons a sense of themselves as a distinct subset of the population. D'Emilio did not explicitly address the constructionist debate in his book. He meant "the making of a minority" in the political sense of a supposedly isolated, invisible group that managed somehow by 1975 to claim more than one thousand organizations in the United States and a surprising measure of political clout. He argued that lesbians and gay men were not so uniformly isolated and invisible before Stonewall as later activists had assumed. In making that argument, D'Emilio built on his earlier article, "Capitalism and Gay Identity," where he presented a materialist argument for the proposition that lesbian and gay identities depended on economic and political developments—especially the separation of production from family relations and urbanization in the late nineteenth century—that are distinctively modern.

The period from 1979 to 1983 thus proved exceptionally productive, with major scholars publishing early work that would establish their reputations as pioneers in the field of LGBT history. As pioneers, they occupied a very sparsely populated frontier; their works served as landmarks for subsequent scholars who would connect early LGBT historical studies to the conceptual grid of the discipline as a whole.

Social, Cultural, and Political History

LGBT history benefited conceptually not only from the emergence of women's history, gender history, and the history of sexuality but also from the increased prominence of social history beginning in the 1970s as well. Martin Duberman, Martha Vicinus, and George Chauncey, the editors of *Hidden from History: Reclaiming the Gay and Lesbian Past* (1989), made this point in introducing their collection of articles, which covered a wide range chronologically as well as geographically, dealing with Europe, Latin America, Asia, Africa, and North America. The driving assumption behind much LGBT history during the 1980s and 1990s was that it could illuminate the experiences of everyday life and ordinary people by exploring their actual thoughts and actions in matters of sexuality, apart from the definitions and expectations of medical and legal authorities. If *Boots of Leather, Slippers of Gold* is the lesbian exemplar of this genre, George Chauncey's *Gay New York: Gender, Urban Culture, and the Making of the Gay Male World, 1890–1940* (1994), perhaps the closest LGBT historians will ever come to producing social history in the conventional mode, is the gay male exemplar. Chauncey demonstrated convincingly that men from working class and racial and ethnic minorities in New York City in the early twentieth century did not operate according to the classifications of sexual identity that medical authorities had been developing since the last third of the nineteenth century. He also cataloged the variations in self-conception and presentation among gay men, including changing meanings of terms such as "gay" and "queer."

Related to this emphasis on social history is what one might broadly think of as a cultural historical approach to issues of sexuality by literary scholars. The same Foucault who gave us *The History of Sexuality* played a major role in the rise of historically influenced literary studies during the 1980s and 1990s, resulting in work by scholars of English literature such as Valerie Traub, Eve Kosofsky Sedgwick, and Jonathan Goldberg using primarily literary sources to explore the significance of sexual classifications. Siobhan Somerville's *Queering the Color Line: Race and the Invention of Homosexuality in American Culture* (2000) is a culmination of all of these trends: a cultural history resting primarily on literary and cinematic texts by a literary scholar, describing "the invention of homosexuality" as related to racial categorizations.

Somerville and other literary scholars used literature to make a historical point that historians also took up using a wider range of sources: observations about the historical variability of LGBT identity led to questions about the historical variability of heterosexual identity, and about the reasons for the existence of such identity categories in the first place. Katz's *The Invention of Heterosexuality* (1995) extended the logic of social constructionism to the supposedly "normal" opposite of "homosexuality," and demonstrated that sexologists created "heterosexuality" only after creating "homosexuality." Jennifer Terry's *An American Obsession: Science, Medicine, and Homosexuality in Modern Society* (1999), takes the obsession with homosexuality in the twentieth-century United States as a peculiar phenomenon in need of explanation. Terry's work illustrates the fascination of LGBT scholars with the political uses of sexual identity classifications, especially insofar as part of their political efficacy derives from their ostensibly medical provenance. Similarly, Lisa Duggan's *Sapphic Slashers: Sex, Violence, and American Modernity* (2000) places sensational accounts of a "lesbian love murder" in Memphis in 1892 into the context of broader anxieties about gender, women's rights agitation, and race. Each of these works is cultural history in that they rely on a wide range of sources in order to discern the meanings of seemingly ordinary categories to the persons who experienced them, especially at times of significant contest over those meanings; they are queer history in that they demonstrate how accusations of impropriety and immorality often serve to conceal underlying political struggles.

In short, for LGBT historians, sexuality is not only historical, it is political as well. Sexuality, like gender, serves in this analysis to transport hierarchy and power differentials into personal relationships while concealing its operation by explaining the effects in terms of "nature." This assumption explicitly undergirds much LGBT historical writing that otherwise falls under the rubrics of social and/or cultural history. It also informs much history that is queer, in the sense not only of examining LGBT persons in the past, but of using historical analysis as the vehicle for raising significant questions about contemporary political and epistemological assumptions, including beliefs about the value of identity-based political movements. William B. Turner explored connections between historical research and queer theory in *A Genealogy of Queer Theory* (2000).

Oddly, however, explicit historical examinations of the LGBT movement remain relatively rare, perhaps because it has only achieved prominence since 1970. Besides D'Emilio's groundbreaking study, *Sexual Politics, Sexual Communities,* the only book-length study thus far that addresses the social movement in detail is Marc Stein's *City of Sisterly and Brotherly Loves: Lesbian and Gay Philadelphia, 1945–1972* (2000). Also in 2000, D'Emilio published *Creating Change: Sexuality, Public Policy, and Civil Rights,* with one historian, William B. Turner, but also one activist, Urvashi Vaid, as coeditors. For many, if not most, LGBT historians, the distinction between historian and activist is so fine as to be nonexistent. D'Emilio served as the founding director of the National Gay and Lesbian Task Force's think tank, the Policy Institute. Bérubé, Duggan, Nestle, Stein, and Turner also claim significant activist as well as scholarly involvements. *Creating Change* contains articles describing the history of the LGBT civil rights movement, but many more of the contributors are political scientists and activists than are historians. The sole effort at a comprehensive account of the LGBT movement since Stonewall, *Out for Good: The Struggle to Build a Gay Rights Movement in America* (1999), comes from two journalists, Dudley Clendinen and Adam Nagourney.

New Directions

Political struggles continue to occur within the social movement and among LGBT scholars, as well as between LGBT persons and the larger society. Only during the 1990s did activists define the categories "bisexual" and "transgender" as distinct political identities ripe for scholarly exploration. Many of the participants in the gay liberation movement of the 1970s and gay rights movement of the 1980s may have acted in ways that one might now categorize as bisexual or transgender, but accepted the rubric "gay" as a broad term encompassing a wide range of identities defined in terms of sexual or gender minority status.

One result is that specifically historical explorations of bisexual or transgender topics remain relatively rare. Attorney and activist Phyllis Randolph Frye's chapter in *Creating Change* on battles to incorporate transgender issues into the lesbian/gay civil rights movement is one example. Transgender historian Susan Stryker, who is executive director of the GLBT Historical Society, has played a major role in defining the emerging field of transgender studies; she edited a 1998 special issue of *GLQ: A Journal of Lesbian and Gay Studies* on transgender studies. It contained contributions from various disciplines and included an article by historian Joanne Meyerowitz, who later published *How Sex Changed: A History of Transexuality in the United States* in 2002.

As with most historical inquiry in the United States, LGBT history has tended to emphasize the Northeast and major urban areas first, with other areas, including places outside the United States, attracting scrutiny only later. Ramón Gutiérrez studied Native American cultures in New Mexico between European contact and U.S. annexation in *When Jesus Came, the Corn Mothers Went Away: Marriage, Sexuality, and Power in New Mexico, 1500–1846* (1991). Recent studies of the South by John Howard (*Men Like That: A Southern Queer History* [1999] and, as editor, *Carrying On in the Lesbian and Gay South* [1997]) and the Pacific Northwest by Peter Boag (*Same-Sex*

Affairs: Constructing and Controlling Homosexuality in the Pacific Northwest [2003]) have significantly broadened the geographic scope of U.S. historians' understanding of LGBT lives. Nan Boyd's *Wide-Open Town: A History of Queer San Francisco to 1965* (2003) extends several trends in queer history to the queerest of American cities.

An early study of a non-U.S. region was Bret Hinsch's *Passions of the Cut Sleeve: The Male Homosexual Tradition in China* (1990). James Green published *Beyond Carnival: Male Homosexuality in Twentieth-Century Brazil* in 1999. Also in 1999, Gregory Pflugfelder published *Cartographies of Desire: Male-Male Sexuality in Japanese Discourse, 1600-1950.* Jeffrey Merrick and Bryant Ragan have edited two volumes on France, *Homosexuality in Modern France* (1996) and *Homosexuality in Early Modern France: A Documentary Collection* (2001). Stephen Murray and Will Roscoe published *Boy-Wives and Female Husbands: Studies in African Homosexualities* in 1998. James Steakley's *The Homosexual Emancipation Movement in Germany* is very important for its early publication date, 1975, but also for describing a social movement that, before World War II, was well ahead of that in the United States.

Conclusion

LGBT historians initially dealt with discrimination within the discipline by staying in the closet and not writing about the LGBT past. As they began to come out and explore LGBT history, they created the Committee for Lesbian and Gay History (CLGH) in 1979. In 1982, CLGH became an affiliate of the American Historical Association. The profession has continued to follow the social movement and the larger society in that LGBT historians are coming out earlier in their careers and increasingly writing dissertations on LGBT topics. Indeed, one way of tracking the expansion of LGBT history is by reviewing the CLGH bibliography of dissertations, http://www.usc.edu/isd/archives/clgh/dissertations.html. New research from LGBT historians is gradually reshaping our understanding of the human past in all respects, and the impact of this research is likely to continue growing in the future.

Bibliography

Boag, Peter. *Same-Sex Affairs: Constructing and Controlling Homosexuality in the Pacific Northwest.* Berkeley: University of California Press, 2003.

Boswell, John. *Christianity, Social Tolerance, and Homosexuality: Gay People in Western Europe from the Beginning of the Christian Era to the Fourteenth Century.* Chicago: University of Chicago Press, 1980.

Chauncey, George. *Gay New York: Gender, Urban Culture, and the Making of the Gay Male World, 1890–1940.* New York: Basic Books, 1994.

Cook, Blanche Wiesen. "The Historical Denial of Lesbianism." *Radical History Review* 20 (1979): 60–65.

D'Emilio, John. *Sexual Politics, Sexual Communities: The Making of a Homosexual Minority in the United States, 1940 to 1970.* Chicago: University of Chicago Press, 1983.

D'Emilio, John, William B. Turner, and Urvashi Vaid, eds. *Creating Change: Sexuality, Public Policy, and Civil Rights.* New York: St. Martin's Press, 2000.

Duberman, Martin Bauml, Martha Vicinus, and George Chauncey, Jr., eds. *Hidden from History: Reclaiming the Gay and Lesbian Past.* New York: New American Library, 1989.

Faderman, Lillian. "The Morbidification of Love between Women by Nineteenth-Century Sexologists." *Journal of Homosexuality* 4 (1978): 73–89.

Green, James. *Beyond Carnival: Male Homosexuality in Twentieth-Century Brazil.* Chicago: University of Chicago Press, 1999.

Katz, Jonathan Ned. *Gay American History: Lesbians and Gay Men in the USA, a Documentary Anthology.* New York: Crowell, 1976. Rev. ed. New York: Meridian, 1992.

Kennedy, Elizabeth Lapovsky, and Madeline D. Davis. *Boots of Leather, Slippers of Gold: The History of a Lesbian Community.* New York: Routledge, 1993.

Licata, Salvatore J., and Robert P. Petersen. *Historical Perspectives on Homosexuality.* New York: Haworth Press, 1981.

Peiss, Kathy, and Christina Simmons, eds., with Robert A. Padgug. *Passion and Power: Sexuality in History.* Philadelphia: Temple University Press, 1989.

Smith-Rosenberg, Carroll. "The Female World of Love and Ritual: Relations between Women in Nineteenth-Century America." *Signs: Journal of Women in Culture and Society* 1 (1975): 1–30.

Stein, Marc. *City of Sisterly and Brotherly Loves: Lesbian and Gay Philadelphia, 1945–1972.* Chicago: University of Chicago Press, 2000.

Terry, Jennifer. *An American Obsession: Science, Medicine, and Homosexuality in Modern Society.* Chicago: University of Chicago Press, 1999.

William B. Turner

See also CLASSICAL STUDIES; ESSENTIALISM AND CONSTRUCTIONISM; HISTORY PROJECTS, LIBRARIES, AND ARCHIVES; LESBIAN HERSTORY ARCHIVES.

HISTORY PROJECTS, LIBRARIES, AND ARCHIVES

Libraries, archives, and history projects have figured prominently in LGBT communities. People with nonmainstream gender or sexual identities often struggle

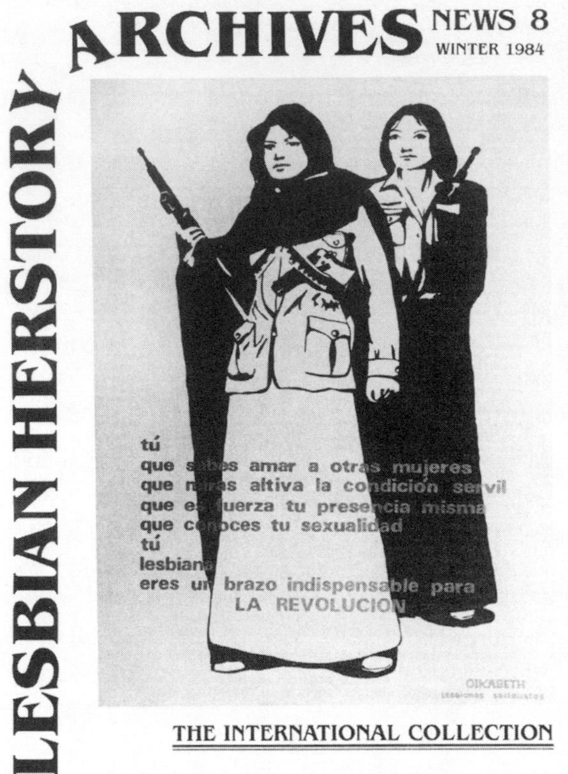

From the International Collection. The cover of the winter 1984 issue (no. 8) of *Lesbian Herstory Archives News* features an illustrated exhortation in Spanish for women to join the Lesbianas Socialistas.

against cultural and individual invisibility, and they usually do not come from families that pass along a positive sense of LGBT life. For these and other reasons, many LGBT people have turned to libraries, archives, and history projects for learning about the LGBT past and present.

Background

Threatened records. Scholars rely on documentary evidence, collected by many libraries, archives, and history projects, to analyze, interpret, and retell histories of gender and sexuality. However, creation of LGBT documents has been limited by many LGBT people's concerns about disclosing their own and other people's sexual and gender identities. Moreover, the diaries, love letters, meeting notes, photographs, flyers, newsletters, and other materials created by LGBT people have often faced insecure futures.

In some notable cases, LGBT records have been systematically destroyed, as when on 6 May 1933, Adolf Hitler's regime in Nazi Germany publicly burned parts of the archives and library of Magnus Hirschfeld's Institute of Sexual Science in Berlin. Martin Duberman discovered when trying to research the sexual history of the nineteenth-century politician James Henry Hammond at the South Caroliniana Library that archivists and donors may also restrict public access to LGBT materials.

Other documents have not survived because, following a person's death, homophobic or transphobic relatives have discarded the documents. In many cases, LGBT people have not thought of offering their records to an archive, and it was not until the late 1980s that professional archives in the United States started actively reaching out to LGBT communities and expressing interest in preserving their histories.

Early collections. Long before this occurred, community-based initiatives worked to preserve LGBT materials. To learn about LGBT role models, foster respect for LGBT people, and know and have access to LGBT history, individuals and groups in a number of cities created history projects, libraries, and archives.

Jim Kepner (1923–1997) began collecting books, articles, and memorabilia "relating directly or indirectly to Gay/Lesbian concerns, sexuality, and morals" in 1942, and ended up creating the first known LGBT archives and library in North America, the International Gay and Lesbian Archives (Carmichael, p. 175). In 1994, it merged with the ONE, Inc., collection, which W. Dorr Legg had started in 1952. ONE/IGLA, now called ONE Institute and Archives, eventually established a relationship with the University of Southern California.

Another early collector was Barbara Grier, who from 1950 to 1972 avidly collected LGBT literature, which she later gave to the San Francisco Public Library. Her collection was the basis for her important bibliography *The Lesbian in Literature,* first published in 1967.

Collections by Region

West Coast. In addition to IGLA and ONE, the West Coast saw the emergence in 1981 of the June L. Mazer Lesbian Archives (originally called the West Coast Lesbian Collections), and in 1985 of the Gay and Lesbian Historical Society of Northern California, renamed the GLBT Historical Society in 2002.

Through the efforts of Willie Walker and other members of the San Francisco Lesbian and Gay History Project, the GLBT Historical Society has done an excellent job of documenting LGBT life in San Francisco and northern California. In 1995, this organization was able to hire the archivist Paula Jabloner, who worked for three years to process key collections, and it has been able to keep paid staff ever since. Walker also helped successfully launch the University of California, San Francisco's AIDS History Project, which spans the first thirteen years of the AIDS epidemic (c. 1981–1994) within the San Francisco Bay area.

In 1996, the San Francisco Public Library opened a Gay and Lesbian Center, later named after the philanthropist James C. Hormel. In addition to collecting new materials on LGBT culture in the Bay Area, it provides physical access to some of the processed collections from the GLBT Historical Society that are on deposit there.

The Gay and Lesbian Archives of the Pacific Northwest was founded in October 1994 by a group of community-based historians in Portland, Oregon.

East Coast. Joan Nestle and Deb Edel started one of the most influential and important community archives projects, the Lesbian Herstory Archives, in New York City in 1973. It opened for use by the lesbian community in 1976 and remained in Nestle's apartment on Manhattan's Upper West Side until 1992, when it moved to a Brooklyn townhouse purchased following a successful fundraising campaign.

The Lesbian Herstory Archives has been a model for other community collections by serving as an agent for political change and community building, and by making contributions to the interpretation of lesbian history while carrying out traditional archival functions. By presenting slide shows and participating in annual pride marches, the Lesbian Herstory Archives has made itself and information about lesbian history visible.

In 1988, the Lesbian and Gay Community Services Center in New York City decided to develop an archival program and start collecting LGBT materials in its National Archive of Lesbian, Gay, Bisexual, and Transgender History.

Midwest. The Gerber/Hart Gay and Lesbian Library and Archives started in Chicago in 1981. Like the Lesbian Herstory Archives and other LGBT libraries and archives, Gerber/Hart conceives of its mission as promoting social change. The Quatrefoil Library, which opened in St. Paul, Minnesota, in 1986, was the realization of a dream for David Irwin and Dick Hewetson, who had been collecting gay books since the mid-1970s.

As with many other community-run projects, both Chicago's Gerber/Hart and St. Paul's Quatrefoil volunteers have focused more on their lending library than on preserving unique primary sources and making them accessible. Preserving and processing manuscript or archival collections is labor- and resource-intensive and reaches a smaller audience. A larger group of people will want to look at an occasional book than come in to do in-depth historical research, so it makes sense that most community-based institutions have organized mainly around libraries.

from the lesbian herstory archives' statement of purpose

(http://www.lesbianherstoryarchives.org/about.htm):

"The Lesbian Herstory Archives exist to gather and preserve records of Lesbian lives and activities so that future generations will have ready access to materials relevant to their lives. The process of gathering this material will also serve to uncover and collect our herstory denied to us previously by patriarchal historians in the interests of the culture which they serve."

Other parts of the United States and Canada. LGBT libraries, archives, and history projects have also been established in other parts of the United States and also in Canada.

The Canadian Lesbian and Gay Archives were formed in 1973 in Toronto and have been run entirely by volunteers. Jearld Moldenhauer, a founding member of the *Body Politic* collective, was instrumental in keeping the newspaper's and other records, which became the initial core of the Canadian Gay Liberation Movement Archives, renamed the Canadian Gay Archives in 1975 and the Canadian Lesbian and Gay Archives in 1993. Other important leaders include Ron Dayman, Ed Jackson, James Fraser, and Alan Miller. This archive has created numerous important bibliographies in addition to its newsletter, and distributes several monographs on Canadian LGBT history.

Collections by Type

Community history projects. Community history projects have had a significant impact not only on the collection and preservation of documents, but also on the interpretation and dissemination of LGBT history. The History Project in Boston, established in 1980, is a group of volunteer historians, activists, and archivists who have concentrated on conducting research and creating forums for educating the general public about LGBT people in Massachusetts. Major accomplishments include an extensive exhibit in 1996, *Public Faces, Private Lives;* a book, *Improper Bostonians,* published in 1998; and the exhibit *Black and Gay in Black and White.* The History Project

From the Graphics Collection. The September 1986 issue (no. 9) of the *Lesbian Herstory Archives Newsletter* shows an unidentified image from the 1960s or 1970s of women embracing, along with a quote from the Greek poet Sappho, on its cover.

has also created online exhibits and helped to record and share Boston's queer history in other ways. Additionally, the project focuses on preserving the documentary record, though it does not house collections itself and is independent of any particular repository. Its volunteers work to shepherd collections into appropriate homes, providing another good model for community archives projects.

Similarly, the Austin Lesbian Activism in the 70's Herstory Project works to facilitate the donation of primary sources about lesbian activity in Austin, Texas, to archives "acceptable to the donor." Project volunteers work primarily with the Center for American History, the Austin History Center, and the Lesbian Herstory Archives. The lesbians in this organization take as their mission preserving their local history, and they work to raise women's awareness of the importance of the records they may have in their closets and attics. They also conduct oral history interviews.

A growing number of studies completed by trained academics can also be considered community history projects. First came Elizabeth Lapovsky Kennedy and Madeline D. Davis's *Boots of Leather, Slippers of Gold,* which appeared in 1993 after a lengthy and careful community study of Buffalo, New York. This was followed by studies by Esther Newton (Cherry Grove, Fire Island), George Chauncey (New York City), John Howard (Mississippi), Marc Stein (Philadelphia), Nan Boyd (San Francisco), and various other studies included in *Creating a Place for Ourselves: Lesbian, Gay, and Bisexual Community Histories,* edited by Brett Beemyn. Based on oral histories as well as archival research, most of these studies depended on the contributions of members of each community studied.

Early collections. The first professional U.S. repository to document sexual minorities intentionally was the Kinsey Institute for Research in Sex, Gender, and Reproduction, founded in 1947 by Alfred Kinsey and affiliated with Indiana University. Sexual practices and attitudes are the focus of its collections. Documents pertinent to histories of sexuality and gender also can be found in many other mainstream archives, although they might not have been collected with this use in mind and might not be described as such. The archivist Elizabeth Knowlton conducted a survey to locate such sources and published her results in a 1987 issue of *Provenance.*

Several initiatives that had been brewing for some time coalesced in the professional archival community in 1988. In Atlanta, at the annual meeting of the Society of American Archivists, members interested in lesbian and gay history met informally and started a petition for the creation of the Lesbian and Gay Archives Roundtable (LAGAR). Since then, LAGAR has reached out to community history projects and archives and has encouraged all archival repositories to take part in documenting LGBT history.

Major public and university collections. In New York City in 1988, the New York Public Library Manuscripts and Archives Division agreed to take and provide access to the accumulated holdings of a community archives project that had gone defunct, the International Gay Information Center Archives. At that time, the library's archives made primary sources about LGBT people and organizations in New York City and the Northeast a collecting focus.

Also in 1988, Cornell University received the library and archives of the Mariposa Education and Research Foundation and established a new program, the Human Sexuality Collection. Mariposa, founded by Bruce R. Voeller in 1970, had been a bicoastal community effort, with apartments in both New York and California filling up with important documents rescued by Mariposa volunteers. Seeing a need for a professional institution to take responsibility for collecting at the national level, the Human Sexuality Collection continued in this vein. Influenced by the activists Voeller and David B. Goodstein and by an advisory committee, Cornell decided to focus on the various ways in which sexuality becomes an issue in society and concentrate on documenting LGBT organizations and individuals, paying particular attention to under-documented people and issues. The Human Sexuality Collection now contains the official archives for numerous national organizations and serves as home to the papers of transgender activists, documentation of how race influences lesbian and gay politics and communities, sources on lesbian writers, and substantial material on the impact of AIDS.

Growth of mainstream LGBT collections. With increased awareness about the importance of documentation about sexual and gender minorities, all kinds of mainstream archives have joined the effort to secure a more complete historical record. The Sophia Smith Collection at Smith College and Harvard University's Schlesinger Library on the History of Women in America have highlighted their important lesbian collections and actively worked to build their holdings. Other repositories have added new collecting subjects. In 1989, Michigan State University started its Changing Men Collections, which document various men's movements and provide different kinds of relevant sources for those studying gender and sexual identity. In 2000, the University of Michigan Library's Labadie Collection accepted the donation of the National Transgender Library and Archives.

At the beginning of the twenty-first century, many regional repositories were collecting local history related to gender and sexual minorities. The University of Oregon, for instance, sought documentation of the numerous lesbian communes and lesbian back-to-the-land activities in Oregon. Duke University's Sallie Bingham Center for Women's History and Culture collected materials on southern lesbian and gay writers and activists and has given a home to the archives of the Atlanta Lesbian Feminist Alliance. Around the same time, Tulane University Libraries' Special Collections started more actively documenting the history of gender and sexual diversity in New Orleans. The Minnesota Historical Society, the Wisconsin Historical Society, and other state repositories have also been preserving important collections from their regions. In 2001, the University of Minnesota Library became home to the Jean-Nickolaus Tretter Collection in Gay, Lesbian, Bisexual, and Transgender Studies, making available materials collected by Tretter since 1982.

from the gerber/hart library website

(http://www.gerberhart.org/):

"Hosting various programs and events which support its beliefs that knowledge is the key to dispelling homophobia and that affirming information about lesbian, gay, bisexual and transgendered persons is critical to fostering pride and self-confidence, Gerber/Hart Library seeks to not only preserve and protect items of LGBT individuals and organizations, but to be a conduit for change."

Advantages and disadvantages. The advantages and disadvantages of community archives and professional archives, as well as the ways these institutions may assist each other and the contributions both can make to better historical understanding, have been regular subjects at archives, library, and LGBT studies conferences. These topics are also explored in *Daring to Find Our Names*, edited by James V. Carmichael, Jr.

Issues discussed include community control, accessibility, mainstream acceptance, professional care, inclusion of controversial topics, and interpretation of sources. In an effort both to assist researchers and to facilitate communication among archives, members of LAGAR have compiled contact, use, and collections information from repositories around North America, and have published *Lavender Legacies: Guide to Sources in North America* (available on the World Wide Web at http://www.archivists.org/saagroups/lagar/home.htm).

Internet and microfilm access. Increasingly in the 1990s and early 2000s, individuals and institutions have explored making information about the history of sexuality and gender identity available to people through the Internet. For instance, Yolanda Retter helped bring attention to the history of lesbians of color through her Web site for the Lesbian History Project (http://www-lib.usc.edu/~retter/main.html). Specific research guides online include Cornell's *Sexuality Research Guide* (http://rmc.library.cornell.edu/HSC/faq/hscfaq.htm) and the New York Public Library's *Gay and Lesbian Studies* (http://www.nypl.org/research/chss/grd/resguides/gay.html). Archives have also worked to make available on the Web more and more of the finding aids that list the contents of individual boxes and folders in their collections. These developments have made the history of sexuality and gender more accessible to a wide audience and make the research process more efficient.

In addition, commercial microfilming companies have produced collections relating to LGBT issues. Microfilming archival collections not only makes them more accessible; it also preserves them in an additional format. The commercial success of such products is a testament to the vitality of LGBT studies.

Preserving the Stories of Their Lives

When the Task Force on Gay Liberation formed at the 1970 American Library Association meeting in Detroit, librarians earned the distinction of having the first nationwide professional organization that included a gay group. Members went on to work for better subject headings, improved indexing for alternative periodicals, and improved public and academic library holdings on LGBT topics. Now, when people go to libraries to look for books on homosexuality or transgenderism, finding suitable sources is not as hard as it once was.

That a band of LGBT activists mobilized early on within the library profession is not at all surprising when one looks at the various ways that LGBT people have cared about books, access to books, and the libraries and archives that preserve the stories of their lives.

Bibliography

Beemyn, Brett. *Creating a Place for Ourselves: Lesbian, Gay, and Bisexual Community Histories.* New York: Routledge, 1997.

Boyd, Nan Alamilla. *Wide-Open Town: A History of Queer San Francisco to 1965.* Berkeley: University of California Press, 2003.

Carmichael, James V., Jr., ed. *Daring to Find Our Names: The Search for Lesbigay Library History.* Westport, Conn.: Greenwood Press, 1998.

Chauncey, George. *Gay New York: Gender, Urban Culture, and the Making of the Gay Male World, 1890–1940.* New York: Basic Books, 1994.

Duberman, Martin Bauml. "'Writhing Bedfellows' in Antebellum South Carolina: Historical Interpretation and the Politics of Evidence." In *Hidden from History: Reclaiming the Gay and Lesbian Past.* Edited by Martin Bauml Duberman, Martha Vicinus, and George Chauncey, Jr. New York: New American Library, 1989.

Gough, Cal, and Ellen Greenblatt, eds. *Gay and Lesbian Library Service.* Jefferson, N.C.: McFarland, 1990.

Grier, Barbara. *The Lesbian in Literature: A Bibliography.* Tallahassee, Fla.: Naiad Press, 1981.

History Project. *Improper Bostonians: Lesbian and Gay History from the Puritans to Playland.* Boston: Beacon Press, 1998.

Howard, John. *Men Like That: A Southern Queer History.* Chicago: University of Chicago Press, 1999.

Kennedy, Elizabeth Lapovsky, and Madeline D. Davis. *Boots of Leather, Slippers of Gold: The History of a Lesbian Community.* New York: Routledge, 1993.

Knowlton, Elizabeth. "Documenting the Gay Rights Movement." *Provenance* 5, no. 1 (1987).

Newton, Esther. *Cherry Grove, Fire Island: Sixty Years in America's First Gay and Lesbian Town.* Boston: Beacon Press, 1993.

Plant, Richard. *The Nazi War against Homosexuals.* New York: Henry Holt, 1986.

Stein, Marc. *City of Sisterly and Brotherly Loves: Lesbian and Gay Philadelphia, 1945–1972.* Chicago: University of Chicago Press, 2000.

Brenda J. Marston

See also GRIER, BARBARA; HISTORY; KEPNER, JAMES; LEGG, DORR; LESBIAN HERSTORY ARCHIVES; *ONE.*

HIV. see AIDS AND PEOPLE WITH AIDS.

HOCKNEY, David **(b. 9 July 1937), artist.**

David Hockney—like Andy Warhol—led a generation of artists who in the 1960s openly affirmed a gay identity forged in relation to popular culture. Born and educated in provincial Yorkshire, England, Hockney won a scholarship to London's Royal College of Art in 1959. Under the influence of city life and an American classmate, Hockney, in his own words, "came out" in 1960. In this "exciting moment," he recalled, he realized that his art could become an expression of his sexual identity (Livingstone, p. 21).

Hockney's paintings from this period record his efforts to align himself with a legacy of homosexual artists. His titles—often written into the paintings as part of the composition—quote or allude to homosexual poets W. H. Auden, Constantine Cavafy, Antonin Artaud, and especially Walt Whitman. Though his imagery recalls Marsden Hartley's coded expressions of homosexuality, the simplicity of Hockney's numeric codes (1=A, 2=B, and so on) and pervading humor mark him as a member of a less secretive and more hopeful generation. The title of one of his paintings, *We Two Boys Together Clinging* (1961), for instance, quotes Whitman's poetry, but also alludes to a newspaper headline, "Two Boys Cling to Cliff All Night Long," a reference to a hiking accident that Hockney chose to imagine as a sexual fantasy involving the handsome pop music star Cliff Richards. According to Hockney's simple numeric codes, Richards is also signified by the number "4.2.":D.B. or "Doll Boy" in reference to his hit song, "Living Doll." Throughout these

David Hockney. The English-born painter and photographer has celebrated aspects of the gay community, especially in New York and Los Angeles, in his artwork since the early 1960s. **[Norman Parkinson Limited/Fiona Cowan/corbis]**

works, Hockney's affirmation of gay identity is suggested by brightly colored cartoonlike figures of lovers that stand out against drab backgrounds scrawled with graffiti, as if to claim the potential for delight even in bleak surroundings.

Hockney's interest in emerging forms of gay community drew him to New York City and California. In the summer of 1961, he used prize money from a printmaking competition to travel to New York City, where he acquired a boyfriend and reveled in the city's gay bars and bookstores. In New York City, Hockney dyed his hair blond as a way, he recalled, to reinvent himself. This episode appears in a series of prints he created that fictionalized his New York City trip after the model of illustrated satires popular in the eighteenth century, which showed young men tempted by wicked city life. Although Hockney's version of *A Rake's Progress* ends, following its eighteenth-century models, in an insane asylum, Hockney himself moved to California in 1963 because, he later explained, "California in my mind was a sunny land of movie studios and beautiful semi-naked people. My picture of it was admittedly strongly colored by physique magazines published there" (Hockney, 1976, p. 93). Reality did nothing to dim Hockney's enthusiasm. His popular paintings of suburban Los Angeles idealize its low-slung houses, mechanically sprinkled yards, palm trees, fancy bathrooms, and swimming pools—these last often populated with attractive men.

Hockney's shower and pool paintings often included figures culled from the physique magazines that had inspired him to move to Los Angeles, combining them with his own snapshots of places and people he knew well. This fusion of documentary veracity with mass-media fantasy associated Hockney with Pop Art. A documentary impulse is reflected in his participation in the film *A Bigger Splash*, a study of the relationship between Hockney's life and work shot in 1971 (released in 1974). Remarkable in that era for its frank, unsensationalized acknowledgment of gay identity, the film documents Hockney's emotional turmoil at the end of a five-year relationship.

Hockney's interest in documentary also helped prompt his move, around 1980, toward photography as a medium. Again insisting on his art's roots in his sexual identity, Hockney claimed that his collages of snapshots of the same scene from different angles derived from his frustration with how "erotic photographs" lacked "life," which he defined as "lived time" (Hockney, 1984, p. 9). His photographic collages expanded far beyond their erotic origins, however, creating a complex visual diary of his corner of the gay community. Here gay identity is enmeshed in other aspects of life. Mainstream newspapers, novels by gay writers, and gay porn magazines mingle in Hockney's interiors, just as portraits of heterosexual couples and children mix with images of Hockney's lovers and his older gay mentors and friends, among them the novelist Christopher Isherwood. The variety of Hockney's interests is reflected in the diversity of his output, which includes not only paintings, drawings, and photo collages, but stage and costume designs as well as a book, *Secret Knowledge* (2001), on the history of artists' use of lenses.

Bibliography

Hockney, David. *David Hockney.* London: Thames and Hudson, 1976.

———. *Cameraworks.* New York: Knopf, 1984.

———. *Secret Knowledge: Rediscovering the Techniques of the Old Masters.* London: Thames and Hudson, 2001.

Livingstone, Marco. *David Hockney.* New York: Holt, Rinehart and Winston, 1981.

Tuchman, Maurice, and Stephanie Barron, eds. *David Hockney: A Retrospective.* Los Angeles: Los Angeles County Museum of Art, 1988.

Christopher Reed

See also PHYSIQUE MAGAZINES AND PHOTOGRAPHS; VISUAL ART.

HOMOEROTICISM AND HOMOSOCIALITY

"Homoeroticism" and "homosociality" designate sometimes opposed but ultimately interdependent concepts. Whereas the notion of the homoerotic refers to same-sex desire, some treatments of homosocial institutions and practices emphasize segregation by sex that lacks or disavows any sexual component. Yet the terms, like the ideas and activities they seek to represent, are often revealingly elusive. If a gay bar, men's bathroom, and college fraternity house are all homosocial male spaces, is it clear that only the first allows for homeroticism? Might spaces and events constructed in part to isolate women from heterosexual interaction, such as girl's schools, slumber parties, and convents, nevertheless encourage homoerotic fantasies, and even sexual relations, between women? Although early-twentieth-century African American lodges or the Chinatown "bachelor societies" created by restrictive immigration policies were most explicitly defined by racial segregation, such same-sex societies may have also served to complicate or clarify the sexual identities of their inhabitants. Investigations of the mutable relationships between the homoerotic and homosocial attempt to illuminate such questions.

Recognizing the Homoerotic

For some critics, homoeroticism is open, explicit, and acknowledged. For example, gay pornography, whose sexual appeal for its consumers is blatant, is obviously homoerotic, although the term "erotic" is often used to distinguish more "sophisticated" and artistic expressions of sexual desire from more ordinary and everyday expressions. Homoerotic art might include the avant-garde films of Barbara Hammer, the photographs of Robert Mapplethorpe, and the poetry of Allen Ginsberg or Thom Gunn, all carefully crafted works that nonetheless directly depict lesbian or gay desire and sexuality. As more popular forms, the beefcake drawings of Tom of Finland, the pulp fiction of Ann Bannon, and the detective novels of Joseph Hansen or Mark Richard Zubro also treat gay or lesbian sexuality openly and sometimes explicitly. Such artifacts of high and popular culture are more or less produced and consumed within or at least on the margins of a culture that recognizes the existence of LGBT people, and in large part defines them, for better or worse, by their sexual desires. Homoeroticism is thus a visible expression of any society that includes homosexuals.

More often, however, homoeroticism has been treated as a covert, indirect, and coded meaning, addressed and available to LGBT audiences but possibly unrecognized by straight society. Most obviously, this sense of homoeroticism as suggestive rather than direct characterizes work from earlier historical periods. In his study of nineteenth-century American fiction, for instance, Scott S. Derrick emphasizes that "homoerotic desire" could not be directly articulated in the work of Nathaniel Hawthorne or Henry James, not only due to social restrictions, but in part because the very concept of the "homosexual" was not yet in place. In a prominent example, most critics and readers now affirm the homoeroticism central to many of Walt Whitman's poems, but this feature of his work was overlooked or ignored for decades by many readers who presumably could not recognize Whitman's expressions of male same-sex desire—much less reconcile it with his status as America's greatest poet. Critics of Emily Dickinson have similarly located expressions of lesbian desire in her poetry that earlier readers may not have suppressed so much as found literally inconceivable: such cases imply that homoeroticism must in some respect be a historical phenomenon. As Thomas Waugh has demonstrated, the long history of male nude photography, which now appears obviously homoerotic, was permitted through the alibis of art (with nude photos evoking classical Greek statues) and health (allowing the exposed male "physique" to be represented as a picture of health rather than an image of transgressive sexuality).

Homoeroticism, then, is often understood to require interpretation, an active reading that mainstream society tends to dismiss or resist as a forced, subjective imposition onto "innocent" texts: a work might only be homoerotic for homosexuals. However, the notion of the homoerotic can also hint that anyone might be susceptible to the desires suggested by certain texts and images. Even a straight man might respond to the physical beauty of a movie star like Montgomery Clift and thus experience a homoerotic charge; a negative response to such unanticipated desire is one way to understand homophobia, as precisely a fear of what one recognizes in oneself. Broadly, of course, the homoerotic is simply a particular manifestation of the erotic, which remains a fundamental but still mysterious and persistently controversial human pleasure. Following a logic explored most diligently by psychoanalysis, homoeroticism may seem more transgressive and so more exciting than socially sanctioned heterosexual desire (which masquerades as "eroticism" itself) precisely insofar as it has been more repressed and censored throughout modern history: the culture that fears homoeroticism might then inadvertently deserve some credit for sustaining its ongoing fascination and appeal.

The Male Homosocial World

Although the term was then nonexistent, "homosociality" summarizes a way of life common in Victorian America that isolated men and women into "separate spheres." The word has been most influentially redirected by the critic Eve Kosofsky Sedgwick to emphasize the continuum between homosocial institutions and homosexual desire, despite the apparent homophobia of many homosocial formations. Before the twentieth century, American men might commonly attend all-male schools and join fraternities, serve in the all-male military, and work in all-male professions and occupations; their increased leisure time could take them to saloons, clubs, fraternal organizations, hunting lodges, and ballparks that encouraged practices of male bonding, shared physical activity, and idealized camaraderie in part by excluding women. While these spaces reinforced patriarchy and often bred misogyny, they sometimes also generated bonds of deep affection and physical intimacy between men. In a culture that viewed marriage and fatherhood as social norms to be achieved eventually, homosocial institutions also allowed many men to remain lifelong bachelors, a category that evoked suspicion but which also offered refuge to men with no sexual interest in women.

Although most men lived as heterosexuals in their homes, their common experience of all-male environments in their working lives and during much of their leisure encouraged intense male bonds that would only weaken when women began to enter these spaces in the first decades of the twentieth century. The sentimental relations that characterized Victorian male friendship were then renegotiated and repressed, so that firm, brief handshakes came to replace the hand-holding common among earlier male friends (as vintage photographs consistently reveal). Nonetheless, remnants of Victorian homosociality remain whenever and wherever men use social systems to remove themselves from women—whether by forming street gangs or joining golf clubs—or retain social rituals, such as the team victory celebration, that still allow them to indulge in physical intimacy. The social assumptions that still segregate college dorms or public toilets and showers also maintain easily overlooked homosocial spaces in our everyday lives. The all-male gay disco and coming-out support group might be recognized as significant post-Stonewall variations on a model in fact established by ostensibly straight males in the previous century.

The Female Homosocial World

In the nineteenth century, the traditional restriction of middle-and upper-class white girls and women to the sphere of the home and church began to slowly break down; if women were not yet allowed access to many public spaces, an exclusive female world of newly established colleges, social clubs, study groups, sewing circles, and political organizations allowed a circulation among women that facilitated close and sometimes fully romantic friendships. Women were commonly allowed more emotional and physical intimacy than even the notably "sentimental" men of the period were, and this closeness could lead to relationships and acts that we would now unhesitatingly designate as "lesbian." Carroll Smith-Rosenberg, among others, has especially highlighted the role that the new women's colleges, established beginning in the 1870s, played in facilitating emotional as well as erotic affiliations between some of the first young women to venture far outside the family home. Educated women trained in a profession could also more easily avoid marriage and motherhood after college and could establish households with other women without arousing the sort of suspicion that would condemn unmarried working-class women. As many feminist historians have emphasized, however, earlier intimate, often lifelong relations between women might not have involved genital contact, and so demand a broader understanding of intimacy and romance than current assumptions allow. Most famously, some women established "Boston marriages," typically long and intense alliances that outsiders might misunderstand as the simple coming together of a couple of "spinsters" or "old maids" choosing cohabitation over loneliness. Other scholars, such as Terry Castle, have cautioned against the tendency to conflate lesbianism with other forms of homosocial bonding by attending too carefully to rare but revealing evidence of libidinal pleasure in some of the private diaries and letters that chronicle early female romances.

By the middle of the twentieth century, women whose romantic and sexual experiences had developed in homosocial environments would begin to form a genuine lesbian subculture, marked in part through the establishment of support organizations like the Daughters of Bilitis, begun in the midst of one of America's most homophobic eras. Like gay men, contemporary lesbians have both perpetuated and radically reinvented the earlier tradition of female homosociality through the establishment of lesbian bookshops, theater troupes, bars, softball leagues, and musical festivals, which attempt to provide safe, communal, male-free zones within a culture that still offers only limited spaces of genuine social tolerance. As lesbian homoeroticism redefined itself through expressions of lust rather than earlier models of affectionate friendship, such homosocial spaces remained important for the ongoing exploration of lesbian desire safely removed from mainstream male surveillance.

While the term homosociality can designate supportive communities as well as exclusive and even oppressive same-sex groups, homoeroticism circulates through both formations, whether as the welcome charge that energizes a gay or lesbian bar, or as the unconscious and repressed attraction that may exist between buddies and girlfriends. Sometimes explicit, but more often suggestive, homoeroticism often slips past the protective borders of social structures that assume sexuality can be excluded within segregated groups.

Bibliography

Carnes, Mark C., and Clyde Griffin, eds. *Meanings for Manhood: Constructions of Masculinity in Victorian America.* Chicago: University of Chicago Press, 1990.

Castle, Terry. *The Apparitional Lesbian: Female Homosexuality and Modern Culture.* New York: Columbia University Press, 1993.

Chudacoff, Howard P. *The Age of the Bachelor: Creating an American Subculture.* Princeton, N.J.: Princeton University Press, 1999.

Derrick, Scott S. *Monumental Anxieties: Homoerotic Desire and Feminine Influence in Nineteenth-Century U.S. Literature.* New Brunswick, N.J.: Rutgers University Press, 1997.

Faderman, Lillian. *Surpassing the Love of Men: Romantic Friendship and Love between Women from the Renaissance to the Present.* New York: Morrow, 1981.

———. *Odd Girls and Twilight Lovers: A History of Lesbian Life in Twentieth-Century America.* New York: Columbia University Press, 1991.

Rothblum, Esther D., and Kathleen A. Brehony, eds. *Boston Marriages: Romantic but Asexual Relationships among Contemporary Lesbians.* Amherst: University of Massachusetts Press, 1993.

Sedgwick, Eve Kosofsky. *Between Men: English Literature and Male Homosocial Desire.* New York: Columbia University Press, 1985.

Showalter, Elaine. *Sexual Anarchy: Gender and Culture at the Fin de Siècle.* New York: Viking, 1990.

Smith-Rosenberg, Carroll. *Disorderly Conduct: Visions of Gender in Victorian America.* New York: Knopf, 1985.

Waugh, Thomas. *Hard to Imagine: Gay Male Eroticism in Photography and Film from Their Beginnings to Stonewall.* New York: Columbia University Press, 1996.

Corey K. Creekmur

See also BOY SCOUTS AND GIRL SCOUTS; FRIENDSHIP; ROMANTIC FRIENDSHIP AND BOSTON MARRIAGE; SAME-SEX INSTITUTIONS; SITUATIONAL HOMOSEXUALITY; SMASHES AND CHUMMING.

HOMOPHILE MOVEMENT

The homophile movement flourished in the United States between 1951 and 1970. This organizationally-based social movement used a variety of tactics in its quest to challenge and change patterns of discrimination against homosexuals within the institutions of the media, law, religion, psychology, and medicine. The participants in the movement came from a variety of backgrounds and across the political spectrum, but the majority of leaders were white gay men and lesbians who were middle class, or at least were college educated and held professional jobs. Homophile organizations were located in cities throughout the United States, with San Francisco, New York City, Los Angeles, and Philadelphia hosting the most active and longest lasting of the groups. Arguably, the most significant homophile organizations were the Mattachine Society, ONE Incorporated, and the Daughters of Bilitis.

Although the movement was led by homosexuals who hoped to better the position of homosexuals in general, the favored term used by the leaders to describe themselves as well as their movement was "homophile," meaning "loving the same." Though derived from Greek, homophile is a modern term. It was first used in Germany in the 1920s, but not until the 1940s did it appear with any regularity. At that time, the burgeoning postwar homosexual civil rights movement in continental Europe, particularly in the Netherlands, Denmark, and Switzerland, adopted the term. Whether or not it was directly imported to the United States in the early 1950s is not known for sure. But shortly before the term was employed and distributed by the Amsterdam-based International Committee for Sexual Equality in the 1950s, it already was being used by U.S. homophile organizations. Homosexual activists in the United States chose this term because it shifted the emphasis away from sex. The decision to use this specific descriptive term caught the attention of subsequent activists and scholars. Many activists and scholars influenced by the gay liberation movement of the 1970s argued that the use of "homophile" demonstrates that the 1950s activists were conservative and that they felt a degree of shame about the sex lives of homosexuals. Beginning in the late 1990s, however, scholars have seen the use of "homophile" as part of a deliberate strategy used by the organizations to assert the common humanity of homosexuals, to remove homosexuality from a medical context, and to provide a word that might replace "pervert" or "deviate" and thus serve as a benign euphemism for homosexuality.

The accepted starting point for the homophile movement in the United States is 1951 with the establishment of the Mattachine Foundation in Los Angeles under the leadership of Harry Hay, Chuck Rowland, Dale Jennings, and others. The short lived Chicago-based Society for Human Rights, founded in 1924, borrowed ideas from the Weimer-era German homosexual civil rights movement and thus can be described as a predecessor to the movement of the 1950s and 1960s. Several founders of the Mattachine Foundation, including Harry Hay, had been members of the Communist Party USA. Although he had his party membership revoked once it was learned he was homosexual, Hay nevertheless remained influenced by both the structure and ideology of the party. Borrowing from Marxist ideology, Hay and the other founders argued that homosexuals must develop a group consciousness as an oppressed class as a prerequesite to ending their oppression. This political perspective has led some historians, John D'Emilio among them, to label the Mattachine Foundation "radical." The founders also borrowed the cell-based organizational structure used by the Communist Party to shield the leadership from public notoriety, though it actually had the effect of making the organization undemocratic and opaque to the rank-and-file members. For the founders, the first step in building a minority consciousness and social movement was to initiate small "discussion groups" in which male and female homosexuals could gather to talk about issues both personal and political.

From its home in Los Angeles, the movement spread along friendship networks throughout urban California. The Mattachine Foundation, however, lasted little more than a year. In early 1953 the leaders of the organization found themselves at the center of a controversy that they were unable to quell because of their secretive structure and because of the deliberate divide between the leaders and members. As a result, in March 1953 a new cadre of leaders, including Hal Call and Ken Burns, was elected and the Mattachine Society was formed. Over the next four years, the organization expanded greatly as new chapters were established in New York, Chicago, and Denver, and as it began publishing a monthly magazine, the *Mattachine Review,* which lasted from 1954 to 1966. Individual chapters, particularly the headquarters in San Francisco, focused on building relationships with local lawyers, ministers, doctors, psychologists, and journalists who were sympathetic to the cause of homosexual civil rights; the chapters also spent an ever-increasing amount of time serving homosexuals who needed help finding a fair lawyer, a good job, an understanding psychologist, and a welcoming place to live.

Shortly before the Mattachine Foundation became the Mattachine Society in January 1953, a multiethnic group of homosexual men, many of whom like Dale Jennings participated in the foundation, started *ONE* magazine. Although the *Review* and *ONE* both fit well within the scope of homophile activism, *ONE* is now and was then generally regarded as more political and more interested in reaching a gay audience than the *Review.* As the main activities of the Mattachine Society migrated to San Francisco between 1953 and 1957, the publishers of *ONE* in Los Angeles started doing work very similar to the work of the Mattachine Society chapters. Included among these activities were educational programs in "homophile studies." The educational program of ONE, sponsored in part by female-to-male transsexual Reed Erickson after 1964, expanded throughout the 1950s and 1960s and resulted in the publication of the *ONE Institute Quarterly of Homophile Studies* from 1968 to 1973 and the establishment of a graduate program in homophile studies, which won approval to grant Master of Arts and Doctor of Philosophy degrees from the California State Department of Education in 1981.

Although lesbians—or, as many preferred to be called at the time, "gay women"—participated in both the Mattachine Society and ONE, in 1955 a small group of women in San Francisco founded the first homophile organization exclusively for lesbians. Initially not a civil rights or publications-oriented organization like the male-dominated Mattachine and ONE, the Daughters of Bilitis began as a social alternative to the lesbian bar scene. Shortly after its founding, however, two members of the group, Del Martin and Phyllis Lyon, took it in a more public direction, arguing that if they were going to help end the isolation of others like themselves, they would need to reach out beyond their immediate friendship circles. Interestingly enough, even though they were located in San Francisco, the founders of the Daughters of Bilitis made their initial moves toward activism and publicity without ever having heard of the Mattachine Society. However, by the end of 1956, the Daughters of Bilitis had established itself within the increasing circle of homophile organizations and had begun publishing a well-respected and widely read magazine, the *Ladder*. Emulating the pattern established by the Mattachine Society, the Daughters of Bilitis established branch chapters in several locations throughout the country. Still, individuals rather than chapters would make the most sustained contribution to the organization. Along with Lyon and Martin, Barbara Gittings in Philadelphia and Gene Damon (Barbara Grier) in Kansas City played key roles in producing the *Ladder* and in spreading the word about the organization.

Research is beginning to shed light on the role sex differences played in the homophile movement. Apparently, the issue was handled in different ways across a range of locales. For example, according to Marc Stein's research, mixed-sex organizations thrived for some time in Philadelphia, where activists believed that such arrangements would counter the perceived disreputability of mostly single-sex homosexual gatherings. In San Francisco, however, home to the national headquarters of both the Mattachine Society and the Daughters of Bilitis, organizations were sex segregated and leaders focused on activism particular to the needs of either male or female homosexuals, but generally not both. What the different locations and organizations appear to have had in common, though, was a primary focus on immediate struggles like arrests and lost jobs and only a secondary concern about philosophical questions such as differences between the sexes. This situation changed in the mid-1960s when lesbian activists, including Del Martin and Phyllis Lyon, started to participate in Second Wave feminism and began to critique the sexism of the male-dominated homophile movement.

Beginning around 1960, what can be characterized as a second-wave of homophile activism emerged. This period, which lasted through the early years of gay liberation, was marked by more aggressive activism but also by activism that still fit within the standard of a liberal civil rights ideology and not a foundation-altering critique and revolutionary practice. The second phase also was more national in scope than the first and it gained more notice from homosexuals and heterosexuals around the globe. The second phase is best evidenced by the appearance of new or reoriented organizations. In San Francisco, for instance, several new organizations were founded between 1960 and 1966 that expanded the work of the Mattachine Society and the Daughters of Bilitis. Included in this group were the Tavern Guild, a mutual-aid organization made up of gay bar employees and owners, and the Council on Religion and the Homosexual, a coalition-building organization that educated the clergy about homosexuality and allowed the clergy to lend their moral authority to the cause of homosexual civil rights. Alongside the new organizations, new and aggressive publications began to appear. In Philadelphia in 1963, Clark Polak took over the leadership of the mixed-sex Janus Society and soon pushed the organization further in the direction of sexual liberation than any other homophile organization had gone. Polak accomplished this largely through the publication of *Drum* magazine from 1964 to 1969. *Drum*, featuring sexological articles by Albert Ellis and fiction by James Barr, in many ways resembled the *Mattachine Review* and *ONE;* however, alongside the standard homophile fare of news, reviews, and reports, *Drum* included articles on sex, provocative gay cartoons, and male physique photography. Within the context of publications like *Drum* and the many that followed, the homophile movement pioneered the joining together of activism, sex, and commerce in the early 1960s.

The second-wave homophile organizations also added public protest to their repertoire of activism. For instance, in 1964 a handful of homophile activists, including Craig Rodwell and Randy Wicker, staged at Whitehall Induction Center in Manhattan what is recognized as the first public protest on behalf of homosexuals, in this case contesting the military's exclusion of homosexuals. Although some activists criticized public protest as brazen, such events became a more common and widely accepted tactic among homophiles through the latter half of the 1960s. The figure most closely associated with the second wave of homophile activism is Franklin Kameny, an astronomer with a Harvard Ph.D. who was fired in 1957 from his job at the U.S. Army map service when it was learned that he had been arrested for lewd conduct in 1956. Kameny actively challenged his dismissal by contesting the Civil Service ban on homosexual employees that was instituted by President Dwight D. Eisenhower in 1953. Unable to regain his job, Kameny focused on changing the discriminatory policies and, eventually, on challenging the American Psychological Association's designation of homosexuality as an illness. Although people like Franklin Kameny and Randy Wicker played key roles in ushering in a new phase of homophile activism, many leaders from the 1950s also continued to push boundaries in the 1960s. In 1967 the Mattachine Society's Hal Call opened the nation's first gay bookstore, and in 1973 Del Martin of the Daughters of Bilitis was the first lesbian elected to the National Board of the National Organization for Women.

Another feature of the second wave of homophile activism was the move toward creating a regional and even a national homophile movement, in contrast to the early homophile organizations, where there was no such attempt. With the founding of two coalition groups, the East Coast Homophile Organizations (ECHO) in 1963 and the North American Conference of Homophile Organizations (NACHO) in 1966, some homophile activists expressed a desire to make a joint effort toward creating a uniform, national agenda while remaining active in their local organizations. However, the successes of these efforts were compromised by the local nature of many of the most pressing battles of the 1960s: police harassment, bar raids, employment and housing discrimination, and bad press in local newspapers.

The period of homophile activism had mostly ended by 1970, following the rise of gay liberation and lesbian feminism and the 1969 Stonewall Riot. Both larger cultural trends, such as the emergence of the counterculture and the New Left, and more specific changes, such as an aging first generation of activists, contributed to the shift in activist generations as well as in activist ideologies and tactics. Since the 1990s, however, scholarship has demonstrated that the divide between homophiles and later activist generations (including, but not limited to, gay liberation) has been somewhat overemphasized and that the continuities within twentieth-century homosexual movements are as pronounced as are the differences. Furthermore, vestiges of homophile activism persisted well into the 1970s with organizations, like San Francisco's Society for Individual Rights, and activists, like Washington, D.C.'s Franklin Kameny, bridging the divide between the eras in a manner that defies easy periodization.

The homophile movement has received a good deal of attention by historians, especially since John D'Emilio wrote about it in his groundbreaking 1983 book, *Sexual Politics, Sexual Communities*. However, many historical discussions of the homophile movement have downplayed the significance and successes of homophile organizations. These accounts have also claimed that the homophiles were assimilationist, accomodationist, conservative, and generally ineffective. Historical research based on newly opened archives and interviews with individuals influenced by the organizations has shown quite clearly that the terms traditionally used to characterize the movement are generally inadequate to account for the complexity of the historical context. It is important to recognize that the first generation of scholars to examine the homophile movement in historical perspective did so from the vantage point of the gay liberation movement. Consequently, many early histories of the homophile movement reveal as much about gay liberationists' need to validate their perspectives in their historical moment, to offer an explanation and justification for their arrival onto the political scene, as they do about the homophile movement itself. While these historical accounts enrich the record as they recover forgotten personalities, organizations, and events, they should also be read as primary documents of the gay liberation movement and movement-influenced scholarship.

So, then, how might scholars begin a new phase of researching and writing about the homophile movement? Along with comparing the movement to the latter gay liberation struggles, many have compared the homophile movement to the contemporaneous black civil rights movement of the 1950s and 1960s. Historians, activists, and other commentators have pointed not only to a common era but also to similar battles with police, psychologists, and a hostile public as well as struggles over the definition of self and group identity. The comparisons between the black civil rights movement and the homophile movement, however, strike some as unfair, not only to black activists but to the homophiles as well. After all, urban homosexual communities in the 1950s are hardly comparable to black communities in urban or rural areas during the same period. If historians must draw comparisons, it might be worthwhile to borrow terms and concepts used to describe the black urban movements of the 1910s and 1920s, such as mutual-aid and self-help activism and strategies of respectability and integration. These and other concepts might better describe the homophile's context and be more appropriate to use when evaluating the relative successes and failures of the homophile movement on its own terms. Such an approach should allow for a more complex picture than that which the rhetorical polarities of "conservative" versus "radical" or "assimilationist" versus "separatist" permit. Moreover, more historically anchored concepts might demonstrate that certain kinds of activism are suited to certain stages of community development and, in fact, are necessary for communities experiencing various forms of discrimination and even oppression to continue to develop. Not only would such perspective provide a better understanding of the homophile movement itself, but it also would provide insight into the relationship between the process of community building and evolving forms of community-based social and political movements.

Bibliography

Boyd, Nan Alamilla. *Wide-Open Town: A History of Queer San Francisco to 1965.* Berkeley: University of California Press, 2003.

D'Emilio, John. *Sexual Politics, Sexual Communities: The Making of a Homosexual Minority in the United States, 1940–1970,* 2d ed. Chicago: University of Chicago Press, 1998.

Marcus, Eric. *Making History: The Struggle for Gay and Lesbian Equal Rights, 1945–1990.* New York: HarperCollins, 1992. This book is a collection of edited oral history interviews, several of which are with individuals who were active in the homophile movement.

Martin, Del, and Phyllis Lyon. *Lesbian/Woman* (1972). Volcano, Calif.: Volcano Press, 1991.

Meeker, Martin. "Behind the Mask of Respectability." *Journal of the History of Sexuality* 10, no. 1 (2001): 78–116.

Sears, James. *Behind the Mask of the Mattachine: The Early Movement for Homosexual Emancipation, the Hal Call Chronicles.* Binghamton, NY: Haworth Press, 2003.

Stein, Marc. *City of Sisterly and Brotherly Loves: Lesbian and Gay Philadelphia, 1945–1972.* Chicago: University of Chicago Press, 2000.

Steitmatter, Rodger. *Unspeakable: The Rise of the Gay and Lesbian Press in America.* Boston: Faber and Faber, 1995.

Timmons, Stuart. *The Trouble with Harry Hay: Founder of the Modern Gay Movement.* Boston: Alyson, 1990.

Martin Meeker

See also BISEXUALITY, BISEXUALS, AND BISEXUAL MOVEMENTS; CALL, HAL; CORY, DONALD WEBSTER; DAUGHTERS OF BILITIS; *DRUM*; ECKSTEIN, ERNESTINE; ERICKSON EDUCATIONAL FOUNDATION; FOSTER, JEANETTE; GITTINGS, BARBARA, AND KAY TOBIN LAHUSEN; GLENN, CLEO; GRAHN, JUDY; GRIER, BARBARA; HAY, HARRY; HOMOPHILE PRESS; HOOVER, J. EDGAR; JANUS SOCIETY; KAMENY, FRANKLIN; KEPNER, JAMES; *LADDER*; LEGG, DORR; LYON, PHILLIS, AND DEL MARTIN; MATTACHINE REVIEW; MATTACHINE SOCIETY; *ONE*; ONE INSTITUTE; POLAK, CLARK; SOCIETY FOR INDIVIDUAL RIGHTS; STONEWALL RIOTS; WICKER, RANDOLFE.

HOMOPHILE MOVEMENT DEMONSTRATIONS

Over the course of the twentieth century, LGBT people led and participated in countless political demonstrations in the United States (including the 1963 March on Washington for Jobs and Freedom, which was organized by Bayard Rustin). The first documented demonstration for LGB rights, however, occurred in New York City on 19 September 1962, when, according to Martin Duberman, Craig Rodwell and Randy Wicker organized a picket line in front of the military draft board on Whitehall Street. (Some sources date this demonstration as having taken place in 1963 or 1964, but Duberman indicates that it took place in 1962.) The purpose of the demonstration was to protest the board's policy of releasing information on sexual orientation to employers. Eight people picketed: Rodwell and Renee Cafiero, who were members of the Mattachine Society of New York, a local homophile group; Cafiero's lover Nancy Garden; Wicker, the founder of the Homosexual League of New York; Wicker's lover Peter; Jefferson Poland, the founder and leader of the New York League for Sexual Freedom; and Poland's girlfriend and her baby. After walking back and forth in front of the building, handing out flyers to passersby in the rain, and receiving minimal attention, the group of three gay men, two lesbians, one straight man, one straight woman, and one child concluded the first known LGB demonstration.

Rodwell and Wicker organized the 1962 demonstration against the wishes of the Mattachine Society of New York, which was concerned about negative public reaction, police backlash, and political repression. In 1965, however, some segments of the national homophile movement, frustrated by the slow pace of change, influenced by the militant politics of the civil rights movement, and led by Washington, D.C., activist Frank Kameny and Philadelphia activist Barbara Gittings, began to support the adoption of direct action tactics (including pickets, demonstrations, and sit-ins). John D'Emilio writes that on 17 April 1965, following reports that the Cuban government was rounding up gay men and imprisoning them in labor camps, the Mattachine Society of Washington, D.C., sponsored a small demonstration at the White House to protest both U.S. and Cuban anti-LGB policies. On 18 April, a similar demonstration, sponsored by Mattachine New York, was held at the United Nations building in New York. Soon thereafter, on 29 May, Mattachine Washington held a demonstration at the White House. In June, East Coast Homophile Organizations (ECHO), made up of the Daughters of Bilitis (DOB) New York chapter, the Janus Society of Philadelphia, and the Mattachine Societies of New York and

Washington, voted to organize a series of demonstrations, including one at the Civil Service Commission building in Washington on 26 June and one at Independence Hall in Philadelphia on the Fourth of July. Marc Stein writes that 44 people, about one-quarter female, participated in the latter. According to D'Emilio, similar demonstrations took place later that year at the Pentagon (31 July), the State Department (28 August), and the White House (23 October).

As the locations of the demonstrations suggest, the main targets of these actions were anti-LGB government policies, and specifically discrimination in federal employment and the military. But as Duberman and Stein have argued, the homophile demonstrators criticized government policies not by attacking American values but by affirming them. Signs such as the one that read "Civil Service Commission is Un-American" and references in press releases and flyers to the Declaration of Independence, the Bill of Rights, the U.S. Constitution, and the Founding Fathers presented the homophile protestors as American patriots. What is particularly striking about this is that this was precisely the moment in history when black power, student, and antiwar protests in the United States were increasingly adopting anti-American rhetoric. Duberman and Stein have also called attention to the conservatism of the dress code imposed by organizers on the picket lines: women were required to wear dresses, men were required to wear business suits, white shirts, and ties. Attempting to challenge stereotypical views of mannish lesbians and feminine gay men and receive maximum favorable publicity in the mainstream press, homophile leaders such as Kameny and Gittings insisted on conformity with conventional gender values as they deployed strategies of what Stein has labeled "militant respectability."

While initial public reaction was minimal, in large part because of a lack of press coverage, homophile activists criticized the demonstrations from various perspectives. Some (including Rodwell) objected to the primary focus on federal employment; others (such as New York's Dick Leitsch) were critical of the dress code. While DOB New York members such as Ernestine Eckstein supported the demonstrations, the DOB national leadership did not, thinking that this was a premature step. Within days of ECHO's June decision to organize demonstrations, DOB withdrew from the regional federation. Nevertheless, militantly respectable homophile demonstrations continued.

Meanwhile, LGBT people began adopting other, more confrontational direct action tactics. On 25 April, after 150 people, many LGBT and many "wearing nonconformist clothing," were refused service at Dewey's restaurant on 17th Street in Philadelphia, two teenage boys and one teenage girl staged an impromptu sit-in. The three were promptly arrested by police, as was local homophile leader Clark Polak, who had come to their assistance. After the four were found guilty of disorderly conduct, the Janus Society, defending the rights of the "masculine woman and the feminine man," organized a five-day demonstration, which culminated in another sit-in on 2 May. Janus claimed that it helped achieve "an immediate cessation of all indiscriminate denials of service" (Stein, pp. 245–246).

After 1965, homophile and transgender protests continued. In 1966, the July Fourth demonstration at Independence Hall became the "Annual Reminder." About 50 conservatively dressed homophile activists marched in 1966, 25–30 in 1967, 75 in 1968, and 45–150 in 1969. Nationally coordinated homophile demonstrations protesting the exclusion of homosexuals from the military took place on Armed Forces Day (21 May) in 1966. Although the details remain murky, in August 1966 another type of confrontational demonstration occurred when transgendered youth, queens, gay hustlers, and others rioted to protest police arrests at Compton's cafeteria in San Francisco's Tenderloin. In the same year, homophile activists in San Francisco who had been denied permission to set up an information booth at the state fair in Sacramento distributed 10,000 leaflets outside the entrance. In 1968, San Francisco LGB people picketed the city's federal office building to protest federal employment discrimination, military discrimination, and laws against private consensual sex. In the late 1960s, Los Angeles picketers protested rules prohibiting entertainers from cross-dressing during performances. The final Annual Reminder in Philadelphia took place just a few weeks after the 1969 Stonewall Riots, which launched a new era in LGBT history.

Bibliography

D'Emilio, John. *Sexual Politics, Sexual Communities.* Chicago: University of Chicago Press, 1983.

Duberman, Martin. *Stonewall.* New York: Dutton 1993.

Gay and Lesbian Historical Society of Northern California. "MTF Transgender Activism in the Tenderloin and Beyond, 1966-1975." *GLQ* 4:2 (1998): 349-372.

Stein, Marc. *City of Sisterly and Brotherly Loves: Lesbian and Gay Philadelphia, 1945–1972.* Chicago: University of Chicago Press, 2000.

Suran, Justin David. "Coming Out Against the War: Antimilitarism and the Politicization of Homosexuality in the Era of Vietnam." American Quarterly 53:3 (September 2001): 452-488.

Thompson, Mark (editor). *Long Road to Freedom: The Advocate History of the Gay and Lesbian Movement.* New York: St. Martin's, 1994.

See also ANTIWAR, PACIFIST, AND PEACE MOVEMENTS; HOMOPHILE MOVEMENT; JANUS SOCIETY; NEW YORK; PHILADELPHIA; RIGHTS OF ASSOCIATION AND ASSEMBLY.

HOMOPHILE PRESS

"Homophile press" usually refers to the dozen or so mid-twentieth-century lesbian and gay newsletters and magazines published before the Stonewall Riots, most of which emphasized the acceptability of homosexuality through intellectual, political, and/or artistic content, and de-emphasized the sexual aspects of homosexuality. Although lesbian and gay organizations did not widely adopt the word "homophile" until 1960, they (and later historians) often applied the term retroactively to groups and publications dating as far back as the late 1940s and early 1950s.

In retrospect, many of the publications of the homophile press may now seem tame and apologetic, but they were radical for their time. In an era when homosexuality was almost universally condemned as a crime, a sin, a mental illness, and a sign of general untrustworthiness, the writers of these publications dared to talk about homosexuality in the first person and say that it was an essentially harmless variation of human nature. Some homophile journalists directly challenged psychiatrists' claims that gay people were sick. Most of the publications argued for decriminalization of homosexuality and an end to police harassment of people in gay bars. They ran articles about police crackdowns, sex-law reform campaigns in other countries, famous homosexuals throughout history, psychiatric research into sexual orientation, and recent homophile events and conferences. Some also included book and film reviews, short stories, and whimsical humor. Even with this relatively tame content, postal authorities of the 1950s sometimes considered the mere fact that a magazine defended "sexual perversion" grounds to impound copies of it as obscene.

In addition to shipping copies to subscribers and organization members, the organizations that published such material often sent free copies to people perceived as having the power to change the treatment of lesbian and gay people in American society: mental health professionals, legislators, law enforcement officers, writers and journalists from mainstream news organizations, radio and television talk show hosts, and so on.

Pre-1960s Publications

The earliest homophile periodicals had very limited press runs, ranging from fewer than twenty copies per issue to about 7,500. Some people have argued that the homophile press had little impact on lesbian and gay people at the time. It is in fact true that most lesbians and gay men did not even know there was a movement afoot for gay equality, much less that gay news periodicals existed. However, these publications were important despite their small circulation. For the movement's writers and activists, the homophile press was a laboratory for developing ideas, political philosophies, and rhetoric, and a way to keep up with what colleagues were accomplishing elsewhere in the country. For nonmovement readers, the periodicals were a source of information, entertainment, and ideas that were at odds with the overwhelming conventional wisdom about homosexuality. For straight mental health professionals and law enforcement officers, they provided an opportunity to understand the perspectives of a type of homosexual person such heterosexuals seldom knowingly met: those neither in therapy nor in trouble with the police. The magazines were also a way of encouraging the mainstream media to occasionally present reports about homosexuality that took into account the perspectives of the people most affected: homosexuals themselves.

When authors write about the history of the homophile press, they usually begin with *Vice Versa,* which published nine monthly issues starting in June 1947. Its editor and main writer, later known as "Lisa Ben," distributed this typewritten, carbon-copied newsletter for women in two Los Angeles lesbian bars. Distributing *Vice Versa* was simple because there were only twelve copies of each issue. *Vice Versa* is the earliest U.S. lesbian and/or gay–equality periodical known to survive. The only earlier documented publications were the 1925 newsletters of the Chicago-based Society for Human Rights, no copies of which are known to still exist.

The "big three" national homophile magazines of the 1950s—*ONE,* the *Mattachine Review,* and the *Ladder*—were the official publications of the era's most prominent homophile groups: ONE, Incorporated; the Mattachine Society; and the Daughters of Bilitis (DOB). All three either launched with or quickly adopted a professionally typeset look. All were monthly publications for most of their run.

ONE was the first to launch, in 1953. Its parent organization, ONE, Incorporated, was founded in Los Angeles the year before for the purpose of creating a lesbian and gay–focused news and literary magazine. *ONE* differed from previous lesbian and gay periodicals in that it was professionally typeset on semigloss paper, was sold openly at several newsstands, and had a comparatively large press run. Editors during the first year were Martin Block and (later) Dale Jennings, who had cofounded the magazine with Bill Lambert (a.k.a. "W. Dorr Legg"). Early contributors included Jim Kepner, Chuck Rowland, and Ann Carll Reid. Although the magazine's content focused more on gay men than lesbians for most of its run, it did often include material by lesbian writers and artists, and for a time it was edited by a woman (Reid). After the magazine's debut, its parent organization developed into a lesbian and gay–equality group and an academic-style research and learning center on lesbian and gay issues. In 1958 *ONE* won a landmark legal battle that benefited all homophile publications: the U.S. Supreme Court unanimously ruled that defending homosexuality did not, in and of itself, make a magazine obscene. That same year, ONE, Incorporated, began to publish America's first lesbian and gay–studies journal, the groundbreaking *ONE Institute Quarterly of Homophile Studies* (1958–1965). It was an unprecedented publication with a limited appeal: it attracted fewer than two hundred subscribers. The group also produced a newsletter for members, *ONE Confidential. ONE* magazine continued publication until 1969, when it fell apart due to internal factionalism.

The *Mattachine Review,* the second major homophile magazine, stood in stark contrast to *ONE.* For much of its 1955 to 1966 run, it was a kind of gay *Reader's Digest,* composed of reprints and summaries of gay-relevant articles originally published elsewhere, interspersed with original reporting and opinion. Whereas *ONE* often published fiction, poetry, and humor, the *Mattachine Review* was primarily a source of news and political views. Even more so than *ONE,* it deemphasized sex. Partly, this approach was a public relations ploy, to counteract the stereotype that gay people were sex fiends who cared little about personal responsibility as members of society. Partly, it was on the advice of the Mattachine Society's lawyers, who worried both about the magazine's potential seizure for obscenity and about its being perceived as promoting a criminal activity (gay sex). Especially in its early years, the *Mattachine Review* advanced a very conformist, middle-class image of gay men, suggesting they are just like everyone else and would blend into society inconspicuously if only society would let them. In addition to this national magazine, there were local Mattachine newsletters in at least eight cities, most of which began publication in the 1960s.

The *Ladder* began as a mimeographed publication. As the official magazine of DOB—a lesbian organization—it focused primarily on news, features, poetry, and fiction for women. However, its readership and writers did include some gay men. DOB cofounders Del Martin and Phyllis Lyon launched the *Ladder* in San Francisco in 1956 as a way to boost the membership of their struggling, year-old organization. In the mid-1960s, under the editorship of Philadelphia-based activist Barbara Gittings, it became the first lesbian or gay magazine to consistently feature photos of actual people (in this case, lesbians) on the covers, thus putting a human face on homosexuality. During this period, the production of the *Ladder* became a battleground for some of the era's key ideological controversies within the homophile movement, and Gittings often had disagreements with the DOB's national headquarters over everything from the magazine's content to the text that appeared on each cover. By the time Barbara Grier (a.k.a. Gene Damon) became the *Ladder*'s final editor in 1968, DOB as an organization was on the wane, eclipsed by more radical organizations with ties to the women's liberation movement. Grier infused the *Ladder* with feminist politics that did not sit well with the DOB's national leadership. In 1970, after a lengthy struggle with DOB, she gained full control of the magazine. Grier published it independently until 1972. Judging from the letters received by the editors throughout the magazine's sixteen years, the publication served as a lifeline for a great many lesbians in remote areas of the United States. The DOB's regional chapters throughout the country also produced newsletters focusing on local events and issues.

Publications That Debuted in the 1960s

Some pre-Stonewall gay-equality periodicals of the 1960s fit firmly into the homophile model established in the 1950s, whereas others employed sexual references and political rhetoric that presaged the sexual liberationist gay lib publications of the early 1970s.

Periodicals following the homophile model included mimeographed newsletters such as the *LCE News* (published in San Francisco by the League for Civil Education starting in 1961), *The Atheneum Review* (published in Florida by the Atheneum Society starting in 1964), and the *Homophile Action League Newsletter* (published in Philadelphia starting in 1968). There were also slicker publications with a magazine format, such as *Tangents* (which split off from *One* in 1965) and *The Homosexual Citizen* (published by the Mattachine Society of Washington, D.C., in collaboration with the Mattachine Society of Florida starting in 1966).

One of the earliest gay news periodicals to incorporate nude photography and a more sex-positive ethos was *Drum,* published in Philadelphia beginning in 1964.

Drum was the brainchild of Clark Polak, head of Philadelphia's Janus Society (formerly the local Mattachine chapter). In *Drum,* Polak created one of the best-selling gay periodicals of the era and used the profits to fund activism and legal challenges. The idea of a homophile organization issuing a borderline soft-porn magazine made Polak and the Janus Society many enemies within the homophile movement. The magazine included serious news (indeed, it was apparently the first gay publication to hire a clipping service to research gay-relevant events in the world), as well as sexually tinged comic strips and essays. However, it was the photographs of young men in bathing suits, shorts, or nothing at all that fueled the ire of many activists. To avoid problems with postal authorities, *Drum* avoided using full frontal nudity (at least not in the version mailed to subscribers), but Polak was nonetheless arrested for distributing obscene literature. In 1969 the magazine folded amid pending legal actions.

In 1967 the Los Angeles–based Personal Rights in Defense and Education (PRIDE) launched a newsletter that would soon become a nationally sold independent gay newspaper: the *Los Angeles Advocate.* A review of its back issues from the late 1960s indicates a tone very different from that of the 1950s homophile publications. Although the *Advocate,* too, contained news and reviews, its playful approach suggested something not obvious in the earlier, more solemn homophile press: that gay people sometimes had fun. In its pages it promoted such clearly nonhomophile events as an ongoing "Advocate Groovy Guy Contest," in which well-muscled young male readers vied to be named the Groovy Guy of the year. The *Advocate,* like other publications such as *Vector* (in San Francisco) and the newspaper *Gay* (in New York), marked a transitional stage between the old homophile press and the imminent explosion of gay liberation publications.

As longtime *ONE* columnist and *Advocate* journalist Jim Kepner once noted, some historians have dismissed the earliest homophile periodicals as amateurish, because they had few professionally trained journalists on their staff. However, as Kepner pointed out, professional journalists were not willing to take the risk of writing for the homophile press. "We did the job," he said, "while the professional journalists stayed in the closet for thirty years" (pp. 6–7).

Bibliography

Cain, Paul D. *Leading the Parade: Conversations with America's Most Influential Lesbians and Gay Men.* Lanham, Md.: Scarecrow Press, 2002.

D'Emilio, John. *Sexual Politics, Sexual Communities: The Making of a Homosexual Minority in the United States, 1940–1970.* Chicago: University of Chicago Press, 1983.

Kepner, Jim. *Rough News, Daring Views: 1950s Pioneer Gay Press Journalism.* New York: Harrington Park Press, 1998.

The Ladder, 1956–1972. New York: Arno Press, 1975.

Marcus, Eric. *Making Gay History: The Half-Century Fight for Lesbian and Gay Equal Rights.* New York: HarperCollins, 2002.

The Mattachine Review, 1955–1966. New York: Arno Press, 1975.

Stein, Marc. *City of Sisterly and Brotherly Loves: Lesbian and Gay Philadelphia, 1945–1972.* Chicago: University of Chicago Press, 2000.

Streitmatter, Rodger. *Unspeakable: The Rise of the Gay and Lesbian Press in America.* Boston: Faber and Faber, 1995.

Tobin, Kay, and Randy Wicker. *The Gay Crusaders.* New York: Arno Press, 1975.

Steven Capsuto

See also *ADVOCATE*; BEN, LISA; CENSORSHIP, OBSCENITY, AND PORNOGRAPHY LAW AND POLICY; *DRUM*; GITTINGS, BARBARA, AND KAY TOBIN LAHUSEN; GRIER, BARBARA; HOMOPHILE MOVEMENT; KEPNER, JAMES; *LADDER*; LEGG, DORR; LYON, PHYLLIS, AND DEL MARTIN; *MATTACHINE REVIEW*; NEWSPAPERS AND MAGAZINES; *ONE*; POLAK, CLARK.

HOMOPHOBIA. see HETEROSEXISM AND HOMOPHOBIA.

HOMOSEXUALITY AND HETEROSEXUALITY

The changing relationship between "homosexuality" (same-sex sexuality) and "heterosexuality" (cross-sex sexuality) lies at the heart of the oppression and liberation of LGB people.

The Medical Model

The French philosopher Michel Foucault, in *The History of Sexuality: Volume One, An Introduction* (1976), declared that before the late nineteenth century, "the sodomite" was "a temporary aberration," but from about 1870 "the homosexual was now a species (p. 43)." Before 1870, the reproductive imperative dominated discourse about sexuality. According to this discourse, it was everyone's responsibility to reproduce, and sexual activities not linked to procreation, like masturbation and same-sex sexual acts, were fleeting phases, dangerous temptations, and moral sins. Although same-sex sexual desires and behaviors may have been common, there was no concept of distinct groups of people ("species") who could be classified on the basis of their sexual orientation. This changed in the late nineteenth century.

In 1868, in a letter to the German sex reformer Karl Heinrich Ulrichs, Karl Maria Kertbeny, a Hungarian writer and journalist, became the first person to use the terms "homosexuality" and "heterosexuality." Although his expression "Heterosexualität," coined in 1880, was initially used in the context of arguments for homosexual reform, the terms "homosexuality" and "heterosexuality" soon came to represent polar opposites, with the former referring to the abnormal and the latter referring to the normal. Together, the words "homosexuality" and "heterosexuality" have defined and policed the boundaries of sexual respectability in the United States.

The homosexuality/heterosexuality conceptual framework took time to stabilize. The earliest mention of the term "heterosexuality" by an American was in "Responsibility for Sexual Perversion," an article by James G. Kiernan that was published in the Chicago Medical Recorder (1892). For Kiernan, heterosexuality was as abnormal as homosexuality because it represented an urge towards nonprocreative sex for pleasure. Kiernan also viewed heterosexuality as abnormal because he defined it as an orientation to different (meaning both male and female) sexes, the equivalent of today's notion of bisexuality. The German doctor Richard von Krafft-Ebing developed a different understanding of the two terms in the late nineteenth century. For Krafft-Ebing, homosexuality was an aberrant attraction for the same sex, a deviation from the norm of opposite sex attraction. It was experienced by "inverts," who displayed the gender style of the opposite sex. Krafft-Ebing's conception thus conflated what today would be regarded as homosexuality and transgenderism. In contrast to Kiernan, the English sex reformer Havelock Ellis stressed the positive nature of heterosexuality, and he viewed sex between a man and a woman as pleasurable in itself rather than a mere vehicle for procreation. But his divorcing of sex from procreation did not prevent him from taking a negative view of homosexuality, which he saw as an instinctual sexual orientation.

The psychoanalyst Sigmund Freud perhaps did more than anyone else to create an antagonistic relationship between homosexuality and heterosexuality. For Freud, sexual desire was socialized. By attaining "heterosexuality," one reached nothing less than full human maturity, having survived a process of fantasizing about incest and patricide. The hard road to maturity might include homosexual fantasy and practice in childhood and adolescence. But for Freud there was always the sturdy upright goal of mature heterosexual relations. Homosexuality was simply the result and the sign of immaturity. According to Freud, sexual object choice was conditioned by family relations and was not innate. But, like Ellis, Freud argued that gender characteristics (masculinity and femininity) were not necessarily related to sexual object choice (homosexuality and heterosexuality). However one appeared, one could be a homosexual.

Many scholars now emphasize that scientific experts were responding to the prior development of LGBT cultures rather than creating something entirely new. Some have also argued that these new sexual categories are best understood in the context of, in dialogue with, and as products of the new racial classification systems that developed in the same period. Most agree, however, that these scientific experts and others played crucial roles in developing modern conceptions of homosexuality and heterosexuality.

The Homosexual/Heterosexual Dichotomy in the Early Twentieth Century

Inspired by Freud and Ellis, a number of early twentieth-century writers popularized heterosexuality as a norm that they self-consciously placed in opposition to homosexuality. Various writers explored changes in sexual mores in terms that were viciously homophobic. For example, in Sinclair Lewis's *Dodsworth* (1929), the American Sam Dodsworth is dragged by the German Kurt into a gay bar. Authors of sex and marriage manuals were often obsessed with the homosexual/heterosexual dichotomy. The psychologist Samuel Schmalhausen warned boys "not to frequent public toilets, for many perverts watch these places as a means of enticing boys ... for aught I know homosexuals may be winning armies of new recruits." Clement Wood scared middle America by stating that 50 percent of twelve-year-old boys were homosexual. Joseph Collins devoted one-third of his book *The Doctor Looks at Love and Life* (1926) to the subject of homosexuality. Collins noted the common view that homosexuals showed effeminate traits. But he insisted that he had known homosexual men who appeared "normal." George Chauncey has shown that in mainstream American society in the 1910s and 1920s, older views that homosexuality was a disorder of gender nonconformity still held sway. According to "Christian Brotherhood or Sexual Perversion?" (1985), as late as 1919, it was possible for "straight" sailors to engage in sexual relations with effeminate "fairy" men without losing their status as "normal" men, if they played the "masculine" role in sex. Chauncey's work suggests that popular discourse diverged from scientific discourse in this period and that the modern homosexual/heterosexual system had not fully solidified. Yet the popular sexual system was changing, as several "straight" men who had volunteered to have sex with and entrap "fairies" were questioned during an investigation at the Newport Naval Training Station.

Lesbians experienced similar changes. Chauncey argued that the shift from models of gender inversion to models of homosexuality also took place in conceptions of female same-sex sexualities, although the shift took place a little later and was not as complete. In 1978, Christina Simmons, in "Companionate Marriage and the Lesbian Threat," argued that the 1920s ideology of happy, egalitarian companionate marriage generated a female heterosexual ideal to counter "the lesbian threat" posed by the visibility of lesbianism in the 1920s (as symbolized by free-loving Greenwich Village bohemians and the mannish lesbians of popular culture). Both women and men faced the social control of the heterosexual/ homosexual dichotomy. Increasingly, intimate same-sex friendships, relationships, and expressions of physical affection were regarded with suspicion, and isolated experiences of same-sex desires or behaviors were seen as evidence of homosexual character. At the same time, heterosexuality was advertised, publicized, encouraged, and celebrated.

Kinsey, the Cold War, and the Sexual Continuum

In *Sexual Behavior in the Human Male* (1948), the sexologist Alfred C. Kinsey revealed, in an extensive study of the sexual habits of 12,000 men, how flawed heterosexuality and homosexuality were as ways of categorizing people (as opposed to sexual acts). Kinsey claimed that 37 percent of American men had had at least one homosexual experience to orgasm in their post-adolescent lives. Ten percent of men had predominantly gay sexual experiences for at least three years in their lives. In other words, homosexuality was extremely common among American men. To capture the complexity of sexual behavior, Kinsey set up a continuum, a seven-point scale, according to which those who were exclusively heterosexual in behavior were rated "0," and those who were exclusively homosexual in behavior were rated "6." Yet very few people actually scored a "0" or a "6." Most people scored somewhere in between, having had both heterosexual and homosexual experiences. "Not all things are black nor all things white," declared Kinsey with deliberate provocation (Kinsey, p. 639). In providing this evidence, Kinsey also completed Freud's work of establishing that sexual preference was a matter of object choice, not gender identity. In 1953, Kinsey followed up his earlier study with *Sexual Behavior in the Human Female,* which showed somewhat lower rates of female homosexuality but nevertheless shocked the U.S. public even more.

In the context of the Cold War, Kinsey was both celebrated (as a rational scientist) and vilified (as an advocate of immorality). While many supporters saw elements in Kinsey's work that could help modernize heterosexual marriage, others saw him as undermining the foundations of American family life. Increasingly in the 1940s and 1950s, conformist heterosexuality was brought into play as a weapon on the Cold War home front. Marriage counsellor Paul Popenoe observed that "Marriage is one of the fundamental institutions which has perpetuated the human race and made civilization possible (Popenoe, p. 192)." For Cold War patriots, strong American marriages confirmed to the world the superiority of U.S. capitalism over Soviet communism. Images of happy families and of heterosexual togetherness abounded in popular culture, from advertising to television shows such as *Leave It to Beaver* and *The Adventures of Ozzie and Harriet.* And Americans conformed en masse: between 1946 and 1957, the birth rate went up by 50 percent; by 1956, the median age of marriage dropped to as low as 20.1 for women and 22.5 for men; and the divorce rate stabilized. Meanwhile, *Playboy* magazine (first published in 1953) and other parts of the sex industry linked the high ideals of consumer capitalism with the pleasures of heterosexuality. The 1950s were the high-water mark for American heterosexuality as an idea, driving countless LGB people into heterosexual marriages and relationships.

The price of this was not only the repression of the homosexual feelings identified by Freud and Kinsey as present among supposed heterosexuals, but the putting down of homosexuals as racial aberrations, psychopathic personalities, and political threats. The sociologist David Reisman (Loosely, p. xii) and other advocates of familial togetherness warned of "the growing homogenization of the sexes" and reacted to old fears of the blurring of gender boundaries between men and women. The government hounded out and weeded out homosexual employees. A U.S. Senate report identified homosexuals as security risks and railed that gay people lacked "emotional stability" and "moral fibre" (Employment of Homosexuals and Other Sex Perverts in Government, 1950, p. 3). Just as Kinsey had opened up a potential blurring of distinctions between homosexuality and heterosexuality, the terms returned in the 1950s as polar and binary opposites to be used as instruments of social control and cultural conformity.

Gay Liberation and the Heterosexual Revolution

Ironically, the dark days of the 1950s contained the seeds of LGBT liberation in the formation of the Mattachine Society, ONE, Inc., and the Daughters of Bilitis, the first homophile movement organizations. These organizations pioneered campaigns for equal rights in the decades before the Stonewall Riots, yet while they railed against the limitations of the homosexuality/heterosexuality system, they fundamentally accepted its principles. Mattachine described homosexuals as "a social minority imprisoned within a dominant culture." The Daughters of Bilitis identified itself as a group of "organised homosexuals . . . for social, not antisocial, ends." Neither Mattachine nor the Daughters of Bilitis rejected the notion of categorizing people as homosexual or heterosexual; they simply wanted those categorized as such to have equal rights.

By the end of the 1960s, however, a number of writers began to more radically redefine the meanings and experiences of homosexuality and heterosexuality. Herbert Marcuse and Wilhelm Reich helped break down the boundaries between homosexuality and heterosexuality by seeking to liberate sexuality from procreation. The birth control pill (launched in the United States in 1960) revolutionized heterosexuality by encouraging more young people to experiment with nonreproductive sex and cohabitation before marriage. The counterculture celebrated the pleasures of sex, drugs, and rock and roll. Following the Stonewall Riots of 1969, gay liberation activists sought to collapse the heterosexual/homosexual dichotomy. For example, in *A Gay Manifesto* (1969–1970), Carl Wittman explicitly rejected the notion that homosexuality was a biological orientation, insisting that "Nature leaves undefined the object of sexual desire. The gender of that object is imposed socially" (Wittman, p. 381). With Kinsey in mind, Wittman then argued that "bisexuality is good; it is the capacity to love someone of the same sex." Noting that "exclusive heterosexuality is fucked up" Wittman wrote that he looked forward to a time when everyone was free to sleep with whomever they liked: men or women.

Wittman tried to liberate the homosexual element in everyone. Similarly, the 1970 statement of the Male Homosexual Workshop at the Revolutionary People's Constitutional Convention declared that "the revolution will not be complete until all men are free to express their love for one another sexually." Everyone ought to come out, the workshop argued. In *Homosexual: Oppression and Liberation* (1971), Dennis Altman predicted "the end of the homosexual" (Altman, p. 225.) because once everyone could express themselves as they wished, sexual boundaries would disappear.

Lesbian feminism in this decade took a similar view. Outraged by Betty Friedan's categorization of lesbian feminists as a "lavender menace," groups such as Radicalesbians put forward a vision of the "woman-identified woman." Radicalesbians declared that "a lesbian is the rage of all women condensed to the point of explosion." In this view, lesbianism was the logical result of feminism, which could free women to explore their feelings for each other as they freed themselves from male tyranny. Lesbian scholars also developed this theme. In the *Straight Mind* (1975), Monique Wittig drew out the links between the homo/hetero dichotomy and the oppression of woman by man. In *Compulsory Heterosexuality and Lesbian Existence* (1981), Adrienne Rich powerfully examined the pressures that influenced women's choices to become heterosexual rather than lesbian. Women should free themselves to love each other, she argued.

The New Right, AIDS, and Queer Theory

Yet by the late 1970s, the homosexual/heterosexual binary had regained much of its power. Many LGB people abandoned or rejected the radicalism of gay liberation and lesbian feminism, adopted the view that they were members of a fixed sexual minority, and turned to efforts to achieve full sexual equality within the terms of the homosexual/heterosexual binary. Whether this represented genuine or strategic essentialism, it became the dominant LGB position. Increasingly, the struggle for LGB pride and integrity took the form of demanding the inclusion of sexual orientation nondiscrimination clauses in human rights legislation to ensure that the rights of LGB people were respected.

Meanwhile, a fierce anti-LGB backlash from the fundamentalist and evangelical Christian New Right sought to reaffirm and strengthen the positioning of heterosexuality as superior to homosexuality as part of a wide-ranging "pro-family" agenda. For right-wing leaders such as Jerry Falwell and Anita Bryant, homosexuality was a condition that could and should be cured when the LGB sinner converted to Christianity. To members of the Christian Right, the fact that AIDS began to affect large numbers of gay men in the 1980s proved that heterosexuality was intrinsically superior to homosexuality.

Yet during the 1980s, distinctions and boundaries between homosexuality and heterosexuality again began to break down. AIDS increased straight people's sympathy for LGB people and made the straight public aware, when public consciousness about AIDS in straight communities increased, that sexual boundaries were oftentimes porous and fluid. AIDS campaigns that targeted "men who have sex with men" rather than "gay men" reflected and promoted the notion that sexual desires, behaviors, and identities did not always correspond in the ways that one might expect. In this same period, LGBT and straight consumerism increasingly appeared to converge, leading Altman to include the phrase "the homosexualization of America" in the title of one of his books.

Challenges to the homosexual/heterosexual binary continued in the early 1990s with the emergence of queer activism and theory. Queer advocates proposed a coalition of all those who were marginal to or excluded from dominant systems of sex, gender, and sexuality. Bisexuals and transgender people, as well as gays and lesbians, joined organizations such as Queer Nation, helping to develop a politics based on sexual and gender multiplicity. Building on the work of scholars who had been examining the social, cultural, and historical construction of sexuality, queer theorists such as Eve Sedgwick and Judith Butler rejected the simplistic division of populations into mutually exclusive homosexual and heterosexual groups and argued instead that human beings were capable of varied and complicated sexual lives that defied straightforward categorization. Meanwhile, queer historians, anthropologists, and other scholars demonstrated that most societies—past and present—have not conceptualized sexuality in terms of the homosexual/heterosexual binary. In doing so, they hoped to deconstruct today's dominant sexual system and construct new and better frameworks for the future.

Bibliography

Altman, Dennis. *Homosexual: Oppression and Liberation.* New York: New York University Press, 1971.

Butler, Judith. *Gender Trouble: Feminism and the Subversion of Identity.* New York: Routledge, 1990.

Chauncey, George, Jr. "Christian Brotherhood or Sexual Perversion? Homosexual Identities and the Construction of Sexual Boundaries in the World War One Era." *Journal of Social History* 19, no. 2 (winter 1985): 189–211.

———. *Gay New York: Gender, Urban Culture, and the Making of the Gay Male World, 1890–1940.* New York: Basic Books, 1994.

Collins, Joseph. *The Doctor Looks at Love and Life.* Garden City, N.Y.: Garden City Publishing, 1929.

Foucault, Michel. *The History of Sexuality: Volume One, An Introduction.* Translated by Robert Hurley. New York: Pantheon, 1978.

Katz, Jonathan Ned. *The Invention of Heterosexuality.* New York: Dutton, 1995.

Kiernan, James G. "Responsibility for Sexual Perversion." Chicago Medical Recorder, vol. 3 (1892): 185–210.

Kinsey, Alfred C. *Sexual Behavior in the Human Male.* Philadelphia: W.B. Saunders, 1948.

Kinsey, Alfred C., et al. *Sexual Behavior in the Human Female.* Philadelphia: W.B. Saunders, 1953.

Loosely, E.W. *Crestwood Heights.* Toronto: University of Toronto Press, 1956.

May, Elaine Tyler. *Homeward Bound: American Families in the Cold War Era.* New York: Basic Books, 1988.

Popenoe, Paul. "What Science Can Do for Matrimony." Address given before the Southern California division of the American Eugenics Society, Los Angeles Public Library. Pasadena, California: Gosney Papers, April 1940.

Rich, Adrienne. *Compulsory Heterosexuality and Lesbian Existence.* London: Onlywomen Press, 1981.

Schalhausen, Samuel. "The War of the Sexes." *Woman's Coming of Age: A Symposium.* ed. V.F. Calverton. New York: Liveright, 1931.

Sedgwick, Eve Kosofsky. *Epistemology of the Closet.* Berkeley: University of California Press, 1989.

Segal, Lynne. *Straight Sex: Rethinking the Politics of Pleasure.* Berkeley: University of California Press, 1994.

Simmons, Christina. "Companionate Marriage and the Lesbian Threat." *Frontiers* 4, no. 3 (fall 1978): 54–59.

Wittig, Monique. *The Straight Mind and Other Essays.* Boston: Beacon Press, 1992.

Wittman, Carl. "*A Gay Manifesto.*" *We Are Everywhere.* ed. Blasius, Mark and Phelan, Shane. New York: Routledge, 1997.

Wood, Clement. *Manhood: The Facts of Life Presented to Men.* Girardi. U.S. 1924.

Kevin White

See also BISEXUALITY, BISEXUALS, AND BISEXUAL MOVEMENTS; ESSENTIALISM AND CONSTRUCTIONISM; GAY LIBERATION; HOMOPHOBIA AND HETEROSEXISM; HOMOEROTICISM AND HOMOSOCIALITY; KINSEY, ALFRED C.; LANGUAGE; LESBIAN FEMINISM; MEDICINE, MEDICALIZATION, AND THE MEDICAL MODEL; PSYCHOLOGY, PSYCHIATRY, PSYCHOANALYSIS, AND SEXOLOGY; RADICALESBIANS; SEX ACTS; SEXUAL ORIENTATION AND PREFERENCE; SEXUAL REVOLUTIONS; SITUATIONAL HOMOSEXUALITY; WITTMAN, CARL.

HOOKER, Evelyn **(b. 2 September 1907; d. 18 November 1996), psychologist.**

Evelyn Hooker was an American psychologist who conducted pioneering research that questioned the assumption that homosexuals were psychologically maladjusted. Her support for LGB rights reflected a lifelong commitment to social justice. She had experienced poverty in her formative years, faced gender discrimination in her early professional life, and witnessed the effects of totalitarianism when she traveled abroad in the 1930s. In 1945, when asked by a gay male friend, she accepted the challenge to study the psychological adjustment of gay men. Based on her life experiences, she was prepared to engage in research that could potentially contribute to eradicating the injustices faced by homosexuals.

Born Evelyn Gentry in 1907 in North Platte, Nebraska, Hooker obtained her bachelor's and master's degrees from the University of Colorado and her doctorate in experimental psychology from Johns Hopkins University in 1932. In 1939 she began her three-decade tenure at the University of California, Los Angeles (UCLA), as a research associate in the psychology department. She also taught in the extension division and, with the exception of one year at Bryn Mawr College, remained at UCLA until 1970, when she went into private practice as a clinical psychologist.

After some preliminary data gathering, Hooker's research with gay men was delayed several years because of her divorce from her first husband and her remarriage to Edward Niles Hooker, a distinguished UCLA professor of English. In 1953 she received a grant to support her research from the National Institute of Mental Health (NIMH). She subsequently obtained a series of NIMH grants and in 1961 was the recipient of an NIMH Research Career Grant. Her major study involved a comparison of thirty homosexual and thirty heterosexual men who were matched for age, intelligence, and education. To test the question of whether homosexuality was pathological, she limited her sample of homosexuals to those who were not referred by a clinical agency, did not seek psychological help, and were gainfully employed. Using indices of psychological adjustment, this group of nonclinical homosexual men could not be distinguished by a panel of expert clinical psychologists from the comparison group of heterosexual men.

Hooker's results produced shockwaves among mental health professionals. She was the first investigator to perform a controlled study in which matched groups of homosexual and heterosexual men were compared on psychological measures of adjustment. Her results dispelled the conventional psychiatric belief that homosexuality was associated with psychological maladjustment. Many mental health professionals, however, criticized her work on the grounds of biased sampling and faulty measures. Nevertheless, her study forced a debate on the question of whether homosexuality constituted maladjustment, and her findings were corroborated in subsequent research in the early 1970s with larger samples and more proven measures of psychological adjustment.

Hooker also pioneered in ethnographic research on the male homosexual subculture in American society. In a series of published papers in the 1960s, she reported on her research as a participant-observer in the gay male homosexual community in Los Angeles. She defined her role as a nonevaluative one in which she strove to see the homosexual world through the eyes of her research subjects. Her in-depth portrayal of the social patterns and institutions of gay life was the first published work of its kind in the scientific literature and it was influential in the subsequent expansion of ethnographic studies of the LGBT subculture in the 1970s.

Reflecting her research achievements, in 1967 she was appointed to head an NIMH Task Force on Homosexuality, which recommended the decriminalization of homosexuality and the removal of employment discrimination against gay men and lesbians. While the Nixon administration ignored the task force report, the report's liberal call for tolerance toward gay men and lesbians and its challenge to the psychiatric orthodoxy of labeling all homosexuals as pathological were influential in the ensuing campaign to remove homosexuality from the roster of psychiatric diagnoses. By the early 1970s, reflecting the impact of the gay liberation movement, gay and lesbian activists and a group of psychiatrists and psychologists who dissented from the canonical medical model challenged the American Psychiatric Association (APA) on the categorization of homosexuality as a mental illness. Hooker's research was heavily cited as scientific evidence refuting the pathologization of homosexuality. In 1974 the APA removed homosexuality from its diagnostic manual.

Bibliography

Bayer, Ronald. *Homosexuality and American Psychiatry: The Politics of Diagnosis.* New York: Basic Books, 1981.

Changing Our Minds: The Story of Dr. Evelyn Hooker. 16mm, 77 min., Intrepid Productions, Los Angeles, 1991.

Hooker, Evelyn. "The Adjustment of the Male Overt Homosexual." *Journal of Projective Techniques* 21 (1957): 18–31.

Minton, Henry L. *Departing from Deviance: A History of Homosexual Rights and Emancipatory Science in America.* Chicago: University of Chicago Press, 2002.

Henry L. Minton

See also ERICKSON EDUCATIONAL FOUNDATION; MEDICINE, MEDICALIZATION, AND THE MEDICAL MODEL; PSYCHOLOGY, PSYCHIATRY, PSYCHOANALYSIS, AND SEXOLOGY.

HOOVER, J. Edgar **(b. 1 January 1895; d. 2 May 1972), longtime Director of the Federal Bureau of Investigation.**

John Edgar Hoover was born to Dickerson Naylor and Annie Hoover in the District of Columbia, the youngest of four children. At sixteen, Edgar (or "Speed," as friends called him, because of his breakneck pace) took his first job as a file clerk at the Library of Congress. While completing a combined college and law degree at George

J. Edgar Hoover. The longtime head of the Federal Bureau of Investigation, whose targets included not only bank robbers, kidnappers, and spies but also homosexuals (despite rumors about his own sexual orientation), civil rights leaders, and alleged communists, testifies before Congress in 1947. **[Bettmann/corbis]**

Washington University night school, on 26 July 1917 Hoover was hired as a clerk at the Department of Justice's enemy alien registration section. By January 1919 Hoover had become an assistant to A. Mitchell Palmer, who was then Attorney General. Later that spring, using a vast set of records he had compiled on radical groups, Hoover was put in charge of arresting and deporting alien radicals in what became known as the "Palmer Raids."

It was this genius at organizing information and a reputation for nonpartisanship that led to Hoover's appointment as Director of the Federal Bureau of Investigation (FBI) on 10 May 1924. Hoover was subsequently reappointed by eight presidents, serving for forty-eight years in this capacity. No contemporary or scholar has explained this longevity, but speculation centers on Hoover's ability to provide personal intelligence that could embarrass or discredit others. A few months before his appointment, he had established the famous OBSCENE file. Here, sexual information about public figures, pornography, and evidence of what the director called "indecent" behavior discovered during an investigation could be kept separate from a case file. Simultaneously, Hoover also established a second file where he kept personal information on public figures that might prove embarrassing to them. During the Church Committee hearings in 1975, it was discovered that some of this information had been obtained through illegal and routine surveillance on liberals, homosexuals, and social justice activists, including Eleanor Roosevelt, Dr. Martin Luther King, Jr., and President John F. Kennedy.

Hoover also used the resources of the bureau to control rumors that he was homosexual, labeling his detractors insane, degenerate, or malicious. Those who spread such gossip often found themselves the target of an FBI investigation and were sometimes forced to recant their claims publicly. Nevertheless, speculation persisted, fed by the fact that he never married, lived with his mother until her death in 1941, and socialized and traveled with handsome agents whose careers benefited from his attention. In 1928 new agent Clyde Tolson would become Hoover's best and perhaps only friend, and by 1936 he was also the Associate Director of the FBI. Although they lived in separate houses, the two vacationed and took their meals together, and used affectionate nicknames ("Speed" and "Eddie" for Hoover, "Junior" for Tolson). In 1993 journalist Anthony Summers published an interview with a woman who claimed to have seen Hoover having sex with boys while dressed as a woman; however, these charges have never been corroborated and no eyewitness has stepped forward to claim more than affectionate behavior between Hoover and Tolson.

These rumors are of more than casual interest. Beginning in the 1950s Hoover targeted homosexuals as national security risks, and endorsed and aided the repression of homophile organizations. Claiming that homosexuals in government could be blackmailed by communist agents, Hoover participated in creating the condition of moral panic that made blackmail possible. When, in 1953, President Dwight Eisenhower made it illegal for any homosexual to hold a federal post, investigations spearheaded by the FBI succeeded in purging hundreds of suspected gays and lesbians from the civil service. But the repression of homosexuals was also part of a larger system of favors rendered and received. Sometimes, as in the case of liberal journalist Joseph Alsop or civil rights activist Bayard Rustin, damaging information about a morals charge became part of a larger campaign of discrediting a government critic. In other cases, such as the arrest of Lyndon Baines Johnson's press aid Walter Jenkins, a morals charge could be covered up as a political favor.

Hoover died in his sleep on 2 May 1972; Tolson was his sole heir. Any evidence of their intimacy that remained was probably destroyed in the hours after Hoover's death, as FBI agents swept his home, and Helen Gandy, his secretary, destroyed files in his office. Ironically, Hoover's crusade against homophile organizations and gay and lesbian activists has left a wealth of information about them in files that have been opened through the Freedom of Information Act. Many of these are available today in the Freedom of Information Act (FOIPA) reading room at the FBI's J. Edgar Hoover Building on Pennsylvania Avenue, NW, Washington, D.C.

Bibliography

Gentry, Curt. *J. Edgar Hoover: The Man and His Secrets.* New York: W.W. Norton, 1991.

Powers, Richard Gid. *Secrecy and Power: The Life of J. Edgar Hoover.* New York: The Free Press, 1987.

Summers, Anthony. *Official and Confidential: The Secret Life of J. Edgar Hoover.* New York: Putnam, 1993.

Theoharis, Athan G. *J. Edgar Hoover, Sex, and Crime: An Historical Antidote.* Chicago: Ivan R. Dee, 1995.

Theoharis, Athan G., and John Stuart Cox. *The Boss: J. Edgar Hoover and the Great American Inquisition.* Philadelphia: Temple University Press, 1988.

Claire Bond Potter

See also FEDERAL LAW AND POLICY; GOVERNMENT AND MILITARY WITCHHUNTS; POLICING AND POLICE; POLITICAL SCANDALS.

HOWE, Marie Jenney **(b. 26 December 1871; d. 28 February 1934), activist, writer.**

Marie Jenney Howe was born in Syracuse, New York, to Marie Saul and Edwin Sherman Jenney, both members of upper-middle-class New York families. At age twenty-two she enrolled at Union Theological Seminary in Meadville, Pennsylvania, where she was introduced to Frederic C. Howe, a young law student at Johns Hopkins University. Although the two had a mutual interest in progressive politics, their views of women's roles clashed—Jenney was a feminist, while Howe had traditional ideas about women as homemakers and thought it bizarre that she was training for the ministry rather than marrying. In 1897 Jenney graduated and took a position in Sioux City, Iowa, as an assistant to Unitarian minister Mary A. Safford, president of the Iowa Suffrage Association and a leading advocate of women ministers in the Unitarian Church. Safford was one of three women ministers who officiated at Jenney's ordination in Syracuse in 1898. Jenney maintained the congregation at Des Moines' First Unitarian Church from 1899 to 1904 while Safford preached throughout Iowa.

After a seven-year correspondence, Jenney and Howe married in 1904. Marie Jenney's enthusiasm for the ministry had cooled during her work in Iowa, and for the rest of her life she officiated only at friends' weddings and funerals. Frederic Howe had become a lawyer and municipal reformer in Cleveland, and after moving there, Marie Jenney continued her work for women's suffrage and joined the new National Consumer's League, which lobbied and organized boycotts in order to change working conditions for women and children. In 1910 the couple moved to New York City, where she helped to form the New York State Suffrage League and became chair of the Twenty-fifth Assembly District division of the local Woman Suffrage Party. She and Fred moved to Greenwich Village, where they became acquainted with some of the leading bohemians and political activists of the day.

In 1912, Marie Jenney Howe founded what became one of the most important and long-lived women's institutions in the United States, Heterodoxy. In its early years membership in the luncheon and debate club grew from twenty-five to sixty, and included most of the major female social, political, intellectual, and artistic leaders of the day, among them writers Charlotte Perkins Gilman and Susan Glaspell, art patron and salon host Mabel Dodge, labor organizers Helen Gurley Flynn and Rose Pastor Stokes, lawyers Crystal Eastman and Inez Milholland, psychologists Beatrice Hinkle and Grace Potter, and anthropologist Elsie Clews Parsons. The only African American member, Grace Nail Johnson, was a civil rights activist in the National Association for the Advancement of Colored People. Speakers at the monthly meetings included anarchist Emma Goldman, socialist writer Helen Keller, lesbian poet Amy Lowell, and birth control advocate Margaret Sanger. Howe introduced a series of "background talks" in which members spoke about their lives as women; this became one of the meetings' most popular features and a predecessor of the consciousness-raising groups of the 1970s women's movement. Heterodoxy members' political attitudes ranged from radical to conservative on various issues, but all members had feminism in common, and most were heavily involved in other social and political reform movements.

Sexual identities, attitudes, and behaviors varied also, from those who advocated free love and open marriage to those who maintained fairly conventional marriages with men or monogamous partnerships with women. At least 10 of the total of 110 club members were lesbians and a number of others had women lovers. Long-term lesbian couples' relationships were acknowledged in much the same way as other members' marriages to men, and Heterodoxy members of all sexual orientations considered their friendships with other women paramount. It is unclear whether Howe had a sexual relationship with her close friend, the lesbian writer and editor Rose Young, but she dedicated her first book to Young, and her letters to friends indicate that her marriage with Frederic Howe was emotionally unsatisfying.

In 1926, Marie Howe journeyed to Paris to stay in the home of lesbian writer Natalie Barney and work on a biography of French writer George Sand, published the following year. Her second book, a translation of Sand's journal, appeared in 1929. By this point Howe was suffering from heart trouble, and she spent her final year corresponding with the well-traveled Heterodoxy members. When she died in her sleep in 1934, club members consoled Rose Young, rather than Frederic Howe, and asked her advice for memorial service arrangements. Heterodoxy continued monthly meetings until the early 1940s, but by then many of the original members had died.

Whatever Marie Jenney Howe's sexual orientation, she created a long-lived feminist organization that never split along political or sexual lines, something that other organizers were not always able to accomplish.

Bibliography

Adickes, Sandra. *To Be Young Was Very Heaven: Women in New York Before the First World War.* New York: St. Martin's Press, 1997.

Schwarz, Judith. *Radical Feminists of Heterodoxy: Greenwich Village, 1912–1940.* Norwich, Vt.: New Victoria, 1986.

Wittenstein, Kate. "The Feminist Uses of Psychoanalysis: Beatrice M. Hinkle and the Foreshadowing of Modern Feminism in the United States." *Journal of Women's History* 10, no. 2 (Summer 1998): 38–62.

Michele Spring-Moore

See also FEMINISM.

HUGHES, Langston (b. 1 February 1902; d. 22 May 1967), writer.

James Langston Hughes was born in Joplin, Missouri, into a family whose ancestors boasted political notables, including a member of John Brown's antislavery party who fought and died with him at Harper's Ferry. Hughes's parents separated in 1903 when his father immigrated to Mexico. Hughes then moved with his mother to Kansas and later to Illinois and Ohio. He was elected class poet in grade school and graduated from high school with the same honor. Hughes published the first of his signature poems, "The Negro Speaks of Rivers," in *Crisis* magazine in 1921, the same year he enrolled at Columbia University in New York.

The Big Sea (1940), the first of his two autobiographies, captures Hughes's excitement upon arriving in New York. In particular, Hughes was energized by the number of black people he saw uptown in Harlem and the thriving culture they were creating. Black intellectuals and artists in New York, like W. E. B. Du Bois, Jessie Fauset, and Countee Cullen, were familiar with the poetry Hughes had published in *Crisis.* They counted themselves, Hughes, and several others as the pioneers of a new black cultural movement, the Harlem Renaissance. Their mission was to harness the post–World War I buoyancy in American culture and channel it into the institutions established to enable black American political, social, and cultural progress. Black art was booming in New York, and also in Washington, D. C., Philadelphia, and Detroit. But no city could boast a talent more impressive than New York's Langston Hughes, who felt an allegiance to the city that he did not feel for Columbia. The combination of his father's unpredictable financial help and the coldness of the almost exclusively white student body resulted in Hughes dropping out after two semesters.

Langston Hughes. The leading poet of the Harlem Renaissance, and one of the most important African-American writers during the period between the two world wars, as well as into the 1960s.

Hughes found a job on a freighter that took him to western Africa, Paris, and Italy. In 1925, while Hughes was in Washington, D.C., living with his mother, his poem "The Weary Blues" won first prize in a contest sponsored by *Opportunity* magazine, and earned him, through Carl Van Vechten, a book contract with the publisher Alfred A. Knopf. In January 1926, Hughes's first book, *The Weary Blues*, appeared. The same year, Hughes enrolled at Lincoln University in Pennsylvania, a historically black college, where he graduated in 1929. Through the Harlem Renaissance luminary Alain Locke, Hughes secured the support of Charlotte Osgood Mason, a wealthy white widow who both doted on Hughes and tried to control his creative output. Mason's support enabled Hughes to complete his first novel, *Not without Laughter* (1930), and to collaborate with Zora Neale Hurston on *Mule Bone*, a play they began about black folk culture in 1929. Hughes's relationships with Mason and Hurston were similarly intense and suffered dramatic breaks that distressed Hughes substantially.

Hughes's secrecy about his sexuality affected his relationships with women and men in multiple ways. Alain Locke's amorous desires for Hughes led Locke to Paris in 1924, where he was gently rebuffed by the poet, who was working there at the time. Several scholars speculate that Hurston's thwarted romantic expectations contributed to the deterioration of her friendship with Hughes, who never had a public, long-term, sexual relationship with a man or a woman. While his autobiographies describe various romantic interactions with women over the years, Hughes's allegiance to gay subcultures is clear. In *The Big Sea*, he describes the pleasure he took in the Hamilton Club Lodge Ball, a popular annual drag ball in Harlem, and in popular lesbian and bisexual performers, like Gladys Bentley and Bessie Smith. In his two-volume biography of Hughes, Arnold Rampersad describes the frustrating lack of evidence about Hughes's sexuality. Even though he concludes that Hughes was asexual, he points out that several of Hughes's contemporary associates attest to his homosexuality as an open secret during the Harlem Renaissance years and beyond. Other scholars definitively identify Hughes as gay. Certainly a persistent, popular appreciation of Hughes as a gay icon contributes to a larger debate about what qualifies as evidence when it comes to histories of marginalized peoples, whose unpopular or controversial identities and affinities may have been deliberately obscured.

Hughes's career suffered dramatically for his public affiliation with left-wing politics in the 1940s. Despite his denials and repudiations, Hughes was identified as a Communist and forced to testify before Senator Joseph McCarthy in 1953. He was criticized by leftists for accommodating red-baiters, but by exonerating himself, Hughes was able to continue a productive and evolving life as a novelist, playwright, columnist, translator, librettist, and anthologer. In 1961, Hughes was inducted to the National Institute of Arts and Letters. He died of cancer in New York City in 1967.

Bibliography

Bernard, Emily, ed. *Remember Me to Harlem: The Letters of Langston Hughes and Carl Van Vechten, 1925–1964.* New York: Knopf, 2001.

Hughes, Langston. *The Big Sea.* New York: Knopf, 1940.

Rampersad, Arnold. *The Life of Langston Hughes.* 2 vols. 2d ed. New York: Oxford University Press, 2002.

Emily Bernard

See also BENTLEY, GLADYS; CULLEN, COUNTEE; HARLEM RENAISSANCE; LITERATURE; LOCKE, ALAIN; THURMAN, WALLACE; VAN VECHTEN, CARL.

THE HUMAN RIGHTS CAMPAIGN

The Human Rights Campaign, known as the Human Rights Campaign Fund until 1995, is the largest lesbian and gay rights organization in the nation, with over one hundred staff and more than 500,000 members in 2003. It was founded in the summer of 1980 as the first national lesbian and gay political action committee, with the aims of supporting LGB-friendly candidates and gaining congressional sponsors for a national lesbian and gay rights civil rights bill. Within twenty years HRC had enlarged its mission to include lobbying Congress and grassroots organizing and had absorbed other groups and programs. At times the organization has been at the center of controversy within the LGB movement because of its lingering image of elitism, and also because of its accomodationist strategy of working within the American political system in traditional ways.

Origins: 1980–1983

By 1980 the United States was experiencing a resurgent conservative movement that attempted to curtail the perceived excesses of the previous two decades in the form of minority civil rights and affirmative action policies; a revitalized women's movement; campus unrest and antiwar protest centered on U.S. involvement in Southeast Asia; and the rapid rise of a visible and organized gay and lesbian movement. The establishment of organizations like the Moral Majority (founded in 1979) signaled the rise of the New Right, as did the landslide 1980 presidential election of Republican Ronald Reagan and the concurrent defeat of key Senate Democrats. Conservatives now challenged, sometimes successfully, ordinances prohibiting discrimination on the basis of sexual orientation passed in several localities during the blossoming of LGB activism and culture in the 1970s. The murder of San Francisco mayor George Moscone and openly gay supervisor Harvey Milk in 1978—and the light sentence given their assassin—further galvanized LGB people toward fighting homophobia.

In the context of these events, Minnesota gay activist Steve Endean became convinced of the need for civil rights protection on the national rather than the state or local levels. He had founded the first lesbian and gay rights political group in his state and been its first lobbyist for that cause. In the mid-1970s he worked toward the adoption of both Twin Cities' LGB rights ordinances and lobbied for a statewide bill, passed in 1993. Moving to Washington, D.C., in 1978 to direct the Gay Rights National Lobby (GRNL), he joined with Jim Foster, Larry Bye, and James Hormel in the planning of the Human Rights Campaign Fund and became its first director, serving from 1980 to 1983.

To achieve its ultimate goal of federal legislation, the HRC established the nation's first LGB fundraising network and cosponsored the landmark study, "Does Support for Gay Rights Spell Political Suicide?" In 1980 HRC made its first contribution to a congressional candidate (who won reelection) and in 1982 sponsored the movement's largest fundraising event yet, a dinner at New York City's Waldorf Astoria, featuring as speaker former Vice President Walter Mondale. The following year, conflicts with other activists led to Endean's resignation from both GRNL and HRC and the latter hired Vic Basile to be executive director, a post he held until 1989.

Expansion of Activities

Under Executive Directors Basile (1983–1989) and Tim McFeeley (1989–1995), HRC broadened its activities and sought to build coalitions, especially with the feminist and African American movements. By the end of 1985, HRC had merged with GRNL, hiring its own lobbyists in the following years. A Field Division for grassroots organizing was added after Endean returned to HRC in 1987 with his constituent mailgram project, the Fairness Fund (renamed Speak Out). In the same year the tax-exempt HRC Foundation was created. The movement's second national March on Washington (11 October 1987) provided an opportunity for HRC to hold the LGB political movement's largest fundraiser yet in the nation's capital. At the end of its first decade, HRC had expanded its lobbying and advocacy activities, made the original political action committee a separate branch, added the Young Leaders Internship Program, and become the first lesbian and gay organization ever to testify at Republican Party platform committee hearings (1988). It also had gained a reputation as an elitist organization—dominated by conservative (and often closeted) wealthy white men—due in part to fundraising through black-tie dinners sponsored by members of HRC called the Insiders Group (later known as the Federal Club). The fifth annual New York City Dinner (1986), however, became memorable when speaker Coretta Scott King declared her "solidarity with the gay and lesbian community."

Responding to AIDS

Once HRC absorbed GRNL in 1985, it turned much of its attention to AIDS-related legislation, forming the AIDS Campaign Trust. (GRNL had begun lobbying for federal funding of AIDS research, education, and prevention in 1983.) Among its more notable efforts in the late 1980s

Human Rights Campaign. Executive Director Elizabeth Birch welcomes President Bill Clinton to the HRC's first National Dinner on 8 November 1997—which was picketed both by demonstrators against gay rights and by AIDS protesters pressing for better policies from the federal government. **[AP Photo/Wilfredo Lee]**

were the Fund's central role, in 1987 and 1988, in increasing the movement's visibility at both major political parties' presidential nominating conventions and successfully lobbying for the passage of several bills, including the Civil Rights Restoration Act (1988), the Fair Housing Amendments Act, and larger AIDS appropriations. Under Executive Director Tim McFeeley, HRC joined other LGB rights and AIDS groups in organizing National AIDS Lobby Days and in pressuring Congress to pass health-related legislation, including the Americans with Disabilities Act (1990) (which included people with AIDS and HIV) and the Ryan White Comprehensive AIDS Resource Emergency (CARE) Act (1990). HRC continued to devote significant energy in the 1990s not only to AIDS but also to women's health and reproductive rights, having already adopted an official pro-choice position on abortion.

Changes in Washington

The 1992 election of President Bill Clinton brought hope to LGB rights groups. Clinton, the first presidential candidate endorsed by the HRC, had included LGB people in his campaign of inclusiveness and in 1993 was the first president to meet with heads of LGB organizations, including McFeeley, in the Oval Office. In light of Clinton's promise to end discrimination in the military—openly LGB people were barred from serving—HRC began Operation Lift the Ban, pouring energy into polling, lobbying, peaceful protest, and constituent pressure on Congress. (HRC members sent over seventy thousand messages to Washington opposing the ban.) Government resistance to changing the policy became the focus of the third March on Washington in April 1993 and spawned coordinated efforts between HRC and the National Gay and Lesbian Task Force.

Despite the efforts of LGB rights organizations, in September Congress passed an uneasy compromise, soon labeled "Don't Ask, Don't Tell." In the wake of this defeat, the passage of Colorado's anti-LGB Amendment 2 in 1992, and public attacks from other activists charging ineffectiveness, HRC conducted an internal review that resulted in a new Plan of Action for 1994. Two issues, hate crimes and job discrimination, became key projects of the organization as it changed leadership in 1995.

New Faces for HRC

When Elizabeth Birch became executive director in 1995, HRC already had entered a new phase that aimed at professionalizing the organization while changing its image. At the same time, it retained Endean's original goal of national LGB civil rights protection but changed its strategy from obtaining sponsors for a national bill (first introduced in Congress in 1974, and again in 1980 and 1991) to supporting piecemeal legislation accomplishing the same protections.

Among the first changes were adoption of a new name ("Fund" was omitted) and a bold, simple logo (a yellow-against-blue equal sign). Birch and the new board sought to alter HRC's lingering Champagne Fund image by emphasizing the diversity of its staff, membership, and activities, and initiating outreach to transgendered people. The other main goal was modernization in terms of hiring professionals in their fields, going online, and adopting corporate-style marketing techniques. HRC made increasing use of celebrities, particularly in its magazine ads and National Coming Out Day (directed by Candace Gingrich, it was adopted as a Project of the HRC Foundation in 1993); spokespeople have included Amanda Bearse, Chastity Bono, and Ellen DeGeneres's mother, Betty.

The usual mix of legislative victory and defeat characterized the 1990s and HRC continued to be at the center of controversy both inside and outside the movement. It laid significant groundwork in 1994 for the introduction in Congress of the Employment Nondiscrimination Act (ENDA, defeated 1996) by launching the Documenting Discrimination Project while obtaining written pledges from a majority of Congress not to discriminate in their offices on the basis of sexual orientation. In 1997 President Clinton addressed the HRC at its first National Dinner and Awards; the same year his nomination of openly-gay James Hormel—a HRC co-founder and Foundation board member—as ambassador to Luxembourg embroiled both in a struggle with homophobic elements in the Senate. Over the next two years HRC drew fire from other activists, first for endorsing the anti-choice New York Republican senator Alfonse D'Amato in his reelection bid, then for its involvement in Millennium March in the year 2000, proposed without consultation among a variety of movement activists. During and since those events, HRC has been more successful in responding to the "Ex-gay" movement's ad campaigns, continuing its ongoing fight against workplace discrimination, and expanding its outreach and programs.

Bibliography

Clendinen, Dudley, and Adam Nagourney. *Out for Good: The Struggle to Build a Gay Rights Movement in America.* New York: Simon and Schuster, 1999.

DeBold, Kathleen, ed. *Out for Office: Campaigning in the Gay Nineties.* Washington, D.C.: Gay and Lesbian Victory Fund, 1994.

D'Emilio, John, William B. Turner, and Urvashi Vaid, eds. *Creating Change: Sexuality, Public Policy, and Civil Rights.* New York: St. Martin's Press, 2000.

Gingrich, Candace, with Chris Bull. *The Accidental Activist: A Personal and Political Memoir.* New York: Simon and Schuster, 1996.

Vaid, Urvashi. *Virtual Equality: The Mainstreaming of Gay and Lesbian Liberation.* New York: Anchor, 1995.

Vicky Eaklor

See also ANTI-DISCRIMINATION LAW AND POLICY; BOYCOTTS; ELECTORAL POLITICS; EMPLOYMENT LAW AND POLICY; FAMILY LAW AND POLICY; FEDERAL LAW AND POLICY; HATE CRIMES LAW AND POLICY; HEALTH AND HEALTH CARE LAW AND POLICY; MILITARY LAW AND POLICY; NATIONAL GAY AND LESBIAN TASK FORCE (NGLTF).

HUMOR. see COMEDY AND HUMOR.

HUNTER, Alberta **(b. 1 April 1895; d. 17 October 1984), singer, composer, actor, nurse.**

One of the most accomplished blues artists of the twentieth century, Alberta Hunter was born into destitute poverty in Memphis at the end of the nineteenth century. Her father, Charles E. Hunter, was a railway porter who abandoned the family soon after her birth. Her strict, reserved mother, Laura (Peterson) Hunter, worked as a maid in a brothel, while her grandmother, Nancy Peterson, took primary responsibility for caring for Alberta and her older sister and younger stepsister. Subjected to sexual abuse as an adolescent by both the white boyfriend of her family's landlady and a black school principal, Hunter also suffered at the hands of a violent stepfather and a social circle that nicknamed her "Pig" for her untidiness and alleged unattractiveness. Strong-minded and fiercely determined to forge her own life, Hunter, at the age of sixteen, ran away to Chicago. After working as a house cleaner and kitchen aide, she began singing in raunchy nightclubs in 1912. She was encouraged and supported by women in the audience as well as by prostitutes working the clubs.

In the 1910s Hunter built a successful career as a blues singer in Chicago, helping to popularize songs by such composers as Maceo Walker ("Sweet Georgia

Brown") and W. C. Handy ("Saint Louis Blues") as well as many songs that she composed herself (such as "I've Got a Mind to Ramble," "Down Hearted Blues," and "I've Had Enough"). In the 1920s she began to sing in New York and to branch out into acting. She starred in shows in Chicago, New York (on Broadway and in Harlem), Philadelphia, and Washington, D.C. In 1927 she sang in France and England and landed a role as Queenie in the 1928–1929 London production of *Show Boat,* starring Paul Robeson. Hunter sang throughout the United States, Europe, and Asia in the 1930s and 1940s. When her singing career began to slow down in the 1950s, she improvised by devoting herself to volunteer work in a Harlem hospital (she was named Volunteer of the Year in 1956), passing elementary school equivalency examinations (she had never finished elementary school), and persuading the YWCA to accept her into its nursing program. To reach her goals, she secretly shaved twelve years off of her age. After twenty years of devoted nursing, Hunter was forced to retire in 1977 because the hospital administration thought she was seventy years old. She was actually eighty-two.

Not ready for retirement, Hunter relaunched her musical career in October 1977 by opening to rave reviews at The Cookery, a new New York nightclub operated by Barney Josephson. She skyrocketed to a star status beyond anything she had previously achieved, appearing on nationally televised talk shows and radio, and in magazines, and newspapers. She opened the Newport Jazz Festival at Carnegie Hall in June 1978; sang at the Kennedy Center; received the Handy Award as Traditional Female Blues Artist of the Year in 1979; and traveled throughout the United States, Europe, and elsewhere. She was particularly pleased when President Jimmy Carter asked her to sing in the White House. She sustained an international singing career until her death in 1984 at the age of eighty-nine.

Love for women was central to Hunter's personal life. (In 1919 Hunter married William Saxby Townsend, but she kicked him out of her home after two months.) She supported her mother, who lived with her in Chicago for a time in 1915 and moved into her Harlem apartment permanently in 1930, until her mother's death in 1954. Although Hunter's stage persona ranged from wryly suggestive and sexually playful to riotously explicit, off-stage she was intensely reserved and refused to smoke, drink, use drugs, or tolerate rough language. She secretly sustained long-lasting lesbian relationships with Carrie Mae Ward in Chicago and later with Lottie Tyler in New York. Evidence suggests she engaged in brief romances with other women as well.

Hunter took care of her voice, got plenty of rest, traveled around the world when she felt like it, and kept a low profile except when performing. She had a reputation for being tight with money and taking care of business. She did not break rules carelessly; she was a disciplined worker and a strong-willed rebel who did things the way she believed they ought to be done. The blues that Alberta Hunter composed and performed helped propel the singer and her audience toward feminist self-affirmation, agency, movement, and change.

Bibliography

Carby, Hazel. "It Jus Be's Dat Way Sometimes: The Sexual Politics of Women's Blues." *Radical America* 20 (1986): 9–22.

Taylor, Frank C., and Gerald Cook. *Alberta Hunter: A Celebration in Blues.* New York: McGraw-Hill, 1987.

Winter, Kari J. "On Blues, Autobiography, and Performative Utterance: The *Jouissance* of Alberta Hunter." In *Creating Safe Space: Violence and Women's Writing,* edited by Tomoko Kuribayashi and Julie Tharp. New York: SUNY Press, 1998.

Kari J. Winter

See also MUSIC: POPULAR.

HUSTLING. see PROSTITUTION, HUSTLING, AND SEX WORK.

I

ICONS

Political regimes, religious institutions, and businesses, particularly those associated with the entertainment industries, create icons to excite the adoration of their citizenry, adherents, and customers. In Western culture since the mid-nineteenth century, many of the most successful iconic images have made the figure appear as both an ordinary person and a person who is unprecedented. Over the course of this period, the number of icons has proliferated at an enormous rate. The growth of consumer culture promoted the marketing of personalities. Promotion was also aided by the development of new media, which resulted in the dissemination of complex images quickly, and which was coupled with the expansion of potential audiences and the time they could devote toward these images. The importance of images to audience members grew as the culture bestowed greater value upon consumption and leisure time, thus upon celebrities and the entertainment world. Many LGBT people, living in a society that strove to deny their love and stigmatize their existence, developed icons as a way to escape the stresses and anxieties of daily life and the limitations and restrictions placed on them by the dominant heterosexual culture.

Several of the first LGBT iconic figures achieved their status because their images and behaviors made them objects of fantasy, figures who were desired romantically or erotically or who were perceived as living the great or passionate life with larger-than-life personalities. The rigidity of gender roles in the culture prompted many gay men to favor women who used wit, camp, and sarcasm to triumph over adversity or to criticize the world. Many lesbians favored independent, forceful figures and women who appropriated men's clothing as icons. Other figures became icons because they were so spectacular that they allowed LGBT people to escape from the troubles of daily life into a more positive environment. Performers also attained iconic status because their transition from ordinary to extraordinary status was a path most LGBT followed or wanted to follow, enabling LGBT people to form strong identifications with them as models of triumph over adversity. Most recently, people who have become icons have lived openly LGBT lives, offering the experience of strength and pride to LGBT communities. Since the Stonewall riots in 1969, the LGBT communities have recognized particular historical figures as icons. These include the poet Walt Whitman, writers Gertrude Stein and Radclyffe Hall, the playwright Oscar Wilde, and performers Ma Rainey and Bessie Smith.

Hollywood's film industry produced some of the first major icons for the LGBT communities. Stars like Bette Davis and Joan Crawford created characters who used bitchiness and limitless satiric powers to control circumstances, their feminine wiles enabling them to triumph while winning the man to their side. They became proxies for many gay men, who often identified with the notion of feminine power and the winning of desirable men. The actresses Greta Garbo and Marlene Dietrich became iconic figures in part because their adoption of masculine clothing both on- and off-screen made them proxies for some LGBT people and gave them an attractiveness that appealed to others within LGBT communi-

Liza Minnelli. A daughter of the legendary icon Judy Garland, she achieved iconic status of her own as the uninhibited, naively hopeful Sally Bowles in the hit musical *Cabaret*. [**The Kobal Collection**]

ties. George Jorgensen, who had failed to break into the movies and went to Denmark in the late 1940s for three sex change operations that received notable media coverage, became Christine Jorgensen. Her triumph over adversity established her as an icon for the transgender community.

Another actress from the classical studio era attained icon status as much for her life off-screen as for her roles in the movies. Judy Garland had major roles in several major Metro Goldwyn Mayer musicals, including *The Wizard of Oz* (1939) and *A Star Is Born* (1954), in which her plaintive songs, "Over the Rainbow" and "The Man That Got Away" summarized many a LGBT person's hopes and disappointments. Her early screen image of the ordinary heterosexual girl next door contrasted with the publicity of her middle and later years, which were filled with troubles and triumphs. This made Garland into a figure that many LGBT people believed represented their lives and experiences.

Many scholars and critics say Garland helped numerous gay men realize they were gay and were members of a larger community. Attending her concerts during the last years of her life became a place to share their love of Garland with others. These concerts served as locations where LGBT people could meet friends and lovers. This connection between Garland's iconic status and LGBT people's ability to meet other LGBT people is epitomized in the question used during the 1950s and 1960s to determine if a person was in the "gay" life: Are you a friend of Dorothy? The question referenced Garland's role in *The Wizard of Oz*. The singer was such an institution that many New York City gay bars draped areas in black crepe in mourning when she died in June 1969. According to folklore, some participants in the Stonewall Riots in June 1969 felt rebellious in part because of their sorrow over Garland's death.

Like Garland, singer Billie Holiday attained a position as an icon because she possessed an enormous talent and because she experienced triumph and tragedy in her life and career. The emotional intensity of her singing enabled black LGBT people, in particular, to feel like she was speaking and living for them. Since the Stonewall Riots, many other performers from the music industry have attained iconic status among LGBT people. Singer and actress Barbra Streisand got her start playing in gay clubs in Greenwich Village in the early 1960s. Along with sensitivity and passion, Streisand showed anger and chutzpah, embodying a sense of strength that many LGBT wanted and possessed. Bette Midler also began her career as a singer and actress in gay environments, playing the Continental Baths in New York. Nicknamed the Divine Miss M, Midler appropriated gay camp sensibilities in her performances. Singing old torch songs, offering off-color impersonations, and telling bawdy jokes, while appearing in outlandish and outrageous costumes,

Midler offered gay male audiences a re-creation of their own appropriation of popular culture. Singer Patti LaBelle and the Bluebelles also played the Continental Baths in the early 1970s. The group's concerts created a place for LGBT people, and especially blacks, to congregate, and spurred many of them to act out their liberation and outrageousness.

Other musicians, including Elton John, Sylvester, and David Bowie, achieved their icon positions through overt discussion of their sexuality and their flamboyance both on and off the stage. Many gay, bisexual, and transgender men identified with or tried to emulate their larger-than-life personalities. Madonna blasted on to the music scene with a high-energy dance sound and outspoken lyrics that played in gay dance bars around the world. Gay males enjoyed her overt sexuality and her focusing attention on both queer styles and past gay icons like Marilyn Monroe. Madonna flirted with lesbian chic, and whether one interpreted lesbian chic as helpful in constructing lesbian identities or hurtful in re-appropriating lesbian imagery for marketing purposes, Madonna's behavior enabled her to become an icon to some lesbians. Singer Boy George illustrated the constructed nature of gender and sexual boundaries with his rebelliously effeminate look. Over the last two decades, Boy George's personal and career resiliency and his appearances on stage and in gay movies, often playing himself, illustrate his iconic status among gay male and transgender people. Similarly, supermodel RuPaul created an image that appealed to both of these communities. Adopting what he called his male and female drags, RuPaul challenged conceptions regarding gender, race, and sex while working in the recording, movie, and television industries throughout the 1990s.

Over the last two decades, several singer-songwriters emerged with music and personal lives that led to iconic status among lesbian communities. k. d. lang songs contained lyrics that spoke to many lesbians. Media images of the singer rejected traditional femininity, providing easy identification for many lesbians, most famously in a *Vanity Fair* cover photo depicting lang being shaved by supermodel Cindy Crawford. Her role as a woman infatuated with another woman in *Salmonberries* (1990), interviews, and public appearances at events such as the Gay Games make her a figure many lesbians see themselves in or view as a role model. Melissa Etheridge made critically successful and popular music with stories that express the feelings of many in the LGBT communities. Etheridge's iconic status grew with her coming out, engaging in a very public relationship with Julie Cypher and advocating social issues, such as same-sex marriage and parental rights.

Barbra Streisand. The iconic superstar, seen here in the hit musical *Hello, Dolly!*, got her start singing in gay clubs in New York City. **[corbis]**

Although not as prolific an arena as either music or the movies, the sporting world has produced several icons. The most dominant female athlete of her era, tennis player Billie Jean King, attained icon status among women after her victory over Bobby Riggs in the "battle of the sexes" in 1973. She gained an iconic position among bisexual and lesbian women after acknowledging her relationship with another woman in 1981. During the early 1970s, Dr. Renee Richards emerged as an icon to transgender people. The transsexual tennis professional insisted on her right to play tennis after her operation. She was denied entry in 1976, but her ability to compete as a woman in the 1977 U.S. Open illuminated the difference between a person's biological sex at birth and their perception of their gender as an adult.

Years later, another tennis star, Martina Navratilova, gained iconic status among lesbians. The mainstream press constructed the tennis player's image in opposition to the femininity of Chris Evert. For lesbian fans, Navratilova's masculinity offered masculinity to women as both an ideal and as ordinary. The tennis star's relationships with several women were so well-known that many lesbians could identify with her. Navratilova came out on national television in 1991 and has worked as an LGBT activist. She has lent her time toward ending discrimination in the military and promoting the Gay Games.

In recent years, the arena of television has represented a new site that has produced icons for LGBT communities. Comedian and actress Ellen DeGeneres assumed icon status with one bellwether moment of television. The "Puppy" episode of *Ellen* represented the experience of coming out and lesbian self-identification to a national audience in 1997. Before and after this episode, Ms. DeGeneres, as her character Ellen, illuminated LGBT life experiences that informed mainstream viewers while offering members of the LGBT communities the ability to see their triumphs and tribulations performed in the popular media on a weekly basis.

Other arenas that have produced icons include theater, painting, and publishing. Harvey Fierstein emerged as an iconic figure for gay males and transgender people with his play *Torch Song Trilogy.* His signature voice and transgender attire have appeared in movies, on television, and in the currently popular Broadway musical *Hairspray.* Sandra Bernhard brought to gay males a sharp tongue and cynical wit to her discussions of relationships and politics, while her amorphous sexuality and lesbian relationships have provided her with iconic status among lesbians. The Mexican painter Frida Kahlo attained iconic status among people of Spanish descent in the United States. Her bisexual lifestyle and struggle through pain and adversity had particular appeal to bisexuals and lesbians. Writers and activists Leslie Feinberg and Kate Bornstein have created award-winning literature and advocated for the rights and recognition of transgender communities.

Some performers' bodies of work, attitudes, and images have seemed particularly important and relevant to LGBT people. While some LGBT icons appealed across gender, racial, and orientation lines, others did not. Since icons are expressions of personal notions of freedom, fantasy, and needs, complex and diverse LGBT communities necessarily have a variety of iconic figures. That most LGBT icons have emerged from the performance arena reflects the appeal of singers, because the individual LGBT listener can develop the sense of a very strong personal relationship or shared group membership with them. A person becomes an icon because their work, attitude, or image appears to reflect the personal experience of the LGBT person. The icon becomes a surrogate for the LGBT community member, acting out that person's desires and fantasies through their personal relationship or shared group membership with the individual LGBT listener. Based upon their work, attitude, or image, these figures seem important and relevant to one's life.

Bibliography

Allen, Louise. *The Lesbian Idol: Martina, kd and the Consumption of Lesbian Masculinity.* London: Cassell, 1997.

Braun, Eric. *Frightening the Horses: Gay Icons of the Cinema.* London: Reynolds & Hearn, 2002.

Bronski, Michael. *Culture Clash: The Making of Gay Sensibility.* Boston: South End Press, 1984.

Dyer, Richard. *Heavenly Bodies: Film Stars and Society.* London: British Film Institute, Macmillan, 1986.

Ehrenstein, David. *Open Secret: Gay Hollywood 1928–1998.* New York: William Morrow, 1998.

Fishwick, Marshall, and Ray B. Browne, eds. *Icons of America.* Bowling Green, Ohio: Popular Press, 1978.

Harris, Daniel. *The Rise and Fall of Gay Culture.* New York: Hyperion, 1997.

Marshall, David P. *Celebrity and Power: Fame in Contemporary Culture.* Minneapolis: University of Minnesota Press, 1997.

Rapper, Toffee. "The Gay Icons Ring." 10 January 2000. http://www.firstuniversal.clara.net/gay-icons-ring.html

Brett L. Abrams

See also ACTORS AND ACTRESSES; FIERSTEIN, HARVEY; FILM AND VIDEO; JORGENSEN, CHRISTINE; KING, BILLIE JEAN; MUSIC: BROADWAY AND MUSICAL THEATER; MUSIC: POPULAR; NAVRATILOVA, MARTINA; RICHARDS, RENÉE; TELEVISION; THEATER AND PERFORMANCE.

IMMIGRATION. see MIGRATION, IMMIGRATION, AND DIASPORA

IMMIGRATION, ASYLUM, AND DEPORTATION LAW AND POLICY

A nation defines itself by whom it excludes. Even before "homosexuality" entered the English language, U.S. immigration policy sought to exclude sexual and gender minorities on the basis of their "criminal" activities or their presumed inclination to become "public charges." In the twentieth century, immigration policy added a medical basis for exclusion: most sexual "inverts" or "deviates" (as they were later called) were presumed to be psychopathic undesirables and were consequently barred from entering the country or becoming citizens. These exclusionary policies ensnared hundreds of sexual and gender minorities, but millions quietly passed through the portals of immigration and citizenship. Nonetheless, it was only after the Stonewall Riots and the beginnings of a LGBT liberation movement that federal immigration policy retreated from its symbolically anti-LGBT stance. Even today, however, the exclusion of people with AIDS reflects the persistence of earlier policies and practices.

Immigration Exclusions Based on Sexual Disease and Incapacity, 1875–1917

From the beginning the federal government in its national immigration policy sought to identify and exclude aliens who would pollute the physical and economic health of the thriving body politic. The Immigration Act of 1875 forbade the "importation into the United States of women for the purposes of prostitution," as such activity would corrupt the morals, health, and even the economy of the United States. Subsequent immigration statutes broadened that prohibition to include "persons suffering from a loathsome or a dangerous contagious disease," such as venereal diseases; "persons who have been convicted of a felony or other infamous crime or misdemeanor involving moral turpitude," including sodomy and gross indecency; and "persons who procure or attempt to bring in prostitutes or women for the purpose of prostitution." Before World War I these exclusions were mostly applied to female sex workers, thousands of whom were barred each year from entering the U.S.

Most male inverts were deported under an entirely different statutory exclusion. In the early twentieth century, Nicholas P., a young Greek immigrant, was arrested for breaking and entering; he allegedly confessed to the Immigration and Naturalization Service (INS) that he had frequented houses of prostitution, had been in the "habit of abusing [him]self, committing masturbation" since age twelve, and had engaged in "unnatural intercourse with men" both in Greece and St. Louis. Based on these admissions, he was deported to Argentina in 1912 as a "public charge." In 1885 Congress had excluded "any convict, lunatic, idiot, or any person unable to take care of himself or herself without becoming a public charge." Nicholas P.'s case reflected the INS's early policy of excluding sexual nonconformists on the grounds that they were physically as well as mentally "degenerate," a condition that would ruin them and leave them to the public welfare system. Consistent with popular and medical opinion that sexual inversion and degeneracy rendered people biologically inferior and even subhuman, such minorities were excludable as public charges until World War I. In 1917 the Solicitor of Labor ruled as a matter of law that "moral perverts" were not public charges under the immigration laws, except when tangible proof of their pauper status existed.

Exclusion of "Psychopathic" Immigrants, 1917–1967

The Immigration Act of 1917 retained the previous exclusions for immigrants afflicted with sexual and other diseases and convicted of crimes of moral turpitude, but added a new basis for exclusion: "constitutional pathologic inferiority." This exclusion was in fact just a more sophisticated version of the public charge basis for barring sexual minorities. It reflected then prevailing medical views that sexual inversion or degeneracy was the product of a serious and permanent psychological defect; the danger posed by this defect was not so much that the immigrant would become a public charge, but that he or she would prey on and corrupt innocent U.S. youth. The INS applied the exclusion to sexual "deviates" it had previously deported under the public charge provision. Between 1918 and 1941 an average of three dozen people per year were excluded under this new provision.

The comprehensive revision of exclusions in the Immigration and Naturalization Act of 1952 retained the medical prohibition and expanded it to include persons "afflicted with a mental disorder, epilepsy, or psychopathic personality." Like the earlier laws, the 1952 statute barred persons "who have been convicted of a crime involving moral turpitude" or who had admitted committing acts constituting such a crime. An initial draft of the statute, not the version later enacted, specifically required the exclusion and deportation of "homosexuals and sex perverts." The INS interpreted the 1952 law as though the earlier language had been included; under its authority, the INS excluded dozens of LGBT people from the country each year. Likewise, the agency applied the "good moral character" requirement of the Immigration and Nationality Act of 1940 to deny the applications of LGBT aliens seeking to become U.S. citizens.

Notwithstanding these rules, thousands of LGBT people entered the United States and became citizens, because the INS was not aware of their minority identities and orientations. But hundreds of LGBT people were prohibited from entry, deported, or denied citizenship because of their illegal sexual activities and the psychopathy ascribed to their identity or orientation. During the Warren Court era of the U.S. Supreme Court (1953–1967), which recognized many new individual rights, a handful of immigrants challenged their exclusions, most of them without success. In *Fleuti v. Rosenberg* (1963), however, the Ninth Circuit Court of Appeals held the term "psychopathic personality" too vague to be constitutionally applied to "homosexuals" generally. An evenly divided Supreme Court affirmed the Ninth Circuit on technical grounds, but none of the justices was comfortable protecting gay and lesbian people from exclusion. In 1965 the U.S. Congress responded to *Fleuti* by amending the 1952 statute to exclude aliens "afflicted with psychopathic personality, or sexual deviation, or a mental defect."

In the 1960s Clive Michael Boutilier, a bisexual Canadian man who admitted to having sex with other men as well as women, challenged his deportation under the original 1952 statute. Affidavits from psychiatrists established that Boutilier exhibited no evidence of psychopathy and thus should not be deported under the medical provision of the law. A divided Supreme Court nonetheless affirmed his deportation in *Boutilier v. INS* (1967). Justice Hugo Black and Chief Justice Earl Warren, the civil libertarians who had sided with the gay immigrant in *Fleuti,* voted against Boutilier, probably because the 1965 amendment persuaded them that Congress had meant to exclude "homosexuals and sex perverts" all along. Boutilier was subsequently deported, ending a loving relationship he had enjoyed with an American. Because it interpreted a vague law in a sweepingly antigay manner and associated "psychopathic personality" with "homosexuality" or even "bisexuality," *Boutilier* was arguably the most damaging antigay U.S. Supreme Court opinion of the twentieth century.

Immigration and Citizenship, 1967–2003

The Stonewall Riots of 1969 revolutionized federal immigration policy. Once lesbians, gay men, and bisexuals came out of their closets in great numbers and mobilized to protest prejudice and false stereotypes against them, the legal and medical professions reevaluated the old exclusions. Two years after Stonewall, Judge Walter Mansfield ruled that the 1940 naturalization statute did not require that gay and lesbian people be denied citizenship because of their private consensual activities. Judge Mansfield reasoned that the right to privacy the Supreme Court had accorded married couples in *Griswold v. Connecticut* (1965) also protected gay and lesbian people's intimate relationships from the prying eyes of immigration officials. Although merely a district court opinion, *In re Labady* (1971) was followed by similar decisions from other judges in the early 1970s. The American Bar Association agreed with Mansfield's interpretation of privacy law when it urged states to repeal their consensual sodomy laws in 1973. Just as the legal community was changing its views on the privacy rights of LGBT people, the medical community was also abandoning its view that LGBT people have inherent mental defects. Empirical evidence had never supported such a viewpoint, and a growing number of respected psychiatrists and medical scientists rejected the notion that sexual orientation is associated with mental dysfunction. Following an unprecedented referendum on the issue among psychiatrists, the president of the American Psychiatric Association (APA) in 1974 wrote the INS, informing the agency of the APA's official action "delisting" homosexuality as a defect or disease and urged the INS to revise its exclusionary policies accordingly.

Bowing to these professional pressures, the INS in 1976 announced that citizenship would not be denied to anyone simply because he or she had been a "practicing sexual deviate," but retained the discretion to deny citizenship to persons convicted of "homosexual act[s]." As for the exclusion of LGBT people from entering the country, the INS felt bound by *Boutilier.* Ironically, then, an immigrant could be stopped at the border or subsequently deported if he or she were gay or lesbian (*Boutilier*), but once permanently living in the United States, that same alien could become a U.S. citizen (*Labady*). This compromise led to confusion and no consistent policy. In August 1979 the Public Health Service, which administered the medical exclusions on the grounds of homosexuality for the federal government, announced that it would no longer conduct examinations or issue certificates to exclude LGBT people on the grounds of psychopathic personalities. The Surgeon General justified the change as reflecting "current and generally accepted canons of medical practice with respect to homosexuality." In response to this new complication, the INS adopted a "don't ask, don't tell" policy in 1980: immigration officials were instructed to make no inquiries with regard to immigrants' sexual orientation, but were required to bar those aliens who made "unsolicited, unambiguous oral or written admission of homosexuality." The INS applied this new policy anemically, but it was invalidated by the Ninth Circuit Court of Appeals in *Hill v. INS* (1983). After *Hill,* the INS continued to take the position that *Boutilier* barred LGBT people from entering the country, but agreed to waive the exclusion for those who sought such waivers. After a decade of limping along in this manner, the U.S. Congress in 1990 repealed the statutory provision mandating exclusion of people "afflicted" with psychopathic personality and sexual deviation.

The 1990 immigration law also gave the Secretary of Health and Human Services discretion to determine which communicable diseases would be the basis for excluding immigrants. This appeared to reverse the 1987 Helms Amendment requiring that people afflicted with AIDS be excluded from entry, but Congress in 1993 amended the immigration statute specifically to exclude

HIV-infected people. To the extent that HIV has been associated with bisexual and gay men, this new exclusion may be viewed to some extent as a replacement for earlier anti-LGBT exclusions; like them, it has excluded certain sexual minorities without actually naming them. Moreover, other indirect exclusions affect LGBT people. American immigration law has long permitted entry and citizenship to aliens who marry U.S. citizens. Although most other industrialized countries are extending similar rights to long-term gay or lesbian partners, the United States has not, as of 2003. While such discrimination does not target gay and lesbian people as previous actions or laws did, it nevertheless affects the lives of thousands of LGBT people.

In a final immigration irony, however, being a despised sexual or gender minority can have one advantage under U.S. immigration law. The INS and the Board of Immigration Appeals have ruled that federal asylum statutes and treaties require the United States to provide asylum to LGBT people and those infected with HIV if they can prove persecution in their home country because of their status. In *Pitcherskaia v. INS* (1997), for example, the Ninth Circuit Court of Appeals ruled that Russian efforts to "cure" a lesbian petitioner—in keeping with the same medical exclusion that was the foundation for U.S. policy for several generations—now formed the basis for granting her asylum. In one sense, therefore, sexual minorities have come full circle: their orientation no longer bars them from entering the United States, but sometimes provides a basis for otherwise ineligible aliens to enter as asylum seekers.

Bibliography

Bayer, Ronald. *Homosexuality and American Psychiatry: The Politics of Diagnosis.* New York: Basic Books, 1981.

D'Emilio, John. *Sexual Politics, Sexual Communities: The Making of a Homosexual Minority in the United States, 1940–1970.* Chicago: University of Chicago Press, 1983.

Eskridge, William N., Jr. *Gaylaw: Challenging the Apartheid of the Closet.* Cambridge, Mass.: Harvard University Press, 1999.

Eskridge, William N., Jr., and Nan Hunter. *Sexuality, Gender, and the Law.* 2nd edition. New York: Foundation Press, 2003.

———. "Challenging the Apartheid of the Closet: Establishing Conditions for Lesbian and Gay Intimacy, Nomos, and Citizenship, 1961–1981." *Hofstra Law Review* 25 (1997): 817, 930–939.

Murdoch, Joyce, and Deb Price. *Courting Justice: Gay Men and Lesbians v. The Supreme Court.* New York: Basic Books, 2001.

William N. Eskridge Jr.

See also DISCRIMINATION; FEDERAL LAW AND POLICY; HEALTH AND HEALTH CARE LAW AND POLICY; MEDICINE, MEDICALIZATION, AND THE MEDICAL MODEL; MIGRATION, IMMIGRATION AND DIASPORA.

INDIANS. see NATIVE AMERICANS.

INDUSTRIALIZATION. see CAPITALISM AND INDUSTRIALIZATION.

INTERGENERATIONAL SEX AND RELATIONSHIPS

Despite the great strides made by the LGBT movement over the past three decades in terms of political power and cultural acceptance, some issues continue to test the limits of straight liberalism and the LGBT movement alike. Public sex and pornography are two, but the issue perhaps most certain to foment serious cultural tensions and political divisions is pedophilia. Pedophilia, or eroticism between adults and young people, is perhaps better and more neutrally understood as but one form of the broader phenomenon of intergenerational sex and relationships, which can also include relations between adults across generations.

Within the LGBT movement in the United States, intergenerational sex involving youth gained widespread public and political attention during the late 1970s. After a decade of gains made by the gay and lesbian liberation movement, coupled with the increasing visibility of LGBT communities, a conservative moral backlash mobilized homophobic cultural fears of homosexuals as recruiters and abusers of children. Anita Bryant's "Save Our Children" crusade, which unleashed the specter of the homosexual teacher as seducer of school children, can be taken as the prime example. Out of this volatile context emerged organizations such as the North American Man/Boy Love Association, formed in Boston in 1978 in response to a moral panic sparked by the arrest of several men on charges of sexual activity with teenage boys. The period also witnessed a slew of writings by apologists for and academics interested in the subject of intergenerational sex. But the 1970s was not the first historical moment in which intergenerational sex and panics about pedophiles prominently figured.

Historical Perspectives on Intergenerational Sex

One of the most powerful arguments for a historical perspective on sex and relationships across generations is its capacity to counter right-wing claims that pedophilia is the relatively recent product of a sexually permissive society run amok. On the contrary, historians have demonstrated that cross-generational sex extends back in time, and that the meanings attached to such relations have changed radically over the decades. For instance, looking at the Horatio Alger tales and Alger's fondness for gentle boys from the "dangerous classes," literary historian Michael Moon has traced what he calls "the pederastic character of much of the 'philanthropic' discourse about boys" during the nineteenth century (p. 90). Moon detects similar man-boy erotics at work in Walt Whitman's 1841 story "The Child's Champion." As these literary examples suggest, nineteenth-century reform work—or "boys' work," as it was sometimes called—furnished a variety of social settings that brought working-class boys and middle-class men together. As John Donald Gustav-Wrathall has demonstrated in his study of the Young Men's Christian Association (YMCA), middle-class men's reform energies were sometimes impelled by elements of homosocial and homoerotic longing. The middle-class man's desire to "take a young stranger by the hand" also points to a recurring theme in the history of cross-generational relationships, that is, the frequent overlap between intergenerational and cross-class relations.

Intergenerational relationships have not been restricted to men and boys. Lesbian historian Martha Vicinus, for instance, has delineated the elements of distance and desire in boarding school friendships between girls and older female teachers or students. During the late nineteenth and early twentieth centuries, "raves" or "crushes" between schoolgirls and older women were intense, emotionally layered relationships in which a language and practice of self-discipline became a means of expressing desire. Crucial here too was the single-sex community of the boarding school, a social setting that nourished same-sex relations between middle-class girls and women.

In addition to nineteenth-century literary visions of man-boy love and schoolgirl "smashes" on admired female teachers, other historical contexts and social settings propped up cross-generational relations. In the early twentieth century, an erotic system of intergenerational sex between older men, known as "wolves," and boys or young men, called "punks," thrived among sailors, hobos, and prisoners. Wolf-punk relations ranged from the casual in nature, involving the exchange of sex for money, treats, or protection, to longer-term relationships in which wolves or "husbands" sometimes referred to their punks as "wives" or "women." As George Chauncey explains in his discussion of wolf-punk relationships, the terminology of wolf and punk, husband and wife, underscored the centrality of gender and age rather than "homosexuality" in early-twentieth-century conceptualizations of male-male sexual practices that also crossed generational lines. It is also significant that while prison officials and moral reformers frowned upon such activity, early-twentieth-century understandings of intergenerational sex were not characterized by notions of predatory male homosexuals and sexually innocent boys.

Moral-Sexual Panics

The mid-twentieth century witnessed a dramatic redefinition of the dominant understandings of intergenerational sex. Profound changes in domestic life, gender norms, and sexuality, brought on by the disruptions of World War II and exacerbated by the Cold War hysteria of the 1950s, prompted widespread cultural anxieties focused on the figure of the "sexual psychopath." Numerous state commissions studied what they termed the problem of the sex deviate, which, combined with sensationalized media reports linking child abuse and murder to sexual psychopaths, produced a postwar sex crime panic. The panic had particularly devastating repercussions for gay men, for it was in this context that the powerful links between male homosexuals and child abuse were forged. As Chauncey has written: "If homosexuals had been relatively invisible before the war, they had also been considered fairly harmless. But press reports in the postwar period created a new, more ominous stereotype of the homosexual as a child molester, a dangerous psychopath likely to commit the most unspeakable offenses against children" (p. 172). To take one example, in his 1966 book, *The Boys of Boise,* journalist John Gerassi documented the 1955–1956 witchhunt in Boise, Idaho, which generated over 150 news stories in the city paper and culminated in a list of the names of over 500 suspected homosexuals compiled by local authorities. In the end, only sixteen charges were laid, but the damage to the city's homosexual subculture had been done as many gay men fled Boise in fear. Associations between gay men and child molestation made during the postwar sex crime panic continue to reverberate in the culture, always ready to be redeployed in subsequent moral-sexual panics. They have also played no small part in pathologizing and policing all forms of intergenerational sex and relationships within same-sex communities.

Beginning in the 1990s, a new series of public scandals—revolving around sexual misconduct between adult male authorities and young people in a host of religious and educational institutions—has threatened to remobilize cultural linkages between homosexuality and child abuse (despite the overwhelming consensus of social scientists that most sexual abuse involves older men and younger girls). Historical analysis can interrupt such politically motivated cultural slippages by demonstrating the historical making of the myth of the homosexual as child molester.

Controversies

Whether in the past or present, intergenerational sex and relationships raise a host of political and ethical issues. For many, discussions of sexual relations between children and adults cannot be separated from issues of child pornography and prostitution. Others have pointed to the failure of much of the literature on intergenerational sex to foreground the voices of the younger partners. But perhaps the most contentious and complex issue relates to consent. Late-1970s political clashes, particularly between lesbians and gay men, were often framed as a debate about the possibility or impossibility of meaningful consent between young people and adults. It is also true that a good deal of the writing on intergenerational sex is marked, many would say marred, by a strong libertarian streak that elides important issues of power. The title of one of the most frequently cited anthologies—*The Age Taboo: Gay Male Sexuality, Power, and Consent*—captures well some of the central issues at stake.

Feminists have been among the most consistent in laying bare the relations of unequal power that often structure intergenerational relations. Indeed, for some feminists, the asymmetries of age and power stamp all intergenerational relationships—but especially those involving youth—as inherently exploitative and thus rule them out of acceptable bounds. Others adopt a position that acknowledges both the problems and the possibilities in such relationships. In the context of the feminist sex wars of the 1980s, for example, Kate Millett offered a rare and thoughtful meditation on "the sexual rights of children," suggesting that prevailing "conditions between adults and children preclude any sexual relationship that is not in some sense exploitative." Millett emphasized that "the main point about children and relationships between adults and children is that children have no rights. They have no money." However, Millett maintained that if society could ever reach a point in which children had sexual, economic, and other rights, "intergenerational sex could perhaps in the future be a wonderful opportunity for understanding between human beings" (p. 222).

Another striking feature of intergenerational sex and relationships has been its almost complete conflation with sexual relations between adults and children or youth. But sex and relationships across generations can, of course, occur between adults. Michel Foucault had something like this in mind when he pointed to the paucity of relationship forms officially recognized by the state. Pointing to the model of child adoption, Foucault wondered why it was not possible for someone officially to adopt a younger or older lover. "Why shouldn't I adopt a friend who's ten years younger than I am? And even if he's ten years older? Rather than arguing that rights are fundamental and natural to the individual, we should try to imagine and create a new relational right which permits all possible types of relations to exist." Commenting on Foucault's proposal, David Halperin notes that "adoption might also provide a mechanism for formalizing differences of wealth or age or education between lovers, acknowledging informal inequality while providing a framework of mutual support in which such inequality, accompanied by clearly marked rights and duties, might not devolve into exploitation or domination" (p. 82). Just how such relationships might look, how they might work, remains difficult to gage, for we know very little about the meaning and dynamics of adult-adult intergenerational relations in present-day same-sex communities. Are LGBT people drawn to them more than their straight counterparts? Within gay men's culture, does the valorization of youthful forms of attractiveness, or a willingness to flout social conventions, set the stage for sex and relationships across the barriers of age? Whatever the case, Foucault and Halperin both radically reverse the pathologizing discourse on relationships across age by suggesting that cross-generational relations might be viewed instead as an opportunity to expand the scope of affectional-sexual relationships and to secure the extension of formal rights.

Attention to cultural and social history suggests that in any discussion of intergenerational sex and relationships it is unwise to ignore or flatten out differences in the historical/social settings of cross-generational relations, each of which generates different structures of power and, hence, a complex and contradictory set of personal and political meanings. Whatever its cultural and historical context, however, intergenerational sex is a useful reminder that age, in addition to race, gender, and class, is a crucial variable of erotic preference and power in same-sex communities—one that will undoubtedly continue to provoke both controversial and creative political and cultural responses.

Bibliography

Chauncey, George. "The Post-War Sex Crime Panic." In *True Stories from the American Past*. Edited by William Graebner. New York: McGraw-Hill, 1993.

———. "Trade, Wolves, and the Boundaries of Normal Manhood." In *Gay New York: Gender, Urban Culture, and the*

Makings of the Gay Male World, 1890–1940. New York: Basic Books, 1994.

Gerassi, John. *The Boys of Boise: Furor, Vice, and Folly in an American City.* New York: Macmillan, 1966.

Gustav-Wrathall, John Donald. *Take the Young Stranger by the Hand: Same-Sex Relations and the YMCA.* Chicago: University of Chicago Press, 1998.

Halperin, David M. *Saint Foucault: Towards a Gay Hagiography.* New York: Oxford University Press, 1995.

Millett, Kate. "Beyond Politics?: Children and Sexuality." In *Pleasure and Danger: Exploring Female Sexuality.* Edited by Carole S. Vance. Boston: Routledge and K. Paul, 1984.

Mitzel, John. *The Boston Sex Scandal.* Boston: Glad Day, 1980.

Moon, Michael. "'The Gentle Boy from the Dangerous Classes': Pederasty, Domesticity, and Capitalism in Horatio Alger." *Representations* 19 (Summer 1987): 87–110.

———. "Rendering the Text and the Body Fluid: The Cases of 'The Child's Champion' and the 1855 *Leaves of Grass.*" In *Disseminating Whitman: Revision and Corporeality in Leaves of Grass.* Cambridge, Mass.: Harvard University Press, 1991.

Tsang, Daniel, ed. *The Age Taboo: Gay Male Sexuality, Power and Consent.* Boston: Alyson, 1981.

Vicinus, Martha. "Distance and Desire: English Boarding School Friendships, 1870–1920." In *Hidden from History: Reclaiming the Gay and Lesbian Past.* Edited by Martin Bauml Duberman, Martha Vicinus, and George Chauncey. New York: New American Library, 1989.

Steven Maynard

See also ALGER, HORATIO; BOY SCOUTS AND GIRL SCOUTS; MILLETT, KATE; NORTH AMERICAN MAN/BOY LOVE ASSOCIATION; SAME-SEX INSTITUTIONS; SEX WARS.

INTERRACIAL AND INTERETHNIC SEX AND RELATIONSHIPS

In his 1995 presidential address to the Organization of American Historians, titled "The Hidden History of Mestizo America," Gary Nash declared, "What we . . . need in our passionate and sometimes violent arguments about American culture and identity . . . is a social and intellectual construction of a mestizo America." Surveying the history of interracial mixing from Pocahontas and John Rolfe in the seventeenth century to debates about multiculturalism in the twentieth, Nash explained he was using the term "mestizo" in "the original sense—referring to racial intermixture of all kinds." "Uncovering the shrouded past of mestizo America," he concluded, "bears on the ongoing pursuit of *e pluribus unum* in this nation—the search for creating commonality out of diversity." Despite this broad vision, and despite the groundbreaking LGBT work on the subject produced by writers such as Cherríe Moraga and Gloria Anzaldúa in *This Bridge Called My Back* (1981) and Anzaldúa in *Borderlands=La Frontera: The New Mestiza* (1987), Nash's address remained silent about the rich history of same-sex ethnic and racial mixing.

This has been the case for most scholarship on interracial and interethnic sex in the United States. Sociologists and historians in particular have explored various aspects of the topic, but their work almost always concentrates on marital, heterosexual, and reproductive forms of sexual expression. Paul Spickard, for example, synthesizes much of this work in his 1989 book *Mixed Blood,* which offers a comparative historical analysis of Jewish American, Japanese American, and African American intermarriage. But by restricting his study to marital relationships, he excludes same-sex ones.

Nevertheless, some of the insights of these scholars have potential applications to LGBT contexts. For example, Spickard points out that what is seen as ethnic and racial mixing within some communities might not be perceived as such outside of those communities. Anglo-Americans might not see a marriage between a Norwegian American and a Swedish American as a mixed marriage, but Norwegian and Swedish communities might think otherwise. The same would be true for Christian versus Jewish views of marriages between Ashkenazi and Sephardic Jews. In LGBT contexts, the same is often the case; the very definition of what constitutes interracial or interethnic same-sex sex depends on constructions of race and ethnicity that are as historically and culturally variable as are constructions of sexuality and gender.

When a Native American *berdache* (sometimes known as a two-spirit person) was born into one Native group but adopted by another, as was the case with Woman Chief in the nineteenth century, should the *berdache*'s sexual relationships with members of the adopted group be conceptualized as part of the history of LGBT interethnic sex? What about when an African American slave descended from one linguistic, religious, and ethnic group in Africa had same-sex sex with an African American slave from another linguistic, religious, or ethnic group in Africa? If the African American slave was the product of a white man's rape of a black woman, was that slave having interracial or interethnic sex when she or he had sex with whites or with blacks? Various studies that examine how and when Irish Americans, Jewish Americans, and Italian Americans became white suggest that what might have been viewed as interracial or interethnic sex in one period might not have been viewed as such in another. Historically changing conceptions of race and ethnicity similarly shape conceptions of the interracial or interethnic status of Jewish-Christian, Chicana-Cubana, Japanese Hawaiian–Chinese Hawaiian, and countless other types of relationships.

To take another example of ideas about interracial and interethnic heterososexuality that can be applied in LGBT contexts, scholars have argued that some racial and ethnic groups with more men than women in a local environment have experienced high rates of male intermarriage. This tends to be the case only when racial and ethnic prejudices do not block such marriages. While such discussions usually ignore the possibility that such contexts might encourage same-sex intraethnic or intraracial sex between men (as may well have been the case, for instance, with Asian Americans on the West Coast in the late nineteenth and early twentieth centuries), demographic scarcity assumptions suggest that LGBT members of ethnic and racial groups that are relatively small in particular local contexts (say, for example, Latinos and Jews in Maine) will likely experience higher levels of interethnic or interracial sex than will members of ethnic and racial groups that are relatively large. Again, this will only be the case when racial and ethnic prejudices do not block these forms of sex.

Spickard offers other insights that may be applicable in LGBT contexts, but only further research will demonstrate if this is the case. For example, he argues that for most American racial and ethnic groups, intermarriage rates increased dramatically two generations after the immigrant generation; intermarriage rates also increased after the 1967 U.S. Supreme Court ruling (in *Loving v. Virginia*) that struck down state laws against interracial marriage. Scholars have not yet determined whether same sex interracial and interethnic sex has followed similar patterns. Nor do we know whether Spickard's finding that intermarriage rates have increased dramatically for almost all racial and ethnic groups in the United States except African Americans are paralleled in LGBT contexts.

Historical Case Studies

Not that much is known about interracial and interethnic same-sex sex in North America before the twentieth century, though such relationships were invariably structured by the dynamics of colonialism, conquest, slavery, and white supremacy. In *Gay American History* (1976), Jonathan Ned Katz provides a translation of a 1567 text that describes the murder by the Spanish in Florida of a French Lutheran who lived with and was loved "very much" by a Native man (pp. 23–25). He also offers a translation of 1646 Dutch records from New Netherland (which later became New York) that refer to the execution of Jan Creoli, "a negro," for committing sodomy with Manuel Congo; in this case, the names suggest a possible crossing of racial or ethnic lines (pp. 35–36). Ramón Gutiérrez (1991) discusses eighteenth-century Spanish Franciscans accused of sodomizing Native servants and mixed-race orphans in New Mexico.

For the nineteenth century, Harriet Jacobs's 1861 autobiographical slave narrative refers to a white male slaveowner who committed on his black male slave "the strangest freaks of despotism" that were "of a nature too filthy to be repeated." Hannah Rosen (1999) has reconstructed the story of Frances Thompson, a black freedwoman who was raped by white men during the Memphis riot of 1866 but whose testimony about those rapes was later discredited when she was revealed to be biologically male. As various literary critics have noted, homoerotic interracial male relationships were major themes in nineteenth-century fictional works by James Fenimore Cooper, Herman Melville, Charles Warren Stoddard, and Mark Twain. Put together, these examples suggest that interracial or interethnic same-sex sex was a source of significant social anxiety and pleasure, often contributing to but sometimes undermining American racial and ethnic hierarchies.

Much more is known about same-sex interracial and interethnic sex in the period from the late nineteenth century through the 1960s, when these forms of sex (and the discourses surrounding them) continued to participate in both constructing and deconstructing white supremacy. Pablo Mitchell (1999) explores the Anglo-Native gay son at the center of an Anglo-Native-Hispano family inheritance dispute in late-nineteenth- and early-twentieth-century New Mexico, using this case to illustrate the ways that "strategic marriage and intermarriage" were central to elite rule (p. 333). Estelle Freedman (1996) examines evidence about interracial lesbian relationships in prisons from 1915 to 1965, focusing on criminologists who "emphasized the ways that race substituted for gender" (p. 425). Siobhan Somerville (2000) analyzes the ways in which "two tabooed types of desire—interracial and homosexual—became linked in early twentieth century sexological and psychological discourse," as well as in the works of various African American writers (p. 34). Eric Garber (1989), George Chauncey (1994), and Kevin Mumford (1997) map the geographical and conceptual terrain of interracial same-sex sex in a variety of early-twentieth-century urban locations, including what Mumford calls the "interzones" of "black/white sex districts."

Various case studies examine interracial and interethnic sex in the 1950s and 1960s. Elizabeth Kennedy and Madeline Davis (1993) discuss interracial same-sex relationships in their work on mid-twentieth century lesbian bar culture in Buffalo, New York, concluding that "interracial couples became quite common" in the 1950s and 1960s (p. 119). Esther Newton's queer history of Cherry Grove, Fire Island (1993), highlights the prejudices that stigmatized interracial and interethnic relationships in that community but also points out that beginning in the 1950s small numbers of African Americans, Hispanics, and Asian Americans found a place in Cherry Grove, often as the lovers of white renters or property owners. In his study of midcentury Philadelphia, Marc Stein (2000) mentions LGB bars that were popular among those looking for interracial sex, coffeehouses that became sites of overlapping LGB and interracial cultures, prisons where interracial same-sex sexual assaults were said to be common, and Quaker-affiliated parties held to encourage socializing across racial and sexual boundaries. (Katz mentions a Los Angeles group called Knights of the Clock, founded in 1950, that apparently had similar aims.) John Howard (1999) argues in his work on Mississippi that "black men and white men participated in markedly similar worlds of desire that rarely overlapped before the 1960s" (p. xiv). He also looks at intersections between interracialism and homoeroticism in the context of the civil rights movement, pulp fiction, and political scandals. Numerous authors have analyzed interracial and interethnic same-sex sex in biographical studies; notable examples are John D'Emilio's book on the civil rights leader Bayard Rustin (2003) and Judy Wu's work on Margaret Chung (2001).

Racial and ethnic prejudice may have discouraged LGB people from forming interracial and interethnic relationships, but they were common enough for LGB people to have developed a variety of terms (regarded as offensive by many) for those who seemed to prefer them. Although it is difficult to date the origins of these terms, they extend back at least several decades. LGB people have described those who prefer Asian Americans as "rice queens," those who prefer South Asians as "curry queens," those who prefer African Americans as "dinge queens," and those who prefer Euro-Americans as "potato queens" or "snow queens." In the case of Asian Americans, the presumed ubiquity of interracial relationships has led to the invention of the term "sticky rice" to describe Asian Americans who partner with Asian Americans. Interracial and interethnic LGB partners have faced not only stigmatizing language, but also unique forms of housing discrimination, family rejection, and representational exoticization. They have also faced racial and ethnic prejudice within their relationships. At the same time, many LGB people involved in these relationships have been in the forefront of antiracist struggles.

Debates in the Late Twentieth Century

While individual voices were raised to defend and criticize interracial and interethnic relationships within LGB communities before the 1960s, a more communal and more public discussion emerged in the 1970s, led primarily by women of color and then taken up by men of color. Anita Cornwell, Audre Lorde, Gloria Anzaldúa, Cherríe Moraga, Joseph Beam, Richard Fung, and David Eng are among the most prominent people of color who have spoken and written about the topic. At times debates about the politics of groups such as Black and White Men Together, Men of All Colors Together, and People of All Colors Together have been heated and intense. The same has been true for debates about representations of interracial and interethnic LGB desire, for example in pornography. For some, interracial LGB relationships invariably reproduce racism. For others, these relationships are key sites of struggle against racism. Still others hope that race can be transcended in interracial relationships or believe that sexual intimacy is profoundly individual and private and that it therefore should not be evaluated in political or social terms. In the end, however, as long as race, ethnicity, sexuality, and gender continue to function as categories of social meaning and markers of political hierarchies in the United States, interracial and interethnic LGB sex will likely remain a subject of controversy and debate.

Bibliography

Anzaldúa, Gloria. *Borderlands = La Frontera: The New Mestiza.* San Francisco: Spinsters, 1987.

Beam, Joseph, ed. *In the Life: A Black Gay Anthology.* Boston: Alyson, 1986.

Chauncey, George. *Gay New York: Gender, Urban Culture, and the Making of the Gay Male World, 1890–1940.* New York: Basic Books, 1994.

Cornwell, Anita. "Letter to a Friend." *Ladder* (December 1971–January 1972): 42–45.

———. "Open Letter to a Black Sister." *Ladder* (October–November 1971): 33–36.

D'Emilio, John. *Lost Prophet: The Life and Times of Bayard Rustin.* New York: Free Press, 2003.

Eng, David L., and Alice Y. Hom. *Q&A: Queer in Asian America.* Philadelphia: Temple University Press, 1998.

Freedman, Estelle B. "The Prison Lesbian: Race, Class, and the Construction of the Aggressive Female Homosexual, 1915–1965." *Feminist Studies* 22, no. 2 (Summer 1996): 397–423.

Garber, Eric. "A Spectacle in Color: The Lesbian and Gay Subculture of Jazz Age Harlem." In *Hidden from History: Reclaiming the Gay and Lesbian Past.* Edited by Martin Bauml Duberman, Martha Vicinus, and George Chauncey. New York: New American Library, 1989.

Gutiérrez, Ramón A. *When Jesus Came, the Corn Mothers Went Away: Marriage, Sexuality, and Power in New Mexico, 1500–1846.* Stanford, Calif.: Stanford University Press, 1991.

Howard, John. *Men Like That: A Southern Queer History.* Chicago: University of Chicago Press, 1999.

Katz, Jonathan Ned. *Gay American History.* New York: Crowell, 1976.

Kennedy, Elizabeth Lapovsky, and Madeline D. Davis. *Boots of Leather, Slippers of Gold: The History of a Lesbian Community.* New York: Routledge, 1993.

Lorde, Audre. *Sister Outsider.* Trumansburg, N.Y.: Crossing Press, 1984.

Mitchell, Pablo. "Accomplished Ladies and Coyotes: Marriage, Power, and Straying from the Flock in Territorial New Mexico, 1880–1920." In *Sex, Love, Race: Crossing Boundaries in North American History.* Edited by Martha Hodes. New York: New York University Press, 1999.

Moraga, Cherríe, and Gloria Anzaldúa. *This Bridge Called My Back: Writings by Radical Women of Color.* Watertown, Mass.: Persephone, 1981.

Mumford, Kevin J. *Interzones: Black/White Sex Districts in Chicago and New York in the Early Twentieth Century.* New York: Columbia University Press, 1997.

Nash, Gary B. "The Hidden History of Mestizo America." *Journal of American History* 82, no. 3 (December 1995): 941–962.

Newton, Esther. *Cherry Grove, Fire Island: Sixty Years in America's First Gay and Lesbian Town.* Boston: Beacon Press, 1993.

Reid-Pharr, Robert. *Black Gay Man.* New York: New York University Press. 2001.

Rosen, Hannah. "'Not That Sort of Women': Race, Gender, and Sexual Violence during the Memphis Riot of 1866." In *Sex, Love, Race: Crossing Boundaries in North American History.* Edited by Martha Hodes. New York: New York University Press, 1999.

Somerville, Siobhan B. *Queering the Color Line: Race and the Invention of Homosexuality in American Culture.* Durham, N.C.: Duke University Press, 2000.

Spickard, Paul R. *Mixed Blood: Intermarriage and Ethnic Identity in Twentieth-Century America.* Madison: University of Wisconsin Press, 1989.

Stein, Marc. *City of Sisterly and Brotherly Loves: Lesbian and Gay Philadelphia, 1945–1972.* Chicago: University of Chicago Press, 2000.

Wu, Judy Tzu-Chun. "Was Mom Chung a 'Sister Lesbian'?: Asian American Gender Experimentation and Interracial Homoeroticism." *Journal of Women's History* 13, no. 1 (Spring 2001): 58–82.

Marc Stein

See also AFRICAN AMERICANS; ASIAN AMERICANS AND PACIFIC ISLANDERS; BLACK AND WHITE MEN TOGETHER (BWMT); NATIVE AMERICANS; RACE AND RACISM.

INTERSEXUALS AND INTERSEXED PEOPLE

Intersexual people have sex chromosomes, external genitalia, or an internal reproductive system that are not considered "standard" for either the male or female sex according to the dominant point of view of modern Western culture. The definition of intersexuality is complex because there is profound disagreement, especially among physicians, intersexual people, and their parents. Physicians mostly identify intersexuality as an "abnormal" condition in which parts characteristic of both sexes are to some extent (really or apparently) combined. However, intersexual people have recently organized to oppose the medical definition, arguing that sex does not constitute a dichotomous phenomenon and that the human population cannot simply be divided into males and females. On the contrary, intersexual organizations believe that variety is predominant among human beings.

According to the prevailing medical view, genitals that cannot clearly be classified as male or female organs mark a disorder and there should be a treatment in order to correct the deficiency. The prevailing medical perspective also pathologizes those whose chromosomes do not fit clearly into the "standard" male (XY) or female (XX) pattern. This point of view encourages genital surgeries, hormonal treatment, and other forms of medical intervention in order to make genitals and/or the body fit into a regular male or female model. Intersexual people, as well as some scholars who specialize in the study of sexuality, have stated that the dominant medical approach is not interested in life-saving or improving the quality of life. On the contrary, intersexual activists think that many physicians want to construct what they identify as an "aesthetic" organ in order to avoid the threat that intersexual people pose to an oppressive culture organized around binary conceptions of sex, gender, and sexuality.

In classical Greece, intersexuals were identified as "hermaphrodites," a term with a mythical origin. According to the myth, Hermaphroditus was the son of Hermes and Aphrodite (or Mercury and Venus in the Roman tradition). The nymph Salmacis fell in love with Hermaphroditus, and as a result of her obsession to possess him, she embraced him tightly and did not let him go. Salmacis asked the gods to fuse their bodies into one. Another representation of sexually ambiguous bodies in classical Greece is Aristophanes's speech in Plato's *Sym-*

posium. Aristophanes describes the original human beings as individuals with four legs, four arms, and two sets of sexual organs. According to this speech, Zeus, the father of all the Olympic gods, decided to cut human beings into halves because they were very arrogant and he wanted to punish them by making them incomplete. This forced men and women to long for their other part, a process that gave birth to love.

The term "hermaphroditism" continued to be used throughout the Middle Ages and is sometimes still used by physicians and others. Historians have studied some of the legal cases involving intersexual people, but very little is known about their lives before the nineteenth century. The term "intersexuality" has been in use since the beginning of the twentieth century, but only recently has its use become widespread.

The Emergence of a Scientific Interpretation

At the end of the eighteenth century, as biology became a modern scientific field of study, it acquired greater legitimacy to claim authority over ambiguous bodies. The French scientist Isidore Geoffroy Saint-Hilaire (1805–1861) founded a new biological subfield named "teratology" (from Greek *teras,* meaning "monster") in order to deal with all kinds of unusual birds. This area of knowledge would explore what he defined as the pathological side of embryology.

According to Saint-Hilaire, nature constituted a whole and every organism was part of a general plan. That plan had begun with no sexual differentiation and later it had evolved toward ambiguously sexual individuals that became genitally dichotomous at the end of the evolutionary scale. This interpretation conceived of a unilinear biological evolution where binary sex difference constituted the final aim of nature's plan. By placing intersexuality into evolution, Saint-Hilaire questioned the belief that identified it as an unnatural phenomenon and instead explained sexual ambiguity as the product of natural history. Under this paradigm, when scientists identified human genitals and/or bodies as having anatomical "pathologies," they would classify them as organisms arrested in their development. Scientists claimed that human intersexuality had to be interpreted through previous organic forms of what they considered older species.

Other nineteenth-century thinkers legitimated this interpretation concerning the relationship between intersexuality and evolution. Charles Darwin, Herbert Spencer, Ernst Haeckel, and other biologists also considered natural history as a process beginning with asexual cells and culminating in complete sexual differentiation between individuals of "opposite" sexes. Evolutionists understood the split between two sexes as a necessary feature of the higher stages of evolution. Using this approach, Haeckel believed that a "normal" embryological history had to "recapitulate" his vision of a natural history, culminating in a binary division between male and female. If recapitulation was not complete and the newborn had ambiguous genitals, then it meant that the body had suffered a halt in its embryological evolution, which was supposed to be "abnormal" for a higher species such as humans.

In her book *Hermaphroditism and the Medical Invention of Sex* (1998), Alice Domurat Dreger explains how, between the late nineteenth century and the beginning of the twentieth, physicians attempted to neutralize genital ambiguity by examining internal sexual organs—named "gonads." Because physicians considered those organs as the criteria necessary for establishing "true" sex, Dregger defines the period as "the age of gonads." Referring to a specific case, this scholar explains how a woman with female sexual organs was forcibly redefined as male because the physician found her gonads to be testes. Medical texts characterized "hermaphroditism" as an "error of sex," and because they thought that gonads could eliminate the ambiguity, they preferred to refer to this biological condition as "pseudo-hermaphroditism." This concept implied that only a clearly defined male or female was "real," while ambiguities of the external sexual organs were "false" manifestations of a "true" gonad to be found through ablation and microscopic analysis of tissue. Only in the second decade of the twentieth century did physicians recognize the existence of individuals with ambiguous gonads named "ovotestes." This contributed to the fall of the "age of gonads." Those intersexuals who had ovotestes, as opposed to the pseudo-hermaphrodites, became known as "true-hermaphrodites."

Twentieth-century Medical Approach

Although the medical approach of distinguishing the "true" sex through gonads was questioned earlier, only in the 1970s was it fully replaced by a new approach. In this decade, John Money argued that there was no "true" biological sex because sex was actually a cultural construction. In 1972, Money took the decision of reassigning the gender of an infant boy, whose penis had been ablated in a routine circumcision gone horribly wrong, through the surgical creation of female genitals. When this case was published, physicians thought it was an interesting experiment because the infant had an identical twin. This situation would allow an evaluation of the role of socialization and biology in the determination of sex. Money claimed that his surgery would provide an anatomical base for the subject's happiness in adulthood. However, Milton Diamond found out later that the child, "Joan," had rejected the assigned female identity. Diamond performed another surgery and provided hormone treatment to help "Joan" become "John."

Money's original reassignment was interpreted as evidence of the primacy of socialization, while the later failure became a point to support biological interpretations of the origin of sex. According to Suzanne Kessler, however, in *Lessons from the Intersexed* (1998), Money's failure does not prove that biology determines sex, because Joan/John was probably raised by parents who provided inconsistent gender messages. Kessler also argues that despite the fact that Money questioned the biological origin of sex, he took for granted the existence of two sexes. According to Money's view, an individual would not be able to lead a "normal" life if his/her genitals were not culturally perceived as either male or female, and thus it was necessary to eliminate ambiguity through surgery. The main difference between Money's view and the previous medical approach was that although Money recommended an early intervention on the infant's body, the criteria for the surgical construction of genitals was not the search for truth in the internal sexual organs. Under the new paradigm it became important to evaluate which sex would be more feasible under the given biological circumstances of a specific body.

In the last quarter of the twentieth century, through the work of John Money and the sanction of the American Academy of Pediatrics, physicians adopted specific treatment protocols. According to these rules, clinicians have to evaluate the genitals and decide which sex would be easier to construct in each specific case. This implies a set of assumptions, including the idea that a boy's gender identity is based on the possession of an adequate penis. In line with this approach, if the penis size does not fulfill physicians' definitions of normality, then it is easier to construct a vagina and to reduce the size of what has now become accepted as a big clitoris.

The Emergence of the Intersexual Movement

In 1993, an episode at the World University Games in Kobe, Japan, brought public attention to discussions about intersexuality. Maria Patiño, Spain's top woman hurdler, had forgotten to take a medical certificate stating that she was a woman, and before competing she had to go through an analysis of some cells obtained from the inside of her cheek. Because Patiño had been born with a condition known as androgen insensitivity, her body did not respond to the hormone that produces a penis and what is understood as male secondary sex characteristics. Even though she had a Y chromosome, she never developed a male body. After the sex test she realized that despite her body and genital appearance, both her chromosomes and her internal sexual organs were read by physicians as male. As a result of the medical exam, she was banned from the games and her entire career was ruined.

In 1993, an intersexual woman named Cheryl Chase founded the Intersex Society of North America (ISNA). Her aim was to make physicians reconsider their approach toward intersexuality in order to prevent unnecessary surgical interventions from happening. Meanwhile, the emergence and evolution of the Internet in the 1990s allowed a group of intersexuals and professionals to share their experiences. Since 1994 the members of ISNA have exposed their views in a newsletter called *Hermaphrodites with Attitude*, and they have contributed to the emergence of a public discussion on intersexuality. In 1996 the ISNA created its own Web page, providing information for the general public and for physicians. Many intersexual persons joined the organization and in 1997 ISNA decided that its main aim would now be to influence the medical profession.

Intersexual activists argue that physicians perform compulsive surgeries on intersexual people not because they want to solve a health problem, but rather because they think that a person without a definite sex would be incapable of dealing with daily life. The members of ISNA have stated that intersex surgeries are comparable to female genital mutilation, and that despite the attention that the latter has received, there is a lack of awareness about the personal and psychological damage that intersex surgery creates. Arguing that intersex surgeries are mutilations, activists claim that they as well as female circumcision should be banned.

The Internet and the writing of texts have not been the only political tools used by the ISNA; they have also resorted to picketing at hospitals that are reluctant to discuss their views and prefer to continue performing intersex surgeries. Chase and other activists have also organized pickets at medical congresses, especially ones whose topic is pediatrics. Through this pressure tactic, the intersexual movement has forced physicians to reconsider their voices. Whereas in the 1990s the criticisms of intersex patients have been mostly disregarded by physicians, in May 2000 the Lawson Wilkins Pediatric Endocrine Society, the largest organization including specialists in children's hormones, invited Chase to participate in its conference and offer her own understanding of how physicians should deal with intersexuality.

By participating in conferences and classes at several universities, intersexual people have counteracted the view that identifies physicians as the experts who have the right to make decisions about bodies with ambiguous genitals. The ISNA has stated, as part of its suggested guidelines for nonintersex individuals writing about intersexuality and intersex people, that it is important to "recognize that you are not the experts about intersex people, intersexuality, or what it means to be intersexed—intersexed people are." This claim becomes especially important in a context in which, as Kessler has pointed out, no real research about the life of surgically and hormonally treated intersexed patients has been conducted by physicians, who actually take for granted what should be questioned. Intersexual activists have tried to overcome their silence by claiming their right to decide about their own lives. They do not oppose surgeries in those cases where some health issue is at stake, but in the majority of the cases, where no real risk is involved, they claim the individual right to choose and then ask physicians to stop making decisions at an early stage of life by manipulating parental fears and misinformation.

The ISNA has promoted an alternative understanding of intersexuality where anatomy is interpreted as complex and variable and there is no distinction made between a normal and an abnormal genital or body. This patient-centered model wants to challenge the idea that difference equals disease. As a result of ISNA's influence, new intersex support groups are emerging in Canada, Europe, Asia, Japan, and New Zealand.

Chase compares the emergence of intersex claims in the 1990s with the lesbian and gay movement of the 1950s. She thinks that the idea of coming out is crucial to inspire legal reforms that limit physicians' power to make decisions about intersex bodies. In this context, ISNA focuses on local activism and has encouraged some activists to come out publicly as intersexuals, showing that they are not just people attached to a certain anatomical condition, but are regular people who hold all kinds of jobs and professions, as in the case of Marge Witty, a psychologist; Hale Hawbecker, an attorney; Martha Coventry, a journalist; and Michael Walker, who is undergoing training as a therapist.

In line with intersexual activists' claims regarding their primacy as experts on the management of their own bodies, some recent scholars who are not intersexual have learned lessons from intersexual people and are challenging the whole dominant sex and gender system while developing a whole new paradigm that defies the traditional medical model.

Bibliography

Domurat Dreger, Alice, *Hermaphrodites and the Medical Invention of Sex.* Cambridge, Mass.: Harvard University Press. 1998.

Fausto-Sterling, Anne, *Sexing the Body: Gender Politics and the Construction of Sexuality.* New York: Basic Books, 2000.

Kessler, Suzanne, *Lessons from the Intersexed.* New Brunswick, N.J.: Rutgers University Press, 1998.

Pablo Ben

See also BENJAMIN, HARRY; GENDER AND SEX; HALL, THOMAS/THOMASINE; MONEY, JOHN, AND ANKE EHRHARDT; TRANSSEXUALS, TRANSVESTITES, TRANSGENDER PEOPLE, AND CROSS-DRESSERS.

ISHERWOOD, Christopher (b. 26 August 1904; d. 4 January 1986), writer.

Christopher Isherwood was born in Cheshire, England, in 1904 to Kathleen and Frank Bradshaw Isherwood. His parents named him Christopher William Bradshaw Isherwood, continuing the family tradition of enshrining the Bradshaw-Isherwood surname in the child's given name. A brother, Richard, was born in 1911. Frank, an officer in the British army, was killed in 1915 in France. Isherwood attended St. Edmund's School in Surrey—where he first met W. H. Auden, who would grow up to be a renowned poet—and then went to Corpus Christi College, Cambridge University (1923–1925). He left without completing a degree. His first novel, *All the Conspirators,* was published in 1928.

Seeking personal and sexual freedom from his mother and from England, Isherwood first visited Berlin, the capital of Weimar Germany, in 1929. As he wrote later in his frank memoir of the period, *Christopher and his Kind* (1976), to him "Berlin meant boys." He lived in Germany intermittently for the next four years. In the 1930s he met and became friends with many leading English literary figures, including E. M. Forster, Stephen Spender, and Somerset Maugham. His second novel, *The Memorial: Portrait of a Family,* was published by Leonard and Virginia Woolf's Hogarth Press in 1932. After leaving Berlin in 1933, Isherwood traveled throughout Europe with his young German lover, Heinz Neddermeyer, who was trying to avoid conscription into the German army. Isherwood wrote his first screenplay, *The Little Friend* (1934), under the guidance of film director Berthold Viertel. He would turn this experience into the novel *Prater Violet* (1945). An early autobiography, *Lions and Shadows: An Education in the Twenties* (1938), presented slightly disguised versions of himself, Auden, and Spender, among others.

Isherwood's early career, and much of his subsequent notoriety, rests on two novels written about Germany, *Mr. Norris Changes Trains* (1935; published in the United States as *The Last of Mr. Norris,* 1935) and *Goodbye to Berlin* (1939). These two novels were reissued in one volume as *The Berlin Stories* (1945). The novels are told from the perspective of a young Englishman, called William Bradshaw in the first novel and Christopher Isherwood in the second, whose seemingly nonsexual persona is part of the coded homosexual context of the novels. Isherwood's most famous character, Sally Bowles, a young English singer-actress in *Goodbye to Berlin,* is sexually scandalous and artistically without talent. The relationship between Sally and Christopher is the centerpiece of the 1951 stage adaptation of Isherwood's German novels, called *I Am a Camera,* by John van Druten. The play was made into a film of the same name and subsequently made into the musical *Cabaret* (Broadway, 1966) by John Kander and Fred Ebb. The subsequent 1972 film by Bob Fosse starred Liza Minnelli as Sally and Michael York as the now bisexual Isherwood character. Through her role as Sally, Liza Minnelli became an icon of gay culture as the film celebrated the "divine decadence" of pre–World War II Germany.

Isherwood emigrated to the United States with Auden in 1939 and settled in Los Angeles, where he began to study Vedanta, a branch of the Hindu religion. He registered as a conscientious objector during World War II and became a U.S. citizen in 1946, when he officially dropped his middle two names. He continued to write novels, autobiographies, screenplays, and translations of Hindu texts such as the Bhagavad Gita. His novel, *The World in the Evening* (1954), includes a bisexual protagonist, a happy gay couple, a discussion of gays in the military, and one of the first published definitions of "camp." Gay and bisexual themes continued in his final three novels: *Down There on a Visit* (1962); *A Single Man* (1964), widely regarded as Isherwood's masterpiece; and *A Meeting by the River* (1967). Isherwood met Don Bachardy in 1953, when Bachardy was just eighteen, and they lived together for the rest of Isherwood's life. Throughout the 1960s and 1970s, Isherwood and Bachardy, an accomplished artist, were openly gay as a couple. In his frank depiction of gay life as well as his elegant, seemingly simple prose, Isherwood provided a model of autobiographical fiction for gay male writers in the late twentieth century. Significant American writers such as Armistead Maupin, Paul Monette, and Edmund White were influenced by Isherwood's life and work.

Isherwood capped his writing career with three honest and elegant autobiographies: *Kathleen and Frank* (1971), a portrait of his parents in which he comes out officially in print; *Christopher and His Kind, 1929–1939* (1976), which tells of the gay life behind the Berlin novels and his meeting Magnus Hirschfeld; and *My Guru and His Disciple* (1980), which details his immersion in Vedanta. Throughout his life Isherwood kept diaries, which are being posthumously published.

Bibliography

Berg, James J., and Chris Freeman. *The Isherwood Century: Essays on the Life and Work of Christopher Isherwood.* Madison: University of Wisconsin Press, 2000.

Isherwood, Christopher. *Diaries, Volume One, 1939–1960.* Edited by Katherine Bucknell. New York: HarperCollins, 1997.

Summers, Claude J. *Christopher Isherwood.* New York: Ungar, 1980.

James J. Berg

See also AUDEN, W. H.; ERICKSON EDUCATIONAL FOUNDATION; LITERATURE.

ISLAM. see MUSLIMS AND ISLAM.

ISLAS, Arturo (b. 24 May 1938; d. 15 February 1991), writer.

A gay Chicano from a working-class family, Islas wrote, with subtlety and humor, three novels that deal with his class background, ethnic/racial identity, and sexuality, as well as the physical handicaps that marked his life: polio in childhood and a colostomy in 1969. Born in El Paso, Texas, Islas grew up in this border and bilingual city. After graduating from high school in 1956, he left the desert for the San Francisco Bay area and Stanford University, where he earned his undergraduate and graduate degrees in English and where in 1970 he became a faculty member. In the 1970s, Islas broke up with his longtime lover, Jay Spears, and then learned in 1985 that Spears was in the hospital with AIDS. The two reconciled before Spears died at the end of 1986. Five years later, Islas also died of complications from AIDS.

Attention is often drawn to the semiautobiographical character of Islas's work as a fictional composite of his own experience and place of birth. In many ways, his fiction is a reflexive and cathartic endeavor to deal with issues of class, racism, and homophobia within the Chicano/a community.

The desert landscape of El Paso, surrounded by stark brown mountains and aromatic sagebrush, is constructed repeatedly in Islas's fiction through characters that are never fully able to break free from their roots and upbringing. The desert is a space of repression (social and sexual) and hypocrisy, a space that keeps pulling back those who escape. Education-as-escape and the compelling desert serve as antagonistic forces that frame his three novels: *The Rain God* (1984), *Migrant Souls* (1990), and *La Mollie and the King of Tears: A Novel,* published posthumously (1996). Islas was working on a fourth novel, *American Dreams and Fantasies,* when he died.

Although identifying as a gay Chicano, Islas did not focus exclusively on the queer experience in his work. In fact, sexuality is not the principal identity or problematic in these narratives, except in one short segment of the section "Rain Dancer" in *The Rain God,* in which we witness the violent death of Felix Angel at the hands of a young soldier who resists the older man's advances. The sexuality of the main character, Miguel Chico, is in the background of both *The Rain God* and *Migrant Souls;* in these novels, being gay serves as one more concealed difference in a family of many secrets and lies. In the third novel, *La Mollie and the King of Tears,* the narrator searches briefly for his brother at an S/M gay bar in San Francisco, but again, sexuality is simply one more cultural difference among many.

The Rain God and *Migrant Souls* deal with three generations of the Angel family, their class status and class pretensions, their religious beliefs and fanaticism, their racial bigotry, and various family "sins," all elements that affect family relations and cause friction between generations, giving rise in the process to a series of family resentments. Miguel Chico's return to Del Sapo (El Paso) from the Bay Area after his colostomy initiates the process of dismantling the family façade and uncovering painful secrets for the reader.

Both novels narrate the migration of the Angel family to the Texas desert from Mexico during the Mexican Revolution. The first novel focuses on the widowed matriarch, Mama Chona, and her children, the first generation in the United States. To create a sense of family, Mama Chona constructs a mythic aristocratic Spanish ancestry that leads her to disdain darker family members, servants, and in-laws, especially if they are anticlerical or atheist. A false sense of superiority and a strict sense of authority serve to mask the social anxieties and antagonisms of this first Angel generation. *Migrant Souls* deals with the rebellious second generation of Angel women and the tensions in Miguel Chico's life as he stands apart from, yet is drawn to, the family. Domestic spaces predominate in both novels; here family members, primarily women, deal with conflictive family or partner relations, murder, suicide, infidelity, disloyalty, illness, and death.

The third novel, *La Mollie and the King of Tears,* provides the first-person narration of Louie Mendoza, a forty-year-old saxophonist from El Paso, who sits in the waiting area of the emergency room in a San Francisco hospital and narrates his entire life and concerns to a sociolinguist researcher while he waits to hear if his lover, Mollie, is going to survive a serious accident. In the process, Louie reconstructs his life in El Paso, in Korea, in a veterans hospital, in Los Angeles, and in San Francisco, where he plays with a band in a night club. Louie is a rather unusual and humorous character, a gifted musician with only a high school diploma, who shifts with ease between colloquial and standard English, quotes from Shakespeare's plays, and philosophizes on the human condition. Like Islas's other novels, *La Mollie* focuses on the complexity of interpersonal relations, especially on difficult interactions between people of different ethnic and class backgrounds.

Bibliography

Burciaga, José Antonio. "A Conversation with Arturo Islas." *Stanford Humanities Review* 2, nos. 2–3 (spring 1992): 158–166.

Islas, Arturo. *The Rain God.* Palo Alto, Calif.: Alexandrian Press, 1984.

———. *Migrant Souls.* New York: Morrow, 1990.

———. *American Dreams and Fantasies.* Unpublished manuscript. Excerpts published in *Stanford Humanities Review* 2, nos. 2–3 (spring 1992): 169–189.

———. *La Mollie and the King of Tears.* Albuquerque: University of New Mexico Press, 1996.

Saldívar, José David. "The Hybridity of Culture in Arturo Islas's *The Rain God.*" *Dispositio: Revista Americana de Estudios Comparados y Culturales/American Journal of Comparative and Cultural Studies* 16, no. 41 (1991): 109–119.

Sánchez, Marta. "Arturo Islas' *The Rain God:* An Alternative Tradition." *American Literature* 62, no. 2 (June 1990): 284–304.

Sánchez, Rosaura. "Ideological Discourses in Arturo Islas's *The Rain God.*" In *Criticism in the Borderlands: Studies in Chicano Literature, Culture, and Ideology.* Edited by Hector Calderón and José David Saldívar. Durham, N.C.: Duke University Press, 1991.

Skenazy, Paul. Afterword to *La Mollie and the King of Tears* by Arturo Islas. Albuquerque: University of New Mexico Press, 1996.

Rosaura Sánchez

J

JANUS SOCIETY

Founded in 1962, the Janus Society was an influential, Philadelphia-based homophile organization that remained active until 1969. Janus featured participation and leadership by lesbians, bisexuals, and gay men; published *Drum,* the most widely circulating homophile magazine of the 1960s; and developed political positions that were among the most militant, radical, and sexually liberated in the LGBT movement of its era. In these respects, Janus challenges histories of the homophile movement that concentrate exclusively on the male-dominated Mattachine Society and the exclusively female Daughters of Bilitis; histories of the homophile press that focus only on the *Mattachine Review,* the *Ladder,* and *ONE* magazine; and histories of pre-Stonewall LGBT organizing that overemphasize the movement's conservatism.

Years of Respectability

The Janus Society was established after the national Mattachine Society, for a variety of financial, administrative, and political reasons, revoked the charters of local Mattachine groups around the United States in early 1961. Philadelphians had just organized a local Mattachine group, not yet officially recognized as a chapter, and in the wake of the national Mattachine's decision these local activists renamed their group the Janus Society of the Delaware Valley (after the two-faced Roman god of beginnings, endings, and doorways). Mae Polakoff, who had led the local Mattachine group, served as the president of Janus in its first two years.

In 1962 and 1963, Janus held regular meetings and social events for its several dozen members; organized public lectures by local psychiatrists and national homophile activists, including Donald Webster Cory; opened an office in Center City Philadelphia; worked with the local branch of the American Civil Liberties Union (ACLU); and published a monthly newsletter that featured articles critical of anti-LGBT psychiatrists, psychotherapists, police, and politicians. In this period Janus members also promoted positive media coverage of LGBT people by appearing on local radio programs and speaking with local journalists, including the author of "The Furtive Fraternity," a groundbreaking article on the local gay world that appeared in *Greater Philadelphia Magazine* in December 1962. In 1963 Janus joined together with three other homophile groups (from New York City and Washington, D.C.) to form East Coast Homophile Organizations (ECHO). Janus hosted ECHO's first convention, which was held in August 1963 at the Drake Hotel in Philadelphia.

In most of its public activities Janus members, like the vast majority of homophile activists in this period, promoted a politics of respectability. To challenge popular negative stereotypes of LGBT people as masculine women and feminine men, Janus encouraged lesbians to embrace femininity, gay men to embrace masculinity, and lesbian and gay activists to embrace heterosocial culture (when presenting themselves to the straight world). For example, at the ECHO conference female participants were encouraged to wear appropriate feminine clothing and male participants were encouraged to wear appropriate masculine clothing. To challenge popular views of LGBT people as excessively focused on sex, Janus downplayed the sexual aspects of LGBT cultures. When they thought it served LGBT interests, Janus members also cultivated ties with respectable scientific and legal experts. While the extent of homophile accommodation to dominant social norms should not be exaggerated, the respectable strategies used by Janus in its early years risked excluding many LGBT people from the gains the group hoped to make.

Years of Militancy

In late 1963 Clark Polak was elected the new president of Janus, quickly taking the organization in new directions. Rejecting the politics of sexual respectability and embracing the values of sexual liberation, Polak transformed the group's monthly newsletter into *Drum* magazine, which offered male physique photographs, the comic strip *Harry Chess,* humorous parodies, news highlights, and aggressively pro-gay and pro-sex editorials and features. For this, Janus was rejected by many homophile leaders elsewhere who feared that *Drum* would provide ammunition for the enemies of the LGBT movement. Some lesbian activists also criticized the male focus of *Drum.* Antagonism to *Drum* led ECHO to expel Janus in 1965 (and welcome instead a new Mattachine Philadelphia group, founded by several Janus lesbians alienated by Polak). But the same features that antagonized many homophile leaders attracted unprecedented numbers of LGBT readers, and *Drum*'s circulation soon was larger than that of all other homophile publications combined. Reflecting the national reach of *Drum,* in late 1964 Janus renamed itself the Janus Society of America.

Meanwhile, in other contexts Janus embraced a politics of militant respectability. In April 1965 Janus organized five days of demonstrations to support a sit-in that teenagers had organized at Dewey's Restaurant in Philadelphia to protest denials of service to gay, cross-dressing, and nonconforming customers. On the Fourth of July in 1965, Janus members participated in an ECHO-sponsored picketing demonstration at Philadelphia's Independence Hall to protest denials of LGBT rights. (The Independence Hall demonstration became the first of five Annual Reminders held each year on the Fourth of July on the same site.) On Armed Forces Day in 1966, Janus held a LGBT rights demonstration at the Philadelphia Navy Yard. In each of these demonstrations, male homophile activists in jackets and ties and female homophile activists in dresses and skirts were as militant about their respectability as they were about their LGBT rights agenda. The politics of militant respectability were also on display as Janus attracted hundreds of people to public lectures held at downtown Philadelphia hotels. The lectures featured, among others, national homophile leaders Cory and Frank Kameny, Kinsey associate Wardell Pomeroy, and psychiatrist Albert Ellis. Meanwhile, Janus supported LGBT people with legal advice, aid, and referrals; intervened on behalf of LGBT people with police and politicians; criticized raids on LGBT bars, clubs, and other LGBT spaces; lobbied for LGBT law reform; and promoted pro-LGBT messages in the local and national media (gaining attention, for example, in *Sexology, Playboy,* the *New Republic,* and the *Wall Street Journal*). Janus also established the Homosexual Law Reform Society (HLRS), which supported LGBT rights cases around the country. HLRS's most significant victory was a 1967 New Jersey Supreme Court case, *Val's Bar v. Division of Alcoholic Beverage Control* (commonly known as *Val's*), that affirmed the right of gay people to assemble in bars. Although HLRS lost when the U.S. Supreme Court, in *Boutilier v. Immigration and Naturalization Service* (1967), upheld a law that labeled gay immigrants "psychopathic personalities" and left them subject to exclusion and deportation, simply reaching the Supreme Court at all and winning three of nine votes did constitute a victory of sorts.

Because of its association with *Drum,* Polak, and Polak's various sex and pornography businesses, Janus activists in Philadelphia and elsewhere were subject to an escalating campaign of surveillance, harassment, and investigation by local, state, and federal law enforcement officials in the late 1960s. After Polak was arrested on federal obscenity charges in 1969, he accepted a 1972 plea bargain that involved closing down his sex businesses. Meanwhile, when Polak relocated to Southern California in 1969–1970, he resisted efforts by some of his former allies to continue Janus's work. Ceasing operations just weeks before the Stonewall Riots of 1969, the Janus Society was soon forgotten and ignored by the post-Stonewall LGBT movement, contributing to the historical amnesia that associates LGBT militancy, radicalism, and sexual liberationism only with post-Stonewall LGBT politics.

Bibliography

Stein, Marc. "'Birthplace of the Nation': Imagining Lesbian and Gay Communities in Philadelphia, 1969–1970." In *Creating a Place for Ourselves: Lesbian, Gay, and Bisexual Community Histories.* Edited by Brett Beemyn. New York: Routledge, 1997.

———. *City of Sisterly and Brotherly Loves: Lesbian and Gay Philadelphia, 1945–1972.* Chicago: University of Chicago Press, 2000.

———. "Sex Politics in the City of Sisterly and Brotherly Loves." *Radical History Review* 59 (1994): 60–92.

Marc Stein

See also *DRUM*; HOMOPHILE MOVEMENT; HOMOPHILE MOVEMENT DEMONSTRATIONS; MATTACHINE SOCIETY; POLAK, CLARK.

JEWETT, Sarah Orne (b. 3 September 1849; d. 24 June 1909), writer.

Theodora Sarah Orne Jewett was born and raised in South Berwick, Maine, the second of three daughters in a close-knit, wealthy New England family. She particularly adored her father, Theodore Herman Jewett, a respected physician who encouraged her wide-ranging intellectual curiosity and love of books, and often invited her to accompany him on his rural rounds. Her relationship with her mother, Caroline Perry, is less well documented but was certainly shaped by Perry's chronic illness; from her, Jewett likely first learned to attend to the feminine intricacies of Victorian social engagement. Jewett herself was unwell for much of her childhood; she suffered from rheumatoid arthritis throughout her life. Pain, in combination with a general disinterest in formal education (she often chided herself for "laziness"), resulted in frequent absences from school and pushed her outside into the fields and woods of Maine. She was, in this and other respects, a tomboy, but never at the expense of her social duties. This combination of individual freedom and female ritual animates the best of her writing; her stories and sketches are populated by intelligent women who are both hardy and independent and, whatever their station, genteel.

Jewett published her first story, "Jenny Garrow's Lovers," in 1868, but her first major work was *Deephaven* (1877), compiled from a series of sketches originally published in *The Atlantic Monthly*. The story concerns two young Boston women, Kate Lancaster and Helen Denis, who spend an unchaperoned summer together exploring a Maine seacoast village. As with most of Jewett's writing, she drew from life to paint the village and its environs, and also the romantic friendship that existed between the work's two protagonists. Throughout her young adulthood, Jewett developed a succession of passionate romantic friendships with other young women; it is widely considered that Kate Birckhead, with whom Jewett was especially close while she was writing the early *Deephaven* sketches, was a significant model for the fictional Kate.

Jewett never seriously considered marriage. On top of her family wealth, she achieved literary success early

Sarah Orne Jewett. The prolific late-nineteenth-century American writer often featured self-reliant women as the protagonists of her fiction. **[Bettmann/corbis]**

enough to be fairly comfortable, and she adeptly managed her own finances. More broadly, Jewett considered it important that women should have a choice whether or not to marry and was a vocal advocate for women's education and entry into the professions. Her novel *A Country Doctor* (1884), considered her most autobiographical, was also the most strongly feminist in this regard; protagonist Nan Prince, following on the heels of her adoptive father, becomes a rural physician but is clearly forced, in the process, to choose career over marriage. Although almost none of Jewett's other major works address these issues so overtly (one exception is the often-anthologized story "A White Heron" [1886]), her writing throughout her life, while conservative on many counts, is filled with independent women protagonists who thrive in female-dominated circles of influence. Her best-known work, *The Country of the Pointed Firs* (1896), contains particularly strong depictions of the vitality and variety of women's relationships in rural Maine society. Indeed, Jewett advised her young friend Willa Cather in 1908 that Cather should avoid writing from a man's point of view altogether.

Jewett was not, as some ill-informed critics claim, a lonely spinster; she was involved, from 1882 until her death, in a "Boston marriage" (some call it *the* Boston marriage) with philanthropist Annie Fields, widow of *Atlantic* publisher James Fields. Although the relationship is not generally understood to have been sexual, there is no doubt that it was committed and intense and sustained both of them emotionally, physically, and spiritually. They wrote passionate letters to one another (Jewett was, unsurprisingly, the more effusive correspondent); they lived and traveled together; they shared literary, political, and personal decisions. As a result, they developed a supportive and strongly egalitarian relationship, each woman complementing the other's talents. In addition, in the famed Victorian library of 108 Charles Street, they were at the center of a formidable international literary and intellectual circle. Many of their close friends also lived in Boston marriages; Fields and Jewett were part of a group of influential women educators, social reformers, authors, artists, and philanthropists, some of whom shared Jewett's particular desire to live a useful life in the company of other women.

Jewett published prolifically despite the fact that she found writing difficult in the midst of her many other activities (she also had to divide her time between Boston and the Jewett home in Maine, where she still held responsibilities), and despite often being in considerable pain. Her other major works include *Country By-Ways* (1881), *A Marsh Island* (1885), *Strangers and Wayfarers* (1890), *The Queen's Twin and Other Stories* (1898), and *The Tory Lover* (1900).

Bibliography

Blanchard, Paula. *Sarah Orne Jewett: Her World and Her Work.* Reading, Mass.: Addison-Wesley. 1994.

Donovan, Josephine. *Sarah Orne Jewett.* New York: Ungar, 1980.

———. "The Unpublished Love Poems of Sarah Orne Jewett." In *Critical Essays on Sarah Orne Jewett.* Edited by Gwen L. Nagel. Boston: Hall, 1984.

Roman, Margaret. *Sarah Orne Jewett: Reconstructing Gender.* Tuscaloosa: University of Alabama Press, 1992.

Catriona Sandilands

See also CATHER, WILLA; LITERATURE; ROMANTIC FRIENDSHIP AND BOSTON MARRIAGE; SMASHES AND CHUMMING.

JEWS AND JUDAISM

Many religious traditions approach homosexuality as a sin, and the legal and mythic texts of ancient Judaism include significant examples of laws and stories that view same-sex erotic attraction and behavior in a negative way. Yet contemporary Jewish culture has responded quite positively to the demands of LGBT people for inclusion and reexamination of ancient textual traditions. The contemporary Jewish community has made it possible for LGBT people to find a place within Jewish life.

Biblical Traditions (1000–165 BCE)

The Hebrew Bible (often referred to by Christians as "The Old Testament") includes a direct reference to some form of male homosexual behavior in the book of Leviticus, 18:22 and 20:13. In these passages, the same interdiction in two variant versions warns that a man must not perform *mishkavei ishah*, translated as "the lying down of a woman," with another man. This act is *to'evah*, an "abomination," and subject to the penalty of death. Traditional Jewish scholarship has understood this to be a prohibition on all male homosexual behavior. But others interpret the text to prohibit only anal intercourse and to sanction only the active partner. Many LGBT biblical scholars suggest that this law must be understood in the context of its time (roughly one thousand years before the common era), when many behaviors commonly accepted today were prohibited by law. They also point out that this is not a prohibition against same-sex love or desire, only against a particular behavior.

The Hebrew Bible also includes other texts that have been understood as "antigay." Homosexuality has been identified by Christian biblical interpreters to be the sin for which the people of Sodom and Gomorrah were punished, but Jewish exegetical tradition generally considers the crime in that story to be inhospitable behavior toward strangers. Often the story of the Garden of Eden, where "God made Adam and Eve, not Adam and Steve," is also used as a text to suggest that heterosexuality is the intended norm of the creator God. The book of Deuteronomy (22:5) includes a prohibition against men or women dressing in the clothes of the other sex. This has been understood as a prohibition against transgender behavior.

But LGBT scholars have pointed out that there are examples of same-sex love in the Hebrew Bible, exemplified in the relationships between David and Jonathan and Ruth and Naomi. The absence of any prohibition against same-sex love between women is also taken in a positive light, although we cannot make any assumptions about what the biblical authors intended, either in the stories of David and Ruth or in the absence of a prohibition against lesbianism.

The Traditions of Ancient Judaism (165 BCE–1700 CE)

The Talmud, the primary text of Jewish law and interpretation (compiled in 500 C.E.), has little to say about homosexual behavior. Lesbianism is defined as a minor transgression. The Talmud raises the issue in reference to whether or not women who commit lesbian acts are nonetheless considered virgins and thus theoretically eligible for marriage with priests (*cohanim*) and their descendants, and the answer is given in the affirmative. Male homosexual behavior is assumed to be rare, and two bachelors are considered so unlikely to be tempted by one another that a minority opinion in the Talmud permits them to sleep together under one blanket if circumstances require, although in general this is prohibited under biblical law. Medieval commentators follow rabbinic law, with little additional commentary. The medieval scholar and legislator Maimonides does recommend that a husband punish his wife if he discovers her to be consorting with women known to engage in homosexual behavior. There are examples of same-sex male erotic poetry by Jewish writers in the Middle Ages, but we do not know the extent to which these poets were merely copying popular Arabic styles or whether the poems indicate the prevalence of male homoeroticism in the era.

Modernity (1700–1969 CE) and After

The modern period saw the rise of the homosexual liberation movement. One of its earliest leaders in Germany, Magnus Hirschfeld (1868–1935), was a Jew. There are also scattered references to lesbian behavior in Yiddish literature from Eastern Europe. A frequent theme in the Yiddish literary tradition depicts cross-dressing women who are thought to have the souls of men in their female bodies, as immortalized in Isaac Bashevis Singer's story "Yentl, the Yeshiva Boy," written in 1962.

The gay and lesbian liberation movement. It was not until Jews involved in the contemporary gay and lesbian liberation movement in the United States began to raise questions about Jewish attitudes that the Jewish community took notice of this issue. At first the reaction was one of disbelief: there simply couldn't be gay and lesbian Jews! But as gay men and lesbians began to come out of the closet they started to ask questions. Some chose to renounce their connections to their Jewish roots, assuming that a religious tradition that included prohibitions of same-sex love was not going to be amenable to change. Orthodox scholars like Norman Lamm published articles reaffirming Judaism's position that homosexuality was an "abomination," although they stopped short of invoking the penalty of death. "Love the sinner, hate the sin" was the basic stance that was taken. Conservative Judaism ignored the issue, except for a few leaders like Herschel Matt who supported the idea that homosexuality was not a choice and that the Jewish community ought to support and welcome gay men and lesbians in their midst.

The women's movement. Many Jewish women who came out as lesbians became actively involved in the secular lesbian-feminist movement. While that community met many of their needs, they found themselves troubled by the anti-Semitism of many in that movement and began to explore their connections to Judaism. Evelyn Torton Beck edited an anthology, *Nice Jewish Girls* (1982), that included essays by more than twenty lesbian feminists, including Irena Klepfisz, Melanie Kaye-Kantrowitz, and Adrienne Rich. Beck was promptly excommunicated (placed in *herem*) by a group of Orthodox rabbis. Secular Jewish lesbians took the lessons they learned about anti-Semitism in the women's movement and translated those lessons into work on social justice issues, asking hard questions about issues such as racism in the United States and working on Israeli-Palestinian dialogue.

The LGBT synagogue movement. Other gay men and lesbians were also not satisfied with walking away from their heritage. In 1972 gay Jews in Los Angeles and New York City formed the first gay and lesbian (only later LGBT) synagogues, Beth Chayim Chadashim, the House of New Life, and Congregation Beth Simhat Torah (the House of Rejoicing over the Torah), respectively. Modeled after the Metropolitan Community Church, the synagogues served a predominantly gay Jewish population. The synagogue that formed shortly thereafter in San Francisco, Sha'ar Zahav (Golden Gate), was led by the first openly gay rabbi in history, Alan Bennett, from 1979 to 1985. Other groups formed in Philadelphia and Washington, D.C. In 2003 there were more than sixty-five LGBT synagogues and groups worldwide, not only in most major cities in the United States but also in Mexico, the United Kingdom, Australia, the Netherlands, South Africa, Canada, Austria, France, Germany, Hungary, Argentina, and Israel. The groups formed a network, the World Congress of Gay and Lesbian Jews, in 1975. Now called the World Congress of Gay, Lesbian, Bisexual, and Transgender Jews, the organization also added the Hebrew subtitle Keshet Ga'avah (Rainbow of Pride) to its name to indicate its connection to Hebrew language and the land of Israel. LGBT synagogues offer all the services of traditional synagogues, often including a Hebrew school for the children of congregants. They welcome members who do not define themselves as LGBT, and that membership has grown over the years. Many of the groups are served by LGBT rabbis, but some are not. The LGBT groups differ from other synagogues only in that they feel an obligation to serve the religious needs of all LGBT Jews from the most to the least traditional and so religious services tend to include traditional as well as nontraditional elements.

Reform and Reconstructionist Judaism. In the 1970s the Reform movement was quick to respond positively to the requests of the gay and lesbian synagogues for affiliation with the movement. Most LGBT synagogues in the United States today belong to the Union of American Hebrew Congregations, the Reform synagogue movement, although a few are affiliated with Reconstructionism and some remain independent.

But synagogue affiliation of LGBT groups was not the major issue confronting Reform and Reconstructionist Judaism. These liberal movements had to deal with the harder questions that gay and lesbian Jews began to pose. Gay men and lesbians wanted to serve in leadership positions as educators, cantors, and rabbis. Some wanted to join Reform and Reconstructionist synagogues as families. And they wanted Reform and Reconstructionist rabbis to agree to perform same-sex marriages and commitment ceremonies and create Hebrew schools where their families would feel welcome.

Lesbian and gay rabbis. There were (and still are) rabbis in every Jewish denomination who are not public about their sexual identities. In the early 1980s, some of those rabbis began to come out. Alan Bennett and Yoel Kahn, graduates of Hebrew Union College (HUC), served as rabbis for the gay congregation in San Francisco. Stacy Offner, another HUC graduate, lost her job in a congregation in the Midwest when she announced that she was a lesbian. Linda Holtzman, a graduate of the Reconstructionist Rabbinical College (RRC), gave up her position in a Conservative congregation and then came out publicly. The presence of these pioneers in the rabbinate made the schools where they were trained reconsider their admissions policies.

In 1979, an openly gay man requested admission to RRC and, after much debate among the faculty and the students, the request was denied. But in 1984 the faculty reversed its decision and began a policy of admitting openly gay and lesbian students for the Reconstructionist rabbinate. In 1989 the HUC also began to admit gay and lesbian students, although some faculty members refused to sign their ordination certificates.

At the beginning of the twenty-first century, more than fifty lesbians and about twenty-five gay men are serving in the rabbinate. These numbers include a few Conservative rabbis, although these individuals do not serve in congregational positions. One Orthodox rabbi, Steve Greenberg, has come out, although he readily admits that he is accepted by only a small number of Orthodox Jews.

Same-sex marriage. The Reconstructionist movement gave official approval for rabbis to perform commitment ceremonies for same-sex couples in 1993, and the Reform movement followed in 2000. Reform, Reconstructionist, and Conservative rabbis have been performing those ceremonies without official approval for many years. All three movements have come out in support of the legalization of same-sex marriage. For the Jewish religious community, supporting couples, especially if those couples intend to raise children, is an important Jewish value, superseding qualms about same-sex relationships. The support of same-sex marriage should therefore not be surprising.

Orthodox and Conservative Judaism. Although no official changes have taken place, the Conservative movement is under great pressure from some of its congregations and rabbis to change policies about ordaining gay and lesbian Jews, and the issue comes up with some frequency to the Law Committee of the Conservative movement and the Jewish Theological Seminary where Conservative rabbis are trained. Orthodox Judaism remains intransigent, although a 2001 documentary film directed by Sandi Dubowski, *Trembling Before G-d*, tells the stories of gay and lesbian Orthodox Jews who have suffered mistreatment in the Orthodox community, and the film has received some attention from Orthodox leaders.

Accepting bisexual and transgender Jews. Despite enormous changes regarding gay men and lesbians, the Jewish community has been slow to recognize the claims and interests of bisexual and transgender Jews. While the liberal Jewish community has been eager to accept gay and lesbian Jews who want to live within traditional family patterns, there has yet to be a serious discussion of bisexuality or the issues raised by those questioning assumptions about the fixed nature of gender. Writings by bisexual and transgender Jews have begun to appear in Jewish LGBT anthologies since 2002, and the Jewish community will face new challenges as bisexual and transgender Jews speak out more forcefully.

Bibliography

Alpert, Rebecca. *Like Bread on the Seder Plate: Jewish Lesbians and the Transformation of Tradition.* New York: Columbia University Press, 1997.

Alpert, Rebecca, Sue Levi Elwell, and Shirley Idelson, eds. *Lesbian Rabbis: The First Generation.* New Brunswick, N.J.: Rutgers University Press, 2001.

Balka, Christie, and Andy Rose, eds. *Twice Blessed: On Being Lesbian or Gay and Jewish.* Boston: Beacon Press, 1989.

Beck, Evelyn Torton, ed. *Nice Jewish Girls: A Lesbian Anthology.* Watertown, Mass.: Persephone Press, 1982.

Lamm, Norman. "Judaism and the Modern Attitude to Homosexuality." In *Encyclopedia Judaica Yearbook.* Jerusalem: Encyclopedia Judaica, 1974.

Matt, Herschel. "Sin, Crime, Sickness, or Alternative Life-Style? A Jewish Approach to Homosexuality." *Judaism* 27 (1978): 13–24.

Olyan, Saul, and Martha Nussbaum, eds. *Sexual Orientation and Human Rights in American Religious Discourse.* New York: Oxford University Press, 1998.

Shneer, David, and Caryn Aviv, eds. *Queer Jews.* New York: Routledge, 2002.

Shokeid, Moshe. *A Gay Synagogue in New York.* New York: Columbia University Press, 1995.

Rebecca T. Alpert

See also ANTI-SEMITISM; CHURCHES, TEMPLES, AND RELIGIOUS GROUPS; CORY, DONALD WEBSTER; MARRIAGE CEREMONIES AND WEDDINGS; MIGRATION, IMMIGRATION, AND DIASPORA.

JOFFREY, Robert (b. 24 December 1930; d. 25 March 1988), dancer, choreographer.

Born Abdullah Jaffa Bey Khan in Seattle, Washington, the only child of an Afghan restaurateur father and an Italian mother, Joffrey began dancing at the age of nine to combat his asthma and bowed-in feet. He took quickly to dance, and started exploring choreography almost immediately. When he was sixteen he met Gerald Arpino, his lifelong partner who was six years his senior, and the couple poured themselves into dance study. He moved to New York in 1948, where he studied briefly at the School of American Ballet and with Alexandra Fedorova, and by 1949 he was performing solo roles in Roland Petit's Ballets de Paris. He also studied modern dance and performed briefly in May O'Donnell's company. He became an accomplished teacher of ballet in New York City and founded his own school in 1953. The next year he formed his first small company, the Robert Joffrey Ballet Concert, drawn from his students, and made a successful new work *Pas des Déesses* to a musical score by gay composer Lou Harrison. The dance was acquired by the London-based Ballet Rambert, and Joffrey's career blossomed. In 1956, he rechristened his company the Robert Joffrey Ballet and appointed Arpino as the company choreographer. Joffrey became the resident choreographer for the New York City Opera from 1957 to 1962.

Through a well-managed series of tours in unlikely venues, the Joffrey company introduced scores of Americans to the art of ballet. Traveling in station wagons to high-school gymnasiums and rotary clubs, the company built an audience through a series of one-night-stands uncommon for ballet. Buoyed by the patronage of wealthy socialite Rebekah Harkness, the company secured a United States State Department sponsored tour of Western Europe and Russia in 1962. Joffrey achieved his greatest choreographic success with the breakthrough work *Astarte* (1967), set to a score by the iconoclastic rock band Crome Syrcus. The mixed-media work featured a film projected on a billowing screen behind a male-female duet. A sensuous experiment that married ballet to rock music, the work attracted national attention to Joffrey's youthful vitality and creative outlook. *Astarte* put the company on the cover of *Time* magazine and confirmed the potential for an uninitiated broad American audience for ballet.

Joffrey choreographed fifteen ballets in his lifetime, but gained more fame as a company director and teacher. He encouraged his young male dancers toward an explosive dynamism on stage that attracted audiences swayed by their brash virtuosity. His company became known internationally for its broad repertory and youthful attack in performances. The company staged reconstructions of important ballets long gone from any active repertory, including several landmark works from gay impresario Serge Diaghilev's Ballets Russes: Léonide Massine's *Le Tricorne* (1919), staged in 1969, and *Parade* (1917), mounted by Joffrey in 1973, both with sets and costumes by Picasso. He also reconstructed bisexual choreographer Vaslav Nijinsky's *L'Après-midi d'un faune* (1912), staged in 1979 with gay ballet star Rudolf Nureyev in the role of the Faun, and *Le Sacre du printemps* (1913), staged in 1987. Joffrey's interest in the past, present, and future of ballet led him to remount Kurt Joos's classic antiwar ballet *The Green Table* (1932) in 1967, offer new productions of work by Sir Frederick Ashton, Agnes de Mille, and Jerome Robbins, and commission new ballets from choreographers then unfamiliar with the idiom, including Alvin Ailey, Laura Dean, William Forsythe, James Kudelka, and Twyla Tharp.

Joffrey's company attracted large LGBT audiences interested in the company's blatant convergence of youth and sensuality. Although Joffrey and Arpino each remained firmly closeted to the press, many LGBT audiences understood them to be lifelong domestic partners, even as they each conducted affairs outside of their relationship. In 1973 Joffrey began a long relationship with gay activist A. Aladar Marberger, and in the 1980s both men contracted HIV. Joffrey died of AIDS in New York City. He received many awards throughout his career, including the Dancemagazine Award, the Capezio Award, and the Handel Medallion of the City of New York. His legacy to the dance world was to harness an unflappable youthful bravado to the idiom of ballet and in the process encourage audiences to imagine an American style of classical dance performance.

Bibliography

Anawalt, Sasha. *The Joffrey Ballet: Robert Joffrey and the Making of an American Dance Company.* New York: Scribner, 1996.

Dunning, Jennifer. "Robert Joffrey, 57, Founder of the Ballet Troupe, is Dead." *New York Times,* 26 March 1988.

Thomas F. DeFrantz

See also DANCE.

JOHNS, Jasper (b. 15 May 1930), artist.

The enigmatic work of Jasper Johns, perhaps America's most respected living artist, invites many interpretations. No line of analysis, however, has proven more controversial than that linking his fascination with masking and codes to his homosexuality. Johns's career offers a case study in debates over the relationship between homosexuality and art, including the potential of minority sexual identity to create community and prompt creative insight, as well as the power of homophobia to limit the recognition and development of these accomplishments.

Born and raised in South Carolina, Johns moved to New York City, planning to study art and poetry. After two years in the Army, he returned to New York and joined the avant-garde circle around the composer John Cage and Cage's lover, the choreographer Merce Cunningham. In 1953, Johns met an artist in this group, Robert Rauschenberg, with whom he would be intimately—though secretly—partnered until 1961. Five years older than Johns, Rauschenberg had already gained art-world attention for work that challenged Abstract Expressionism's emphasis on expressive mark making. Quickly extrapolating from Rauschenberg's ideas, Johns in the "Flag" and "Target" series mounted a powerful critique of Abstract Expressionism's claims to have developed an American form of individualistic self-expression. Flags and targets are clearly learned symbols, not personally imagined abstract marks. Their connotations—the American-ness of the American flag, the emotions of aggression and vulnerability associated with the target—reveal the formulaic quality of the values Abstract Expressionism claimed as original inventions.

Johns's flag and target paintings rocketed him to fame. Throughout his career, however, Johns lashed out at critics who read their own personal meanings into his work. At the same time, his art returned repeatedly to codes and hidden meanings. One controversial analysis of this dynamic is that Johns's influential art expresses that the price of fame for gay men of his generation is to accept the condition of keeping their sexuality secret.

Jasper Johns. The American artist's enigmatic work since the 1950s, which had its origins in a challenge to the dominance of Abstract Expressionism, is subject to various and sometimes controversial interpretations. **[Christopher Felver/corbis]**

Kenneth Silver's and Jonathan Katz's studies of Johns's early work relate both his subject matter and his techniques to his sexual identity. Johns's targets, especially as they were often combined with plaster casts of body parts in little closet-like boxes, are described by Silver as a "portrait of a homosexual man of the postwar period . . . The besieged gay body—and gay psyche—is fragmented and sorted into compartments, each one capable of being alternately closeted or exposed."

Johns's paintings invoking the gay poets Frank O'Hara and Hart Crane allude even more clearly to the intertwined history of art and homosexuality. Johns's *In Memory of My Feelings—Frank O'Hara,* which includes its full title stenciled across the bottom of the image, was painted in 1961, immediately after his break-up with Rauschenberg. O'Hara was among the most openly gay men in the New York art world, a poet, art critic, and curator who championed Johns's career. Johns's title quotes the title of an O'Hara poem, and this painting also includes the words "DEAD MAN" almost obscured by paint. Jill Johnston's analysis concludes, "It was O'Hara's *human nature* that Johns wanted, the fearless homosexual poet . . . open to Walt Whitman and Hart Crane before him." Johnston's analysis extends to Johns's later work, which juxtaposes collaged newspaper articles about the AIDS crisis with quotations from his earlier works (quotations that, given the nature of his work, themselves quote other kinds of imagery, most prominently a sixteenth-century altarpiece for the victims and caregivers of an earlier plague).

Interpretations of Johns's work in relation to homosexuality rely, however, less on subject matter than on how this imagery is presented. Silver describes Johns's early use of a thick wax encaustic embedded with shreds of newspaper as a way to "mummify" Abstract Expressionist "marks of vitality, so that we sense ourselves distanced from both the work as a record of activity and from the artist whose activity is recorded." The complex layering of Johns's later works has, likewise, been seen as a strategy of masking or veiling, not to obscure the secret of homosexuality, but to perform the habits of dissembling and coding adopted by homosexuals in the public eye. Jonathan Weinberg, while skirting the issue of Johns's homosexuality, has analyzed the dynamics of anal and autoeroticism in his work.

Johns' resistance to such interpretations—notably his refusal to allow reproductions of his art to be printed in Johnston's book—does not undermine their validity. On the contrary, as Johnston's accounts of her conversations with the artist show, his verbal strategies of silence, distraction, and intimidation echo the visual effects of his work, consciously or unconsciously confirming her portrait of a man for whom sexual identity is experienced as secret and expressed as code.

Bibliography

Harrison, Charles and Fred Orton. "Jasper Johns: 'Meaning What you See.'" *Art History* 7, no. 1 (March 1984): 76–99.

Johnston, Jill. *Jasper Johns: Privileged Information.* New York: Thames and Hudson, 1996.

Katz, Jonathan. "The Art of Code: Jasper Johns and Robert Rauschenberg." In *Significant Others: Creativity and Intimate Partnership.* Whitney Chadwick and Isabelle de Courtivron, eds. London: Thames and Hudson, 1993.

Katz, Jonathan. "Dismembership: Jasper Johns and the Body Politic." In *Performing the Body/Performing the Text.* Amelia Jones and Andrew Stephenson, eds. London: Routledge, 1999.

Silver, Kenneth E. "Modes of Disclosure: The Construction of Gay Identity and the Rise of Pop Art." In *Hand-Painted Pop.* Russell Ferguson, ed. Los Angeles: Museum of Contemporary Art, 1992.

Weinberg, Jonathan. "It's in the Can: Jasper Johns and the Anal Society." *Genders* 1 (Spring 1988): 40–57.

Christopher Reed

See also ART HISTORY; CAGE, JOHN; CRANE, HART; CUNNINGHAM, MERCE; RAUSCHENBERG; ROBERT; VISUAL ART.

JOHNSTON, Jill **(b. 17 May 1929), essayist and art critic**

Jill Johnston, the daughter of Cyril Frederick Johnston and Olive Margaret Crowe Johnston, began life in London, England. Raised to believe that her father was an English aristocrat who had died in her early childhood, Johnston discovered during college that he actually had been a bell maker who died much later and that her parents had never married. In *Mother Bound,* the first volume of Johnston's two-volume *Autobiography in Search of a Father,* she explores the psychological turmoil of growing up under the cloud of a massive deception and without a father. Hospitalized twice for schizophrenia, Johnston has attributed some of her troubles with mental illness to the difficulties of such a childhood.

Johnston's early history showed no signs of the radicalism that she would later espouse. She attended an exclusive girl's boarding school and then graduated from Tufts University in Medford, Massachusetts, with a B.S. in 1951. In 1958 she married Richard Lanham. The couple had two children, a son and a daughter, but divorced in 1964. With Johnston's approval, Lanham retained custody of their children. After she came out as a lesbian, Johnston's ability to parent her offspring was further complicated. Angered by Johnston's openness about her sexuality, Lanham tried to block her from contact with the children. Ambivalent about motherhood, the lesbian feminist Johnston would later call for a family form based on communities of women.

Before her marriage to Lanham, Johnston worked first as a dancer and then, in 1957, became an art and dance critic, a career that eventually provided her with enormous public visibility. Two years later, in 1959, Johnston joined the then-underground New York newspaper, the *Village Voice,* as its "Dance Journal" columnist. The newspaper, much more radical than its later incarnation, reported on the New York City avant-garde. Johnston would write for the *Voice* until 1978, covering dance, painting, sculpture, multimedia, and other "happenings." She also served as a critic and columnist for the New York City–based publications *Art News* (1959–1965) and *Art in America* (1983–1987).

In 1965 Johnston began incorporating personal anecdotes into her criticism. The use of the autobiographical form enabled her to connect the personal to the political and artistic. This highly subjective approach, which represented a radical departure from existing norms and from standard conceptions about the role and function of art criticism, shocked the art establishment.

By the early 1970s Johnston had adopted a neo-Dadaist style of writing that would become her trademark. She broke the rules of syntax and used free association to create an open-ended form of expression that allowed a reader to freely enter or exit her world. Like Gertrude Stein, the lesbian writer whom she regarded as her intellectual and stylistic forerunner, Johnston deliberately violated literary conventions. Her essays would often run on for pages without capitalization or paragraphs, and in their attempts to interpret, describe, and analyze in such a format, they came to symbolize the tumultuous social changes of their time.

Whereas Stein remained quiet about her sexuality, Johnston very publicly tied the innovations of her writing style to her identity as a lesbian. Johnston came out personally around 1969. She came out publicly in the 4 March 1971 *Village Voice* essay "Lois Lane Is a Lesbian," a piece that is reprinted in her 1973 collection, *Lesbian Nation.* The book, the title of which soon became part of the lexicon, includes a diverse assortment of essays: a lesbian wedding ceremony is discussed in "The Wedding," new family structures in "Lesbian Mothers Ltd.," and the undoing of male artistic privilege in "Zelda, Zelda, Zelda."

Lesbian Nation also asserted the centrality of lesbianism to the feminist revolution. Famously arguing that all women are lesbians and that a feminist revolution is not possible without a lesbian one, Johnston participated in the ferocious struggles within the women's liberation movement of the early 1970s. She advised women to retreat from men and build a lesbian nation at the grassroots level.

Johnston became more moderate with age. She dropped the antifamily, antimonogamy leitmotif of her earlier work and distanced herself from her earlier radicalism. In 1980 she began living with Ingrid Nyeboe, a Danish citizen. Taking advantage of a 1989 act passed by the Danish Parliament that granted lesbians and gay men the right to marry, Johnston and Nyeboe married in Odense, Denmark, on 26 June 1993. Johnston now lives in Massachusetts as part of a family that includes her son, daughter, and grandchildren.

Bibliography

Gilmore, Leigh. *Autobiographics: A Feminist Theory of Women's Self-Representation.* Ithaca, N.Y.: Cornell University Press, 1994.

Johnston, Jill. *Marmalade Me.* New York: Dutton, 1971.

———. *Admission Accomplished: The Lesbian Nation Years (1970–75).* London: Serpents Tail, 1998.

Caryn E. Neumann

See also FAMILY ISSUES; LESBIAN FEMINISM.

JONES, Bill T. (b. 15 February 1952) dancer, choreographer and ZANE, Arnie (b. 1948; d. 1988), dancer, choreographer, photographer, media artist.

Bill T. Jones (William Tass Jones), like other choreographers of his generation, is concerned with reevaluating and refiguring the dancing body as a site of personal and cultural agency and political expression rather than (only) a source of visual pleasure. Jones is known for his charisma and skill as a solo performer and improviser, for the evening-length works he creates for his Bill T. Jones/Arnie Zane Dance Company, and for his articulate discourse about life and artistic process. Although his choreography varies in size and approach, Jones's work is marked by personal revelation or frank confrontation—delivered in movement and spoken text—as part of a broader exploration of human difference and dignity. Arnie Zane, who died in 1988, shared his partner's postmodern sensibilities and brought skills and insights, developed through his work in photography and media studies, and a vital physicality to their dancing and choreography.

Jones was born in Bunnell, Florida, and raised in upstate New York, part of a large family of Baptist-Methodist migrant farm workers. Zane, whose family included Italian Catholics and Lithuanian Jews, was born in the Bronx, New York. They met at the State University of New York at Binghamton in 1971. Their first collaborations mixed Jones's athleticism and love of spoken text with Zane's interest in photography and media studies. Their movement was grounded in contact improvisation, a technique that emphasizes ongoing touch and weight sharing between two or multiple bodies. Their use of contact was muscular and physically daring, more purposeful than sexual. Part of the appeal of their work was in their physical differences: one tall, muscular, fluid, and black, the other, short, wiry, intense, and white. Jones's interests in contact improvisation and postmodernism, both largely practiced by white artists, initially set him apart from choreographers such as Alvin Ailey, who made more accessible dances related to African American experience. The trilogy *Monkey Run Road, Blauvelt Mountain,* and *Valley Cottage* (1979–1980) brought Jones and Zane international recognition.

Bill T. Jones. A performance of the dancer-choreographer's *Still/Here* (1993) at the annual Edinburgh International Festival. [© Johan Elbers 1997]

The partners created Bill T. Jones/Arnie Zane Dance Company (then Bill T. Jones/Arnie Zane & Company) in 1982. In the next few years, their choreography broadened and became more overtly political. Jones created *Swamp Fever* (1983) for six male members of the Alvin Ailey American Dance Theater. Their *Secret Pastures* (1984) featured Jones as the Fabricated Man, the brainchild of Zane's Mad Scientist, a comment about an African American artist's role in the primarily Euro-American postmodern performance world. After Zane's early death, Jones continued the company as a tribute to his partner.

Jones's concern with human agency and identity as centered in the body is evident in the large group works he created for his company in the 1990s and in his independent collaborations with other artists. In his *Last Supper at Uncle Tom's Cabin/The Promised Land* (1990), Jones explores identity and faith. Inspired by personal and family history, Jones develops these themes through references to Harriet Beecher Stowe's *Uncle Tom's Cabin*, Martin Luther King's "I Have a Dream" speech, and the biblical story of Job. Jones has men play women, women play men, blacks play whites, and whites play blacks. The difference between performer and role is overt to suggest that people may lead other than prescribed lives. In the final section, *The Promised Land*, a large cast of company members and performers newly recruited at each performance site dance naked, giving them a common vulnerability. *Still/Here* (1993), based on a series of workshops Jones did with gravely ill people, is an exploration of devastating illness and healing. Jones combines exquisite dancing performed by his varied, athletic company members with sound collages and digital imagery, especially images of workshop participants and medical slides. Jones does not appear as a dancer, but presents himself on videotape as a workshop participant. *Ghostcatching* (1999) is a collaboration between Jones and media artists Paul Kaiser and Shelley Eshkar. Jones's movement was recorded using motion capture technology, and then used to inform the movement of digital line drawings dancing in an eight-and-one-half minute digital video. The virtual dancers are like Jones—the viewer sees Jones in their movement—but a Jones stripped of his usual identity markers, especially skin color. The piece works as a commentary about the preciousness of the body and its corporeal immediacy. The video is also used in Jones's 1999 solo *The Breathing Show* (1999).

Jones and Zane received several important awards during their partnership. Jones received a MacArthur Fellowship in 1994.

Bibliography

Foster, Susan. "Simply (?) the Doing of It, Like Two Arms Going Round and Round." In *Continuous Replay: The Photographs of Arnie Zane*. Edited by Jonathan Green. Cambridge, Mass., and Riverside, Calif.: MIT Press and UCR/California Museum of Photography, 1999.

Jones, Bill T., with Peggy Gillespie. *Last Night on Earth*. New York: Pantheon Books, 1995.

Zimmer, Elizabeth, and Susan Quasha. *Body Against Body: The Dance and Other Collaborations of Bill T. Jones and Arnie Zane*. Barrytown, N.Y.: Station Hill Press 1989.

Ann Dils

See also DANCE.

JONES, Prophet (b. 24 November 1907; d. 12 August 1971), preacher, religious leader.

Born in Birmingham, Alabama, James F. Jones, popularly known as Prophet Jones, achieved national prominence as a flamboyant religious leader in Detroit during the 1940s and 1950s. He became one of the few African Americans featured regularly in the mainstream, white-controlled mass media of his era, only to have his acclaim tarnished at the height of his fame with a morals arrest for propositioning an undercover policeman.

Jones arrived in Detroit in 1938 and soon began preaching and prophesying on a weekly radio program. Through his broadcast pulpit, he attracted predominantly African American working-class followers to rousing all-night services, first at a wood frame church in the city's slums and in subsequent years at a converted movie house complete with a $5,300 throne.

Jones's devoted following bestowed him with such lavish gifts as a fleet of expensive automobiles, a wardrobe of fine suits, and a fifty-four-room mansion. He displayed his finery on shopping sprees at downtown department stores, accompanied by an entourage of handsome valets and assistants. His appeal echoed that of Little Richard and other gender-bending performers on the black drag circuit of the 1940s and 1950s, when the so-called freakish man occupied an accepted queer social role in Jones's native South.

Jones achieved local notoriety through a mixture of opulence, faith healing, and predictions, which sometimes bordered on the fantastical. Each November on his birthday, Jones treated members of the press to a lavish banquet at which he announced prophesies for the coming year, prophesies published with fanfare in the next day's newspapers. He predicted that anyone alive in the year 2000 would live forever and also claimed to have foreseen the dropping of the first atomic bomb in a puff of smoke from a piece of fried chicken.

In November 1944 Jones's sashaying extravagance drew national attention when *Life* magazine featured him in a multipage photo spread showcasing his luxurious home, quoting prices for various fixtures, and suggestively showing his young assistant James Walton reading to him at bedside. In 1953, after Jones had supposedly healed their mother with a folk cure of sips from a water fountain at the Gary, Indiana, bus station, two schoolteachers presented the prophet with a full-length white mink coat worth over $12,000. The gift garnered another appearance in *Life.* In the decade after World War II, Jones received similar exposure in *Time, Newsweek,* and the *Saturday Evening Post,* which dubbed him the "Messiah in Mink."

Jones's rise to fame came in the midst of Cold War attacks on visible homosexuality and as African Americans pushed to end legal segregation in Dixie and de facto segregation in the North. Middle-class black critics, skeptical of Jones's clairvoyance, attributed his popularity to superstition. Writing in *Ebony* in 1951, Adam Clayton Powell Jr. insinuated that Jones and Walton had been lovers and that their relationship was an open secret.

While rumors of homosexuality complicated his celebrity, white reporters followed Jones when he attended Dwight Eisenhower's first presidential inauguration in 1953 and tagged along on an evangelical trip he made to New York City in 1954. A year later, Jones purchased a time slot for a short-lived series on WXYZ-TV, becoming the first African American preacher with a regular show on Detroit area television.

On 20 February 1956, Detroit police arrested Jones at his home for an alleged indecent act with a black rookie vice officer who had been planted among the prophet's followers. Jones immediately lost his radio program, forcing him to sell his vehicles and spacious home within weeks to pay his debts. The morals arrest sparked a frenzy in the three Detroit dailies, the two local African American weeklies, and the national gossip press. The scandal magazine *Whisper* unabashedly asked whether Jones was "seer or queer?"

As African Americans in postwar Detroit battled racial inequality in housing and employment, middle-class blacks—striving for improved material conditions and social status—heralded the downfall of Jones. Meanwhile, his working-class supporters rallied behind him, filling the courtroom for the six-day trial in July 1956 and cheering when an all-white jury found him not guilty.

Despite his acquittal, the specter of homosexuality remained with Jones for the rest of his life. The *Detroit News,* the *Detroit Free Press,* and the *Advocate* all noted the arrest in their obituaries when Jones died. Although diminished in stature and wealth, Jones remained a noteworthy figure in Detroit, continuing his bold flamboyance in the decade before the rise of the gay liberation movement. When he died in 1971, 2,700 mourners attended his funeral, where his white mink coat lay draped over his coffin.

Bibliography

Brean, Herbert. "Prophet Jones: Detroit Evangelist Preaches Good Faith and Gleans Its Happy Rewards." *Life,* 27 November 1944, 57–63.

Kobler, John. "Prophet Jones: Messiah in Mink." *Saturday Evening Post,* 5 March 1955, 20–21, 74–77.

MacIntire, Dal. "Flamboyant Prophet Jones Goes to His Reward at 63." *The Advocate,* 15–28 September 1971, 11.

Retzloff, Tim. " 'Seer or Queer?': Postwar Fascination with Detroit's Prophet Jones." *GLQ* 8 (2002): 271–296.

Tim Retzloff

See also AFRICAN AMERICAN RELIGION AND SPIRITUALITY.

JORGENSEN, Christine (b. 30 May 1926; d. 3 May 1989), celebrity, entertainer, memoirist.

The first internationally known transsexual personality of the twentieth century, Christine (*née* George) Jorgensen was not only a pioneer in the field of sex reassignment surgery, but she provided an unprecedented example for the thousands of gender dysphoric individuals who followed in her footsteps.

George Jorgensen was born 30 May 1926 to working-class parents of Danish descent in the Throggs Neck section of the Bronx in New York City. In an interview with *Time* magazine reporters in February 1953, Jorgensen described her early years of confusion and solitude as the "no man's land of sex." After graduating from high school, Jorgensen entered the army in August 1945 and served as a clerk at Fort Dix, New Jersey, for fourteen months. With money earned from the G. I. Bill, Jorgensen studied at photography school in New Haven, Connecticut, with the intent of becoming a professional photographer.

In 1948, Jorgensen read *The Male Hormone*, the best-selling book by science journalist Paul de Kruif, and wondered if his own gender confusion might be the result of a deficit of testosterone, or a surfeit of estrogen, in his body. Jorgensen had heard about endocrinologists who could chemically correct hormonal imbalances. Following the advice of his physician and supportive friends, Jorgensen sailed to Copenhagen, Denmark, in 1950 to undergo experimental estrogen therapy and six operations. George rechristened himself with the name "Christine" in tribute to Dr. Christian Hamburger, the Danish physician who supervised Jorgensen's treatments.

In late November 1952, while recovering from surgery, the story of Jorgensen's transformation was leaked to the New York *Daily News*, which ran the headline "Ex-GI Becomes Blonde Beauty." Because there were no widely known precedents for Jorgensen's transformation, she was understood alternately as an ex-soldier, a glamorous *femme fatale*, and an upwardly mobile success story. The medical community generally responded favorably to Jorgensen's story, but the media catapulted Jorgensen's celebrity status to epic proportions and made her "the most talked about girl in the world." In early 1953, the twenty-seven-year-old Jorgensen published an autobiographical sketch in Hearst's *American Weekly* for the reputed sum of thirty thousand dollars. The sketch was reprinted in newspapers around the world and translated into approximately eighty languages.

In April 1953, Jorgensen suffered a minor setback when the media announced that she was not a "real woman" but instead only a "castrated male." Apparently, surgeons did not have the capacity to surgically construct a vagina for Jorgensen until 1954. In the early 1950s, Jorgensen was held to the standard, propagated by many influential psychologists, that anyone who experienced confusion about their sexual identity and their gender role was a "sex pervert," a common phrase used to describe those who engaged in transvestism or abnormal sexual activities. Yet despite this negative publicity—or perhaps because of it Jorgensen continued to be a popular celebrity. In 1953, Jorgensen accepted an offer to perform in Las Vegas for a salary of twelve thousand dollars per week. Her early act consisted of talking about her transformation, changing in and out of designer gowns while standing behind a screen, and narrating a photographic slide show of her two years spent in Copenhagen. She told an interviewer in 1957:

Transsexual Pioneer. A portrait of George Jorgensen during the period of surgical transformation in the early 1950s in which he became Christine Jorgensen. **[Bettmann/corbis]**

> When I first started in the business I told a few jokes, very nice jokes, but I didn't get any response from the audience. And I remember one evening [Jimmy Durante] looked at me and he said, "You know, Christine, you could tell the funniest joke ever written on stage in the first fifteen minutes of your act and you won't get a laugh. *They're too busy looking at you.*" And this I understand and accept. (*Christine Jorgensen Reveals*)

Later managers commissioned professional comedians to write jokes for Jorgensen and even encouraged her to do burlesque parodies of *Madame Butterfly* and the Ballet Russe, but she had only marginal success with this material. Throughout the 1950s and 1960s, she toured the United States, South America, the Philippines, Cuba, and Western Europe.

Christine Jorgensen. The world-famous transsexual agrees to pose for a "cheesecake" photo at the Hotel Sahara in Las Vegas during a two-week engagement there in November 1953. **[Bettmann/corbis]**

Jorgensen regarded herself as a role model for individuals who we might now identify as transgender. She encouraged people to seek out medical professionals who might help them reconcile their physical bodies with their gender identities. In addition, Jorgensen challenged the widely held belief that homosexuality was a social problem and in the late 1950s declared that "it is society's way of thinking toward homosexuality which is the problem" (*Christine Jorgensen Reveals*). Jorgensen also made headlines when in March 1959 she and her then-fiancé, Howard Knox, applied for a marriage license in Manhattan. The New York City Board of Licenses refused to grant the couple their wish because Knox did not have the appropriate papers to prove he had been divorced from his first wife. While they waited for the papers to be delivered from Knox's hometown of Chicago, Jorgensen and Knox decided to call the wedding off, preferring instead to remain just good friends.

In 1967, the book *Christine Jorgensen: A Personal Autobiography* was published to great acclaim. The book foreshadowed the transsexual autobiography as a new literary genre. But in the late 1960s, the momentum of the women's and sexual liberation movements, as well as the widespread study of gender dysphoria in professional clinical contexts, made Jorgensen's femme version of a 1950s glamorous starlet seem reactionary to some. In her later years, Jorgensen showed a more liberated attitude that was in keeping with the spirit of the sexual revolution of the era. In a 1975 interview in *People*, for example, she announced that she was able to have orgasms, though "whether it's like that of a man or a woman I can't say." Yet Jorgensen spent most of her remaining years as a self-described "old maid" in her house in Laguna Beach, California, emerging occasionally for public appearances in such programs as *Good Morning America* and *The Tom Snyder Show*, and some cabaret performances in the Los Angeles area during the early 1980s. She died of bladder cancer on 3 May 1989, three weeks short of her sixty-third birthday.

Bibliography

Jorgensen, Christine. *Christine Jorgensen Reveals.* Audio recording. New York: J Records, 1957.

Jorgensen, Christine. *Christine Jorgensen: A Personal Autobiography.* New York: Paul S. Ericksson, 1967.

Meyerowitz, Joanne. *How Sex Changed: A History of Transsexuality in the United States.* Cambridge, Mass.: Harvard University Press, 2002.

Serlin, David Harley. "Christine Jorgensen and the Cold War Closet." *Radical History Review* 62 (Spring 1995): 136–165.

David Serlin

See also COMEDY AND HUMOR; ERICKSON EDUCATIONAL FOUNDATION; ICONS; TRANSSEXUALS, TRANSVESTITES, TRANSGENDER PEOPLE, AND CROSS-DRESSERS.

JOURNALISM. see MEDIA STUDIES AND JOURNALISM.

K

KAMENY, Franklin (b. 21 May 1925),

homophile, gay rights activist.

Frank Kameny was born in Queens, New York, to a middle-class Jewish family. A precocious child, Kameny took an early interest in science and by the age of seven had decided on a career in astronomy. Graduating from Richmond Hill High School at the age of sixteen, he studied physics at New York's Queens College. After a tour of duty during World War II as a U.S. Army mortar crewman, Kameny won a fellowship to Harvard University, where he earned a Ph.D. in astronomy in 1956.

After a year as a research and teaching assistant in Georgetown University's Astronomy department, Kameny transferred to the Army Map Service, where he managed astronomical observation projects to map accurate distances between the earth's land masses. But when a routine government security screening in 1957 revealed that he had been arrested on a morals charge in a known gay cruising area, he was dismissed from his civilian job. Unable to obtain a security clearance and thus unable to work as an astronomer, Kameny became dependent on charity. Unlike the thousands of other victims of the "lavender scare," Kameny decided to fight his dismissal. When administrative appeals failed and the U.S. Court of Appeals ruled against him, his attorney abandoned the case. In his own brief to the U.S. Supreme Court, Kameny compared the government's antigay policies with discrimination based on religious or racial grounds. Adopting the rhetoric of civil rights, he asserted that he and fifteen million other Americans were being treated as second-class citizens because of their homosexuality.

In 1961, when the Supreme Court refused to hear his case, Kameny enlisted others in the cause and founded the Mattachine Society of Washington (MSW). As the group's president (1961–1965), Kameny was one of the few homosexuals in America willing to appear publicly using his own name. Calling his group the "NAACP of the homosexual minority," Kameny introduced traditional tactics of political reform to the LGBT movement—distributing press releases, testifying before committees, lobbying government officials, and filing legal challenges. In MSW's 1963 dispute with the District of Columbia over a license to raise charitable donations, Kameny became the first openly gay person to testify publicly before a congressional committee. In the spring and summer of 1965 he organized a series of historic LGBT pickets in front of the White House and other government buildings in Washington, D.C. Through speaking engagements around the country and leadership roles in groups such as the East Coast Homophile Organizations (ECHO), Kameny spread his message of activism, radicalizing existing gay organizations and helping new groups form in other cities.

Acting as a paralegal, Kameny represented hundreds of gay and lesbian military personnel, civil servants, and contractors in disputes with the federal government. With the aid of the local American Civil Liberties Union (ACLU) chapter, which he helped found in 1961, Kameny encouraged a series of test discrimination cases in the courts to challenge the Civil Service Commission's exclusion of gays and lesbians, forcing a reversal of policy in 1975. Kameny was also involved in the first legal steps to

Franklin Kameny. The outspoken and energetic early gay rights activist, who founded the Mattachine Society of Washington in 1961 and organized numerous legal and lobbying efforts, leads a procession of the Gertrude Stein Democratic Club in Washington, D.C. **[Joan E. Biren]**

challenge the U.S. military's policy of discharging gay and lesbian service members, including the case of gay Air Force Sergeant Leonard Matlovich. And by the late 1970s he succeeded in forcing the federal government to begin granting gays and lesbians security clearances.

In addition, Kameny led a sustained lobbying effort aimed at undoing the official position of the American Psychiatric Association (APA) that homosexuality was a mental illness. As a scientist, he appeared in public debates with professional psychiatrists, asserting that their understanding of homosexuality was based on a skewed sampling of psychiatric patients. In 1965 he led the MSW to declare that homosexuality was not a sickness but an orientation equivalent to heterosexuality. After watching Stokley Carmichael on television in 1968 chanting "black is beautiful" to enthusiastic crowds of African Americans, Kameny coined the slogan "gay is good," hoping that it would help his community overcome years of internalized homophobia. At the 1971 APA convention in Washington, D.C., Kameny joined members of the Gay Liberation Front (GLF) in storming the convention and taking over the proceedings. Under pressure from LGBT activists and psychiatrists, the APA voted in 1973 to remove homosexuality from its *Diagnostic and Statistical Manual of Psychiatric Disorders* (DSM).

In 1971, when the U.S. Congress permitted the District of Columbia to elect a nonvoting delegate to the House of Representatives, Kameny ventured into local politics and became the first openly gay person to run for Congress. Coming in fourth in the six-way race, he succeeded in garnering publicity for his "personal freedoms" platform and in politicizing the local LGBT community. After the election, Kameny's campaign committee reorganized into a local Gay Activists Alliance (GAA), a nonpartisan political group dedicated to securing full rights and privileges of citizenship for the gay and lesbian community of the District of Columbia. Kameny and the GAA were instrumental in securing passage of the D.C. Human Rights Law in 1973, one of the nation's first laws to ban discrimination against gays and lesbians. In 1975 he was appointed to the District's Human Rights Commission, the first openly gay mayoral appointee in the nation's capital. After serving for seven years, he was appointed to the city's Board of Appeals and Review. For over three decades, Kameny had served as an active member of, and elder statesmen to, the Gay and Lesbian Activists Alliance, a powerful advocate for the gay and lesbian community with local officials, the media, the police, and the school system.

In recognition of his long-time activism, Kameny was asked to serve on the board of the National Gay Task Force (NGTF) in 1973. As a NGTF board member, he was among a group of LGBT leaders who met with officials of the Carter administration in 1977—the first such White

House meeting in U.S. history. At the local level, Kameny was an outspoken defender of civil liberties on all matters sexual, leading fights against D.C.'s antisodomy law and defending the rights of bars featuring nude dancers. For over forty years, he has remained a formidable voice in the movements for LGBT rights and sexual freedom.

Bibliography

Bayer, Ronald. *Homosexuality and American Psychiatry: The Politics of Diagnosis.* New York: Basic Books, 1981.

Clendinen, Dudley, and Adam Nagourney. *Out for Good. The Struggle to Build a Gay Rights Movement in America.* New York: Simon & Schuster, 1999.

D'Emilio, John. *Sexual Politics, Sexual Communities: The Making of a Homosexual Minority in the United States, 1940–1970.* Chicago: University of Chicago Press, 1983.

Johnson, David K. *The Lavender Scare: The Cold War Persecution of Gays and Lesbians in the Federal Government.* Chicago: University of Chicago Press, 2003.

Marcus, Eric. *Making History: The Struggle for Gay and Lesbian Equal Rights 1945–1990: An Oral History.* New York: HarperCollins, 1992.

Murdoch, Joyce, and Deb Price. *Courting Justice: Gay Men and Lesbians v. The Supreme Court.* New York: Basic Books, 2001.

Tobin, Kay, and Randy Wicker. *The Gay Crusaders.* New York: Paperback Library, 1972.

David K. Johnson

See also AMERICAN CIVIL LIBERTIES UNION (ACLU); ANTI-DISCRIMINATION LAW AND POLICY; CORY, DONALD WEBSTER; ELECTORAL POLITICS; EMPLOYMENT LAW AND POLICY; FEDERAL LAW AND POLICY; GAY ACTIVISTS ALLIANCE; HOMOPHILE MOVEMENT; MATTACHINE SOCIETY; MEDICINE, MEDICALIZATION, AND THE MEDICAL MODEL; MILITARY LAW AND POLICY; NATIONAL GAY AND LESBIAN TASK FORCE (NGLTF); PSYCHOLOGY, PSYCHIATRY, PSYCHOANALYSIS, AND SEXOLOGY.

KENNY, Maurice (b. 16 August 1929), writer.

Maurice Kenny was born in Watertown, New York, his father Mohawk and his mother part-Seneca. When he was thirteen, his parents separated, and he moved with his mother to New Jersey. Unhappy at school, his truancy led a juvenile judge to recommend that he be placed in reform school. His father intervened and brought him back to upstate New York, where he completed high school.

Kenny began writing poetry as a teenager. He was especially influenced by Walt Whitman, whose natural language and rhythm were qualities he later found in Native American oral literature. He enrolled in Butler University in 1952 and received a B.A. in English literature. In 1956, he entered St. Lawrence University in Canton, New York, and with the encouragement of novelist Douglas Angus wrote the poems published in his first chapbook, *The Hopeless Kill* (1956). At his father's urging, he enrolled at New York University in 1958, where he studied with poet Louise Bogan. His first full length collection, *Dead Letters Sent and Other Poems,* appeared that year. A hiatus followed, during which he traveled in the United States, Mexico, and the Caribbean, and also began drinking heavily. Eventually, friends brought him back to New York, and soon thereafter he moved to Chicago, where he wrote obituaries for the *Chicago Sun-Times,* and, in his free time, began writing poetry again. After a year, he returned to New York in 1967, and a Brooklyn Heights apartment became his home for the next two decades.

Kenny's career coincided with a period of political and cultural upheaval for Native Americans. In 1969 Native American activists occupied Alcatraz Island, garnering international attention. Two years later, the American Indian Movement was formed, and a series of confrontations with federal authorities ensued, culminating in the violent face-off at Wounded Knee, North Dakota, in early 1973. Less visible, but more lasting, was a growing trend among Indians to reject assimilation and embrace their traditional cultures. The 1970s renaissance in Native American literature was in large part the result of native writers and poets seeking to chronicle these events and articulate authentic Native American identities. Poets especially were able to draw on the native oral heritage to produce a creative synthesis of tradition and modernity in their work.

Kenny credits his late 1960s poem, "First Rule," with leading him back to this heritage. This exploration came to fruition in the long poem, "I Am the Sun" (1973), written in response to the Wounded Knee events. Consciousness of his native heritage is also evident in *North: Poems of Home* (1977), his first full-length collection in nineteen years, and *Dancing Back Strong the Nation* (1979). Kenny's style has been described as oracular and incantatory, leading some to refer to his poems as chants. Kenny, however, reserves the term "chant" for writings of a ritual nature.

In 1976, Kenny asserted his gay identity with the publication in *Gay Sunshine* of the poem, "Winkte," and an essay, "Tinselled Bucks: An Historical Study in Indian Homosexuality." In his essay, Kenny claimed the *berdache,* or two-spirit, tradition as an exemplar for contemporary Indians. He was among the first nationally recognized American Indians to come out publicly.

With *Blackrobe: Isaac Jogues* (1982) Kenny ventured into the genre of historical poetry, telling the story of a Jesuit missionary martyred by the Mohawks in 1646. It was nominated for a Pulitzer Prize and received the National Public Radio Award for Broadcasting (1984). The death of his mother led him to write about his childhood and family in *The Mama Poems* (1984), which received the American Book Award of the Before Columbus Foundation. In *Rain and Other Fictions* (1985; reprinted 1990) he made yet another departure, publishing short stories and a one-act play. Kenny returned to historical poetry with *Tekonwatonti/Molly Brant* (1992), which recreates the voice of a prominent Mohawk woman who married an Englishman. In this and other historical works, he portrays individuals who are multiply located. Like himself, they cross (and sometimes transgress) boundaries between cultures and ways of being, whether as Indians in a white world, missionaries among Indians, Indian women married to white men, or gay men in a heterosexual world. This interest in historically grounded storytelling distinguishes his work from the mythico-poetic style of feminist Native authors such as Paula Gunn Allen.

The search for historical Native American voices eventually led Kenny to re-evaluate the legacy of Walt Whitman. In "Whitman's Indifference to Indians" (1992), he criticized the poet's silence on U.S. Indian policies and argued that Whitman's failure to include Native Americans among his subjects was a tragic loss. Kenny himself promoted diverse authors throughout his career, establishing Strawberry Press in 1976 to publish Native Americans' work, editing collections of Native American writings, and encouraging writers of color as editor of the journal *Contact/II.*

In 1986, he moved to Saranac Lake in upstate New York. He continued to travel frequently to lecture and teach. He has been poet-in-residence at North Country Community College and the State University of New York at Potsdam. In 1995, he received an honorary doctorate from St. Lawrence University. Kenny has published over thirty collections of poetry, fiction, and essays, and his works have appeared in nearly a hundred journals, magazines, and anthologies in several languages. Joseph Bruchac has ranked him among "the four or five significant Native American poets."

Bibliography

Bruchac, Joseph. *Survival This Way: Interviews with American Indian Poets.* Tucson: Sun Tracks/University of Arizona Press, 1987.

Swann, Brian, and Arnold Krupat, ed. *I Tell You Now: Autobiographical Essays by Native American Writers.* Lincoln: University of Nebraska Press, 1987, 1989.

Will Roscoe

KEPNER, James (b. 1923; d. 15 November 1997), writer, activist.

Los Angeles resident Jim Kepner was a major writer, activist, and intellectual in the gay rights movement for over four decades. Kepner's voice dominated the homophile press of the 1950s, shaping gay political identity in the McCarthy era. By the 1990s, Kepner had contributed over two thousand essays, articles, poems, and fictional stories to the gay press, which he wrote under several pseudonyms.

Born in January 1923, Kepner was discovered under an oleander bush in Galveston, Texas. Nine months later he was adopted by a strict, religious couple in an unhappy marriage. After graduating from high school near the top of his class, Kepner contemplated entering the clergy or the military but, as he became aware of his desire for other men, embraced atheism and pacifism instead. Looking for signs of gay life, Kepner worked odd jobs—as a factory worker, taxi driver, bookstore operator, soda jerk, and sand shoveler—for the next several years in New York, Miami, Los Angeles, and San Francisco. While living in San Francisco in 1943, as Kepner prepared to enter a gay bar (The Black Cat) for the first time, a brutal police raid ensued, leaving him speechless and horrified across the street. The raid politicized Kepner, and he devoted the rest of his life to understanding and combating social injustice against gay and lesbian people.

Kepner was a prolific, skillful, and impulsive writer, but a literary focus eluded him for years. During the 1940s, Kepner wrote movie reviews for the Communist Party's *Daily Worker* and dabbled in science fiction. Kepner's experience with the Communist Party was mixed—it helped him conceive of gay people as an oppressed minority in the abstract, but the party expelled Kepner when his homosexuality was discovered. A similar scandal exiled Kepner from a network of science fiction discussion groups in San Francisco. Upon settling down in Los Angeles in 1951, Kepner gravitated to the homophile movement, attending his first Mattachine Foundation meeting in 1952. Although overjoyed to find a community of gay activists, Kepner found Mattachine's purge of former Communist Party members disturbing. Kepner's energy, personality, and writing talents found a warmer reception at the newly created *ONE* magazine, which, unlike Mattachine, required no loyalty oath denouncing past Communist Party affiliation.

ONE soon dominated Kepner's life, and Kepner's calm, analytical, yet outraged voice dominated the magazine for over a decade, as he wrote under pseudonyms such as Lyn Pedersen and Dal McIntire. His debut article, "The Importance of Being Different," appeared in March

1954 under the pseudonym Damon Pythias. Kepner's monthly roundup of gay news around the country, called "Tangents," was *ONE*'s most popular feature during the 1950s. In addition to his work on the magazine, Kepner taught several classes at the ONE Institute, including one on homophile history and a popular seminar on Walt Whitman. Kepner also edited the ONE Institute's quarterly journal *Homophile Studies*. Kepner's historical writing, derived from years of tireless archival accumulation, established a framework for gay history adopted by most subsequent gay and lesbian historians, consciously or unconsciously. Although never accepted in the academic mainstream during his lifetime, Kepner deserves the distinction of being regarded as both the first U.S. gay historian and the first U.S. gay archivist.

During the 1960s, Kepner withdrew from ONE, Inc., as he was frustrated by its limitations, yet he was excited by the explosion of new gay publications. Aside from publishing several of his own newsletters, Kepner contributed regularly to the *Advocate* and numerous gay publications during the 1960s, 1970s, and 1980s. A seasoned activist by the late 1960s, Kepner helped found several prominent gay liberation groups in Los Angeles, including PRIDE and the Los Angeles chapter of the Gay Liberation Front. He also helped organize local contingents for mass marches on Washington, D.C. The soft-spoken Kepner claimed that his biggest frustration as an activist was watching groups be taken over by publicity-driven egomaniacs, resulting in his frequent resignations from groups he had helped start.

In 1972, Kepner opened the first official gay archive, the National Gay Archives (later renamed the International Lesbian and Gay Archives) in his Torrance, California, apartment and moved the collection to Hollywood shortly thereafter. Maintaining the collection and assisting scholars consumed his later years. Upon ONE colleague Dorr Legg's death in 1994, Kepner integrated his archive with the vast materials the ONE Institute accumulated over the years. When Kepner died at the age of seventy-three, his life's work was a core collection at the world's largest gay archive, the ONE Institute and Archive.

Bibliography

Bullough, Vern. *Before Stonewall: Activists for Gay and Lesbian Rights in Historical Context.* New York: Harrington Park Press, 2002.

Kepner, Jim. *Rough News—Daring Views: 1950s Pioneer Gay Press Journalism.* New York: Haworth Press, 1998.

Marcus, Eric. *Making History: The Struggle for Gay and Lesbian Equal Rights 1945–1990: An Oral History.* New York: Harper Perennial, 1992.

Craig Loftin

See also *ADVOCATE*; GAY LIBERATION FRONT; HISTORY PROJECTS, LIBRARIES, AND ARCHIVES; HOMOPHILE MOVEMENT; *MATTACHINE REVIEW*; *ONE*; ONE INSTITUTE.

KIM, Willyce **(b. 18 February 1946), writer.**

Willyce Kim, recognized as the first Asian lesbian to have her work published in the United States, is best known as a poet and writer who helped forge the emerging West Coast lesbian feminist movement and culture in the 1970s. Her participation in and contribution to the lesbian feminist movement counter the image of this movement as solely white and middle-class. Kim published three books of poetry, *Curtains of Light* (1970), *Eating Artichokes* (1972), and *Under the Rolling Sky* (1976), that depicted love and friendship between women, were frank in their description of sex and passion between women, and provided examples of a women-centered world.

Kim, who was born in Honolulu, Hawaii, to second-generation Korean American parents, was raised in a Catholic home with two younger siblings, a brother and a sister. From the age of seven to thirteen, Kim lived with her family in San Francisco's Richmond district, where her father attended the University of San Francisco and then Hastings Law School. The family eventually moved back to Hawaii so that her father could practice law in Honolulu.

She left Hawaii in 1964 to attend San Francisco College for Women, where she graduated with a BA in English in 1968. She attended college during the height of the hippie, flower power, and anti–Vietnam War era and lived about eight blocks from the Haight-Ashbury section of the city, which was then the epicenter for the counterculture lifestyle. Kim describes this period as an amazing time during which she became intoxicated with the possibilities of change and believed that people's ideas about, perceptions of, and treatment of women would also change.

After college, Kim held several jobs but soon abandoned conventional employment to begin work primarily on women's issues. In the early 1970s she moved from San Francisco to Oakland and became part of the Women's Press Collective, founded by Judy Grahn and Wendy Cadden. At the Woman's Place bookstore, Kim befriended Grahn and Cadden, who took an interest in her self-published book of poems and invited Kim to work with the collective.

Through this collective, Kim learned much about the publication, printing, and distribution of books by and about women, particularly lesbians. One aspect of her work included trips across the country to distribute books at alternative and women's bookstores. Kim also participated in numerous readings with Grahn and Pat Parker in various states, including California, Washington, and Oregon, and in spaces such as colleges, bookstores, and lesbian bars. In a later interview with Kim (conducted by Alice Y. Hom), Kim recalled one event at which she had read her work standing atop a pool table, which was covered with a board to serve as a makeshift stage. Asked if she had observed other Asian American lesbians at these same events, Kim remembers seeing none in the spaces that she frequented in the early 1970s.

This notable absence of Asian American lesbians in public settings changed in the late 1970s when groups such as Unbound Feet, a collective of Asian American women writers that included lesbians Merle Woo, Canyon Sam, and Kitty Tsui, emerged. For quite a few Asian American lesbian authors who published in the early 1980s (including Woo and Tsui), Kim's visibility as a writer who was lesbian and Asian American made her an invaluable and affirming role model, precisely because there were few Asian Americans publishing or visible to others in the lesbian feminist movement of the 1970s.

Although the content and themes of Kim's work do not directly address the intersection of race and sexuality, or draw on the unique experiences of Asian American lesbians, her work is important because it clearly reflects the time period and historical context during which it was written. In the 1970s lesbian feminists created a woman-centered world, and Kim was very much a part of establishing lesbian culture and building its institutions. She has described her writing as open-ended in that a lesbian audience may interpret her work however it wishes to describe or define itself.

In the 1980s Kim began working at the University of California, Berkeley, where she remained through 2003 as the manager of the main stacks at Doe Library. During that decade she published two well-received novels, *Dancer Dawkins and the California Kid* (1985) and *Dead Heat* (1988). She continued to write, and in the early 2000s, she returned to short stories and poetry, with her work appearing in the *Harrington Lesbian Fiction Quarterly*. Just as she did in most of her earlier works, Kim remained steadfast to the goal of presenting lesbian characters with complexity and in all their contradictions.

Bibliography

Tsui, Kitty. "Willyce Kim." In *Contemporary Lesbian Writers of the United States: A Bio-Bibliographical Critical Sourcebook.* Edited by Sandra Pollack and Denise D. Knight. Westport, Conn.: Greenwood Press, 1993, 283–286.

Alice Y. Hom

See also ASIAN AMERICAN LGBTQ ORGANIZATIONS AND PERIODICALS; GRAHN, JUDY; PARKER, PAT.

KING, Billie Jean (b. 22 November 1943),

tennis champion, women's rights activist, feminist, promoter of women's professional and amateur sports at all levels.

Billie Jean Moffitt was born in Long Beach, California. Her mother, Betty Jerman Moffitt, was a housewife and her father, Willis B. Moffitt, a fireman. She was the older of two children (her brother Randy Moffitt pitched for the San Francisco Giants). As a youth Billie Jean played softball, baseball, and football, and earned the tag of tomboy. She was not comfortable with this label since it implied masculinity and suspicious sexuality. At her parents' urging she tried the "girl's sport" of tennis at age eleven and took to it unequivocally; that first year she handily defeated a college junior in straight sets.

In 1959 King's impressive loss to Wimbledon champion Maria Bueno at the eastern grass court championships convinced coach Frank Brennan to lure her to his Saddle River, New Jersey, tennis school. In 1961 King teamed with Karen Hantze to win the women's doubles at Wimbledon, the youngest team ever to do so. That was the first of twenty-one Wimbledon titles King won between 1961 and 1979.

King was ranked first in women's tennis in the late 1960s and early 1970s. She earned $100,000, unprecedented for a female tennis player, but bemoaned the far greater prize monies available to male professionals. She co-organized the Virginia Slims tournament in opposition to the regular tour to raise salaries and administrative control. Her own game was unparalled: she won singles titles at Wimbledon in 1966–1968, 1972, 1973, and 1975; at the U.S. Open in 1967, 1971, 1972, and 1974; at the French Open in 1972; and at the Australian Open in 1968.

In 1965 King married Larry King, a college boyfriend. In 1973 King accepted the challenge posed by Bobby Riggs, age fifty-five and a former Wimbledon champion, to compete at the Houston Astrodome in the much ballyhooed "Battle of the Sexes." He had already defeated one female tennis star and King fully understood the symbolic meaning of their match amid mid-1970s gender equity political struggles. He appeared wearing a pig snout (as in male chauvinist pig) and she, playing to the media, was carried in on a platform by four beefcake men dressed as slaves. She beat him soundly and became the spokesperson for parity issues of pay, opportunity, and respect in women's sports.

On 5 May 1981, King was outed as a lesbian by her former hairdresser/secretary and former lover, Marilyn Barnett, with whom she had been involved since 1972. Using love letters and her life as a part of a romantic couple with King on the tour as proof of their bond, Barnett argued in a now-infamous palimony suit that she was entitled to economic compensation as a spouse. Larry King learned of their affair in 1978 when Billie Jean confided her problems with Marilyn to him. He stayed loyal to her while, by Billie Jean's recounting, Barnett's monetary and personal demands grew increasingly unreasonable; Barnett refused to move out of King's Malibu home or return the love letters from years earlier. When Billie Jean called a press conference on 8 May 1981 she cried before the press and admitted to her lesbian affair, calling it a regrettable mistake. With Larry at her side, she laid claim to heterosexuality and portrayed Barnett as unstable. This posture disappointed and infuriated many gay and lesbian activists as well as feminists who had come to respect her as a leader and an outspoken advocate of social change. King was openly ridiculed for her unwillingness to assume a defiantly lesbian-and-proud posture. Her concerns lay with the damage that would be done to the blossoming women's tennis tour and the shadows of doubt about "hetero-normalcy" that would further surround women athletes. She preferred then to claim temporary bisexuality and swear her marital loyalty to Larry. She was also fully aware of how rapidly her own endorsements would disappear (and they did). She was a subject of ridicule and tawdriness in numerous tabloid newspapers, all which used her lesbian affair to discredit women's tennis and women's sports in general. She bore this strain and harassment with grace and fortitude. She retired from professional tennis in 1984.

Scorned in large part by the lesbian and gay communities for her unwillingness to be openly gay, she reversed that posture in 1994 when during a Gay [Olympics] Games fundraising event she acknowledged tennis champion Martina Navratilova—openly lesbian for years—for Navratilova's acceptance of her own sexuality. King divorced her husband in 1981 and in 1998 embraced the lesbian (versus bisexual) label at age fifty-five. Her public yet closeted struggle with her lesbian identity was by King's own evaluation the most difficult issue in her life.

King's legacy to the LGB community is immense: she founded the proactive Women's Sports Foundation, openly advocates for increased opportunities for girls and women in sports (pre– and post–Title IX legislation), and serves as an understated example of the personal pressure, economic loss, and personal coming-to-terms that embracing a public lesbian identity necessitates. Her honors continue to mount: she was a 1987 inductee into the International Tennis Hall of Fame and a 1990 inductee into the National Women's Hall of Fame. In 1998 she founded the Billie Jean King Foundation, which provides grant monies to women, gays, lesbians, and multicultural groups and works to raise monies and consciousness about AIDS. She also coached the 1996 and 2000 Olympic women's tennis teams.

Billie Jean King. Though perhaps best known for her 1973 "Battle of the Sexes" with Bobby Riggs, King dominated women's tennis in the late 1960s and early 1970s, and later ended a long, difficult internal struggle by declaring herself a lesbian.

Bibliography

Johnson, Anne Janette. *Great Women in Sports.* New York: Visible Ink, 1996.

King, Billie Jean, and Kim Chapin. *Billie Jean King.* New York: Harper, 1974.

King, Billie Jean, and Frank DeFord. *Billie Jean King.* New York: Viking, 1982.

Taylor, Anne. "The Battles of Billie Jean King." *Women's Sports and Fitness* (September/October 1998): 131–34, 168–171.

Susan E. Cayleff

See also ICONS; SPORTS.

KINSEY, Alfred C. (b. 23 June 1894; d. 25 August 1956), biologist, sex researcher.

Alfred Kinsey ranks as one of the most influential sex researchers (sexologists) of the twentieth century. Born in Hoboken, New Jersey, Kinsey later married Clara Bracken McMillen; they had four children, one of whom died just before his fifth birthday. Kinsey was a graduate of Bowdoin College and the Bussey Institute at Harvard. He became an assistant professor of zoology at Indiana University in 1920, where for twenty years he specialized in research on the gall wasp.

Kinsey and his associates at the Institute for Sex Research at Indiana University (later named the Kinsey Institute for Research in Sex, Gender, and Reproduction) are best known for the two volumes popularly dubbed the Kinsey Reports. *Sexual Behavior in the Human Male* (1948) and *Sexual Behavior in the Human Female* (1953) gave the postwar nation a glimpse into American sexual lives while also underscoring the chasm between sexual norms and actual behavior. His pioneering research played a significant role in the transition from religious to scientific authority over matters of sexuality in the United States.

Despite its shortcomings, Kinsey's research represented a significant departure from earlier sex research, particularly that of the case study method of psychoanalysis. Both Kinsey reports were based upon extensive sex histories conducted with almost twelve thousand white women and men. His subjects were often members of particular institutions he visited, such as prisons, schools, or workplaces. The Kinsey team did not include the interviews they conducted with African Americans because the team believed its sample was not large enough. The average interview lasted from ninety minutes to two hours, covering hundreds of items. Although based on large numbers of adults, the Kinsey findings on sexuality could not accurately be generalized to the population at large because he used volunteers in his research rather than a representative random sample.

Kinsey viewed sexual behavior as the result of a complex interplay of biological, psychological, and social influences. Although he studied how social variables such as class, gender, and religion shaped an individual's "total sexual outlet," he generally viewed these as constraints on a "natural" sexuality rooted in "our mammalian heritage." His focus on the "natural" led Kinsey to criticize social institutions or customs that he saw as impeding sexual expression. For example, he harshly condemned sex laws, especially the sexual psychopath laws that frequently targeted gay men. His insistence that he was an objective scientist translated into a refusal to condemn minority sexual groups. This led postwar LGBT communities to perceive him as an ally.

Methodology and Conclusions

Kinsey's significant legacy in the study of LGB people is largely conceptual and political rather than empirical. He challenged the notion of fixed sexual identities that nineteenth- and early-twentieth-century sexologists had advanced, arguing that "The world is not to be divided into sheep and goats" (1948, p. 639). The well-known Kinsey Scale suggested that individuals might be located on a 0–6 continuum ranging from exclusively heterosexual to exclusively homosexual in both sexual involvement and interest. Although the scale was unsuccessful as a research tool, it helped destabilize the cultural acceptance of rigid sexual categories. Kinsey believed that everyone had the capacity for homosexuality, and so he spoke only of homosexual behavior, not about distinct identities or persons. As opposed to early sexologists such as Richard Krafft-Ebing and Havelock Ellis, who categorized types of behavior as "abnormal" or "perverted," Kinsey eschewed both the moralism of religion and the pathologizing gaze of psychiatry.

Kinsey reported that, regardless of their sexual identities, many men and women in his study had participated in homosexual behavior during their lives. The popular belief that one in ten adults is gay is commonly attributed to the Kinsey research. His actual findings, however, are more complicated than this simple claim. Although he found that 10 percent of males were "more or less exclusively homosexual" (that is, they would be located as a Kinsey Scale 5 or 6) for at least three years between the ages of sixteen and fifty-five, he also found that 4 percent of males were exclusively homosexual throughout their lives. The frequency of exclusive homosexual behavior was lower for women: 1–3 percent of unmarried women in his sample rated a 6 on the Kinsey Scale between the ages of twenty-five and thirty-five. Still, Kinsey's finding that 50 percent of men and 28 percent of women had some type of homosexual experience further stimulated postwar anxieties about sexuality and gender.

Controversy

A mark of Kinsey's enduring significance as an icon of the sexual revolution is the unremitting controversy about him and his research. Although both of his books became immediate bestsellers, the publication of *Sexual Behavior in the Human Female* during the height of McCarthyism triggered public outrage. Kinsey was denounced in the popular media as well as by the scientific community. The

Alfred Kinsey. His institute's Kinsey Reports, two major studies published after World War II, revolutionized scientific research into, knowledge of, and societal attitudes toward sexual behavior. **[Getty Images]**

Rockefeller Foundation terminated his funding in 1954, on the brink of congressional hearings. Decades after his death Kinsey remains the target of social and religious conservatives who see him as the leading architect of the liberal changes they despise in the sexual culture. They are particularly incensed by Kinsey's acceptance of homosexuality. Conservative activist Judith Reisman has waged the most vehement campaign to discredit Kinsey. Her two books, *Kinsey, Sex, and Fraud* (1990) and *Kinsey: Crimes and Consequences* (1998), lodge a series of personal attacks against Kinsey and his associates, alleging that they were closet homosexuals and pedophiles whose research was corrupted by their own sexual perversions. These attacks reinforced those brought by James H. Jones's controversial 1997 biography, *Alfred C. Kinsey: A Public/Private Life,* in which Jones suggests that Kinsey's critiques of sexual guilt and repression were driven by his own "bizarre behavior," including a range of sexual compulsions.

Perhaps the most provocative allegation against Kinsey is Reisman's charge that he and his associates advocated incest and child molestation. This claim is elaborated in the Family Research Council's 1994 video documentary, *The Children of Table 34,* which charges that Kinsey's research was based on cruel and illegal sexual experimentation on hundreds of children. Although the Kinsey Institute issued a public refutation of these charges, they served in 1995 as the basis for House Resolution 2749, introduced by one-term conservative U.S. representative Steve Stockman to investigate whether Kinsey's research involved any fraud or criminal wrongdoing. The bill died in committee. However, Kinsey's vulnerability to attacks on his personal sexual behavior vividly illustrates the persistent culture of sexual shame that he worked so hard to disrupt.

Bibliography

Gathorne-Hardy, Jonathan. *Sex the Measure of All Things: A Life of Alfred C. Kinsey.* Bloomington: Indiana University Press.

Irvine, Janice M. *Disorders of Desire: Sex and Gender in Modern American Sexology.* Philadelphia: Temple University Press, 1990.

Jones, James H. *Alfred C. Kinsey: A Public/Private Life.* New York: Norton, 1997.

Kinsey, Alfred C., Wardell B. Pomeroy, and Clyde E. Martin. *Sexual Behavior in the Human Male.* Philadelphia: W. B. Saunders, 1948.

Kinsey, Alfred C., Wardell B. Pomeroy, Clyde E. Martin, and Paul H. Gebhard. *Sexual Behavior in the Human Female.* Philadelphia: W. B. Saunders, 1953.

Janice M. Irvine

See also BISEXUALITY, BISEXUALS, AND BISEXUAL MOVEMENTS; FOSTER, JEANNETTE; LAWRENCE, LOUISE; PSYCHOLOGY, PSYCHIATRY, PSYCHOANALYSIS, AND SEXOLOGY; SADOMASOCHISM, SADISTS, AND MASOCHISTS; SEX ACTS.

KIRSTEIN, Lincoln **(b. 4 May 1907; d. 5 January 1996), writer, impresario, art patron.**

Lincoln Kirstein was a writer, patron, and important impresario of the visual and performing arts in the United States in the middle decades of the twentieth century. Family money allowed him to avoid a life of paid work and concentrate on promoting and organizing the creative work of others. He was closely associated with a number of artistic, literary, and intellectual figures of the 1930s and 1940s, especially the largely homosexual circle gathered around the Magic Realist artists. His most important legacy is undoubtedly the School of American Ballet and the New York City Ballet, whose continuing presence realizes Kirstein's desire for a permanent, internationally respected American national ballet. In 1941 he married Fidelma Cadmus (sister of Paul Cadmus), but had frequent and open affairs with men throughout his life.

Kirstein, a prolific author, wrote more than thirty books and hundreds of articles on a wide array of topics including poetry and fiction, modern art, film and photography, and the history and technique of dance. Of special relevance here are his books on the Magic Realist artists Paul Cadmus and Pavel Tchelitchev and the Russian dancer Vaslav Nijinksy—all homosexual or known to have had homosexual affairs. As a Harvard University undergraduate he cofounded the literary journal *Hound and Horn* for which he reviewed dance and theater. He also cofounded the Harvard Society for Contemporary Art, which organized well-received exhibitions of modern European and American art in Boston.

Kirstein was exposed to the famous Ballets Russes, with its avant-garde productions directed by Sergei Diaghilev, during an early trip to Europe, but became truly enamored of dance while living in Paris in the early 1930s. There he attended performances of Les Ballets 1933 directed by George Balanchine. When the company collapsed, Kirstein secured an invitation from the directors of Hartford, Connecticut's, Wadsworth Athenaeum for Balanchine and company to come to America and found a ballet school and company. Upon his arrival Balanchine concluded Hartford could never support a permanent company and Kirstein quickly secured funding from friends and family to establish the School of American Ballet in New York in 1934 with Balanchine as artistic director.

Lacking a permanent performance space and secure funding base, Kirstein organized dancers from the school into the American Ballet, which performed at the Metropolitan Opera. In summers it toured as the Ballet Caravan, presenting modern ballets on American themes. In 1936 Kirstein's friendship with Walker Evans led to his appointment as the head of the Works Progress Administration Federal Dance Theater Project. He served as a private in the army during World War II and afterward was attached to the government's division of Monuments, Fine Art, and Archives, working in Europe to recover art looted by the Nazis. In 1946 he and Balanchine organized the subscription-based Ballet Society, which reassembled many dancers from his prewar companies. Its 1948 breakthrough performance of *Orpheus* (commissioned by Kirstein from Igor Stravinsky with sets designed by sculptor Isamu Noguchi) at the New York City Center for Music and Drama led to the establishment of a permanent ballet company, the now-legendary New York City Ballet. In the mid-1950s Kirstein was instrumental in launching the annual American Shakespeare Festival in Stratford, Connecticut, which he hoped would be the beginning of a national theater.

Kirstein had a particular genius for interweaving his friend's creative talents through his numerous projects. Tchelitchev designed ballet sets, while George Platt Lynes was the semiofficial photographer of Kirstein's ballet school and companies. Paul Cadmus designed sets for the American Ballet Caravan work *Filling Station* and provided drawings for Kirstein's book *Ballet Alphabet.* A number of Cadmus's paintings from the 1940s are set in the School of American Ballet and feature its premier dancers. Kirstein's friendship with Nelson Rockefeller and Gaston Lachaise led to the inclusion of the sculptor's work at Rockefeller Center, and Rockefeller underwrote Ballet Caravan's 1941 tour of Latin America. Kirstein later toured the southern continent, purchasing art for the Museum of Modern Art of which Rockefeller was a trustee. Kirstein was also instrumental in securing Museum of Modern Art exhibitions of Elie Nadelman's sculptures and Walker Evans's photographs. He was a frequent subject in the work of his friends and commissioning his portrait was a favorite form of patronage.

In recognition of his contributions to the arts, Kirstein was awarded the U.S. Presidential Medal of Freedom in 1984 and the National Medal of Arts in 1985.

Bibliography

Jenkins, Nicholas. "Reflections: The Great Impresario." *The New Yorker* 74, no. 8 (13 April 1998): 48–61.

Leddick, David. *Intimate Companions: A Triography of George Platt Lynes, Paul Cadmus, Lincoln Kirstein, and Their Circle.* New York: St. Martin's Press, 2000.

Kirstein, Lincoln. *Mosaic: Memoirs.* New York: Farrar, Straus & Giroux, 1994.

Simmonds, Harvey. *Lincoln Kirstein, the Published Writings, 1922–1977: A First Bibliography.* New Haven: Yale University Library, 1978.

Weber, Nicholas Fox. *Patron Saints: Five Rebels Who Opened America to a New Art, 1928–1943.* New York: Knopf, 1992.

Michael J. Murphy

See also DANCE; FORD, CHARLES HENRI.

KLAH, Hastíín **(b. December 1867; d. 2 March, 1937), medicine man, weaver, ethnographic consultant.**

Klah (Lefthanded) is more accurately transcribed as *tl'ah;* Navajos refer to him as Hastíín Klah using the Navajo term of respect equivalent to "mister" or "sir." Klah was born near Fort Wingate, New Mexico, shortly after the Navajos had been released from three years of confinement by the U.S. army. He belonged to a large and influential family; his great-grandfather was the prominent chief Narbona.

Klah's status as a *nádleehí* (lit., one who is constantly changing, used for both male and female *berdaches*, that is, "two-spirit" men and women) was acknowledged by his family sometime in his early teens. Although Navajo tradition portrays *nádleehí* as hermaphrodites, most probably were not. Klah's male anatomy was vouched for by Father Berard Haile, a self-trained anthropologist who observed him undressed during sweat lodge ceremonies. Cross-dressing was also a variable trait among *nádleehí*; Klah himself wore men's clothes. Described as "unmarried" by anthropologists and white friends, oral tradition remembers him as having sexual relations with both men and women.

Navajo mythology sanctioned the *nádleehí* role and an important deity was *nádleehí*. Consequently, *nádleehí* were believed to have special aptitude for religious pursuits, and many became medicine men (a male role). By engaging as well in such female pursuits as farming, sheepherding, pottery making, and basketry, they were often among the wealthier members of the tribe.

Klah's aptitude for memorizing the prayers, myths, and images used in religious ceremonies was apparent by the age of ten. With his family's support, he pursued extensive training as a medicine man. Not until 1917, at the age of forty-nine, did he consider his education complete. Whereas most medicine men mastered one or two ceremonies in a lifetime, Klah was qualified to perform eight; knowledge of several of these was lost with his death.

Klah also learned the women's art of weaving. During his lifetime, manufactured clothing replaced the traditional use of woven goods, but women continued weaving blankets for sale to a white market as rugs. In the 1920s and 1930s, as the aesthetic value of Navajo weaving came to be recognized, these items made the transition from the floor to the walls of museums and collectors' homes.

In 1914, Arthur and Franc Newcomb began operating a trading post near Klah's home in western New Mexico. Franc Newcomb, who dedicated one of her books to Klah and wrote his biography, became interested in the intricate designs of mythological scenes that he made from colored sand and other materials during ceremonies. With Klah's permission, she learned to memorize these and reproduce them on paper, eventually preserving hundreds of images. In 1919, at her suggestion, Klah produced a weaving with a sandpainting design. Such images were normally destroyed at the end of a ceremony, and to make them in permanent form was considered sacrilegious and dangerous. Klah, however, believed that his power as a medicine man could protect him, and he made over twenty of these large-scale tapestries, while his nieces made even more under his direction. Most were sold to museums and collectors. The attention they drew from collectors and the exceptional quality of Klah's work contributed to the transition of Navajo weaving from craft to fine art.

One of these collectors was the wealthy Bostonian, Mary Cabot Wheelwright. Her interest in Navajo religion led her to propose transcribing Klah's extensive repertoire of Navajo oral literature. This, too, was controversial from a Navajo point of view, but Klah was convinced of the value of preserving his knowledge. He collaborated as well with anthropologists Gladys Reichard and Harry Hoijer.

Klah traveled widely in the white world. In 1893, he demonstrated weaving at the World's Columbian Exposition in Chicago. At Wheelwright's behest he made trips to her homes in Maine, Santa Barbara, and northern New Mexico. In 1934, he returned to Chicago, where his demonstration of sandpainting at the Century of Progress Exhibition was observed by President Franklin D. Roosevelt. The arts proved to be one of the first areas in which Euro-Americans were able to perceive native people as equals, and exhibitions like these, featuring displays of native arts, marked a turning point in popular views of Native Americans.

When Klah's assistant died unexpectedly in 1931, he was too old to begin training another. Consequently, when Wheelwright suggested that his weavings and ceremonial paraphernalia be placed in a museum that she planned to build in Santa Fe, he agreed. These became the core holdings of the Museum of Navajo Ceremonial Art, later renamed the Wheelwright Museum of the American Indian. The museum opened in 1937, a few months after Klah's death from pneumonia at the age of 70.

Klah made a lasting contribution by seeking the preservation of his cultural expertise. His familiarity with so many ceremonies enabled him to synthesize divergent Navajo religious traditions and present them as a coherent system and a source of tribal unity. As Gladys Reichard observed, he had an intuitive and imaginative mind, which was receptive to new ideas and was orthodox without being conservative. He was very much a figure of the twentieth century, an avant-garde *berdache*.

Bibliography

Newcomb, Franc Johnson. *Hosteen Klah: Navaho Medicine Man and Sand Painter.* Norman: University of Oklahoma Press, 1964.

Roscoe, Will. *Changing Ones: Third and Fourth Genders in Native North America.* New York: St. Martin's Press, 1998.

Will Roscoe

See also TRANSSEXUALS, TRANSVESTITES, TRANSGENDER PEOPLE, AND CROSS-DRESSERS; TWO-SPIRIT MALES.

KLUMPKE, Anna (b. 28 October 1856; d. 9 February 1942), painter.

Anna Elizabeth Klumpke was the first of five daughters and two sons born in San Francisco to John Gerald Klumpke, a German-born Roman Catholic cobbler turned real estate dealer, and Dorothea Mathilda Tolle, a German-speaking Protestant. After a childhood knee injury, Klumpke used a crutch or cane for the rest of her life. From age nine to eleven, Klumpke, with her mother and her sisters, lived in Europe, seeking help for her lame leg. After a divorce in 1872, mother and children returned to Europe, where the Klumpke sisters excelled academically. One became a physician, another an astronomer with a doctorate in mathematics. The next to youngest became a pianist and the youngest was a violinist, composer, and tenured professor of music and theory.

Klumpke studied traditional painting at the Académie Julian in Paris for ten years (from about 1877–1887) under William-Adolphe Bouguereau, Tony Robert-Fleury, and Jules-Joseph Lefebvre. She excelled in portraiture and peasant genre scenes. Klumpke needed to earn her own living. Beginning in 1882 at age twenty-five, she gained portrait commissions by winning admission to and awards at annual juried salon shows. Her sisters were often the subject of her paintings, which increased their fame as well as her own. In 1889, she painted a dignified image of the American women's rights activist Elizabeth Cady Stanton.

Anna Klumpke had a gift for languages and often translated for students and instructors in the Académie Julian. In 1889 she was asked to translate for a U.S. horse dealer when he visited Rosa Bonheur (b. 1822), the award-winning French painter of animals. Bonheur's life companion and studio helpmate, Nathalie Micas, had died earlier in 1889, and Bonheur was in mourning when Klumpke met her. In the ensuing years, a warm correspondence developed.

In 1891, Klumpke moved to Boston. The following year, she exhibited thirty-eight oils and pastels. Her portraits found a favorable clientele in the Boston area and, by the end of her first year, her earnings equaled a Harvard University professor's. In 1893 her paintings were shown at the World's Columbian Exposition in Chicago. In 1897 she exhibited at the Gillespie Gallery in Pittsburgh and at the Mark Hopkins Institute in San Francisco. In 1898, her portraits were included in the Albany Historical and Art Society show.

In early 1898 Klumpke wrote to Rosa Bonheur asking to paint the older artist's portrait, and Bonheur acquiesced, inviting Klumpke to stay with her and use her studio. Klumpke arrived at Bonheur's home near Fontainebleau, outside of Paris, on 16 June 1898. Forty-four days later, Bonheur proposed, asking her if she would "like to stay with me and share my existence?" Despite objections from both families, Klumpke agreed to a "divine marriage of two souls." During the next year, Klumpke painted at least three formal portraits of Bonheur and also took photographs of her. Especially significant are photographs showing Bonheur flaunting conventions by smoking a cigarette and wearing her work smock with men's trousers.

Bonheur died 25 May 1899 in Klumpke's arms. They had had nine months together. The year before, Klumpke had photographed Bonheur wearing a laurel crown that she, Klumpke, had made. Bonheur called it "Old Europe crowned by young America" and asked to be buried wearing it. Her wish was granted.

Bonheur had willed her home and complete control of her estate to Klumpke, freeing Klumpke of the need to seek portrait commissions. Nevertheless, Klumpke continued to paint for the rest of her life. For the first nine years after Bonheur's death, Klumpke worked on a biography of the older artist, sifting through notes and letters and cataloging works of art. This effort was published as *Rosa Bonheur: Sa Vie, Son Oeuvre* (1908).

In her fifties and sixties, Klumpke received the Order of Chevalier (1913) and the Order of Officier (1921) of the French Legion of Honor. In 1937, in anticipation of World War II, Anna Klumpke, then in her late eighties, returned to the United States to live in San Francisco. She died there on 9 February 1942. Her ashes were added to the tomb in the Père Lachaise cemetery in Paris that already held the remains of Bonheur, Bonheur's lover Nathalie Micas, and Micas's mother.

Klumpke's paintings are in the Metropolitan Museum of Art (New York); the M. H. De Young Museum (San Francisco); the National Portrait Gallery (Washington, D.C.); the Rosa Bonheur Studio Museum, Château de By (Thoméry, France); and the Walker Art Museum (Brunswick, Maine).

Bibliography

Dwyer, Britta C. *Anna Klumpke: A Turn-of-the-Century Painter and Her World.* Boston: Northeastern University Press, 1999.

Klumpke, Anna. *Memoirs of an Artist.* Boston: Wright and Potter, 1940.

———. *Rosa Bonheur: The Artist's (Auto)biography.* Translated by Gretchen van Slyke. Ann Arbor: University of Michigan Press, 1997.

Tee A. Corinne

See also VISUAL ART.

KOPAY, David (b. 28 June 1942), athlete.

David Kopay was born in Chicago, Illinois, the second of Anton and Marguerite Kopay's four children. When Kopay reached fourth grade, his family moved to North Hollywood, California. In his biography, *The David Kopay Story,* Kopay recalls an unhappy home environment: "I do not remember a time in our house when there was not some kind of fight going on between my parents. Not once do I remember them exchanging any kind of love words. What I most often heard them call each other was 'You son of a bitch' " (p. 25). After attending a Claretian seminary for eighteen months and graduating from Notre Dame High School, Kopay won a football scholarship to the University of Washington (Seattle) in 1961. In 1964 Kopay co-captained his squad to a Rose Bowl berth. During his college years he also discovered sex, first with a woman and later with a fellow male athlete.

Despite Kopay's impressive college career, football's professional leagues did not draft him upon graduation. But he found his way onto the San Francisco 49ers as a free agent in 1964 and played on five National Football League teams during the next ten years (often as a member of the "suicide squad" or special teams). As a professional he knew his limitations, observing later, "I was ... a good ballplayer, but I wasn't any star" (Kopay, p. 11). Toward the end of his professional career, at his therapist's suggestion, David married a female friend, but their brief union proved unfulfilling. The couple soon separated. (Divorce occurred only many years later.)

In 1975, following Kopay's football retirement, *Washington Star* reporter Lynn Rosellini wrote several articles about homosexuality in sports. Several athletes willingly acknowledged being gay, but only off the record. Kopay rejoiced at Rosellini's series and was finally ready to acknowledge publicly his homosexuality. He contacted Rosellini, and with her story on 11 December 1975 became the first openly gay professional athlete. He told Robert McQueen in an interview for the *Advocate* (10 March 1976), "I'd been thinking about it for a long time. Many people in the sports world already knew I was gay. My family knew. And I knew how difficult and frustrating it is to try to lead a double-life. I was tired of compromising myself" (p. 19). People from many professions came out as LGBT in the 1970s, but perhaps none startled society as much as the macho footballer.

Sadly, Kopay paid a steep price for his admission. Coaching and sales representative jobs, typical for retired players, never materialized. Kopay's public disclosure also initially strained several family relationships (since mended). However, with Perry Deane Young, Kopay wrote his autobiography; published in 1977, it became a *New York Times* best-seller for over two months, a first for any sports-oriented book.

Despite his good intentions, Kopay's relationship with gay movement leaders often was strained. Some inaccurately perceived Kopay as a "dumb jock" when his apolitical background highlighted an excusable naiveté. Writer Rita Mae Brown lamented that David "could have been so important to us, in so many ways. And instead, all the guys did was hit on him.... The movement made a tremendous mistake with Dave" (Brown, p. 10).

After completing his autobiography, Kopay briefly relocated to several cities before accepting a job from his Uncle Bill at Hollywood's Linoleum City, where he has worked as a sales manager for many years. David remains hopeful that someone will film his life's story, but no one has yet accepted the challenge.

Kopay oiled the hinges to professional sports teams' closets in 1975, but still almost no active team sport participant has followed him through that door. Kopay muses, "I don't know why [other athletes] haven't come out. I know I felt so desperate that I needed to come out" (Kopay, p. 16). Perhaps money plays a crucial role. Kopay confesses, "If I'd had a lot more money, possibly I would have never spoken out" (p. 20).

Kopay's revelation changed attitudes regarding homosexuality. If one gay man could become a professional football player, perhaps another would not feel relegated to a stereotypic gay job—or life. Of his biography, Kopay told Michael O'Connor in a 1989 *Torso* interview, "it's done a lot of good for *me,* but it's also *legitimized* so many people in a way.... I know it's the best thing I've ever done and maybe ever *will* do!" (pp. 31–32)

Bibliography

Brown, Rita Mae. Interview by Paul D. Cain. Unpublished transcript, 19 August 1995.

Cain, Paul D. *Leading the Parade: Conversations with America's Most Influential Lesbians and Gay Men.* Lanham, Md.: Scarecrow Press, 2002.

Kopay, David. Interview by Paul D. Cain. Unpublished transcript, 16 July 1994.

Kopay, David, and Perry Deane Young. *The David Kopay Story.* New York: Arbor House, 1977.

McQueen, Robert I. "Dave Kopay Interview." *Advocate,* 10 March 1976, pp. 19–20.

Marcus, Eric. *Making History: The Struggle for Gay and Lesbian Equal Rights, 1945–1990, an Oral History.* New York: HarperCollins, 1992.

O'Connor, Michael E. "The David Kopay Story ... A Decade Later." *Torso,* October 1989, pp. 30–35, 82, 86.

Paul D. Cain

See also SPORTS.

KRAMER, Larry (b. 25 June 1935), activist, screenwriter, dramatist.

Larry Kramer was born in Bridgeport, Connecticut, the son of George Leon Kramer and Rea Sara Wishengrad. When he was eight years old, Kramer went to the National Theatre in Washington, D.C., to see a puppet play, an experience that transformed him into an instant theater buff. Kramer's mother supported his love of the theater, but his father dismissed Kramer as a "sissy" because of his interest in the arts.

College and Early Work

In September 1953 Kramer began his undergraduate education at Yale University, where he struggled to fit in. After his brother, Arthur, married in November 1953, Kramer tried to kill himself. He was put in the care of a psychiatrist, as a condition for remaining at Yale. The following April, Kramer's male German professor seduced him. When he confessed the affair to his family, Arthur convinced their parents that Kramer should continue analysis. Meanwhile, at Yale—from which Kramer graduated in 1957—he found singing and dramatic performances a welcome release from the pressures of dealing with his sexuality and psychoanalysis.

In 1961 Kramer moved to London to work for Columbia Pictures before branching out as producer and screenwriter for an adaptation of D. H. Lawrence's sexually explicit novel *Women in Love* (1920). The 1969 film garnered four Academy Award nominations, including one for Best Screenplay for Kramer.

Kramer's first play, *Sissies' Scrapbook,* was produced in 1973 by New York City's Playwrights Horizons. Drawn from Kramer's personal experiences as a homosexual, it involved the friendship of a gay man with three straight men who have known each other since college days. Encouraged by positive response, Kramer revised the play under the title *Four Friends* for production at the Theatre de Lys in 1974. In this new form it had little success either critically or commercially.

After his therapist suggested that he write a novel, Kramer spent three years working on *Faggots* (1978), a satire revolving around four days in the life of New York City's gay community. With its pointed admonitions against promiscuity among homosexuals, the book anticipated the controversial nature of Kramer's AIDS activism over the next two decades. Fred Lemish, the novel's central character, cannot fulfill his longing for a permanent relationship in a gay culture focused on fleeting sexual encounters. *Faggots* received positive critical response, but some reviewers were offended by its frank depiction of gay sex.

The AIDS Epidemic

With the outbreak of AIDS, Kramer was among the first to campaign for research and treatment, stridently demanding immediate action from public officials and institutions. He was a founder of Gay Men's Health Crisis, the first organization to confront the epidemic, in 1982. Disenchanted, however, with what he considered the organization's slow progress, he withdrew to start, in 1987, the AIDS Coalition to Unleash Power (ACT UP), an organization aimed at generating a more vigorous response to the ravages of AIDS.

Kramer was an outspoken political catalyst from the beginning of the AIDS epidemic. Accused of being an "anti-erotic" alarmist (with *Faggots* frequently cited as "evidence"), Kramer used confrontational tactics that focused sharply on assaulting the conscience of American society and the unresponsive Reagan administration. Despite growing media attention and highly publicized AIDS-related deaths, including that of movie star Rock Hudson, response to AIDS continued to be slow. Kramer, however, was undaunted and kept on agitating.

As his relationship with Gay Men's Health Crisis deteriorated, Kramer turned the experience into a play. On 21 April 1985 *The Normal Heart* made its debut at New York City's Public Theatre to much acclaim and controversy. Set between 1981 and 1984, the play leavens the bleakness of the accumulating horror of the epidemic with sarcasm and humor, despite its unmistakable indictment of a whole society's apathy in the face of the specter of AIDS.

The Normal Heart deals with the experiences of several gay men, but the connecting thread of this episodic

Larry Kramer. The outspoken playwright and AIDS activist, who cofounded the Gay Men's Health Crisis in 1982 and the more confrontational ACT UP in 1987, has influenced—and antagonized—large segments of the LGBT community and society at large in his unrelenting crusade against the disease. **[Marc Geller]**

work is the central character, Ned Weeks. When he begins to understand the mounting crisis, Ned is stunned to learn from Dr. Emma Brookner that the mysterious illness may be transmitted sexually. Ned's outbursts, directed at various officials and even those close to him, alienate Ned from the world around him. He has an uneasy relationship with his distant older brother, Ben, a father figure representing society's disapproval of the "gay lifestyle." Ultimately, Ben grows past his prejudices to accept Ned, an outcome Kramer clearly wants straight America to emulate. Audiences were drawn to the play's dramatic intensity, but its content made it the most controversial and pivotal gay-themed drama to emerge in the late twentieth century.

Kramer's next theatrical work, *Just Say No: A Play about a Farce* (1988), was not well received by critics. Dealing with the ways sexual hypocrisy in high places (during the height of the Reagan presidency) allowed AIDS to develop into a plague, it features a First Lady, her flamboyantly gay son, and the closeted gay mayor of Appleburg. The Reagans and Ed Koch, the mayor of New York City, were the thinly veiled targets, but Kramer weaves in many satiric references to contemporary American life. Critics found the blending of farce with the tragedies of the AIDS crisis an uneasy combination.

Later Work and Life

The Destiny of Me, the sequel to *The Normal Heart,* premiered at New York City's Circle Repertory Company on 20 October 1992. *The Destiny of Me* is a significantly more personal work, in the style of the family-oriented dramas of the American lyric realism tradition. It deals with the Kramer-Weeks family and social history, using AIDS as the catalyst for a searing exploration of the main character's life, sexual orientation, and sense of purpose. Various times in Weeks' life overlap as different characters, used to present key situations, float in and out of the action. The ability to view his experiences from the dual perspectives of his youthful and present-day selves permits Weeks to arrive at significant revelations about his life. His past is set against a present in which he vehemently argues with his doctor about his health and about the complex relationship between AIDS and activism. Critical response to this melancholy work was mixed, but critics respectfully acknowledged Kramer's historic significance in the fight against AIDS.

Kramer, who is HIV-positive, has at times been dangerously ill: in 2001 he received a liver transplant. With his longtime lover, architect David Webster, he divides his time between homes in New York City and Connecticut. He is currently at work on "The American People," a monumental novel he has been writing for over twenty years, which deals with the AIDS epidemic and continues where his early novel, *Faggots,* leaves off. In 1998 Lawrence D. Mass, who along with Kramer founded Gay Men's Health Crisis, edited a massive volume of essays in tribute to Kramer's influence, featuring contributions from a diverse group of writers and activists, some of whom had had serious and acrimonious differences with Kramer in the past. It is a tribute to the far-reaching impact Kramer has had on gay life in America that even Kramer's adversaries admire his activism.

Bibliography

Kramer, Larry. *Faggots.* New York: Random House, 1978.

———. *Reports from the Holocaust: The Making of an AIDS Activist.* Updated and expanded edition. New York: Cassell, 1995.

———. *The Normal Heart and the Destiny of Me.* New York: Grove, 2000.

———. *Women in Love and Other Dramatic Writings: Women in Love, Sissies' Scrapbook, A Minor Dark Age, Just Say No, The Farce in Just Saying No.* New York: Grove, 2003.

Mass, Lawrence, ed. *We Must Love One Another or Die: The Life and Legacies of Larry Kramer.* London: Cassell, 1997.

James Fisher

See also AIDS AND PEOPLE WITH AIDS; AIDS COALITION TO UNLEASH POWER (ACT UP); AIDS SERVICE ORGANIZATIONS; LITERATURE; RUSSO, VITO; THEATER AND PERFORMANCE.

KUROMIYA, Kiyoshi (b. 9 May 1943; d. 10 May 2000), activist.

Kiyoshi Kuromiya was a Japanese American civil rights, antiwar, gay liberation, and AIDS activist whose personal political history demonstrates the importance of the cross-fertilization of social movements in the making of queer politics.

Born at Heart Mountain, Wyoming, in a World War II internment camp for people of Japanese ancestry, Kuromiya became politicized as a civil rights, antiwar, and gay liberation activist in the 1960s. He participated in the Congress of Racial Equality restaurant sit-ins on Route 40, Aberdeen, Maryland, in 1962; participated in the 1963 March on Washington when Martin Luther King Jr. gave his "I Have a Dream" speech; and was injured in an act of police violence at the State Capitol building in Montgomery, Alabama, while leading black high school students in a voter registration march in 1965.

In 1968, as an architecture student at the University of Pennsylvania, Kuromiya protested the use of napalm in Vietnam by first announcing that a dog would be burned alive in front of the university's Van Pelt Library, and then, when thousands came to protest, he distributed a pamphlet reading, "Congratulations on your anti-napalm protest. You saved the life of a dog. Now, how about saving the lives of tens of thousands of people in Vietnam."

Kuromiya participated in an early homosexual rights demonstration at Independence Hall, Philadelphia, in 1965. He was one of the founders of Gay Liberation Front–Philadelphia in 1969 and, in an important act of cross-movement solidarity, served as an openly gay delegate to the Black Panther Party's Revolutionary People's Constitutional Convention, held at Temple University in Philadelphia in 1969. It was during this convention that the Black Panther Party endorsed the gay liberation struggle.

In the 1980s and 1990s, Kuromiya was a pioneering AIDS activist whose participation in the AIDS mobilization effort helped to redefine the nature of social movement activism and to reinvigorate LGBT politics in the AIDS era. He was at the forefront of AIDS activist efforts at cross-race and cross-class coalition building. Throughout the late 1980s and 1990s, he was a long-standing member of the direct action group ACT UP Philadelphia. He participated in some of ACT UP's most dramatic and influential protests in the United States and abroad and was an active member of the ACT UP People of Color Caucus. In a parallel effort to overcome class- and race-based divisions among people living with HIV and AIDS in Philadelphia, he helped to found the multiracial and multiclass People with AIDS (PWA) coalition We the People Living with AIDS/HIV. In the early 1990s, the activities of this group became one of the most significant avenues for political participation among low-income sexual minorities of color.

Together with other activists across the United States and the world, Kuromiya helped to challenge the authority of biomedicine in AIDS research and treatment. In the self-help style of the PWA movement, he directed significant attention to the education and empowerment of people living with HIV and AIDS. He was an internationally recognized treatment activist who participated in the struggle for community-based research and for research that mattered to the variety of groups affected by AIDS, including people of color, drug users, and women. He also edited the ACT UP *Standard of Care,* the first standard of HIV care written by and for people living with HIV.

Kuromiya is perhaps best known as the founder of the Critical Path Project, a newsletter, 24-hour telephone hot line, Web page, and free Internet service for people living with HIV and AIDS in the Philadelphia region and beyond. He developed Critical Path to be an organizing tool and a comprehensive source of HIV treatment information in the Internet era. Accordingly, he was the lead litigant for a U.S. Supreme Court challenge to overturn the 1995 Communications Decency Act on Internet Censorship. In 1999, Kuromiya sued the United States in a class action suit to decriminalize medical use of marijuana.

Kuromiya's personal and political influences were eclectic. In the late 1970s and early 1980s, he worked with architect R. Buckminster Fuller, helping Fuller to complete many of his books. Kuromiya is credited as Fuller's "adjuvant," meaning, roughly, "catalyst," on *Critical Path* (1981), one of Fuller's apocryphal ruminations on technology and human history, and Kuromiya edited another of Fuller's books, *Cosmography* (1992), after Fuller's death. Kuromiya's interest in and commitment to digital democracy were derived in part from Fuller's philosophy.

Kuromiya died on 10 May 2000 due to complications from AIDS.

Bibliography

Forster, Evan M. "Philadelphia's Kiyoshi Kuromiya Lights Up." *POZ Magazine* (February/March 1996).

Jeff Maskovsky and Julie Davids

See also AIDS AND PEOPLE WITH AIDS; AIDS COALITION TO UNLEASH POWER (ACT UP); ANTIWAR, PACIFIST, AND PEACE MOVEMENTS; HOMOPHILE MOVEMENT; NEW LEFT AND STUDENT MOVEMENTS.

abcdefghijk**l**mnopqrstuvwxyz

L

LABOR MOVEMENTS AND LABOR UNIONS

The Stonewall Riots in New York City in 1969 opened the doors to agitation by LGBT people for their rights in the workplace. This activism was always part of the larger LGBT rights movement but took on a more organized life of its own as U.S. sexual minority trade unionists and their allies took up the cause starting in the 1970s. Daily discrimination and institutionalized prejudice in the one place all LGBT people went, the workplace, spurred the need for a large-scale movement for workers' rights.

Early Alliances

Homophobia resulted in discrimination for many LGB workers at their places of employment, which in turn led to organizing. Most of the sexual minority rights and workers' rights alliances were built after Stonewall, but the earliest account of gay men out and organizing at work can be found in Allan Bérubé's research on the Marine Cooks and Stewards union from the 1930s to the early 1950s. In the 1950s U.S. senator Joseph McCarthy labeled gay civil service workers a threat to national security and thousands were fired because of their sexual orientation. The first large-scale attempts in the 1970s to protect LGB people at work were organizing campaigns to include sexual orientation in nondiscrimination language in union contracts. National campaigns included the American Federation of Teachers, which at its 1973 convention passed a resolution protesting employment discrimination based on sexual orientation. That same year, the National Education Association came out against employment discrimination founded on sexual orientation. Union locals held rank-and-file campaigns to get protection from discrimination based on sexual orientation in their union contracts. In 1974 sexual minority employees at the Seattle Public Library, unionized by the American Federation of State, City and Municipal Employees, fought successfully to gain protective language in their contract, one of the first victories in the country. The independent Transportation Employees Union in Michigan negotiated similar provisions in Ann Arbor the same year. These small workers' rights battles to get sexual orientation recognized as a protective category began in the 1970s and were soon in the national spotlight.

In the Spotlight

Burgeoning LGB and labor alliances had their first high-profile campaign in 1974 with the Coors boycott. Coors, a beer manufacturer, was known to have fired gay employees and forced prospective employees to take lie detector tests about their sexual orientations. Started in California by two Teamsters, the boycott successfully crippled Coors sales in LGB bars and grocery stores in California. The news about the anti-LGB policies soon reached the East Coast and spurred similar boycotts in New York City. The boycott was eventually led by Harvey Milk and Howard Wallace and, with the support of LGB unionists in the San Francisco Bay area, they forced the company to cease anti-LGB employment policies. More than just a beer boycott, the Coors campaign created an awareness of employment discrimination based on sexual orientation.

Teachers were disproportionately affected by anti-LGB discrimination at work. Accusations of homosexuality were often accompanied by wrongful allegations of child sexual abuse. If there was even a rumor that a teacher or school counselor was gay, administrators and school boards often fired them immediately. In 1975 Bay Area Gay Liberation (BAGL) was founded in San Francisco to combat increasing homophobia. BAGL, along with the Gay Teachers Caucus, picketed the Board of Education, calling for fairness at work. In 1978 California's Briggs Initiative, Proposition 6, was an attempt to bar LGB teachers from public schools. A coalition of labor unions, including the state American Federation of Teachers and National Education Association affiliates and the California American Federation of Labor-Congress of Industrial Organizations (AFL-CIO), rallied their members to vote "no on 6" and ultimately defeated the prejudicial initiative. Activists fought similar anti-LGB ballot initiatives around the country in the 1970s in Miami, Wichita, Seattle, and Eugene, but none had the strong backing of labor unions like the San Francisco campaign. Anti-LGB gay political movements that targeted homosexuals in employment, housing, and public accommodations won in Eugene but were narrowly defeated in the other cities.

Labor Unions and the Age of AIDS

In the 1980s HIV and AIDS devastated the LGB community and presented LGB workers with even more challenges. Sexual minority workers were particularly vulnerable to homophobic and AIDSphobic discrimination on the job, which ranged from wrongful termination to the denial of benefits for family members. AIDS made LGB employees more aware of the discrimination they faced when it came to family health insurance benefits and bereavement leave. Gay employees' partners were often ineligible for health insurance and gay employees were denied bereavement leave when partners or other family members died. Employees at the *Village Voice* newspaper in New York City were among the few workers in the early 1980s to have successfully negotiated spouse-equivalent benefits in their employee benefits package (which they did in 1982).

AIDS also changed the ways that employers treated the education of their employees, LGB or otherwise. New policies on workplace safety, health insurance benefits, and disability discrimination had to be established in order to educate employees and provide for their basic rights. In the mid-1980s, the San Francisco Service Employees International Union (SEIU) Local 250, a group of mostly hospital workers, formed a coalition of health care professionals to educate each other about HIV and AIDS. This educational network provided one of the only ways to get and disseminate accurate information about AIDS and served as a model for other union training programs throughout the rest of the country. Rank-and-file unionists were responsible for this innovative information, long before national branches of unions dealt with the problem of AIDS. Lane Kirkland, president of the national AFL-CIO, finally made an official statement in 1990 that union members with HIV/AIDS have a right to work without discrimination.

Sexual Minorities and Union Caucuses

As shown with the response to the HIV/AIDS crisis, sexual minority rights activism within unions came from the bottom up in the form of caucuses, small groups of employees with similar interests. As Miriam Frank's work shows, local, statewide, and national LGB caucuses were instrumental in spreading the message about the effectiveness of gay workers in their workplaces and beyond. In 1979 in San Francisco, the LGB caucus of Hotel and Restaurants Employees (HERE) Local 2 published a newspaper, *Dishrag,* which they used as an organizing tool by publishing stories about workplace problems concerning wages and benefits that LGB employees were having all around the city. They also publicized organizing drives and pickets, bringing the LGB community out to rallies for workers' rights at restaurants and hotels.

Another group, the SEIU Lavender Caucus, introduced LGB-friendly resolutions at its international convention in 1984. This set the pace for individual locals to take action on gay issues. For instance, Oregon's Local 503 network of LGB workers organized to push the local to negotiate for the addition of sexual orientation protection to its contract in 1987. This local also organized the group Lesbian and Gay Unionists to fight the antigay ballot measure 9 in Oregon in 1992, which would have made employment discrimination against LGB people legal.

Boston's Gay and Lesbian Labor Activists' Network (GALLAN), founded in 1986 by state and health care workers, was a union caucus with two aims. Its mission was to bring union and class politics into the LGB movement and to fight homophobia and bring LGB issues into the workplace and the labor movement. GALLAN and the Gay Lesbian Concerns Committee (GLCC) worked in coalition with other public employee unions to lobby for domestic partnership bills in Massachusetts throughout the 1980s and 1990s. Many other small union caucuses formed around the country to achieve workers' rights for sexual minorities. This organizing effort became recognized by national unions in the 1990s.

Setting the National Agenda

Until the early 1990s, sexual minority labor networks did not have an organized national voice. The group Pride at Work had its first conference in New York City in 1992, at which smaller groups like GALLAN and SEIU's Lavender Caucus did national networking. Pride At Work published its first pamphlet in 1991, describing collective bargaining strategies for negotiating LGB issues such as domestic partnership benefits and nondiscrimination language. To achieve maximum visibility for LGB issues in the union, members of Pride At Work voted in 1996 to affiliate with the AFL-CIO. With the support of AFL-CIO vice president Linda Chavez-Thompson, Pride At Work was recognized as an official constituency group in 1997 and began to set a national agenda for sexual minority workers' rights. The group focused on organizing sexual minority workers in their unions and bargaining for nondiscrimination clauses and domestic partnership benefits. This group also lobbied for the proposed Employment Non-Discrimination Act (ENDA) that, if passed, would have provided federal protections for sexual minority workers. At the end of the twentieth century, Pride At Work became even more inclusive, addressing transgender workers' rights, such as accommodations for transitioning at work. Pride At Work also created coalitions with other AFL-CIO groups, such as the Asian Pacific Labor Alliance (APALA), to lobby for the rights of all workers.

Bibliography

Bérubé, Allan. *Coming Out Under Fire: The History of Gay Men and Women in World War Two.* New York: Free Press, 1990.

Hollibaugh, Amber, and Nikhil Pal Singh. "Sexuality, Labor, and the New Trade Unionism: A Conversation." In *My Dangerous Desires: A Queer Girl Dreaming Her Way Home.* Durham, N.C.: Duke University Press, 2000.

Hunt, Gerald, ed. *Laboring for Rights: Unions and Sexual Diversity across Nations.* Philadelphia: Temple University Press, 1999.

Johnson, David K. "'Homosexual Citizens': Washington's Gay Community Confronts the Civil Service." *Washington History* 6, no. 2 (Fall–Winter 1994–1995): 44–63.

Krupat, Kitty, and Patrick McCreery, eds. *Out At Work: Building a Gay-Labor Alliance.* Minneapolis: University of Minnesota Press, 2001.

Christa M. Orth

See also ANTIDISCRIMINATION LAW AND POLICY; BOYCOTTS; ECONOMICS; EMPLOYMENT AND OCCUPATIONS.

LADDER

Launched in October 1956 by the lesbian rights group Daughters of Bilitis (DOB) as a membership recruitment tool, the *Ladder* magazine was for sixteen years the pioneering publication by and for lesbians. It stands today as one of the most important and enduring products of the homophile movement. Through the artwork on its covers and the content of its pages, the *Ladder* helped develop lesbian identity, promote lesbian visibility, and construct lesbian community during the 1950s and 1960s. It joined two other fledgling gay magazines—*ONE* and *Mattachine Review*—in launching a revolution in the publishing world by developing the homophile press. The *Ladder* helped make gay and lesbian periodicals accessible, attractive, and indispensable to a growing social movement.

The magazine's title reflects the thinking of the times. The typed, mimeographed newsletter was named the *Ladder* because its creators saw it as a vehicle for lesbians to lift themselves out of the depths of self- and societal hatred. In the first issue, editor "Ann Ferguson" (the short-lived pseudonym of Phyllis Lyon, one of DOB's founders) wrote, "With this first issue, we enter a field already ably served by *ONE* and *Mattachine Review.* We offer, however, that so-called 'feminine viewpoint' which they have had so much difficulty obtaining. It is to be hoped that our venture will encourage the women to take an ever-increasing part in the steadily-growing fight for understanding of the homophile minority."

Most of the women involved in DOB in 1956 protected themselves by using pen names in the newsletter. Being openly homosexual at that time exposed a lesbian or gay man to possible dismissal from employment, loss of family and friends, harassment, and arrest. From the first issue of the *Ladder* on, the leaders of DOB sought to reassure their readers that involvement in the organization would help, not harm, them. They also appealed for both financial support and original artwork, fiction, poetry, and essays.

Their calls were answered. Over the years they received a wealth of responses. In May and August 1957 the magazine received laudatory letters from Lorraine Hansberry, the African American playwright who made Broadway history with her award-winning 1959 drama *A Raisin in the Sun.* (The letters were signed "L.H.N." and "L.N.," reflecting her married name, Nemiroff, although she separated from her husband in that same year.) The *Ladder* also debuted numerous lesbian and feminist authors and artists, such as the humorist and mystery writer Rita Mae Brown and the science fiction author Marion Zimmer Bradley. The magazine featured early works by researchers such as Jeannette Foster, who worked with the Kinsey Institute and was the author of *Sex Variant Women in Literature* (1956). Each issue also

Ladder. Featured on the cover of the October 1965 issue—along with the added label "A Lesbian Review"—is a photograph with the headline "Homophile Groups Picket in Nation's Capital." **[GLHS (Gay and Lesbian Historical Society)]**

included political commentary, reports on homophile conferences and meetings, and the Daughters of Bilitis's "statement of purpose." The *Ladder* was the one reliable source where lesbians could find information about homophile activities; read reviews of the growing numbers of works dealing with lesbianism and homosexuality; order LGB-themed records, books, and magazines; and find a sense of connection to other lesbians. In this era before LGBT bookstores and community centers, it was a virtual meeting space for lesbians.

DOB leaders also used the publication as a tool for research. They conducted their own demographic surveys of their readership, in 1958 and again in 1963. While the sample sizes of both surveys were small, these studies nonetheless were the first ones done by lesbians about lesbians, including information on family histories, education, employment, and relationships. As such, they aided the homophile groups' groundbreaking efforts to counter the prevailing medical, legal, and religious views that portrayed homosexual women and men as "deviant."

In the early 1960s, the *Ladder* underwent a dramatic transformation. Among other major changes—such as adding the words "A Lesbian Review" to the front cover—a new editor, Barbara Gittings, began publishing photographs of lesbians taken by her partner, Kay Tobin Lahusen. The black-and-white photographs ranged from "back of head" shots, in which no faces are visible, to close-ups of attractive women, singly and in couples. For example, the June 1966 issue of the *Ladder* featured Ernestine Eckstein (a pseudonym), an African American woman active with DOB in New York, who argued for public demonstrations and litigation as a means of securing basic rights for lesbians and gay men.

The *Ladder* in the mid-1960s was a forum where an evolving movement could debate tactics and strategies at a time when dissent and agitation for change were becoming more pronounced. In addition, by 1965 the *Ladder* was regularly monitoring and reporting on the print and electronic media's treatment of homosexuality and was reporting on the increasingly strategic uses of the media by gay men and lesbians, especially as guests on local radio and television talk shows around the country.

By 1968, the *Ladder* had a paid subscription list of about one thousand. It began to move from a focus on lesbian and gay liberation to lesbian feminist issues under the editorship of Barbara Grier ("Gene Damon"). But by 1970, increasingly fractious organizational disagreements over governance and ideology—for example, questions of local autonomy and the growing importance of the women's movement to many of the DOB's leaders—led Grier and then-DOB president Rita Laporte to abruptly sever the magazine's ties to the Daughters of Bilitis. They took the subscription list and production materials from DOB's headquarters in San Francisco and moved them to Grier's home in Nevada. Grier began to publish the *Ladder* independently as a lesbian-feminist journal, and it lasted for two more years. But DOB could not survive the loss of its magazine. It had been the glue that held the national organization together. While chapters continued their local activities throughout the 1970s, DOB as a national entity was dissolved in 1970.

During its sixteen years of existence, the *Ladder* drew on the talents and visions of numerous women, including editors Phyllis Lyon, Del Martin, Barbara Gittings, Helen Sandoz, and Barbara Grier. It evolved from a typed, mimeographed twelve-page newsletter into a professionally printed, high-quality magazine sold at selected newsstands and bookstores in major cities. It is fondly remembered today by lesbians who were looking for love or friendship or just accurate information about homosexuality in the 1950s and 1960s, and old copies are still treasured by former subscribers. Each of them—and countless others, who gave their time and talent or simply shared copies at work or at the bars—helped create a publication that was a landmark in the development of modern LGBT culture and community.

Bibliography

Bullough, Vern, ed. *Before Stonewall: Activists for Gay and Lesbian Rights in Historical Context.* New York: Harrington Park Press, 2002.

Grier, Barbara and Coletta Reid, eds. *The Lavender Herring: Lesbian Essays from the "Ladder."* Baltimore: Diana Press, 1976.

Katz, Jonathan Ned, ed. *The Ladder.* Arno Series on Homosexuality. New York: Arno Press, 1975. (A complete, bound photo reprint of the magazine from its first issue.)

Kepner, Jim. *Rough News, Daring Views: 1950s' Pioneer Gay Press Journalism.* New York: Harrington Park Press, 1998.

Martin, Del, and Phyllis Lyon. *Lesbian/Woman.* San Francisco: Glide, 1972. Rev. ed. Volcano, Calif.: Volcano Press, 1991.

Terry, Jennifer. *An American Obsession: Science, Medicine, and Homosexuality in Modern Society.* Chicago: University of Chicago Press, 1999.

Marcia M. Gallo

See also BROWN, RITA MAE; ECKSTEIN, ERNESTINE; FOSTER, JEANNETTE; GITTINGS, BARBARA, AND KAY TOBIN LAHUSEN; GRAHN, JUDY; GRIER, BARBARA; HANSBERRY, LORRAINE; HOMOPHILE MOVEMENT; HOMOPHILE PRESS; LESBIAN FEMINISM; LYON, PHYLLIS, AND DEL MARTIN; RULE, JANE; SHELLEY, MARTHA.

LAHUSEN, KAY TOBIN. see GITTINGS, BARBARA, AND KAY TOBIN LAHUSEN.

LAMBDA LEGAL DEFENSE

The Lambda Legal Defense and Education Fund is a nonprofit, tax-exempt, public interest law firm, dedicated to the protection of lesbian and gay rights. Its stated mission is to "achieve full recognition of the civil rights of lesbians, gay men, and people with HIV/AIDS through impact litigation, education, and public policy work." Lambda has participated, either as counsel or as amicus curiae (friend of the court), in some of the most important cases of the modern lesbian and gay civil rights movement. More recently it has represented transgender litigants as well. Headquartered in New York City since its incorporation in 1973, Lambda has established four regional offices and a national network of cooperating attorneys, making it the largest lesbian and gay legal organization in the country.

Formation of Lambda

In the early 1970s, William Thom, E. Carrington Boggan, and several other gay lawyers gathered informally in New York City to discuss the possibility of forming a public interest law firm whose purpose would be to further the cause of gay rights. New York State law at the time forbade the practice of law by a corporation or association unless the organization was "organized for benevolent or charitable purposes, or for the purpose of assisting persons without means in the pursuit of any civil remedy." Basing its charter and petition on that of the recently approved Puerto Rican Legal Defense and Education Fund, Thom applied to the Appellate Division of the New York Supreme Court for approval.

Lambda's purposes, as stated in its application to the court, were to provide

> without charge legal services in those situations which give rise to legal issues having a substantial effect on the legal rights of homosexuals; to promote the availability of legal services to homosexuals by encouraging and attracting homosexuals into the legal profession; to disseminate to homosexuals general information concerning their legal rights and obligations, and to render technical assistance to any legal services corporation or agency in regard to legal issues affecting homosexuals.

In 1972 the Appellate Division unanimously rejected the application, proclaiming that the stated purposes were "neither benevolent nor charitable." The New York Court of Appeals, New York State's highest court, reversed the lower court. On 18 October 1973, the lower court approved Thom's application and the Lambda Legal Defense and Education Fund was officially incorporated and authorized to practice law. In July 1974 the Internal Revenue Service granted Lambda tax-exempt status under Section 501(c) (3) of the Internal Revenue Code, making it the first gay rights organization to gain tax-exempt charitable status from the federal government.

Lambda's Early Days

In the early days, Lambda was short on staff and money and thus not in a position to offer direct representation to aggrieved lesbians and gay men. Its primary activity was to file appellate briefs as amicus curiae in cases dealing with lesbian and gay issues, particularly in those cases in

in re thom

301 n.e.2d 542 (N.Y. 1973) (reversing lower court and holding that Lambda should be granted corporate charter).

people v. onofre

415 n.e.2d 936 (n.y. 1980), cert. denied, 415 u.s. 987 (1981) (holding that state criminalization of consensual private sodomy violated federal constitution).

bowers v. hardwick

478 u.s. 186 (1986) (upholding georgia's sodomy statute against claim by gay man that constitutional right to privacy should protect consensual sodomy in private home).

baehr v. lewin

(holding that state's restriction of marriage to opposite sex couples was sex discrimination and remanding for trial on state's justification for restriction). on remand, trial court held state statute unconstitutional. baehr v. miike, 65 uslw 2399 (1996), but the decision was mooted by a constitutional amendment that authorized the state legislature to restrict marriage to opposite sex couples.

which positive arguments on behalf of gay men and lesbians had not been presented by legal counsel.

Despite the paucity of funds, Lambda did provide direct representation in some key early cases. In 1977, when the ACLU decided not to appeal the case of Sergeant Leonard Matlovich, which challenged the military's ban on homosexuals, Lambda's general counsel, E. Carrington Boggan, agreed to handle the case himself, provided Matlovich could forward the necessary costs of litigation. And in 1979 Lambda's president, Margot Karle, served as co-counsel in *People v. Onofre*, a case in which the New York Court of Appeals declared New York State's sodomy statute unconstitutional under the federal Constitution.

Lambda operated with minimal staff and on a shoestring budget until the early 1980s. Under the leadership of Tim Sweeney, executive director from 1981 to 1986, Lambda's financial situation improved significantly. The annual budget grew from approximately $70,000 to over $350,000 in just four years. Sweeney pushed to add full-time professional staff to the organization. In 1983 Abby Rubenfeld joined the Lambda staff as its first managing attorney (renamed "legal director" several years later). In 1984 Nancy Langer was appointed as Lambda's first full-time public information director. With the growth in financial support, Lambda began to focus on transforming itself from a New York organization to a more national one. In 1980 a new national board of directors was elected, with an emphasis on geographical diversity.

After Sweeney announced his resignation in 1985, Tom Stoddard was selected as executive director. From 1986 to 1992 Stoddard transformed Lambda from a $350,000-a-year public interest law firm with a staff of six to a firm with a $1,800,000 annual budget and a staff of twenty-two. Under Stoddard's leadership, Lambda also opened its first regional office in Los Angeles.

As Lambda's first legal director (1983–1988), Abby Rubenfeld handled Lambda's growing docket of cases and worked to make the docket consistent with Lambda's image as a national organization. Rubenfeld's tenure with Lambda coincided with *Bowers v. Hardwick*, a case challenging Georgia's sodomy statute that reached the U.S. Supreme Court in 1986. While the *Hardwick* case was on appeal, Lambda was working on another sodomy case, *New York v. Uplinger*, challenging a state loitering statute that had been used to arrest a gay man for soliciting sodomy from an undercover policeman. The Supreme Court had granted certiorari in *Uplinger*, raising concerns that Lambda's earlier victory in *Onofre*, striking down the New York sodomy statute on federal constitutional grounds, was at risk. At the same time, a Texas sodomy case, *Baker v. Wade*, was pending before the Fifth Circuit. To help coordinate litigation challenging sodomy statutes nationwide, Lambda organized the Ad Hoc Task Force to Challenge Sodomy Laws.

Because gay rights litigation included issues in addition to sodomy challenges, the original Task Force quickly grew to become the National Lesbian and Gay Civil Rights Roundtable. The group met three times a year in different locations. Before long it expanded to include academics and researchers who were also interested in national strategies to obtain equal rights for lesbians and gay men. In addition to the Roundtable, Lambda organized a monthly conference call for lawyers at lesbian and gay rights organizations around the country. Known as the National Litigators Strategy Project (later known as the Litigators' Roundtable), the conference call enabled each legal organization to stay abreast of the others' docket and to stay informed about precedents that would negatively or positively affect other cases.

Lambda at the Beginning of the Twenty-First Century

In 1992 Kevin Cathcart became the new executive director of Lambda, following Tom Stoddard. Over the next ten years, under Cathcart's leadership, the Lambda staff tripled in number and the annual budget grew to over $6 million. Cathcart guided Lambda through the opening of its second, third, and fourth regional offices, based in Chicago (1993), Atlanta (1997), and Dallas (2002).

In addition to bringing groundbreaking cases, Lambda continued its role from the 1980s as a key organizer of the national network of lesbian and gay rights litigators. It also educated the public about discrimination against LGBT people and people with AIDS by working with the media, publishing educational pamphlets, participating in conferences, and providing guest speakers for schools and similar groups.

High-Profile Cases

Lambda's most important cases have been those with nationwide impact. For example, the 1993 Hawaii marriage case, *Baehr v. Lewin,* changed the national conversation about same-sex marriage, even though the litigation failed to establish same-sex marriage rights in Hawaii. Lambda attorney Evan Wolfson was co-counsel in the case. His work on *Baehr v. Lewin* led to the creation of Lambda's Marriage Project.

Lambda's first appearance before the U.S. Supreme Court occurred on 18 January 1983 in *New York v. Uplinger.* Lambda cooperating attorney, William Gardner from Buffalo, argued the case. In 1984 the Court voted five to four that certiorari had been improvidently granted, thereby preserving the state court decision in favor of Uplinger, which held that solicitation for sodomy was a constitutionally protected activity. While *Uplinger* was under consideration, Lambda worked behind the scenes on *Bowers v. Hardwick.*

Lambda lawyer Suzanne Goldberg was co-counsel in *Romer v. Evans,* in which the U.S. Supreme Court struck down an amendment to the Colorado constitution that discriminated against lesbians, bisexuals, and gay men. *Romer* was the first Supreme Court case to strike down an antigay law under the equal protection clause. Lambda also represented James Dale in his legal battle against the Boy Scouts of America. Lambda senior attorney Evan Wolfson argued before the Supreme Court that the Boy Scouts did not have a first amendment right to be exempt from New Jersey's antidiscrimination laws. The Supreme Court disagreed and upheld the decision of the Boy Scouts to remove Dale from its membership.

In 2003, Lambda won a sweeping victory in the case of *Lawrence v. Texas.* This case began as a challenge in state court to Texas's same-sex sodomy statute. On facts very similar to the *Bowers v. Hardwick* case from 1986, the Texas courts, relying on *Bowers,* held that it was constitutionally permissible to criminalize consensual private same-sex sodomy. On 26 June 2003, the U. S. Supreme Court disagreed and reversed the convictions of the Texas men charged under the statute. Of greater import, however, was the court's pronouncement that "*Bowers* was not correct when it was decided and it is not correct today. It ought not to remain binding precedent. *Bowers v. Hardwick* should be and now is overruled." Many commentators claim that the victory in *Lawrence* is as important to the LGBT movement as *Brown v. Topeka Board of Education* was to the civil rights movement for race equality in the 1950s.

new york v. uplinger

467 u.s. 246 (1984) (writ of certiorari dismissed in sodomy statute challenge because of "uncertainty regarding precise federal question decided" by new york appellate court).

romer v. evans

467 u.s. 246 (1984) (holding that colorado anti-gay constitutional amendment violated federal equal protection clause).

dale v. boy scouts of america

528 u.s. 1109 (2000) (recognizing first amendment right of boy scouts to exclude gay scout members).

lawrence v. texas

2002 wl 1611564 (granting certiorari in challenge to texas sodomy statute).

Bibliography

Cain, Patricia A. *Rainbow Rights: The Role of Lawyers and Courts in the Lesbian and Gay Civil Rights Movement.* Boulder, Colo.: Westview Press, 2000.

Keen, Lisa, and Suzanne Goldberg. *Strangers to the Law: Gay People on Trial.* Ann Arbor: University of Michigan Press, 1998.

Lambda Legal Defense and Education Fund. *The Lambda Update Newsletter Archives.* New York: Lambda Legal Defense and Education Fund, Winter 1976–Spring 1992.

Lawrence v. Texas, 539 US _____, 123 S. Ct. 2472 (2003).

Patricia A. Cain

See also ANTI-DISCRIMINATION LAW AND POLICY; BOY SCOUTS AND GIRL SCOUTS; DISABILITY, DISABLED PEOPLE, AND DISABILITY MOVEMENTS; FAMILY LAW AND POLICY; FEDERAL LAW AND POLICY; MILITARY LAW AND POLICY; PRIVACY AND PRIVACY RIGHTS; RIGHTS OF ASSOCIATION AND ASSEMBLY; SODOMY, BUGGERY, CRIMES AGAINST NATURE, DISORDERLY CONDUCT, AND LEWD AND LASCIVIOUS LAW AND POLICY; YOUTH AND YOUTH GROUPS.

LANGUAGE

Over the course of U.S. history, the language used to describe, criticize, and affirm same-sex sexuality and gender variance has exhibited great complexity. The terms used have varied greatly across time, space, and social and cultural groups (defined, for example, by class, race, gender, and sexuality). Scholars have generally concluded that rather than representing different names for the same phenomena, these terms are associated with the existence of multiple systems of sexual and gendered meanings.

Key Terms in Early America

In *Changing Ones,* Will Roscoe presents documentation for 157 Native American groups ("tribes") with male gender-mixing or gender-crossing roles and fifty with female ones. In some instances there were distinct terms for the male and female transgender roles; in others a generic term was used. Europeans and Euro-Americans applied the word *berdache* (originally an Arabic and Iranian word meaning "slave" and lacking any sex or gender meaning) to Native Americans who would now be categorized as *transgender* but not to their sexual partners, who were conventional in appearance and sexual role.

Until the second half of the nineteenth century, Euro-Americans most frequently used terms derived from Judeo-Christian religious traditions when referring to same-sex sexuality and gender variance. "The abominable sin not to be named among Christians" was the long label; *sodomy* and *buggery* were the short ones for what were considered crimes against nature. Sodomites, according to interpretations of the Judeo-Christian Bible, were men of the city of Sodom who sought to violate a seemingly male angel; *buggerers* were heretics (the original heresy was Albigensian, but the term was generalized and in 1533 began to be used in English law in the sense of illicit sexual acts). Sodomy and buggery referred to different sexual practices in different contexts (including, at times, oral sex, anal sex, and bestiality), but generally encompassed a variety of nonreproductive sexual acts. The terms were generally used to refer not to distinct types of people but rather to sinful behaviors that anyone might commit.

New Language

In the late nineteenth and early twentieth centuries, a variety of English-language terms came into use, many of which conflated sexual and gender meanings, drew on ancient historical references, and were associated with identities as well as behaviors. Scientific experts invented and used a variety of terms, including *inverts* and *inversion,* to refer to what many conceptualized as psychological *hermaphroditism* (combining elements of the male and female in one person) and *transvestism.* Some believe that *dyke* derived from the *dite* in *hermaphrodite.* The *verto* root in *inversion, perversion, invert,* and *pervert* means "turning," which conveyed the sense of turning away from sexual and gender norms.

As far as can be determined, the term *homosexuality* was first used in the United States in James Kiernan's 1892 translation of work by European sexologists. The initial diffusion of the word *homosexual* (applicable to those born female or male) remained linked to conceptions of gender deviance, though some scholars argue that over time the term lost those associations and came to refer exclusively to same-sex sexual orientation. Similarly, while *bisexual* was initially used to refer to what would later be called *androgyny* (combining masculine and feminine elements), some scholars argue that over time it lost those associations and came to refer to a sexual orientation to both males and females. In contrast to the heavy weight of religious and legal opprobrium carried by *inversion* and *perversion* in medical discourse, *homosexual* was a more neutral descriptive term.

Lesbian had a vaguely positive etymology, linked as it was to the pre-Christian "cradle of western culture," ancient Greece, and more specifically to the island (Lesbos) where the great female poet Sappho lived. (The French word *lesbienne* was used for females sexually engaged with females in the seventeenth century, but not in English until the late nineteenth century.) A similar grasping for an ancient Greek analog for males was

Dorian. Oscar Wilde's unnatural character, Dorian Gray, may have been an allusion to the Dorians as supposed inventors of pederasty; Wilde's highly visible trial in the 1890s made the label insufficiently covert for those who saw themselves as continuing the tradition of "Greek love" but not wishing to share Wilde's fate. Karl Ulrich's mid nineteenth century contrast of *Urning* (from Aphrodite Urania in Plato's *Symposium*) for homosexuals and *Dioning* for heterosexuals was partially carried from German into English as *Uranian,* but—with the common pronunciation of the distant planet as a homonym for "your anus"—did not provide adequate camouflage.

According to George Chauncey, in New York City by the 1910s and 1920s the men who identified themselves as part of a distinct category of men primarily on the basis of their homosexual interest rather than their womanlike gender identity and self-presentation usually called themselves *queer.* They rejected the terms *fairy* and *pansy* (commonly used for feminine men). Both *queer* and *fairy* referred to the sexually receptive partner and stood in contrast to *normal,* a category that included *trade,* males who, though available as insertors to be serviced, preferred sex with women or told their male sexual partners that they did. Chauncey asserts that *gay* began to be used in the 1920s and began to catch on in the late 1930s: "By the late 1940s, younger gay men were chastising older men who still used *queer,* which the younger men regarded as demeaning" (*Gay New York,* p. 19). Typically, the earlier history was unknown to a new generation: "Younger men rejected *queer* as a pejorative name that others had given them," rather than having been advanced to distinguish masculine men from *fairies.* Even for those involved in male-male sex, the gender-variant sense of *fairy* had seeped into what had been the contrasting term *queer.* The then-young generation wanted to narrow their contrast with *normal* and to downplay effeminacy as an inextricable part of homosexuality: "In calling themselves *gay,* a new generation of men insisted on the right to name themselves, to claim their status as men, and to reject the 'effeminate' styles of the older generation" (p. 19).

Similarly, the hero of the gay-affirmative 1933 novel *Better Angel* specified his objection to the term *homosexual:*

> "I don't like that word."
>
> "It's highly scientific."
>
> "Oh, I know that, but it makes me sound like a biological freak of some sort—to be classed with morons and cretins and paranoiacs"
>
> (cited in Meeker, p. 174).

Movement Language

After World War II, *gay* and *homosexual* continued to be used for both men and women, but when the homophile movement developed in the 1950s, new terms came into use. Under an ancient Greek aegis, the Daughters of Bilitis served as a euphemism for (the already euphemistic) "lesbian" in the name of the first American female homophile group. *Bilitis* was appropriated from nineteenth-century lesbian-themed French poetry (written by a man, Pierre Louys, in the poem "Chansons de Bilitis").The first sustained male homophile group used the similarly obscure label *mattachine,* a kind of European masked dancer, when it named itself the Mattachine Society. *Daughters of Bilitis* and *Mattachine* were used within and for the homophile movement; *gay* continued to be the favored popular term. Meanwhile, in the late 1940s David O. Cauldwell was the first American to use the term *transsexual* to refer to a person who wanted to change their sex surgically.

In the early 1970s, gay liberationists more forcefully rejected the term *homosexual,* breaking with what they perceived as the abjection-embracing reformers of the earlier homophile movement and the medical experts who had coined *homosexuality.* Some elders, however, sneered at the desexualization of *gay* and others decried erasing differences between outlaw/rebel *queers* and *straights* (persons conventional in all ways, including heterosexual partnering). One letter-writer to *Fag Rag* complained in 1977 that "movement gays want to persuade people that *gay* is a 'homosexual whose heterosexuality is expressed through homosexuality'." In this same period, lesbian feminists criticized the use of *gay* and *homosexual* for women and pressed for the use of terms (such as lesbian) that distinguished women from men.

Valorizing general nonconformity beyond identification with homosexuality was central to the challenge by a younger generation who attempted to reclaim and revalue *queer* during the 1990s. Although fashionable in academia, where claims about inclusively and transformations of negative meanings are common, on the streets and playgrounds of America *queer* continues to be a slur, in particular a slur on apparent departures from gender orthodoxy. The venerable conflation of gender unorthodoxy and same-sex sexual desire has also seeped into the use of *gay* by children and adolescents as a general-purpose insult. Similarly, in its international diffusion, the word *gay,* borrowed to differentiate "modern"/egalitarian homosexuality from traditional heterogender homosexuality, often devolves into being a new synonym for the gender-variant participant in same-sex relations.

Hostile Terms

The labels so far mentioned range from pejorative ones deployed primarily by those hostile to homosexual relations (*abomination, sodomite*) through originally hostile terms taken up by those involved in homosexual relations (*homosexual, lesbian, queer, dyke*) to those proposed by those involved in homosexual relations (*gay, Uranian, Dorian*).

There are many more derogations, including ethnically specific ones such as the African American *punk* (for weak, dominated males sexually used by more aggressive and masculine males called *jockers/wolves* in prison argot) and *bull-dagger* (for a bulky and masculine woman impaling others with dildos or with a protruding clitoris). Derogatory Hispanic terms include *maricón* (for weak, dominated, and sexually used males), *marimacho* (a macho María, for a mannish lesbian), and *cachapera* (for a female who splits open female sex partners). In Spanish, the gender-conventional sexual partner often goes unlabeled, though labels do exist and include *mayate* and *vampirio,* for masculine males who are "serviced" by males, and *tortillera* (making tortillas is a metaphor for rubbing together, a widely shared view of what two lesbians must do together in bed perpetuated in a culture that has difficulty conceiving of "sex" that does not involve a penis).

Within postwar homosexual networks and subcultures, particularly gay bars, a large lexicon of disparagements for the specialized tastes of gay men developed. The *x* + *queen* construction was and is particularly generative, with *x* being a metaphor for the kind of male the queen seeks. For example, the "chicken" queen desires the young, the "rice" queen desires Asians and Pacific Islanders, the "dinge" queen desires black-skinned partners, the "potato" queen desires white-skinned partners, and the "size" queen desires men with large penises. That construction also extended to passions other than a particular "type" of sex partner, for example, *drama queen* for those who makes every event and relationship in "her" life a major dramatic production, *fire queen* for activists (metaphorically on fire to bring about better regard and treatment for homosexuals), and *opera queen* for those with an inordinate fascination (in the view of the labeler) for opera (and usually for diva sopranos). Many terms disparaging particular ethnicities have been attested, including *boogaloo* for eager-to-dance blacks, *Nubian* for subservient blacks, *Samurai Sue* for gay Japanese males, *flip* for Filipinos (with the connotation of being easily flipped into a sexually receptive position), and so forth. *Breeder* is a contemptuous term for heterosexuals (including those who have not procreated); *pussy-pusher* is a more graphic sneer at heterosexual males that may have been inspired by *fudge-packer,* a straight (and prototypically black) sneer at an anal penetrator (*fudge* being slang for feces).

Although many of the pejorative labels that were flung about by *queens* of the preliberation era have fallen into disuse, most of the somewhat or very contemptuous labels still in use date back to that time. As the foreword to *The Queens' Vernacular* put it, the flamboyant and often hostile lexicon was "the street poetry of queens, . . . invented, coined, dished, and shrieked by the gay stereotypes," those who could not or would not *pass* (for straight). Those who were *out* (of the closet) were very aware of and resentful toward others regularly engaging in same-sex sex who *passed* and avoided the high price of harassment and most of the public stigma borne by the obvious queens and dykes. Pretensions—especially pretensions to superiority by males who sought male sexual partners and who looked and acted straight—were vigorously shredded in sneering comments from queens.

Wit and verbal agility were highly valued in queenly circles and were turned on straight harassers as well as on those who sought to pass as straight. In contrast, dykes got into fistfights with those verbally disrespecting them and their partnerships with femme females. Dyke verbal agility was not distinctively valued (either by femmes or by other butches). The normative model of a dyke was strong, silent, and able to prevail in physical fights. (Already in 1941 Legman attributed the relative paucity of lesbian slang to a "tradition of gentlemanly restraint among lesbians [that] stifles the flamboyance and conversational cynicism in sexual matters that slang coinage requires" [p. 1156].) Protected by their butches, the femmes did not need to fire back disparagements. Wit and verbal agility was similarly not a part of the role of the "real man" who was desired and sometimes snared by queens (but who often disappointed the queens when they were physically attacked). Seeming to be slow in comprehension and not skilled at verbal retorts was part of the *trade* role. Such *catches* were desired for unspoiled/"natural" masculinity and scoffed at as "unevolved" by those with highly developed repartee skills who sometimes wanted their mouths stuffed with more tangible objects than witty barbs.

Dichotomies of Sexual Behavior

The dichotomization *fem[me]/butch* for the gendered appearance of lesbian pairs seems to have originated among participants in lesbian bar culture. That sexual conduct does not necessarily follow heterosexual analogs, however, is clear from the characterization "butch in the streets, femme in the sheets." Gay men similarly seem to have made the distinction between dominating/penetrating *tops* and submissive/penetrated *bottoms*. Contrary to the fantasies of some seeking to be penetrated by hypermasculine thugs, however, those who look masculine are not necessarily tops, and those in drag frequently report topping males who are masculine in appearance and heterosexual in self-identification. The term *versatile* has long been adopted by those who are not committed to being either tops or bottoms (*activos* or *pasivos* in Spanish, with *gay* having the meaning of sexual versatility).

Changing Terms for Lesbians

At least for a time during the late 1970s and early 1980s apogee of lesbian feminism, it was widely considered archaic to present oneself as *butch* or *femme* or to seek a partner who was butch or femme. The word *dyke* temporarily fell out of use in politically correct circles (joking about "political correctness" seems to have begun among lesbians laughing at themselves or their slightly more zealous *sisters*). Changing terms (history to *herstory*, women to *wimmin*) was also embraced as a political project (or in place of political projects) by believers in linguistic determinism. In this period there were also feminist women who called themselves *lesbian* and *woman-identified* but who did not have sex with other women. Such women were classified by women who had sex with other women as *political lesbians*, and the large rank of women who later renounced college-age lesbian identification have been dubbed *hasbyterians* (abbreviating "has been lesbian" plus the suffix -ian for a class of persons).

Ways of Speaking

Research on language and homosexuality published before 1970 was almost entirely vocabulary lists without consideration of who used or understood the argot of the underworld/subculture. Research slowly turned toward use of a specialized lexicon and eventually to how homosexual identity and desire were performed by whom and to whom. In a path-breaking 1970 article, Julia Stanley argued that "homosexual slang" beyond a few basic terms was unknown to many of those heavily or even exclusively involved in same-sex sexual relations. Women who had sexual relationships with women but did not go to gay bars were especially unlikely to know most of the terms. From this, Stanley concluded that there was not a distinct speech community of all homosexuals. Stanley also stressed that there were particular terms used by some (especially queens) in ways that were unintelligible to most straights, and that there were standard ways to generate new terms. *Noun* + *noun* combinations are particularly common with rhyming components regarded as especially felicitous (e.g., *fag hag, frou-frou*); truncation is recurrent (e.g., *DiFi* for San Francisco politician Dianne Feinstein, *bi* for "bisexuals"); and the diminutive *-ette* (e.g., in *dykette*) is applied to nouns beyond the loanwords from French that arrived already having the suffix.

LGBT Ways of Speaking

It is widely supposed (and not just by straight people) that gay males speak at a higher pitch than straight males, that lesbians speak at a lower pitch than straight women, and that the range of pitches (intonational contour) is similarly greater among gay men than among straight men and lesser among lesbians than among straight women. Although research has failed to sustain such hypotheses, some intonational patterns are heard as "gay" or "lesbian" by hostile others and are produced to make characters in mass media representations register as gay or lesbian, especially the stereotypical *screaming queen* (the "scream" referring more to pitch than to volume). Lisping is also culturally coded as effeminate (and homosexual) to the extent that native speakers of Spanish from Mexico hear native speakers of Spanish from Spain as *faggy* because of Spanish speech patterns that sound like lisping to Mexicans. A more generalized "sounding mannish" stereotypes some females as *dykes*.

During the 1970s, some feminist scholars such as Robin Lakoff posited the existence of "woman's language," which she argued was characterized by various features such as using tag questions (transforming a statement into a request for confirmation by appending "right?" or something similar to the end). Examination of the speech of men and women found some men using the features more than some women. The propounders of the "woman's language" thesis failed to address the way sexuality is read into what is regarded as crossing from conventionally gendered speech patterns, so that a man using what is stereotypically feminine language is assumed to be gay and a woman who "talks like a man" is perceived as lesbian. Most proponents retreated from claiming distinctive features to tabulating higher frequencies for these features among women than among men; in other words, they retreated from making categorical claims and made statistical ones instead.

Lesbian and gay language scholars similarly sought to find and categorize lesbian ways of speaking and "gayspeak," especially any that seemed to promote group solidarity rather than castigate fellow sufferers of society's denigration of homosexuals. The project was daunting for lesbian separatists trying to identify a distinct "mother tongue." Dorothy Painter concluded that "lesbians do not possess a repertory of verbal and nonverbal cues they can explicate or knowingly use to interpret lesbianism" (p. 73).

Though she pioneered in questioning the universality and uniqueness of "homosexual slang," Stanley sought to celebrate women bonding through a shared and distinguishable way of speaking ("mother wit") even while acknowledging that its distinctness was not conceived by most lesbians, that many did not participate in it, and that intentions were frequently misunderstood (not just jokes failing): "Some of those lesbians who fail to recognize lesbian humor as such fail to do so because they lack awareness of themselves as a community with shared experiences" (p. 305). (Understanding this statement required the background knowledge of the lesbian feminist project to change the social world rather than to describe the existing one, and to raise the consciousness of the mass of lesbians who lacked the vanguard's sense of how social relations should be arranged.)

Objections to Joseph Hayes's 1976 positing of "gayspeak" were less utopian. Hayes tried to incorporate both the politically hypercorrect ways gay liberationists influenced by lesbian feminism spoke and the wildly politically incorrect (or parodistic) ways traditional queens spoke into a singular "gayspeak." This made describing and analyzing a distinctive way of speaking particularly difficult, though the two could be considered two separate registers in which some gay men spoke with each other. The more fundamental problem, as James Darsey pointed out, was that none of the ways of speaking identified as "gayspeak" was "exclusively a product of the gay subculture, or universal within that subculture. . . . Hayes fails to provide us with any words or word patterns that have a constant function and usage across settings which might illuminate something uniquely and universally gay" (p. 63). Those who command the queenly register do not always talk that way; many openly gay men (and almost all lesbians) never do; and some straight men and women do. Even within the ranks of gay rights advocates, there is a divide between assimilationists who argue that "we're just like straight people, except for what we do in bed" and romantics who see gay specialness, a distinctive "gay sensibility," or even a special mission to challenge conventions of all sort (not just sexual and gender ones).

Language to Promote Community

As for challenges to using the term *community*, the standard for a gay or a lesbian way of speaking seems to be unfairly elevated. Not all of the words in what is labeled "the English language" are known to all speakers. Moreover, much of the lexicon and the particular sounds used in English are also used in other languages. Nor is the prototypical subject-verb-object order unique to English. Still the range of sound, knowledge of specialized lexicon, and syntactic and pragmatic devices (ways of constructing sentences and of communicating) among gay or lesbian speakers of English do not differ substantially from the range among straight speakers of English. The same is true for speakers of other languages. Lesbians and gays use the same language devices to signal solidarity and to cooperate in building coherence in conversation as straights do. A distinctive "gay English" is dubious and there is probably more similarity in the ways of speaking of American Masons (to take a somewhat secret organization historically famous for covert signals of membership) than among those who consider themselves *gay* or those who consider themselves *lesbian*. Claims about ways of speaking that are recognized by participants continue, despite the lack of objective features.

During the 1970s, many supposed that queen-speak would disappear, that it was a self-hating response to external oppression, so that both were destined for oblivion as oppression ended. LGB movement activists criticized the perceived misogyny of using "she" in reference by queens to gay males (especially ridiculing those striving not to appear feminine). Such denigrations were also abhorrent to *clones*, whose simulation (or parody) of hypermasculinity devalued verbal display and who developed elaborate nonverbal codes (placement of key rings, placement and colors of handkerchiefs in back pockets) for communicating specific kinds of desire (and, coincidentally, gay identity) on the streets and in discos where the music was too loud for conversation. *Clones* undertook much of the style, including the nonarticulateness of *trade*, without pretending to be uninterested in having sex with men and sought homogender (butch-butch) relations and relationships. The "bitchy" speech style did not, however, disappear, and the general exhortation to "accept being who you are" eventually extended to those who enjoyed and excelled at camp humor. Those men with exaggerated feminine features were reconceptualized as fearless social critics of the naturalness of gender (performing the glamour and toughness of women who excelled in "a man's world" rather than stereotypically feminine demureness and domesticity) rather than as perpetuators of denigration of women.

The Celebration of Queenspeak

"Queenspeak" has not died out and it is now celebrated as part of the academic fascination with gender as the key to most everything, including homosexuality and "gay language." Similarly, a revival and rationalization of femme/butch lesbian relationships emerged after some years of insisting on abandoning or transcending role dichotomization among (homogender) woman-loving/woman-identified women. Like the once demonized *queens*, the lesbian *butches* and *femmes* (present and past) were reconceptualized at playing with and parodying gender rather than being victims of false consciousness.

Linguistics

The science of linguistics that differentiated itself from the study of literature during the decades between the World War I and the launching of Sputnik focused primarily on the patternings of sound contrasts in particular languages (for example, the contrast between "vat" and "bat" that does not register with monolingual speakers of Spanish). No one has ever maintained that LGBT speakers differ from non-LGBT speakers in the significant sound contrasts (phonology) of their language. Similarly, although as already noted, some ways of (re)forming words are more used by gay or by transgender persons, most of the words they use are performed, that is, already in use (albeit a few with somewhat different meanings).There is not a distinctive morphology unique to transgender, lesbian, or gay persons.

American linguistics, funded as never before by the National Defense Act following the Soviet satellite Sputnik's launch, turned from phonology and morphology to syntax, the study of sentence-formation. Gay English is as much an SOV (subject-object-verb) order language as the English of straight people. There are no syntactical patterns unique to LGBT speakers or any serious claims of syntactical specialties by any category of the nonheterosexual. Insofar as there is an LGBT linguistics, it is concerned with specialist vocabulary and with performing identity in speech, especially with performing in covert ways recognized by the like-minded. Performativity is a concept developed by British speech-act philosopher John Austin and deployed particularly to ways of doing gender (with a special focus on those performing a gender discordant with their natal sex) in the theorizing of Judith Butler and others. The most influential American linguist, Noam Chomsky, has always cast the variabilites of "performance" by individuals or by those included in any social categories as outside linguistics, the latter being the study of underlying syntactic principles (and phonological and morphological principles, though these are not separate levels in Chomskian linguistics). Thus, there is no LGBT linguistics within the dominant tradition of what is "linguistics." In the Chomskian view, what LGBT linguists analyze is "only performance" and thus not worth consideration.

Intra-language variability by social categories has been central to sociolinguistics and some linguists have dubbed their study of language use "pragmatics" (a "level" above syntax). The results of inquiry by sociolinguists and scholars of communication are drawn on in discussions of LGBT "ways of speaking." Although bisexual ways of speaking would seem an interesting topic for those asserting distinctive or recognizable gay/lesbian ways of speaking, little research has examined three categories of sexual identity/orientation.

Bibliography

Chauncey, George. *Gay New York.* New York: Basic Books, 1994.

Darsey, James. "'Gayspeak': a response." In *Gayspeak.* Edited by James Chesebro. New York: Pilgrim Press, 1981.

Dynes, Wayne R. *Homolexis.* New York: Gay Academic Union, 1995.

Hayes, Joseph J. "Gayspeak." *Quarterly Journal of Speech* 62 (1976): 256–626.

Hofstader, Richard. *The Paranoid Style in American Politics.* New York: Knopf, 1966.

Kulick, Don. "Gay and Lesbian Language." *Annual Review of Anthropology 29* (2000): 243–325.

Kulick, Don. "Transgender and Language." *GLQ* 5 (1999): 605–22.

Lakoff, Robin T. "Language and Woman's Place." *Language in Society* 2 (1973): 45–79.

Leap, William L. *Word's Out: Gay Men's English.* Minneapolis: University of Minnesota Press, 1996.

Legman, Gershorn. "The Language of Homosexuality: An American Glossary." Appendix to George W. Henry, *Sex Variants.* New York: Hoeber, 1941.

Meeker, Richard [Forman Brown]. *Better Angel.* Boston: Alyson, 1990 [1933].

Murray, Stephen O. "Stigma Transformation and Relexification in the International Diffusion of *Gay.*" In *Beyond the Lavender Lexicon.* Edited by William Leap. New York: Gordon & Breach, 1995.

Murray, Stephen O. *Theory Groups in the Study of Language in North America.* Amsterdam: Benjamins, 1994.

Nestle, Joan. "Butch-fem Relationships." *Heresies* 12 (1981):21–24.

Painter, Dorothy S. "Recognition Among Lesbians in Straight Settings." In *Gayspeak.* Edited by James Chesebro. New York: Pilgrim Press, 1981.

Rogers, Bruce. *The Queens' Vernacular.* San Francisco: Straight Arrow Books, 1972.

Roscoe, Will. *Changing Ones: Third and Fourth Genders in Native North America.* New York: St. Martin's Press, 1998.

Stanley, Julia P. "Homosexual Slang." *American Speech* 45 (1970):45-59.

Stanley, Julia P., and Susan Robbins. "Mother Wit." In *Lavender Culture*. Edited by Karla Jay and Allan Young. New York: Jove, 1979.

Weston, Kathy. *Render Me, Gender Me*. New York: Columbia University Press, 1997.

Stephen O. Murray

LATINAS AND LATINOS

The U.S. Census Bureau estimates that by 2005, "Hispanics," including "Black Hispanics," will be the largest ethnic/racial group in the United States after non-Hispanic whites. Thus, it is likely that LGBT Latinas and Latinos (people of Latin American and Hispanic Caribbean descent) will also be the largest LGBT ethnic/racial group after non-Hispanic whites.

The many terms used by Latinas and Latinos to identify themselves vary according to cultural and political identity, degree of assimilation, and other factors. Some are umbrella terms like "Latina" and "Latino" (which may or may not include people from Brazil) and the official government term "Hispanic." Other terms are specific to the country of origin (i.e., Peruvian, Guatemalan). Some people of Mexican descent who were born in the United States prefer the term "Chicana/o," while some Puerto Ricans refer to themselves as *Boricuas*. Often left out of the mix are LGBT people of Afro/Latina/o, Asian/Latina/o, Judeo/Latina/o, and multicultural descent. Spanish terms (including pejorative ones) for LGBT identities vary from country to country and include *joto, maricón, pato, tortillera, marimacha, de ambiente, mariposa, manflora, del otro lado, transvesti,* and *cachapera*.

Issues

The complex of cultural, political, and personal issues faced by LGBT Latinas and Latinos includes the homophobia, transphobia, classism, and colorism of non-LGBT Latinas/Latinos; the racism and classism of LGBT whites; lateral prejudice and classism from other people of color; and classism and colorism within LGBT Latina/Latino communities. Latina lesbians must also deal with sexism in GBT and non-GBT communities of all ethnicities. Also relevant are the ways in which an individual's family relates to her or his LGBT identity and the ways in which the larger world relates to an individual's language ability and immigration status. In analyzing the Latina/Latino LGBT experience, one must consider race, class, sexuality, and gender in relation to many other variables, such as where an individual grew up, how long she or he has been in the United States, what the ethnicities of her or his parents are, how much formal education the individual has, and so forth. (For an identity model that considers a number of these permutations, see Yolanda Retter's "Identity Development of Lifelong vs. Catalyzed Latina Lesbians" [1987].)

Identity

In the introduction to *Compañeras: Latina Lesbians,* Mariana Romo Carmona explains, "For many of us the process of acquiring an identity as a lesbian is closely tied to coming to terms with our racial and cultural identity" (Ramos, p. xxii). The same has been the case for GBT people. Attempts by white LGBT people to use an ethnic analogy to explain the oppression of all LGBT people are often met with the argument that the structural power differentials associated with race, class, and gender are asymmetrically different from those associated with LGBT identity.

The literature on identity issues among LGBT Latinas/Latinos includes published and unpublished material by Hilda Hidalgo (1984), Edward Morales (1983), Oliva Espin (1987), and Retter (1987). Because of Latino cultural attitudes toward women, some lesbians like writer Cherríe Moraga negotiate the stresses of identity development, sexism, and misogyny by gravitating toward a butch persona and assuming a malelike stance toward other women (Almaguer, p. 268). Moraga says that at first "I didn't really think of myself as female or male. I thought of myself as this hybrid or something" (Almaguer, p. 268). Activist and writer Jeanne Córdova felt a similar incongruity until her butchness met feminism: "I wasn't cut out to be a girl. Before feminism came along and said 'girls can be anything they want to be,' I had no mental options save thinking I was a boy" (p. 274). She continues, "My parents and Catholicism had taught me to accept the gender dichotomy. By this definition, my little girl-bodied, male-behaving self was 'sick.' Feminism healed the contradictions of my life" (pp. 280–282).

Latina lesbian activists seem to be more accepting of femme/butch culture than their white feminist counterparts and Latina femmes (some of whom identify as bisexual) seem to struggle less with sexual identity issues than Latina butches do. Almaguer has proposed some reasons why many Chicanos do not readily identify as LGBT:

> Chicanos have never occupied the social space where a gay or lesbian identity can readily become a primary basis for self-identity. This is due in part to their structural position at the subordinate ends of both the class and racial hierarchies and in a context where ethnicity remains a primary basis for group identity and survival. They are not as free

> as individuals situated elsewhere in the social structure to redefine their sexual identity in ways that contravene the imperatives of minority family life and its traditional gender expectations. (p. 264)

Gender expectations lead some segments of Latin American and U.S. Latino culture to divide men who have sex with men into *pasivos* and *activos;* the former are *jotos* (homosexual/passive/femalelike) while the latter are *chingones* (aggressive/virile/not homosexual). Some of the consequences of this dichotomy and the sexism prevalent in Latino culture are that *pasivos* are devalued, while *activos,* who may deny their homosexual activities, practice unsafe sex, and be in relationships with women, put their female partners at risk for HIV and other sexually transmitted diseases.

Racism

LGBT Latinas/Latinos are both the targets and perpetrators of race-based prejudice. Due to racism in white-dominated LGBT organizations and projects, people of color often stay away from these groups. Racism in personal relationships is another issue. Most LGBT people of color have experienced the problematic behavior of white "color collectors," who exoticize people of color and intentionally seek them out as sexual partners. In discussing this dynamic, Almaguer has argued that "class coded lust reflects the middle class white or Latino man's colonial desire for the *pasivo.*" Meanwhile the *activo* is exoticized as a "potent ethnic masculinity that titillates the middle class white man who then plays the passive role" (Almaguer, p. 265).

A variation of racist practices is found in *colorism,* a complex dynamic whereby many Latinas/Latinos look more favorably upon their light-skinned brethren, while many Anglos favor darker-skinned Latinas/Latinos. In cross-cultural encounters and relationships, the effects and stereotypes of centuries of colonialism and power differentials (what Almaguer calls a "hierarchy of dominance and submission") are often at play and yet are frequently ignored. Although Latina lesbian literature consistently affirms that gender, sexuality, race, and class are inextricably intertwined, white lesbian feminists focus on sexism as the root oppression and ignore how power relations related to race, ethnicity, and class affect women of color. Latino GBT people face similar problems in white-dominated GBT movements where sexual orientation is the focus.

Religion and *Familia*

Many LGBT Latinas/Latinos come from a Roman Catholic (or, increasingly, a fundamentalist Christian) tradition. Historically, the homophobia and misogyny of the Roman Catholic Church requires that women be subservient, a notion that many Latina lesbians have resisted. In Retter's study, one respondent comments on this dual oppression: "The culture valued males and undervalued females; the role that women play in relation to men was not acceptable [to me; there was] a conscious rejection of that role; I felt the Catholic church was extremely invested in womyn being subservient—a part of me always turned away from handing my power over" (Retter 1987, p. 117).

Bésame Mucho. The cover of a 1999 book of "New Gay Latino Fiction," edited by Jaime Manrique with Jesse Dorris. **[Latinfocus.com]**

Catholics like Maria Dolores Díaz and Jeanne Córdova followed their spiritual inclinations into the convent but left after realizing that these communities of women were too closely tied to the hierarchy and misogyny of the Vatican. They found another kind of community as lesbian activists in Los Angeles. However, the Roman Catholic Church exerts long and deep influence, and feelings of guilt and sinfulness are common among LGBT Latinas and Latinos who are trying to come to terms with their sexual and gender identities. Religion and *familia* are cornerstones of many Latina/o psyches and rejection by one or both of these institutions has significant effects on LGBT people. One respondent in the Retter study notes, "When *familia* rejects us it is devastating, because we are brought up to think that *familia* is forever" (Retter 1987, p. 114).

Sometimes, to avoid shaming their families, LGBT Latinas and Latinos choose to leave home. One U.S.-born gay man of Mexican descent explains, "I would never want to hurt my parents so I left my hometown so they won't find out" (Kirk, p. B3).

Misogyny and Sexism

Heterosexual commitment by a Latina to a Latino is interpreted as proof of her fidelity to her people. Thus, lesbianism challenges the foundation of *la familia* and *La Raza* (the race). Those women who do not adhere to the culture's gender norms are considered traitors and become targets for the kind of collective animus aimed at "La Malinche" (an Indian woman who by force or choice consorted with Hernando Cortés and who was later attacked as a betrayer of her people). In Chicano movement groups during the 1960s and 1970s, independent women were held in check by others who called them "lesbians," "*vendidas*" (sellouts), and "traitors" to *La Raza.* Thus Moraga, who is of Chicana/Anglo descent, explains, "Resisting sex roles . . . was far easier in an Anglo context than in a Chicano one" (Almaguer, p. 267).

Other perceived transgressors include women whose calling is outside the bounds of motherhood. Emma Pérez and Deena González were two of the first U.S. Latinas to earn Ph.D.s in history. For several decades, as both Latinas and lesbians, they have served as role models, mentors, and multi-issue advocates. Like a number of other strong Latinas, they have at times been the target of homophobic attacks by Latina/Latino colleagues. Pérez calls these behaviors "invasive or invasionary politics [that] are most often practiced under the guise of sisterhood or brotherhood" (Pérez, p. 110). Even in male-dominated LGBT Latino groups, Latina lesbians must choose to overlook the sexism of their *hermanos* (brothers) in favor of the benefits and leverage that larger numbers can bring. Others choose to form Latina lesbian groups and then work in alliance with a variety of LGBT and non-LGBT lesbian, cogender, and progressive groups. Although few lesbians of color identify as lesbian separatists, Juana Maria Paz and Naomi Littlebear Morena both contributed to the lesbian separatist anthology *For Lesbians Only* (1988) and one Latina lesbian separatist was a panelist on the *Oprah Winfrey Show* in 1988.

Homophobia and Transphobia

Before and after the Stonewall Riots of 1969, LGBT people worked in Latina/Latino causes such as César Chávez's farm workers' movement, but many, with good reason, stayed in the closet. Frank Mendiola helped organize a number of boycotts against growers who exploited farm workers. His good relations with another organizer couple soured after they learned that he was gay. In her study of Puerto Rican lesbians, Hilda Hidalgo found that there were many closeted lesbians in leadership positions in major Puerto Rican organizations (p. 110).

Feelings toward those who contravene cultural expectations are harsh and can be inferred from how Latinas/Latinos in a 1992 poll ranked LGBT people. Mexicans and Cubans in the United States ranked lesbians and gays as the fourth most disliked group after communists, Nazis, and the Ku Klux Klan. Puerto Ricans ranked them as third most disliked (21 percent) since only 10 percent disliked Nazis (Aponte/Merced, p. 300). These attitudes have proven lethal to some LGBT Latinas and Latinos. In 1980 Fred Paez, a gay activist investigating police brutality in Houston, was shot in the back of the head and his death was ruled an accident. Ana Maria Rosales was murdered in front of a Washington, D.C., gay bar in 1993, while Eddie Araujo, a seventeen-year-old transgender youth, was murdered in California in 2003. Some, like California high school student Alana Flores, have successfully fought back. Flores was a plaintiff in a lawsuit that in 2003 won the right for LGBT students to be protected from harassment at school. She was the only plaintiff willing to reveal her name.

In spite of widespread homophobia and transphobia in the Latina/Latino community, some non-LGBT Latina and Latino notables have been publicly supportive, thus helping to reduce negative attitudes. César Chávez spoke at the 1987 March on Washington for Lesbian and Gay Rights, and show host Cristina Saralegui has helped raise consciousness about Latina/Latino LGBT issues on her popular television show *"El Show de Cristina."* Collaborative and supportive relationships between LGBT Latina/Latino and non-LGBT Latina/Latino groups and organizations have developed more slowly. Martha Duffer, the executive director of ALLGO (Austin Latina/o Lesbian Gay, Bisexual and Transgender Organization), has noted that mainstream Latino groups hesitate to align with LGBT Latinas and Latinos because they fear alienating homophobic sectors of their constituencies. As an example, in 2003 *Hispanic Magazine* ran a cover story on Cuban American playwright Nilo Cruz (who is "out") and who won the first Pulitzer Prize awarded to a Latino. The article did not mention that he is gay.

Immigration

The late sociologist Lionel Cantú points out in an article on gay and lesbian immigration that "immigration restrictions and exclusions are organized along five distinct but intersecting dimensions: race, class, gender, ideology and sexuality" (p. 446). Research on the exclusion of LGBT people seeking to immigrate to the United States has been carried out by, among others, ethnic studies scholar Eithne Luibheid, who has examined "the organization of sexual monitoring at the United States–Mexican border," focusing on the case of Sara Harb Quiroz, who was deported from the United States in the early 1960s for "looking like a lesbian" (p. 477).

While LGBT immigrants may come to the United States for economic or political reasons, they may also come because of their sexual orientation or gender identity. They may wish to avoid shaming their families or may want to escape from violent homophobia and transphobia in their countries. In 1980, when Cuba's president Fidel Castro announced that he would allow open emigration, an estimated 10,000 self-identified lesbians and gays left Cuba. Until the late 1980s, the U.S. Immigration and Naturalization Service (INS) did not consider sexual orientation a valid reason for granting asylum. In 1986 a Houston judge barred the INS from deporting a gay Cubano who claimed that were he returned to Cuba he would be persecuted due to his sexual orientation. In 1990 the INS suspended its policy of barring LGBT people who declared an LGBT identity. Three years later, a San Francisco judge granted the asylum petition of a gay Brazilian. In 1994 the INS granted asylum to a gay Mexicano, and Attorney General Janet Reno announced that LGBT people could henceforth qualify for asylum status. However, since 1987 people who are HIV positive cannot immigrate to the United States and, while exceptions are made for non-transgender heterosexual spouses, no such exemption exists for LGB and known-transgender partners and spouses.

Health

LGBT Latinas and Latinos may lack the ability to access health care due to their immigration status and may lack health insurance due to their economic status. Some may avoid health care providers due to a fear of homophobic, transphobic, and racist attitudes. Research and outreach are slowly changing the attitudes of non-LGBT care providers and health organizations. Recent examples include Roland(o) Palencia, a former Gay and Lesbian Latinos Unidos president who has served as the director of Clinica Monseñor Oscar Romero in Los Angeles. Clinica is one of few sources of medical care for noninsured Latina/os in Los Angeles. Another is the March of Dimes, which chose a Latina lesbian couple and their twins (who were born prematurely) as its Ambassador Family for 2003.

AIDS has had a deep impact on the GBT Latino community. In 2000 the rate of AIDS among Latinos was 22.5 per 100,000 (representing 19 percent of U.S. AIDS cases at a time when Latinos were 13 percent of the U.S. population). According to one study, socioeconomic status and sexual orientation are contributing factors to these rates. According to Erika Hayasaki, "Gay Latino men living in poverty and subjected to racism and homophobia are more likely to engage in high-risk sexual behavior and have higher rates of HIV" (2001). Programs to provide culturally sensitive services to Latina/os dealing with HIV/AIDS include Proyecto Contra Sida Por Vida (PCPV) in San Francisco and Bienestar in Southern California.

Mixed Agendas

Most Latina/Latino LGBT people do not separate their ethnic identity from their LGBT identity. Playwright Luis Alfaro recalls being asked, "Are you a gay Latino or a Latino gay?" His response: "As if these parts of oneself could be separated" (Glitz). The pluralistic agenda of LGBT Latinas/Latinos is problematic for white-dominated LGBT groups. Martha Duffer notes that "Mainstream [LGBT] groups are not interested in working with people of color beyond tokenism, particularly when [they bring in] economic and other social justice issues, which [mainstream LGBT groups] tend to mistakenly believe to be unrelated to their focus" (Smith, 2003). Recently, the National Latina/Latino Lesbian, Gay, Bisexual and Transgender Organization (LLEGÓ) was the only LGBT organization to attempt significant outreach to Latinos in Dade County, Florida, where an anti-LGBT measure was on the ballot. Although the measure was defeated in 2002, 62.9 percent of Latinos voted in favor of it. Martin Ornelas-Quintero, LLEGÓ's executive director, notes that the same pattern (a lack of outreach to Latinos on the part of other LGBT organizations) was seen in California, where the anti–same-sex marriage Knight Initiative easily won in 2000.

Some Latinas/Latinos have resolved these political and cultural conflicts and paradoxes by choosing to work in multi-issue organizations that are LGBT friendly. Olga Vives, a Cubana, has worked in the National Organization for Women (NOW) where she can focus on the mix of issues that affect her life as a "Latina, immigrant, mother and lesbian from the Midwest" (Smith, 2002). In 2000 she was elected NOW Vice President of Action. She says she "sees the needs of Latinas-Latinos as extending beyond a unilateral focus on LGBT issues" (Smith, 2002).

As white-dominated LGBT groups have developed a need to gain support from people of color in governmental and non-governmental organizations, they have sought help from LGBT Latinas and Latinos. Ingrid Durán, the leader of the Congressional Hispanic Caucus Institute, has been approached by LGBT groups that historically have done little outreach to LGBT people of color. One example is the Human Rights Campaign, which asked Durán to help it develop connections to people-of-color groups and lobbies on Capitol Hill. Durán also works to increase tolerance in non-LGBT Latina/Latino organizations. She helped persuade the influential National Hispanic Leadership Agenda (NHLA) to help vote LLEGÓ into NHLA.

LLEGÓ Director Martin Ornelas-Quintero notes that for LGBT and non-LGBT Latinas/Latinos, one "point of convergence" is the Permanent Partners Immigration Act. In 2003 the Mexican American Legal and Education Fund endorsed the legislation. Another point of convergence is leverage activism whereby LGBT Latinas/Latinos help elect LGBT–friendly politicians, thereby collecting political goodwill. Their support has been a key factor in several elections and appointments. Attorney and activist Elena Popp was among a group of LGBT Latinas/Latinos that helped elect former California State Assembly Speaker Antonio Villaraigosa to a seat on the Los Angeles City Council (2003). Sam Zamarripa, Georgia State Senator, acknowledged in 2002 the help he received from LGBT constituents, including the organization Latino Gay Community of Atlanta. *Ellas en Acción* helped promote the appointment of lesbian Susan Leal to the San Francisco Board of Supervisors in 1993. In Massachusetts, Jarrett Barrios put together a coalition of LGBT and non-LGBT supporters and became the first out gay Latino to be elected a state senator (2002). In New York City, Margarita López, a former housing rights organizer, was elected to the City Council (1997).

History

Without benefit of a social movement or support groups, few LGBT Latinas and Latinos before the 1970s left overt evidence of their affectional-sexual orientations or gender identities. Historians must often read between the lines of scientific, religious, legal, and photographic materials to infer the presence of LGBT Latinas/Latinos. What exists is slowly being uncovered and examined by researchers, scholars, students, and historians.

Literature on the subject includes Pablo Mitchell's exploration of an Anglo-Native gay son at the center of an Anglo-Native-Hispano family inheritance dispute in late-nineteenth and early-twentieth-century New Mexico. Mitchell uses this case to illustrate the ways that "strategic marriage and intermarriage" were central to elite Anglo and Hispano rule (p. 333). Louis Sullivan has researched the life of Jack Bee Garland (1869–1936), born Elvira Mugarrieta to a Mexican diplomat in San Francisco. Garland passed as a male, worked as a journalist during the Spanish–American War, as a nurse after the San Francisco earthquake, and with homeless men in his native city. George Chauncey's book on gay life in New York argues that, "in the 1940s and 1950s, African-Americans and Puerto Ricans would become the primary targets of sodomy prosecutions," a continuation of earlier patterns that targeted "immigrants in the poorest sections of the city" (pp. 140–141).

Marc Stein's book on Philadelphia refers to local media stories that suggested that there was a "sex angle" to the murder in 1950 of Mexican American Robert Prado; Puerto Rican men were accused, though not convicted, of the murder (p. 119). The Latina Lesbian Oral History Project at the ONE Institute and Archives (Los Angeles) includes an interview with Nancy Valverde, who remembers the 1950s as a time when Los Angeles police harassed and arrested her on numerous occasions and charged her with masquerading (not wearing the required number of articles of female clothing). According to Esther Newton's study of Cherry Grove, Fire Island, small numbers of Hispanics began coming to this LGB resort in the 1960s, but generally as "hotel and restaurant workers, entertainers, or friends/lovers of whites who were renters or property owners" (p. 154). Joanne Meyerowitz's book on the history of transsexuals mentions a late 1960s New York counseling group for female-to-male transsexuals that included several Puerto Ricans, one Colombian, and one Cuban. Horacio Roque Ramírez's study of San Francisco Queer Latinas/Latinos in San Francisco (1960s–1990s) examines the formation of LGBT/queer community, while Yolanda Retter's study of lesbian activism in Los Angeles (1970–1990) includes material on Latina lesbians. In John Preston's *Hometowns,* Jessie Monteagudo and Michael Nava reminisce about their experiences growing up gay in Miami and Sacramento.

Part of the effort to make LGBT Latina/Latino history visible includes the collection and preservation of Latina/Latino LGBT historical materials, which then must be made accessible to the public. Over the years Juanita Díaz-Cotto in New York and Yolanda Leyva in Arizona have gathered materials on Latina lesbian history. At the ONE Institute and Archives in Los Angeles,

Yolanda Retter is compiling an historical LGBT Latina/Latino database. Northeastern University sponsored an exhibit and online chronology that highlights Boston-area LGBT Latina/Latino history. A unique archive is the Berkeley-based Archivo Rodrigo Reyes, named after the late activist and artist. The Archivo includes LGBT Latino (and some Latina) photographs and ephemera from the San Francisco Bay Area, which Reyes began collecting in the 1970s. While many LGBT and non-LGBT archives and collections have some materials related to Latina/Latino LGBT history (for example, Princeton has an extensive collection on writer Reinaldo Arenas), none has a major general collection on LGBT Latinas/Latinos. Meanwhile Latina/o archives and collections fail to focus on LGBT materials. This reflects both a lack of research on the subject and a lack of interest on the part of most archives and collections.

Future Directions

LGBT Latinas/Latinos continue to struggle against prejudice within their ethnic cultures, within other LGBT communities, and within their own diverse LGBT Latina/Latino communities. These unresolved struggles are part of a collective crisis. In the first part of the twenty-first century, the melting pot mentality in the United States is still unable to process the pressures created by unassimilatable "difference." Yet adapting to the pressures created by difference is something that colonized people learned how to do long ago. Preferring acculturation to assimilation, Gloria Anzaldúa's "new *mestiza*" uses her experience of both belonging and not belonging to create new paradigms:

> As a mestiza I have no country, my homeland cast me out, yet all countries are mine because I am every woman's sister or potential lover. (As a lesbian I have no race, my own people disclaim me; but I am all races because there is the queer in me in all races). I am cultureless because as a feminist, I challenge the collective cultural/religious male-derived beliefs of Indo-Hispanics and Anglos; yet I am cultured because I am participating in the creation of yet another culture, a new story to explain the world and our participation in it. (Anzaldúa, pp. 80–81)

Bibliography

Almaguer, Tomás. "Chicano Men: A Cartography of Homosexual Identity and Behavior." In *The Lesbian and Gay Studies Reader.* Edited by Henry Abelove, Michèle Barale, and David Halperin. New York: Routledge, 1993.

Anzaldúa, Gloria. *Borderlands=La Frontera.* San Francisco: Spinters/Aunt Lute, 1987.

Aponte Parés, Luis, and Jorge Merced. "Páginas Omitidas: The Gay and Lesbian Presence." In *The Puerto Rican Movement: Voices from the Diaspora.* Edited by Andrés Torres and José Velázquez. Philadelphia: Temple University Press, 1998.

Brinkley, Sydney. "Gay Latinos, 'La Raza,' and the New 'Familia'." www.blacklightonline.com/gaylatinos.html. Retrieved 1992.

Cantú, Lionel. "Gay and Lesbian Immigration." In *Encyclopedia of American Immigration.* Edited by James Ciment. Armonk, N.Y.: M. E. Sharpe, 2001.

Chauncey, George. *Gay New York.* New York: Basic Books, 1994.

Coffman, Janet. "Gay Latinos Face Problem of Double Discrimination." *Phoenix,* 29 November 1979, p. 9.

Córdova, Jeanne. "Butches, Lies, and Feminism." In *The Persistent Desire: A Femme-Butch Reader.* Edited by Joan Nestle. Boston: Alyson, 1992.

Espin, Oliva. "Issues of Identity in the Psychology of Latina Lesbians." In *Lesbian Psychologies: Explanations and Challenges.* Edited by the Boston Lesbian Psychologies Collective. Urbana: University of Illinois Press, 1987.

Fernández, Charles. "Undocumented Aliens in the Queer Nation." *OUT/LOOK* (spring 1991): 20–23.

Glitz, Michael. "Luis Alfaro." In "Our Best and Brightest Activists: The Arts." *The Advocate,* 17 August 1999, p. 1.

Hayasaki, Erika. "Task Force Studies the Effects of Poverty and Racism on Gay Latinos." *Los Angeles Times,* 13 July 2001, np.

Hidalgo, Hilda. "The Puerto Rican Lesbian in the United States." In *Women-Identified Women.* Edited by Trudy Darty and Sandee Potter. Palo Alto, Calif.: Mayfield, 1984.

Hoagland, Lucia, and Julia Penelopee, eds. *For Lesbians Only: A Separatist Anthology.* London: Onlywoman, 1988.

Hodes, Martha, ed. *Sex, Love, Race: Crossing Boundaries in North American History.* New York: New York University Press, 1999.

Kirk, Robin. "Between Two Worlds: Gay Latinos Struggle with Their Identities."

Luibheid, Eithne. "'Looking Like a Lesbian': The Organization of Sexual Monitoring at the United States–Mexican Border." *Journal of the History of Sexuality* 8, no. 3 (1998): 477–506.

Meyerowitz, Joanne. *How Sex Changed: A History of Transsexuality in the United States.* Cambridge, Mass.: Harvard University Press, 2002.

Moraga, Cherrie. *Loving in the War Years: Lo que nunca pasó por sus labios.* 2d ed. Cambridge, Mass.: South End, 2000.

Moraga, Cherríe, and Gloria Anzaldúa, eds. *This Bridge Called My Back. Writings by Radical Women of Color.* 3d ed. Berkeley: Third Woman, 2001.

Morales, Eduardo. *Third World Gays and Lesbians: A Process of Multiple Identities.* Paper presented at the 91st APA Convention, 1983.

Newton, Esther. *Cherry Grove, Fire Island: Sixty Years in America's First Gay and Lesbian Town.* Boston: Beacon, 1993.

Pérez, Emma. "Irigaray's Female Symbolic in the Making of Chicana Lesbian *Sitios y Lenguas* (Sites and Discourses)." In *The Lesbian Postmodern.* Edited by Laura Doan. New York: Columbia University Press, 1994.

Preston, John. *Hometowns.* New York: Penguin, 1992.

Ramos, Juanita, ed. *Compàneras: Latina Lesbians.* New York: Latina Lesbian History Project, 1987.

Retter, Yolanda. "Identity Development of Lifelong vs. Catalyzed Latina Lesbians." Master's thesis, University of California, Los Angeles, 1987.

———. "On the Side of Angels: Lesbian Activism in Los Angeles, 1970–1990." Ph.D. dissertation, University of New Mexico, 1999.

Roque Ramirez, Horacio Nelson. "Communities of Desire: Queer Latina/Latino History and Memory, San Francisco Bay Area, 1960s–1990s." Ph.D. dissertation, University of California, Berkeley, 2001.

Smith, Jeniffer. "Gay Latinos Stepping Out of the Shadows." *Southern Voice,* 3 February 2003, np.

Smith, Rhonda. "From outside the Movement, Latina Lesbians Push for Change." *Southern Voice,* 1 April 2002, np.

Stein, Marc. *City of Sisterly and Brotherly Loves.* Chicago: University of Chicago Press, 2000.

Sullivan, Louis. *From Female to Male: The Life of Jack Bee Garland.* Boston: Alyson, 1990.

Yolanda Retter Vargas

See also ALARCON, FRANCISCO; ANZALDÚA, GLORIA; ARENAS, REINALDO; BACA, JUDY; BOURBON, RAY (RAE); CÓRDOVA, JEANNE; DIAZ-COTTO, JUANITA; ISLAS, ARTURO; LATINA AND LATINO STUDIES; MIGRATION, IMMIGRATION, AND DIASPORA; MORAGA, CHERRÍE; PIÑERO, MIGUEL; POMA, EDGAR; PUERTO RICO; RACE AND RACISM; RECHY, JOHN; REYES, RODRIGO; RIVERA, SYLVIA; SARRIA, JOSÉ; SOLANAS, VALERIE; TAVERA, HANK; ZULMA.

LATINA AND LATINO LGBTQ ORGANIZATIONS AND PERIODICALS

Fear of homophobic rejection by families and communities of origin has kept many LGBT Latinas and Latinos from engaging in LGBT activism, while racism has reduced LGBT Latina and Latino participation in white-dominated LGBT organizations. This historical pattern tends to obscure the presence and contributions of those LGBT Latinas and Latinos who have created and/or participated in LGBT groups and projects. In addition, the lack of coverage of issues important to LGBT people of color in the mainstream LGBT press has exacerbated problems of Latino and Latina invisibility. According to Lydia Otero, *Unidad,* the newsletter of the Gay and Lesbian Latinos Unidos in Los Angeles, was created in part "because we can't rely on the [mainstream] gay and lesbian press to document our history for us," (Podolsky, p. 6).

Homophile, Gay Liberationist, and Lesbian Feminist Activism

As the process of uncovering the history of LGBT Latinas and Latinos in the United States has progressed, evidence of an LGBT Latina and Latino presence has been found in homophile-era organizations. The first homophile group, the Mattachine Society, was formed in Los Angeles in 1950. Its New York City chapter was cofounded in 1955 by Cubano Tony Segura. When ONE, Inc., was founded in 1952, Tony Reyes, an entertainer, was a signer of the articles of incorporation. The Daughters of Bilitis (DOB), the first known U.S. lesbian organization, was founded in San Francisco (1955) by four couples, including a Chicana and her Filipina partner.

In 1961, San Francisco Cubano drag show entertainer José Sarria ran for the city's board of supervisors as an out gay man, and although he lost, he received six thousand votes. In the 1960s, Cubana Ada Bello joined DOB Philadelphia and edited first the chapter's newsletter and later the newsletter of the Homophile Action League. In the DOB, Bello used a pseudonym because she did not want to jeopardize her application for U.S. citizenship. When the Cuban Revolution proved unfriendly to homosexuals, homophile activists gathered in front of the United Nations in 1965 and staged one of the earliest public LGBT protests.

The generational marker for many LGBT baby boomers was the 1969 Stonewall Riots, and at least one Latino actively participated in that historic event. Puerto Rican–Venezuelan drag queen and transgender activist Ray (Sylvia Lee) Rivera later recalled: "To be there was so beautiful. It was so exciting. I said, 'Well, great now it's my time. I'm out there being a revolutionary for everybody else, and now it's time to do my thing for my own people'" (Rivera, p. 191). Rivera and others later formed STAR (Street Transvestite Action Revolutionaries), and decades later Rivera was credited with helping amend New York City's antidiscrimination statutes to include transgender people.

Following Stonewall, gay liberation and lesbian feminist groups proliferated, but few Latinas/Latinos (or people of color) actively participated in the new wave of white dominated groups. One exception was Gay Liberation Front Philadelphia; Kiyoshi Kuromiya, a Japanese

American, recalls that 30 percent of the membership in 1970 was Latino. In Los Angeles the Lesbian Feminists, a radical political group of the early 1970s, counted a handful of lesbians of color (including several Latinas) as members. In Oakland, California, the Third World Gay Caucus (1976) included Latinos, who sponsored a Tardeada (afternoon social event). In 1972 a group of New York Latino gay men published a Spanish language literary magazine called *Afuera.*

Early LGBT Latina and Latino Organizations

Beginning in the 1970s, LGBT Latina and Latino organizations were formed to deal with the specific concerns of Latinas and Latinos. LGBT Latina and Latino groups provide a support system and opportunities for socializing in a culturally sensitive environment as well as opportunities for learning organizing skills. Regardless of geographic location, most LGBT Latina and Latino organizations have engaged in a dual approach to activism, working on behalf of both Latina-Latino and LGBT causes.

In Los Angeles, the organizing pattern for many Latina lesbians was to join Chicano movement groups and find them to be sexist and homophobic (1960s and 1970s); move into the LGBT community and find themselves facing sexism and racism (1970s); form Latina-specific groups and collaborate with activist groups of various ethnicities and sexual orientations (1970s); join Latino and Latina LGBT cogender groups (1980s); and form a new wave of Latina lesbian groups while collaborating with LGBT, people of color, and progressive groups (1980s–2000s).

The first known LGBT Latino group in Los Angeles was Unidos, organized by Chicano Steve Jordan (also called Jordon) in 1970. Other early groups include Greater Liberated Chicanos (cofounded by Rick Reyes as Gay Latinos in 1972) and United Gay Chicanos. In Puerto Rico, Rafael Cruet and Ernie Potvin founded Comunidad de Orgullo Gay in 1974. The group published a newsletter, *Pa'fuera,* and established Casa Orgullo, a community services center. The earliest known Latina lesbian group, Latin American Lesbians, met briefly in Los Angeles in 1974. Jeanne Córdova, a lesbian of Mexican and Irish descent, joined DOB Los Angeles and transformed the chapter newsletter in the *Lesbian Tide* (1971–1980), a national publication. Although it published little material on lesbians of color, *Lesbian Tide* is arguably the newspaper of record of the lesbian feminist decade of the 1970s.

Most recovered LGBT Latina and Latino history is from urban areas. However, in the early 1970s two Latino gay men joined gay activists Harry Hay and John Burnside to fight what archivist and writer Jim Kepner called a "water rip-off scheme" in New Mexico. During the 1970s, a group of Latina lesbians negotiated an agreement that permitted them to occupy a portion of white lesbian land in Arkansas, and they named the parcel Arco Iris. Juana Maria Paz, a welfare activist, lived on that and other "womyn's" land and later wrote about her experiences.

The Late 1970s

In the late 1970s, as more LGBT people of color activist groups formed, white-dominated groups and publications began to pay some attention to LGBT people of color issues. Organizers of the founding conference of the National Lesbian Feminist Organization (NLFO, 1978) invited few women of color as delegates, but white delegates insisted that those women of color who were present (mostly Latinas from San Francisco and Los Angeles) be credentialed as delegates. The reconstituted delegate body approved a measure declaring that half the seats on the NLFO Steering Committee must be lesbians of color of diverse class backgrounds. Five Latinas were elected to the Steering Committee. Although the NLFO did not last long, the ethnic parity policy set a precedent.

After the NLFO conference, lesbians of color in Los Angeles and San Diego formed groups with the same name, Lesbians of Color (LOC). In 1980, Latinas in Los Angeles Lesbians of Color formed a subgroup (Lesbianas Latina Americanas). Los Angeles LOC members also collaborated with white lesbian groups. For example, they led the antiracism workshop at retreats organized by the Califia Collective. In 1983, Los Angeles LOC organized the first National Lesbians of Color Conference. Over two hundred lesbians and progressive women of color attended this event in Malibu, California.

Toward the end of the 1970s, Latina lesbians in Seattle contributed to the single published issue of the *Lesbians of Color Caucus Quarterly* in 1979, and in the same year, Latinas and Latinos in Austin, Texas, formed what was probably the only LGBT chapter of the Brown Berets. In New York City, twelve lesbians and gays marched openly in the 1979 Puerto Rican Day parade. Ten years later, there were over fifty marchers.

Religion is a major theme in the psyches of many Latinas and Latinos. Some of those who felt uncomfortable with the homophobia of the Catholic Church found an alternative in pastor Fernando Martinez's Latin Church of Christian Fellowship, founded in Los Angeles in 1979. Others, including Vilma Torres, joined Troy Perry's Metropolitan Community Church (MCC), where

Torres later served as a minister. Another alternative was Dignity, a Catholic LGBT organization formed in 1969.

As the 1970s came to a close, a lesbian and gay march on Washington was proposed. Several large mainstream LGBT groups felt that the time was not right for such a momentous event. Ignoring those concerns, grassroots LGBT activists met in Houston and began to plan for a 1979 march. They voted to have lesbians of color lead the march, followed by men of color. Juanita Ramos (Juanita Diaz-Cotto), a member of COHLA (Comité Homosexual Latinoamericano), served on both the national planning committee and the New York committee and was a speaker at the March on Washington rally. Twenty-four years later, Lizbeth Menendez, an activist and labor organizer, was a regional coordinator for the 1993 March on Washington.

In conjunction with the first March on Washington, the first National Third World Lesbian and Gay Conference was held near Howard University. Latina/Latino groups participating included Latinos Unidos (Los Angeles), COHLA (New York City), Latins for Human Rights (Miami), Comité Latino de Lesbianas y Homosexuales de Boston, Gay Alliance of Latin Americans (San Francisco), and Houston Gay Chicano/a Caucus. Although elated about participating in this historical gathering, attendees also struggled over the lack of attention that the numerically superior Latina/Latino and African American groups paid to Asian, Pacific Islander, and Native American issues. Solidarity prevailed, however, as the People of Color contingent came together to participate in the march and rally.

The 1980s

In 1980 thousands of Cubans, including LGBT people, were allowed to leave their homeland, embarking from the port of Mariel (thus their name, Marielitos). Boston activists formed the Boston Area Coalition for Cuban Aid and Resettlement (BACCAR) and obtained funding for La Casa Amarilla, a halfway house for the immigrants. The Metropolitan Community Church, with parishes in many U.S. cities, also organized a network of MCC members willing to serve as host families.

During the early 1980s, the Gay Hispanic Caucus in Houston sponsored cultural and social activities and published a newsletter, *Noticias.* In Long Beach, California, Raices Latinas offered social and cultural events. In Los Angeles, Gay Latinos Unidos, later Gay and Lesbian Latinos Unidos (GLLU), was formed in 1981. The group became a significant political presence in Los Angeles LGBT activist circles under presidents like Roland(o) Palencia, Laura Esquivel, and Lydia Otero. In 1983, GLLU lesbians formed Lesbianas Unidas (LU) but remained affiliated with GLLU until the 1990s. LU's activities illustrate the dual political and cultural commitment of Latina/Latino LGBT groups: LU sponsored a popular annual retreat, participated in the planning of the first Lesbianas Feministas Encuentro (conference) in Mexico in 1987, marched against the SimpsonMazolli anti-immigration legislation in 1984, participated in the twentieth anniversary commemoration of the Chicano Moratorium march in 1990, and offered financial support to a hospital in Nicaragua.

LU women also participated in the Connexxus Women's Center/Centro de Mujeres (CX) in West Hollywood. At its peak (1984–1990), CX was a $200,000-a-year operation. Initially, few women of color were invited to participate in planning the center. However, Latina lesbians called a meeting with key CX organizers Adel Martinez and Loren Jardine and, after negotiations, Latinas became an integral part of CX. (All three CX board presidents were Latinas.) CX sponsored a Latina lesbian outreach program in East Los Angeles at a Latino social services agency and cosponsored the first Latina Lesbian Mental Health Conference in 1987. It also sponsored photographer Laura Aguilar's groundbreaking Latina Lesbian Series.

In Texas, the Gay and Lesbian Tejanos Conference was held in 1986, and participating groups included the Gay Hispanic Coalition of Dallas, Gay and Lesbian Hispanic Unidos (Houston), and Ambiente (San Antonio). Also participating was ALLGO (Austin Latina/Latino Lesbian and Gay Organization), an organization formed in 1985, which continues to offer support groups, cultural events, and health education programs. In Washington, D.C., ENLACE was formed in 1987 as a Latino gay and lesbian political support group. Members marched in the District of Columbia's annual Hispanic Parade and set up Hola Gay, a Spanish language hotline. In Chicago, Lesbianas Latinas en Nuestro Ambiente was formed in 1988. In the same year, the Los Angeles–based, nationally circulated *Lesbian News* published a column of information and news of interest to Latinas ("La Plaza"). Since that time columns by comedian Monica Palacios and journalist Vicki Torres have appeared in *Lesbian News.*

The International Lesbian and Gay People of Color Conference was held in Los Angeles in 1986, and both Latinas and Latinos served on the steering committee. After the conference, a group met to found a Latino caucus, which eventually evolved into LLEGÓ, now the premier LGBT Latino organization in the United States.

LLEGÓ's programs include lobbying, sponsoring national encuentros in the United States and Mexico, and organizing community capacity-building training programs. When Lesbianas Latinas de Tucson in Arizona organized the first Latina Lesbian Conference in the fall of 1994, LLEGÓ provided funding. LLEGÓ also provided a grant to Lesbianas Unidas to conduct interviews for the Latina Lesbian Oral History Project in Los Angeles.

In the 1980s, AIDS began to decimate the gay male community. In 1989, Los Angeles LGBT Latino activists were awarded a grant to address issues of neglect toward HIV/AIDS in the Latino community. Under the leadership of CEO Oscar de la O, the organization evolved into a multiservice organization with ten locations in southern California. Recently, it has sponsored LUNA (Latinas Understanding the Need for Action), a women's program. Other Latino HIV/AIDS programs and health services providers include PCPV (Proyecto Contra Sida Por Vida) in San Francisco, which offers health care outreach to the transgender community; GALAEI (Gay and Lesbian AIDS Education Initiative) in Philadelphia; and Mano a Mano, a coalition of New York City Latino gay organizations that uses HIV/AIDS funding to run programs like SOMOS, which works against homophobia in the Latino community, and the Capacity-Building Project, which provides grants to gay Latino groups. The 1980s was also the decade when LGBT people began to address publicly the issues of substance abuse. Lapis, an outreach and prevention program aimed at Latina and African American lesbians, was funded in the late 1980s through the Alcoholism Center for Women in Los Angeles.

Recent Developments

During the last decade of the twentieth century and into the first decade of the twenty first century, LGBT Latina and Latino organizations continued to emerge to address both the changing and ongoing needs of the community. Among these were SOL (Somos Orgullo Latino, Oregon, 1993); HOLA (Homosexuales Latinos, St. Louis, Missouri); GLACE (Gay and Lesbian Association of Cuban Exiles, Miami); ALMA (Association of Latin Men for Action, Chicago, 1993),which has marched in Chicago's Puerto Rican and Mexican Independence Day Parades; Amigas Latinas (Chicago, 1996), a support, education, and advocacy group; and Ellas en Acción (San Francisco, 1993), a lesbian advocacy, arts, and educational organization that played a role in the election of a Latina lesbian, Susan Leal, to the city's Board of Supervisors in 1993. LLUNA (Latina Lesbians United Never Apart, Boston, 1993) has organized an International Women's Day event and participated in gay pride and Columbus Day events. Las Buenas Amigas (New York City, 1993), an educational, cultural, political, and social organization, promotes safe space and visibility for Latina lesbians. Groups for monolingual Spanish speakers include Dos Espiritus, a support group for gay men in Elgin, Illinois, and a chapter of PFLAG (Parents, Families, and Friends of Lesbians and Gays) in Tucson.

Progressive grassroots organizations with a strong Latina and Latino LGBT presence include the Esperanza Peace and Justice Center founded in 1987 in San Antonio by Graciela Sanchez. After homophobic pressures led the city to cut Esperanza's funding, the center sued and won. *La Voz,* Esperanza's magazine, is edited by Gloria Ramirez.

Arts advocacy organizations include Viva (founded in the 1980s in Los Angeles), which promotes the work of LGBT Latina and Latino artists; the MACHA Theatre Company (Mujeres Advancing Culture, History, and Art), also in Los Angeles; and QUELACO (Queer Latino/a Artists Coalition) in San Francisco, which promotes queer Latina and Latino art and produces an annual art, cultural, and performance festival.

In the 1990s, Colombiana writer, activist, and librarian Tatiana de la Tierra published three Latina lesbian magazines—*Conmoción, Esto No Tiene Nombre,* and *Telaraña.* In 2003, *Tongues* is an arts magazine and Web 'zine published by a Los Angeles lesbians of color group of the same name. Many of the active members are Latina lesbians, including artist Alma López, whose image *Our Lady*—a controversial depiction of Our Lady of Guadalupe—caused a furor in New Mexico in 2001. Two LGBT Latino publications with a national readership are *QV,* established in 1997, and *Tentaciones,* created in 2000. In 2003, *Tentaciones* published a list of the sixteen most influential LGBT Latinas and Latinos in the United States, which caused some consternation in Chicago, since none of its longtime Latina and Latino activists made the list. "En La Vida," the Latina/Latino section of Chicago's *Windy City Times* (which is available online) promptly published a list of Chicago LGBT notables.

LGBT Latinas and Latinos continue to struggle against homophobia and racism, along with sexism, class oppression, linguistic discrimination, and immigration status. Organizations and publications that focus on their issues serve as a counter to prejudice and as a source of support, advocacy, and *orgullo* (pride).

Bibliography

Aponte-Parés, Luis, and Jorge Merced. "Páginas Omitidas: The Gay and Lesbian Presence." In *The Puerto Rican Movement:*

Voices from the Diaspora. Edited by Andres Torres and José Velázquez. Philadelphia: Temple University Press, 1998.

D'Emilio, John. *Sexual Politics, Sexual Communities: The Making of a Homosexual Minority in the United States, 1940–1970.* 2d ed. Chicago: University of Chicago Press, 1998.

Kepner, Jim. "Lesbian Gay Latino History Project Emerges from National Gay Archives." *NGA Newsletter,* 1983, pp. 4–5.

Leyva, Yolanda. "Breaking the Silence: Putting Latina Lesbian History at the Center." In *The New Lesbian Studies: Into the Twenty-first Century.* Edited by Bonnie Zimmerman and Toni A. H. McNaron. New York: Feminist Press, 1996.

Martin, Del, and Phyllis Lyon. *Lesbian/Woman.* San Francisco: Glide, 1972.

Podolsky, Robin. "Linkage." *LA Weekly,* 23 December 1988, p. 6.

Retter, Yolanda. "On the Side of Angels: A History of Lesbian Activism in Los Angeles, 1970–1990." Ph.D. diss., University of New Mexico, 1999.

Rivera, Ray ("Sylvia Lee"). "The Drag Queen." In *Making History: The Struggle for Gay and Lesbian Rights, 1945–1990, an Oral History.* Edited by Eric Marcus. New York: HarperCollins, 1992.

Roque Ramirez, Horacio. "Communities of Desire: Queer Latina/Latino History and Memory, San Francisco Bay Area, 1960s–1990s." Ph.D. diss., University of California at Berkeley, 2001.

Sanchez, Edwin. "Reclaiming a Birthright." *New York Native,* 17 July 1989, p. 11.

Stein, Marc. *City of Sisterly and Brotherly Loves: Lesbian and Gay Philadelphia, 1945–1972.* Chicago: University of Chicago Press, 2000.

Yolanda Retter

See also ANZALDÚA, GLORIA; CORDOVA, JEANNE; DIAZ-COTTO, JUANITA; LATINAS AND LATINOS; LATINA AND LATINO STUDIES; MORAGA, CHERRÍE; PUERTO RICO; REYES, RODRIGO; RIVERA, SYLVIA; SARRIA, JOSÉ; TAVERA, HANK.

LATINA AND LATINO STUDIES

Since the early 1990s, the most thriving subfield of Latino studies in the United States has been queer studies. Finding its strongest anchor in literary studies, Latino studies scholarship that addresses LGBT gender roles and sexualities has challenged many of the heterosexual assumptions embedded in much Latino-American writing. Queer Latino studies has simultaneously placed the lives and cultures of queer Latinas and Latinos within mainstream LGBT studies. Queer Latino studies has thus had the dual role of making race and ethnicity necessary categories of analysis in LGBT studies and of bringing questions of gender, sexuality, and desire to the center of Latino studies. The authors building a queer Latino studies literature have come from Chicana and Chicano (Mexican American), Puerto Rican, Cuban, and several other national and ethnic backgrounds, and from varied disciplinary and interdisciplinary contexts. They have produced fiction, essays, poetry, plays, performance art, film, video, and academic writing in the social sciences, the humanities, and the arts. Many of them began their work not in universities but in community-based coalitions of artists, writers, and activists committed to making connections between racial and ethnic conditions and sexual consciousness. While a great deal of queer Latino studies has focused attention on the U.S. mainland, often the writings cross national borders in their content, politics, and audience. Given Latinos' ongoing transnational economic, cultural, and political relationships with Latin America, U.S.-based LGBT Latino studies often investigates relationships between sexualities "at home" and abroad. Given these ongoing transnational relations, queer Latino studies has also differed along national lines. Queer Chicanos and Chicanas, for example, have explored their racialization in the United States while simultaneously exploring the historical legacies of patriarchy in their Mexican ideological roots. Likewise, queer Puerto Ricans have investigated their ongoing historical relations "at home" in the United States and "at home" in the island, addressing the ways in which race, language, and class mark insider and outsider statuses in both locations. Queer Cubans and Cuban Americans, on the other hand, having a different relation as "exiles" from a country deemed an enemy by the United States, have explored in part lesbian and gay Cubans' experiences in the islands during the revolutionary period.

Historical and Political Contexts

The growth of social protest movements in the 1960s and 1970s gave birth to what can be considered the first writings linking Latino and LGBT studies. Though sporadic, early publications—such as New York City's Spanish-language *Afuera* (1972)—discussed Third World liberation, Marxist thought, and patriarchy from a gay Latin American perspective. Over time, newsletters and occasional articles from organizations such as San Francisco's Gay Latino Alliance (GALA, 1975–1983), New York City's El Comité de Homosexuales Latinoamericanos (COHLA, around the mid-1970s), and Boston's El Comité Latino de Lesbianas y Homosexuales (about 1979) began to create a small corpus of writings.

Despite the fact that Chicano and Puerto Rican studies began to take institutional form at this time at several East Coast and West Coast colleges and universities, the few writings circulating outside the academy that brought together LGBT studies and Latino studies did not shape the curriculum in any significant way. Homophobia and rigid heterosexist nationalist positions in these early programs argued for national liberation without making space for feminist and LGBT critiques of patriarchy and heterosexuality. Yet despite the lack of institutional support, a growing body of work addressing queer sexuality from Latina and Latino perspectives began to take form in the late 1970s.

Latina and Latino Literary Challenges

Well-known gay author John Rechy, who is of mixed Scottish and Mexican descent, could be considered the first contributor to what would eventually take form as queer Latino studies. In his classic *City of Night* (1963) and the more politically engaged *The Sexual Outlaw* (1977), Rechy addressed sexuality and gay oppression. Because his writings have not always explicitly marked the intersection of sexual and racial identities, the first generation of Chicano literary scholars refused to consider him a Chicano author, given his gay sexuality and his mixed-race background. In his *Miraculous Day of Amalia Gomez* (1991), Rechy brought closer the relationship between gay and Latino lives in Los Angeles, the most recurrent location for his novels. Despite Latino critics' homophobia and racial essentialism regarding Rechy's background, a cross-generational LGBT and Latino audience has become aware of his work. More recent LGBT Latino critics have returned to his writings and placed him alongside other well-known Latino writers. These critics have been more appreciative of the ability of mixed race writers like Rechy to contribute to dialogues about multiracial identity and sexuality.

Chicana and Latina lesbians initiated more explicitly political discussions linking sexuality, race, gender, and nationality in Latino studies. The groundbreaking first edition of *This Bridge Called My Back: Writing by Radical Women of Color* (1981) gave a national platform to many Latina authors addressing lesbian sexuality. Conceived in 1979 by Cherríe Moraga and Gloria Anzaldúa, *This Bridge* mixed poetry, nonfictional narratives, personal letters, and political manifestos to create a multiracial dialogue among Third World women. Followed by other foundational publications from Moraga and Anzaldúa, *This Bridge* remains the most important intervention into LGBT studies from a Latino perspective.

Two important Chicana and Latina lesbian anthologies in the 1990s continued to address Queer and Latino studies from lesbian positions. Representing many writers from the Southwest, *Chicana Lesbians: The Girls Our Mothers Warned Us About* (1991) broke important political and theoretical ground in Chicana and Chicano studies. Mixing poetry and essays with more academic treatises, *Chicana Lesbians* offered powerful critiques of Chicano patriarchy. With strong East Coast Latina representation, *Compañeras: Latina Lesbians* (1994) similarly explored identity, nationality, liberation, and sexuality in Latina lesbian lives. More transnational in its scope than *Chicana Lesbians*, *Compañeras* offered important historical and political discussions on the forging of cultural, political, and social Latina lesbian networks in the Americas.

Queer Latino men's anthologies have been fewer and less politically focused than those of Latina lesbians. *Ya Vas Carnal* (Go Head On, Brother), a 1995 poetry compilation by three gay Chicano cultural workers and writers in San Francisco, was one of the first gay Latino men's anthologies to address queer sexuality openly from a Chicano perspective. Subsequently, the 1999 publications *Virgins, Guerrillas, and Locas: Gay Latinos Writing about Love* and *Bésame Mucho* (Kiss Me a Lot) offered personal fictional and nonfictional accounts of love, desire, family life, and health. Along with the contributions of the Colombian Jaime Manrique, the Cuban Rafael Campo, the late Cuban exile Reinaldo Arenas, and the Chicano novelist Arturo Islas, gay Latino men's writing is slowly becoming a significant body of work addressing male gender roles and sexualities.

Theater and Performance

A strong component of queer Latino studies has been the work of creative performers and artists and the scholars who write about their productions. Foremost in the list of Chicana lesbian playwrights has been Cherríe Moraga, who has produced three collections of plays. In her work, Moraga has consistently explored spirituality, sexuality, family, and the home. A younger generation of playwrights including Ricardo A. Bracho and Jorge Ignacio Cortiñas continues to challenge assumptions about queer and racial and ethnic identities in the United States. Long-established performance artists Monica Palacios, Luis Alfaro, Marga Gómez, and Carmelita Tropicana have brought to the stage queer Latino and Latina life in dramatic and hilarious fashion. Their collective work has received wide acclaim from varied audiences, including non-Latinos. Filmmakers Frances Negrón-Muntaner and Mary Guzman have explored identity, migration, gender, and sexuality from lesbian Latina perspectives. Also active in video and filmmaking have been Teresa "Osa" Hidalgo-de la Riva, Janelle Rodriguez, and Veronica Majano, all members of a new generation of Latina lesbian filmmakers from the San Francisco Bay Area.

Questions of language and nation have been central in most of these artists' and performers' work. They have consciously made bilingualism and "Spanglish" the preferred mode for queer studies. Often bridging immigrant and post-immigrant Latino communities, these artists reveal the tensions in their lives as they straddle at least two different cultural positions. While their work explores the painful experience of leaving their racial and ethnic communities in hopes of finding a sense of place in the white-dominant lesbian and gay enclaves and institutions that often stereotype and denigrate them, they just as often delve into the process of returning home.

History and the Social Sciences

Historical examinations of queer Latina and Latino communities have been largely missing in queer studies, with only one extensive study of the San Francisco Bay Area having appeared as of the early twenty-first century. As this study, by Horacio N. Roque Ramírez, demonstrates, the making of queer Latina and Latino communities has been multinational and multigendered. Queer Latina and Latino history in San Francisco has grown out of the social, political, and cultural lives of both queer migrants and individuals already established in the Bay Area. The impetus to head for the Bay Area involved a combination of the desire to live more open sexual and political lives and the attraction of the region and its famous countercultures. María Cora and Karla E. Rosales have explored Latina lesbian cultures in this region as well. Respectively, their work has examined black Puerto Rican lesbians and self-identified butch Latina lesbians. Despite these contributions to the history of queer Latinas and Latinos in the Bay Area, there has been little comparable study elsewhere in the nation, which has meant that queer studies in general lacks the racial and cultural complexity that more local histories would bring. Some scholarly works, however, have shed light on individual Latina and Latino contributions to gay and lesbian history. These include Martin Duberman's work on the Puerto Rican Sylvia Rivera in New York; Marc Stein's work on the Cuban American Ada Bello in Philadelphia; and Michael R. Gorman's work on José Sarria in San Francisco. The historical scholarship of Ramón A Gutiérrez, Emma Pérez, and Antonia I. Castañeda also addresses the relationship between gender and sexuality among Latinas and Latinos.

More extensive has been the work of sociologists and other social scientists. Tomás Almaguer's 1991 essay "Chicano Men: A Cartography of Homosexual Identity and Behavior" is one the most extensively anthologized. Generally, Almaguer argued that, in the "Mexican/Latin American male sexual system," it is not the object of attraction but the question of who penetrates or gets penetrated in anal sex that defines homosexuality. He also argued that "there is no cultural equivalent to the modern 'gay man' in the Mexican/Latin American sexual system" (p. 75). The essay, published at a moment when there was no existing sociological research on gay Latinos, overemphasized the top-bottom reductionist hypothesis. It also reduced the experience of gay Chicano and Latino men to one of stigma and shame within their communities, and failed to acknowledge the variety of gay experience throughout the Americas. A more ethnographic discussion of gay Latinos is that of the late sociologist Lionel Cantú, who "queered" migration studies by demonstrating the central role of sexuality in the experience of gay Mexican immigrant men in Los Angeles. Cantú also explored transnational relations between these immigrant men and the ways in which their lives are culturally and socially connected to both sides of the U.S.-Mexico border. Along these lines of investigating migration and sexuality, Oliva M. Espín has explored the process of healing in the lives of Latina lesbian migrants in the United States. Arguing for the need to recognize the diverse class, racial, and sexual backgrounds of Latina immigrants, Espín offers a framework that explores but also critiques dominant (white) feminist theories of identity. Finally, the research of Barbara V. Marín, Héctor Carrillo, George Ayala, Lourdes Arguelles, Horacio N. Roque Ramírez, and Rafael M. Díaz on AIDS in Latino communities explores the racial, class, gender, and cultural factors that must be acknowledged more overtly to respond to the epidemic more successfully.

Cultural Studies

One of the strongest areas in queer Latino studies, and in queer studies in general, has been cultural studies. Generally based in large research universities, this work is part of the burgeoning tendency since the early 1990s toward theoretical exploration of the meaning and production of various cultural texts: novels, films, television, plays, music, and other kinds of popular media. Yvonne Yarbro-Bejarano, José Esteban Muñoz, José Quiroga, Juana María Rodríguez, Alberto Sandoval-Sánchez, David Román, and others have written on multiple levels about the politics of identity expressed in Latino cultural forms.

These scholars have probed the intersecting, multiple ways that gender, sexuality, and culture find expression in Latino life. Usually in conversation with work in performance studies, American studies, Latin American studies, and ethnic studies, queer Latino cultural studies expands the national and temporal borders of queer studies. Though largely based in the United States, this work takes up questions of imperialism, conquest, and patriarchy in Latin America as they relate to Latino life, culture, and sexuality in the United States. In this sense, they explore the notion of Latinidad—that is, the formation and expression of identity among Latinas and Latinos—and queer Latinidad, specifically. In exploring queer Latinidad, they make more explicit the heterogeneous historical, cultural, and regional roots of Latinos and their queer sexualities. The field has been successful also in making visible white racial assumptions in queer cultural studies. In addition it has shed light on the difficult negotiations queer Latinas and Latinos carry out to claim visibility, language, space, identity, and rights.

Works in Latino studies that address transgender and bisexual sexualities have been few. With the exception of AIDS health research addressing risk factors and behaviors associated with bisexual and transgender identities, Latino studies has yet to focus critical attention on the politics and cultures of bisexual identity and transgender Latino communities.

With the exception of the well known writings of Moraga and Anzaldúa and a handful of other essays, few contributions from Latino studies have found their way into the center of LGBT studies. Often relegated to superficial discussions of "diversity" and "difference," queer Latino studies has nevertheless challenged many assumptions about what constitutes LGBT community, sisterhood, brotherhood, and history. At the same time, various scholars and artists have strengthened Latino studies in the last three decades by expanding notions of culture, identity, and liberation.

Bibliography

Almaguer, Tomás. "Chicano Men: A Cartography of Homosexual Identity and Behavior." *Differences: A Journal of Feminist Cultural Studies* 3, no. 2 (summer 1991): 75–100.

Cantú, Lionel, Jr. "Border Crossings: Mexican Men and the Sexuality of Migration." Ph.D. diss., University of California, Irvine, 1999.

Moraga, Cherríe, and Gloria Anzaldúa, eds. *This Bridge Called My Back: Writings by Radical Women of Color.* 3d ed. Berkeley: Third Woman Press, 2002.

Negrón-Muntaner, Frances. "When I Was a Puerto Rican Lesbian: Meditations on 'Brincando el charco: Portrait of a Puerto Rican'." *GLQ: A Journal of Lesbian and Gay Studies* 5 (1999): 511–526.

Ramos, Juanita, ed. *Compañeras: Latina Lesbians.* New York: Latina Lesbian History Project, 1987.

Reyes, Rodrigo, Francisco X. Alarcón, and Juan Pablo Gutiérrez. *Ya Vas Carnal: Poetry by Rodrigo Reyes, Francisco X. Alarcón, and Juan Pablo Gutiérrez.* San Francisco: Humanizarte, 1985

Rodríguez, Juana María. *Queer Latinidad: Identity Practices, Discursive Spaces.* New York: New York University Press, 2003.

Roque Ramírez, Horacio N. "Communities of Desire: Queer Latina/Latino History and Memory, San Francisco Bay Area, 1960s–1990s." Ph.D. diss., University of California at Berkeley, 2001.

Trujillo, Carla, ed. *Chicana Lesbians: The Girls Our Mothers Warned Us About.* Berkeley: Third Woman, 1991.

Horacio N. Roque Ramírez

See also ANZALDÚA, GLORIA; ISLAS, ARTURO; LATINAS AND LATINOS; LATINA AND LATINO LGBTQ ORGANIZATIONS AND PERIODICALS; MORAGA, CHERRÍE; RECHY, JOHN.

LAW. See Antidiscrimination Law and Policy; Censorship, Obscenity, and Pornography Law and Policy; Employment Law and Policy; Family Law and Policy; Federal Law and Policy; Hate Crimes Law and Policy; Health and Health Care Law and Policy; Immigration, Asylum, and Deportation Law and Policy; Military Law and Policy; Rape, Sexual Assault, and Sexual Harassment Law and Policy; Sexual Psychopath Law and Policy; Transgender and Gender Impersonation Law and Policy.

LAWRENCE, Louise (b. 1912; d. 1976), educator.

Louise Lawrence was a male-to-female transvestite who cross-dressed from an early age. She grew up as a boy named "Lew" in an upper middle-class family and worked in a bank after she graduated from high school. In the 1930s, while still living as a man, she began corresponding with other cross-dressers, and in 1944, after her second marriage had failed, she moved from Berkeley to San Francisco and started to live full time as a woman. From the late 1940s on, she lived with a female partner, Gay, who worked as a nurse. To support herself, she managed an apartment building for working women and sold some of her own artwork.

Lawrence had an abiding belief in science, and she devoted herself to educating doctors and researchers about transvestism. From the mid-1940s she worked with Karl M. Bowman, the psychiatrist who directed San Francisco's Langley Porter Clinic, to help doctors understand transvestism. Eventually, the doctors at Langley Porter presented her as a role model to some of their transgendered patients. Lawrence met Alfred C. Kinsey in 1948 when he was visiting San Francisco, and she began a concerted campaign to convince him that transvestism was a relatively common condition worthy of scientific study. Over the next several years she introduced Kinsey to numerous cross-dressers, professional female impersonators, and eventually transsexuals. She encouraged her friends and acquaintances to give their life histories to Kinsey, and she sent him clippings and books for his library.

In 1950 Kinsey started paying Lawrence for typing the life histories of the cross-dressers she knew and for copying fictional accounts of transvestism, especially stories of petticoat discipline, an erotic genre in which cross-dressed men were humiliated by sadistic women. Lawrence sent Kinsey stacks of manuscripts, letters, life histories, and scrapbooks of clippings and photographs. She also donated the diary of the year she began to live as a woman and other autobiographical writings and compiled a list for Kinsey of the 152 transvestites she knew in the United States. (All of these items reside in the archives of the Kinsey Institute for Research in Sex, Gender, and Reproduction.)

In the late 1940s Kinsey introduced Lawrence to Harry Benjamin, a sexologist and endocrinologist soon to become the nation's foremost expert on transvestism and transsexualism. Benjamin relied heavily on Lawrence for advice and information on transvestism. In face-to-face visits and through years of correspondence, he bounced ideas off of her, even though the two differed in their hypotheses about the underlying causes of cross-gender identification. While Benjamin searched for biological causes of transvestism and transsexualism, Lawrence focused on early childhood experience. In 1951, with Benjamin's encouragement, Lawrence published an article, "Transvestism: An Empirical Study," under the pseudonym Janet Thompson, in the *International Journal of Sexology.*

After the male-to-female transsexual Christine Jorgensen made the news in 1952, Lawrence extended her educational efforts to include transsexuals as well as transvestites. In the 1950s she was at the center of, and to a certain extent created, a transsexual social network. Lawrence had Benjamin introduce her to his patients, including Jorgensen, and she made additional contacts on her own. She corresponded with transsexuals, introduced them to each other and to Kinsey, met with them, and counseled them informally. Lawrence considered herself a "permanent transvestite," not a transsexual. She did not seek transsexual surgery but experimented with female hormones under Benjamin's guidance.

Lawrence established herself as an expert on and a champion of transvestites, but she also had an interest in other sexual minorities. Earlier in her life, when living as a man, she had experimented with homosexuality but discovered that she did not derive satisfaction from sexual relations with men. She continued, though, to socialize with gay men, lesbians, and female impersonators. In the 1950s she established contacts with homophile (or early gay rights) activists, especially in the San Francisco chapter of the Mattachine Society.

Bibliography

Lawrence, Louise. Collection. Kinsey Institute for Research in Sex, Gender, and Reproduction, Indiana University, Bloomington, Ind.

Meyerowitz, Joanne. "Sex Research at the Borders of Gender: Transvestites, Transsexuals, and Alfred C. Kinsey." *Bulletin of the History of Medicine* 75 (2001): 72–90.

———. *How Sex Changed: A History of Transsexuality in the United States.* Cambridge, Mass.: Harvard University Press, 2002.

Joanne Meyerowitz

See also BENJAMIN, HARRY; KINSEY, ALFRED C.; PRINCE, VIRGINIA; TRANSGENDER ORGANIZATIONS AND PERIODICALS; TRANSSEXUALS, TRANSVESTITES, TRANSGENDER PEOPLE, AND CROSS-DRESSERS.

LE GUIN, Ursula K. (b. 21 October 1929), writer.

Ursula Kroeber Le Guin was born in Berkeley, California. Her mother was the writer Theodora Kroeber and her father the anthropologist Alfred L. Kroeber. She graduated from Radcliffe College in 1951 and, after earning an M.A. at Columbia University in 1952, she received a Fulbright scholarship to start her doctoral studies in French literature in France. She abandoned her academic career to become a writer, but was not successful at first, in part because her prose broke the rules of literary genres. Although science fiction has historically been dominated by male writers and readers, Le Guin found a place for herself in this genre while continuing to write poetry, works for children, political essays, fantasy, and other types of literature. She has also produced audio recordings of some of her writings and a film based on her novel *The Lathe of Heaven* (1971).

Le Guin's writing became influential in feminist circles because of her critique of male power and its social consequences, including violence, authority, and competition. The political ideas expressed in her fiction include elements from varied sources, including anarchism, taoism, feminism, and anthropological theory, combined in creative ways. Le Guin is known for her ability to listen to criticism and for criticizing herself, and this attitude has influenced the development of her work. Le Guin's approach to writing involves taking responsibility for the impact of words, instead of using language for profit or to control others. She considers writing a craft that she is proud to have developed through hard work, and this is why she continues coordinating writing workshops. Through writing, the author has developed a prose and poetry that critiques all forms of oppression, with an especially sensitive consciousness about gender and sexuality.

In 1969 came the publication of *The Left Hand of Darkness*, in which Le Guin puts forward the notion of an anarchic "female principle" that governs through custom rather than force or constraint. The novel's innovations brought radical feminist thinking into science fiction. Genly Ai, a young black male anthropologist, travels to planet Winter as a representative for the League of the Planets. Planet Winter is inhabited by the Gethens, an intelligent species whose members develop either male or female sexual organs in the context of an estrus period that takes place each month. When two members of this species are ready to reproduce, one develops female organs while the other develops male ones. In a later self-critical comment, Le Guin states that by imagining this heterosexual complementarity she erased same-sex sexuality from the narrative. In spite of this denial of homosexual practices, Ai develops a homoerotic friendship with a Gethen. Moreover, the novel develops an imaginative account of the influences of sex and gender identity in society. This complex representation of a society invented as a result of Le Guin's sensibility about trans sexuality offers insights that few feminists or LGB readers perceived at the time the novel was published.

In her texts, Le Guin constructs main heterosexual characters, but she frequently includes queer people who are either integrated in their societies or fight against homophobia. One clear example of this is the novel *The Dispossessed,* which features a planet named Urras, where anarchists were allowed to constitute their own world on Anarres, the nearby satellite. In this novel, several characters with homosexual identities are not labeled or differentiated from those who have a heterosexual orientation. On Anarres, the frontiers between homosexuality and heterosexuality are blurred; although individuals tend to develop a specific sexual orientation, this only constitutes a tendency and sexual practices can vary. The main male character, a physicist called Shevek, leans toward heterosexual desire, but he has a sexual friendship with another man.

Le Guin's sensibility toward queer identities is expressed in self-conscious feminist narratives. Using her female identity as a tool to observe and criticize various forms of oppression, Le Guin deals with class, ethnicity, gender, sexuality, and age. Other science fiction works by the author include *Rocannon's World* (1966), "Vaster than Empires and More Slow" (1971), and *The Word for World is Forest* (1976). Her most famous fantasy prose is the books of Earthsea, a series she began in 1968 with *A Wizard of Earthsea* and completed in 2001, with the fifth novel and sixth book, *The Other Wind.*

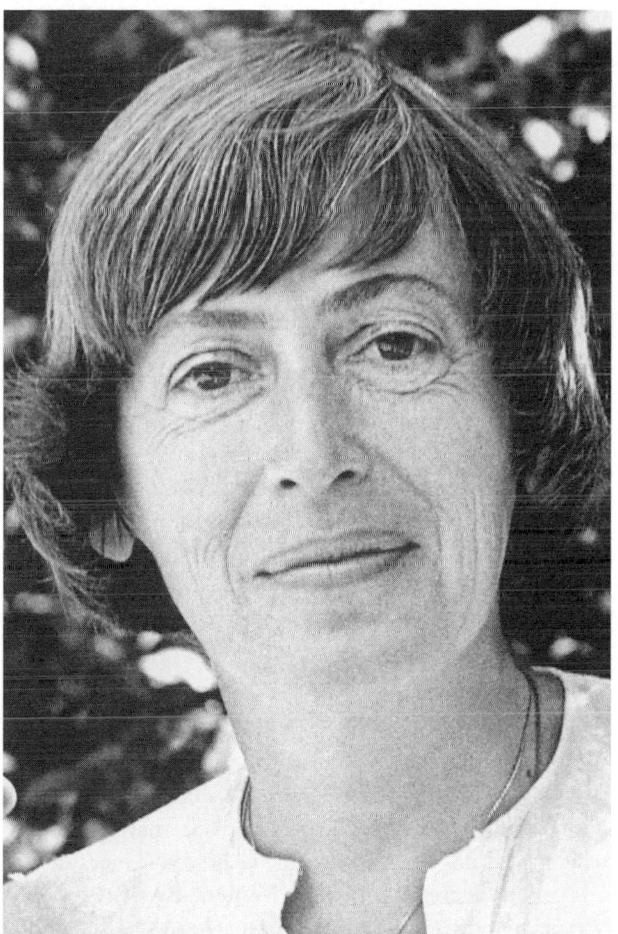

Ursula K. Le Guin. This innovative feminist writer has focused mainly, though far from exclusively, on the traditionally male-dominated genre of science fiction, including *The Left Hand of Darkness* (1969) and her Earthsea series of several books between 1968 and 2001. **[Bettmann/corbis]**

Bibliography

Bratman, David S. *Ursula K. Le Guin: A Primary Bibliography.* Oakland, Calif.: Potlatch 4, 1995.

Le Guin, Ursula K. *Dancing at the Edge of the World.* New York: Grove Press, 1989.

White, Donna R. *Dancing with Dragons: Ursula K. Le Guin and the Critics.* Columbia, S.C.: Camden House, 1999.

Pablo Ben

LEATHERSEX AND SEXUALITY

The modern leathersex community is a pansexual, diverse subculture united not so much by common practice or ideology as by a shared commitment to a particular aesthetic, a tradition that is inextricably tied up with post–World War II images of American manhood. While sadomasochism (S/M), bondage, sexual discipline, and fisting are popular within the leathersex world and the history of leathersex is intimately linked with the history of gay S/M, the term *leathersex* should not be taken as synonymous with S/M. Part of leather's sexual appeal, in fact, speaks to a broad sense of community, a safe space where one's fantasies and inclinations (whether or not they involve S/M) can be nonjudgmentally realized. Many have also commented on leather's connotations of toughness; donning black leather is an assertion of power and strength in a society that is often eager to cast men who have sex with men, women who have sex with women, and nonconformists of all sexual preferences as sissies, perverts, and outcasts.

Modern S/M and leathersex have only the vaguest historical continuity with anything that developed before the twentieth century. While fragments of such ideas persisting from the Victorian era can be found and such past luminaries as the Marquis de Sade may be idolized within S/M and leathersex world, these instances do not add up to a credible history. Walter, the diarist of the Victorian erotic classic *My Secret Life,* mentions that establishments catering to those with a taste for sadism or masochism were in operation in nineteenth-century London; similar houses operated in New York City. Likewise, late-nineteenth-century and early-twentieth-century scientific experts such as Richard Krafft-Ebing, Havelock Ellis, and Sigmund Freud mentioned the existence of S/M practices, and networks of sadomasochists—acquaintances who felt safe with each other and who referred other acquaintances with similar interests—were already active at the turn of the century.

However, the problem remained that S/M practitioners of all sexual orientations, faced with a disapproving society, had to find safe ways of identifying themselves to others who shared their proclivities. As dual transgressors, homosexual S/M practitioners had particular difficulty doing this. While nightclubs and social organizations that served heterosexuals with a taste for "deviant" sex may have been established in major cities, stories of gay men being excluded from these clubs are more common than stories of their being welcomed. This led to the growth of separate, underground homosexual S/M networks. Meanwhile, women who sought S/M or fetish sex with other women were often accommodated in heterosexual circles. This possibly exploitative accommodation retarded the development of distinct women's leather, S/M, and fetish communities.

Motorcycle Culture and Early Clubs

Underground S/M networks, especially those involving gay men, experienced a sea change as waves of American boys came home from World War II, bringing with them restless energy, military-surplus riding apparel, and a love for the machines (especially motorcycles and aircraft) that they had used to defeat the Axis powers. There were nongay motorcycle gangs all over the country by the late 1940s, and very few of them included women; thus, the motorcycle gang was a perfect model for homosexual male groups. Looking like heterosexual biker clubs meant that no one stopped to think why there were no women with them when they roared through town. Moreover, the fierce reputation such clubs enjoyed was simultaneously a form of protection against homophobic harassment, a means of self-identification in a society that rejected homosexuals, and a turn-on for those who liked their trade rough.

In 1954, one of the homosexual motorcycle groups in Los Angeles organized itself into an official club, the Satyrs. The bikes, like the leather, were mostly war surplus. In naming themselves, the group followed a tradition established by fighting divisions in the army. They made back patches like the battalion patches they had brought home and called them colors as warriors have done for centuries. They even had medals made, imitating not medals of honor and valor but the sortie pins that were common during the war. In the beginning, the pins were distributed at out-of-town motorcycle runs only. They quickly became proof of longevity and brotherhood, just as wartime sortie pins had been.

The dual influence of the military and the motorcycle gang launched the attitudes and institutions that became the essential features of the modern leather community. According to anthropologist Gayle Rubin, the military and biker influences led to two stylistic poles for leathermen: the military style emphasized "formality, hierarchy, order, and discipline," while the biker was associated with the "celebration of disorder, rebelliousness, and individualism." Both styles have had an enduring effect on leather culture. The constructs of respect and mannered protocols in many early male clubs were more or less military, some requiring formal apprenticeships as part of their initiation. Others were less strict, but all were organized for the purpose of facilitating S/M sex. In describing the founding of Second City Motorcycle Club of Chicago, Chuck Renslow states that "motorcycle" was simply code for S/M.

In the 1960s, the motorcycle clubs led to the establishment of bars, some of which were owned by clubs or club officers. From their beginning, the motorcycle clubs stopped at bars on their runs, and members often gathered in bars in town. There were at least two bars in New York intentionally serving leathermen as early as the mid-1950s. In the 1960s, the clubs settled on the idea of having "home bars" in which to hang their "colors" or logos, and leather bars quickly spread across the country. Almost immediately, the bars became community centers for leathermen. Clubs had been only very slightly less private than the networks; bars were many degrees more public, but did not, in the beginning, have a genuine open-door policy. Nonetheless, by the time these gangs moved off their bikes and into clubs, bars, and other organizations, leather fashion had become firmly established, having taken on the mantle of a tribal identifying mark and having been adopted by lesbians and others in the S/M scene.

By the end of the 1960s, many leather bars had backrooms, commonly painted black and thus often called black rooms, where gay and S/M sex of all kinds took place. The black rooms flourished, attracting little more legal attention than the bars themselves. A companion development for the black rooms was an S/M-tolerant attitude in some newly available gay bathhouses and sex clubs. Bathhouses amounted to backrooms without the bar. Sex clubs often were said to be bathhouses without the bath. Also in the 1960s, leather clubs, bars, baths, and sex clubs became more visible to the general public. In June 1964, for instance, the editors of *Life* magazine used a mural of leathermen painted by Chuck Arnett in San Francisco's infamous Tool Box bar as a two-page illustration in an article called "Homosexuality in America." In contrast, S/M-seeking heterosexuals and lesbians still had only social networks, which continued to function for gay men as well.

In the postwar years, another powerful force changed the face of leathersex. Physique magazines and their related mail-order films, art folios, and photo sets were both feeding and helping to form the appetites of leathermen. In 1945, these were joined by the newsstand publication *Justice Weekly*, out of Toronto, Canada. For twenty-seven years, Justice Weekly allowed S/M strangers to meet without being introduced and vetted by other members of a network of acquaintances. Its usefulness to gay men in America was probably slight in the beginning, but grew by the late 1960s. In the 1950s, magazines like *Bizarre* and *Exotique* also appeared, but they intentionally did not facilitate contacts, and they were for the heterosexual trade, including the women seeking women who were accommodated in that realm. Meanwhile, the photography and art—especially the Nazi-uniform influenced art of Tom of Finland and the masochistic fantasy art of George Quaintance—found within both newsstand and mail-order publications defined styles of appearance and liberated sexual fantasies. In this context, biker-style black leathers, which were featured both in the new gay media and in a mainstream culture industry that was quick to appropriate and commodify any and all symbols of rebelliousness and dissent, began to eclipse the brown leathers of both the war-surplus and the Western or cowboy model of masculinity.

Growth of the Leather Community

The increased visibility of leathermen in the 1960s continued and accelerated through the end of the century. Magazines for gay men flourished in the 1970s, including many for leathermen. Among them, *Drummer* magazine, first published in Los Angeles in June 1975, stands out. Not only did *Drummer* last for twenty-four years, it also launched the careers of many of the leather community's most important writers, photographers, artists, and thinkers. Perhaps most significantly, Larry Townsend, author of the groundbreaking gay man's guide to S/M, the *Leatherman's Handbook* (1972), came to the attention of an international population in the pages of *Drummer.*

Motorcycle clubs became increasingly independent of the motorcycle in the 1970s, often choosing to call themselves leather/Levi clubs as they grew, multiplied, and became increasingly liberal about allowing guests. When visitors began to attend both in-town and out-of-town runs, some of the events grew to unexpected scale. As events developed, the emerging businesses supplying leathersex needs—everything from bondage gear and whips to videos and magazines—became a migrating marketplace set up wherever leathermen and leatherwomen gathered. Leathersex aesthetics also began to spill over into other, not necessarily LGBT, subcultures, such as the science fiction/fantasy/neo-medieval demimonde. One such group is the aggressively heterosexual Tuchux, founded some time in the early 1970s, which based itself on an imaginary tribe described by John Norman in his *Gor* series of S/M science-fiction novels.

Driven by the energies of a single bisexual woman, the late Cynthia Slater, another important new element was added to the leather community's resources. As a call-taker and sometime trainer for the San Francisco Sex Information Hotline (SFSI), Slater recognized a need for the people working the hotline to be better informed about S/M. Her efforts resulted in the 1974 formation of

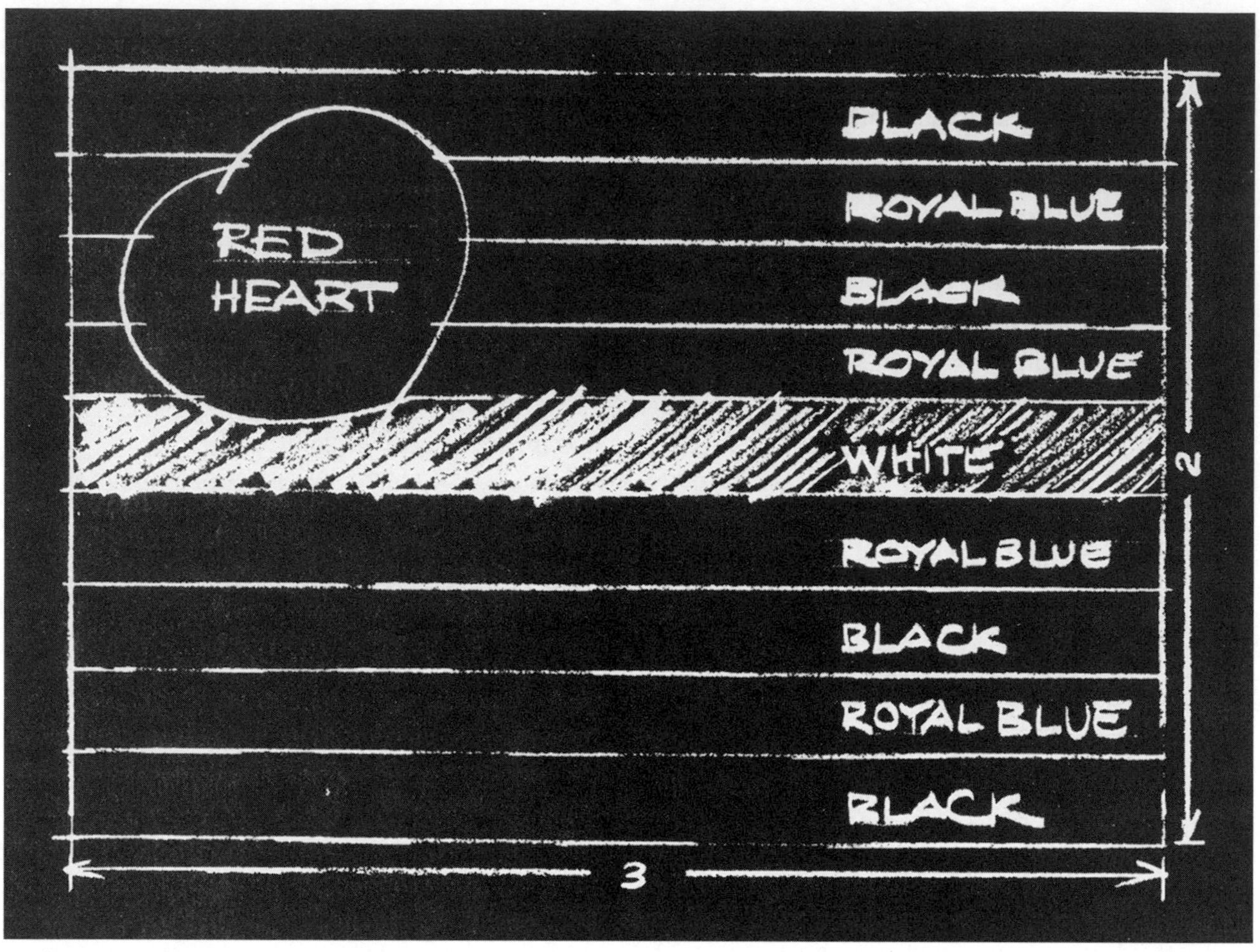

Leather Pride Flag. Tony DeBlase's design, shown here, was presented to the leather community at the International Mr. Leather event in Chicago, 28 May 1989, and within a month the flag had already been seen in several Gay Pride parades.

the Society of Janus, a pansexual S/M education and support group. About this time, while leatherman groups remained, perforce, exclusively male, some heterosexual groups began experimenting with inclusion or outreach. In New York City, the Eulenspiegel Society (TES) was also inclusive. Founded in 1971 by Pat Bond as a support group for masochists, TES welcomed people of all sexualities. The masochists-only portion of the early mandate was soon left behind, but TES continued to welcome all kinky people, submissive and dominant, switches and the curious, men and women, gay, lesbian and straight, and eventually transsexuals.

In 1975, a fisting club called Catacombs opened in San Francisco. At around the same time, a group of thirteen gay male sadomasochists in Chicago organized the Chicago Hellfire Club (CHC), one of the first clubs formed for the purpose of facilitating S/M sexual encounters that used no code or façade of any sort. CHC chose to use instruments of S/M and torture in its colors and to state plainly that the group was made up of gay sadomasochists seeking others like themselves for sexual purposes. Some gay S/M clubs were formed in reaction to the adoption of leather garb as a sort of gay male uniform by homosexuals who were not involved in S/M.

For clubs, 1978 was a boom year. In his *Leather History Timeline,* Tony DeBlase lists twenty-five clubs founded that year, two in Canada and the remaining twenty-three scattered in thirteen different states. Among them, Samois was established in San Francisco in 1978 to serve the interests of women who do S/M with women. It was the first lesbian S/M club and was followed by others, such as Leather and Lace in Los Angeles. In 1980 in New York, Gay Male S/M Activists (GMS/MA) was organized as a direct result of a letter by Brian O'Dell published in *Gay Community News.* The group became one of the major forces in the S/M technique-training movement, which dominated the development of the leather community in the 1980s.

The National Leather Association (NLA) was different in intent and effect. When Steve Maidhof and a few friends in the Seattle area formed NLA in 1986, they intended to bring together gay men and lesbians in one club and to serve all of the various purposes of clubs: entertainment, education, social interaction, and activism. Before NLA's second anniversary, it had already become, like Janus and TES, a congregation of all sexualities.

By the late 1980s, the constituency that called itself "the leather community" comprised hundreds of leather, motorcycle, and explicitly S/M clubs, along with leather bars and businesses serving leather, S/M, and fetish needs as well as a growing calendar of special events and a rapidly changing roster of stars. In the absence of any formal governing body, leather people—starting, as was often the case, with gay men—organized socially and to some extent politically around events featuring leather title contests. The phenomenon, which began in 1973 with a Mr. Scene and Machine Contest in Washington, D.C., became stable with the founding of International Mr. Leather (IML) in 1979. Contests provided a forum in which leather men from across the country could communicate and interact with the sexual atmosphere charged but, unlike most club runs, not quite the central reason for the gathering.

The Era of National Organizing

With the advent in Chicago of IML, the leather title idea became a "system," national in scope and international in appeal. Bars could have local contests, as could clubs and businesses. The contest weekends provided opportunities for political meetings, vendor fairs, sexual interactions, and network development. In the early 1980s, the lesbian S/M group Samois sponsored the first Women's Leather Dance, the first Ms. Leather Contest, and the first Lesbian Pride Leather Dance. Besides the sixty-five or more contests around the country and internationally that feed into the IML system and those that also recently fed into a similar Mr. Drummer contest (1981–2001), there are now or have been regional, national, and international leather title contests for self-described leather boys, deaf men and women, black men and women, dykes, dads, cowboys, and mommies, to mention only a few.

The previously slight cooperation of gay men and lesbians in leather increased significantly in the 1980s when women joined men in the grassroots AIDS movement. The leather community suffered a high mortality rate, and its radical sex practices were among the targets in the effort to blame the start or spread of AIDS on someone or something. Consequently, leathermen took a prominent lead in the fight for AIDS services and funding. Almost immediately, they were joined by women in leather who often served as caregivers, but no less significantly contributed to the style and energy of the movement as coworkers and allies.

All the elements, institutions, celebrities, and coalitions developed through the mid-1980s were sorely tested toward the end of the decade when the leather community tried to assert its legitimacy within the LGBT community and also attempted to achieve a coordination that would amount to national leadership. Though no longer willing to see themselves as fringe-dwellers, leatherpeople were considered a liability by leaders in the increasingly successful LGB rights movement, which often attempted to put a non-threatening public face on the LGB community. For instance, leather contingents had to fight to get themselves included in the LGB marches on Washington in 1987 and 1993. This attitude was a major obstacle to large-scale organizing in the leather community.

In fact, the overall out leather community, though increasingly unified by just such pressures from outside, was no longer LGB in the majority. Three organizations founded in the 1990s exemplify the current mode of community building. In the fall of 1991, Chuck Renslow and acquaintances founded the Leather Archives and Museum (LA&M), and in April 1996, a coalition of leather people from New York S/M Activists led by Susan Wright started The National Coalition for Sexual Freedom (NCSF) to "fight for sexual freedom and privacy rights for all adults who engage in safe, sane and consensual sexual expression." In 1997, Jon Weis, again assisted by New York S/M Activists and inspired by the gay community's Creating Change Conferences, founded the Leather Leadership Conference (LLC). These three pansexual organizations are examples of grassroots organizing, but they also provide the leather community with the means to preserve its history, prepare future leaders and activists, and meet current legal challenges. Meanwhile, no major institutional form developed in the leather community has been discarded: the old networks continue to function for those who need them and some of the earliest clubs continue as well, contributing to the ongoing development of the leather community.

Bibliography

Bean, Joseph. *Leathersex: A Guide for the Curious Outsider and the Serious Player.* Los Angeles: Daedalus, 1994.

———. *Leathersex Q & A: Questions About Leathersex and the Leather Lifestyles Answered.* Los Angeles: Daedalus, 1996.

Baldwin, Guy. *Ties That Bind: The S/M/Leather/Fetish Erotic Lifestyle, Issues, Commentaries and Advice.* Los Angeles: Daedalus, 1993.

Bienvenu, Robert V., II. "The Development of Sadomasochism as a Cultural Style in the Twentieth-Century United States." Ph.D dissertation, Department of Anthropology, Indiana University (Bloomington), 1998.

Carney, William. *The Real Thing.* New York: Putnam's Sons, 1968.

———. *The Rose Exterminator.* New York: Everest House, 1982.

DeBlase, Anthony F. *Leather History Timeline.* 4th ed. Chicago: Leather Archives and Museum, 1999.

Rubin, Gayle, "Elegy for the Valley of the Kings: AIDS and the Leather Community in San Francisco, 1981–1996." In *In Changing Times: Gay Men and Lesbians Encounter HIV/AIDS*, edited by Martin P. Levine, Peter M. Nardi, and John H. Gagnon. Chicago, University of Chicago Press, 1997.

———. "The Leather Menace." In *Coming to Power,* edited by Samois. Boston, Alyson, 1982.

———. "The Miracle Mile: South of Market and Gay Male Leather in San Francisco, 1962–1996." In *Reclaiming San Francisco: History, Politics, Culture.* Edited by James Brook, Chris Carlsson, and Nancy Peters. San Francisco: City Lights Books, 1998.

———. "Old Guard, New Guard." *Cuir Underground* 4, no. 2 (Summer 1998).

———. "Sites, Settlements, and Urban Sex: Archaeology and The Study of Gay Leathermen in San Francisco, 1955–1995." In *Archaeologies of Sexuality,* edited by Robert Schmidt and Barbara Voss. London: Routledge, 2000.

———. "The Valley of the Kings: Leathermen in San Francisco, 1960–1990." Ph.D. dissertation, Department of Anthropology, University of Michigan, 1994.

Thompson, Mark, ed. *Leatherfolk: Radical Sex, People, Politics and Practice.* Boston: Alyson Publications, 1991.

Townsend, Larry. *The Leatherman's Handbook.* Los Angeles: LT Publications, 1972.

Joseph W. Bean

See also FETISHES; SADOMASOCHISM, SADISTS, AND MASOCHISTS; SEX CLUBS.

LEGG, Dorr **(b. 12 December 1904; d. 26 July 1994), activist, publisher.**

Primarily associated with the first openly gay magazine, *ONE,* Dorr Legg also influenced the shaping of gay studies in U.S. colleges and universities by creating the first gay educational institution, the ONE Institute. Legg remained an important gay activist and educator up until the time of his death.

William Lambert Dorr Legg grew up in Ann Arbor, Michigan, the son of a piano manufacturer. Intellectually gifted, he studied piano and architecture at the University of Michigan. After graduating in 1928, Legg spent the next two decades working as a private landscape architect in New York, Miami, and Detroit, and also taught architecture at the University of Oregon from 1935 to 1942. His architecture career was cut short, however, when an interracial affair in Detroit led to police harassment and professional jeopardy. In 1948, Legg and his lover ventured to Los Angeles seeking a more tolerant atmosphere.

Hardly a paradise of acceptance or inclusivity during the late 1940s, Los Angeles nonetheless offered opportunities for gay life and activism not available elsewhere in the country. Legg began attending Mattachine Foundation meetings, and in 1950 he helped organize the Knights of the Clock, a small group dedicated to interracial homosexual solidarity. On 15 October 1952, Legg officially embarked on his second career when a small group of disgruntled Mattachine activists concocted *ONE* magazine (1953–1967), the first national gay magazine, in Legg's kitchen. For the next fifteen years, under the pseudonym "William Lambert," Legg managed *ONE*'s business affairs, performed editorial duties, contributed hundreds of articles and editorials, answered *ONE*'s mail, and spent the majority of his waking hours in *ONE*'s cramped office space. Thousands of gay men and women who visited *ONE*'s offices in the 1950s and 1960s were greeted (and often put to work) by Dorr Legg.

The magazine remained the principal activity of ONE, Inc., until the 1960s, but many of the activists, Legg included, had larger ambitions for the organization. A book press was created—Legg's involvement included editing ONE Press's second book, *Homosexuals Today* (1956), the first extensive account of American and European homophile movement achievements. ONE Press never quite took off, but the idea of an educational institution where gay people could conduct research and take classes on gay culture and history seemed the ideal remedy for what Legg considered gay people's chief problem in the postwar years: ignorance about themselves. This led to the creation of the ONE Institute, which offered its first class in 1956 called "The Homophile in Society," taught by Legg. During the next several years, Legg taught several courses, recruited instructors, and developed the ONE Institute into a stable intellectual bedrock of the gay rights struggle.

As ONE, Inc., took on more projects, bitter disputes arose over the organization's direction and purpose. During the early 1960s, Legg was increasingly devoted to the ONE Institute, seeking more resources to fund its educational programs, annual meetings, and quarterly journal. *ONE* magazine editor Don Slater, meanwhile, felt the original magazine should remain the organization's focus, claiming that Legg's projects drained resources necessary to improve the magazine's quality. By 1965, Legg and Slater were battling each other in court, attempting to gain control of the name "ONE." A compromise awarded Legg the name ONE while allowing Slater the resources necessary to start a rival magazine, which became *Tangents* (1967–1970). *ONE* magazine disappeared from newsstands, but for the next three decades, under Legg's firm control, the ONE Institute continued offering classes and facilitating research from its Los Angeles facilities, adding a graduate school in 1981.

Legg was an unusual gay activist in many respects. Commencing his "second career" (in his own words) at age forty-eight, Legg was considerably older than many of his colleagues. He was a staunch Republican throughout his life, and deeply libertarian. His tough-love, pull-yourself-up-by-the-bootstraps philosophy rubbed some left-leaning gay activists the wrong way. His advocacy of homosexuality as a method of population control also outraged many fellow activists. Legg disapproved of militant gay activism such as street protests during the late 1960s and 1970s, preferring a more intellectual approach that branded him old-fashioned to many younger activists. Legg's stubborn use of the word "homophile," rejected by gay liberation activists during the 1960s and 1970s, also damaged his credibility within the gay movement in his later years. When Legg died at age eighty-nine on 26 July 1994, survived by longtime partner John Nojima, the resources of the ONE Institute merged with Jim Kepner's International Lesbian and Gay Archives, creating the largest gay archive in the world, the ONE Institute and Archives in Los Angeles. This facility is Legg's chief legacy. In an era when gay organizations form and fold almost daily, ONE has survived for fifty years, primarily due to Legg's tenacious, and sometimes domineering, leadership.

Bibliography

Bullough, Vern, ed. *Before Stonewall: Activists for Gay and Lesbian Rights in Historical Context.* New York: Harrington Park Press, 2002.

Bullough, Vern, Dorr Legg, Barry Elcano, et al., eds. *An Annotated Bibliography of Homosexuality.* New York: Garland, 1976.

Cutler, Marvin, ed. (psuedonym for W. Dorr Legg). *Homosexuals Today: A Handbook of Organizations and Publications.* Los Angeles: ONE, Inc., 1956.

D'Emilio, John. *Sexual Politics, Sexual Communities: The Making of a Homosexual Minority in the United States, 1940–1970.* Chicago: University of Chicago Press, 1983.

Legg, W. Dorr. *Homophile Studies in Theory and Practice.* San Francisco: GLB Publishers and ONE Institute Press, 1994.

Craig M. Loftin

See also HOMOPHILE MOVEMENT; HOMOPHILE PRESS; *ONE*; ONE INSTITUTE.

LESBIAN AVENGERS

Formed in 1992, the Lesbian Avengers is an informal network of grassroots organizations that use street theater and direct action to increase lesbian visibility, challenge oppression, and resist queer assimilation into the dominant culture. Although accurate tracking is difficult because chapters appear and disappear quickly, in 2000 there were about fifty-five Lesbian Avenger chapters in the United States and at least five operating in other countries. There is no national organization or structure, and each chapter is locally founded and operated, but chapters often collaborate on major national protests and events such as annual "dyke marches."

Objectives

The Avengers was established in New York City in 1992 by six longtime lesbian activists who were concerned that the "gay movement" was failing to nurture the next generation of lesbian activists. They felt that academia was too theoretical; gay institutions were too conservative—lesbian visibility needed the same jolt that the AIDS Coalition to Unleash Power (ACT UP) had provided for AIDS activism.

Not long after the group was founded, it adopted as its logo a bomb with a lit fuse, an image that set the tone for the Avengers' activities. Several chapters drew new members with the boast, "We Don't Recruit, We Reload." Others used posters featuring gun-toting women in action. Critics saw these as calls to violence, but Lesbian Avengers describes them as theater, as symbolic ways of voicing outrage and confronting power.

The desire for such an aggressive strategy was stimulated in part by the 1991 murder of a lesbian and a gay man in Oregon. In that incident, neo-Nazi skinheads threw Molotov cocktails into the victims' home in an attack spurred on by a heated battle over an (ultimately defeated) ballot initiative that would have overturned statewide protections against discrimination based on sexual orientation and blocked passage of future protections.

That deadly event sparked the Lesbian Avenger trademark fire-eating, a staple stunt at carnivals that involves putting a lit torch into one's mouth and removing it with the flame still blazing. Saliva and lack of oxygen suppress the flame, which then reignites as it exits the flame-eaters' mouth. The Lesbian Avenger handbook describes its use of fire-eating as a symbolic act of reclaiming the element used against them: "The fire will not consume us—we take it and make it our own. . . . Lesbian Avengers eat fire to show that they can conquer their fears, and that they will not be intimidated. The bomb symbolizes the fact that we take the violence . . . consume it and turn this energy into positive non-violent action."

That attitude, coupled with its use of outrageous, often humorous street theater, has made the Lesbian Avengers a magnet to younger radical lesbians. Although membership is relatively small, the chapters have drawn a generally more diverse, multicultural group than most LGBT movement organizations can claim.

As a Moderate Response

The emergence of the Lesbian Avengers follows a cycle that social justice movements have traditionally experienced whereby a period dominated by assimilationist reformers is followed by the rise of liberationist radicals, who in turn are criticized by activists with more moderate politics. In this case, the more moderate homophile movement of the 1960s was followed by the more militant post-Stonewall Riots politics of the 1970s, which favored visibility over respectability. In turn, this gave way to more moderate politics that, for example, favored lobbying to street theater in the late 1970s. The late 1980s witnessed the revival of militancy as AIDS decimated queer communities in the context of governmental indifference. ACT UP was born out of that rage and an unwillingness to wait for slow reform while the death toll rose. By the early 1990s, however, more moderate politics were again ascendant, and the creation of Lesbian Avengers was part of an effort to challenge the new assimilationism.

Critics of radical liberationism dismiss the tactics of Lesbian Avengers and other direct action groups as irrational, unproductive, narcissistic, and more interested in mocking than in changing the system. Liberationists, in turn, dismiss reformers as collaborators who allow a narrow slice of the community access to the illusion of power while making life more difficult and more dangerous for the rest.

Actions

One of the most visible early actions of Lesbian Avengers, the Dyke March, coincided with the 1993 March on Washington. The event, which involved a separate march held before the general march, drew some twenty thousand women. The Dyke March was conceived as a protest march to increase lesbian visibility, spotlight issues unique to the lesbian community, and express outrage about being the targets of harassment, discrimination, and violence. In the following years, dyke marches were organized in various locations, mobilizing thousands in San Francisco, Chicago, New York and Los Angeles. Dyke marches have also been held in British Columbia and Toronto, and more than two hundred people participated in the "Dyke March, Tokyo" in 1997.

The tactics of Lesbian Avengers are as varied as the participants. Although members engage in traditional activities such as writing protest letters and cooking food at women's shelters, more original, outrageous tactics are the hallmarks of an Avenger zap. Examples include the following:

- In its first action in New York in 1992, Lesbian Avengers responded to a takeover of the education system by far right religious ideologues by going to a conservative religious school and handing out rainbow balloons emblazoned with the phrase "Ask about Lesbian Lives."
- In 1995, the San Francisco chapter of the Lesbian Avengers zapped Exodus International, a notorious anti-LGB religious organization that claims to "cure" homosexuality. Five Avengers stormed the Exodus headquarters in San Rafael, California, climbed onto the reception desk, shouted "We don't need to be cured," and released a thousand crickets.
- The Boston Avengers held a Lesbian Avenger "Eat Out" outside of a Jenny Craig weight loss branch to fight sizeism and fat-phobia in 1995.
- In 1997, the Lesbian Avengers protested a Promise Keepers rally in Washington, D.C.
- On Valentine's Day, the Avengers sent a message to the Family Research Council with the poem "Roses are Red / Violets are Violet / Don't knock sodomy / Least til you've tried it" and handed out leaflets at a Massachusetts elementary school that read "Girls who love girls, and women who love women are OK."

Sarah Schulman, a member of ACT UP and one of the Lesbian Avengers founders, says the group exceeded expectations: "The original motive for the Lesbian Avengers was to find some kind of training ground to teach younger lesbians organizing skills because male dominated groups were not allowing them to develop. It became a cultural phenomenon no one expected."

Bibliography

Lesbian Avengers Website. http://www.lesbian.org

Retter, Yolanda. "Dyke Marches: A Herstory." *New Internationlist Magazine,* 22 November 22, 2001.

Schulman, Sarah, and Urvashi Vaid. *My American History: Lesbian and Gay Life During the Reagan/Bush Years.* New York: Routledge, 1994.

Nadine Smith

See also MARCHES ON WASHINGTON; PRIDE MARCHES AND PARADES.

LESBIAN CONNECTION

Lesbian Connection is the longest-running lesbian publication in the United States. Launched in October 1974 by the Ambitious Amazons, a Lansing, Michigan, collective, the magazine was designed to create grassroots networks and to provide a forum for all lesbians.

Editorial contributions are solicited and welcomed from all lesbians, and the magazine is written in great part by its readers. In *Lesbian Connection*'s premiere issue, the collective's members urged readers to contribute to future issues. They requested event announcements, letters, and personal reactions, and they solicited any and all items that might be of interest to lesbians (excluding literary contributions such as poetry and short stories).

Its founders conceived of *Lesbian Connection* as a national clearinghouse of information and ideas, and themselves as caretakers of that information, rather than as editors or publishers who might speak with a single editorial voice. Instead, they encouraged the inclusion of a wide variety of voices, drawn from their readers.

Humble Beginnings

The magazine began as a mimeographed, ten-page publication in an 8½-by-11 single-staple format. Its original print run was four hundred, and its budget $110. It was free of charge and distributed by mail to individuals and organizations throughout the country. To keep costs down, the Ambitious Amazon collective urged groups that received issues to reproduce and distribute them to lesbians on their own mailing lists.

The collective's members also tried to stretch dollars as much as possible, attempting, for instance, to make a one-thousand-copy mimeograph master last for three thousand copies. During the first several years, the collective held fundraisers and sponsored lesbian potluck dinners and dances to raise operating funds.

Lesbian Connection, also known as LC or Elsie, was a success from its first issue. In the two months between the printing of the first and second volumes, circulation tripled to 1,200. By 2003 the collective was printing twenty-five thousand copies of every issue, and the cost of producing and mailing a single twenty-eight-page issue had risen to $70,000.

With success came the challenges of producing an ever-larger magazine and maintaining an ever-changing mailing list. For nearly ten years, the staff worked with only a donated typewriter, until a special fund drive raised enough money to buy two computers. For several years, collective members trained themselves to do the printing in-house on a donated (but ancient) offset printing press. *Lesbian Connection* was produced completely by volunteer labor for its first seven years. In 1981 the collective began to pay a handful of workers to help produce it, while others continued to donate their time.

Founded on Feminist Principles

Lesbian Connection was launched at a time when lesbian feminist activism was emerging, and both the gay and lesbian and feminist movements were beginning to find greater voice. The first *Ms. Magazine* had been published in 1973, a year earlier, marking a new direction for feminism in periodical publications. *Lesbian Connection* joined other 1970s lesbian publications such as *Lavender Woman, The Furies, Amazon Quarterly, Lesbian Tide,* and *Sinister Wisdom* in creating a means for building networks and a safe place for lesbians to learn about themselves and their communities.

From the beginning, the Ambitious Amazons collective insisted on adhering to lesbian feminist principles in the creation and production of its magazine. Members were committed to the magazine's being inclusive in its content and to providing an open forum for all lesbian experience. Reader submissions are edited only for clarity and length, and the sole restriction on content is that it be lesbian-positive. When members of the previously all-volunteer staff began receiving a salary in 1981, all workers were paid the same wage, whether they were responsible for filing, typing, editing, printing, or distributing. Each was considered equally valuable to the production of the magazine.

The magazine has also been egalitarian in its outreach. It has been "free to lesbians" since its first volume. By 2003 the suggested annual donation was $27 ("more if you can, less if you can't"), but no one is required to pay. Adhering to the "pay if you can" principle, the publishers have emphasized in every issue that the subscription price is a voluntary contribution.

Reader-Created Content

The lesbian feminist principles of its founders is what drove the decision to have the magazine written primarily by its readers. In the Ambitious Amazons' view, all women are experts at their own lives, and their individual expertise can be shared to create a greater good for all lesbians.

Lesbian Connection prints information about music festivals, conferences, and cultural events, as well as reader reviews of books, music, films, and television shows. The magazine also runs reader-written articles about issues and problems of concern to its audience. Over the years, the magazine has published numerous articles addressing health issues, alcoholism, lesbian parenting. child custody, legal problems, and many other relevant topics.

After receiving a great number of submissions concerning lesbians in the military, the magazine launched a regular section entitled "Uncle Sam Doesn't Want You." Another regular section, called "How To," prints reader-written articles explaining how to do nearly anything, from caulking a bathtub to artificially inseminating.

Lesbian Connection also strives to build national and international lesbian networks through its "Contact Dykes" section, which lists lesbian-friendly establishments such as restaurants and hotels, as well as the names, addresses, and telephone numbers of women who are willing to help other lesbians traveling in their area.

Lasting Impact

Since its inception, the magazine has aimed not to turn a profit, but to reach out to a wide variety of lesbians and provide them with information that can improve their lives. For longer than any other national publication, *Lesbian Connection* has nurtured a grassroots network that has allowed lesbians from around the world to communicate and connect, and throughout its history, the magazine has provided a lifeline to women who are isolated from lesbian communities.

Lesbian Connection is a continuing example of lesbian feminist principles in action. From its egalitarian treatment of its staff to its insistence on allowing readers to control its content, the magazine's success has demonstrated that publications founded on principle can coexist with slick for-profit magazines—and even thrive.

Bibliography

Gross, Larry P., and James D. Woods, eds. *Columbia Reader on Lesbians and Gay Men in Media, Society, and Politics.* New York: Columbia University Press, 1999.

National Museum & Archives of Lesbian and Gay History. *The Lesbian Almanac.* New York: Berkley Books, 1996.

Streitmatter, Rodger. *Unspeakable: The Rise of the Gay and Lesbian Press in America.* Boston: Faber and Faber, 1995.

Jane R. Ballinger

LESBIAN FEMINISM

Lesbian feminism emerged during the second wave of feminist activism in the United States. Beginning in the 1970s, lesbian feminists challenged homophobia and heterosexism in the women's movement, fought against sexism in the LGBT movement, struggled against antilesbianism and antifeminism in other social movements, and carved out political, social, and cultural niches for themselves. Many lesbian feminists advocated separatism, living whenever and wherever possible in lesbian feminist communities and spending money and time only with other lesbian feminists. Lesbian feminists also developed radical critiques of patriarchy, sexism, misogyny, homophobia, heterosexism, and the social construction of sex, gender, and sexuality. For many lesbian feminists, lesbianism was the logical outcome of feminism—as one lesbian feminist put it, "feminism is the theory, lesbianism is the practice."

Early History

Historians often trace the beginning of lesbian feminism to the founding of Radicalesbians in New York in 1970 and the Furies in Washington, D.C., in 1971–72. The establishment of these two groups represents a vital and crucial turning point in the history of lesbian feminism and—along with the writing of various manifestos, the organizing of various political actions, and the creation of various groups in the late 1960s and early 1970s—marks the beginning of an organized lesbian feminist movement that called itself lesbian and feminist. However, the history of lesbian feminism in terms of building, fostering, and developing identities and politics that can be classified as both lesbian and feminist follows the course of the nineteenth and twentieth centuries.

Many nineteenth-century women who formed same-sex romantic, passionate, and intimate friendships, established Boston marriages, or even passed as men, believed in and fought for women's rights, women's equality, and women's empowerment. When sexologists created new sexual taxonomies in the late nineteenth and early twentieth centuries, the people they labeled inverts and homosexuals included women who resisted sex and gender oppression. Among the women who fought for female suffrage, embraced the cause of free love, labeled themselves New Women, wore men's clothing, advocated for the advancement of "colored" women, and adopted the new term "feminist" in the early twentieth century are women who considered themselves lesbians or who have been identified as lesbians by historians. As urban lesbian cultures—often centered in bars, speakeasies, house parties, and softball leagues and frequently organized through femme/butch dyads—began to take shape in the first half of the twentieth century, many participants viewed themselves and were viewed by others as strong proponents of female resistance and female strength. Lesbians who broke down barriers against women working in traditionally male jobs and serving in the traditionally male military can also be regarded as both lesbian and feminist.

Lesbians played important roles in the women's movement in the years before and after World War II, but only in the 1950s did a formally organized lesbian movement begin. Of the first major homophile organizations, the Daughters of Bilitis (DOB) was the most widely known and influential group for women. Founded in 1955 by lesbian partners Del Martin and Phyllis Lyon, DOB soon had chapters in major urban centers across the United States. Inspired by the predominantly male Mattachine Society, Lyon and Martin sought to create an organization and a publication, *The Ladder,* dedicated to changing public attitudes toward lesbians and lesbianism. While some DOB lesbians (including, for example, Barbara Gittings) were opposed to or ambivalent about feminism, others explored the effects of sexism on lesbians, criticized gay men for being sexist, and expressed interest in forming alliances with women's movement organizations. In the late 1960s, several DOB members and other homophile leaders strongly embraced feminist politics. Martin joined the National Organization for Women (NOW) in 1967; DOB president Rita Laporte and *The Ladder* editor Barbara Grier attempted to take the organization and the magazine in feminist directions; and writer Anita Cornwell published groundbreaking work that explored intersections of gender, sexuality, and race in their publication. Conflicts over feminism, however, helped precipitate the collapse of the national DOB in the early 1970s.

Meanwhile, following the transformative Stonewall Riots of 1969, which launched the gay liberation movement, lesbians began to feel increasingly alienated from gay men, gay communities, and gay politics. In 1970, Martin said good-bye to gay men in a statement published in various periodicals, including *The Ladder* and *The Advocate.* Citing philosophical, moral, and political differences, Martin wrote a scathing critique of sexism in gay political organizations, public spaces such as bars and bathhouses, and gay publications and then announced that she was turning her attention to the feminist movement: "I must go where the action is—where there is still hope, where there is still possibility for personal and collective growth. It is a revelation to find acceptance, equality, love, and friendship—everything we sought in the homophile movement—not there but in the women's movement" (Martin). In spite of their common ground of oppression based on same-sex sexual orientation, many lesbians felt that gay men did not treat them with mutual respect or a sense of equality. Many women felt this way not only about older homophile collectives such as the Mattachine Society but also about younger gay liberationist ones such as the Gay Liberation Front.

The women's movement that Martin and other lesbians embraced gave rise to many feminist organizations, liberal and radical, and lesbians played key roles in countless feminist groups. Many lesbians, however, experienced tremendous conflict within organized feminism as talk of women's liberation and women's equality occurred alongside actions excluding, avoiding, and attacking lesbianism and lesbians. One of the most volatile and notable examples of this happened in NOW. Conflict between lesbians and heterosexuals had been brewing, especially in its largest chapter, New York City NOW. With the emergence of the gay liberation movement, lesbians demanded recognition and support from the women's movement. Within the chapter, feminists began to identify lesbianism as a key feminist issue. After Rita Mae Brown, a member of this NOW chapter, came out as a lesbian, she claimed that NOW national president Betty Friedan pushed her out. Other lesbians in the chapter, including chapter president Ti-Grace Atkinson, were voted out of or unilaterally removed from office—incidents many referred to as being purged. In 1969, Friedan lamented that lesbians in NOW were threatening its pursuit of women's equality, constituting what she called a "lavender menace." In response to this epithet, forty-plus lesbians, many from the New York City chapter of NOW, stormed the stage at the 1970 Congress to Unite Women—wearing purple shirts bearing Friedan's words—and insisted that lesbianism was a women's-rights issue. Despite fears among national NOW board members that a strong and visible lesbian presence would diminish the organization's political clout, many rank-and-file members supported the protest and its message. In the same year as the Lavender Menace protest, the Northern California chapter of NOW passed a resolution identifying lesbians' rights as women's rights. Mobilizing from the grassroots within NOW's federated structure, women pushed the resolution to the state chapter of NOW, then to a regional conference. In 1971, the national NOW passed the resolution and, on paper at least, acknowledged lesbian rights as part of its national agenda.

Lesbian Feminist Organizing

Implementing inclusivity, however, was another story altogether. Some lesbians, scorned by the purges and faced with the task of changing many heterosexual women's hearts and minds, abandoned liberal feminist groups such as NOW for radical feminism and women's liberation. In spite of the paeans to sisterhood and revolution, however, many radical feminist organizations did not openly discuss lesbianism or welcome lesbians with open arms. While lesbians began participating more actively and openly in contemporaneous radical movements, especially black power, they also began to pen manifestos about lesbian separatism and the unique oppression faced by lesbians. In 1970, Radicalesbians, a group founded in New York and made up of women who had participated in gay liberation, women's liberation, or both, invented a new political definition of what it meant to be a lesbian: "What is a lesbian? A lesbian is the rage of all women condensed to the point of explosion." Different from male homosexuality and certainly different from female heterosexuality, lesbianism, according to the Radicalesbians' manifesto, "The Woman-Identified Woman," was a source of political and cultural power. According to Radicalesbians, all women who were women-identified could consider themselves lesbians, and Radicalesbians called upon all such women to deepen their commitments, sexual and otherwise, to other women.

Alienated from a feminist movement that openly sought women's liberation, but had broken its promise to represent all women, and discouraged by sexism among men in gay liberation, many lesbians now founded their own, separate organizations. Radicalesbians groups were established in several cities beyond New York, including Philadelphia. The Furies, one of the most influential, formed as a residential, publishing, and political collective in Washington, D.C. Other groups sprang up in a variety of U.S. cities, including New York, Chicago, San Francisco, and Boston, and in many of these, lesbian feminists and separatists proposed that lesbianism was the most complete form of feminism, the ultimate expression of "the personal is political." Revising conservative essentialist and biologically determinist views about women, they argued that *all* women were born lesbians but that male privilege and dominance in U.S. (and Western) society destroyed women's capacity to love women and instead pitted them against one another. In this framework, women who threw off the yoke of male domination and openly loved women, in sexual and/or nonsexual ways, were lesbians. Describing lesbianism as a political identity and not just a sexual choice, many lesbian feminists advocated overthrowing heterosexual marriage and the nuclear family as institutions oppressive to women.

Such commentary was often expressed through the lesbian feminist press, which exploded in the 1970s as more and more women published and distributed newsletters, newspapers, magazines, and journals across the United States. Lesbian feminist publications varied widely in form, content, and distribution; some journals continued for years, while others lasted only for a single issue. While collectives such as the Furies published journals that have received significant scholarly attention, other collectives formed for the sole purpose of publishing a single newsletter, many of which have been overlooked. Most of these publications were typed, mimeographed, and either distributed through mail subscriptions or sold in independent women's bookstores.

By helping women to address feelings of isolation and providing a source of news and commentary on lesbian experiences, these publications fostered the development of urban and rural lesbian feminist communities. Some publications, such as *Spectre: Paper of Revolutionary Lesbians* (Ann Arbor, Michigan) and *The Furies,* focused on socio-political aspects of lesbian life; others emphasized lesbian art and culture. For example, African American lesbian poet Audre Lorde served as poetry editor for *Chrysalis* and *Amazon Quarterly*, contributing to the papers' political and cultural forums. Although many lesbian feminist publications did not enjoy a long publication run, they introduced political, social, and cultural issues to other lesbians and feminists and promoted discussion about what it meant to be a lesbian. Among the better known periodicals were *Furies, Spectre, Lesbian Tide* and *Chrysalis* (both in Los Angeles), *Amazon Quarterly* (Oakland, California), *Lesbians Fight Back* and *Wicce: A Lesbian/Feminist Newspaper* (both in Philadelphia), and *Lavender Woman* (Chicago). All boasted a variety of features, including political manifestos and statements, photographs, cartoons, calendars of events, cultural reviews, and fiction.

In addition to producing publications dedicated to lesbian liberation, lesbian feminists cultivated multiple political strategies. Using the radical feminist practice of zap actions, lesbian feminists targeted venues of traditional womanhood and heterosexuality, protesting beauty pageants and bridal stores. In addition to practices of zap actions and consciousness-raising, lesbian feminists critiqued heterosexuality and patriarchy through unique lenses. They invented and modified language to challenge patriarchal power, replacing "women" with "wimmin" or "womyn," and dropping birth names in favor of woman-identified names. They also forged gynocentric spiritualities, writing about and embracing traditions that preceded Judeo-Christianity and taking up witchcraft and goddess worship.

Many lesbian feminists also advocated and, whenever possible, practiced separatism, living in communities that did not include heterosexual women or men. In

"Creating Community!" This poster, featuring a drawing of three women joining hands to form a circle over the words "a coming together," advertises a lesbian feminist conference.

some contexts, lesbian separatists broke off from lesbian feminist groups when their agenda of total separation from men and heterosexual women was met with resistance. In their own economically independent communities, lesbian separatists pursued the political project of creating and maintaining feminist, women-only space. Urban and rural collectives disassociated themselves from the population at large in locations ranging from major metropolitan areas such as Washington, D.C., to rural parts of Kansas and Mississippi. The collectives tended to be short-lived as conflicting life choices, political objectives, and personal values came to the fore. While they lasted, however, these groups practiced innovative forms of cooperative living, egalitarianism, and an ethic of caring. Lesbian feminist values were also institutionalized in longer-term creations, including feminist bookstores, coffeehouses, and the women's music industry. In the 1970s, lesbians and feminists came together to establish the annual Michigan Womyn's Music Festival, still in existence and functioning in the new century as a weeklong event featuring singers, poets, artists, and their supporters. Other festivals that celebrate women's music, art, and culture later sprang up across the United States; these include Camp Sister Spirit's Womyn's Festival in Ovett, Mississippi, the Bay Area Women's Festival, and the Ohio Lesbian Festival.

Criticism and Conflict

In spite of their commitment to eradicating injustice for all women, lesbian feminists and their theories of lesbian feminism came under fire in the mid-1970s. Many lesbian feminist groups adopted the tools of other revolutionary movements: consciousness-raising, action, criticism, and self-criticism. However, lesbian feminists faced factionalism and criticism from both within and outside their communities. Though women of color such as Ernestine Eckstein, Cleo Glenn, Ada Bello, Jeanne Cordova, and Anita Cornwell played important (though underexamined) roles in the homophile movement of the 1960s and the lesbian feminist movement of the early 1970s, lesbian feminist groups, especially separatist communities, tended to be made up primarily of white, university-educated, middle-class women. Those women who were older or younger, of color, working-class, disabled, radical or socialist, overweight or otherwise non-conforming to traditional ideas of beauty all charged various lesbian feminist groups with reproducing discrimination and oppression. Class and color became the main factors that produced division.

Lesbian feminists advocated the inclusion of women of color in their groups, but such inclusion was never widespread in practice. Many women of color outside of lesbian feminism criticized the radical doctrine for overlooking their interests and agendas. A key moment of conflict took place in 1970 at the Black Panthers' Revolutionary People's Constitutional Convention in Philadelphia, where black women confronted white lesbians. Over the next several years, radical lesbians of color charged "mainstream" lesbian feminists with being racist and classist. Audre Lorde, Barbara Smith, and Cherríe Moraga, among others, offered important critiques of feminism, especially its whiteness, while refusing to become antifeminist in the process. In so doing, they articulated important lesbian feminist stances, offering complicated, radical positions on the intersections of race, class, gender, sexuality, and other factors in women's lives. In 1977, the Combahee River Collective published its influential "Black Feminist Statement," which evinced the group's commitment to fighting the integrated and interlocking forces of racism, sexism, heterosexism, and class oppression. The collective also challenged the idea of separatism, recognizing that although they were feminists and lesbians, they felt solidarity with progressive black men, straight feminists, and other allies. By the mid-1970s, African American lesbians were organizing as lesbians, feminists, and women of color in such groups as the National Black Feminist Organization (founded in 1973), the Combahee River Collective, and the National Coalition of Black Lesbians and Gay Men (founded in 1978).

Within lesbian feminist groups, accusations of classism, ageism, and racism were common. Chicana author Cherríe Moraga pointed out that the structure of lesbian feminism excluded women of color even though lesbian feminist groups claimed to be open to all women. Rita Mae Brown's memoir of her time in the Furies collective, *A Plain Brown Rapper* (1976), documents some of the clashes related to class that arose within this collective. There were differences of opinion over how and where money should be spent, who should work at what types of jobs, and how best to communicate with other collective members, all of which Brown attributes to class divisions. The 1970s also marked the beginning of Native American lesbian publishing. Influenced by the 1960s native revivalism, gay and lesbian Native Americans began to publish essays, poetry, and novels. Paula Gunn Allen's essay "Beloved Women: Lesbians In American Indian Cultures" marked her public coming out and her challenge to the tribal and church-influenced homophobia she experienced. Asian and Pacific Island American (API) lesbians were particularly active in larger Asian communities, such as San Francisco, where API lesbian and feminist activist organizations rallied for access to health care, entry to bars, and provided support networks.

Other critics accused lesbian feminists of being anti-sex, suggesting that when lesbian feminists attacked sex between women and men as the primary basis of women's second-class status, they were being prudish and not recognizing that sex for women could be pleasurable, empowering, and liberating. In print, many lesbian feminist publications offered contemptuous analyses of heterosexuality, often condemning pornography, heterosexual satisfaction, and acts and displays of heterosexuality. In the process, some lesbian feminists discouraged sexual definitions of lesbianism, identifying such definitions as male and heterosexual in origin. Influential theorists such as Catherine MacKinnon and Andrea Dworkin equated pornography and rape, which fuelled intense debates over the role of sex, pornography, violence, and sexuality in feminism and lesbian feminism. Eventually these debates erupted into the full-fledged feminist "sex wars" of the late 1970s and 1980s. Many lesbian feminists, including Joan Nestle, Amber Hollibaugh, Pat Califia, Ann Snitow, and Dorothy Allison, resisted the so-called anti-sex feminists in print and in person. For example, Joan Nestle's essay "My Mother Liked to Fuck" challenged the notion that all heterosexual intercourse and sexual penetration were forms of legalized rape. Though many lesbian feminists took the pro-sex side, critics of lesbian feminism equated the movement with the anti-sex faction.

Lesbian feminists also came under fire for not accepting male-to-female transsexuals as women and for denying the legitimacy of bisexual desire and politics. By the 1990s, the Michigan Womyn's Music Festival was a main cultural and political site of tension among feminists, lesbians, and transsexuals. In 1991, a festival security guard expelled a transsexual woman. Afterward, festival organizers instituted a "womyn-born womyn"–only policy, stipulating that only women who were born physically female could attend the festival. While preserving the ideals of women-only spaces and safe spaces for women that were advocated by many lesbian feminist groups, the festival was attacked for the way it dealt with a controversy sometimes referred to as the "Transgender Menace." By the end of the decade, transsexual activists (through Camp Trans, their counterfestival demonstrations across the street from the Womyn's Festival) garnered more allies at the festival. While Michigan Womyn's Festival organizers did relax their policies somewhat regarding some transsexuals, Camp Trans is still ongoing, operating as a vital force for trans politics, activism, and awareness and demonstrating the grip that the male/female dichotomy has had on feminism, lesbian and otherwise, in theory and practice. By 2003, Camp Trans publicized their goal to have a greater presence of MTF activists to directly challenge the womyn-born womyn policy. The protest highlights that while the festival does not set policy for other women-only organizations and support services, they act as the transphobic standard of such spaces.

Although lesbian feminism emerged in the 1970s in response to sexism in the LGBT movement and homophobia and heterosexism in the women's movement, the movement remains both influential and controversial in the twenty-first century. While caricatured in U.S. mainstream culture, lesbian feminism remains popular among its core of believers as an explicit political commitment and an implicit set of beliefs and practices. Serial and monographic publications, music festivals, women-only spaces, art, pornography, and bookstores continue to express and develop the tenets of lesbian feminism while also incorporating and responding to critiques. Lesbian feminism generated a radical legacy through political mobilization, social activism, intersectional analysis, and new perspectives on the power of patriarchy; the social construction of sex, gender, and sexuality; and the route to liberation and empowerment.

Bibliography

Brown, Rita Mae. *A Plain Brown Rapper.* Baltimore: Diana Press, 1976.

Echols, Alice. *Daring to Be Bad: Radical Feminism in America, 1967–1975.* Minneapolis: University Of Minnesota Press, 1989.

Jay, Karla. *Tales of the Lavender Menace: A Memoir of Liberation.* New York: Basic Books, 1999.

Nestle, Joan. "My Mother Liked to Fuck." In *The Eight Technologies of Otherness.* Sue Golding Ed., London: Routledge, 1997.

Martin, Del and Phyllis Lyon. *Lesbian/Woman.* San Francisco: Glide Publications, 1972.

Moraga, Cherríe and Gloria Anzaldúa Eds. *This Bridge Called My Back: Writings By Radical Women Of Color.* Watertown, Mass: Persephone Press, 1981.

Stein, Arlene. *Sex and Sensiblity: Stories of a Lesbian Generation.* Berkeley: University Of California Press, 1997.

Stephanie Gilmore and Anne Collinson

See also ANTI-SEMITISM; ANZALDÚA, GLORIA; ATKINSON, TI-GRACE; ATLANTA; BROWN, RITA MAE; COMBAHEE RIVER COLLECTIVE; CORNWELL, ANITA; FEMMES AND BUTCHES; FURIES; GRAHN, JUDY; JOHNSTON, JILL; LESBIAN CONNECTION; LYON, PHYLLIS, AND DEL MARTIN; LORDE, AUDRE; MILLETT, KATE; MORAGA, CHERRÍE; MORGAN, ROBIN; MUSIC: WOMEN'S; MUSIC: WOMEN'S FESTIVALS; RADICALESBIANS; RICH, ADRIENNE; SHELLEY, MARTHA; SMITH, BARBARA; SOLANAS, VALERIE; WOO, MERLE.

LESBIAN HERSTORY ARCHIVES

The Lesbian Herstory Archives in New York City is the world's largest and oldest lesbian archive. It originated in 1973, emerging out of a lesbian consciousness-raising group formed by members of the Gay Academic Union—a post-Stonewall organization consisting mostly of City University of New York graduate students.

Cofounders Deborah Edel and Joan Nestle believed that mainstream institutions, including libraries and archives, did not care about lesbian culture. To ensure the preservation of lesbian culture and history, they established their own archive, run by lesbians.

Planning began in 1974 and in 1976 the Lesbian Herstory Archives opened in the cofounders' Upper West Side apartment in Manhattan. The collection began with the donation of Nestle's and Edel's personal papers and books. Soon others began contributing materials. The Archives has consistently adhered to the principle of being a grassroots, all-volunteer organization dependent on community members.

In 1975 the Archives published its first newsletter, containing the statement of purpose that continues to guide the Archives today. This statement declares that the Archives exists to "gather and preserve records of lesbian lives and activities so that future generations will have ready access to materials relevant to their lives. The process of gathering this material will also serve to uncover and collect our 'herstory' denied to us previously by patriarchal historians in the interests of the culture that they serve." Lesbians, using these materials, can then examine and reassess the lesbian experience. The statement expressed the commitment to preserve materials, regardless of format or dimension, related to the lives and experiences of lesbians.

In the first years of the twenty-first century, the Archives houses a huge range of material, including over 20,000 volumes; 2,000 photographs; 300 special collections; 600 periodical titles; 1,300 organizational and subject files; thousands of feet of film and video footage; art and artifacts; musical recordings; posters and T-shirts; memorabilia; and objects from bars, bookstores, and protests.

By 1978 the collection occupied most of the space in the apartment where it was housed and a campaign was underway to help spread the word about the Archives through a traveling slide show. The coordinators took it to all homes and public places where they were asked to speak. It built a feeling of pride in LGBT people and communities and—according to the statement of purpose—"helped . . . to remove the stigma of formality and exclusivity from the concept of an 'archive'."

Many of the Archives' principles are a radical departure from conventional archiving practices. They are inclusive and informal and reveal the Archives' commitment to living history, to housing the present along with the past. The Archives has become a mixture of library, museum, and family album. It is a sacred, open, inviting place cultivated and cared for by lesbians. No lesbian or non-lesbian woman is excluded (men are allowed in by special arrangement), and the goal is to represent every lesbian life. Consequently, the collection reflects the experiences of women, regardless of race and class, who have the courage to touch other women. It includes material from passing women; transgender individuals; femmes and butches; lesbians who have been married; and women who are bisexual, celibate, or polyamorous. The principles insist that a lesbian life is a valuable life and that treasuring lesbian lives is a political act. They take seriously the dangers of homophobia and reject the divisive agenda of oppressive thinkers who put pressure on lesbians to accommodate themselves to cultural norms. Government funding is refused because it might facilitate the seizing of material deemed in violation of federal obscenity laws: the choice of an individual to deposit her truth in diaries, photos, letters, and recordings is viewed as too precious to run the risk of confiscation. By turning down offers of purchase from academic or traditional research institutions (which often require certain forms of identification or credentials to gain entry) the Archives maintains its independence and accessibility. By not policing the content of collections from or about lesbians it maintains its inclusivity. It is a home not just for intellectuals, but for all.

The Archives was incorporated as the Lesbian Herstory Educational Foundation Inc., a not-for-profit foundation. In the mid-1980s the internal structure was revamped to create a volunteer coordinating committee that augments the leadership of the Archives' veteran coordinators. In addition to attending to specific areas of responsibility, coordinators perform the everyday functions needed to keep the Archives in operation. In 1992 the Archives relocated to a home of its own in the Park Slope section of Brooklyn. The location was selected for the large population of lesbians living in the community, for accessibility by public transportation, and for space considerations.

Lesbian culture is inseparable from the legacy of social activism and the social change and justice that activism has achieved. The collection of the Archives demonstrates that where there have been social movements, there have been lesbians. For thirty years the Archives has continued to serve as a living example of the kind of collective organizing that makes conviction an invitation and community inevitable.

Bibliography

Nestle, Joan. "Radical Archiving: A Lesbian Feminist Perspective." *Gay Insurgent,* nos. 4–5 (spring 1979): 10–12.

Schwartz, Judith. "The Archivist's Balancing Act: Helping Researchers while Protecting Individual Privacy." *Journal of American History* 79 (1992): 179–189.

Thistlethwaite, Polly. "The Lesbian and Gay Past: An Interpretive Battleground." *Gay Community News,* winter 1995, pp. 10, 24.

Amy Beth

See also HAMPTON, MABEL; HISTORY; HISTORY PROJECTS, LIBRARIES, AND ARCHIVES.

LGBTQ STUDIES

Lesbian, gay, bisexual, transgender, and queer studies is a broad, diverse, diffuse, and contentious field, with significant contributions generated through activist politics as well as within academic institutions. Defined as the study of LGBTQ populations—in history, culture, and politics—the field in the United States began in the twentieth century, with the first emergence of these populations into public visibility. But defined as the study of normative and nonnormative human bodies and minds—including their gender, race, class, and sexual characteristics—the field in the United States appeared as a branch of European sexology during the mid-nineteenth century.

Early History of Sexology

The figure most identified with the field of sexology from the middle to the end of the nineteenth century is Richard von Krafft-Ebing, whose *Psychopathia Sexualis* appeared in twelve German editions between 1886 and 1903. During his career as an insane-asylum physician, a neurologist in private practice, a university professor of psychiatry, and a director of an exclusive private clinic, Krafft-Ebing collected case histories of the sexual "perversions" of interest to forensic psychiatrists, lawyers, and other medical professionals. But the text circulated well beyond this audience, which expanded further with each edition.

During the mid-nineteenth century and subsequently, the categories deployed to classify sexual variation have shifted; they have always been open to conflict, debate, and change in basic definitions. In presenting his overall classificatory system for the major sexual "perversions," Krafft-Ebing defined sadism, masochism, fetishism, and antipathetic sexuality, which he also called contrary sexual instinct, and drew on the work of prominent theorists of hereditary biological "degeneration." He accepted a distinction between "primitive" races and the "lower" orders of European populations, among whom perverted behavior might be characteristic of the entire group, and "civilized" or privileged Europeans, among whom perverted behavior indicated individual pathological degeneration or arrested development. The result was a hazy, unstable distinction between vice or immoral perversity, most characteristic of those on the lower end of the "development" of race and class hierarchies, and the condition of perversion, which might be found without hint of vice at the higher end of these hierarchies. Krafft-Ebing then equivocated about whether the conditions of perversion among the "higher" types might be considered diseases to be treated or natural anomalies to be understood and tolerated.

The ambivalence lodged within Krafft-Ebing's texts characterizes the biological and psychological study of LGBTQ populations to this day. Controversies continue over whether sexual difference from an assumed heterosexual norm is pathological or benign, fixed or variable, nature or nurture, vice or virtue. Since the mid-nineteenth century, homophile as well as homophobic attitudes have permeated the study of human sexuality, mixed up in contradiction-ridden texts, as well as the fields of biology and psychology in general. Many texts in these fields also generally replicate the invidious racial, class, and gender hierarchies, distinctions, and exclusions that mark Krafft-Ebing's studies.

Krafft-Ebing's ambivalence toward the condition of "civilized" sexual perversion drew on, for its positive valence, the pioneering theories of Karl Ulrichs and the extensive research and polemics of Magnus Hirschfeld. Ulrichs's writings, published between 1865 and 1879, described a variety of man-manly love and defined its practitioners as Urnings, or members of a third, intermediate sex characterized by male bodies with female psyches. Urnings, including Ulrichs himself, represented nonpathological anomalies of nature whose sexual feelings were not immoral, but often spiritual and noble. Ulrichs, and later John Addington Symonds and Edward Carpenter, as well as Hirschfeld, resisted the pathologizing evolutionary accounts of sexual deviance as arrested or degenerative, but they mounted their defenses primarily on behalf of privileged Anglo-European men. All of these writers retained the primitive/civilized distinction to some degree, however, and based their defenses of Urnings, or intermediate types, on the alleged fine qualities, high achievements, and sensitive natures of "civilized" men.

The place of women in both the pathologizing and the naturalizing frameworks for the "perversions" was profoundly vexed. The development of civilized femininity was considered a marker of evolutionary progress, and the term "women" tended to reference privileged Anglo-European groups (those considered lower on the evolutionary scale were more likely to be called "females"). But even the most prosperous "civilized" women were believed to be less evolved than men of their nation, class, race, and ethnicity. So when women appeared in sexology texts, their positioning was especially contradictory. For a woman's physiology, psyche, or behavior to be described as in any way "like" a man's raised a conundrum: Was she like a man of her class and therefore a "higher" type than other women? Or was she like a man of a lower position and therefore a degraded female? Or was she a freak of nature, an anomaly, or a benign quirk, like an Urning?

The texts of the European sexologists, as they traveled and profoundly influenced the study of sexuality in the United States, were thus expansive, contradictory, and politically ambivalent. They contained pathologizing attacks on "perverts," imagined and real, but they also contained a naturalizing if not normalizing homophile discourse right from the start. And they included some ethnographic investigation of the populations described, along with the individual clinical case studies. The American sexologists of the late nineteenth century—including especially James Kiernan and Charles Hughes—contributed little original work to this field. Their influence was overwhelmed by the impact first of British sexologist Havelock Ellis, whose *Sexual Inversion* (1901) displaced Krafft-Ebing's *Psychopathia Sexualis* as the most important text in the field during the early twentieth century, and then of the German founder of psychoanalysis, Sigmund Freud. When Freud published "The Psychogenesis of a Case of Homosexuality in a Woman" in 1920, his emphasis on fantasy and desire more fully psychologized sexuality, and more fully naturalized and normalized the sexual "perversions" than had any of the sexologists' frameworks. But Freud's theories still invoked an evolutionary model, referred to the biological basis of the sexual "drives," applied almost exclusively to privileged Anglo-European populations, and depended on a fixed and hierarchical gender division.

Twentieth-Century Studies

The clinical psychological, empirical/sociological, and biological study of LGBTQ populations (under various changing historical categories, including "sexual inverts," "homosexuals," "deviants," and so on) continued through the twentieth century in a complex stew of interactions and distinct developments in each of these areas. Beginning with the early work of Magnus Hirschfeld, the sexual survey became a significant mode of investigation. From Katherine Bement Davis's study of twenty-two hundred women, among whom homosexual experience was found to be widespread (1929), to George Henry's report on one hundred "socially well adjusted men and women whose preferred form of libidinous gratification is homosexual" (1937), to Alfred Kinsey's sensational and notorious studies of male and female sexuality published during the 1950s and Shere Hite's provocative report on three thousand women (1976), sexual surveys have repeatedly both reproduced and challenged the contradictory biological and psychological conclusions of twentieth-century sexual science.

Though the sexual sciences continued to reflect the ambivalences and contradictions embedded in nineteenth-century sexology, during the twentieth century the homophile impulse grew within this field. Since the 1973 removal of homosexuality from the list of pathologies included in the psychological/psychiatric profession's *Diagnostic and Statistical Manual of Mental Disorders*, scientific consensus settled on the treatment of homosexuality as a benign variation, rather than as a disease or aberration. But conflict and contradiction continue over whether to consider homosexuality biologically fixed or environmentally shaped. The emergence of the study of transsexual and transgendered populations in the mid-twentieth century further expanded and complicated these discussions. From the publicity during the 1950s and 1960s surrounding the "sex change" operation of Christine Jorgensen, to the controversies generated by the emerging work of researchers and physicians, including Harry Benjamin and John Money, to the important distinctions between "transsexual" and "transgender" identities, the relation of the gendered mind and body has come under renewed scrutiny and revived politicization. Debates such as those over the existence of a "gay gene" or the implications of studies of identical twins have periodically reignited the nature versus nurture controversy as well—as has the development of so-called conversion therapies (closely aligned with fundamentalist Christianity) designed to promote heterosexual behavior in repentant homosexuals. But the entire field, including its homophile as well as homophobic projects and publications, has continued to reflect many of the assumptions, hierarchies, and exclusions of nineteenth-century sexology. Within the sexual sciences, assertions of the naturalness or normality of gay or homosexual people generally focus on privileged Western white men, and distinctions are often made between involuntary, and thus defensible, "conditions" and voluntary or "situational" immorality—often attributed to racial minorities, "lower" classes, or institutionalized populations. This history and the implications of these controversies and debates are contextualized and analyzed in science studies work, including books by the biologist Anne Fausto-Sterling, the philosopher Edward Stein, the sociologist Janice Irvine, and the historian Jennifer Terry.

In the arts, humanities, and the softer social sciences, occasional studies of lesbian and gay or homosexual life were published during the decades prior to the 1969 Stonewall Riots in New York City and the growth of gay liberation and lesbian feminism during the 1970s. A few groundbreaking works appeared during these years, including Clellan Ford and Frank Beach's *Patterns of Sexual Behavior* (1951) and Jeannette Foster's *Sex Variant Women in Literature* (1956). During the 1950s and 1960s, the organized homophile movement also supported public discussions, and publications focused on issues of concern to their memberships. In addition, major figures, such as Sappho or Oscar Wilde, and controversial issues, such as sexual tensions in single-sex institutions, were addressed in college courses, biographies, essays, films, and theater. But the field of LGBTQ studies did not take visible and institutionalized form until the 1970s, when the political energies of several social movements coalesced to generate a steady stream of new studies of LGBTQ life. The gay liberation movement produced new periodicals and book-length studies, along with energetic new audiences. Some of these publications were polemical and ephemeral, but much of this work survived to influence subsequent generations, including Dennis Altman's *Homosexual Oppression and Liberation* (1971); the essays in Karla Jay and Allen Young's widely circulated anthologies, *Out of the Closets: Voices of Gay Liberation* (1972) and *Lavender Culture* (1979); Jonathan Ned Katz's pioneering collection of historical documents, *Gay American History* (1976); and Vito Russo's cult classic *The Celluloid Closet: Homosexuality in the Movies* (1981). Early lesbian feminism and ongoing social movements for racial justice provided the context for an equivalent and related avalanche of publications during the 1970s and early 1980s, such as Gayle Rubin's widely reprinted essay "The Traffic in Women" (1976), Monique Wittig's 1981 essays "The Straight Mind" and "One Is Not Born a Woman" (translated from the French), Audre Lorde's *Sister Outsider: Essays and Speeches* (1984), Barbara Smith's *Home Girls: A Black Feminist Anthology* (1983), and Cherríe Moraga and Gloria Anzaldúa's prescient, field-altering anthology *This Bridge Called My Back: Writings by Radical Women of Color* (1981).

This new work of the 1970s and early 1980s was generated primarily in social movement–supported institutions, created outside of the academic professions and without the support of colleges and universities. New presses and publications, such as Kitchen Table or the *Gay Community News* in Boston, published work that mainstream presses would not touch. Newly founded archives and history projects, such as the Lesbian Herstory Archives and the San Francisco History Project, collected materials that traditional libraries disregarded; collectively supported slide shows, such as Allan Bérubé's "She Even Chewed Tobacco"; and circulated research findings to excited new audiences. The determination to challenge the pathologizing theories and beliefs of homophobic sexual science, religion, cultural representation, law, and public policy infused these projects and their constituencies with energy and political passion. But not all of the new work in LGBTQ studies challenged every hierarchy and exclusion—much debate persisted over basic definitions of "gay," "lesbian," and "bisexual," as well as over inclusiveness, especially along lines of gender, race, class, and ethnicity.

Activists and Intellectuals

This social movement context also generated and supported new work within academic institutions during these decades, including anthropologist Esther Newton's now classic ethnography, *Mother Camp: Female Impersonators in America* (1972); Lillian Faderman's *Surpassing the Love of Men: Romantic Friendship and Love between Women from the Renaissance to the Present* (1981); Carroll Smith-Rosenberg's *Disorderly Conduct* (1985); and John D'Emilio's authoritative history *Sexual Politics, Sexual Communities: The Making of a Homosexual Minority in the United States, 1940–1970* (1983)—an achievement influenced by the earlier work of British historical sociologists Mary McIntosh ("The Homosexual Role" [1969]) and Jeffrey Weeks (*Coming Out: Homosexual Politics in Britian from the Nineteenth Century to the Present* [1977]). These publications collectively produced a body of theory now referred to as "social constructionism"—the argument that sexuality is not primarily a biologically fixed reality, but rather is historically shaped and politically inflected. Social construction theory, influenced by both U.S. feminism and the British gay left, critically engaged the sexual sciences in an effort to reframe basic conceptions about the meanings of sexual difference.

The new academic publications in LGBTQ studies and the work published and circulated outside the universities remained in close conversation during the 1970s and 1980s. Institutions such as the Gay Academic Union, founded in 1972, and the Center for Lesbian and Gay Studies, founded in 1986, worked to combine and integrate the work of academic scholars and activist intellectuals, who were sometimes the same people. This overlap was especially pronounced during the efflorescence of engaged research and writing generated by the AIDS crisis beginning in the early 1980s. Activists and academics collaborated extensively in producing analysis for this health emergency. Perhaps most emblematic is the work of Cindy Patton, who produced *Sex and Germs* (1985) while working as an HIV-prevention educator and journalist for the *Gay Community News*, and then wrote *Inventing AIDS* (1990) as she completed a Ph.D. in communications—a course of study motivated by the need to make sense of the epidemic. Other publications, by Douglas Crimp, Cathy Cohen, and David Roman, show similar deep interactions among activist and academic intellectuals in LGBTQ studies.

Academic and activist energies coalesced in the feminist/lesbian "sex wars" of the mid-1980s with a broad range of thinkers and writers assembled in the pages of anthologies, including *Take Back the Night* (1980), edited by Laura Lauderer; *Against Sadomasochism* (1982), edited by Robin Linden; and *Powers of Desire* (1983), edited by Ann Snitow and others (which includes the now classic essay by Cherríe Moraga and Amber Hollibaugh, "What We're Rollin' around in Bed With"); and *Pleasure and Danger* (1984), edited by Carole Vance (which includes Gayle Rubin's "Thinking Sex: Notes for a Radical Theory of the Politics of Sexuality," an essay that shifted the ground within LGBTQ studies dramatically).

Rubin's essay was a response to the challenges of the "sex wars" debates over pornography, prostitution, sadomasochism, and lesbian femme/butch roles, and to the growing influence of the English translation of Michel Foucault's *History of Sexuality: An Introduction.* Foucault's poststructuralist arguments, which echoed social construction theory in some respects, profoundly influenced LGBTQ studies beginning in the mid-1980s. The first publications in the category designated "queer theory" clearly demonstrated this influence: Eve Sedgwick's *Between Men* (1985) and *Epistemology of the Closet* (1990), David Halperin's *One Hundred Years of Homosexuality* (1990), Judith Butler's field altering *Gender Trouble* (1990), and Michael Warner's edited anthology *Fear of a Queer Planet* (1993). This new work in queer theory, also profoundly influenced by a new queer activist politics, shifted the terrain of inquiry from documenting the lives of LGBT populations to critiquing the structures of sexual normativity pervasively embedded in the institutions and languages of everyday life. But like other work in lesbian and gay studies, queer theory did not always challenge the embedded exclusions of race, gender, and class that have been a legacy of nineteenth-century sexology. Much of the new work also assumed a white, Western, and often male "queer" subject.

The new work in queer theory exceeded the boundaries of the academic disciplines and often offered incisive critiques of disciplinary knowledges. But within the university, this work achieved its influence primarily within the literary humanities. In history, anthropology, and sociology much new work proceeded within the boundaries of lesbian and gay studies and worked to expand the disciplines from within. An expanding bibliography of new work was generated by historians, including George Chauncey, Martin Duberman, Leila Rupp, Marc Stein, and Estelle Freedman, as well as by the sociologists Steven Epstein, Arlene Stein, Joshua Gamson, and Suzanna Walters; the anthropologists and ethnographers Esther Newton, Elizabeth Kennedy and Madeline Davis, Kath Weston, Walter Williams, Sue-Ellen Jacobs, and Wesley Thomas and Richard Parker; the political and legal scholars Cathy Cohen, Jacqueline Stevens, Mark Blasius, Joan Tronto, and Ruthann Robson; and by numerous others in a spectrum of interdisciplinary locations, such as the film theorist Richard Dyer, the visual arts critic Richard Meyer, the religious studies scholars Janet Jakobsen and Ann Pellegrini, and the performance studies analysts Jill Dolan and Sue-Ellen Case.

Since the mid-1990s, critiques of lesbian and gay identity politics have fomented productive change in activism and scholarship. Bisexual, pansexual, polymorphous, and transgender writers and organizers, such as Susan Stryker, Brett Beemyn, and Leslie Feinberg, interacted with queer as well as lesbian and gay intellectuals to produce a second generation of queer-inflected advocacy, research, and scholarship across the disciplines and in nonacademic public arenas beginning in the mid-to-late 1990s. Judith Halberstam's *Female Masculinity* (1998), John Howard's *Men Like That* (1999), and Carolyn Dinshaw's *Getting Medieval* (1999) challenged both lesbian and gay studies and queer theory to move beyond the history/theory, social science/humanities splits that shaped so much of the field of LGBTQ studies since the 1980s. But perhaps the deepest challenge to the field, and the most promising new direction within it, is the new scholarship now appearing from within the overlapping fields of transnational and postcolonial studies, feminist and race theory, and LGBTQ studies. Building on the pioneering work of established scholars such as Jacqueline Alexander, recent publications by younger scholars are expanding the horizon of LGBTQ studies in the United States to include the global context, and are serving to connect work across disciplines with significant global economic and political issues. José Muñoz's *Disidentifications* (1999), David Eng's *Racial Castration* (1999), Martin Manalansan's *Global Divas* (2003), Juana Rodriguez's *Queer Latinidad* (2003), and the essays collected in Manalansan and Arnaldo Cruz's *Queer Globalizations* (2002), are charting expansive, ambitious new directions for LGBTQ studies in the twenty-first century. These new approaches within the field of LGBTQ studies presage the development of a more comprehensive challenge to the embedded assumptions of nineteenth-century sexology—its reflection of the hierarchies of global imperialism; its primitive/civilized binary; its gender, race, and class distinctions and exclusions; its erasure of the impact of political economy—than the field of LGBTQ studies has yet produced.

Bibliography

Abelove, Henry, Michèle Aina Barale, and David M. Halperin, eds. *The Lesbian and Gay Studies Reader.* New York: Routledge, 1993.

Altman, Dennis. *Homosexual: Oppression and Liberation.* New York: Outerbridge and Dienstfrey, 1971.

Bayer, Ronald. *Homosexuality and American Psychiatry: The Politics of Diagnosis.* New York: Basic Books, 1981.

Beemyn, Brett, and Mickey Eliason, eds. *Queer Studies: A Lesbian, Gay, Bisexual, and Transgender Anthology.* New York: New York University Press, 1996.

Bérubé, Allan. *Coming Out under Fire: The History of Gay Men and Women in World War Two.* New York: The Free Press, 1990.

Bérubé, Allan, with the San Francisco History Project. "She Even Chewed Tobacco." In *Hidden from History: Reclaiming the Lesbian and Gay Past.* Edited by Martin Bauml Duberman, Martha Vicinus, and George Chauncey Jr. New York: New American Library, 1989.

Blasius, Mark. *Gay and Lesbian Politics: Sexuality and the Emergence of a New Ethic.* Philadelphia: Temple University Press, 1994.

Boswell, John. *Christianity, Social Tolerance, and Homosexuality: Gay People in Western Europe from the Beginning of the Christian Era to the Fourteenth Century.* Chicago: University of Chicago Press, 1980.

Butler, Judith. *Gender Trouble: Feminism and the Subversion of Identity.* New York: Routledge, 1990.

Carpenter, Edward. *Intermediate Types among Primitive Folk: A Study in Social Evolution.* London: M. Kennerley, 1921.

Case, Sue-Ellen. *Domain Matrix: Performing Lesbian at the End of Print Culture.* Bloomington: Indiana University Press, 1996.

Chauncey, George. *Gay New York: Gender, Urban Culture, and the Making of the Gay Male World, 1890–1940.* New York: Basic Books, 1994.

Cohen, Cathy J. *The Boundaries of Blackness: AIDS and the Breakdown of Black Politics.* Chicago: University of Chicago Press, 1999.

Cohen, Cathy J., Kathleen B. Jones, and Joan C. Tronto, eds. *Women Transforming Politics: An Alternative Reader.* New York: New York University Press, 1997.

Crew, Louie, ed. *The Gay Academic.* Palm Springs, Calif.: ETC Publications, 1978.

Crimp, Douglas. *AIDS: Cultural Analysis/Cultural Activism.* Cambridge, Mass.: MIT Press, 1988.

Cruikshank, Margaret, ed. *Lesbian Studies: Present and Future.* Old Westbury, N.Y.: The Feminist Press, 1982.

Cruz-Malavé, Arnaldo, and Martin F. Manalasan. *Queer Globalizations: Citizenship and the Afterlife of Colonization.* New York: New York University Press, 2002.

Davis, Katherine Bement. *Factors in the Sex Life of Twenty-Two Hundred Women.* New York and London: Harper and Brothers, 1929.

D'Emilio, John. *Sexual Politics, Sexual Communities: The Making of a Homosexual Minority in the United States, 1940–1970.* Chicago: University of Chicago Press, 1983.

D'Emilio, John, and Estelle B. Freedman. *Intimate Matters: A History of Sexuality in America.* New York: Harper and Row, 1988.

Dinshaw, Carolyn. *Getting Medieval: Sexualities and Communities Pre- and Postmodern.* Durham, N.C.: Duke University Press, 1999.

Dolan, Jill. *Presence and Desire: Essays on Gender, Sexuality, Performance.* Ann Arbor: University of Michigan Press, 1993.

Duberman, Martin Bauml, Martha Vicinus, and George Chauncey Jr.*Hidden from History: Reclaiming the Lesbian and Gay Past.* New York: New American Library, 1989.

Duggan, Lisa. *Sapphic Slashers: Sex, Violence, and American Modernity.* Durham, N.C.: Duke University Press, 2000.

Duggan, Lisa, and Nan D. Hunter. *Sex Wars: Sexual Dissent and Political Culture.* New York: Routledge, 1995.

Dyer, Richard. *Now You See It: Studies on Lesbian and Gay Film.* New York: Routledge, 1990.

Ellis, Havelock. *Sexual Inversion.* Philadelphia: F.A. Davis, 1901. First U.S. edition.

Eng, David L. *Racial Castration: Managing Masculinity in Asian America.* Durham, N.C.: Duke University Press, 1999.

Eng, David L., and Alice Y. Hom, eds. *Q and A: Queer in Asian America.* Philadelphia: Temple University Press, 1998.

Epstein, Steven. *Impure Science: AIDS, Activism, and The Politics of Knowledge.* Berkeley: University of California Press, 1996.

Faderman, Lillian. *Surpassing the Love of Men: Romantic Friendship and Love between Women from the Renaissance to the Present.* New York: William Morrow, 1981.

Fausto-Sterling, Anne. *Sexing the Body: Gender Politics and the Construction of Sexuality.* New York: Basic Books, 2000.

Feinberg, Leslie. *Transgender Warriors: From Joan of Arc to RuPaul.* Boston: Beacon Press, 1996.

Ford, Clellan Stearns, and Frank Beach. *Patterns of Sexual Behavior.* New York: Harper, 1951.

Foster, Jeannette H. *Sex Variant Women in Literature: A Historical and Quantitative Survey.* New York: Vantage Press, 1956.

Foucault, Michel. *The History of Sexuality, Vol. 1: An Introduction.* Translated by Robert Hurley. New York: Pantheon, 1978.

Freud, Sigmund. "The Psychogenesis of a Case of Homosexuality in a Woman (1920)." In *The Standard Edition of the Complete Psychological Works of Sigmund Freud.*Edited by James Strachey. London: Hogarth Press, 1955.

Gamson, Joshua. *Freaks Talk Back: Tabloid Talk Shows and Sexual Nonconformity.* Chicago: University of Chicago Press, 1998.

Gay Academic Union. *The Universities and the Gay Experience: Proceedings of the Conference Sponsored by the Women and Men of the Gay Academic Union, November 23 and 24, 1973.* New York: Gay Academic Union, 1974.

Halberstam, Judith. *Female Masculinity.* Durham, N.C.: Duke University Press, 1998.

Halperin, David. *One Hundred Years of Homosexuality: And Other Essays on Greek Love.* New York: Routledge, 1990.

Hamer, Dean, and Peter Copeland. *The Science of Desire: The Search for the Gay Gene and the Biology of Behavior.* New York: Simon and Schuster, 1994.

Henry, George. *Sex Variants: A Study of Homosexual Patterns.* New York and London: P. B. Hoeber, 1941.

Hite, Shere. *The Hite Report: A Nationwide Study on Female Sexuality.* New York: Macmillan, 1976.

Hollibaugh, Amber L. *My Dangerous Desires: A Queer Girl Dreaming Her Way Home.* Durham, N.C.: Duke University Press, 2000.

Howard, John. *Men Like That: A Southern Queer History.* Chicago: University of Chicago Press, 1999.

Hutchins, Lorraine, and Lani Kaahumanu, eds. *Bi Any Other Name: Bisexual People Speak Out.* Boston: Alyson, 1991.

Irvine, Janice. *Disorders of Desire: Sex and Gender in Modern American Sexology.* Philadelphia: Temple University Press, 1990.

Jacobs, Sue-Ellen, Wesley Thomas, and Sabine Lang, eds. *Two Spirit People: Native American Gender Identity, Sexuality, and Spirituality.* Urbana: University of Illinois Press, 1997.

Jakobsen, Janet, and Ann Pellegrini. *Love the Sin: Sexual Regulation and the Limits of Religious Tolerance.* New York: New York University Press, 2003.

Jay, Karla, and Allen Young, eds. *Out of the Closets: Voices of Gay Liberation.* Reprint, New York: New York University Press, 1992. Originally published in 1972.

———. *Lavender Culture.* Reprint, New York: New York University Press, 1994. Originally published in 1979.

Katz, Jonathan Ned. *Gay American History.* New York: Crowell, 1976.

Kennedy, Elizabeth Lapovsky, and Madeline Davis. *Boots of Leather, Slippers of Gold: The History of a Lesbian Community.* New York: Routledge, 1993.

Kennedy, Hubert. *Ulrichs: The Life and Work of Karl Heinrich Ulrichs, Pioneer of the Modern Gay Movement.* Boston: Alyson, 1988.

Kinsey, Alfred, Wardell B. Pomeroy, and Clyde E. Martin. *Sexual Behavior in the Human Male.* Philadelphia: W. B. Saunders, 1948.

———. *Sexual Behavior in the Human Female.* Philadelphia: W. B. Saunders, 1953.

Krafft-Ebing, Richard von. *Psychopathia Sexualis with Especial Reference to Contrary Sexual Instinct.* Translated from the 12th and final ed. by Brian King. Burbank, Calif.: Bloat, 1999.

Lederer, Laura, ed. *Take Back the Night: Women on Pornography.* New York: Morrow, 1980.

Lesbian Herstory Archives. Available from http://www.lesbianherstoryarchives.org.

Linden, Robin, ed. *Against Sadomasochism: A Radical Feminist Analysis.* East Palo Alto, Calif.: Frog in the Well, 1982.

Lorde, Audre. *Sister Outsider: Essays and Speeches.* Trumansburg, N.Y.: Crossing Press, 1984.

Manalansan, Martin. *Global Divas: Filipino Gay Men in the Diaspora.* Durham, N.C.: Duke University Press, 2003.

McIntosh, Mary. "The Homosexual Role." *Social Problems* 16, no. 2 (1968).

Meyer, Richard. *Outlaw Representation: Censorship and Homosexuality in Twentieth-Century America.* New York: Oxford University Press, 2002.

Meyerowitz, Joanne. *How Sex Changed. A History of Transsexuality in the United States.* Cambridge, Mass.: Harvard University Press, 2002.

Moraga, Cherríe, and Gloria Anzaldúa, eds. *This Bridge Called My Back: Writings by Radical Women of Color.* New York: Kitchen Table Press, 1981.

Muñoz, José Esteban. *Disidentifications: Queers of Color and the Performance of Politics.* Minneapolis: University of Minnesota Press, 1999.

Newton, Esther. *Mother Camp: Female Impersonators in America.* Englewood Cliffs, N.J.: Prentice Hall, 1972.

———. *Cherry Grove, Fire Island: Sixty Years in America's First Gay and Lesbian Town.* Boston: Beacon, 1993.

Parker, Richard, Regina Maria Barbosa, and Peter Aggleton. *Framing the Sexual Subject: The Politics of Gender, Sexuality and Power.* Berkeley: University of California Press, 2000.

Patton, Cindy. *Sex and Germs: The Politics of AIDS.* Boston: South End Press, 1985.

———. *Inventing AIDS.* New York: Routledge, 1990.

———. *Globalizing AIDS.* Minneapolis: University of Minnesota Press, 2002.

Robson, Ruthann. *Lesbian (Out)law: Survival under the Rule of Law.* Ithaca, N.Y.: Firebrand Books, 1992.

Rodriguez, Juana Maria. *Queer Latinidad: Identity Practices, Discursive Spaces.* New York: New York University Press, 2003.

Román, David. *Acts of Intervention: Performance, Gay Culture, and AIDS.* Bloomington: Indiana University Press, 1998.

Rosario, Vernon A., ed. *Science and Homosexualities.* New York: Routledge, 1997.

Rowbotham, Sheila, and Jeffrey Weeks. *Socialism and the New Life: The Personal and Sexual Politics of Edward Carpenter and Havelock Ellis.* London: Pluto Press, 1977.

Rubin, Gayle. "The Traffic in Women: Notes on the 'Political Economy' of Sex." In *Toward an Anthropology of Women.* Edited by Rayna R. Reiter. New York: Monthly Review Press, 1975.

———. "Thinking Sex: Notes for a Radical Theory of the Politics of Sexuality." In *Pleasure and Danger: Exploring Female Sexuality.* Edited by Carole Vance. Boston: Routledge and Kegan Paul, 1984.

Rupp, Leila J. *A Desired Past: A Short History of Same-Sex Love in America.* Chicago: University of Chicago Press, 1999.

Russo, Vito. *The Celluloid Closet: Homosexuality at the Movies.* New York: HarperCollins, 1981.

San Francisco History Project. Available from http://ww.glbthistory.org.

Sedgwick, Eve Kosofsky. *Between Men: English Literature and Male Homosocial Desire.* New York: Columbia University Press, 1985.

———. *Epistemology of the Closet.* Berkeley: University of California Press, 1990.

Smith, Barbara, ed. *Home Girls: A Black Feminist Anthology.* New York: Kitchen Table Press, 1983.

Smith-Rosenberg, Carroll. *Disorderly Conduct: Visions of Gender in Victorian America.* New York: Knopf, 1985.

Snitow, Ann, Christine Stansell, and Sharon Thompson, eds. *Powers of Desire: The Politics of Sexuality.* New York: Monthly Review Press, 1993.

Stein, Arlene. *Sex and Sensibility: Stories of a Lesbian Generation.* Berkeley: University of California Press, 1997.

Stein, Edward. *The Mismeasure of Desire: The Science, Theory, and Ethics of Sexual Orientation.* New York: Oxford University Press, 1999.

Stein, Marc. *City of Sisterly and Brotherly Loves: Lesbian and Gay Philadelphia, 1945–1972.* Chicago: University of Chicago Press, 2000.

Stevens, Jacqueline. *Reproducing the State.* Princeton, N.J.: Princeton University Press, 1999.

Storr, Merl, ed. *Bisexuality: A Critical Reader.* New York: Routledge, 1999.

Stryker, Susan, and Stephen Whittle, eds. *The Transgender Reader.* New York: Routledge, 2003.

Symonds, John Addington. *A Problem in Modern Ethics, Being an Inquiry into the Phenomenon of Sex Inversion.* London: [s.n.], 1896.

Terry, Jennifer. *An American Obsession: Science, Medicine, and Homosexuality in Modern Society.* Chicago: University of Chicago Press, 1999.

Vance, Carole. *Pleasure and Danger: Exploring Female Sexuality.* Boston: Routledge and Kegan Paul, 1984.

Walters, Suzanna Danuta. *All the Rage: The Story of Gay Visibility in America.* Chicago: University of Chicago Press, 2001.

Warner, Michael, ed. *Fear of a Queer Planet: Queer Politics and Social Theory.* Minneapolis: University of Minnesota Press, 1993.

Weeks, Jeffrey. *Coming Out: Homosexual Politics in Britain from the Nineteenth Century to the Present.* London: Quartet Books, 1977.

Weston, Kath. *Families We Choose: Lesbians, Gays, Kinship.* New York: Columbia University Press, 1991.

Williams, Walter. *The Spirit and the Flesh: Sexual Diversity in American Indian Culture.* Boston: Beacon, 1986.

Wittig, Monique. *The Straight Mind and Other Essays.* Boston: Beacon, 1992.

Wolff, Charlotte. *Magnus Hirschfeld: A Portrait of the Pioneer in Sexology.* London: Quartet Books, 1986.

Zimmerman, Bonnie, and Toni A. H. McNaron, eds. *The New Lesbian Studies: Into the Twenty-First Century.* New York: The Feminist Press, 1996.

Lisa Duggan

See also CULTURAL STUDIES AND CULTURAL THEORY; HISTORY PROJECTS, LIBRARIES, AND ARCHIVES; LEGG, DORR; LESBIAN HERSTORY ARCHIVES; ONE INSTITUTE; QUEER THEORY AND QUEER STUDIES; WOMEN'S STUDIES AND FEMINIST STUDIES.

Liberace. The ostentatiously outfitted and bejeweled entertainer performs at New York's Radio City Music Hall in 1984, three years before his AIDS-related death (though he always publicly denied both his medical condition and his sexual orientation). **[AP/Mario Cabrera]**

LIBERACE **(b. 16 May 1911; d. 4 February 1987), pianist, entertainer.**

Born Wladziu Valentino Liberace, to a musical family in working-class West Allis, Wisconsin, this musical prodigy developed from these roots his devotion to Catholicism, his working-class conservatism, and his ability to speak directly to his audiences. An excellent musician by most accounts, he was most noted for his flamboyant costumes and presentations.

Liberace won several classical music competitions and it is said he played piano with the Chicago Symphony, under Dr. Frederick Stock, when he was only fourteen. Despite disapproval from his parents, who wanted him to stay with classical music, in the 1940s Liberace moved to New York and into popular music because of the money and the joy of pleasing large audiences. He promoted himself relentlessly and, while playing the cabaret rooms of prestigious hotels in major American cities, developed a gimmick, placing a candelabra on the piano as Chopin had. Liberace solidified his career in the early 1950s with a local television program in Los Angeles, presenting an image of himself as the good son, which endeared him to a certain type of older woman. The show started as a summer replacement for Dinah Shore, but became a syndicated success and earned Liberace two Emmys.

Over the course of his career, Liberace won the hearts of large audiences; he was especially popular with women. Before Liberace, other homosexual stars, such as Ramon Novarro, used a similar image of flirtatiousness toward women to cover their sexual interests. Liberace linked this image to the spectacle of his performances and the enjoyment of the material successes of the American Dream.

Liberace played in venues ranging from nightclubs to Carnegie Hall, Madison Square Garden, and the Hollywood Bowl. In addition, he appeared in three royal performances in London, the third in 1972, and toured Australia successfully in 1971. Three books were published about him, and he was named three times the Pop

Keyboard Artist of the Year by *Contemporary Keyboard* magazine. His flashy clothes, pianos (often mirrored), classic cars, and jewels were part of his persona and fascinated his audiences.

Like many LGB people of the era, Liberace strove to keep his homosexuality a secret. He went on staged dates with women, including a few with actress Mae West, and like other entertainers sought media coverage of concocted heterosexual romances. During the mid-1950s, he fought in the courts to control his image. He won a libel suit on a technicality against *Confidential,* a tabloid that labeled the entertainer a homosexual. A few years later, Liberace won the largest British libel settlement up to that time against the *London Daily Mirror,* which he said implied he was a homosexual. The pianist denied his homosexuality in court. As was the case with other homosexuals in U.S. society, compulsory heterosexuality forced Liberace to be dishonest about his sexual interests.

Liberace did not embrace gay liberation after the Stonewall Riots of 1969. Yet on stage, his shows contained flamboyance and innuendoes that suggested his homosexual interests. Off stage, he lived the hedonistic Hollywood/Palm Springs lifestyle of the 1970s, engaging in sexual promiscuity without the ideological perspective of sexual liberation that energized some LGBT people during this era. After 1969 he had three primary lovers, the second of whom, Scott Thorson, brought a palimony suit after the pianist left him. The courts ruled that Thorson's palimony clause, based on Liberace's alleged commitment to adopt and take care of Thorson financially, was an unenforceable contract for sexual services. (Only with a 1988 California court of appeals decision did palimony rights become extended to same-sex couples.)

Like so many men of his generation, Liberace contracted AIDS. The entertainer denied this condition as vociferously as he had his sexual orientation. While actor Rock Hudson admitted that he had the disease at a press conference in 1984, Liberace continued to perform and make regular public appearances without disclosing his illness. Even after Liberace's death, members of his entourage and others with vested interests struggled to keep the pianist's sexual orientation hidden from the public. His doctors told the public that Liberace died of cardiac arrest due to heart failure, but the Riverside County, California, coroner announced that analysis showed that the pianist died of pneumonia due to AIDS.

Bibliography

Berrett, Jesse. "Liberace: Behind the Music," *Rethinking History* 4 (2000): 77–79.

Ehrenstein, David. *Open Secret: Gay Hollywood 1928–1998.* New York: William Morrow, 1998.

Mitchell, Mark. *Virtuosi: A Defense and a (Sometimes Erotic) Celebration of Great Pianists.* Bloomington: Indiana University Press, 2000.

Pyron, Darden Asbury. *Liberace: An American Boy.* Chicago: University of Chicago Press, 2000.

Brett L. Abrams

See also MUSIC: POPULAR.

LINGUISTICS. see LANGUAGE.

LIQUOR CONTROL LAW AND POLICY

Gay bars and saloons became popular gathering places, more for gay men than for lesbians, as early as the 1900s. In large cities like New York these gathering places flourished even during Prohibition. The repeal of Prohibition in 1933, however, brought with it closer scrutiny of public bars to guarantee that patrons were orderly and that establishments did not encourage immorality. State alcoholic beverage control boards or licensing agencies, with the help of local police, were a constant threat to the existence of gay and lesbian bars. Up until the late 1960s, even in the most progressive cities, like San Francisco and New York, police raids were frequent.

Prohibition

In 1851 Maine adopted a statewide law that banned the sale of alcoholic beverages. Thirteen states, mostly in the north, followed; New York did not pass a statewide prohibition law. Its bars and saloons were nonetheless affected by the temperance movement of the late 1800s. In 1896 the New York Legislature enacted the Raines Law, which shut down saloons on Sundays, except for bars and saloons that were located in hotels. As a consequence many bars in New York City began to offer rooms for rent in a sufficient number (ten) to qualify as a hotel. Known as "Raines Law hotels," more than a thousand such institutions were in operation in the early 1900s. Moral reformers in New York City, concerned that these "hotels" were primarily operated for immoral sexual encounters and commercial prostitution, decided that the best way to cure the problem was for the bars to forbid women on the premises. One consequence of this "men only" rule was that a number of these bars in "Raines Law hotels" developed into popular spots for gay men.

By the early 1900s at least half the states had declared themselves "dry." Battles between the Drys and the Wets moved to the national level. In 1913, Congress passed the

Interstate Liquor Act, which prohibited the shipping of alcohol into dry states. In 1917, Congress proposed to amend the United States Constitution by adding an amendment that would prohibit the "manufacture, sale, or transportation of intoxicating liquors . . . for beverage purposes." This amendment (the Eighteenth) was ratified and became effective in 1920.

During the thirteen years (1920–1933) that Prohibition existed at the national level, countless illegal bars and speakeasies operated, especially in large cities. Regulated male-only saloons were replaced by unregulated speakeasies in which the sexes mingled freely. This was the era of the Harlem Renaissance, during which time lesbians and gay men frequented clubs where bootleg whiskey was served and illicit sexual activity was the norm.

After Prohibition

When the twenty-first amendment to the U.S. Constitution repealed prohibition in 1933, control of liquor sales was returned to the states. Most states opted for strict control of liquor sales and authorized cities and counties to determine whether such sales should occur within their boundaries. In many large cities, establishments were prohibited from selling drinks to the public in barrooms or saloons, even after World War II. State and local restrictions on liquor sales made the opening of public gay bars, like the ones in New York City, San Francisco, and Los Angeles, impossible in many other cities.

The repeal of prohibition had another effect. Even in cities where drinking in public was legal, the rules of appropriate bar behavior were suddenly changed. Legalization of alcohol sales carried with it a fear of return to the saloons of the nineteenth and early twentieth centuries that the temperance movement had fought so hard to destroy. The compromise was to allow bars and saloons to operate so long as they did not turn into "disorderly houses." To enforce these new standards of behavior, state licensing boards were created and given the power to terminate an owner's license to sell liquor if the new standards were not met.

State licensing agencies, often called Alcohol Control Boards (ABC), or, in New York, the State Licensing Agency (SLA), engaged in undercover work to determine whether certain bars and saloons were operating properly. Police officers or others hired by the agency would typically visit a bar on a nightly basis to determine whether or not the bar was operated in an orderly fashion. These agents understood a "disorderly house" to include any bar that was frequented by prostitutes, homosexuals, or other sexual perverts. Once a bar was identified as a hangout for homosexuals, it risked losing its liquor license.

An early legal challenge to these harassing tactics occurred in New York in 1939. Gloria's Bar and Grill argued that its license should not be revoked merely because homosexuals frequented the establishment. Rather, some offensive conduct must be shown to have occurred before the determination of a "disorderly house" could be made. The SLA asserted that such conduct had occurred and also that it had the power to close any bar that welcomed homosexuals, even without proof of disorderly conduct. Not until the 1960s were arguments such as those made by Gloria's successful in the New York courts.

Post–World War II New York

Prior to 1967, New York court opinions on the propriety of revoking or suspending an establishment's liquor license because of homosexual activity on the premises were mixed. Because the New York statute allowed revocation only if the proprietor permitted the premises to become disorderly, the arguments made on behalf of bar owners were (1) that insufficient conduct existed to constitute disorder, and (2) even if disorderly conduct occurred, such conduct was so isolated that the owner could not possibly have had sufficient knowledge that the conduct was occurring on the premises. In most cases, the SLA acted only after a police arrest of a bar patron for solicitation. In those few cases in which courts reversed SLA decisions, they found either that the solicitations were too few in number to constitute disorder or that they occurred in private without the knowledge or constructive knowledge of the bar owner. In 1959 the SLA announced a campaign to revoke the licenses of all bars "patronized by prostitutes and homosexuals." Shortly thereafter, the gay bars of New York City were shut down. Rather than challenge the closings in court, the owners typically reopened either in a new location or sometimes even in the same location under new management.

By the 1960s, even before the Stonewall Riots, political organizers were challenging the SLA's position that the mere presence of gay patrons was sufficient to revoke a bar's license for being "disorderly." In 1966, Dick Leitsch, then-president of the Mattachine Society of New York, organized a "sip-in." The plan was for a group of three gay men to appear at various bars in the city, announce that they were gay, and order a drink. If any bar refused to serve them out of concern about its liquor license, then Leitsch was prepared to sue the bar in order to establish the right of gays to congregate in the bar of their choice. Apparently, the first bars that the three men visited (with the press in attendance) readily served them. Only when they went to a well-known gay bar were they denied service. Under threat of suit, the SLA voluntarily changed its policy.

In 1967, the New York Court of Appeals issued an important progay ruling in a case against a gay bar whose license had been revoked prior to the 1966 change in policy. The court explicitly ruled that the fact that gay persons were allowed to congregate was not sufficient to convict a bar owner of the knowing operation of a disorderly house. Furthermore, although some of the gay patrons were dancing with each other and kissing each other, that conduct was not sufficient to find the place "disorderly."

Liquor Law in California

In post–World War II San Francisco, The Black Cat was probably the most well-known watering hole for gay men on the west coast. A bohemian bar from before World War II, and made more famous by its role in Jack Kerouac's *On the Road* and the patronage of poet Allen Ginsberg, The Black Cat drew the attention of the San Francisco vice squad when it became a hangout for gay clientele. In 1949, after a year-long police investigation, the Board of Equalization revoked The Black Cat's license on grounds that it was being used as a "disorderly house." The specific charge was that "persons of known homosexual tendencies patronized said premises and used said premises as a meeting place." The owner of the bar, Sol Stoumen, challenged the revocation in court. The trial court sustained the revocation of the license, explaining that it "would be a sorry commentary on the law . . . to find that persons holding liquor licenses could permit their premises to be used month after month as meeting places for persons of known homosexual tendencies" (*Stoumen v. Reilly*). An intermediate appellate court affirmed the decision in 1950, and Stoumen appealed to the California Supreme Court. In 1951, the Supreme Court ruled in favor of Stoumen and reinstated The Black Cat's liquor license, holding that the state could not revoke a liquor license solely on grounds that a bar caters to a gay clientele.

The state legislature responded to the *Stoumen* case by enacting a statute that authorized the revocation of a liquor license if the premises were a "resort for illegal possessors or users of narcotics, prostitutes, pimps, panderers, or sexual perverts." Relying on this, statute, police continued their harassment of gay bars. The constitutionality of the new statute was tested in 1959 in *Vallerga v. Department of Alcoholic Beverage Control*, a challenge to the closing of the popular lesbian bar, Mary's First and Last Chance. The California Supreme Court struck the statute down, not based on a finding that gay and lesbian people have a constitutional right to gather in public, but rather on the more narrow rationale that the provision in the California constitution giving the liquor board the ability to revoke a license for "good cause" did not authorize revocation solely because the establishment catered to homosexuals.

While the *Vallerga* decision was a positive one for gay and lesbian bars, it did not end police harassment. The 1959 mayoral election in San Francisco created a particularly hard time for gay bars. Mayor George Christopher was up for reelection. His opponent charged him with providing too much support for the gay and lesbian community and with turning San Francisco into a gay mecca. Although Christopher denied the allegations and won the election, the charges caused him to institute a crackdown on gay bars.

These attacks led to the formation of the Tavern Guild in 1962. The Tavern Guild was formed by a group of gay bar owners and employees who decided that, if they banded together, they could better fight the assaults. All the gay and lesbian bar cases had distinguished between places that were mere hangouts for gay men and lesbians and premises on which "homosexual conduct" occurred. The police in the early 1960s claimed to observe much indecorous behavior. Not only were patrons arrested, licenses were lost. The Tavern Guild provided a lawyer and a bail bondsmen for every individual arrested on or near the premises of bars and taverns owned by guild members. In 1964 a new homophile rights organization, Society for Individual Rights, was formed. That group worked with the Tavern Guild to become a political force in San Francisco that ultimately led to San Francisco's image in the 1970s as the "gay capital" of the United States.

Liquor Law in Other States

New Jersey's experience was similar to that of New York. After years of legal battles over the right of bars to serve a predominately homosexual clientele, the New Jersey Supreme Court held in 1967 that the "asserted rights of the homosexuals to assemble in and patronize licensed establishments are intertwined with the asserted rights of licensed establishments to serve them" (*One Eleven Wines and Liquors, Inc. v. Division of Alcoholic Beverage Control*). While bar patrons continued to experience harassment after 1967, the decision made it clear that the mere congregation of gay men and lesbians on the premises was not a sufficient justification for revoking a liquor license.

By contrast, a Miami ordinance declaring it unlawful for a business licensed to sell intoxicating beverages to "knowingly sell to, serve to or allow consumption of alcoholic beverages by a homosexual person, lesbian or pervert . . . or to knowingly allow two or more persons who are homosexuals, lesbians or perverts to congregate or remain in his place of business," was upheld by the Florida courts in 1967 (*Inman v. City of Miami).*

Some states continued to apply rules that jeopardized the liquor licenses of gay and lesbian bars well into the 1970s and 1980s. In Las Vegas, Nevada, the county code authorized revocation of licenses of "each licensee, who shall permit his licensed premises to be frequented by or to become the meeting place, hangout, or rendezvous for known prostitutes, homosexuals, vagrants, known hoodlums." In 1975, the Supreme Court of Nevada held the provision unconstitutional, saying that it "is established beyond peradventure that the mere presence of prostitutes, homosexuals or other 'undesirable' classes of persons in the licensed premises is not an adequate ground upon which to revoke a liquor license" (*Cline v. Clark County Liquor and Gaming Licensing Board).*

Since the 1980s, gay and lesbian bars have flourished throughout the country as centers of gay and lesbian culture. Police harassment of owners and patrons is rare and, when it does occur, is considered an abuse of power subject to legal redress.

Bibliography

Chauncey, George. *Gay New York: Gender, Urban Culture and the Making of the Gay Male World 1890–1940.* New York: Basic Books, 1994.

Cline v. Clark County Liquor and Gaming Licensing Board. 535 P.2d 783 (Nev. 1975).

D'Emilio, John. *Sexual Politics, Sexual Communities: The Making of a Homosexual Minority in the United States, 1940 1970.* Chicago: University of Chicago Press, 1983.

Eskidge, William M., Jr., *Gaylaw: Challenging the Apartheid of the Closet.* Cambridge, Mass.: Harvard University Press, 1999.

Faderman, Lilliam. *Odd Girls and Twilight Lovers: A History of Lesbian Life in Twentieth-Century America.* New York: Columbia University Press, 1991.

Inman v. City of Miami, 197 So.2d 50 (Fla. 1967).

Kerma Restaurant Corp. v. State Liquor Authority. 233 N.E.2d 833 (N.Y. 1967).

One Eleven Wines and Liquors, Inc. v. Division of Alcoholic Beverage Control. 235 A.2d 12 (N.J. 1967).

Stoumen v. Reilly. 234 P.2d 969 (Cal. 1951).

Vallerga v. Department of Alcoholic Beverage Control. 347 P.2d 909 (Cal. 1959)

Patricia A. Cain

See also ALCOHOL AND DRUGS; BARS, CLUBS AND RESTAURANTS; CRIME AND CRIMINALIZATION; DISCRIMINATION; FEDERAL LAW AND POLICY; RIGHTS OF ASSOCIATION AND ASSEMBLY; TRANSGENDER AND GENDER IMPERSONATION LAW AND POLICY.

LISA BEN, *see* BEN, LISA

LITERARY CRITICISM AND THEORY

Literature's impact on LGBT people, culture, politics, and history cannot be overestimated. Numerous writers such as Sappho, Emily Dickinson, Walt Whitman, Oscar Wilde, André Gide, Marcel Proust, Hart Crane, Alice Walker, Jeanette Winterson, among many others, tantalize LGBT imaginations. Whether or not these writers "actually" belong to the LGBT "family," the pantheon of "queer" literary icons is important: the language they cultivated rearticulates, challenges, and transforms the worlds of sexual and gender minorities. The scenarios, plots, images, and ideas found in imaginative writing produce possibilities of reading about "queer" characters, actions, and themes, giving audiences opportunities to identify with, enjoy, identify against, and criticize what they discover on the page. And if LGBT plots or figures do not explicitly appear, there are always creative ways to "queer" what is being read. "Made-up" worlds are readily remade and will often yield to the desires of interested readers. Literature can and does provide pleasurable escape from worlds that have not historically valued LGBT lives. At the same time, it can provide alternatives to sexual conventions and gender traditions and can provide new ways to think about culture, society, and politics.

At least since the rise of new social movements, including gay liberation and lesbian feminism, in the late 1960s and early 1970s, literary critics and theorists concerned with sexuality and gender have done important work in the United States. After the 1960s, literature scholars could no longer pretend to be innocent about the ways in which their work was deeply embedded and implicated in the sexual, gender, and other struggles of their eras. In the early 1980s, the tragic advent of the AIDS epidemic added a specific kind of urgency to the academic and institutional knowledge about sexuality and gender that had begun to thrive in U.S. college and university literature departments. Within such a politically charged climate, open to the serious study of marginalized and neglected groups, more and more academic institutions began to include sustainable sexuality and gender curricula. Literary critics and theorists played key roles in these developments, publishing groundbreaking scholarship and training large numbers of students dedicated to exploring LGBT perspectives on art, culture, literature, history, and politics.

LGBT literary criticism and theory has developed beyond its initial focus on recovering "lost" and neglected queer texts (such as Herman Melville's *Moby-Dick* and Djuna Barnes's *Nightwood*), establishing a queer literary canon (with texts such as James Baldwin's *Giovanni's Room* and Rita Mae Brown's *Rubyfruit Jungle*), and confirming or speculating about the sexualities and genders of various writers (such as Emily Dickinson, Walt Whitman, and Langston Hughes). Over time, the sustained study of LGBT literature has yielded much more than additions of major works to established national canons, though this has been an important accomplishment. The field has also increasingly engaged in more than just exercises in literary appreciation; it has inspired critiques of dominant heterosexual and gender-normative societies and cultures and has interrogated the ways in which sexuality and gender are often used as vehicles for expressing ideas about ourselves, our cultures, our histories, and our futures. Literary artifacts, including poems, plays, novels, and short stories, provide readers with opportunities to be deeply concerned about the language and representation of characters, lives, societies, and contexts filled with sexual and gender complications.

Literature, by definition, is concerned with language—its symbols, images, ideologies, effects, and historical references and influences. From the dialogues of Plato's *Symposium* and the intricacies of Marcel Proust's *A La Recherche du Temps Perdu* to the spare and urbane poems of Frank O'Hara and the harsh conditions of Dorothy Allison's *Bastard Out of Carolina*, the "wordy" presentations of diverse sexualities and genders have provoked literary scholars to focus their reading talents on the topics of sexuality and gender. The major skills of literary study—inventive and imaginative practices associated with being careful, attentive, and slow readers—allow for the excavation of the rhetorical devices, images, associations, and implications of sexuality and gender. Sexuality and gender, in turn, are linked with a virtually limitless array of topics, including love, desire, power, politics, identity, community, society, nationality, internationality, birth, death, health, disease, science, technology, and art. As a consequence and in line with developments in other literary fields, in the past thirty years LGBT literary criticism and theory have moved beyond a fairly exclusive focus on analyses of canonical literary texts and now contribute greatly to various cultural studies domains. Exploring all sorts of items that can be read for their rhetorical and linguistic properties and effects, LGBT literary critics and theorists today examine, for example, political rhetoric, government documents, court records, film, music, art, advertising, television, sermons, diaries, and letters, not to mention noncanonical literature. The queer study of literature now tends to function as a form of intellectual inquiry that explores the ways words about sexuality and gender describe, code, shape, evaluate, and transform the worlds in which we live. One does not simply read about LGBT sexuality and gender anymore—one reads for what representations of sexuality and gender illuminate about life on and off the page.

Major Influences, Methodologies, and Thinkers

The dominant reading protocols of literary criticism and theory are often shifting and are influenced by a variety of disciplines, movements, and theories that are not simply literary. These include history, anthropology, and philosophy; African American, Native American, Latina and Latino, and Asian American movements; and Marxism, psychoanalysis, poststructuralism, and postmodernism. Perhaps more than any other discipline, movement, and theory of the late twentieth century, feminist studies, feminism, and feminist theory initiated the kinds of analyses and conversations that developed into LGBT literary criticism and theory. Although not all critics and theorists of sexuality and gender are feminists and are free of misogynist tendencies, the field's indebtedness to feminist studies and women's studies is undeniable. Feminism's interrogation of sex differences and gender hierarchies helped scholars think about the ways that "gender," despite its foundation in seemingly natural categories of anatomical sex difference, was not merely biological fact. Instead, gender reflected and produced uneven and unequal social, cultural, and political arrangements. Because of its "constructed" and constructing qualities, gender could be considered a category of experience open to interrogation and transformation.

Yet while feminist knowledge developed, various women who did not identify with white and heterosexual definitions of feminist experience challenged feminist biases about the "natural and universal character" of sexual desire; they questioned whether women automatically desired men as sexual and emotional partners and in what ways violations of what it means to be a "woman" transforms the definition of "woman." From their insights, LGBT literary critics and theorists learned about the ways in which sexuality, like gender difference, is open to scrutiny and revision. Debates about pornography, about lesbian sadomasochist practices, about men's place in feminism, about gay men's relationship with feminism, among other issues, further fractured unified ideas about feminist consciousness and inspired important interventions and sophisticated analyses of sexuality that made their ways into literary scholarship. Texts such as Monique Wittig's *The Lesbian Body*, Susan Sontag's "Notes on Camp," Adrienne Rich's "Compulsory Heterosexuality and Lesbian Existence," Gayle Rubin's "The Traffic in Women" (1975) and "Thinking Sex" (1993), Shulamith Firestone's *A Dialect of Sex* (1971), Audre Lorde's *Zami: A New Spelling of My Name* (1984), Cherríe Moraga and Gloria Anzaldúa's edited collection *This Bridge Called My Back: Writings by Radical Women of Color* (1981), Barbara Smith's edited collection *Home Girls: A Black Feminist Anthology* (1983), Carol Vance's edited volume *Pleasure and Danger: Exploring Female Sexuality* (1989), and Michel Foucault's *History of Sexuality*, volume 1 (1980) helped build on and transform feminism's crucial insights and were particularly important for the development of the reading protocols that sustained LGBT literary scholarship.

With the publication of the massive *The Lesbian and Gay Studies Reader* in 1993 (Routledge), LGBT theory and criticism established itself as a more recognizable field of inquiry. The striking number of literary essays and essays by literary critics and theorists in this collection is notable; the numbers demonstrate just how influential the study of literature and literary methods have become in sexuality studies—and vice versa. A quick list of other titles by literature scholars also demonstrates some of the ways in which LGBT criticism has had a dramatic impact on the study of most major literary periods, genres, and national literatures: D. A. Miller's *The Novel and the Police* (1988) and *Bringing Out Roland Barthes* (1992); Teresa de Lauretis's *Technologies of Gender: Essays on Theory, Film, and Fiction* (1987); Paul Julian Smith, *The Body Hispanic: Gender and Sexuality in Spanish and Spanish-American Literature* (1992); Emily Apter's *André Gide and the Codes of Homotextuality* (1987); Jonathan Goldberg's *Sodometries* (1992); Diana Fuss's edited collection, *Inside/Out: Lesbian Theories, Gay Theories* (1991); Michael Moon's *Disseminating Whitman* (1991); Michael Warner's edited volume *Fear of a Queer Planet* (1993); Susan Wolfe and Julia Penelope's edited volume *Sexual Practice, Textual Theory: Lesbian Cultural Criticism* (1993), Lee Edelman's *Homographesis* (1994), Carolyn Dinshaw's *Getting Medieval* (1999), Leo Bersani's *Homos* (1995) and *The Culture of Redemption* (1990); Gloria Anzaldúa's *Borderlands=La Frontera: The New Mestiza* (1987); Lauren Berlant's *The Queen of America Goes to Washington City: Essays on Sex and Citizenship* (1997); Josiah Blackmore and Gregory Hutcheson's *Queer Iberia: Sexualities, Cultures, and the Crossings from the Middle Ages to the Renaissance* (1999); Mary Pat Brady's *Extinct Lands, Temporal Geographies: Chicana Literature and the Urgency of Space* (2002), among numerous other important titles.

In these works, one can see that literary criticism and theory today focuses on more than "literature" or literary texts. These works explore larger ideas about culture, conceptions of selves and others, and the ways that power, race, class, gender, religion, and nation all join sexuality in making the story of desire and identity that much more complicated. Much of this work is strongly influenced by what is now called "queer theory," a method of thinking about LGBT politics, arts, and culture that synthesizes the insights of multiple disciplines, particularly those fields engaged in philosophical, linguistic, and psychoanalytic work.

Anthropologist Gayle Rubin's landmark essay "Thinking Sex" (1993), for example, was a call to make sexuality an intellectual and political priority; her thoughts—influenced by historical and cultural analyses of power offered by Michel Foucault—are paradigmatic and helped inspire scholars to interrogate social arrangements organized by conservative hierarchies of sexuality and gender. Numerous other critics followed suit, most notably Judith Butler, who, in her popular *Gender Trouble* (1989), linked together continental philosophy, French feminism, and Freudian and Lacanian psychoanalysis in order to explore the ways that sex, gender, and sexuality differences are not natural, but rather are performed through complicated repetitions of legal, political, medical, and artistic words, rules, ideas, practices, and anxieties. Although a philosopher by training, Butler's work galvanized literary theory and criticism, especially with its attention to the ways that acts of language and speech can provide further insights into the constructed quality and politically charged nature of sex, gender, and sexuality.

The other major scholar that made LGBT literary criticism into what is now commonly called "queer theory" is Eve Kosofsky Sedgwick. The author of books such as *Between Men* (1985) and *Epistemology of the Closet* (1990), Sedgwick produced literary readings, readings that explored links and relationships between homoeroticism and heterosexuality in numerous literary genres. But her work consisted of more than just studies of major canonical writers such as Henry James, though it was also that. Especially in *Epistemology*, Sedgwick offered contagious speculations about the ways that the secrecy of the "closet"—and specifically the secrecy of the "homosexual" closet—grounds much of Western knowledge and much of how we know what we know.

Although the name "queer theory" stuck, notable queer studies scholars Lauren Berlant and Michael Warner, in a column that in 1995 appeared in the official publication of the literature and language professional guild, the Modern Language Association (MLA), described what they saw developing in literature departments as a kind of theory specifically inflected by literary training. They argue that what was actually being created in the 1990s would more accurately be named "queer criticism," by which they meant cultural studies practices that did not offer sweeping theories about sexuality and gender as much as they offered particular analyses of a whole range of important literary texts, films, political developments, and media that are important for queer subcultures. As Berlant and Warner's column notes, this kind of literary criticism has found a vibrant home in the literature departments that gave rise to its creation. In 1976 the MLA Gay and Lesbian Caucus was formed, reflecting the notion that the deep study of sexuality and gender from an LGBTQ perspective is not merely a fad but a vital part of the profession's scholarly activities. And each year, the best essay in lesbian and gay studies is given an endowed honor by the MLA, the Compton-Noll Prize.

"Other" and Future Issues

Given LGBT literary criticism and theory's place within a lineage of post-1960s politicized fields of knowledge, it is perhaps not surprising that study of the links between race, class, religion, nationality, sex, gender, and sexuality is a goal. But goals are not always met. Although women of color had been calling attention to the ways that race and class complicate any analysis of sexuality at least since edited volumes such as *This Bridge Called My Back* and *Home Girls,* extensive engagement with race and class analyses has been lacking, and not exclusively because of white critics' neglect. The articulation of antihomophobic criticism has faced opposition among a number of more heterosexually conservative racial and ethnic minority groups. The work of a number of LGBT literary critics of color, however, has made notable contributions to this project, especially Philip Brian Harper and his analysis of masculinity and race in *Are We Not Men?: Masculine Anxiety and the Problem of African-American Identity* (1996). Robert Reid-Pharr's collection of essays, *Black Gay Man* (2001), performs similarly useful moves in exploring vexing relations between race, sexuality, and gender. José Esteban Muñoz's *Disidentifications: Queers of Color and the Performance of Politics* (1999) describes the manner in which those outside of mainstream culture negotiate norms of race, gender, class, and sexuality by identifying with film, art, performance, photography, and television. In 2000, Dwight McBride and Jennifer Brody edited a volume of *Callaloo,* a journal of African and African American literature and arts, calling for a more rigorous conversation to happen between critical race studies, literary studies, and queer criticism. And David Eng's *Racial Castration: Managing Masculinity in Asian America* (2001) is a helpful inquiry into the specifically Asian American dynamics of racial embodiment in the United States.

The study of queer sexuality is increasingly complicated, especially when we take into account the issues posed by bisexual, transgender, and disability perspectives. For all of its complexity of method and thought, sexuality studies is often reliant on the notions of stable and able bodies, with clearly articulated sexual preferences. Bisexuality is certainly a sexuality position that often does not receive enough critical attention. Two helpful anthologies have set out the particular terrain of inquiry: Elizabeth Reba Weise's *Closer to Home: Bisexuality and Feminism* (1992) and Loraine Hutchins and Lani Kaahumanu's *Bi Any Other Name: Bisexual People Speak Out* (1991). Marjorie Garber's *Vice Versa: Bisexuality and the Eroticism of Everyday Life* (1996) is a detailed literary and historical account that challenges the easy oppositions between heterosexuality and homosexuality, arguing that bisexuality is not a sexual orientation as much as it is a sexuality that undoes sexual orientation as a category.

Exciting new work about trans and transgender sexuality, identity, and desire makes the practice of LGBT literary criticism and theory more difficult and more productive. Urgent questions arise: What does it mean when one's anatomical sex does not correspond with the gender identity one feels one has or one wants to acquire? How do psychiatric definitions and medical procedures transform the story one tells about sex, sex difference, and sexuality? Pat Califia's *Sex Changes: The Politics of Transgenderism* (1997) and Kate Bornstein's *Gender Outlaw* (1996) are particularly important, initial responses to such questions. But while such trans work might not be so transgender oriented; the play and flow of different gender roles and positions makes traditional oppositions between masculine and feminine, between male and female, harder to assume. Literary scholar Judith Halberstam's *Female Masculinity* (1998) is a crucial study to consider. Halberstam interrogates the diverse experiences of masculine expressions of female identity and sexuality from the nineteenth century to the present. Using novels such as Radclyffe Hall's *The Well of Loneliness* and exploring topics such as femme/butch roles, transgender dykes, boxing, and film, Halberstam transforms our understanding of masculinity and the ways we think about gender and sexuality categories.

And the interest in the large concept of "disability" also provokes new directions in the critical repertoire: What does it mean when a body is immediately distinguished from "normal" sexual abilities and sometimes requires prosthetics and other devices in order to function? A 2003 special of issue of *GLQ: A Journal of Lesbian and Gay Studies,* "Desiring Disability: Queer Theory Meets Disability Studies," organized a number of essays that question the particular challenges and crises when desire and embodiment can no longer assume physical dexterity and health. The issue encouraged thinking about "crip theory" and the performance art of queer and disabled artists and activists. Mobility devices, fitness, prostheses, transformed abilities, disease, access to public places and institutions all influence and transform what often is taken for granted: functioning bodies and conventional sexualities.

What these even newer variations on LGBT literary criticism and theory reveal is that queer criticism is still a relatively young field. Although the success of its impact on the scholarship of literature departments and disciplines worldwide is impressive, the conceptual and curricular problems it faces are important and familiar. Faculty positions exclusively in LGBT literature or queer theory in literature departments are still rare, and many institutions have not programmed substantial numbers of LGBT literature classes. It remains to be seen how the literary study of LGBT sexualities and genders will continue to develop beyond assertions of identity difference into even more nuanced arguments that push our thinking about the status of sexuality, gender, and literature. What, for instance, will LGBTQ texts tell us about the study of literature in general—is there a specifically queer form of language, a queer form of speech? It also remains to be seen what will happen once the now-familiar gestures of queer literary criticism and theory are mainstreamed and assumed as basic starting points for literature scholars. Whatever the horizon, sexuality and gender most certainly will surprise us, and no doubt there will be a book and a critic waiting to describe, analyze, and challenge new revelations.

Bibliography

Abelove, Henry, Michèle Aina Barale, and David M. Halperin, eds. *The Lesbian and Gay Studies Reader.* New York: Routledge, 1993.

Anzaldúa, Gloria. *Borderland = La Frontera: The New Mestizo.* Berkeley, Calif.: Third World Press, 1987.

Anzaldúa, Gloria, and Cherrie Moraga, eds. *This Bridge Called My Back: Writings by Radical Women of Color.* New York: Kitchen Table Press, 1981.

Apter, Emily. *André Gide: And the Codes of Homotextuality.* Saratoga, Calif.: Anma Libri, 1987.

Berlant, Lauren. *The Queen of America Goes to Washington City: Essays on Sex and Citizenship.* Durham, N.C.: Duke University Press, 1997.

Berlant, Lauren, and Michael Warner. "What Does Queer Theory Teach Us About X?" *PMLA* 110, no. 3 (May 1995): 343–349.

Bersani, Leo. *The Culture of Redemption.* Cambridge, MA: Harvard University Press, 1990.

———. *Homos.* Cambridge, Mass.: Harvard University Press, 1995.

Blackmore, Josiah, and Gregory S. Hutcheson, eds. *Queer Iberia: Sexualities, Cultures, and Crossings from the Middle Ages to the Renaissance.* Durham, N.C.: Duke University Press, 1999.

Bornstein, Kate. *Gender Outlaw.* New York: Routledge, 1996.

Brady, Mary Pat. *Extinct Lands, Temporal Geographies: Chicana Literature and the Urgency of Space.* Durham, N.C.: Duke University Press, 2002.

Butler, Judith. *Gender Trouble.* New York: Routledge, 1989.

Califia, Pat. *Sex Changes: The Politics of Transgenderism.* San Francisco: Cleis Press, 1997.

De Lauretis, Teresa. *Technologies of Gender: Essays on Theory, Film, and Fiction.* Bloomington: Indiana University Press, 1987.

Dinshaw, Carolyn. *Getting Medieval: Sexualities and Communities, Pre- and Postmodern.* Durham, N.C.: Duke University Press, 1999.

Dollimore, Jonathan. *Sexual Dissidence.* Oxford, U.K.: Clarendon Press, 1991.

Eng, David. *Racial Castration: Managing Masculinity in Asian America.* Durham, N.C.: Duke University Press, 2001.

Firestone, Shulamith. *The Dialect of Sex: The Case for the Feminist Revolution.* Rev. ed. New York: Bantam, 1971.

Foucault, Michel. *The History of Sexuality.* Vol. 1: *An Introduction.* New York: Random House, 1980.

Fuss, Diana, ed. *Inside/Out: Lesbian Theories, Gay Theories.* New York: Routledge, 1991.

Garber, Marjorie B. *Vice Versa: Bisexuality and the Eroticism of Everyday Life.* New York: Simon and Schuster, 1996.

Goldberg, Jonathan. *Sodometries.* Stanford, Calif.: Stanford University Press, 1992.

Halberstam, Judith. *Female Masculinity.* Durham, N.C.: Duke University Press, 1998.

Harper, Philip Brian. *Are We Not Men?: Masculine Anxiety and the Problem of African-American Identity.* New York: Oxford University Press, 1996.

Hutchins, Loraine, and Lani Kaahumanu, eds. *Bi Any Other Name: Bisexual People Speak Out.* Boston: Alyson, 1991.

Lorde, Audre. *Zami: A New Spelling of My Name.* Trumansburg, N.Y.: Crossing Press, 1984.

McRuer, Robert, and Abby Wilkerson, eds. "Queer Theory Meets Disability Studies." *GLQ* 9, nos. 1–2 (March 2003).

Miller, D. A. *The Novel and the Police.* Berkeley and Los Angeles: University of California Press, 1988.

———. *Bringing Out Roland Barthes.* Berkeley: University of California Press, 1992.

Moon, Michael. *Disseminating Whitman: Revision and Corporeality in Leaves of Grass.* Cambridge, Mass.: Harvard University Press, 1991.

Muñoz, José Esteban. *Disidentifications: Queers of Color and the Performance of Politics.* Minneapolis: University of Minnesota Press, 1999.

Reid-Pharr, Robert. *Black Gay Man.* New York: New York University Press, 2001.

Rich, Adrienne. "Compulsory Heterosexuality and Lesbian Existence." *Signs* 5, no. 4 (1980): 631–660.

Rubin, Gayle. "The Traffic in Women." 1975.

———. "Thinking Sex: Notes for a Radical Theory of the Politics of Sexuality." *The Lesbian and Gay Studies Reader.* Edited by Henry Abelove, Michele Aina Barale, David M. Halperin. New York: Routledge, 1993.

Sedgwick, Eve. *Between Men.* New York: Columbia University Press, 1985.

———. *Epistemology of the Closet.* Berkeley and Los Angeles: University of California Press, 1990.

Sinfeld, Alan. *Cultural Politics—Queer Reading.* Philadelphia: University of Pennsylvania Press, 1994.

Smith, Paul Julian. *The Body Hispanic: Gender and Sexuality in Spanish and Spanish American Literature.* New York and London: Oxford University Press, 1992.

Sontag, Susan. "Notes on Camp." *Against Interpretation.* New York: Delta, 1979.

Vance, Carol, ed. *Pleasure and Danger: Exploring Female Sexuality.* London and Sydney, Wellington: Pandora, 1989.

Warner, Michael, ed. *Fear of a Queer Planet.* Minneapolis: University of Minnesota Press, 1993.

Weise, Elizabeth Reba, ed. *Closer to Home: Bisexuality and Feminism.* Seattle, Wash.: Seal, 1992.

Wittig, Monique. *The Lesbian Body.* New York: Avon, 1976.

Michael L. Cobb

See also BEATS; CULTURAL STUDIES AND CULTURAL THEORY; FOSTER, JEANNETTE; HARLEM RENAISSANCE; LANGUAGE; LITERATURE; PULP FICTION: GAY; PULP FICTION: LESBIAN.

LITERATURE

This is a composite entry; it is composed of the following three parts:

LITERATURE: EIGHTEENTH AND NINETEENTH CENTURIES

The only term that is easy to define in a brief survey of American LGBT literatures of the eighteenth and nineteenth centuries is the time span. Between 1700 and 1899, what it meant for women to express love and passion for one another, for men to write of mutual affection and desire, and for writers to represent these and other emotions in something called literature varied greatly by person, place, period, and document.

A review of LGBT literary works should not imply that each writer under discussion conceived of his or her sexuality and gender in the same way, nor that we who read these works a century or two later see their sexuality and gender in the same light. Even the words in these documents that appear to imply sexual intimacy might originally have denoted exclusively spiritual, platonic friendships, and references to the latter might have served as coded references to erotic relationships. Carefully interpreting pre-twentieth-century queer literary works requires knowledge concerning individual writers' histories, hidden connotations of words, definitions of "romantic friendship," authors' motives for writing texts, and our motives for reading them.

Early Writings, Religious and Otherwise

Condemnation. Much early American literature on LGBT issues takes the form of prohibitions voiced by theologians in sermons, warnings issued by moralists, and significant silences in other texts. Many early American authorities likened England to the biblical Sodom for its supposed degeneracy and imagined America as a refuge from Old World "sodomy." The term applied to sexual relations between members of the same sex, between unmarried members of different sexes, and between humans and animals. Without differentiating between these acts, authorities harshly condemned them all. In one sermon, "The Cry of Sodom Enquired Into" (1674), Samuel Danforth sought to justify the state's recent execution of a youth accused of sodomy, invoking the biblical language of "abomination" and describing both sodomy and bestiality as "going after strange flesh."

"A Christian in His Personal Calling," Cotton Mather's sermon of 1701, has as its concluding lines, "The sin of Sodom was abundance of idleness. All the Sins of Sodom will abound Where Idleness is Countenanced." Sinful sexuality, as far as Mather was concerned, inevitably began with idleness and sloth. An anonymous work, *Onania, or the Heinous Sin of Self-Pollution* (1720), went further, insisting that "wasting seed" not only encouraged sodomy but also caused physical harm. These prohibitions and dire warnings, which Jonathan Ned Katz has gathered in the *Gay and Lesbian Almanac*, often applied only to men, neglecting women's desires, let alone conceptions of lesbian identity then evolving.

Affirmation. Though this climate offered scant incentive for people to write potentially self incriminating accounts of unorthodox lives, colonial literature does include some affirmative LGBT images. Women and men alike, thought the Puritans, were "brides of Christ"; women and men alike, by the same logic, possessed an immortal soul that abided in the afterlife without a conventional gender designation.

Some spiritual autobiographers described a deity who male writers wished would "ravish" them. They invoked the language of fleshly desires to symbolize spirituality. An example is the poet Edward Taylor's exhortation in his "Preparatory Meditations" to "Bring forth a birth of keys t' unlock love's chest." Taylor begs, "Lord, ope the door: rub off my rust, remove / My sin, and oil my lock." "Enlivened" and lubricated, the speaker would then be united with the Lord. In a second symbol of such a union, Taylor places himself within traditionally feminine domesticity, writing in the famous poem "Huswifery," "Make me, O Lord, Thy spinning wheel complete." Transforming spools of thread into glorious holy robes, the speaker becomes a household instrument God would lovingly, sternly manipulate.

Similar homoerotic desires, felt by Michael Wigglesworth, evidently led to various self-castigating diary entries and to the cathartic, millennial poem "The Day of Doom." The poet—who had, as he put it, lusted after his male parishioners—attempted to banish his desires in his prolonged epic of brimstone.

Three men who lived decades later and dubbed one another "Lorenzo," "Leander," and "Castillo" seem not to have banished desires but instead found allusive means of expressing them. In the journals of two of the men, John Fishbourne Mifflin and James Gibson—journals that Caleb Crain has unearthed—the men preserve locks of one another's hair and conspire to spend their nights together. We do not know if they expressed their love sexually on the nights in question, but we do know that their contemporaries struggled to find the right words and actions for fulfilling their own desires. As Alexander Hamilton wrote to John Laurens, a fellow aide-de-camp to George Washington during the Revolutionary War, "I wish, my dear Laurens . . . it might be in my power, by action rather than words, [to] convince you that I love you."

Romantic Friendships and Boston Marriages

Expressions of love and desire from the nineteenth century cover a wider range of representations while posing interpretive challenges to readers. The cross-dressing in Catharine Maria Sedgwick's *Hope Leslie* (1827) and Theodore Winthrop's *Cecil Dreeme* (1861) initiates a transgender tradition in American letters. Nathaniel Hawthorne's *The Scarlet Letter* (1851) hints at bisexuality in the relationship between Hester Prynne and her husband, Roger Chillingsworth; between Prynne and her erstwhile lover Arthur Dimmesdale; and between the two men, whose pursuit of one another's secrets becomes oddly erotic.

Arrangements that strike us as amorous but unusual might be better understood in light of what Lillian Faderman terms "romantic friendships" and what Carroll Smith-Rosenberg has called "The Female World of Love and Ritual." The persistence of single-sex educational and vocational institutions through the century, the loss of many marriageable men in the Civil War, and the strict limitations placed upon women's spheres meant that many deemed by the outside world to be spinsters, old wives, or widows formed romantic and passionate attachments with one another. These arrangements, which Henry James parodied in another early narrative of bisexuality, *The Bostonians* (1886), came to be known late in the century as "Boston marriages." Twenty-first-century readers can find it difficult to determine whether or not these relationships were sexual and whether or not they should be labeled as lesbian.

Readers of Emily Dickinson's poetry engage many of these interpretive complications in reviewing her rich, often ambiguous sexual imagery, and in studying the sexually charged letters she wrote to clergyman Charles Wadsworth, Judge Otis Lord, and, most notoriously, Susan Gilbert Dickinson, her neighbor and sister-in-law. Her professions of love to Sue in letters and poems—later collected and edited by Ellen Louise Hart and Martha Nell Smith in *Open Me Carefully*—suggest that the poet's willingness to express her affections went unrequited. Readers once grouped her poems into tidy categories and conventionalized her verse, but a more innovative Dickinson, who placed her writings in enigmatic manuscript collections called fascicles and who wrote verses that defy categorization, keeps modern readers at work. Readers conventionally picture the poet as retiring and reclusive, but a more engaged and social Emily Dickinson, who actively participated in the social circle of her family and in the sexual politics of her world, emerges from later studies.

Studies of Sarah Orne Jewett, conventionally viewed as a local-color writer and remembered for "Deephaven" (1894) and *The Country of the Pointed Firs* (1910), show that she lived in a romantic friendship for more than twenty years with Annie A. Fields, widow of an important editor who had once published Jewett's work. Jewett lent encouragement to the aspiring young writer Willa Cather, who depicted LGBT relationships in settings that ranged from the East Coast to Nebraska and who brought Boston marriages into the next century.

Interracial and Interclass Same-Sex Relations

Admiration and exploitation. Nineteenth-century gay male literary images embrace domestic, exotic, frontier, and cosmopolitan settings. Herman Melville's novels of the 1840s and 1850s openly depict the exotic sexuality of Polynesian men and women, and suggest that sailors' camaraderie included mutual or even group masturbation. Though interpretations of Melville's sexuality become complicated by questions about his family relationships, his marriage, his iconoclasm, and the varying social codes of life at home and at sea, readers tend to agree that Melville was not alone in locating queer sexuality in maritime and distant settings.

Writing before Melville and influencing his work, particularly *Typee* (1846) and *Omoo* (1847), Richard Henry Dana set his novel *Two Years before the Mast* (1841) in the same locales and depicted the same ambiguous friendships between comrades. Writing after Melville and following in this Polynesian tradition, Charles Warren Stoddard depicted a kind of sensual, same-sex utopia in works with telling titles, *South-Sea Idylls* (1874) and *The Island of Tranquil Delights* (1904).

In domestic settings, accounts of interracial same-sex relations include those by Anglo-American diarists who admired the physiques of Indian warriors or squaws, as well as slave-owners who carefully noted slaves' muscles and supposedly sculpted physiques. In one mid-century memoir, *Army Life in a Black Regiment* (1870), Thomas Wentworth Higginson leads a battalion of African American soldiers fighting for the Union cause but frequently pauses, as Christopher Looby has shown, to describe his delight at watching his men bathing, resting, and preparing for battle.

In another memoir, *Incidents in the Life of a Slave Girl* (1861), Harriet Jacobs mentions a cruel slave master, who, Jacobs tells us, "took into his head the strangest freaks of despotism." A slave named Luke was at the despot's mercy, and, Jacobs observes, "some of these freaks were of a nature too filthy to be repeated." In a narrative that supplies graphic details of the sexual and physical abuse of other slaves, her reluctance to detail these "filthy" acts suggests their homosexual, forced, and sadistic character. Desire in these instances did not always correspond with egalitarian relationships so much as it reveals tendencies to objectify, idealize, and manipulate those who held less power.

A loving but manly interracial fraternity. The country's classic literary canon, as Leslie Fiedler was the first to point out, seems indeed to include a great many fraternal but socially unequal relationships that cross racial and ethnic lines. James Fenimore Cooper's frontier hero Natty Bumpo and Chingachgook in *The Last of the Mohicans* (1826); the Anglo-American and Christian Ishmael and Queequeg, his exotic, "pagan" companion aboard ship—and in bed—in Melville's *Moby Dick* (1851); and the conscience-stricken rascal and the fugitive slave in Mark Twain's *The Adventures of Huckleberry Finn* (1884), show the prevalence in nineteenth-century American letters of masculine interracial bonds. Even Henry David Thoreau interrupts his critique of New England economics in *Walden* (1854) to remark admiringly on the graceful, self-sufficient woodchopper Alek Therien, "A more simple and natural man it would be hard to find."

To read Walt Whitman's most famous poem, "Song of Myself" (1855), without noticing how much of its eroticism falls outside of the sphere of conventional, heterosexual matrimony, is to miss much of the work's startling erotic imagery. Celebrating masculine and feminine bodies alike, the poem's inclusive voice expresses wide varieties of longing and loving, encouraging readers to act upon the poem's words by touching the lives and bodies of others. Whitman depicted same-sex love in the erotic, corporeal, and phallic imagery of the "Calamus" poems, and added songs celebrating heterosexual coupling in the "Children of Adam" sequence. Whitman himself, we now know, enjoyed either romantic partnerships or extremely close, physically affectionate friendships with younger, working-class intimates Fred Vaughan and Peter Doyle, and played a nurturing role in Civil War hospitals, where, as a nurse, he would treat, embrace, and kiss the wounded.

If nineteenth-century Americans were preoccupied with the taboo subject of interracial cross-sex sexuality, which by mid-century they began to call "miscegenation," interracial bonds between men began to offer an imagined literary and mythic alternative. While heterosexual unions, to this way of thinking, could lead to children of mixed racial backgrounds, homosocial bonds allowed for platonic relationships and recast nationhood as a loving but manly interracial fraternity.

Increasing Ambiguity

If manly brothers helped shape the nation at the frontiers, socialite dandies helped shape it in the parlor rooms. The tales and novels of Henry James show how the dandy figure grew increasingly sexually ambiguous, until writers and fans, as in "The Author of Beltraffio" (1884), and teachers and students, as in "The Pupil" (1891), express amorous, mutual admiration. Fellow portrait artists work in a kind of erotic camaraderie and competition in *The Tragic Muse* (1890), James's counterpart to Oscar Wilde's *The Picture of Dorian Gray* (1891), and aging observers admire the talents and ambitions of younger men in James's *Roderick Hudson* (1875) and *The Ambassadors* (1904).

An aging Horatio Alger admired the ambitions of the young men who appear so repeatedly in Alger's classic "rags to riches" novels. The novelist Bayard Taylor fictionalized the life of Fitz-Greene Halleck, known as the "American Byron," in a subtle story of bisexuality and marriage, *Joseph and His Friend* (1870); and Alfred J. Cohen, who wrote as Alan Dale, penned another bisexual narrative in *A Marriage below Zero* (1899), a melodramatic account of a gay male affair, told from an abandoned wife's point of view.

Subtle codes for conveying rarer passions. By this time, however, clinical definitions of homosexuality had begun to take hold in Europe, Wilde had endured his public trial, and Edward Carpenter had begun writing pamphlets that spoke positively of "homogenic love." For many, literary depictions of same-sex relationships began to look more like potential perversity than benign brotherhood.

The British essayist and memoirist John Addington Symonds even asked Whitman if his poems actually depicted sexual contact between men, and if he enacted in life what he represented in verse. Whitman's famous denial (that in a kind of brawling, reckless heterosexuality he had fathered six illegitimate children), his revisions of the more explicit passages in some of his poems, and his written reminiscences prompted readers to ask how literally and biographically they should read his poems.

Women's amorous relationships also seemed more suspicious to Willa Cather's readers than they had to previous generations; their representation in literature seemed increasingly taboo. Cather and her contemporaries, from pioneering autobiographers Claude Hartland and Earl Lind to the novelist Henry Blake Fuller to the early feminist theorist Charlotte Perkins Gilman, made literary careers out of pushing the limits of such taboos ever further.

The stories that queer literature has to tell from before the twentieth century flirt with these subtly shifting taboos. This literature finds subtle codes for conveying rarer passions, works with or against the negative attitudes that words like "sodomy" and "deviancy" implicitly convey, and awaits the conscientious sympathy readers of a latter day, such as ourselves, can supply.

Bibliography

Bergman, David. *Gaiety Transfigured: Gay Self-Representation in American Literature.* Madison: University of Wisconsin Press, 1991.

Crain, Caleb. *American Sympathy: Men, Friendship, and Literature in the New Nation.* New Haven, Conn.: Yale University Press, 2001.

D'Emilio, John, and Estelle B. Freedman. *Intimate Matters: A History of Sexuality in America.* New York: Harper, 1988.

Dickinson, Emily. *The Poems of Emily Dickinson.* Edited by Thomas H. Johnson. 3 vols. Cambridge, Mass: Harvard University Press, 1955.

———. *The Letters of Emily Dickinson.* Edited by Thomas H. Johnson. 3 vols. Cambridge, Mass: Harvard University Press, 1958.

———. *Open Me Carefully: Emily Dickinson's Intimate Letters to Susan Huntington Dickinson.* Edited by Ellen Louise Hart and Martha Nell Smith. Ashfield, Mass.: Paris Press, 1998.

Faderman, Lillian. *Surpassing the Love of Man: Romantic Friendships and Love between Women from the Renaissance to the Present.* New York: Morrow, 1981.

Farr, Judith. *The Passions of Emily Dickinson.* Cambridge, Mass: Harvard University Press, 1992.

Fiedler, Leslie. *Love and Death in the American Novel.* New York: Criterion Books, 1960.

Godbeer, Richard. *The Sexual Revolution in Early America.* Baltimore: Johns Hopkins University Press, 2002.

Habegger, Alfred. *My Wars Are Laid Away in Books: The Life of Emily Dickinson.* New York: Random House, 2001.

Higginson, Thomas Wentworth. *The Complete Civil War Journal and Selected Letters of Thomas Wentworth Higginson.* Edited by Christopher Looby. Chicago: University of Chicago Press, 2000.

Jacobs, Harriet. *Incidents in the Life of a Slave Girl.* Edited by Nellie Y. McKay and Frances Smith Foster. New York: Norton, 2001.

Katz, Jonathan Ned. *Gay and Lesbian Almanac.* New York: Harper, 1983.

———. *Love Stories: Sex between Men before Homosexuality.* Chicago: University of Chicago Press, 2001.

Leavitt, David, and Mark Mitchell, eds. *Pages Passed from Hand to Hand: The Hidden Tradition of Homosexual Literature in English, 1748–1914.* London; Vintage, 1999.

Moon, Michael. *Disseminating Whitman: Revision and Corporeality in "Leaves of Grass."* Cambridge, Mass: Harvard University Press, 1991.

Pollak, Vivian R. *The Erotic Whitman.* Berkeley: University of California Press, 2000.

Reynolds, David S. *Walt Whitman's America: A Cultural Biography.* New York: Knopf, 1995.

Rupp, Leila J. *A Desired Past: A Short History of Same-Sex Love in America.* Chicago: University of Chicago Press, 1999.

Schmidgall, Gary. *Walt Whitman: A Gay Life.* New York: Dutton, 1997.

Smith-Rosenberg, Carroll. "The Female World of Love and Ritual: Relations between Women in Nineteenth Century America." In *Feminism and History.* Edited by Joan Wallach Scott. New York: Oxford University Press, 1996.

Whitman, Walt. *Leaves of Grass: Authoritative Texts, Prefaces, Whitman on His Art, Criticism.* Edited by Sculley Bradley and Harold W. Blodgett. New York: Norton, 1973.

Adam Sonstegard

See also ALGER, HORATIO; COLONIAL AMERICA; DICKINSON, EMILY; GILMAN, CHARLOTTE PERKINS; INTERRACIAL AND INTERETHNIC SEX AND RELATIONSHIPS; JEWETT, SARAH ORNE; ROMANTIC FRIENDSHIP AND BOSTON MARRIAGE; SLAVERY AND EMANCIPATION; STODDARD, CHARLES WARREN; WHITMAN, WALT; WIGGLESWORTH, MICHAEL.

LITERATURE: 1890–1969

Scholarship since the Stonewall Riots (1969) has continually pushed and expanded the understanding of homosocial identity and its genealogical ancestors. Many nineteenth-century literary figures have been put under new lenses, while new visions of familiar texts by innovative scholars and ever-curious readers have augmented the list of cultural ancestors. As novelist Richard Hall pointed out in a *New Republic* article (1979) about Henry James: "Lives, like carpets, have many strands. They may be perceived in many designs. What the biographer picks out depends not only on the keenness of his vision but on what he is empowered to see." Twenty-first-century scholars, students, and literary aficionados know that nineteenth-century writers such as Herman Melville, Walt Whitman, and Emily Dickinson are only the beginning of a rich American heritage.

Turn-of-the-Century Literature

The fiction of Henry James (1843–1916) is a prime example of how post-Stonewall literary criticism explored the canon and reconfigured readings of turn-of-the-century literature. The traditional scholarship of Leon Edel (written between 1950 and 1972) and the work of other Jamesians posited that James's grief over the death of his beloved cousin Minny Temple in 1870 had left the author a confirmed bachelor. But starting with Richard Hall's perceptive questioning in the *New Republic* of James's "life unlived, the beast forever crouched," queer theorists soon uncovered a different set of readings.

Even the most traditional of male critics such as Leon Edel, Irving Howe, and Lionel Trilling could not ignore the lesbian overtones in James's *The Bostonians* (1886). Other critics, including Michael Moon and Eve Sedgwick, ventured beyond the more obvious homoerotic connections. In *Between Men: English Literature and Male Homosocial Desire* (1985) and *Tendencies* (1993), Sedgwick explored more subtle and coded homoerotic references in *Wings of the Dove* (1902) and *The Golden Bowl* (1904).

None of the scholars who have reread James suggest that he consciously saw himself as a homosexual. James was horrified by the 1895 conviction and imprisonment on sodomy charges of Oscar Wilde in England, but refused to sign an 1896 petition supporting a pardon. In fact, like a good many other writers, James may have taken Wilde's downfall as a dire warning against writing that could be deemed too provocative. He therefore relied on exploring friendship between older and younger men, which still had benign connotations at the turn of the century.

American Expatriates in Europe

James moved to England permanently in the 1870s after traveling around Europe and living in Paris. Like many other American writers and painters, he viewed Europe as a place to learn his craft, to earn a living, and to view his native land at a distance with some dispassion and clarity.

The subsequent generation of literary expatriates who followed James to England, France, and Italy was much more cognizant of their homosexuality or "inversion." Their sexual difference became a significant factor in their decision to emigrate. By the turn of the century, for example, Natalie Clifford Barney was calling herself "naturally unnatural." Far ahead of her contemporaries, she rejected the "third sex" theories of Richard von Krafft-Ebing and Havelock Ellis and tried to claim her place as a beautiful woman in search of others. Barney looked to lesbian prototypes—however negative—in the French literature of Théophile de Gautier, Charles Baudelaire, and Émile Zola that were lacking in her own literary heritage. For Barney as well as for other lesbian expatriates such as Gertrude Stein, Djuna Barnes, and Janet Flanner, the cultural reality was that the native French paid little attention to the morality of foreigners as long as it did not affect their own daughters. Americans were less liberal-minded. Barney's first book, *Quelques portraits-sonnets de Femmes* (Some Portrait-Sonnets of Women, 1900), a collection of French poetry praising the beauty of women, was savaged in the American press. Her distraught father, Alfred Barney, purchased all the copies of the book that he could find and destroyed the plates. In contrast, the French critics were more appalled by her lapses in rhyme and meter.

With the harsh criticism of her work in America, Barney developed several strategies for expressing lesbian subject matter with impunity. The first was to create a series of plays, poems, and pseudo-Socratic dialogues about the life of Sappho, a figure from ancient Greece who was simultaneously still popular yet removed and exempt from contemporary values. Nineteenth-century poets and historians generally portrayed Sappho as a heterosexual mother who had leapt over the Leucadian cliffs after she had been spurned by the sailor Phaon. Barney and her lover, British-born poet Renée Vivien (born Pauline Mary Tarn) recast the Greek poet as a lover of women. By recreating Sappho in their own likeness, Barney and Vivien established a literary foremother who validated both their writing and lifestyle; for Barney, these two elements were inseparable.

Literary Amnesia

Barney was Gertrude Stein's friend and neighbor on the Left Bank of Paris, but their philosophical differences were many. Unlike Barney, Stein was reticent about her private life. Stein's first novel, *Q.E.D.,* written as early as 1903, was published posthumously and privately in 1950. In *The Autobiography of Alice B. Toklas* (1933), Stein claims that she placed the work in a desk drawer and forgot about it—a rather unlikely explanation for the "genius" she has Toklas label her in the same work.

Compared to Stein's major works, however, *Q.E.D.* is best forgotten. The lesbian triangle in the novel is largely of interest for what it reveals about Stein's early life and her unfortunate involvements. In *Q.E.D.* a character named Adele (Stein) becomes passionately attached to Helen (in real life, May Bookstaver), only to discover that she is financially and romantically controlled by Mabel (in real life, Mabel Haynes).

This bitter triangle of Stein's college days haunted her for many years, and the breakup played some part in her expatriation. Stein eventually found a way to voice this story by heterosexualizing it, first in *Fernhurst* (written c. 1904–1905) and later in "Melanctha" in *Three Lives* (1909). References to lesbianism were retained, but they were intricately coded, such as the repeated refrain of Melanctha biblically "knowing" Jane Harden.

The Gay Grotesque

The 1920s and 1930s ushered in a golden age of LGB writers, artists, and filmmakers. Their talents spanned the Atlantic and embraced the black as well as the white communities, as the Harlem Renaissance blossomed in New York and beyond.

One common trope of LGB writing is the "carnivalesque." Although the roots of the grotesque may be traced back to writers of all sexual persuasions and nationalities, including Rabelais, Laurence Sterne, and James Joyce, the carnivalesque has a special place for deviant writers who perhaps instinctively identify with its rebellious traditions. In the twentieth century, "monstrosity" in its many forms was often analyzed according to moral, medical, and psychological models, but some writers and artists refused to be cowed or defined by modern systems of labeling and limitation as they rebelliously explored and reclaimed the carnivalesque.

Two salient examples of this form are *Strange Brother* (1931) by Blair Niles (born Mary Blair Rice Beebie), and *The Young and Evil* (1933), coauthored by Charles Henri Ford and Parker Tyler. Little is known of Niles, except that she was a white author who was interested in not only writing but also personal exploration. Ford, born in Mississippi, and Tyler, born in New Orleans, migrated to Greenwich Village in New York City.

Both novels use Greenwich Village and Harlem as the setting for the gay grotesque. The rich, creative spirit of black LGB writers, artists, and musicians who populated Harlem during the 1920s and 1930s was in and of itself an inversion and subversion of the social order as the ruling class of the United States envisioned it. Harlem, like Greenwich Village, was a place to flee to, a fertile city of the imagination where African Americans gathered, leaving their native towns for a place where their artistic aspirations would not be considered abnormal.

In both novels, the protagonists wander the nocturnal landscape of New York City in search of sex, cigarettes, and illegal alcohol. They sample many of the seamy offerings of the thriving homosexual world: the characters cruise bars, pick up strange men in the streets or public bathrooms, and attend a drag ball in Harlem.

Lesbian Carnivalesque

The literary expatriates continued to flourish in Paris, which remained another primary site for American authors. Salons run by Natalie Clifford Barney, Gertrude Stein, and Mina Loy reopened at the close of World War I. These salons and a Left Bank Anglo bookstore run by lesbian Sylvia Beach embraced those members of the

"Lost Generation" who remained in Europe, as well as new arrivals, such as Harlem Renaissance poet Claude McKay.

One of the new émigrés was Djuna Barnes. As someone who had to earn a living, Barnes realized that lesbian content was literary suicide, especially in the wake of the obscenity trials regarding *The Well of Loneliness* (1928) by Radclyffe Hall, whom Barnes knew and even satirized in *Ladies Almanack* (1928). Barnes resorted to several strategies to protect her name from the legal dangers of censorship and the threat of public condemnation. First, she did not identify herself as a lesbian. Although she is generally considered bisexual, she doggedly refused to label herself as either lesbian or bisexual. She imagined herself as a heterosexual writing on a controversial subject with a long literary history. Furthermore, the hermetic quality of her work, especially her modernistic riffs and mock historical narratives such as *Ladies Almanack,* kept her works out of the hands of the general nonliterary public (those most likely to find her work offensive).

Influenced by her friend Charles Henri Ford, Barnes embraced the grotesque. In *Nightwood* (1936), Nora Flood meets Robin Vote at the circus. Nora's passion for Robin seems relatively palatable when set against an inverted twilight world of "monstrous" freaks, including tattooed circus performers and the eccentric and verbose transvestite Matthew O'Connor. As Carolyn Allen points out in *Following Djuna: Women Lovers and the Erotics of Loss* (1996), Barnes, like Stein and Barney, discouraged attempts to read her lesbian characters (Robin and Nora) as a couple in which one is the "congenital invert" while the other is more traditionally feminine—that is, a couple that would be more like Stephen Gordon and Mary Llewellen in *The Well of Loneliness.*

Encoded Longings

Few accounts of the Harlem scene by black writers were as open as *Strange Brother,* with the noteworthy exception of Richard Bruce Nugent's infamous story "Smoke, Lilies and Jade," which was printed in the first and only issue of the magazine *Fire!!* (1926). In this impressionistic story, punctuated only by ellipses (which often mark the space for something that cannot be said), the character Alex longs for Beauty, "because his body was beautiful . . . and white and warm." Nugent daringly celebrates both interracial relationships and bisexuality: "one can love two at the same time."

Nevertheless, although many of the most celebrated writers of the Harlem Renaissance were homosexual or bisexual, their works were deeply encoded. Gloria Hull (1993) has demonstrated, for instance, that some of the love poems of Angelina Weld Grimké contained a feminine pronoun in the manuscript that was altered to the masculine form for publication purposes. A few poems have been published, such as "Brown Girl" and "Naughty Nan," that extol feminine beauty. Grimké's scant literary production was due, Hull posits, to the restraints resulting from widespread homophobia.

Post-Stonewall critics such as Hull and Barbara Smith have begun to explore the intersections of sexuality and race in order to reevaluate the texts of acknowledged bisexual poets such as Countee Cullen and the possibly bisexual Langston Hughes. The latter's work exhibited very little homosexual content and whose sexual tastes seemed a mystery even to those closest to him. In the context of new scholarship, Hughes's "dream deferred" (in "Harlem") and Cullen's lack of "peace / Night or day, no slight release / . . . Walking through my body's street" (in "Heritage") take on a new resonance, though for some, a homosocial interpretation of these poems might seem strained.

The same conundrum applies to *Passing* (1929) by Nella Larsen, a novel that has received much attention due to the implicit similarities in the ways femme lesbians, masculine homosexual men, and light-skinned blacks have passed in the dominant culture. Just as many lesbians married men who virulently hated homosexuals, Larsen's passing protagonist Clare Kendry married a malicious racist. Whether Larsen intended this dual reading is not entirely clear, although Deborah E. McDowell, in introducing the 1986 edition of *Passing,* makes a strong argument for reading lesbianism into the text. McDowell points to Irene's (the narrator's) erotic descriptions of Clare as a "lovely creature" with a "tempting mouth," as well as the repeated images of heat and fire that Clare's presence conjures up.

Reflections in Southern Eyes

By the 1940s, southerners were the most influential writers in the United States. Many of them, including Carson McCullers, Gore Vidal, Truman Capote, and Tennessee Williams were also homosexual or bisexual.

The presentation of what has often been called a "homosexual sensibility" is often subtle. Though there is no blatant homosexuality or lesbianism in the works of Capote or McCullers, homosexuality is often hinted at through role reversal. The two authors employed the southern Gothic tradition (as envisaged by William Faulkner) and transformed it to investigate the "freakish" quality of their own existence. Role reversals include the girl who is a tomboy and the boy who is too feminine. Both Capote and McCullers successfully employ this strategy. In Capote's *Other Voices, Other Rooms* (1948), Joel does not look like a "real boy." "He was too pretty, too delicate and fair-skinned." His playmate, Idabel, calls him "sissy-britches," and she is so filthy and rough that Miss Roberta, the proprietor of the café in Noon City, tells Idabel not to come into her store. McCullers uses tomboys as the protagonists of two important novels—Mick in *The Heart Is a Lonely Hunter* (1940) and Frankie Adams in *Member of the Wedding* (1946).

Both Capote and McCullers see their characters as outsiders. In *Other Voices, Other Rooms,* the paralyzed father, the eccentric Randolph with his effeminate ways, the bird-killing Amy, the centenarian Jesus Fever, and the mutilated Zoo form a household of outcasts. In *The Heart Is a Lonely Hunter,* all the characters are "freaks" of sorts, including the deaf mute John Singer, the dwarflike Jake Blount, and the awkward and tomboyish Mick Kelly. Although homosexuality is not mentioned amid all this Faulkner-inspired Gothic grotesqueness (something pointed out by Tennessee Williams), the most tender relationship in the novel exists between Singer and his mute friend Antonapoulos, who is confined to a mental institution for most of the story.

World War II

The major catalyst of the 1940s was World War II, which transformed the way homosexuals were portrayed in literature, a change best represented by Gore Vidal in *The City and the Pillar* (1948). Vidal's protagonist, Jim Willard, is the epitome of a southern gentleman: a tall, blond, polite tennis player from Virginia. He, too, turns out to be an outcast. He falls in love with the boy next door, Bob Shaw, and one sultry idyllic night while camping out together in an old slave cabin by the river, they wrestle and make love.

Despite their individual quirks, the central male figures are doggedly "normal" men who pass effortlessly in the heterosexual world. Their masculinity is underscored by their participation in World War II: Jim enters the army, Shaw serves in the navy. Homosexual servicemen in uniform are in the background of every bar and party, perhaps suggesting the impact that World War II had on the development of homosexual consciousness.

The novel was a breakthrough in presenting Jim's obsession with Bob, not his homosexuality per se, as the problem. Nevertheless, in his work Vidal replicates the homophobic Freudian wisdom of the day: Jim's father "represent[s] bleakness and punishment," while his mother is overly doting and protective. One could interpret Jim's fixation on Bob as his failure to develop beyond adolescent fantasies.

The McCarthy Era

The political backlash of the 1950s that often lumped "commies" and "queers" into a single category created frightening times for many writers and artists. Material that could be construed as leaning to the Left might be banned or earn its creator an unwelcome subpoena to be questioned by a congressional committee. As anticommunism, as promulgated by Senator Joseph McCarthy and his political allies, spread across the United States and as far away as New Zealand, many writers found it safest to disguise their material or, at the very least, to distance themselves from it in some way so that they could claim it was truly a "fiction" in every sense of the word. When the political climate of the era is considered, it is amazing to see how much overt gay and lesbian material was nonetheless published during this period.

McCarthyism's emphasis on the holiness of the nuclear family unit as the antidote to "pinko commie queers" affected most literary output, all the way down to dime store novels such as lesbian pulp fiction. After wartime restrictions on paper were lifted, Gold Medal began to publish heterosexual thrillers and lesbian pulp novels with tawdry, suggestive covers. Many of the lesbian pulps were actually written by men or homophobic women, and they portrayed lesbian life as desperate and unhappy, but others by Paula Christian, Vin Packer, Valerie Taylor, and Ann Bannon presented more positive images and won an abiding place in lesbian culture, so much so that some of these authors are still in print.

One of the most famous pulps was *Women's Barracks* by Tereska Torrès, translated from the French by her husband, Meyer Levin; it had sold millions of copies by the 1960s. The novel focuses on the lives of a half dozen women in the Free French forces living in London during World War II. In "Making the World Safe for the Missionary Position" (1990), Kate Adams aptly summed up the plot of the novel as "the sexual revelations of four or five young women soldiers who, if the novel's word is taken literally, did nothing during their army years except have affairs with men, have affairs with women, talk to each other about the affairs they were having, and try to get over the affairs they had already had." Although the novel seemed to support post–World War II ideology that the best and safest place for women was in the home, not the armed forces, *Women's Barracks* was singled out by the Gathings Committee of the U.S. Congress in 1952 as one of sixty paperback novels that included "obscenity, violence, lust, use of narcotics, blasphemy, vulgarity, pornography, juvenile delinquency, sadism, masochism, perversion, homosexuality, lesbianism" and descriptions of a host of other sins.

Although the government worried that cheap paperbacks were spreading perversion, lesbians became concerned with the negative tilt of many of these works. For example, one nonfiction book, Ann Aldrich's *We Walk Alone* (1955), provoked a debate at the May 1957 meeting of the Daughters of Bilitis (DOB) in San Francisco. Helen Sanders, then DOB president, attacked the book for its "undue stress on the obvious and bizarre 'types' of Lesbians" and suggested the author "seek the 'cure' she believes possible since she so obviously hates and resents her lot" (*Ladder,* vol. 1, no. 9, June 1957). The titles of other pulp novels—for example, *Warped Women* by Janet Pritchard (1956)—made their prejudices clear. With negative paperbacks available in every drugstore while Jeannette H. Foster had to contract with a vanity press to publish her groundbreaking *Sex Variant Women in Literature* (1956), lesbian readers must have felt extremely frustrated indeed.

Nevertheless, some lesbian pulp novels were more positive in their characterizations and images, and served a useful social function. Laura, Ann Bannon's central character in *Odd Girl Out* (1957), *I Am a Woman* (1959), and *Women in the Shadows* (1959), runs away to New York City, where she dates Jack, a homosexual man, to cover up her "deviance." He, in turn, takes her to the homosexual haunts of Greenwich Village, where Laura meets up with Bannon's most memorable lesbian, Beebo Brinker. Although Bannon's Village was not geographically accurate, it provided readers with a travel guide of sorts, along with tips on what to wear, how to stand, how to cruise, and how not to make a sexual pass at a heterosexual roommate.

Lesbians Write Gay Men

Although pulp novels far outnumbered more serious endeavors, a few classics emerged in the 1950s. In order to be taken seriously, the authors of these novels took great pains to distance themselves from their subject matter, a strategy that gave their works the cache of objective and dispassionate interest. It was no accident, therefore, that at mid-century two lesbian novelists—Mary Renault (born Mary Challans) and Marguerite Yourcenar (born Marguerite Antoinette Jeanne Marie Ghislaine Cleenewerck de Brayencourt)—became two of the most important voices on male homosexuality. Yourcenar, who was born in Belgium, lived in Maine with her lifelong companion and translator Grace Frick. Her *Memoires d'Hadrien* (1951; *Memoirs of Hadrian,* 1954) became her most successful novel. In Yourcenar's book, Hadrian evokes the glory of ancient Greece, in particular the emperor's passion for the young and handsome Antinous, and this couple often compare themselves to Achilles and his beloved friend Patrocles. Thus, the novel establishes what appears to be a historical timeline tracing homosexuality back to ancient Greece and beyond that, to the mythological times before Homer. Although Hadrian drives Antinous to suicide by his affairs with other men and women, homosexuality was presented as an accepted form of love, even for those in power. Obviously, such a work had enormous appeal for male homosexuals, who could escape through fiction into a better reality and forget for a moment the malodorous politics of the present.

Even Mary Renault's *The Charioteer* (1953), set during World War II in bomb-ravaged London, was replete with images drawn from antiquity. Though Renault was not an American, the novel—a rare and serious look at homosexuality—was one of the most enduring and popular books in the United States in the 1950s.

Baldwin's Homosexual Masterpieces

James Baldwin's distancing strategy in *Giovanni's Room* (1956) is to make David, the American narrator, and Giovanni, his Italian lover, both white and to set the novel in gay Paris, where, many Americans assumed, anything goes for "five dirty minutes in the dark." While several critics have posited that Baldwin's choices of setting and race are geared to elude homophobic critics, the transposition may also be a sensible way to keep the focus on homosexuality and American values rather than race. It would be unfair, however, to suggest that Baldwin created only white homosexuals. During the same decade he addressed the desires of black protagonists for other black males in "The Outing," (1951), *Go Tell It on the Mountain* (1952), and *Another Country* (1962).

Whereas Baldwin's works about his upbringing are often laced with biblical references, *Giovanni's Room* is a trove of allusions to a hidden canon of homosexual texts. They are symbolically held in Giovanni's room, a "maid's room" (thus not intended for someone of Giovanni's gender) that is not centrally located, but is in fact "far out. It is almost not Paris." The room becomes the site of David's physical initiation into adult homosexuality, but it also holds Giovanni's "regurgitated life," "boxes of cardboard and leather," out of which peep "sheets of violin music," a hint of the artistic contents hidden within. The novel is a catalog of quotes and allusions, deftly referred to throughout the book starting with the names of the central characters and their reference to the biblical David and Jonathan. The purpose of so many allusions is to bestow a long homosexual literary heritage on *Giovanni's Room* and to claim in an oblique way that imaginative ground was actually broken long before Baldwin's novel.

A Woman on Women

Not all novelists felt the need to displace race or gender, but for Patricia Highsmith, a daring lesbian novel, *The Price of Salt* (1952), caused her to adopt a nom de plume. Author of the successful novel *Strangers on a Train* (1950), which she then adapted for a film directed by Alfred Hitchcock, Highsmith claimed to have used the pseudonym Claire Morgan so she would not be pigeonholed as a lesbian writer; the disguise protected her true identity. Like Baldwin, Highsmith alludes to other texts and incorporates theories from other fields, most particularly psychology. But instead of using them to buttress her characters or her theme, Highsmith satirizes them in order to move beyond their limitations. For instance, Highsmith embeds and then deconstructs a number of references to popular psychology of the day. She has one of her protagonists, Therese, work in the toy department of a store, selling dolls, and as if that were not enough to suggest infantilism, Therese is a quasi-orphan abandoned at an institutional home, where she becomes fixated on Sister Alicia. Carol, older and richer with a child of her own, more or less "adopts" Therese by inviting the young woman to her home, where Therese winds up tucked in bed and fed hot milk while Carol smokes a cigarette.

As the novel develops, however, Carol and Therese take off on a cross-country journey that leads Carol away from her marriage and Therese into adulthood; it is not just a picaresque road story in which neither character grows. At the end, Carol loses her child to her ex-husband. Although these may seem dire consequences to contemporary lesbians, they actually represented an improvement over the usual fictional denouement in which the runaway mother—whatever her sexual proclivities—was killed by a speeding train like Anna Karenina or driven to suicide like Emma Bovary. Even more amazing, Therese and Carol are reunited at the end of the novel. While the ending is indeterminate—and not the happy conclusion some lesbians have read into it—the possibility exists, perhaps for the first time in a serious lesbian novel, of at least a fulfilling and equal relationship, one that may be worth more than the modest "price of salt" of the book's title.

The Beat of a Different Drummer

In the 1950s the Beat generation rebelled against everything post–World War II America tried to represent. Mostly products of an Ivy League education, they embraced poetry, poverty, and, in some cases, crime and insanity in a capitalist society that valued financial success, hard work, and conventional careers. They were rootless travelers at a time when most Americans wanted to migrate no further than the suburbs. And in a predominantly Christian society, they embraced Eastern religions and exalted mysticism over ritual, meditation over prayer. In a culture where "real men" drank beer, they smoked pot and used other mind-altering drugs. And more than was evident during their heyday, they rebelled against sexual normativity by engaging in "free sex" with multiple female sexual partners, other men, and each other.

The Beatniks were spawned by an eclectic set of ancestral inheritances, including Arthur Rimbaud's synesthesia, Baudelaire's *mal du siècle,* Walt Whitman's emotional intensity, and the language and drug culture of jazz musicians. According to Steven Watson in *The Birth of the Beat Generation: Visionaries, Rebels, and Hipsters* (1995), Allen Ginsberg and Jack Kerouac (born Jean-Louis Lebris de Kerouac) defined their "new vision" of writing as early as 1944. This "new consciousness" had three main premises: "1) Uncensored self-expression is the seed of creativity. 2) The artist's consciousness is expanded through nonrational means: derangement of the senses, via drugs, dreams, hallucinatory states, and visions. 3) Art supersedes the dictates of conventional morality" (p. 40).

By the 1950s, the Beat generation (a term coined by Kerouac) had become a major force in American literature. Seminal works included William S. Burroughs's *Junky: Confessions of an Unredeemed Drug Addict* (1953), *Naked Lunch* (1959), *The Wild Boys: A Book of the Dead* (1971), and *Queer* (1985); Jack Kerouac's *On the Road* (1957), *The Subterraneans* (1958), *The Dharma Bums* (1958), *Big Sur* (1962) and *Visions of Cody* (1971); and the poetry of Gary Snyder, Gregory Corso, and Robert Duncan. The Beat circle also included Herbert Huncke, Neal Cassady, Carl Solomon, Diane di Prima, and LeRoi Jones (Amiri Baraka). West Coast poet Lawrence Ferlinghetti opened City Lights Books in San Francisco, which was the first U.S. bookstore to sell only paperbacks and which published Allen Ginsberg's *Howl* in 1956. Ferlinghetti and Shigeyoshi Murao, the manager of his store, were arrested on obscenity charges for selling *Howl,* but on 3 October 1957, Judge Clayton W. Horn found them not guilty despite the poem's raw language and obvious homosexuality. The acquittal was a major stepping stone for the publication of works with homoerotic content. Although Ginsberg lived quite openly with his partner and fellow poet Peter Orlovsky, some of the other Beat writers typically downplayed their homosexual acts by transposing them into heterosexual couplings within their novels.

The Beats left behind a body of spontaneous, raw, introspective poetry and prose that revolutionized American writing and turned the Beats into cult figures.

Places for Us

Despite the contention of the gay liberationists of the following decade, the 1960s were a relatively rich time for LGB culture. Several prominent authors wrote books with major gay or lesbian characters.

In her nonfiction work *Lesbian Images* (1975), Jane Rule recounts—with some dismay—the publication saga of Alma Routsong's "gentle" novel *A Place for Us* (1969). Unable to find a publisher for her new novel, despite the fact that she had previously published two others, Routsong privately printed the work at the Bleecker Street Press and sold it at DOB meetings and similar venues. Despite such careful control of her audience, Routsong still felt compelled to employ a pseudonym, Isabel Miller, which combined an anagram of "lesbia" with her mother's surname, Miller.

Routsong dared to place lesbians in new landscapes and plots where the conflict was something other than a woman-loving identity. Her *A Place for Us* is an interesting case in point. According to Routsong, her novel "was suggested by the life of the painter Mary Ann Wilson and her companion Miss Brundidge, who lived and farmed together for many years . . . [in] Greene County, New York State, in the early part of the nineteenth century" (Miller, 1972). Having found evidence of their "romantic attachment" to one another, Routsong researched the period and imagined the circumstances that brought the two women together. *A Place for Us* transforms the real-life women into Patience White, a painter, who falls in love with her neighbor, Sarah Dowling, a woman raised in a family of daughters to fulfill the role of the son on her father's farm. Out of scant historical material, Routsong was able to spin a convincing tale of two lesbians from very different social and economic classes, who knew no other women like them and thus had to proceed with absolutely no role models.

Rule's *Desert of the Heart* (1964) focused not on history, but on contemporary psychological conventions about lesbians. In her opening lines, Rule warns the reader that "conventions, like clichés, have a way of surviving their own usefulness." Rule then proceeds to turn those very clichés on their heads, first presenting Evelyn Hall, an English professor in Reno awaiting a divorce, and Ann Childs, a casino employee, as tempting doubles. "Ann was almost young enough to be her own child. But only a parent could be allowed to feel tenderness for his own likeness. In a childless woman such tenderness was at best narcissistic." Rule dares the readers to measure the couple against contemporary psychological profiles of homosexuals as "narcissistic," and then she presents a warm and thoroughly normal romance, beset with differences in social class and lifestyle that many heterosexual couples face as well. Still, some critics, blinded by their prejudices, were not convinced and judged the novel by the characters' unhappiness, which they thought was the lesbians' due. Thus, in the end, when Rule declines to kill off her protagonists in a sandstorm or to have Evelyn return to her wimpish husband, George, the critics viewed Ann and Evelyn's attempt to build a life together in Reno (if only "for the while then . . . for an indefinite period of time") as a borrowed heterosexual plot.

At the time, there were few gay and lesbian publications to counteract mainstream homophobia, yet groups such as the DOB and its publication the *Ladder*, along with word of mouth, ensured that these all-too-rare novels got into the hands of grateful lesbian readers who developed an enduring affection for them. Other lesbians read against the grain of mainstream reviews and rushed to buy any book that hinted, however negatively, at lesbian content.

The Changing Tide

While Rule expatriated herself to Canada, by World War II many European writers began to immigrate to the United States. Among the most prominent was Christopher Isherwood, who moved to southern California in 1939 and became a citizen in 1946. Beginning with *The World in the Evening* (1954) and continuing with *Down There on a Visit* (1962), Isherwood set much of his work in the United States, whereas the bulk of his earlier work takes place in Berlin. One of his American novels, *A Single Man* (1964), is perhaps his finest work. The almost Aristotelian structure of the novel, which takes place in Los Angeles in one day, presents George's homosexuality as a state of being rather than as a premise for development. George's day in various milieus around Los Angeles—from the university to a friend's hospital bed to a gay bar to his midnight dip in the surf—bears an implicit comparison with James Joyce's *Ulysses*, although Leopold Bloom's journey through Dublin on foot is replaced by a car trip on the Los Angeles freeway, just as George's homosexuality stands in for Bloom's outsider status as a Jew. As Claude Summers points out in *Gay Fictions* (1990), "rather than being subject to overt persecution, George most commonly experiences attitudes of condescending tolerance or studied indifference to his sexuality." As an aging gay man, he feels alienation from the denizens of the bars and to a degree from his own students. George mostly suffers in his "singleness": his past relationship with Jim has been so private and discreet that after Jim's death, he cannot mourn publicly. Though his grief should (through its very commonality) tie him to the rest of humanity, it separates him all the more.

Not Your Average Man

Not all writers, however, presented homosexuality as simply another facet of a normal life. Indeed, some reveled in the seamier sides of gay existence, as did Samuel M. Steward, writing pornography under the name of Phil Andros (his most notable work being *Stud,* 1966), and Latino writer John Rechy. Published in 1963 by Grove Press—the same year as the American publication of Jean Genet's *Our Lady of the Flowers*—Rechy's *City of Night* follows the adventures of the unnamed narrator, who, as Rechy himself did, migrates from El Paso, Texas, to New York City's Times Square and eventually to the gay haunts of New Orleans and Los Angeles as well. As much an Everyman as Isherwood's George, the narrator lives not for relationships but for paid sex that proves his worth as well as his heterosexuality. The narrator, like an inverted saint subjecting himself to temptations, allows dozens of men he spurns to pay for sexual acts with him—only to avoid the dreadful temptation each time to recognize that he is gay too, thus uniting with them. Unlike the novels of Rule, Routsong, and Isherwood, Rechy revels in presenting the grimiest details of a hustler's life. The most outlandish customers, including one man who rents an apartment to house his leather collection and another who invites the narrator home only to mother him, are the ones who catch the narrator's eye. Normality is not of interest here.

Rechy's next novel, *Numbers* (1967), follows the adventures of Johnny Rio (whose name perhaps pays homage to Tennessee Williams's "Joy Rio"), a former hustler, who now obsessively cruises in Griffith Park and other areas of Los Angeles as he tries to have sex with enough gay men to somehow extract his own identity from them. Here the reader is presented with another outsider, someone who moves closer to accepting his gay identity through anonymous sexuality. Thus, Rechy (as did Steward) embraces in a rather revolutionary way the very promiscuity that was downplayed and whispered about by political groups of the era. His unapologetic passion for the seamiest and most secretive sides of homosexual life almost presages the "anything goes" sexuality of the gay liberationists of the next decade.

Rechy's and Steward's works remind us that the literary road to the Stonewall Riots of 1969 was both long and well-paved. The richness of the LGB literary heritage of the first seven decades of the twentieth century is particularly astonishing when one takes into account the lack of public acceptance for the thematic material that inspired its authors. When the Oscar Wilde Memorial Bookshop, the first gay and lesbian bookstore in the country, opened its doors in Greenwich Village in 1967, such works found themselves, for the first time (with the exception of private collections), side by side on bookshelves, joined in what would later be deemed a queer literary canon.

Bibliography

Abelove, Henry, et al. *The Lesbian and Gay Studies Reader.* New York: Routledge, 1993.

Abraham, Julie. *Are Girls Necessary?: Lesbian Writing and Modern Histories.* New York: Routledge, 1996.

Adams, Kate. "Making the World Safe for the Missionary Position: Images of the Lesbian in Post–World War II America." In *Lesbian Texts and Contexts: Radical Revisions.* Edited by Karla Jay and Joanne Glasgow. New York: New York University Press, 1990.

Allen, Carolyn. *Following Djuna: Women Lovers and the Erotics of Loss.* Bloomington: Indiana University Press, 1996.

Bronski, Michael. *Culture Clash: The Making of Gay Sensibility.* Boston: South End Press, 1984.

———. *Pulp Fiction: Uncovering the Golden Age of Gay Male Pulps.* New York: St. Martins Press, 2003.

Castle, Terry. *The Apparitional Lesbian: Female Homosexuality and Modern Culture.* New York: Columbia University Press, 1993.

Daughters of Bilitis. *Ladder.* Vols. 1–16 (1956–1972). Reprinted New York: Arno Press, 1975.

Faderman, Lillian. *Odd Girls and Twilight Lovers: A History of Lesbian Life in Twentieth Century America.* New York: Columbia University Press, 1991.

Farwell, Marilyn R. *Heterosexual Plots and Lesbian Narratives.* New York: New York University Press, 1996.

Ferguson, Blanche E. *Countee Cullen and the Negro Renaissance.* New York: Dodd, Mead, 1966.

Fetterley, Judith. *The Resisting Reader: A Feminist Approach to American Fiction.* Bloomington: Indiana University Press, 1978.

Foster, Jeannette H. *Sex Variant Women in Literature: A Historical and Quantitative Survey.* Reprint. Tallahassee, Fla.: Naiad, 1985.

Haggerty, George E., and Bonnie Zimmerman, eds. *Professions of Desire: Lesbian and Gay Studies in Literature.* New York: Modern Language Association, 1995.

Hall, Richard. "An Obscure Hurt: The Sexuality of Henry James, Part I." *New Republic,* 28 April 1979: 25–29.

Hoogland, Renée C. *Lesbian Configurations.* Cambridge, U.K.: Polity Press, 1997.

Hull, Gloria T. "'Lines She Did Not Dare': Angelina Weld Grimke, Harlem Renaissance Poet." In *The Lesbian and Gay Studies Reader.* Edited by Henry Abelove et al. New York: Routledge, 1993.

Jay, Karla, ed. *Lesbian Erotics.* New York: New York University Press, 1995.

Jay, Karla, and Joanne Glasgow, eds. *Lesbian Texts and Contexts: Radical Revisions.* New York: New York University Press, 1990.

Lewis, David Levering, ed. *The Portable Harlem Renaissance Reader.* New York: Penguin, 1995.

Lilly, Mark. *Gay Men's Literature in the Twentieth Century.* Basingstoke, U.K.: Macmillan, 1993.

Mattachine Society. *Mattachine Review.* Vols. 1–13 (1955–1966). Reprint. New York: Arno Press, 1975.

Miller, Isabel. Afterword in *Patience and Sarah.* New York: McGraw-Hill, 1972.

Pollack, Sandra, and Denise D. Knight, eds. *Contemporary Lesbian Writers of the United States: A Bio-Bibliographical Critical Sourcebook.* Westport, Conn.: Greenwood Press, 1993.

Roof, Judith. *Come As You Are: Sexuality and Narrative.* New York: Columbia University Press, 1996.

Rule, Jane. *Lesbian Images.* Garden City, N.Y.: Doubleday, 1975.

Sarotte, Georges-Michel. *Like a Brother, Like a Lover: Male Homosexuality in the American Novel and Theater from Herman Melville to James Baldwin.* Garden City, N.Y.: Doubleday, 1978.

Sedgwick, Eve Kosofsky. *Between Men: English Literature and Male Homosocial Desire.* New York: Columbia University Press, 1985.

———. *Tendencies.* Durham, N.C.: Duke University Press, 1993.

Summers, Claude J. *Gay Fictions, Wilde to Stonewall: Studies in a Male Homosexual Literary Tradition.* New York: Continuum, 1990.

Summers, Claude J., ed. *The Gay and Lesbian Literary Heritage: A Reader's Companion to the Writers and Their Works, from Antiquity to the Present.* New York: Holt, 1995.

Vicinus, Martha, ed. *Lesbian Subjects: A Feminist Studies Reader.* Bloomington: Indiana University Press, 1996.

Watson, Steven. *The Birth of the Beat Generation: Visionaries, Rebels, and Hipsters, 1944–1960.* New York: Pantheon, 1995.

———. *The Harlem Renaissance: Hub of African-American Culture, 1920–1930.* New York: Pantheon, 1995.

Zimmerman, Bonnie. *The Safe Sea of Women: Lesbian Fiction 1969–1989.* Boston: Beacon Press, 1990.

Karla Jay

See also ANDERSON, MARGARET, AND JANE HEAP; AUDEN, W.H.; BALDWIN, JAMES; BANNON, ANN; BARNES, DJUNA; BARNEY, NATALIE; BEATS; BOWLES, PAUL AND JANE BOWLES; BURROUGHS, WILLIAM S.; CAPOTE, TRUMAN; CATHER, WILLA; CHEEVER, JOHN; CULLEN, COUNTEE; DELANEY, SAMUEL; DUNBAR-NELSON, ALICE; FORD, CHARLES HENRI; FOSTER, JEANETTE; FUGATE, JAMES BARR; GINSBERG, ALLEN; GRIMKÉ, ANGELINA WELD; GOODMAN, PAUL; GUNN, THOM; HARLEM RENAISSANCE; HIGHSMITH, PATRICIA; HUGHES, LANGSTON; ISHERWOOD, CHRISTOPHER; MCCULLERS, CARSON; MCKAY, CLAUDE; NILES, BLAIR; NUGENT, RICHARD BRUCE; PRIME-STEVENSON, EDWARD I.; PULP FICTION: GAY; PULP FICTION: LESBIAN; SARTON, MAY; SMITH, LILLIAN; STEIN, GERTRUDE, AND ALICE B. TOKLAS; THURMAN, WALLACE; VIDAL, GORE; WILHELM, GALE; WILLIAMS, TENNESSEE; YOURCENAR, MARGUERITE.

LITERATURE: 1969–PRESENT

From the last decades of the nineteenth century onward, literary works—and their writers—have been key to the development of both mainstream understandings of homosexuality and transgenderism, and of modern LGBT cultures themselves. However, the development of the gay liberation and lesbian feminist movements in the years immediately following the late 1960s upheaval that is signaled with the shorthand "Stonewall" produced in the United States a particularly intensified focus on literary works. The Stonewall Riots of 1969 also marked fundamental changes in both the content of the literature produced and the places in which it was published; the new publishing venues that appeared were inseparable from the new ideas. At the same time, there were significant continuities across the cultural divide represented by Stonewall—within the careers of individual writers and in terms of reader expectations—in the ways in which homosexuality and transgenderism might be represented in literature.

In the decades after Stonewall, LGBT literature continued to be shaped by developments in LGBT politics, as well as by changes in the economic and social options available to white women and women and men of color and by changes in public discussions of gender and racial difference. The development of LGBT literature, like the development of LGBT politics, was also profoundly affected by the HIV/AIDS epidemic that, beginning in the early 1980s, took away a host of writers and readers, became the subject of a trove of extraordinary artistic work, and irreversibly heightened the cultural visibility of LGBT people in the United States. Consequently, by the end of the twentieth century, literature—in the form of novels, poetry, plays, and memoirs—had become part of a broader array of forms for cultural work available to a very diverse group of LGBT-identified artists, including many different combinations of class, racial, gender, and sexual identifications.

New Ideas, New Forms of Publication

In the late 1960s and early 1970s, gay liberationists and lesbian feminists challenged mainstream views that regarded homosexuality as either an illness or a moral failing and of heterosexuality as the norm and ideal. They challenged conventional understandings of gender (masculine and feminine) and conventional understandings of lesbians and gay men as confused about their gender, as illustrated by masculine women and effeminate men. Alongside activists in other social movements, including the civil rights movement, the antiwar movement, and the women's liberation movement, gay liberationists and lesbian feminists rejected the authorities who had traditionally controlled public opinion; in the case of homosexuality these were, in particular, doctors, legislators, and religious leaders. Instead, they advocated listening to ordinary people speaking about their own experiences. This shifting of authority was especially crucial for lesbians and gay men because, as they had faced significant penalties for making themselves visible by speaking on their own behalf, the public discussion of homosexuality had been almost exclusively the province of hostile social authorities. Gay liberationists and lesbian feminists argued that gays and lesbians, whenever possible, should come out, and come out with things to say.

They should, moreover, create new records. Multiple social movements promoted the idea that everyone—even those who for reasons of education, gender, race, ethnicity, and so on did not fit the conventional cultural model of the "writer"—could write meaningfully about their lives. People were encouraged to take up poetry, drama, and fiction. But autobiographical writing, and coming out stories in particular, became particularly important forms of lesbian and gay writing in the 1970s.

Independent journals, magazines, and newspapers (*Aphra*, *Sinister Wisdom*, *Conditions*, *Christopher Street*, *Gay Community News*, and others), independent small presses (Daughters Inc., Alyson Press, Naiad Press, Firebrand Books, and Kitchen Table: Women of Color Press, for example), a network of lesbian and gay and women's bookstores, and reading series and conferences for LGBT writers sprang up across the country, accompanying the spread of gay liberation, women's liberation, and lesbian feminist groups and providing contexts, publishers, and distributors for all of this new writing. Such work was also often anthologized in collections of stories, poems, and plays; collections of particular types of writing, such as coming out stories; or combinations of political and literary writings. While some of these newspapers, journals, magazines, presses, and bookstores lasted for years and others for decades, and while some of the anthologies stayed in print, new newspapers, journals, and (often glossier) magazines appeared and new bookstores opened as older ones faded. New anthologies also appeared, offering new ways of thinking about LGBT literature and experience. By the 1990s mainstream newspapers, journals, magazines, and bookstores also began to publish or stock LGBT writing.

LGBT writers' networks have been maintained over the years by conferences and literary awards, such as the now annual Outwrite conferences and the Lambda Literary Awards. Increasingly, the lesbian and gay writers of the 1990s—Paul Monette, Tony Kushner, Dorothy Allison, and Michael Cunningham, for example—were nominated for, and sometimes won, national literary awards.

New Writers

By the time of Stonewall, there were already many lesbian and gay writers—mostly white, many from elite backgrounds—with established careers, including novelists such as Christopher Isherwood, Truman Capote, and James Baldwin; poets such as Elizabeth Bishop, Muriel Rukeyser, and May Swenson; and playwrights such as Tennessee Williams and Edward Albee. In many cases their homosexuality had become an open secret. Many of them had written—though sometimes briefly, grimly, or without anyone noticing—about homosexuality. But as it became possible, after Stonewall, to come out in a newly public fashion, new types of gay or lesbian writers could emerge—those for whom same-sex desire might be an ongoing subject and for whom LGBT cultures explicitly provide a perspective for their work. Some of these were writers who had already begun their careers, such as the poets Allen Ginsberg and Adrienne Rich; influenced and taken up by gay liberation and lesbian feminism, they developed broad new audiences. Others were writers who emerged out of the flux of the civil rights movement and women's liberation movements, as well as gay liberation and lesbian feminism, including Judy Grahn, Audre Lorde, Pat Parker, Kate Millett, Jill Johnston, June Arnold, Bertha Harris, or in the next generation Jewelle Gomez, Dorothy Allison, Essex Hemphill, and Melvin Dixon.

Place/Space: Class, Race, and Gender

While literary works are most often focused on, directed toward, and accessible to middle-class and elite persons, the novels dealing with homosexuality available before Stonewall were sought out by a wide range of people, whether from neighborhood lending libraries in urban centers in the 1920s and 1930s or as pulp paperbacks available in gas stations and drugstores across the country in the 1950s and 1960s. Such novels most often focused on either elite individuals—often living abroad—or persons who, by virtue of their homosexual-

This Bridge Called My Back. The cover of the influential collection of "Writings by Radical Women of Color" edited by Cherríe Moraga and Gloria Anzaldúa. **[Arte Publico Press]**

ity, were downwardly mobile. Homosexuality could thus be distanced from the everyday reality of the middle class—located in a shadowy social underworld, for example, or a foreign capital, or both—as in the Parisian bars of Baldwin's *Giovanni's Room* (1956) or among the hustlers and queens of John Rechy's *City of Night* (1963).

After Stonewall, poets and novelists wrote more attentively about working-class life, from Judy Grahn's *The Common Woman* (1969) and *A Woman Is Talking to Death* (1973) and Maureen Brady's *Folly* (1982) to Dorothy Allison in *Trash* (1988) and *Bastard Out of Carolina* (1992). It likewise became possible for both literary authors such as Jane Rule and Edmund White and popular writers such as Armistead Maupin and E. Lynn Harris to represent complex middle-class LGBT lives. Everyone could represent social worlds in which LGBT and heterosexual stories and lives were integrated.

The city was a central setting and subject in LGBT literature before and after Stonewall. That gay men and lesbians needed to leave the rural, small-town, or suburban places in which they had grown up for urban centers where they could comfortably be lesbian or gay was the common message. Frequent locations were Paris and, in the United States, New York City and San Francisco—as in Andrew Holleran's *Dancer from the Dance* (1978) and Armistead Maupin's *Tales of the City* (1978). This pattern was especially important in the work of male writers, though there were such notable exceptions as George Whitmore's *Nebraska* (1987). But LGBT life outside of northern urban centers and away from the East and West coasts gradually became more visible, beginning with women's work and work published by small presses, such as the writings of June Arnold in the 1970s and Mab Segrest and Minnie Bruce Pratt in the 1980s. In the 1990s a range of African American and white, working- and middle-class LGBT novelists, story writers, playwrights, and essayists focusing on the South—such as Dorothy Allison, Randall Kenan, and Jim Grimsley—began to be published by mainstream presses.

During the 1970s and 1980s, lesbians and gay men developed distinct public cultures and distinct literary worlds. This was especially the case among whites. These divisions broke down socially, politically, and in literary terms over the course of the 1980s in response to the HIV/AIDS epidemic, when women and men began working together to a greater extent. Lesbians began appearing more frequently in the writings of white gay men, such as Edmund White's *A Boy's Own Story* (1982) and David Leavitt's *Lost Language of Cranes* (1986), and gay men in white women's fiction, often at first in fiction about the epidemic, such as Sarah Schulman's *People in Trouble* (1990) and Rebecca Brown's *The Gifts of the Body* (1994).

Mainstream publication opportunities appeared earliest—beginning in the late 1970s—for white gay male writers, such as the members of the Violet Quill Club, including most notably Edmund White and Andrew Holleran. White gay male writers have consequently developed the broadest array of literary voices among LGBT writers, from the middlebrow comedy of Stephen McCauley to the shock tactics of Dennis Cooper to the literary experiments of Dale Peck. Nevertheless, as literature, especially the novel, has historically been the most accessible cultural form for those with the least economic as well as cultural capital, literary works remained culturally central longer for white lesbians and lesbians and gay men of color than for white gay men, for whom a wider range of opportunities for cultural representation—in theater, film, television, and so on—also became available soonest.

Despite exceptions—for example, African American women writing about lesbianism in the late 1970s and 1980s, including Ann Allen Shockley, Alice Walker, and Audre Lorde—the development of a large body of LGBT writing by women of color began largely in the small press arena, where the work of Native American writers such as Paula Gunn Allen and Asian American writers like Kitty Tsui first appeared. That development was significantly shaped by expanded discussions of race within feminism by lesbians of color in the 1980s, which was a consequence of the groundbreaking work of African American writer and activist Barbara Smith and Latina writers and activists Cherríe Moraga and Gloria Anzaldúa. African American gay men working to develop a literature through small press publication—including Joseph Beam and Essex Hemphill, who created anthologies and collections of poems—were very much influenced by their female peers. African American gay male novelists who emerged into mainstream publications, including Melvin Dixon in the 1980s and Randall Kenan in the 1990s, invariably had to contend with being compared to Baldwin. Popular African American writers published by mainstream presses, such as E. Lynn Harris, only emerged in the 1990s. Like their white counterparts, the newest generation of LGBT writers of color, such as Alexander Chee and Achy Obejas, appear both in small press and mainstream contexts, and those who are politically self-conscious most likely have been influenced by the queer politics of the 1990s.

Genre

The novel, the literary form from which most readers expect a chronicle of social, sexual, and emotional experience and the one accessible to the widest audience, has been the central source of literary representations of LGBT lives. At the same time, the form of the novel has been a central problem in LGBT literature. Most readers expect a narrative, a story, from a novel and, in addition, a more-or-less familiar story. Certainly before Stonewall, and to a large degree since, that familiar story has most often been a story of heterosexual lovers, in which LGBT persons have appeared as deviant, whether the deviation is presented as tragic or benign.

For LGBT writers the form of the novel as a story of growing up meshed most easily with the form of the coming out story, as demonstrated first and most effectively by the great success of Rita Mae Brown's *Rubyfruit Jungle* (1973). Consequently, the story of growing up gay or lesbian has been a persistent subject of LGBT literature. The drawback of this pattern is that it still allows for, even requires, the persistent representation of homosexuality as a problem that must be dealt with.

In pursuit of alternative patterns, some LGBT writers chose to bypass the need for a story, a narrative, altogether. In the 1970s, for example, Bertha Harris and June Arnold, and in the 1980s and 1990s, Rebecca Brown, Carole Maso, and Randall Kenan, drew on the modernist tradition of experimental work by such early twentieth-century LGBT writers as Gertrude Stein and Djuna Barnes. Many other LGBT fiction writers have instead chosen to focus their work in a particular genre, such as detective fiction (Joseph Hansen, Mary Wings) or science fiction (Samuel Delaney, Joanna Russ). In detective fiction, homosexuality—or homophobia—can be the key to the mystery, or the writer can treat the detective's homosexuality quite neutrally, because the plot of the novel is determined by the unfolding of the mystery rather than the details of the detective's life. Science fiction offered to LGBT as to feminist writers opportunities for playing with sex, gender, and sexuality and for drawing on the social possibilities of new worlds or commenting on this one, but doing all of this free of assuming homosexuality as a problem. Historical fiction has also been a significant genre in LGBT writing, allowing the exploration of LGBT history in such novels as David Leavitt's *While England Sleeps* (1993) and Mark Merlis's *American Studies* (1994).

Autobiography has been a form of special importance in post-Stonewall LGBT literature, from the work of Kate Millett and Audre Lorde to the responses to the HIV/AIDS epidemic by writers such as Paul Monette and Mark Doty, even as a broader interest in memoir developed across the culture. Autobiography provides a form capacious enough to capture kinds of experience not usually the focus of literature. Homosexuality can be a given rather than a problem; that is, it need not be at the center of the writer's attention.

Poetry, while a less popular literary form than the novel in the United States in the twentieth century, has been a significant medium for LGBT writers after Stonewall. LGBT poets from Ginsberg, Rich, and Lorde to Marilyn Hacker, Essex Hemphill, and Mark Doty have had an unusually broad public audience. Poets are free from the conventions of narrative—of having to "tell a story" that anyone can understand—that constrain writers of fiction. Like memoirists, they can attempt to convey a wider range of experience and feeling than fiction often allows. Some LGBT poets, especially those influenced by the social movements of the 1960s, have seen themselves in the role of witnesses testifying to their own experience as LGBT persons and that of others in their communities, as in Pat Parker's *Movement in Black* (1978), Judy Grahn's *Work of a Common Woman* (1978), and Cheryl Clarke's *Narratives: Poems in the Tradition of*

Black Women (1982). There is, however, no thematic unity among LGBT poets, nor is there any formal consistency. This is a group whose practices range from the formalism of Marilyn Hacker to the open forms and prosy colloquialism of Edward Field.

Mart Crowley's *The Boys in the Band* (1968), explicitly focused on a group of New York City gay men, was a theatrical breakthrough for gay playwrights. Following Crowley's work, more plays explicitly identified as lesbian or gay began to appear in the 1970s. Particularly significant, however, in terms of the theater being produced during the 1970s and 1980s, was the development of the camp tradition by men such as Charles Ludlam with his Ridiculous Theater Company and by the women's experimental theater associated with the WOW Cafe in New York City, where Lois Weaver and Peggy Shaw were central figures. Plays addressing the HIV/AIDS epidemic, from Larry Kramer's *The Normal Heart* (1985) to Tony Kushner's *Angels in America* (1993), contributed significantly to shaping public discourse about the epidemic and establishing explicitly gay theater in the cultural mainstream. Individual lesbian and gay playwrights who have by now developed substantial careers include Terence McNally and Paula Vogel. Also during the 1980s and 1990s, LGBT writers and performers such as Holly Hughes, Danitra Vance, Luis Alfaro, Tim Miller, and the Pomo Afro Homos theater troupe had very visible roles in the development of the new field of performance art.

Cultural Politics: Art, Community, Expectations, Boundaries

Some post-Stonewall LGBT writers have had explicit political agendas and have seen it as their responsibility to represent their group, while others have not. Reviewers seeking to validate LGBT work that impresses them are prone to praise the literature in question for addressing "universal" subjects rather than "merely" LGBT concerns—implying that LGBT concerns are not a sufficient subject for truly impressive writing. At the same time, all openly LGBT writers have had to contend, as all "minority" writers have in the American context, with the tendency of reviewers to see each LGBT writer as representative of the group rather than as an individual with particular skills and goals. LGBT writers have also had to contend, again like all so-called minority writers, with the expectation on the part of some readers that they will present only positive images of, in this case, LGBT life. The demand for positive images can be intensely felt—born out of frustration at mainstream distortions of LGBT life and the belief that fully realized images would dispel homophobia and transphobia. But no one writer or work can be expected to represent all LGBT people. And in practice, realistic images will not always be positive.

The organizing principles of LGBT social worlds are, moreover, continually being revised. In response to the work of bisexual and transgender activists, there has been growing recognition of bisexual and transgender identities within and in relation to lesbian and gay communities. LGBT literature has long contained stories of women and men choosing between homosexual and heterosexual relationships, as well as portraits of masculine women and feminine men. But certainly before and, still, after Stonewall there was in the literature an emphasis on deciding between heterosexual and homosexual desires. Accepting both was rarely presented as an option. Moreover, masculinity in women and femininity in men were historically understood to be evidence of homosexuality rather than expressions of gender identifications that might be understood as separable from sexual orientation. In the past two decades, however, numerous anthologies of writings about bisexuality have been published, as well as explorations of the subject by established writers such as novelist and essayist Jan Clausen. Transgender literature now includes memoirs of changing gender and cross-gender identifications such as Jan Morris's *Conundrum* (1974); fiction like Leslie Feinberg's *Stone Butch Blues* (1993); and writing for the theater, most notably the work of performance artist Kate Bornstein. There has also been a great deal of theoretical writing on bisexuality and transgender identities.

One underlying question that has taken different forms over the decades has been definitional, namely, what is LGBT literature? Is it work by LGBT persons, about LGBT subjects, or including LGBT characters? Such questions, of course, lead immediately to questions about who or what constitutes an LGBT person, subject, or character. At base, the significant question is, probably, why do we care?

That question has two dimensions. Why do we care about the sexual and gender identifications of the authors or the characters in the works we read? (Literary works themselves are not usually understood to have sexual or gender identifications, though sometimes that is not apparent when we discuss gay or lesbian or transgender novels, for example.) And why do we care about policing the borders of sexual and gender identity categories and, by extension, the literature identified with those categories?

On the one hand, there is a legitimate desire for cultural visibility—an aspiration for an identifiable LGBT literature—that has been fulfilled in the decades since

Stonewall broached the possibility of coming out, and then of living LGBT lives in public, in ways not previously imaginable. On the other hand, there is often the concern about misidentifying an author or work, perhaps because after decades of social stigma, identifying someone or something as LGBT, when they or it might not be, still seems like an insult—or liable to produce insults. It does seem to be the case that, once the possibility of establishing a group or culture emerges, some people become deeply invested in the nature of that group, and their investment takes the form of a desire to control the meaning of group identification.

There is also real anxiety among writers and readers about being shut off from the universal, being ghettoized. There has long been in the United States a broad cultural proscription against identification with any group that is understood as socially, culturally, or politically marginal—women, African Americans, Asian Americans, Latinos, Native Americans, lesbians and gay men—much less any combination of marginal positions. Writers are subtly encouraged to see themselves as marginalizing themselves by such identifications, even when they might in fact belong to one of those groups. That proscription was somewhat weakened in the 1970s and 1980s, but came back with increasing force in the 1990s—just as LGBT writers were gaining more mainstream recognition.

If, however, accepting the idea that to identify oneself as an LGBT writer is to establish oneself as marginal, claiming a somehow less valuable perspective from which to view the world than the perspectives of those who are heterosexual, means not only agreeing to second-class status, but propping up the cultural assumption that gender-normative heterosexuals do not have their own, equally specific, perspectives. Perhaps there is no universal literature after all.

Julie Abraham

See also ALBEE, EDWARD; ALLEN, PAULA GUNN; ANZALDÚA, GLORIA; ARENAS, REINALDO; BEAM, JOSEPH; BISHOP, ELIZABETH; BOOKSTORES; BRANT, BETH; BROWN, RITA MAE; CENSORSHIP, OBSCENITY, AND PORNOGRAPHY LAW AND POLICY; CHRYSTOS; CORNWELL, ANITA; CRISP, QUENTIN; DALY, MARY; DELANEY, SAMUEL; DÍAZ-COTTO, JUANITA; FIERSTEIN, HARVEY; GIDLOW, ELSA; GRAHN, JUDY; ISLAS, ARTURO; JOHNSTON, JILL; KENNY, MAURICE; KIM, WILLYCE; KRAMER, LARRY; LE GUIN, URSULA K.; LORDE, AUDRE; MILLETT, KATE; MONETTE, PAUL; MORAGA, CHERRÍE; MORGAN, ROBIN; NEWSPAPERS AND MAGAZINES; NODA, BARBARA; PARKER, PAT; POMA, EDGAR; PRESTON, JOHN; PUBLISHERS; RECHY, JOHN; REYES, RODRIGO; RICH, ADRIENNE; RULE, JANE; SHOCKLEY, ANN ALLEN; SMITH, BARBARA; TAYLOR, VALERIE; TSUI, KITTY; WHITE, EDMUND; WOO, MERLE.

LITTLE SISTER. see LOZEN.

LOBDELL, Lucy Ann (b. 1829; d. 1890/1891?), hunter, writer.

Lucy Ann Lobdell has the distinction of being one of the first subjects of an American medical article on female–female sexual relations, Dr. P. M. Wise's "Case of Sexual Perversion" (1883). Lobdell, a nineteenth-century cross-dresser, would perhaps have dubbed herself "transgender" had she lived in the modern era. Wise described her as having a "coarse voice and masculine features" and observed her "dressed in male attire" and "declar[ing] herself to be a man." He claimed too that Lobdell insisted she "possesses [the] virility . . . of a male" and "has the power to erect [her clitoris] in the same way a turtle protrudes its head."

What Wise failed to observe in the 1880s, when he was a doctor and she an inmate at the Willard Asylum for the Insane in New York, was what a vibrant person she had been before the onset of severe manic depression, which kept her in the asylum for more than ten years until her death. Fortunately, Lobdell had already recorded the story of her younger years in a forty-seven page self-published autobiography, *Narrative of Lucy Ann Lobdell, the Female Huntress of Delaware and Sullivan Counties* (1855).

Lobdell, born in Westerlo in upstate New York, was the daughter of a lumberman. From her earliest years she was a wanderer in the woods and a hunter. She also regarded herself as an accomplished violinist and something of an intellectual, who loved debating with the neighborhood ministers. In her autobiography Lobdell describes several suitors to whom she had been sympathetic, including George Washington Slater, whom she finally married and with whom she had a daughter, Helen. (In Lobdell's much later interviews with Dr. Wise she denied ever being attracted to a man.)

In any case, her first experience of transvestism occurred in the course of Slater's courtship of her. Because Lobdell's father disapproved of him, Lobdell ran away from home to see him, stealing her father's horse and donning her brother's clothes. In her autobiography, she presents her situation as high adventure. She is exhilarated later when a gentleman comes across her in the woods where she goes to hunt and mistakes her for a young man. She quotes his newspaper article about their encounter at length: "Her nether limbs were encased in a pair of snug-fitting pants, and a pair of Indian moccasins were upon her feet. She had a good-looking rifle upon her shoulder, and a brace of double-barreled pistols in the side-pockets of her coat, while a most formidable hunting knife hung suspended by her side." The writer attests to her astonishing shooting skills as well as her phenomenal energy and strength. He describes her inviting him to the family home, changing into a dress, serving tea, and "plying her needle in the most ladylike manner."

In her later life, Lobdell clearly eschewed those latter activities. When her husband became abusive, she left him, though she was pregnant with their daughter. She lived for a time with her parents, then left the daughter with them and went out into the world to earn a living. Her explanation of her transvestitism at this time is a strong early feminist statement: "I made up my mind to dress in men's attire to seek labor, as I was used to men's work. And as I might work harder at housework, and get only a dollar per week, and I was capable of doing men's work, and getting men's wages, I resolved to try.... If [a woman] is willing to toil, give her wages equal with that of man.... Secure her to her rights." Lobdell spent several years as a trapper and hunter in northern Minnesota, living among Native Americans as a man.

The rest of her story can only be gleaned from medical accounts. In ill health, Lobdell left her life in the woods and went to Pennsylvania, where she ended up in an almshouse because she was unable to support herself. There she met Maria Perry, a woman "of good education," according to Dr. Wise, who had been deserted by her husband and was destitute. The two women left the almshouse together. Lobdell assumed the name "Joseph Israel Lobdell" and passed as a man (sometimes as the Reverend Joseph Lobdell, a Methodist minister). Lobdell and Perry lived together "as husband and wife," Wise says, for twelve years, making a home in the woods where Lobdell worked as a hunter and trapper.

Contradictory stories are extant about how Lobdell's sex was discovered, but the record is clear that she was arrested in a village and sent to jail as a "vagrant." She was released after four months, according to one version of the story, because Perry petitioned for her freedom in an eloquently penned plea. Two or three years later, Lobdell was again in an almshouse, from which she was committed to the Willard Asylum. Wise claimed that when she was admitted "she was in a state of turbulent excitement... of an erotic nature and her sexual inclination was perverted. In passing the ward, she embraced the female attendant in a lewd manner and came near overpowering her before she received assistance." He also observed during her incarceration at Willard that she had "repeated paroxysmal attacks of erotomania [excessive sexual desire] and exhilaration . . . followed by corresponding periods of mental and physical depression."

Ten years later, in 1890, shortly before her death, a doctor's log book at the Willard Asylum recorded that "she has gotten over her old ideas. Has been quiet and orderly for some months past."

Bibliography

Katz, Jonathan Ned. *Gay American History: Lesbians and Gay Men in the United States.* New York: Harper and Row, 1985. Originally published in 1976.

Kiernan, James G. "Original Communications . . . Sexual Perversion." *Detroit Lancet* 7, no. 11 (May 1884): 482–483.

Lobdell, Lucy Ann. *Narrative of Lucy Ann Lobdell, the Female Huntress of Delaware and Sullivan Counties.* New York: 1855.

Wise, P. M. "Case of Sexual Perversion." *Alienist and Neurologist* 4, no. 1 (January 1883): 87–91.

Lillian Faderman

See also MEDICINE, MEDICALIZATION, AND THE MEDICAL MODEL; PRISONS, JAILS, AND REFORMATORIES: WOMEN'S; PSYCHOLOGY, PSYCHIATRY, PSYCHOANALYSIS, AND SEXOLOGY; TRANSSEXUALS, TRANSVESTITES, TRANSGENDER PEOPLE, AND CROSS-DRESSERS.

LOCKE, Alain (b. 13 September 1886; d. 10 June 1954), teacher, writer, philosopher.

A powerful editor, scholar, and teacher, Alain LeRoy Locke is best known for his crucial role in inaugurating the New Negro Movement, or Harlem Renaissance, of the 1920s and 1930s. In 1925, Paul Kellogg, editor of *Survey Graphic* magazine, asked Locke to serve as editor for a special issue on race and black New York. Locke subtitled the special March issue *Harlem: Mecca of the New Negro*, and in it he included essays, poems, drawings, plays, and short stories by young intellectuals who would become some of the century's best-known African American artists and writers, including James Weldon Johnson, W.E.B. DuBois, Countee Cullen, Langston Hughes, Claude McKay, Jean Toomer, and Angelina Grimké. The issue was an unprecedented success, and eight months later Locke published a revised and expanded version called *The New Negro.* With Locke's essay "Enter the New Negro," *Survey Graphic* and *The New Negro* announced an emerging cultural, political, and aesthetic vision for black Americans. *The New Negro* remains the central text of the Harlem Renaissance, and it launched the careers of its most famous participants.

Locke was born in Philadelphia, the only child of Pliny Ishmael Locke and Mary Hawkins Locke. His parents were a well-established part of Philadelphia's black elite. Locke attended Central High School and then the

Philadelphia School of Pedagogy, where his father was a teacher. He entered Harvard University in 1904 and graduated magna cum laude and Phi Beta Kappa in 1907. As the first African American Rhodes Scholar, Locke studied at Oxford University in England. After graduating from Oxford, he spent a year studying philosophy at the University of Berlin. In 1912, he returned to the United States to teach English and philosophy at Howard University, a historically black institution in Washington, D.C. Locke took leave of Howard to return to Harvard, where he completed his doctorate in philosophy in 1918. He rejoined the faculty at Howard as a professor of philosophy and maintained his position until his retirement in 1952.

Although Locke's outstanding scholarship and his role in educating the black elite at Howard are noteworthy, he remains most celebrated for his role in the Harlem cultural world. Many of the major artists of the decades associated with the Harlem Renaissance were LGB; among the most notable were Cullen, "Moms" Mabel Hampton, Nella Larsen, McKay, Richard Bruce Nugent, Bessie Smith, Billy Strayhorn, and Wallace Thurman. At the time, Locke was the most prominent. Locke published Nugent's first short story, "Sadhji," in *The New Negro*, and Nugent, then known as Richard Bruce, became the first African American author to publish an openly gay story, "Smoke, Lilies, and Jade," in the 1926 issue of *Fire!!*, a journal he established with the painter Aaron Douglas, Hughes, Zora Neale Hurston, and Thurman. Locke also fostered the careers of many younger, gay poets including Cullen, Hughes, and Thurman, the latter of whom published the gay-themed novel *Infants in the Spring* in 1932. A devoted supporter of black artists, Locke also helped several authors, among them Hughes, Hurston, and McKay, secure patrons so that they could continue their literary careers. About Locke, Nugent once said, "Almost everybody listened to his dictates" (Garber, p. 216).

One of Locke's protégés, Cullen, taught high school English to another young gay author, James Baldwin. Some critics argue that Locke and Cullen sustained a love affair at one time. If so, their relationship may have been a short one; Cullen married Yolande DuBois (daughter of W.E.B. DuBois) in 1928, though it should be noted that on his honeymoon Cullen brought along his best man and lover, Harold Jackman. His marriage ended in 1929. The white, gay socialite and patron of the arts Carl Van Vechten was also among Locke's friends, and the two helped to bring Harlem and its cultural offerings to the world.

Besides promoting literature, Locke was also known as a staunch advocate of the visual arts and theater. In his essay "The American Negro Artist" (1931), he named the painter Aaron Douglas "the pioneer of the African style among the American Negro artists." In drama, he celebrated the future of black playwrights who drew their work from black culture. There is no other senior intellectual of the era who matched Locke's commitment to meeting and encouraging younger artists. Beyond his role in the Harlem Renaissance, his philosophy, which many associate with pragmatism, has illuminated American philosophical studies, especially as he introduced new ways of thinking through questions of race and culture.

Bibliography

Harris, Leonard. *The Philosophy of Alain Locke: Harlem Renaissance and Beyond.* Philadelphia: Temple University Press, 1989.

Locke, Alain LeRoy. The Cultural Temper of Alain Locke: A Selection of His Essays on Art and Culture. Edited by Jeffrey C. Stewart. New York: Garland, 1983.

———. *The New Negro.* New York: Macmillan, 1992.

Washington, Johnny. Evolution, History, and Destiny: Letters to Alain Locke (1886–1954). New York: Peter Lang, 2002.

Shelly Eversley

See also CULLEN, COUNTEE; GRIMKÉ, ANGELINA WELD; HARLEM RENAISSANCE; HUGHES, LANGSTON; MCKAY, CLAUDE; NUGENT, RICHARD BRUCE; THURMAN, WALLACE; VAN VECHTEN, CARL.

LORDE, Audre (b. 18 February 1934; d. 17 November 1992) writer, activist.

Born in Harlem at the height of the Great Depression, Audre Lorde was the youngest of three daughters of immigrant parents from the Caribbean island of Grenada. Startled by the unexpected and blatant racism they encountered in the United States, her parents attempted to shield their children by never mentioning it. Rejected and isolated in her predominantly white Catholic elementary school, Lorde handled racism alone. In high school she found a few friends but Genevieve, the only other black student was her best friend. "Genny" committed suicide at age sixteen. For the next four years, Lorde wrote a memorial poem to her each spring, and in speeches and writings throughout her life, mourned her loss. Five of the twenty-five poems in her first book are written to Genny. *The Collected Poems of Audre Lorde* (1997) contains ten of her eleven books of poetry (*Undersong* [1992] is not included).

At four years of age Lorde spoke her first words: "I want to read." (Tate, p. 23). She began writing in a journal when she was about twelve (an almost daily habit

Audre Lorde. This black, lesbian feminist, a prolific poet and professor of literature, spread her mantra of inclusiveness—"Embrace difference"—to a variety of audiences, within and outside the women's movement. **[Audre Lorde]**

throughout her life), and when she was fifteen, her first love poem (to a boy) was published in *Seventeen* magazine. Her first book, *The First Cities* (1968), brought her to the attention of feminists, who invited her to read the work to female audiences, thus launching her into women's movement activities, where she became a spokeswoman and bridge builder. She was also invited to become a writer-in-residence at Tougaloo, an historically black college in Mississippi, where she discovered her passion for teaching, and in 1968 began her lifelong career as a professor of literature at City College in New York (CCNY).

Lorde married Edward Rollins, a white lawyer, in 1962. They had two children, Elizabeth (b. 1963) and Jonathan (b. 1965). Her poem, "And what about the Children," is an ironic statement about relatives' "dire predictions," "wild grim speculations," and comments on the texture of their hair (*The Collected Poems of Audre Lorde*, p. 45). Lorde separated from Rollins in 1970 and divorced him a few years later. By then she had entered a partnership with Frances Clayton, a white professor whom she had met at Tougaloo college, and who "othermothered" Lorde's children equally. In the mid-1980's Lorde moved to St. Croix to live with her final partner, Gloria I. Joseph, Ph.D., who described herself in the same manner as Lorde did: a black woman of West Indian parentage, born and raised in the United States. Lorde died there in 1992 of breast cancer, which had metastasized to her liver.

Lorde's influence within women's movement politics was huge and immediate; her charismatic speaking and writing filled an obvious but unarticulated need for just such a black feminist presence. Women of all colors considered her their own, and she willingly became anchor and bridge, encouraging everyone's contributions to the movement, urging women not to fear, but rather to *discover* one another's differences so that they could be shared and used productively for collective growth. "Embrace difference" became her mantra. Lorde's embrace of her "black," her "woman" and her "lesbian" selves was in keeping with the identity politics of the time. "The personal is political" meant that as marginalized people began to voice respect for their own identity, they would embrace their right to struggle against the powers that held them down. A 1978 statement by a black women's collective states, "the most radical politics come directly out of our own identity, as opposed to working to end somebody else's oppression" (Combahee River Collective, p. 16). But where many people addressed their struggles separately, according to the group they were working with (race, *or* gender, *or* sexual orientation *or* class), Lorde submerged none, carrying all of her identities into whichever group she was working with, declaring that differences were valuable tools to share and that grappling with the differences would strengthen each struggle. Her lifelong interactions with white women were advantageous also, allowing her to interrelate unabashedly: critiquing, loving, castigating, urging, and embracing—in the same way she desired to be treated herself.

She treated black men whom she engaged about sexism in the same manner. Her stinging rebuke to a black sociologist who had attacked black feminists appeared in the *Black Scholar* (1979); it was the leadoff essay among those by several women who were invited to respond in the following issue, among them June Jordan and Ntozake Shange. Her rebuke to James Baldwin in 1985 was equally firm but gentler in tone, perhaps resulting from her understanding that Baldwin was not hostile to women or black feminism but simply unaware of the United States feminist movement and the battles it generated, having spent a decade in Europe. In a "conversation" in *Essence,* a black women's magazine, she admonished him that his silence and that of other prominent black men about the violence against black women by black men, including murder and rape, gave tacit consent to the violence, and was destroying black communities. The previous year she had written that "sexual hostility against black women is practiced not only by the whole racist society but implemented within our black communities as well. It is a disease striking the heart of black nationhood, and silence will not make it disappear" (*Sister Outsider,* pp. 119-120).

Aware of her attraction to women from a young age, Lorde moved beyond "cuddling and kissing" (*Zami,* p. 19) when she was eighteen. Challenged and seduced by a woman friend and co-worker at her temporary job in Connecticut, she proved to both the young woman and herself that she was a more-than-adequate, naturally "dykely" lover (*Zami,* pp. 135–140). Thereafter, Lorde reveled in her lesbian sexuality, considering it a central force driving her literary work, providing energy for her various life activities, and shaping her roles in three intersecting U.S. social movements of the 1950s to 1990s: black liberation, women's liberation, and black lesbian and gay liberation. Lorde had published overtly lesbian love poems since 1970 (see, for example, *Cables to Rage,* pp. 51, 53), but they were not widely distributed. The 1974 publication of her explicitly sexual "love poem" in *Ms. Magazine,* however, brought her lesbianism dramatically front and center in a nationwide venue. Her lesbianism might have been less problematic in black liberation circles had she practiced but not preached it, as many black women did. However, by determining to focus consistent attention on lesbianism as an identity equal to "black" and "woman," she forced friction within the groups she entered, creating dialectical exchanges that helped expand the demand for a more inclusive vision within each of the three movements.

Lorde's involvement in gay liberation was focused more on black lesbian and gay liberation than on the largely white gay/lesbian liberation movement. After the Stonewall Riots (1969), gay liberation groups proliferated throughout the country. In Washington, D.C., black gay men broke away from the predominantly white gay group in the 1970s, forming The National Coalition of Black Lesbians and Gays (NCBLG) in 1978. In 1979 NCBLG held a National Conference for Third World Lesbians and Gays to coincide with the 1979 March on Washington for Lesbian and Gay Rights. Lorde electrified six hundred lesbians and gay men of color with her keynote speech and became a standard bearer for various ethnic groups that were mobilized by the conference. Latinos, American Indians, and Asians formed separate mixed-gender groups of lesbians and gay men that would also work in coalition with the other groups of color on certain issues, including socializing men of color in learning how to share power with women; combating racial/ethnic discrimination by the predominantly white gay and lesbian community in gay nightclubs and restaurants; and insisting on an equal place on the stage as speakers and presenters at public events, as well as participation in planning such events. Third World lesbians and gays would coalesce with the larger gay and lesbian community on issues that affected them all, such as legislative initiatives, protests against sodomy laws, actions for AIDS funding, and achieving and maintaining abortion rights. Lorde joined the board of NCBLG, while remaining "cheerleader" for all the groups. NCBLG became defunct in 1991. Many black gay feminist men, including Joseph Beam, editor of *In the Life,* the first anthology of writing by black gay men, and award-winning filmmaker Marlon Riggs explicitly acknowledged and followed her courageous example. Audre Lorde organizations, awards, and scholarships proliferate; a film, *A Litany for Survival* and a video, *The Edge of Each Other's Battles: The Vision of Audre Lorde* are widely used; and her books are reprinted, translated, and taught in classrooms worldwide.

Bibliography

Bowen, Angela. *Who Said It Was Simple: Audre Lorde's Complex Connections to Three U.S. Liberation Movements, 1952–1992.* Ph.D. diss., Clark University, 1997.

Combahee River Collective. "A Black Feminist Statement." In *But Some of Us Are Brave.* eds. Gloria T. Hull, Patricia Bell Scott, and Barbara Smith. New York: Feminist Press, 1982.

Lorde, Audre. *The First Cities* (New York: Poets Press, 1968). New York: W.W. Norton, 1997.

———. *Cables To Rage* (London: Paul Bremer, 1970). New York: W. W. Norton, 1997.

———. *From A Land Where Other People Live* (Detroit: Broadside, 1973). New York: W.W. Norton, 1997.

———. "Love Poem." *Ms. Magazine* 2, no. 8 (1974): 53.

———. *New York Head Shop And Museum* (Detroit: Broadside, 1974). New York: W. W. Norton, 1997.

———. *Between Our Selves.* Point Reyes, Calif.: Eidolon, 1976, 1997.

———. *Coal.* New York: W.W. Norton, 1976, 1997.

———. *The Black Unicorn.* New York: W. W. Norton, 1978, 1997.

———. *The Cancer Journals.* San Francisco: Aunt Lute Books, 1980.

———. *Chosen Poems: Old And New.* New York: W. W. Norton, 1982, 1997.

———. *Zami: A New Spelling Of My Name.* (Watertown: Persephone, 1982). Freedom, Calif.: Crossing Press, 1997.

———. *Sister Outsider: Essays And Speeches.* Freedom, Calif.: Crossing Press. 1984.

———. *Our Dead Behind Us.* New York: W. W. Norton, 1986, 1997.

———. *A Burst Of Light.* Ithaca: Firebrand, 1988.

———. *Undersong: Chosen Poems, Old and New, Revised.* New York: W. W. Norton, 1992.

———. *The Marvelous Arithmetics of Difference.* New York: W.W. Norton, 1993.

———. *The Collected Poems of Audre Lorde.* New York: W. W. Norton, 1997.

Tate, Claudia. *Black Women Writers at Work.* New York: Continuum Press, 1984.

Angela Bowen

See also LITERATURE; PARKER, PAT; RICH, ADRIENNE.

LOS ANGELES AND WEST HOLLYWOOD

While populations of native Californians, Spanish- and Mexican-descended Californios, immigrant laborers from the Far East, and migrants from the eastern United States all inhabited the region now identified as metropolitan Los Angeles long before the turn of the twentieth century, the city of Los Angeles emerged as a major U.S. population center only as the twentieth century dawned. While earlier the city had preserved the longer name, applied by eighteenth-century Spanish settlers, of Our Lady the Queen of the Angels of Porciúncula, by 1900 Anglo U.S. settlers favored the shortened version, Los Angeles ("the Angels" in Spanish). This was part of the ongoing process of colonizing the city's cultural identity and history, and eventually Los Angeles was shortened to the Anglo-friendly initials L.A., by which the city came to be known in common parlance. From its unsettled beginnings, L.A. has always named and misnamed far more than a strictly geographically defined municipal entity; L.A. has historically if informally referred to a far-flung region incorporating not only the city of Los Angeles (which includes most of the San Fernando Valley) but also the Inland Empire to the east and Orange County to the south. L.A. has also itself been historically misidentified as and by "Hollywood," the district within its borders most directly identified with the film and entertainment industry.

The Early Twentieth Century

Documentation of LGBT experience in early twentieth-century L.A. survives in part thanks to the colonies of artists and craftspeople that developed in and around Hollywood. As biographies of major film figures like directors George Cukor and James Whale, actors Ramon Novarro and Marlene Dietrich, and costume designer Orry-Kelly make clear, LGBT people were tolerated in Hollywood as long as they maintained strict public silence about their sexual identities. At least as early as 1929, members of the Hollywood film community began to patronize LGBT-identified establishments, like Jimmy's Back Yard (a nightclub on Ivar Street in downtown Hollywood) and several so-called pansy clubs, which featured transvestite entertainment and enjoyed a brief period of popularity in the early 1930s. Depression-era L.A. also reflected the larger national tolerance for leftist politics, which allowed early gay activists like Harry Hay the opportunity to make contacts with others who, like the actor Will Geer, were starting to see connections between their sexual and political marginality. The relative sexual and political tolerance of L.A. in this period also attracted gay cultural figures like the English novelist Christopher Isherwood, who arrived in L.A. in 1939 and remained there for the rest of his life. Another migrant to L.A. in the 1930s was Dr. Evelyn Hooker, who, while not homosexual herself, went on to do groundbreaking research on gay psychology, in part thanks to her enduring friendship with Isherwood.

World War II and the Cold War

L.A. in the 1940s was dominated, as was the world, by World War II and its aftermath. On weekend passes and furloughs, LGB military personnel enjoyed gay bars such as Bradley's in Hollywood and lesbian bars such as the If Club in L.A. Many military personnel discharged for LGB-related reasons and others uprooted by wartime mobilization settled in L.A. In the mid-1940s, Hooker embarked on the research, based at the University of California at Los Angeles (UCLA) that would lead her to conclude that homosexuality was not a mental illness. In 1945, Bob Mizer founded the Athletic Model Guild, thus establishing one of the first but by no means the last of L.A.'s outlets for the production and distribution of beefcake pictorials. Two years later Lisa Ben (née Edythe Eyde) began issuing *Vice Versa,* a series of typescripts whose very limited circulation did not prevent it from acquiring significance as one of the earliest instances of public writing for and by lesbians in the United States. Ben and others also reported on emerging lesbian social circles in the same period and on the existence of lesbian-friendly clubs like the If Club, Flamingo Club, Paradise Club, and the Star Room. Gay Angelenos from the same period report the significant evolution of a gay male subculture as well, especially in and around the cruising grounds of downtown L.A.'s Pershing Square, the gay- and drag-friendly bars along downtown's Main Street, and the gay beach in Santa Monica. In gay Hollywood proper, the social scene revolved in part around the very popular (and "mixed") Café Gala, which was gay owned and whose bar area was renowned as a watering hole for gay (and straight) men in the industry.

Late 1940s L.A. was also enshrouded, like the rest of the nation, in the paranoia and anxieties of the early Cold War and atomic age. LGBT activists with leftist politics, like Hay, were targeted for harassment by the House Un-American Activities Committee, which held public meetings in southern California. These meetings primarily targeted entertainment figures based in McCarthy-era Hollywood, who were often accused of being both gay and communist.

The Homophile Movement

This climate did not, however, prevent a small group of gay Angelenos, led by Hay, from forming the Mattachine Society in 1950. Mattachine, named after troupes of masqueraded dancers who performed in medieval European courts, was one of the earliest LGBT activist groups in the United States and is often credited with inaugurating the modern U.S. LGBT political movement. While some L.A.-based social clubs (including the Knights of the Clocks, formed by a group of interracial, black-white gay couples) predated Mattachine, the latter was the first to embrace an explicitly political, and cautiously public, set of goals.

Tensions among early Mattachine members led quickly to a split, however, which resulted in the creation of ONE, Inc. in 1952 and, in 1953, of its magazine, *ONE* (and later the ONE Institute). The founders included W. Dorr Legg, Don Slater, and Tony Reyes. Both ONE, Inc. and the Mattachine Society contributed to the greater visibility and efficacy of an organized LGBT movement in mid-century L.A. and the nation. Among their accomplishments was a successful challenge to the 1952 arrest of Mattachine member Dale Jennings on "lewd and dissolute" behavior charges for soliciting sex in public from a police officer engaging in entrapment. Another was the landmark 1958 U.S. Supreme Court ruling in *ONE, Inc. v. Olesen,* which allowed the circulation of gay-themed materials via the U.S. mail. The latter case came about because of attempts by ONE Inc. to distribute its successful magazine to an ever-growing readership. While the early Mattachine's membership was predominantly male (Marilyn Rieger was an influential, significant exception), *ONE* benefited from the contributions of its cogendered staff, which included several dedicated lesbian writers and editors. Beginning with the historic publication in February 1954 of its first special issue, called "The Feminine Viewpoint," *ONE* featured material relevant to the lives and interests of lesbians and drew on the talents of a staff that included Ann "Corky" Carll Reid, Joan Corbin (pseudonym Eve Elloree), Stella Rush (Sten Russell), and Helen "Sandy" Sandoz. Sandoz was also the first president of L.A.'s chapter of the Daughters of Bilitis (DOB), the lesbian organization, founded in San Francisco in 1955 and extended to L.A. in 1958. Because of the risks that all homophile activists and writers faced in the intensely homophobic climate of the 1950s and 1960s, many used aliases and pseudonyms. Meanwhile, and with good reason, 1950s Hollywood remained a deeply closeted and paranoid place, but it also remained relatively hospitable, within strict limits, to its LGBT denizens, from directors like Vicente Minnelli and Charles Walters to writers like Arthur Laurents and Gore Vidal, as well as to countless actors, musicians, choreographers, set and costume designers, and others employed at the major studios.

By the mid-1960s, ONE, Inc. had suffered its own schism, as differences in vision alienated members of the leadership from one another. Don Slater left *ONE* magazine to start his own short-lived publication, *Tangents;* Stella Rush and other female staffers transferred their energies to the DOB's publication, the *Ladder;* and ONE Inc.'s remaining organizer, Dorr Legg, grew increasingly isolated and conservative. After this period, ONE Inc. survived primarily thanks to the financial support of millionaire southerner Reed Erickson (née Rita), a transgender person with whom Legg maintained a volatile connection. In 1994, what remained of ONE Inc. combined its rich collection of documentary materials with those organized by archivist James Kepner's International Gay and Lesbian Archives. Together they formed the ONE/IGLA Institute, a vital resource center located near and affiliated with the University of Southern California.

Cultural Figures in the 1960s

In the early 1960s, L.A. witnessed the arrival of another set of significant LGBT cultural figures. These included the novelist John Rechy, whose experiences hustling other men in Pershing Square and nearby hustler bars (and his more general sexual cruising in L.A.'s enormous Griffith Park) became the subject matter of much of his early fiction, notably in his groundbreaking first novel, *City of Night* (1963). Rechy's published work, along with Isherwood's novel *A Single Man* (1964) and his *Diaries* (covering the mid-century but published much later), constitute a rich, detailed cultural history of twentieth-century gay L.A from the perspectives of two of its most accomplished inhabitants. Rechy remains one of gay

L.A.'s most important social and sexual historians; one of his lasting legacies can be found at the Numbers bar and restaurant, whose name is the title of a 1967 novel by Rechy. Numbers, established in Hollywood in 1979, has traditionally and notoriously catered to a high-priced sex trade, even after its move to a more sanitary West Hollywood address in 1998.

The sexual researcher and historian Vern Bullough arrived in L.A. in 1959. A straight ally whose work complemented Hooker's in treating homosexuality and gender variation as noncontroversial manifestations of human psychology and behavior, Bullough dedicated himself to both intellectual and political activism, dividing his energies between his academic work at California State University at Northridge, his collaborations with ONE, Inc. and Mattachine, and his work with the emerging transvestite-transgender movement led by activists such as Erickson and Virginia Prince.

David Hockney, one of the major figures of late-twentieth-century painting and visual art, came to L.A. in the early 1960s. He famously fell in love with both its cultural and natural topographies and has in the course of a long career documented across diverse media (including, for example, Polaroid montages of Isherwood with his lover Don Bachardy) many aspects of L.A. life, gay and otherwise.

Late 1960s to Late 1970s

While the narrative of U.S. LGBT history has been dominated since the late 1960s by developments (like the Stonewall Riots of 1969) that took place in New York City and San Francisco, LGBT Angelenos continued to make their own vital contributions to both local and national LGBT life. These contributions include the founding of the *Los Angeles Advocate* newsletter in 1967 by PRIDE members Dick Michaels and Bill Rand; two years later, Michaels and Rand bought the newsletter (by then a magazine) from PRIDE, renamed it the *Advocate,* and watched its circulation and popularity continue to grow. By the time the magazine was sold to San Francisco millionaire David Goodstein in the mid-1970s, its circulation had risen from five hundred to forty thousand; by the time Goodstein died in 1985, the *Advocate* was a national publication, and it continued into the twenty-first century as a premiere national LGBT newsmagazine.

Just a year after the founding of the *Advocate,* activist Troy Perry established the Metropolitan Community Church (MCC) in Los Angeles and in doing so planted the seed for what would also become a national movement, this one spiritual, as LGBT communities across the country started their own chapters of MCC. By the time the elderly Reverend Perry dedicated MCC's national center (its "mother" church) in L.A. in 1999, both he and the organization he founded had become legendary in, and vital to, the larger national and even international LGBT scene.

As the 1960s veered into the 1970s, and as LGBT America veered into its modern, post-Stonewall period of cultural emergence and political consolidation, the L.A. community kept stride. In 1969, activist Morris Kight established the L.A. Gay Liberation Front (GLF) in 1969, which organized protests against homophobic establishments like West Hollywood's Barney's Beanery (which notoriously sported signs reading "No Fagots [sic] Allowed") and also initiated L.A.'s first gay pride parade down Hollywood Boulevard in 1970. In 1971, Kight created L.A.'s Gay Community Services Center (GCSC). (The Center added "Lesbian" to its name in 1984.) While L.A.'s GLF chapter did not last long, its parade became an enduring southern California institution, known best for its annual Christopher Street West celebration. By the time L.A.'s renamed Gay and Lesbian Center celebrated its thirtieth anniversary in 2001, it was one of the largest such centers in the United States, with an operating budget in the many millions of dollars and an impressive headquarters offering an equally impressive array of services.

While both the GLF and Kight's nascent GCSC drew fire for being too male centered, L.A.'s growing lesbian community (which was taking hold in enclaves centered in West Hollywood and Long Beach) found strength and support in the feminist movement. Lesbians were instrumental in the establishment and maintenance of L.A.'s Woman's Building (located for much of its life near L.A.'s Chinatown), which enjoyed prominence as a feminist institution from its founding in 1973 to its closing in 1991. The Sisterhood Bookstore was established in 1972. The following year, UCLA hosted the highly successful and turbulent West Coast Lesbian Conference. Over the course of the 1970s, lesbian nightlife revolved around bars like the Seventh Circle, Bacchanal, Joanie Presents, and the Cork Room.

In the 1970s, as national attention continued to be directed toward more visibly evolving LGBT communities, especially that of San Francisco, L.A.'s continued to make its own important if less flashy strides. The year 1973, for example, witnessed the establishment (in what is now L.A.'s Koreatown) of Jewel's Catch One, which by its thirtieth anniversary enjoyed the status of being the oldest black-owned LGBT nightclub-community center in the country. The long-running *Lesbian News* was first published in 1975, and in 1979 a bookstore called A Different Light opened in the city's Silverlake District. In

1983 it opened a branch in New York City's Chelsea neighborhood and additional outlets opened in San Francisco's Castro District in 1987 and West Hollywood in 1990. In these years, both Rechy and Hockney continued to produce work dedicated to the exploration, in words and images, of L.A.'s complex gay life. Among their more significant works were Rechy's "documentary" fiction *Sexual Outlaw* (1977), which radically expanded the scope and variety of the author's explorations of L.A.'s sexual undergrounds and sexual politics, and Hockney's legendary (and homo-coded) pool paintings, many of which are featured in the documentary film *A Bigger Splash* (1974).

Recent Developments

By the late 1970s and early 1980s, it had become clear that LGBT L.A. had two significant population centers, one in West Hollywood and the other in Silverlake. The former, an unincorporated part of Los Angeles County and therefore a safe haven from the aggressively homophobic Los Angeles Police Department, was geographically situated between Hollywood and Beverly Hills and attracted primarily white, middle-class residents who could afford the rents. The latter, located between Hollywood and downtown L.A., was historically more ethnically and economically diverse, welcoming not only working-class LGBT people and people of color but also more specialized sexual communities and clubs. Since the early 1970s, West Hollywood and Silverlake together have come to symbolize the increasing complexity of LGBT L.A.'s culture. If West Hollywood was wealthier, more mainstream, and the center of L.A.'s burgeoning pleasure industry (bars, nightclubs, bathhouses, porn studios), Silverlake was the center of much that was more genuinely alternative, more aptly queer, about L.A.'s homosexual culture and sexual cultures in general. While the balance between these two districts tipped, in part because of the 1984 political incorporation of West Hollywood into its own independent municipality, Silverlake continued to provide a healthy counterweight to its higher-profile sister community.

In any case, the political and cultural importance of the incorporation of West Hollywood at the same time that AIDS was starting to devastate L.A.'s gay community cannot be underestimated. Since 1984, the city of West Hollywood has proved an important anomaly on the local and national gay scene; it began its life with the first-ever LGBT-majority city council in the nation and has since that moment been a model of what LGBT-sensitive city politics can do when LGBT people are no longer a small minority in a given voting population. As important AIDS research began to be conducted at UCLA, and as AIDS started to affect some very high profile (and often closeted) gay celebrities like Rock Hudson, the consolidation of the local LGBT political movement in West Hollywood helped LGBT Angelenos address the many demands that the AIDS emergency made on them. LGBT activists formed organizations such as AIDS Project Los Angeles (APLA) and Project Angel Food, both of which were instrumental in delivering much-needed services to all L.A. communities affected by AIDS. While it took mainstream Hollywood (with very few exceptions) a good decade after AIDS's initial appearance to devote significant funds to its representation in feature films (*Philadelphia,* 1993) and television (*And the Band Played On,* 1993), L.A.-based writers like Paul Monette (in his memoir *Borrowed Time,* 1988) and independent filmmakers like Tom Joslin (in his indispensable documentary *Silverlake Life,* 1993) managed to record in more detailed, realistic, and compelling terms their own experiences battling AIDS, both by nursing their dying lovers and by confronting their own HIV status as well.

While AIDS in its first decade arguably dominated gay experience in L.A., it did not entirely monopolize it. On the positive side were Dr. Virginia Uribe's establishment of Project 10 (in support of gay, lesbian, questioning, and allied youth) at Fairfax High School, where she taught and where she witnessed too often the disturbing harassment of LGBT teens by their homophobic and transphobic peers; the establishment in 1984 of Connexxus, an organization designed to support the needs of L.A.'s lesbian community (first opened in West Hollywood, Connexxus also briefly operated a Centro in East Los Angeles for Latina lesbians before both offices closed in 1990); and the historic emergence in 1991 of a renewed grassroots LGBT political movement provoked by anger over Governor Pete Wilson's veto of a bill to protect LGBT people from employment discrimination that he had promised to sign as he courted LGBT voters during his 1990 gubernatorial campaign. The mostly spontaneous protests against Wilson's veto continued nightly for two weeks, swelling to thousands of marchers by the end and shutting down traffic along some of L.A.'s and West Hollywood's busiest streets.

In the 1990s and the first decade of the new century, the LGBT community experienced a sea change as members and allies of its earliest generations started to pass away. These included Legg in 1994, Hooker in 1996, Kepner in 1997, Hay in 2002, and Kight in 2003. Nevertheless, the L.A. community, now reflecting its own greater sexual and gender diversity in the initials "LGBTQ," continues to evolve and diversify further. More cultural figures (including L.A.–based performance artists like Vaginal Cream Davis, Luis Alfaro, and Monica Palacios) are producing work that explores in particular the LGBT and queer experience in L.A.'s communities of color. And even mainstream entertainment has begun more fully to embrace defiantly "out" LGBT artists like comic Ellen DeGeneres, musician Melissa Etheridge, and writer-director Alan Ball (all L.A. residents).

Challenges like AIDS, hate crimes, and homophobic and transphobic discrimination still face the L.A. as well as the national LGBT community in the first years of the twenty-first century, but LGBT L.A. continues to contribute to that larger community in its own uniquely Angeleno manner. And if LGBT L.A. once had trouble distinguishing itself from its alter egos of Hollywood and West Hollywood, it has come in its long evolution to embrace those two identities, among others. As a truly metropolitan and cosmopolitan community, LGBT L.A. continues to extend its reach beyond West Hollywood to include other LGBT communities, old and new, from Silverlake to Long Beach to Orange County's Laguna Beach, as well as many points in between.

Bibliography

Bérubé, Allan. *Coming Out under Fire: The History of Gay Men and Women in World War Two.* New York: Free Press, 1990.

Bullough, Vern, L., ed. *Before Stonewall: Activists for Gay and Lesbian Rights in Historical Context.* Binghamton, N.Y.: Harrington Park Press, 2002.

D'Emilio, John. *Sexual Politics, Sexual Communities: The Making of a Homosexual Minority in the U.S., 1940–1970.* 2d ed. Chicago: University of Chicago Press. 1998.

Kenney, Moira Rachel. *Mapping Gay L.A.: The Intersection of Place and Politics.* Philadelphia: Temple University Press, 2001.

Retter, Yolanda. "The Lesbian History Project." Available from http://www-lib.usc.edu/~retter/main.html.

———. "On the Side of Angels: A History of Lesbian Activism in Los Angeles, 1970–1990." Ph.D. diss., University of New Mexico, 1999.

Timmons, Stuart. *The Trouble with Harry Hay.* Boston: Alyson Books, 1990.

Ricardo L. Ortiz

See also ACTORS AND ACTRESSES; *ADVOCATE*; AILEY, ALVIN; AMERICAN CIVIL LIBERTIES UNION (ACLU); ANGER, KENNETH; BACA, JUDY; BEN, LISA; BENEDICT, RUTH; BENTLEY, GLADYS; BOURBON, RAY (RAE); COMEDY AND HUMOR; COMMUNITY CENTERS; CORDOVA, JEANNE; CUKOR, GEORGE; ERICKSON, REED; GOODSTEIN, DAVID; HAY, HARRY; HOCKNEY, DAVID; HOOKER, EVELYN; ICONS; ISHERWOOD, CHRISTOPHER; JEWS AND JUDAISM; KEPNER, JAMES; LATINA AND LATINO LGBTQ ORGANIZATIONS AND PERIODICALS; LEGG, DORR; *MATTACHINE REVIEW*; MATTACHINE SOCIETY; MIZER, ROBERT; MONETTE, PAUL; *ONE*; ONE INSTITUTE; PERRY, TROY; PRINCE, VIRGINIA; RECHY, JOHN; VIDAL, GORE.

LOZEN

(a.k.a. Lizah, Losa, Little Sister) (b. ca. 1840; d. June 1889), medicine person, warrior, mediator.

Lozen was born in the Chihennes or Warm Springs Band of Chiricahua Apaches. Her brother was Chief Victorio (Bi-duyé). Although Lozen is well known among Apaches, many of the accounts documenting her role in the Apache wars of the 1870s and 1880s were not published until the late twentieth century. These show her to have been a leading figure in the final episode of Native American armed resistance to the invasion that began with the arrival of Columbus.

Although a female *berdache* ("two-spirited") status has not been documented among the Apaches, Lozen's career parallels those of such women in other tribes. During a vigil at the time of her puberty feast, she received the power to heal wounds and locate the enemy. She subsequently studied with older shamans and undertook additional vision quests. Her skills in riding, fighting, shooting, roping, and horse stealing were legendary and favorably compared to exploits of men. In camp, she continued to do women's chores, but also tended horses. She was called "Dextrous Horse Thief" and "Warrior Woman." As a fighter, she was as formidable as Victorio, who once said, "Lozen is as my right hand. Strong as a man, braver than most, and cunning in strategy, Lozen is a shield to her people" (Ball, *In the Days of Victorio,* p. 15).

In 1871, the U.S. government offered to establish a reservation for the Apaches under Cochise and Victorio at Warm Springs, New Mexico. After consulting with his sister, Victorio agreed. But the tribe was subsequently moved to less favorable locations, and, in 1876 they fled from the San Carlos reservation in Arizona, eluding capture for the next three years. In the period of extended conflict that ensued, Apache leaders relied on Lozen's predictions. She joined Victorio on raids, attended war dances, and participated in councils. Contemporaries described her as sacred and respected above all other women.

In the fall of 1880, Victorio was being pursued in Texas when a woman in his band entered labor. Lozen remained behind with her, until she had given birth, then escorted mother and infant across New Mexico to the Mescalero Apache reservation, eluding American and Mexican forces along the way. Meanwhile, Victorio was trapped by the Mexican military and killed along with seventy-eight others. Lozen now joined Victorio's seventy-year-old successor, Nana, and the medicine man, Geronimo (Goyankla).

In the summer of 1881, Lozen captured a herd of horses bearing valuable ammunition. Soon after, she

" Warrior Woman." Lozen (front, left), sister of Chief Victorio, sits with Dahteste and other Chiricahua Apaches after their capture in 1886. **[Arizona Historical Society/Tucson, neg. no. 19,796]**

joined Geronimo when he left the San Carlos reservation to resume raiding. In a battle with Mexican troops, Lozen calmly retrieved a mule carrying ammunition while under direct fire. In the spring of 1883, she filled another role, as mediator, when she and a woman named Dahteste (Tah-das-te) arranged a meeting with General George Crook. (Married to one of Geronimo's followers, Dahteste was also an excellent fighter.) At this meeting, Geronimo and Nana agreed to return to Fort Apache—but by the spring of 1885 they were in flight once again.

In March 1886, Lozen and Dahteste arranged another conference with Crook. Geronimo almost surrendered, then changed his mind and fled. Lozen joined him. Meanwhile, to prevent the four hundred Chiricahuas who had remained on the reservation from joining the renegades, General Nelson Miles, Crook's replacement, had them incarcerated in Florida. In late summer 1886, Lozen and Dahteste appeared at a camp of American soldiers in Mexico and announced that Geronimo was willing to meet. His followers had been reduced to some three dozen men, women, and children. Undefeated in battle, they were nonetheless tired and homesick. Joining the Chiricahuas in Florida, they remained prisoners of war until 1913.

Apache accounts describe Lozen and Dahteste as regular companions at this time. They appear huddled together in a famous photograph taken of the Chiricahuas shortly after capture. In the 1930s, Apache informants told anthropologist Morris Opler about two unnamed women who lived together during imprisonment and had sexual relations—undoubtedly Lozen and Dahteste.

From Florida, the tribe was moved to Mount Vernon, Alabama, where Lozen contracted tuberculosis and died in 1889 at about the age of fifty. She was buried in an unmarked grave along with 250 other Apaches. Dahteste was among those eventually allowed to return to the

Mescalero reservation in New Mexico. She remarried, but was said to have mourned Lozen's death the rest of her life.

Bibliography

Ball, Eve. *In the Days of Victorio.* Tucson: University of Arizona Press, 1970).

Buchanan, Kimberly M. *Apache Women Warriors.* El Paso: Texas Western Press, 1986.

Robinson, Sherry. "Lozen: Apache Woman Warrior." *Wild West* (June 1997): 52–56, 81–82.

Roscoe, Will. *Changing Ones: Third and Fourth Genders in Native North America.* New York. St. Martin's Press, 1998.

Will Roscoe

See also TRANSSEXUALS, TRANSVESTITES, TRANSGENDER PEOPLE, AND CROSS-DRESSERS; TWO-SPIRIT FEMALES.

LUDLAM, Charles **(b. 12 April 1943; d. 28 May 1987), playwright, director, actor.**

Charles Braun Ludlam was born in Floral Park, Long Island. His parents were almost a stereotype of the gay artist's progenitors: a supportive mother and a father who despised his son's love of theater. Ludlam claimed that his love of theater began when he saw a Punch and Judy show at a local fair; his later work certainly seems to be inspired by the artifice and slapstick farce of such traditional theatrical presentations.

After studying drama at Hofstra University, Ludlam moved into Greenwich Village, where he would spend the rest of his life, and became part of the new gay theater and film scene that was flourishing in the mid-1960s. He found his first artistic home at the Playhouse of the Ridiculous, run by playwright Ronald Tavel and director John Vaccaro. The Playhouse group was allied with a number of key figures of the avant-garde. Jack Smith, remembered for his film, *Flaming Creatures*, was a central figure in the troupe. Some of Andy Warhol's entourage worked with the group and Warhol was a supporter of the "ridiculous" movement. The Playhouse of the Ridiculous went beyond absurdist drama to promote a bawdy theater of nonsense. Drag was central to the group's performances, which were often send-ups of B movies. Though productions began with a script, much of each performance was improvised. This was the middle 1960s and drugs were central to the creation, performance, and reception of the troupe's work. Always ambitious, Ludlam started performing and writing for the company. Eventually Vaccaro saw him as a threat and fired him. Eight of the actors walked out in protest and joined Ludlam's new company, which would become the Ridiculous Theatre Company (1967).

Like his idol, Molière, Ludlam was the producer, director, playwright, and diva of his company from its inception in 1967 until his death. Some performers feuded with the imperious impresario and left the company; however, it remained quite stable over its history. Though on and off welfare himself, Ludlam successfully raised money to keep his company alive. He wrote at least one play a year. The company moved from venue to venue in its early years, usually playing late-night shows, until it found a permanent home in a former nightclub at One Sheridan Square in 1967.

Ludlams's plays were built from trash culture, particularly B movies (such as *Conquest of the Universe* [1967]) and high art (such as his version of Wagner's ring cycle, *Der Ring Gott Farblonjet* [1977]). It is difficult to separate the most successful works from Ludlam's famous performances in them: his adaptation of *Camille* (1973); his version of the life of Maria Callas, *Galas: A Modern Tragedy* (1983); and the "Victorian penny dreadful," *The Mystery of Irma Vep* (1984), in which he and Everett Quinton played seven male and female roles. *Irma Vep* has become a repertory staple in theaters across America.

Ludlam rebelled against all labels. He did not want to be considered avant-garde because he thought many who were so labeled were frauds. He saw his female impersonation as serious acting, not mere drag. Though his work involved parody and farce, he wanted it taken seriously. And though most of his performers were gay, he eschewed labels like "gay theater" or "camp." While his work often mocked gay stereotypes, it also celebrated the glory of being a flaming queen. Since he disdained the mainstream, he was indifferent to a politics that fought for gay men's right to be in the mainstream. These different textures—male-female, character-actor, artifice-reality, pathos-farce—were at the heart of Ludlam's performances. One could say that an awareness of and celebration of the absurdity of these binary oppositions is at the heart of much LGBT art and that Ludlam was one of the most important queer theater artists of his time.

In addition to his work for the Ridiculous Theatre Company, Ludlam acted occasionally on television and in feature film. He taught playwriting at Yale and New York University and guest directed for the Santa Fe Opera. He was preparing to direct Shakespeare's *Titus Andronicus* in Central Park for the New York Shakespeare Festival when he succumbed to HIV-related infections. Ludlam's death in 1984 merited a front-page story in the *New York Times.* He was considered a theatrical eminence. The street in front of his theater was renamed Charles Ludlam Lane. For a number of years, the company continued under the direction of Ludlam's lover and protégeé, Everett Quinton, and Ludlam remains an influence on many theatrical figures.

Bibliography

Kaufman, David. *Ridiculous! The Theatrical Life and Times of Charles Ludlam.* New York: Applause Theatre & Cinema Books, 2002.

Ludlam, Charles. *The Complete Plays of Charles Ludlam.* New York: Perennial Library, 1989.

———. *Ridiculous Theatre: Scourge of Human Folly: The Essays and Opinions of Charles Ludlam.* Edited by Steven Samuels. New York: Theatre Communications Group, 1992.

John M. Clum

See also EICHELBERGER, ETHYL; THEATER AND PERFORMANCE.

LYNES, George Platt **(b. 15 April 1907; d. 6 December 1955), photographer.**

George Platt Lynes dedicated his formidable technical expertise and extraordinary imagination to the visualization of homoeroticism, creating a visual vocabulary of gay desire that continues to influence art and fashion. His career is significant, as well, for its reflection of the institutional history of the arts in relation to homosexual identity.

The son of an Episcopalian minister, Lynes emulated Aesthetic precedent and aspired to be a poet. Sent to Paris to study French in 1925, Lynes visited Gertrude Stein. His good looks and self-confidence helped integrate him into Stein's influential circle and into the avant-garde in New York, which by the 1920s had developed semisecret LGB networks under the influence of medical theories of homosexuality as a personality type characterized by, among other things, artistic sensitivity. Regardless of whether such theories are true, they helped attract homoerotically inclined individuals to these networks, where they developed their artistic talents.

After returning from Paris in 1925, Lynes published pamphlets of avant-garde prose, including Stein's work, and later opened a bookstore specializing in modern literature. In New York's literary circles, he met the novelist Glenway Westcott and his lover Monroe Wheeler, who later became director of exhibitions at the Museum of Modern Art in New York City. This threesome began an erotic and intellectual partnership that lasted for fifteen years and was crucial to the development of Lynes's career. While traveling together in France in 1928, Westcott and Wheeler convinced Lynes to abandon writing and to concentrate on what had been a hobby: photography. Lynes's earliest photographs document a social network strongly determined by homosexual identity. His first pictures include portraits of Jean Cocteau and Stein with her companion, Alice B. Toklas. Portraiture remained an important aspect of Lynes's photography, and he later made striking images of the writers André Gide and Christopher Isherwood, the arts patron Lincoln Kirstein, the painters Marsden Hartley, Paul Cadmus and Jared French, among others.

Lynes's portraits are remarkable for their use of Surrealist-inspired costumes, poses, and settings, always for an effect that enhances the glamour of the sitter. This skill brought Lynes to the attention of fashion magazines, which were rapidly increasing both their readership and their use of photograph illustrations in this period. Lynes, without sacrificing elegance, imbued fashion models with an eye-catching novelty that made his images stand out in the magazine format, earning commissions from major New York fashion magazines and the retailers that advertised in their pages. His theatrical lighting and minimal sets on which models pose with a few carefully chosen props became a standard for fashion photography in the thirties. The theatricality of Lynes's fashion photography reflected his lifelong interest in ballet, and another important body of his work documents the innovative costumes and choreography of ballet troupes associated with George Balanchine.

As Lynes's career developed, he became increasingly committed to another category of work: nude—often explicitly homoerotic—photography. From the first, his portraiture had included photographs of his intimate friends, including frankly homoerotic images of couples like Cadmus and French, which have only recently been made public. Some of the female models and certain props and poses from Lynes's fashion shoots reappear as nudes, and he was rumored to charge his commercial clients for sets primarily intended for his late-night erotic studio sessions. Lynes's commercial ballet imagery expanded the borders of acceptable public presentations of the male body. And again, models, props, and costumes from his ballet images reappeared in more frankly erotic work. Taken together, Lynes's nude photography records with great beauty and visual wit his community of handsome men erotically engaged with one another. It was this accomplishment that, around 1950, prompted Alfred Kinsey to collect Lynes's erotic photographs; today the Kinsey Institute holds the definitive collection of

Lynes's work, with over six hundred photographs and hundreds of negatives. Ultimately, Lynes decided that it was by his erotic imagery that he wished to be remembered, and he destroyed records of much of his commercial work.

Lynes's career exemplifies several developments in the relationship between art and homosexuality during the twentieth century. His trajectory from would-be poet to successful commercial photographer coincides with the rise of mass-media imagery as an influential source of ideas about eroticism. His participation in a variety of homosexual networks points to the growing importance of these subcultures both within and outside the avant-garde. Lynes's concealment of his large body of homoerotic art, however, reflects the limitations on expressions of sexual identity outside his immediate social context. Lynes's collaboration with Kinsey contributed to the pioneering effort to document homosexuality at a time when such work was actively discouraged. Only recently has more open interest in visual expressions of homosexual identity allowed widespread recognition and appreciation of Lynes's art. His reemergence as a focus of both popular and scholarly interest suggests the prescience of his vision of homoerotic desire.

Bibliography

Crump, James. *George Platt Lynes: Photographs from the Kinsey Institute.* New York: Little Brown, 1993.

Ellenzweig. Allen. *The Homoerotic Photograph.* New York: Columbia University Press, 1992.

Leddick, David. *George Platt Lynes.* Cologne: Taschen, 2000.

———. *Intimate Companions: A Triography of George Platt Lynes, Paul Cadmus, Lincoln Kirstein and their Circle.* New York: St. Martin's 2000.

Christopher Reed

See also HARTLEY, MARSDEN; VISUAL ART.

LYON, Phyllis (b. 10 November 1924), and Del MARTIN (b. 5 May 1921), activists, feminists.

In 1955 Phyllis Lyon and Del Martin were part of a small group of women in San Francisco who started the first known national lesbian organization in the United States, the Daughters of Bilitis (DOB). They provided daily leadership to the DOB through its first decade of existence and were identified with it throughout its more than twenty-year history. Lyon and Martin were responsible for insisting that the lesbian experience be given particular attention within the homophile movement of the 1950s and 1960s. Later they also helped shape the ideas and actions of the feminist, family violence, sex education, and pro-aging movements of the late twentieth century, while playing significant roles in San Francisco electoral politics.

Lyon was born in Tulsa, Oklahoma. She and her family moved a good deal during her youth and she attended schools in three different parts of California. She majored in journalism at the University of California at Berkeley in the 1940s and was on the staff of the school's newspaper, the *Daily Californian.* In 1946, after several years as a reporter in California, she took a position in Seattle, Washington, as associate editor with *Pacific Builder and Engineer* magazine. It was here that she met Martin.

Martin grew up in San Francisco and also attended Berkeley and wrote for the *Daily Californian.* After transferring to San Francisco State University, she became managing editor of its newspaper, the *Golden Gator.* In 1940, she married a college classmate and two years later gave birth to her daughter Kendra. After her divorce, Martin worked at odd jobs in the San Francisco Bay Area. She worked as a reporter for *Pacific Builder* in San Francisco before accepting a job in Seattle as editor of *Daily Construction Reports,* the sister publication to *Pacific Builder and Engineer,* in 1949. She and Lyon became close friends and, after three years, lovers.

When Lyon returned to San Francisco to celebrate her sister's graduation from Berkeley with an automobile tour of the United States, Martin followed, and on Valentine's Day 1953 they set up their first home and their new lives together. They immediately opened a joint bank account and established themselves as a couple. But they had a difficult time finding other lesbians to socialize with and were too shy to approach women in the lesbian bars in San Francisco. Introduced by a mutual friend to Noni Frey, they attended a meeting held in September 1955 to discuss forming a secret lesbian social club. "They found us," Martin remembers. "We didn't get involved to fight for any causes. We just wanted to meet lesbians" (interview with author, September 1997, San Francisco). The new group soon split, however, over the club's purpose, with several of the women wanting it to be strictly social and a few others, notably Lyon and Martin, wanting that, and more. Half of the original eight members left the group.

But they had laid an organizational foundation in the first year, and Lyon and Martin were determined to keep the new group, called the Daughters of Bilitis, going. Under Martin's leadership as president (with Lyon as sec-

Phyllis Lyon and Del Martin. The couple, and others, cofounded the Daughters of Bilitis and helped to lead the social and activist organization—among their many roles in a half century of activism on a wide variety of issues, in the San Francisco area and nationwide. **[Del Martin]**

retary) the DOB was redirected toward social activism as well as social activities. Education and exploration were key components of their new programs and a series of private discussions and public meetings were held. In 1956, the members agreed that the best way to publicize their efforts was through a newsletter. That year the first ongoing lesbian publication was created, and the *Ladder* proved to be a vital voice for the growing gay and lesbian movement until 1972. Lyon—initially writing as "Ann Ferguson," until the fourth issue, when she dropped the pseudonym—was its first editor. She served in that position until July 1960, when Martin assumed the responsibility for the next three years.

Both women have been outspoken advocates and passionate proselytizers for lesbian issues, as well as savvy activists. In addition to their work with the DOB, Lyon and Martin saw the potential for positive social change in working with diverse groups of people in San Francisco and throughout the country. They were among the founders of the Council on Religion and the Homosexual, a groundbreaking San Francisco coalition of clergy and homophile activists, in 1964. They helped launch Citizens Alert, an organization of civil rights and minority groups dealing with police brutality in 1965. In 1968, they became the first lesbians to join the National Organization for Women as a couple and became active leaders of the Northern California chapter, helping pass national pro-lesbian rights policies at a time when the "Lavender Menace" was seen as a threat by conservative forces within the women's movement.

The publication of their book *Lesbian/Woman* in 1972 catapulted Lyon and Martin to national attention, and they subsequently appeared throughout the country on college campuses, radio, and television shows (including the *Phil Donahue* show). In San Francisco, they helped create the Alice B. Toklas Memorial Democratic Club in 1972. Martin served on the city's Commission on the Status of Women for three years and was president from 1976–1977. Lyon was on the Human Rights Commission for almost twelve years, and chaired it from 1982–1983. From the mid-1960s on, Lyon was actively involved in human sexuality education, working with the National Sex Forum to produce pro-sex booklets and films and helping to establish the International Museum of Erotic Art. She was one of the founders of the Institute for Advanced Study of Human Sexuality, a graduate school. Martin published *Battered Wives* in 1976, one of the first books about violence against women. She became a spokesperson for the nascent battered women's shelter and family violence prevention movements. Martin and Lyon had also became increasingly active in local and national Democratic Party electoral campaigns and continue to urge women's participation in the world of politics.

Their activism continues in the early twentieth century. As of 2003, they devote their energies to issues of aging and are members of Old Lesbians Organizing for Change. Lyon and Martin attended the 1995 White House Conference on Aging to represent older lesbians and gay men, and they are organizing for the 2005 White House

Conference on Aging. They are determined that a large and vocal delegation of old LGBT people be part of it.

To celebrate their fiftieth anniversary in 2003, the couple were honored in San Francisco at the premiere of the film *No Secret Anymore: The Times of Del Martin and Phyllis Lyon.* This documentary by filmmaker Joan E. Biren (JEB) shows the combined century of activism these two women have contributed to so many movements for equality and justice.

Bibliography

Abbott, Sydney, and Barbara Love. *Sappho Was a Right-On Woman.* New York: Stein and Day, 1972.

Bullough, Vern, ed. *Before Stonewall: Activists for Gay and Lesbian Rights in Historical Context.* New York: Haworth Press, 2002.

Cain, Paul. *Leading the Parade: Conversations with America's Most Influential Lesbians and Gay Men.* New York: Scarecrow Press, 2002.

D'Emilio, John. *Sexual Politics, Sexual Communities: The Making of a Homosexual Minority in the United States, 1940–1970.* 2nd ed. Chicago: University of Chicago Press, 1998.

Faderman, Lillian. *Odd Girls and Twilight Lovers: A History of Lesbian Life in Twentieth-Century America.* New York: Columbia University Press, 1991.

Martin, Del, and Phyllis Lyon. *Lesbian/Woman.* San Francisco: Gilde Publications, 1972; rev. ed., Volcano, Calif.: Volcano Press, 1991.

Miller, Neil. *Out of the Past: Gay and Lesbian History from 1869 to the Present.* New York: Random House, 1995.

Mixner, David, and Dennis Bailey. *Brave Journeys: Profiles in Gay and Lesbian Courage.* New York: Bantam Books, 2000.

Tobin, Kay, and Randy Wicker. *The Gay Crusaders.* New York: Paperback Library, 1972.

Marcia M. Gallo

See also DAUGHTERS OF BILITIS; HOMOPHILE MOVEMENT; HOMOPHILE PRESS; *LADDER*; LESBIAN FEMINISM.

abcdefghijkl**m**nopqrstuvwxyz

M

McCULLERS, Carson (b. 19 February 1917; d. 29 September 1967), writer.

Lula Carson Smith was born in Columbus, Georgia, the eldest of three children of Lamar Smith, a jewelry-store owner, and Vera Marguerite Waters. After graduating from high school in 1935, she studied creative writing at Columbia University and New York University. In the fall of 1936 McCullers began work on her first novel, *The Heart Is a Lonely Hunter.* The story of a deaf mute to whom the lonely and isolated people of a southern town turn for silent solace, the novel (published by Houghton Mifflin in June 1940) considered the themes of loneliness and isolation that recur in much of McCullers's work. It was an immediate and much-praised success.

Reflections in a Golden Eye, McCullers's second novel, was published by Houghton Mifflin in 1941. Readers who expected a book like the author's first novel were shocked by the story of voyeurism, obsession, repressed homosexuality, and infidelity set on a peacetime army base.

McCullers third major work, *The Ballad of the Sad Café,* a story of jealousy and obsession in a triangular love relationship involving an Amazon-like woman, a hunchbacked dwarf and an ex-convict, set in a small southern mill town, appeared in the August 1943 *Harper's Bazaar.* The work was later published in *"The Ballad of the Sad Café": The Novels and Stories of Carson McCullers* (1951).

March 1946 saw the publication of McCullers's fourth major work, *The Member of the Wedding,* the story of a lonely adolescent girl, Frankie Addams, who wants to find her "we of me" by joining with her older brother and his bride. McCullers's theatrical adaptation of the novel opened on Broadway in 1950 to near unanimous acclaim and enjoyed a run of 501 performances.

The final fifteen years of McCullers's life saw a decline in the writer's health and in her creative abilities. Bedridden by paralysis from a series of strokes, McCullers was devastated by the failed production of her second play *The Square Root of Wonderful,* which closed after only forty-five performances on Broadway in 1957, and the mixed reception of her final novel *Clock Without Hands* (1961). Her final book-length publication was a book of children's verse, *Sweet as Pickle and Clean as a Pig* (1964). *The Mortgaged Heart,* a collection of short stories, essays, and poetry, edited by McCullers's sister Margarita Smith, was published in 1971. At the time of her death she was at work on an autobiography, *Illumination and Night Glare,* which was posthumously published in 2000.

McCullers lived a complex and difficult personal and professional life. In September 1937, Carson married James Reeves McCullers, Jr., a native of Wetumpka, Alabama (born 11 August 1913), whom she met when he was in the army stationed at Fort Benning, near her hometown. The marriage was simultaneously the most supportive and destructive relationship in her life, and was from its beginning plagued by the partners' shared difficulty with alcoholism, their sexual ambivalence, and the tension caused by Reeves's envy of McCullers's writing abilities. The couple divorced in 1941, but reconciled and remarried in 1945. Reeves committed suicide in a Paris hotel room in November 1953.

During a separation from her husband in 1940, McCullers shared a house in Brooklyn Heights with

Carson McCullers. The poetic Southern writer explored the loneliness, love, and obsession of people on the outskirts of conventional society, especially in four major works of fiction (one of them subsequently a long-running Broadway play, and all of them turned into films).

George Davis (an editor at *Harper's Bazaar*) and the British poet W. H. Auden. This house, located at 7 Middagh Street, became the center of a bohemian, sexually liberated, literary and artistic group including Gypsy Rose Lee, Benjamin Britten, Peter Pears, Richard Wright, and Oliver Smith. Following her father's sudden death in August 1944, McCullers, along with her mother and sister, moved to Nyack, New York. She spent most of the rest of her life in this house on the Hudson River.

McCullers's life was blighted by a series of cerebral strokes caused by a misdiagnosed and untreated childhood case of rheumatic fever. On 15 August 1967, McCullers suffered a final stroke. Comatose for forty-seven days, she died on 29 September 1967 in the Nyack Hospital and was buried in Nyack's Oak Hill Cemetery.

As part of a general renaissance of interest in her life and work, much of the consideration of McCullers since the 1980s has focused on her sexuality, the representation of LGBT characters in her work, and the consideration of McCullers's work vis-à-vis queer theory and LGBT aesthetics. Although she did not self-identify as a lesbian or as bisexual, McCullers was emotionally and sexually involved with both men and women during her life. Her personal philosophy regarding sexuality that was reflected in her work—that the gender of the person whom one loves is irrelevant to that love—complicates and transcends traditional, restrictive understandings of sexual and gender identity.

Bibliography

Adams, Rachel. "'A Mixture of Delicious and Freak': The Queer Fiction of Carson McCullers." *American Literature: A Journal of Literary History, Criticism, and Bibliography* 71 (1999): 551–583.

Carr, Virginia Spencer. *The Lonely Hunter: A Biography of Carson McCullers.* Garden City, N.Y.: Doubleday, 1975.

———. *Understanding Carson McCullers.* Columbia: University of South Carolina Press, 1990.

Evans, Oliver. *The Ballad of Carson McCullers: A Biography.* New York: Coward-McCann, 1966.

James, Judith Giblin. *Wunderkind: The Reputation of Carson McCullers, 1940–1990.* Columbia, S.C.: Camden House, 1995.

Kenschaft, Lori J. "Homoerotics and Human Connections: Reading Carson McCullers 'As a Lesbian.'" In *Critical Essays on Carson McCullers.* Edited by Beverly Lyon Clark and Melvin J. Friedman. New York: G. K. Hall, 1996.

Kiernan, Robert F. *Katherine Anne Porter and Carson McCullers: A Reference Guide.* New York: G. K. Hall, 1976.

McDowell, Margaret B. *Carson McCullers.* Boston: Twayne, 1980.

McKinnie, Betty E., and Carlos L. Dews. "The Delayed Entrance of Lily Mae Jenkins: Queer Identity, Gender Ambiguity, and Southern Ambivalence in Carson McCullers's *The Member of the Wedding.*" In *Southern Women Playwrights: New Essays in Literary History and Criticism.* Edited by Robert L. McDonald and Linda Rohrer Paige. Tuscaloosa: University of Alabama Press, 2002.

Mukherjee, Srimati. "The Impoverishment of the Female Hero in *The Ballad of the Sad Café.*" *Proceedings of the Philological Association of Louisiana* (1992): 105–109.

Portada, Arleen. "Sex-Role Rebellion and the Failure of Marriage in the Fiction of Carson McCullers." *Pembroke Magazine* 20 (1988): 63–71.

Savigneau, Josyane. *Carson McCullers: A Life.* Translated by Joan E. Howard. Boston: Houghton Mifflin, 2001.

Shapiro, Adrian M., Jackson R. Byer, and Kathleen Field. *Carson McCullers: A Descriptive Listing and Annotated Bibliography of Criticism.* New York: Garland, 1980.

Sosnoski, Karen. "Society's Freaks: The Effects of Sexual Stereotyping in Carson McCullers' Fiction." *Pembroke Magazine* 20 (1988): 82–88.

Westling, Louise. "Tomboys and Revolting Femininity." In *Critical Essays on Carson McCullers.* Edited by Beverly Lyon Clark and Melvin J. Friedman. New York: G. K. Hall, 1996.

Whatling, Clare. "Reading Miss Amelia: Critical Strategies in the Construction of Sex, Gender, Sexuality, the Gothic and the Grotesque." In *Modernist Sexualities.* Edited by Hugh Stevens and Caroline Howlett. Manchester, U.K.: Manchester University Press, 2000.

Whitt, Jan. "'The We of Me': Carson McCullers as Lesbian Novelist." *Journal of Homosexuality* 37, no. 1 (1999): 127–140.

Carlos L. Dews

See also AUDEN, W.H.; LITERATURE.

McKAY, Claude (b. 15 September 1889; d. 22 May 1948), writer.

Though often associated with the Harlem Renaissance, Claude McKay began his literary career well before his arrival in Harlem and, despite the success he found there, held a deep mistrust of the most celebrated artists and intellectuals associated with that renowned movement. His literary efforts in Harlem were consistently eschewed or explicitly rejected by established black publications, and his personal and professional affiliations were almost exclusively with white editors and mentors.

Born the last of eleven children to farmers Thomas McKay and Hannah Edwards, McKay grew up in rural Jamaica. His upbringing was marked by poverty but inculcated in him unaffected values that he considered an indispensable alternative to the racism, anti-Semitism, and materialism that he would later discover in the United States.

At eighteen McKay formed a friendship with the English writer and aesthete, Walter Jekyll. A man in his mid-fifties, Jekyll took an interest in the samples of poetry McKay shared with him and, over several years, nurtured the young writer's evident talent. By age twenty-three, McKay had published two volumes of poetry, *Songs of Jamaica* (1912) and *Constab Ballads* (1912), both written in Jamaican patios. Largely overlooked by later critics, these collections so impressed his countrymen that McKay became the first black to receive a medal from the Jamaican Institute of Arts and Sciences. His winning of this prize coincided with a move to the United States, where McKay planned to study agronomy at Tuskegee Institute. Dissatisfaction with the curriculum there prompted a move to Kansas State College, where McKay engaged in a two-year course of study, interspersed with visits to Kansas City, Wichita, and Denver. Despite the college's benefits, McKay found its setting an isolating environment. In 1914 a gift from his old mentor provided him with the means to depart Kansas for New York City, where he reunited with Jamaican girlfriend Eulalie Edwards, married, and fathered a daughter—and then separated from his wife without ever meeting his child.

The collapse of his marriage notwithstanding, McKay found New York City an ideal setting, on account of Harlem's many distractions and large black population—particularly its Jamaicans and other West Indians. The National Association for the Advancement of Colored People and a nascent National Urban League, both headquartered in New York, helped define the city as a center of black activism. McKay joined a throng of black artists, musicians, and writers, many of whom were finding an outlet for their creative energies for the first time. Dividing his energy between several of the various jobs open to black men—waiter, porter, bar-boy—and writing, McKay searched for a U.S. audience, abandoning dialect for more conservative verse and writing under male and female pen names. He eventually garnered the attention of first Frank Harris, publisher of *Pearson's Magazine,* and then Max Eastman, publisher of *The Liberator.*

In New York, McKay found literary and sexual release, but while his poetry occasionally featured romantic affairs between partners of unspecified gender, his prose very rarely hinted at homosexual desire. With few exceptions, he adhered to the general prohibition against public treatment of homosexuality in his writing, in part, perhaps, because his own sexual identity was in perpetual flux. McKay had long-term affairs with men and women and, had the term been in vogue, he likely would have self-identified as bisexual.

Stung by racism since his arrival in the United States, McKay left New York in 1919 for a two-year stay in London, where he worked for the Marxist periodical *Worker's Dreadnought* and published *Spring in New Hampshire* (1920). After returning to the United States, he worked as an editor at *The Liberator* and published *Harlem Shadows* (1922). Then came a pilgrimage to Russia and the start of "the expatriate years." While living first in various cities throughout France and Spain (1923–1930) and then in northern Africa (1930–1934), McKay found his muse and generated his best prose: *Home to Harlem* (1928), *Banjo* (1929), *Gingertown* (1932), and *Banana Bottom* (1933).

A return to Harlem in 1934 reestablished friendships with Countee Cullen and James Weldon Johnson among others, but the Great Depression and personality clashes with African American leaders severely limited his employment prospects. Although McKay would go on to publish *A Long Way from Home* (1937) and *Harlem: Negro Metropolis* (1940), commercial success and fame were behind him. In 1944 he moved to Chicago, where he died of congestive heart failure at age fifty-seven.

Bibliography

Cooper, Wayne F. *Claude McKay: Rebel Sojourner in the Harlem Renaissance.* Baton Rouge: Louisiana State University Press, 1987.

———, ed. *The Passion of Claude McKay: Selected Poetry and Prose, 1912–1948.* New York: Schocken, 1973.

Giles, James R. *Claude McKay.* Boston: Twayne, 1976.

Hathaway, Heather. *Caribbean Waves: Relocating Claude McKay and Paule Marshall.* Bloomington: Indiana University Press, 1999.

James, Winston. *A Fierce Hatred of Injustice: Claude McKay's Jamaica and His Poetry of Rebellion.* New York: Verso, 2000.

McKay, Claude. *Harlem Shadows: The Poems of Claude McKay.* New York: Harcourt, Brace, 1922.

———. *Gingertown.* New York: Harper, 1932.

———. *Harlem: Negro Metropolis.* New York: Dutton, 1940.

———. *Banjo: A Story without a Plot.* New York: Harvest, 1970.

———. *Banana Bottom.* New York: Harvest, 1974.

———. *Home to Harlem.* Boston: Northeastern University Press, 1987.

———. *A Long Way from Home.* New York: Harvest, 1989.

McLeod, A. L., ed. *Claude McKay: Centennial Studies.* New Delhi, India: Sterling, 1992.

Peter Taylor

See also HARLEM RENAISSANCE.

McNALLY, Terrence (b. 3 November 1939), playwright.

Terrence McNally was born in St. Petersburg, Florida, grew up in Corpus Christi, Texas, and received his B.A. degree in English at Columbia University. From the start of his career with *And Things That Go Bump in the Night* (1965), McNally's goal as a playwright has been to do work that matters to the audience and to himself, even at the risk of provoking critics. Autobiographical and emotionally raw, with two gay men included in the cast of characters, that first play prompted one enraged reviewer unprepared to accept gay characters in family dramas to write, "The American theatre would be a better place today if Terrence McNally's parents had smothered him in his cradle" (McNally, 1998, p. 26). McNally's relationship with Edward Albee around this time no doubt inflamed homophobic critics even more.

McNally did not let hostile reviews stop him and soon proved his early critics wrong, particularly with one-act plays featuring antic humor and healthy doses of sex that attracted enthusiastic audiences. Although success may have been the best revenge on hateful critics, McNally's reputation for liveliness during the late 1960s and early 1970s did have a peculiar downside. He was dogged by a preconception that he could produce riotously funny short plays but could not write longer ones of equal impact, despite the fact that *The Ritz* (1975), a farce set in a gay bathhouse owned by the Mafia, was a comedy hit that addressed issues of stereotyping and homophobia. Commenting on the relationship between truth and humor, McNally has said,

> Why the truth is not supposed to be funny is one of the rules someone must have come up with somewhere along the line and everyone believed him (or her). . . . Whoever he or she was, I would like to thank him or her for making my life very difficult. Everyone agrees that comedy is supposed to be truthful. But hardly anyone agrees that the truth can be treated humorously. (McNally, 1990, p. x)

In 1986 McNally's professional life became a little less difficult when he was offered a home base at the Manhattan Theatre Club. In spite of reeling after the deaths of close friends actor James Coco from heart disease and actor-director Robert Drivas from AIDS, he promptly delivered the romantic comedy *Frankie and Johnny in the Clair de Lune* (1987) and has continued to produce his most accomplished work there. In *The Lisbon Traviata* (1989), McNally combined his lifelong love of opera, and specifically the artistry of Maria Callas (also celebrated in *Master Class* [1995]), with a study of the passions that can arise between gay men in both friendships (the very funny Act One) and sexual relationships (a darker, more violent Act Two).

McNally integrates personal truth telling with humor more seamlessly in *Lips Together, Teeth Apart* (1991) and *A Perfect Ganesh* (1993), plays that explore the ways we face our own mortality at the same time we grieve for loved ones. Whether looking at two heterosexual married couples over the Fourth of July holiday at a Fire Island beach house inherited from a brother who had died of AIDS, or following two elderly women touring India's sacred places, he introduces contemporary gay issues (casual sex, committed relationships, illness, mortality, and perceptions that heterosexuals have of gay men) smoothly into works with wide appeal.

Even if he had not written *Love! Valour! Compassion!* (1994) next, these two poignant, engagingly funny plays would provide ample support for McNally's self-assessment, "I agree there's laughter in my plays, and that I have a comic sensibility. But *I* don't think I write comedies" (Zinman, p. 13). *Love! Valour! Compassion!*, a bittersweet play about eight gay men who spend three holiday weekends at a country house over a summer, won almost universal approval while serving up male nudity. McNally's greatest success to date in attracting diverse audiences and winning multiple awards, it also reflects McNally's grief over continuing to lose friends and lovers to AIDS. Besides that, the Broadway production's stellar direction showed another important McNally trait: his ability to find, hire, and develop new talent like director Joe Mantello, as he had with actors Nathan Lane, Christine Baranski, and Anthony Heald.

In *Corpus Christi* (1998), McNally returned to exploring friendship and loyalty among gay men. Vocal religious factions got word that the men in this modern-day passion play were disciples of a charismatic spiritual leader and, before seeing it, branded it "the gay-Jesus play." McNally was again in the middle of a media firestorm that had little to do with his actual work. Characteristically, he soldiered on, this time concentrating on his successful sideline as a writer of the books and librettos for musicals and operas (*The Full Monty* [2000] and *Dead Man Walking* [2000]). He accomplished this during a personally demanding time when his companion, Gary Bonasorte, was dying from AIDS. However, it was expected that McNally would return imminently to braving the risks of producing new dramatic work that matters.

Bibliography

Clum, John M. *Acting Gay: Male Homosexuality in Modern Drama.* New York: Columbia University Press, 1992.

Franklin, Nancy. "Resurrection: 'Corpus Christi's' Tortured Route to the Stage." *The New Yorker* 74, no. 33 (26 October 1998–2 November 1998): 244–256.

McNally, Terrence. *Three Plays: The Lisbon Traviata, Frankie and Johnny in the Clair de Lune, and It's Only a Play.* New York: Plume, 1990.

McNally, Terrence. "What I Know about Being a Playwright." *American Theatre* 15, no. 9 (November 1998): 25–26.

Savran, David. *The Playwright's Voice: American Dramatists on Memory, Writing, and the Politics of Culture.* New York: Theatre Communications Group, 1999.

Zinman, Toby S. "The Muses of Terrence McNally: Music and Mortality Are His Consuming Themes." *American Theatre* 12, no. 3 (March 1995): 12–17.

John McFarland

See also ALBEE, EDWARD; COMEDY AND HUMOR; LITERATURE; MUSIC: OPERA; THEATER AND PERFORMANCE.

MAPPLETHORPE, Robert

(b. 4 November 1946; d. 9 March 1989), artist, photographer.

The work and name of Robert Mapplethorpe have become synonymous with issues of censorship and homosexuality. In June 1989, the Corcoran Gallery of Art in Washington, D.C., cancelled a Mapplethorpe retrospective entitled *The Perfect Moment,* which was scheduled to open a few weeks later. The cancellation, which occurred amid conservative attacks on the National Endowment for the Arts (NEA), which had partially funded *The Perfect Moment,* provoked a national controversy over creative freedom and homoerotic art. That controversy led, in turn, to content restrictions on federally funded art and the attempted dismantling of the NEA.

Robert Mapplethorpe. A 1980 self-portrait by the photographer, many of whose more explicit works were the targets of condemnation and censorship. **[Gillian Cuthill, Foundation manager, The Robert Mapplethorpe Foundation, 120]**

Mapplethorpe had died of AIDS-related causes in March 1989, three months prior to the Corcoran cancellation. By the time of his death, he had emerged as one of the most successful U.S. art photographers of the post–World War II era. His elegant prints commanded critical attention (if not always praise) and high prices within the burgeoning market for art photography in the late 1970s and 1980s. In order to augment the market value of his work, Mapplethorpe often presented his photographs as luxury objects, whether by printing them on linen, surrounding them with fabrics such as silk, velvet, or leather, or enclosing them in unique frames of his own design.

Throughout his career, Mapplethorpe organized his photography into three major themes: still lifes, portraits, and homosexuality—or, as one magazine put it, "flowers, faces, and fetishes" (Fritscher, p. 15). Each of these themes was filtered through a signature style that emphasized formal symmetry, intricate tonal gradations, and an utter clarity of texture and visual detail. Mapplethorpe delighted in presenting wildly different subjects as equally stylized forms of photographic delectation. "I don't think there's that much difference," he once said, "between a photograph of [a] fist up someone's ass and a photograph of carnations in a bowl" (Hodges). Mapplethorpe's pictures of sadomasochism were no less aesthetic than his still lifes, and his pictures of flowers could be as erotically suggestive as his portraits of leathermen.

Although Mapplethorpe's reputation as an artist rests almost entirely on his photographic output, he studied painting and sculpture (not photography) at Pratt Institute in Brooklyn, New York, from 1963 to 1969. As a student, Mapplethorpe favored psychedelic paintings and drawings based loosely on French surrealism and the engravings of William Blake. In 1967, Mapplethorpe met Patti Smith, an aspiring poet and singer, and the two moved in together in an apartment near Pratt. Smith became one of Mapplethorpe's best friends and frequent models. In 1969, Mapplethorpe dropped out of Pratt and moved, with Smith, into the Chelsea Hotel in Manhattan.

At this time, Mapplethorpe was creating collages and mixed media objects, many of which incorporated male nude photographs appropriated from pornographic magazines. These works, which bore titles such as *Ah Men*, *Cowboy*, and *Untitled (Blow Job)*, sexualized the male body while simultaneously suggesting, through the use of obscuring bars and spray paint, the censorship to which such homoerotic images had historically been subjected. For all their visual wit, Mapplethorpe's collages were not considered commercially viable by the galleries he approached at the time. Perhaps because of this, Mapplethorpe moved away from collage and mixed media work and increasingly focused on photography.

In 1972, Mapplethorpe met Sam Wagstaff, a wealthy art collector and curator who became his mentor and, briefly, his lover. With Wagstaff's help, Mapplethorpe landed his first one-man show at the Light Gallery in New York in 1973. The exhibition featured Polaroid photographs, several of which were self-portraits. Following the show, Mapplethorpe turned to large-format press camera and, ultimately, to a Hasselblad.

In 1975, Smith signed a contract with Arista records and Mapplethorpe shot the cover for her first LP, *Horses.* Mapplethorpe's stark portrait of the singer in a man's shirt and suspenders, standing against a blank white wall, marked one of the aesthetic highpoints of his early career. Between 1977 and 1980, he produced a series of intense and impressive photographs of gay sadomasochism, of its practitioners and paraphernalia, while continuing to create pictures of flowers and celebrities. During this time, Mapplethorpe was taken on by the Robert Miller Gallery in New York and developed an international reputation, with one-man shows in Chicago, Los Angeles, San Francisco, Paris, Amsterdam, and Brussels.

Around 1980, Mapplethorpe began to photograph black men, some of whom he met at gay bars and pursued for both sexual and photographic purposes. Unlike the men in the sadomasochistic pictures, Mapplethorpe's black male nudes are always muscular, youthful, and well endowed. The nudes have been cut to the very pattern of Mapplethorpe's desire for them. In 1986, Mapplethorpe published *The Black Book,* a controversial collection of black male nudes, which continues to stand as one of his signature projects. Later that same year, Mapplethorpe was diagnosed with AIDS. In 1988, his health on the decline, he established the Robert Mapplethorpe Foundation, a charitable organization that funds both AIDS research and photography exhibitions and research.

Bibliography

Danto, Arthur C. *Playing with the Edge: The Photographic Achievement of Robert Mapplethorpe.* Berkeley: University of California Press, 1996.

Fritscher, Jack. "The Robert Mapplethorpe Gallery." *Son of Drummer* [special issue of *Drummer* magazine] (1978): 15.

Hodges, Parker. "Robert Mapplethorpe: Photographer." *Manhattan Gaze* (10 December 1979–6 January 1980).

Kardon, Janet. *Robert Mapplethorpe: The Perfect Moment.* Philadelphia: Institute of Contemporary Art, 1988.

Marshall, Richard, Richard Howard, and Ingrid Sischy. *Robert Mapplethorpe.* New York: Whitney Museum of American Art, 1988.

Meyer, Richard. "The Jesse Helms Theory of Art." *October* 104 (Spring 2003): 131–148.

Richard Meyer

See also ART HISTORY; CENSORSHIP, PORNOGRAPHY, AND OBSCENITY LAW AND POLICY; NEW RIGHT; VISUAL ART.

MARCHES ON WASHINGTON

Marches on Washington have played significant roles in social justice movements, increasing visibility, reducing isolation, highlighting agendas, pressuring elites, and invigorating grassroots organizing. These mass gatherings in the nation's capital are rites of passage, signals of movements whose time has come. By taking grievances to the center of government, a broad range of movements have sought to expose the contradiction between the ideals of the U.S. Constitution and the realities of discrimination, inequality, injustice, and oppression.

The 1963 March on Washington for Jobs and Freedom made famous by Dr. Martin Luther King's "I Have A Dream" speech but organized by Bayard Rustin (an African American gay man), ignited the imagination of other social justice movements including the LGBT movement. Gay, lesbian, bisexual and transgender activists who cut their activist teeth in the anti-war, civil rights, and women's movements began to imagine the power of incorporating mass demonstration into the burgeoning movement for gay liberation. Just days after the 1963 march, *Confidential* magazine reported on a homophile conference in Philadelphia, where one Washington, D.C., gay activist declared, "There are 15 million of us in the United States. This makes us the second largest minority in the country, second only to the Negroes." According to *Confidential*, "The boys and girls aren't quite ready to stage a Gay March on Washington yet, but from the looks of things at their convention, they may work up to it in a couple of years." The article concluded, "If we ever do see the day when 200,000 homos march down Constitution Avenue, though, the capital had better watch out. Those handsome Washington cops will be facing a new form of hazardous duty" (Stein, 224).

The first LGBT public protest in Washington D.C. was not a mass gathering but a small demonstration in April 1965. After press reports indicated that the Cuban government was imprisoning homosexuals in labor camps, homophile activists organized protests against U.S. and Cuban policies at the United Nations headquarters in New York and the White House in Washington. In May seven men dressed in suits and three women in conservative dresses picketed in front of the White House. The Mattachine Society of Washington organized the picket to protest the government's discriminatory employment practices. Later that year, similar demonstrations were held at the Civil Service building, the Pentagon, the State Department, and again at the White House. In this last protest, the number of demonstrators grew to 45.

Over the next decade, the Stonewall Riots in New York City, the growing visibility of the LGBT movement across the country, and the declassification of homosexuality as a mental illness by the American Psychiatric Association were significant milestones in LGBT history. Then came Anita Bryant's anti-LGBT campaign, the anti-LGBT Briggs initiative in California, and the assassination of San Francisco Supervisor Harvey Milk in 1978. Milk had been the most prominent voice in support of a LGBT march on the nation's capital, believing that LGBT visibility would help put an end to discrimination. After Milk's death, organizers took up his call.

A national organizing structure was quickly created with a national office and two regional offices. A march was to be organized by a committee of 128 delegates selected from across the country to ensure that rural as well as urban centers had a voice in the process. The organizers also made a commitment to ensure at least 50% women and 25% people of color held leadership positions in the effort. Advisory committees of other traditionally underrepresented groups (including seniors, people with disabilities, youth, etc.) were formed. The organizers also created a list of demands that included a broad range of civil rights issues including opposition to racism, sexism and classism.

On 14 October 1979, less than a year after the assassination of Harvey Milk and just 10 years after the Stonewall riots, about 100,000 marchers participated in the first March on Washington for Lesbian and Gay Rights. The impact was profound for those who had traveled from urban centers and small towns across the country. On the day before the march, hundreds attended the first National Third World Gay and Lesbian Conference, which stimulated political organizing by African Americans, Latinos/as, Native Americans, and Asian Americans (and the establishment of such groups as the National Coalition of Black Lesbians and Gays). The day after the march was designated Constituent Lobbying Day and all participants were asked to visit their Senators and Representatives. Opponents of the march lined parts of the route, cursed the marchers, and warned tourists to stay off the streets. Evangelical Jerry Falwell led prayers in the Rayburn House Office building, saying "God made Adam and Eve, not Adam and Steve." When the march concluded, many of the organizing structures transformed into local groups pushing for social change in communities across the country.

The second march on Washington was held on 11 October 1987. Fueled in large part by fury at the lack of government response to AIDS and the homophobic *Bowers vs. Hardwick* 1986 Supreme Court decision upholding sodomy laws, the march drew what organizers said were more than 500,000 to 600,000 participants. In a widely criticized action, the U.S. Park Police estimated the crowd size first at 50,000 and then 200,000. The larger estimate suggests that this was the country's largest civil rights demonstration to date. One of the highlights of the

Text continued on page 227

the 1987 march on washington demands and statements

1. The legal recognition of lesbian and gay relationships.

   > Changes must be made in the courts and in the legislatures to provide homosexual couples the same privileges and benefits as heterosexuals who commit themselves to similar relationships. Changes must also be made in public opinion so that society recognizes and celebrates the diversity in family relationships.

The changes sought included rights of inheritance, visitation and custody rights, insurance rights, and parenting and adoption rights. Also listed under this demand were calls for lesbian and gay youth to be provided "social services"; government-funded alternative housing, foster care, counseling, and legal aid; "sex information and health care services"; and "sexuality and anti-homophobic curriculum in the schools, access to lesbian and gay publications in public and school libraries, and freedom to participate in related school activities.

2. The repeal of all laws that make sodomy between consenting adults a crime.

   > Like Jim Crow laws of the American South which sanctioned and promoted racism, sodomy laws give the government's stamp of approval to individual people's hatred of lesbian and gay people. To single out lesbian and gay people for special prosecutorial attention stigmatizes all who are gay and lesbian whether or not they are ever arrested or charged with sodomy.

3. A Presidential order banning anti-gay discrimination by the Federal Government. This referred to an Executive Order banning discrimination on the basis of sexual orientation in federal employment, the military, federally contracted private employment, and all federally funded programs.

   > Eliminating employment discrimination based solely on sexual orientation in the government sector would send a signal to the rest of the country that this discrimination is immoral and should be illegal.

4. Passage of the Congressional lesbian and gay civil rights bill.

   > The government should provide protection from discrimination based on sexual orientation in employment, public accommodations and education just as protection is provided on race, creed, color, sex, or national origin.
   >
   > The government should ensure all public education programs include programs designed to combat lesbian/gay prejudice. . . . Institutions that discriminate against lesbian and gay people should be denied tax exempt status and federal funding.

5. An end to discrimination against people with AIDS, ARC, HIV positive status, or those perceived to have AIDS. The statement called for massive increases in funding for AIDS education, research, and patient care as well as federal funding for:

   > . . . a massive AIDS education and prevention program that is explicit, culturally sensitive, lesbian and gay affirming and sex positive. . . . The government must provide safe sex education to all youth.
   >
   > Compassionate, comprehensive health care services must be available for patients without regard to ability to pay. . . . There must be a complete federal funding of all health and social services for all people with AIDS/ARC. . . . The federal government must underwrite and insure all research for a cure and a vaccine. Funding for these programs must come from the military budget, not already existing appropriations in the social services budget.

6. Reproductive freedom, the right to control one's own body, and an end to sexist oppression.

   > All people must have access to birth control. . . . Those who wish must have the right to artificial insemination by donor. Public and private institutions should support parenting by lesbian or gay couples. . . . All people must have access to free abortions and contraceptives on demand regardless of age.

   The march also called for passage of the Equal Rights Amendment.

7. An end to racism in this country and apartheid in South Africa.

As members of the lesbian and gay movement, we too are affected by rising racism and sexism which oppresses People of Color and women; thereby the liberation of lesbians and gay is intricately linked to the struggle against racism, sexism and anti-Semitism. We realize that none of us are free until we are all free. We, therefore, call upon all of our sisters and brothers to actively confront racism and sexism on all levels both within our movement, and in the larger society. We demand an end to racist and sexist oppression. We demand an end to all social, economic, judicial, and legal oppression of lesbians and gays, and people of every race.

platform of the 1993 march on washington for lesbian, gay, and bi equal rights and liberation

Action Statement Preamble to the Platform

The Lesbian, Gay, Bisexual, and Transgender movement recognizes that our quest for social justice fundamentally links us to the struggles against racism and sexism, class bias, economic injustice, and religious intolerance. We must realize if one of us is oppressed we all are oppressed. The diversity of our movement requires and compels us to stand in opposition to all forms of oppression that diminish the quality of life for all people. We will be vigilant in our determination to rid our movement and our society of all forms of oppression and exploitation, so that all of us can develop to our full human potential without regard to race, religion, sexual orientation, identification, identity, gender and gender expression, ability, age, or class.

Platform Demands and Related Items

1. We demand passage of a Lesbian, Gay, Bisexual, and Transgender civil rights bill and an end to discrimination by state and federal governments including the military; repeal of all sodomy laws and other laws that criminalize private sexual expression between consenting adults.

   Passage of "The Civil Rights Amendment Act of 1991" (HR1430 & S574).

   Repeal of Department of Defense directive 1332.14.

   Repeal of laws prohibiting sodomy, cross-gender expression (dress codes) or non-coercive sexual behavior between adults.

   Amendment of the Code of Federal Regulations to recognize same-sex relationships.

   Passage of the Equal Rights Amendment.

   Implementation of, funding for, and enforcement of the Americans with Disabilities Act of 1991.

   Passage and implementation of graduated age-of-consent laws.

2. We demand massive increase in funding for AIDS education, research, and patient care; universal access to health care including alternative therapies; and an end to sexism in medical research and health care.

   The provision of responsive, appropriate health care for people with disabilities, deaf and hard of hearing people.

   Revision of the Centers for Disease Control definition of AIDS to include infections particular to women.

   Implementation of the recommendation of the National AIDS Commission immediately.

   A massive increase in funding for AIDS education, research and care—money for AIDS, not for war. This money should come from the defense budget, not existing social services.

   An increase in funding and research to provide an independent study of HIV infection in women, People of Color, Bisexuals, Heterosexuals, children, and women/to/women transmission.

   Access to anonymous testing for HIV.

   No mandatory HIV testing.

   A cure for AIDS.

   The development and legalization of a national needle exchange program.

   Free substance abuse treatment on demand.

   The re-definition of sexual re-assignment surgeries as medical, not cosmetic, treatment.

   The provision of appropriate medical treatment for all transgendered people in prisons and hospitals.

   An increase in funding and research for chronic illness, including breast ovarian, and other cancers particular to women.

   The right of all people with chronic illness, including HIV/AIDS, to choices in medical treatment as well as the right to end such treatment.

continued on next page

continued from previous page

3. We demand legislation to prevent discrimination against Lesbians, Gays, Bisexuals, and Transgendered people in the areas of family diversity, custody, adoption, and foster care and that the definition of family includes the full diversity of all family structures.

   The recognition and legal protection of the whole range of family structures.

   An end to abuse and exploitation of and discrimination against youth.

   An end to abuse and exploitation of and discrimination against older/old people.

   Full implementation of the recommendations contained in the report of the Health and Human Services Task Force on Youth Suicide.

   Recognition of domestic partnerships.

   Legalization of same-sex marriages.

4. We demand full and equal inclusion of Lesbians, Gays, Bisexuals, and Transgendered people in the educational system, and inclusion of Lesbian, Gay, Bisexual, and Transgender studies in multicultural curricula.

   Culturally inclusive Lesbian, Gay, Bisexual and Transgendered Studies program; and information on abortion, AIDS/HIV, childcare and sexuality at all levels of education.

   Establishment of campus offices and programs to address Lesbian, Gay, Bisexual and Transgender students' special needs.

   The ban of all discriminatory ROTC programs and recruiters from learning institutions.

   An end to discrimination at all levels of education.

5. We demand the right to reproductive freedom and choice, to control our own bodies, and an end to sexist discrimination.

   The right to control our bodies.

   Unrestricted, safe and affordable alternative insemination.

   An end to sterilization abuse.

   That access to safe and affordable abortion and contraception be available to all people on demand, without restriction and regardless of age.

   That access to unbiased and complete information about the full range of reproductive options be available to all people, regardless of age.

6. We demand an end to racial and ethnic discrimination in all forms.

   Support for non-racist policies and affirmative action.

   An end to institutionalized racism.

   Equal economic opportunity and an end to poverty.

   Full reproductive rights, improvement of pre-natal services, availability of alternative insemination for Lesbians and Bisexual women of color.

   Repeal of all "English Only" laws and restore and enforce bilingual education.

   Repeal all discriminatory immigration laws based on race and HIV status.

   A commitment to ending racism, including internalized racism, sexism and all forms of religious and ethnic oppression in our communities and in this country.

   An end to the genocide of all the indigenous peoples and their cultures.

   Restoration of the self-determination of all indigenous people of the world.

7. We demand an end to discrimination and violent oppression based on actual or perceived sexual orientation/identification, race, religion, identity, sex and gender expression, disability, age, class, AIDS/HIV infection.

   An end to anti-Semitism.

   An end to sexist oppression.

   An end to discrimination against people with disabilities, deaf and hard of hearing people.

   An end to discrimination based on sexual orientation in all programs of the Boy Scouts of America.

   An end to economic injustice in this country and internationally.

   An end to discrimination against prisoners with HIV/AIDS.

   An end to discrimination against people with HIV/AIDS, and those perceived as having HIV/AIDS.

   An end to consideration of gender dysphoria as a psychiatric disorder.

   An end to hate crimes including police brutality, rape and bashing.

   An end to censorship.

Gay Rights March. What had begun as a small, single-issue demonstration in 1965 evolved into large-scale and broadly based events in the nation's capital in 1979, 1987 (shown here), 1993, and 2000. **[Lee Snider/corbis]**

Continued from page 223

march was the first display of the NAMES Project AIDS Memorial Quilt, featuring, 1,920 panels remembering those who had died from AIDS. Two days after the march 600 to 800 people were arrested at a civil disobedience action at the Supreme Court. One measure of the march's success was the number of organizations that were founded as a result—including BiNet U.S.A., the National Latino/a Gay & Lesbian Organization (LLEGÓ), AT&T's LGBT employee group LEAGUE, and various AIDS activist groups. Following the grassroots organizing structure of its predecessor, the march also dramatically expanded the network of local organizations working for change in rural areas and gave birth to National Coming Out Day that is marked each year on the march's anniversary.

The third march, officially "The 1993 March on Washington for Lesbian, Gay, and Bi Equal Rights and Liberation," was held on 25 April 1993 and drew approximately one million participants. The march took place in the midst of the national debate about "gays in the military," which was precipitated by U.S. President Bill Clinton's promises to lift the ban on LGBT military service. The AIDS Quilt was displayed on the Mall as part of a weeklong series of conferences, workshops, protests, lobbying activities, dances, readings, and religious ceremonies. An autonomous Dyke March organized by the Lesbian Avengers featured approximately 20,000 female participants. Unlike the 1979 and 1987 marches, organizers focused on gaining massive media attention to the gathering. This time the national media provided extensive coverage of the march.

LGBT groups were driven to organize the 1993 march because the demands of the 1987 march had not been fulfilled, the presidency of George Bush had triggered no meaningful change in the country's AIDS policy, and because presidential candidate Bill Clinton's inclusive discourse about the gay community fueled an optimism that helped draw the hopeful as well as the angry to Washington, D.C.

The hope generated by President Clinton's election also began a debate about whether the nation's capital was the best place to focus the LGBT communities' collective energies. State capitals and local municipalities were increasingly where anti-LGBT groups were focusing their resources and strategies. More conservative LGBT groups began to challenge the platform of the march calling for a single focus rather than a broad vision of social justice.

Division among LGBT groups had widened by the time organizing for the Millennium March on Washington began. Many national organizations objected to the manner in which the march had been called, without a debate and a broad coalition in place such as those that had preceded previous marches. Under-funded state organizations saw the timing of the event as a drain at a time when resources were desperately needed to fight anti-LGBT initiatives flooding states. March organizers attempted to ease the controversy by "pausing" the organization process to hear from the community and endorsed a plan to march on state capitals in 1999. The march on state capitals, called Equality Begins at Home, was sponsored by the National Gay and Lesbian Task Force and the Federation of Statewide LGBT Advocacy organizations made up of dozens of state groups.

However, many saw these steps as too little too late. The organizing structure had not changed and whether or not to march was not up for discussion. National groups that initially supported the event withdrew their endorsement, opponents demanded a debate on the wisdom of another national march, and a vocal list of critics challenged the process, timing, and message of the event calling it undemocratic. The power wielded by the small group of organizations that had launched the effort for the Millennium March and deep concerns that the social justice principles that undergirded the preceding marches had been abandoned in favor of a neatly packaged media image were also primary concerns of the march's opponents.

Supporters of the Millennium March saw the event as a necessary means to rally the community in a vital election year. The changes in organizing tactics they argued for were an acknowledgment of a changing society and a maturing movement. Corporate sponsors were not evidence of selling out a community but rather a testament to the movement's arrival in the mainstream. Finally they argued the controversy, while visible in the media, was a tempest in a teapot to the larger community. The masses ultimately would vote with their feet and ignore the controversy.

On 30 April 2000 more than 200,000 attendees gathered for the Millennium March. The weekend included a two-day street festival, a variety of conferences, a star-studded rock concert, and many affiliated events. Both President Clinton and Vice President Al Gore addressed the crowd on the National Mall via video. The event and the controversy that surrounded it drew strong media coverage and lengthy analysis in the mainstream press. Those who attended experienced the thrill of suddenly being in the majority in the nation's capital, the power of being visible in large numbers, and the joy of gathering in safety.

Activists who supported the Millennium March and many who opposed it agreed on the importance of returning to Washington, D.C., for mass gatherings so that new generations of LGBT people could experience first hand the transformative power of marching on the nation's capital.

Bibliograhphy

D'Emilio, John. *Lost Prophet: The Life and Times of Bayard Rustin.* New York: Free Press, 2003.

D'Emilio, John. William B. Turner, and Urvashi Vaid, eds. *Creating Change: Sexuality, Public Policy, and Civil Rights.* New York: St. Martin's Press, 2000.

Stein, Marc. *City of Sisterly and Brotherly Loves: Lesbian and Gay Philadelphia, 1945-1972.* Chicago: Chicago University Press, 2000.

Thompson, Mark, ed. *Long Road to Freedom: The Advocate History of the Gay and Lesbian Movement.* With a forward by Randy Shilts. New York: St. Martin's Press, 1994.

Nadine Smith

See also AIDS MEMORIAL QUILT—NAMES PROJECT; DÍAZ-COTTO, JUANITA; HOMOPHILE MOVEMENT DEMONSTRATIONS; MARRIAGE CEREMONIES AND WEDDINGS; RODWELL, CRAIG.

MARKS, JEANETTE. see WOOLLEY, MARY, AND JEANETTE MARKS.

MARRIAGE. see FAMILY ISSUES.

MARRIAGE CEREMONIES AND WEDDINGS

In September 2002, the *New York Times* began including same-sex commitment ceremonies in its Sunday wedding announcements section. While this change in policy reflects a significant social shift and may reveal an underlying increase in same-sex weddings, same-sex marriage is not a new phenomenon. Historian John Boswell provides evidence of same-sex unions in ancient Greece. Marriage between men, Boswell argues, was sanctioned in early Rome, and the Emperor Nero is reported to have married a man in a public ceremony. However, by the fourth century, same-sex sexual relationships were less accepted, and the Romans passed laws prohibiting same-sex marriage and homosexual activity.

Prior to the nineteenth century in the Western World, marriage often functioned as a primarily economic arrangement that had little to do with love. However, increasing industrialization and urbanization reduced the economic necessity of the institution, and marriage began its transformation into a relationship based on love. These and other social changes provided more opportunities for same-sex sexual relationships and opened the door to modern same-sex marriage.

Pre-Stonewall Marriage

In the Americas, evidence suggests that same-sex marriages existed among many Native American tribes. Numerous Native American societies accepted and even celebrated individuals who assumed a third gender, that of the *berdache* or two-spirit person. According to anthropologist Will Roscoe, at least 155 North American tribes included men who dressed as women, fulfilled female roles, and often had sex with men. A third of these tribes also had female *berdaches,* who dressed as men, hunted, fought in wars, and even married other women. For example, in the mid-nineteenth century, a female member of the Crow tribe, Woman Chief, led men into battle and was known for her brave deeds. She eventually had four wives.

During the eighteenth and nineteenth centuries, other same-sex couples occasionally married or lived in socially recognized marital relationships. Many female couples of the nineteenth century lived together in what were known at the time as Boston marriages. Although the women involved in these relationships did not necessarily hold a marriage ceremony, they stayed together in long-term relationships that were marital unions in virtually all respects. Jonathan Katz provides evidence of a number of women who passed as men and married other women. Women were motivated to do so partially in an effort to gain greater financial independence. For example, in the late nineteenth century, one woman took the name Murray Hall, settled in New York City, and opened an employment service. She married twice and had a reputation for drinking, playing cards, and being sweet on women. One especially famous case is that of jazz musician Billy Tipton (born Dorothy), who married Kathleen Flaherty in the late 1950s. Together they raised several adopted children.

In New York City in the 1920s and 1930s, some same-sex couples had public wedding ceremonies and viewed

Wedding Ceremony. Standing at a pulpit, a couple are pronounced "man and man." **[AP/Wide World Photos]**

their relationships as marriages. Lillian Faderman describes elaborate weddings of femme/butch couples in Harlem. The couples sometimes secured real marriage licenses by masculinizing one partner's first name or by having a male friend apply for the license. George Chauncey describes how long-term relationships or marriages between older and younger working-class men were common, especially among the hoboes who frequented the streets of New York City in the 1920s. Some gay male couples referred to each other as husband and wife because their relationships so closely mirrored a heterosexual marriage.

Post-Stonewall Marriage

Same-sex weddings and interest in legal marriage have become more prevalent since the Stonewall Riots of 1969 and the emergence of the modern LGBT movement. Same-sex marriage was a concern of the post-Stonewall movement from its inception. In the 1970s, three same-sex couples filed for marriage licenses. However, the topic

In Support of Same-Sex Marriage. Demonstrators in November 1998 respond to protests by the virulently homophobic Reverend Fred Phelps at Broadway Methodist Church in Chicago, the site of same-sex marriage ceremonies. **[Ralf-Finn Hestoft/corbis SABA]**

was controversial in the 1970s, with many lesbian and gay liberation activists agreeing with the critique of traditional marriage advanced by the women's movement. Marriage was seen by some as an institution promoting monogamy and domesticity and ultimately reinforcing male dominance and heterosexual privilege. Some argued that gays and lesbians would not gain equality until marriage was abolished altogether.

In the late 1970s and early 1980s, discussions of legalizing same-sex marriage all but disappeared from queer politics. Gretchen Stiers suggests that this may be due to the influence of antimarriage arguments in the gay liberation and women's movements, or because other issues took center stage as gays and lesbians increasingly faced attacks from the right, such as Anita Bryant's antigay campaign.

The issue again returned to center stage in the LGBT rights movement on October 10, 1987, when over one thousand same-sex couples participated in a same-sex wedding ceremony in front of the Internal Revenue Service building on the day before the National March on Washington. The April 24, 1993, March on Washington also included a same-sex union ceremony, with two thousand couples sharing nuptial vows. Vermont became the first state to extend many of the legal, social, and economic benefits of heterosexual marriage to same-sex couples in 2000, when the state legislature created a new legal category of "civil unions." However, the benefits the law provides include only those offered by the state and exclude the thousand-plus federal benefits available to married heterosexual couples. Reaction to the Vermont initiative and pro-gay marriage court rulings in Hawaii was largely negative, with thirty-eight states and the federal government passing laws and amendments to state constitutions explicitly prohibiting same-sex marriage under "Defense of Marriage" acts by early 2003. Following the landmark Supreme Court decision (*Lawrence v. Texas)* striking down anti-sodomy laws in June 2003, conservative members of the U.S. Congress, including the senate majority leader, discussed amending the Constitution to ban same-sex marriage.

Same-sex marriage has faced less resistance in Canada and European nations such as the Netherlands and Belgium, which recently became the first countries to legalize fully equitable same-sex marriage. A 2003 decision by the Ontario appeals court has paved the way for fully legal same-sex marriage throughout Canada. The level of controversy in the United States suggests that it is likely to take many years for the U.S. to follow the lead of Canada, the Netherlands, and Belgium.

"If the club won't allow us as members, why would we want to join?"

Given the fact that same-sex marriages in the United States generally carry no legal force, why have growing numbers of couples decided to hold ceremonies? Same-sex couples wish to marry for both personal and political reasons. On a personal level, motivations are often comparable to the reasons heterosexual couples marry. Couples may wish to demonstrate their commitment to the relationship and love for one another, and many may see their union as a spiritual or religious one. Holding a marriage ceremony is also a rite of passage that can signify entrance into adulthood. In contrast to heterosexuals, same-sex couples are not generally subjected to external pressures to enter their unions and are more likely to encounter familial and social resistance. In such a climate, celebrating a wedding with friends and/or family can be a particularly powerful signifier of support for the relationship.

Unlike most heterosexual couples, same-sex couples may also have political motivations for holding a ceremony. Just as being out to friends, family, and coworkers can be a powerful political statement, seeking public affirmation of a same-sex relationship is also a way to raise awareness and create dialogue about the discriminatory nature of the marital institution. As having children becomes more prevalent among same-sex couples, they are interested in the protections and legal rights afforded to married couples, such as adoption and health insurance. The AIDS crisis also has fostered increased recognition among same-sex couples of the need for the medical rights denied them by the state, including health insurance and hospital visitation rights. Thus, increasing outrage and politicization over the discriminatory nature of state-sanctioned heterosexual marriage may underlie some couples' decisions to have a wedding.

Stiers and Ellen Lewin argue that same-sex weddings are simultaneously acts of resistance and accommodation. They are acts of accommodation because they reflect an acceptance of the institution of marriage and a desire to share in its benefits. At the same time, however, they are acts of resistance in that they challenge straight and male dominance. Nan Hunter argues that same-sex marriage challenges the power hierarchy in heterosexual relationships. Through decisions over the years, federal courts have established that marriage is an authority/dependence relationship based on biological male and female differences. When a couple of the same sex marries, this undermines the gendered hierarchy of marriage.

How Modern Couples Tie the Knot

Stiers suggests that the accommodation-resistance dynamic inherent in same-sex marriage is also visible in the content of same-sex wedding ceremonies. There is great variation in the content of the wedding ceremonies chosen by same-sex couples. Because same-sex weddings challenge the gender dichotomy of marriage, they exist partially outside of the institution, and participants are thus less bound by social expectations. Same-sex couples are freer to pick and choose how to express their love and commitment. Thus, ceremonies often include some combination of traditional aspects similar to those in heterosexual weddings as well as unique elements that reflect queer culture or personal beliefs and values. For example, while many same-sex wedding ceremonies include religious practices, such as vows, prayers, and hymns, same-sex couples may give these elements a new twist by altering the gender pronouns or otherwise personalizing them. A lesbian Jewish couple might both break the ceremonial glass, whereas in cross-sex weddings this task is traditionally the man's. Some couples draw from feminist or pagan spirituality to challenge the institutions of both marriage and patriarchy while also expressing personal religious beliefs.

Other, more cultural, facets of heterosexual ceremonies are also found in same-sex celebrations, such as wedding cakes, special dances, festive attire, showers, and gift registries. However, same-sex couples might incorporate unique aspects into their cultural repertoire by having a simple same-sex cake topper or, more elaborately, an all-gay wedding party with a lesbian best man dressed in a tuxedo and a gay maid of honor wearing the finest satin and tulle gown. Other cultural variations include actively supporting gay-owned or gay-friendly businesses or "registering" for guests to give donations to a favorite charity (for example, one advocating equal marriage rights for same-sex couples). Queer culture can also be reflected by involving drag queens in aspects of the ceremony or by holding the reception at a favorite gay nightclub.

Regardless of how modern same-sex weddings are celebrated, their increased prevalence and visibility signify varying degrees of progress on cultural, religious, and familial fronts. At the same time, the ceremonies, with their lack of legal recognition, vividly serve as reminders for how far same-sex couples still must travel to gain political, economic, and legal equality with heterosexuals.

Bibliography

Boswell, John. *Same-Sex Unions in Premodern Europe.* New York: Villard Books, 1994.

Chauncey, George. *Gay New York: Gender, Urban Culture, and the Makings of the Gay Male World, 1890–1940.* New York: Basic Books, 1994.

D'Emilio, John, and Estelle Freedman. *Intimate Matters: A History of Sexuality in America.* New York: Harper & Row, 1988.

Faderman, Lillian. *Odd Girls and Twilight Lovers: A History of Lesbian Life in Twentieth-Century America.* New York: Columbia University Press, 1991.

Hunter, Nan D. "Marriage, Law and Gender: A Feminist Inquiry." In *Sex Wars: Sexual Dissent and Political Culture.* Edited by Lisa Duggan and Nan D. Hunter. New York: Routledge, 1995.

Katz, Jonathan. *Gay American History: Lesbians and Gay Men in the USA.* New York: Crowell, 1976.

Lewin, Ellen. *Recognizing Ourselves: Ceremonies of Lesbian and Gay Commitment.* New York: Columbia University Press, 1998.

Roscoe, Will. *Changing Ones: Third and Fourth Genders in Native North America.* New York: St. Martin's Press, 1998.

Sherman, Suzanne, ed. *Lesbian and Gay Marriage: Private Commitments, Public Ceremonies.* Philadelphia: Temple University Press, 1992.

Stiers, Gretchen A. *From This Day Forward: Commitment, Marriage and Family in Lesbian and Gay Relationships.* New York: St. Martin's Press, 1999.

Nella Van Dyke and Irenee R. Beattie

See also BENTLEY, GLADYS; FAMILY ISSUES; FAMILY LAW AND POLICY; HALL, MURRAY; JEWS AND JUDAISM; JORGENSEN, CHRISTINE; MARCHES ON WASHINGTON; MITCHELL, ALICE; ROMANTIC FRIENDSHIP AND BOSTON MARRIAGE; WOMAN CHIEF.

MARTIAL ARTS. see GYMS, FITNESS CLUBS, AND HEALTH CLUBS.

MARTIN, DEL. see LYON, PHYLLIS, AND DEL MARTIN.

MASAHAI Amatkwisai (b. 1850s?; d. 1890s), healer, *hwame:*.

Masahai Amatkwisai, also known as Sahaykwisa, was a Mohave healer and *hwame:* (a female with an alternative gender status) who lived in the late nineteenth century. Masahai specialized in treating venereal diseases, a common specialty for *hwame:* healers and a sign of great spiritual power. He was highly successful in hunting and planting, as well as in his work as a doctor, and was wealthy by Mohave standards. Masahai took several wives, all of whom eventually left him. At the age of about twenty-five, he was raped and underwent an identity crisis. He started to drink heavily and apparently reverted to a female gender identity. After this, Masahai increasingly behaved in ways that, within Mohave culture, marked her as a witch who used spiritual powers to harm others. She was drowned by her two male lovers in the 1890s at about forty-five years of age.

The Mohave formerly resided along the Colorado River, cultivating crops and hunting, in an area that now includes parts of California, Arizona, and Nevada. When Masahai was a child, much of the tribe was placed on the Colorado River Reservation in west central Arizona, but his family remained at Fort Mohave with a conservative Mohave group. He belonged to a large, prominent, and highly respected family of the Huttoh branch of Mohave. No information has been preserved about Masahai's childhood. When he reached adulthood, he looked feminine and had developed breasts, but is said never to have menstruated. His society regarded him as a *hwame:* and twentieth-century Mohave referred to him in English with the male pronoun. His full name was a man's name, Masahai Matkwisa Manye:, meaning "Alluring Young Girl Who is Pleasing." It was designed to increase luck in attracting women. As was typical for Mohave healers, he gained his power to cure sexual diseases through dreams. The same power was believed to make him lucky in love, a trait that was assigned to *hwame:* in general.

Masahai had at least three wives during his young adulthood, when he was fully identified with the *hwame:* status. All the wives endured relentless teasing, a standard Mohave practice with the spouses of cross-gender individuals. The first two wives left Masahai in part because the taunting became unbearable for them. But Masahai found another wife each time, being known as a good provider who ensured that his wives were well-dressed. When searching for a new wife, Masahai went to dances where he joined the men outside and exhibited typical Mohave male behavior such as flirting with women and talking explicitly about his former wife's body.

When his second wife left, a disappointed Masahai painted his face like a warrior. But instead of going to his rival's camp, he went to another woman's lodge and began to woo her, highlighting his skill as a hunter. On his third visit, the woman agreed to leave her husband and elope with Masahai. But this last wife returned to her husband. Masahai repeatedly stood at the edge of their camp in a manner that implied intent to bewitch someone. After several such visits, the husband ambushed him in the woods and raped him.

After the rape, Masahai began to drink heavily and turned to prostitution, an occupation in which he had occasionally engaged before. He began to desire men, although the Mohave believed that he was also having sex in his dreams with the ghosts of women he had previously bewitched. Masahai was now perceived as a full-fledged witch. His end came when he boasted to his two current lovers, Suhura:ye and Ilykutcemidho:, about having killed Suhura:ye's father by witchcraft. The two men then threw him in the Colorado River to drown. This occurred in the 1890s, when Masahai was in his mid-forties. The Mohave believed that witches deserved death, but also that they wished to be killed, as only murder would allow their souls to join bewitched lovers in the afterlife. Masahai's boasting behavior was seen as an attempt to goad others into killing him.

Masahai Amatkwisai lived in a time of great stress for the Mohave people as they coped with U.S. expansion into their territory. He conformed to his society's expectations for a *hwame:* and healer, but apparently concluded that his position as *hwame:* had become untenable. Although Mohave culture provided an institutionalized alternative gender role for women, Masahai was ridiculed and insulted behind his back, suggesting that acceptance of *hwame:* status was declining in his time. Family descendants say that he "tired of this life" (Roscoe, p. 97) because he had captured so many souls through his shamanism, and was ready to die.

Bibliography

Blackwood, Evelyn. "Sexuality and Gender in Certain Native American Tribes: The Case of Cross-Gender Females." *Signs: Journal of Women in Culture and Society* 10 (1984): 1–42.

Devereux, George. "Institutionalized Homosexuality of the Mohave Indians." *Human Biology* 9, no. 4 (1937): 498–527.

Lang, Sabine. *Men as Women, Women as Men. Changing Gender in Native American Cultures.* Translated from the German by John L. Vantine. Austin: University of Texas Press, 1998.

Roscoe, Will. *Changing Ones: Third and Fourth Genders in Native North America.* New York: St Martin's Press, 1998.

Robin Jarvis Brownlie

See also TRANSSEXUALS, TRANSVESTITES, TRANSGENDER PEOPLE, AND CROSS-DRESSERS; TWO-SPIRIT FEMALES.

MATTACHINE REVIEW

In January 1955 the *Mattachine Review* became the nation's second widely circulated magazine published by and for the fledgling gay and lesbian community. *ONE,* a magazine established two years earlier by a handful of Mattachine Society members, operated independently of the society and its ideological foundation. Although the two publications shared the common goal of eradicating political injustice and social prejudice aimed at homosexuals, the *Review* adopted a milder tone in keeping with the noncombative, assimilationist perspective of the Mattachine Society. In the August 1956 issue, for example, writer Ken Burns admonished gays that they must blame themselves for much of their plight. "When will the homosexual ever realize that social reform, to be effective, must be preceded by personal reform?" he asked (p. 27). From its inception, the magazine reflected the Mattachine Society perspective that homosexuals would gain social acceptance through education. It sought to build bridges by publishing the work of progressive experts.

Each issue contained a mix of original essays on the homosexual experience; reprints of scientific studies related to homosexuality; poetry with a homosexual theme; reviews of books related to homosexuality; and letters to the editor to give readers "the true facts of the Mattachine Society and the place of the sex variant in the life of the community" (*Mattachine Review,* p. 2). The first issue included reprints of the poem "Hate" by Bertrand Russell and a scientific study by Dr. Evelyn Hooker, a Los Angeles psychologist whose research had determined that "inverts are not a distinct personality type" (Hooker, p. 22). Hooker's landmark study argued that homosexuals were equally well adjusted as heterosexuals, but since the study received little attention in the mainstream press, it was virtually unknown to vast numbers of homosexuals before appearing in the *Review.*

The *Mattachine Review* began publication during the anticommunist and antigay hysteria of McCarthyism, testimony to the determination of its organizers to confront the social intolerance of that era. When its first issue went to press, *ONE* magazine was locked in a fierce legal battle with postal officials who had confiscated the October 1954 issue on the grounds that it was obscene. Even so, the *Mattachine Review* went out through the mail, as the case against *ONE* wound through the courts. Its masthead listed the names of business manager Don Lucas, art director Mel Betti, and production manger Rod Holiday, but did not name the magazine's editor, Harold "Hal" Call, who was also president of the Mattachine Society, until August 1956.

Given the difficulty in finding printers who would produce a magazine that might subject them to prosecution, Call established Pan-Graphic Press to handle typesetting, graphic design, printing, and binding. A former publisher of several small midwestern newspapers, Call had also worked as an advertising executive for the *Kansas City Star* until the newspaper learned of his 1952 arrest on morals charges in Chicago involving a sexual encounter with another man.

This arrangement placed Call in sure control of the magazine and its content, ensuring that it would reflect the official views of the Mattachine Society and not fall to the "whims of the membership" (Marcus, p. 67). Call wrote many of the articles in the *Review's* early days, using pseudonyms for his bylines to provide the illusion of a larger staff of writers and a variety of voices. The magazine refused to print articles and letters advocating confrontational tactics that found a ready home on the pages of the more provocative *ONE.*

Circulation climbed from 2,942 in January and February 1955 to nearly five thousand the following November when it became a monthly publication. The actual readership was thought to be much greater since subscribers tended to circulate the magazine among friends and colleagues. Newsstands carried the magazine in several cities, ranging from the major metropolitan centers of New York City, Los Angeles, and San Francisco to smaller cities such as Buffalo, New York, and Cleveland, Ohio. It was also sold at a bookstore in the Virgin Islands and through a mail-order company in Copenhagen.

The five-by-eight inch magazine published between thirty-two and fifty-six pages each month. Professionally typeset, its graphics consisted of sketch drawings, but none of a homoerotic nature. Along with *ONE* and the *Ladder,* published by the lesbian organization Daughters of Bilitis, the *Mattachine Review* played an important role in the founding of a nascent gay community in the 1950s by providing access to information and perspectives that readers could not find elsewhere. James Barr, the pseudonymous author of the gay-themed novels *Quatrefoil* in 1950 and *Derricks* in 1951, contributed several original articles.

In 1957 *Mattachine Review* became the first gay publication to draw attention to the Wolfenden Report, in which the British government recommended the limited decriminalization of homosexual acts by consenting homosexual males in private. Its ongoing coverage was particularly significant since the report was virtually ignored by other newspapers and magazines in the United States. In 1958 the *Review* heralded the unanimous U.S. Supreme Court decision that exonerated *ONE* from obscenity charges, which is widely viewed as the most important legal victory for homosexuals during the 1950s.

By the late 1950s the political atmosphere had relaxed to such a degree that, beginning in August 1958, the *Review* printed a series of articles featuring the individuals responsible for the publication, including their photographs. In 1960 it carried the transcript of a groundbreaking series on Pacifica Radio's KPFA in Berkeley, California, that featured Call among a panel of guests. The broadcast was one of the first to permit a homosexual to speak firsthand about the realities of the homosexual experience. Topics covered on the broadcast ranged from social and employment discrimination to police harassment.

By the mid-1960s the magazine's strict adherence to the Mattachine Society's conservative social philosophy proved to be its downfall. The *Mattachine Review* was seen as increasingly out of step at a time when combative forces in the movement were confronting police harassment and government employment discrimination with picketing and public protests. Upheaval in the movement's leadership ranks only exacerbated problems at the magazine. The Mattachine Society disbanded as a national organization in 1960, although several independent organizations continued using the name, and the schism spilled over to the *Mattachine Review.* Continued in-fighting at the Mattachine Society and competition from an increasing number of publications for the homosexual market took their toll. The *Mattachine Review* appeared only sporadically during the mid-1960s and then ceased publication altogether in 1967, a victim of the shift in gay political sentiment from the conservatism of the 1950s to radicalism of the 1960s. In effect, the political activism that the *Mattachine Review* helped create by providing a platform for dialogue ultimately killed the publication when it failed to change with the times.

Bibliography

Alwood, Edward. *Straight News: Gays, Lesbians and the News Media.* New York: Columbia University Press, 1996.

Burns, Ken. "The Homosexual Faces a Challenge." *Mattachine Review* (August 1956).

D'Emilio, John. *Sexual Politics, Sexual Communities: The Making of a Homosexual Minority in the United States, 1940–1970.* Chicago: University of Chicago Press, 1983.

Gross, Larry P. *Up from Invisibility: Lesbians, Gay Men, and the Media in America.* New York: Columbia University Press, 2001.

Hooker, Evelyn. "Inverts Are Not a Distinct Personality Type." *Mattachine Review* (January/February 1955).

Marcus, Eric. *Making History: The Struggle for Gay and Lesbian Equal Rights.* New York: HarperCollins, 1992.

Mattachine Review, Editorial, January/February 1955.

Streitmatter, Rodger. *Unspeakable: The Rise of the Gay and Lesbian Press in America.* Boston: Faber and Faber, 1995.

Edward Alwood

See also CALL, HAL; FUGATE, JAMES BARR; HOMOPHILE MOVEMENT; HOMOPHILE PRESS; KEPNER, JAMES; MATTACHINE SOCIETY.

MATTACHINE SOCIETY

The Mattachine Society is perhaps the best known but also among the least understood organizations of the homophile movement. This is largely because the organization existed in several different manifestations, some of which were antagonistic to the others, and because of the tendency of historical scholarship to evaluate past social movements according to contemporary beliefs and strategies.

The Mattachine Society experienced three distinct stages in its organizational history that can be categorized along the following lines: the Mattachine Foundation (1951–1953); the Mattachine Society as a national organization with local chapters (1953–1961); and the national headquarters and local chapters of the Mattachine Society as several independent organizations (1961–1970s).

The Mattachine Foundation was formed in Los Angeles in 1951 and the process of incorporation was initiated in 1952, but it can date its origins as far back as 1948. That year Harry Hay, a Los Angeles–based actor who was active in the Communist Party, met with a group of like-minded gay men and suggested that they mobilize support for presidential candidate Henry Wallace, with whom they had political sympathies. Although the gathering never moved beyond coining a name ("Bachelors for Wallace"), it did provide the impetus for Hay and others to found a group of gay men three years later. Hay suggested the name Mattachine—the term used to describe traveling performers in medieval Europe who staged satires while wearing masks—because he thought that their performances resonated with the experiences of many American homosexuals who also were forced to hide behind masks. Many of the founders shared Hay's leftist politics, including Rudi Gernrich, Bob Hull, and Chuck Rowland. The founders agreed that the foundation should be organized along the lines of the secretive, cell-like structure of the Communist Party, which also needed to protect the identities of its members. Hay also took from the Communist Party and Marxism in general the idea that homosexuals must develop a group consciousness as an oppressed class as a prerequisite to ending their oppression.

The leaders of the organization sponsored discussion groups for homosexuals as one method for fomenting a group identity and minority consciousness. Between 1951 and early 1953 the organization grew throughout Southern California and in the San Francisco Bay Area. The leadership made tentative steps into the arenas of public relations and the law. The Mattachine Foundation claimed a modest victory when a member who had been arrested for solicitation in a public restroom, Dale Jennings, pled not guilty to the charge, admitting his homosexuality but also declaring his innocence. The case was dismissed and the man set free, although the judge's decision did not establish any real legal precedent.

The foundation pursued an ambiguous path of publicity. Leaders of the foundation contacted local politicians and journalists in an effort to elicit their opinions on homosexuality. The same leaders, however, preferred to remain anonymous. This basic inconsistency proved to be problematic. In March 1953 a journalist who had received a foundation mailing did some research on the organization and uncovered little information; playing on the widespread fear of communism, he wrote a somewhat sensationalist article in which he suggested that the organization, with its secretive leadership, might be a front organization. The article surprised and worried many of Mattachine's rank-and-file participants, who started asking questions and demanding answers of their leaders. In a pair of membership conventions in April and May of 1953, the leadership of the foundation abandoned its secretive structure and opened the organization to democratic elections. In a climate of suspicions about everything from financial improprieties and personal misrepresentations to communist infiltration and the aims of the organization, the membership elected a new slate of leaders. Some historians have claimed that the newly elected leaders (such as Ken Burns and Marilyn Rieger of Los Angeles and Harold "Hal" Call of San Francisco) were "conservative," whereas the ousted leaders (such as Harry Hay and Chuck Rowland) were "radical." However, most fail to note that the original leftist leaders were reluctant to publicly identify themselves with the organization or as homosexuals themselves, while the new leadership did so readily and without the use of pseudonyms. This discrepancy begs the question of how "conservative" and "radical" should be defined in the context of the 1950s homophile movement.

At the Mattachine Society's May 1953 convention, the leaders of the foundation signed a document that officially dissolved the Mattachine Foundation and recognized the establishment of the Mattachine Society. Some participants in the foundation shifted their energies to work on the homophile magazine, *ONE*, which had first appeared in January 1953, shortly before the demise of the foundation. The next two years witnessed a great deal of change within the Mattachine Society. As the organization sought to establish itself, some members dropped away, new ones took their place, and some rose to positions of influence. Chief among the latter group were Call and Donald Stewart Lucas, both from San Francisco. Call had moved to San Francisco in 1952 and shortly thereafter became involved in the Berkeley chapter of the foundation. With his aggressive personality, Call easily assumed a leadership role and began to notice what he perceived as significant problems within the small organization—chief among them were secrecy and a lack of communication. Call was trained as a journalist and, before coming to San Francisco, had even owned a small daily newspaper.

Immediately after the May 1953 convention, Call set out to establish a "publications chapter" of the organization in San Francisco and to become the chair of its publications committee. From that institutional position, Call published newsletters and proposed that the organization publish a journal in order to provide a public voice for homosexuals and to end what he called the "conspiracy of silence" surrounding the objective discussion of homosexuality. The journal, which came to be known as the *Mattachine Review,* first appeared in February 1955. As it became the central activity of the society, the publication of the *Review* in San Francisco played an important role in shifting the locus of power within the organization to that city. The national headquarters of the organization officially moved to San Francisco in January 1957, albeit not without some wrangling between leaders in Los Angeles and those in San Francisco.

In addition to publishing the *Review,* the San Francisco chapter of the society, first as a local chapter and then as the national headquarters, greatly expanded the educational activities of the organization. Lucas claims that education was the main priority of the society, but the group's leaders defined "education" very broadly. That is, education encompassed not merely the transmission of information about specific items of interest, but also the complete enlightenment of society, including both heterosexuals and homosexuals, about the scientific, objective facts of homosexual behavior and identity. Although scientists and psychologists had long offered their own "truths" about homosexuality, the leaders of the society were heavily influenced by the decidedly nonhomophobic research of Alfred Kinsey and Evelyn Hooker. To achieve these ends, the society pursued an education program through the *Review* as well as through the publications of Pan-Graphic Press (a small press owned by Call and Lucas); the research sponsored and aided by the society; public relations activities and work with journalists, broadcasters, and photographers on a local and national scale; exchanges with social workers, clergy, parole officers, lawyers, and psychologists; and the hosting of conventions and meetings addressing the topic of homosexuality.

Between 1953 and 1961 active chapters of the Mattachine Society also flourished at various times in Boston, Chicago, Denver, Detroit, New York City, Philadelphia, and Washington, D.C. Although a few of the chapters amounted to not much more than one-man shows (as was the case with Prescott Townsend in Boston), other chapters, like New York City's, pursued a wide-ranging program of education not unlike the one run by the society's leaders in San Francisco. In New York, Curtis Dewees, Joe McCarthy, John LeRoy, and author Donald Webster Cory (Edward Sagarin) established a regular series of lectures and discussion groups and lent their voice to the occasional radio program that wished to interview a homosexual. Throughout the second half of the 1950s, however, a sense of dissatisfaction arose among the branch chapters, particularly in New York and Washington, D.C. The struggle largely centered on questions of autonomy, control, funding, visibility, and personality, and resulted in the dissolution of the society's national structure in 1961.

Following that formal dissolution, several of the branch chapters continued their work and some even thrived. The national chapter in San Francisco became known simply as the Mattachine Society, Inc., while some branch chapters retained their original names (e.g., the Mattachine Society of New York) and others changed theirs (e.g., the Philadelphia chapter evolved into the Janus Society, under the leadership of Mae Polakoff and Mark Kendall). The Washington, D.C., offshoot, known as the Mattachine Society of Washington, was arguably the most active and committed to political change among the former chapters. Franklin Kameny, the leader of the Mattachine Society of Washington, challenged the discriminatory policies of the U.S. Civil Service and worked to change the designation by the American Psychological Association that homosexuality was an illness. The Mattachine Society of New York outlasted both the Los Angeles and San Francisco groups and played a role in activism in the gay liberation era.

In San Francisco, Call and Lucas continued to lead the organization, which by 1960 had become less a membership group and more of an education and social service organization. A mixture of increased demand for services from the organization (partially due to the vastly expanded public visibility of the society) along with diminishing financial and human resources resulted in the decline of the group between 1965 and 1967. Not coincidently, a new generation of homophile organizations that assumed many of the society's prior functions appeared between 1960 and 1966 in San Francisco, including the Council on Religion and the Homosexual (1964), the Tavern Guild (1962), the Coits (1962), the Imperial Court (1966), Vanguard (1966), and the Society for Individual Rights (1964). Although the Mattachine Society continued to exist as a paper organization until Call's death in 2000, it all but ceased operation in 1967 when Call opened the Adonis Bookstore and when Lucas began doing community organizing and antipoverty work with President Johnson's Great Society programs.

Bibliography

Boyd, Nan Alamilla. *Wide-Open Town: A History of Queer San Francisco to 1965.* Berkeley: University of California Press, 2003.

D'Emilio, John. *Sexual Politics, Sexual Communities: The Making of a Homosexual Minority in the United States, 1940–1970*, 2nd edition. Chicago: University of Chicago Press, 1998.

Marcus, Eric. *Making History: The Struggle for Gay and Lesbian Equal Rights, 1945–1990.* New York: HarperCollins, 1992.

Meeker, Martin. "Behind the Mask of Respectability." *Journal of the History of Sexuality* 10, no. 1 (2001): 78–116.

Stein, Marc. *City of Sisterly and Brotherly Loves: Lesbian and Gay Philadelphia, 1945–1972.* Chicago: University of Chicago Press, 2000.

Streitmatter, Rodger. *Unspeakable: The Rise of the Gay and Lesbian Press in America.* Boston: Faber and Faber, 1995.

Timmons, Stuart. *The Trouble with Harry Hay: Founder of the Modern Gay Movement.* Boston: Alyson, 1990.

Martin Meeker

See also ANARCHISM, SOCIALISM, AND COMMUNISM; BREWSTER, LEE; CALL, HAL; CHICAGO; COLORADO; GRAHN, JUDY; HART, PEARL; HAY, HARRY; HOMOPHILE MOVEMENT; HOMOPHILE MOVEMENT DEMONSTRATIONS; HOMOPHILE PRESS; JANUS SOCIETY; KAMENY, FRANKLIN; KEPNER, JAMES; LATINA AND LATINO LGBTQ ORGANIZATIONS AND PERIODICALS; MATTACHINE REVIEW; ONE; ONE INSTITUTE; STONEWALL RIOTS; TRANSGENDER ORGANIZATIONS AND PERIODICALS.

MATTHIESSEN, F. O. **(b. 19 February 1902; d. 1 April 1950), literary scholar, political activist.**

Trained at Yale and Harvard Universities as a scholar of European Renaissance literature, Francis Otto Matthiessen became one of the preeminent scholars of American literature of his generation. His *American Renaissance: Art and Expression in the Age of Emerson and Whitman* (1941), which established the works of Ralph Waldo Emerson, Henry David Thoreau, Walt Whitman, Nathaniel Hawthorne, and Herman Melville as evidence of a genuinely American literature in the mid-nineteenth century, remains a critical touchstone for American literary historians and students. *American Renaissance* serves as the title not only for countless college and university courses, but also for numerous studies of antebellum American literature. In addition to being recognized for his influential literary criticism, which includes one of the first studies of T. S. Eliot (1935) and books on Henry James and the James family, Sarah Orne Jewett, and Theodore Dreiser, Matthiessen exemplifies for LGBT and queer studies scholars, students, and teachers a tradition of political activism and persistent attention to the world outside the "ivy-covered walls" of the academy. Matthiessen may have written about—some would even say, produced—a distinctly American literary tradition, but he was also always concerned with issues beyond the boundaries of the literary.

Although he spent nearly his entire career teaching history and literature at Harvard (1930–1950), among Matthiessen's lesser-known writings are essays in news magazines calling attention to the plight of Mexican American coal miners in the American Southwest, which he visited in the 1930s. Likewise, as one of the founders of the Harvard Teachers' Union, and as a Christian socialist (a descriptive phrase he sometimes used to encapsulate his guiding beliefs), Matthiessen lobbied repeatedly on behalf of labor and in support of fair and comprehensive union representation. In 1948 he seconded the nomination of Henry Wallace at the national Progressive Party Convention. In the late 1940s, Matthiessen helped to found the Salzburg Seminar in American Civilization—what some called an "intellectual Marshall Plan"—which he hoped would serve as an opportunity to discuss with Europeans the possibilities of American culture and democracy and "to enact anew the chief function of culture and humanism, to bring man again into communication with man" (*From the Heart of Europe,* 1948, p. 13).

In 1923, while aboard the ocean liner *Paris* en route to England as a Rhodes scholar, Matthiessen met the painter Russell Cheney; for the next twenty years, they were partners and shared their lives across America and Europe, at homes in Boston and in Kittery, Maine, and in a voluminous correspondence. These letters (selected and published posthumously in 1978 by Louis Hyde in *Rat and the Devil*) chronicle the lives of two gay men in the first half of the twentieth century and reveal a side of Matthiessen not typically visible in the literary criticism. If, from our point of view, *American Renaissance* treats five authors all of whose sexual orientations have been the subjects of scrutiny among modern LGBT critics, sexual orientation is not, by and large, a category that Matthiessen addresses either openly or favorably in his book. Indeed, in a famous passage from *American Renaissance* treating section five of "Song of Myself," Matthiessen disparages Whitman's "regressive, infantile fluidity": "In the passivity of the poet's body," he writes, "there is a quality vaguely pathological and homosexual" (p. 535). Among its other effects, this discussion marks the virtual impossibility in 1941 of publicly discussing homosexual themes or content in other than pejorative terms.

In Matthiessen and Cheney's private correspondence, however, one finds another Matthiessen, urging Cheney to come to terms with his sexual orientation, and insisting upon its naturalness: "No, accept it, just the way you accept the fact that you have two legs," he writes. In part, Matthiessen's life with Cheney demonstrates the public/private divide within which sexual minorities in the immediate pre– and post–World War II years often lived. In the same letter to Cheney (7 February 1925), Matthiessen makes clear a distinction between the rest of the world and those "close friends" with whom he thinks it safe to share the fact of their relationship. Within these constraints Cheney and Matthiessen forged a remarkable, long-standing relationship of tremendous mutual support.

Five years after Cheney's death, when Matthiessen committed suicide in April 1950, his suicide note mentioned a range of concerns and motives. Among these, the increasing East/West tensions of an incipient Cold War played a role, as did the demand some months before that he, like so many others, justify his political beliefs and activism before the House Un-American Activities Committee. Although Cheney is not mentioned in the note, a few years earlier Matthiessen had memorialized him when he described, upon returning to Salzburg, "a city of ghosts. . . . I am pierced with the realization of how much [Russell] taught me to see, of how life shared with him took on more vividness than I have ever felt in any other company." But at the last, Matthiessen worried that he could no longer "continue to be of use to my profession and my friends." To the very end, then, his attention was directed toward a larger, worldly sense of usefulness, and of participation in the central debates of his place and time. This may remain his central, crucial lesson for LGBT and queer readers and writers today.

Bibliography

Chauncey, George. *Gay New York: Gender, Urban Culture, and the Making of the Gay Male World 1890–1940.* New York: Basic Books, 1994.

Corburn, Robert J. *Homosexuality in Cold War America: Resistance and the Crisis of Masculinity.* Durham: Duke University Press, 1997.

Grossman, Jay. "The Canon in the Closet: Matthiessen's Whitman, Whitman's Matthiessen." *American Literature* 70, no. 4 (December 1998): 799–832.

Hyde, Louis, ed. *Rat and the Devil: Journal Letters of F. O. Matthiessen and Russell Cheney.* Hamden, Conn.: Archon Books, 1978.

Matthiessen, F. O. *Russell Cheney, 1881–1945: A Record of His Work.* New York: Oxford University Press, 1947.

Jay Grossman

See also LITERARY CRITICISM AND THEORY.

MAUPIN, Armistead (b. 13 May 1944), writer.

A southern son and graduate of the University of North Carolina at Chapel Hill, Maupin grew up in a conservative, religious, and traditional environment in the relatively small city of Raleigh, North Carolina. After graduating with a major in English, he abandoned law school, joined the U.S. Navy, and fought in the Vietnam War. He received a commendation from President Richard Nixon for his involvement in rebuilding housing in Vietnam for disabled Vietnamese veterans of the war. Back in the United States, Maupin began a career in journalism and even spent some time working for North Carolina senator Jesse Helms. However, with a move to San Francisco to work for the Associated Press in 1971, everything changed.

In the spring of 1976, the first brief installment of his daily column "Tales of the City" appeared in the *San Francisco Chronicle* (it had started earlier at the *Pacific Sun* and moved to the *Chronicle* when the *Sun* folded). These commentaries would become some of the most widely read and widely praised texts of gay literature over the following thirty years. Consisting of six novels published between 1978 and 1989, the *Tales* are surely Maupin's great contribution to the literature of contemporary U.S. culture. The novels have been likened to the works of Charles Dickens in their initial newspaper serialization and as documentaries of the social, political, and ethical zeitgeist.

The first novel, *Tales of the City* (1978), introduces the principal characters: Mary Ann Singleton, fresh into San Francisco from Cleveland; her landlady at 28 Barbary Lane, the inscrutable and marvelous Anna Madrigal; her gay neighbor, Michael (Mouse) Tolliver; and the elite but scandal-ridden Halcyon family. The adventures continue in the second installment, *More Tales of the City* (1980), and the third, *Further Tales of the City* (1982). The fourth book, *Babycakes* (1984), has a more somber tone, as it is one of the first fictional chronicles of the earliest days of the AIDS crisis, which hit San Francisco—and especially Maupin's Castro district—so hard in the first half of the 1980s. Maupin's account of AIDS and its implications in *Babycakes, Significant Others* (1987), and *Sure of You* (1989), the final installment in the series, represents an important social and literary record of ground zero of the AIDS pandemic, and the entire series is also an insightful and beautiful representation of queer families, love, loss, and the glories of the mundane, all described with great wit, intelligence, and passion. In a review of *Sure of You* in the *New York Times Book Review* (22 October 1989), gay novelist David Feinberg wrote, "AIDS pervades the book.

Armistead Maupin. The author of the "Tales of the City" newspaper column and resulting series of novels, chronicling the San Francisco gay community in the 1970s and 1980s, relaxes on Macondray Lane, on Russian Hill. **[Catherine Karnow/corbis]**

The mood is rawer, tenderer, sadder than the earlier books in the series, with an undercurrent of anger" (p. 26). It is clear that the devastation of the gay community of the 1980s finally overtook the author of *Tales,* and his series is likewise important because of its perhaps unconscious rage against that decade of silence and death.

The popularity of the *Tales* has made Maupin something of a celebrity, and he has used his fame, such as it is, to be an advocate for gay and lesbian causes as well as to point out hypocrisy in the media and in Hollywood. Beginning in the late 1980s, for example, Maupin became a loud voice in support of outing gay people in high places. His work has had another impact on the media as well. Several of the *Tales* books have been filmed for television, prompting some censorship battles with the Public Broadcasting System and other venues. Maupin penned the screenplay for the award-winning 1995 documentary *The Celluloid Closet* (by Rob Epstein and Jeffrey Friedman, based on Vito Russo's *The Celluloid Closet: Homosexuality in the Movies* [1981], a study of homosexuality in Hollywood). Maupin is one of the film's interviewees, along with such notables as Gore Vidal, Susie Bright, Susan Sarandon, Tom Hanks, Shirley MacLaine, Quentin Crisp, and Whoopi Goldberg.

In the dozen years after closing the door at 28 Barbary Lane, Maupin published what is perhaps his least successful novel, *Maybe the Moon* (1992), and what may be his best ever, *The Night Listener* (2001). The latter book chronicles Maupin's breakup with his longtime lover and business partner, Terry Anderson, as well as his correspondence with the elusive Tony Johnson, purported author of the autobiographical *A Rock and a Hard Place* (1993). Maupin's novel is a stunning portrait of the aftermath of a long-term relationship and a beautiful, moving depiction of father-son relationships. Arguably, *The Night Listener* mixes fiction and reality as well as any book ever has.

Bibliography

Feinberg, David. Review of *Sure of You,* by Armistead Maupin. *New York Times Book Review,* 22 October 1989, 26.

Gale, Patrick. *Armistead Maupin.* Bath, England: Absolute Press, 1999.

"Life and Works of Armistead Maupin." Available from www.literarybent.com, Maupin's website.

Maupin, Armistead. *28 Barbary Lane: A Tales of the City Omnibus.* New York: HarperCollins, 1990.

———. *Back to Barbary Lane: The Final Tales of the City Omnibus.* HarperCollins, 1991.

———. *The Night Listener.* New York: HarperCollins, 2000.

Chris Freeman

See also COMEDY AND HUMOR; COMING OUT AND OUTING; LITERATURE; RUSSO, VITO.

MAYNE, XAVIER. see PRIME-STEVENSON, EDWARD I.

MEAD, Margaret (b. 16 December 1901; d. 15 November 1978), anthropologist.

Margaret Mead was an anthropologist and the best-selling author of numerous books, including the controversial *Coming of Age in Samoa: A Psychological Study of Primitive Youth for Western Civilisation* (1928), *Sex and Temperament in Three Primitive Societies* (1935), and *Male and Female: A Study of the Sexes in a Changing World* (1949). These books were controversial at the time of publication for their forthright, frank, and comparative discussions of sexual behavior such as teenage sexual experimentation, homosexual practices, and masturbation in nonwestern societies and in the United States. One of them—*Coming of Age in Samoa*—again raised a stir some fifty years later when Australian anthropologist Derek Freeman argued that Mead's analysis of Samoan culture as "sexually liberated" was completely wrong (although Freeman's arguments themselves have been severely critiqued).

Margaret Mead. The popular and influential cultural anthropologist (right) explored sexuality and other aspects of human behavior in Samoa and elsewhere during her half-century-long career.

Born into an academic family, Mead completed her doctor of philosophy degree at Columbia University as a student of the influential American anthropologist Franz Boas. She was appointed assistant curator in the Department of Anthropology at the American Museum of Natural History in 1926 and remained associated with the museum for the rest of her life—more than fifty-two years. She was one of the key intellectuals involved in the development of the Culture and Personality theoretical school, which contested the then-popular biological, racist theories of nonwestern peoples by arguing that individual human behavior is primarily shaped through the cultural environment in which it is located. (This group also included anthropologists Ruth Benedict and Edward Sapir.) Mead and Ruth Benedict were among the first anthropologists to discuss homosexuality not as a deviant behavior but as a universal practice that some cultures were better prepared than others to accommodate. These were radical statements at the time they were published because of their defense of homosexual practices as "normal" in certain cultural contexts. Much later they were criticized in anthropological writing on sexuality, albeit for different reasons. One reason is that identifying "the homosexual" in other cultural contexts imposes an assumption of a presocial, universal "homosexual identity," which reflects a particular Anglo-European, early-twentieth-century psychiatric logic that constructed coherent identities out of complex sexual desires and practices.

That Mead is often identified by historians of social science as one of the first anthropologists to theorize sexuality from a relativist, cross-cultural perspective may be true, but this perspective also reflects a selective, post–gay liberation reinterpretation of her work. Mead did not see herself primarily as a pioneering sexologist or anthropologist of sexuality; rather, her observations about sexuality often provided a point of entry to other issues that she cared about deeply, such as childhood development, racial inequality, population growth, and the limits of human malleability.

One of the most interesting aspects of Mead's posthumous career has been the outing of her lesbian relationship with Benedict, whose best-selling books include *The Chrysanthemum and the Sword* (1946) and *Patterns of Culture* (1934). Recent biographies of Mead—including *With a Daughter's Eye: A Memoir of Margaret Mead and Gregory Bateson* (1984), by Mead's anthropologist daughter, Mary Catherine Bateson, and *Margaret Mead and Ruth Benedict: The Kinship of Women* (1999), by Hilary Lapsley—have focused on the personal correspondence between Mead and Benedict, noting Mead's relatively open-minded and self-accepting attitude toward her same-sex relationships (some of which took place during her three marriages to men) despite the absence of any overt discussion of her sexuality, theoretically or descriptively, in any of her published work, including her autobiography, *Blackberry Winter: My Earlier Years* (1972). This public silence is most likely partly attributable to the general social and political climate surrounding homosexuality in America at this time, but it may also have been due to the objectivist, positivist model of social science pervasive in anthropology during the first half of the twentieth century. According to this model, anthropology was the "science" of human nature, and theoretical frameworks need not and should not be connected to the social scientist's personal experiences in any way, at least in relation to the ethnographic data. Yet another possibility, suggested by her daughter, is that Mead did not view either "homosexual" or "heterosexual" as sufficient or appropriate labels to represent her choices and actions, making her a forerunner of the queer movement that emerged some fifteen years after her death.

Margaret Mead was a pioneering feminist in anthropology and inspired many women to enter the field. Esther Newton, one of the first anthropologists to have written about homosexual cultures in America, remembered reading in Mead's *Coming of Age in Samoa* the argument that gender "norms" were subject to cultural forces. This was an epiphany for Newton, who was then struggling to accept her homosexuality. "Mead's work," she writes in *Margaret Mead Made Me Gay* (2000), "taught me that the smug high school peacocks whose dating/popularity values had rated me so low . . . were not lords of the world but only of one nasty barnyard" (p. 2). During her life, Mead became so popular as a writer, teacher, and public speaker on issues of human behavior that *Time* magazine declared her "Mother of the World" in 1969. Although aspects of her research and writing have at times been subjected to harsh criticism, Mead continues to be recognized as an innovative and original thinker on cross-cultural differences pertaining to gender, sexuality, and other aspects of human behavior.

Bibliography

Lapsley, Hilary. *Margaret Mead and Ruth Benedict: The Kinship of Women.* Amherst: University of Massachusetts Press, 1999.

Newton, Esther. *Margaret Mead Made Me Gay: Personal Essays, Public Ideas.* Durham, N.C.: Duke University Press, 2000.

Weston, Kath. *Long Slow Burn: Sexuality and Social Science.* New York: Routledge, 1998.

David A. B. Murray

See also ANTHROPOLOGY; BENEDICT, RUTH.

MEDIA STUDIES AND JOURNALISM

Media studies explores the production, nature, and consequences of electronic and print media messages and involves a highly interdisciplinary approach, drawing from the fields of communication, journalism, sociology, anthropology, history, and literary studies. It utilizes a number of different theoretical perspectives and research methodologies, including empirical and textual analysis, behavioral- and ethnographic-based studies of media impact, and empirical and historical case studies of media production processes. What unites these disparate approaches and efforts is an agreement on research as a critical project whose aim is to raise questions about the role of media in society.

The LGBT movement in the United States has emerged in the context of a rapidly expanding and powerful media environment, and media images are an important source of information in defining LGBT identity and community. Historians have used media sources to document the growth of the LGBT community. Although not properly a part of media studies, such work explores the close relationship between the media and the developing sexual communities in America. George Chauncey (1994) showed in his pre–World War II history of gay New York that while the mainstream press typically ignored the LGBT community, tabloids and neighborhood periodicals covered the emergence of the gay communities in Greenwich Village and Harlem. John D'Emilio's 1983 history of the post–World War II homophile movement chronicles the interaction between mainstream media coverage and the development of the LGBT media, which countered many of the negative images. As he notes, positive mainstream media visibility was a goal of the many homophile activists. Marc Stein's history of the LGBT community in Philadelphia (2000) and Gary Atkins's history of Seattle (2003) draw upon the local press coverage and show the important role of both visibility in the mainstream media and the establishment of a community LGBT media played in community building.

Within the field of media studies since the 1980s, the study of LGBT people and the media has emerged as a defined subfield with its own literature and research agenda. The basic research questions concern how LGBT media images are created and what are the consequences. The field has moved from an earlier focus on criticizing media invisibility and homophobic representations to a concern about the nature and significance of seemingly affirmative LGBT media images.

One major area of research is LGBT representations in the news media. As news media purports to give a factual account of social reality, key topics in research are the nature of authoritative news sources, the process of news gathering and writing, the frames used to interpret events, issues of balance and "objective" reporting, and overall questions of social power associated with the construction of meanings and news narratives. Prior to the 1960s, news media images of LGBT people were typically shaped by narratives of crime and perversion. Edward Alwood's study *Straight News* (1996) provides a general history of how, starting in the 1960s, major news organizations such as the *New York Times* and the television networks responded to LGBT media activists, LGBT media professionals within the news organizations, and growing LGBT political activity, and how they began framing the LGBT community as a minority seeking equality and inclusion into the social mainstream. Timothy Cook and Kevin Hartnett's 2001 empirical analysis of network broadcast news in the 1970s documents how a 1977 Dade County, Florida, referendum provided the LGBT political movement with a presence in national television news. James Kinsella (1989) and Paula Treichler (1987), however, showed how news reporting in the 1980s of the AIDS epidemic revitalized many of the homophobic narratives of gay male sexuality as a sickness. Marion Meyer's 1993 study of coverage of the gays-in-the-military issue in the 1990s revealed a male, heterosexist news narrative reinforcing homophobic myths and stereotypes. While election year coverage on National Public Radio in the 1990s of the LGBT community grew more positive, Kevin G. Barnhust (2003) found a greater reliance on professional LGBT sources and voices to represent the community and a growth in the number and intensity of negative comments to provide news balance. Overall, while the amount of positive news coverage has increased, news narratives still have yet to give LGBT concerns the same legitimacy and status as those of other minorities.

Although entertainment media typically is not given the same authority as news narratives, given its ubiquity and popularity, media scholars regard it as a discourse with far more powerful consequences. The economic and legal environment and audience characteristics are different among the major entertainment media of film, broadcast television, and cable television. Typically, film and cable television have more freedom than broadcast television in depicting LGBT characters and topics. While LGBT content was evident in film since its early days, prior to the late 1970s, there were few neutral, much less positive LGBT images in broadcasting entertainment. However, media scholars like Alexander Doty (1993) have explored the rich possibilities existing for queer readings of nominally straight characters and situations in this period of broadcasting. Responding to LGBT activists, entertainment professionals in the late 1970s began to incorporate more positive LGBT images in programming, and by the late 1990s LGBT visibility had increased.

LGBT visibility on broadcast television is always a few steps behind film and cable television, and breakthroughs in LGBT images occurred first in films like *Boys in the Band* (1970), *Making Love* (1982), and *Torch Song Trilogy* (1988), and on cable television shows such as *And the Played On* (1993). While media scholars happily acknowledge the decline in explicitly homophobic characterizations in the entertainment media, they nonetheless regard the new visibility as fraught with problems. In spite of the increase in positive images, the mainstream entertainment media is programmed for a heterosexual audience. Popular television talk shows typically represent LGBT sexuality as marginal. Although a number of popular prime-time shows have LGBT central characters, (for example, *Ellen* and *Will and Grace*), such portrayals typically present a narrow image of LGBT sexuality and community that does not challenge dominant heterosexual assumptions. And while cable television shows such as *Queer as Folk* present a broader image of gay male sexuality and community, such programming is aimed more at creating a specific viewing audience demographic (young, white, urban, typically male) and less at reflecting the broad characteristics and concerns of the LGBT community. Nonetheless, research by Rodger Streitmatter (2003) suggests that such images have a positive benefit both for LGBT and non-LGBT adolescents.

The LGBT Media

Along with the study of mainstream news and entertainment media, media scholars have also examined the LGBT media. Streitmatter (1995) chronicles the rise of the LGBT press from the early 1950s to its current stage, showing its important role in the formation of LGBT identity and community. On a smaller scale, there has been also the growth of LGBT broadcast programming. LGBT-based community media have been instrumental in community development, both in the past when mainstream media ignored the community and currently in providing a particular LGBT perspective.

Because much of both the mainstream and community media is advertising based, another area of scholarly interest is the development of the LGBT market for advertisers and its impact on media images. As the LGBT market becomes more attractive to advertisers, LGBT media representations are being shaped by the need to reach those groups with the most disposable income, primarily white, Anglo, middle-class, young males. As a result, LGBT community media are functioning less as a "minority media" providing representation of the broad community and more as a lifestyle/market niche media, assembling primarily one segment of the LGBT community as its audience. As a result, many segments of the LGBT community are again becoming "invisible" or marginalized. A focus on LGBT concerns and topics continues to grow as an area of research within media studies. The major media studies scholarly organizations, such as the National Communication Association, the International Communication Association, and the Association for Education in Journalism and Mass Communication, have LGBT studies division and LGBT research panels at their annual meetings. The LGBT advocacy organization Gay and Lesbian Alliance Against Defamation (GLAAD) provides funding for research through its Center for the Study of Media and Society.

Bibliography

Alwood, Edward. *Straight News: Gays, Lesbians, and the News Media.* New York: Columbia University Press, 1996.

Atkins, Gary L. *Gay Seattle: Stories of Exile and Belonging.* Seattle: University of Washington Press, 2003.

Barnhurst, Kevin G. "Queer Political News: Election Year Coverage of the Lesbian, Gay, Bisexual, and Transgendered Community in National Public Radio, 1992–2000." *Journalism* 4, no. 1 (2003): 5–28.

Capsuto, Steven. *Alternate Channels: The Uncensored Story of Gay and Lesbian Images on Radio and Television.* New York: Ballantine, 2000.

Chauncey, George. *Gay New York: Gender, Urban Culture, and the Making of the Gay Male World, 1890–1940.* New York: HarperCollins, 1994.

Cook, Timothy, and Kevin Hartnett. "Splitting Images: The Nightly Network News and the Politics of the Lesbian and Gay Movement, 1969–1978." In *Sexual Identities, Queer Politics.* Edited by Mark Blasius. Princeton, N.J.: Princeton University Press, 2001, pp. 286–318.

D'Emilio, John. *Sexual Politics, Sexual Communities: The Making of a Homosexual Minority in the United States, 1949–1970.* Chicago: University of Chicago Press, 1983.

Doty, Alexander. *Making Things Perfectly Queer: Interpreting Mass Culture.* Minneapolis: University of Minnesota Press, 1993.

Dow, B. J. "Ellen, Television, and the Politics of Gay and Lesbian Visibility." *Critical Studies in Media Communication* 18, no. 2 (June 2001): 123–140.

Duggan, Lisa. *Sapphic Slashers: Sex, Violence, and American Modernity.* Durham, N.C.: Duke University Press, 2000.

Fejes, Fred. "Murder, Perversion, and Moral Panic: The 1954 Media Campaign Against Miami's Homosexuals and the Discourse of Civic Betterment." *Journal of the History of Sexuality,* 9, no. 3 (July 2000): 344–398.

———. "The Political Economy of Lesbian and Gay Identity." In *Sex and Money: Feminism and Political Economy in the Media.* Edited by Eileen R. Meehan and Ellen Riordan. Minneapolis: University of Minnesota Press, 2002.

Fejes, Fred, and Kevin Petrich. "Invisibility, Homophobia, and Heterosexism: Lesbians, Gays, and the Media." *Critical Studies in Mass Communication* 10 (1993): 396–422.

Gamson, Joshua. *Freaks Talk Back: Tabloid Talk Shows and Sexual Nonconformity.* Chicago: University of Chicago Press, 1998.

Gross, Larry. *Up From Invisibility: Lesbians, Gay Men, and the Media in America.* New York: Columbia University Press, 2001.

Gross, Larry, and James D. Woods, eds. *The Columbia Reader on Lesbian and Gay Men in the Media, Society, and Politics.* New York: Columbia University Press, 1999.

Johnson, Phylis, and Michael C. Keith. *Queer Airwaves: The Story of Gay and Lesbian Broadcasting.* Armonk, N.Y.: M. E. Sharpe, 2001.

Kinsella, James. *Covering the Plague: AIDS and the American Media.* New Brunswick, N.J.: Rutgers University Press, 1989.

McCarthy, Anna. "Ellen: Making Queer Television History" *GLQ: A Journal of Lesbian and Gay Studies* 7, no. 4 (2001): 593–620.

Meyers, Marion. "Defining Homosexuality: News Coverage of the Repeal the Ban Controversy." *Discourse and Society* 5, no. 4 (July 1994): 321–344.

Montgomery, Kathryn. *Target Prime Time: Advocacy Groups and the Struggle Over Entertainment Television.* New York: Oxford University Press, 1989.

Penaloza, Lisa. "We're Here, We're Queer, and We're Going Shopping! A Critical Perspective on the Accommodation of Gays and Lesbians in the U.S. Marketplace." *Journal of Homosexuality* 31, no. 1/2 (June 1996).

Russo, Vito. *The Celluloid Closet: Homosexuality in the Movies.* New York: Harper and Row, 1987.

Sender, Katherine. "Gay Readers, Consumers, and a Dominant Gay Habitus: 25 Years of the *Advocate* Magazine." *Journal of Communication* 51 (2001): 73–99.

———. "Business not Politics: Gays, Lesbians, Bisexuals, Transgender People, and the Consumer Sphere." New York: GLAAD Center for the Study of Media and Society, 2002.

Stein, Marc. *City of Sisterly and Brotherly Loves: Lesbian and Gay Philadelphia, 1945–1972.* Chicago: University of Chicago Press, 2000.

Streitmatter, Rodger. *Unspeakable: The Rise of the Gay and Lesbian Press in America.* Boston: Faber and Faber, 1995.

———. "How Youth Media Can Help Combat Homophobia Among American Teenagers." New York: GLAAD Center for the Study of Media and Society, 2002.

Treichler, Paula. "AIDS, Homophobia, and Biomedical Discourse: An Epidemic of Signification." *October* 43 (1987): 31–70.

Walters, Suzanna Danuta. *All the Rage: The Story of Gay Visibility in America.* Chicago: University of Chicago Press, 2002.

Fred Fejes

See also ADVERTISING; FILM AND VIDEO STUDIES; NEWSPAPERS AND MAGAZINES; TELEVISION.

MEDICINE, MEDICALIZATION, AND THE MEDICAL MODEL

One of the most dramatic revolutions in lesbian and gay history, and perhaps the greatest victory of the gay rights movement, is the transformation in medical attitudes toward homosexuality. Many historians, such as Michel Foucault, argue that nineteenth-century physicians constructed the modern concept of homosexuality. "Sodomy" and "pederasty" had long been studied by legal, religious, and medical forensics experts as criminal or immoral acts. However, it was only in Victorian medical literature that the "sexual invert" or "homosexual" emerged as a distinct category of human being with characteristic anatomical, physiological, and neuropsychiatric pathology. In light of many earlier documents attesting to same-sex relationships and identities before and during this period, historians have debated the relative importance of nineteenth-century doctors in constructing homosexual identity. Nevertheless, it does seem clear that the medicalization of homosexuality brought the issue to broad public attention and continues to be a rallying point for homosexual activists.

Contrary Sexual Sensation

Victorian doctors certainly believed that they had discovered a new phenomenon that perplexed, if not terrified, them. The emerging leaders in psychiatry and sexology believed same-sex attraction had to be a profound mental aberration with a biological causation. Initially, German neuropsychiatrists dominated the study of homosexuality. In 1869, Dr. Karl Westphal first described a female patient with "contrary sexual feeling" (*conträre Sexualempfindung*), which consisted of masculine behavior and dress during childhood, and sexual attraction toward women as an adult. Westphal's interest had been sparked in part by a Hanoverian jurist, Karl Heinrich Ulrichs. In a series of pamphlets published from 1864 to 1879, Ulrichs argued that Uranism (as he called it) was congenital, natural, and, therefore, undeserving of legal persecution. Like many of the liberal physicians who studied homosexuality, Ulrichs trusted that science could dispel legal, religious, and cultural prejudice.

Ulrichs was aware of recent discoveries that all mammalian embryos at an early point in development are "bisexual." In other words, they possess both male and female primordial genital tissue before differentiating in either a female or male direction. This original hermaphroditic state suggested that some degree of male and female elements might persist in adults. Ulrichs described himself and others of his kind as possessing "a female soul in a male body." It was the persistent female psychic element of "Urnings" that stimulated their attraction to men. This "psychosexual hermaphroditism" model of homosexuality remained current into the twentieth century. It still underlies neurobiological and endocrinological hypotheses that gay men's brains or the hormonal balance of gay men is more feminine than that of heterosexual men.

The psychosexual inversion model was criticized by European doctors such as Richard von Krafft-Ebing. In *Psychopathia Sexualis* (1886), his ever-expanding encyclopedia of sexual perversities, Krafft-Ebing emphasized that most inverts did not display cross-gendered anatomy. Nevertheless, he believed that homosexuality was an innate neuropsychiatric disorder resulting from hereditary degeneration. Many of the homosexuals who corresponded with him were educated, masculine men, and his stance on their degenerate nature softened in his later years. He even testified on behalf of homosexual men and opposed German anti-sodomy laws.

Magnus Hirschfeld, who lived in Germany, was the first openly homosexual physician to promote biological studies of homosexuality. He conceptualized it as an intermediate state between complete maleness and complete femaleness and attributed it to the balance of sex hormones. Until the Nazis closed his Institute for Sexual Science in 1933, Hirschfeld lobbied tirelessly on behalf of homosexual rights. Hirschfeld usually encouraged his patients to accept their sexual variation, yet on several occasions he did refer distressed homosexual patients to Dr. Eugen Steinach for experimental castration and transplantation with heterosexual testes. In most of the published medical cases, distraught homosexuals voluntarily subjected themselves to painful and dangerous medical procedures hoping to conform to familial and social norms.

Pathologization Versus Biologization

Many of the doctors who engaged in biological research of homosexuality hoped this work would provide a means of detecting and potentially treating what they regarded as inversion. Following humoral conceptions of illness, some nineteenth-century physicians recommended dietary therapies and exercise just as they did for the treatment of masturbation. Steinach's endocrinological approach gained credibility after the discovery of the sex hormones in the 1920s. Claims that male homosexuals had low levels of male hormones, however, proved false. This did not stop some clinicians from using androgen shots—which tended to increase homosexual behavior, not transform it into heterosexual behavior.

The biologization of homosexuality, however, did not necessarily imply its pathologization. From the mid-nineteenth century until today, homosexual researchers and heterosexual scientists sympathetic to the social plight of gays have tried to prove that homosexuality is "natural," biological, and unalterable, hoping that this might result in homosexuality's wider acceptance. Like Ulrichs or Hirschfeld, these gay-friendly scientists have insisted that homosexuality is not a pathology but a natural biological variant. Particularly from the Roaring Twenties until World War II, there were numerous positive depictions of homosexuality in the medical literature (see sidebar).

Freudian Views of Inversion

Sigmund Freud's groundbreaking *Three Essays on the Theory of Sexuality* (1905) introduced the fundamental psychoanalytic notions of infantile sexuality: the oral, anal, and phallic stages of psychosexual development; the castration complex; and penis envy. Despite his lack of clinical experience with homosexuals until then, Freud made sexual inversion the subject of the first essay as well as the final section, entitled the "Prevention of Inversion." Freud disagreed with Krafft-Ebing's neurodegenerative model of the sexual perversions. Instead, Freud argued that "sexual aberrations" were universal, primitive, infantile capacities. The newborn could potentially find any part of the body erotogenic; furthermore, all children went through a phase of "latent homosexuality" until conventional heterosexual object choice developed at puberty. Although Freud was surprisingly radical in suggesting the universality of homosexuality, he was nonetheless a man of his time, since he believed that heterosexual, reproductive sexuality was the only normal, healthy developmental outcome. For Freud, homosexuality was a form of arrested, infantile sexual development resulting from pathological parent-child dynamics. However, Freud did not believe that homosexuals were necessarily unhappy or dysfunctional people, nor did they need to be "cured." Indeed, he was not optimistic about the psychoanalytic treatment of homosexuality per se.

Dr. Abraham Brill, one of Freud's early American promoters, was even more adamant about this. He noted that "Homosexuality is a very wide-spread manifestation.... [I]t affects persons from every stratum of society and every walk of life.... Homosexuality is not a sign of insanity or of any mental deficiency" (p. 249). He claimed to have been consulted by over five hundred homosexuals, few of whom sought treatment "with the idea of becoming sexually normal" (p. 250). Those who did were either neurotics with deep conflicts about their sexuality or were forced into treatment by their families. Brill argued that psychoanalysis of homosexuals who were coerced into therapy and did not want to be cured was a waste of time and money. It was more useful to encourage the family to be broad-minded: "[Homosexuals] should be allowed to follow their own existence, and very often you will find that some of them will turn out to be persons of the highest types, who will contribute much to the understanding and welfare of mankind" (p. 252).

Screening Out Homosexuals

In print, American analysts did not criticize Freud's liberal stance on homosexuality. Privately, however, many harbored a moralistic disdain for homosexuality and American analytical institutes refused to admit openly homosexual candidates into training. Upon Freud's death in 1939 and with the U.S. entry into World War II, the psychoanalytic literature on homosexuality took a vocal turn toward pathologization—if not demonization. In 1940, psychoanalyst Sandor Rado challenged Freudian orthodoxy by denying the universality of infantile bisexuality and insisting that homosexuality was distinctly pathological and potentially curable. Typically, analysts found a pathological family dynamic behind homosexuality: a "close binding," overprotective mother and a detached, hostile father. Some psychoanalysts even advocated the use of hormone and shock therapies to break down the resistance of recalcitrant homosexual patients.

Psychoanalysts also gained enormous professional clout thanks to their involvement in the war effort. The Selective Service wanted to screen out homosexual inductees who might falter under pressure and later be a burden on the veteran health system available to veterans of the U.S. armed forces. "Homosexual proclivities" was one category of the mental handicaps to be referred for expert scrutiny and exclusion. Psychiatrists also assessed for "reclaimability" (i.e., the capacity to return to service) the thousands of servicemen diagnosed with "pathological sexuality" (most of whom were accused of homosexuality).

Homosexual Panic and Schizophrenia

The stresses of war and crowded all-male living conditions seem to have prompted numerous cases of panic or

in defense of homosexuality

William J. Robinson was Chief of the Department of Genito-Urinary Diseases and Dermatology at the Bronx Hospital in New York City. He was a friend of homosexual sexologist Magnus Hirschfeld, whose work he frequently praised. As editor of the *American Journal of Urology and Sexology,* Robinson often published items on homosexuality, including a touching letter from an anonymous "invert," who wrote in 1919:

> [It] is my belief that two men who love each other have as much right to live together as a man and a woman have. Also that it is as beautiful when looked at in the right light and far more equal! . . . May I not have as high an ideal in my love towards men, as a man towards a woman? Higher no doubt, than most men have toward women! (p. 455)

Dr. Florence Beery, who relied on the biological model of congenital bisexuality, was positively enthusiastic about homosexuals. Writing in the *Medico-Legal Journal* of 1924, she declared:

> Homo-sexuals are keen, quick, intuitive, sensitive, exceptionally tactful and have a great deal of understanding. . . . Contrary to the general impression, homosexuals are not necessarily morbid; they are generally fine, healthy specimens, well developed bodily, intellectual, and generally with a very high standard of conduct" (p. 5).

She ridiculed doctors' desperate search for cross-sexed anatomical traits and insisted that generally the "homogenic woman" had a thoroughly feminine body. It was the lesbian's temperament that was "active, brave, originative, decisive," Beery asserted. "Such a woman is fitted for remarkable work in professional life or as a manageress of institutions, even as a ruler of a country" (p. 7).

psychotic reactions associated with homosexual anxiety. Dr. Edward Kempf first called this "homosexual panic" and subsequent psychiatrists sometimes referred to it as "Kempf's disease." In Kempf's textbook on *Psychopathology* (1921), he described typical cases in which a young soldier became convinced that friends or comrades believed he was homosexual, stared at him oddly, whispered insults like "cock sucker," "woman," "fairy," and tried to engage him in fellatio or sodomy. Kempf explained that homosexual panic resulted from repressed "perverse sexual cravings" (p. 477). In the most severe cases, it became chronic and was indistinguishable from dementia or schizophrenia.

Freud (1911) had proposed earlier that paranoia was frequently the result of repressed homosexuality being transformed through the defense mechanisms of reaction formation ("I hate him") plus projection ("he hates me"). Analysts suspected that homosexuality was at the root of all cases of schizophrenia. One analyst even called schizophrenia the "twin brother" of homosexuality. Homosexuality increasingly became the culprit for much other psychopathology, such as neurotic disorders, alcoholism, even promiscuous heterosexuality. Thus, homosexuality was a central problem for psychoanalysis as well as a common reason for lengthy treatment.

Sexual Inversion and Transsexualism

The psychosexual hermaphroditism or inversion model focused on same-sex loving men with supposedly feminine temperaments, behavior, and bodily traits. Conversely, lesbians were characterized as mannish in personality, dress, and anatomy. Some inverts, such as Ulrichs, endorsed these stereotypes because they genuinely seemed accurate. However, some homosexuals and experienced doctors noted that many "inverts" were completely unremarkable in their gender presentation. Early-twentieth-century doctors began to separate the different components of sexuality and gendered behavior and identity. Freud in 1905 made the distinction between "sexual object" and "sexual aim": the object being the type of person or fetish one found erotic, the aim being the type of acts that were erotic.

In *The Transvestites* (1910), Hirschfeld coined the term "transvestitism" to describe the erotic impulse to cross-dress. However, sexologist Havelock Ellis noted that for some people cross-dressing was not titillating, but the natural expression of their sexual identity. Indeed, many of Hirschfeld's cases would be characterized today as "transsexual." Hirschfeld was the first to use this term, but he did so in connection with "intersexual" or hermaphroditic constitution. He was also the first physician to refer patients for partial sex reassignment surgery, beginning in 1912. The first complete male-to-female "genital transformation" surgeries were performed in Berlin in 1931 on two patients classified as "homosexual transvestites."

The matters of sexual object, sexual aim, dress, and gender identity continued to be jumbled together until the 1950s. For example, George Jorgensen made world headlines in 1952 when she returned from Denmark as Christine, yet her doctors had diagnosed her with "genuine transvestitism." It was only in the 1960s that specialists, such as endocrinologist Harry Benjamin, began to distinguish transsexualism from homosexuality or transvestitism. Sex reassignment surgery and hormones became legitimized as a treatment for transsexualism after the Johns Hopkins Hospital began to offer them in 1966. The diagnoses of "transsexualism" and "gender identity disorder of childhood" were first included in the third edition of the *Diagnostic and Statistical Manual of Mental Disorders* (DSM)—the official classification manual published by the American Psychiatric Association (APA)—in 1980. It remains a contested diagnosis, like that of homosexuality, which was listed in the DMS-I (1952) as a type of sociopathic personality disturbance.

Challenges to the Medical Model

The pathologization of homosexuality was undermined with the publication of *Sexual Behavior in the Human Male* (1948) by Alfred C. Kinsey, Wardell Pomeroy, and Clyde Martin. Popularly known as the "Kinsey Report," this survey of over five thousand men revealed astoundingly high rates of homosexual behavior (as well as masturbation and other extramarital sex) among white American men. Kinsey found that 37 percent of his subjects had engaged in at least one homosexual act to the point of orgasm at some time between adolescence and old age (p. 650). This statistic spurred activist Harry Hay to organize the hidden gay population, forming the first "homophile" group—the Mattachine Society in Los Angeles.

Many psychiatrists and sexologists objected to Kinsey's findings and were offended by his stinging critiques of both hormonal and psychoanalytic theories of homosexuality. Most notably, Kinsey argued that sexual orientation was not binary (either hetero- or homosexual) or fixed over one's lifespan. He introduced a 0 to 6 scale to classify behavior on a continuum from exclusively heterosexual (0) to exclusively homosexual (6). He found that 10 percent of men are "more or less exclusively homosexual (i.e., rate 5 or 6) for at least three years between the ages of 16 and 55" (p. 651). This became the oft quoted "10 percent" figure of gays in the population. If indeed homosexuality was so prevalent, it was either the most common psychiatric disorder or not a disorder at all.

Further challenges to the pathological view of homosexuality came from psychologist Evelyn Hooker at the University of California, Los Angeles. One of her homosexual students introduced her to the gay community of Los Angeles and urged her to examine non-clinical subjects. Previous research had been skewed by its reliance on prison cases or homosexuals seeking psychiatric treatment. In the 1940s, Hooker began conducting psychological testing of non-patient homosexuals and found that they did not significantly differ in their psychological adjustment from heterosexual controls matched for age and educational level. She started to publish her findings in the late 1950s and was a welcome speaker at homophile meetings. Hooker chaired a National Institute of Mental Health research panel on homosexuality that ultimately criticized the widespread mistreatment of homosexuals. Rather than recommending conversion, the panel suggested that the best way of improving homosexuals' mental health was by decriminalizing homosexuality and promoting social acceptance.

Analysts Defend Their Practice

Psychoanalysts reacted with skepticism, if not outright fury, to research suggesting that homosexuality was not a severe disorder. Edmund Bergler, a Viennese analyst who emigrated to New York in 1937, was the most strident critic of Kinsey. Bergler insisted that homosexuality was intrinsically a severe neurotic disease; therefore, if Kinsey's percentages were to be believed, homosexuality would be the most common psychopathology in the U.S. He feared that any public acceptance of homosexuality would only promote it. Writing in the midst of the Cold War, Bergler warned that Kinsey's work would be exploited to stigmatize the image of the U.S. Bergler was a tireless self-promoter whose publications and media statements reiterated his conviction that homosexuals were "psychic masochists" with an aggressive oral compulsion that fueled promiscuous, self-destructive sex. Analysts found a scientific validation of sorts in a large survey by Irving Bieber titled *Homosexuality: A Psychoanalytic Study,* and published in 1962. Members of the Society of Medical Psychoanalysts answered a long questionnaire about their homosexual patients; these were compared to results on heterosexual patients. Bieber made no attempt to study non-patient homosexual men. He interpreted the findings as reinforcing analytic dogma that homosexuality was an irrational defensive reaction to a pathological, emasculating childhood. Bieber was nevertheless optimistic that younger homosexuals who persevered in analysis (beyond 350 hours) could achieve a "heterosexual adaptation."

Gays Revolt

A variety of behaviorist conversion therapies were being actively promoted in the 1950s and 1960s. Electrical shock aversion therapy (first used to treat alcoholism in the 1920s), chemical aversion therapy with emetics (developed in the 1950s), covert sensitization, and other conditioning techniques all tried to reorient erotic attraction by associating homoerotic images with discomfort. Like other forms of "treatment" for homosexuality, they generally failed in the long run and provoked visceral opposition by homophile activists in the 1950s and 1960s, proponents of gay liberation, lesbian feminists, and gay rights activists who had become more vocal after the Stonewall riots of 1969. At the 1970 annual meeting of the APA, Dr. Nathaniel McConaghy's presentation on aversive conditioning exploded in gay pandemonium as gay activists accused him of being a vicious torturer.

The work of Kinsey, Hooker, and others all emboldened a new generation of post-Stonewall gay liberation activists ready to engage in dramatic and confrontational tactics, including disrupting APA meetings and demanding equal time to refute the theories of pathologizers. With the assistance of key supporters within the APA, a panel of non-patient gays spoke at the 1971 APA meeting. At the association's 1972 meeting, a gay psychiatrist appeared in disguise to discuss the prejudice he faced within the profession. That year the APA's Nomenclature Committee began considering the pathological status of homosexuality as presented in the second edition of the DSM in 1968. There was extensive debate on the subject at the 1973 meeting, and more psychiatrists supported reform. After much behind-the-scenes lobbying both for and against depathologization, the APA Board of Trustees voted on 15 December 1973 to delete homosexuality from the DSM. Sensitive to many psychoanalysts' deep theoretical and emotional commitment to the pathological status of homosexuality, the Board added the diagnosis of "sexual orientation disturbance" (later named "ego-dystonic homosexuality") for individuals who are distressed by their homosexuality. Newspapers around the world reported on the decision, with one journalist wryly noting that it was the single greatest cure in the history of psychiatry.

Many prominent psychoanalysts, such as Charles Socarides and Irving Bieber, were outraged and mounted a vocal battle against the change, ultimately forcing it to a vote among the APA membership. In 1974, a majority of APA members ratified the declassification of homosexuality as a mental illness. The American Psychological Association followed suit in 1975 and the National Association of Social Workers in 1977. Gay and lesbian caucuses were formally recognized within all these organizations. The American Psychoanalytic Association proved most resistant to such changes, and only in 1992 did this organization officially reversed its long-standing policy of excluding homosexuals from advancement in psychoanalytic institutes. However, in 2002 it defended gay/lesbian parenting rights before the APA took an identical stance.

Continuing Challenges

The emergence in 1981 of a new and mysterious immunodeficiency syndrome among gay men reassociated homosexuality and disease in the public discourse. Acquired Immunodeficiency Syndrome (AIDS) would soon become a global epidemic. Because it particularly devastated a generation of gay men, AIDS impelled gay activists to create community-based systems of care and to lobby for greater government attention to gay health. While numerous lesbian and gay doctors and researchers have focused their attention onto AIDS, many others have explored related issues affecting the community, such as the coming-out process, queer adolescents, alcoholism and substance abuse, gay parenting, and lesbian health.

In the 1990s there was a resurgence of scientific research on the causes of homosexuality—although now conducted by openly gay scientists. In a study of twins, Richard Pillard and J. Michael Bailey claimed to have found evidence of a hereditary factor in homosexuality. Dean Hammer sought evidence of the maternal transmission of homosexuality and presented data suggesting an association between homosexuality and the X chromosome in men. Relying on a small sample, Simon LeVay found suggestive evidence of neuroanatomical differences between homosexual and heterosexual men's hypothalami. Although these studies still await further confirmation (and they have been criticized in many quarters), they received great amounts of media attention and were prematurely accepted as conclusive by some. Research into the biology of transsexualism has been quite limited, but small studies from the Netherlands suggest characteristic neuroanatomical differences between transsexuals and non-transsexuals.

While many transsexuals, like many lesbians and gay men, favor biological models of gender and sexuality, some transsexual activists in the 1990s argued that the medical model was rigid and prescriptive in its insistence on full hormonal and surgical sex transition as a means of "curing" transsexuals. Many activists preferred the term "transgender" to designate a broad range of nonconformist gender identities and roles where sex reassignment surgery may or may not be desired. Transgendered professionals have become increasingly active in health care associations. Thanks to their input the Harry Benjamin International Gender Dysphoria Association's

"Standards of Care for Gender Identity Disorders" have evolved significantly since their first version of 1979. The suggested guidelines for treatment of transgenderism are now less pathologizing, more focused on overall psychological self-fulfillment, and they have reduced the time delays and evaluation costs of obtaining sex reassignment hormones and surgery. The inclusion of Gender Identity Disorder in the DSM has also been contested. Many activists argue that this pathologizes transgenderism, whereas others see the diagnosis as a pragmatic necessity for justifying insurance coverage for sex reassignment hormones and surgery.

In the span of a century, the diagnosis of homosexuality has come full circle: from being "discovered" as a profound psychiatric illness to being declared nothing of the sort. Furthermore, people with a diversity of sexualities (such as bisexuals, transgenders, queers, and intersexuals) have gained a political voice and public attention in the process. While mainstream healthcare associations have condemned homophobia, antigay attitudes still persist in society and some clinicians continue to promote "reparative" therapy of homosexuality. As long as cultural bias persists, scientific research on homosexuality and transgenderism will undoubtedly continue to be an object of scientific and social controversy.

Bibliography

Abelove, Henry. "Freud, Male Homosexuality, and the Americans." In *The Lesbian and Gay Studies Reader.* Edited by Henry Abelove et al. New York: Routledge, 1993.

Bayer, Ronald. *Homosexuality and American Psychiatry: The Politics of Diagnosis.* Princeton, N.J.: Princeton University Press, 1981.

Beery, Florence. "The Psyche of the Intermediate Sex." *The Medico-Legal Journal* 41 (1924): 4–9.

Brill, Abraham Arden. "The Psychiatric Approach to the Problem of Homosexuality." *The Journal-Lancet* 55 (1935): 249–252.

Foucault, Michel. *The History of Sexuality. Volume I: An Introduction.* Translated by Robert Hurley. New York: Vintage Books, 1990.

Freud, Sigmund. "Three Essays on the Theory of Sexuality" [1905]. In *Standard Edition,* Vol. 7, pp. 125–243. London: Hogarth Press, 1955.

———. "Psychoanalytic Notes upon an Autobiographical Account of a Case of Paranoia (Dementia Paranoides)" [1911]. In *Standard Edition,* Vol. 12, pp. 1–84. London: Hogarth Press, 1955.

Kempf, Edward John. *Psychopathology.* St. Louis, Mo.: C. V. Mosby, 1921.

Kinsey, Alfred C., Wardell B. Pomeroy, and Clyde E. Martin. *Sexual Behavior in the Human Male.* Philadelphia: W. B. Saunders, 1948.

"Letter from an Invert, A." *American Journal of Urology and Sexology* 15 (1919): 454–455.

LeVay, Simon. *Queer Science: The Use and Abuse of Research into Homosexuality.* Cambridge, Mass.: MIT Press, 1996.

Lewes, Kenneth. *The Psychoanalytic Theory of Male Homosexuality.* New York: Simon and Schuster, 1988.

Meyerowitz, Joanne. *How Sex Changed: A History of Transsexuality in the United States.* Cambridge, Mass.: Harvard University Press, 2002.

Oosterhuis, Harry. *Stepchildren of Nature: Krafft-Ebing, Psychiatry, and the Making of Sexual Identity.* Chicago: University of Chicago Press, 2000.

Rosario, Vernon A. *Homosexuality and Science. A Guide to the Debates.* Santa Barbara, Calif.: ABC-Clio Press, 2002.

Stein, Edward. *The Mismeasure of Desire: The Science, Theory, and Ethics of Sexual Orientation.* New York: Oxford University Press, 1999.

Terry, Jennifer. *An American Obsession: Science, Medicine, and Homosexuality in Modern Society.* Chicago: University of Chicago Press, 1999.

Vernon A. Rosario

See also AIDS AND PEOPLE WITH AIDS; BENJAMIN, HARRY; BIOLOGY AND ZOOLOGY; CRIME AND CRIMINALIZATION; DISABILITY, DISABLED PEOPLE, AND DISABILITY MOVEMENTS; HOMOSEXUALITY AND HETEROSEXUALITY; HOOKER, EVELYN; IMMIGRATION, ASYLUM, AND DEPORTATION LAW AND POLICY; INTERSEXUALS AND INTERSEXED PEOPLE; JORGENSEN, CHRISTINE; KAMENY, FRANKLIN; KINSEY, ALFRED C.; LOBDELL, LUCY ANN; NATIONAL GAY AND LESBIAN TASK FORCE (NGLTF); PSYCHOLOGY, PSYCHIATRY, PSYCHOANALYSIS, AND SEXOLOGY; SEXUAL ORIENTATION AND PREFERENCE; TRANSSEXUALS, TRANSVESTITES, TRANSGENDER PEOPLE, AND CROSS-DRESSERS.

MEMPHIS

Founded in 1819, the city of Memphis sits on the bluffs overlooking the Mississippi River. Its history is often associated with racial conflict and strife. Race riots after the Civil War marred its Reconstruction history, and in the 1890s Memphis journalist Ida B. Wells-Barnett publicized the horrors of lynchings in her town and across the South, focusing in particular on how African American men were terrorized in the name of protecting white women's sexual virtue. Throughout the twentieth century, Memphis saw the rise of, and resistance to, the African American civil rights movement. When one of the movement's most prominent leaders, Dr. Martin Luther King, Jr., came to Memphis to help negotiate an end to the long-standing sanitation workers' strike, he was assassinated at the downtown Lorraine Motel on 4 April 1968.

Although these episodes in Memphis's history are well documented, the city's LGBT past has also found its way into the historical record. One of the most widely known moments of Memphis's pre-Stonewall past is the sensationalized 1892 Alice Mitchell–Freda Ward murder case. The 26 January 1892 *Memphis Appeal-Avalanche* suggested that Mitchell slashed Ward's throat because "her erstwhile bosom friend . . . treated her coldly." The case was conducted as a lunacy inquisition rather than a criminal trial, and the testimony of expert medical witnesses, friends, family, and even Mitchell was published in the local newspaper. In the end, Mitchell was declared insane and committed to the Tennessee State Asylum, where she died in 1898. The way this case was sensationalized is an early example of the social construction of same-sex sexuality as deviant.

Around the same time as the Mitchell–Ward case, the *Memphis Public Ledger* published the story of Marie Hinkle, a professional male impersonator. When Hinkle's engagement at the Broome Variety Theater in Memphis ended, she made plans to travel to New York for another engagement. Two female admirers, Ione and Lizette, wanted to accompany Hinkle to her train and ended up in a fight for Hinkle's attention. In its coverage, the media focused on links between violence and cross-dressing, concepts sexologists routinely employed to make sense of same-sex sexuality at the turn of the twentieth century.

Since Memphis is bordered on the west by the Mississippi River and on the south by the state of Mississippi, urban development concentrated in the east. By World War II two main sites of popular gay life emerged in the downtown and midtown areas of the city. The earliest gay-straight mixed bars included the Rathskeller, the Rendezvous (a landmark barbeque restaurant), and such private bars as the Aristocrat and Raven, all of which were located in the downtown area. In the 1970s and 1980s gay bars opened their doors both downtown and midtown—an area east of downtown where Rhodes College and the University of Memphis are located. Public parks—Court Square and Confederate Park in downtown and Overton Park in midtown—also emerged as sites for cruising and sexual encounters. Building gay and lesbian communities was possible in these milieus—bars and parks—but creating a political community in a conservative atmosphere was considerably more difficult.

Despite public activism on the West Coast with the Mattachine Society and Daughters of Bilitis in the 1950s or on the East Coast with the Stonewall Riots in 1969, gay Memphians displayed little or no political activism during these eras. Prior to the mid-1970s, references to gay community in Memphis likely meant circles of friends, private socializing, and cruising in public parks. Eventually, more public gay institutions emerged. By 1975 Memphis boasted a gay newspaper, a Metropolitan Community Church, public social organizations such as The Queen's Men, and at least five gay bars. With the onset of the AIDS epidemic in the early 1980s, local gay men founded the Aid to End AIDS Committee (ATEAC). Memphis was also home to a thriving drag and female impersonator community.

Although many issues could bring the gay communities in Memphis together, race and gender seemed to keep them apart. As Buring notes in her 1997 study of gay and lesbian Memphis, gay institutions may have appeared to be racially integrated, but blacks maintained a considerable distance because they recognized that the more publicly identifiable gay community mirrored the larger, segregated society. They were a part of the larger black community, but homophobia kept them slightly apart, and as a result, they founded such organizations as the Memphis Committee and Black Gays and Lesbians Allied for Dignity (B-GLAD).

Lesbians in pre-Stonewall Memphis created social networks through local gay and mixed bars and the city's softball leagues, which enabled women to socialize and form relationships with other women, many of whom were also lesbians. Memphis lesbians during this time adopted femme/butch roles. With the rise of gay liberation occurring at the same time as the women's liberation movement, many lesbians in Memphis also joined local feminist organizations, particularly the Memphis chapter of the National Organization for Women (NOW). Through NOW, ongoing softball activities, the Memphis Gay Switchboard, and such community institutions as the Bread and Roses delicatessen and the Meristem feminist bookstore, local lesbians created their own communities, but they were never fully racially integrated and black lesbians never developed organizations or bars to cater exclusively to their needs.

Memphis lesbians and gay men boast a history of being socially "out" in the sense that there have been clearly gay spaces, but political activism does not have a strong history among members of the community. Buring suggests that "the force of social conservatism . . . keeps Southern lesbians and gay men from getting involved or 'rocking the boat'" (p. 226). However, gay men and lesbians did move from a marginal existence to an institutional presence in the mid- to late-twentieth century, changing the social, cultural, and political landscape of the city of Memphis.

Bibliography

Buring, Daneel. *Lesbian and Gay Memphis: Building Communities behind the Magnolia Curtain.* New York: Garland Press, 1997.

Duggan, Lisa. "The Trials of Alice Mitchell: Sensationalism, Sexology, and the Lesbian Subject in Turn-of-the-Century America." *Signs* 18, no. 4 (1993): 791–814.

Duggan, Lisa. *Sapphic Slashers: Sex, Violence, and American Modernity.* Durham, N.C.: Duke University Press, 2000.

Gilmore, Stephanie. "The Dynamics of Second-Wave Feminism in Memphis, 1971–1982: Rethinking the Liberal/Radical Divide." *NWSA Journal* 15, no. 1 (2003): 94–117.

Lindquist, Lisa J. "Images of Alice: Gender, Deviancy, and a Love Murder in Memphis." *Journal of the History of Sexuality* 6, no. 1 (1995): 30–61.

Stephanie Gilmore

See also HUNTER, ALBERTA; MITCHELL, ALICE.

MEN OF ALL COLORS TOGETHER. see BLACK AND WHITE MEN TOGETHER (BWMT).

MENOTTI, GIAN CARLO. see BARBER, SAMUEL, AND GIAN-CARLO MENOTTI

MICHIGAN

With its scenic countryside and decaying cities, its union-supported liberalism and church-based conservatism, and its strife and cooperation between African Americans and whites, Michigan has mirrored significant trends in U.S. history. A Midwestern state shaped and defined by the automobile, which also shaped and defined American life in the twentieth century, Michigan has likewise mirrored important trends in America's queer past. Since World War II, the experiences of LGBT Michiganders have reflected and often influenced major social and political developments among LGBT people nationwide.

Pre-Stonewall LGBT Life

As the state's largest city and the "Arsenal of Democracy" during World War II, Detroit served as an early focal point of gay life in Michigan. By the 1950s, the Ten Eleven, the Gold Dollar, the Sweetheart Bar, La Rosa's, the Palais, and other white working-class bars clustered near the downtown radius from which the city's main roadways fanned out of the city. As the African American population grew and many whites migrated to the suburbs, gay bars such as the Woodward and the Brass Rail spread out along the city's thoroughfares. The Escape Lounge, a dance club that opened in a shopping center miles from the city center in the mid-1960s, attracted a more middle-class crowd. The Interchange, with easy access to the nearby Lodge Freeway and Interstate 94, opened in 1969 and soon became home to Detroit's first leather groups, the Tribe and the Selectmen.

In the deeply segregated city, African American LGB people developed a separate queer culture. Black gay men found safe space in female impersonation revues at popular nightspots like the Club Casbah and Uncle Tom's Plantation during the drag craze of the early 1950s. From the 1940s through the 1960s, lesbian Ruth Ellis provided an important social outlet for black women and men "in the life" through private house parties at her Oakland Avenue home.

During the 1950s in Flint, at the time Michigan's second largest city, widely dispersed gay and bisexual men utilized the very automobiles they helped manufacture to reach downtown gay meeting places like the tearoom at the Greyhound bus station, the parking lot of Herrlich's Drug Store, and Melva Earhart's State Bar on Union Street. The car functioned not only as a vehicle for reaching queer locales, but also as an important gay site itself, used for cruising pedestrians and other drivers, its cushy seats a convenient place for sexual encounters. By the late 1950s and early 1960s, less populated Michigan cities proved large enough to support such long-lived lesbian and gay bars as the Flame in Ann Arbor, Papa Joe's in Grand Rapids, and Dutch's in Saginaw. The small town of Saugatuck, an old artist's colony on the coast of Lake Michigan, became a popular summer retreat for gays from Chicago.

As with Cold War attacks on homosexuality throughout the United States, Michigan politicians and police targeted still largely hidden LGB communities during the 1950s. As part of a nationwide sex crime panic, Democratic Governor G. Mennen Williams appointed the Governor's Commission on the Deviated Criminal Sex Offender, which recommended harsher laws for sex crimes—laws promptly enacted by the state legislature. Detroit police harassment of gay men culminated in the high profile "morals" arrests of African American cult leader Prophet Jones at his home in 1956 and pop singer Johnnie Ray outside the Brass Rail in 1959.

Meanwhile, administrators at the University of Michigan (UM) in Ann Arbor pressured lesbian students to withdraw from the university and cooperated with police in widely reported raids on homosexual activity in campus rest rooms. Similar crackdowns took place at Michigan State University (MSU) in East Lansing and at

Wayne State University in Detroit. Despite the harassment by university officials, Michigan college campuses proved to be crucial settings for the creation of LGB friendship networks of students and faculty alike and, consequently, for organizing for social change. Ten years before the Stonewall Riots, Wayne State students Hal Lawson, David Brewer, and Jai Moore led a short-lived Detroit chapter of the Mattachine Society from 1958 to 1960.

Gay Liberation and Lesbian Separatism

Inspired by the explosion of radical activism that followed the Stonewall Riots, gay liberation groups achieved noteworthy institutional and legal breakthroughs in Michigan in the early 1970s. LGB campus organizations emerged at smaller public universities such as Western Michigan in Kalamazoo, Central Michigan in Mount Pleasant, and Grand Valley State in Allendale, as well as the larger Wayne State, MSU, and UM.

Ann Arbor, the home of Students for Democratic Society and a sizable anti–Vietnam War movement, was a particularly fertile ground for the Gay Liberation Front (GLF). In defiance of UM President Robben Fleming, GLF held a conference on homosexuality on campus in 1970, followed over the next few years by various protests, guerilla theater, and "zaps" of unfriendly bars, all aimed at ending the silence of LGB life. In November 1971, activists helped secure the establishment at UM of the Human Sexuality Office, reportedly the first such office in the country, with GLF member Jim Toy and Radicalesbian Cyndi Gair hired as the first "gay advocates."

Collegiate rival cities Ann Arbor and East Lansing enacted pioneering nondiscrimination ordinances in 1972, the same year that Nancy Wechsler and Jerry DeGriek, Human Rights Party members of the Ann Arbor City Council, came out of the closet and became two of the earliest openly lesbian and gay elected officials in the United States. Gay hippie activists in Detroit founded the *Gay Liberator* in 1970 and in June 1972 held the state's first queer march down Woodward Avenue. Two years later, Detroit voters approved a new city charter that included civil rights protections for lesbians and gays.

Separate from the male-dominated gay liberation movement, influential pockets of lesbian feminists in several Michigan cities engaged in community building throughout the 1970s, founding cooperative businesses such as A Woman's Bookstore in Ann Arbor, starting publications such as *Lesbian Connection* in Lansing, and advancing women's music through radio programs such as "Face the Music" in Flint. In 1974, Marilyn Frye began teaching a feminist philosophy course at MSU, and in 1978, lesbians across the state mobilized financial support for the successful court battle of Margareth Miller to keep custody of her daughter Jillian. Inspired by the Boston Women's Music Festival, Lisa Vogel and friends organized the first Michigan Womyn's Music Festival (MWMF) in 1976. The internationally renowned celebration of women's culture drew thousands of pilgrims to 650 acres of land in northern Michigan each summer.

Political schisms within LGB communities demonstrated that community beliefs were far from uniform. How best to challenge patriarchy was highly contested: for example, many Radicalesbians in Ann Arbor decried the prevalent use of drag by gay men as sexist, yet others did not. Some lesbians who worked in a local massage parlor mobilized local sex workers in the late 1970s to protest working conditions and to decriminalize prostitution; other lesbians found this objectionable. Two decades later, the MWMF saw its policy of admitting only biologically born women come under fire. In response to the expulsion of transsexuals, a number of transsexual women and their allies set up Camp Trans outside the gate to the festival in 1993 to protest. The following year, festival producers altered their stance, announcing that the decision of whether attendees were womyn-born womyn would be left to the individual. This, in effect, permitted entrance to transsexuals who felt they had always been female.

Into the Mainstream

The liberation impulse subsided in the mid-1970s as LGB people in Michigan increasingly entered the mainstream. The Association of Suburban People, founded in 1975, became the first notable post-liberation LGB organization in the Detroit metro area. As the number of LGB bars in Detroit doubled in the 1970s—several, like Bookie's and Menjo's, locating along Six Mile Road—white gay men created a gentrified enclave next to Palmer Park. Then, over the next two decades, gays all but abandoned the area as many gay men died of AIDS and others moved to suburbs such as Royal Oak and Ferndale, returning to the Motor City only to bar hop. Ferndale emerged as the new nucleus of Detroit-area LGB life by the late 1980s, when Affirmations Community Center, the Midwest AIDS Prevention Project, and *Cruise* magazine all located on the other side of Detroit's Eight Mile Road boundary.

Elsewhere in Michigan, LGB people asserted a more visible presence within smaller municipalities through Metropolitan Community Church congregations, chapters of Dignity and Integrity, and various political social organizations like the Lansing Association of Human Rights, the Celery City Men's Club, Ann Arbor Frontrunners, and Friends North. Following the 1987 March on Washington, a group of Grand Rapids organizers founded a community center called the Network, soon hosting weekly discussion groups and raising funds for a building on the city's northeast side. One Grand Rapids lesbian remade her neighborhood by purchasing and renovating nearby houses, then renting them to lesbian and straight female friends. She discreetly reshaped her residential street based on a vision of sexual identity and community while purposely resisting white flight to the suburbs.

In October 1977, gay men and lesbian women from across the state came together to form the Michigan Organization for Human Rights (MOHR), which during the 1980s targeted oppression through traditional political mechanisms such as a partially successful court challenge to the state sodomy law and an unsuccessful effort to include sexual orientation in the state's civil rights laws. When MOHR disbanded in the early 1990s, the Triangle Foundation stepped in to continue the quest for equal rights. Triangle's executive director Jeffrey Montgomery played a national role in fighting hate crimes, lobbying Congress, and monitoring the 1995 Oakland County trial of Jonathan Schmitz for the murder of Scott Amedure after the two appeared together on the *Jenny Jones Show*.

The first known cases of AIDS appeared in Michigan in 1982. A year later Evelyn Fisher, an infectious disease specialist at Henry Ford Hospital, joined with a group of concerned gay men to form Wellness Networks, later AIDS Partnership Michigan. Volunteerism and government funding soon supported HIV and AIDS service organizations elsewhere in the state. Responding to the need for AIDS services specifically targeted to African American gay and bisexual men, the Detroit Health Department initiated the Community Health Awareness Group in 1985.

Leaving behind the invisibility afforded by private house parties, Detroit's African American LGB people during the 1980s and 1990s created numerous formal organizations, from the Men of Color Motivation Group and the A. Lorde Collective to the annual celebration Hotter Than July and *Kick!* magazine. In 1984, Off Broadway East opened on Harper. Renee McCoy, executive director of the National Coalition of Black Lesbians and Gays, became founding pastor of Full Truth Unity Fellowship Church in 1989. Still largely segregated from their white counterparts, queer blacks nonetheless pursued similar avenues to mainstream acceptance through social, cultural, and religious institutions.

As fear of AIDS and stigmatization of LGB people gave way to increasing, often begrudging, tolerance, Michigan queers gained new political savvy. In the early 1990s, a Colorado-like anti-LGB ballot proposal launched by a Bay City fish farmer failed through a successful counterattack by the Michigan Campaign for Human Dignity and because Republican Governor John Engler opposed the measure; he feared a loss of tourist dollars. Although Lansing and Ferndale voters overturned nondiscrimination ordinances in the late 1990s, Ypsilanti's ordinance twice survived efforts to repeal it by ballot initiative in 1997 and 2002.

Perhaps the most significant mainstreaming of LGB life in Michigan occurred in the workplace, particularly within the automobile industry due to the shifting attitudes of corporate brass and within the United Auto Workers. While a few gay and bisexual men expressed their sexuality in the shop even before Stonewall—through cross-dressing, flirtation, and trysts—most gay and bisexual men remained closeted at work throughout the 1970s and 1980s. A series of events, including the coming out of retired Ford Vice President Alan Gilmour in Michigan's LGBT newspaper *Between the Lines* in 1996, persistent agitation by queer employees like Ron Woods, and pressure from shareholders, led the industry to include nondiscrimination clauses in union contracts in the late 1990s. In 2000, the big three automakers went a step further, extending domestic partnership benefits to its white-collar and blue-collar workforce throughout the United States.

Bibliography

Allison, April. "A Rich Heritage: The History of Lesbians and Gay Men at Michigan State University." In *Moving Forward: Lesbians and Gay Men at Michigan State University*. Vol. 1. East Lansing: Michigan State University, 1992.

Chauncey, George. "The Postwar Sex Crime Panic." In *True Stories from the American Past*. Edited by William Graebner. New York: HarperCollins, 1993.

Frank, Miriam. "Coming Out at the Point of Production: Queer Male Auto Workers." Paper presented at the 21st Annual North American Labor History Conference, Wayne State University, 17–19 October 2002.

Lavender Information and Library Association. *Artifacts and Disclosures: Michigan's Lesbian, Gay, Bisexual, and Transgender Heritage*. Ann Arbor: University of Michigan School of Information, 2000 [cited 1 November 2002]. Available from www.lgbtheritage.org

Peake, Linda. "'Race' and Sexuality: Challenging the Patriarchal Structuring of Urban Social Space." *Environment and Planning D: Society and Space* 11 (1993): 415–432.

Retzloff, Tim. "Cars and Bars: Assembling Gay Men in Postwar Flint, Michigan." In *Creating a Place for Ourselves: Lesbian,*

Gay, and Bisexual Community Histories. Edited by Brett Beemyn. New York: Routledge, 1997.

Retzloff, Tim. "Gay Liberation: When Michigan Tore Out of the Closets and Into the Streets." *Between the Lines* (June 1994): 10–11.

Rubin, Gayle S., with Karen Miller. "Revisioning Ann Arbor's Radical Past: An Interview with Gayle S. Rubin." *Michigan Feminist Studies* 12 (1997–98): 91–108.

Thorpe, Rochella. "'A House Where Queers Go': African American Lesbian Nightlife in Detroit, 1940–1975." In *Inventing Lesbian Cultures in America.* Edited by Ellen Lewin. Boston: Beacon Press, 1996.

Thorpe, Roey. "The Changing Face of Lesbian Bars in Detroit, 1938–1965." In *Creating a Place for Ourselves: Lesbian, Gay, and Bisexual Community Histories.* Edited by Brett Beemyn. New York: Routledge, 1997.

Tsang, Daniel. "Ann Arbor Gay Purges." *Midwest Gay Academic Journal* 1, no.1 (1977): 13–19.

Tim Retzloff

See also BRANT, BETH; FEMMES AND BUTCHES; HART, PEARL; JONES, PROPHET; LEGG, DORR; *LESBIAN CONNECTION*; MUSIC: WOMEN'S FESTIVALS; TSANG, DANIEL.

MIGRATION, IMMIGRATION, AND DIASPORA

Until quite recently a remarkable paradox has existed at the very center of the study and writing of LGBT and queer history. For while it is nearly impossible to read even a single account of the emergence and development of LGBT identities, communities, and cultures without encountering the usually offhand reference to migration (from the rural to the urban, from the periphery to the metropolis, from the family residence to the private domicile) as the precondition for the existence of these dissident sexualities and genders, LGBT history has for the most part failed to define migration, historicize its different expressions, or theorize the relationship between this phenomenon and non-LGBT practices and identities.

To be sure, there have been significant exceptions. Colonial historians of sexuality and gender have emphasized the critical importance of cultural encounters between three migrating groups: Native American, African American, and Euro-American. John D'Emilio long ago discussed the roles that capitalism, urbanization, and migration played in the emergence of LGBT identities and communities in the late nineteenth century. George Chauncey situates his consideration of gay life in early-twentieth-century New York in the context of working-class immigrant cultures. Nayan Shah analyzes same-sex sexualities within Chinese immigrant bachelor cultures in early-twentieth-century San Francisco. Eric Garber's work on LGBT dimensions of the Harlem Renaissance underscores the importance of the Great Migration of African Americans from the rural South to the urban North. Esther Newton's study of Cherry Grove, Fire Island, analyzes the shorter distances traveled by LGB people who established the first LGB resort in the first half of the twentieth century. D'Emilio and Allan Bérubé, in their work on mass mobilization during World War II, argue that wartime migration helped precipitate a nationwide coming out experience. Manuel Castells, Kath Weston, and Marc Stein have all discussed the LGBT migration streams that created LGBT neighborhoods in many U.S. cities after World War II. Challenging the urban focus of LGBT history, John Howard's study of gay life in Mississippi argues that "circulation is as important as congregation" (p. 14). Joanne Meyerowitz and David Serlin have examined the movement of U.S. transsexuals who traveled to Europe for sex change surgeries in the 1950s and 1960s. And William Eskridge Jr. and Eithne Luibhéid, among others, have written about U.S. immigration restrictions adopted in the 1950s and 1960s to prohibit sexual psychopaths and deviants from entering the United States.

Nevertheless, much work in LGBT studies deemphasizes and de-centers migration, immigration, and diaspora. Why has this been the case? What has enabled LGBT studies to marginalize a phenomenon so intimately bound up with the emergence of homosexuality and transgenderism in the United States? And finally, what are the consequences of situating the emergence and development of perverse sexualities and genders within the political economy of migration?

Marginalizing Migration in U.S. LGBT History

The failure to theorize migration within LGBT studies is all the more remarkable when examining, in particular, U.S. LGBT history. If one considers work on LGBT issues within the domain of literary practice, one discovers that the frequently cited LGBT literati—from Herman Melville, Henry James, Djuna Barnes, and Gertrude Stein to James Baldwin, Paul Bowles, Audre Lorde, and Reinaldo Arenas—were famous for their fictional and nonfictional migrations. Indeed, the long chain of U.S. migrants and emigrants who wrote of matters relating to gender and sexuality has produced the shadow of gender and sexual dissidence behind the "expatriate" whenever that figure is summoned in the United States. And as historians of gender and sexuality have noted, the existence of dissident forms of gendered and sexualized embodiment in everyday life, including the "fairy," the "invert," the "bulldagger," the "intermediate sex," and the "homosexual," in major U.S. cities at the turn of the twentieth century, is inextricable from unprecedented international and internal labor migrations. In other words, both global and local migrations have been and continue to be the fulcrum on which U.S. LGBT genders and sexualities have been invented, sustained, and transformed. And yet much U.S. LGBT historiography and political activism disregards the centrality of migration as the material foundation for the emergence and development of LGBT genders and sexualities.

Metaphors of Migration in LGBT History and Politics

If one tendency has been to ignore the constitutive role of labor migrations in the formation and development of LGBT and queer identities and practices, another marginalizing tendency has been the metaphorizing and appropriation of terms and paradigms specific to the history of migration, immigration, and diaspora for describing LGBT identity and experience. Within academic writing, LGBT identities have often been studied and theorized as an "ethnicity," appropriating a model developed for the study of twentieth-century U.S. communities and social groups formed as a result of European labor migrations. Within popular writing, including the collection *Gay Seattle: Stories of Exile and Belonging* (2003), the dialectic of "exile" and "belonging" has often been taken up to characterize LGBT experiences with family and natal communities. Even the most popular metaphor for organizing and narrating LGBT experience, that of "coming out of the closet," is predicated on a spatial logic of inside and outside space that is both discretely bounded and rigorously enforced, recalling and building upon the existence of national borders and spatially constituted identities.

The appropriation and metaphorizing of paradigms specific to migration and immigration to characterize a predominantly white U.S. experience of LGBT desire and social life have only further displaced the historical experience of those people whose genders and sexualities were and continue to be formed through and intertwined with the historical experience of migration. The use of the ethnicity model for talking about LGBT identity has contributed little to discussions about ethnic working-class communities and the forms of LGBT embodiment and desire that circulate within and through those communities. LGBT studies scholars who use the ethnicity model rarely turn to an analysis of the institutions that generated, regulated, and cemented ethnic working-class culture, such as labor unions, religious organizations, and immigration law. They tend to rely instead on the study of institutions such as psychiatry and psychoanalysis, which, comparatively speaking had little influence on working-class ethnic lives (though, to be sure, many influential psychiatrists and psychoanalysts were themselves immigrants). Similarly, the metaphorizing of "exile" in LGBT popular culture to describe the experience of LGBT life outside of traditional kinship and heterosexual community networks has had the concomitant effect of eschewing knowledge about the sexual and gendered lives of actual modern political and (post)colonial exiles.

The Politics of Migration in LGBT Politics

Only in more recent work in LGBT studies have the circumstances and contexts of migration been theorized and engaged on a more consistent basis. This work, historical, legal, literary, and political in scope, has had the effect of disrupting and pluralizing the LGBT moniker and the organization and meanings of desire that this moniker has tended to stabilize and homogenize. Most centrally, this work has moved to the foreground the centrality of race and class as defining elements within a European capitalist settler-colonial society such as the United States. Most simply, at the core of the work examining questions of migration, immigration, and diaspora in U.S. LGBT historical and contemporary life has been an interrogation of the racialized and classed constraints that form LGBT identities. Twentieth-century U.S. LGBT culture figures the "urban" as the origin point for its historical emergence. And yet, the racialized labor migrations through which U.S. urbanization occurred have supported more heterogeneous "perverse desires" than allowed for by many urban-focused narratives.

Migration, Spatialization, and Alternative Genders and Sexualities

The beginning of the twentieth century was marked in the United States by unprecedented labor migrations. In the decades between 1880 and 1920, between eight and nine million migrants arrived per decade, transforming U.S. life. Along with the industrialization of agriculture and the failure of Reconstruction in the U.S. South, these migrations helped to transform the United States into a majority urban country for the first time. Indeed not only did cities hold the majority of the U.S. population by the beginning of the twentieth century, but also port cities such as New York, whose industries relied heavily on immigrant labor, soon found themselves with immigrant populations that comprised up to 40 percent of their total population. In addition, African American migration to cities in the South and the North, which would later be called the Great Migration, transformed U.S. urban space and public culture, generating racially codified responses from the white urban elite. Within this context the city became a complex field of conflict and contestation between an immigrant and nonwhite laboring class and a mostly native white middle-class bourgeoisie that sought to organize and control the new migrants.

Sexuality and gender figured centrally within elite tactics, often producing a racialized geography that spatially organized sexualized and gendered cultures and practices. Red-light districts, commercial sex resorts, and dance halls and bars within which working-class immigrants and black and other nonwhite migrants invented cultures of embodied pleasure were some of the mainstays of these geographies. Mapped by the activities of reformers, journalists, and vice squads and concentrated within working-class sectors of the city, these geographies, or what Kevin Mumford terms "interzones," contained forms of same-sex and transgender desire that were minimally defined by or produced through dominant cultural groups. As George Chauncey suggests in *Gay New York*, "The institutions and social forms of the gay subculture were patterned in many respects on those of the [immigrant] working class culture in which it took shape: the saloons, small social clubs, and large fancy-dress balls around which fairy life revolved were all typical elements of working-class life" (p. 41). Coinciding with the rise of a white middle-class LGB culture in U.S. urban life, then, was the persistence, within racialized working-class space, of other forms of LGBT desire and embodiment. The "fairy," the "wolf," the "bulldagger," and the "male impersonator" all found expression and legibility within the constraints of the sexualized, gendered, and racialized spaces produced by the intersection of racialized labor migrations and urban reform and policing.

The Sexualization of Citizenship

If the sexualized and gendered spatial organization of urban life operated as one means by which both LGBT and non-LGBT perverse formations emerged simultaneously, immigration policy functioned similarly to expand non-LGBT sexual perversities while simultaneously regulating homosexuality and transgenderism.

As a settler society, the United States relied heavily on international migration as a means for reproducing and increasing its domestic labor force. Yet as a nation-state it maintained a compelling interest in defining its population through citizenship. Immigration law and policy became a powerful apparatus that addressed the differing needs of the economy and the state in defining the national population. And immigration law and policy, in turn, deployed discourses and practices of sexuality and gender, functioning as a means for the state to regulate the sexualities and genders of immigrants, especially immigrants of color. On the one hand, non-"heterosexual" and non-gender-normative immigrants were constituted as an excludable population; on the other hand, racially excludable populations (such as Asian immigrants) were constituted as nonheterosexual and non-gender-normative.

In a series of immigration laws passed in the late nineteenth century, the U.S. government began to incorporate the regulation of sexual and gender difference into the functions of immigration policy. As early as 1875, the U.S. Congress passed the Page Act, which restricted the immigration of both contract workers from Asia and women suspected of engaging in prostitution. Designed to restrict Chinese migration and settlement through gendered and sexualized exclusion, this act and subsequent laws transformed Chinese immigration into a primarily male migration stream from the 1870s to the 1940s. In turn, the predominantly single-sex composition of Chinese immigrant communities, especially in highly visible "Chinatowns," became the object of racist discourses that justified the continued disenfranchisement of Chinese immigrants in part based upon their status as single, unmarried, presumptive sexual deviants. Hence, since the late nineteenth century, immigration policy has functioned to expand both the representations and conditions of sexual and gender variance beyond the modern "homo/hetero" binary naturalized by heterosexual culture. At various moments in the twentieth century, racial discrimination in immigration policy operated through the sexualized and gendered exclusion of female immigrants of color and the unequal right of "white" immigrants to petition for the admission of kin or to have sanctioned sexual relations within the nation.

In addition to these episodes of immigration policy-making during which racial exclusion was effected through sexual exclusion and legitimated through the dissemination of sexualized ideologies, in the 1950s the United States incorporated homophobia as a more explicit orientation of that policy. Earlier immigration laws had excluded those who had been convicted of "crimes of moral turpitude" and those marked by "constitutional psychopathic inferiority." In 1952, the Walter-McCarren Act excluded those "afflicted with psychopathic personality," a phrase generally understood to refer to homosexuality. In 1965, the U.S. Congress passed an amendment to the Walter-McCarren Act, adding "sexual deviation" to the list of grounds for exclusion. The ban on "homosexual" immigration lasted until 1990, at which point new laws were passed to exclude people with AIDS.

While there may be no way of accurately gauging the entire spectrum of effects that the formal exclusion of homosexuality has had on the immigration process, it appears that these regulations, even after their repeal in 1990, constituted the border as a heteronormative space and disproportionately affected in particular the mobility of transgender migrants of color.

Globalization and Diasporic Politics

By 1990, following the modification of racialized immigration restrictions in the 1960s, immigration to the United States had again reached historic proportions. Outpacing the levels reached at the beginning of the century, immigrant arrivals to the United States spiked to ten million people per year for the decades between 1980 and 2000. Even more significant than the sheer size of this migration stream was its composition. Unlike the situation at the turn of the twentieth century, when non-Western migration was racially restricted by legislation, the "new" immigration of the 1980s and 1990s was composed primarily of Latino, Asian, and Caribbean migrants. Concentrated in specific urban cities, including Los Angeles, New York, Miami, Houston, and Chicago, the new immigration of the late twentieth century has been critical in the formation of new transnational economic and cultural spaces in the United States. If turn-of-the-century migration to the United States facilitated the rise of cities within a national economy, "new" immigration has contributed to the rise of the city within a "global" economy. Sutured to the national political economies from which they immigrated—aided by the rise of new media, modes of transportation, and methods of capital transfer—while at the same time marginalized from dominant U.S. culture, new migrants to U.S. cities formed diasporic cultural communities that have intensified connections worldwide.

The effects of the Asian, Latino, and black diasporas of the 1980s and 1990s on LGBT urban politics and culture were numerous and substantive. Within the political sphere there emerged local diasporic LGBT groups such as the South Asian Lesbian and Gay Association (SALGA) and the Colombian Lesbian and Gay Association (COLEGA) in New York City, which maintained political and organizing ties with other groups in the Asian and Latino diaspora and LGBT organizations in their homelands. In addition, pan-diasporic and people of color groups formed coalitional organizations such as the Audre Lorde Project in New York and the Esperanza Project in Texas, which developed specific "Queers of Color" political platforms that distinguished the specificities of racialized homophobia for immigrant, diasporic, and people of color communities. Within the terrain of culture, through the work of diasporic and immigrant of color artists such as Luis Alfaro, Margo Gomez, Brian Freeman, Alina Troyana (a.k.a. Carmelita Tropicana), Richard Fung, Isaac Julian, Shani Mootoo, and many others, a broader expression of LGBT cultural politics developed within the U.S. public sphere. Within these diasporic cultural politics, or what queer black diasporic theorist Kobena Mercer calls "cultures of hybridity," terms such as "lesbian," "gay," "bisexual," "transgender," and even "queer" tend less to refer to a U.S. notion or referent and operate instead like life "rough sketches" that outline the point of imbrication between unevenly mixed cultural systems of non-LGBT desire (Gopinath, 1998). The rise of late-twentieth-century black, Asian, and Latino diasporas within the United States has radically pluralized the referent of non-LGBT desire, while tying U.S. immigrant of color sexual politics and practices to cultural spaces and mediascapes that exceed the limits of the nation-state.

In the ordinary lives of queer diasporics living in the United States, the narratives and logics that organize U.S. LGBT identities have been denaturalized. In his book *Global Divas* (2003), the queer Filipino anthropologist Martin Manalansan has shown how a U.S. LGBT popular culture that continues to center the Stonewall Riots of June 1969 in New York City as the origin point of a "global gay" movement—commemorated annually across U.S. cities in LGBT pride parades—has encountered its limit with diasporic LGBT migrants who, in the very same city, do not identify with that event as the "origin" of their cultural emergence. Instead the emergence of queer diasporic cultural and political formations at the end of the twentieth century continues to be another instance in which U.S. national LGBT identities have been de-centered as the locus of perverse desires within the context of international labor migrations.

Bibliography

Atkins, Gary. *Gay Seattle: Stories of Exile and Belonging*. Seattle: University of Washington Press, 2003.

Bérubé, Allan. *Coming Out under Fire: The History of Gay Men and Women in World War Two*. New York: The Free Press, 1990.

Castells, Manuel. *The City and the Grassroots: A Cross-Cultural Theory of Urban Social Movements*. Berkeley: University of California Press, 1983.

Chapin, Jessica. "Closing America's 'Back Door.'" *GLQ* 4, no. 3 (1998): 403–422.

Chauncey, George. *Gay New York: Gender, Urban Culture, and the Making of the Gay Male World, 1890–1940*. New York: Basic Books, 1994.

D'Emilio, John, "Capitalism and Gay Identity." In *Powers of Desire: The Politics of Sexuality*. Edited by Ann Snitow,

Christine Stansell, and Sharon Thompson. New York: Monthly Review Press, 1983.

———. *Sexual Politics, Sexual Communities: The Making of a Homosexual Minority in the United States, 1940–1970*. Chicago: University of Chicago Press, 1983; 2d ed., with a new preface and afterward, 1998.

Epstein, Steven, "Gay Politics, Ethnic Identity: The Limits of Social Constructionism." *Socialist Review* 43/44 (1987): 9–49.

Eskridge, William N., Jr. *Gaylaw: Challenging the Apartheid of the Closet*. Cambridge, Mass.: Harvard University Press, 1999.

Ferguson, Roderick A. *Aberrations in Black: Toward a Queer of Color Critique*. Minneapolis: University of Minnesota Press, 2003.

Garber, Eric. "A Spectacle in Color: The Lesbian and Gay Subculture of Jazz Age Harlem." In *Hidden from History: Reclaiming the Gay and Lesbian Past*. Edited by Martin Bauml Duberman, Martha Vicinus, and George Chauncey, Jr. New York: New American Library, 1989.

Gopinath, Gayatri. "Homo-Economics: Queer Sexualities in a Transnational Frame." In *Burning Down the House: Recycling Domesticity*. Edited by Rosemary Marangoly George. New York: Westview, 1998.

Howard, John. *Men Like That: A Southern Queer History*. Chicago: University of Chicago Press, 1999.

King, Anthony. *Re-Presenting the City: Ethnicity, Capital, and Culture in the Twenty-First-Century Metropolis*. New York: New York University Press, 1996.

Luibhéid, Eithne. *Entry Denied: Controlling Sexuality at the Border*. Minneapolis: University of Minnesota Press, 2002.

Manalansan, Martin. *Global Divas: Filipino Gay Men in New York City*. Durham, N.C.: Duke University Press, 2003.

Mercer, Kobena. *Welcome to the Jungle: New Positions in Black Cultural Studies*. New York: Routledge, 1994.

Meyerowitz, Joanne. *How Sex Changed: A History of Transsexuality in the United States*. Cambridge, Mass.: Harvard University Press, 2002.

Mumford, Kevin J. *Interzones: Black/White Sex Districts in Chicago and New York in the Early Twentieth Century*. New York: Columbia University Press, 1997.

Muñoz, José Esteban. *Disidentifications: Queers of Color and the Performance of Politics*. Minneapolis: University of Minnesota Press, 1999.

Newton, Esther. *Cherry Grove, Fire Island: Sixty Years in America's First Gay and Lesbian Town*. Boston: Beacon, 1993.

Shah, Nayan. *Contagious Divides: Epidemics and Race in San Francisco's Chinatown*. Berkeley: University of California Press, 2001.

Stein, Marc. *City of Sisterly and Brotherly Loves: Lesbian and Gay Philadelphia, 1945–1972*. Chicago: University of Chicago Press, 2000.

Weston, Kath. "Get Thee to a Big City: Sexual Imaginary and the Great Gay Migration." *GLQ* 2, no. 3 (1995): 253–277.

Chandan Reddy

See also AFRICAN AMERICANS; ARAB AMERICANS; ASIAN AMERICANS AND PACIFIC ISLANDERS; CLASS AND CLASS OPPRESSION; JEWS AND JUDAISM; LATINAS AND LATINOS; NATIVE AMERICANS; RACE AND RACISM; URBAN, SUBURBAN, AND RURAL GEOGRAPHIES.

MILITARY

Life in the U.S. military has long created opportunities for intimacy between service personnel of the same sex, including many who were not primarily homosexual. For more than half a century, many soldiers, sailors, flyers, and others in the armed forces have been relatively open about their same-sex attraction. However, the more common experience is of living under regular threat of punishment by prosecution or discharge, designed to enforce the heterosexual orthodoxy of the military. There seemed briefly a chance that the ban on lesbians and gays serving openly in the military would be lifted during the early days of the Clinton presidency, but hopes were quickly dashed. The United States now stands as one of a rapidly diminishing cluster of countries in the industrialized world where military effectiveness is presumed to be at risk in the absence of such a ban.

The retention of the ban illustrates the daunting challenge facing sexual diversity activists in the United States. Despite the considerable gains in LGBT visibility achieved since the 1960s and the substantial organizational vitality of political activism on sexual orientation issues, the impediments to removing even such basic policy discrimination are imposing. Sexual minority activists confront a strong religious right, a battery of Republican politicians (with a minority of Democrats) prepared to play anti-LGBT cards, a fragmented political system making any legislative progress difficult, and a constitutional rights framework not offering much defense. On this issue in particular, they face armed services united in their opposition to lifting the ban, in a country whose military wields extraordinary political power—with substantial popular support. Admitting that openly lesbian or gay service personnel could remain in the military would challenge an institution with male dominance, hypermasculinity, and heterosexual supremacy at its cultural core. Acceptance of LGBT service people would undermine this important tenet.

Pre-1940s History

The discharge of military personnel for homosexual behavior dates from at least the continental army of the revolutionary period. Prohibitions on homosexual behavior were formulated more explicitly as provisions in the Articles of War prepared in 1916 and 1920, prohibiting sodomy and treating homosexual behavior as criminal. Such policy formally targeted behavior, but the concept of the homosexual person was becoming more widely embraced at the time and formed the basis of recurrent witchhunts. It was at this time that the military began psychological screening to keep out those deemed unfit, including those who displayed "the stigmata of degeneration" or who showed other signs of "sexual perversion," though implementation was halting and uneven. In 1919, an investigation and entrapment strategy was launched at the Naval Training Station in Newport, Rhode Island, not coincidentally timed to take place directly after the end of World War I (during which all available personnel were retained). The result was the courts-martial and imprisonment of sailors presumed to be homosexual, though the national publicity given the episode led to much criticism of the entrapment methods employed. In 1920, a U.S. Senate subcommittee condemned the Newport operation, calling unsuccessfully for an end to prison sentences for "perverted acts" and for medical response instead. This would be the last sustained reformist voice for some decades.

World War II and Its Aftermath

In a period of accelerating registration for military service, the Selective Service in 1941 added "homosexual proclivities" to the list of disqualifiers guiding volunteer physicians working at draft boards, effectively shifting formal policy toward the exclusion of a category of person with homosexual tendencies, and framing it as an illness rather than a sin or crime. These policies were aimed initially at men; only in 1944 did the Women's Army Corps develop policies that explicitly included homosexuality as a disqualifier. For all those who were pursued, the punishment meted out for transgression was generally a dishonorable discharge rather than imprisonment. Some leeway was created for those thought "treatable" or whose transgression was thought momentary, though within a context of more uniformly exclusionary policy.

That said, the need to maximize recruitment during wartime created semi-official laxness in the ban, and there were innumerable cases of service members known to be homosexuals retained throughout the war. The isolation of military personnel from family and home community increased the capacity to experiment. Even if official norms about sexuality inside the military were unwelcoming of homosexuality, here and elsewhere the crucible of war expanded the range of social and cultural tolerance. Anecdotal evidence compiled by Alan Bérubé (1990) and Randy Shilts (1993) reveals the many settings in which same-sex activity and sustained relationships were frequently given room by comrades and officers.

Wartime mobilization also saw the recruitment of women into otherwise male-dominated manufacturing jobs. This challenged traditional gender norms and created a degree of independence for women now being paid much better wages than before and often geographically dislodged from their home communities. The explosion of military and industrial activity during this time fueled the growth of commercial establishments in large cities catering to diverse clientele. A port city like San Francisco, with a large military presence, was fertile ground for bars known to have queer patronage.

The war years nurtured expectations for social and political change, and particularly for greater equity. The reform pressures intensified by the deprivations and demands of war included those focused on race and led in 1948 to U.S. President Harry Truman's executive order paving the way for racial desegregation in the military. This flew in the face of persistent claims from the military's own high ranks that such a move would compromise cohesion and effectiveness. The same year saw U.S. congressional action aimed at integrating women more thoroughly into the armed services (short of combat roles). The short-lived surge of progressive ideas soon included calls for change on sexual diversity fronts, made by homophile groups like the Mattachine Society.

But no shift in military policy on sexuality would come soon. The integration of policies for the separate armed services following World War II led to more uniform policies that prohibited sodomy ("unnatural carnal copulation") and effectively excluded lesbians and gay men. The intensification of public rhetoric aimed at communism entrenched such policies more deeply than ever. In the military, the U.S. State Department, and other branches of government, homosexuals were portrayed as ideal prey for spies. Military discharges increased dramatically through this period, and grew further in the 1960s, except during the Korean War (and later the Vietnam War), precisely the times when the argumentation behind the discharges would be at their most forceful, but also the periods when military personnel needs were at their greatest.

The wave of activism on sexual diversity in the period beginning in the late 1960s did not at first include much attention to the military ban, informed as it was by deep suspicion of the armed forces as embodying an essentially irretrievable culture of oppression. Even as the movement developed a larger mainstream current in the 1980s, challenging military exclusion was not a priority.

But service members and their allies had by then mounted challenges to the military's policy. Air Force

Sergeant Leonard Matlovich did so in the mid-1970s, spurred by a public call by veteran activist Franklin Kameny for a test case to challenge the military's policy and aided by a lawyer associated with the Military Law Project of the American Civil Liberties Union (ACLU). He and others who followed had no effect on policy, but they made gay and lesbian military personnel visible, and helped embolden further activism.

By the 1980s, reform pressures and internal conflict had led the military to confront the extent to which blacks and women were harassed and otherwise marginalized in the services. But there was only token change in the outlook on sexual diversity. The rationale behind exclusion shifted from the language of security risk to unit cohesion and morale. Over the 1980s, an average of 1,500 discharges a year were based on this rationale, though there were far fewer during the U.S.-led 1991 offensive in the Persian Gulf. There were more men than women among the victims of the ban, but the proportion of women in the services subject to such discharge was higher.

By the time of the Gulf War, women were more visible in the military and occupied a wider variety of roles. Congress lifted the formal exclusion of women from combat roles in 1991, and while this accelerated internal debates over male-female relations inside the military, there could be no real question that the attitudinal environment into which more women were being integrated was being seriously challenged on gender or sexuality dimensions. The Tailhook scandal of 1991, in which a large military convention saw widespread harassment and assault directed at women, provided national exposure to a culture that appeared to have changed little over a period of ostensible reform.

The Clinton Period

When Bill Clinton was vying for the Democratic presidential nomination in the fall of 1991, he responded to a question on the military ban by committing to an executive order lifting it. The issue was still not a front-burner issue for most sexual diversity activists, though the turn of the decade had seen some increased attention to it. In 1988, the National Gay and Lesbian Task Force created the Military Freedom Project, partly in response to an anti-lesbian witchhunt at the military's Parris Island base. Around that time, cracks seemed to appear in the military's own defense of the ban. Between 1989 and 1991, three Pentagon studies admitted that homosexuals were qualified for military service and questioned some of the rationales behind the ban. Openly gay U.S. Representative Gerry Studds publicized those findings, giving the issue additional media coverage. Clinton's promise helped further shift the issue to the front burner.

When Clinton secured the nomination and then won the November election, expectations for greater equity in national policy across a range of fields ran exceedingly high. On the military ban, they were fueled by assurances from the transition team that action would be taken very quickly after the president's inauguration.

However, several factors began undermining the commitment in January 1993. Republicans and conservative Democrats in Congress immediately displayed a willingness to publicly oppose the move. The religious right, veterans groups, and other conservatives also began to mobilize public opposition, creating an extraordinary firestorm of protest immediately after the president's inauguration.

Public opinion surveys over the previous fifteen years had shown steady increases in support for allowing lesbians and gays to serve, up to 69 percent. But such support had always coexisted with substantial majority disapproval of homosexuality and as a result was soft and volatile. The anti-LGBT mobilization following Clinton's January inauguration dropped public support for his proposal to less than 50 percent and increased impatience at the new president spending time on this issue rather than on the economy.

With General Colin Powell as chair of the Joint Chiefs of Staff, military commanders whipped up opposition to the plan among service personnel. The military had long enjoyed political prestige in the United States, and relative immunity to the skepticism so widely shown toward public sector institutions. The Persian Gulf War in fact had heightened the military's standing, and General Powell's. This allowed for near-insurrectionary mobilization against the presidential initiative. Powell personally and publicly opposed lifting the ban, and his African American background gave him undeserved credibility in countering claims that the military's opposition to the president's proposal had parallels to the military's resistance to racial desegregation in the 1940s.

It was not hard to demonstrate that most military personnel were angrily opposed to lifting the ban. Artfully reproduced images of close sleeping quarters on submarines and shared shower facilities in various military branches evoked visceral insecurities and prejudices. The demographics of the military ensured that opinion would in any event be more socially traditional than in the public. Surveys had always shown that anti-LGBT sentiment was relatively more widespread among men, those with less education, and those from smaller cities and towns. In other words, the population sectors providing the military's most important recruitment pools were those most likely to breed social conservatism.

Democratic Senator Sam Nunn led the charge from his powerful position as chair of the Armed Services Committee. In the spring, his committee held hearings on the matter, heavily tilted toward opponents of Clinton's proposal. By then it was clear that a removal of the ban would not survive congressional action, and an administration already perceived as having low credibility on military issues began to pull back.

Openly gay Democratic House member Barney Frank, sensing total defeat in Congress, suggested a compromise in May that was dubbed "don't ask, don't tell," meaning that members of the military could not be queried about their sexual orientation and should not speak about being lesbian or gay, voluntarily or in response to questions. This dismayed activists who still believed that the ban could be lifted. By the summer, the administration acquiesced in a proposal from Sam Nunn that was also labeled "don't ask, don't tell," but effectively gave the military more leeway. The ban was effectively still in place, more rigidly so because it was soon to be encoded in statute (and not just regulations). Clinton made matters worse by pretending that the ultimate version was a compromise when it was a defeat, thereby helping to deceive many observers (including much of the mainstream media) that the new policy constituted a noticeable step in the right direction.

LGBT activists never had a chance. They may well have been ill-prepared for a campaign on the military and too optimistic about the president's capacity to effect change. But such optimism was reinforced by a number of Democratic insiders who offered assurances of immediate action. By March 1993, the best marshaling of activist resources could not have halted the slide.

In theory, the new policy barred asking service personnel about sexual orientation. But any acknowledgment of being gay or lesbian, any sign of a "propensity to engage in homosexual acts," were and remain grounds for discharge. The criminalization of sodomy for military personnel encoded in the Uniform Code of Military Justice also remained intact. After a brief slowdown, discharges rebounded to about a thousand per year. The cost of training replacements was estimated in the late 1990s to be over $150 million a year.

The Post-Clinton Years

Many lesbians and gay men have been able to serve with relative openness and acceptance within their units and divisions. But harassment and violence remained widespread across all services. A policy that some naïvely imagined would end the active investigation of military personnel suspected of being gay or lesbian did not. From the mid-1990s on, there were regular reports of antigay witchhunts, some involving undercover agents visiting bars and other LGBT establishments.

In 1999, Private Barry Winchell, a twenty-one-year-old based at Fort Campbell, Kentucky, who was presumed to be gay, was bludgeoned to death by a fellow soldier. In the wake of this grisly crime and after years of prompting, the Defense Department conducted a survey pointing to widespread antigay harassment and persistent inaction by senior officers.

In 2002, with increasing talk of a new war in the Persian Gulf, the military's policy gained renewed notoriety with news that seven service members with Arabic language skills had been discharged. Soon thereafter, a "stop-loss" order that otherwise prevented marines from leaving the service for the next twelve months omitted any relief on the discharge of homosexuals. In fact, leeway was probably increased during the most intense hostilities in 2003, but the military was intent on not formally admitting so.

The Service Members Legal Defense Network, formed in 1993, regularly focused attention on these and other forms of institutionally sustained discrimination, generating media coverage and an increase in critical editorializing. The 2003 U.S. Supreme Court decision in *Lawrence v. Texas* increased expectations of successful challenges to exclusionary policies, though traditional Court deference to the military made rapid change unlikely. U.S. military leaders have remained strikingly insulated from the pressure for change and from increased abandonment of exclusionary policies among their NATO allies.

Bibliography

Bérubé, Allan. *Coming Out Under Fire: The History of Gay Men and Women in World War Two.* New York: Free Press, 1990

Evans, Rhonda. "U.S. Military Policies Concerning Homosexuals: Development, Implementation, and Outcomes." Report prepared for the Center for the Study of Sexual Minorities in the Military, University of California at Santa Barbara, November 2001. Available from http://www.gaymilitary.ucsb.edu

Hebert, Melissa S. *Camouflage Is Not Only for Combat: Gender, Sexuality, and Women in the Military.* New York: New York University Press, 1998.

Herek, Gregory M., Jared B. Jobe, and Ralph M. Carney, eds. *Out in Force: Sexual Orientation and the Military.* Chicago: University of Chicago Press, 1996.

Rayside, David. *On the Fringe: Gays and Lesbians in Politics.* Ithaca, N.Y.: Cornell University Press, 1998.

Rimmerman, Craig A., ed. *Gay Rights, Military Wrongs: Political Perspectives on Lesbians and Gays in the Military.* New York: Garland, 1996.

Shilts, Randy. *Conduct Unbecoming: Gays and Lesbians in the U.S. Military.* New York: St. Martin's Press, 1993

David Rayside

See also AMERICAN CIVIL LIBERTIES UNION (ACLU); ANTIWAR, PACIFIST, AND PEACE MOVEMENTS; CHEEVER, JOHN; FEDERAL LAW AND POLICY; GERBER, HENRY; GRAHN, JUDY; NATIONAL GAY AND LESBIAN TASK FORCE (NGLTF); O'HARA, FRANK; WALKER, MARY; WAR.

MILITARY LAW AND POLICY

Homosexuals and other sexual minorities have served in the U.S. armed forces since the colonial period. Beginning in the early twentieth century, however, the military adopted a series of policies intended to uncover and eliminate homosexuals. While inconsistency in enforcement and frequent revisions in the military's discriminatory laws and practices permitted some LGBT people to serve even during periods of aggressive repression, the military's hostility toward homosexuals also led to courts-martial, administrative discharge hearings, and witchhunts that ended the careers of thousands of servicemembers.

The armed forces' discrimination against sexual minorities affected more than the lives of individual servicemembers. Military service has played a key role in the history of disfranchised groups seeking full citizenship. Laws that restrict LGBT people from military service also deny access to the privileges that accompany participation in a fundamental obligation of citizenship. As a result, civil rights advocates as well as lesbian and gay servicemembers have challenged antigay military policies.

The Crimes of Sexual Orientation

Since the founding of the United States, military leaders have controlled their own systems of crime and punishment. Under the U.S. Constitution, military justice is a separate system that operates under different rules than federal and state criminal justice systems. Congress and the President are responsible for the laws that govern criminal and administrative action in the military. After World War II, court-martial procedure began to converge with civilian criminal procedure. But military justice retains its own rules, judges, crimes, and courts.

Sodomy, the crime most associated with homosexuality, was first made explicitly criminal under military law in 1916, when a new article of war prohibited assault with intent to commit sodomy. By 1920, a revised article of war specified sodomy itself as a separate offense, and the Manual for Courts-Martial, the official guide to military criminal procedure, defined the crime as anal or oral copulation between men or between a man and a woman. Although the sodomy article made some homosexual (and some heterosexual) sex a serious crime, sodomy prosecutions were not an easy way to expel suspected homosexuals. Convincing evidence was hard to find, witnesses were rare, physical evidence was often inconclusive, and victims or participants were reluctant to cooperate with investigators. Servicemembers suspected of being gay were also prosecuted for other vaguely worded military crimes.

Major reforms of military law after World War II increased the costs of prosecuting servicemembers for sodomy or other crimes. The Uniform Code of Military Justice (UCMJ), adopted by Congress in 1950 to standardize criminal law and procedure across the armed forces, granted accused servicemembers basic procedural rights, including access to counsel and the opportunity to appeal cases to a court of civilian judges, for the first time. But sodomy remained criminal, punishable by up to five years' confinement and a dishonorable discharge, under Article 125 of the UCMJ. Other military rules were also used to prosecute homosexuality, including Article 133, which prohibited "conduct unbecoming an officer and a gentleman," and Article 134, which made criminal "all disorders and neglects to the prejudice of good order and discipline in the armed forces" and "all conduct of a nature to bring discredit upon the armed forces." Because women had become a significant presence in the armed forces during World War II, interpretations of the new code attempted to define military crime in gender-inclusive fashion. For instance, female officers could be charged with the crime of "conduct unbecoming an officer and a gentlewoman," and two women could be convicted of committing sodomy.

In 2000, in recognition of the fiftieth anniversary of the UCMJ, an independent blue-ribbon commission issued a report recommending significant changes in military law. One of those recommendations was that sodomy be decriminalized. Though criminal prosecution for adult, consensual homosexual acts is unlikely in the post-*Lawrence v. Texas* climate, the crime of sodomy remains on the books in the military.

Pre-Enlistment Screening and Administrative Discharge

The military relied on courts-martial to eliminate some suspected gays and lesbians throughout the twentieth century, but the expense, public embarrassment, and harsh penalties that resulted from criminal trials led commanders to look for other ways to get rid of sexual minorities. After World War I, the military tried to identify homosexuals by their physical appearance. The army instructed its doctors to screen recruits for characteristics identified as "feminine," including sloping shoulders, broad hips, or little or no facial or body hair. Despite an official policy that required criminal prosecution for suspected homosexual acts, administrative discharges were routinely used to force out suspected homosexuals. These discharges sent servicemen back into the civilian world with the stigma of a less-than-honorable "blue" or "Section VIII" discharge, which was considered an unwelcome and public badge of homosexuality.

The trend toward screening and administrative rather than criminal sanction became official before the United States entered World War II, when military leaders directed that suspected gays be discharged without court-martial so long as aggravating factors, such as sexual relations with minors or forcible sexual relations, were not involved. As the historian Allan Bérubé has described, the military tried to identify homosexuals and bar them from service, relying on the advice of medical and psychiatric experts in a failed effort to stem the growth of a vibrant gay subculture in the armed forces. During and after the war the military repeatedly revised its guidelines on how to deal with suspected homosexuals.

Military regulations focused on identifying male homosexuals, but servicewomen's lives were profoundly altered by officials' fear that lesbians and promiscuous women populated their ranks. Witchhunts, beginning in World War II and peaking in the 1950s, attempted to expose and get rid of women who might be gay. As the historian Leisa Meyer has pointed out, the 350,000 women in uniform during World War II had to manage a myriad of restrictions on their professional, social, and sexual opportunities because of concerns about female sexuality. The most notorious investigation of female homosexuality during the war took place at Fort Oglethorpe, a Women's Army Corps (WAC) training camp. It was triggered by a letter from the mother of a twenty-year-old WAC that cast Fort Oglethorpe as a den of homosexual iniquity and prompted the army to begin an investigation that uncovered a handful of lesbian couples—and recommended discharge for just one woman.

Shortly after the war, the Department of Defense standardized a harsh antigay policy across the armed forces. A 1949 memorandum directed that "homosexual personnel" should be barred from service "in any capacity," and that "known homosexuals" should be promptly separated. In 1953, the Dwight D. Eisenhower administration codified "sexual perversion" as grounds for dismissal from federal jobs, increasing the rate of discharge from the military as well as other forms of federal employment. The Department of Defense issued its first directive specifying "sexual perversion," including homosexual acts and sodomy, as grounds for administrative discharge in 1959. Servicemembers accused under this directive rarely contested their discharges, hoping to avoid court-martial and protect friends who might be vulnerable to military investigation. In 1965 the regulations were revised to permit hearings before discharge boards and representation by counsel, reforms that enabled many more accused persons to challenge their discharges. Approximately two thousand persons per year, the same rate as during World War II, were discharged for homosexuality from 1950 through 1965.

a 1945 war department memorandum

"The mere confession by an individual to a psychiatrist that he possesses homosexual tendencies will not in itself constitute sufficient cause for discharge; the individual . . . will be hospitalized and, depending upon the results of the observation and treatment, will be either restored to duty or separated from the service."

Allegations of inconsistency in the administration of discharges led to a comprehensive review of military policy during Jimmy Carter's presidency. In 1981, during the Reagan administration, a new directive made discharge mandatory if a servicemember engaged in, attempted to engage in, or solicited a homosexual act. The discharge could be honorable, however, if it was not related to specific misconduct. The 1981 directive also notoriously stated that "homosexuality is incompatible with military service," listing a series of rationales for the ban on homosexuals. Arguments that had been made in support of earlier regulations prohibiting homosexual acts—that homosexuals were a risk to security because of the stigma associated with public disclosure of their sexual orientation and that gay men and lesbians were mentally unstable—had been discredited by both military and civilian studies of homosexuality. The military correspondingly altered its rationale for the new policy, emphasizing the privacy rights and morale of heterosexual servicemembers. Approximately 1,400 discharges per year between 1980 and 1991 were attributed to homosexuality.

the case of tom dooley

The military's pursuit of Navy doctor and Catholic icon Tom Dooley reveals its aggressive attitude toward ousting certain gay men during the early years of the Cold War. Touted as the next Surgeon General of the Navy after gaining notoriety through celebrated humanitarian missions to Vietnam and Laos, Dooley was forced to resign in 1956 for "homosexual tendencies." Naval intelligence officers had followed Dooley around the world, tapped his phones, and repeatedly set him up for sexual encounters with informants. (James T. Fisher, *Dr. America: The Lives of Thomas A. Dooley, 1927–1961* pp. 82–88.)

In 1992 soon-to-be president Bill Clinton made a campaign promise to end the ban on homosexual servicemembers. But after encountering military and congressional resistance, the Clinton administration adopted a policy that was later codified into a federal statute: the 1993 "don't ask, don't tell, don't pursue" policy no longer requires that homosexuals be discharged, but it permits the military to exclude sexual minorities who violate rules about behavior, speech, or marriage. A servicemember who engages in, attempts to engage in, or solicits a homosexual act is to be discharged, unless he can prove that such act was an aberration and is unlikely to recur. Colloquially known as the "queen for a day" exception, this policy retains a loophole initially codified in the World War II regulations. Discharge is also mandated for a servicemember who states that he or she is a homosexual or bisexual (unless she can rebut the presumption that he or she is likely to engage in homosexual acts). Those who marry or attempt to marry a person of the same sex are also subject to discharge. Under "don't ask, don't tell," more than 7,800 servicemembers were discharged through 2001.

The Battle to Serve

Servicemembers accused of homosexuality-related crimes, or who were targeted for separation because of their perceived sexual orientation, did not always exit quietly. In the early 1950s, few challenged their discharges. But after the U.S. Supreme Court held in 1958 that administrative separations were subject to judicial review, servicemembers could and did bring their claims to federal court. In 1961, Fannie Mae Clackum, a former air force corporal, won a legal victory in the U.S. Court of Claims. The air force had accused her of being a lesbian and sought to discharge her, but she denied the allegation and demanded a court-martial instead. The air force refused and simply discharged her, without convening a court-martial or informing her of any charges. Like other servicemembers whose discharges were later held invalid by civilian courts, Clackum won because the military had violated her right to due process. In the 1960s, more servicemembers used similar tactics to resist military discrimination, bringing procedural challenges to military administrative action. Their efforts were aided by reforms in military law and the support of the gay rights movement.

Until the 1970s, few servicemembers accused of being homosexuals were willing to admit that they were gay or lesbian (if in fact they were), and none challenged the military's legal right to discharge them on the basis of homosexuality. But the advent of gay liberation, symbolized by the Stonewall Riots in 1969, encouraged lesbian and gay service personnel to fight their exclusion from military service. In 1975 air force Sergeant Leonard Matlovich, a highly decorated veteran of three tours in Vietnam, came out as a gay man in a letter to the secretary of the air force, hoping to convince the military to grant him an exception to its policy against homosexuals. Instead, he was discharged—honorably, but against his wishes. Matlovich's courage in announcing his homosexuality and his commitment to challenging the basis for the military policy in court attracted media and public attention. Like most of the servicemembers who brought claims against the military in court, Matlovich failed to win reinstatement. But he forced the military to defend its reasons, in public, for separating a gay sergeant with an exemplary service record. He argued that his right to due process had been violated by the air force's arbitrary action, but also that the military had violated his right to privacy and to equal protection of the laws.

Miriam Ben-Shalom, an army drill sergeant who successfully challenged her 1976 discharge for homosexual tendencies, relied on similar arguments and added claims about substantive due process (that the military's policy was unconstitutionally unfair) and free speech. A federal district court found that there was no connection between Ben-Shalom's sexual orientation and her ability to serve in the military. The court ordered Ben-Shalom reinstated—which the army finally did, eleven years after her discharge. When the army refused her request for reenlistment, Ben-Shalom sued again. This time, the U.S. Court of Appeals for the Seventh Circuit held that her status as a homosexual alone (she had admitted only that she was a lesbian, not that she had committed any homosexual acts) was enough evidence of a propensity to engage in prohibited conduct to warrant discharge.

Many other servicemembers in the 1980s and 1990s tried to overturn the military's policy against homosexuality in the courts, but met with limited success. Judges have largely deferred to the military despite the fact that neither the military's internal reports (like the navy's Crittenden Report in 1957) nor studies completed by outside agencies (such as the RAND-sponsored National Defense Research Institute study in 1993) have found any connection between sexual orientation and fitness for military duty.

Bibliography

Bérubé, Allan. *Coming Out under Fire: The History of Gay Men and Women in World War Two.* New York: Plume, 1990.

D'Emilio, John. *Sexual Politics, Sexual Communities: The Making of a Homosexual Minority in the United States, 1940–1970.* Chicago: University of Chicago Press, 1983.

Eskridge, William N., Jr. "Privacy Jurisprudence and the Apartheid of the Closet, 1946–1961." *Florida State University Law Review* 24, no. 4 (1997): 703–838.

Karst, Kenneth L. "The Pursuit of Manhood and the Desegregation of the Armed Forces." *UCLA Law Review* 38, no. 3 (1991): 499–581.

Meyer, Leisa D. *Creating G.I. Jane: Power and Sexuality in the Women's Army Corps During World War II.* New York: Columbia, 1996.

National Defense Research Institute. *Sexual Orientation and U.S. Military Personnel Policy: Options and Assessment.* Santa Monica, Calif.: National Defense Research Institute, 1993.

Rivera, Rhonda R. "Our Straight-Laced Judges: The Legal Position of Homosexual Persons in the United States." *Hastings Law Journal* 30 (March 1979): 799–955. Reprinted in *Hastings Law Journal* 50, no. 4 (1999): 1015.

Servicemembers' Legal Defense Network. *Conduct Unbecoming: Annual Reports on "Don't Ask, Don't Tell, Don't Pursue."* 1994–2003. Available from http://www.sldn.org (see "Law Library").

Shilts, Randy. *Conduct Unbecoming: Lesbians and Gays in the U.S. Military: Vietnam to the Persian Gulf.* New York: St. Martin's Press, 1993.

Elizabeth Lutes Hillman

See also CRIME AND CRIMINALIZATION; DISCRIMINATION; EMPLOYMENT LAW AND POLICY; FEDERAL LAW AND POLICY; GOVERNMENT AND MILITARY WITCHHUNTS; KAMENY, FRANKLIN; MILITARY; POLICING AND POLICE; SULLIVAN, HARRY STACK; WAR.

MILK, Harvey **(b. 22 May 1930; d. 27 November 1978), San Francisco supervisor, gay rights activist.**

Harvey Milk was born in Woodmere, New York, to William and Minerva Karns Milk. He graduated from New York State College for Teachers in Albany in 1951, and joined the navy, becoming a deep-sea diver. After his discharge, Milk worked in New York and Texas at jobs ranging from teaching to investment banking before becoming the producer for a friend's Broadway plays. He followed a production of *Hair* (1967) to San Francisco, moving between San Francisco and New York for several years before settling in San Francisco in 1972 with Scott Smith, who would become his campaign manager. They opened a camera shop, Castro Camera, in March 1973.

The Watergate scandal, a special tax on small-business owners, and a teacher who borrowed a projector from the camera shop because her district could not afford one propelled Milk into politics in 1973. Milk ran for the Board of Supervisors, the consolidated city council-county commission for San Francisco, with a campaign that emphasized his outsider status—gay, Jewish, hippie, and newcomer to politics and to San Francisco. He ran without the support of the Alice B. Toklas Memorial Democratic Club, the city's LGB political organization, which believed in supporting liberal straight candidates sympathetic to gays and lesbians, but not gay or lesbian candidates themselves. Milk made an impressive showing, coming in tenth out of thirty-two candidates.

Milk ran again for supervisor in 1975, winning the endorsement of labor unions for successfully implementing a Coors beer boycott by LGB bars after Coors refused to sign a Teamster's contract. The Toklas Club openly opposed Milk in this election, believing he gave gays a bad name. Milk finished the race in seventh place after the six incumbents. The newly elected mayor, George Moscone, appointed Milk to the Board of Permit Appeals in 1976, making Milk the first openly gay commissioner in the United States.

Milk's third campaign began two months after he took his seat on the Board of Permit Appeals. He decided to seek the Democratic nomination for a seat in the California Assembly after learning that the Democratic leadership had agreed on Art Agnos as its choice for nominee in advance of the primary. Though once again he did not earn the endorsement of the Toklas Club, a cadre of Milk supporters in the club managed to ensure that Agnos did not win its endorsement either. Labor was afraid to oppose the Democratic Party leadership, so Milk was officially endorsed by only a few unions, although privately he had considerable labor support. Despite his lack of support from the groups normally in Milk's camp—LGB organizations, unions, and Democrats—Milk won seventeen thousand votes and lost to Agnos by only four thousand votes.

Milk ran again for supervisor in 1977, and this time his persistence paid off. He was the top vote getter of the

Harvey Milk. Finally elected in 1977 as the first openly gay San Francisco supervisor, he served only eleven months before being assassinated, along with Mayor George Moscone; in death, he has become a lasting symbol of gay liberation. **[AP/Wide World Photos]**

seventeen candidates, winning 30.5 percent of the vote. During his tenure as supervisor, he was responsible for the passage of a LGB rights bill in 1978 and a pooper-scooper law that required pet owners to clean up after their pets. He campaigned across the state against Proposition 6, a measure on the California ballot that would prevent anyone who talked about, advocated, or practiced homosexuality from teaching in the schools. The measure—ultimately defeated—allowed Milk to give LGB rights issues center stage. Milk's pooper-scooper bill was equally important to Milk's view of government, according to biographer Randy Shilts: "Harvey's political philosophy was never more complicated than the issue of dogshit; government should solve people's basic problems" (p. 203).

Milk served only eleven months in office. He was killed, along with Mayor George Moscone, on 27 November 1978, by fellow supervisor Dan White. A conservative member of the board, White had resigned his seat and then asked for it back. On the day of the killings, Moscone was planning to announce that he would not reappoint White. White was convicted of involuntary manslaughter with the infamous "Twinkie" defense—that junk food exacerbated his depression—and was sentenced to five years in prison. On 21 October 1985, within a year of his release, he committed suicide.

Harvey Milk remains a powerful symbol of gay liberation whose lasting message was openness, honesty, pride, and hope. Gay historian John D'Emilio summarizes what Milk has left behind: "The legacy that I think he would want to be remembered for is the imperative to live one's life at all times with integrity" (Cloud).

Bibliography

Cloud, John. "Why Milk is Still Fresh." The *Advocate,* 10 November 1998. Available from http://www.findarticles.com/m1589/1998_Nov_10/5487936/pl/article.jhtml.

Foss, Karen A. "Harvey Milk: 'You Have to Give Them Hope.'" *Journal of the West* 27, no. 2 (April 1988): 75–81.

Foss, Karen A. "The Logic of Folly in the Political Campaigns of Harvey Milk." In *Queer Words, Queer Images: Communication and the Construction of Homosexuality.* Edited by R. Jeffrey Ringer. New York: New York University Press, 1994.

Shilts, Randy. *The Mayor of Castro Street: The Life and Times of Harvey Milk.* New York: St. Martin's Press, 1982.

The Times of Harvey Milk. 16 mm, 87 minutes. San Francisco: Black Sands.

Weiss, Mike. *Double Play: The San Francisco City Hall Killings.* Reading, Mass.: Addison-Wesley, 1984.

Karen A. Foss

See also AIDS MEMORIAL QUILT—NAMES PROJECT; BOYCOTTS; DEMOCRATIC PARTY; ELECTORAL POLITICS.

MILLAY, Edna St. Vincent

(b. 22 February 1892; d. 18 October 1950), poet.

Edna St. Vincent Millay, born to Cora and Henry Millay in Rockland, Maine, was the oldest of three daughters (her sisters were Norma and Kathleen). Her father was sent away by her mother when she was eight. Her mother went to work as a nurse to support herself and her girls, who, left on their own, developed both the independence and the strong mutual bonds that would characterize their relationships in the future. Millay, called not Edna but "Vincent," earned early notice as a poet with childhood successes, including publications in *St. Nicholas* children's magazine.

Her first great triumph, the long poem *Renascence*, elicited much comment when it appeared in the 1912 *Lyric Year*. Critic Jessie Rittenhouse thought the poem "the freshest, most distinctive in the book" (Milford, p. 76). At age twenty, Millay was a girl who wrote like a man, "a brawny male," Arthur Davidson Ficke joked. Impressed by her talent, her mentor Caroline B. Dow sent Millay to Vassar College.

During the Vassar years, Millay participated widely in theatrical and literary life, developing a performative style that would later structure her poetry and her readings as she became both the most well-known female poet and the representative "new woman" of the 1920s. She edited the *Vassar Miscellany Monthly*, which published some poems she had written earlier, such as "The Suicide" and "Interim." The years at Vassar were marked by strong female friendships and also by a legacy of strong poems about women, such as the "Memorial to D. C." that prefigured a later six-poem sequence written for Elinor Wylie.

At Vassar, she had a long and intense relationship with Elaine Ralli. Both of Millay's recent biographers, Nancy Milford and Daniel Epstein, portray her as involved in a number of lesbian relationships, perhaps beginning with her sisters. The very icon of free love, Millay had many sexual encounters with both male and female partners—some of them quite transitory, and all within the framework of a capacity to arouse passionate attachments that sometimes created bitterness and grief.

As the culture of the moderns developed in Greenwich Village, Millay was in the middle of it, wildly popular, involved with the Provincetown Players, writing plays, and reciting poems that college students knew by heart long before they were published. With a memorable presence, she attracted serious attention from a number of admirers, male and female, some of whom found it hard to get over her. Critic and lover Edmund Wilson was one of those. After Millay died, Wilson's 1952 "Epilogue" in his *The Shores of Light* called her an "exceptional being." "One never forgot the things she noticed, for she charged them with her own intense feeling" (p. 745). He thought her perhaps more interested in the poetic emotion her affairs aroused than in the individuals.

Millay was especially well-known for her intense poetry about love, often defiant love, like the entire volume titled *A Few Figs from Thistles* (1920). She reversed the expectations of female poets in many respects. Sometimes she played with the gender of her persona, speaking in a voice that would have seemed masculine to her readers, addressing a lover as "she." Even the casual flippancy of "First Fig" was decidedly unfeminine: "My candle burns at both ends; / It will not last the night; / But ah my foes and oh my friends / It gives a lovely light!" (Millay, p. 19). In perfectly formed sonnets, she theatricalized identity.

Millay's politics were progressive. She supported feminists and wrote a commemorative sonnet (Number lxvii) on behalf of equal rights for women. She demonstrated against the execution of Sacco and Vanzetti, protesting to the governor in a personal letter that he ought to stay the execution, and then wrote not only a protest poem, "Justice Denied in Massachusetts," and sonnets dedicated to them, but also an essay, "Fear," accusing readers of fearing anarchists when they ought rather to fear injustice. She helped make the United States tour of Emma Goldman possible in the thirties.

Perhaps in part because of her immense popularity, Millay came under attack. John Crowe Ransom's "The Poet as Woman" (1937) implied that her femininity had undermined her critical faculties. As a Poundian "make it new" aesthetic came to prevail, her very success in renewing the formal musicality of the sonnet tradition worked against her. Married to Eugen Jan Boissevain, she wrote from their farm at Steepletop, New York. But her extraordinary ability to make poetic language call attention to the experiences of everyday life and the drama of plants, birds, hills, and seasons shared little with the difficult poetics of T.S. Eliot, Ezra Pound, or Wallace Stevens. Furthermore, like others who made gender identity and sexuality central to their stylistic work, Millay lost credibility with modernist and Cold War critics who demanded more universality.

Nonetheless, there is now renewed interest in Millay, and two major biographies appeared in 2001. Her incorporation of both musicality and drama into poetic style and her mastery of form make her one of the chief lyric poets of the twentieth century.

Bibliography

Clark, Suzanne. "Jouissance and the Sentimental Daughter: Edna St. Vincent Millay." In *Sentimental Modernism: Women Writers and the Revolution of the Word*. Bloomington: Indiana University Press, 1991.

Epstein, Daniel Mark. *The Loves and Love Poems of Edna St. Vincent Millay*. New York: Henry Holt, 2001.

Freedman, Diane, ed. *Millay at 100: A Critical Reappraisal*. Carbondale: Southern Illinois University Press, 1995.

Milford, Nancy. *Savage Beauty: The Life of Edna St. Vincent Millay*. New York: Random House, 2001.

Millay, Edna St. Vincent. *The Letters of Edna St. Vincent Millay*. Edited by Allan Ross Macdougall. New York: Grossett and Dunlap, 1952.

———. *Selected Poems: The Centenary Edition*. Edited by Colin Falck. New York: HarperCollins, 1992.

Ransom, John Crowe. "The Poet as Woman." *Southern Review* 2 (Spring 1937): 784.

Wilson, Edmund. "Epilogue, 1952: Edna St. Vincent Millay." In *The Shores of Light*. New York: Random House, 1952.

Suzanne Clark

See also LITERATURE.

MILLETT, Kate **(b. 14 September 1934), artist, writer.**

Katherine Murray Millett was born in St. Paul, Minnesota. In 1956 she earned a bachelor of arts degree with honors from the University of Minnesota. Two years later she was awarded a master's degree with first class honors from Oxford University. She taught English at the University of North Carolina in Greensboro before moving to New York City to begin a career in art. She supported herself by teaching kindergarten in Harlem. In 1961 Millett moved to Tokyo. There she studied sculpting and again supported herself through teaching, this time as an English instructor at Waseda University. Millett married Japanese sculptor Fumio Yoshimura in 1965 in New York City, but the two established an open marriage that enabled Millett to have a series of relationships with women. During these years, Millett taught English and philosophy at Barnard College while finishing her doctorate at Columbia University. She found time to join the National Organization for Women (NOW) and subsequently New York Radical Women in 1969. In 1970 she was awarded her Ph.D. with distinction. Her dissertation was published as *Sexual Politics* that same year, bringing her instant fame and thirty thousand dollars, most of which she used to establish the Women's Art Colony Farm in Poughkeepsie, New York, where she lived as of 2003.

Sexual Politics was innovative, comprehensive, and sharply argued. Millett was one of the first modern feminists to define patriarchy as a cultural, psychological, political, and economic system of gendered and sexualized power relationships. At the same time that other radical feminists worked to make radical criticism speak to the experiences of women, Millett situated women deeply in Western cultural traditions that, she argued, spoke in one voice about the difference between men and women. For patriarchy to exist, she insisted, sexual difference between men and women had to be maintained and continuously elaborated upon. She identified the very figures most celebrated for their sexually liberating impact—Sigmund Freud, D. H. Lawrence, Henry Miller, Norman Mailer, and Jean Genet—as promoting the sexual repression of women. Millett's history of expanding sexual freedoms forcefully argued that so-called revolutionary eras were defined as such through men's shifting access to women, and not by their success in liberating women from social and sexual repression. Millett's understanding of sexuality as the central feature of American gender relations proved to be an extremely productive conception for second-wave feminists. Unlike those who complained that sexuality was a diversion from politics, Millett viewed sexuality as politics. She saw the intersection of sexuality and gender as the most important feature of women's identities and thus their oppression.

Sexual Politics propelled Millett into a leadership role in the women's liberation movement not only for its brilliance but by the sheer amount of media attention she received for it. As with many leading feminists of the late 1960s, Millett's relationship with the media was a mixed blessing. For example, *Time* magazine, in its 31 August 1970 issue, dubbed her the "Mao Tse-tung of Women's Liberation" and later focused the nation's attention on her bisexuality. Feminists Ti-Grace Atkinson, Gloria Steinem, Susan Brownmiller, and Florynce Kennedy held a press conference to show their support for Millett, for gay liberation, and for feminist sisterhood. Nonetheless, an emerging gay-straight split quickly divided New York City feminists along radical and liberal lines, and NOW, under the direction of Betty Friedan, purged the New York City chapter of its lesbian officers in the wake of Millett's outing.

Celebrity was difficult for Millett, as she discussed in a 1974 autobiographical novel, *Flying*. Becoming a lightning rod for feminists and antifeminists alike, coupled with her ongoing struggles with bipolar depression, led to a period of psychological breakdown. Millett was institutionalized by her family against her will, all of which she

Kate Millett. The American radical feminist and political activist—who first won widespread acclaim for her groundbreaking 1970 book, *Sexual Politics*—is photographed in Paris in 1979, shortly after her expulsion from Iran for protesting the revolutionary regime's oppressive policies against women. [Bettmann/corbis]

recounted in *The Loony Bin Trip* (1990). Other autobiographical works include *Sita* (1977) and *A.D.: A Memoir* (1995). *The Basement,* published in 1979, marked Millett's turn to issues of violence, torture, and cruelty not only against women but also more widely. *Going to Iran* (1982) recounts the political oppression in Iran after the rise of Ayatollah Khomeini, and *The Politics of Cruelty* (1994) deals with the issue of cruelty globally.

Millett's celebrity faded as 1970s feminism became both more academic and less radical. In 1999, Millett published a piece in the magazine *On the Issues* about her difficulty keeping *Sexual Politics* in print and her invisibility to a newer generation of feminists. She told of supporting herself by selling Christmas trees in upstate New York, being turned down for adjunct teaching positions, and struggling to keep the Women's Art Colony Farm afloat. Millett continues to show her art internationally and to write. Most recently, she wrote about caring for her elderly mother in *Mother Millett* (2001). She is active in the antipsychiatric movement, the prison reform movement, and the campaign against torture.

Bibliography

Freely, Maureen. "What Kate Did Next." *Observer,* 3 January 1999.

Wandersee, Winifred. *On the Move: American Women in the 1970s.* Boston, 1988.

Jane Gerhard

See also INTERGENERATIONAL SEX AND RELATIONSHIPS; LITERARY CRITICISM AND THEORY; LITERATURE.

MISSISSIPPI

The nation's poorest state, Mississippi upsets dominant notions of LGBT community and history. Less a matter of migration to cities, queer life more commonly has been characterized by careful negotiation of local institutions—home, church, school, and workplace. Although often assumed hostile to sexual and gender nonconformity, these very sites are where they have flourished. Elder LGBT Mississippians recall meeting sexual partners at church socials and family reunions, in classrooms and on shop floors, on athletic fields and at roadside rest areas. While households, employers, and educational and religious organizations sometimes condemned "deviant" sexualities and genders, their buildings and grounds became the most common sites for queer sexual activity.

Finding friends and partners across a largely rural landscape, queer Mississippians have relied on various means of transportation, on circulation as much as congregation. The state has long harbored queer networks but only recently lesbian and gay cultures. Before the 1960s, same-sex play between adolescents was tacitly condoned, and queer sex among adults was clandestine but commonplace. Although oral and anal sex were criminalized by the 1839 sodomy law and seven men were imprisoned under the statute as of 1880, homosexual activity was quietly accommodated with a prevailing pretense of ignorance. By the 1970s, however, LGBT identity politics and organized Christian resistance grew hand in hand.

For women in particular, education and separatist organizations have proved critical in the forging of same-sex worlds and relationships. In the early 1890s, famed suffragist Pauline Orr and Miriam Paslay created a life together as professors at the first state-funded women's college in the United States, what would become the Mississippi University for Women. The two sparked feminist resistance to corrupt male college presidents in Columbus, Mississippi. They promoted a broad curriculum for women instead of domestic sciences. And they advocated equal pay for equal work at other state universities. Following in that tradition, in the early 1990s, Brenda and Wanda Hinson founded Camp Sister Spirit near Ovett. Despite death threats, the couple developed their feminist rural retreat for women-only, lesbian, and gay male events. They further cultivated a nonprofit organization for the alleviation of hunger, poverty, and bigotry in the region. Though anchored in state and local struggles for social change, Orr and Paslay and the Hinsons became key figures in national and international women's reform movements.

For at least a hundred years, mainstream media generated queer scandal around male public figures implicated in homosexual acts. In the 1890s, newspapers exposed Professor William Sims, who was kicked off the faculty at the University of Mississippi, as well as planter-politician Dabney Marshall, who murdered his accuser. In the 1980s, TV and press reporters hounded U.S. Representative Jon Hinson and Governor Bill Allain, who nonetheless clung to elective office. While oppressive discourses continually cast homosexuality as new or as only occurring outside the state, a number of Mississippi writers produced queer narratives with local settings—from playwrights Mart Crowley and Tennessee Williams to novelists Hubert Creekmore and Thomas Hal Phillips, from poet and memoirist William Alexander Percy to physique artist and pulp novelist Carl Corley.

Scandals involving black civil rights activist Aaron Henry and white advocate Bill Higgs marked a crucial turning point in regional queer history. When accused in the early 1960s of intercourse with younger men, the two movement leaders inevitably denied the allegations. Such dissembling was second nature, given the cultural climate. But the linkage of queer sexuality to racial equality was thereby established, both in alarmist rhetoric and in practice. Thus, a strident legal-political crackdown against LGBT Mississippians emerged not in the 1950s, as elsewhere, but in the 1960s, as part of the massive resistance to African American freedom struggles.

LGBT bars date back at least to the 1940s; there were friendly or accommodating establishments even earlier, most with markedly mixed clienteles of young and old, women and men, the gender normative and non-normative. Mirroring larger divides, however, they often have remained racially segregated. When towns and cities achieved the critical mass to support more than one queer bar, separate black and white establishments usually resulted. In Jackson in the 1970s and 1980s, the two were located directly across the street from one another.

Although fundamentalist preachers from Mississippi founded some of today's most retrograde vehicles of homophobia (Donald Wildmon's American Family Association and Fred Phelps's God Hates Fags), many queer Mississippians, black and white, have retained strong commitments to Christian spirituality. While the Mississippi Gay Alliance, founded in 1973, and its longtime leader, Eddie Sandifer, often advocated a radical political agenda linking various left causes, the most successful organizing, Sandifer concedes, has been through LGBT congregations such as the Metropolitan Community Church, first opened in Jackson in 1983. Today the political struggle is largely led by Equality Mississippi and its executive director, Jody Renaldo. An annual Mississippi LGBT Summit, uniting a variety of university student groups and other social and political organizations, is hosted by Camp Sister Spirit.

Transgender persons have occasionally found amenable physicians, including gay doctor Ben Folk, and hospitals for treatments, as at the University Medical Center in Jackson. More frequently they have traveled—as far as Brussels—for lower-cost sex reassignment surgery.

Interestingly, relatively few queer Mississippians over the years have moved to the LGBT enclaves of major cities. Of those who have, many have returned to the state regularly throughout their lives and permanently in retirement. Ironically, as mainstream media fixate on rural prejudice and brutality, American AVPs, or antiviolence projects, report a far greater incidence of homophobic assault and murder in urban centers, with their high LGBT visibility. Thus, some LGBT people find greater safety in Mississippi, whereas many queer urbanites consider the form of selective visibility practiced there an ideological impossibility. Often belittled as backward or exceptionally repressive, Mississippi continues to hold a deep emotional grip upon its queer natives.

Bibliography

Greene, Kate. "Fear and Loathing in Mississippi: The Attack on Camp Sister Spirit." *Women and Politics* 17, no. 3 (1997).

Howard, John. *Men Like That: A Southern Queer History.* Chicago: University of Chicago Press, 1999.

———. "The Talk of the County: Revisiting Accusation, Murder, and Mississippi, 1895." In *Queer Studies: An Interdisciplinary Reader.* Edited by Robert J. Corber and Stephen Valocchi. Oxford: Blackwell, 2003.

Howard, John, ed., *Carryin' On in the Lesbian and Gay South.* New York: New York University Press, 1997.

Wilkerson-Freeman, Sarah. "Love and Liberation: Southern Women-Loving-Women and the Power of the Heart." Paper presented to the Organization of American Historians, Memphis, Tenn., April 2003.

John Howard

See also FORD, CHARLES HENRI; WALKER, A'LELIA; WILLIAMS, TENNESSEE; WOMACK, H. LYNN.

MITCHELL, Alice (b. 1873; d. 1898).

Alice Mitchell, age nineteen, was committed to an asylum for the notorious murder of her "girl lover" Freda Ward, age seventeen, on 25 January 1892 in Memphis, Tennessee. She then unwittingly became a central figure in debates over the meaning of lesbian love that continued, in the United States and Europe, until the middle of the twentieth century.

Born to George and Isabella Scott Mitchell in 1873, Mitchell grew up alongside her three surviving siblings (of seven children born to her mother) in a prosperous and well-known Memphis family. She attended the private, all-white Higbee School for Girls, where she met Freda Ward. The close friendship that developed between Mitchell and Ward at the Higbee School was considered, by teachers, students, and other observers, to be typical of the "chumming" relationships common among schoolgirls there. But when Mitchell and Ward concocted a plan to elope and marry, Ward's relatives expressed alarm and forbade Ward to continue her friendship with Mitchell. The plan was revealed when Ward's older sister read letters that she had confiscated, which detailed Mitchell's plan to dress as a man and go by the name of Alvin Ward, take a boat to St. Louis with Ward, and marry her there. Mitchell then intended to set up a household and work to support Ward.

After Mitchell was separated from Ward, she withdrew into a deep depression and began to lose weight and lose hope for future happiness. Ward, in contrast, continued the life that she and Mitchell had once shared. They had both corresponded with boys under fictitious names, occasionally meeting them at public places in the city. Ward continued to do so. Mitchell's feelings of abandonment and betrayal, expressed in letters that were later read at trial and published in the Memphis newspapers, led her to increasingly desperate attempts to contact Ward and resume their relationship. When these efforts failed, Mitchell planned to kill Ward in order to prevent her from marrying one of the boys.

On 25 January 1892, Mitchell slit Ward's throat on her way to board a Mississippi riverboat. Ward died, and Mitchell was arrested and placed in a special section of the jail reserved for privileged, white inmates. Mitchell was not tried for murder, but examined at an inquisition of lunacy, to determine whether she was insane and unfit for trial. At the inquisition, the many conflicting and confused theories about the meaning of her love for Ward were aired and publicized. Mitchell's lawyers, in consultation with her father and various prominent Memphis physicians, argued that Mitchell was "presently insane" and unable to stand trial for murder. Family members and neighbors testified. Some believed that her love for Ward was an ordinary girlish passion, not an indication of insanity, and that the murder was probably motivated by envy of or competition for boys. Some argued, in the press or on the stand, that the plea of present insanity was a legal trick to protect her from a murder trial. Others believed that Mitchell's passion and marriage plan were an indication of a suspicious and possibly dangerous peculiarity that might indicate insanity or might be more straightforwardly a sign of bad character.

Doctors and asylum superintendents testified, presenting and explaining a wide range of theories and possible diagnoses of Mitchell—erotomania, hermaphroditism, paranoia, monomania, imperative impulse or emotional morbid impulse, contrary love, or perverted sexual attachment. Some physicians argued that Mitchell's love for Ward was in itself insane, while others argued that it was not insane, but only eccentric or perhaps immoral.

The testimony at the lunacy inquisition in Mitchell's case was widely publicized in the new mass circulation daily newspapers in the United States, and to a lesser extent in Europe as well. The newspaper reports drew upon French novels featuring erotic passion between women, newly available in cheap editions in the United States during the 1890s. These newspaper reports in turn fed the imaginations of twentieth-century novelists, who reworked the various "stories" of the Mitchell/Ward case into new fiction. At the same time, the medical press published various case studies of Mitchell, and compared an avalanche of new cases of "sexual inversion" or "lesbianism" to Mitchell's. She appeared in the internationally influential work of sexologists Richard von Krafft-Ebing and Havelock Ellis, and persisted as a central figure in sexological writing on lesbianism into the 1950s.

The character and life story of Alice Mitchell, as represented in fiction, the press, and the medical literature of the first half of the twentieth century, bore little relation to the living historical person. Her "case" was appropriated within these fields of publication, to forward the development of a notion of "the lesbian" or "the homosexual" as a unique kind of character. Mitchell's story most often became a template for representations of masculine, predatory, potentially violent lesbians who constituted a danger to the gender and sexual order of the family and the nation. But her story also became a starting point for defenses of "the lesbian," and for critiques of the oppressive constraints on her freedom that might lead to tragedies if not reformed. Radclyffe Hall's 1928 novel, *The Well of Loneliness,* recapitulates and rewrites central elements of the Mitchell/Ward story, converting it from a central mode of attack on sexual love between women into the most widely circulated defense of that love available before World War II.

Alice Mitchell, the living historical person, was committed to the state mental hospital where she died in 1898, at the age of 25. Reports in the press claimed she died of tuberculosis, then widespread in such institutions. But an interview with one of her attorneys, published in a Memphis newspaper during the 1930s, revealed that she killed herself by jumping into a water tower. She is buried in Memphis, Tennessee.

Bibliography

Duggan, Lisa. *Sapphic Slashers: Sex, Violence and American Modernity.* Durham, N.C., and London: Duke University Press, 2000.

Katz, Jonathan Ned. *Gay American History.* New York: Thomas Y. Crowell, 1976.

———. *Gay/Lesbian Almanac: A New Documentary.* New York: Harper and Row, 1983.

Lindquist, Lisa. "Images of Alice: Gender, Deviancy, and a Love Murder in Memphis." *Journal of the History of Sexuality* 6, no. 1 (Winter 1995): 30–61.

Lisa Duggan

See also TRANSSEXUALS, TRANSVESTITES, TRANSGENDER PEOPLE, AND CROSS-DRESSERS; VIOLENCE.

MIZER, Robert (b. 27 March 1922; d. 12 May 1992), photographer, filmmaker, publisher.

Robert Mizer was among the most prolific and influential of the artists who advanced male physique photography during the middle years of the twentieth century. Mizer was born in Haley, Idaho, in 1922 and moved to Los Angeles as an infant with his widowed mother. He took up photography as a hobby while a teenager and would photograph bodybuilders on his frequent visits to "Muscle Beach" in Venice. In 1945, at the age of twenty-three, he founded the Athletic Model Guild (AMG), a studio dedicated to celebrating youthful male beauty. Working out of his childhood home, he photographed thousands of models between 1945 and 1992. Mail order sales of still photos supplied Mizer's income. In order to promote those sales he published, beginning in 1951, the magazine *Physique Pictorial.* Doubling as a catalog, his magazine was widely distributed in the United States and endured far beyond the heyday of physique photography, continuing until 1990. Starting in 1958 Mizer also produced hundreds of short homoerotic films, which he marketed through *Physique Pictorial.*

Mizer was one of dozens of photographers and entrepreneurs who in the years following World War II expanded the availability of homoerotic images for purchase through newsstands and mail order. Mizer pursued his work despite federal obscenity laws designed to prohibit the circulation of erotic material through the U.S. Postal Service. Earlier in the century Bernarr McFadden had successfully fended off federal charges that *Physical Culture* magazine was obscene by disavowing its potential for erotic interpretation and claiming that visual presentation of muscular strength inspired athleticism, good health, and solid moral character. Mizer's work built upon the legal disclaimers and visual codes of his prewar predecessors. Many of his photographs and films, whether of individuals, pairs, or groups, suggested athletic scenarios (wrestling was a particular favorite) and healthful recreation, often in forested or other natural settings. In addition, he posed models with props to suggest classical statuary, and he developed an aesthetic that, while often campy, laid claim to the artistic merits of the nude male. Athleticism and art provided Mizer and his peers with a line of defense against charges of obscenity, although this defense was tested by surveillance, intimidation, arrest, and prosecution.

Mizer was convicted and served time on an obscenity charge, but won his case on appeal. During the 1960s other physique publishers were similarly prosecuted and also won on appeal, so that by the end of the decade the federal courts effectively established the legal right to produce and sell erotic images of men in the United States.

The modern pornography industry began to develop in earnest, offering full nudity and explicit sex acts. Mizer made some efforts to produce sexually explicit material, but for the most part he left this field to others and continued to produce innocent and playful boy-next-door scenarios, including fantasy scenes of bondage and discipline. Most of his models in the 1940s and 1950s were white, although in the 1970s African American and Latino models began to appear regularly in *Physique Pictorial.* In his magazine, Mizer would include editorial comments on contemporary issues alongside information about his models (name, age, hobbies, etc.). Mizer also inscribed next to many portraits an obscure symbol, which indicated his impressions of the model's personality traits.

Scholars Thomas Waugh and Christopher Nealon argue that Mizer and his peers definitively shaped the history of sexuality through their art. Purchase of physique photography from newsstands and through the mail allowed men not only to stimulate their personal erotic interest in male bodies, but also to know that similar desires were shared by a vast audience. In the years leading up to Stonewall, physique photography helped to create a sense of community through mass consumption. Mizer's films and photos encouraged allegiance to a collective sexual identity, although the predominance of white models limited by race the range of possible identifications and desires within that collective.

Mizer's place in history is secured by the sheer volume of his output (nearly one million print negatives and between one and three thousand short films), by the longevity of *Physique Pictorial,* and by his trademark aesthetic. Interest in Mizer's work revived in the 1990s shortly after his death in Los Angeles. The German publisher Taschen reprinted the entire run of *Physique Pictorial,* and Campfire Video assembled five volumes of his films for release on video. In 1999 Canadian director Thom Fitzgerald produced the film *Beefcake,* which imaginatively recreates the AMG Studio and celebrates the camp sensibility Mizer brought to male erotica in an age that, in retrospect, appears both more repressive and more innocent than the early twenty-first century.

Bibliography

Nealon, Christopher. "The Secret Public of Physique Culture." In *Foundlings: Lesbian and Gay Historical Emotion Before Stonewall.* Durham, N.C.: Duke University Press, 2001.

Stanley, Wayne. "Introduction." In *The Complete Reprint of Physique Pictorial: 1951–1990.* Cologne: Taschen, 1997.

Waugh, Thomas. "Strength and Stealth." In *Hard to Imagine: Gay Male Eroticism in Photography and Film from Their Beginnings to Stonewall.* New York: Columbia University Press, 1996.

Greg Mullins

See also PHYSIQUE MAGAZINES AND PHOTOGRAPHS; PORNOGRAPHY; VISUAL ART:PHOTOGRAPHY.

MONETTE, Paul (b. 16 October 1945; d. 10 February 1995), writer, activist.

Paul Monette is a complex figure who combined love and anger, talent and ambition, insecurity and arrogance to forge a rich life and a significant body of work. Though he will be remembered as a central voice of the AIDS crisis, AIDS did not make his career. He had produced a number of books, in particular the promising first novel *Taking Care of Mrs. Carroll* (1978), before AIDS became the primary reality of his life and work in the mid-1980s.

Monette divided his life into two parts, as his National Book Award–winning memoir *Becoming a Man: Half a Life Story* (1992) indicates. His early life—until his mid-twenties—was a suffocating time, full of torment and hiding. He was the product of the repressive Puritan culture of New England. Born into a lower-middle-class family in Lawrence, Massachusetts, at the end of World War II, Monette saw himself as the quintessentially repressed child of the 1950s and 1960s: "Until I was twenty-five, I was the only man I knew who had no story at all. . . . That's how the closet feels, once you've made your nest in it and learned to call it home. Self-pity becomes your oxygen" (*Becoming a Man,* p. 1). As a day student on scholarship at Phillips Academy in Andover, Massachusetts, and at Yale University, Monette subjugated his body's urges to his mind's queries, excelling as a student but growing little as a man. He watched the Adonis culture of prep school as an outsider, and his chronicling of that experience in *Becoming a Man* makes that book a useful, enlightening contribution to contemporary understandings of the gay male experience in the second half of the twentieth century.

The second part of Monette's life began when he met Roger Horwitz in Boston in September 1974. Horwitz, who grew up in an upper-middle-class Jewish household in suburban Chicago and earned both a Ph.D. in comparative literature and a law degree from Harvard University, was an unassuming, brilliant man who supported Monette emotionally and who believed in him and his work unflinchingly. The two men left Boston for Los Angeles in 1977, in part so that Monette could pursue a career as a Hollywood writer. The twelve-year relationship with Horwitz was the great touchstone in Monette's life in his struggle to become an actualized, functioning gay man. Monette expresses this at the end of *Becoming a Man,* taking an inventory of his life before meeting Horwitz from the point of view of a decade after losing him to AIDS: "That much fate I believe in, the tortuous journey that brings you to love, all the twists and near misses. Somehow it's all had a purpose, once you're finally real" (*Becoming a Man*, pp. 277–278).

That second act of Monette's life developed into the horror, loss, and intensely lived struggle of the first wave of the AIDS crisis. *Love Alone: Eighteen Elegies for Rog* (1988) and *Borrowed Time: An AIDS Memoir* (1988), eulogizing and documenting the death of Horwitz, are surely two of the most moving and important works on the early AIDS era. They are among the earliest and most eloquent personal testimonies of the epidemic, putting the faces of gay men on the cold, impersonal statistics of AIDS. As Monette emerged as a public figure, especially with the "crossover" success of *Borrowed Time*, his life and work became more politicized. He wrote in the preface for *Love Alone*, "What is written here is only one man's passing and one man's cry, a warrior burying a warrior. May it fuel the fire of those on the front lines who mean to prevail, and of the friends who stand in the fire with them. We will not be bowed out or erased by this. . . . Pity us not" (*Love Alone*, p. xiii).

Monette had two major relationships after Roger Horwitz's death, and those bonds—with Stephen Kolzak and Winston Wilde—allowed Monette to combine his life and his work, as he wrote two AIDS-focused novels, *Afterlife* (1990) and *Halfway Home* (1991), which are partly based on his life with Kolzak, and two memoirs, *Becoming a Man* and *Last Watch of the Night* (1994), while he was with Wilde. Perhaps the overarching questions of the last decade of Monette's life are these: How did the battleground of AIDS come to dominate his life, and how did the urgency of "dying by inches" (*Becoming a Man*, p. 2) shape his creativity and his emotional life as a gay man struggling with the ravages of illness?

Monette died at his home in Los Angeles in February 1995 of complications from AIDS, a few months before his fiftieth birthday. The last years of his life have been chronicled in an award-winning documentary, *Paul Monette: The Brink of Summer's End*.

Bibliography

Bramer, Monte, director. *Paul Monette: The Brink of Summer's End*. Home Box Office, 1997.

Monette, Paul. *Borrowed Time: An AIDS Memoir*. New York: Harcourt Brace, 1988.

———. *Becoming a Man: Half a Life Story*. New York: Harcourt Brace, 1992.

Chris Freeman

See also AIDS AND PEOPLE WITH AIDS; LITERATURE.

MONEY, John (b. 8 July 1921), and Anke EHRHARDT (b. 20 Feb 1940), medical psychologists, sex researchers.

The controversial work of John Money and Anke Ehrhardt has had a profound effect on sex research as well as on the humanities and social sciences since the late 1960s. Money was born in Morrinsville, Waikato, New Zealand, into a conservative evangelical Christian family, a fact that, some claim, influenced his future research interests. He completed his undergraduate degree in psychology at Victoria University in 1943 and, in the mid-1940s, moved to the United States. He earned his Ph.D. in social relations from the Psychological Clinic at Harvard University in 1952. Since 1951, Money has been on the faculty of the Johns Hopkins University Medical School, where he founded the Psychohormonal Research Unit. In 1966, following his increasing interest in the phenomena of transsexualism and gender dysphoria, the term attributed to those individuals who believe that they were assigned the wrong gender at birth or who have the physical and psychological experience of being born into the wrong body, Money founded Hopkins's Gender Identity Clinic, the first of its kind in the United States.

Ehrhardt was born in Hamburg, Germany. Between 1962 and 1964 she earned degrees in psychology from the Universities of Munich and Hamburg. In 1966, while a doctoral student at the University of Düsseldorf, Ehrhardt traveled to the United States to work with Money at Johns Hopkins. Given Money's interest in the hormonal basis of gender dysphoria and Ehrhardt's interest in the relationship between sex hormones and gender, the established scientist and the budding graduate student made a highly compatible interdisciplinary research team.

Ehrhardt completed her Ph.D. in psychology in 1969 and, three years later, she and Money coauthored the groundbreaking book *Man and Woman, Boy and Girl* (1972). The book's centerpiece, for which it garnered international praise, was its study involving a set of fraternal twin boys from Canada. In 1966, at eight months, the boys underwent routine circumcisions, but one of the boys suffered a freak accident that destroyed his penis. Shortly thereafter, Money counseled the family and recommended that the parents raise their son, "John," as a girl, "Joan," complete with estrogen treatments and a surgically-constructed vagina to replace the damaged penis.

The supposed transformation of a biological-born male into a person with a female gender role affirmed Money and Ehrhardt's theories about the potential malleability of gender identity through sex hormones and behavioral training. Many feminists in the 1970s embraced Money and Ehrhardt's ideas as scientific proof of how gender roles, far from being solely determined by biology, are socially constructed. Not everyone was satisfied with the results of the "John and Joan" case, however. In the mid-1970s, biologists like Milton Diamond were not entirely convinced by the malleability of gender through surgical or hormonal intervention. Money and Ehrhardt had argued that it would have been impossible for a child without a penis to grow into a psychologically and developmentally healthy male and that the only reasonable option was raising the boy as a girl. Diamond, by contrast, believed that an individual's sense of gender identity was hardwired into the human brain and did not, as Money and Ehrhardt argued, rely on one's relationship to external physical traits such as the size or shape of one's genitalia. Despite Diamond's skepticism, Money and Ehrhardt's theories flourished, and even today they still influence pediatric surgeons confronted with ambiguous genitalia.

Following the scientific and professional triumphs of the twins study, Money authored such memorable treatises as *Sexual Signatures* (1975) and *The Destroying Angel* (1985), the latter of which described the secret antimasturbatory origins of Graham crackers and Kellogg's breakfast cereals. His later books included psychological interpretations of sexual behavior such as *Venuses Penuses* (1986) and *The Breathless Orgasm* (1991). Meanwhile, Ehrhardt continued her research on prenatal sex hormones, but she also became increasingly interested in health care issues within LGBT populations. Since 1977, Ehrhardt has been associated with the Department of Psychiatry at Columbia University, where she studies the psychological repercussions of sexual risk behavior among varied populations. She also serves as director of the HIV Center for Clinical and Behavioral Studies at the New York State Psychiatric Institute.

Since the 1980s, sex hormone research pioneered by Money and Ehrhardt has been increasingly challenged by new brain- and gene-based models for thinking about the origins of gender identity and sexual orientation. Biologists like Anne Fausto-Sterling and Ruth Hubbard, for instance, have advocated the acceptance of a much wider continuum of hormonal and genetic possibilities in human beings that calls for complexity rather than following a binary either-or system of gender identity. Furthermore, Money and Ehrhardt's ideas have also been challenged by intersex individuals and organizations seeking to prevent doctors from "correcting" individuals whose genitals do not conform to a two-note system of gender identity. The advent of queer theory has also confronted much of the scientific and ideological bases of gender identity and sexual orientation on which Money and Ehrhardt's theories were founded.

In 1997 journalist John Colapinto tracked down "Joan," only to discover that the adjustment to a female gender identity Money and Ehrhardt had described was not, in fact, permanent. Colapinto found that by the early 1980s, "Joan" had rejected the female role assigned to her and was now living as David Reimer, a man with a wife, adopted children, and a fully reconstructed penis. Apparently, for years Reimer's parents had complained that their son's gender reassignment was not working. But Money, according to Colapinto, had ignored any evidence that might contest his theories. For many, these revelations have undermined the authoritative stance for which Money and Ehrhardt's work had been originally celebrated.

Bibliography

Colapinto, John. *As Nature Made Him: The Boy Who Was Raised as a Girl.* New York: HarperCollins, 2000.

Fausto-Sterling, Anne. *Myths of Gender: Biological Theories about Women and Men.* New York: Basic Books, 1985.

Kessler, Suzanne J. *Lessons from the Intersexed.* New Brunswick, N.J.: Rutgers University Press, 1998.

Money, John, and Anke A. Ehrhardt. *Man and Woman, Boy and Girl: The Differentiation and Dimorphism of Gender Identity from Conception to Maturity.* Baltimore: Johns Hopkins University Press, 1972.

David Serlin

See also BIOLOGY AND ZOOLOGY; ERICKSON EDUCATIONAL FOUNDATION; ERICKSON, REED; INTERSEXUALS AND INTERSEXED PEOPLE; PSYCHOLOGY, PSYCHIATRY, PSYCHOANALYSIS, AND SEXOLOGY; TRANSSEXUALS, TRANSVESTITES, TRANSGENDER PEOPLE, AND CROSS-DRESSERS.

MONOGAMY AND NONMONOGAMY

The standard definition of monogamy refers to a kinship system in which a person can be married to only one other person at a time. In anthropology, monogamy is typically counterpoised to polygamy, a system in which a person may marry more than one other person, most often a man having more than one wife. In Western societies influenced by Judeo-Christian traditions, monogamy carries a strong moral valuation and is associated with a great many virtues such as stability, maturity, trust, and fidelity.

Today, monogamy is often opposed to promiscuity in the popular imagination, and promiscuity is inevitably constructed as a reserve of many unwholesome things such as irresponsibility, hedonism, failure to care or love, and even sexual exploitation. The contemporary binary opposition with promiscuity has meant that monogamy increasingly has come to be equated with the idea of sexual exclusivity with just one partner over a significant period of time.

Patterns in the Past

Recent scholarly work has brought to light a lengthy history of male and female same-sex couples and romantic friendships in Western societies. According to Alfred Kinsey's 1948 and 1953 studies of male and female sexual behavior in the United States, 71 percent of females and 51 percent of males who reported any same-sex sexual activity claimed that they had had only one or two same-sex sexual partners.

An equally long history of specifically male nonmonogamous sexual networks has become evident from studies that range from Guido Ruggiero's 1985 work on fourteenth-century Venice to George Chauncey's 1994 account of early twentieth-century New York. These works document the existence of extensive and well-developed "undergrounds" of male cruising sites in urban spaces where men have sought each other out for often fleeting encounters.

While some early twentieth-century sexologists linked lesbians with promiscuous sex as well, most evidence suggests that promiscuity has been less common among lesbians than among gay men. Elizabeth Kennedy and Madeline Davis's 1993 study of mid-century Buffalo, New York, argues that while "cheating" may have been common in working-class femme/butch lesbian bar culture, monogamy remained the articulated ideal. According to Kinsey, 22 percent of males who reported any same-sex sexual activity claimed more than 10 male partners, while the comparable figure among females was 4 percent.

Lesbians and gay men contrasted. Distinctive modes of sexual organization and experience have often been the grounds for very different political agendas among lesbians and gay men. The homophile activist Clark Polak argued in the 1960s that, insofar as men were naturally promiscuous and women were naturally monogamous, lesbians and gay men had a great deal in common because they, unlike heterosexuals, could be true to their natures in the context of their same-sex sexual relationships.

More commonly, these differences have led to misunderstandings and conflict. While gay men have often been concerned about the clash between their sexual transit through public space and the actions of antigay police and perpetrators of antigay violence, lesbians have been more concerned about sexual harassment and reproductive rights. The sexual libertarianism of many men in the gay movements of the 1960s and 1970s contrasted with the antipornography and rape crisis initiatives pursued by many women in the same era.

These differences and debates became more complex in the 1980s "sex wars" among feminists, when many lesbians critiqued the traditional lack of sexual agency reproduced in some feminist rhetoric and called for nonmonogamous exploration. Gay men, in the same period, began to seek ways to have "safe sex" and became preoccupied with caregiving and relationship rights, as friends and lovers succumbed to the AIDS epidemic. In other words, sizeable constituencies of lesbians and gay men spoke up for concerns that had been associated with the other gender.

The gay marriage debate. All of these trends have become further embroiled in the "gay marriage" debates of the 1990s and 2000s. While the plea for same-sex relationship recognition has broad-based support in most LGBT communities, the demand for marriage raises many questions regarding the degree to which LGBT people wish to adopt the full range of traditions and expectations associated with this quintessentially heterosexual institution.

One of the primary debating points of advocates for gay marriage is that marriage would have a salutary effect on LGBT people precisely because it would give greater visibility to existing practices of monogamy among many same-sex couples and would further promote monogamy in LGBT communities. Opponents fear the imposition of heterosexist regulations upon the indigenous practices of LGBT people who feel little affection for the strictures of conventional, monogamous heterosexuality.

Patterns in the Early Twenty-first Century

So what are LGBT people doing in the early twenty-first century? The research literature shows that for gay men as a whole, monogamy, understood as the practice of sexually exclusive long-term relationships, is a minority model. But far from simply falling into the promiscuity camp as imagined by the larger society, gay men typically seek romantic, caring, and mutually supportive relationships with another man, along with sexual adventure and plural partnering. Most male couples construct their relationships without many of the guidelines or regulations, such as monogamy, that are used within heterosexual relationships. Among the options that male couples may adopt is sexual exclusivity, but it is by no means a given.

Philip Blumstein and Pepper Schwartz's 1983 study of male couples found that 82 percent had been nonmonogamous at some time during their relationships. For many, this occurred in a context of open relationships characterized by mutually agreed-upon nonmonogamy. Blumstein and Schwartz also found, however, that behavior often varied considerably from overt policy. Many of the men in open relationships, in fact, acted on their agreement infrequently, while a significant number (43 percent) of men in relationships with no mutual understanding on monogamy had additional sexual partners beyond their primary partner. These findings have been confirmed by other research on gay male relationships.

Studies of white and black men, as well as studies of gay men in Britain and Canada, arrive at similar conclusions. Most men in couples do not impose a sexually exclusive rule upon themselves or their partners; nevertheless, sexual openness or inclusiveness may or may not be practiced with any great frequency. At the same time, men in tacitly or overtly monogamous relationships also report engaging in some degree of sexual nonmonogamy at rates of 41 to 65 percent, depending on the study and the time period examined.

What these findings suggest is that the indigenous form of relationship development that has arisen in gay male cultures does not organize itself around the monogamy-promiscuity binary. Rather, if a modal form of relationship formation can be identified, it is that gay men typically enter into relationships with primary partners, and then with their primary partner retain the option to pursue secondary sexual adventures.

Having identified a modal form, it is important to note that there is no singular or dominant form of relationship system that characterizes GBT men as a whole. Many enter into sexually exclusive relationships in the early stages of forming a primary partnership. Some continue with monogamy; others add episodic partners after several years have elapsed. These secondary partners may be pursued either together as a couple or separately. And finally, some couples abandon sexual openness and adopt exclusivity later in their relationship. Monogamy, then, is an option rather than a requirement of gay relationships.

Nonmonogamy is not an indicator of relationship failure among gay men. Lawrence Kurdek and J. Patrick Schmitt found that "partners in open and closed gay relationships were equivalent in intimacy, security, satisfaction, and commitment" (p. 230), a finding confirmed by other researchers. More important than monogamy itself is a couple's understanding of the meaning of sex with another partner. For those who equate sexual exclusivity with the communication of the value of the relationship, sex with another may be read as an indicator of "infidelity" or "betrayal." However, polyamorous female or male couples may rely on other indicators of mutual affection and have tacit or explicit understandings that additional partners are, for example, "just sex" and thus do not jeopardize the primary relationship.

Though there has been a good deal of speculation on the effect of the AIDS epidemic on the rate of sexual exclusivity among gay men, there is very little firm evidence in the area. Sexual openness does pose additional challenges to the consistent practice of safe sex necessary to prevent HIV transmission.

Research on monogamy in lesbian relationships is much more unsystematic and anecdotal. It suggests that lesbians are much more likely than gay men to endorse monogamy in their relationships but less likely to do so than married, heterosexual women. Both lesbians and gay men (along with heterosexual women) are less likely to equate sex outside the relationship with relationship breakdown than are heterosexual men. As Weeks et al. remarked, "the principle of 'co-independence' that structures the operation of same sex relationships, the break from heterosexual assumptions, and the *abstract* possibilities of separating sex from emotional ties, mean that nonmonogamy is always (at the abstract or practical level) a possibility for non-heterosexual relationships" (p. 150).

Same-sex sexual relationships often draw on cultural understandings regarding friendship (which are usually nonexclusive) as much as they do on marriage (which traditionally demands exclusivity). They draw upon the larger (heterosexual) society for understandings of successful relationship development, but at the same time are disconnected from the social mechanisms that reproduce monogamy as a relationship ideal. It is only recently that LGBT communities have come to document and value the relationships that have grown up as autonomous and authentic cultural formations, rather than viewing them through the lens of heterosexist demands and aspirations. Monogamy and nonmonogamy are among the issues that LGBT people consider in their own relationships, often developing innovative alternatives to heterosexual models.

Bibliography

Blumstein, Philip, and Pepper Schwartz. *American Couples.* New York: Morrow, 1983.

Chauncey, George. *Gay New York: Gender, Urban Culture, and the Making of the Gay Male World, 1890–1940.* New York: Basic Books, 1994.

Kennedy, Elizabeth Lapovsky, and Madeline D. Davis. *Boots of Leather, Slippers of Gold: The History of a Lesbian Community.* New York: Routledge, 1993.

Kinsey, Alfred. *Sexual Behavior in the Human Female.* Philadelphia: Saunders, 1953.

Kinsey, Alfred, Wardell Baxter Pomeroy, and Clyde E. Martin. *Sexual Behavior in the Human Male.* Philadelphia: Saunders, 1948.

Kurdek, Lawrence, and J. Patrick Schmitt. "Relationship Quality of Gay Men in Closed or Open Relationships." In *Gay Relationships.* Edited by John De Cecco. New York: Haworth, 1988.

Ruggiero, Guido. *The Boundaries of Eros.* New York: Oxford University Press, 1985.

Sheets, Virgil, and Marlow Wolfe. "Sexual Jealousy in Heterosexuals, Lesbians, and Gays." *Sex Roles* 44, nos. 5–6 (March 2001): 255–276.

Stein, Marc. *City of Sisterly and Brotherly Loves: Lesbian and Gay Philadelphia, 1945–1972.* Chicago: University of Chicago Press, 2000.

Terry, Jennifer. *An American Obsession: Science, Medicine, and Homosexuality in Modern Society.* Chicago: University of Chicago Press, 1999.

Weeks, Jeffrey, Brian Heathy, and Catherine Donovan. *Same Sex Intimacies.* London: Routledge, 2001.

Barry D. Adam

See also CRUISING; KINSEY, ALFRED C.; TRICKING.

MORAGA, Cherríe (b. 25 September 1952), lesbian writer, feminist.

Cherríe Moraga, born in Whittier, California, grew up in San Gabriel, a suburb of Los Angeles. Her mother Elvira Moraga is a Chicana, her father Joseph Lawrence an Anglo. Moraga's writing explores her identity as a mixed-heritage, working-class Chicana lesbian, particularly the meanings associated with light skin and a butch sexual identification. Moraga and her brother and sister were the first generation in their family to attend college. She received her B.A. in English from Immaculate Heart College in Hollywood, California, in 1974 and an M.A. in feminist literature from San Francisco State University. Moraga came of age in the context of 1970s movements—Chicano, feminist, and gay—that influenced her commitment to writing for social change. As of 2003, Moraga is an artist-in-residence at Stanford University.

In Moraga's first intervention in feminist scholarship and theory, *This Bridge Called My Back: Writings by Radical Women of Color* co-edited with Gloria Anzaldúa (1981), the writers refused to identify one aspect of identity as more important than another. Moraga's writing explores the complex and contradictory ways that race, gender, class, and sexuality shape identity in an ongoing, open-ended process.

Moraga's collage of poems, essays, and diary entries, *Loving in the War Years: Lo que nunca pasó por sus labios* (That which never passed her lips), is the first book on Chicana lesbianism (1983). The autobiographical essay "A Long Line of Vendidas" (female sell-outs) critiques Mexican/Chicano cultural attitudes toward women's roles, bodies, and sexualities, and the male domination and homophobia of the Chicano movement. The essay analyzes *La Malinche,* the indigenous woman who aided the conquistador Cortés and symbolically gave birth to the mestizo (mixed-race) Mexican people. For Moraga, *La Malinche* is used to contain and coerce female sexuality: any woman who fails to conform to the feminine ideal or organizes her desire independently from Chicano men is labeled a traitor, a *malinchista.* The book traces Moraga's journey from childhood, through coming-out experiences in a white lesbian community, to her political and sexual connection with Latinas and Chicanas. The title poem, "Loving in the War Years," addresses the dangers of lesbian existence. This collection was reprinted in 2000, with new poems and essays added.

In 1985 Moraga studied with Maria Irene Fornes at the Hispanic Playwrights-in-Residence Laboratory at the Intar Theatre in New York City. Moraga's first three plays, *Giving Up the Ghost* (published in 1986, premiered in 1989), *Shadow of a Man* (premiered in 1990), and *Heroes and Saints* (premiered in 1992), were published in *Heroes and Saints and Other Plays* (1994). *Ghost* marks the first staging of Chicana lesbian desire in theater history. *Shadow* is set in the context of the Chicano family; *Heroes* dramatizes a community's response to pesticide poisoning, embodied in the protagonist's deformity. A recurring theme in Moraga's work is the cultural value placed on men and Chicanas' betrayal of themselves and other mestizas as a result of their unquestioning acceptance of male superiority. Moraga's use of bilingual language captures the beauty and rhythms of Chicano speech; her views about lesbian identity and desire are always linked to Chicano culture and the working-class Chicano family.

Moraga's subsequent published plays include *Heart of the Earth: A Popol Vuh Story* (2000), *A Circle in the Dirt: El Pueblo de East Palo Alto* (2001), *Watsonville: Some Place Not Here* (2000), and *The Hungry Woman: A Mexican Medea* (2000). This last play critiques heterosexist and sexist aspects of cultural nationalism, combining the character of Medea with that of another child-killer, *La Llorona* (weeping woman) of the Mexican oral tradition.

Exiled from a futuristic Chicano state for her sexuality, Medea sacrifices her son to keep him from growing to manhood.

Chicano Nation, or Aztlán (the legendary Aztec place of human origin, now the southwestern United States), also appears in Moraga's second volume of poetry and prose, *The Last Generation* (1993). Therein, the essay "Queer Aztlán" envisions more utopian possibilities than *The Hungry Woman:* a nation that chooses to embrace sexual and racial diversity. The book also examines the racial category of "whiteness" within the context of cultural nationalism, the family, and lesbian desire.

The memoir *Waiting in the Wings: Portrait of a Queer Motherhood* (1997) chronicles Moraga's decision to have a child. Themes include grappling with the child's maleness, the politics of lesbian motherhood, the need for both "blood" and "queer" family, and the relationship, at times conflicted, between her roles as mother and writer. Through her writing, Moraga invents a new identity, (butch) lesbian mother (terms usually seen as mutually exclusive in the dominant culture) and contributes to the acknowledgment of sexuality as empowering and important for intellectual and political work.

Bibliography

Alarcón, Norma. "Making 'Familia' from Scratch: Split Subjectivities in the Work of Helena María Viramontes and Cherríe Moraga." In *Chicana Creativity and Criticism: Charting New Frontiers in American Literature.* Edited by María Herrera-Sobek and Helena María Viramontes. Houston: Arte Público Press, 1988.

Romero, Lora. "'When Something Goes Queer': Familiarity, Formalism, and Minority Intellectuals in the 1980s." *The Yale Journal of Criticism* 6, no. 1 (1993): 121–141.

Yarbro-Bejarano, Yvonne. *The Wounded Heart: Writing on Cherríe Moraga.* Austin: University of Texas Press, 2001.

Yvonne Yarbro-Bejarano

See also ANZALDÚA, GLORIA; FORNES, MARIA IRENE; LITERATURE.

MORGAN, CLAIRE. see HIGHSMITH, PATRICIA.

MORGAN, Robin **(b. 29 January 1941), writer, activist.**

Robin Morgan was born in Lake Worth, Florida. She was raised by her mother and her aunt, who relocated to Mount Vernon, New York, a working-class suburb of New York City, when she was very young.

A precocious and pretty child who could act, Morgan was soon the primary breadwinner of her family. By age five she had her own radio show. Radio launched her into television, through which she became known to millions as Dagmar in *Mama,* a hit show about a family of Norwegian immigrants living in San Francisco in the early 1900s. Morgan seemed such a model child that in 1954 the starchy General Federation of Women's Clubs of America named her the "Ideal American Girl."

By age sixteen Morgan, who was already writing poetry on the side, had grown weary of acting. She longed to go to college, but her mother prevented her from attending the University of Chicago, which had admitted her to a special program for talented and intelligent teenagers. Foiled by her mother, she devised a fail-safe exit from show business—she gained weight. Morgan subsequently found work in a literary agency and later became an editor at Grove Press, which was known for its publication of the radical and outré. In 1962 she married the up-and-coming poet Kenneth Pitchford, despite the fact that he was homosexually inclined. Their marriage was held together by a shared love of poetry, their son Blake, and a bit of a dare given her husband's sexual preference.

In 1967, when the first women's liberation group, New York Radical Women, began meeting in New York City, Morgan was among the participants. She was already involved with the Yippies, the leftist group whose slapstick-style politics and guerrilla theater tactics she brought to the women's movement and to another group, WITCH (Women's International Terrorist Conspiracy from Hell), that she helped form. Its members conducted a number of "actions," such as disrupting bridal fairs and hexing the New York Stock Exchange while dressed in full witch drag.

Morgan was among the new movement's most effective polemicists and organizers. She played a pivotal role in organizing the movement's first national demonstration, the 1968 protest at the Miss America Pageant in Atlantic City. Her 1970 anthology of women's liberation writing, *Sisterhood Is Powerful,* was among the best-selling feminist books of the decade. Morgan was initially a feminist "politico," which is to say that her allegiance was more to the Left than to feminism. However, by 1970 she had grown disenchanted with the Left and repudiated it in an inflammatory and widely read essay, "Goodbye to All That," published in the newspaper *Rat.* In it, she suggested that if leftist men refused to give up their "cock privilege," they might be divested of their cocks. She published in feminist newspapers and magazines and devised many memorable, if controversial, one-liners. Many of these essays were published in her 1977 collection, *Going Too Far.*

Morgan was among those feminists who began to redefine radical feminism in ways that were sometimes antithetical to its original formulation—a strand some called cultural feminism. She embraced essentialist explanations of gender and encouraged feminists to build a woman-centered counterculture rather than wasting their time in futile confrontations with male dominance. Morgan was among the first to support the lesbian feminist notion of women-loving women, but her support was conditional. In 1971 she argued that lesbians who supported nonmonogamy and accepted transvestites and transsexuals as their allies had adopted a male style that could destroy the women's movement. This theory is explained in the essay "Lesbianism and Feminism" in *Going Too Far,* which was the keynote speech at the West Coast Lesbian Feminist Conference in Los Angeles in 1973. The vigilance with which she and other like-minded feminists patrolled the borders of feminist and lesbian desire provoked a rebellion in the early 1980s as growing numbers of women began to question whether "woman-identified" sexuality was any less affected by cultural norms than the sort of "male-identified" sex—sadomasochist, femme-butch—regularly denounced by cultural feminists.

After twenty years of feeling sexually obliterated in her marriage, she fell in love with another woman. According to her autobiography, her significant relationships since 1982 have been lesbian. Morgan has remained a tireless activist and prolific writer. She is a prominent player in the effort to internationalize feminism. From 1990 until 1993 she was the executive editor of *Ms.* magazine. She has written five books of nonfiction, two novels, and six books of poetry as well as editing three anthologies of feminist writing. Morgan helped legitimize lesbianism in the women's movement, but the terms of that legitimation were challenged by sexual minorities in the 1980s and beyond.

Bibliography

Alpert, Jane. *Growing Up Underground.* New York: Morrow, 1981.

Echols, Alice. *Daring to Be Bad: Radical Feminism in America, 1967–1975.* Minneapolis: University of Minnesota Press, 1989.

Morgan, Robin. *Saturday's Child: A Memoir.* New York: Norton, 2001.

Alice Echols

See also LESBIAN FEMINISM.

MURPHY, Frank **(b. 13 April 1890; d. 19 July 1949), U.S. Supreme Court justice.**

Although no United States Supreme Court justices are known for certain to have been gay, lesbian, bisexual, or transgender, Frank Murphy is the most likely possibility. The lifelong bachelor successfully maintained heterosexual appearances throughout his remarkable career, impressing gossip columnists with a cavalcade of attractive girlfriends. All the while, however, he kept suspiciously close company with a key adviser (also a bachelor). Suspicions about Murphy's sexual orientation were restricted to whispers and offhand remarks during his life, but it was common during the 1930s and 1940s for men to conceal their homosexuality in order to have successful careers. It is likely that Murphy's careful discretion allowed him access to one of the nation's highest positions of power, an impressive feat during a period when social paranoia over homosexuality reached unprecedented heights.

Historians describe Frank Murphy as an ardent New Dealer and Democrat, faithful to President Franklin D. Roosevelt's policies and political vision. Murphy was born and raised in Michigan and studied law at the University of Michigan in Ann Arbor. After brief stints as a private attorney and judge, he was elected mayor of Detroit in 1930. As mayor, he created innovative relief programs for the unemployed during the worst years of the Great Depression. These programs captured the attention of the Democratic Party leadership, and in 1933 President Roosevelt, newly elected, appointed Murphy governor general of the Philippines. During the next three years, Murphy oversaw the transition of the Philippines from an American colony to an independent commonwealth.

Upon his return to the United States in 1936, he was elected governor of Michigan. His two-year term was dominated by contentious (and often bloody) labor battles between General Motors and the United Auto Workers. As the United Auto Workers pioneered labor militancy through its use of sit-down strikes, business leaders demanded a swift crackdown on the rebellious laborers. Murphy's refusal to send in troops in 1937 was a significant boost to the American labor movement, provoking critics to condemn his handling of the situation as "feminine." After losing his reelection bid in 1938, Murphy served as U.S. attorney general until his successful nomination to the U.S. Supreme Court in 1940, where he served until his death in 1949. As a Supreme Court justice his decisions consistently defended free speech, freedom of religion, and minority rights. Perhaps his most famous—and controversial—defense of minority rights

> The most extensive discussion of Murphy's sexual orientation appears in *Courting Justice: Gay Men and Lesbians v. The Supreme Court,* pp. 18–21, by Joyce Murdoch and Deb Price.

came during the 1946 *Yamashita* case. In a climate of racist anti-Japanese hysteria, Murphy argued in a dissent to the majority opinion that war crimes trials being conducted against Japanese generals after World War II were unconstitutional.

Although Murphy's sexuality was never a source of public discussion during his lifetime, diaries of contemporary figures such as the columnist Drew Pearson and presidential advisor Harry Hopkins reveal that many people assumed that Murphy was homosexual. In addition to his theatrical mannerisms and flamboyant fashion sense, Murphy's lifelong companionship with aide and adviser Edward G. Kemp raised many eyebrows. Kemp and Murphy met while undergraduates at the University of Michigan. They served together in World War I and, after completing their military service, formed a law practice together. As Murphy's career took off, Kemp remained Murphy's primary adviser and closest confidante until Murphy's death in 1949. The two lifelong bachelors frequently shared living quarters. Their relationship had many characteristics in common with the famous relationship between Federal Bureau of Investigation director J. Edgar Hoover and his lifelong assistant, Clyde Tolson. Ironically, prevailing social prejudices protected both couples. Because homosexuals were thought to be criminals, degenerates, and psychopaths according to the logic of the day, the American public assumed that persons of Murphy's or Hoover's stature simply could not be homosexual.

The press never hinted that Murphy and Kemp's relationship was anything other than professional. In fact, newspapers frequently printed stories describing the supposed girlfriends of Murphy who accompanied him to social functions. Murphy kept a busy social calendar, and as was the case with many gay movie stars of the same era, the girlfriends served to deflect suspicions about his private life. Murphy announced two engagements late in his life, but did not follow through on either of them. One frustrated fiancée called off her engagement to Murphy after repeated postponements on his part, even after she had converted to Catholicism to please him. The other engagement included plans for a secret wedding service, to be attended only by Kemp and a personal secretary (all four would then live together), but Murphy died a month before the wedding date.

Bibliography

Fine, Sidney. *Frank Murphy.* 3 vols. Ann Arbor: University of Michigan Press, 1975–1984.

Howard, J. Woodford. *Mr. Justice Murphy: A Political Biography.* Princeton, N.J.: Princeton University Press, 1968.

Lunt, Richard D. *The High Ministry of Government: The Political Career of Frank Murphy.* Detroit, Mich.: Wayne State University Press, 1965.

Murdoch, Joyce, and Deb Price. *Courting Justice: Gay Men and Lesbians v. the Supreme Court.* New York: Basic Books, 2001.

Craig M. Loftin

See also FEDERAL LAW AND POLICY.

MURRAY, Pauli (b. 20 November 1910; d. 1 July 1985), lawyer, activist.

As an activist, feminist, lawyer, and socialist, Pauli Murray was involved in some of the key social justice movements in the United States during the twentieth century. She voted for socialist candidate Norman Thomas in 1932, served in the ranks of the Works Progress Administration (WPA), and briefly joined a little-known Marxist-Leninist political faction led by a former Communist Party leader, Jay Lovestone. In the civil rights arena, Murray was an organizer for A. Philip Randolph's World War II–era March on Washington Movement, staged sit-in protests while attending Howard University Law School, and was active with the pacifist Fellowship of Reconciliation when it sponsored the first freedom rides in 1947. Murray also had a powerful voice in the burgeoning feminist movement. She served on the Committee on Civil and Political Rights of the Presidential Commission on the Status of Women in 1962 and 1963, coauthored an influential 1965 article in the *George Washington Law Review* on sex discrimination titled "Jane Crow and the Law," and was a founding member of the National Organization for Women (NOW) in 1966.

The broad spectrum of Murray's interests and activities tell only part of the story of her importance as a historical figure. In all of the spaces in which she operated, Murray sought to express the full complexity of her person as a southern-raised self-supporting African American woman radical who built lasting intimate relationships with women yet struggled with her same-sex desires and gender identity. Murray's efforts to embrace the multiple aspects of her identity, although not always visible or spoken, intertwined with and informed her political engagement.

Murray was born Anna Pauline Murray in Baltimore, Maryland, the fourth of William H. Murray and Agnes

Fitzgerald Murray's six children. Both of her parents were of mixed ancestry and members of the black educated elite, but Murray lost both at an early age: Agnes Murray died suddenly in 1914, and William Murray faced continued bouts with mental illness that led him three years later to be involuntarily committed to Crownsville State Hospital in Maryland. As a result, Murray moved south to live with her maternal grandparents and her mother's oldest sister, Pauline Fitzgerald Dame, who formally adopted her.

Raised in Durham, North Carolina, Murray spent her formative years negotiating the racial limitations of Jim Crow segregation. In 1926, as a high school graduate determined to gain an education outside of the constraints of southern segregation, Murray moved to New York City to live with her extended family in Queens. In 1928, Murray entered the then all-female Hunter College. In her second year, Murray moved out on her own. Residing at the 137th Street Young Women's Christian Association and working in a variety of jobs, these years marked a crucial period of transformation in her life.

In 1930 the economic chaos of the Great Depression forced Murray to place her college ambitions on hold. In this period, she continued to build significant political and personal relationships with men and women. After a brief unsuccessful marriage, Murray took to traveling the nation. She hitchhiked with female friends throughout New England and, sharing the driving responsibilities with a friend who owned a car, traveled across the country to Vallejo, California, just outside of San Francisco. Murray later published a fictionalized account of her adventures passing as a young boy and illegally riding the railroad in the *Negro Anthology* (1934), compiled by Nancy Cunard.

In 1933, Murray graduated from Hunter. After a period with the WPA and a variety of progressive organizations, Murray joined the staff of the Socialist Party–affiliated Workers' Defense League. In 1940 she served as the main organizer of a campaign to prevent the execution of Odell Waller, a black Virginia sharecropper accused of killing his white landlord. In 1941, fueled by the Waller case and a growing interest in civil rights justice, Murray entered Howard Law School. She graduated three years later, the first in her class and the only woman.

Reliant solely on her income to support herself and her elderly aunts, Murray struggled to make a living as a lawyer. Murray often turned to publishing projects, including *The State Laws on Race and Color* (1951), which she edited, and *Proud Shoes: The Story of an American Family* (1956), which she wrote, to support herself. From 1956 to 1960, Murray practiced law at a New York City legal firm that provided some financial security and marked the beginning of a sixteen-year friendship with coworker Irene Barlow. At the urging of her friend Maida Springer, Murray left the firm in 1960 to teach constitutional law for a year at the newly established Ghana Law School in Accra. In 1965, Murray earned a doctorate of juridical science from Yale University Law School and in 1967 moved to Columbia, South Carolina, to work as an administrator at Benedict College. A year later she accepted a faculty position at Brandeis University to teach American civilization and help develop the Afro-American Studies Program, which placed her in the midst of the black power student movement.

In 1973, following the death of her dear friend Barlow, Murray's life shifted profoundly. She resigned her full professorship at Brandeis University and entered an Episcopal seminary. In 1977 she became the first African American in the United States to be ordained as an Episcopalian priest. Murray died in Pittsburgh, Pennsylvania.

Bibliography

"Dialogue. Pauli Murray's Notable Connections." *Journal of Women's History* 14, no. 2 (Summer 2002): 54–82.

Murray, Pauli. Papers. Arthur and Elizabeth Schlesinger Library on the History of Women in America. Radcliffe Institute for Advanced Study. Harvard University, Cambridge, Mass.

———. *Song in A Weary Throat: An American Pilgrimage.* New York: Harper and Row, 1987.

Dayo Folayan Gore

MUSIC: BROADWAY AND MUSICAL THEATER

The American musical has long been a utopic place to explore new themes and ideas while simultaneously championing community. Within what is typically a two and one-half hour time period, characters fall in love, undergo stress and hardship, find ways to negotiate their identities and desires within society, experience loss, and ultimately celebrate life despite its complex, ephemeral, and occasionally tragic nature. Audiences are sent forth from musical theater performances with what is known as an eleven o'clock lift—a final number designed to stick in one's head, usually encompassing the major ideals of the show and occasionally even suggesting a way to make life a little better. Musical theater, historically, has been an arena of LGBT hope, whether for generations of homosexuals forced to remain closeted, those oppressed by McCarthyism and political profiling, or any who have lived and died under the specter of AIDS.

Form and Structure

Musical theater, traditionally a larger-than-life performance form that finds its characters responding to life's problems (no matter how insignificant) through song and dance, is distinctly and perhaps irrevocably marked by its irregular and comprehensive structure. Often, a show's music belies its origins in folk music and operetta, but the show may also feature variations on pop and rock. Musical theater's choreography often draws from a wide range of movement vocabularies, ultimately featuring an amalgam of ballet, tap, modern, and jazz dance. Depending on the director and the performers in any given role, a musical's acting style shifts rapidly between gritty realism and the broadest of melodrama, sometimes within the span of a single song. When these elements are assembled into a musical, even if perfectly integrated, the sum total of the performance event will almost always seem odd and contrived next to any other play or film, and certainly the musical's distant cousin, real life.

Owing to its idealistic themes, its counternormative form and structure, and the large numbers of gay and bisexual creators and performers that make up its family tree, it perhaps is not surprising that conventional culture has reduced this art form to a simple formula: musical theater equals gay. Theater historians and theorists—homosexual and heterosexual—continue to explore the history of this stereotype, but despite serious research done on behalf of the musical, popular culture continues to reify the idea that knowledge of musicals is an indicator of a person's sexuality. Just as there is no singular type of musical theater (endless structural variations exist—the rock musical, the book musical, the dance-based musical, the sung-through musical), there is clearly no sense in affixing a gay label to all musical theater. A careful look, though, at some of the musical's gay and bisexual creators, the success of musicals with LGBT characters and plots, and the openness and potential that musical theater affords to anyone wishing to read it queerly speaks volumes as to why musical theater is a haven for LGBT practitioners and audiences.

The Musical's Creators

Musical theater has been primarily composed, written, directed, and choreographed by white men. Although women have been finding more of a place in musical theater since the late twentieth century, the musical has for decades been a boy's club that allowed performance rights, but not necessarily membership, to women. Male composer-lyricist teams like Rodgers and Hammerstein, Lerner and Loewe, Kander and Ebb, and even Lloyd-Weber and Rice have dominated the industry for decades, and although none of these partnerships have ever been proven to be sexual, the homosociality of the musical's creative teams cannot be denied.

The American musical grew up in New York City, fostered by a host of men wrestling publicly and privately with their sexual identities. As the gay mecca in the early part of the twentieth century, New York City afforded a place to work and play for all sorts of people looking for different lifestyles. At a crossroads of the arts, musical theater offered a safe venue for many to labor where the closets were slightly more ajar. Theater practitioners, knowing that many of their colleagues were gay, were able to be as out or as unobservable as they wanted to be (or at least more so than in most other professions), snapping up the spotlight and amassing celebrity or quietly blending into the chorus. Ornate sets, opulent costumes, and row after row of beautiful men and women singing and dancing offered spectators and practitioners a chance to participate in fabulous displays of color and life, the spectacle for which musical theater has come to be known. A subculture emerged around witnessing these performances among gay men, whose visibility in Manhattan and whose sexual and social identities were being solidified during the same era as the musical.

Charting the sexualities of the creators of musicals has been a major preoccupation of scholars, but this information is only useful when it transcends mere gossip and is used to ascertain how a composer, lyricist, author, director, or choreographer's sexuality affected their work. For instance, composer-lyricist Cole Porter's *Anything Goes* (Broadway, 1934) and *Kiss Me Kate* (Broadway, 1948) both contain numerous witty (and often naughty) references to the pleasures of gay sexuality, carefully coded so as not to offend the general public. Porter's own relative comfort with his sexuality and his large social circle of gay and lesbian friends find a happy home within his musicals. Lyricist Lorenz Hart, however, a longtime collaborator with composer Richard Rodgers, found his own homosexuality distasteful and debilitating. His own self-loathing and loneliness informed the songs of *Babes in Arms* (Broadway, 1937) and *Pal Joey* (Broadway, 1940), where characters struggle with the impossibility of love and the inevitable heartbreak that it causes. Similar analyses can be done with other musicals, such as *West Side Story* (Broadway, 1957), that lack any overtly homosexual characters or story lines but have been partially or wholly conceived by gay men. *West Side Story*'s major collaborators, director-choreographer Jerome Robbins, composer Leonard Bernstein, book writer Arthur Laurents, and lyricist Stephen Sondheim, were all gay, which sheds light on why Tony and Maria's hetero-

Rent. The cast of Jonathan Larson's 1996 version of the opera *La Bohème* stops the show. [Getty Images]

sexual ballad, "Somewhere," is often read as expressing a longing to find a paradise where lovers of all orientations can find peace and happiness.

Gay and Lesbian Characters

Even more interesting than the sexualities of musical theater's creators are the LGBT characters who have appeared within the shows and what their presence in the musical has in common with contemporary perceptions of sexuality in society. Predictably, gay characters are easily visible from the politically liberating 1960s onward, as evidenced by musicals like *Hair* (Broadway, 1968) and *A Chorus Line* (Broadway 1975), both about young people sharing their hopes, dreams, and identities with each other. In the various incarnations (Broadway, 1966; film, 1972; Broadway, Roundabout Theatre revival, 1998) of *Cabaret*—a musical, based on a story by gay novelist Christopher Isherwood—the central male love interest is played as a heterosexual, a bisexual, and a mostly closeted homosexual, respectively. *La Cage Aux Folles* (1983) is arguably Broadway's first homosexual musical; the play on which it was based was later adapted to become the much more mainstream film *The Birdcage* (1996). It is a story about two middle-aged lovers, one who owns a drag-queen nightclub and the other who is its star. Within the course of this musical, one of the main characters has to defend his lifestyle and sings "I Am What I Am," a defiant song that has since become a queer anthem. Three one-act musicals by William Finn, *In Trousers* (Off-Broadway, 1979), *The March of the Falsettos* (Off-Broadway, 1981), and *Falsettoland* (Off-Off-Broadway, 1990), are similarly about the collision of family values and sexual identity. The central character in these three musicals learns he is gay, and yet still desires to keep his wife and son and lover together as a happy family.

Falsettoland is especially remarkable as it is one of the earliest mainstream musicals to feature a character with AIDS. It paved the way for Jonathan Larson's *Rent* (Broadway, 1996), a musical adaptation of Puccini's opera *La Bohème* (Turin, Italy, 1896) that follows a group of young starving artists in New York City, many of whom are gay or have AIDS. Based on Manuel Puig's novel, John Kander and Fred Ebb's *Kiss of the Spider-woman* (Broadway, 1993) visits the fantasy world that a gay window dresser inhabits while incarcerated in a South American prison. The syndication of the television sitcom *Will and Grace* (which first aired in 1998) heralds an era where there is growing mainstream comfort with gay identities (within stereotypical roles, of course), and this phenomenon has translated to the stage, both in new

A Chorus Line. The cast unites to create one singular sensation in this landmark 1975 show on the yearnings of Broadway's supporting players. **[Getty Images]**

musicals and in frequent revivals of older shows with gay characters. Although the increased volume of gay characters is a welcome change to musical theater, practitioners, critics, and audiences need to examine how these themes and identities function politically. What ideologies does this increased gay visibility support or seek to change?

An example of this tension between presence and politics is the way that lesbians have been represented in musicals. As of the first years of the twenty-first century, lesbian characters have primarily been relegated to smaller roles such as the next-door neighbors in *Falsettoland* or as party goers in *The Wild Party* musicals (two different shows, Broadway and Off-Broadway, which both opened in 2000). Even the lesbian relationship in *Rent* seems merely a diversion until the central heterosexual plot is resumed. Often, these women's bodies are objectified or are only present as tokens: a nod to another minority without any real thematic or political substance. Hopefully, this increased onstage representation of lesbians in musical theater starting in the later part of the twentieth century will result in a more significant incorporation of lesbian characters and themes in subsequent decades of musical theater.

Drag and the Musical

In part because of its ties to spectacle, drag has long figured as a prominent part of many musicals, with historical antecedents as far back as American minstrelsy, English pantomime, and even Romantic ballet. Small character parts in musicals like *South Pacific* (Broadway, 1949) find humor in characters temporarily donning clothes meant for the opposite sex. *The Rocky Horror Picture Show* (London, 1973; film, 1975) deals with the subject more overtly, featuring a bisexual "sweet transvestite from Transsexual, Transylvania" and the pleasures that a young engaged couple finds in his mansion. The year 1975 saw two Broadway musicals that further explore drag performance. In *A Chorus Line* one of the characters recounts the day his parents discovered him performing in a drag show, and in *Chicago* one male character convincingly masquerades as a female socialite until his performance is unmasked (a subplot that was cut from the 2002 film). Since the 1970s, many more musicals have featured men in drag as highly sympathetic characters. In *La Cage aux Folles* the put-upon drag queen Albin tries desperately to keep his family together, and in *Rent* some of the most moving love songs and dialogue are given to Angel, the streetwise drag queen dying of AIDS. Two movie musicals with cross-dressing as their central plot device were subsequently adapted as stage shows; the 1959 film *Some Like it Hot* was reincarnated as the Broadway stage musical *Sugar* in 1972, and the 1982 film *Victor/Victoria* starring Julie Andrews was revived as a play on Broadway in 1995. Musical theater clearly has a longstanding relationship with drag; in recent musicals on stage and screen, it has become an acceptable place to examine not just the performance of gender but also the performance of sexuality.

One example of a show that explores transgender issues is *Hedwig and the Angry Inch* (Off-Broadway, 1998), a musical about an East German transsexual rocker whose botched sex change operation and immigration to the United States leads to loneliness and confusion. In 2001 its cult popularity led to a film, perhaps an indicator of how musical theater is becoming increasingly willing and able to examine explicitly the construction of gender and sexuality and to help create a forum for more mainstream discussions of such issues.

Queering the Musical

Prior to the 1960s, few overtly nonstraight characters appeared onstage, and certainly very few pieces of theater deviated from the heteronormative standards of the day. Bearing this in mind, it seems almost incongruous that many older musicals that reinforce cultural stereotypes or keep gay and lesbian characters and issues out of the spotlight are now or have always been enjoyed (even worshipped) by homosexual communities. As these audiences have done for years, scholars and critics are finding the musical a complex and useful site to examine an array of queer themes and identities—even when not originally intended by a show's creators.

Celebrity culture does much to explain the ties between the musical and its gay or lesbian fans. Stars of the musical theater often establish a following because of the performance conventions of the musical; songs of hope and support are sung directly to audience members, by some performers as often as eight times a week. These performers, mostly female, become well loved (and sometimes deified) by audiences. They are subsequently cast in similar role after role, usually as someone queer audiences can relate to or would like to be, such as a romantic lead character or as someone who continually perseveres despite life's obstacles. Their love ballads and showstopping numbers, such as "I'm Still Here" from *Follies* (Broadway, 1971) and "Over the Rainbow" from the film *The Wizard of Oz* (1939), even though sung by heterosexual characters, have frequently been adopted by the queer community because they speak to queer history, aesthetic, and sentiment. Divas of the stage and screen are celebrated further in piano bars, karaoke nights, and revues, where the musical's songs are performed as are the stage personas and vocal styles of its major celebrities, such as Judy Garland, Chita Rivera, Liza Minnelli, Ethel Merman, Barbra Streisand, and Betty Buckley.

Another strategy for queering the musical is to consider its marginalized parties. Whom does the greater community of heterosexuals exclude, oppress, or ignore? Gays and lesbians can identify with the characters who do not find happiness in the same things or share the same values that the greater society does. Characters that are villainized, made to seem excessively feminine or masculine, or who are not allowed a fair chance in life can be read as queer characters—those who regardless of their actual sexualities are different enough from the general public that they seem to have traits or experiences in common with gays and lesbians in the audience. For instance, the hyper-masculine character, Jud Fry, in *Oklahoma* (Broadway, 1943) and the delicate Harry Beaton in *Brigadoon* (Broadway, 1947) both fail as romantic suitors and are punished for their counternormative approaches to masculinity and heterosexuality. The structure of the musical itself can push some characters to the margins; characters are similarly queerable who are not allowed to sing or dance with the rest of the chorus, who are not allotted much dialogue or stage time, or who are either killed off (like Jud Fry and Harry Beaton) or left out of the musical's traditional happy ending (where the stage is often packed with happy heterosexual couples). Those characters marked as different because of religion, ethnicity, or race (such as the Polynesian character, Bloody Mary, in *South Pacific* or the Puerto Rican, Chino, in *West Side Story)* may also be attractive or sympathetic to gay and lesbian audiences because of the characters' inability or refusal to fit in.

In theatrical circles, the shorthand for dramatic literature is straight theater. It is not surprising, therefore, that musical theater has maintained a queer identity. LGBT characters, plots, and themes are undoubtedly growing more socially acceptable and sought after. Theater practitioners are becoming more able to openly assert their sexualities and apply them to their craft. As long as these trends continue, the American musical will remain a popular, meaningful, and unquestionably queer form of theater.

Bibliography

Clum, John M. *Something for the Boys: Musical Theater and Gay Culture.* New York: St. Martin's Press, 1999.

Dyer, Richard. *Only Entertainment.* New York: Routledge, 1992.

Kislan, Richard. *The Musical: A Look at the American Musical Theatre.* Rev. ed. New York: Applause Books, 1995.

Marra, Kim, and Robert A. Schanke, eds. *Staging Desire: Queer Readings of American Theater History.* Ann Arbor: University of Michigan Press, 2002.

Mast, Gerald. *Can't Help Singin': The American Musical on Stage and Screen.* Woodstock, N.Y.: Overlook Press, 1987.

Miller, D. A. *Place for Us: Essay on the Broadway Musical.* Cambridge, Mass.: Harvard University Press, 1998.

Most, Andrea. "'You've Got to Be Carefully Taught': The Politics of Race in Rodgers and Hammerstein's *South Pacific.*" *Theatre Journal* 52 (2000): 307–337.

Román, David. *Acts of Intervention: Performance, Gay Culture, and AIDS.* Bloomington: Indiana University Press, 1998.

Sandoval-Sanchez, Alberto. *José, Can You See?: Latinos on and off Broadway.* Madison: University of Wisconsin Press, 1999.

Wolf, Stacy. *A Problem Like Maria: Gender and Sexuality in the American Musical.* Ann Arbor: University of Michigan Press, 2002.

Zachary A. Dorsey

See also ACTORS AND ACTRESSES; BERNSTEIN, LEONARD; CHORUSES AND BANDS; HART, LORENZ; ICONS; PORTER, COLE; SONDHEIM, STEPHEN; THEATER AND PERFORMANCE; WATERS, ETHEL.

MUSIC: CLASSICAL

Although it is possible but not provable that the songwriter Stephen Foster (1826–1864) preferred the company of men to women—he had an unhappy marriage and was the inseparable companion of painter George Cooper for the last two years of his life—the demonstrable LGBT impact on American classical music begins with the twentieth century. Charles Tomlinson Griffes (1884–1920) studied in Germany from 1903 to 1907 and while there he learned of Magnus Hirschfeld, Oscar Wilde, and other open practitioners of homosexuality. He recorded his own affairs in a German-language diary. Influenced by late German romanticism, French impressionism, and Asian motifs, Griffes is most noted for his art songs, piano compositions, and the tone poem *The Pleasure Dome of Kublai Khan.*

Beginning in the 1920s, LGBT musical composers, performers, and writers formed a number of interlocking, close communities that have endured for more than eighty years. They have nurtured youthful prospects, written scores for texts by LGBT writers, and established a vigorous performance tradition that now calls attention to the AIDS crisis. This flourishing scene, without which most of twentieth-century American classical music would be inconceivable, developed from circles in Paris, New York, and California.

Early Influence of Boulanger and Copland

The French composer and composition teacher Nadia Boulanger (1887–1979)—who, according to composer Ned Rorem (b. 1923) is "so far as musical creation is concerned, the most influential person who ever lived"—met the American expatriate community of Paris at the salons of lesbian writers Natalie Barney (1876–1972) and Gertrude Stein (1874–1946). Boulanger, who never married, was the first woman to conduct the New York, Philadelphia, and Boston Symphony Orchestras. She conducted the first performance of homosexual Russian expatriate Igor Stravinsky's *Dumbarton Oaks* Concerto in 1938. Among her pupils were Virgil Thomson (1896–1989), Aaron Copland (1900–1990), Marc Blitzstein (1905–1964), Gian-Carlo Menotti (b. 1911), and Ned Rorem. All shared a respect for tonality and interest in relating their work to American popular culture. They all settled in or near New York City, and in turn inspired and collaborated with other gay composers.

Virgil Thomson is most famous for two operas for which Gertrude Stein wrote the libretti, *Four Saints in Three Acts* (1934) and *The Mother of Us All* (1947), the latter an ironic take on American history combined with the story of Susan B. Anthony. Thomson's companion, painter Maurice Grosser, collaborated in the production of these works. As music critic for the *New York Herald Tribune* (1940–1954), Thomson was noted for his frequently vitriolic prose. His writings are collected in several volumes.

Aaron Copland studied with Boulanger—she was the soloist in the first performance of his *Organ Symphony* (1935)—and was influenced by Thomson. Unlike the sardonic Thomson, Copland's greatest works treated the American tradition with affection. His ballets *Billy the Kid* (1938), *Rodeo* (1942), and *Appalachian Spring* (1944) remain classics. *A Lincoln Portrait* (1942) and *Fanfare for the Common Man* (1943) are frequently performed by leading orchestras, the former with celebrities taking the speaking part of Lincoln. Copland's settings of American hymns and folksongs, especially "Shall We Gather at the River," are among the most moving pieces of those that regularly appear at AIDS benefits. In 1964, a decade after Copland was interrogated, to no avail, by U.S. senator Joseph McCarthy for his involvement in leftist activities, he was awarded the Presidential Medal of Freedom.

Marc Blitzstein (1905–1964), although from a wealthy Philadelphia family, was an active member of the

American Composers. Gathered at the home of Virgil Thomson (seated at left) are, seated, Gian-Carlo Menotti (center) and William Schuman, and, standing, Samuel Barber (left) and Aaron Copland—all major figures in twentieth-century classical music. **[Bettmann/corbis]**

Communist Party. He wrote articles for *The New Masses* as well as music journals. His most famous work, *The Cradle Will Rock* (1936), told the story of the oppression and resistance of steel workers. Supported by New Deal money from the Federal Theater Project, the first production was directed by Orson Welles on a shoestring budget because the opera's controversial subject caused Congress to cut the agency's funds. Blitzstein was married to writer Eva Goldbeck for three years before her death in 1936, but he preferred the company of men. He was murdered in Martinique after he tried to pick up three Portuguese sailors.

Gian Carlo Menotti is noted for bringing American immigrant and working-class communities to life in melodic works such as *The Medium* (1945), *The Consul* (1949), *The Saint of Bleeker Street* (1954), and his touching Christmas story, *Amahl and the Night Visitors* (1951). He founded the Festival of Two Worlds at Spoleto, Italy, in 1958; he expanded it to include performances in Charleston, South Carolina, in 1977, which he continued directing until 1993.

Menotti's life partner was the composer Samuel Barber (1910–1981). Barber is best remembered for his vocal music: two beautiful song cycles, *Knoxville: Summer of 1915* (1947), written at the request of soprano Eleanor Steber, and the *Hermit Songs*, premiered by Leontyne Price (1953), are performed far more frequently than are his effective operas *Vanessa* (1958)—libretto by Menotti—and *Antony and Cleopatra* (1966; rev. 1975). Barber's orchestral music, especially the *Adagio for Strings* (1938), and concerti for cello, violin, and piano are established elements of the symphonic repertoire.

Ned Rorem, who studied with both Copland and Boulanger, has fashioned hundreds of melodic art songs out of poems by homosexuals including Sappho, Walt Whitman, Paul Goodman, W. H. Auden, and (perhaps) William Shakespeare and Emily Dickinson. His diaries, lectures, and music criticism, which comprise thirteen volumes, are characterized by the same elegance as his music.

Leonard Bernstein

Boulanger's pupils, in turn, mentored a second generation of gay composers. Most notable is Leonard Bernstein (1918–1998), who led a performance of Blitzstein's *The Cradle Will Rock* while a student at Harvard University in 1938. He also studied with Copland and championed his works. Bernstein was most noted in his lifetime as a conductor, especially of the New York Philharmonic from 1958 to 1969, and for his efforts to bring music to new audiences, as in his Young People's Concerts and Norton Lectures at Harvard. His major compositions are well regarded, too. They include three symphonies, the second subtitled and inspired by a poem of W. H. Auden, "The Age of Anxiety"; the Broadway plays *Candide* (1956) and *West Side Story* (1957); and *Chichester Psalms* (1965). *Mass* (1971), which opened at the Kennedy Center, in Washington, D.C., incorporated lyrics stressing the composer's opposition to the Vietnam War. Bernstein espoused radical politics, as in his support of the Black Panthers, yet was discreet about his homosexuality. He married Chilean actress Felicia Montealgre in 1951, had three children with her, and remained married to her despite his affairs until her death in 1978. Only in 1983, with the opera *A Quiet Place,* did he deal with a bisexual man who provides the emotional center for a group of unstable heterosexuals.

Henry Cowell and the Avant-Garde Movement

Unlike the Boulanger circle, Californian Henry Cowell (1897–1965) and his pupils John Cage (1912–1992), Lou Harrison (1917–2003), and (indirectly) Harry Partch (1901–1974) consciously set themselves up as an avant-garde movement that employed atonality, novel instruments, sounds previously considered nonmusical, and Asian influences. Cowell's anarchist parents acquainted him with Asian and folk music: as early as 1912 he employed tone clusters in a piano composition. Later works used an electronic keyboard (the "Rhythmicon"), the East Asian gamelan, and a "string piano"—plucking strings inside the piano—and offer performers the freedom to improvise based on a nontraditional notation that Cage more fully developed. Although he wrote twenty symphonies and numerous other works, Cowell is best known for his indefatigable championing of modern American music—he was an early publicist for Charles Ives—through organizations he founded such as the New Music Society of California (1925), the quarterly *New Music* (1927), and the Pan American Association of Composers. His manifesto, *New Musical Resources* (1930), is probably more famous than his compositions are. In 1936, Cowell was convicted of having sex with a seventeen-year-old youth; at his trial, he confessed to other contacts as well. He served four years in San Quentin State Prison. He was pardoned in 1942, moved to the East Coast, married ethnomusicologist Sidney Hawkins Robertson, and continued to teach composition until his death.

Cowell's most famous pupil, Los Angeles native John Cage, rejected composition techniques that University of California at Los Angeles Professor Arnold Schoenberg taught him in favor of Cowell's methods. Cage incorporated various "noises" (which he refused to separate from music) such as radio and audience sounds (the latter most famously in *4′33″* [1952]—of silence, that is), along with Asian philosophy and indeterminacy, into his works. He adopted the Zen Buddhist notion that music existed to "sober the mind" rather than to communicate ideas, and relied on the pattern of chance provided by the *I Ching* to determine in what order his musical fragments would constitute a whole. Many of Cage's works accompanied ballets performed by the company founded by and named after his lifetime partner, Merce Cunningham (b. 1919), who also pioneered in physical movement that same pattern of chance expressed through the dancers' improvisations.

Lou Harrison, a student of Cage, was especially interested in Asian music. With his life partner, William Colvig, he designed an American gamelan that was inspired by Mexican and Navajo music as well as East Asian music. The author of three symphonies, Harrison was also active in the movements for ecology, peace, and gay rights. His opera *Young Caesar* (1971) explores the protagonist's attraction to men. In 1995, Harrison's "Parade for MTT" welcomed the openly gay conductor Michael Tilson Thomas (b. 1944), a champion of twentieth-century American music, as musical director of the San Francisco Symphony.

Harry Partch liked people to believe he was a self-taught composer and former hobo, but he knew Harrison and was aware of musical currents in California. Partch took experimentation to new heights: among other things, he invented a 43-note scale and instruments containing forty-four strings, glass rods, and percussion created from such items as hubcaps, liquor bottles, glass jars, and airplane fuel tanks. Much of Partch's work deals with loners or the western American desert: for example, in *Barstow* (1941), which he called a "Hobo Concerto," he sets eight pieces of hitchhiker graffiti from that California town to music. *Oedipus* (1951) and *Delusion of the Fury* (1966) are large-scale masterpieces that employ instrumental music, song, dance, and theater.

Contributions by Lesbian Composers

American lesbian composers are not as well known as their male counterparts are—with three exceptions. Mrs. H. H. A. Beach (b. Amy Maria Cheney, 1867–1944) was a child prodigy pianist. Her family moved in the highest circles of Boston society, and she became acquainted with leading composers and conductors on her trips to Europe, especially Germany. At the age of 18, she married a man twenty-five years her senior (using his initials for concert programs, becoming known as Mrs. H. H. A. Beach throughout the world) and did not remarry after his death in 1910. Of her approximately 150 compositions, the early *Grand Mass* (1892) and *Gaelic Symphony* (1896) are still occasionally performed, but her later works repeated rather than developed her early successes, and are almost never played in concert.

Pauline Oliveros (b. 1932) began as a composer, accordianist, and college professor in California, but gave all that up in the early 1980s. She then explored and set up workshops on the practice of Deep Listening (careful attention to all of the sounds produced in an environment). In 1985, she established the Pauline Oliveros Foundation, devoted to creating a worldwide community of creative artists in various media, using the latest technology to exchange their creations. Her work stresses collaboration and improvisation. She has also written extensively on the need to appreciate and develop women composers. In 1994 she composed *Epigraphs in the Time of AIDS.*

Diamanda Galás's (b. 1955) combination of original and adapted music and performance art is perhaps the most searing critique of homophobia and the First World's inadequate response to AIDS to date. Her electronically modified voice, encompassing several octaves and ranging from the nearly inaudible to intolerable screeching, has been deployed in the *Plague Mass* (1990), a setting of the traditional requiem interspersed with other poems; *Vena Cava* (1993), which depicts the isolation of a person dying from AIDS; and other works written after the death of her brother, playwright Philip-Dimitri Galás (1954–1986). Mixing classical, jazz, spiritual, folk, and rock music, she sometimes appears half-naked in the form of an AIDS virus covered in blood. Her works that do not deal with AIDS denounce genocide, torture, and the oppression of women.

Performers, Musical Groups, and Choruses

Unlike composers, prominent performers have usually concealed their homosexuality. Much of the criticism received from the press by Bernstein's predecessor at the New York Philharmonic, the gifted Dmitri Mitropoulos (1896–1960), may have stemmed from his homosexuality. Thomas Schippers (1930–1977) conducted the premier of Barber's *Antony and Cleopatra* to open the new Metropolitan Opera House in 1966 and was a successful conductor of opera and also the Cincinnati Symphony. James Levine, conductor and general music director of the Metropolitan Opera since 1974, has been discreet about his sexuality following early allegations about improprieties with underage boys. Lesbian conductors include Kary Gardner (b. 1941), who founded the short-lived New England Women's Symphony in the late 1970s, and the Jewish Dutch refugee Frieda Belinfante (1905–1995), founder of the Orange County, California, Symphony Orchestra. It is hard to locate well-known "out" classical singers and instrumentalists; among the former are soprano Patricia Racette and countertenor Brian Asawa, among the latter is the pianist Van Cliburn. For countertenor David Daniels, being gay is "a huge part of me" that "affects my singing," and he has criticized the "conservative" opera queens who "love the voices and the costumes but they're not willing to stand anything different. . . . There's a lot of negativity from the gay community because I'm open, and proud, and honest" (Kettle, "Get Back in the Closet").

Despite the reluctance of celebrity musicians, LGBT people throughout the nation (and world) have been forming musical groups, especially choruses, since the 1970s. Lesbian musical groups came first. The Anna Crusis Women's Choir, begun in Philadelphia in 1975, is the oldest member of the Gay and Lesbian Association of Choruses (GALA), which now numbers more than 170 choruses, with some eight thousand members. The Gotham Male (later Gay Men's) Chorus in New York (founded 1977) and San Francisco Gay Men's Chorus (founded 1978), one of several gay musical organizations founded by John Reed Sims (1947–1984), soon followed. Beginning in 1982, when fourteen choruses performed concomitantly with the Gay Games in San Francisco, similar festivals have been held annually.

GALA choruses frequently perform benefits for people with AIDS, sometimes commisioning new works and drawing support from famous singers and instrumentalists, who perform with them. David Del Tredici (b. 1937) and John Corigliano (b. 1938) are two leading composers who have made AIDS their subject. A student of Copland best known for compositions based on *Alice in Wonderland,* Del Tredici has set to music poems by gay writers Paul Monette, Allen Ginsberg, and Alfred Corn (*Dracula,* 1999). Michael Tilson Thomas and the San Francisco Symphony gave the first performance of his cantata *Gay Life* in 2001. Corigliano's *First Symphony* (1990), commissioned by Sir George Solti and the Chicago Symphony, was dedicated to the memory of people with AIDS. He adapted the third movement into the choral work "Of Rage and Remembrance," which mentions the names of his deceased friends, for the gay male choruses of Chicago, New York, and Seattle. Perhaps most moving is the *AIDS Quilt Songbook* (1992), which was conceived by baritone Will Parker (1943–1993) as an ongoing, collaborative effort—a musical version of the physical AIDS quilt. Different songwriters and poets contributed to the first version, which has since been performed in its entirety or with some songs omitted and new ones added. As it grows, it reflects the democratic governance of LGBT chorus organizations and the community of LGBT performers without which modern American classical music would hardly exist.

Bibliography

Brett, Philip, Elizabeth Wood, and Gary C. Thomas, eds. *Queering the Pitch: The New Gay and Lesbian Musicology.* New York: Routledge, 1994.

Hadleigh, Boze. *Sing Out! Gays and Lesbians in the Music World.* New York: Barricade Books, 1998.

Kettle, Marvin, "Get Back in the Closet." *The Guardian,* 23 August 2001. Interview with David Daniels. Available at http://www.guardian.co.uk/edinburghfestival2001

Nicholls, David, ed. *The Whole World of Music: A Henry Cowell Symposium.* Sydney: Harwood Academic Press, 1997.

Rosenstiel, Léonie. *Nadia Boulanger: A Life in Music.* New York: Norton, 1982.

Schwartz, K. Robert. "Composers' Closets Open for All to See." *New York Times,* 19 June 1994, Section H, pp. 1–2.

———. "Cracking the Classical Closet." *The Advocate* no. 784 (11 May 1999): 48–49.

Ward, Keith. "Musical Responses to HIV and AIDS." In *Perspectives on American Music since 1950.* Edited by James Heintze. New York: Garland, 1999.

William Pencak

See also BARBER, SAMUEL, AND GIAN CARLO MENOTTI; BARNEY, NATALIE; BERNSTEIN, LEONARD; CAGE, JOHN; CHORUSES AND BANDS; COPLAND, AARON; OLIVEROS, PAULINE; STEIN, GERTRUDE, AND ALICE B. TOKLAS; THOMSON, VIRGIL.

MUSIC: OPERA

Opera, Wayne Koestenbaum has persuasively argued, has attracted LGBT people because so many of them have been silenced, afraid to express their passions in homophobic society. The grand gestures, elaborate costumes, and larger-than-life utterances of the great operatic characters speak to and compensate for the repressed sexuality of the opera queen, both giving voice to hidden desire and witnessing, sorrowfully, to love unfulfilled. Erotic excess has always been the driving force behind opera—most of which deal with people trapped in loveless marriages or other hopeless relationships. They tend either to die magnificently or finally achieve happiness. LGBT people also identify with the frequent gender transgressions in opera. The heroic male roles of baroque operas—notably those of Monteverdi (Orpheus, for example) and Handel (such as Julius Caesar)—were performed by castrati in the seventeenth and eighteenth centuries and taken by women until the advent of countertenors (some of whom are handsome, gay men in the late twentieth century). Great mezzo sopranos in the early nineteenth century sang parts such as Romeo (Bellini) and numerous generals and kings (Rossini), whereas youths such as Cherubino in Mozart's *Marriage of Figaro* and Octavian in Richard Strauss's *Der Rosenkavalier* are "trouser roles" played by women dressed as men; in a further twist, these male characters sometimes disguise themselves as women.

Whereas opera has symbolized glamor and social rituals such as galas and opening nights for the upper classes who foot the bill, for many LGBT people it has meant fanatic attachment to particular singers—whose own personal lives acquire a fascination comparable to those of their stage creations—and participation in a community of largely LGBT opera lovers who follow the details of performances with critical enthusiasm. As Walt Whitman noted, in the mid-nineteenth century, he and his companions would head for "the 25-cent place in the theatre" where he "used to meet and make new friends in the galleries." Unlike the "average man [who] doesn't object to high prices because be only wants to go to the theatre about twice a year . . . for the Bohemians we are—many, many times are not too many" (Schmidgall, p. 131). In the late twentieth century, standing rooms and cheap seats were still meeting places and cruising zones for LGBT people, especially gay men. Their zeal occasionally produces headlines, as when in 1965 Metropolitan opera standees waited in line for days for tickets to Maria Callas's comeback, or when fights broke out between her partisans and those of Renata Tebaldi.

Walt Whitman may well have been America's first opera queen. Opera inspired his poetry, prose, and criticism for the *Brooklyn Daily Eagle*; overall, he cited thirteen grand operas by contemporary favorites Verdi, Bellini, and Donizetti and referred to singers and songs hundreds of times. Whitman sought to model his work on opera and called on American writers and composers to be inspired by the "superb suggestions of the Grand Opera" (Schmidgall, p. 25). He entitled collections of his poetry the "Song of Myself" and "Chants Democratic." Only "some moments at the opera" and being "in the woods" could put Whitman's "soul in high glee all out" (Schmidgall, p. 68). Juxtaposing the sound of the "great Italian singers" with "the voices of the native substrata of Manahattan young men," he regarded both as uniquely seductive (Schmidgall, p. 16). Whitman none-too-subtly praised the erotic attraction of the male operatic voice: "I want that tenor, large and fresh as the creation, the orbed parting of whose mouth shall lift over my head the sluices of all delight yet discovered for our race." He rhapsodized over his favorite tenor, Geremia Bettini—"a beautiful, large, robust, and friendly young man"; "never before did I realize what an indescribable volume of delight the recesses of the soul can bear from the sound of the human voice" (Schmidgall, p. 18). With opera providing the peak emotional experience offered by culture, Whitman believed that indigenous opera was needed for the United States to escape the foreign cultural domination. Opera needed to rank highly among the "democratic fetes . . . highly original" with which the nation would make its mark (Schmidgall, p. 25).

Whitman viewed opera variously as erotic stimulant, fulfillment of larger-than-life fantasies through worship of particular singers, inspiration for literature, and symbol of American culture, planes on which it has continued to intersect with LGBT history in the United States. Whitman's optimism about opera soon yielded to the concerns of lesbian authors Edith Wharton and Willa Cather in the early twentieth century. Wharton's novel *The Age of Innocence* (1920) opens in a box at the New York Academy of Music, predecessor of the Metropolitan Opera, where opera has been reduced to the ornament of an elite seeking social exclusivity. It neutralizes or covers the passions and excludes the national pulse that Whitman hoped it would express. Willa Cather loved and wrote extensively about opera. *The Song of the Lark* (1915) is based on the life of Olive Fremstad, a midwestern diva who must lose her innocence and succumb to the rigors of serious vocal training to gain the bittersweet victory of success in a corrupt and affected world. (Cather's *Lucy Gayheart* [1935] has a similar plot; she substituted singers for herself in these semi-autobiographical works.) She writes of the opera fanatic in her short story "A Gold Slipper" (1905), where a man left unmoved by a diva's performance is mesmerized by her lost slipper—that is, the glamour of her self-presentation. In Cather's "Paul's Case" (1905), a young man, introduced to the social whirl and high society associated with opera, kills himself because he runs out of money and can no longer endure normal life.

As with turn-of-the-century writers and political activists, several of the most eminent female singers in the United States spoke about their preference for female companionship. Fremstad's lifetime companion Mary Watkins Cushing wrote about her slavish devotion to her mistress; she spoke of how the diva would touch her "flat and heaving bosom," and she slept with a string attached to her toe from Fremstad's bedpost so she could be summoned at will in the middle of the night. Mary Garden wrote in her autobiography of her physical attraction to her first teacher and to Mme. Lily Debussy, adding "sometimes I wonder why I've never been crazy about men." Frances Alda, Emma Eames, and Grace Moore also spoke of strong attachments to female role models who influenced their career choices (Kostenbaum, p. 99).

Homosexuals and Homosexual Stand-ins

Many of the most important U.S. opera composers of the twentieth century were homosexuals, but none expressed the sensitivity and tragedy of unrequited homosexual longing as did the Englishman Benjamin Britten in the operas *Peter Grimes* (1945), *Billy Budd* (1951), and *Death in Venice* (1973). These are among the most frequently performed post–World War II works in major opera houses in the United States. Until the 1990s, among American composers, only Paul Bowles and Virgil Thomson, twice in collaboration with author Gertrude Stein, touched on homosexual themes in their works for the stage, and even they did not deal explicitly with the subject. Better known as a writer, Bowles wrote two operas based on the works of gay Spanish poet Federico García Lorca: *The Wind Remains* (1941), which explores the fantasies of a young man who cannot find heterosexual love but has no alternative, and *Yerma* (1958), the story of a woman who murders her husband because he cannot give her children. Thomson met Stein in Paris in 1926. Together they wrote *Four Saints in Three Acts*, which premiered in 1934 with an all-black cast directed by John Houseman. The saints—Teresa of Avila and her confessor Saint Settlement and Ignatius of Loyola and his mentor Saint Chavez—and the production suggest the composer and librettist's concern, typical of the New Deal era, with displaying the virtues of cultures regarded as inferior by mainstream U.S. culture. The African American cast and the saints whose celibacy and interior spiritual struggles they portray may be regarded as socially acceptable stand-ins for homosexuals. In *The Mother of Us All*, begun shortly before Stein's death in 1946 and posthumously premiered the following year, lesbian Susan B. Anthony and her companion Anne are introduced by narrators playing the parts of Thomson and Stein themselves. Although Susan B., as she is called, is not a sexual being, she stands head and shoulders above male politicians such as John Adams (implausibly reduced to a hopeless romantic) and Ulysses S. Grant. Thomson wrote a third opera, *Lord Byron* (1972), which is less well known. It consists of a series of flashbacks following Byron's death in which his unhappy affairs with women are stressed; only several fellow male poets appreciate him.

Sympathy for the Dispossessed

Perhaps to compensate for the love that dared not be spoken, most homosexual opera composers have dealt sympathetically with the plight of other underprivileged groups. George Gershwin wrote of black life in Charleston, South Carolina, in *Porgy and Bess* (1935). The most famous of Gian Carlo Menotti's numerous operas, including *The Old Maid and the Thief* (1939), *The Medium* (1946), *The Consul* (1950), and *The Saint of Bleecker Street* (1954), are set in poor urban neighborhoods. The most popular of his several children's operas, *Amahl and the Night Visitors* (1951), tells of a crippled boy's response to Jesus's birth. Leonard Bernstein's major works for the stage straddled the line between opera and Broadway. *West Side Story* (1957) was a rewritten version of *Romeo and Juliet* in which Puerto Ricans and Italians fight and fall in love in a neighborhood on New York City's Upper West Side (ironically soon to be displaced for Lincoln Center, a home for the performing arts). *Candide* (1956) is based on Voltaire's short novel of the hapless lad victimized by the incompetent evildoers who dominate the world. Marc Blitzstein, a mentor for Bernstein, composed *The Cradle Will Rock* (1937), a New Deal drama based loosely on actual events, in which a prostitute and druggist organize Steeltown against the tyrannical Mister Mister and his so-called Liberty Committee. Blitzstein's other notable opera, *Regina* (1953), was based on Lillian Hellman's play *The Little Foxes* (1939), a tale of avarice and corruption in a southern family. Aaron Copland's only opera, *The Tender Land* (1954), deals with a small midwestern community that, suspicious of two itinerant workers, considers them murderers; a young woman, dissuaded from leaving with the man she loves, leaves anyway. An extremely successful opera, by gay composer Jake Heggie, is *Dead Man Walking* (2000), the story of a nun and the convicted murderer she befriends on death row.

Mainstream Themes

Gay composers have also written operas on more conventional themes. Menotti's companion, Samuel Barber, has worked mostly in symphonic and chamber music. His two major operas, *Vanessa* (1953) and *Antony and Cleopatra* (1966), deal with love among the upper classes. Both were premiered at the New York Metropolitan Opera, the latter opening the new house in Lincoln Center in a gargantuan production whose awkwardness eclipsed the work's real virtues, which were far more evident in the revised version staged first at the Julliard School in 1975. John Corigliano's *Ghosts of Versailles* (1991) is a pastiche in which both the music and characters from Mozart's *Marriage of Figaro* (1786) interact with members of Marie Antoinette's court as they observe their lives from eternity. The Russian Igor Stravinsky composed *The Rake's Progress* (1951), with a libretto by the Englishman W. H. Auden and his companion Chester Kallman. Both Auden and Stravinsky were longtime permanent residents of the United States. The story, based on eighteenth-century English engraver William Hogarth's series of prints depicting a young man's moral degeneration when he comes to London, adds a transgender element in the form of a bearded lady, Baba the Turk, invented by the librettists, who is by far the opera's most sympathetic and decent character.

Maria Callas. The revered diva of the 1950s to 1970s adopts a placid pose at odds with her tempestuous style, personality, and life. **[Getty Images (formerly Archive Photos, Inc.)]**

Recent Opera and Its Gay Fans

As of 2003, only two operas by American composers dealing explicitly with homosexuality have attained wide notice. Stewart Wallace's opera *Harvey Milk* (1991) tells the story of the San Francisco supervisor, the first openly gay official in the United States, based on *The Life and Times of Harvey Milk* (1984), the first gay film to win an Academy Award (Best Documentary, 1984). The first scene takes place at New York City's Metropolitan Opera,

La Gran Scena. The female impersonators of this New York City–based opera company have parodied the opera world and its divas since 1981.

where a fifteen-year-old Milk finds his love of opera reciprocated by numerous older men. For much of the first act, he wears handcuffs to symbolize both his unexpressed desires and the persecution of LGBT people. Milk is arrested after entrapment by a policeman, but the handcuffs do not come off until the Stonewall Riots of 1969, which are depicted, lead to their removal. Milk moves in with his lover, gay activist Scott Smith, and subsequently runs for public office. A gay pride parade and a memorial service for Milk are staged, and the motivations of his assassin, Dan White, are brought out.

Harold Blumenfeld's work *A Season in Hell* (1994) is based on the life of the nineteenth-century French poet Arthur Rimbaud. Set at the moment when Rimbaud gives up poetry to sell guns and slaves in Abyssinia, the opera looks both forward and backward in the writer's life. A highlight of the opera is Rimbaud's tempestuous love affair with the older poet Paul Verlaine, which leads to the latter's imprisonment after he wounds Rimbaud with a pistol shot.

For many gay Americans—mostly males—at the turn of the millennium, opera matters less as a creative, contemporary art form in which homosexuals are writing, composing, or acting and more as a means of enjoying masterpieces of the past and the singers associated with them. Opera queens worship their divas much as film buffs adore movie stars. Maria Callas, whose career resembled her contemporary Judy Garland's, has attracted a huge gay following. After her transformation from a fat woman into an Audrey Hepburn look-alike glamor queen, her tempestuous personality, riveting acting, flawed yet thrilling singing, and tragic personal life combined to give her recordings and several biographies large sales. The leading literary works about opera in our time deal with Callas and her mystique. Albert Innaurato's play *Magda and Callas* (1988)—the former referring to Magda Olivero, another gay icon who sang into her eighties—is about the perils of young singers imitating a diva before becoming one. Terrence McNally, the librettist for Heggie's *Dead Man Walking*, has written *The Lisbon Traviata* (1985, rev. 1989)—which compares the gay fetishization of Callas to that of young male models and treats the AIDS epidemic as well—and *Master Class* (1995), in which actresses including Zoe Caldwell, Patti LuPone, and Faye Dunaway have brought to life a Callas who sacrificed her youth to become a great singer before throwing her career away for the false paradise represented by Aristotle Onassis and the glitter of high society.

LGBT opera fans do not always take themselves so seriously, and in fact some do an excellent job of satirizing their own enthusiasm. James McCourt's novel *Mawdrew Czgowchwz* (1975; pronounced "Mardu Gorgeous," although the initials match those of Maria Callas) is about a fictional superdiva who can sing anything and is involved in murder, mayhem, and witchcraft. Since 1981 the female impersonators of La Gran Scena, founded and directed by Ira Siff (Vera Galupe-Borszkh) and based in New York City, have delighted audiences with their parodies of the operatic world, especially the personalities and (with remarkable accuracy) vocal traits of leading divas. The leading singers include Sylvia Bills, Fodor Szedan, Alfredo Sorta-Pudgi, and the world's oldest diva, Gabriella Tonnoziti-Casseruola. *Parterre: A Queer Opera Zine* (www.parterre.com) offers reviews, interviews with singers, gossip, and musical selections both outstanding and outrageous primarily for the edification of opera queens. Through composition, literature, fanatic devotion, and parody, LGBT Americans have established themselves as a significant part of the American opera scene.

Bibliography

Dizikes, John. *Opera in America: A Cultural History.* New Haven, Conn.: Yale University Press, 1993.

Galatopoulos, Stelios. *Maria Callas: Sacred Monster.* New York: Simon and Schuster, 1998.

Giannone, Richard. *Music in Willa Cather's Fiction.* Lincoln: University of Nebraska Press, 1968.

Kirk, Elise K. *American Opera.* Urbana: University of Illinois Press, 2001.

Koestenbaum, Wayne. *The Queen's Throat: Opera, Homosexuality, and the Mystery of Desire.* New York: Poseidon Press, 1993.

Montgomery, Maureen E. *Displaying Women: Spectacles of Leisure in Edith Wharton's New York.* New York: Routledge, 1998.

Sadie, Stanley, ed. *New Grove's Dictionary of Opera.* London: Macmillan, 1992.

Schmidgall, Gary. *Walt Whitman: A Gay Life.* New York: Dutton, 1997.

Watkins, Mary Fitch. *Behind the Scenes at the Opera: Intimate Revelations of Backstage Musical Life and Work.* New York: Stokes, 1925.

William Pencak

See also ANTHONY, SUSAN B.; AUDEN, W. H.; BARBER, SAMUEL, AND GIAN CARLO MENOTTI; BARNEY, NATALIE; BERNSTEIN, LEONARD; BOWLES, PAUL AND JANE BOWLES; CAGE, JOHN; CATHER, WILLA; CHORUSES AND BANDS; COPLAND, AARON; ICONS; MCNALLY, TERRENCE; MILK, HARVEY; OLIVEROS, PAULINE; STEIN, GERTRUDE, AND ALICE B. TOKLAS; THOMSON, VIRGIL; WHITMAN, WALT.

MUSIC: POPULAR

LGBT artists and audiences have consistently created and consumed popular music, but for much of the past their regular participation in this area of mainstream entertainment was hidden or obscured. "Popular music" may be broadly defined as music produced and consumed in the context of a commercial entertainment industry, increasingly disseminated through recordings and the mass media (radio, cinema, television, the Internet) rather than live performance. Pop music encompasses a range of distinct but intertwining genres, such as blues, jazz, country, and rock and roll, and their many variants, such as disco, punk, and rap. Popular music is therefore defined by musical styles and forms (such as discrete "songs" marketed as "singles") as well as by modes of production and consumption, rather than literal popularity (itself usually established by sales rather than artistic success). Though obviously faddish and often dismissed as ephemeral, pop music can acquire a cultural resonance that helps define historical periods and events, and it often plays an important role in the personal lives of its consumers, as individuals and especially as members of social groups whose identities are often established and reinforced by shared musical tastes.

Securing its location at the heart of mainstream entertainment, the content of popular song has been dominated by the language and images of heterosexual romance and, increasingly, the direct expression of straight sexuality. Along with Hollywood cinema, the popular music industry has directed heterosexuals on how to speak, feel, and act in their emotional and erotic lives. As music commonly produced for dancing, popular music has also defined forms of socially acceptable physical contact between couples in public spaces. Given this pervasive, explicitly heterosexual context, gay and lesbian musicians seeking a place in popular music often have had to suppress their sexualities or carefully encode them, perhaps for unacknowledged audiences "in the know," while gay and lesbian listeners have persistently performed creative acts of translation and appropriation to make popular songs speak to and about them. Since the 1970s, the increased prominence and power of gay and lesbian musicians, record producers, and music fans have finally forced the entertainment industry and mainstream audiences to acknowledge—and in some cases even affirm—LGBT contributions to popular music. Increasingly, openly gay and lesbian performers speak to audiences without the evasion that heretofore characterized the history of pop songwriting and performance.

Recovering Gay and Lesbian Popular Musicians

Gays and lesbians since the late twentieth century have wished to recover artistic predecessors in order to construct a previously unwritten history of gay and lesbian musical creativity. However, it remains difficult to identify popular gay or lesbian musicians prior to the twentieth century and the advent of recorded music. Identifying a performer's sexuality often relies on rumors and hints rather than direct statements or convincing evidence. Frequently an artist's sexual identity was known within a musical community, but hidden from the public; in many cases, such knowledge only comes to light after the performer's career or life is over. The assumption has been that public knowledge of an artist's homosexuality would harm if not destroy that person's career; while less firmly entrenched than in the past, this fear persists into the twenty-first century, even as artists challenge and disprove it. In any case, the understandable desire to identify past gay and lesbian role models must always be set against the historical and social factors that prevented these performers from openly declaring their sexual identities to a potentially hostile public and (perhaps even more) intolerant music industry.

The dominant popular musical form of the nineteenth century, the blackface minstrel show, portrayed the iconic figure "Zip Coon" as a flamboyant black dandy and often featured comic female impersonation, but such gender play remains overshadowed by minstrelsy's more pervasive (and now much more offensive) racial masquerade. The first clear acknowledgment of homosexuality in popular music may be on risqué blues records from the 1920s released in the context of the Harlem Renaissance, which supported a vital gay and lesbian subculture. Alongside "dirty blues" celebrating straight copulation, songs about "sissy men" and "bull dykers" (or "bulldaggers") were recorded by performers who often were applying such terms to themselves. Ma Rainey's "Prove It On Me Blues" affirms the narrator's lesbian preferences, and her "Sissy Blues" decries a straying husband's dalliance with another man. Rainey's famous (and bisexual) protégée Bessie Smith also sang about "mannish-acting" women and "womanish-acting" men, while the unabashed lesbian Gladys Bentley greeted visitors to Harlem's Clam House in her trademark tuxedo and top hat. If blues lyrics often ridiculed "sissies" and "B.D. women," they at least acknowledged the existence of such figures when mainstream culture seemed oblivious to them, and often with bemused tolerance rather than the hateful disgust that would infect homophobic rap lyrics decades later.

At the same time, the culture of early jazz established itself as a much more intolerant fraternity, and only a few figures in the history of jazz, including the vibraphonist Gary Burton and the pianist Dick Voynow, have had the courage to publicly reveal their homosexuality. However, among the crucial figures in jazz history, the gay composer, arranger, and pianist Billy Strayhorn played a fundamental role as Duke Ellington's intimate collaborator for decades. Among Strayhorn's enduring compositions are two of the most famous in jazz, "Lush Life" and "Take the A Train." His example suggests that the history of gay participation in jazz may have been central, but remains obscured. (When jazz musician Billy Tipton was found, upon his death in 1989, to have been a woman who spent her entire professional and personal life as a man, another neglected facet of the unwritten history of jazz was revealed.)

As African American musical cultures, blues and jazz were still relatively marginal forms in the first decades of the twentieth century. In the musical mainstream known as Tin Pan Alley, popular singers of love songs often shifted pronouns so that the same lyrics could be addressed to a male or female listener. Some of the earliest recorded expressions of gay desire are due to singers simply refusing that change: male voices singing Broadway hits like "Can't Help Lovin' That Man" or "What Wouldn't I Do for That Man?" now raise questions about how such records were heard by their original listeners. Early novelty songs like "Masculine Women, Feminine Men" (with origins in the cross-dressing English musical hall) more brazenly suggested a sexually flexible demimonde to be found in some urban nightclubs. Simultaneously, the late-1920s vogue for "crooning" (the intimate vocal style encouraged by the invention of microphones and radio) led to frequent condemnations of effeminate, "pansy" male singers such as Rudy Vallee and Russ Columbo before more "manly" big band singers displaced them.

Tin Pan Alley was defined by its great songwriters rather than singers. Among the ranks of Irving Berlin, Jerome Kern, and George Gershwin, the gay songwriter Cole Porter and the lyricist Lorenz Hart (collaborating with the composer Richard Rodgers) produced some of America's best-known love songs, which critics now suggest reveal their authors' jaundiced views of conventional (heterosexual) romantic sentiment through witty or deeply ironic lyrics. For instance, Hart's "My Funny Valentine" or "Bewitched, Bothered, and Bewildered" are among America's favorite treatments of the torment in adoring another person. Decades later, some of Porter's enduring tunes, such as "Every Time We Say Goodbye" or "I've Got You Under My Skin," revealed their uncanny relevance in the era of AIDS, frequently through performances by gay choirs celebrating Porter's legacy.

Rock and Roll and Androgyny

The rise of rock and roll as America's dominant popular music in the late 1950s accompanied a larger shift in social and sexual mores. Exploiting the postwar baby boom, rock and roll established an almost exclusive association of pop music with a youth audience. The transitional period leading to rock's dominance allowed a few then-closeted gay performers to succeed, including Johnnie Ray, Johnny Mathis, and, most astonishingly, the flamboyant pop-classical pianist Liberace, who in 1959 successfully sued a British newspaper gossip columnist for implying that he was gay. Although one of the chief architects of early rock and roll was the gay and outrageous Little Richard, figures such as Elvis Presley and James Brown established rock as an overwhelmingly male and heterosexual domain, despite the regular contributions of female artists. Nevertheless, by including attractive young males, including Presley, among its main commodities, rock has persistently promoted "pretty boys," usually adored by young female (and gay) fans and dismissed by the older male musicians, fans, and critics who tend to define the genre (though not always its sales). Among pop's most successful acts, teen idols from Frankie Avalon in the 1950s to "boy bands" like the Back Street Boys in the 1990s represent a continuous aspect of

American pop's sexual economy that has been repressed by its main critics.

As rock developed in the 1960s its aggressive masculinity seemed to become even more secure, although the social rebellion that rock represented also took the form of androgynous visual and performance styles. Long hair, make-up, "feminine" clothing, and camp mannerisms marked otherwise macho rockers from Mick Jagger to Jimi Hendrix (as well as their many heirs, such as Steven Tyler of the band Aerosmith and Prince). This consciously outrageous style reached its zenith in the 1970s, when British rock stars like Marc Bolan, Gary Glitter, and especially the influential David Bowie presented themselves as "glam" or "glitter" rockers. Along with American counterparts like Alice Cooper, the New York Dolls, Iggy Pop, and the Velvet Underground (featuring Lou Reed), these performers teased audiences and the media with flirtatious suggestions of "deviant" bisexuality. (Lou Reed's "Walk on the Wild Side" was perhaps the first pop song depicting a transsexual makeover to reach mainstream radio.) In retrospect, glam style, which in the United States never achieved its British success, simply served rock's ongoing desire to shock rather than actually to affirm alternative sexualities, and many of these stars even suggested that only "real men" would have the nerve to adopt such blatantly effeminate images. By the time similar styles were perpetuated by interchangeable heavy metal bands apparently lacking camp sensibilities, any potential subversion of heterosexual norms seemed abandoned. Nevertheless, the freedom to play with conventional gender images encouraged by glam had a lasting impact on major pop stars from Elton John to Boy George, themselves flamboyant fashion plates who, unlike most of their predecessors, would after periods of evasion declare themselves gay.

From Disco to Homocore

While mainstream rock generally ignored the rise of the gay liberation movement in the decade following the 1969 Stonewall riots, the alignment of pop music and a growing pride in gay identity and community came from another direction. In 1975 the South Shore Commission released the progay "Free Man," and Carl Bean recorded "I Was Born This Way" for Motown in 1977, but the communal soundtrack for urban gay life in the 1970s was provided by the dance-driven music called disco. Disco linked black and Latin musical sources to the affirmation of an expanding gay subculture, factors that played a role in the backlash against disco from mainstream rock fans in a few years. The openly gay artist Sylvester forcefully emphasized the link between disco and gay sexuality with "You Make Me Feel (Mighty Real)" in 1978. Soon disco divas like Donna Summer and Gloria Gaynor generated large gay followings, but disco's most unusual success came in the form of the Village People, a group of singers and dancers chosen to embody gay stereotypes while performing thinly veiled anthems to gay life like the 1978 hits "Y.M.C.A." and "Macho Man." While the group's members seemed to flaunt their sexuality, their brief mainstream popularity suggested that many still did not get the joke.

By the time straight white males decided "disco sucks," the form had been widely appropriated by heterosexuals and stripped of its gay origins. Rather than disappearing, the music being played in gay clubs was by then mutating into other categories of dance music, including "house," "techno," and "hi-NRG," all more or less derivatives of disco but supporting their own subcultural variants. (House music especially provided the background for critically aware drag performances by black and Hispanic gays, captured in the 1990 documentary *Paris is Burning*; the postdisco gay underground also produced RuPaul, America's first superstar African American drag queen.) For a time, however, disco posed a genuine challenge to mainstream rock, in part because its success was determined by disc jockeys and the response of clubgoers rather than radio airplay or established artists. More significantly, disco contributed to the construction of a visible, increasingly political gay community. The decline of disco also coincided with the first wave of deaths from AIDS. Among the many gay musicians who would soon be mourned were Sylvester, the cabaret singer Peter Allen, Liberace, the Village People creator Jacques Morali, Freddie Mercury of the band Queen (wildly popular with straight audiences), and Ricky Wilson of the camp new wave group the B-52s.

The era's other major challenge to mainstream rock was punk (and its less aggressive variant, new wave). Although they presented themselves as an enraged alternative to macho male rockers and the superbands that filled stadiums, punk's most prominent figures still tended to reinforce heterosexual norms and aggressive male perspectives, though a few figures, like Wayne County (soon to transform into Jayne County), resisted this pressure. When punk's initial fury could not be sustained, post-punk bands and performers effected a kind of glam revival, which now included artists who retrieved the old insult "queer" as a badge of honor. British groups like Culture Club (featuring Boy George), Erasure (Andy Bell and Vince Clarke), the Smiths (featuring Morrissey), the Pet Shop Boys (Neil Tennant and Chris Lowe), and Bronski Beat and the Communards (both including singer Jimmy Somerville) all drew upon gay life and tra-

Melissa Etheridge. This singer is one of several to achieve a wide following beyond the lesbian community, especially since the late 1980s. **[Getty Images (formerly Archive Photos, Inc.)]**

ditions, from Oscar Wilde to the recently displaced disco subculture, in their lyrics, concerts, and music videos (the latter a new and influential venue for pop performers).

Some of these musicians annoyed fans by evading personal revelations in interviews when their music seemed to otherwise affirm gay lifestyles. Most often, the eventual coming out of MTV-era stars like Boy George or George Michael (earlier half of the duo Wham!) did not generate the hostile response early performers feared it must. The queer activism motivating some of these acts announced itself even more forcefully through the later merger of militant politics and post-punk aesthetics tagged homocore or queercore. Loud and fast bands like Pansy Division signaled the final rejection of the long-standing stereotype of greater gay affiliation with Broadway than hard rock. If homocore's impact has remained limited, it at least finally proved that homosexuality and hard rock can coexist.

From Women's Music to Riot Grrrls

Although powerful female performers from Janis Joplin to Patti Smith have regularly broken into the boy's club of rock, in the 1970s lesbian musicians, inspired by the separatist ideology of radical feminism, established a culture of women's (or "womyn's") music almost completely independent of the commercial mainstream. Strongly rooted in 1960s folk traditions, the acoustic guitar was the favored instrument for singer-songwriters like Holly Near, Cris Williamson, Teresa Trull, and Alix Dobkin, whose 1973 *Lavender Jane Loves Women* was the first out lesbian album. Women's music explicitly confined its audience to the "lesbian nation" served by independent record companies like Olivia, founded in 1973, and through live performances at women-only events like the annual Michigan Womyn's Music Festival, the "lesbian Woodstock."

Other performers who emerged from this context, such as Phranc and Two Nice Girls, appeared on mainstream labels, while similar artists like Tracy Chapman, Michelle Shocked, Indigo Girls, and especially Melissa Etheridge achieved even wider success within and (sometimes controversially) beyond the lesbian community. Certainly the most popular artist to emerge through lesbian support was the androgynous k.d. lang, who also challenged perhaps the most sexually conservative of all popular genres, country music. Lang attained a large lesbian following before she came out and has moved away from her base in country music, although the rise of gay and lesbian rodeo and country dancing has maintained the queer presence in country she initiated, as has the relatively unique contribution of Doug Stevens and the Outband. Among others, lesbian artists like lang and Etheridge have come out without harming their careers or reducing their popularity.

Like homocore, a younger generation of female musicians challenged the codes of women's music through their affiliation with the Riot Grrrl movement, which emphasized vocals screamed over loud and fast punk-derived music. Groups like Tribe 8 and Team Dresch explicitly acknowledged women's music traditions, but Tribe 8 also confronted those traditions when they appeared (amid protests) at the 1994 Michigan Womyn's Musical Festival. For a short while Riot Grrrls were treated as a cute novelty by the mainstream press, so some participants in the movement in the late 1990s revived the separatist strategies of their older sisters. If women's music asserted its difference from the mainstream music industry, "postfeminist" musicians have strongly rejected the notion that music produced by and for women should follow any specific style or form.

Listening Queerly: Gay and Lesbian Audiences

While gay and lesbian musicians have been important in the production and performance of pop music, queer audiences have arguably been even more prominent in pop music history. Though the observation lends itself to stereotype, gay men have been identified as passionate fans of opera and show tunes for decades, and in the period before Stonewall, gay men often built affiliations through their shared adoration of singers such as—most famously—Judy Garland. After Stonewall, gay male fans continued to embrace icons such as Barbra Streisand, Diana Ross, Donna Summer, Cher, and Madonna. This diva worship has certainly included camp appreciation (all have inspired drag performers), but the function of such singers to articulate translatable emotions and to encourage group identification should not be underestimated. Meanwhile, women's music offered lesbian fans more direct role models and musical representations of their lives and desires in a protective environment. Now lesbian and gay musicians can finally speak directly to their peers openly and through mainstream media. Although explicit homophobia was also more audible in some rock, reggae, and rap recordings at the end of the twentieth century, gay and lesbian popular music was finally, proudly out and unlikely ever to retreat to its sonic closet.

Bibliography

Allen, Louise. *The Lesbian Idol: Martina, KD, and the Consumption of Lesbian Masculinity.* London: Cassell, 1997.

Bradby, Barbara. "Lesbians and Popular Music: Does It Matter Who Is Singing?" In *Outwrite: Lesbianism and Popular Culture.* Edited by Gabriele Griffin. London: Pluto Press, 1993.

Burns, Lori, and Mélisse Lafrance. *Disruptive Divas: Feminism, Identity, and Popular Music.* New York: Routledge, 2002.

Carby, Hazel. "'It Jus Be's Dat Way Sometime': The Sexual Politics of Women's Blues." *Radical America* 20, no. 4 (1986): 9–22.

Creekmur, Corey K., and Alexander Doty, eds. *Out in Culture: Gay, Lesbian, and Queer Essays on Popular Culture.* Durham, N.C.: Duke University Press, 1995.

Currid, Brian. "'We Are Family': House Music and Queer Performativity." In *Cruising the Performative: Interventions into the Representation of Ethnicity, Nationality, and Sexuality.* Edited by Sue-Ellen Case, Philip Brett, and Susan Leigh Foster. Bloomington: Indiana University Press, 1995.

Dawson, Ashley. "'Do Doc Martens Have a Special Smell?': Homocore, Skinhead Eroticism, and Queer Agency." In *Reading Rock and Roll: Authenticity, Appropriation, Aesthetics.* Edited by Kevin J. H. Dettmar and William Richey. New York: Columbia University Press, 1999.

Fuchs, Cynthia. "If I Had a Dick: Queers, Punks, and Alternative Acts." In *Mapping the Beat: Popular Music and Contemporary Theory.* Edited by Thomas Swiss, John Sloop, and Andrew Herman. Malden, Mass.: Blackwell, 1998.

Gill, John. *Queer Noises: Male and Female Homosexuality in Twentieth-Century Music.* Minneapolis: University of Minnesota Press, 1995.

Hamer, Diane, and Belinda Budge, eds. *The Good, the Bad, and the Gorgeous: Popular Culture's Romance with Lesbianism.* London: Pandora, 1994.

Mockus, Martha. "Queer Thoughts on Country Music and K. D. Lang." In *Queering the Pitch: The New Gay and Lesbian Musicology.* Edited by Philip Brett, Elizabeth Wood, and Gary C. Thomas. London: Routledge, 1994.

Reynolds, Simon, and Joy Press. *The Sex Revolts: Gender, Rebellion, and Rock 'n' Roll.* Cambridge, Mass.: Harvard University Press, 1995.

Smith, Richard. *Seduced and Abandoned: Essays on Gay Men and Popular Music.* London: Cassell, 1995.

Stein, Arlene. "Androgyny Goes Pop: But Is It Lesbian Music?" In *Sisters, Sexperts, Queers: Beyond the Lesbian Nation.* Edited by Arlene Stein. New York: Plume, 1993.

Whiteley, Sheila. *Women and Popular Music: Sexuality, Identity, and Subjectivity.* London: Routledge, 2000.

———, ed. *Sexing the Groove: Popular Music and Gender.* London: Routledge, 1997.

Corey K. Creekmur

See also BENTLEY, GLADYS; CHORUSES AND BANDS; HART, LORENZ; HUNTER, ALBERTA; ICONS; LIBERACE; MUSIC: WOMEN'S; MUSIC: WOMEN'S FESTIVALS; OLIVIA RECORDS; PORTER, COLE; RAINEY, MA; SMITH, BESSIE; STRAYHORN, BILLY; TIPTON, BILLY; WATERS, ETHEL.

MUSIC: WOMEN'S

Also referred to as womyn's music or women-identified music, women's music emerged around 1970 as part of the second wave of the feminist movement. Generally understood as music by, for, and about women, the majority of performing artists, producers, and listeners of women's music are lesbians. Women's music is rooted in earlier musical traditions of the women's suffrage movement; African American blues queens of the 1920s and 1930s such as Gladys Bentley; and the protest songs of Anglo-American folk music, especially those of Malvina Reynolds and Peggy Seeger.

Characteristics

Women's music has been shaped by several social, political, musical, and economic factors. Socially, women's music created and nourished lesbian culture and communities throughout North America, much like women's softball leagues. Women's music venues themselves attest to this: women's coffeehouses and women's music festi-

Bessie Smith. A sexual icon of the Harlem Renaissance, changing tastes, alcoholism, and racial prejudice took their toll on her career.

vals are the usual sites for live performances and enthusiastic performer-audience interactions. Disgruntled by the sexism of mainstream, male-dominated popular music of the late 1960s and early 1970s, women's music both reflected and energized feminist commitments to confront institutionalized misogyny and homophobia. In addition, women's music was notable for the many songs that engaged lesbian life, desire, and sexuality. For this reason, women's music is often understood among cultural insiders as a euphemism for lesbian music. Largely a vocal genre, women's music practitioners commonly write autobiographical lyrics that feature a range of women's relationships with women—as mothers, grandmothers, daughters, friends, lovers, and workers. As a musical genre, women's music is eclectic: it draws primarily from the acoustic folk tradition, although it also incorporates the sounds of pop, rock, jazz, funk, reggae, and classical music. Most women's music features guitar or piano as the main instruments, while percussion, strings, or winds create secondary accompaniments. The voice and words of the singer comprise the most important elements.

Economically, women's music attempted to function as an anticapitalist feminist enterprise by creating a network of women-owned and operated record labels, distribution companies, and festival producers. Intentionally avoiding the mainstream recording industry, radio, and television, this community-based, low-budget effort gave women an unprecedented opportunity to design, record, engineer, produce, and distribute recordings in a feminist context and to apprentice with more experienced women in all aspects of the music industry. The best-known women's music label was Olivia Records, founded in 1973 by Mary Watkins and Linda Tillery in Washington, D.C.; Olivia relocated to Oakland, California, in 1977. With over forty albums recorded, Olivia's shining moment was the production of *Lesbian Concentrate: A Lesbianthology of Songs and Poems* in 1977, a collective musical response to Anita Bryant's antigay campaign in Florida, and one of the first recordings to use the word "lesbian" in the title. The proceeds were directed to the Lesbian Mothers' National Defense Fund. Other women's music labels that thrived during the 1970s and early 1980s are Women's Wax Works, Sister Sun, Redwood Records (founded by Holly Near in 1973), Urana Records (founded by Kay Gardner in New York City), and Pleiades Records (founded by Margie Adam and Barbara Price in Berkeley, California). Ladyslipper in Durham, North Carolina, was established in 1977 and remains the largest distributor of women's music (as well as other related genres). The economic downturn of the late 1980s forced most of these companies to change direction or go out of business. In 1990, Olivia Records expanded into Olivia Cruises and Resorts, selling all-women vacations to lesbians and bisexual women.

Performers

African American women are among the most prominent leaders in the women's music genre as songwriters, performers, and producers. Mary Watkins, a classically trained pianist, incorporates jazz, rhythm and blues, gospel, and soul music into her compositions. Some of her recordings are *Something Moving* (Olivia Records, 1978), *Winds of Change* (Palo Alto Records, 1982), *Spiritsong* (Redwood Records, 1985), and *Dancing Souls* (Ladyslipper, 2000) with Kay Gardner. She has performed and co-produced extensively with Linda Tillery, one of the most highly respected composers, arrangers, producers, and performers of women's music. Inspired mostly by funk and rhythm and blues, Tillery's best recordings are *Linda Tillery* (Olivia Records, 1977), *Secrets* (411 Records, 1986), and *Good Time, A Good Time* (Tuizer Music, 1995), a collection of blues and spirituals with the Cultural Heritage Choir directed by Tillery. Her own

Indigo Girls. Amy Ray and Emily Saliers are two of the women musicians whose personalized views of life and love have been recorded on mainstream labels. **[AP/Wide World Photos]**

songs are marked by recurrent themes of political and economic oppression, liberation, and Christian hypocrisy. Both Watkins and Tillery—along with Filipina American sisters Jean and June Millington—can be found on the album credits for numerous women's music artists throughout the 1970s and 1980s.

Working in the folk music tradition, Deidre McCalla is a guitarist and songwriter within women's music as well as on out lesbian. Her recordings include *Fur Coats and Blue Jeans* (Roulette, 1973), *Don't Doubt It* (Olivia Records, 1985), *With a Little Luck* (Olivia Records, 1987), and *Everyday Heroes and Heroines* (Olivia Records, 1992). Ubaka Hill remains an extremely popular artist in women's music circles; she performs as a percussionist—on conga and *djembe*—and storyteller. Faith Nolan of Toronto continues to perform in the women's music network; she is a folk-blues guitarist and singer-songwriter whose music often addresses the lives of black Canadians. Her recordings include *Africville* (1986) and *Sistership* (1987), both on the Multi Cultural Women in Concert label, and a collection of protest songs called *Freedom to Love* (Redwood Records, 1989).

Although not devoted exclusively to the women's music network, Sweet Honey in the Rock should be included in this genre for their feminist commitments to a wide range of issues, women-oriented themes (including sexuality), and musical stamina. Founded in 1973 by Bernice Johnson Reagon, a former worker with the Student Nonviolent Coordinating Committee, Sweet Honey in the Rock is a Grammy Award–winning all-female a cappella ensemble well-known for reinvigorating African American spirituals and political songs; their music has inspired many other women's music artists. Among Sweet Honey's seventeen albums are *Sweet Honey in the Rock* (Flying Fish, 1976), *B'lieve I'll Run On . . .* (Redwood Records, 1978), *Good News* (Flying Fish, 1981), and *We All . . . Everyone of Us* (Flying Fish, 1983).

Other pioneering artists in women's music are Alix Dobkin, Kay Gardner, Cris Williamson, Tret Fure, Meg Christian, Holly Near, and Margie Adam. Alix Dobkin is credited with recording the first album of women's music, *Lavender Jane Loves Women* (Women's Wax Works, 1973), with Kay Gardner. Still active on the festival circuit, Dobkin performs in the folk music tradition, and in addition to being an openly lesbian feminist also involves herself with Jewish political groups. Dobkin has recorded *Living with Lesbians* (1976), *XXAlix* (1980), *Never Been Better/These Women* (1986), and *Love and Politics: A 30-Year Saga* (1992), all with the Women's Wax Works label.

Cris Williamson's first album, *The Changer and the Changed* (Olivia Records, 1975), is considered a classic and is the best-selling record in women's music (over 250,000 copies). Her musical style blends folk, country, and pop sounds with impassioned lyrics of lesbian desire and spirituality. In addition to maintaining an active touring schedule, Williamson has made numerous recordings throughout her career, including *Blue Rider* (1982), *Prairie Fire* (1985), and *Wolf Moon* (1985) on the Olivia label. With her longtime partner Tret Fure, she recorded *Postcards from Paradise* (1993) on Olivia Records and *Between the Covers* (1997) and *Radio Quiet* (1998) on Wolf Moon/Goldenrod Records. Working solo in the first years after the century's turn, Williamson released *Ashes* in 2001 on Wolf Moon Records.

Meg Christian holds a degree in music from the University of North Carolina and is an accomplished guitarist in the classical, folk, and Appalachian styles. On her first album, *I Know You Know* (Olivia Records, 1974), she recorded both original music and songs by other artists. Her music is celebrated for its humorous depictions of lesbian life, as exemplified by her anthem "Ode to a Gym Teacher." Like other veterans of women's music, Christian collaborated on many other albums, including *Meg/Chris at Carnegie Hall* (Second Wave Records, 1985). In 1985 she left the United States to study Syda Yoga with Guruyami Chidvilasananda in India, and in 1986 she recorded *The Fire of Love: Songs for Guruyami Chidvilasananda* on the Ladyslipper label. Along with Williamson, Near, Adam, and Bonnie Raitt, Christian appears in Olivia's 1990 documentary, *The Changer: A Record of the Times*, an excellent source of the early days of women's music.

Holly Near is an important pioneer in women's music and political activism; she has been incredibly productive as a songwriter, performer, activist, and recording artist. She is one of the few women's music artists who criticized anti-bisexual sentiments in the lesbian community. With twenty-five recordings to her credit in a variety of musical styles, her work in women's music is best represented by *Hang in There* (Redwood Records, 1973); *This Train Still Runs* (Abbe Alice Music, 1996), with Ronnie Gilbert; and *Simply Love: The Women's Music Collection* (Calico Tracks Music, 2000).

Conclusion

By the mid-1980s a network of economic, political, and aesthetic shifts had altered the scope of women's music and the women-identified culture it spawned. Economically, women's music artists and producers found it increasingly difficult to stay afloat in a low-budget arena. Several women musicians in a variety of genres emerged in the late 1980s and 1990s, earned their way into the mainstream music industry, and recorded on major labels: Tracy Chapman, the Indigo Girls, Michelle Shocked, Melissa Etheridge, k.d. lang, Shawn Colvin, Suzanne Vega, and Sinéad O'Connor. These artists' unconventional expressions of gender and sexuality attracted listeners from the women's music scene while also making the Top Forty, winning awards and critical acclaim from mainstream audiences. Although women's music is often criticized for lacking musical originality, its fan base of queer feminist women contributed to the success of mainstream women musicians. Furthermore, younger women artists such as Ani DiFranco and the Riot Grrrl bands who produce their own records, espouse pro-queer feminist politics, and actively eschew the corporate music industry are clearly indebted to the earlier generation of women's music.

Bibliography

Buffalo, Audreen. "Sweet Honey: A Cappella Activists." *Ms.* (March–April 1993): 25–29.

Lont, Cynthia M. "Women's Music: No Longer a Small Private Party." In *Rockin' The Boat: Mass Music and Mass Movements.* Edited by Reebee Garofalo. Boston: South End Press, 1992.

Morris, Bonnie J. *Eden Built by Eves: The Culture of Women's Music Festivals.* Los Angeles: Alyson, 1999.

Pollock, Mary S. "The Politics of Women's Music: A Conversation with Linda Tillery and Mary Watkins." *Frontiers: A Journal of Women's Studies* 10:1 (1988): 14–19.

Post, Laura. *Backstage Pass: Interviews with Women in Music.* Norwich, Vt.: New Victoria, 1997.

Martha Mockus

See also LESBIAN FEMINISM; MUSIC: POPULAR; MUSIC: WOMEN'S FESTIVALS; OLIVIA RECORDS.

MUSIC: WOMEN'S FESTIVALS

Beginning in the mid-1970s, women's music festivals have served as North America's lesbian Woodstocks, gathering together women's music fans and political activists for several days of concerts, comedy, workshops, and crafts. The form such festivals have taken has been very much influenced by the lesbian-feminist rhetoric and politics of the 1970s and 1980s, making them a distinct and separate entity from gay men's musical events such as Wigstock, Radical Faerie gatherings, and circuit parties, as well as from "straight" but "rad" festivals such as Burning Man and Rainbow Gathering.

In 1974, Kristin Lems, a heterosexual feminist activist, initiated the first large women's music festival—the National Women's Music Festival (NWMF), which has met annually on university campuses in Illinois or Indiana ever since. NWMF's significance and daring in showcasing many new lesbian artists was soon matched by the even more radical Michigan Womyn's Music Festival (MWMF), founded in 1976 by the then nineteen-year-old Lisa Vogel, her sister Kristie Vogel, and friend Mary Kindig. (Barbara "Boo" Price served as coproducer through 1994.)

MWMF quickly gained notoriety as "the" lesbian festival due to its enormous size (almost ten thousand women attended in 1982), its wooded camping environment of private, clothing-optional land, and its long-standing policy of excluding all males over age five. While the NWMF permitted men to attend (although this was contested at first), MWMF accommodated boy children over five in a separate camp, "Brother Sun" (on its own section of festival land), and requested that all festivalgoers be born female, that is, not transgender. These issues have fostered considerable debate and continue to do so. Two other festivals, Campfest and the East Coast Lesbian Festival (ECLF), also required participants to be woman-born and to leave older boy children at home. ECLF was the first and almost only festival to use the word "lesbian" in its title; NWMF and other festivals, while upholding the political value of woman-only space, did not advertise as being for lesbians only.

As women's music culture blossomed in the climate of lesbian separatism and women-only institutions during the 1970s and early 1980s, recording companies and distribution networks made the music and comedy of lesbian artists available to fans in isolated towns where performers rarely toured. The option of a summer pilgrimage to a large-scale festival of lesbian culture attracted thousands of women eager to see and mingle with their favorite artists. In the years before greater media visibility of lesbians—before the comedian Ellen DeGeneres, the singer Melissa Etheridge, and the actress and talk-show host Rosie O'Donnell had come out publicly—festivals offered an alternative lesbian "star" system and the unusual opportunity to see key technical labor roles performed by female sound, light, carpentry, and production crews.

Within a fifteen-year period after the establishment of MWMF, similar, if smaller, festivals were established in more than twenty states, filling the calendar from Mother's Day weekend in May through Labor Day in September. Some of the most popular regional festivals were Campfest (Pennsylvania/Delaware/New Jersey); ECLF (upstate New York); the Gulf Coast Womyn's Festival (Mississippi); the Northeast or New England Women's Music Retreat (NEWMR, often in Connecticut); Rhythmfest (Georgia); Sisterfire (Washington, D.C.); the Southern and West Coast Women's Music and Comedy festivals produced by Robin Tyler (held in Georgia and Yosemite Park, respectively); and Wimminfest (New Mexico). Other festivals were held in Alaska, Arizona, Hawaii, Illinois, Nevada, Ohio, Texas, and Virginia; in Northampton, Massachusetts; in the Pacific Northwest; and in the Poconos.

Most festivals followed a similar format, presenting a day stage introducing lesser-known, typically unpaid performers, followed by workshops, a night stage of better-known headliners, disco and country/western dances, and goddess-centered spiritual rituals and drum circles. Basic vegetarian fare was usually provided as part of the camping package. Often a two-to-four-hour work shift was expected of campers in addition to their ticket payment, and a sliding scale reduced fees for low-income women, older women, and children—with day care available, but restrictions on boy children, even as infants.

As well as showcasing primarily lesbian artists, whose works were often considered too controversial for mainstream radio play, festivals such as MWMF promoted an extraordinary range of political views, emphasizing visibility for women of color and the obligation of white festiegoers to unlearn racism. Stage lineups at MWMF and other festivals were balanced carefully to include a range of styles, from rock to folk to jazz to blues to drumming, and the originally appearing slate of white performers from the mid-1970s such as Margie Adam, Meg Christian, Holly Near, and Cris Williamson expanded to include Asian American, Quebecoise, African Canadian, Jewish, Latina, and African American artists such as Alix Dobkin, Maxine Feldman, Marga Gomez, June Millington, Vicki Randle, Toshi Reagon, Sweet Honey in the Rock, Lucie Blue Tremblay, Mary Watkins, and Karen Williams, to name but a few. Edwina Lee Tyler and Ubaka Hill brought African drum performance to a new level of appreciation and vitality, and MWMF staff, in particular, labored to attract younger fans by steadily updating their lineup with punk, grunge, and riot-grrl bands like Tribe 8, the Butchies, Bitch and Animal, as well as the spoken-word "slam" poet Alix Olsen.

While the Indigo Girls, Melissa Etheridge, and Tracy Chapman all appeared at festivals before attaining enormous mainstream popularity, few festival performers won this same level of visibility or financial success beyond the lesbian folk/rock audience, and as the range of festivals began to shrink after 1992, performers dependent upon the festival fan base were often in competition for a decreasing number of stage slots. The lack of public familiarity with many popular lesbian festival artists was exacerbated by Sarah McLachlan's highly successful Lilith Fair. Promoting mostly corporate-backed straight female performers to mixed male and female audiences during 1997 and 1998, Lilith Fair was billed falsely as the first-ever women's festival.

For the thousands of women who have spent nearly thirty summers under the stars at MWMF and elsewhere, festival culture wins praise for providing "safe" and "healing" space, for popularizing the use of American Sign Language interpreters onstage, and for offering an affordable medley of concerts. Still unresolved are a host of controversies, particularly with regard to the woman-born-woman policy at MWMF; since 1994, an unofficial "Camp Trans" near the admission gates at the festival has been a staging ground for protests, and some artists, including Melissa Ferrick, have elected to boycott the festival. Others, including the Queens, New York, duo Bitch and Animal, have chosen to affirm transgender rights and identities from the Michigan stage, while also affirming the festival as a celebration for nontransgender women.

Other conflicts concern stage content. With more and more lesbian couples bringing children, are some shows too sexual? How can the gap between youth and the graying population of loyal, original festivalgoers be bridged? Longtime workers at many festivals acknowledge the enormous amount of unpaid work time spent "processing" other issues behind the scenes, such as alcohol and smoking on the land, sadomasochism (S/M) displays, boy children, male backup vocals, accommodation of women with disabilities, and international artists hassled at the U.S. border.

Regardless of these controversies, festivals including NWMF, MWMF, and Gulf Coast have moved successfully into the twenty-first century but must now compete for the lesbian entertainment dollar with other events, including urban poetry slams and Olivia Cruises. That festival culture is old enough to have acquired a history is evident in the flurry of films, Ph.D. dissertations, and books paying homage to MWMF and to the legacy of women's music as a social movement.

Bibliography

Armstrong, Toni, Jr., ed. *Hot Wire: A Journal of Women's Music and Culture.* Published three times per year, 1984–1994.

Edwalds, Loraine, and Midge Stocker, eds. *The Woman-Centered Economy: Ideals, Reality, and the Space In Between.* Chicago: Third Side Press, 1995.

Morris, Bonnie J. *Eden Built by Eves.* Los Angeles: Alyson, 1999.

Mosbacher, Dee. *Radical Harmonies: The Story of Women's Music.* Woman Vision, 2002. Documentary.

Near, Holly, and Derk Richardson. *Fire in the Rain, Singer in the Storm: An Autobiography.* York: Morrow, 1990.

Post, Laura. *Backstage Pass: Interviews with Women in Music.* Norwich, Vt.: New Victoria, 1997.

Van Gelder, Lindsay, and Pamela Robin Brandt. *The Girls Next Door: Into the Heart of Lesbian America.* New York: Simon and Schuster, 1996.

Bonnie J. Morris

See also LESBIAN FEMINISM; MICHIGAN; MUSIC: POPULAR.

MUSIC STUDIES AND MUSICOLOGY

Despite the widespread presence of LGBT people in the world of music as creators, performers, and listeners, musical scholarship avoided consideration of sexualities and genders and the possibility of their impact on musical work until fairly recently. This can be ascribed to musicology's roots in a formalist transcendental aesthetic (rooted in nineteenth-century German pedagogy), as well as to the homophobic and transphobic panic embedded in attitudes toward such a suspiciously emotional and sensual activity as music. Since the late 1980s, however, a dramatic wave of increasingly self-assured writings have firmly established the topic in music as well as in associated disciplines.

Early Work

Beginning in the post-Stonewall Riots context of the mid-1970s, several works of scholarship on LGBT topics began to appear. Some of these, especially those focusing on rock music, were associated with the rise of cultural studies; scholars in the then-new area of popular culture found it natural to pay a great deal of attention to popular music, especially in terms of lyrics, images of performers, and audience reception. However, most of these writers were not associated with academic music departments, nor did their writings tend to use the technical languages or formal methods associated with musicology.

The first person to present and publish LGBT studies in the smaller and more conservative world of academic musicology was Philip Brett, a scholar at the University of California at Berkeley. His first writings in the area, beginning in the late 1970s, focused on gay British composer Benjamin Britten. Not limited to the biographical, they also considered social and philosophical aspects of the "open secret" that characterized Britten's public career, a concept that continued to interest Brett throughout his professional life. From the beginning, Brett wrote in a carefully modulated blend of technical musical rhetoric, history, cultural theory, and subjective analysis, establishing an unusually broad-based model for musicological inquiry that became highly influential.

Breakthroughs

LGBT music studies remained relatively uncommon for some years; it took musicology's general breakthrough into cultural theory in the late 1980s and early 1990s (in the form of the so-called "new musicology"), instigated by feminist musicologist Susan McClary, among others, for more extensive work to appear. At the 1988 meeting of the American Musicological Society (AMS), Maynard Solomon presented evidence suggesting that Franz Schubert might have participated in male homosexual circles in early nineteenth-century Vienna. This initiated a highly charged, ongoing debate over social and musical interpretation, which has involved numerous scholars writing for a number of newspapers and journals, most significantly a special issue of the journal *Nineteenth-Century Music* in 1993. At the 1989 meeting, Brett was again an agent of change; having organized informal gatherings in previous years, he finally and officially founded the Gay and Lesbian Study Group (GLSG) of the AMS.

The 1990 AMS meeting in Oakland, California, included a session called "Composers and Sexuality," with papers presented by Brett, McClary, and Gary C. Thomas, and received a standing ovation. At the same gathering, a second organizational meeting of the GLSG established an organizational structure with equal representation of women and men, a regular series of meetings with presentations, and the *GLSG Newsletter* under the editorship of Frances Feldon and Paul Attinello. Notable scholars associated with this group included Elizabeth Wood, Mitchell Morris, Suzanne Cusick, Byron Adams, and Lydia Hamessley, among many others. The immediate influence of the group on its parent organization can be seen in Malcolm Hicks's 1991 article in the *Journal of the American Musicological Society*—the first of its kind to appear in that relatively conservative periodical—and in 1996 the establishment of the Philip Brett Award for lesbian or gay scholarly publications.

The inclusion of articles on LGBT topics by Brett, Wood, and Morris in R. A. Solie's *Musicology and Difference,* published in 1993, as well as the 1994 publication of the anthology *Queering the Pitch* under the joint editorship of Brett, Wood, and Thomas, permanently established the subdiscipline in the academic world. In fact, attention to gender included queer topics from the outset, perhaps because feminism and queer theory struck musicology at the same time, but also because of the various androgynies deeply embedded in the gender discourse of music. In the 1990s increasing publicity led to dramatic public arguments about revered historical figures (such as Schubert and George Frideric Handel) and problems in musical meaning, fanned by indignant newspaper debates. Other professional organizations for music scholars, including the Society for Ethnomusicology (notably Carolina Robertson and Brian Currid) and the Society for Music Theory (notably Fred Maus and Nadine Hubbs), began to expand their activities in LGBT studies.

In the twenty-first century, Brett and Wood were again responsible for a turning point in the history of the subdiscipline, writing an article, "Gay and Lesbian Music," for the monumental second edition of the *New Grove Dictionary of Music and Musicians* in 2001. The dictionary's editors were evidently not entirely comfortable with the topic; they cut the entry a great deal, and chief editor Stanley Sadie singled it out from over six thousand others as having given him "a great deal of trouble." Brett published a spirited defense in the *BBC Music Magazine* in early 2002; it was his last major act, as he abruptly fell ill, dying of cancer later that year.

Major Themes

Since the late 1980s, methodology, rhetoric, and research in LGBT musicology have developed with remarkable speed. Scholars have now published work in areas such as history, biography, anthropology, and sociology and have adopted a wide variety of approaches to aesthetics and interpretation. Significant projects have been concerned with the sexual and gender behaviors of canonic figures, ranging from the composers and performers of twelfth-century Notre Dame polyphony to twentieth-century Americans such as Aaron Copland, Marc Blitzstein, and Ned Rorem. In these types of projects, musicologists have explored not only what sexuality and gender can tell us about music but what music can tell us about sexuality and gender. The rediscovery and reevaluation of the work of obscured historical figures, especially lesbian composers, has been part of the larger work by feminist scholars of returning women composers to history.

Popular music studies have generally started from solid evidence, including biographical information, interviews, performance images, and lyrics. A number of essay collections, both by single and multiple authors, have not only compared works, genres, and events involving LGBT artists such as k.d. lang and Jimmy Somerville, but have also looked at the root systems of queer culture that wind through the world of music; examples include books by John Gill (1995) and Lee Fleming (1996). More recently, studies have begun to take many of these tropes apart, attempting to follow the rapidly changing and increasingly complex gender roles and sexual identities disseminated all over the world by the music industry.

The methods and ideas that were once identified with ethnomusicology have become so intertwined with other aspects of the new musicology that it is now impossible to separate them. In addition to many of the above types of studies, scholars who define themselves as ethnomusicologists have also worked on sophisticated explorations of alternate genders and sexualities in non-Eurocentric cultures (such as Carolina Robertson's work on Polynesian cultures) and have consistently applied concepts of cultural and gender relativism.

Since music, through the involvement of performers and audiences, tends to be a social art, reception is another important area of study, encompassing both collective constructions of identity and personal subject positions (as in Cusick's influential article published in *Queering the Pitch*). This area includes investigations of such contexts as the establishment of women's music in the 1970s, the gay and lesbian choruses, and public reception of performers such as Phranc and Boy George.

Reexamined biographies have led to the question of why such studies might be significant—a particularly tricky discussion in music, where it is often more difficult to show evidence of LGBT meanings in the artwork than in, say, literature or the visual arts. Rethinking the tricky territory between formal and symbolic interpretations of sounds and scores has resulted in studies that connect constructed experience, musical creation, performance, and reception in a semiotic chain of queered meanings. Groundbreaking work of this type has included a number of articles about women, especially Cusick's contribution to *Queering the Pitch,* and work by the contributors to *En Travesti,* with their flamboyant exposure of the labyrinthine traditions linked to the "trouser roles" of opera. Wayne Koestenbaum's *The Queen's Throat* (1993) significantly opened up discussions about the personal experience of divas and voices, social-subcultural uses of images, and technical-historical knowledge. Among the most sophisticated studies of this kind is D. A. Miller's *Place for Us* (1998), which explores the ways that musical theater depicts the narcissistic pride and insecurity common to many gay men, implying a feedback between music and audience in a manner that recalls the work of Roland Barthes.

Ultimately, these studies have contributed to an increasingly common realization of the most obvious, and most startling, fact of all: that music is, and has always been, deeply and complexly associated with alternate sexualities and genders of every kind. LGBT studies have helped to revive discussion of the most difficult and most exciting conflicts that have existed in every musical culture—those that appear when the discipline faces the sensual, those endless battles between the formal and the flamboyant.

Bibliography

Blackmer, Corinne E., and Patricia Juliana Smith, eds.. *En Travesti: Women, Gender Subversion, Opera.* New York: Columbia University Press, 1995.

Brett, Philip. "Britten and Grimes." *Musical Times* 117 (1977): 995–1000.

———. "A Matter of Pride." *BBC Music Magazine,* February 2002, pp. 28–32.

Brett, Philip, Elizabeth Wood, and Gary C. Thomas, eds. *Queering the Pitch: The New Gay and Lesbian Musicology.* New York: Routledge, 1994.

Fleming, Lee, ed. *Hot Licks: Lesbian Musicians of Note.* Charlottestown, Prince Edward Island, Canada: Gynergy Books, 1996.

Fuller, Sophie, and Lloyd Whitesell, eds. *Queer Episodes in Music and Modern Identity.* Urbana: University of Illinois Press, 2002.

Gill, John. *Queer Noises: Male and Female Homosexuality in Twentieth-Century Music.* Minneapolis: University of Minnesota Press, 1995.

Hicks, Malcolm. "The Imprisonment of Henry Cowell." *Journal of the American Musicological Society* 44 (1991): 92–119

Ibars, Eduardo Haro. *Gay Rock.* Madrid: Ediciones Júcar, 1975.

Koestenbaum, Wayne. *The Queen's Throat: Opera, Homosexuality, and the Mystery of Desire.* New York: Poseidon, 1993.

Kramer, Lawrence, ed. "Schubert: Music, Sexuality, Culture." *Nineteenth-Century Music* 17, no. 1 (1993).

Miller, D. A. *Place for Us: Essays on the Broadway Musical.* Cambridge, Mass.: Harvard University Press, 1998.

Solie, Ruth A., ed.: *Musicology and Difference: Gender and Sexuality in Music Scholarship.* Berkeley: University of California Press, 1993.

Paul Attinello

See also MUSIC: BROADWAY AND MUSICAL THEATER; MUSIC: CLASSICAL; MUSIC: OPERA; MUSIC: POPULAR; MUSIC: WOMEN'S.

MUSLIMS AND ISLAM

The faith of Islam and its adherents who call themselves Muslims have complicated relationships to homoeroticism and same-sex sexual relations. Many have interpreted the Koran, the sacred scripture that serves as the primary source of authority for Muslims, as condemning sex between men and as silent about lesbianism. The same is true for the Hebrew Bible. However, Islam has been more tolerant in practice than most types of Christianity and some branches of Judaism.

The Koran approaches the issue as a rhetorical question aimed at a male audience: "How can you lust for males, of all creatures in the world, and leave those whom God has created for you as your mates?" (Surah 26:165–166). The prophet Muhammad is also said to have addressed the issue in his farewell sermon, adding a prohibition also against anal intercourse with a woman, which indicates that the underlying assumption is that sex was regarded by him as procreative, not recreational.

The Shari'a, Muslim law based on the Koran and the Hadith (recollections of the prophet's sayings and deeds, a secondary source of authority for Muslims), makes male sex acts with males a punishable offense, but without stated punishments. A large scope for interpretation is therefore possible.

One reason for the relative silence on the issue throughout most of Muslim history is that pre-Islamic Arabia and Persia both practiced a type of male-to-male mentoring similar to ancient Greece, in which an older man would act as a mentor to a young protégé, with whom he would also act as sexual initiator. Such men would be expected to marry women and produce families, and would not have identified as alternative in their sexuality at all.

Another reason might be the sexual segregation (*purdah*) of Muslim societies. Engaging in illicit sexual relations with another man's wife or his daughter would constitute a serious offense, because a family's honor rested on the reputation of its women. Same-sex relations would be more difficult to detect in such a system, and might afford more opportunities, particularly for adolescent experimentation.

Islam's mystical tradition, Sufism, has long been an exception on matters of same-sex sexual expression and eroticism. Sometimes the master-disciple relationship in Sufism became particularly close. Jalāl al-Dīn al-Rūmī (c. 1207–1273), probably the best known of Sufi poets and founder of the Mawlawiyah order (whirling dervish), wrote some of his most moving love poetry to a disciple of his named Shams al-Dīn, but the poetry always carries a double meaning because the beloved one is, at the same time, the earthly Shams and Allah (God). Shams, whose name means "sun of religion," became, to Rūmī, an embodiment of the divine beloved, a symbol of divine-human relationship. He used his passion for Shams to give voice to his wild longing after Allah. Rūmī became so wrapped up in Shams that his other followers became jealous. They murdered Shams, hid his body in a well, and lied to Rūmī about his disappearance. Late in his life, another disciple, Husām al-Dīn Chelebi, became close to him and succeeded Rūmī as head of the order when Rūmī died. For some Sufi poets, a woman could represent the transcendent love of Allah. Rūmī had one poem in which he said that "Woman is a ray of God," but his strongest attachments were always to his male disciples.

Secular poetry also developed a homoerotic tradition in the cosmopolitan court of the Abbasid empire, centered at Baghdad, beginning in the eighth century. The most famous poet writing in Arabic was Abū Nuwās (c. 747 to 762–c. 813 to 815), who wrote love poems in praise of anal intercourse with adolescent boys. As Everett Rowson points out, once the boy became fully adult, signified by being able to grow a beard, he lost his allure, according to some poets, while others wrote in praise of the fully bearded youth. In either case, the hierarchical pattern was similar that found in ancient Greece. For adult males, the idealized status of penetrator validated his masculinity and authority. So for an adult male to be the recipient in anal sex was regarded as shameful, because the passive partner was seen as being in the female role.

The best-known poet writing secular homoerotic poetry in Persian was Sa'īd al-Shirāz (c. 1213–1292). Like Rūmī, he wrote mystical religious poetry in Persian as well, in which the beautiful boy offers a glimpse of the transcendent divine. His secular poems imply that boys offer a richer range of sexual pleasures than do women.

Lesbianism has never been emphasized positively or negatively in Islam. Homoerotic attachments may have developed in the homosocial atmosphere of the harems, but since female authorship was rare in pre-nineteenth-century Muslim worlds, an extensive literature paralleling the male tradition did not develop. However, there are important literary examples of love between women among twentieth-century women writers. Perhaps the most famous was the fiction and film screenplay writer Ismat Chutgai, who ranked among the most important writers in the 1940s Urdu literary scene. In 1942 she published *Lihaaf* (The Quilt), which narrated the mysterious intimacy of an older woman and her maidservant, who are observed entangled beneath bedcovers by a visiting niece. The story aroused public controversy and led to an obscenity trial in Lahore, Pakistan.

The fairly tolerant legacy of Islam is rapidly disintegrating because of the rise of Muslim fundamentalism. As a reaction to colonialism, Islamic cultures are trying to define themselves against Western "decadence." The recent tendency is to define anything but reproductive sex as immoral and rooted in Western influence, even though Islamic tradition has always had a high view of the role of pleasure in sex.

LGBT Muslims in America

Muslims first arrived in the United States in significant numbers as African slaves and later, in the nineteenth century, as sailors and migrants from Syria, Lebanon, Turkey, and India. In the 1920s and 1930s, missionary movements including the Ahmadīya sect from India sent missionaries who developed mosques and converted African Americans in Philadelphia, Chicago, Detroit, and St. Louis. The black-dominated Nation of Islam also emerged during this period. Since the 1960s, Muslims have been part of the large migration streams of Arabs, South Asians, and Southeast Asians and have exhibited growing strength in black communities. Among the migrant groups have been members of many different Islamic sects and traditions. For example, the Ismāʿīlī sect (also known as the Aga Khan movement) was originally dominant in Southwest Asia and India. When Indians in East Africa fled their homes in the 1960s, many came to Canada and the United States. Ismāʿīlīs believe Islam to be a continuously evolving faith that must be reinterpreted to adapt to modern-day society and culture. Their spiritual leader, Prince Aga Khan, who is thought to be a direct descendent of the prophet Muhammad, has been open to dialogue and communication with progressive movements within Islam, although he has not officially made any gay-affirming statements. Beginning in the 1990s, LGB Muslims began to organize various types of groups and networks in the United States. There are currently several organizations, primarily concentrated in major cities, for LGB Muslims, who often find themselves outside of the mainstream of Islam. If they come out, LGB Muslims often face expulsion from their mosques and rejection from their families. Forming groups and networks is a way for LGB Muslims to deal with homophobia in Muslim communities; religious, ethnic, and racial prejudice in American society; and other local, national, and global issues.

In August 2003, a group of about seventy LGBT Muslims and their supporters met in New York City for a national conference, Our Individual Lives; Our Collective Journey, to discuss LGBT Muslim life in the wake of the attacks on the World Trade Center and the Pentagon on 11 September 2001 and other world events. Speakers at the conference discussed what has come to be called the progressive Muslim movement as a location where LGBT Muslims can find acceptance. Sufism, because of its long history of LGBT acceptance, is another way that LGBT Muslims can reconcile with their religion, according to one speaker. A panel also discussed *In the Name of Allah,* a new documentary about LGBT Muslims.

The conference was sponsored by the Al-Fatiha Foundation, a Washington, D.C.–based support and advocacy group for LGBT Muslims. Al-Fatiha (Arabic for "the opening") started in November 1997 when its founder, Faisal Alam, created a listserv (an Internet-based e-mail discussion group). In 2003 the listserv hosted more than 275 subscribers from more than twenty countries around the world. Subscribers of the listserv decided soon after its establishment to meet in person at what became the First International Retreat for LGBT Muslims, held in Boston, Massachusetts, in October 1998. More than forty participants attended, representing thirteen ethnicities and nationalities and including participants from South Africa, Canada, Belgium, and the Netherlands. At the end of the three-day retreat, participants formally decided that an international organization was needed in order to address the specific issues and problems facing the "gay" Muslim community. Since the retreat, Al-Fatiha has grown to include chapters in the United States in Atlanta, Houston, Los Angeles, Philadelphia, New York City, San Diego, San Francisco, and Washington, D.C. Local chapters hold social events, discussion groups, parties, and regional retreats and participate in local LGBT and Muslim events. The international perspective of LGBT Muslims has broadened and deepened through networks of affiliate and sister organizations. In London, Al-Fatiha UK and the Safra Project work with local LGBT Muslims. In Canada, there is Salaam Toronto, Salaam Halifax, and Salaam Vancouver.

Another international organization that often focuses on Muslim issues is the Gay and Lesbian Arabic Society (GLAS), established in 1988 in the United States, but with chapters in other countries as well. GLAS serves as a networking organization for LGB people of Arab descent and LGB people living in Arab countries. It aims to promote positive images of LGB people in Arab communities worldwide and to combat negative portrayals of Arabs within the LGB community. The group also provides a support network for members, fighting for human rights wherever oppression exists. It regards itself as a part of the global LGB movement seeking an end to injustice and discrimination based on sexual orientation. GLAS added a lesbian division, Lazeeza, which has its own Web home page that features information about its mailing list, news of interest to Arab lesbians, articles, poetry, and other relevant material.

The Internet has proven to be a valuable means of communication and organization among LGBT Muslims. An important online source for Muslim Arab lesbians is *Blint al Nass*, a cultural e-zine. Ahbab is a more general online community for LGBT Arab Muslims. Queer Jihad, another online community of support, is not a formal organization or a movement. Its home page states that Queer Jihad is an "idea." Recognizing the difficulty of being queer and Muslim in America (and elsewhere), Queer Jihad is interested in "encouraging queer people to remain true to their Creator, to grapple with the issues, to come to terms with who they are in whatever manner and fashion they are capable of." The issue of Islam and homosexuality, the home page declares, is complicated, requiring struggle within oneself and within the community. Queer Jihad is defined as "the queer Muslim struggle for acceptance: first, the struggle to accept ourselves as being exactly the way Allah has created us to be; and secondly, the struggle for understanding among Muslims in general."

"Jihad" is a misunderstood word in the West. It means to struggle, to endeavor. Traditionally, the first and most important jihad is the struggle with one's self and one's desires. Queer jihad refers in part to the internal struggle with sexuality, with accepting it, dealing with it, and moving on, but it is also an endeavor to provide knowledge and foster understanding with the larger community. Both tasks are difficult for queer Muslims in the United States, but through Web sites and organizations like Al-Fatiha, GLAS, Lazeeza, Ahbab, and Queer Jihad, LGBT Muslims are breaking down the barriers that keep them isolated.

Bibliography

Denny, Frederick M. *An Introduction to Islam.* New York: Macmillan, 1994.

Duran, Khalid. "Homosexuality and Islam." In *Homosexuality and World Religions.* Edited by Arlene Swidler. Valley Forge, Pa.: Trinity Press International, 1993.

Khan, Badruddin. *Sex, Longing, and Not Belonging: A Gay Muslim's Quest for Love and Meaning.* Oakland, Calif.: Floating Lotus, 1997.

Murray, Stephen O., and J. Will Roscoe, eds. *Islamic Homosexualities: Culture, History, and Literature.* New York: New York University Press, 1997.

Rowson, Everett K. "Middle Eastern Literature: Arabic." In *Gay and Lesbian Literary Heritage.* Edited by Claude J. Summers. New York : Henry Holt, 1995.

Schmitt, Arno, and J. Jehoeda Sofer, eds. *Sexuality and Eroticism Among Males in Moslem Societies.* New York: Haworth, 1991.

Skjaervo, Prods Oktor. "Middle Eastern Literature: Persian." In *Gay and Lesbian Literary Heritage.* Edited by Claude J. Summers. New York: Henry Holt, 1995.

Woods, Gregory. *A History of Gay Literature: The Male Tradition.* New Haven, Conn.: Yale University Press, 1998.

Lori Rowlett

See also AFRICAN AMERICANS; ANTI-SEMITISM; ARAB AMERICANS; ASIAN AMERICANS; CHURCHES, TEMPLES, AND RELIGIOUS GROUPS.

N

NAMES PROJECT. see AIDS MEMORIAL QUILT—NAMES PROJECT.

NATIONAL BLACK LESBIAN AND GAY LEADERSHIP FORUM. see AFRICAN AMERICAN LGBTQ ORGANIZATIONS AND PERIODICALS.

NATIONAL COALITION OF BLACK LESBIANS AND GAYS. see AFRICAN AMERICAN LGBTQ ORGANIZATIONS AND PERIODICALS.

NATIONAL GAY AND LESBIAN TASK FORCE (NGLTF)

The National Gay and Lesbian Task Force, originally called the National Gay Task Force, was formed in October 1973 by a group of New York City activists—Bruce Voeller, Nathalie Rockhill, and Ron Gold—who had met in the Gay Activists Alliance. At the time, virtually all gay and lesbian movement organizations were local in nature. Voeller, Rockhill, and Gold were interested in creating a national organization with full-time paid staff. With the support of Howard Brown, a former New York City health commissioner whose coming out was a front-page story in the *New York Times* in 1973, they raised money and constructed a board of directors drawn mostly from the Northeast.

Based in New York, NGLTF turned its attention to national campaigns beyond the scope of local groups. It quickly amassed a number of significant victories. In 1974 it played a key role in the referendum within the American Psychiatric Association that removed homosexuality from its list of mental disorders. It elicited from the National Council of Churches a resolution condemning antigay discrimination. It prodded the American Bar Association into going on record in favor of sodomy law repeal. In Washington, D.C., it successfully lobbied in 1975 the federal Civil Service Commission to lift its blanket ban on the employment of lesbians, gay men, and bisexuals. That same year, it persuaded U.S. Representative Bella Abzug, Democrat from New York, to introduce a bill in Congress to amend federal civil rights statutes to include sexual orientation. It also won reversal of an Internal Revenue Service ruling that denied tax-exempt status to groups that argued for the acceptability of homosexuality. Concerned about negative portrayals of homosexuality in the mainstream media, NGLTF initiated the first coordinated nationwide action against network television to protest the airing of a homophobic episode of the ABC series *Marcus Welby, M.D.* It established a "Gay Media Alert!" to keep local activists appraised of homophobic programming.

From the beginning, women on the staff and board of NGLTF lobbied for gender parity in the organization. Board membership was divided equally between men and women, and in 1975, NGLTF hired Jean O'Leary to serve as coexecutive director with Bruce Voeller. With the support of board members such as Frances Doughty and Charlotte Bunch, O'Leary pressed successfully to add new priorities to the work of the Task Force. NGLTF worked within the mainstream women's movement to win support for lesbian rights. In 1975, the convention of the National Organization for Women passed a lesbian rights

National Gay and Lesbian Task Force. Urvashi Vaid, one of this ambitious group's many executive directors since the late 1980s, addresses a rally, speaking behind a sign that reads, "Mr. President, our country has AIDS." **[Patsy Lynch]**

resolution. Two years later, O'Leary and the other women of NGLTF spearheaded a successful national campaign for adoption of a lesbian rights plank at the International Women's Year Conference U.S. called by President Jimmy Carter and held in Houston. O'Leary also pushed NGLTF to be involved in mainstream party politics, which, in the 1970s, essentially meant the Democratic Party. In 1976, she organized a national convention project that pressed candidates for the presidential nomination to take a stand on gay issues and attempted to get openly gay or lesbian delegates elected in the states. O'Leary was one of only four such delegates at the Democratic Convention in New York City.

The rise of the New Right, the spread of antigay ballot referenda, and the election of Ronald Reagan to the presidency in 1980 posed a new set of challenges for the organization. Voeller and O'Leary both left NGLTF in 1979. Their replacements, Charles Brydon and Lucia Valeska, worked poorly together and could not adapt to the more hostile political climate. In 1982, Ginny Apuzzo became executive director. An inspirational speaker, she traveled around the country trying to restore NGLTF's credibility among local activists. She hired Kevin Berrill to direct an antiviolence project and Jeff Levi as a Washington-based lobbyist.

Most of all, Apuzzo turned the resources of the Task Force toward the emerging AIDS epidemic. Though the national caseload in 1982 was still below a thousand, Apuzzo sensed that a crisis of massive proportions was in the making, and, with Levi, she tried to craft a national response. NGLTF worked closely with friendly members of Congress, such as Representatives Henry Waxman (a California Democrat) and Ted Weiss (a Democrat from New York State), to organize congressional hearings. She strove to bring local organizations together into a national effort, helping to create what later became the AIDS Action Council and a much larger coalition, National Organizations Responding to AIDS. The emphasis on AIDS made a strong presence in Washington, D.C. ever more important and, in 1986, when Jeff Levi became the executive director, he moved the organization to Washington, D.C.

Meanwhile, the configuration of the lesbian and gay movement was changing. The Human Rights Campaign, concerned with electing to Congress supporters of gay rights, was becoming a stronger presence in Washington while the AIDS epidemic was provoking a whole new wave of local militant activism. The Christian right was targeting the gains of the gay movement all over the country. By the late 1980s, NGLTF decided to shift its focus to building support for grassroots activism in communities across the country. Organizing itself into a series of issue-oriented projects—privacy, antiviolence, family, campus organizing, fight-the-right, lesbian health—NGLTF began to provide training and technical assistance to local groups in every region. Under the leadership of Urvashi Vaid, who became executive director in 1989, NGLTF's annual Creating Change conference was quickly recognized as the premier gathering of lesbians, gays, and bisexuals and, eventually, transgender activists in the United States.

In the wake of the devastating "gays in the military" debate of 1993, NGLTF decided that a more explicitly progressive voice needed to be heard within the LGBT movement. It began to refer to itself as the "progressive voice of the queer movement" and "the queer voice of the progressive movement." Intent on pursuing coalition politics, it started to speak out on issues such as welfare reform, immigration restriction, affirmative action, and the death penalty. It rewrote its mission statement to make explicit the inclusion of bisexual and transgender concerns. It established a policy institute in 1995, a think tank designed to produce research and progressive analysis that could be used by activists around the country. In the late 1990s, it began to add to its work with local activists an emphasis on statewide organizing. NGLTF has provided support and helped to seed statewide coalitions around the country and was a founding sponsor of a national federation of statewide LGBT organizations.

For all its important work, NGLTF has been plagued by difficulties throughout its history. Trying to be too many things to too many people, it has often overreached itself and repeatedly faced serious budget crises that have forced staff cutbacks and failure to follow through on its work. It has picked up issues for a time, such as antiviolence work and campus organizing, and then dropped them as it has moved on to newer issues. It has also been plagued by rapid turnover of its leadership. Between 1993 and 2003 it had seven different executive directors. The change in leadership has made it difficult to maintain continuity and establish a strong continuing public presence. As a result, NGLTF has seen itself eclipsed in size by other national organizations, like the Human Rights Campaign and Lambda Legal Defense and Education Fund, and has watched as newer national organizations, such as GLSEN and GLAAD, have grown and carved out important missions for themselves. Nevertheless, NGLTF remains an active and distinctive advocate for LGBT liberation.

John D'Emilio

See also ANTIDISCRIMINATION LAW AND POLICY; BOYCOTTS; DEMOCRATIC PARTY; DISABILITY, DISABLED PEOPLE, AND DISABILITY MOVEMENTS; ELECTORAL POLITICS; EMPLOYMENT LAW AND POLICY; FAMILY LAW AND POLICY; FEDERAL LAW AND POLICY; FEMINISM; HEALTH AND HEALTH CARE LAW AND POLICY; KAMENY, FRANKLIN; MEDICINE, MEDICALIZATION, AND THE MEDICAL MODEL; MILITARY; POOR PEOPLE'S MOVEMENTS; PSYCHOLOGY, PSYCHIATRY, PSYCHOANALYSIS, AND SEXOLOGY.

NATIONALISM

During broadcasts of the Olympics and other international sporting events, television coverage often includes brief documentaries on the people and culture of the host nation. Australians, we were told in 2000, are open and friendly people living on a vast expanse of arid land; Koreans, we were told in 1988, are proud of their ancient traditions yet dedicated to rapid modernization. These representations uphold the popular understanding of a nation as "an extensive aggregate of persons . . . closely associated with each other by common descent, language, or history" who "form a distinct race or people, usually organized as a separate political state and occupying a definite territory" (from the *Oxford English Dictionary,* quoted in Stein, p. 253).

However, as Benedict Anderson has noted, this definition is a fiction of sorts, an imagined (but powerful) reality that belies a complex, relatively recent form of social organization. Nationalism can more accurately be defined as a set of discourses and practices that work to solidify the ideals of bounded communities constituted as nations. Nationalism often does this work by promoting notions of insiders and outsiders, by suppressing internal divisions, and by positioning different groups of insiders in distinct but complementary roles. It is a particularly powerful ideology in the United States and has been invoked in multiple ways since the country's inception as a nation.

Nationalism and Sexuality

George Mosse and others have observed that LGBT people have troubled nationalism for a long time. Mosse argues that sexuality has long been a part of nationalist discourses. Within nationalist frameworks, relations between men are conceptualized through metaphors of brotherly homosocial love; women are positioned as wives and mothers whose primary functions are to care for men and produce the nation's next generation. In such frameworks, male homosexuality becomes the taboo, the line that must not be crossed, as it marks an "incestuous" turn in brotherly bonds. Lesbianism becomes invisible since the nation's male rulers cannot imagine relationships that do not require their presence.

These insights can help explain the many ways in which heterosexism and transphobia in the United States establishes the reproductive heterosexual couple as the national ideal. They can help account for differences in the nation's treatment of LBT females and GBT males. And they can provide a starting point for exploring the nation's treatment of LGBT "insiders" and "outsiders" in such realms as immigration law, citizenship rights, military institutions, and national security policy. When U.S. immigration law has excluded LGBT people as "psychopathic personalities" and "sexual deviants" (as it did through much of the twentieth century), when citizenship rights to privacy have been denied to LGBT people (as they were until 2003), when military institutions have attempted to exclude LGBT people from the forces that defend the nation (as they have done through the early 2000s), and when law enforcement officials have targeted LGBT people as security risks (which they did in particularly significant ways during the McCarthy era), the

United States has continually demonstrated opposition to LGBT people.

LGBT Nationalisms

At the same time, nationalist discourses, sentiments, and images have been adopted by numerous minority groups to further their own objectives and to fight oppression. When ethnic and racial nationalists within the United States have endorsed conservative visions of the family, gender roles, and sexual identities, they, too, have defined themselves in opposition to LGBT people. As Marc Stein has observed, LGBT people have also often adopted tropes of nationalism, sometimes for strategic reasons, sometimes because they are true believers in nationalism, and sometimes for a combination of reasons. One way that they have done this is by imagining themselves as a nation, articulating a sense of collective identity. This occurred, for example, when lesbians promoted the notion of the "lesbian nation" in the 1970s and when activists in the 1990s constituted themselves as "Queer Nation." Similar though less explicit developments took place when, in the 1960s, homophile magazines such as *Drum* "imagined the existence of a national community of gay men entitled to autonomous cultural space and a shared network of politics and desire" (Stein, p. 255).

Another way that U.S. LGBT activists have appropriated discourses of nationalism is by anchoring their arguments for rights in U.S. patriotic traditions. This occurred, for example, when LGBT activists marched at Independence Hall on the Fourth of July in the 1960s, advocated for military nondiscrimination policies so that LGBT people could better serve the nation, and defended LGBT rights with language found in the U.S. Declaration of Independence, Constitution, and Bill of Rights. Since the 1950s, LGBT activists have worked with two national political languages to further their cause: "a libertarian discourse," which "drew on the long tradition of resistance to state infringements of individual rights," and "a minority rights discourse," which was built on the strategies of the African American civil rights movement (Stein, pp. 259–260). The first discourse may help explain the success of LGBT legal advocates in convincing a Republican-dominated U.S. Supreme Court to recognize LGB privacy rights in 2003, but it has been criticized for promoting antigovernment attitudes. The second, while often successful, has been criticized for promoting conflict between LGBT and African American communities.

Recent Nationalisms

These discourses are found in two opposing trajectories of nationalism utilized in recent U.S. LGBT activism. The assimiliationist trajectory utilizes libertarian and/or minority rights discourse to argue for acceptance as equal, patriotic, upstanding American citizens. LGBT people supporting this trajectory want to be recognized as equal to their fellow Americans and as citizens who uphold the values and ideals of the American nation. Their "difference," they argue, should not take away from them any of the privileges and rights of being American. Assimilationist nationalism is found in recent court challenges attempting to legalize same-sex marriage. Lesbian and gay couples are demanding the right to marry and enjoy the same state-sanctioned privileges and rights as heterosexual couples currently enjoy. Advocates of the legalization of same-sex marriage have argued that their desire to have this particular kind of relationship (a monogamous couple) recognized and protected by the state demonstrates identification with and similarity to their fellow Americans' values.

A second recent trajectory of LGBT nationalism is separatist and builds more exclusively on discourses of minority rights. It argues that LGBT people form a distinct social, cultural, and political community (or communities) whose values are not reflected in American nationalist discourses (which are heteronormative and rigidly gendered). LGBT people, according to this view, should strive to develop separate, self-contained communities that reflect and support their "way of life." Lesbian separatist promoters of the "lesbian nation" adopted this type of politics in the 1970s. "Queer Nation," an activist network that arose in the early 1990s, manifested the separatist nationalist trajectory in many of its public performances and statements of resistance. Polemical slogans such as "I Hate Straights," which were emblazoned on t-shirts and posters at LGBT pride parades in New York City and Chicago in 1990, deliberately provoked anti-assimilationist sentiments in order to communicate the collective anger and frustration felt by many LGBT people and people with AIDS (PWAs) over ongoing marginalization within, and rejection by, the United States. Queer Nation activists also often demonstrated nationalist sentiment through their policing of the literal and figurative boundaries of LGBT communities, defending the physical territories of LGBT neighborhoods while also attempting to define who was queer and who was not. However, as Lauren Berlant and Elizabeth Freeman (1992) have pointed out, Queer Nation tactics were never completely separatist, as they recognized that PWAs required state support for medications and health services and that LGBT communities could never fully disregard state laws and policies (pp. 154–155).

Though popular among many LGBT activists, the nationalist politics of Queer Nation were criticized in many quarters and for many reasons. Perhaps the most significant objection raised was that, like all forms of nationalism, queer nationalism homogenized complex LGBT communities, downplayed and suppressed internal divisions and differences, and failed to acknowledge the fluid boundaries of sex, gender, and sexuality. While there are shared experiences across different LGBT communities in the United States, there are also important divergences and divisions based on ability, class, ethnicity, gender, language, region, religion, sex, sexuality, and other factors. Thus, while it is important to acknowledge the power of nationalist discourses in terms of their potential to both oppress and liberate U.S. LGBT and queer people, we must also always remember the rich diversity that exists in ways of being an LGBT or queer "American." Finally, as Henry Abelove has pointed out, while queers may appropriate discourses and practices of the nation-state, many also are antinationalist in the ways in which they reject narratives of history framed by the nation-state and prefer instead narratives that are framed "either by some sub-national entity or by the globe" (Abelove, p. 53).

Bibliography

Abelove, Henry. "The Queering of Lesbian/Gay History." Radical History Review, no. 62 (Spring 1995): 44-57

Anderson, Benedict. *Imagined Communities: Reflections on the Origin and Spread of Nationalism. Revised edition. London and New York: Verso, 1991.*

Berlant, Lauren, and Elizabeth Freeman. "Queer Nationality." Boundary 2 19, no. 1 (1992): 149–180.

D'Emilio, John. "The Homosexual Menace: The Politics of Sexuality in Cold War America," in *Passion and Power: Sexuality in History*, ed. Kathy Peiss and Christina Simmons (Philadelphia: Temple Univ. Press, 1989): pp. 226-240.

Duggan, Lisa. "Making it Perfectly Queer." Socialist Review 22 no.1 (1992): 11-31.

Luibhéid, Eithne. *Entry Denied: Controlling Sexuality at the Border* Minneapolis : University of Minnesota Press, 2002.

Mosse, George. *Nationalism and Sexuality.* Madison: University of Wisconsin Press, 1988.

Parker, Andrew. *Nationalisms and Sexualities.* New York: Routledge, 1992.

Stein, Marc. "Birthplace of the Nation: Imagining Lesbian and Gay Communities in Philadelphia, 1969–70." In *Creating a Place for Ourselves: Lesbian Gay and Bisexual Community Histories.* Edited by Brett Beemyn. New York: Routledge, 1997.

David A. B. Murray

See also JOHNSTON, JILL; LESBIAN FEMINISM; QUEER NATION.

NATIVE AMERICANS

The existence of androgynous shamans from the earliest peopling of the Americas is part of a long history of respect for transgenderism and same-sex love and affection in many indigenous Native American cultures. Although a wide variety of cultures existed among the aboriginal peoples of the Western Hemisphere, many accepted sexual and gender diversity.

It is difficult to say what proportion of aboriginal cultures took an accepting attitude toward sexual and gender diversity, in part because of the paucity of historical sources that document sexual and gender behaviors. The evidence that does exist suggests that the most accepting North American Native societies were those located in the Great Lakes region, the Northern Plains, the Southwest, California, and Alaska. However, scattered information for Northwest, Subarctic, and Eastern Woodlands cultures indicates similar acceptance in these areas. Because the eastern area of North America was so thoroughly dominated by European invaders in the colonial era, same-sex and transgender traditions may have been suppressed before adequate documentation was made. Statements by European American explorers, frontiersmen, Christian missionaries, and anthropologists are not to be trusted when they claim that homosexuality and transgenderism were denigrated by aboriginal cultures. Many such claims were more a reflection of the European and European American writers' heterosexism and gender normativity than an accurate depiction of Native American values and practices. The preponderance of evidence, both from early documentary sources and from Native oral histories, indicates that the vast majority of the indigenous cultures of North America were accepting of same-sex love and transgenderism.

Sex, Gender, and Religious Values

This acceptance was a product of several factors, most notably because sex was not seen as sinful in Native American religions. With some exceptions, sex was not restricted to its reproductive role, but was seen as a major blessing from the spirit world, a gift to human and animal species to be enjoyed freely from childhood to old age. Among cultures that practiced matrilineal kinship, women were particularly free in their behavior, since their child's family status depended on the mother's relatives rather than on the child's father; every child was automatically a member of the mother's kin group. In matrilineal societies a woman's status was not dependent upon her having a husband, and the status of the child was not dependent upon the mother being married to a man. Consequently, in matrilineal kinship groups, which were common in North America, denigrating terms such as "bastard" did not have any meaning. In such societies, female sexuality was considerably more free and open than in societies where a woman was only supposed to have sex with her husband.

For males as well as females, most American Indian religions emphasized the freedom of individuals to follow their own inclinations, based on guidance from their personal spirit guardians, and to share generously what they had with others. With such freedom-loving attitudes, children's sexual play was more likely to be regarded by adults as an amusing activity rather than as a cause for alarm. This casual attitude toward child rearing continued to influence aboriginal people as they grew up and married. Yet while sex was certainly much more accepted than in the Judeo-Christian tradition, it was not the major emphasis of Native societies. The focus was instead on the individual person's "spirit," which was defined as their basic character and was believed to come directly from the spirit world. Thus, if a person was androgynous or transgender, their personality was accepted as the result of the spirits combining both masculine and feminine characteristics within one person. Such two-spirit persons, referred to by early French explorers as *berdaches,* were honored as the possessor of twice as much spirituality as the average masculine man or feminine woman.

Family, Friendship, Marriage, and Reproduction

Native American societies were built upon two types of interpersonal relations: family (tying an individual to multiple people of other genders) and friendship (tying an individual to others of the same sex). The cultural value placed on extremely close friendships between two "blood brothers" or two women friends created contexts in which private homosexual behavior could occur without attracting attention. Because sex in the context of friendship was casually accepted, there is relatively little documentation about it. But the evidence that does exist suggests that the role of sex in promoting close interpersonal ties within various societies may be just as important as the role of sex as a means of reproduction. While Christian ideology emphasizes that the purpose of sex is reproduction, that is not the view of Native American (and other) religions.

Beyond their role in same-sex friendships, homosexual behaviors among many aboriginal Native American cultures were also recognized in the form of same-sex marriages. The usual pattern among American Indians focused not on two masculine men or two feminine women getting married, but instead on encouraging a masculine man to marry a feminine two-spirit male or a feminine woman to marry a masculine two-spirit female. Feminine males often had special roles as shamans, artists, or teachers, while masculine females often took on hunter-warrior roles. For example, in the 1840s a frontier trader who lived among the Crow Indians described the prominent role of a masculine female named Woman Chief. She was known for her skill in hunting buffalo and for her bravery as a warrior. She became so successful as a hunter that she became attractive to potential wives. Among the Plains tribes of the nineteenth century, wealthy husbands typically had several wives. By the 1850s, Woman Chief had four wives and a large herd of horses and was ranked among the highest status warriors of the Crow tribe.

Androgynous or transgender two-spirit roles were seen as different and distinct from the regular gender roles of men and women. Some scholars have called this tradition "gender mixing," while others have seen it as an alternative gender role. In the context of Native cultures that allowed for more gender flexibility than was the case in its Western counterpart, there was room for diverse types of persons (including transsexual, transgender, and androgynous types). Most cultures accepted the fact that these alternative gendered individuals could be sexually attracted to a person of the same biological sex, but there have also been rare instances of heterosexual attractions and behavior as well. There was a strong economic motivation for a feminine person (of either sex) to marry a masculine person (of either sex). The complementary advantages of persons filling different gender roles meant that two masculine hunters would not get married, nor would two women farmers. In aboriginal economies, a husband-wife team needed to perform different labor roles to provide the household with a balanced subsistence.

Accordingly, the husband of a two-spirit male was not defined as a "homosexual" merely because his spouse was male. The community defined him on the basis of his gender role as a man, since he was a hunter, rather than on his sexual behavior or the sex of his partner. Likewise, the wife of a two-spirit female was not defined as a "lesbian," but continued to be defined as a woman because she performed women's labor roles of farming, plant gathering, cooking, and craftwork. These cultural systems did not categorize people as "heterosexual" or "homosexual," but permitted individuals to follow their sexual and gender tastes and attractions. In tribes that accepted marriage for the two-spirit person, the clan membership of that person's spouse was much more important than their sex.

Gay American Indians. Members of this group, one of several that serve as a liaison between the LGBT community and other Native Americans who live in cities, take part in a Gay Pride March in San Francisco. **[Jill Posener]**

This also meant that a person who had married a two-spirit person was not stigmatized as different and could later marry heterosexually. With the exception of the two-spirit persons, who were relatively few in number, social pressure emphasized that most people should beget children. After they had done so, it did not matter much if they had homosexual or other nonprocreative relationships. Indeed, even the two-spirit people contributed to the future growth of the tribe through their important roles as adoptive parents for orphaned children.

In many native cultures' conceptions of spirituality, the person who was different was seen as having been created that way by the spirit world. Even though they were different from the norm, two-spirit people were respected. They were considered to be exceptional rather than abnormal. For example, in the late nineteenth century a two-spirit person named We'wha was a prominent leader of the Zuni people. An early anthropologist reported that We'wha was prominent in religious ceremonials and was considered the most intelligent person in the pueblo. We'wha's word was considered law. When the Zuni sent representatives to Washington, D.C., to meet U.S. president Grover Cleveland, We'wha was presented as a Zuni princess and was thought by the whites to be a masculine-looking female.

Suppression, Continuation, and Revival of Native Traditions

Beginning in the sixteenth century, respectful attitudes toward two-spirit persons changed drastically due to the influence of Europeans in America. Bringing with them their homophobic and transphobic Christian religion, Spanish conquerors in Florida, California, and the Southwest justified conquest and plunder on the basis of the Indians' acceptance of "sodomy." This, they argued, was evidence that Native Americans were uncivilized heathens in need of Christian conversion or extermination. English and other European settlers were similarly condemning as they gained control over more and more North American territory. British, Spanish, U.S., Canadian, and Mexican government policies suppressed Native American sexuality and religion. Over time, two-spirit traditions went underground, and sex that was persecuted by Christian missionaries and government officials became secretive.

In the twentieth century, while European and European American condemnation of homosexuality and transgenderism influenced many Indian people, those who retained their traditions continued to respect two-spirit persons. This accepting attitude had a significant impact on the white founders of the homophile, gay liberation, and lesbian feminist movements in the United

States. For example, the views of Harry Hay, a founder of the Mattachine Society in 1950, were very much affected by his encounters with sexual and gender diversity within southwestern aboriginal cultures. In turn, LGBT Indians have been influenced by the LGBT movement to stand up openly and take pride in their accepting Native traditions. Like traditionalist Indians, they feel an appreciation for the strength and the magic of human diversity. They accept people as they are, rather than expect everyone to conform to a dualistic gender and heterosexual norm.

In LGBT-friendly cities such as San Francisco, Native groups like Gay American Indians (founded in 1975 by Randy Burns and Barbara Cameron) have effectively served as a liaison between the large urban Indian community and the LGBT community. As such, they have been recognized as valuable by the non-LGBT Indian community. On many Indian reservations in conservative parts of the nation, however, homophobic and transphobic attitudes are still common. Especially among Christianized Indians who were converted by missionaries, anti-LGBT attitudes are evident. Just as in the non-Indian population, many young LGBT and questioning people suffer from prejudice and discrimination, either from their relatives and the Indian community or from non-Indian neighbors. Some two-spirit persons have been shunned, thrown out of their homes, driven to suicide, or even murdered because of their sexualities and genders.

In response and also as a reflection of the larger LGBT movement, a number of Native American LGBT activist groups have been formed in different cities, with names like Two Spirit People of the First Nations. Prominent native writers like Paula Gunn Allen (Laguna) and Wesley Thomas (Navajo) have publicized traditions of acceptance within Native cultures. As they help to reduce homophobia and transphobia, more non-LGBT Indian relatives and friends have joined in the effort to challenge heterosexism and gender normativity. As a result, greater acceptance of sexual and gender minorities has become a part of contemporary Native American social movements. Most Native people accept the reality that people differ and that these differences provide valuable complementarities to make the world whole. Sexual diversity and gender variation are seen as part of the spiritual plan of the universe to provide benefit for all living things.

Bibliography

Allen, Paula Gunn. *The Sacred Hoop: Recovering the Feminine in American Indian Traditions.* Boston: Beacon, 1986.

Jacobs, Sue-Ellen, Wesley Thomas, and Sabine Lang, eds. *Two-Spirit People: Native American Gender Identity, Sexuality, and Spirituality.* Urbana: University of Illinois Press, 1997.

Katz, Jonathan. *Gay American History: Lesbians and Gay Men in the U.S.A., a Documentary.* New York: Crowell, 1976.

Lang, Sabine. *Men as Women, Women as Men: Changing Gender in Native American Cultures.* Translated from the German by John L. Vantine. Austin: University of Texas Press, 1998.

Roscoe, Will. *The Zuni Man-Woman.* Albuquerque: University of New Mexico Press, 1991.

———. *Changed Ones: Third and Fourth Genders in Native North America.* New York: St. Martin's, 1998.

Roscoe, Will, ed. *Living the Spirit: A Gay American Indian Anthology.* New York: St. Martin's, 1988.

Williams, Walter L. *The Spirit and the Flesh: Sexual Diversity in American Indian Culture.* Boston: Beacon, 1986.

Walter L. Williams

See also ALLEN, PAULA GUNN; BRANT, BETH; BURNS, RANDY; CAMERON, BARBARA; CHRYSTOS; GAGE, ELMER; KLAH, HASTÍÍN; MASAHAI AMATKWISAI; NATIVE AMERICAN RELIGION AND SPIRITUALITY; NATIVE AMERICAN LGBTQ ORGANIZATIONS AND PERIODICALS; NATIVE AMERICAN STUDIES; OSH-TISCH; PI'TAMAKAN; QÁNQON-KÁMEK-KLAÚLA; RACE AND RACISM; TWO-SPIRIT FEMALES; TWO-SPIRIT MALES; WE'WHA; WOMAN CHIEF.

NATIVE AMERICAN LGBT ORGANIZATIONS AND PERIODICALS

The history of Native American LGBT organizations began in 1975 with the founding of Gay American Indians (GAI) in San Francisco by Barbara Cameron (Hunkpapa Lakota) and Randy Burns (Northern Paiute). The two were seeking to address the double discrimination faced by Native American gays and lesbians resulting from racism within the mainstream lesbian and gay movement and the homophobia of Christianized Native societies. GAI started as a social group that offered Native gays and lesbians opportunities to meet each other in a safe, welcoming environment. But it quickly evolved into an organization that provided a wider range of services to its constituency and also functioned as a lobby group working to bring its members' concerns to nongay Native groups and non-Native gay groups. By the 1980s GAI was a thriving group that had made gains in raising the profile of Native gays and lesbians. It had also made progress in encouraging Native, mainstream, and gay organizations to improve their outreach to Native American gays and lesbians. By the time it celebrated its tenth anniversary in 1985, it had about six hundred members nationwide.

GAI engaged in many other roles and activities as well. As young Native American gays and lesbians continued migrating to San Francisco to connect with others like themselves, GAI helped them find housing, jobs, student loans, and social opportunities. It also involved itself in the quest to learn and publicize more about the history of alternate gender roles (formerly called *berdache*) in Native American societies. One of Randy Burns's inspirations in co-founding GAI was his discovery of this history through a gay newspaper, and other group members were interested as well. GAI collaborated with historian Will Roscoe in compiling a bibliography of sources on alternative gender statuses, which was published in 1985 as *A Bibliography and Index of Berdache and Gay Roles among North American Indians.* Not long after, it compiled the very first anthology of writing by Native American gays and lesbians, titled *Living the Spirit: A Gay American Indian Anthology* (1988). Over twenty writers contributed to this groundbreaking collection of stories, poems, artwork, and essays.

GAI was the only Native American lesbian and gay group for more than a decade after its founding. Only in 1987 was it joined by American Indian Gays and Lesbians (AIGL), based in Minneapolis. The Minneapolis group began with goals similar to those of GAI, wishing to offer gay and lesbian Native people safe spaces in which to meet and to provide culturally appropriate support grounded in an understanding of Native traditions. AIGL rapidly made its mark by establishing a new institution for Native gays and lesbians in the form of an annual gathering. In 1988 AIGL hosted a gathering called the Basket and the Bow: A Gathering of Lesbian and Gay Native Americans at the Minneapolis American Indian Center, drawing over sixty participants from Canada and the United States. This gathering was so successful that it became an annual event, later renamed the International Two-Spirit Gathering. After its inaugural celebration in Minneapolis, the gathering began to shift location each year; gatherings were subsequently held in Manitoba, Oregon, Arizona, Kansas, New Brunswick, and British Columbia, among other places. For the tenth annual event, the temporarily dormant AIGL was revitalized to organize and host the International Two-Spirit Gathering in Minneapolis. Subsequently, it continued to change venues annually, hosted by local two-spirit groups in various places in the United States and Canada.

The HIV/AIDS Challenge and the Proliferation of Groups

By the late 1980s new Native gay and lesbian organizations began to spring up in cities throughout the United States and Canada. At the same time, a vitally important new issue had arisen, one to which GAI was also turning its attention: the HIV/AIDS epidemic. GAI members founded the Indian AIDS Project in 1987, and the next year they joined a larger group to establish the American Indian AIDS Institute, focused on providing support services to those affected by HIV/AIDS and on public education as well. By the early 1990s many members of AIGL were so busy organizing around HIV/AIDS that the group decided to become dormant for a time, only to reemerge in 1997 to host the International Two-Spirit Gathering.

In New York City in 1989, WeWah and BarChee-Ampe was established by Native lesbians and gays, taking its name from two historical alternate-gender individuals discussed in GAI's publication, *Living the Spirit.* Facing the alarming rate of HIV/AIDS infections in New York City, the group immediately became involved in dealing with AIDS-related issues among Native people, working with the American Indian Community House to create the HIV/AIDS Project in 1990. It also organized a new type of conference in 1991, Two Spirits and HIV: A Conference for the Health of Gay and Lesbian Native Americans.

Also including services for HIV-infected Aboriginal people among its primary goals was Gays and Lesbians of the First Nations (GLFN), founded in Toronto in 1989. The group was the first of its kind in Canada and it grew quickly. GLFN offered a wide range of activities for its members, including talking and healing circles, a newsletter, drag shows, award shows, and the Two-Spirits Softball Team, in addition to HIV/AIDS services. By 1992 the organization had grown to three hundred members hailing from sixteen Aboriginal nations. The same year it changed its name to 2-Spirited People of the 1st Nations, reflecting the newly developed terminology of the Native LGBT community.

The period between the late 1980s and the early 1990s generally witnessed a blossoming of gay and lesbian Native organizations in cities across North America. In Winnipeg, Nichiwakan was formed, and in Seattle, Tahoma Two-Spirits. Vancouver Two-Spirits was founded in Vancouver, and San Diego activists formed Nations of the Four Directions. In the next few years, organizations also arose in Washington, D.C., and Nashville, Tennessee.

A New Concept for Self-Understanding

One of the most significant developments of this period, in addition to the growth of Native lesbian and gay groups, was the emergence of new language and understandings of self. When the Third Annual International Gathering of Gay and Lesbian Native Americans was held in Winnipeg in 1990, a new term for Native lesbians and gays was suggested and enthusiastically taken up. The term was "two-spirit" (or "two-spirited"), an English translation of the Ojibway *niizh manitoag,* expressing the idea that Native gays and lesbians were people who united the spirits of both sexes in one person. The term and the idea have proven immensely popular for a variety of reasons. Perhaps most importantly, the language and concept of two-spirit were generated by two-spirit people themselves, providing an alternative to the adoption (yet again) of Western, colonizing discourses on sexuality. The term "two-spirit" builds on Aboriginal worldviews and philosophies and is a powerful reminder of the affirmation and integration historically experienced by two-spirit people within most Native American societies. In addition, as Will Roscoe has suggested, the word "two-spirit" conveys both racial and sexual identity and avoids the gendered division embodied in the non-Native terminology "lesbian and gay." In celebrating and reviving their Native traditions, two-spirit people can simultaneously embrace their own heritage and draw strength from a past in which their predecessors were accorded cultural honor, spiritual value, and social acceptance.

The Contributions of Native Two-Spirit Writers

The proliferation of Native LGBT two-spirit organizations has occurred in a symbiotic relationship with the establishment and expansion of a network of Native two-spirit writers, artists, and intellectuals willing to be open about their sexual identity. The first Native American writer to come out as gay was Mohawk poet Maurice Kenny, whose pathbreaking article "Tinselled Bucks: An Historical Study of Indian Homosexuality" appeared in the periodical *Gay Sunshine* (Winter 1975–1976) and was reprinted twelve years later in *Living the Spirit* (1988). In the spring of 1981 an article by mixed-blood Laguna Pueblo writer Paula Gunn Allen, "Beloved Women: Lesbians in American Indian Cultures," was published in the journal *Conditions;* it was reprinted in her book *The Sacred Hoop* in 1986. Both were taking a considerable risk, given the widespread problem of homophobia in Native communities, especially on some reservations. But as Paula Gunn Allen later stated, it was profoundly important to speak out on behalf of the many young Native two-spirit people living on those reservations: "I decided I could take the risk—I don't live there. But there are young gay Indians who do and they have to hear this" (Roscoe, 1998, p. 101).

Other Native lesbian and gay writers also went public about their sexual orientation in the 1980s. Two Native lesbians, Barbara Cameron and Chrystos, published writings in the now-classic 1981 feminist collection edited by Cherríe Moraga and Gloria Anzaldúa, *This Bridge Called My Back: Writings by Radical Women of Color.* In 1984 Mohawk writer Beth Brant's collection, *A Gathering of Spirit: Writing and Art by North American Indian Women,* included the work of eleven Native lesbians. Brant herself was open about her sexuality from the outset of her writing career. In 1988 *Living the Spirit* greatly expanded the list of open lesbian and gay Native writers. Since then many more writers, artists, and intellectuals have come out, including Canadian Cree playwright Tomson Highway, Cree actor Billy Merasty, Six Nations writer Daniel David Moses, Odawa actress Gloria Eshkibok, and Métis writer Gregory Scofield.

The work of so many dedicated LGBT two-spirit writers and activists has had a significant impact on the acceptance of two-spirit people in Native communities. This process has also been facilitated by the revival and revitalization of Native traditions that began in the 1960s, a project to which those same writers and activists have contributed enormously. In addition, the publication of academic research into alternate gender statuses in historic Native societies has helped to further understanding and acceptance of two-spirit people in their own communities. The most important of these publications include Walter L. Williams's widely read *The Spirit and the Flesh: Sexual Diversity in American Indian Culture* (1986) and GAI's *Living the Spirit.* Subsequently, historian Will Roscoe's *Changing Ones: Third and Fourth Genders in Native North America* (1998), provided another detailed exploration of historic Native alternate gender roles. All of this has helped to create a climate of greater acceptance for Native people who identify as LGBT, or two-spirit.

The State of Two-Spirit Organizations

At the turn of the twenty-first century, two-spirit organizations are more numerous and robust than ever. GAI still exists in San Francisco, as does American Indian Gays and Lesbians in Minneapolis. The New York City group has changed its name to Gay and Lesbian Indigenous People, NY, while retaining the name *WeWah/BarChee-Ampe* for its newsletter. Toronto's 2-Spirited People of the 1st Nations remains active and is preparing to host the 2003 International Two-Spirit Gathering to be held in Ontario, Canada, near Mnjikaning First Nation (Rama). In Seattle the Northwest Two-Spirit Society is active, offering monthly meetings and a separate drumming group along with other activities. The Two Spirit Society of Denver meets twice a month at the Denver Gay and Lesbian Center, maintains its own drum group, and organizes musical events, picnics, and other social gatherings. San Francisco now boasts a second two-spirit group, Bay Area American Indian Two-Spirits (BAAITS), which meets twice monthly, alternating its location between San Francisco and Oakland. The mission statement posted on its Web site expresses ideas common to most of these groups: "Bay Area American Indians Two-Spirits (BAAITS) exists to restore and recover the role of Two-Spirited people within the American Indian community by creating forums for the spiritual, cultural and artistic expression of Two-Spirit people."

By the beginning of the twenty-first century, Native American LGBT organizations had made tremendous gains in forging a unique identity centered largely around the two-spirit model. A number of these organizations maintain Web sites, and the Internet offers several online forums for two-spirit people to discuss issues of interest. In addition to the annual International Two-Spirit Gathering, several smaller-scale, local and regional gatherings are held. Three decades of Native LGBT organizing and publishing have created a flourishing two-spirit community across North America that declares, affirms, and reinforces the pride of its members.

Bibliography

Allen, Paula Gunn. *The Sacred Hoop: Recovering the Feminine in American Indian Traditions.* Boston: Beacon, 1986.

"Bay Area American Indians Two-Spirits." Available from http://www.geocities.com/WestHollywood/Castro/8260.

Brant, Beth, ed. *A Gathering of Spirit: A Collection by North American Indian Women.* Rockland, Me.: Sinister Wisdom Books, 1984.

Moraga, Cherríe, and Gloria Anzaldúa, eds. *This Bridge Called My Back: Writings by Radical Women of Color.* Watertown, Mass.: Persephone Press, 1981.

Roscoe, Will. *Changing Ones: Third and Fourth Genders in Native North America.* New York: St Martin's Griffin, 1998.

Roscoe, Will, ed. *A Bibliography and Index of Berdache and Gay Roles among North American Indians.* San Francisco: Gay American Indians, 1985.

———. *Living the Spirit: Gay American Indian Anthology.* Compiled by Gay American Indians (GAI). New York: St. Martin's Press, 1988.

Williams, Walter L. *The Spirit and the Flesh: Sexual Diversity in American Indian Culture.* Boston: Beacon, 1986.

Robin Jarvis Brownlie

See also ALLEN, PAULA GUNN; BRANT, BETH; BURNS, RANDY; CAMERON, BARBARA; CHRYSTOS; KENNY, MAURICE; NATIVE AMERICANS; NATIVE AMERICAN RELIGION AND SPIRITUALITY; TWO-SPIRIT FEMALES; TWO-SPIRIT MALES.

NATIVE AMERICAN RELIGION AND SPIRITUALITY

The history and role of LGBT peoples within Native American religious and spiritual traditions is not well known. Such information is frequently concealed in the primary historical sources. Often, this knowledge is considered by Native Americans to be secret and powerful, knowledge that is generally kept from outsiders. In other cases, information about Native American religious traditions is rendered unreliable by the nature of the source from which it is derived. Such problematic sources include the records of Spanish conquistadors, Jesuit missionaries, and French traders. These Europeans considered the existence of what would later be termed homosexuality and transgenderism to be proof of the uncivilized nature of the Native Americans. They therefore tended to ignore the actions of LGBT people or to describe their activities as "sinful," emphasizing the "savage" nature of the Native Americans.

The role of LGBT peoples within Native American spiritual traditions varied from group to group. Because each Native culture possesses distinct religious beliefs and traditions and because these beliefs and traditions changed over time, it is impossible to assert that there was one overarching Native American tradition, and what is true for one group or era might not be true for another. However, it is possible to speak of general trends and commonalities between groups. Gays, lesbians, and transgender peoples, referred to by many contemporary Native Americans as two-spirit people, played active and important roles in the religion, cosmology, and rituals of many different Native American cultures. Two-spirit people may be biologically male or female. However, little is known about two-spirit females. Often, two-spirit people and other LGBT peoples are viewed as special or set apart by nature, and thus are seen as spiritually powerful. In a majority of Native American cultures, two-spirit people are healers. Some use herbal medicine to cure; others engage in chanting, dance, prayer, or other remedies in order to heal their patients. Two-spirit people also often serve as gravediggers and mourners for the dead of the community.

Often, gays, lesbians, and two-spirit people are called to be shamans, individuals who have greater access to the realm of the spiritual. Some groups, including the Navajo and the Lakota Sioux, consider two-spirit shamans to be more powerful than either male or female shamans, as the two-spirit shaman has elements of both genders. Other groups view two-spirit people as seers or visionaries who may be able to foretell the future. Among many groups, two-spirit people are often seen as the recipients of supernatural gifts of some kind.

Lesbians who serve as shamans are also vested with great power, which derives from both their femininity (a power possessed by all women) and from their personal identification with a divinity or spirit. These women, known among the Lakota as *koskalaka,* can be endowed with the power to influence both the tangible and intangible worlds.

In several Plains groups, two-spirit people play an active role in the Sun Dance, an important ceremony. Two-spirit people are called on to raise and bless the poles used in the dance. In some groups, two-spirit people may also be expected to cook special ceremonial meals or to bless food. Two-spirit people can also be called on to perform particular tasks for individuals. Among the Cherokee and Navajo, two-spirit people serve as matchmakers for young men and women. Among the Oglala Lakota and the Papago, two-spirit people are called upon to give secret names to men or boys. These names are usually sexual or funny in nature, but are considered to be powerful and to ensure spiritual protection, long life, and health for the individual who receives the name. Sitting Bull, Black Elk, and Crazy Horse all were said to have received secret names from two-spirit people.

Gays, lesbians, and two-spirit people also play a role in the stories that make up the oral traditions of many different cultures. Their presence in these stories shows that they hold an important and valid place in Native American society and cosmology. In many cases, supernatural beings appear in oral tradition as two-spirit people.

The creation story of the Navajo includes a set of two-spirit twins named Turquoise Boy and White Shell Girl, who taught the first man and first woman to farm. The twins also taught the people to make other important items such as pottery, baskets, grinding stones, and hoes. A second part of the story demonstrates the value of the labor of two-spirit people. When the men and women of the group quarrel and separate, the twins go with the men, taking their grinding stones and other tools. With the help of the twins, the men live comfortably, while the women are surrounded by turmoil. Finally, the twins help the first man, the first woman, and their children to escape from a flood that is consuming the world by leading them into the Fourth World.

The sexuality of two-spirit people and themes of same-sex love are also examined in oral tradition. In a story of the Michahai Yokuts, a group of young wives who are actually homosexual desire to run away together. They formulate a plan to escape their married life. The women run to a high cliff, where they make ropes of eagle's down that carry them into the sky. There, they became the constellation Pleiades. The women's husbands try to follow them, but are kept from their wives even in the heavens; they become the constellation Taurus.

Today, many LGBT Native Americans identify themselves as two-spirit and freely participate in the religious and spiritual traditions of their group. Currently, the role of two-spirit people in the religious and spiritual traditions of the Native Americans is the focus of many anthropologists and a few historians, who seek to reconstruct this role more completely.

Bibliography

Allen, Paula Gunn. *The Sacred Hoop: Recovering the Feminine in American Indian Traditions.* Boston: Beacon, 1986.

Gutiérrez, Ramón A. *When Jesus Came, the Corn Mothers Went Away: Marriage, Sexuality, and Power in New Mexico, 1500–1846.* Stanford, Calif.: Stanford University Press, 1991.

Lang, Sabine. *Men as Women, Women as Men: Changing Gender in Native American Cultures.* Austin: University of Texas Press, 1998.

Roscoe, Will. *Changing Ones: Third and Fourth Genders in Native North America.* New York: St. Martin's Press, 1998.

Trexler, Richard C. *Sex and Conquest: Gendered Violence, Political Order, and the European Conquest of the Americas.* Ithaca, N.Y.: Cornell University Press, 1995.

Williams, Walter L. *The Spirit and the Flesh: Sexual Diversity in American Indian Culture.* Boston: Beacon Press, 1986.

Tamara Shircliff Spike

See also CHURCHES, TEMPLES, AND RELIGIOUS GROUPS; KLAH, HASTÍÍN; MASAHAI AMATKWISAI; NATIVE AMERICANS; NATIVE AMERICAN LGBTQ ORGANIZATIONS AND PERIODICALS; NATIVE AMERICAN STUDIES; OSH-TISCH; PI'TAMAKAN; QÁNQON-KÁMEK-KLAÚLA; TWO-SPIRIT FEMALES; TWO-SPIRIT MALES; WE'WHA; WOMAN CHIEF.

NATIVE AMERICAN STUDIES

Native American Studies is a new academic field that has grown out of research in several disciplines, mainly anthropology, history, and literary criticism. Until the 1960s most historians ignored Native Americans, except as they could be used as foils for European American expansion, and left Indian history to anthropologists. For their part, some anthropologists turned to early accounts written by European explorers and missionaries on the frontier as their major sources. Anthropologists who utilized historical sources became known as ethnohistorians. Since the 1960s, as ethnic studies programs were founded in various colleges and universities, scholars devoting attention to the indigenous peoples of North America took on the mantle of American Indian Studies or Native American Studies.

Initially, homosexual and transgender behavior was a topic that most scholars ignored, except for a few anthropologists who wrote brief articles about the acceptance of same-sex sexual and transgender behavior in many Native American societies. However, after the pioneering generation of early twentieth-century ethnographers, which included Matilda Coxe Stevenson, Waldemar Bogoras, George Devereux, Margaret Mead, and Ruth Underhill, most anthropologists who wrote about sexual and gender variance were content to simply quote the early historical primary sources and not undertake original analysis. That approach worked well in terms of the early history. The independent historian Jonathan Ned Katz (with the help of gay studies pioneers like Harry Hay, Jim Kepner, W. Dorr Legg, James Steakley, and Sue-Ellen Jacobs) gathered together many of these documents on early Native Americans in his pathbreaking book *Gay American History.* The first scholarly book that devoted significant attention to Native Americans was by historian Vern Bullough, *Sexual Variance in Society and History.*

Dependence upon these early primary sources, however, was problematic for anthropologists who tried to write about homosexuality and transgenderism among recent American Indians. Many claimed, inaccurately, that traditions of acceptance of same-sex sexual relationships and transgender phenomena had disappeared. However, Native American literary scholar Paula Gunn Allen suggested in a 1981 essay, "Lesbians in American Indian Cultures," that same-sex sexual and gender variant traditions continued into the present. When she published her book *The Sacred Hoop: Recovering the Feminine in American Indian Traditions*, she included a call for more research on a vibrant lesbian and gay native heritage.

Meanwhile, ethnohistorian Walter L. Williams grew distrustful of claims by anthropologists that homosexuality had "disappeared" among modern Indian people. After several years of archival research, he spent 1982 and 1983 living on various reservations in the Great Plains and the Southwest, as well as visiting the Maya Indians in Yucatan, Mexico, to interview native people who were homosexually identified. His research was published as *The Spirit and the Flesh: Sexual Diversity in American Indian Culture*, which was the first book on this topic that utilized both historical sources and ethnographic fieldwork.

At the same time, the Native activist group Gay American Indians, which was founded by Randy Burns (Northern Paiute) and Barbara Cameron (Lakota Sioux) in San Francisco, published a valuable collection of personal narratives of gay and lesbian Native Americans, *Living the Spirit: A Gay American Indian Anthology.* Independent scholar Will Roscoe, who worked on this project, later wrote *The Zuni Man-Woman* as well as a number of journal articles and other books relating to homosexual and transgender Native Americans.

By the 1990s Native American sexual and gender diversity had become a "hot topic" attracting a number of anthropologists to write on the subject. German anthropologist Sabine Lang, who wrote her Ph.D. dissertation at the University of Hamburg, published it in German as *Männer als Frauen–Frauen als Männer: Geschlechtsrollenwechsel bei den Indianern Nordamerikas* and later revised in English under the title *Men as Women, Women as Men: Changing Gender in Native American Cultures.* Lang joined University of Washington anthropologist Sue-Ellen Jacobs and her Navajo graduate student Wesley Thomas to co-edit *Two-Spirit People: Native American Gender Identity, Sexuality, and Spirituality.*

The main methodological change in recent Native American Studies has involved increased focus on the perspectives and words of Native people themselves. More Native interviews and autobiographies have been written, rather than just depending upon the perspectives of anthropologists and historians. Another methodological advance in recent years has been the entry of archaeologists who have begun to do research on gender and sexual variance. By analyzing differences in dress and burial goods in pre-Columbian burials, they have found evidence that suggests the ancientness of gender diversity. The main theoretical differences among scholars revolve around whether such variance is best conceived as "gender mixing" or "alternative genders." Most scholars accept that these choices are not either/or opposites.

With this outpouring of scholarship by openly LGBT researchers, commentary on homosexuality and transgenderism among native people began to find its way into general textbooks on Native American Studies. While the tendency among some older scholars working in the field was to ignore or dismiss the subject, a new generation of Native American Studies scholars seems comfortable incorporating sexual and gender diversity into its research and teaching. Especially due to the influence of feminist and gender studies scholars, who have highly emphasized gender variance and transgenderism cross-culturally, the topic has been further publicized.

Bibliography

Allen, Paula Gunn. "Lesbians in American Indian Cultures." *Conditions* 7 (1981): 67–87.

———. *The Sacred Hoop: Recovering the Feminine in American Indian Traditions.* Boston: Beacon, 1986, 1992.

Bullough, Vern L. *Sexual Variance in Society and History.* New York: Wiley, 1976.

Gay American Indians. *Living the Spirit: A Gay American Indian Anthology.* Will Roscoe, coordinating editor. New York: St. Martin's Press, 1988.

Jacobs, Sue-Ellen, Sabine Lang, and Wesley Thomas, eds. *Two-Spirit People: Native American Gender Identity, Sexuality, and Spirituality.* Urbana: University of Illinois Press, 1997.

Katz, Jonathan Ned. *Gay American History: Lesbians and Gay Men in the U.S.A.: A Documentary.* New York: Crowell, 1976.

Lang, Sabine. *Männer als Frauen, Frauen als Männer: Geschlechtsrollenwechsel bei den Indianern Nordamerikas* (Hamburg): Wayasabah, 1990.

———. *Men as Women, Women as Men: Changing Gender in Native American Cultures.* Trans. by John L. Vantine. Austin: University of Texas Press, 1998.

Rosco, Will. *The Zuni Man-Woman.* Albuquerque: University of New Mexico Press, 1991.

Williams, Walter L. *The Spirit and the Flesh: Sexual Diversity in American Indian Culture.* Boston: Beacon, 1986.

Walter Williams

See also ALLEN, PAULA GUNN; BURNS, RANDY; CAMERON, BARBARA; NATIVE AMERICANS; NATIVE AMERICAN LGBTQ ORGANIZATIONS AND PERIODICALS; NATIVE AMERICAN RELIGION AND SPIRITUALITY; TWO-SPIRIT FEMALES; TWO-SPIRIT MALES.

NAVRATILOVA, Martina (b. 18 October 1956), tennis player, activist.

Martina Navratilova was born in Prague, Czech Republic (then part of Czechoslovakia), where her grandmother was a member of the Czech national tennis team and her parents were administrators for Czech tennis. Thus, it was no surprise when young Navratilova excelled at tennis. At the age of eight, she entered her first tournament, and by sixteen, she was the number one ranked player in Czechoslovakia. After competing in the United States, Navratilova realized that she would never achieve her full potential as a tennis player in communist Czechoslovakia. In 1975 she defected to the United States. This daunting decision by the eighteen-year-old Navratilova led to her rise in fame within the tennis world and paved the way for her future political activities; nonetheless, it also meant she could not return to Czechoslovakia nor see her family for many years. On 21 July 1981 Navratilova took the oath of American citizenship.

Early in her career, it was evident that Navratilova was different from other tennis players, particularly the U.S. women. She was more muscular than was considered socially acceptable and had a more powerful style of play. Although initially suspect, Navratilova's training techniques eventually transformed women's tennis as other women began strength training to remain competitive. Navratilova also became the first openly lesbian professional athlete, which very likely cost her millions of dollars in endorsements. During her career, she amassed an incredible record, winning 170 career singles matches, 9 Wimbledon singles titles, 19 total Wimbledon championships (including doubles matches), a streak of 74 matches in 1984, and the Grand Slam (the U.S., Australian, and French Open events and Wimbledon) in 1987. Navratilova's professional tennis career earnings surpassed $20 million. She was named the Female Athlete of the Decade (in the 1980s) by the *National Sports Review* and was inducted into the International Tennis Hall of Fame in 2000.

Though initially outed as a lesbian by the press, Navratilova ultimately became a champion of LGBT rights and frankly challenged sexism and heterosexism. She confronted the press about their portrayal of basketball legend Magic Johnson as a hero when he admitted that he contracted HIV through countless heterosexual contacts. Navratilova asserted that an HIV-positive woman admitting to similar sexual escapades would be labeled immoral and lose her corporate sponsorships. Navratilova also publicly responded to homophobic comments within the tennis community, such as Margaret Court's 1990 proclamation that lesbians were bad role models and Jelena Dokic's father Damir's 2002 statement that he would commit suicide if his daughter was a lesbian. In both cases, Navratilova expressed indignation and condemned the homophobic nature of such comments.

In one of her most visible political actions, in 1992 Navratilova avidly campaigned against Colorado's Amendment 2, which outlawed antidiscrimination ordinances protecting LGB people. Although voters in that state approved the amendment, the American Civil Liberties Union (ACLU) and Navratilova filed a lawsuit challenging the initiative. In 1996 the U.S. Supreme Court ruled that the ordinance was unconstitutional.

Navratilova's involvement in LGBT culture included participation at historic and significant gatherings. As a keynote speaker at the 1993 March on Washington, the first major LGBT event in which she participated, Navratilova emphasized the importance of being open about one's sexual orientation. This event inspired Navratilova's vision for the Visa "Rainbow Card," which

Martina Navratilova. The first openly lesbian professional athlete, she is a longtime activist for LGBT and other causes, as well as one of the best women's tennis players of all time. [Duomo/corbis]

raises funds for LGBT nonprofit causes, such as civil rights issues and HIV/AIDS and breast cancer research. In its first year, the Rainbow Card raised $50,000, and by 2002 it had accumulated over $1.5 million for LGBT causes. Additionally, Navratilova welcomed participants during the opening ceremonies at the 1998 Gay Games in Amsterdam and was a keynote speaker at the Millennium March. For the first time in her storied career—twenty years after first achieving the number one world ranking—she finally became a spokesperson for a major company when she appeared in a national advertising campaign for Subaru. She was the first out lesbian athlete to appear in such a campaign.

Navratilova works for many local causes in Colorado, her home since 1989. She regularly raises funds for women's support centers, the Susan G. Komen Breast Cancer Foundation, and female political candidates. She has also been a visible supporter of the environment and People for the Ethical Treatment of Animals (PETA). Navratilova conducts workshops for the top-ranked children in tennis as well as for children from Denver's inner-city parks program. As of 2003, she has come out of retirement to compete in doubles, becoming the oldest person to win a Women's Tennis Association title. She has also written several mystery novels set in the tennis world, is a commentator for major tennis tournaments, and continues her LGBT activism.

Bibliography

Allen, Louise. *The Lesbian Idol: Martina, kd, and the Consumption of Lesbian Masculinity.* Washington, D.C.: Cassell, 1997.

Blue, Adrianne. *Martina: The Lives and Times of Martina Navratilova.* Secaucus, N.J.: Carol Publishing Group, 1995.

Silvas, Sharon. "Martina! Serving On and Off the Court." *Colorado Woman News* 2, no. 18 (June 30, 1992): 17.

Spencer, Nancy E. "'America's Sweetheart' and 'Czech-mate.' A Discursive Analysis of the Evert-Navratilova Rivalry." *Journal of Sport & Social Issues* 27 (2003): 18–37.

Vikki Krane

See also COLORADO; ICONS; RICHARDS, RENÉE; SPORTS.

NEIGHBORHOODS. see GHETTOS AND NEIGHBORHOODS.

NEW LEFT AND STUDENT MOVEMENTS

In June 1962 several dozen white student activists from East Coast and Midwestern colleges gathered in Michigan to discuss their shared concerns about racism, poverty, the nuclear arms race, and the prevailing Cold War culture of complacency. These students, gathering under the aegis of Students for a Democratic Society (SDS), issued the Port Huron Statement, in which they outlined their vision for rejuvenating U.S. politics and society through participatory democracy. Focusing on the intertwined problems of racial and economic injustice, SDS members sought to organize a white student movement parallel to the civil rights struggle. They also positioned SDS to serve as the nexus of this New Left in a role comparable to that claimed by the Student Nonviolent Coordinating Committee (SNCC), organized in 1960 by students from historically black colleges in the Jim Crow South.

The New Left of the 1960s staked out a politics of anti-anticommunism, distinguishing it from the Old Left of the interwar and Cold War decades. Whereas Old Leftists drew upon Marxist-Leninist analyses and models of organizing, New Leftists refused to be drawn into the Cold War communist-anticommunist dichotomy. Instead, they argued that anticommunism distracted citizens from the genuine ills of U.S. society and condemned the reigning corporate liberalism that served the interests of the wealthy rather than the economically disadvantaged.

Along with the questions of race and class that dominated early New Left community projects, student activists addressed local concerns, as when the Free Speech Movement organized in Berkeley in response to attempts by University of California officials to regulate political activity on campus property. As the decade wore on, however, the escalating Vietnam War took precedence for the New Left. Draft resisters organized across the nation, using the famed slogans, "Hell No, We Won't Go!" and "Girls Say Yes to Guys Who Say No" (to the draft, that is). Increasingly, movement leaders shifted from condemning the "evils in America" to the "evils of America," SDS historian Kirkpatrick Sale has noted, and began advocating violent means to social change. New Leftists cheered on North Vietnamese leader Ho Chi Minh and the National Liberation Front of South Vietnam. White students led major rebellions at Columbia University and many other campuses, while rifle-toting black power activists took over the student union at Cornell University in 1969. As anger about the war and other policies of the Johnson and Nixon presidential administrations brought hundreds of thousands of students into the movement, the New Left became increasingly decentralized. SDS eventually disintegrated as a series of Marxist-Leninist factions battled to take control over the organization's national leadership. Nonetheless, New Left organizers continued to address the Vietnam War, racism, and newer concerns such as feminism, the ecology, and gay liberation through the early 1970s.

LGB People in the New Left

Throughout the 1960s, lesbians, gay men, and bisexuals played critical roles in local and national student movement politics. Following the Stonewall Riots, the gay liberation movement's sweeping vision of democratic social transformation and ardent espousal of "coming out" derived directly from its members' experiences in the New Left and from attempting to live out what movement historian Doug Rossinow described as "the politics of authenticity." However, the student movement often offered an uncomfortable home to those men and women for whom authentic living included acting upon one's sexual attraction to the same or both sexes.

Student activists of all sexualities shared similar goals: ending poverty and racism; organizing disenfranchised Americans to assert the power to improve the material conditions of their lives; stopping the Vietnam War; and curbing the excesses of the military-industrial complex. But despite the self-proclaimed radicalism of many heterosexual men in the New Left, they frequently shared the antigay attitudes of the Cold War society in which they grew up. Generally dominating New Left organizations, these men often gay-baited their opponents and cajoled male recruits into proving their masculinity. They frequently organized women in and out of the movement based on whom they were dating at a given moment, effectively dividing New Left women into girlfriends who mimeographed and made coffee on the one hand and desexualized leaders who were essentially accepted as "one of the boys" on the other. Frequently, these men justified their own antigay and antifeminist rhetoric and practices by identifying as authentic revolutionary attitudes the homophobia and misogyny that they perceived as inherent to white working-class, black power, and Third World movements and cultures. Antigay movement cultures were further exacerbated by infiltrators from the Federal Bureau of Investigation and other state and local government authorities, whose agents spread rumors about the sexual orientation of specific activists in order to discredit them. Gay-baiting took its toll upon unknown numbers of lesbians, gay men, and bisexuals, compelling some to lie and hide their sexual orientation while driving others from the movement altogether.

Homophobia in the New Left

Carl Wittman's experiences in the New Left illustrate the challenges experienced by LGB movement activists. A pioneering student leader at Swarthmore College, Wittman authored "An Interracial Movement for the Poor?" with Tom Hayden, the lead author of the Port Huron Statement. This document, which became the template for SDS's Economic Research and Action Project (ERAP), outlined the strategy of social movement building through local community organizing around racism and poverty. Wittman and Hayden led the ERAP organizing in Newark, New Jersey, but after Hayden reportedly declared that homosexuals were not welcome on the project, Wittman—then closeted about his sexual orientation—withdrew and launched a similar venture in nearby Hoboken.

Greg Calvert, another longtime SDS leader, reported the extensive harassment he received as a semi-openly bisexual man in the New Left. Before he joined the staff of the SDS national office in Chicago, Calvert's experiences with homophobia in the campus movement at Iowa State University left him quite wary of taking even more visible positions. Nonetheless, when his then-partner Jane

Era of Protest. A large crowd in the 1960s demonstrates against the war in Vietnam and for racial and social justice—but during that period, homophobia was often a problem within the movement rather than one of its targets. [corbis]

Adams became the interim SDS national secretary, he followed her to Chicago to take over as editor of the organization's weekly newspaper, *New Left Notes*, and eventually succeeded Adams as national secretary. Once on the national office staff, Calvert immediately encountered macho, homophobic posturing and frequent "queer" jokes from the male national leadership. As movement infighting steadily escalated, the antigay potshots accelerated accordingly. One woman on the national office staff sought to discredit Calvert by publicly comparing him to Bayard Rustin, the gay civil rights and pacifist organizer who continued to support the Democratic Party despite its position on the Vietnam War. At one regional SDS meeting, an organizer in the Chicago JOIN (Jobs or Income Now) Community Union told the audience—looking at Calvert as he walked down the aisle—that "you've got to realize that poor people and working people aren't ever going to take students seriously. If you came down and tried to organize in our community, folks would think you're nothing but a bunch of faggots" (Calvert, p. 197). This homophobia, combined with the SDS national leadership's new advocacy of violent insurrection, eventually drove Calvert out of SDS altogether. From there, he turned to organizing active-duty servicemen against the war near military bases in Texas and Massachusetts and joined the antinuclear and Central American solidarity movements after the end of the Vietnam War.

Calvert's story was repeated frequently across the New Left as heterosexual men mocked their male rivals as homosexuals, bragged about their prowess with women, and joked about pretending to be gay to avoid the draft. As the modern feminist movement emerged, women who challenged male chauvinism in the New Left risked being slurred as lesbians, though very few women came out as such until after immersing themselves in feminist consciousness-raising groups. Women such as Charlotte Bunch and Leslie Cagan cut their organizing teeth in the New Left before becoming renowned lesbian-feminist activists—though like many of their future feminist sisters, they dated heterosexually during the years of their involvement in the New Left and Bunch even married a male movement comrade. When Amber Hollibaugh, another veteran movement organizer, became romantically involved with one of her female housemates in the Red Family commune in Berkeley, she and her housemate were told that their behavior was unacceptable and were asked to leave the commune.

While most New Leftists brought to the movement the antigay attitudes instilled in them as children of the Cold War 1950s, the trust and candor earned during the ongoing work of discussing, planning, and carrying out social change provided some heterosexual activists with the experiential knowledge necessary to challenge these homophobic assumptions. Helen Garvy (who became the first woman elected to the SDS national leadership) recalled how the importance of gay liberation became tangible to her by watching the difficulties her colleague Carl Wittman had coming out to his Old Left parents. Similar transformations of consciousness took place during the Chicago Seven conspiracy trial following the 1968 Democratic National Convention. Government prosecutor Thomas Foran's relentless gay baiting of the white defendants and defense witness Allen Ginsberg directly prompted Tom Hayden and other movement leaders to reconsider how sexual diversity was integral to their overarching vision of social transformation.

The New Left and Gay Liberation

As he immersed himself in San Francisco's gay culture in the spring of 1969, Carl Wittman began writing "Refugees from Amerika: A Gay Manifesto." In this essay, arguably the seminal theoretical outline of the new gay liberation movement, Wittman applied the lessons learned by New Left organizers to the issues facing lesbians and gay men. Begun before the Stonewall Riots (though published afterwards), Wittman denounced gay male chauvinism; rejected marriage and mimicry of other heterosexual institutions; and condemned discrimination by legal, psychiatric, and government authorities. He called for forming coalitions with the women's, black, and Chicano movements, other white heterosexual radicals, homophiles, and members of the counterculture, and issued a call to "free ourselves: come out everywhere; initiate self defense and political activity; [and] initiate counter community institutions" (Wittman).

In the wake of Stonewall, and as the protest movements of the decade became increasingly decentralized and splintered, LGB New Leftists began organizing gay liberation groups across the United States. In taking the name Gay Liberation Front, GLF members paid homage to Vietnam's National Liberation Front. From then through the early 1970s, GLF activists such as Kiyoshi Kuromiya, a onetime SDS leader in Philadelphia, took part in antiwar demonstrations in New York City, Washington, D.C., San Francisco, and elsewhere under banners such as "Gays Unite against the War." In Berkeley, for example, the Gay Liberation Theater debuted during the October 1969 Vietnam Moratorium protests, proclaiming it "queer, unnatural, and perverse" to send soldiers to fight communists in Vietnam while in the U.S. men were tormented, raped, jailed, and murdered for loving their brothers.

The GLF involvement at antiwar demonstrations spoke to the broad vision of social transformation that queer New Leftists brought to the nascent gay liberation movement. Similarly, impressed by Cuba's advances in education, housing, health, and other material conditions of living since the 1959 Revolution, numerous GLF activists took part on the Venceremos Brigades. On these, delegations of young Americans were originally organized by SDS to defy the anticommunist ban on travel to Cuba, otherwise pro-Cuban gay liberation activists condemned the work camps established by Castro's government for male homosexuals and other dissidents. In response, Brigade organizers charged the GLF activists with belonging to an anti-Cuban "cultural imperialist offensive" and finally instituted what amounted to a "don't ask, don't tell" policy demanding that gay participants remain silent about their sexuality.

Such battles over the place of gays and lesbians in the making of a revolutionary society repeated themselves throughout the already contentious final years of the New Left. Those Marxist-Leninist organizations such as Progressive Labor that relied upon recruiting members from the student movements adhered to Stalinist definitions of morality that dismissed homosexuality, and thus rejected gay liberation, as the products of bourgeois capitalist society that would disappear after the triumph of communism. Early in the 1970s, when Amber Hollibaugh helped activists from the armed revolutionary wing of the movement elude authorities, these fugitives turned and lectured her on the alleged capitalist decadence of her lesbianism. Hollibaugh's parents, who had joined a Maoist cell in Vancouver, were even expelled from the group for having a lesbian daughter.

Black Panther leaders, to whom many white radicals looked for role models, divided over the question of homosexuality. In his 1968 book, *Soul on Ice,* Eldridge Cleaver venomously attacked James Baldwin and other black gay men "acquiescing in this racial death-wish . . . bending over and touching their toes for the white man" (p. 102). In 1970, however, Black Panther Party leader Huey Newton declared his support for the gay liberation movement, and exhorted his comrades to reject their antigay attitudes and eliminate words such as "faggot" and "punk" from their everyday vocabularies.

Lesbians also struggled with the hostility of some of their heterosexual sisters in the women's liberation movement. Betty Friedan of the National Organization for Women raised the specter of a "lavender menace" threatening that movement. Meanwhile, Amber Hollibaugh and Charlotte Bunch helped organize a 1971 conference in Toronto designed to bring together U.S. and Canadian women with their counterparts from Vietnam, Cambodia, and Laos. In the planning for this conference, pacifist and radical women battled over whether the agenda should include lesbian issues, with some anti-imperialist women claiming that participants were imposing decadent bourgeois Western values on the Southeast Asian women by raising the question of lesbianism.

Early accounts of the New Left dated the demise of the movement to 1969, when the armed revolutionaries of the Weathermen faction seized control of the SDS national leadership. This chronology, however, obscures what was actually the rapid expansion of antiwar, feminist, environmental, gay liberation, and black, Chicano, Puerto Rican, and Native American power organizing well into the 1970s, long after SDS's collapse. While lesbians, gay men, and bisexuals often struggled to reconcile their political and personal identities through the 1960s, they embraced the feminist philosophy that "the personal is political" and applied this insight to their subsequent political organizing. The dedication of gay liberation and lesbian-feminist activists, and LGBT/queer activists in later decades, to multi-issue social justice organizing can be traced directly to the experiences of LGB activists working against war, racism, and poverty in the 1960s.

Bibliography

Bunch, Charlotte. *Passionate Politics: Feminist Theory in Action, Essays, 1968–1986.* New York: St. Martin's Press, 1986.

Calvert, Gregory Nevala. *Democracy from the Heart: Spiritual Values, Decentralism, and Democratic Idealism in the Movement of the 1960s.* Eugene, Ore.: Communitas Press, 1991.

Carson, Clayborne. *In Struggle: SNCC and the Black Awakening of the 1960s.* Cambridge, Mass.: Harvard University Press, 1981.

Chafe, William H. *Never Stop Running: Allard Lowenstein and the Struggle to Save American Liberalism.* New York: Basic Books, 1993.

Cleaver, Eldridge. *Soul on Ice.* New York: Dell, 1968.

Evans, Sara. *Personal Politics: The Roots of Women's Liberation in the Civil Rights Movement and the New Left.* New York: Knopf, 1979.

Gitlin, Todd. *The Sixties: Years of Hope, Days of Rage.* New York: Bantam, 1987.

Hollibaugh, Amber L. *My Dangerous Desires: A Queer Girl Dreaming Her Way Home.* Durham, N.C.: Duke University Press, 2000.

Jay, Karla. *Tales of the Lavender Menace: A Memoir of Liberation.* New York: Basic Books, 1993.

Kissack, Terence. "Freaking Fag Revolutionaries: New York's Gay Liberation Front, 1969–1971." *Radical History Review* 62 (1995): 104–134.

Lekus, Ian. "Losing Our Kids: Queer Perspectives on the Chicago Seven Conspiracy Trial." In *The New Left Revisited.* Edited By John McMillian and Paul Buhle. Philadelphia: Temple University Press, 2003.

Rossinow, Doug. *The Politics of Authenticity: Liberalism, Christianity, and the New Left in America.* New York: Columbia University Press, 1998.

Sale, Kirkpatrick. *SDS.* New York: Random House, 1973.

Wittman, Carl. "A Gay Manifesto." In *Out of the Closets: Voices of Gay Liberation.* Edited by Karla Jay and Allen Young. New York: Douglas, 1972.

Ian Lekus

See also ANARCHISM, SOCIALISM, AND COMMUNISM; ANTIWAR, PACIFIST, AND PEACE MOVEMENTS; COLLEGES AND UNIVERSITIES; GAY LIBERATION FRONT; KUROMIYA, KYOSHI; LESBIAN FEMINISM; WITTMAN, CARL.

NEW ORLEANS

The Queen of the South, New Orleans, is the oldest center of gay and lesbian life in the southern United States. The origins of New Orleans's gay and lesbian communities are linked to its history as a port city and its laissez-faire attitudes toward sexuality. In 1724, for example, Captain Beauchamp of the frigate *Bellone* was charged with having an affair with his cabin boy. No sooner had the French Superior Council, the colony's ruling assembly, transferred the lad to another ship than Captain Beauchamp rescued the cabin boy and escaped down the Mississippi River to the Gulf of Mexico.

Also in the eighteenth century, prostitution flourished in New Orleans because of the large number of sailors and bachelors in the city. Male and female prostitutes were readily available in the houses on Basin Street at the rear of the French Quarter and on the two-block boulevard of brothels on Gallatin Street, located strategically close to the waterfront. One of the more notorious houses of assignation was the home of Madam Carole and her staff of boys with names like Lady Richard and Miss Big Nellie. In 1897 city fathers attempted to regulate prostitution by creating a restricted vice district dubbed Storyville. Under wartime pressure from the U.S. Navy, Storyville closed in 1917, ending a colorful chapter of New Orleans history.

In contrast to the activities of many sailors and prostitutes, some men and women entered committed relationships with same-sex partners. At the turn of the century, two women living in a committed relationship ran the Little Courtyard Coffee Shoppe on Royal Street. Wild gossip circulated about the pair, and the shop enjoyed a thriving business attracted by the curiosity of tourists and locals alike. New Orleans men had a tradition of keeping mistresses: when the arrangement was with a young male, it was known as an uptown marriage. Typically, the gentleman lived along St. Charles Avenue or in the Garden District with his wife and family while spending his free time in the French Quarter with his male lover.

Mardi Gras. Nick Rippen (left) and his friend Robbie Joy dress up as peacocks on March 7, 2000, for the annual anything-goes festivities in and around the French Quarter in New Orleans. **[Reuters NewMedia Inc./corbis]**

From the 1920s through World War II

In the 1920s and 1930s, gay New Orleans carved out many of the social spaces that persisted through the end of the twentieth century. The ironic effect of Prohibition in New Orleans was to allow gay bars to develop without harassment from police or public scrutiny. By the time Prohibition ended, mixed and gay bars were a mainstay of Quarter nightlife. An old New Orleans saying declared: "New Orleanians don't care what you do. They just want to know about it, but they don't care." The French Quarter attracted a bohemian community drawn by cheap rents, easy liquor, and its history as a haven for pirates, prostitutes, and artists. Notable gay bohemians lured to New Orleans included Lyle Saxon, William Spratling, Tennessee Williams, and Truman Capote.

In the 1930s, bars and restaurants continued as important meeting places of the gay community in New Orleans. Early mixed bars included the Old Absinthe House, Pat O'Brien's, and Café Lafitte, which was run by lesbian Mary Collins. Working-class males associated in the less respectable bars of the French Quarter, including the Society Page on Exchange Alley, the Starlight Lounge at Charters and St. Phillip Streets, and the Greek sailor bars on lower Decatur Street. New Orleans also contained numerous restaurants catering to the gay community. Among these, Victor's Café and James Beer Parlor became important gathering places for the gay community.

Although gay New Orleanians were in the process of creating common spaces, lines of race, class, and gender still trumped those of sexual identity. This became especially evident during carnival season, when black New Orleanians claimed their own space, protested racial inequalities, and burlesqued white New Orleans society. Notable among these carnival protests were the parades of the Black Zulu Aid and Pleasure Club. Regular features of the early parades were gangs of female impersonators who followed the rolling floats along the parade route. The leader of one of these groups was Corinne the queen, called "The Gay Cat," crowned Queen of Zulu in 1931. Transvestism demonstrated the uncertainty of multiple identity categories, and in the case of carnival, black cross-dressers challenged not only categories of sex, gender, and sexuality but also categories of race. While confusing male and female, they also brought into question differences between white and black.

In the 1940s cross-dressing for reasons other than carnival became popular parts of New Orleans nightlife. Drag queens performed for tourists at the lakefront's My-Oh-My Club. If one was particularly adventurous, one could cross the color line and visit the Dew Drop Inn, where interracial liaisons were common. In these clubs many cross-dressers found acceptance.

The Postwar Years to 1970

Following World War II, homosexuality became much more visible in New Orleans. City Park, Audubon Park, and Jackson Square were important spaces in the city's sexual geography where men could find quick and indiscriminate sex. The Lee Circle Young Men's Christian Association (YMCA) and the segregated Dryades YMCA were notorious among residents and visitors alike, and in the 1950s and 1960s, several bars, including the Galley

House, Café Lafitte In Exile, Dixie's House of Music, Tony Bassina's, Brady's, and Charlene's served a growing gay and lesbian community. Both men and women frequented these clubs and everyone dressed well.

Police harassment accompanied the emergence of a visible homosexual community. On a single night in 1953, the New Orleans Police Department raided several gay and lesbian bars. At the Golden Rod, forty-three women and one man were arrested for obscenity. In September 1962 the vice squad arrested twenty-nine individuals in four raids, and from 1959 to 1961 a single bar was raided seventy-eight times. Following these arrests, the arrestees' names appeared in the *New Orleans Times-Picayune,* as did the charges and the incidentals of the arrests. Such revelations often resulted in job loss and eviction. Some committed suicide rather than face the devastating consequences to both self and family of public exposure. The most notorious case of harassment occurred between 1967 and 1969, when New Orleans district attorney Jim Garrison targeted respected businessman Clay Shaw as a conspirator in the John F. Kennedy assassination because of Shaw's open homosexuality. The once-wealthy Shaw died in 1974 after suffering financial and physical distress.

Growing Political Activism

In the 1970s, New Orleans reached the height of its gay political activism. In the 1960s, the homophile movement had attracted a small following in the city, which resulted in marches through the Quarter. In January 1970, New Orleans's first militant gay political organization, the New Orleans Gay Liberation Front (GLF), campaigned for six days in front of City Hall to protest police harassment. The GLF was soon succeeded by other groups, including the Metropolitan Community Church, the Daughters Of Bilitis, the Gertrude Stein Democratic Club, the Crescent City Coalition, and the Louisiana Lesbian and Gay Political Action Caucus.

Increasing political activism in New Orleans coincided with the Upstairs Lounge tragedy. On the evening of 24 June 1973, an arsonist ignited a fire in the stairwell of the second-floor Upstairs Bar. For protection, the lounge had installed bars on its windows, and in the ensuing blaze, thirty-two men and women lost their lives. Memorial services were held at St. Marks United Methodist Church, where mourners proudly exited to the glare of local television cameras.

In the spring of 1977, Human Equal Rights for Everyone (HERE) organized a political march for 18 June to protest Anita Bryant's first public appearance since the repeal of a Florida ordinance prohibiting discrimination based on sexual orientation nine days earlier. The planned march attracted hundreds on the day of Bryant's performance and represented the pinnacle of popular activism in New Orleans.

Celebration and Tragedy

Traditionally, political issues in New Orleans have found expression in social activity. As the homophile movement spread across America in the 1950s and 1960s, New Orleanians formed the first gay carnival krewes (social clubs dedicated to the celebration of Mardi Gras). The earliest, the Krewe of Yuga, debuted in 1959 and folded in 1962 when police raided the krewe's carnival ball and arrested ninety-six participants. The longest-running krewe is Petronius, which held its first ball in 1962 and is the largest gay krewe in New Orleans. At the height of gay Mardi Gras in 1984, eleven krewes held balls. However, in the 1980s New Orleans's gay community endured the onslaught of AIDS. As an epicenter for the disease, New Orleans suffered devastating losses among the gay male population, and by the mid-1990s only four krewes remained, including Petronius, Amon Ra, Armenius, and the Lords of Leather. An important part of gay carnival is the Bourbon Street Awards, hosted since the early 1960s at various locations on either Bourbon or St. Ann Streets and showcasing the costumes and tableaux painstakingly created by New Orleanians. In the 1990s Southern Decadence became the center of New Orleans Labor Day revelries and has come to rival Mardi Gras as the gay carnival. The celebration began as a private party in 1972 and has evolved to attract visitors from around the world. The third major festival in New Orleans is Gay Halloween. Like Southern Decadence, Halloween New Orleans began as a small gathering of friends in 1984 and evolved into a major event in the 1990s. Since 1987, the proceeds from Halloween New Orleans have benefited Lazarus House, a hospice established in response to the AIDS epidemic.

Bibliography

Coyle, Katy, and Nadiene Van Dyke. "Sex, Smashing, and Storyville in Turn-of-the-Century New Orleans: Reexamining the Continuum of Lesbian Sexuality. In *Carryin' on in the Lesbian and Gay South.* Edited by John Howard. New York: New York University Press, 1997.

Holditch, W. Kenneth. "William Spratling, William Faulkner, and Other Famous Creoles." *Mississippi Quarterly* 51, no. 3 (Summer 1998): 423–434.

———. "The Last Frontier of Bohemia: Tennessee Williams in New Orleans, 1938–1983." *The Southern Quarterly* 23, no. 2 (Winter 1985): 1–37.

Kirkwood, James. *American Grotesque: An Account of the Clay Shaw-Jim Garrison Affair in the City of New Orleans.* New York: Simon and Schuster, 1970.

Mitchell, Reid. *All on a Mardi Gras Day: Episodes in the History of New Orleans Carnival.* Cambridge, Mass.: Harvard University Press, 1995.

Thomas, James W. *Lyle Saxon: A Critical Biography.* Birmingham, Ala.: Summa Publications, 1991.

Richard D. H. Clark

See also CAPOTE; TRUMAN; DUNBAR-NELSON, ALICE; GENTRIFICATION; WILLIAMS, TENNESSEE.

NEW RIGHT

The social movement known as the New Right emerged in the United States in the 1950s and 1960s. In the decades before that time, conservatives could be found in a number of organizations and in the Republican Party, and right-wing movements can clearly be identified in earlier periods of U.S. history. But it was not until the late 1960s and 1970s that the New Right coalesced into a coherent social movement that ultimately pushed the United States toward the Right, not just politically and economically but socially as well.

Two Strains of Conservatism

Opposition to New Deal liberalism and anticommunism motivated much early New Right activism. Yet two strains of conservatism have been important throughout the movement's history. One branch has essentially espoused a political and economic conservatism and a return to laissez-faire capitalism. These conservatives reject collectivism and see capitalism in its pure form as the best defense of freedom and liberty. A second branch—and one crucial to understanding the ways the New Right organizes against LGBT people—is based on social traditionalism and religious conservatism. According to social traditionalists, who have dominated the New Right since the 1980s, late-twentieth-century trends such as the legalization of abortion, the high divorce rate, the emergence of a women's liberation movement, and the gains of the gay and lesbian movement signal moral decay and a decline in traditional values. Traditionalists have thus sought policies that would bolster "traditional" family life, turning back the trend toward social liberalism and bringing religion to the center of civic life.

The Emergence of Anti-Lesbian and Gay Organizing

Anti–lesbian and gay organizing by the New Right dates to the 1970s, shortly after the emergence of an active lesbian and gay movement in the late 1960s. One of the first highly publicized antihomosexual campaigns occurred in Dade County, Florida, in 1977, when the former beauty queen and born-again Christian Anita Bryant led a successful petition drive to overturn an ordinance that would have barred discrimination on the basis of sexual orientation. Although local in scope, this drive sparked a wave of organizing against lesbian and gay civil rights measures, including the passage of an Oklahoma law forbidding lesbians and gays from teaching in schools and repeals of lesbian and gay rights legislation in Wichita, Kansas; Eugene, Oregon; and elsewhere.

Bolstered by success in Dade County, the Save Our Children campaign moved its attention to California in 1978. There, state senator John Briggs gathered enough signatures to place on the ballot a measure that would bar lesbians and gay men from teaching in public schools. Although Proposition 6 (also known as the Briggs Initiative) ultimately did not pass, it galvanized both lesbian and gay activists and conservative Christians. Some activists in this campaign, such as Lou Sheldon of the Anaheim-based Traditional Values Coalition, were to remain active in anti–lesbian and gay movements for the next several decades.

Around the same time, the Reverend Jerry Falwell, pastor of the fundamentalist Thomas Road Baptist Church in Lynchburg, Virginia, was persuaded by New Right activists Richard Viguerie, Paul Weyrich, and Ed McAteer to found the Moral Majority in 1979. Opposition to homosexuality was only one of the stated aims of the Moral Majority, which Falwell established as a "pro-family" organization. Other issues included prayer in schools, opposition to state-sponsored gambling, the evils of rock and roll, and voter registration, with the aim of influencing the Republican Party platform. During its heyday, the Moral Majority was influential in mobilizing thousands of Christians to vote for conservative candidates and causes. Although the Moral Majority folded in the late 1980s, Falwell created a new, more broadly based organization, the Liberty Federation, in 1986, and he continued to extend his influence as the host of a popular nationwide television program and as chancellor of Liberty University in Lynchburg.

The Emergence of the New Religious Right

Despite early successes in Dade County and elsewhere, the New Right did not make homosexuality a central focus of its organizing in the early 1980s. Homosexuality was only one of many issues motivating right-wing activists; opposition to abortion and the Equal Rights Amendment were also key issues. During the late 1970s and early 1980s, however, the religious arm of the New Right became prominent, such that some scholars refer to the evolving movement as the New Religious Right or the

Christian Right. The Right experienced a number of important successes in this period, including the election of President Ronald Reagan to office in 1980 and 1984 and the election of President George H. W. Bush in 1988. Religious Right activists created a number of conservative "pro-family" organizations, including the Christian Coalition, the Family Research Council, and Focus on the Family, and sought—with great success—to turn out conservative Christians to vote.

During this period, conservative Christian activists made clear inroads into party politics, developing strong ties with the Republican Party at both the national and local levels. One of the staunchest supporters of the New Right in the U.S. Congress was Senator Jesse Helms of North Carolina. Over his thirty-year career, which lasted from 1972 to 2002, Helms routinely introduced legislation against abortion and for school prayer. Helms also led the national opposition to gay and lesbian rights, including a widely publicized attack on the National Endowment for the Arts in 1989 to protest NEA funding of what he perceived as "obscenity" in art, including homoerotic photographs by the artist Robert Mapplethorpe. Helms also led opposition to federal funding for AIDS prevention and sexuality research, arguing that such programs encouraged homosexual behavior.

Both in and outside of Washington, D.C., a number of right-wing grassroots organizations became influential during this time, most notably the Christian Coalition, founded by the Reverend Marion "Pat" Robertson in 1989. The Christian Coalition has arguably been one of the largest and most effective New Religious Right organizations. With its Christian Broadcasting Network and popular *700 Club* television ministry, the Christian Coalition has been able to reach a much broader membership base than did the Moral Majority. Although membership accounts may well be inflated, the organization boasted more than one million members in the 1990s and nine hundred chapters in fifty states. Perhaps more than other organizations, the Christian Coalition has played an important role in making the Religious Right appeal to more mainstream voters. A second organization influential in anti–lesbian and gay organizing is Focus on the Family. Founded in 1977 by James Dobson, a psychologist, Focus on the Family has been a leader in anti-lesbian and gay organizing campaigns, priding itself on providing materials to local groups and cultivating support in its numerous publications. Focus on the Family has also been active in promoting "ex-gay" ministries such as Exodus International, which seek to convert lesbians and gay men to heterosexuality.

Pat Robertson. The founder of the Christian Coalition has used that organization, his *700 Club* television ministry, and various other means to spread the message of the Religious Right—including virulent opposition to homosexuality. **[Getty Images]**

By the late 1980s and early 1990s, opposition to homosexuality had become a centerpiece of New Religious Right activity. As gays and lesbians made gains in public acceptance and visibility, including protection against discrimination in employment and housing in some locales, the Religious Right fought back. One of the main strategies used by right-wing activists in the late 1980s and early 1990s was the ballot initiative. These initiatives sought to repeal legislation that prohibited discrimination on the basis of sexual orientation. In areas where no such legislation existed, the campaigns sought, in a preemptive strike, to amend state constitutions to prohibit state and local governments from passing laws that would outlaw discrimination against lesbians, gays, and bisexuals.

Ballot Initiatives

The first successful statewide anti–lesbian and gay ballot initiatives appeared in Colorado and Oregon in 1992. The Colorado initiative (Amendment 2) sought to outlaw lesbians' and gays' attempts to end discrimination on the basis of sexual orientation. The Oregon initiative

(Measure 9) went even further, requiring any organization that received government funding to present homosexuality as "abnormal, wrong, unnatural, and perverse." Although sponsored by state-level groups Colorado for Family Values and the Oregon Citizens Alliance, both of these initiatives received substantial support from national right-wing organizations, including the Christian Coalition, Focus on the Family, and the Traditional Values Coalition.

Oregon voters rejected Measure 9 by a narrow margin. Yet much to the surprise of Colorado activists and pollsters, Amendment 2 was approved by 53 percent of Colorado voters in November 1992. Although the amendment was never put into effect—it was declared unconstitutional by the Colorado Supreme Court in 1994 and by the U.S. Supreme Court in 1996—the two ballot initiatives nonetheless had a major impact on Religious Right organizing tactics and strategies. The two test cases made clear that large numbers of people were willing to mobilize and vote against lesbians and gays. Subsequently, in numerous communities, including Cincinnati, Ohio, and many Oregon counties, Religious Right groups worked to pass local-level ballot initiatives and to repeal city and local-level civil rights protections for lesbians and gays. In 1994, Religious Right activists attempted to introduce statewide ballot initiatives in eleven states.

Gays in the Military and the Emergence of "Don't Ask, Don't Tell"

The question of homosexuality and military service erupted at about the same time, in 1993, when newly elected Democratic president Bill Clinton announced that he would repeal the ban on lesbians' and gays' service in the military. Religious Right groups sprang into action, spreading the fear that gay men and women would be sharing showers, foxholes, and latrines with heterosexual soldiers, and that good, honest soldiers would be the objects of sexual harassment and be unwittingly exposed to the threat of AIDS. Military cohesion, they argued, would be irrevocably torn. The issue died down when Clinton crafted a policy known as "don't ask, don't tell," in which lesbians and gays would be ejected from the military only if their sexual orientation became known. Essentially a codification of previous practices, this controversial policy would eventually be responsible for the ejection of thousands of men and women from military service.

Same-Sex Marriage and the Redefinition of Family

The 1996 Supreme Court ruling essentially signaled the end of the ballot initiative as a right-wing strategy. Yet homosexuality did not recede from conservative Christian organizing. Instead, the debate shifted to other "hot button" issues, especially gay marriage and domestic partnerships. Perhaps no other issue has been as forcefully opposed by Religious Right activists as the attempt by lesbians and gays to redefine the family to include same-sex couples.

The issue of same-sex marriage rose to the forefront in 1990, when three same-sex couples in Hawaii sued for the right to marry, arguing that the denial of marriage licenses was unconstitutional under the Hawaiian state constitution. Although winning in the courts, the Hawaiian couples did not ultimately gain the right to marry, as a constitutional amendment passed by Hawaiian voters in 1998 (and vigorously supported by the Christian Right) restricted marriage to one man and one woman. As of 2003, no state has legalized same-sex marriage, although the state of Vermont began in 1999 to offer civil unions providing many of the benefits of legal marriage. The Religious Right responded to these efforts to liberalize marriage laws by organizing a National Campaign to Protect Marriage, with leaders from major right-wing groups participating, including Colorado for Family Values, the Traditional Values Coalition, Pat Robertson's Family Research Council, and Concerned Women for America (the group established in 1972 by Phyllis Schlafly, who is best known for her organizing against the Equal Rights Amendment).

Spreading the specter of the decline of the American family, Religious Right activists made same-sex marriage a central issue in the 1996 Republican primary, asking all GOP candidates to sign a pledge to oppose same-sex marriage. Religious Right activists quickly moved to pass legislation in a number of states to restrict same-sex marriage. Opposition to same-sex marriage was not wholly a Republican issue, however, and President Bill Clinton proposed a bill (the so-called Defense of Marriage Act), quickly passed by both House and Senate, that would define marriage as between one man and one woman. As of 2003, same-sex marriage, and the concern that the Supreme Court decision in *Lawrence vs. Texas* will lead to greater liberalitation of existing laws, are still very contentious issues, mobilizing both New Right and LGBT activists.

Bibliography

Crawford, Alan. *Thunder on the Right: The "New Right" and the Politics of Resentment.* New York: Pantheon, 1980.

Diamond, Sara. *Roads to Dominion: Right-Wing Movements and Political Power in the United States.* New York: Guilford Press, 1995.

———. *Not by Politics Alone: The Enduring Influence of the Christian Right.* New York: Guilford Press, 1998.

Esterberg, Kristin, and Jeffrey Longhofer. "Researching the Radical Right: Responses to Anti-Lesbian/Gay Initiatives." In *Inside the Academy and Out: Lesbian/Gay/Queer Studies and Social Action.* Edited by Janice L. Ristock and Catherine G. Taylor. Toronto: University of Toronto Press, 1998.

Himmelstein, Jerome L. *To the Right: The Transformation of American Conservatism.* Berkeley: University of California Press, 1990.

Hull, Kathleen E. "The Political Limits of the Rights Frame: The Case of Same-Sex Marriage in Hawaii." *Sociological Perspectives* 44, no. 2 (2001): 207–232.

Klatch, Rebecca E. *A Generation Divided: The New Left, The New Right, and the 1960s.* Berkeley: University of California Press, 1999.

McGirr, Lisa. *Suburban Warriors: The Origins of the New American Right.* Princeton, N.J.: Princeton University Press, 2001.

Miller, Neil. *Out of the Past: Gay and Lesbian History from 1869 to the Present.* New York: Vintage, 1995.

Moen, Matthew C. "From Revolution to Evolution: The Changing Nature of the Christian Right." *Sociology of Religion* 55, no. 3 (1994): 345–357.

Smith, Anna Marie. "The Politicization of Marriage in Contemporary American Public Policy: The Defense of Marriage Act and the Personal Responsibility Act." *Citizenship Studies* 5, no. 3 (2001): 303–320.

Stein, Arlene. *The Stranger Next Door: The Story of a Small Community's Battle over Sex, Faith, and Civil Rights.* Boston: Beacon, 2001.

Kristin G. Esterberg

See also ANTIDISCRIMINATION LAW AND POLICY; ART HISTORY; COLORADO; EDUCATION LAW AND POLICY; ELECTORAL POLITICS; FAMILY LAW AND POLICY; FEDERAL LAW AND POLICY; FLORIDA; MAPPLETHORPE, ROBERT; MILITARY LAW AND POLICY; REPUBLICAN PARTY; RIGGS, MARLON.

NEW YORK CITY

Although historians have uncovered evidence of same-sex sexual and cross-gender acts and desires dating back to the earliest days of European settlement, no evidence has yet suggested that New York City was home to the kinds of "sodomitical subcultures" scholars have identified in pre-modern European cities. It is clear, however, that, by the middle of the nineteenth century, men interested in same-sex erotic and romantic relationships in the bustling port city of New York found plenty of opportunity. The industrializing urban economy drew men away from their families and afforded them an unprecedented degree of anonymity. In a largely homosocial world of factories and boarding houses, wage-earning men pursued fleeting sexual encounters as well as more sustained same-sex relationships. Men of the burgeoning middle class, often employed as clerks in the city's offices and ships, also sought out sex with other men. The journals of the poet Walt Whitman, who referred to Manhattan as the "city of orgies, walks and joys" offer ample evidence of the erotic possibilities of the expanding city (Whitman, "City of Orgies," in *Leaves of Grass*). Whitman roamed through the city's streets and docks, where he met countless working-class men, many of whom he would ask to spend the night.

The end of the nineteenth century saw the emergence of a gay male subculture centered on the Bowery, the wide avenue in lower Manhattan that offered commercial attractions—including saloons, dance halls, and penny museums—for the city's growing working-class and immigrant populations. By the 1890s, some of these establishments began to cater to men interested in same-sex relations. As early as the 1870s, Bill McGlory, the proprietor of a Lower East Side dance hall, hired effeminate men—referred to as "female impersonators" or "fairies" —to entertain the clientele. Soon thereafter, other "fairy resorts" opened on or near the Bowery. These included Paresis Hall, named after the term for insanity related to venereal disease, and the Slide, which, according to the *New York Herald* (5 January 1892) featured "depravity of a depth unknown in the lowest slums of London or Paris. . . ." These resorts also appealed to more prosperous New Yorkers and tourists interested in "slumming" in the city's notorious tenement districts.

George Chauncey argues that working-class fairies—who were identified as such because of their inversion of gender roles rather than their engagement in same-sex relations—stood at the center of "a highly visible, remarkably complex, and continually changing gay male world [that] took shape in New York City" and flourished until the beginning of the Second World War (p. 1). Although fairies were, at the outset, its most recognizable denizens, this world encompassed many other New York City men of all social classes, who engaged in a variety of types of same-sex relationships and occupied a broad range of subjectivities (for example, "queers," "trade," "wolves," and "punks") that are not equivalent to the modern categories of "homosexual" and "heterosexual."

Fairies were not the only figures to invert gendered order in New York City in the nineteenth century. Some biological females (often, but not always working-class) adopted male gendered identities and lived much of their lives as men; many forged sexual relationships with women and some even married. The most famous such individual was Murray Hall, an employment bureau proprietor who became a respected and influential politician associated with Tammany Hall, the city's Democratic political organization. Hall was well known for his homosociability; he played poker and drank along with the other Tammany men. Hall married twice and adopted a daughter. Hall's biological sex was not revealed until his death in 1901.

By the time of Hall's death, many New Yorkers had encountered sensationalized accounts of "passing women" in the press, the most publicized of which concerned Alice Mitchell, who was tried and convicted for the 1892 Memphis murder of her "girl lover." Informing and legitimating such accounts were newly popularized understandings of sexuality, pioneered by medical professionals, which associated gender "inversion" with same-sex desire and ultimately figured the "invert"—and later the "homosexual" and "lesbian"—as distinct and socially undesirable types. Influenced by this discourse, elite and middle-class social reformers and allied urban sociologists increasingly defined "moral perversion" as a problem worthy of their attention. In New York City, anti-vice organizations including the Society for the Suppression of Vice, founded by Anthony Comstock in 1872, the Committee of Fifteen (established 1900), and its successor the Committee of Fourteen (established 1905) considered the city's homosexual culture a sign of social disorder. These organizations encouraged the city's police department to prosecute same-sex sodomy cases; indeed the number of such prosecutions increased exponentially after 1880. Later, anti-vice reformers directed their energies toward rooting out same-sex content in artistic productions. Among the theatrical works targeted were two plays with lesbian themes, Sholem Asch's *The God of Vengeance,* which premiered on Broadway in 1923 and was the first play ever to be declared obscene under New York criminal statutes, and Edouard Bourdet's *The Captive,* first staged in New York City in 1926.

Not all of New York City's social reformers joined in these anti-vice crusades, however. Indeed, many of the leading figures in the city's reform movements of the late nineteenth and early twentieth centuries formed primary erotic and romantic attachments with members of the same sex. Among them were Lillian Wald, founder of the Henry Street Settlement on the Lower East Side, Staten Island photographer Alice Austen, and activist Crystal Eastman. The prevalence of same-sex partnership among these influential reformers was accompanied by a rejection of the gendered limitations that so often excluded women of their class from participating in public life. A number of male reform colleagues shared in this critique of the traditional gender order and also organized their lives around same-sex relationships. These included settlement leaders John Lovejoy Elliott of the Hudson Guild in Hell's Kitchen and Charles B. Stover of the University Settlement on the Lower East Side. Both of these men, who counted Socrates and Whitman as their greatest influences, eschewed marriage and family and instead formed primary relationships with working-class men.

In the early twentieth century, many of the more progressive members of this reform-minded group found themselves drawn to the burgeoning bohemian culture centered in Greenwich Village. The Village was home to a vibrant intellectual and artistic community whose members tended to embrace leftist political ideologies, including socialism and anarchism. Many Village radicals espoused a liberationist sexual and gender politics that encompassed such causes as the critique of state-sanctioned marriage and the promotion of legalized birth control. Same-sex love received little condemnation in this anti-bourgeois milieu; indeed some prominent Village figures, most notably Emma Goldman, developed vigorous arguments in support of homosexual rights. The Village served as home to Heterodoxy, a social club for self-professed "unconventional" women opposed to orthodoxy of all kinds. Founded by suffrage activist Marie Jenney Howe in 1912, Heterodoxy counted among its members an array of intellectual, artistic, and political visionaries, including feminist author Charlotte Perkins Gilman, labor organizer Rose Pastor Stokes, anthropologist Elsie Clews Parsons, and National Association for the Advancement of Colored People (NAACP) activist Grace Nail Johnson, the club's only African American member. Judith Schwarz reveals that at least ten of the "Heterodites" were lesbians, who received "strong emotional support" from other club members (p. 36).

By the 1920s, according to Chauncey, "Greenwich Village hosted the best-known gay enclave in both the city and the nation—and the first to take shape in a predominantly middle-class (albeit bohemian) milieu" (p. 227). At first drawn to the unconventional atmosphere established by bohemian denizens, LGBT people became a distinct presence in the 1920s. The neighborhood was home to a number of popular commercial establishments—including speakeasies and tea rooms—frequented by "long-haired men" and "short-haired women" (p. 229). Among the best known were The Flower Pot, on the corner of Christopher and Gay, and the Jungle, on Cornelia Street. Often the success of these establishments stemmed from the popularity of the proprietor; one of the most famous was a lesbian from Poland named Eva Kotchover, who took the name Eve Addams and opened the Black Rabbit on MacDougal Street. Like many other Village gathering places catering to a queer clientele, the Black Rabbit found itself subject to frequent police raids. Addams was convicted on an obscenity charge in 1926 for publishing a collection of short stories entitled *Lesbian Love*, served prison time, and was eventually deported.

Another feature of Village gay life were popular drag balls held at Webster Hall on East 11th Street. At these gala events, tuxedo-clad women and men wearing make-up and gowns danced until dawn. An advertisement for the fifteenth annual ball, held in 1926, suggested the open and festive atmosphere of the event, beckoning ball-goers to "come when you like, with whom you like—wear what you like." Drag balls were even more prominent in Harlem, the uptown African American neighborhood that was also a hub of LGBT life by the 1920s. The largest of these events were held at the Hamilton Lodge, which could accommodate six thousand people. Smaller affairs were hosted at the elegant Savoy Ballroom, at which, according to Eric Garber, "the highlight of the event was the beauty contest, in which the fashionably dressed drags would vie for the title of Queen of the Ball" (p. 325). Although organized by Harlem residents, other New Yorkers, among them Village LGBT people and high-society "slummers," often attended. According to Kevin Mumford, such movement worked in reciprocal directions; Harlem LGBT people, including artist Richard Nugent, traveled downtown to partake of Village spectacles as well.

Drag balls were only one hallmark of a rich and varied queer world of early twentieth-century Harlem. This LGBT world—in many ways even more dynamic and expansive than that of the Village—emerged as part of the explosive growth of the larger African American population in Harlem—part of the "great migration" of southern blacks to northern cities. As was the case in the Village, Harlem's queer enclave developed against the backdrop of bohemian intellectual and artistic ferment, in this case the Harlem Renaissance. Among the luminaries who participated in this world were the writers Langston Hughes, Countee Cullen, and Claude McKay. These figures drew inspiration from the popular artistic culture in Harlem, a central feature of which was the blues. A number of popular and influential blues artists—who performed in nightclubs like the Drool Inn and the Clam House—established transgressive gendered personas and performed lyrics that reflected a range of same-sex desires and experiences. The singer Gladys Bentley, who married her girlfriend in a civil ceremony, performed in tuxedo and top hat. A popular song in her repertoire bore the title "Sissie Man's Blues." Other performers, including Ma Rainey and Bessie Jackson (formerly Lucille Bogan) sang of same-sex relationships. Rainey's "B.D. [bulldagger] Blues" offered the lyrical pronouncement: "Comin' a time, BD women, they ain't gonna need no men."

During the 1920s, the Times Square neighborhood emerged as another prominent queer enclave; gay men, in particular, found affordable housing and accessible spots for cruising and socializing in and around the city's premiere entertainment district. This period also saw the emergence of a "pansy craze" in Times Square clubs and speakeasies. According to Chauncey, Prohibition had the unintended consequence of labeling all those who consumed alcohol as criminal, thereby blurring the boundaries of respectability. Thus, middle-class visitors to Times Square proved more likely to seek out entertainment previously considered illicit. Responding to this new market, nightclub impresarios began to feature performances by effeminate and cross-dressing men for middle-class audiences. Although such performances illustrated the extent to which the gay world had become visible to the larger city, such visibility was quickly followed by a backlash. With the end of prohibition in the early 1930s, the State Liquor Authority achieved far greater control over the city's bars and clubs. Pressured by reformers and public officials, authorities used this power to shut down clubs catering to LGBT clientele. As a result, LGBT people found themselves forced to the margins of New York City's public culture in the 1930s.

From World War II to the Stonewall Riots

Mobilization for World War II was accompanied by an expansion of New York's LGBT population. Soldiers passing through the city experienced LGBT life in Harlem and the Village. Others came to New York to pursue war-related job opportunities. Many decided to remain in or move to New York after the war rather than return to their hometowns. Veteran Maxwell Gordon, who hitchhiked to New York in 1946, searched for the gay camaraderie he had discovered in the military. When he arrived in New York, he "found out that literally there were hundreds and thousands of people just like me, who'd been in either Europe or the Pacific" (Bérubé, p. 246). After the war, new LGB communities emerged in Brooklyn Heights, in Jackson Heights, and on Manhattan's East Side. New bars and nightclubs opened, too, including the string of men's bars on Third Avenue known as the "Bird Circuit." Femme/butch lesbian bars also proliferated, especially in the Village. These included the Pony Stable, Kooky's, and the Sea Colony. Often controlled by organized crime and frequently raided by the police, these bars could be risky places. Same-sex dancing, wearing clothing belonging to the "opposite sex," and serving alcohol to homosexuals were all illegal. Many patrons caught in police raids were beaten, sexually assaulted, and imprisoned.

In the face of such harassment and in opposition to the broader persecution of homosexuality in the postwar era, some LGBT New Yorkers began to organize. In 1955, Tony Segura and Sam Morford established a branch of the Mattachine Society, the homophile organization founded in California. A prominent early member of the group was Donald Webster Cory (Edward Sagarin), whose influential 1951 book, *The Homosexual in America,* characterized gays and lesbians as a minority group deserving of civil rights protections. In its first years, the New York Mattachine focused on education and advocacy. After breaking with the national organization in 1960, members boldly protested police raids of gay bars as well as the entrapment of men cruising for sex. The largest homophile organization in the United States, New York Mattachine remained active through the 1960s. In 1958, Barbara Gittings formed a chapter of the Daughters of Bilitis (DOB), New York's first incorporated lesbian organization. As editor of the DOB publication the *Ladder,* Gittings criticized the homophile movement as passive and unduly reliant on the approval of medical experts and advocated the adoption of a more activist stance.

Postwar New York was also home to a vibrant countercultural scene. The Beat writers Allen Ginsberg and William Burroughs produced work that railed against conventional sexual morality and celebrated homoerotic desire in bold and unapologetic fashion. Literary figures James Baldwin and Audre Lorde produced work that linked calls to sexual freedom to a politics of anti-racism. In the 1960s, artist Andy Warhol and his collaborators produced radical films that aggressively flaunted bourgeois conventions and featured LGBT actors and characters.

The famous Stonewall Riots of June 1969 galvanized these impulses toward radical protest and launched a militant liberation movement. Incited by a police raid on a Christopher Street bar, the Stonewall riots lasted for several days and brought together a diverse group of protesters who demanded "Gay Power!" Shortly thereafter, a group of energized LGBT New Yorkers founded the Gay Liberation Front (GLF). Influenced by the New Left, antiwar, and civil rights movements, GLF linked the gay liberation cause to other fights against oppression and sought to build alliances with other movement groups. Disaffected GLF members who believed that such alliances distracted from the primary cause of gay liberation broke off and formed the Gay Activists Alliance in December 1969.

Other GLF members objected to white male domination of the organization; they too formed their own groups. These included Radicalesbians, authors of the influential lesbian feminist document "The Woman-Identified Woman," and Third World Gay Revolution, which objected to "the inherent racism found in any white group with white leadership and white thinking" (in *Becoming Visible,* p. 166). Transgender activists also felt alienated from the GLF. In 1970, a group led by Sylvia Rivera, who was at the Stonewall Inn the night it was raided, and Marsha P. Johnson formed STAR (Street Transvestite Action Revolutionaries). Among other causes, the group devoted itself to assisting young street queens. Also in this period, Lee Brewster, famous for the drag balls he hosted at the Diplomat Hotel, formed an organization known as the Queens Liberation Front, which worked to overturn New York City laws that criminalized cross-dressing.

Post-Stonewall Developments

The post-Stonewall liberation movements counted some significant achievements in New York City, including the revocation of unfavorable municipal ordinances and a reduction in the level of police harassment. LGBT organizations and businesses flourished in this less restrictive climate. The 1970s saw the opening of a host of new lesbian bars—including Bonnie and Clyde's and the Dutchess—as well as women's bookstores and coffeehouses. New lesbian political organizations also proliferated in the 1970s and early 1980s. These include Salsa Soul Sisters (later African Ancestral Lesbians United for Societal Change), founded by Dolores Jackson, and Las Buenas Amigas, a Latina lesbian group. In 1973, Joan Nestle and Deborah Edel founded the Lesbian Herstory Archives, a volunteer-run organization now headquartered in the lesbian enclave of Park Slope, Brooklyn.

In the 1970s, businesses and institutions catering to gay men opened throughout the city. New York City grew famous for its gay nightlife; men could choose from a whole host of establishments catering to niche markets. The disco crowd could choose among dance clubs, including the Loft, the Sanctuary, and the Paradise Garage. Popular destinations for the leather and Levi set included the Eagle, the Spike, and the legendary Mineshaft, all on the West Side. Many of these establishments provided opportunities for sexual contact; even small bars featured "backrooms." Social organizations—including gay bowling leagues, choruses, and political organizations—also abounded.

LGBT publishing also expanded in the 1970s and 1980s. Among the important publications produced in New York City were *Come Out!* (1969), *Christopher Street* (1976), *New York Native* (1980), and *Outweek* (1989). In December 1983, the Gay and Lesbian Community Services Center (now Lesbian, Gay, Bisexual and Transgender Community Center) opened its doors at 208 W. 13th Street. The Center proved to be an invaluable resource for LGBT New Yorkers; among the groups to be born there were the AIDS Coalition to Unleash Power (ACT UP), Lesbian Avengers, and The Gay and Lesbian Alliance Against Defamation (GLAAD).

In the 1980s, LGBT New Yorkers confronted the disease that came to be known as Acquired Immune Deficiency Syndrome (AIDS), which was first identified in New York City in 1981. AIDS, which initially predominantly struck gay men, created a crisis almost immediately. The first organization to respond to the epidemic, the Gay Men's Health Crisis (GMHC), was founded in 1981 under the leadership of playwright Larry Kramer. GMHC, which became the largest organization of its kind, worked to educate gay men about AIDS prevention and provided legal, medical, and other forms of support services to those living with the disease. In response to a skyrocketing death toll and government inaction, angry AIDS activists adopted more militant and confrontational tactics. In the mid-1980s, for example, the Lavender Hill Mob staged a number of direct actions protesting government AIDS policy. ACT UP was founded in March 1987. This group, comprised mostly of white men, staged dramatic demonstrations and direct actions, including the disruption of the New York Stock Exchange. ACT UP chapters soon became established throughout the country and internationally. The organization exercised significant influence on the ways in which the government and the medical profession responded to the disease.

Organizations influenced by ACT UP emerged in the early 1990s. Queer Nation, founded in 1990, employed direct action to challenge the politics of gay and lesbian assimilation and to respond to a rising tide of anti-LGBT violence. The Lesbian Avengers, founded in 1992, embraced similar tactics to promote "lesbian survival and visibility." The group also introduced the "Dyke March," now an annual event.

By the end of the twentieth century, the activist culture of the 1980s and early 1990s had lost some of its vibrancy. Still, LGBT New Yorkers could count some successes. 1993 saw the passage of a domestic partnership law. Several openly gay and lesbian candidates were elected to public office in the 1990s. In April 2002, the New York Association for Gender Rights Advocacy (NYAGRA), under the leadership of Pauline Park, led a successful campaign to amend the city's human rights ordinance to protect the rights of all transsexual, transgendered, and gender-variant people. The group continues to fight for coverage under state law. In 2003, the New York City Department of Education and the Harvey Milk School, a collaborative endeavor between the Hetrick-Martin Institute and the New York City Board of Education, became the country's first accredited public school designed to meet the needs of LGBT youth.

Bibliography

Bérubé, Allan. *Coming Out Under Fire: The History of Gay Men and Women In World War Two.* New York: The Free Press, 1992.

Chauncey, George. *Gay New York: Gender, Urban Culture, and the Making of the Gay Male World, 1890–1940.* New York: Basic Books, 1994.

D'Emilio, John, and Estelle B. Freedman. *Intimate Matters: A History of Sexuality in America.* Chicago: University of Chicago Press, 1997.

D'Emilio, John. *Sexual Politics, Sexual Communities: The Making of a Homosexual Minority in the United States, 1940–1970.* Chicago: University of Chicago Press, 1983.

Duberman, Martin. *Stonewall.* New York: Dutton, 1993.

Faderman, Lillian. *Odd Girls and Twilight Lovers: A History of Lesbian Life in Twentieth-Century America.* New York: Penguin, 1991.

Friedman, Andrea. *Prurient Interests: Gender, Democracy, and Obscenity in New York City, 1909–1945.* New York: Columbia University Press, 2000.

Garber, Eric. "A Spectacle in Color: The Lesbian and Gay Subculture of Jazz Age Harlem." In Martin Duberman, Martha Vicinus, and George Chauncey, Jr., eds. *Hidden from History: Reclaiming the Gay and Lesbian Past.* New York: New American Library, 1989.

Kaiser, Charles. *The Gay Metropolis. The Landmark History of Gay Life in America Since World War II.* Boston: Houghton Mifflin, 1997.

Katz, Jonathan. *Gay American History: Lesbians and Gay Men in the U.S.A.* New York: Crowell, 1976.

Kissack, Terence. "Freaking Fag Revolutionaries: New York's Gay Liberation Front, 1969–1971," *Radical History Review* 62 (Spring 1995): 104–134.

Kramer, Larry. *Reports from the Holocaust: The Making of an AIDS Activist.* New York: St. Martin's Press, 1989.

Marotta, Toby. *The Politics of Homosexuality.* Boston: Houghton Mifflin, 1981.

McGarry, Molly, and Fred Wasserman. *Becoming Visible: An Illustrated History of Lesbian and Gay Life in Twentieth-Century America.* New York: Penguin Studio, 1998.

Mumford, Kevin J. *Interzones: Black/White Sex Districts in Chicago and New York in the Early Twentieth Century.* New York: Columbia University Press, 1997.

Nestle, Joan. *A Restricted Country.* Ithaca, NY: Firebrand Books, 1987.

Schwarz, Judith. *Radical Feminists of Heterodoxy: Greenwich Village, 1912–1940.* Norwich: VT: New Victoria Publishers, 1986.

Whitman, Walt. *Poetry and Prose.* New York: Library of America, 1982.

Kevin Murphy

See also HARLEM RENAISSANCE; LESBIAN HERSTORY ARCHIVES; STONEWALL RIOTS.

NEWSPAPERS AND MAGAZINES

The lesbian and gay press began quietly in California cities where gay men and lesbians congregated after World War II. The first known publication, *Vice Versa,* was distributed in Los Angeles in 1947 and 1948 by a young lesbian who used the pseudonym Lisa Ben (an anagram of lesbian). She produced the fifteen-page newsletterlike magazine on carbon paper on her typewriter at work and gave copies to her friends and other women in Los Angeles bars.

The first lesbian and gay publications with a national reach were launched in the 1950s, a time when the mainstream press virtually ignored gay and lesbian issues. What little coverage there was focused on crime and on homosexuality as a threat to society. *ONE* magazine was established in 1953 by a group of Los Angeles men who were frustrated with the lack of mainstream press attention to gay concerns. The magazine's founders aimed to promote civil rights for homosexuals, but they chose not to affiliate with the nation's largest homophile organization, the Mattachine Society, because they were not satisfied with the group's assimilationist approach. *ONE* magazine continued publication for fourteen years, and its circulation of five thousand was among the largest of all pre-Stonewall homophile publications.

The *Mattachine Review* was founded in San Francisco in 1955 by members of the Mattachine Society, a homophile group that sought to gain acceptance by encouraging homosexuals to conform to the standards of the dominant heterosexual society. Like *ONE* magazine, the *Mattachine Review* was not written with a female audience in mind. It was aimed primarily at homosexual men and reached a circulation of one thousand.

In 1956, Phyllis Lyon and Del Martin, members of the San Francisco–based homophile organization Daughters of Bilitis (DOB), founded the first widely distributed lesbian publication, the *Ladder.* Like the *Mattachine Review,* the *Ladder* took a conciliatory tone in its early years, educating its readers and reassuring them with legal and medical advice. The *Ladder* was published for sixteen years, with circulation reaching a high of seven hundred, considerably less than the gay men's publications. The influence of the magazine was reflected, however, in the many new publications it inspired in DOB chapters around the country.

All three of the flagship publications of the lesbian and gay press were subjected to government scrutiny and threats of censorship. The Federal Bureau of Investigation (FBI) investigated them in search of obscene material or supporters of communism. FBI agents regularly harassed editors, contacting their employers and seriously damaging more than one career. Periodically, postal officials seized the magazines and claimed that sending homosexual materials through the mail was illegal because they were obscene. *ONE* engaged in a four-year court battle with U.S. postal officials, losing in district and federal courts, until the U.S. Supreme Court in 1958 ruled in favor of the magazine, deeming that the subject of homosexuality was not by definition obscene and that *ONE* could be sent through the mail.

All of the pre-Stonewall publications were published by volunteers working on tight budgets. The content of the magazines was a mix of personal essays, poetry, fiction, letters to the editor, and referrals to journal articles and books dealing with homosexual issues. They also reported news from around the country, particularly news that documented the denial of civil rights to gay men and lesbians. Because they functioned to inform readers of the nascent political stirrings among gays and lesbians, these publications are widely credited with making possible the birth of the gay and lesbian movement that was to follow.

A Move to Militancy in the 1960s

Reflecting social upheavals taking place throughout the United States in the 1960s, gay and lesbian publications began to exhibit a more activist and militant stance. Inspired by the civil rights, antiwar, and women's movements, many called for their readers to demand their civil rights. The content of publications in the 1960s shifted away from fiction and poetry and began to place greater emphasis on politics and news.

The 1960s spawned the first publications outside of the West Coast. *Drum* was founded in Philadelphia in 1964 by a gay rights organization called the Janus Society. Subtitled *Sex in Perspective,* the magazine aimed to entertain as well as inform its readers. The magazine took a militant stance, soon to be seen in other publications of the 1960s, arguing against the sort of homophile accommodationism that was typical of the publications of the 1950s. *Drum* was also the first gay publication to turn a significant profit. The magazine was the first news publication to include homoerotica in its pages, in the form of photographs of handsome, scantily clad men. Circulation of the magazine soared, reaching ten thousand within two years, more than all other existing gay and lesbian publications combined.

In 1966 Frank Kameny, an activist who had written for the *Ladder,* launched *Homosexual Citizen,* the first gay and lesbian magazine in Washington, D.C. The publication carried the subtitle *News of Civil Liberties and Social Rights for Homosexuals,* an indicator of its goal to fight aggressively for homosexual rights. One of the most activist and militant publications of the time, it had a small circulation of four hundred, but it explicitly aimed to influence public policy rather than simply inform its readers. Kameny had the publication mailed to Washington decision makers, including President Lyndon Johnson, members of the U.S. Congress, and FBI chief J. Edgar Hoover.

The *Ladder,* still published by the Daughters of Bilitis, also took a more militant stance in the 1960s. In 1963 Barbara Gittings of Philadelphia became the *Ladder*'s editor. She added the subtitle *A Lesbian Review* to the publication and began calling for its readers to engage in political activism.

Editors of these East Coast publications were not above making news themselves. In addition to urging readers to fight for their rights, most also engaged directly in political activism, carrying picket signs in protests and extensively covering the demonstrations in their publications. Such coverage informed readers nationwide about the gay and lesbian movement and helped to expand its message beyond the East Coast.

The *Los Angeles Advocate,* which was to become the largest gay and lesbian publication in history, was launched in 1967 in Los Angeles. It developed from *PRIDE Newsletter,* the publication of the gay rights organization Personal Rights in Defense and Education. Under the leadership of its first editor, Richard T. Mitch, it was renamed the *Advocate* and became an independent newspaper when the gay rights organization disbanded in 1968.

The *Advocate* was the first gay newspaper in the United States, and it was the first publication to operate as a business with a paid staff and revenues solely from advertising, subscriptions, and newsstand sales. The publication was wildly successful, with its circulation quickly skyrocketing in two years to 23,000 and distribution expanding to East Coast cities.

Another publication that had an impact on the gay and lesbian community in the 1960s was Al Goldstein's sex tabloid *Screw,* launched in 1968 in New York City. Although it was not a gay publication, it carried a column, *Homosexual Citizen,* written by gay activists Jack Nichols and Lige Clark, who borrowed the name from the by-then defunct magazine. The column educated countless people, gay and heterosexual alike, and had a far greater reach than the gay and lesbian publications of the time, with the circulation of *Screw* reaching 150,000.

After Stonewall

By mid-1969 the combined circulation of all lesbian and gay publications was 55,000, and gay men and lesbians were learning from these publications about the growing movement for civil rights. The militant stance of the lesbian and gay press during the mid-to-late 1960s is widely credited with setting the stage for what came later.

In June 1969 vice officers raiding the Stonewall Inn in New York City's Greenwich Village were met with resistance from hundreds of gays and lesbians, leading to riots that lasted for four nights. Mainstream media coverage of the event focused on its criminal nature, with no mention of the political dimension of the riots. Members of the gay and lesbian press, however, were present to chronicle the developments that would eventually come to be regarded as the beginning of the gay and lesbian liberation movement. Publications such as the *Advocate* and the *Homosexual Citizen* column in *Screw* devoted extensive space to the Stonewall rebellion, and gays and lesbians throughout the country, many for the first time, were inspired to speak out and demand their civil rights.

The activism inspired by Stonewall led to an explosion of lesbian and gay publications, among them a number of street newspapers that took a radical stance, calling for gay nationalism, socialism, anarchy, and revolution. This radical burst of publications inflamed an ongoing debate in the lesbian and gay press as to whether the movement should take a moderate approach to politics or whether it should follow the example of groups such as the Black Panthers and call for an overthrow of the U.S. government.

A number of publications called for the gay and lesbian movement to join forces and form coalitions with other revolutionary groups. Among them were *Come Out!,* a Greenwich Village publication founded in November 1969 that was affiliated with the Gay Liberation Front. *Gay Sunshine, Gay Times,* and *Gay Flames,* all launched in 1970, also called for a revolutionary approach to gay rights. A number of the radical political publications of the early 1970s also took an extreme approach to sexual liberation. Among the most prominent was *Fag Rag,* founded by a Boston collective in 1971. The sensationalistic tabloid published graphic articles and explicit sexual images and defined gay sex as a political statement. The burst of radical publications had subsided by 1973, and more moderate voices soon won out. Among the best known were the *Advocate* and *GAY,* founded by Nichols and Clarke of the *Homosexual Citizen* column, both of which argued against coalitions with radical groups.

The early 1970s also saw the birth of a number of regional weekly newspapers. The most prominent included *Gay Community News* in Boston, the *Washington Blade,* the *Philadelphia Gay News,* the *Bay Area Reporter* for San Francisco and vicinity, and the *DRUMMER* of San Francisco. *Christopher Street,* an upscale monthly magazine, was launched in New York City in 1976 with the aim of attracting a sophisticated audience with extensive coverage of the arts.

The Lesbian Feminist 1970s

Inspired by the reemergence of the feminist movement in the 1970s, a variety of lesbian feminist publications were launched. With the exception of Boston's *Gay Community News,* which included both men and women on its staff and strove for equal coverage, most of the post-Stonewall publications were aimed primarily at men. Feeling that the gay press was not meeting their needs, lesbians created a press of their own. These lesbian newspapers and magazines were generally published by collectives. Adhering to feminist principles, they often operated on a pay-if-you-can basis. Because their publications were free of charge, many were quickly in financial trouble and most were short-lived.

Amazon Quarterly, which published from 1973 to 1975, boasted a circulation of nine thousand, the largest of the lesbian publications at the time. The magazine focused on literature, art, and culture. *Lesbian Connection,* a publication written by its readers, is the longest-running lesbian publication. It was launched in 1974 and was still being published in 2003. The magazine began with a circulation of 400, which had increased to 25,000 in the latter year.

A number of publications identified themselves as lesbian feminist and espoused a separatist philosophy. *Lesbian Tide,* launched in Los Angeles in 1971 by Jeanne Córdova, was the first all-news lesbian publication. Before its demise in 1980, the magazine reached a circulation of three thousand.

The Furies was founded by a Washington, D.C., collective in 1972, and while lasting for only a year, it inspired countless individual lesbians and many other publications as well with its cogent rendition of a lesbian feminist ideology and its advocacy of class consciousness. Members of the founding collective included writers Rita Mae Brown and Charlotte Bunch and photographer Joan E. Biren (JEB). After the magazine folded, former collective members went on to found the lesbian publishing house Diana Press and Olivia Records.

By 1975 there were some fifty lesbian publications in existence, with a combined circulation of fifty thousand. Among the most influential were *Sinister Wisdom, off our backs, Lavender Woman, Ain't I a Woman, Dyke, Sisters, Tribad,* and *Azalea: A Magazine by Third World Lesbians.*

AIDS in the 1980s

The first article on the disease that would soon be known as AIDS ran in May 1981 in the *New York Native,* a biweekly tabloid launched two years earlier. Dr. Lawrence Mass, an unpaid contributor to the *Native,* broke the story and tried in vain to get the information out quickly to the rest of the gay press. With the exception of the *Washington Blade,* however, most other gay publications were reluctant to pick up the story. Like the mainstream press, many in the gay press ignored the threat of AIDS, and some even trivialized its importance. Critics have charged that the refusal of gay publications to cover the crisis in its early years was due to a combination of their reluctance to question the freewheeling gay sexual revolution that many had championed in their pages and their dependence on bathhouses and clubs for advertising revenue.

By the late 1980s, the AIDS crisis had spawned a resurgence of militancy in the lesbian and gay community, represented by organizations such as ACT UP and Queer Nation. *OutWeek,* launched in New York in 1989, reflected the radical politics of these organizations. Hearkening back to the militant press of the early 1970s, *OutWeek* vociferously criticized those it deemed to be enemies of the LGBT community—pharmaceutical companies, the advertising industry, Congress, organized religion, and even the LGBTQ press itself. The magazine made its biggest splash, however, with its relentless outing of celebrities and public figures such as publisher Malcolm Forbes.

The majority of 1980s publications were targeted to men, although a few, such as *Gay Community News, OutWeek,* and *The News* in Los Angeles gave an equal voice to men and women. A number of lesbian publications arose during the decade, among them *Big Apple Dyke News, Conditions,* and *Lesbian Ethics.* As the decade drew to a close, new lesbian publications reflected the militant shift in the movement. *Lesbian Contradiction* served as the radical political voice of lesbians. And a new genre of lesbian erotica appeared, with sexually explicit publications such as *On Our Backs, Yoni,* and *Bad Attitude.* By the end of the decade there were more than eight hundred lesbian and gay publications in circulation, reaching more than one million readers.

Specialty Publications

In the 1990s a number of specialty magazines joined the ranks of the LGBTQ press. *POZ* magazine is targeted to the HIV/AIDS community. *BLK* offers content specifically targeted to African American lesbians and gay men. *XY* is aimed at gay and lesbian teens.

Members of the transgender, bisexual, and queer communities, who have experienced mixed coverage in lesbian and gay publications, have created magazines of their own. *Anything That Moves,* a bisexual magazine with a radical perspective, began publishing in San Francisco in 1991. *Transgender Community News* and *Transgender Tapestry* offers news and support not found in most LGBTQ publications.

As the needs of LGBTQ communities change, publications arose to meet specific needs. *In The Family* is a magazine for LGBTQ families, written primarily by family therapists, and *Alternative Family Magazine* is a publication for LGBTQ parents and their children.

Lifestyle Magazines

From its very beginning, the gay press has struggled with the complications associated with paid advertising. Gay men's magazines and newspapers have historically been supported in large part by sex-oriented ads, while lesbian publications, particularly in the 1970s, have found it difficult to drum up sufficient advertising revenue in the lesbian business community. The centrality of advertising for LGBTQ publications grew substantially in the 1990s, with a greater presence of advertisements for mainstream consumer products. During that decade the first national advertisements began to appear in their pages. Drawn to the allure of DINKS (double incomes, no kids), companies bought ad space in LGBTQ magazines for such products as Absolut vodka and Miller beer, and other companies soon followed. The financial windfall provided by these advertisers gave birth to a new type of LGBTQ publication: glossy lifestyle magazines that focused on culture, fashion, and celebrity. *Out, Genre,* and *Frontiers* targeted gay men, and *Curve, GirlFriends,* and *Lesbian News* in Los Angeles targeted lesbians. *Square Peg* and *10 Percent* were aimed at both men and women.

These lifestyle publications are often criticized for shunning politics and avoiding content that might lower circulation or offend advertisers. Their publishers, however, argue that they provide a service to the LGBTQ community and are driven by more than the profit motive. While publications with a more radical voice find it difficult to attract national advertising, the popularity of lifestyle magazines is undeniable. The number of LGBTQ publications has grown only slightly since the 1980s, but circulation has skyrocketed to more than two million, led by *Out,* with 100,000 readers.

Nationally distributed lifestyle magazines are the most visible and have by far the widest circulation of LGBT periodicals. But hundreds of LGBTQ newspapers and magazines continue to provide news to their local and regional communities.

Bibliography

D'Emilio, John. *Sexual Politics, Sexual Communities: The Making of a Homosexual Minority in the United States, 1940–1970.* Chicago: University of Chicago Press, 1983.

Fitzgerald, Mark. "Farewell to the Gay '90s." *Editor and Publisher* 2 (October 2000): 32–35.

Gross, Larry, and James D. Woods, eds. *The Columbia Reader on Lesbians and Gay Men in Media, Society, and Politics.* New York: Columbia University Press, 1999.

Miller, Alan V., comp. *Our Own Voices: A Directory of Gay and Lesbian Periodicals, 1890–1990, Including the Complete Holdings of the Canadian Gay Archives.* Toronto: The Archives, 1996.

Miller, Neil. *Out of the Past: Gay and Lesbian History from 1869 to the Present.* New York: Vintage Books, 1995.

National Museum and Archive of Lesbian and Gay History, comp. *The Lesbian Almanac.* New York: Berkley Books, 1996.

Streitmatter, Rodger. *Unspeakable: The Rise of the Gay and Lesbian Press in America.* Boston: Faber and Faber, 1995.

Jane R. Ballinger

See also *ADVOCATE*; AFRICAN AMERICAN LGBTQ ORGANIZATIONS AND PERIODICALS; ASIAN AMERICAN LGBTQ ORGANIZATIONS AND PERIODICALS; BEN, LISA; BREWSTER, LEE; CENSORSHIP, OBSCENITY, AND PORNOGRAPHY LAW AND POLICY; *DRUM*; *GAY COMMUNITY NEWS*; HOMOPHILE PRESS; *LADDER*; LATINA AND LATINO LGBTQ ORGANIZATIONS AND PERIODICALS;

LESBIAN CONNECTION; *MATTACHINE REVIEW*; MEDIA STUDIES AND JOURNALISM; NATIVE AMERICAN LGBTQ ORGANIZATIONS AND PERIODICALS; *ONE*; PHYSIQUE MAGAZINES AND PHOTOGRAPHS; PORNOGRAPHY; RADICAL FAERIES; TRANSGENDER ORGANIZATIONS AND PERIODICALS; WICKER, RANDOLFE.

NILES, Blair (b.1880; d. 1959), writer.

A noted explorer, travel writer, ethnographer, and popular novelist who, though heterosexual, wrote sympathetically about gay life, Niles was born Mary Blair Rice in 1880 in Coles Ferry, Virginia. She was the daughter of Henry Crenshaw Rice and Gordon (Pryor) Rice and the granddaughter of the ardent secessionists and authors Roger A. Pryor and Sara Pryor.

In 1902, at the age of 22, Niles married explorer and naturalist William Beebe (best remembered for his 1934 world record ocean descent in the Bathysphere with Otis Barton). The couple took up residence in New York City, where they lived when not on expedition, a pattern Niles maintained for her entire life. Immediately following their marriage, the couple set out for Mexico to study and obtain animal specimens for New York City's Zoological Park (now the Bronx Zoo). They published an account of their experience, *Two Bird Lovers in Mexico,* in 1905. Later they visited Trinidad, Venezuela, and British Guinea, publishing an account of that voyage as well (*Our Search for a Wilderness*). In 1909 Niles and Beebe accepted an offer to lead an expedition to study pheasants around the world in their natural habitats. After a seventeen-month globe-trotting expedition, they returned to New York and published their research in the massive four-volume *A Monograph of the Pheasants.*

Niles's marriage to Beebe was not destined to last. Niles obtained a Nevada divorce from Beebe on the grounds of "cruelty" (the *New York Times* headline read, "Naturalist Was Cruel"). However, in 1913, the day after the divorce was final, Blair married architect Robert L. Niles Jr. and changed her name to Blair Niles. She and her second husband collaborated on several projects. One of the most popular was a four-part series of articles on "Devil's Island," published as a serial in July–August 1927 in the *Sunday New York Times Magazine.* Niles was said to be the only woman ever to have set foot on the Devil's Island penal colony in French Guiana. She and her husband, who acted as photographer for the project, were also said to be the only foreigners ever to have voluntarily visited the island. They were given full access to the prison and conducted extensive interviews of the men imprisoned there.

Niles also wrote two books based on her Devil's Island research: a hugely popular exposé titled *Condemned to Devil's Island: The Biography of an Unknown Convict* and a fictional work called *Free. Condemned to Devil's Island* was translated into many European languages, bringing foreign investigators to the penal colony and spurring prison reforms. The book was also made into the film *Condemned,* an early black and white "talkie." During this period, Blair enjoyed the company of such Hollywood luminaries as actress Mary Pickford.

The 1920s and 1930s were prolific years for Niles. From 1923 to 1939 the inveterate traveler authored twelve diverse books, ranging from travelogues such as *Columbia, Land of Miracles* to *Strange Brother,* a 1931 novel depicting gay life in Harlem, and a history of Virginia's James River (*The James: From Sea to Iron Gate,* 1939). In 1925 Niles also cofounded the Society of Woman Geographers (SWG), which is still in existence. In 1938 she received a Gold Medal from the City of Lima, Peru; in 1941 she received the Constance Lindsay Skinner Medal from the Women's National Book Association and the Bookseller's League; and in 1944 she received the SWG's highest honor.

Although significant, Niles' impact on the LGBT community seems to have been unintentional on her part. Niles approached LGBT life in Harlem as she did the tribes in South America about which she wrote—as an explorer and observer of human behavior. (The 1942 edition of *Twentieth Century Authors* describes *Strange Brother* as a sociological study of "male inverts," as homosexuals were then called.)

That Niles was well acquainted with LGBT life in New York despite being heterosexual is beyond doubt. *Strange Brother* explores in vivid detail both the world of Greenwich Village bohemians and urban speakeasies in the latter days of the Harlem Renaissance, and as such it is considered to be an extremely accurate portrayal of 1930s New York City LGBT life. For example, *Strange Brother*'s fictional speakeasy, the Lobster Pot, was based on Harry Hansberry's legendary Clam House on 133rd Street where African American lesbian Gladys Bentley, "the bulldagger who sang the blues," performed in a tuxedo and top hat.

Strange Brother is significant because it was the first widely read American account of openly gay men, drag balls, and antigay police raids. Published just two years after Radclyffe Hall's *Well of Loneliness* (1929), it is arguably the first popular novel to portray a gay man in a positive light. The novel chronicles the story of Mark Thornton, a young man who escapes his "shadow world" of homosexuality by losing himself in the black jazz joints of Harlem. Treated sympathetically by Niles, Thornton comes to Harlem from a small Midwestern town, not to find adventure or make assignations, but because he identifies with those he believes are also outcasts from American life.

Niles could not have anticipated the effect *Strange Brother* would have in the formation of LGBT identity. The book was widely distributed and read among gay men in the 1930s, and was listed by author Anthony Slide as one of fifty seminal "lost gay novels" of the first half of the twentieth century. It was still in print as of 2003.

Bibliography

Mumford, Kevin J. "Homosex Changes: Race, Cultural Geography, and the Emergence of the Gay." *American Quarterly* 48, no. 3 (1996): 395-414.

Slide, Anthony. *Lost Gay Novels: A Reference Guide to Fifty Works from the First Half of the Twentieth Century.* New York: Harrington Park Press, 2003.

Lea Pierce

See also BENTLEY, GLADYS; HARLEM RENAISSANCE; LITERATURE.

NIN, Anaïs (b. 21 February 1903; d. 14 January, 1977), writer.

Anaïs Nin was born in Neuilly-sur-Seine, France. Her father abandoned the family when she was ten years old. The following year, her mother moved the family to New York, where Nin lived until 1925. During the voyage to New York, Nin began her diary. Over the next fifty years, she would write over 150 volumes.

In 1923, Nin met Hugh Guiler. They married in 1925, and moved to Paris where Guiler worked in finance. Nin was at first shocked by the greater French openness in matters of sexuality and dedicated herself to being a loyal wife. At the same time, she continued to read novels that provided her with other models of relationships and began to feel frustrated with the lack of artistic ambition in her husband. In 1931, Nin met the writer Henry Miller and his wife June. Nin was captivated by June, and the two women began a passionate friendship. After June left Paris, Nin and Henry began an affair that was both sexual and creative, as the two writers shared their work and their ideas. In 1940, Nin returned with her husband to New York. She continued her affairs with men and in 1947 met Rupert Pole. When Pole moved to California that same year, Nin, dividing her time between the two men, began a bicoastal life that continued until her death.

Nin published her first works in the 1930s. Her study, *D.H. Lawrence: An Unprofessional Study* (1932) sought to emphasize the "feminine" element in the controversial writer's work. *The House of Incest* (1936), a novel, explored a major theme in Nin's work and life: the search for the self through relationships with another. Over the next forty years, Nin published several more works of fiction as well as multiple volumes of her diary.

Early critics regarded much of Nin's work as scandalous, both for its open treatment of women's sexuality and for its focus on women's inner lives. They also criticized the influence of surrealism on her work and the excessive "femininity" of her writing style. Her novels were not widely available until the 1950s. Her reputation as a writer grew in the 1960s, as critics and readers became more receptive to her style and subject matter. The publication of the first volume of her diary (which covers the years 1931–1934) in 1966 gained her praise and celebrity.

In the 1930s, Nin underwent psychoanalysis. The impact this had on her can be seen in her fiction and her diaries, both of which are concerned with exploring how the individual persona, one often influenced by the demands of society and culture, masks the true self underneath. Nin believed that an examination of the inner life could lead to the revelation and realization of the true self.

This emphasis on the inner life runs throughout Nin's work. Nin appeared to explore her own inner life not only in her diaries, but in her fiction as well, much of which drew its inspiration from the diaries. The continued examination of her life served as an inspiration for women in the late 1960s and 1970s when Nin's work was seen as a model for the sorts of questions women were asking in consciousness-raising groups.

While feminist discussion of Nin in the 1970s emphasized the authenticity of Nin's struggle for self-discovery, some have since argued that the diaries are highly fictionalized. Others, including feminists, have criticized Nin for an excessive concern with the inner life and a lack of interest in larger political and economic struggles.

In several of her fictional works, in her diaries, and in her life, Nin explored the topic of homosexuality. She examined the relationship between male homosexuals and female heterosexuals, a relationship that she saw as being based in a mutual rejection of authority. She also explored lesbianism, most notably in *Ladders to Fire* (1946). Claimed by some to be based on her relationship with June Miller, this work tells the story of two women who seek in each other that which they are missing. Nin described this impulse as a search for "twinship" and saw it as part of an attempt to understand one's true self. Nin insisted, however, that relationships with women could never substitute for having to come to terms with the "other," that is, the man. At the same time, she argued that one should be free to love whomever one wished.

Bibliography

Bair, Deirdre. *Anaïs Nin: A Biography.* New York: Putnam, 1995.

Fitch, Noël Riley. *Anaïs: The Erotic Life of Anaïs Nin.* Boston: Little, Brown, 1993.

Zaller, Robert, ed. *A Casebook on Anaïs Nin.* New York: New American Library, 1974.

Victoria E. Thompson

See also LITERATURE.

Elaine Noble. A legislative pioneer in 1974, as the first openly lesbian or gay candidate in the United States to win electoral office at the state level, she served one term in the Massachusetts House of Representatives. **[AP/Wide World Photos]**

NOBLE, Elaine **(22 February 1944–), legislator.**

In November 1974, Elaine Noble won a seat in the Massachusetts House of Representatives, thereby becoming the second openly lesbian or gay candidate to win electoral office in the United States and the first to do so at the state level. (In Ann Arbor, Michigan, openly lesbian Kathy Kozachenko won a city council seat in April of that year, six months after sitting councilors Nancy Wechsler and Jerry deGrieck had come out.) In 1961, Jose Sarria had been the first openly gay person to run for electoral office, and a full decade passed before Frank Kameny in Washington, D.C., became the second. Inspired in part by Noble's victory, Minnesota State Senator Allan Spear came out as gay in late 1974. But at the decade's end, fewer than ten individuals held electoral office in the United States while fully out as lesbian or gay.

Noble was born in Pennsylvania, her father a longtime union and civil rights activist. Her schooling took her to Boston University, Emerson College, and Harvard University. While later teaching at Emerson, she became active in sexual diversity politics. In the early 1970s, she joined the Daughters of Bilitis and the National Organization for Women (NOW), speaking out against anti-lesbian sentiments within NOW. She addressed hundreds of participants at Boston's first official gay pride march, in 1971, and a year or two later broadened her profile by co-producing and moderating the weekly radio show "Gaywire."

In 1972, Noble became a leader of the Women's Political Caucus and campaigned for Barney Frank's successful race for a seat in the state House. In 1974, she won a Democratic nomination for her own seat, in Boston's Back Bay area. This nomination came in the midst of a furor over school busing, and Noble remained outspoken on the side of desegregation.

Noble won the November election with a comfortable majority and became a national celebrity among LGB people. She fought hard to avoid being labeled a single issue politician, an image that almost all openly LGB candidates had to combat in the years to follow. Alongside Barney Frank, she worked hard, but unsuccessfully, to secure passage of a sexual orientation antidiscrimination bill. She also responded to countless requests for help on sexual orientation issues arising in her own district and far beyond. In 1977, she was in the first LGB delegation to ever meet with officials at the White House.

In the same year, the standard-bearing pressures on Noble increased as Anita Bryant began spearheading religious right campaigning against nondiscrimination measures. She felt increasingly that the LGB community was unrealistic and unrelenting in its demands on her and quick to condemn what were perceived as shortcomings—that she did not devote even more time than she did to sexual diversity causes. As others in her footsteps would discover, she faced great difficulties in balancing her roles as a district representative and as a spokesperson for a marginalized community that extended far beyond her district boundaries.

In 1978, Noble decided against running for reelection, partly from disillusionment, and also because major redistricting would pit her against Barney Frank, as well as put her in a disadvantaged position. Noble reentered electoral politics in 1980, trying unsuccessfully to gain the Democratic nomination for a U.S. Senate seat in Massachusetts. She worked in the administration of Boston Mayor Kevin White, which soon was entangled in a corruption scandal. She was not one of the accused, but it still dealt her political career a serious blow.

In the following years Noble retained an interest in health issues, cofounding a LGB alcohol and drug treatment center in Minneapolis and trying unsuccessfully to establish similar institutions in the Boston area. In 1991 and again in 1993, she ran for a city council seat in Cambridge, across the Charles River from her one-time electoral district, but lost both times. Noble then began working in mutual fund management, and for a time in the mid- and late 1990s, she managed the Meyers Pride Value Fund, which invested in firms with pro-LGB records.

Noble's pioneering entry into legislative politics was weighted with the aspirations of a community that was in those early days beyond the fringe of the formal political process. At times, she was a victim of the tendency for those on the margins to "eat their own," and she spoke out against that pattern. She found herself buffeted by competing and sometimes incompatible pressures, still a common experience of elected representatives who come from marginalized communities.

Bibliography

DeBold, Kathleen. *Out for Office: Campaigning in the Gay Nineties.* Washington, D.C.: Gay and Lesbian Victory Fund, 1994.

Rayside, David. *On the Fringe: Gays and Lesbians in Politics.* Ithaca, N.Y.: Cornell University Press, 1998.

Thompson, Mark. *Long Road to Freedom: The Advocate History of the Gay and Lesbian Movement.* New York: St. Martin's, 1994.

Yeager, Ken. *Trailblazers: Profiles of America's Gay and Lesbian Elected Officials.* New York: Haworth, 1999.

David Rayside

See also BOSTON; FRANK, BARNEY; DEMOCRATIC PARTY; ELECTORAL POLITICS.

NODA, Barbara (b. 14 January 1953), writer.

Barbara Noda was born in Stockton, California, and grew up in the Salinas Valley. A third-generation Japanese American (*sansei*), Noda was the youngest child and only daughter of *nisei* (second generation) parents. Her father cultivated strawberries in the Salinas Valley. In her poem, "The Hills around Salinas," Noda describes her experiences growing up in this rural, agricultural region:

> As a lonely young girl, growing up in an alien town,
> I raced down those graveled and dirt roads on a shiny orange bicycle and the wheels turned and turned; like the dreams of a feverish child. (*Strawberries*, 1979)

Noda's consciousness of race, class, and gender were based on her childhood experiences of witnessing her father's long days in the fields, her mother's role in maintaining an agricultural household economy, and her own experiences as an only daughter of a Japanese American family living in a region predominantly divided between white landowners and Filipino and Mexican laborers. In the same poem, Noda describes her response to these experiences as

> endless hours of writing,
> writing,
> the same delirious motion to be free.

After graduating from the University of California at Santa Cruz, Noda moved to San Francisco to be a writer. There she contributed to a body of writing, art, and political expression that had emerged out of an era of social ferment and change in the United States.

Noda's poems and writings capture a pivotal time in gay and lesbian, Asian American, and feminist history. The late 1960s and early 1970s marked the emergence of new waves of Asian American, feminist, worker, and LGBT movements nationwide. Greater community consciousness was articulated subsequently in numerous independent publications and journals. Along with other writers, Noda challenged any universal conception of feminists and lesbians. She published her poem "Strawberries" in the spring 1978 issue of *Conditions:*

Three, a journal founded by Elly Bulkin and others that featured writing by women, particularly lesbians, of diverse backgrounds. Noda's book of poetry, *Strawberries,* was published in 1979 by Shameless Hussy Press, a prominent second wave feminist press. These poems paint lyrical, gentle, and almost nostalgic images of growing up: her father in the fields; her mother writing her a bedtime story; her coming out to her mother. In "Mother and Daughter," Noda writes,

> there is a difference there is a difference
> it has taken years for the shine to come through
> now we both know that mornings for you
> are different for me.

Her poems evoking erotic desire are similarly entwined with evocations of Japanese culture and Asian American identity. In "The Woodblock of My Dreams," Noda writes:

> And then I found her—
> like a geisha flapping to my side
> with a steaming hot cup of tea,
> her smile the smile of smiles
> she giggled and disappeared.
> I chased her in my blue and white yukata
> the stripes rippling through a breeze
> ecstatic—my moans filled me like a mountain.

Together, the poems illustrate the multiple subjectivities that Noda negotiated in her relationships with her parents, lovers, and self. Noda also examined these multiple subjectivities within a three-part conversation between lesbians White, Pink, and Green about monetary success, intimacy and love, drugs, and religion in her experimental play *Aw Shucks! (Shigata Ga Nai),* which she directed at San Francisco's Asian American Theater Company in May and June 1981. For example, Pink addresses her complex social location as both an ethnic and sexual minority when she talks about being a lesbian daughter of parents who had been interned in a concentration camp (referring to the U.S. government's internment of persons of Japanese descent in 1942). Noda's poetry and fiction were published in numerous anthologies and journals, including the poem "One, Two, Three!" in the inaugural issue of *Yellow Silk,* a journal dedicated to erotica, in 1981.

In her prose writings, Noda draws upon her experience as a Japanese American lesbian and feminist in addressing the experiences of Asian American women and lesbians within the Asian American community. Noda contributed to two special issues of *Bridge: An Asian American Perspective,* the winter 1978–1979 and spring 1979 issues, dedicated to Asian American women and edited by Genny Lim and Judy Yung. In the spring 1979 issue, "Coming Out: We Are Here in the Asian American Community: A Dialogue with Three Asian Women" by Barbara Noda, Kitty Tsui, and Zee Wong, addresses the silences within the Asian American community regarding homosexuality and specifically lesbians. Noda called for an Asian American movement inclusive of all members of the community regardless of sexual orientation and gender and for a political awareness that addressed the intersections of gender, race, and sexuality. In the summer of 1980, Noda provided a further critique of Asian American articulations of identity in her review of these issues for *Conditions: Six.* Identifying herself as "an Asian woman," she addresses the problem of bicultural identity, likening the assumed loss of identity to "being a woman in a male-dominated society" (pp. 203–204). Besides highlighting the diversity among Asian American women, Noda also calls for more attention within the community of Asian American writers to their "Asian roots" across the Pacific, an expression of identity not limited to defensive responses to the dominant society's negative images of Asian Americans. Finally, she says that Asian Americans "do not have to define themselves as feminists or lesbians, but where in their words do they acknowledge wholeheartedly the strength, assertiveness, and success in their lives as women?" (p. 211). This review motivated a spirited response by Nellie Wong in *Conditions: Seven,* highlighting key issues of debate within the Asian American and feminist communities. In 1983, Noda criticized the internal dynamics of second-wave feminism in her contribution to *This Bridge Called My Back: Writings by Radical Women of Color,* called "Lowriding through the Women's Movement." Although she has not published further works of poetry, Noda has written for the *New Phoenix Rising* about Asian American and Pacific Islander lesbian issues and has continued to be active in the San Francisco Bay area LGBT community.

Bibliography

Noda, Barbara. *Strawberries.* Oakland, Calif.: Shameless Hussy Press, 1979.

———. *Aw Shucks! (Shigata Ga Nai).* Unpublished play. Asian American Theater Company Archives, California Ethnic and Multicultural Archives, University of California at Santa Barbara, 1980.

———. Review of "Asian American Women, two special issues of *Bridge: An Asian American Perspective* (Vol. 6, No. 4, Winter 1978–9; Vol. 7, No. 1, Spring 1979)." *Conditions: Six* 2, no. 3 (Summer 1980): 203–211.

———. "Response." *Conditions: Seven* 3, no. 3 (1981): 185.

———. "Lowriding through the Women's Movement." In *This Bridge Called My Back: Writings By Radical Women of Color.* Edited by Cherríe Moraga and Gloria Anzaldúa. New York: Women of Color Press, 1983.

Noda, Barbara, Kitty Tsui, and Zee Wong. "Coming Out: We Are Here in the Asian American Community: A Dialogue with Three Asian Women." *Bridge: An Asian American Perspective* 7, no. 1 (Spring 1979): 22–24.

Wong, Nellie. "Asian American Women, Feminism, and Creativity." *Conditions: Seven* 3, no. 3 (1981) 177–184.

Karen Leong

NORTH AMERICAN MAN/BOY LOVE ASSOCIATION (NAMBLA)

Among LGBT groups, few can claim the degree of name recognition accorded to the North American Man/Boy Love Association (NAMBLA). Founded in 1978, NAMBLA has been among the most controversial groups in LGBT history. The group was initially inspired by the work of the Boston/Boise Committee, which formed in 1977 to defend a group of men indicted for running a boy prostitution ring based in Massachusetts. After the charges against all but one of the men were dismissed, the committee disbanded and NAMBLA was created. NAMBLA chapters have existed in New York City, Boston, Los Angeles, San Francisco, and Toronto; total membership has never been confirmed, but is estimated to have never been larger than one thousand.

It is difficult to determine the politics of NAMBLA, though by most accounts it supports consensual intergenerational relationships between men and teenage boys and opposes age-of-consent laws. NAMBLA has often resisted defining its politics, in part because many members fear police repression, in part because many members are anarchists who resist authoritarian structures, in part because many members are more interested in exposing the politics of their opponents, and in part because members do not always agree on the group's goals. Some who have belonged to or supported NAMBLA are motivated primarily by free speech, rights of assembly, and civil libertarian concerns. Others are motivated principally by visions of youth rights and youth liberation. A number of members see NAMBLA as a vehicle for challenging antisexual values that insist children are nonsexual. Some argue for the right and ability of post-pubescent teenagers to consent to sex with adults. Others extend this further to cover pre-pubescent children. And some, often using historical examples, defend the desirability, for both men and boys, of man-boy love.

NAMBLA's history includes a long string of hostile attacks and legal defenses involving both the organization and its supporters. Critics charge that the power differences between adults and minors exceeds those of most other relationships, that sex between adults and minors is intrinsically exploitative, that minors do not have the physical and psychological capacity to consent to sex with adults, and that sex between adults and minors constitutes sexual abuse. NAMBLA meetings have been kept under police surveillance; the Federal Bureau of Investigation has launched investigations; politicians, journalists, and religious leaders have attacked the organization; right-wing and left-wing activists have targeted the group; states have refused to allow NAMBLA to incorporate as a nonprofit agency; publicly identified members have been fired from their jobs; and public institutions have refused to allow the group to meet on their premises. LGBT groups, including community centers, pride march organizing committees, and the International Lesbian and Gay Association have struggled about whether to include or exclude NAMBLA. Most have favored exclusion.

As even some critics acknowledge, NAMBLA members have not been secretive about their beliefs and practices. On the contrary, the group maintains a formidable list of publications, available in many bookstores and libraries. The Harvard University Library, as well as several other prominent repositories, carry runs of the group's publications, including *NAMBLA News, NAMBLA Bulletin, NAMBLA Journal,* and *Gayme.* A series called NAMBLA Topics addresses mostly legal issues, although number 4 is called *Boys Speak Out on Man/Boy Love* (1986); number 5 offers an anthology, *Poems of Love and Liberation* (1996); and number 8 (1998) carries a short story, "Voodoo," by Ken Esser. The group also published *A Witchhunt Foiled: The FBI vs. NAMBLA* (1985). Nor has NAMBLA shied away from appropriate public venues, including LGBT pride parades, radio and television programs, and protest marches.

Despite its controversy, the organization has had a remarkable group of supporters, members, and defenders. Allen Ginsberg spoke at a NAMBLA conference in the 1980s. The American Civil Liberties Union has defended NAMBLA; the *New York Times* has criticized the firing of group members; and Camille Paglia has criticized NAMBLA's critics. Member Edward Hougen and his wife Margaret Hougen ministered to the Metropolitan Community Church in Boston and also published the popular international biweekly *Guide.* Bob Rhodes, a federal government attorney, provided NAMBLA with essential legal advice. David Thorstad, formerly active in the Socialist Workers Party and the Gay Activists Alliance, offered NAMBLA experienced leadership. John Mitzel wrote *The Boston Sex Scandal* (1980), which novelist and critic Edmund White called "irreverent, hilarious, and hard-hitting." Tom Reeves was active in the civil rights and antiwar movements, neighborhood organizing, and housing advocacy. Perhaps the youngest member of the group, Bill Andriette—who joined when he was fifteen years old—became a key NAMBLA writer, thinker, worker, and spokesperson.

At the beginning of the twenty-first century, the final chapter on NAMBLA has yet to be written, but none can question the fact that debates about love and conflict between the generations will not soon disappear. Historians and psychologists have recently attempted to understand the social construction of childhood sexuality, pedophilia, and abuse. Michel Foucault, in his introduction to *The History of Sexuality* (1978), identified the "masturbating child" and the "homosexual" as sources of anxiety in the modern age. Expanding on Foucault and others, James R. Kincaid, in *Child-Loving: the Erotic Child and Victorian Culture* (1992), maintained: "By insisting so loudly on the innocence, purity and asexuality of the child, we have created a subversive echo experience, corruption, eroticism."

Bibliography

Kincaid, James R. *Child-Loving: The Erotic Child and Victorian Culture.* New York: Routledge, 1992.

Levine, Judith. *Harmful to Minors: The Perils of Protecting Children from Sex.* Minneapolis: University of Minnesota Press, 2002.

Mitzel, John. *The Boston Sex Scandal.* Boston: Glad Day Books, 1980.

Thorstad, David. *A Witchhunt Foiled: The FBI vs. NAMBLA.* New York: NAMBLA, 1985.

Tsang, Daniel. *The Age Taboo: Gay Male Sexuality, Power, and Consent.* Boston: Alyson Publications, 1981.

Charles Shively

See also CHUA, SIONG-HUAT; INTERGENERATIONAL SEX AND RELATIONSHIPS.

NORTHAMPTON

Called "The Happy Valley" by some, the "Lesbian Capital of the Northeast" by others, and "Lesbianville, USA" by the *National Enquirer,* Northampton, Massachusetts, has a rich and varied history that has only become widely known as a haven for LGBT people in the post-Stonewall era. However, the town's diversity and tolerance, not just for LGBT people, stretches back over many years. Incorporated in 1654, the town is home to a community made up of a varied cross-section of people; many artists and musicians live and work alongside farmers, professors, students, young professionals, and others. The town's history reflects this assortment of people. In the eighteenth century, Jonathan Edwards preached in Northampton for twenty-three years, until his parishioners handed him his walking papers; Shays's Rebellion took place in the area from 1786 to 1787; and philanthropists of all stripes have played a huge part in shaping the town's direction, whether that was by donating money to local schools or helping fund large concert halls. Northampton is home to the nation's first municipal theater, the Academy of Music, built in 1890. Some of the many notable people who have passed through the town include Daniel Webster, Ralph Waldo Emerson, Sojourner Truth, and Ethel and Lionel Barrymore. Significant parts of John Irving's *The Cider House Rules* were filmed in Northampton, as was a section of the 1966 film version of Edward Albee's play *Who's Afraid of Virginia Woolf?*

Residents of the town have included an amazingly wide range of people as varied as Sylvester Graham, who invented the graham cracker in addition to promoting innovative ideas about healthy living and eating habits. United States President Calvin Coolidge practiced law in an office on Main Street that is now home to Fitzwilly's restaurant (as much a landmark as Thorne's Marketplace, which opened in 1979 just before the downtown economic boom Northampton experienced during the early to middle 1980s). Coolidge, elected president in 1923, served as Northampton's mayor for two years prior to his stint as State Senator. Author and poet Sylvia Plath attended Smith College during the early 1950s (and wrote about it in her quasi-autobiographical novel *The Bell Jar*). In the 1980s local cartoonists Kevin Eastman and Peter Laird launched the wildly famous Teenage Mutant Ninja Turtles. In 1990, Eastman founded the Words and Pictures Museum, also on Main Street, which stayed open from 1992 to 1999, when it was transformed into an online virtual museum.

Economically, Northampton sat in an ideal location for early industry, as it is situated almost equidistant from Boston, New York City, and Albany. Initially limited by the very few transportation options over the Connecticut River (just one, in fact: the ferry), bridges, canals, and the railroad all appeared within forty years of one another. Fittingly, an industrial boom resulted, and Northampton developed with an emphasis on the silk trade.

Northampton is also well known as a site for education, primarily because of the prestigious all-women's Smith College, whose campus is a very brief walk from the bustling commerce of Main Street, where galleries, funky shops, and restaurants rub proverbial elbows with one another. In addition, there are four other colleges and a university not far from Northampton: Amherst, Hampshire, Mount Holyoke, and the University of Massachusetts at Amherst. Not far from UMass Amherst, in fact, is the Stonewall Center, which was one of the nation's first LGBT centers on college and university campuses. Northampton is where a number of off-campus students from these nearby institutions of higher learning make their homes. This link with education is not by any means limited to college and university involvement with the town. Northampton's long history includes some of the best-known prep schools for girls in the 1800s, as well as the Clarke School for the Deaf, which is widely considered progressive in its methods and educational mission.

Primarily known for being LGBT friendly (with the possible exception of the issue of FTM transmen who enroll as women at Smith and later transition to men during their time at the all women's college), Northampton has long been—and remains to this day—politically progressive. A Free Congregational Society was first organized in Northampton in 1863; this was a group that called for racial equality, radical change in education, women's rights, and the reform of child labor standards, in addition to temperance. In 2002 Northampton was one of very few cities in Massachusetts to pass resolutions resisting and urging the repeal of the USA Patriot Act.

Smith's inclusion within the town has encouraged an atmosphere friendly to feminism and to women's concerns. As such, it seems unsurprising that lesbians would want to live, work, and settle in the area. By the early 2000s a substantial LGBT population existed in Northampton, one of the largest LGBT groups found outside of a major city, and the lesbian population in the town was dramatically larger than the population of gay men. This gender disparity is fairly unusual in LGBT communities, which may be part of why Northampton earned the "Lesbian Capital of the Northeast" moniker. The annual Northampton Lesbian Festival, held during the summer, may be another.

Like Smith's students, LGBT people are readily visible in Northampton, though they certainly do not dominate the town's population. In fact, no one group does: the town's population is generally balanced, diverse, and tolerant. It is queer-friendly, obviously, but anyone coming to Northampton to see nothing but lesbians in the streets will be sorely disappointed. Still, due to the high numbers of visible LGBT people, one may well see same-sex displays of affection at any given time (not just during a Pride festival), and there are out LGBT people who hold offices within city government (including openly lesbian Mayor Mary Claire Higgins). In addition, the Political Alliance is based in Northampton. This group makes sure LGBT issues are being addressed by local politicians, researches and sponsors candidates, and holds voter registration drives and public forums on Hate Crimes (and other topics) in addition to pushing for domestic partnership benefits for Northampton city employees—not something a person would expect to find in the average American city.

Bibliography

Gay.com. http://www.gay.com.

Northampton Chamber of Commerce. Available from http://www.northamptonuncommon.com.

Northampton, Massachusetts. Available from http://www.noho.com.

Van Vorhis, Jacqueline. *The Look of Paradise: A Pictorial History of Northampton, Massachusetts, 1654 to 1984.* Northampton, Mass.: Phoenix Publishing, 1984.

Anne N. Thalheimer

NUGENT, Richard Bruce (b. 2 July 1906; d. 27 May 1987), gay writer, artist.

Richard Bruce Nugent was born in Washington, D.C., to Pauline Minerva Bruce Nugent and Richard Henry Nugent, Jr. His father, a Pullman porter and messenger for the U.S. Supreme Court, died when Nugent was thirteen, leaving his widow and children in difficult financial circumstances, despite the Bruce family's prominence in Washington's African American elite. Nugent's mother relocated to New York to find employment. Nugent and his younger brother, Gary Lambert "Pete" Nugent, who became a renowned tap dancer in the 1930s, joined her there several months later.

Nugent attended Washington's distinguished Dunbar High School for one year in 1919–1920. The move to New York, however, ended his formal education, rendering his subsequent literary and artistic achievements all the more remarkable. Nugent found work as a delivery boy, a bellhop, and, more important to his future, an art apprentice at the catalog house Stone, Van Dresser. He also took classes at the New York Evening School of Industrial Arts and the Traphagen School of Fashion.

Returning to Washington in 1925, Nugent frequented the salon of the poet Georgia Douglas Johnson, where he met Langston Hughes and attracted the attention of Howard University professor and Harlem Renaissance leader Alain Locke. Locke included Nugent's story "Sahdji" in his important 1925 anthology, *The New Negro.* Nugent's first published poem, "Shadow," appeared in *Opportunity,* the monthly magazine of the National Urban League, at about the same time.

In 1926, back in New York, Nugent joined the informal group of younger African American artists—Wallace Thurman, Zora Neale Hurston, Hughes, and Aaron Douglas among them—that produced *FIRE!!*, a short-lived but important literary quarterly. *FIRE!!*'s first and only issue contained Nugent's "Smoke, Lilies and Jade," a modernist prose composition that quite openly expressed Nugent's homosexual sensibility. He was the first black writer to reveal his same-sex interests unambiguously in print. During this same period Nugent wrote a novella, *Geisha Man,* that was even more explicit; it remained unpublished during Nugent's lifetime. Also dating from the late 1920s are Nugent's transgressive "Bible stories," in which same-sex desire is woven into the Gospels. One of his most powerful pieces, "Pope Pius the Only," a first-person, stream-of-consciousness narrative of being lynched, appeared in the "little magazine" *Challenge* in 1937. Nugent found employment with the Federal Writers' Project around this time.

Nugent was as much an artist as a writer. His drawings appeared in *Opportunity* and were featured in the important anthology *Ebony and Topaz* (1927). In 1930 he created the "Salome Series" of watercolor drawings of male and female bodies named for biblical figures and rendered in the art deco style; like *Geisha Man,* they were published posthumously. The touring Harmon Foundation exhibit of 1931 included four Nugent pieces.

Also involved in the theater, Nugent appeared in the 1927 production of *Porgy,* the play that preceded George Gershwin's opera *Porgy and Bess.* After its Broadway run, the play toured for over two years with Nugent in the cast. In 1933 Nugent appeared on Broadway again, this time as a dancer, in *Run, Little Chillun.*

In subsequent decades, Nugent continued to write, draw, and paint, but little of his work was published or shown publicly. Stylistically, his visual art reached an apex of elegance and refinement in the 1940s. He wrote several unpublished novels exploring relationships between men; he was particularly fascinated with men who considered themselves "straight," but who found emotional and sexual succor with homosexuals like himself. The transgressive nature of his work, his bohemian lifestyle, and his aversion to systematic self-promotion inhibited public recognition of his creative talent.

Nugent's early writing was influenced by Carl Van Vechten's mannered novels of America's upper-class bohemia—especially by the first, *Peter Whiffle,* which was, in turn, inspired by Joris-Karl Huysmans's notorious 1884 novel, *À rebours.* The English aesthetes of the fin de siècle also influenced Nugent, as did Erté and other artists featured in *Harper's Bazaar* and *Vogue.* Nugent's open association with this "decadent" tradition generated criticism from African American intellectuals—including even his former patron Alain Locke, a homosexual himself but more closeted than Nugent, who believed that it was the duty of the African American artist to represent the black community and express its cultural essence.

In 1952, much to the surprise of his friends, Nugent married Grace Marr, a nurse-educator and daughter of a prominent Pittsburgh minister. Their platonic marriage lasted until her death in 1969; they had no children. Nugent died eighteen years later in Hoboken, New Jersey.

Bibliography

Garber, Eric. "Richard Bruce Nugent." In *Dictionary of Literary Biography.* Volume 51: *Afro-American Writers from the Harlem Renaissance to 1940.* Edited by Trudier Harris and Thadious M. Davis. Farmington Hills, Mich.: Gale Group, 1987, pp. 213–221.

Garber, Eric. "A Spectacle in Color: The Lesbian and Gay Subcultures of Jazz Age Harlem." In *Hidden from History: Reclaiming the Gay and Lesbian Past.* Edited by Martin B. Duberman, Martha Vicinus, and George Chauncey. New York: NAL Books, 1989, pp. 318–331.

McBreen, Ellen. "Biblical Gender Bending in Harlem: The Queer Performance of Nugent's Salome." *Art Journal* 57, no. 3 (Fall 1998): 22–28.

Nugent, Richard Bruce. *Gay Rebel of the Harlem Renaissance: Selections from the Work of Richard Bruce Nugent.* Edited by Thomas H. Wirth. Durham, N.C.: Duke University Press, 2002.

Thomas H. Wirth

See also HARLEM RENAISSANCE; LITERATURE; LOCKE, ALAIN; THURMAN, WALLACE; VISUAL ART.

O

O'HARA, Frank **(b. 27 March 1926; d. 24 July 1966), poet, playwright, art critic.**

Frank O'Hara was a highly innovative postmodern poet whose work was unusual in its stylistic diversity. One of the members of the New York School of poets (a group that also included Kenneth Koch, James Schuyler, and John Ashbery), he was a contemporary of the Beats and the Black Mountain poets. His poetry shows an eclectic array of influences and interests: European symbolism and surrealism; the American poetic tradition of Walt Whitman, William Carlos Williams, and Hart Crane; Abstract Expressionist painting; Pop Art; cinema; and classical and contemporary music. His work ranges from early surrealist pieces to his exuberant and highly original "I do this I do that" poems, which chart his walks around New York during his lunch hour. Above all an urban poet, O'Hara wrote poems that are notable for the way they map New York in the 1950s and 1960s, but also link it to wider global, historical, and psychological spaces.

Born in Baltimore, O'Hara attended St. John's High School in Worcester, Massachusetts, and then served as a sonarman third class on the destroyer U.S.S. *Nicholas* in World War II. He graduated from Harvard College in 1950, having changed his major from music to English, and was also one of the founders of the Poet's Theatre in Cambridge, Massachusetts. He was awarded a Master of Arts degree at the University of Michigan, Ann Arbor, in 1951 and then moved to New York, where he published his first book, *A City Winter, and Other Poems* (1952). He was employed briefly on the front desk of the Museum of Modern Art but resigned to become editor of *Art News* (1953–1955).

O'Hara rejoined the Museum of Modern Art in 1955 as special assistant in the International Program and became associate curator in 1960. During this period he organized many seminal exhibitions by Abstract Expressionist painters such as Willem de Kooning, Franz Kline, Barnett Newman, Mark Rothko, and Robert Motherwell, as well as the sculptor David Smith and painters of the New York School, including Grace Hartigan and Michael Goldberg. He was an astute art critic and wrote an influential monograph on Jackson Pollock. His art criticism was collected posthumously in *Art Chronicles* (1975) and *Standing Still and Walking in New York* (1983), both edited by Donald Allen. From 1957 to 1965 he published five volumes of poetry: *Meditations in An Emergency* (1957); *Odes*, with five serigraphs by Mike Goldberg (1960); *Second Avenue* (1960); *Lunch Poems* (1964); and *Love Poems (Tentative Title)* (1965). O'Hara also wrote a number of plays, gathered retrospectively in *Selected Plays* (1978).

O'Hara was an improvisational writer who often dashed off poems on his lunch hour or in the company of other people. His poems are very intense but at the same time humorous, talk based, gossipy, and poetically subversive. The focal point of an artistic coterie, O'Hara was also a prolific collaborator: his co-produced works include poems with Kenneth Koch and Bill Berkson, a series of lithographs with Larry Rivers, poem-paintings with Norman Bluhm, and a film with Alfred Leslie. A devotee of all the arts, O'Hara had an enormous appetite for films, concerts, and dance performances, references to which saturate his poems.

O'Hara was gay, and the intensity of his friendships was legendary. The range of his relationships was also immense, as he pursued close friendships with several women, most notably Bunny Lang, Jane Freilicher, Grace Hartigan, and Patsy Southgate. These women, as well as male lovers including Larry Rivers, Joe LeSueur, and Vincent Warren; and male friends such as Bill Berkson and Kenneth Koch figure prominently in his poems. O'Hara died at the age of forty, when he was hit by a beach-buggy on Fire Island, a well-known gay resort near New York City. His *Collected Poems* (1971), *Selected Poems* (1974), *Early Writing* (1977), and *Poems Retrieved* (1977) were edited by Donald Allen and published after his death.

O'Hara's poetry contains many allusions to gay culture and activities, such as cruising and cross-dressing, and his poems sometimes adopt attitudes that are campy or ethically transgressive. His poetry, nevertheless, is not as unambiguously gay as that of Allen Ginsberg; in some O'Hara poems it is not even apparent that the poet's lover is male. His homosexuality is arguably most obvious in the vocabulary and style of some of his poems: it has a linguistic, as much as a thematic, presence in his work. This more implicit referencing of his sexuality does not, however, stem from political or social evasiveness about his sexual identity. In fact, O'Hara was ahead of his time in his attitude toward his gayness. His poems convey a fluid and open sense of gender and sexual boundaries, creating a "morphing" sexuality that is more reflective of today's discourses and practices than of those most visible in the 1950s and 1960s.

Bibliography

Berkson, Bill, and Joe LeSueur, eds. *Homage to Frank O'Hara.* Berkeley: Creative Arts Book Company, 1980.

Diggory, Terence, and Stephen Paul Miller. *The Scene of My Selves: New Work on New York School Poets.* Orono, Maine: National Poetry Foundation, 2001.

Gooch, Brad. *City Poet: The Life and Times of Frank O'Hara.* New York: Knopf, 1993.

Perloff, Marjorie. *Frank O'Hara: Poet among Painters.* 2d ed. Chicago: University of Chicago Press, 1998.

Smith, Hazel. *Hyperscapes in the Poetry of Frank O'Hara: Difference, Homosexuality, Topography.* Liverpool, U.K.: Liverpool University Press, 2000.

Hazel Smith

See also CRANE, HART; JOHNS, JASPER; THEATER AND PERFORMANCE; VISUAL ART; WHITMAN, WALT.

OBSCENITY LAW AND POLICY. see CENSORSHIP, OBSCENITY, AND PORNOGRAPHY LAW AND POLICY.

OCCUPATIONS. see EMPLOYMENT AND OCCUPATIONS.

OLIVEROS, Pauline (b. 30 May 1932), composer, musician.

Pauline Oliveros is an out lesbian and avant-garde U.S. composer. She uses her musical compositions to challenge the prevailing stereotypes of sexuality that support the belief that only men can make music.

Born in Houston, Texas, into a musical family, Oliveros and her older brother grew up with two strong role models of women in music. Her father, John B. Oliveros Jr., abandoned the family in 1941. To make ends meet, Oliveros's mother and her maternal grandmother gave piano lessons. Her mother, Edith Oliveros Gutierrez, later became a composer of some note.

In light of her family background, it is not surprising that Oliveros displayed an early interest in music. She spent her childhood years mastering piano, French horn, and the accordion. The last instrument became Oliveros's lifelong passion, and it introduced her to a man who helped to shape her pioneering compositions.

Oliveros's accordion teacher taught the budding musician to listen to combination tones, the added sounds that are sometimes heard when two or more tones are played together. Both combination tones and the very act of listening later served as important elements of Oliveros's musical pioneering.

Oliveros's interest in the concept of deep listening, the practice of hearing everything possible as well as the sounds of music, grew out of a childhood experience.

In the 1940s, the teenage Oliveros played accordion in a polka band to earn extra income. One day, the group attempted to play German polkas in a Polish hall. Unfortunately for the band, the German invasion of Poland during World War II did not make German music a particularly popular choice among the Poles, and an angry audience forced the musicians to abandon the stage. The experience alerted Oliveros to the many ways in which music can affect people.

Determined to make a career as a musician, Oliveros entered the University of Houston as an accordion major in 1949. She became interested in composition and, dissatisfied with the conservative approach at Houston, decided to leave the university in 1952 for a more innovative program. Packing her accordion, Oliveros headed to San Francisco. From 1952 to 1960, she supported herself there as a composer and performer. In 1957, San

Francisco State College awarded Oliveros a B.A in composition studies, an unusual achievement for a woman.

Few women composers existed in the 1950s and 1960s, making Oliveros acutely aware of sex-based discrimination within the field. Such prejudice limited her career trajectory and led her to design compositions that act as feminist statements about artistic freedom and self expression. She subsequently listed the advancement of women in music alongside composition as her chief areas of professional focus.

In 1958, Oliveros began experimenting with digital delay and the expanded accordion, part of a form of music known as electronic music that subsequently became commonplace in academic and industrial circles. In the late 1960s, the faculty of the Music Department at the University of California at San Diego decided to establish a graduate course in electronic music, and Oliveros was one of the few people on the West Coast qualified to teach it. In 1967 she joined the department as a non-tenure-track lecturer. Her credentials included service at the San Francisco Tape Music Center as cofounder and codirector from 1961 to 1966 and work at the Mills College Tape Music Center in Oakland as inaugural director in 1966 and 1967. She eventually won tenure at San Diego but resigned her professorship in 1981. Exhausted by dealing with the politics of academia and frustrated by the academic preference for baroque and classical music, she decided to resume freelance composing and performing.

Of the more than one hundred diverse compositions Oliveros has produced, the most important include *To Valerie Solanas and Marilyn Monroe in Recognition of Their Desperation* (1970) and *Sonic Meditations* (1971). The first piece is one of the earliest attempts to relate music to feminism. Oliveros came out publicly as a lesbian upon releasing *Sonic*, a collection of twenty-five short guides for improvisation that require no formal musical training to perform. Like *Sonic*, many of Oliveros's works are developed collaboratively with lesbian and bisexual women artists. Her musical recordings include *The Roots of the Moment* (1988), *Deep Listening* (1989), and *Crone Music* (1989).

In 1985, Oliveros established in Kingston, New York, the Pauline Oliveros Foundation for research in art and technology. She remained with this organization while frequently accepting academic appointments as a composer in residence and visiting professor.

Bibliography

Gagne, Cole. *Soundpieces 2: Interviews with American Composers.* Metuchen, N.J.: Scarecrow Press, 1993.

Oliveros, Pauline. *Software for People: Collected Writings 1963–80.* Baltimore: Smith Publications, 1984.

Taylor, Timothy D. "The Gendered Construction of the Musical Self: The Music of Pauline Oliveros." *Musical Quarterly* 77 (1993): 385–396.

Von Gunden, Heidi. *The Music of Pauline Oliveros.* Metuchen, N.J.: Scarecrow Press, 1983.

Caryn E. Neumann

See also MUSIC: CLASSICAL.

OLIVIA RECORDS

The lesbian-feminist record label Olivia Records released its first "fund-raiser" 45 rpm single in 1974, featuring Meg Christian singing "Lady" by Carole King on one side and Cris Williamson singing her composition "If It Weren't for the Music" on the other. Olivia Records went on to become one of the most successful of several women-owned-and-operated record labels that emerged during the women's movement of the 1970s, releasing over forty albums in twenty years. Declining record sales, due in part to a shift in the politics and musical tastes of younger lesbians, forced Olivia to supplement and, eventually, replace music with another business enterprise. In 1990, Olivia transformed itself into a lesbian vacation company, Olivia Cruises and Resorts; over the next decade the company phased out its recording enterprise altogether.

Olivia Records began as an attempt to put lesbian separatist ideology into practice. In the early 1970s in Washington, D.C., a separatist collective calling itself The Furies published an influential eponymous newspaper that frequently articulated the goals of "cultural feminism": the development of women-identified arts, religions, communities, and economic institutions. The May 1973 issue of *The Furies* featured a bold and controversial article entitled "Building Feminist Institutions" by Helaine Harris and Lee Schwing, which advocated feminist entrepreneurship and businesses (euphemistically called "institutions"). Theoretically, feminist institutions would offer economic self-sufficiency to the women's community, which would allow structural economic and social changes. Harris, along with two other Furies members Ginny Berson and Jennifer Woodul, were casting about for an appropriate feminist institution to found; eventually, they joined forces with local folk singer Meg Christian and members of the Radical Lesbians of Ann Arbor to create the Olivia Records collective in January 1973. The idea of a record company apparently grew from a chance remark made by Cris Williamson during a radio

selected discography of olivia and second wave records, 1975–1984

Meg Christian, *I Know You Know* (Olivia, 1975)

Cris Williamson, *The Changer and the Changed* (Olivia, 1975)

BeBe K'Roche, *BeBe K'Roche* (Olivia, 1976)

Various Artists, *Lesbian Concentrate* (Olivia, 1977)

Meg Christian, *Face The Music* (Olivia, 1977)

Trish Nugent, *Foxglove Woman* (Olivia 1977)

Woody Simmons, *Oregon Mountains* (Olivia, 1977)

Teresa Trull, *The Ways A Woman Can Be* (Olivia, 1977)

Linda Tillery, *Linda Tillery* (Olivia, 1978)

Mary Watkins, *Something Moving* (Olivia, 1978)

Cris Williamson, *Strange Paradise* (Olivia, 1978)

Teresa Trull, *Let It Be Known* (Olivia, 1980)

Meg Christian, *Turning It Over* (Olivia, 1981)

Cris Williamson, *Blue Rider* (Olivia, 1982)

Meg Christian and Cris Williamson, *Meg and Cris At Carnegie Hall* (Second Wave, 1983)

Alicia Bridges, *Hocus Pocus* (Second Wave, 1984)

Meg Christian, *From the Heart* (Olivia, 1984)

Tret Fure, *Terminal Hold* (Second Wave, 1984)

Cris Williamson, Prairie Fire (Olivia, 1984)

interview with Christian and Berson, but it was Christian who, in 1974, recorded Olivia's first full-length album of songs, *I Know You Know,* released in 1975.

The First Recordings of Women's Music

Two important feminist recording projects preceded Olivia's first album. In 1972, the Chicago Women's Liberation Rock Band and New Haven Women's Liberation Rock Band joined forces to release *Mountain Moving Day* (on the independent label Rounder Records), with each band recording one side of the album. Despite choosing the idiom of rock music, dubbed and spurned as sexist "cock rock" by feminists in the middle 1970s, both bands promoted the establishment of an alternative women-identified culture and worked to open up previously closed opportunities for women as musicians and musical technicians. One year later, folk singer Alix Dobkin, along with flautist Kay Gardner and bassist Patches Attom, formed the group Lavender Jane and within the year released the first album entirely produced and nationally distributed by women. *Lavender Jane Loves Women* first hit lesbian turntables in early 1974, at the same time Olivia Records released its inaugural single.

By the 1970s stylized or "urban" folk music had a strong association with grassroots leftist politics, established by activist musicians such as Woody Guthrie, Phil Ochs, Joan Baez, and the young Bob Dylan. This musical idiom, with its emphasis on sing-along refrains and message-laden lyrics over musical virtuosity, became a powerful consciousness-raising and community-building device for the Old and New Left, and later for cultural feminism. Christian's *I Know You Know* follows this tradition of political music, although her classical guitar training remained a prominent feature of her arrangements and a selling point for the album. On the back cover of the album and in interviews for feminist presses, Olivia Records publicized Christian as a serious performer "with a degree in music" and the album as "high quality women's music." The company also disclosed its ideological goals to provide technical training, decent and equal pay, and nonoppressive working conditions to women. However, as was evident in the marketing of its first album, the tension between professionalism and profitability on one hand and activism and equanimity on the other plagued Olivia Records throughout its early years.

I Know You Know unexpectedly sold more than ten thousand copies within the first year. A grassroots network of fans, resulting from Christian's rigorous cross-country tour of women-only venues, volunteered to act as regional distributors. About six months after the release of *I Know You Know,* Olivia Records released its second album, Williamson's *The Changer and the Changed* (1975), which remains the company's best-selling album. Williamson had recorded a commercial album in 1971 on the Ampex label that had become an underground hit in lesbian-feminist circles due in part to Christian's performances of those songs in concert. In contrast to the acoustic guitar-based style of Christian, Williamson's piano and rhythm-section ballads expanded "women's music" into soft rock styles. Furthermore, whereas most of Christian's songs on *I Know You Know* provided realistic details of lesbian desire and relationships—a youthful crush on a gym teacher, the gray area between shared and separate property within a lesbian relationship, secrecy within the family, and scars from social oppression—Williamson's more abstract lyrical themes on *The Changer and the Changed* largely concerned women's spirituality, internal emotional lives, and connection to the environment and cosmos. Within the first year of its release, Williamson's album for Olivia sold well over twice as many copies as Christian's and became the financial cornerstone of the Olivia Records catalog.

Problems with Success

In 1976 the four "big names" in women's music—Meg Christian, Margie Adam, Holly Near, and Cris Williamson—launched a "Women on Wheels" tour that began drawing audiences in the thousands, consolidating a sizeable niche market that would later that same year attend the first separatist Michigan Womyn's Music Festival. But by this time Adam, the pianist for Olivia Record's first two releases, had formed her own label, Pleiades Records, and Near had several years earlier formed Redwood Records with her parents. The women's music "industry" soon became mired in capitalistic competition. At one point Olivia Records even attempted to monopolize the network of volunteer distributors, who eventually formed their own separate organization, the Women's Independent Label Distributors (WILD). More important, however, within the next several years Olivia had to scale down its effort to produce the work of an array of unknown struggling female musicians and concentrate on its top-selling "stars." Despite the steady attempt to integrate African- and Latin-derived musical styles in the company catalog, the market for Olivia Records in the late 1970s and early 1980s remained largely white, middle-class, and aesthetically conservative. African American Olivia artists such as Mary Watkins and Linda Tillery, composing in the idioms of jazz, soul, and funk, sold poorly in comparison to the staple recordings of Christian and Williamson.

By the early 1980s a financially shaky Olivia Records reorganized into a more efficient, hierarchical corporate structure and created the subsidiary label Second Wave Records, featuring nonseparatist artists who often used male musicians, wrote less political lyrics, and composed more mainstream pop and rock songs. Ironically, the first release on Second Wave Records was a return to Olivia's roots: the double-album live recording of Christian and Williamson in concert at Carnegie Hall, celebrating Olivia Records' tenth anniversary. Second Wave's catalog notably includes three albums by the veteran sound engineer and studio musician Tret Fure (*Terminal Hold,* 1984; *Edges of the Heart,* 1986; *Time Turns the Moon,* 1990) and *Hocus Pocus* (1984) by Alicia Bridges, who had previously recorded the 1978 disco hit "I Love the Night Life." Despite the intention to produce mainstream-friendly artists under its Second Wave subsidiary, Olivia Records still shied away from harder-edged rock sounds, rejecting an audition tape sent to them, for instance, by a then-little-known Melissa Etheridge.

Although Olivia Records struggled with and ultimately succumbed to mainstream capitalist pressures, the artists and ideology of its early years had a profound impact on the landscape of popular music, especially in the middle to late 1980s with the rise of androgynous and lesbian-coded female folk-based singer/songwriters who recorded on major labels or healthy independents. These included "out and proud" artists such as Phranc (Island), Two Nice Girls (Rough Trade), Indigo Girls (Epic), and bisexual Ani DiFranco (who followed Olivia Records in creating her own label, Righteous Babe Records), as well as "keep 'em guessing" artists such as Tracy Chapman (Elektra) and Michelle Shocked (Polygram). The short-lived Riot Grrrl scene that developed in Washington, D.C., and Olympia, Washington, in the early 1990s also deserve mention. These women musicians, playing a furious punk- and grunge-derived rock and preaching feminist and antihomophobic messages, formed support networks and independent labels maintained through underground publications ('zines) and mini-festivals, reviving the grassroots feminist spirit of The Furies and the economic/musical activism of their foremothers at Olivia Records.

Bibliography

Armstrong, Tony. "Olivia Turns Twenty." *Hot Wire* 10, no. 1 (January 1994): 24–26, 46–47, 62.

Dlugacz, Judy. "If It Weren't for the Music: 15 Years of Olivia Records (Part 1)." *Hot Wire* 4, no. 3 (July 1988): 28–31, 52.

Dlugacz, Judy. "If It Weren't for the Music: 15 Years of Olivia Records (Part 2)." *Hot Wire* 5, no. 1 (January 1989): 20, 22–23.

Grimstad, Kirsten, and Susan Rennie, eds. *The New Woman's Survival Sourcebook.* New York: Knopf, 1975.

Kort, Michele. "Sisterhood Is Profitable." *Mother Jones* 8, no. 4 (1983): 39–44.

Lont, Cynthia M. "Women's Music: No Longer a Private Party." In *Rockin' the Boat: Mass Music and Mass Movements.* Edited by Reebee Garofalo. Boston: South End Press, 1992, pp. 241–253.

Moira, Fran. "The Muses of Olivia: Our Own Economy, Our Own Song." *Off Our Backs* 4 (August/September 1974): 2–3.

Peraino, Judith A. *Listening to the Sirens: Musical Technologies of Queer Identity.* Berkeley: University of California Press (forthcoming).

Pollock, Mary. "The Politics of Women's Music: A Conversation with Linda Tillery and Mary Watkins." *Frontiers: A Journal of Women Studies* 10, no. 1 (1988): 14–19.

Schwing, Lee, and Helaine Harris. "Building Feminist Institutions." *The Furies* (May/June 1973): 2–3.

Woodul, Jennifer. "Olivia Records." In *The New Woman's Survival Sourcebook*. Edited by Susan Rennie and Kirsten Grimstad. New York: Knopf, 1975, pp. 177–178.

Judith A. Peraino

See also BUSINESSES; FURIES; MUSIC: WOMEN'S; TRANSGENDER ORGANIZATIONS AND PERIODICALS.

ONE

ONE magazine was the premiere publication of the homophile movement. The first issue was published in January 1953 by a group of homosexual men and women in Los Angeles. The magazine witnessed changes in content, format, and editorial staff over the following fifteen years until it ceased publication in 1968 (although it reappeared briefly in 1972).

The beginning of *ONE* magazine is attributed to a group of women and men who participated in the Mattachine Foundation. The main activity of the foundation was sponsoring discussion groups in which gay men and some lesbians gathered to discuss a variety of issues of particular relevance to sex variance. A favorite topic of the discussion groups—and, ultimately, a key concern of the homophile movement overall—was the problem of communication. Participants in the discussion groups wondered how they might help distribute objective, nonjudgmental information about law, religion, and psychology as it related to homosexuality when the only avenue of communication available was the mainstream press, which in 1953 was interested in homosexuality only if the story was sensational. The resolution of this quandary seemed clear to several discussion group participants at a meeting in October 1952: publish a magazine in which homosexuals (and experts sympathetic to the cause of the homophile movement) could create a meaningful and influential counterdiscourse. Rather than start a magazine under the auspices of the Mattachine Foundation, which at the time was beginning to experience some internal problems, a group that included Dale Jennings, Don Slater, Martin Block, and Dorr Legg started the independent magazine *ONE*. The title of the magazine was derived from a Thomas Carlyle poem celebrating fraternity, which declared "a mystic bond of brotherhood makes all men one."

Although *ONE* magazine was independent of the Mattachine Foundation, it was a project of ONE, Inc., which was founded simultaneously with the magazine in late 1952. Publications was only one of four "divisions" of

ONE. This cover shows blind Justice and the quote "Cheap Pornography . . . Vulgar & Indecent—says the Court"—apparently before the magazine's de facto U.S. Supreme Court victory.

ONE, Inc.; the other three divisions were education, research, and social service. Although the magazine and the social services divisions were for the most part moribund by the early 1970s, the ONE Institute continues to exist in 2003 as an archive and research institute.

One of the reasons that *ONE* can be described as the premiere homophile magazine is that its standards were at a level somewhat higher (although inconsistently so) than its chief competitors in the 1950s and early 1960s: the *Mattachine Review* and the *Ladder*. *ONE* featured articles by respected writers like Norman Mailer, James Barr, and Donald Webster Cory; it regularly published the research findings of nonhomophobic psychologists like Evelyn Hooker and Blanche Baker; it contained numerous, detailed accounts of news related to homosexuals around the world, many of which were collected and excerpted by Jim Kepner; it was the one homophile publication to strive for a degree of balance (but never equality) between articles about male and female homosexuals; and it printed scores of essays that discussed the emerging gay culture from the perspective not of a lawyer or a psychologist but of an insider, a participant. Typical, for example, was the July 1958 article, "The Gay Beach," in which the reader is treated to a lively but reasonably realistic conversation between two gay men as they visit a gay beach in Southern California. Not only do the two men gossip and cruise, but they muse about the unfortunate divisions between homosexuals and heterosexuals as well as among homosexuals and they pine for a time when such divisions might be merely benign variations or preferences. In addition to mostly intelligent, often sensitive articles, *ONE* contained photographs and drawings that, while tame even by the standards of the 1950s and 1960s, celebrated the gay male body and hinted at the more controversial physique publications then in circulation. The magazine also included advertising for other homophile organizations and publications and occasionally for presumably gay-owned or managed businesses.

Another *ONE*. This issue focuses on "Homosexual Rights" and features photographs of Thomas Hennings Jr. and Robert Hutchins on the cover.

It was precisely this sort of content that attracted the attention of U.S. postal authorities in Los Angeles. The authorities had delayed the distribution of the August 1953 issue, but they confiscated the October 1954 issue, declaring it "obscene, lewd, lascivious and filthy." With the future of the magazine (as well as other homophile publications) hanging in the balance, the editors of *ONE* appealed the action to the Federal District Court, the Ninth Court of Appeals, and, eventually, the U.S. Supreme Court. In its 13 January 1958 decision, the Supreme Court, without comment, overruled the decisions of the lower courts, thus making a de facto declaration that the issue of *ONE* in question was not obscene. In his book *Sexual Politics, Sexual Communities,* historian John D'Emilio describes this as the gay movement's "only significant victory during the 1950s" (p. 115).

Factionalism and personality conflict were features of the homophile movement from its very inception, but the ONE Institute and *ONE* magazine were at the center of one of the more sensational clashes, which has since come to be known as "The Heist." At the center of the conflict were Dorr Legg, who was the director of the institute and primarily interested in educational programs, and Don Slater, who was the editor of *ONE*. The quarrel was based on matters both ideological and personal, but was sufficiently contentious to drive Slater to an extreme action. Along with the help of a few supporters, in April 1965 Slater removed the contents of *ONE*'s Los Angeles office to a separate location and subsequently named it the Homosexual Information Center. As a result, for a four-month period, between May and August 1965, two separate *ONE* magazines were published: Slater's breakaway edition and the official ONE Institute version, edited by Richard Conger. Slater's *ONE* died quickly, but the edition published by the ONE Institute did so more slowly, lasting until early 1968.

The reasons for the demise of *ONE*, however, have as much to do with internal battles as they do external developments. The world of homosexual publications changed by the middle 1960s. All-in-one journals such as *ONE* and the *Mattachine Review* were losing favor to more specialized publications such as Guy Strait's bar-oriented newspapers in San Francisco (including *Citizen's News*), gay-male lifestyle magazines like Clark Polak's *Drum,* and, soon, more politically oriented publications like the *Los Angeles Advocate.* As the gay world grew and diversified in the 1960s, so did the requirements of its print culture.

Bibliography

D'Emilio, John. *Sexual Politics, Sexual Communities: The Making of a Homosexual Minority in the United States, 1940–1970,* 2nd edition. Chicago: University of Chicago Press, 1998.

Hansen, Joseph. *A Few Doors West of Hope: The Life and Times of Dauntless Don Slater.* Los Angeles: Homosexual Information Center, 1998.

Kepner, Jim. *Rough News—Daring Views: 1950s Pioneer Gay Press Journalism.* New York: Haworth Press, 1998.

Legg, Dorr, ed. *Homophile Studies in Theory and Practice.* Los Angeles: ONE Institute Press, 1994.

Marcus, Eric. *Making History: The Struggle for Gay and Lesbian Equal Rights, 1945–1990.* New York: HarperCollins, 1992.

Streitmatter, Rodger. *Unspeakable: The Rise of the Gay and Lesbian Press in America.* Boston: Faber and Faber, 1995.

Martin Meeker

See also CENSORSHIP, OBSCENITY, AND PORNOGRAPHY LAW AND POLICY; HOMOPHILE MOVEMENT; HOMOPHILE PRESS; LEGG, DORR; MATTACHINE SOCIETY; ONE INSTITUTE; PULP FICTION: GAY.

ONE INSTITUTE

Since its founding in 1955, the ONE Institute of Los Angeles has been a cornerstone institution for gay research. In 1956 the Institute offered the first college-level course on homosexuality from a gay-affirmative perspective on the premise that gay men and lesbians familiar with their group history, sociology, and anthropology could more effectively fight for their civil rights. Under the banner "homophile studies," the Institute's interdisciplinary curriculum challenged deeply embedded academic biases against homosexuality, laying the groundwork for present-day gay studies in universities across the country. In addition to its innovative classes, the Institute's library, subject files, and archival collections have offered a research base for a wide range of foundational gay research. Still in operation at the start of the twenty-first century, the ONE Institute remains the oldest and most enduring gay organization in the United States.

Founding

The ONE Institute was a staple institution of the Los Angeles–based homophile movement of the 1950s. It spun off from the Mattachine Foundation (later the Mattachine Society) when, in 1952, members of a Mattachine discussion group became frustrated with the Mattachine's "secret society" approach to mobilizing the gay minority. In an effort to boost the visibility and image of gay men and lesbians, these members abandoned Mattachine to found the nation's first openly homosexual national publication, whose first issue appeared in January 1953. Daring to print "The Homosexual Magazine" on the cover at the peak of the repressive McCarthy era, *ONE* magazine became the key voice of the homophile movement until its demise in 1967.

From *ONE* magazine's inception, however, several founders had more ambitious plans for the organization (operating under the name ONE, Inc.). The abysmal quality of published information about homosexuality during the 1950s compelled the group to consider education, research, and publishing high priorities. (Educational goals also allowed the magazine to operate under tax-exempt status.) During 1953 and 1954 the ordeal of writing, editing, assembling, and distributing the nation's first gay monthly kept the staff members busy, but once the magazine's operations ran smoothly, they conceived the ONE Institute in 1955 to handle the group's research and education goals.

The activists behind the ONE Institute sought to position themselves as official experts on homosexuality, wrestling the distinction away from psychiatrists, police chiefs, politicians, and other ill-informed, so-called experts widely quoted in the popular press. The psychiatrist Edmund Bergler, for example, often quoted in *Time* magazine and the *New York Times* as the nation's foremost expert on homosexuality, regularly horrified gay men and lesbians by insisting that homosexuality was a curable disease caused by "psychic masochism." The ONE Institute offered an official "homosexual viewpoint" to challenge such theories, supported by research produced from its libraries and classes. ONE's experts appeared in magazine articles and panel discussions criticizing prejudicial social attitudes throughout the 1950s and 1960s. ONE fell short of its ambition to become as respected as the Kinsey Institute, but the erudite, academic tone of ONE's representatives impressed both homosexual and heterosexual audiences. More importantly, the knowledge generated at the ONE Institute offered an intellectual foundation for the gay movement and gay consciousness.

Central Figures

The key figure behind the ONE Institute was W. Dorr Legg. In 1953 he became the business manager for *ONE* magazine under the fictitious name William Lambert; he also wrote articles for the magazine under several pseudonyms. Previously a landscape architect and college professor, Legg immersed himself in gay activism upon moving to Los Angeles in 1952, and in 1956 the ONE Institute became his life's work. Over the years, Legg's formidable intellect had mastered most college disciplines, reflected in hundreds of lectures on homosexual issues spanning the academic spectrum. In addition to teaching dozens of courses, Legg also handled most of the Institute's administrative work until his death in 1994.

Another important figure was Merritt Thompson, a retired University of Southern California School of Education professor with over fifty years of experience in education. Thompson assisted Dorr Legg in conceiving and structuring an interdisciplinary curriculum for the systematic study of homosexuality, which they called "homophile studies." Under the pseudonym Thomas Merritt, Thompson served as the Institute's first dean and taught several courses until ending his association with ONE in 1963.

In 1964 millionaire philanthropist and female-to-male transsexual Reed Erickson befriended Dorr Legg and, under the moniker of the Institute for the Study of Human Resources, funded the majority of the ONE Institute's activities for the next fifteen years. In 1981, upon the accreditation of ONE's graduate school, Erickson promised a new campus in a sprawling Los Angeles mansion, but unexpectedly rescinded his offer shortly after signing the papers, triggering a ten-year estate dispute that drained the ONE Institute of its resources, nearly destroying the organization.

Activities

ONE's classes were usually held in its cramped offices, limiting attendance until a move to more spacious quarters in 1961 gave the organization breathing space to expand its classes and curriculum. Any adult could enroll in a class regardless of college experience. Enrollment ranged from two or three people in its seminars to thirty in its more popular classes. While most classes were taught in Los Angeles, ONE conducted extension classes in San Francisco, Denver, Detroit, and other large cities. ONE had no formal degree-granting powers until the establishment of its graduate school in 1981, whereby the state of California sanctioned the Institute to give master's degrees and Ph.D.s in homophile studies. Access to ONE's library and files enabled students to produce a substantial body of research over the years, while ONE's monthly public lectures drew crowds into the hundreds. Guest speakers included the activists Del Martin of the Daughters of Bilitis and Hal Call of the Mattachine Society; the psychologists Albert Ellis and Evelyn Hooker; the writers Christopher Isherwood, Ann Bannon, and Donald Webster Cory; and religious, legal, and other experts.

In most years the ONE Institute held a Midwinter Institute in January, consisting of speeches, lectures, research reports, and special events spread out over several days. Attendance ranged from 150 to 500 participants and observers. Themes of early Midwinter Meetings included "The Homosexual Answers His Critics" (1958), "Mental Health and Homosexuality" (1960), "The Homosexual in the Community" (1960), and "New Frontiers in the Law" (1963). Aside from intellectual purposes, the meetings offered opportunities for homophile activists to meet, strategize, and argue with each other. An attempt to construct a homosexual Bill of Rights during the 1961 Midwinter Institute, for example, rocked the homophile world when the Daughters of Bilitis rejected the idea as extremist and unnecessary. The fallout of the disastrous meeting was felt for years, leading to increased tension in the movement between male and female homophile factions.

Beginning in 1958, the ONE Institute published a quarterly journal titled *ONE Institute Quarterly: Homophile Studies,* the first English-language academic-style journal devoted to homosexuality. Reflecting the Institute's interdisciplinary orientation, lesbian and gay scholars contributed a wide range of articles. Essay topics included homosexuality in Native American cultures, the homosexuality of the Russian composer Pyotr Tchaikovsky, the legal rights of homosexuals, homosexuality in the Bible, and summaries of the latest scientific research. Although circulation never rose higher than a few hundred, the twenty-two issues of the irregularly published quarterly (the last issue was published in 1969) have influenced subsequent gay research.

Later Years

In 1965 an explosive dispute between Dorr Legg and the longtime *ONE* magazine editor Don Slater ripped the organization apart. Legg and Slater battled each other in court for the rights to the name "ONE"—Legg prevailed, though *ONE* magazine soon disappeared from newsstands. The split represented a deeper schism among gay activists in the 1960s as a younger generation incorporated tactics of the black power and anti–Vietnam War movements, to the chagrin of older homophile activists (such as Legg) who preferred a tone of assimilation and moderation. As new groups emerged by the hundreds during the late 1960s and early 1970s, ONE lost its vanguard position in the gay movement. However, despite the considerable strides in gay visibility, the study of homosexuality remained academically marginalized during these years, so ONE's classes continued to serve an important intellectual function for the gay community.

Until the early 1990s, despite the severe financial strains caused by the Reed Erickson estate dispute, the Institute still offered homophile studies classes much as it had since the 1950s.

By the early 1990s, partly because of the ONE Institute's efforts over the decades, gay research earned greater mainstream academic acceptance. Legg passed away on 26 July 1994 at the age of eighty-nine, ending the Institute's program of homophile studies. Under the leadership of a new generation of activists, the ONE Institute dropped its classes, merged with Jim Kepner's International Gay and Lesbian Archives, and moved into an abandoned fraternity house owned by the University of Southern California. In May 2001 the revamped ONE Institute and Archives opened, offering its vast resources to yet another generation of gay scholars and activists.

Bibliography

Bullough, Vern, ed. *Before Stonewall: Activists for Gay and Lesbian Rights in Historical Context.* New York: Harrington Park Press, 2002.

Cutler, Marvin [W. Dorr Legg], ed. *Homosexuals Today: 1956.* Los Angeles: ONE Inc., 1956.

D'Emilio, John. *Sexual Politics, Sexual Communities: The Making of a Homosexual Minority in the United States, 1940–1970.* Chicago: University of Chicago Press, 1983.

Gregory, Robert. "ONE Institute: 1955–1960, a Report." *Homophile Studies* 3 (1960): 214–220.

Kepner, Jim. *Rough News—Daring Views: 1950s' Pioneer Gay Press Journalism.* New York: Haworth Press, 1998.

Legg, W. Dorr. *Homophile Studies in Theory and Practice.* San Francisco: GLB Publishers and ONE Institute Press, 1994.

Craig M. Loftin

See also DAUGHTERS OF BILITIS; ERICKSON EDUCATIONAL FOUNDATION; ERICKSON, REED; HOMOPHILE MOVEMENT; LEGG, DORR; LGBTQ STUDIES; MATTACHINE SOCIETY; *ONE*.

OSH-TISCH (Finds Them and Kills Them, a.k.a. *Maracota* [or Woman], Jim [from mi:akà:te, "girl"]), (b. 1854; d. 2 January 1929), medicine man, warrior, artisan.

Osh-Tisch (a more accurate transcription is *ó:tsikyap dapés*) was the most famous *boté,* or *berdache* (a word used by early French explorers for an androgynous Native American male), of the Crow Indians. He grew up at a time when the tribe freely roamed the plains in pursuit of buffalo and was a leading figure during the period of transition to reservation life.

The visibility of Crow *berdaches* was commented on by observers as early as the 1830s. By reputation, *boté* excelled in women's work, such as cooking, butchering, and hide-tanning, and in the use of hides to make clothing, lodges, and other items. The Crow sun dance ceremony required the participation of a *boté,* who cut down the tree used for the central pole of the ceremonial lodge.

By his own account (thanks to a rare instance of a transcribed interview with a *berdache* made by retired U.S. Army General Hugh Scott), Osh-Tisch was "inclined to be a woman, never a man" and cross-dressed at an early age despite initial parental opposition. By the time he reached adulthood, his skills in hide-tanning and constructing lodges were legendary. The lodge he made for Chief Iron Bull was the largest in the tribe's history. Crows stated, "Iron Bull's lodge is like the lodge of the Sun" (Curtis, p. 51).

When interviewed by Scott, Osh-Tisch denied that a vision or spiritual calling had led him to adopt women's clothes. At the time, however, the Crows were under pressure to abandon traditional beliefs, and Osh-Tisch may have been reticent to speak for this reason. In fact, he had become a medicine person based on a vision he had experienced while young. (A record of this transformation survives in a lodge he made with decorative elements symbolic of the vision.)

Osh-Tisch's name refers to an event that occurred in June 1876. Some 175 Crow warriors fought with General George Crook against the Sioux and Cheyenne at the Battle of the Rosebud—an engagement that could have been as disastrous as General George Custer's last stand eight days later were it not for Crow aid. Among the Crow warriors was Osh-Tisch, dressed in male clothing, fighting alongside a woman named "The Other Magpie." Together, they rescued a fallen Crow, and Osh-Tisch killed and scalped an enemy. The episode was long remembered in the region. A photograph taken not long after shows Osh-Tisch seated with a woman, probably "The Other Magpie."

By the late 1870s the Crows were confined to their reservation in Montana, dependent on the government for food and other necessities. Government agents, missionaries, and teachers discouraged traditional Crow culture, frequently singling out *boté.* In the late 1880s one agent rounded up Osh-Tisch and others, cut their hair, and forced them to do manual labor. The Crow response is indicative of their attitude toward *berdaches*: the tribe's chief personally intervened and demanded that the agent leave the reservation.

In the early 1900s a Baptist missionary began to denounce Osh-Tisch from his pulpit, urging congregants to shun him and other *boté.* Osh-Tisch, however, continued to cross-dress—because, as he told Scott in 1919,

Osh-Tisch. The most famous Crow *boté*—who usually dressed and behaved as a woman but also fought in male garb—stands in front of his cabin in 1928, wearing clothes he made for his burial. **[National Anthropological Archives, Smithsonian Institution, neg. no. 88-134]**

"That is my road." According to Scott, he still enjoyed an "enviable position" in the tribe.

Osh-Tisch received an allotment of land in the 1880s, and census records show him as the head of a household that included relatives and an adopted child, whose gender was originally recorded as male and later as female. In the early 1900s Osh-Tisch's relations with agents improved. According to Scott, one agent's daughter remembered "Maracota Jim" as pleasant and good-natured, calling on the family to sell native crafts. He visited friends at reservations in Montana and Idaho, and acquired a reputation as the best poker player in the region (in many tribes, *berdaches* were believed to be lucky). In place of hidework, Osh-Tisch took up sewing and in the 1920s won ribbons at the local county fair for his quilts.

Photographs taken in 1928 at Scott's request show Osh-Tisch wearing elaborately decorated clothing he had made for his own burial. He died the following year, having outlasted and outwitted efforts over several decades to change his "road."

Bibliography

Curtis, Edward S. *The North American Indian,* vol. 4. New York: Johnson Reprint Corporation, 1970.

Riebeth, Carolyn R. *J.H. Sharp among the Crow Indians 1902–1910: Personal Memories of His Life and Friendships on the Crow Reservation in Montana.* El Segundo, Calif.: Upton and Sons, 1985.

Roscoe, Will. *Changing Ones: Third and Fourth Genders in Native North America.* New York: St. Martin's Press, 1998.

Scott, Hugh Lenox. "Berdache," "Notes on Sign Language and Miscellaneous Ethnographic Notes." MS 2932, National Anthropological Archives. Smithsonian Institution, Washington, D.C.

Williams, Walter L. *The Spirit and the Flesh: Sexual Diversity in American Indian Culture.* Boston: Beacon, 1986.

Will Roscoe

See also TRANSSEXUALS, TRANSVESTITES, TRANSGENDER PEOPLE, AND CROSS-DRESSERS; TWO-SPIRIT MALES.

OUTING. see COMING OUT AND OUTING

P

PACIFIC ISLANDERS. see ASIAN AMERICANS AND PACIFIC ISLANDERS.

PACIFISM. see ANTIWAR, PACIFIST, AND PEACE MOVEMENTS.

PARAPHILIAS. see SADOMASOCHISM, SADISTS AND MASOCHISTS.

PARENTING. see FAMILY ISSUES.

PARENTS, FAMILIES AND FRIENDS OF LESBIANS AND GAYS (PFLAG)

Parents, Families and Friends of Lesbians and Gays is a unique organization that reflects the adaptation of LGBT persons and their allies to the practices of social movement advocacy in the United States. Its mission is to "promote the health and well-being of gay, lesbian, bisexual and transgendered persons, their families and friends" through support, education, and advocacy. At the end of 2002 the group claimed eighty thousand members and 460 affiliates in the United States. What makes PFLAG unique is that it exists to facilitate participation in the movement for LGBT civil rights by persons who are not themselves LGBT.

LGBT persons are unusual among identity-based social movements because the vast majority do not share the relevant identity characteristic with their parents. Thus, while racial and ethnic minorities have no need for a "Parents, Families and Friends of" Organization, PFLAG plays an extremely important, albeit often intangible, role in the LGBT social movement. It is difficult to specify the exact psychological characteristics that give rise to active political engagement on one's own behalf, but the highly conflicted relationships many LGBT persons have with their families of origin can significantly diminish their capacity for activism. On the other hand, a significant and growing number of family members and friends of LGBT persons find discrimination against LGBT persons outrageous. PFLAG members acknowledge these issues in various ways. They include "support" along with "advocacy" in their mission. At the 1993 March on Washington, PFLAG parents fanned out into the crowd in front of their exhibitor tent for the express purpose of bestowing hugs on any passersby who wanted one. In general, PFLAG has become adept at leveraging the esteem with which American culture regards parents, especially mothers, on behalf of LGBT civil rights claims.

PFLAG's history is closely intertwined with that of the LGBT movement and its advocacy work from the outset. According to the organization's own history, its conception resulted from Jeanne and Jules Manford's 1972 experience of watching on television as counter-protestors attacked their son Morton during a gay rights demonstration in New York City. The Manfords were horrified to see that the police did nothing to intervene. Later that year Jeanne Manford marched with her son in the annual Pride Day parade in Greenwich Village and found that many participants asked her to speak with their parents. In March 1973, Parents and Friends of

PFLAG. At the 1993 March on Washington, members and supporters carry a banner reading, "Parents and Friends of Lesbians and Gays: The Real Meaning of Family Values." **[Cathy Cade]**

Gays, as the organization was originally named, held its first meeting in a church.

Throughout the 1970s, parents of lesbian and gay children formed individual local support groups. These different groups often communicated with each other, but they would not create a national structure to unify local groups until the end of the decade. In 1974 the Manfords visited Los Angeles and encouraged Adele and Larry Starr to form such a group. The Starrs' Los Angeles group, founded in 1976, was the first in the nation to apply for tax-exempt status with the Internal Revenue Service (IRS). A PFLAG representative spoke on issues that parents of lesbians and gay men face at the first-ever meeting of lesbian and gay activists at the White House in March 1977, organized by the National Gay Task Force.

In 1979, at the first national lesbian/gay rights march in Washington, D.C, a group of parents held a press conference to express support for their lesbian/gay children. They also met to organize what was now termed Parents-FLAG at the national level. Two more years elapsed before another meeting in the Starrs' living room brought about the creation of the national group. Adele Starr volunteered to serve as president of the board of directors. PFLAG's primary activities during this period consisted of creating and supporting local chapters, responding to requests for information, and contacting public officials to oppose discriminatory policies.

PFLAG moved its national office to Denver, Colorado, when Elinor Lewallen became board president in 1987, and hired its first paid staff member that same year. In 1988, boasting two hundred local chapters across the nation, PFLAG moved to rented office space in Washington, D.C., where its headquarters have remained. In addition, the organization hired its first paid executive director at that time. In this respect, PFLAG reflects the increased professionalization of American politics during the last third of the twentieth century. Its activities during the 1990s also indicated the increasing prominence of LGBT civil rights issues in national politics.

Board President Paulette Goodman created a stir in 1990 when a letter she wrote to First Lady Barbara Bush, and Bush's response, were made public. Bush, whose husband had always aroused suspicions among conservative Christians, wrote to Goodman, "I firmly believe we cannot tolerate discrimination against any individuals or groups in our country" as cited on the PFLAG website. Activists on the Republican right responded with outrage, claiming that Bush supported "the gay agenda."

Conservative activists would later pay PFLAG a backhanded compliment by creating Parents and Families of Ex-Gays (PFOX). The "ex-gay" movement—Christian ministries dedicated to converting lesbians and gay men through various combinations of psychotherapy and Christian faith—languished largely unnoticed by the rest of the conservative Christian movement until the late

1990s, when conservative activists recognized it as the means to convey their opposition to LGBT civil rights in a seemingly compassionate manner. PFOX exists to offer support for parents and family members of "ex-gay" persons and claims that its members suffer discrimination and harassment.

Also during 1990, PFLAG endured significant internal tensions over the appropriate role of its national staff. In August, dissident board members revealed calls for votes of no confidence in both the executive director and the board president, along with a detailed report of significant management failures at the main office. In part, the disagreements reflected the organization's rapid growth, from two hundred to over four hundred chapters in a matter of months. In part, they reflected conflicts over the relative importance of the headquarters' two main tasks of supporting chapters and conducting advocacy in Washington, D.C. Nancy McDonald, board president at the time, identified both PFLAG's key strength and the tension inherent in the organization's self-definition when she claimed, "'I look at PFLAG as a continuum. You enter needing support. We're hoping you'll gain enough information and knowledge about the topic to be able to educate others. Then maybe you'll write that letter or speak at that committee. All three are important'" (Gideonse, p. 32).

The organization ultimately resolved its difficulties. In a further reflection of U.S. society and social movements, during the late 1990s PFLAG supported the creation of subsidiary groups specifically for African American and Asian American parents—implicit recognition of the difference that race and ethnicity make in individuals' experiences of their or their children's sexuality. It has also mirrored the larger movement in explicitly supporting the civil rights claims of bisexual, transgender, and intersexed persons. PFLAG thus continues to play a unique, and uniquely necessary, role in the social movement for LGBT civil rights.

Bibliography

Gideonse, Ted. "PFLAG's Family Crisis." *The Advocate* (October 28, 1997): 32.

PFLAG website. Available from www.pflag.org/about/history.html

Schwartz, Harriet. "The Ex Files." *The Advocate* (June 10, 1997): 44.

Stefanakos, Victoria Scanlan. "Does Your Mother Know?" *The Advocate* (August 28, 2001): 36.

William B. Turner

See also FAMILY ISSUES; FAMILY LAW AND POLICY; SUICIDE.

PARKER, Pat (b. 20 January 1944; d. 4 June 1989), poet.

The first and most influential African American working-class poet who was also a lesbian and feminist of the post-Stonewall generation, Pat Parker was born as a premature baby in Houston, Texas, the youngest of four daughters. At the urging of her father, she focused on education as a way to improve her circumstances. She moved to California after graduating from high school in 1962 and completed undergraduate and graduate degrees at Los Angeles City College and San Francisco State College. Her political activism began during the middle 1960s when she became a member of the Black Panther Party. Parker's career as a poet began with her first public reading in 1963, during her first marriage to the playwright Ed Bullins. Parker used poetry as an escape from Bullins's unremitting criticism of her prose, which was possibly a factor in their divorce in 1966 and her subsequent marriage to Robert F. Parker. Her early experiences honed a willingness to develop a separate voice of her own and to write about contemporary issues ranging from the Vietnam War to civil rights.

Parker's move to San Francisco in 1969 placed her in a position to assist in the foundation of the Women's Press Collective in Oakland, through which she met the white working-class poet Judy Grahn, whose later lengthy poem *A Woman Is Talking To Death* was modeled on Parker's work. Throughout the early 1970s, Parker and Grahn (along with other lesbian feminist writers such as Susan Griffin) gave public readings of their work in many cities on the West Coast at women's festivals, bookstores, bars, and coffee houses, spreading both the concept of lesbian feminism and an awareness of its literature. Her readings broke existing stereotypes, claiming and asserting the reality and validity of lesbian women of color. She also served as medical coordinator of the Oakland Feminist Women's Health Center from 1978 to 1987 (when she retired to have more time for her writing) and founded the Black Women's Revolutionary Council in 1980. Her death from breast cancer was deeply felt by the women's movement. After her passing, numerous prominent feminist and lesbian writers such as Audre Lorde and Jewelle Gomez addressed the relative lack of public dialogue about her work by acknowledging her pioneering influence on not only their decisions to come out, but also the evolution of their approaches to speaking honestly about race, class, and sexual identity within women's poetry.

The complex simplicities of Parker's poetry represent the intersection of the multiple communities in which she claimed citizenship and whose imagery and issues were combined in powerful and striking ways. Her work also articulates black lesbian experience through the expression of her own life in her poetry. Despite the general recognition of her diverse array of community identifications, the arguments over how to view Parker's legacy exhibit certain common themes. Her poems pungently address often hidden or unpopular issues of class, sexism, and gender, reflecting her unwillingness to participate in any social reform movement, whether African American, feminist, or gay liberation, whose tenets did not acknowledge all aspects of her identity. By refusing to diminish herself to secure a voice, Parker broke with the alternative literary establishment of the 1960s and 1970s, and spoke openly of controversial issues such as abortion, wife abuse, domestic violence, murder, and the myriad levels of discrimination practiced by women upon and against each other. The best examples of this are her lengthy autobiographical poem "Goat Child," recalled by Judy Grahn as offering the then-revolutionary idea that a woman's life was suitably complex subject matter for artistic creation, and "Womanslaughter," the poem dedicated to her murdered sister Shirley, read by Parker in 1976 in Brussels at the International Tribunal on Crimes Against Women.

Critical reception and analysis of her writing both within and outside the lesbian community has been somewhat more limited than might be expected, due in part to the fact that her three original chapbooks (small collections of writings similar to a pamphlet), *Child of Myself* (1974), *Pit Stop* (1974), and *Womanslaughter* (1978), have all gone out of print. However, their contents were reissued in her signature collection *Movement in Black* (1978). Her final 1985 collection, *Jonestown and Other Madness,* is a volume of longer poems focusing on topics from then-contemporary headlines. Much of the scholarship about Parker is comparative in nature, examining both the many layers of meaning contained in her writings and the poetic techniques (particularly her use of African American patterns such as call and response—the responsive patterns of singing characteristic of many black congregations) she employed to meld them into a vibrant whole. This work often links her to feminist poets such as Sylvia Plath and Adrienne Rich. Her emphasis on oral performance is reflected in the styles of language she used, which have caused some critics outside of the lesbian community to see her poems as more political statements than artistic creations. However, the importance of Parker's work to lesbian feminist poetry lies in her proving that a black lesbian could articulate a powerful and unique viewpoint on social issues through blending the values of all her communities and thus serve as an inspiration to achieving solutions acceptable to each.

Bibliography

Annas, Pamela. "A Poetry of Survival: Unnaming and Renaming in the Poetry of Audre Lorde, Pat Parker, Sylvia Plath, and Adrienne Rich." *Colby Library Quarterly* 18, no. 1 (March 1982): 9–25.

Callaghan, Dympna. "Pat Parker: Feminism in Postmodernity." In *Contemporary Poetry Meets Modern Theory.* Edited by Antony Easthope and John O. Thompson. Toronto: University of Toronto Press, 1991.

Garber, Linda. *Lesbian Identity Poetics: Judy Grahn, Pat Parker and the Rise of Queer Theory.* Ph.D. dissertation, Stanford University, 1995.

Oritz, Ana T. "Pat Parker: Revolutionary Spirit." *Sojourner: The Women's Forum* 14, no. 2 (August 1989): 3A.

Robert B. Ridinger

See also GRAHN, JUDY; LITERATURE; LORDE, AUDRE.

PEACE MOVEMENTS. see ANTIWAR, PACIFIST, AND PEACE MOVEMENTS

PEDOPHILIA. see INTERGENERATIONAL SEX AND RELATIONSHIPS.

PEOPLE OF ALL COLORS TOGETHER. see BLACK AND WHITE MEN TOGETHER (BWMT).

PERFORMANCE, THEATER, AND DANCE STUDIES

As noted by Peggy Phelan in *Mourning Sex* (1997), "one of the deepest challenges of writing about performance is that the object of one's meditation, the performance itself, disappears" (p. 3). Performance, theater, and dance scholarship is thus often uniquely situated as among the only material artifacts of an otherwise ephemeral event. Scholarly and popular books, journals, and essays, as well as editorials, feature articles, and performance reviews in mainstream, independent, and special interest press (including LGBT media), serve as forums for the political, critical, theoretical, and historiographical debate and acclaim of performance works. The original performance, theater, or dance event, made indelible through the subsequent distribution of criticism that it provokes, serves as the basis for the writing of history.

Scholarship on the Pre-Stonewall World

Much theater, dance and performance scholarship marks the Stonewall Riots (1969) as a turning point in American cultural history. Prior to 1967, in fact, explicit representations of LGB people were often prohibited on the American stage, due to the enforcement of the Comstock

Laws of 1873 ("act for the suppression of trade in, and circulation of, obscene literature and articles of immoral use"), as well as the Wales Padlock Act of 1927, which gave explicit power of arrest to the New York police department for the suppression of "homosexual" representations on the American stage. Notwithstanding violent police raids, often resulting in arrests and imprisonment, many theater works dealing with LGBT desire were produced in the late nineteeth and early twentieth century. Kaier Curtin's *We Can Always Call Them Bulgarians: The Emergence of Lesbians and Gay Men on the American Stage* (1987) offers a critical analysis of gay and lesbian representation before Stonewall and, in particular, during this period of extreme moral censorship that has come to define this first part of the century. Curtin notes that more than two dozen "illegal" LGB plays were produced from 1920 to 1940, though some received limited runs—Mae West's *Sex* (1926) and Edouard Bourdet's *The Captive* (1926), for example, experienced police raids on the very same night. Curtin notes that plays with lesbian themes were often overlooked by legal authorities as such desire was unrecognizable to a large part of the theater-going public. Female impersonation, moreover, existed almost entirely unscathed, as queer desire was not attached to popular vaudeville performance traditions. When Mae West's comedy *The Pleasure Man* (1928) appeared on Broadway with cross-dressing male characters, however, it was quickly banned.

Long before the LGBT liberation movements of the post-Stonewall era, a progressive advocacy movement existed, promoting that free speech be extended to the American stage. Don Shewey notes in *Out Front: Contemporary Gay and Lesbian Plays* (1988) that as gay and lesbian characters began to emerge in more plays, the continued repression of homosexuality in American culture produced a queerness often only intelligible "between the lines" and often consisting of largely negative representations of homosexual characters as "unhappy" and "pathetic" (p. xiii). Many scholars observe that, in early century works, gay and lesbian characters were often killed or killed themselves at the end of a play, reinforcing the notion that GLB people were isolated and hopeless. Lillian Hellman's *The Children's Hour* (1934), for example, concludes with a suicide, as one woman professes her love for another woman and then promptly takes her own life. A large part of the historiography of early LGB desire in performance thus centers on examining dialectical relationships between censorship, repressive imagery, pubic feelings about LGB people and LGB resistance. Alan Sinfield, author of *Out on Stage: Lesbian and Gay Theatre in the Twentieth Century* (1999), quoting scholar Richard Dyer, notes, "How anything is represented is the means by which we think and feel about that thing, by which we comprehend" (p. 3). Sinfield argues that "theatre was one of the places where psychological ideas about sex circulated" (p. 75). Though usually covert and often negative, public representations of same-sex desire contributed to the creation of public consciousness about homosexuality and the emergence of queer discourse.

The establishment of the "House Un American Activities Committee" (HUAC) and the ensuing witch-hunts of the McCarthy era in the 1950s placed homosexuals, communists, and other so-called "un-American" groups under even greater pressure and more serious national suspicion. LGB plays continued to emerge in this era, but some LGB artists, particularly playwrights, created increasingly veiled representations of LGB themes to protect their reputations. Some scholarship, such as David Savran's *Communists, Cowboys, and Queers* (1992), has been devoted to unveiling the queer tropes in historically mainstreamed mid-century works by such artists as Tennessee Williams, Arthur Miller, Robert Anderson, Lanford Wilson, Lorraine Hansberry, and Edward Albee. Other scholarship charts the relationship between the culture of moral censorship and the emergence of a "downtown" and regional theater scene. Shewey, for example, notes that when in 1958 Joe Cino opened the now famous Café Cino (which featured works by Oscar Wilde, William Inge, Noel Coward, Jean Genet, Tennessee Williams, Doric Wilson, Lanford Wilson, and Robert Patrick, to name a few), it was also "the accidental birth of Off-Off Broadway" (p. xiv), paving the way for such downtown venues as Judson Poets Theater, La Mama Experimental Theatre Club, The Other Side of Silence (TOSOS), The Glines, as well as countless organizations outside of New York.

Scholarship on the Stonewall and Post-Stonewall Eras

Many scholars agree that Mart Crowley's landmark play *The Boys in the Band* (1968) is to gay theater what the Stonewall Riots are to the LGB liberation movement. In *Boys in the Band*, a game of truth facilitates revelations of gay desire as well as gay self-loathing. Despite its pathologizing perspective on gay life, *The Boys in the Band*, like the LGB liberation movement, marks a turning point in queer cultural history after which being openly LGB is increasingly valued. In this sense, queerness, notes Sinfield, follows a Freudian trope, as something a person *is*, and "coming out" is what a person *does* to mark this passage in self-actualization. As *Boys in the Band* enjoyed unparalleled popularity in its time, many scholars have focused attention on the ways in which *Boys in the Band* affected the emerging genre of gay and lesbian theatre as well as a changing landscape of American culture.

If *Boys in the Band* represents the first "out" characters on the American stage, then The Theater of the Ridiculous, founded by Charles Ludlam (hailed "our great antecedent" by playwright Tony Kushner), represents perhaps American's first "out" aesthetic. Kate Davy's essay, "fe/male impersonation" (1994), uses the case of The Theater of the Ridiculous to distinguish "gay theater," which attempts to stage representations of homosexuality or gay couples, from a "gay aesthetic." Ludlam and his colleagues, with their famously camp sensibility, inhabit classical heterosexual narratives with their gay, costumed bodies. Camp is an intentional political strategy that employs parody and nuanced layers of signification to construct a counter-normative discourse and celebratorily queer self-representation. Davy notes that the nature of camp allows performers to play their characters with utmost earnest sincerity while simultaneously "winking" at the audience, thereby boldly inserting themselves into public discourse. Camp tactics have been adopted by other performance groups such as The Cockettes, Hot Peaches, Bloolips, Ballet Trockadero, and countless others studied by theater and performance studies scholars.

Theater and performance scholars, particularly female academics, have attempted to distinguish lesbian performance from gay male performance, as well as to historicize the marginalization of lesbian performance. Influenced by second wave feminist politics, a flowering of feminist theater collectives occurred between the early 1970's and late 1980's in New York City, as well as throughout the regional theater scene. Although these collectives varied in approach, scholars note that many collectives shared overtly political missions, as well as egalitarian and ad-hoc governing structures. Style and aestethic were equally varied, including agitational propoganda theater, or agit-prop; (such as It's Alright to Be a Woman Theater); revisionist canonical drama (such as Women's Experimental Theater, or WET); non-linear and absurdist drama (such as Maria Irene Fornes's New York Theater Strategy); and lesbian camp and parody (such as Women's One World, or WOW, Café). While many of the collectives that emerged in the 70's and 80's have since disappeared, scholars note, WOW Café stands out as still producing lesbian feminist work. Like Ridiculous Theater, WOW's lesbian performance often presents parodied versions of popular texts to knowing, insider audiences. What distinguishes much of this lesbian performance from its male counterparts, Davy notes, is the fact that the performers do not engage in "traditional" drag, but rather insist that all of the characters are female and thus lesbian. WOW lesbian performance often employs a femme/butch aesthetic, radically reconstituting drag and embodying strategies of resistance. Describing WOW performance artist Carmelita Tropicana (Alina Troyano) as a lesbian performer dragged as a feminine woman, scholar Jill Dolan, writing in *The Feminist Spectator as Critic* (1988), points out that "femininity, in the lesbian context, is foregrounded as drag, the assumption of an 'unnatural' gender role" (p. 69). The use of a femme/butch aesthetic, Dolan and others argue, is not a mirroring of heterosexual society, but rather a rejection of the (heterosexist) gender binary offered by mainstream culture through a kind of dragging within rather than across gender constructs. Similar arguments can be found in Sue-Ellen Case's article, "Towards a Butch-Femme Aesthetic" (1988), as well as other lesbian feminist works.

AIDS: Challenging Political and Performance Practices

Due in part to the AIDS epidemic in the mid-1980s and early 1990s, American culture experienced an increased visible presence of gay men in the public arena. In his landmark book *Acts of Intervention: Performance, Gay Culture, and AIDS* (1998), David Roman engages the relationship theater and performance scholarship has with aids, aids activism, and human rights advocacy. Roman carves out a new definition of performance criticism that discourages critical analysis based purely on virtuosity and instead reconstitutes performance and performance scholarship as part of a larger discourse aimed at social change. He coins the term "critical generosity" to describe a new praxis of criticism that exists "more than simply a procedure of critique or means for qualitative analysis" but as a "cooperative endeavor and collaborative engagement with a larger social mission" (p. xxvii).

In noting that dominant theater historiography positions Tony Kushner's *Angels in America: A Gay Fantasia on National Themes* and Jonathan Larson's *Rent* as the official exemplars of AIDS performance activism, David Savran, in his book *A Queer Sort of Materialism: Recontextualizing American Theater* (2003), argues that these works are being privileged based upon their commercial success (*Angels in America* won a Tony Award for "Best Play," and *Rent* a Tony for "Best Musical," both in 1994) while earlier and less mainstreamed works, such as Larry Kramer's *The Normal Heart* (1985), are marginalized despite their political significance. Savran argues that the relative success of Kushner's and Larson's works is due, in part, to their deliberate reconstitution of the gay male as normative rather than perverse. Historically, heterosexuality was aligned with normativity and thus the universal subject. These millennium musicals, however, recast the gay (white) man as universal subject, rendering "homosexual," as Monique Wittig has observed, "the axis of categorization from which to universalize" (Savran, p. 66). Since "the new queer remains a white, middle-class subject," however, these millennium spectacles, in spite of their more obvious political import, reaffirm the status quo by perpetuating a "counterfeit universal" (p. 66).

In an article entitled "Discussing the Undiscussable," which appeared in *The New Yorker* (December 26, 1994), dance critic Arlene Croce describes why she refused to see the performance of choreographer Bill T. Jones's *Still/Here,* a ballet that includes video documentary of real men living with HIV and AIDS. Since Jones is African American, gay, and HIV-positive, Croce asserts that *Still/Here* represents the experience of an overly particularized minority community, lacks universalism, and supports a LGB "agenda." Solo performance artist Holly Hughes, best known for her legal struggle with the National Endowment of the Arts after they defunded her award due to the "obscene" nature of her work, has been similarly accused of propagandizing. David Roman and performance artist Tim Miller, in their *Theatre Journal* article "Preaching to the Converted" (1995), note that the frequent accusation that queer artists make political propaganda, not art for the masses, is a dismissal deeply entrenched in a homophobic cultural paradigm and serves to perpetuate the ghettoization of LGB performance.

Reclaiming the Queer and Building Radical Multiculturalism

Queer Nation, a LGBT activist group (founded in 1990) that employed street-theater tactics in LGBT liberation advocacy, represents the public recuperation of the long-stigmatized term "queer" as a sign and symbol of empowerment. In accordance with the tenets of queer theory, which draws largely upon notions of "performativity" advanced chiefly by the fields of theater and performance studies, gender and sexuality are socially constructed "performances," and thus entirely fluid, subjective and unstable identity categories. In *Geographies Of Learning* (2001), Dolan distinguishes "gay and lesbian" from "queer," when she writes, "To be queer is not who you are, it's what you do, it's your relation to dominant power, and your relation to marginality, as a place of empowerment" (p. 98). Ostensibly, queer, unlike "gay" and "lesbian," is gender neutral, transgender inclusive, and an attractive alternative to some of the exclusionary identity politics linked with LGB liberation. Kate Bornstein's *Gender Outlaw: On Men, Women, and the Rest of Us* (1994), for example, chronicles Bornstein's life as an MTF transgender performance artist and scholar, and further suggests the fluidity and performativity of gender and sexuality.

As "queerness" is defined less by sexual practice than by active resistance to marginalization, and "performativity" suggests that identity is a social construct, some scholars in theater and performance studies have begun to include issues of race and ethnicity, as well as gender and sexuality, in queer performance analysis and criticism. Particular attention has been given to historicizing performance by and about queers of color and cultural hybrids, including Hansberry, Wilson, Fornes, Troyano, Edgar Poma, Rodrigo Reyes, Hank Tavera, Marga Gomez, Chay Yew, Brian Freeman, the Pomo Afro Homos, Cherríe Moraga, Lisa Kron, Luis Alfaro, and others. In his article "Queer Theater, Queer Theory" (2002), Jose Munoz describes how Alfaro uses memory performance to situate himself between two worlds (Latino and queer) and, in so doing, construct his bicultural identity. Munoz points out that in Alfaro's performance *Cuerpo Politizado* (Politicized Body), "the family is more than just a site to run from or a source of irony" (p. 241). For a queer person of color, Munoz notes, a person's ethnic or racial identity may be as significant as one's sexual identity. Thus, a clean break from one's heterosexual family unit, signaled by a simple replacement with a gay and lesbian "family," runs the queer of color at risk of erasing an equally significant part of his or her cultural identity.

Providing a history of the Split Britches ensemble comprised of Peggy Shaw, Lois Weaver, and Deb Margolin, Case, writing in *Split Britches: Lesbian Practice/Feminist Performance* (1996), notes that Margolin, though not a lesbian, participates in queer performance praxis, reinforcing the notion of queer as an action, a mode of performance, not a state of being. Furthermore, Margolin is Jewish American, an identity highlighted in such Split Britches performances as *Upwardly Mobile Home,* in which Margolin sings "I Want to Be in America" (from the popular musical *West Side Story)* in Yiddish. In this sense, Margolin challenges notions of what Munoz has called "universal whiteness" (p. 244) by performing the role of the "white Other." Margolin's uniquely situated cultural hybridity is marked by her contribution to queer and multicultural performance, in spite of her personal identity positions as heterosexual and white.

Future of the Field

Dolan's recent article, "Performance, Utopia, and the Utopian Performative" (2001), in conversation with her earlier works, argues that performance is a place of possibility. Dolan writes that she attends performance to catch a momentary glimpse of how the world could be.

Through a complex process of identification and desire, she as a spectator is alerted to her co-presence with strangers and to their collective powers of creativity, resistance, and hope.

Theater and performance scholarship has the awesome task of historicizing, theorizing, and critiquing, among other things, LGBT theater and performance. Traditional definitions of "community" are themselves queered as performance scholarship attempts to disrupt mythic notions of "a gay community" and seeks to investigate modes of performance with particular attention to such intersecting factors as race, gender, class, citizenship, and geography, as well as sexuality. At the same time, theater and performance scholarship, through its ability to reach a wider scope of people than a given performance event, creates a community of public discourse.

Bibliography

Bornstein, Kate. *Gender Outlaw: On Men, Women, and the Rest of Us.* New York: Routledge, 1996.

Case, Sue-Ellen. *Split Britches: Lesbian Practice/Feminist Performance.* New York and London: Routledge, 1996.

———. "Towards a Butch-Femme Aesthetic." *Discourse* 11 (Winter 1988-1989). (Reprinted in *The Lesbian And Gay Studies Reader.* Eds. Abelove, et al. New York: Routledge, 1993.)

Curtin, Kaier. *We Can Always Call Them Bulgarians: The Emergence of Lesbians and Gay Men on the American Stage.* Boston: Alyson Publications, 1987.

Davy, Kate. "Fe/male Impersonation: The Discourse of Camp." In *The Politics and Poetics of Camp.* Edited by Moe Meyers. New York and London: Routledge, 1994.

Dolan, Jill. *Geographies of Learning: Theory and Practice, Activism and Performance.* Middletown, Conn.: Wesleyan University Press, 2001.

———. *The Feminist Spectator as Critic.* Ann Arbor: University of Michigan Press, 1988.

———. "Performance, Utopia, and the 'Utopian Performative.'" *Theatre Journal* 53 (2001): 455–479.

Munoz, Jose. "Queer Theatre, Queer Theory." In *The Queerest Art.* Edited by Alisa Solomon and Framji Minwalla. New York: New York University Press, 2002.

Phelan, Peggy. *Mourning Sex: Performing Public Memories.* New York and London: Routledge, 1997.

Roman, David. *Acts of Intervention: Performance, Gay Culture, and AIDS.* Bloomington and Indianapolis: Indiana University Press, 1998.

Roman, David, and Tim Miller. "Preaching to the Converted." *Theatre Journal* 47 (1995): 169–188.

Savran, David. *A Queer Sort of Materialism: Recontextualizing American Theater.* Ann Arbor: University of Michigan Press, 2003.

———. *Communists, Cowboys, and Queers.* Minneapolis: The University Of Minnesota Press, 1992.

Shewey, Don, ed. *Out Front: Contemporary Gay and Lesbian Plays.* New York: Grove, 1988.

Sinfield, Alan. *Out on Stage: Lesbian and Gay Theatre in the Twentieth Century.* New Haven and London: Yale University Press, 1999.

Jaclyn Iris Pryor

See also AIDS AND PEOPLE WITH AIDS; ALBEE, EDWARD; CHAMBERS, JANE; DANCE; EICHELBERGER, ETHYL; FIERSTEIN, HARVEY; FORNES, MARIA IRENE; HANSBERRY, LORRAINE; JONES, BILL T., AND ARNIE ZANE; KRAMER, LARRY; KUSHNER, TONY; LUDLAM, CHARLES; MCNALLY, TERRENCE; MORAGA, CHERRÍE; POMA, EDGAR; REYES, RODRIGO; THEATER AND PERFORMANCE; WILLIAMS, TENNESSEE; WILSON, LANFORD.

PERRY, Troy **(b. 27 July 1940), religious leader, minister.**

Troy D. Perry was born in Tallahassee, Florida, the son of Troy D. Perry, Sr., and Edith Allen Perry. After his father's death in an automobile accident in 1952 and his mother's subsequent remarriage, Perry's family moved to Daytona Beach. Shortly thereafter, Perry ran away from home and spent two years living with relatives in southern Georgia and El Paso, Texas. He returned after his mother's separation from her husband, and lived with the family in Winter Haven, Florida, and Mobile, Alabama.

Perry was drawn to religion from childhood. Though his parents attended their Baptist church only on special occasions, Perry attended frequently, and his commitment only increased upon his arrival in Georgia. There, he lived with relatives who were involved in Pentecostal and Holiness churches, including a particularly fervent aunt who handled serpents as part of her worship practice. When Perry was thirteen, this aunt prophesied that he had been called to the ministry. Her congregation, believing the prophecy to be the direct word of God, encouraged Perry to begin preaching in their church. In Texas he continued to preach, this time in his relatives' congregation of the Assemblies of God, and upon his return to Florida at the age of fifteen, he was licensed to preach by the local Baptist church.

Believing preaching to be more important than formal schooling, Perry dropped out of high school before his senior year and became a traveling evangelist for the Church of God. After marrying a woman from his local congregation, he relocated to Chicago, where he attended Bible college (after passing the General Educational Development exam as an alternative to his high school diploma) and served as pastor to a small Church of God congregation. It was also in Chicago that Perry's sexual orientation, of which he had been aware since childhood, began to be known to those around him.

Recounting his childhood in *Don't Be Afraid Anymore* (1990), Perry recalls his first sexual experience with another boy his age as "magical," characterized by "wonderful pleasure and happiness" (p. 2). By his later teenage years, however, he found his attraction to men "troublesome and very disturbing" (p. 14). Nevertheless, before marrying he had a clandestine relationship with another young man from his Alabama church. A few years later, this lover told Perry's superiors in the church about their relationship, and Perry was summarily excommunicated from the Church of God. He appealed the following year and was denied, but soon thereafter he became involved in a rival denomination, the Church of God in Prophecy. When the company where he worked during the week offered him a job in the Los Angeles area, he agreed to go and concurrently applied and was accepted for the pastorate of a congregation in that area.

Moving to the Los Angeles vicinity in the early 1960s gave Perry greater access to information about homosexuality, and he soon came to the conclusion that he was gay. Though his district overseer advised him to destroy the books he had been reading and return to his congregation, the local bishop defrocked him. Perry's wife returned with their two sons to her family in Alabama.

Following this crucial turning point in his life, Perry became increasingly involved in the gay social world of 1960s Los Angeles. A two-year military tour from 1965 to 1967 (Perry was drafted despite his avowed homosexuality) only reinforced his identity further, while continuing to keep him marginally connected to Pentecostal Christianity through services and prayer meetings at his base in Germany. Upon returning home to Los Angeles, Perry was less involved with the church, but an unsuccessful suicide attempt after the unexpected end of a relationship renewed his "acquaintance with God" (Perry, 1990, p. 30) and affirmed God's love for him as a "practicing" gay man. Soon after this, a conversation with a friend who had been arrested in a bar raid convinced Perry that his call to the ministry was still valid, and that his mission was to found a church that would minister to gay and lesbian (and later, bisexual and transgender) Christians. The first service of the Metropolitan Community Church was held on 6 October 1968, with a conregation of twelve people in attendance.

As of 2003, the Reverend Elder Troy Perry heads an international denomination that claims over forty thousand members. Encompassing from its first service a diverse group of Christians, the denomination is characterized more by doctrinal flexibility than by any particular teachings—aside from the truth of Christianity and the equality of LGBT people, and heterosexual in the eyes of God.

Bibliography

Perry, Troy D., with Thomas L. P. Swicegood. *Don't Be Afraid Anymore: The Story of Reverend Troy Perry and the Metropolitan Community Churches.* New York: St. Martin's Press, 1990.

Perry, Troy D. "Gays and the Gospel: An Interview with Troy Perry." *Christian Century* 113 (1996): 896–901.

Perry, Troy D., as told to Charles L. Lucas. *The Lord is My Shepherd and He Knows I'm Gay.* Los Angeles: Nash, 1972.

Melissa M. Wilcox

See also CHURCHES, TEMPLES, AND RELIGIOUS GROUPS.

PHILADELPHIA

Philadelphia through the eighteenth and early nineteenth centuries was the largest and most important city in the British North American colonies and then in the early American republic. For more than one hundred years thereafter, it was among the greatest manufacturing centers in the country. One of its nicknames, "Workshop to the World," was entirely justified. With economic readjustments after World War II, however, Philadelphia began a long decline and slipped from being the third largest U.S. city to its ranking as fifth in the 2000 census. Although the economy of the region remains strong, the contemporary urban core shares many of the problems common to postindustrial cities. The downtown area, however, known in Philadelphia as Center City, is thriving, in no small part due to the presence of the many LGBT residents and businesses that were committed to the area long before there were signs of economic revival. This broad picture is necessary to contextualize the history of sexual and gender minorities in Philadelphia.

There are few sources upon which to base a detailed LGBT history before the late nineteenth century. With most of that early period, all that exists, or has been discovered so far, are legal documents, so little social or cultural history is possible. What antigay laws there were, as was the case with many laws on other subjects, completely ignored women. Pennsylvania was probably the most tolerant colony in general, and its relatively light penalties for sodomy reflected that ethos, though other crimes that were perceived as being of a moral nature, such as adultery, fornication, and lying, were criminal there (but not in other colonies or in England) and could have severe sentences. The death penalty for sodomy was abolished by a 1676 English law that applied the ultimate sanction only to murder. Later statutes did apply the death penalty, but only to cases of "buggery" by "negros." In 1718 it was once again applied to whites as well. True to its original position, Pennsylvania, after joining the union, became the first state to revoke the death penalty for sodomy. Obviously, there are many gaps in the LGBT record. One topic that bears investigation is the role of sexual minorities among Pennsylvania Germans. According to the 1790 census, this group made up 31 percent of the new state's population, just slightly less than the Anglo-American plurality.

Two events, one obscure, one well-known, typify the place of gay men in late-nineteenth-century Philadelphia (and are emblematic of the larger American experience). A young effeminate man was sent by his mother to the Insane Department of Philadelphia's public hospital in 1886 largely because he was suffering from extreme delusions. What is unclear from the report of the case is whether or not it was the delusions that got him there or the fact that he was inclined to masturbate and fondle or fellate other men. This example of the medicalization of a lower-class individual stands in contrast with the meeting of two gay artistic titans. Oscar Wilde was not yet at the pinnacle of his career when he visited the United States in 1882, but he was well on his way. At first the American poet Walt Whitman was not particularly interested in Wilde. Wilde, however, extravagantly praised him in a public speech in Philadelphia, and Whitman invited him to Camden, New Jersey, just across the Delaware River from Philadelphia. They talked of prosody, the future of literature, and the contrasts between the United States and England. For his part, Wilde was deeply moved by visiting "the grand old man," and, according to his companion, was mostly deep in thought on his trip back to Philadelphia.

Whether or not Whitman's presence nearby was responsible, Philadelphia seems to have had more than its share of artists who were either attracted to members of the same sex or whose work was homoerotically charged. Whitman's close relationship with the artist Thomas Eakins is well documented, not least in Eakins's portrait (said to be Whitman's favorite) and photographs of the poet. The Charlotte Cushman Club, founded originally by the famous nineteenth-century actress, provided hotel space for visiting actresses and other social venues for lesbians beginning in 1907.

The record broadens and grows much more detailed after 1900. With it comes a broader perspective on LGBT life. Clues to the lives of ordinary people become more abundant. Rittenhouse Square in central Philadelphia is mentioned many times in various early-twentieth-century sources as being a location for gay cruising and socializing. Social workers and newspapers began to note the growing presence of gender nonconformists. Even various LGBT folk customs are recorded, including dress habits, cruising techniques, and argot. One of historian Jonathan Ned Katz's more striking examples involves a straight detective and his friends being solicited on a Philadelphia street by a male cross-dresser. Though some early-twentieth-century writers were struck by the differences that were displayed by inverts in various U.S. cities, the detective recognized their commonalities.

Katz also made translations of relevant passages from pioneer scholar and activist Magnus Hirschfeld's monumental *The Homosexuality of Men and Women* (1914). In the early twentieth century, Hirschfeld comprehensively covered what was known about homosexuality in his day. In addition to surveying the literature, he did a world tour to discover what he could. In the United States, he was told that Philadelphia had a hidden but active world available to sexual minorities. A letter he received from a Colorado professor corroborated this perception in describing a Turkish bathhouse frequented by about sixty homosexuals in Philadelphia every Saturday night.

The scattered references to same-sex desire continued through the 1930s and deserve fuller investigation. One of the most intriguing is a photograph of Ray St. Clare and Sepia Mae West that appeared in the *Philadelphia Tribune*, the city's African American newspaper, on 13 February 1936. Headlined "Funny what love will do," its subject is a couple in wedding attire. Sepia is described in the caption as being one of Philadelphia's most prominent female impersonators. Evidently, the wedding was the "largest ever given in any nite [*sic*] club." There are accounts of similar ceremonies from that era and for the next few decades as well.

World War II was a dividing line in Philadelphia, just as it was elsewhere in the United States. Though not as important an embarkation point for returning veterans as New York City, New Orleans, and San Francisco, it was nonetheless a large navy and army city with enough of an institutional and commercial base to provide support for LGBT returning veterans. The focus of the emerging LGBT community was in Center City, where most of the nightlife was concentrated. Though some LGBT bars were established before the war, many more can be documented from the 1950s and later periods. The majority of them were in Center City, but some were located in North Philadelphia, a predominantly African American neighborhood; on the docks; and even in some suburbs.

Characteristically, many late-night restaurants catered to the LGBT bar crowd. The most well-known of these was Dewey's, which in 1965 was also the site of one of the first, if not the first, demonstrations for equal treatment of LGBT people in a commercial establishment. The management there refused to serve LGBT people, fearing they drove away other customers. A local activist group, the Janus Society, sponsored two sit-downs, the first leading to several arrests.

Walt Whitman remained controversial even long after his death in 1892. John Wanamaker, the department store founder, refused to stock Whitman's work early in the twentieth century, but the poet did not really become an irritant until mid-century. A new bridge spanning the Delaware River (separating Philadelphia from New Jersey) was scheduled to be named for him. For the burgeoning conservative Roman Catholic movement of the 1950s, it was a disgrace to name the bridge after someone these Catholics thought degenerate. There were, however, also pressures supporting the name. Several scholars wrote to the river's governing body in favor of Whitman's name, and some religious officials did so as well. The two-year controversy had ended by 1957, the year the structure opened as the Walt Whitman Bridge, but it was long remembered by Philadelphians. Subsequently, Whitman, by virtue of having the bridge named after him, became a source of pride for gays. Three decades after the bridge's completion, a public service announcement produced by the Philadelphia Lesbian and Gay Task Force presented a young man (with the bridge prominently in the background), who, shortly after coming out, wondered why his teachers had never told him that Whitman was gay.

During the 1960s, there were more important developments than the bridge controversy. The establishment of several LGBT activist organizations during that decade provided staying power, visibility, and continuity for the community that enhanced its long-term viability. Of course, they created tension as well. The Mattachine Society came to the city in 1960, about a decade after its founding in Los Angeles. Ultimately, the local group changed its name to the Janus Society of the Delaware Valley. Over time, Philadelphia was distinguished in at least two ways from the homophile movement elsewhere. At least in the early years, there seemed to be better relations between men and women there than in other cities. And ultimately, those attached to the movement by the mid-1960s became more radicalized than was the norm. After conflicts developed between men and women, most lesbians left the Janus Society to devote their energies instead to a revived Mattachine chapter, a chapter of the Daughters of Bilitis, and a local Homophile Action League. The most visible signs of radicalization in Philadelphia, if the sit-ins at Dewey's are not provocative enough, were the protests at Independence Hall, Philadelphia's global symbol of freedom, on the Fourth of July from 1965 through 1969.

The social life of LGBT people was also enlarging considerably. Spruce Street was becoming the "main street" of "the life" in the city. Most of the bars and restaurants were there or nearby. The Allegro, between Broad and Fifteenth, was very popular for more than two decades until it closed in 1983. The corner of Spruce and Broad Streets was the LGBT assembly point for the New Year's Mummers Parade, a major Philadelphia event. Henri David's drag parties were well known. Henry McIlhenny, who was from a wealthy and socially prominent Philadelphia family, held famous gay parties at his mansion just off of Rittenhouse Square. Atlantic City became, more than ever, a resort destination with a "gay beach" for Philadelphia men and women. The annual June parades celebrating LGBT pride became regularized in the early 1970s.

Philadelphia during the 1960s and 1970s also had one of the most repressive police commissioners in the country. Frank Rizzo, who later became mayor, was notorious for turning a blind eye to violations of everyone's civil rights. For sexual and gender minorities, police abuse took the form of the usual tactics of raiding bars and petty harassment of any street activity that could be considered a misdemeanor, no matter how insignificant. The police were especially virulent on the so-called merry-go-round, a cruising circle that was partly located on Spruce Street, near Schuylkill River Park. So closely is the park identified with the LGBT community that many people, including straights, still know the park as Judy Garland Park, after the gay icon.

The Eromin Center ("Eromin" for erotic minorities) was established in 1973. It was a clearinghouse to serve the psychological needs and sexual health concerns of LGBT people and was one of the first of its kind. With an outpatient clinic that provided group and individual therapy, among other services, its importance to the community was greater than the numbers it served (which were considerable). In a sense, it was like a glue for the community and a safety net. It lasted until the late 1980s. About the same time, an early manifestation of an LGBT community center occupied a small building on Kater Street, near Fifth. Another locale for service was the Christian Association on the University of Pennsylvania campus. During the 1970s and 1980s it housed a peer education group for LGBT people and was also the venue of an annual cultural festival that drew performers and speakers from all over the world.

AIDS consumed most of the community's energies in Philadelphia, as it did elsewhere, in the 1980s and after. The AIDS Coalition to Unleash Power (ACT UP) was the locus of action on a variety of fronts. It applied pressure on medical and social service institutions in the city to provide for people with AIDS. Once governmental and private organizations were established, ACT UP held them to account on a variety of points, including race, gender, and class issues. In Philadelphia its protest function was most dramatically evident on 12 September, 1991, when an estimated 7,500 people from many constituencies demonstrated outside the Hotel Atop the Bellevue, where President George H. W. Bush was attending a Republican fund-raising dinner. When ACT UP protestors staged their signature die-in, an ersatz coffin inadvertently fell over the barricades. The police then charged the crowd with nightsticks and arrested eight protesters. A civilian panel condemned the police tactics. The city itself would settle a separate federal suit filed by ACT UP on behalf of fourteen people and five other groups who alleged that the police had violated their civil rights during the demonstration.

Though not a project of ACT UP in the formal sense, AIDS activist Kiyoshi Kuromiya's Critical Path AIDS Project was a cutting-edge adjunct to the group's work. His long, creative, activist credentials were put to good use in the struggle against AIDS. Critical Path was a newsletter for those with AIDS that combined practical information with serious scientific articles. Recognizing that "information is power," Kuromiya was among the first to use the Web to disseminate information about AIDS, and www.critpath.org became internationally famous. Though the print version ceased when Kuromiya died in 2000, the Web site continued to be maintained.

Early-twenty-first-century Philadelphia has a large LGBT population, and though it is not as prominent on the national scene as the LGBT communities in many other cities are, it is substantial enough to support a variety of institutions and activities. The "gayborhood," as it has come to be called here, is centered east of Broad Street, on Thirteenth Street, between Walnut and Pine.

The William Way Community Center was founded in 1996 and in 1997 purchased the Engineers' Club building in Center City. Even before purchasing the building, the center had been awarded a $300,000 grant by the federal government's Department of Housing and Urban Development, for renovations. The four-story building houses the Philadelphia LGBT Library and Archives and has offices for more than ten organizations, in addition to sponsoring its own support and social service groups. Today nearly three thousand people use the building each month.

Another center serves the LGBT community at the University of Pennsylvania. Founded in 1982, it became the first such center in the nation to have its own building. David Goodhand and Vincent Griski met at the university in 1983 and became early Microsoft employees. In 2000 they made a substantial gift to the university. The university administration decided to use the funds to provide a committed building to the center.

The Equality Forum began as Pridefest America in 1993 and is held every year in late April and early May. Programming has included seminars on the entire gamut of LGBT topics, from the arts and cinema to political and health issues. Performances and exhibits of all kinds are also part of its mission. Over the years, it has gone from a three-day to a week-long event.

Philadelphia has long languished, caught in an awkward place in the Northeast Corridor. With the nation's financial capital to the north, its governmental capital to the south, and its star on the national stage long past, the city could have easily gone into irreversible, permanent decline. That it has not done so is due, at least in part, to the vibrant LGBT population that has made up a large part of the city's urban center for more than fifty years.

Bibliography

Azzolina, David S. "The Circle Always Grew: Folklore and Gay Identity, 1945–1960." Ph.D. diss., University of Pennsylvania, 1996.

Ellmann, Richard. *Oscar Wilde.* New York: Knopf, 1988.

Katz, Jonathan Ned. *Gay/Lesbian Almanac: A New Documentary.* New York: Harper, 1983.

———. *Gay American History: Lesbians and Gay Men in the U.S.A: A Documentary History.* New York: Meridian, 1992.

Nickels, Thom. *Gay and Lesbian Philadelphia.* Charleston, S.C.: Arcadia, 2002.

Philadelphia Gay News, 3 January 1976–3 December 1982.

Stein, Marc. *City of Sisterly and Brotherly Loves: Lesbian and Gay Philadelphia, 1945–1972.* Chicago: University of Chicago Press, 2000.

Weigley, Russell F., ed. *Philadelphia: A 300-Year History.* 2d ed. New York: Norton, 1982. The best history of the city.

David Azzolina

See also BARBER, SAMUEL, AND GIAN CARLO MENOTTI; BENTLEY, GLADYS; CORNWELL, ANITA; CUSHMAN, CHARLOTTE; *DRUM*; EAKINS, THOMAS; ERICKSON, REED; GITTINGS, BARBARA, AND KAY TOBIN LAHUSEN; HART, ALAN; HOMOPHILE MOVEMENT DEMONSTRATIONS; JANUS SOCIETY; KUROMIYA, KYOSHI; LOCKE, ALAIN; POLAK, CLARK; RADICALESBIANS; RIGHTS OF ASSOCIATION AND ASSEMBLY; TSANG, DANIEL; WHITMAN, WALT; WITTMAN, CARL.

PHILOSOPHY

The modern discipline of philosophy has resisted the explicit inclusion of LGBT areas of inquiry. Official recognition of LGBT scholarly work was initiated in 1988, when John Pugh organized the first newsletter of the Society for Lesbian and Gay Philosophy. Pugh and Claudia Card were the initial cochairs of this pioneering organization, which first offered a program at the 1990 American Philosophical Association (APA) meeting in New Orleans. In 1997 an official APA Committee on the Status of Lesbian, Gay, Bisexual, and Transgender People in the Profession was formed. Its "Newsletter on Philosophy and Lesbian, Gay, Bisexual, and Transgender Issues," first edited by Timothy Murphy, was regularly published in the *APA Newsletter* beginning in 1999. The APA Committee was cochaired by Edward Stein and Jacob Hale for its first three years, and then by Mark Chekola and Christopher Horvath. Card celebrated the opening of philosophy's closet by proclaiming:

> This committee differs from all of the other committees in the APA in backing outlaws. . . . Being outlaws means we risk censure for being shameless enough not to hide, or else we lead a life of duplicity that produces real shame because it makes us dishonest in acquiescing in others' false assumptions and accepting trust we might not otherwise have been given. (*APA Newsletter*, Spring 1999)

Card also called for the collection of narratives about LGBT philosophers' experiences in the discipline, which were later published in the *APA Newsletter*.

Lesbian Feminist Philosophy

While the formation of the APA Committee was a milestone in the history of professional philosophy in the United States, there was prior to this a groundswell of lesbian feminist philosophy that emerged in the 1970s and 1980s in the Society for Women in Philosophy (SWIP). Especially in the midwestern SWIP, lesbian feminist philosophy took root and flourished in a set of distinctive theoretical works first published after nearly a decade of conference presentations and discussions. These include Sara Lucia Hoagland's *Lesbian Ethics* (1988), Claudia Card's *Adventures in Lesbian Philosophy* (1994) and *Lesbian Choices* (1995), Marilyn Frye's *Politics of Reality* (1983) and *Willful Virgin* (1992), Joyce Trebilcot's *Mothering* (1983) and *Dyke Ideas* (1994), and Jeffner Allen's *Lesbian Philosophies and Cultures* (1990) and *Lesbian Philosophy* (1986). While influenced by second wave feminism in the 1970s, these feminist philosophers attempted to place female heterosexuality at the center of feminist analyses of the oppression of women, foregrounding the institution of heterosexuality and women's sexual subordination to men as major impediments to a more fully emancipated female sex. Many lesbian feminist philosophers attempted to theorize "lesbian" as a site of resistance to male heteronormative sexual oppression.

According to Frye and Monique Wittig, for example, restricting male access to women is the first act of challenging male power, as the social construction of male dominance relies on nearly unconditional access to women's sexual, reproductive, spiritual, and physical energies. Wittig argued that "women" constitute a class of people appropriated by men and that "lesbian" offers a site of resistance to sexual captivity. She offered the provocative claim that if lesbians are not "women" to men, then lesbians are not "women." This highlighted the social construction of gender as a sexual project and the social appropriation of female anatomy and sexuality as phenomena that serve heterosexualized male hegemony. Lesbian feminist philosophy and practice created a renaissance in writing and new social organizations that prioritized the ontology and values of lesbian sex, love, and community. While the more recent emergence of queer theory has largely overshadowed these feminist philosophical writings (even while building on their insights), lesbian feminist philosophy still offers a challenging paradigm for thinking about the oppression of women; its entanglements with sexual violence, misogyny, lesbophobia, and compulsory heterosexuality; and the possibilities of female agency, sexual liberation, and alternative communities of resistance.

The enclaves of SWIP chapters and the disruptions caused by early lesbian feminist philosophy linked feminist movements and artistic literatures with academic philosophy, but lesbian feminist influence in the APA was limited. Meanwhile, the paradigm of lesbian feminist philosophy was complicated in the 1980s by questions about race, class, culture, status, and sexual differences, which challenged some of the universalizing claims made by lesbian feminist philosophers. In the same period, the AIDS crisis disrupted allegiances to lesbian separatist trajectories and offered instead new and more inclusive social movements engaging in civil rights struggles for LGBT people and in transgressive queer politics.

Philosophical Queer Theory

In the early 1990s, postmodern queer theory emerged as a more exciting hot spot for philosophical work on the body, sex, gender, sexuality, desire, and agency. Queer theory quickly overshadowed lesbian feminism philosophy, largely by replacing feminism's growing commitment to exploring social differences with a new emphasis on desire, pleasure, and—despite claims to the contrary—

new forms of humanist individualism centered on the body. Queer theory, however, was not initially embraced in the circles and societies of academic philosophy in the United States, despite the fact that some of the most influential queer theorists such as Judith Butler are philosophers. This is partially a reflection of U.S. philosophical traditions that swing mostly counter to continental philosophy and the philosophical metaphysicians used in high queer theory, such as Jacques Lacan, Jacques Derrida, Michel Foucault, Sigmund Freud, Georg Hegel, Louis Althusser, and Slavoj Zizek. Although queer theory has influenced philosophical analyses of postmodernity, it has had much greater influence in providing philosophical animation for work in areas outside of academic philosophy, such as literary criticism, film studies, cultural studies, rhetoric, speech communication, sociology, political science, history, and anthropology. Queer theory has also been very influential in interdisciplinary areas such as women's and gender studies, LGBT and sexuality studies, and more recently transgender and gender identity studies. This has had the effect of situating profound philosophical challenges related to sex, gender, and sexuality in places where this type of thinking is allowed, which encouraged and reinforced the separation of queer theory from academic philosophy.

The durable resistance of U.S. academic philosophy to lesbian feminist, queer, and transgender theory can also be seen in the fragile "love of knowledge" practices that define the discipline itself. Identified by some scholars (Evelyn Fox Keller, Eve Kosofsky Sedgwick, and David M. Halperin) as remarkably homoerotic, the practices of philosophy's love of wisdom (stretching back to the Greeks) have traditionally involved intense textual exchange and an intimate dialectic between aged male philosophers and their aspiring male students. Academic philosophy pictures itself as a discipline based on the preservation and reading of canonical philosophical texts, a highly regulated analytic method of inquiry, writing, and critique, and on a recurring set of unanswerable questions that ignore or sidestep more contemporary questions about sex and gender in all of their variations. The notion that philosophy commonly takes place on the streets or in the sheets is only of remote professional interest to a largely Cartesianized priesthood of philosophical experts practicing the mind's labors of abstraction. While normative bodies present challenges to American philosophy's mind-centered practices, queering the body is even more deeply unsettling.

Social Justice and State Politics

What one finds more commonly in contemporary U.S. academic philosophy is a different kind of heretical courage, one that has emerged in new LGBT philosophical inquiry into the foundational values and policies of social justice and liberal state politics. These new explorations, influenced by developments in political philosophy, differ from earlier, more conventional modes of sex inquiry (such as Roger Baker and Frederick Elliston's *Philosophy and Sex,* 1975) that focused on the morality of specific sexual acts, the nature of perversion, and the cogency of scientific etiological accounts of homosexuality. In addition to exploring these topics, new LGBT philosophical work tends to focus on issues of social justice and the erotic rights of individuals, largely in response to the growing visibility of LGBT movements. These topics are often framed by a "queering" of liberal politics. Examining identity politics, the empirical truth of sexuality for the self, and the representation of LGBT minoritarian suffering, these analyses circulate around issues of rights, responsibilities, and discrimination against LGBT people. Published work includes legal, ethical, and civil rights arguments for and against same-sex marriage, same-sex parenting, same-sex adoptions, surrogacy rights and responsibilities, rights to privacy and outing practices, military and Reserve Officer Training Corps regulations concerning homosexuality, state regulation of sex acts and pornography, sex education in the schools, homophobia and institutional practices, desire and obligation in the age of AIDS, and other questions related to the personal ethics of relationships and the incursions of state and institutional disciplinary power into personal life.

Many of these philosophical controversies query the relationship of the state to the individual and explore the rights, responsibilities, and harms of calling on the state or the higher powers of law to protect or prohibit human sexual behaviors and to regulate the lives of sexual subjects. Typically, philosophical journals have cast these questions as controversies, allowing for the anti-LGBT positions of, for example, John Finnis, Michael Levin, and Roger Scruton, to be matched with the supportive LGBT positions exemplified in the work of Timothy Murphy, David Mayo, Elizabeth Daumer, Frederick Suppe, Mark Chekola, Richard Mohr, Claudia Card, Edward Stein, Lisa Heldke, Jacob Hale, John Corvino, and Abby Wilkerson.

Conceptual and Normative Philosophy

Alan Soble, in "The Fundamentals of the Philosophy of Sex" (2002), makes a primary distinction between conceptual and normative philosophical analysis. In LGBT philosophy, "conceptual analysis" refers to the analysis and clarification of central notions, such as what counts as "a sex act," "sexual activity," "sexual desire," "homosexual acts," "homoeroticism," and "sex difference."

Examples include Frye's analysis of "lesbian sex"; Heldke's, Peg O'Connor's and Amanda Udis-Kessler's writings on bisexuality; Hale's and Jacquelyn N. Zita's work on transgender concepts; and Butler's work on the ontology of sex, gender, and resistance. In contrast, "normative analysis" is concerned with the value and evaluation of sexual activities and sexual pleasures, as exemplified by the work of Murphy, Janice Moulton, Michael Slote, Graham Priest, and Linda LeMoncheck, all of whom interrogate the values of various sexual practices and the cogency of normative judgments regarding "sexual perversions."

Alan Soble contrasts "moral evaluations" with "nonmoral evaluations" of sex: "Nonmorally good sex is sexual activity that provides pleasure to the participants or is physically or emotionally satisfying, while nonmorally bad sex is unexciting, tedious, boring, unenjoyable, or even unpleasant" (*Philosophy of Sex).* In other words, good sex can be morally bad or good, depending on the value and ethical systems deployed in a philosophical analysis. These value inquiries can be further separated from "pragmatic considerations" related to sexual practices and questions about what is safe, useful, and effective, both at the level of physical sex acts and in the intersubjective sexual encounters of emotional intimacy. Alongside these types of analyses, political and social philosophy take up questions related to the state and social regulation of human sexuality: legal permissibility; civic rights and responsibilities; privacy entitlements; institutional regulations; and individual and community rights to erotic self-determination and access to space, resources, and protection from harm.

The Natural and Unnatural

The question of the "naturalness" of LGBT activities, including various sexual practices such as sadomasochism and fetishism, and the "naturalness" of transgender and transsexual bodies still produces an annual harvest of academic philosophical work that draws upon queer, intersex, transgender, and sex theory developed mostly outside of academic philosophy. In traditionally conservative philosophy, what is "unnatural" in human sexuality is based on appeals to the ontology of human nature or its normative imprinting on the body (in particular, on sexual organs and the uses to which they can be put). Given that LGBT bodies, desires, and practices have been considered "unnatural" in many, but not all, human cultures, the question of the natural versus the unnatural is recast in philosophy as a moral controversy grounded in a normative ontology of the body's nature. In these controversies, LGBT critics have often invoked the naturalistic fallacy to argue against any easy alignment between what is (in nature) and what should be (in cultural practices).

A second line of philosophical analysis interrogates the cogency of biological explanations for LGBT bodies, practices, and desires. In these inquiries, nature is often positioned as a limit-concept, establishing what the body cannot but otherwise do. Inquiry into the ontology of sex, gender, and sexuality—the question of whether sexed bodies, gendered identities, or sexual orientations are culturally constructed categories or expressions of deeply personal and hence revealing facts of constitutional being—remains a lively and interminable domain of philosophical debate between social constructionists and essentialists of various types. Edward Stein has argued philosophically that the relevance of scientific research into the origins of sexual orientation does not imply any conclusions about moral entitlements or civil rights.

Conclusion

Philosophy as a discipline has always prided itself in asking the grand and mostly indeterminate questions of human existence: What can I/we know? How should I/we live? What exists? What is the good? What is right? What has been done to me/us? What can I/we hope for? What is to be done? Philosophy offers a palette of the grandest of the grand human universals, often pondering the meaning of value, truth, being, meaning, self, personhood, subject, agency, power, matter, and reality. To challenge the construction of these universals in the name of particularity or in the name of identitarian interests such as those emerging in LGBT philosophy is to make note of a possible contaminant in philosophy's closet. When the contaminants speak, this also calls attention to the (phallicized) male heterosexual body—the hidden body of the mind-body dualism that has determined the endgame of philosophy in Western culture. Queer philosophical writing about the body offers challenges to the austerely kept body of philosophy, a challenge articulated in the feel of the slimy holes in Christine Pierce's analysis of Jean-Paul Sartre, the oozing drips in Elizabeth Grosz's analysis of women's bodies, the gaping holes in Leo Bersani's anal writing, and the melancholic velvet in Judith Butler's theorization of the heteronormative bodily ego. In this movement of LGBT theorizing, difference over deviance, fluidity over rigidity, plurality over dualism, and bodily pleasure over disdain show signs of emerging in the future of philosophical writing, most assuredly when queer philosophers acquire the securities of post-tenured life.

At this time, however, emergent LGBT work in feminist theory, race theory, queer theory, and intersex and transgender theory has not reshaped the categorical paradigms of mainstream academic philosophy. However, LGBT academic philosophers have made some inroads using traditional methods to frame new questions and queries. This new work in conceptual, normative, ethical, ontological, social, and political philosophy has made its own mark. The slow but steady emergence of LGBT philosophy on the sidelines of this long-standing and largely somatophobic discipline is a remarkable moment in U.S. philosophy, often making dangerous demands on those who "risk censure for being shameless enough not to hide." Within new LGBT academic philosophy, the philosopher's body and the place from which she or he thinks are changing and becoming visible. Standpoint theory and the partial and subjugated knowledges that have been articulated in the work of LGBT theorists may someday help bring about a new period of philosophical thought, perhaps not a future that will turn philosophy on its head, but one that will enable philosophy to embrace the sex and gender variant body.

Bibliography

Butler, Judith. *Gender Trouble: Feminism and the Subversion of Identity.* New York: Routledge, 1990.

———. *Bodies that Matter: On the Discursive Limits of "Sex."* New York: Routledge,1993.

———. *Excitable Speech: A Politics of the Performance.* New York: Routledge, 1997.

Card, Claudia. *Lesbian Choices.* New York: Columbia University Press, 1995.

Card, Claudia, ed. *Adventures in Lesbian Philosophy.* Bloomington: Indiana University Press, 1994.

Corvino, John, ed. *Same Sex: Debating the Ethics, Science, and Culture of Homosexuality.* Lanham, Md.: Rowman and Littlefield. 1997.

Frye, Marilyn. "Lesbian Sex." In her *Willful Virgin: Essays in Feminism 1976–1992.* Freedom, Calif.: Crossing Press, 1992.

———. *The Politics of Reality.* Trumansburg, N.Y.: Crossing Press, 1983.

Hale, Jacob. "Are Lesbians Women?" *Hypatia* 12 (Spring 1997): 94–121.

Halperin, David M. "Is There a History of Sexuality?" In his *One Hundred Years of Homosexuality: And Other Essays on Greek Love.* New York: Routledge, 1990.

Hoagland, Sara Lucia. *Lesbian Ethics: Toward New Value.* Palo Alto, Calif.: Institute of Lesbian Studies, 1988.

Keller, Evelyn Fox. "Love and Sex in Plato's Epistemology." In her *Reflections on Gender and Science.* New Haven, Conn.: Yale University Press, 1985.

Mohr, Richard D. *Gays/Justice: A Study of Ethics, Society, and Law.* New York: Columbia University Press, 1988.

Murphy, Timothy F., ed. *Gay Ethics: Controversies in Outing, Civil Rights, and Sexual Science.* New York: Haworth Press, 1994.

Sedgwick, Eve Kosofsky. *Between Men: English Literature and Male Homosexual Desires.* New York: Columbia University Press, 1985.

Soble, Alan. *Philosophy of Sex: Contemporary Readings.* 4th ed. Lanham, Md.: Rowman and Littlefield, 2002.

Stein, Edward. *The Mismeasure of Desire: The Science, Theory, and Ethics of Sexual Orientation.* New York: Oxford University Press, 1999.

Trebilcot, Joyce. *Dyke Ideas: Process, Politics, Daily Life.* Albany, N.Y.: SUNY Press, 1994.

Wittig, Monique. *The Straight Mind and Other Essays.* Boston: Beacon, 1992.

Zita, Jacquelyn N. *Body Talk: Philosophical Reflections on Sex and Gender.* New York: Columbia University Press, 1998.

Jacqueline N. Zita

See also QUEER THEORY AND QUEER STUDIES.

PHYSICAL EDUCATION

Questions of sexuality and gender have been central to the history of physical education since the introduction of the discipline into U.S. colleges and universities in the late nineteenth century. The deeply entrenched cultural association between athletic prowess, heterosexual masculinity, and the male body has helped position the discipline as a key site for the analysis of LGBT identities and as a vehicle through which normative sexualities have been variously reinforced and transgressed.

With the emergence of capitalist industrial society in the nineteenth century, the distinction between leisure time and labor time became increasingly pronounced, and newly waged laborers and the middle and upper classes took to organized sport and exercise in large numbers. This trend was mirrored in the rapidly expanding higher education system where competitive intercollegiate athletics programs were complemented by the creation of physical education departments in which exercise specialists introduced young men to military drill and gymnastics. In each of these realms, sport was designed to cultivate a virile, tough, and implicitly heterosexual manhood that could sustain itself within what was widely viewed as artificial and effete urban society.

Women in Sport

Concern over the frailty of middle- and upper-class white women, whose enrollment in higher education was increasing during the same period, enabled women physical educators to enter the world of academe for the first time. From the 1890s onward, physical education departments for women created degree-granting majors as well as providing oftentimes mandatory physical exercise courses for female students.

Susan K. Cahn's *Coming on Strong* (1994), which examines the history of women in sport in the twentieth century, reveals that from the beginning, concerns about the sexual appetites and persuasions of physically active undergraduate women abounded. In the early decades of the century, concern focused on the belief that "mannish" female athletes might acquire masculine sexual behaviors and find their feminine inhibitions giving way to uncontainable heterosexual desire. But by the 1930s, female athleticism began to connote failed rather than excessive heterosexuality and physical educators worried that "mannish" athletes might have a propensity for same-sex desire. In the 1950s, at the height of the Cold War "homosexual panic," physical educators responded to the "crisis" of the "mannish lesbian athlete" by developing a curriculum that undertook an activist approach to heterosexuality: beauty and charm were emphasized over rigorous health and fitness, and mixed-sex "co-recreation" over what were formerly strictly segregated activities for men and women.

As white women largely deserted "manly" sports such as track and field in the 1930s, African American women, trained in segregated high schools and colleges in the South, began to blaze a trail of national and international success. In the early days of their participation, African American women were not constrained by the same stereotypes as their white counterparts, since ideal versions of black womanhood were not tied to a similarly limited set of characteristics and practices. This is not to say that their participation was entirely a positive development, however: African American women's participation did not produce high levels of anxiety among the white physical education establishment because they did not view African Americans as "real women" in the first place. This assumption, in addition to formal and informal racial segregation across the United States, meant that African American women, like other women of color, remained largely invisible in the dominant culture of physical education. This was to change with the sporting rivalries of the Cold War and a concerted effort on the part of both the black and white athletic establishments to cultivate black women athletes who were both more feminine (that is, more heterosexual) and more successful than their Russian counterparts. While white sports officials came to rely on black women to keep pace with Eastern European bloc athletes and to disprove Soviet charges of pervasive racial discrimination in the United States, black officials approached women's track and field as a measure of black cultural achievement and as a vehicle by which to insert into the public sphere carefully cultivated images of black women who were both feminine and morally virtuous.

physical education as charm school

In *Coming on Strong: Gender and Sexuality in Twentieth-Century Women's Sport* (1994), Susan Cahn describes a 1956 conference for directors of college women's physical education at which guest speaker Dr. Josephine Renshaw advised those in the audience to do all they could to encourage heterosexual interest among these women because the "muscular Amazon with unkempt hair, clod-hopper shoes, and dowdy clothing" might "revert to friendships with [her] own sex if disappointed with heterosexual attachments" (p. 164).

New Scholarly Perspectives: 1970–2000

In the 1970s, with the emergence of the sociology of sport as a field of study within physical education, critical perspectives on gender, sexuality, physical education, and sport began to appear. Early work in this area focused on the "lesbian stigma" and the negative effect of "role conflict" and homophobic stereotypes on straight women in sport. Scholars of this era were particularly concerned about the "female apologetic," or the tendency for women athletes to perform traditional displays of heterosexual femininity in order to counter the lesbian stigma.

As the lives of LGBT people were increasingly taken to be legitimate subjects of study in the university at large, scholars in the sociology of sport became less fearful and euphemistic in their treatment of antinormative sexualities and genders. This shift manifested itself in life history and ethnographic research aimed at reclaiming the experiences of lesbian educators, coaches, and athletes in order to reduce their invisibility and the oppressive silence that surrounded issues of lesbian identity in the world of sport. Pat Griffin's *Strong Women, Deep Closets: Lesbians and Homophobia in Sport* (1998) exemplifies this line of work with its detailed accounts of the harassment, discrimination, and silencing experienced by lesbian teachers and coaches, along with stories of their resistance to such oppression.

The pervasive cultural disjuncture between homosexuality and masculinity and thus homosexuality and sport meant that gay and bisexual men in this period remained largely invisible as scholars, teachers, or students of physical education. This absence was challenged in the 1990s by scholars seeking to make evident and to interpret the experiences of gay men in sport and to understand how male homoeroticism is enabled and constrained in heterosexual and homosexual men's sport cultures.

Inspired by Michel Foucault's work on the history of sexuality, Freudian and Lacanian psychoanalysis, and feminist theories of "biological" sex as the product of regimes of gender and compulsory heterosexuality, what would most appropriately be termed "queer" scholarship in the sociology of sport also began to emerge in the 1990s. Queer studies of sport are characterized by a move away from both essentializing research about "lesbian experience" and from a deviance model in which sexual orientation is only made visible when LGBT people are the focus of discussion, thus leaving heterosexuality as the unexamined norm. Instead, queer studies seeks to understand the ways in which sport and physical education function as sites through which sexual identities are produced and naturalized as normal or deviant, but also through which apparently stable categories are disrupted and transgressed. Such work shares an assumption that sport and physical education are particularly potent realms for queer research because they are centered on the body and because of the continuing segregation of competitive sports along lines of gender. Through examples ranging from the *Pumping Iron* films, through the controversy surrounding transsexual professional tennis player Renée Richards, to "gender verification" testing at international athletic events, poststructuralist scholars have sought to displace notions of the body in sport as natural—and hence naturally sexed—and instead to explore the contingency and fluidity of sexuality and gender as they are manifested in sporting practices, cultures, and texts. In the context of the ongoing commodification of sport, researchers have placed particular emphasis on the effect of commercial pressures in the public presentation of activities that are viewed as gay (for example, men's figure skating) or lesbian (such as women's golf).

Although certain work in sport studies is attuned to the necessity of analyzing the intersection of sexuality with relations of race, class, gender, nation, and so on, categories such as "lesbians in sport" or "gay athletes" are still frequently deployed without consideration of their universalizing and thus exclusionary functions. While there exists a range of approaches to queer issues in the intersecting fields of physical education, the sociology and psychology of sport, and sport studies, the implicit subject of the discipline—American, white, and middle class—is yet to be decentered.

Bibliography

Adams, Mary Louise. "To Be an Ordinary Hero: Male Figure Skaters and the Ideology of Gender." In *Men and Masculinities: A Critical Anthology.* Edited by T. Haddock. Toronto: Canadian Scholars Press, 1993.

Birrell, Susan, and Cheryl L. Cole, eds. *Women, Sport, and Culture.* Champaign, Ill.: Human Kinetics, 1994.

Cahn, Susan K. *Coming on Strong: Gender and Sexuality in Twentieth-Century Women's Sport.* New York: Free Press, 1994.

Connell, Robert. *Gender and Power.* Palo Alto, Calif.: Stanford University Press, 1987.

Griffin, Pat. *Strong Women, Deep Closets: Lesbians and Homophobia in Sport.* Champaign, Ill.: Human Kinetics, 1998.

Messner, Michael A., and Don F. Sabo, eds. *Sport, Men, and the Gender Order.* Champaign, Ill.: Human Kinetics Press, 1990.

Pronger, Brian. *The Arena of Masculinity: Sport, Homosexuality, and the Meaning of Sex.* New York: St. Martin's Press, 1990.

Sykes, Heather. "Turning the Closets Inside/Out: Towards a Queer Feminist Theory in Women's Physical Education." *Sociology of Sport Journal* 15 (1998): 154–173.

Samantha J. King

See also SPORTS.

PHYSIQUE MAGAZINES AND PHOTOGRAPHS

Featuring photographs and drawings of young men posing and flexing their muscles, usually in small posing straps, physique magazines flourished from the mid-1950s to the early 1960s. They were the major source of print and visual culture for gay men before Stonewall; at the height of their popularity, the physiques outcirculated homophile magazines by almost ten to one. Distributed through the mail and sold on newsstands in some major cities, they combined editorials, readers' letters, and photos and drawings to create an early form of gay public culture through which gay men could experience themselves as part of a collective—a particularly important development at a time when homosexuality was still primarily understood in individual, psychological terms.

Thomas Waugh's monumental study of gay male visual culture, *Hard to Imagine* (1996), provides a thoroughgoing account, not only of the history of the physique magazines, but of the forms of popular visual representations of the male body that preceded them. Waugh traces the origins of the physiques back to the late nineteenth and early twentieth centuries. Emphasizing the importance of movements like the Young Men's Christian Association (YMCA) and scouting in the United States, as well as German naturalist and gymnasium movements, he suggests that depictions of naked or partly clothed male bodies emerged at least in part from a need to resist the dehumanization of industrial work. He also describes the significance of technological and marketplace advances to the development of physique photography, focusing on the popularity of postcards, magazines, and relatively cheap cameras at the turn of the twentieth century. Though the audience for this early form of beefcake photography was overwhelmingly male, the orientation of "physical culture" in this period was predominantly heterosexual. Magazines like Bernarr Macfadden's *Physical Culture* stressed a Victorian ideal of the muscleman as the model for a virility that could resist the draining influences of urban life and middle-class gentility. However, Waugh is able to show that even in this period gay men were using heavily coded personal ads in *Physical Culture* to meet each other and were avid collectors of physique photos from the magazines.

By the 1930s some of the conditions for a print-based, gay physique culture were in place, though its infrastructure was not yet discernibly gay. Bodybuilding and gym-based weightlifting were becoming more popular. *Strength and Health* magazine, linked to the York Barbell Company in York, Pennsylvania, began publishing in this period, and the first Mister America bodybuilding contest was held in 1939. Here and there, gay photographers like Al Urban started up regional mail-order services for their photos of muscular young men, but no one had yet thought of assembling photos into a magazine format.

The Heyday of Physique Photography

Physique photography in magazine form, the form that became truly popular, began in the 1950s with men like Bob Mizer, an amateur photographer in Los Angeles who began to see that the mail order catalogs sent to prospective purchasers of physique photos were themselves a potential source of profit. (As Waugh points out, an entrepreneurial impulse drove both straight and gay men involved in the world of physique photography from the very start.) Soon the catalogs evolved into simple magazines with editorials, letter columns, and feature articles alongside advertisements and the photos themselves. It was in this format that the physique magazines reached their widest circulation.

Though at the peak of physique photography's popularity there were more than one hundred muscle magazines on the market, Mizer's *Physique Pictorial* was among the longest-running and best known. The photos, editorials, and letters in *Physique Pictorial* offer an exemplary record of the emergence of a popular gay male visual culture as well as a record of the difficult conditions in which such a culture could develop. As Mizer and his cohorts began to photograph muscular men who were not necessarily bodybuilders, turning instead to fresh-faced boys next door, athletes, and young soldiers, they implicitly signaled that it was male beauty, rather than male strength, that the magazines were offering. This was an aesthetic turn that got Mizer, along with a whole generation of physique photographers, into constant trouble with the police and the state. Indeed, one way to understand the history of physique photography is as the struggle of the photographers trying to produce representations of an erotic male body that would nonetheless escape censorship.

The primary visual and rhetorical strategies photographers and publishers used in order to avoid police harassment and the censors at the U.S. Postal Service were what Waugh has called the "artistic and athletic alibis." By insisting that they were taking pictures of muscular young men as part of a coolly aesthetic pursuit of photographic art or as a service to young men in need of inspiration in their own exercise regimes, Mizer and his cohort hoped to convince police and postal censors that magazines like *Physique Pictorial* did not encourage the sort of prurience that could classify them as obscene and therefore illegal. Mizer's editorials in *Physique Pictorial* are frequently aimed at what he saw as the hypocrisy of labeling the naked or erotic male body "obscene," and his photographs, which depict young athletes in Greek or Roman costume, in gyms, or in military gear are an argument for both the classical purity and the dailiness and normality of male beauty.

Twined together with the history of the artistic and athletic alibis in physique culture is its history of racial representation. Greg Mullins has shown the ways in which early-twentieth-century physique magazines used photos of African men to offset the possibility of overtly eroticizing men's bodies, adopting a cool, anthropological stance toward those men that attempted to displace the lure of male beauty with an idea of muscular development as a kind of evolution. And Tracy Morgan has shown that 1950s physique photographers, though they abandoned any pretense to anthropological distance in photographing men of color, nonetheless kept them at a remove, often separating photos of them into special issues or preserving a hint of the anthropological alibi by photographing men with racially coded props like straw hats or chains.

Physique Photography Becomes Obsolete

Overall, the strategy of the alibi was only marginally successful. Many physique photographers, collectors, and a few models were harassed by the police and by the U.S. Postal Service in the 1950s and 1960s, and a few of them—Mizer included—served prison sentences. After a police raid on physique collectors in Northampton, Massachusetts, Smith College English professor Newton Arvin was forced to testify against friends and colleagues and attempted suicide. In 1962, though, the U.S. Supreme Court heard an obscenity case centered on physique magazines in *MANual Enterprises v. Day*, and ruled 6-1 in the magazines' favor, thereby easing restrictions on what could be distributed in the mail. Though the Supreme Court maintained that the magazines were aimed at the "prurient interests" of readers, it asserted that "prurient interest" was not a sufficient criterion for defining obscenity, insisting that truly "obscene" materials were also "patently offensive"—and that the physique magazines were not.

The ruling in *MANual Enterprises* opened the door for the physique magazines to become more open about the erotic lure of physique photos as well as the specifically gay sexuality they were addressing. Slowly over the course of the 1960s, physique photography grew more overtly sexual as artists depicted their models nude and chose younger, slimmer men—and boys—to photograph. Though Mizer's photographs retained their 1950s atmosphere of playful, boyish romping, most other photographers quickly moved to take advantage of what they saw as both more expressive and more profitable sexual nudes. Other magazines, meanwhile, like Philadelphia's *Drum*, began to be more explicitly political, adopting the idiom of camp and the rhetoric of gay liberation in its editorials and photo captions.

By the 1970s the popularity of the physique magazines was on the wane: the loosening of obscenity law, helped along by the *MANual Enterprises* decision, opened the field to more explicit and more profitable pornography. The physiques were also surpassed by political change: the rise of a self-identified gay movement abruptly made them seem closeted and antiliberatory. It was not until the 1990s, as lesbian and gay activists, collectors, and historians took to reclaiming the byways of pre-Stonewall gay eros, that the physiques became interesting to large numbers of gay men again—this time as a slightly campy reflection of what was regarded as a more innocent, pre-AIDS sexuality as well as a precursor to the politics of gay liberation. Scholarly books like Waugh's *Hard to Imagine*, coffee-table books like Hooven's *Beefcake* (1998), and films like Thom Fitzgerald's *Beefcake* (1999) all established connections between the 1960s muscle culture and subsequent gay sexuality. By drawing such connections, historians of physique culture have made it clear that the closet it built—the alibi around the display of the male body—is still with us in advertising, in contemporary men's fitness magazines, and on the Internet, almost as though the closet is erotic in itself. The sheer variety of sexual representations of men in contemporary visual culture makes it hard to know.

Bibliography

Fitzgerald, Thom. *Beefcake.* 16mm, 93 min. Santa Monica, CA: Strand Releasing, 1999.

Hooven, F. Valentine III. *Beefcake: The Muscle Magazines of America, 1950–1970.* Cologne, Germany: Taschen, 1995.

Meyer, Richard. *Outlaw Representation: Censorship and Homosexuality in Twentieth-Century American Art.* Oxford: Oxford University Press, 2002.

Morgan, Tracy. "Pages of Whiteness: Race, Physique Magazines, and the Emergence of Gay Public Culture, 1955–1960." *Found Objects,* no. 4 (Fall 1994): 109–126.

Mullins, Greg. "Nudes, Prudes, and Pigmies: The Desirability of Disavowal in *Physical Culture.*" *Discourse* 15, no. 1 (Fall 1992): 27–48.

Waugh, Thomas. *Hard to Imagine: Gay Male Eroticism in Photography and Film from their Beginnings to Stonewall.* New York: Columbia University Press, 1996.

Christopher Nealon

See also CENSORSHIP, OBSCENITY, AND PORNOGRAPHY LAW AND POLICY; HOCKNEY, DAVID; MIZER, ROBERT; PORNOGRAPHY.

PI'TAMAKAN (b. c. 1810s; d. c. 1850s), warrior.

Pi'tamakan, or Running Eagle, was born into the Pikuni or Piegan tribe of what is now northern Montana sometime in the early 1800s and came to prominence sometime around the middle of the century. The Piegan are the southernmost of the three tribes of the Blackfoot Confederacy, whose traditional territory extended from central Montana to the North Saskatchewan River in central Alberta. She was known as Young Weasel Woman when she was a child. Her father encouraged her when, at around the age of twelve, she exhibited an interest in men's activities and preferred to play with boys instead of girls.

Pi'tamakan's career as a warrior began in her teens, when her small hunting party was attacked by the Assiniboine. She is said to have saved her father's life during the fight. When she joined another raiding party against the Crow, she stole eleven horses and killed a Crow warrior. After this victory she was allowed to sing the Victory Song and a Scalp Dance was done in her honor. After a major battle with the Pend d'Oreille, she became the only woman in the tribe's history to receive a male name and was invited to join the all-male Braves Society. Because of her skills and good fortune, she was soon leading raiding parties and many Piegan warriors were happy to follow her.

It was not unheard-of among Northern Great Plains tribes like the Piegan for a woman to participate in warfare. In these androcentric horse cultures, the greatest individual prestige came through the masculine arenas of warfare, hunting, and horse raiding. Therefore, it was not unusual for women to seek such prestige for themselves, and among the Piegan they were called manly-hearted women. Manly-hearted women were generally older, married to men, and did not wear men's clothing; it was rare for an interest in warfare to involve more extensive adoption of the masculine role.

Pi'tamakan starting wearing men's clothing in her teens, likely around the same time that her career as a warrior began. Until her father's death, however, she had to perform the women's work for the family because her mother was often sick. When her father was killed by the Crow, she took his place at the head of the family and brought a young widow into the family to perform the necessary domestic labor. It is unclear whether she married the widow or if a sexual relationship existed between them. One account of her life says that she had married a Piegan man when she was younger but that he was killed in battle with the Crow. After his death she sought help from the Sun to avenge him and received a vision in which the Sun promised to give her great power in war so long as she never had intercourse with a man again. Another account of her vision, which says that she had always rejected male suitors and fasted to receive a spiritual guardian emphasizes that her vision of the Sun added credence to her gender role change and made her a holy person among the Piegan. One account of her behavior while leading war parties suggests that, although she was the leader and always wore men's clothing, she would also do the cooking for her men and repair their moccasins. When one of her warriors objected, she is said to have replied, "I am a woman. Men don't know how to sew" (Ewers, p. 199). This account, however, does not accord with the rest of her behavior, particularly her permanent adoption of masculine dress as a teenager and her decision to bring the young widow into her family so that she did not have to do the domestic work anymore.

There are two different accounts of Pi'tamakan's death. One says she was killed during a raid on the Flathead Indians west of the Rockies, a common target for horse raids by the Piegan. The Flatheads had heard that a woman was leading the raids against them and were on the lookout for a strange woman. She was shot dead when she was spotted by a Flathead warrior. Another account says she was killed when she led a large war party against the Pend d'Oreille in retaliation for an attack on a group of Piegan warriors. Some Blackfeet claim that her good luck finally ended and she was killed because she had broken her vow to the Sun by having intercourse with one of the men in her party.

Bibliography

Ewers, John C. *Plains Indian History and Culture: Essays on Continuity and Change.* Norman and London: University of Oklahoma Press, 1997.

Lang, Sabine. *Men As Women, Women As Men: Changing Gender in Native American Cultures.* Translated from the German by John L. Vantine. Austin: University of Texas Press, 1998.

Lewis, Oscar. "Manly-Hearted Women among the Northern Piegan." *American Anthropologist* 43 (1941): 173–187.

Medicine, Beatrice. " 'Warrior Women'—Sex Role Alternatives for Plains Indian Women." In *The Hidden Half: Studies of Plains Indian Women.* Edited by Patricia Albers and Beatrice Medicine. Washington, D.C.: University Press of America, 1983.

Roscoe, Will. *Changing Ones: Third and Fourth Genders in Native North America.* New York: St. Martin's Press, 1998.

Roscoe, Will, ed. *Living the Spirit: A Gay American Indian Anthology.* New York: St. Martin's Press, 1988.

Schaeffer, Claude E. "The Kutenai Female Berdache." *Ethnohistory* 12 (1965): 193–236.

Sheila McManus

See also TRANSSEXUALS, TRANSVESTITES, TRANSGENDER PEOPLE, AND CROSS-DRESSERS; TWO-SPIRIT FEMALES.

PIERCINGS, TATTOOS, AND SCARS

For some LGBT communities, piercing, tattooing, and scarification play important roles as forms of investment in the erotic and somatic potential of the body and as physical markers of social difference and marginalization. Body modification has become a zone of interest for scholars seeking to understand how and why certain groups define themselves through modifications of their bodies. While essentially an individual activity, body modifications like piercing, tattooing, and scarification have come to be recognized as having particular meanings in marginalized subcultures. As markers of difference, celebrations of pride, and, vehicles for embodied pleasure, body modifications in LGBT communities are best read in relation to each community's understanding of the symbols of the physical markings and their relationship to marked bodies. Reading marked bodies must take into account the body, its links to group identity, the symbolism of the markings, and the historical moment at which these markings emerged. While piercing, tattooing, and scarification have come to have similar meanings for LGBT communities in North America, they have different genealogies insofar as they migrated into and were then utilized by those communities in distinct ways.

Tattooing

In Western societies, tattooing is traditionally a form of body expression for male-dominated groups like sailors, bikers, and soldiers. The tattoo has, according to Clinton R. Sanders, been used to inscribe the working-class male body with a kind of rebellious masculinity. As North American bourgeois culture sought to define the appropriate middle-class body in the nineteenth century, individuals who remained outside of this project because of their occupation or status sought to define themselves with body markings in opposition to the middle-class idealized unmarked body. In the twentieth century, the emergence of gay male (and some masculinized forms of lesbian) identity has been closely tied to these representations of masculinity.

The tattoo as a form of self-decoration and self-expression for masculine groups that were ostracized by mainstream society became for many gay men a symbol of hypermasculinized sexuality. The early beefcake photographs of the 1950s and 1960s attest to the gay male desire for the tattooed bodies of sailors, bikers, and soldiers. Such tattooed bodies were desired because of their coding as hypermasculinized males who remained rebelliously outside the confines of mainstream society. Samuel M. Steward's personal musings on the relationship between gay male desire and tattooing address the transition of the tattoo from an object on the bodies that gay males desired to an object of self-identification among the emerging LGBT communities of the 1960s and 1970s.

While the tattoo has come to be an accepted form of self-expression in LGBT communities, it has also come to be a means of expressing both resistance to mainstream society and pride in a sexualized identity. This can be seen especially in the number of LGBT tattoos making use of symbols of LGBT identity (female-female and male-male symbols, lambdas, pink triangles, and so on). During the height of the AIDS epidemic, from the early 1980s into the 1990s, this form of rebellious self-identification reached its height with many HIV-positive individuals tattooing themselves with symbols of their status (the biohazard symbol, the acronym for Person with AIDS, and others). While LGBT communities have integrated the tattoo as a mark of difference, sometimes based on resistance or pride, the tattoo has in popular culture witnessed what Arnold Rubin terms a "tattoo renaissance," making the tattooed body more acceptable to mainstream society.

Piercing

Piercing in LGBT communities in North America emerged, like the tattoo, as a form of resistance, pride, and eroticism. However, unlike the hypermasculinized symbolism associated with mid-century forms of the tattoo, piercing in early LGBT communities was favored by young gay men who adapted feminized forms of ear piercing into their ideal of a feminized gay male image. Young gay men in the 1950s and 1960s pierced their ears to ornament themselves in a more feminine manner. Given the prevailing atmosphere of the preliberation period, these acts were charged with transgressive symbolism in that pierced male bodies were read as feminine and/or homosexual by mainstream culture.

With the flowering of lesbian and gay liberation in the 1970s, body piercing and body play (a term denoting the mutability and erotic potential of the body to explore pain, pleasure, desire, and transgression) became more important among the LGBT sadomasochism (S/M) subcultures of larger urban centers. Borrowing body piercing from so-called primitive cultures, in which the piercing was usually part of a rite of passage, LGBT S/M subcultures integrated it into their sexualized body play as a form of sexual and erotic exploration. Jim Ward, a body piercer in San Francisco, is often credited with the growth and popularity of piercing in these communities.

While LGBT S/M communities were exploring the erotic potential of body piercing, the "modern primitives"—part of an emerging Western subculture that uses practices, techniques, and modifications from so-called primitive cultures to explore the modern body and its relationship to the modern world—began utilizing body piercings as a form of spirituality, physical transgression, and ritual of passage. In the late 1970s the emerging punk movement in Great Britain and the U.S., which emphasized the rejection of modern Western cultural values, borrowed these symbols from the LGBT S/M and "primitive" communities to use body piercing as a form of defiance and resistance to the middle-class idealized unmarked body. In the late 1970s and early 1980s, body piercing again crossed cultural lines, this time from the punk and S/M communities into popular LGBT culture, as non–S/M LGBT people began piercing their bodies for public display. These piercings were a celebration of the erotic potential of different erogenous zones like ears, nipples, or genitals with designated names emerging for specific piercings. Like tattooing, body piercing had a renaissance in the 1990s as mainstream society accepted and integrated pierced bodies into popular culture.

Scarification

Scarification or branding, like body piercing, emerged from the subcultures of the LGBT S/M and "primitive" communities in the 1970s. However, there is also another, more covert, tradition of physical self-mutilation that emerged in the 1970s and 1980s among young LGBT individuals who marked their bodies with scars as physical outlets for and manifestations of their psychological pain. Like the physical markings of tattoos and piercings of the body, scarification and ritual branding have come to be seen as a rite of passage, a form of physical play with the body's erotic and transgressive possibilities, and a marker of difference, defiance, and celebration. Although never experiencing the popular acceptance and approval of mainstream society that has been accorded to tattooed and pierced bodies, scarification and branding has in LGBT communities come to be recognized as a form of body play that is heavily invested with a transgressive spiritual and erotic power.

Bibliography

DeMello, Margo. *Bodies of Inscription: A Cultural History of the Modern Tattoo Community.* Durham, N.C.: Duke University Press, 2000.

Rubin, Arnold, ed. *Marks of Civilization: Artistic Transformations of the Human Body.* Los Angeles: Museum of Cultural History, University of California Press, 1988.

Sanders, Clinton R. *Customizing the Body: The Art and Culture of Tattooing.* Philadelphia: Temple University Press, 1989.

Steward, Samuel M. *Bad Boys and Tough Tattoos: A Social History of the Tattoo with Gangs, Sailors, and Street-Corner Punks, 1950–1965.* London: Haworth Press, 1990.

Thompson, Mark, ed. *Leatherfolk: Radical Sex, People, Politics, and Practice.* Boston: Alyson, 1991.

R. J. Gilmour

See also EICHELBERGER, ETHYL; LEATHER SEX AND SEXUALITY; SADOMASOCHISM, SADISTS, AND MASOCHISTS.

PIÑERO, Miguel (b. 19 December 1946; d. 16 June 1988), poet, playwright, actor.

Born in Puerto Rico, Piñero migrated to New York City with his family as a child. One of seven children, Piñero was seven when his father walked out on his mother. Life was difficult for Piñero. Growing up poor on the streets of New York and suffering from sexual abuse, he turned to drugs and became a mugger, thief, and shoplifter. Piñero was convicted of armed robbery in 1971 and was sent to the Ossining Correctional Facility (Sing Sing) for armed robbery. It was there that he met Marvin Felix Camillo, who was running a drama workshop.

The talented people Camillo found at Sing Sing would later become "The Family," an acting troupe of ex-convicts of whom Piñero was the most successful. Camillo and Piñero became friends, and Camillo submitted Piñero's poem "Black Woman with the Blonde Wig On" to a contest, which it won. He was paroled in 1973.

Piñero's first and most successful play was *Short Eyes: The Killing of a Sex Offender by the Inmates of the House of Detention.* The play tells the story of men trapped in a prison system with its own code of conduct and laws, and how they survive. The climax of the play is the murder of Clark Davis, the incarcerated child molester. In the prison hierarchy, sexual offenders are considered the lowest of the low, and Clark's death is carried out with brutal efficiency. The character Cupcakes, youthful and handsome, is the prize desired by the love-starved men.

Short Eyes opened on 23 May 1974 at New York's Public Theater, with Joseph Papp as producer and Camillo directing. Many in the cast were members of The Family. *Short Eyes* won the Obie Award for best off-Broadway play of 1973–1974, and Camillo won for distinguished direction. That same year, *Short Eyes* won the New York Drama Critics Circle Award for best American play.

Piñero became friends with Miguel Algarin, another "NuYorican" poet. Together they founded the Nuyorican Poets Cafe in 1974 on Manhattan's Lower East Side. The marginalization of poor people of color, excluded from the mainstream American artistic community, served as the political focus for their creative voices. The Nuyorican Poets Cafe was born of the political radicalism of the 1960s, and the cafe has served as a laboratory for cultural and political art ever since. Piñero's poetry, collected in *La Bodega Sold Dreams* (1980), influenced many other artists. Piñero is cited as being a forerunner to rap and hip-hop music. In 1993, the Nuyorican Poets Cafe was recognized by the Municipal Society of New York as one of the "living treasures" of the city. It is still at the heart of poetic life in New York City.

Many of Piñero's characters blur the line between gay and straight. *Paper Toilet* takes place in a subway toilet and deals in part with characters cruising. *Irving* deals with the coming out of a closeted Jewish man—and the discovery that he and his sister have been dating the same man.

Piñero was a commercial success, writing plays and television scripts; he also appeared in episodes of the television series *Miami Vice, Kojak,* and *The Equalizer*, as well as movies, among them *Fort Apache, The Bronx* (1981) and *Breathless* (1983). In the movie adaptation of *Short Eyes* (1977), Piñero played the minor character GoGo.

Piñero was briefly married to Juanita Lovette Rameize (1977–1979) and adopted a son, Ismael Castro. Even with all of his success, Piñero remained a heroin addict. (He used to scalp tickets to *Short Eyes* for money with which to buy heroin.) He continued an on-and-off life of crime and was arrested periodically. Piñero died in New York City from liver disease in 1988. His friend Algarin led the procession in which Piñero's ashes were scattered across the Lower East Side. He then read a poem Piñero had written for the occasion of his own death.

Piñero was bisexual. Many of the characters in his plays were sexually ambiguous. However, it is doubtful that he identified in any way with the gay and lesbian community. The Latin idea of machismo, which every man is supposed to aspire to, may have caused tension in Piñero's life. The idea of being passive during sex challenges masculinity. Gay identity often takes into account both masculine and feminine roles—something that Piñero might have found objectionable.

Perhaps actor Benjamin Bratt's assessment of Piñero is the most realistic. Bratt played the complex Piñero in the film *Piñero* (2001) and concluded that Piñero was a sensualist: he would indulge in whatever felt good to him at that particular moment. To be labeled gay or bisexual would have had little meaning to Piñero.

Bibliography

Camillo, Marvin Felix. "Introduction." *Short Eyes: A Play*, by Miguel Piñero. New York: Hill and Wang, 1975.

Duralde, Alonso. "Unspoiled Bratt." *The Advocate,* issue 858, (February 5, 2002): 40–45.

Michael Handis

See also THEATER AND PERFORMANCE.

POLAK, Clark (b. 15 October 1937; d. 18 September 1980), activist.

One of the most important homophile activists of the 1960s, Clark Phillip Polak was the president of the Philadelphia-based Janus Society (1963–1969); the founder, publisher, and editor of *Drum* magazine (1964–1969); and the leader of the Homosexual Law Reform Society (1965–1969). Also the owner of several sex and pornography businesses, Polak consistently challenged the homophile movement to join the sexual revolution and affirm gay sexual culture. Relentlessly pursued by local, state, and federal authorities who accused him of violating obscenity laws, Polak was forced to relocate in the early 1970s, beginning a second career as a gay activist, real estate investor, and art collector in Southern California.

Polak was born in 1937 to middle-class Jewish parents in Philadelphia. Years later he claimed that he began having sex with boys at age five and was known as queer at Central High School. After flunking out of Pennsylvania State University, Polak became a businessman in Philadelphia, doing quite well as the owner of Frankford Personnel and Northeast Advertising Service. By the late 1950s Polak was living in Center City, the heart of gay Philadelphia. In 1957 he was arrested and released on disorderly conduct charges; the circumstances surrounding that arrest remain unclear.

Having encountered Donald Webster Cory's influential book *The Homosexual in America* (1951) in the 1950s, Polak joined the Janus Society in 1962. In 1963 he organized a Janus-sponsored lecture by Cory at the Essex Hotel, attracting an audience of approximately 125 people. Later in 1963, when the Drake Hotel attempted to withdraw from its agreement to rent space for a conference of East Coast Homophile Organizations (ECHO), Polak reportedly made violent threats to the hotel managers. For this Polak was censured by ECHO, but his actions may have helped persuade the Drake to honor its agreement.

In late 1963 Polak was elected president of Janus, a position that he held for six tumultuous years. In many respects, Polak's work as a homophile leader paralleled that of other homophile activists. He organized public lectures on LGBT topics; raised money for LGBT causes; supported LGBT research projects; advocated for LGBT people with local, state, and federal authorities; worked with the American Civil Liberties Union (ACLU) to support LGBT civil rights; published and distributed LGBT materials; organized LGBT demonstrations; and presented pro-LGBT positions in mainstream newspaper, magazine, radio, and television media (including various Philadelphia outlets as well as *Sexology, Playboy,* the *Wall Street Journal,* and the *Phil Donahue Show*).

In other respects, Polak struck out in new directions, urging the homophile movement to become more militant, more radical, more pro-gay, and more sex-positive. Perhaps his greatest achievement was *Drum* magazine.

While the *Mattachine Review, ONE* magazine, and the *Ladder* are often cited as the most significant homophile publications of the 1950s and 1960s, *Drum* had a circulation (approximately fifteen thousand, according to a 1968 *Wall Street Journal* article) that was larger than that of all of the others combined. It achieved this success by combining male physique photography (which the other main homophile periodicals rejected) with political news and commentary, cultural features, humorous comic strips, and an editorial stance that celebrated free gay sexual expression.

Meanwhile, Polak developed several sex businesses, including LARK Enterprises, which published personal advertisements; Trojan Book Service, which published and distributed gay pornographic materials that sometimes featured Polak's lover James Mitchell; and Beaver Book Service, which catered to the straight male market. Later in the 1960s Polak purchased and ran three pornographic bookstores in Philadelphia.

While leading Janus, publishing *Drum*, and running his sex businesses, Polak also founded the Homosexual Law Reform Society (HLRS). Taking the profits earned from *Drum* and his sex businesses, Polak used the HLRS to fund a variety of important LGBT rights cases, including a 1967 New Jersey Supreme Court case, *Val's v. Division of Alcoholic Beverage Control,* commonly referred to as *Val's*, that established the right of LGBT people to assemble in bars and a 1967 U.S. Supreme Court case, *Boutilier v. Immigration and Naturalization Service,* that unsuccessfully challenged a federal immigration law that excluded homosexuals as "psychopathic personalities."

Over the course of the 1960s, Polak was criticized by many homophile activists who objected to his difficult and contentious personality, criticized his dictatorial leadership style, opposed the overwhelmingly male focus of his homophile activities, and rejected his radical sex politics. Meanwhile, Polak was targeted by federal, state, and local officials, who routinely harassed him, his allies, and his employees for alleged violations of obscenity laws. Ultimately, Polak was convicted on federal charges and in 1972 accepted a plea bargain under which he agreed to abandon his pornography businesses. By this time he had already moved to California, closing down Janus and HLRS.

In Southern California, Polak helped establish the Stonewall Democratic Club and the ACLU Gay Rights Chapter, supported the Los Angeles gay community center, funded the International Gay and Lesbian Archives, ran an art gallery and wrote art criticism, and made a second fortune in real estate. By the late 1970s Polak apparently was involved with rough hustlers, using drugs, and losing money. In September 1980 he committed suicide.

With his death, the LGBT movement lost one of its most colorful figures from the pre–Stonewall Riots era. For a variety of reasons, most scholars of homophile politics have paid little attention to Polak's activities, describing the movement as much more sexually, culturally, and politically conservative than it actually was. When Polak's activities are placed at the center, rather than the margins, of the history of the homophile movement, that history will have to be rewritten.

Bibliography

Kepner, Jim. "A Farewell to Friends Departed." *National Gay Archives Bulletin* (Fall 1983): 16.

Stein, Marc. "'Birthplace of the Nation': Imagining Lesbian and Gay Communities in Philadelphia, 1969–1970." In *Creating a Place for Ourselves: Lesbian, Gay, and Bisexual Community Histories.* Edited by Brett Beemyn. New York: Routledge, 1997.

Stein, Marc. *City of Sisterly and Brotherly Loves: Lesbian and Gay Philadelphia, 1945–1972.* Chicago: University of Chicago Press, 2000.

Stein, Marc. "Sex Politics in the City of Sisterly and Brotherly Loves." *Radical History Review* 59 (1994): 60–92.

Marc Stein

See also CENSORSHIP, OBSCENITY, AND PORNOGRAPHY LAW AND POLICY; *DRUM*; HOMOPHILE MOVEMENT; HOMOPHILE PRESS; JANUS SOCIETY.

POLICING AND POLICE

In a narrow sense, policing refers to the actions of the police, that is, organized civil and military forces responsible for enforcing laws, preventing and detecting crime, and maintaining social order. In a broad sense, policing refers to any actions taken to regulate and control a community. LGBT desires, acts, identities, communities, and movements have been intensively policed in both senses.

Policing in the Broad Sense

In the broad sense, religion, the state, and science have played key roles in policing genders and sexualities, as have families, schools, and media. Religious discourses of sin (as in Christian views of sodomy), state discourses of crime (as in police perspectives on disorderly conduct), and scientific discourses of disease (as in medical conceptions of mental illness) have all been used in attempts to control same-sex sexualities and cross-gender behaviors. And discourses of sexuality and gender, in turn, have been deployed in projects of race and class control (as in the labeling of people of color, immigrants, and working-class people as hypersexual or hyposexual).

While some have identified a shift in the locus of authority from religious elites in the colonial era to political officials in the nineteenth century and scientific experts in the twentieth, others have emphasized intersections and overlaps between these forms of regulation in every era of U.S. history. In the colonial period, for instance, religious conceptions of sodomy as a sin were the basis of legal definitions of sodomy as a crime. In the twentieth century, scientific conceptions of homosexuality as a psychopathology were encoded and institutionalized in sexual psychopath and immigration statutes, and these laws remained in place long after the scientific consensus shifted away from the view that homosexuality is intrinsically psychopathological. Those who think that religious conceptions lost all power after the disestablishment of religion in the eighteenth century need only consider the influence of the Christian Right on twentieth century discourses of sexuality and gender and the ongoing power of Christianity in certain regions of the country. Cultural authority to police sexualities and genders has shifted over the course of U.S. history, but authority remains fragmented, diffuse, and pervasive.

There have also been debates and disagreements about whether to focus attention on the policing of the dominant or the deviant. While some have highlighted the effects of regulation on LGBT people and phenomena, others have emphasized the ways in which policing attempts to control not only that which is defined as abnormal but also that which is defined as normal. Attacking "sissies" and "tomboys," for example, polices not only those who are defined as gender deviants but also those who are seen as "boyish" boys and "girly" girls. Labeling women man-hating lesbians is a way of keeping straight women in line as much as it is a way of taunting deviant women. Expressing disapproval of certain types of physical displays of same-sex affection is a method of establishing strict boundaries between the appropriately homosocial and the transgressively homoerotic, policing both sides of that border.

Where there perhaps is more agreement, at least among scholars, is that because LGBT identities and communities did not exist before the late nineteenth century, it is not really possible to talk about the policing of these identities and communities before this period. And because organized LGBT movements did not exist until the mid-twentieth century, it is not really possible to talk about the policing of these movements before this period. That said, same-sex sexual desires and acts and cross-gender behaviors predate the late nineteenth century, and these were policed, in the broad and narrow sense, from the moment that Europeans first invaded North America.

Policing in the Narrow Sense

In the narrow sense, LGBT people and phenomena have been policed by a wide range of police forces. Local and state police have enforced laws against buggery, crimes against nature, cross-dressing, disorderly conduct, indecency, lewd and lascivious behavior, obscenity, prostitution, sexual psychopathy, solicitation, and a wide variety of other crimes, and they have often done so with disproportionate impact on LGBT people and phenomena. They have also enforced anti-LGBT public health and liquor control laws (for example, through raids on bathhouses, bars, and clubs) and have enforced anti-LGBT court rulings in adoption, child custody, foster care, and inheritance cases. Military police have enforced laws against LGBT sexual acts, identities, and speech in all branches of the armed forces. Federal immigration and customs officials have policed the nation's borders to exclude LGBT people, LGBT materials, and people with HIV/AIDS. Federal postal officials have enforced laws against mailing LGBT materials defined as obscene. And the Federal Bureau of Investigation (FBI) has spied on LGBT individuals and groups and has actively supported local, state, and federal officials in the enforcement of anti-LGBT laws.

Police forces in the United States, which exercise elements of the state's monopoly on the legitimate use of force, have also acted in extralegal and quasi-legal ways against the interests of LGBT people. Even when entrapment has been ruled illegal, they have set up sexual situations in which LGBT people break laws that they might not otherwise break, sometimes by flirting, pursuing, touching, and having sex with undercover police officers (who are often selected on the basis of youth and good looks). Even when courts have limited application of obscenity laws against LGBT materials, police have harassed and arrested the producers of such materials. Even when they have known that arrests of LGBT bar patrons, political activists, and public demonstrators would not be held up in court, they have brought in LGBT people for questioning, held them overnight in jails, informed their families and employers, and then released them. In the course of doing so, they have often committed physical and sexual assaults on LGBT people. Even when it has been illegal for police to collect payoffs from local businesses, they have done so with LGBT bars in exchange for protection from or information about police raids.

In both their legal and extralegal activities, police forces have been supported and aided by a variety of nongovernmental organizations that have been given unique powers by state authorities. Examples from the late nineteenth and early twentieth centuries include the Society for the Prevention of Cruelty to Children, the Society for the Suppression of Vice, the Committee of Fifteen, the Committee of Fourteen, the City Vigilance League, the Watch and Ward Society, and the Law and Order League. Mid-twentieth-century organizations include the Legion of Decency, the National Organization for Decent Literature, Citizens for Decent Literature, and the Churchmen's Commission for Decent Publications. These groups and others played critical roles in policing sexualities and genders in the broad and narrow sense.

All of which is not to say that police forces in the United States have never acted in line with LGBT interests. Especially in the last thirty years but also in earlier periods, police have investigated and arrested those who murdered, raped, and assaulted LGBT people, those who damaged and stole LGBT property, those who attempted to blackmail LGBT people, and those who committed other crimes against LGBT people. Nevertheless, in important respects LGBT people in the United States lived much of the twentieth century in what can be described as a police state, deprived of basic civil rights and targeted by police authorities. To this day, many LGBT people believe, and significant evidence supports their claims, that police forces do not treat crimes against LGBT people as seriously as they treat crimes against others.

Historical Patterns

The best documentation of pre-1969 police actions against LGBT people and phenomena has come in five forms: collections of primary texts, case studies and broad monographs on the colonial era, works that deal with military policing, historical and anthropological local studies, and studies by legal scholars. In the first three categories, the most notable works are by Jonathan Ned Katz; Kathleen Brown and Richard Godbeer; and Allan Bérubé and Leisa Meyer. In the fourth group, Nan Boyd's book on San Francisco, George Chauncey's on New York, John Howard's on Mississippi, Elizabeth Kennedy and Madeline Davis's on Buffalo, Marc Stein's on Philadelphia, and Brett Beemyn's collection of various local studies offer detailed examples and analyses of larger patterns. Legal scholar William Eskridge's book *Gaylaw* is perhaps the most comprehensive and synthetic national account of anti-LGBT policing, though works such as Ruthan Robson's book *Lesbian (Out)Law* offer important perspectives on the distinctive aspects of antilesbian policing.

Some have been tempted to make generalizations about national patterns of anti-LGBT law enforcement before there is sufficient evidence to do so. As Boyd has pointed out, for example, in part because of different systems of liquor control, the post-Prohibition crackdown on LGBT commercial establishments that Chauncey sees occurring in New York City in the 1930s did not occur in San Francisco. Stein's evidence suggests that Philadelphia, New York, and Washington, D.C., were close enough geographically that when anti-LGBT policing increased in one city, many LGBT people shifted some of their social activities to less-intensively policed cities nearby. If this is true, care must be taken when generalizing about national patterns of policing on the basis of local studies. Many have claimed that anti-LGBT policing reached its height during the 1950s, but the evidence that has been gathered thus far by no means establishes that the 1960s were any better than the 1950s in this regard, and significant evidence suggests the reverse. And with the exception of Howard's work, little research has been done on nonurban policing.

Based on evidence from various locations, Eskridge argues that sodomy arrests were quite rare before the 1880s, but then increased dramatically (especially in the years surrounding World War I), at precisely the time that sodomy was being redefined in many states to include oral sex (instead of just anal sex) and to include same-sex female as well as same-sex male sex. Eskridge observes another dramatic increase after World War II. In terms of reported "sodomy" cases (which may or may not correspond to arrests), the total number peaked in the period from 1971 to 1985, but the number involving consenting same-sex adults peaked in the period from 1956 to 1970. These figures mask significant local variations. Though figures are missing for key years, Eskridge's statistics suggest that for the period from 1875 to 1920, "sodomy" arrests peaked from 1906 to 1910 in Boston and Chicago, from 1911 to 1915 in Philadelphia and San Francisco, and from 1916 to 1920 in Los Angeles and New York. During the period from 1920 to 1965, they appear to have peaked in the late 1940s in Washington, D.C., the late 1950s in New York, and the early 1960s in San Francisco. Far larger numbers of LGBT people were arrested for crimes such as disorderly conduct; in New York, arraignments for "degenerate" disorderly conduct peaked at more than 3000 per year from 1947 to 1949, though penalties were less severe than they had been in earlier years. Eskridge's figures suggest that the number of soldiers receiving anti-LGBT military discharges, as a percent of total forces,

"Lesbians against Police Violence." Protesters in San Francisco march against violence and hostility by police toward lesbians, 24 June 1979. **[Roger Ressmeyer/corbis]**

peaked in the period from 1957 to 1961 and then declined, but in absolute terms discharges peaked in the 1960s, declined in the mid-1970s, peaked again in the early 1980s, declined to a low point in 1994, and then began rising again (after the "don't ask, don't tell" policy was adopted during the Clinton presidency). Much more research and analysis will be necessary before a more definitive periodization of anti-LGBT policing can be established.

More research will also have to be conducted to understand race, class, and gender differences in anti-LGBT policing, but what is known thus far is highly suggestive. Katz reports that Pennsylvania's 1700 sodomy law made sodomy a capital crime for blacks but not whites; Virginia's 1800 sodomy law removed the death penalty for free persons but not for slaves. According to Eskridge, of the sixty-three prisoners reported incarcerated for crimes against nature in the 1880 U.S. Census, thirty-two were men of color in the South and one-third of the white prisoners were immigrants from Europe. Chauncey writes that most sodomy prosecutions in early-twentieth-century New York involved poor immigrants and in the 1940s and 1950s involved African Americans and Puerto Ricans. Statistics on sodomy arrests and sexual psychopath commitments from Philadelphia and Pennsylvania in the 1950s also suggest disproportionate impact on working class people and people of color.

Some have argued that lesbians have been less policed than gay men, and if policing is conceptualized narrowly (for example, in terms of sodomy arrests) there is evidence to support this position. However, if lesbians have restricted their public activities because the police have not protected them from rapes, sexual assaults, and physical violence, then lesbianism has been policed in the broader sense. Rendering lesbianism invisible in the public sphere is a form of social policing, as is conceptualizing lesbians as less sexual than gay men. Economic discrimination against women, to the extent that it encourages women's dependence on men, is also a form of anti-lesbian policing. In the realms of adoption, child custody, and foster care, lesbians have probably been policed more intensively than have gay men. And in proportion to their numbers, the same has been the case in the military. To the extent that it diminishes lesbians and conceptualizes them only in comparative relation to gay men, the claim that lesbians have been less policed than gay men is itself a form of anti-lesbian policing.

Most anti-LGBT policing, whether directed against males or females, has been aimed at social and sexual activities, but police forces have also targeted political activities. While the policing of the organized LGBT movement began with the crackdown on the Society for Human Rights in the 1920s and continued with the attempt in the 1950s to ban distribution of *ONE* magazine through the U.S. postal system, it appears that the most intense period of anti-LGBT movement policing may have taken place in the 1960s and 1970s. In these decades, homophile activist meetings and events were raided by local and state police (in Greater Philadelphia and San Francisco); the FBI spied on and disrupted homophile, gay liberation, and lesbian feminist groups in various locations; and local, state, and federal officials, through a coordinated campaign of surveillance, harassment, and prosecution, effectively destroyed the Janus Society, *Drum* magazine, and the Homosexual Law Reform Society. Ironically, some of the best evidence that documents the activities of these and other LGBT political groups comes from police records obtained by researchers through Freedom of Information Act requests.

Recent Developments

Given the important role that police forces have played in policing LGBT communities, it is perhaps not surprising that the most well-known episode in LGBT history, the New York City Stonewall Riots of 1969, was precipitated by a confrontation between police and LGBT people. And given the ability of LGBT people to eroticize almost any relationship of power that exists in society, it is perhaps not surprising that a major genre of gay pornography features characters who appear (at least briefly) in police uniform.

In the last thirty years, in large part because of the work of LGBT activists, police regulation of LGBT sexualities and genders in the narrow sense has changed dramatically. By most accounts, raids on LGBT bars and clubs have declined, sexual psychopath laws have been overturned, overt immigration exclusions of LGBT people have been removed, and, as of 2003, sodomy laws have been declared unconstitutional. Police in many jurisdictions now collect statistics on hate crimes against LGBT people. Various towns, cities, and states have appointed officers and committees to serve as official liaisons between LGBT communities and the police. The nonhiring of LGBT persons seeking employment with police forces and the firing of openly LGBT police officers has decreased, and some police forces have declared their interest in hiring LGBT people. Many police departments are now covered by laws prohibiting discrimination on the basis of sexual orientation, and some by laws prohibiting discrimination on the basis of gender identity. Since the founding of the Gay Officers Action League in New York in 1982, many organizations of LGBT law enforcement professionals have been established.

Anti-LGBT policing, however, continues. In the narrow sense, local and state police continue to enforce laws against prostitution, public sex, and solicitation, they continue to use zoning laws to displace sex businesses, and they continue to discriminate against LGBT people and phenomena in the enforcement of disorderly conduct laws. Police authorities continue to be called upon to enforce discriminatory decisions in adoption, custody, and inheritance disputes. Since the advent of AIDS, public health laws have been used aggressively to police LGBT commercial establishments (such as bathhouses). Since the introduction of the internet, obscenity laws have been used in new ways by those opposed to LGBT representations. Military police have arguably stepped up their anti-LGBT practices, and immigration officials now police the nation's borders to exclude people with HIV/AIDS. Reports of reprehensible police conduct continue to circulate in cases where LGBT people are murdered, raped, sexually assaulted, or otherwise victimized. And in the broad sense, cultural authorities continue to police transgressive and normative sexualities and genders, changing tactics and strategies but still attempting to impose order on the most disorderly of human desires.

Marc Stein

Bibliography

Beemyn, Brett. *Creating a Place for Ourselves.* New York: Routledge, 1997.

Bérubé, Allan. *Coming Out Under Fire.* New York: Free Press, 1990.

Boyd, Nan Alamilla. *Wide Open Town.* Berkeley: University of California Press, 2003.

Brown, Kathleen. " 'Changed . . . into the Fashion of Man.'" *Journal of the History of Sexuality* 6 (1995): 171–193.

Chauncey, George. *Gay New York.* New York: Basic, 1994.

D'Emilio, John. *Sexual Politics, Sexual Communities.* Chicago: University of Chicago Press, 1983.

D'Emilio, John, and Estelle Freedman. *Intimate Matters.* New York: Harper and Row, 1988.

Eskridge, William N., Jr. *Gaylaw.* Cambridge: Harvard University Press, 1999.

Foucault, Michel. *The History of Sexuality.* Volume 1. Translated by Robert Hurley. New York: Vintage, 1978.

Godbeer, Richard. *Sexual Revolution in Early America.* Baltimore: Johns Hopkins University Press, 2002.

Howard, John. *Men Like That.* Chicago: University of Chicago Press, 1999.

Katz, Jonathan Ned. *Gay/Lesbian Almanac.* New York: Harper and Row, 1983.

Kennedy, Elizabeth Lapovsky, and Madeline D. Davis. *Boots of Leather, Slippers of Gold.* New York: Routledge, 1993.

Meyer, Leisa D. *Creating G.I. Jane.* New York: Columbia University Press, 1996.

Newton, Esther. *Cherry Grove, Fire Island.* Boston: Beacon, 1993.

Robson, Ruthann. *Lesbian (Out)law.* Ithaca: Firebrand, 1992.

Rupp, Leila J. *A Desired Past.* Chicago: University of Chicago Press, 1999.

Stein, Marc. *City of Sisterly and Brotherly Loves.* Chicago: University of Chicago Press, 2000.

Marc Stein

See also CENSORSHIP, OBSCENTIY, AND PORNOGRAPHY LAW AND POLICY; CRIME AND CRIMINALIZATION; FEDERAL LAW AND POLICY; HATE CRIMES LAW AND POLICY; IMMIGRATION, ASYLUM, AND DEPORTATION LAW AND POLICY; MILITARY LAW AND POLICY; RIGHTS OF ASSOCIATION AND ASSEMBLY; SODOMY, BUGGERY, CRIMES AGAINST NATURE, LEWD AND LAW AND POLICY; STONEWALL RIOTS.

POLITICAL SCANDALS

Homosexuality has been a central theme in many American political scandals. Historically, gay political scandals have evolved from quiet, whispered affairs into sensational, media-saturated public dramas. Dismissed by some scholars as trivial or inappropriate to study, a growing number of scholars contend that scandals involving sex and sexuality serve an important social function, stimulating public discussion of normative values and taboo subjects. This has been especially true since the 1970s, as the rise of gay visibility in American society has forced a reevaluation of the political relevance of sexual identity. Since 1980, a high incidence of gay political scandals suggests persistent anxiety in certain segments of society regarding open gay and lesbian participation in the American political system.

Scandals vary in their details, but most include the same components: an alleged transgression of public morality occurs (sometimes real, sometimes fabricated by political rivals or the media), followed by some combination of rumor, cover-up, denial, confession, and a ruined career. In addition to these components, three variables are important to consider in all gay political scandals. The first variable is the role of the media. Sensational coverage in newspapers, magazines, and radio and television news programs can transform trivial rumors into full-blown scandals. However, media exposure is not essential to damage or ruin a person's career. Sometimes scandals are not reported until years after they have occurred, even if they had devastating consequences at the time. Prior to the 1970s, the mainstream press rarely reported anything unfavorable about the private lives of politicians, so there are fewer known gay scandals compared to recent decades. The second variable is the role of partisan politics. Both Democrats and Republicans (though more often Republicans) have exploited social prejudices against gay men and lesbians in order to embarrass rival candidates. As a result, scandals regularly break out during election campaigns. In some cases, campaign advertisements repeatedly remind voters of a rival's past sexual transgressions. In other cases Republican or Democratic Party officials invent rumors outright. The third variable is the role of hypocrisy. The consequences of hypocrisy are more severe than the consequences of alleged or actual sexual transgressions. Since the early 1980s, several congressmen have survived gay scandals by making forthright, honest public statements about their sexual preferences. Politicians discovered in homosexual affairs who have endorsed antigay legislation or who repeatedly deny they are gay despite evidence to the contrary usually end up with wrecked careers.

There are few known lesbian scandals. Persistent gender bias in American politics has effectively shut out most women seeking prominent positions as U.S. senators, representatives, or governors. The few women who attain these high offices usually guard their private lives carefully. Because of this secrecy, along with a misogynist backlash among social conservatives against women's political advances, female politicians are more likely than their male counterparts to be faced with rumors that they are homosexual. Such lesbian rumors are, too often, spread in a hostile spirit. First ladies assuming important leadership roles, such as Hillary Clinton, seem especially prone to unsubstantiated lesbian rumors. (Occasionally, as in Eleanor Roosevelt's case, the rumors have turned out to have some foundation in reality.)

Early Scandals and Nonscandals

A mislabeled painting perpetuated the long-standing myth that Edward Hyde (better known as Lord Cornbury), royal governor of colonial New York and New Jersey (1702–1708), was so loyal to Queen Anne that he regularly donned women's clothing to imitate her. There is little evidence that Cornbury ever actually dressed in women's clothes—the charge was apparently invented by political rivals. In *The Lord Cornbury Scandal* (1998),

> The sexual preferences of George Washington and Alexander Hamilton have also been the source of debate. As with many historical cases, the evidence is open to many interpretations.

Patricia U. Bonomi concluded that politicians of colonial America regularly besmirched their rivals with suggestions of effeminacy and gender inversion. Cornbury is the first known example of such a smear, but even George Washington was not immune to such attacks, as cartoonists drew caricatures of him in women's clothing. These scandals of the eighteenth century established the pattern for gay scandals in the following years by associating a politician's lack of "manliness" with his lack of leadership abilities, exposing the masculinist pretenses of American political power throughout the centuries.

During the nineteenth century, the American press avoided reporting political scandals involving homosexuality or sodomy, although at least one president—Democrat James Buchanan, who served from 1857 to 1861—preferred male company. Distinguished in American history as the only bachelor president, Buchanan's close male companions were the objects of rumor, curiosity, and the occasional snide remark, but these had no noticeable effect on his political career—a remarkable fact considering how controversial a suspected gay or lesbian presidential candidate would subsequently become. Historians debate whether the so-called romantic friendships of the nineteenth century, such as Buchanan's, involved sexual gratification and caution that such intimate relationships were not necessarily sexual. Abraham Lincoln, for example, has also been the object of modern-day speculations about his sexual orientation, but his bed sharing as a young man with a close male friend was not unusual in a frontier environment with scarce resources for bedding. Buchanan's same-sex intimacies, in contrast, were a well-established pattern throughout his life, even during his presidential term. Regardless of Lincoln's or Buchanan's actual sexual behavior, these debates 150 years later have achieved scandal-like dimensions for even suggesting that an American president—especially one as revered as Lincoln—might have been sexually attracted to other men.

The Roosevelt Era

In 1920 future president Franklin Delano Roosevelt became the target of a misfired gay scandal while campaigning as the Democratic vice-presidential candidate. Rhode Island publisher John Rathom, a longtime Roosevelt family foe, alerted several newspapers to Roosevelt's regrettable decision, while assistant navy secretary, to approve a plan to entrap suspected homosexuals using navy soldiers as decoys in Newport, Rhode Island, in 1919. Rathom also hinted that Roosevelt himself was gay, but newspapers heavily censored the story because homosexuality was still a taboo topic for the press, and the scandal failed to spread. The remainder of Roosevelt's career was unfettered by gay rumors, but ironically his wife, Eleanor Roosevelt, was likely a lesbian, according to her biographer, Blanche Wiesen Cook. Eleanor Roosevelt had her first Boston marriage with an older woman in college, and throughout her life enjoyed intimate, romantic relationships with other women, carefully balancing a secretive private life with a long, successful—and very public—career as a political activist.

A prominent member of the Roosevelt administration, Assistant Secretary of State Sumner Welles, lost his career to scandal after he propositioned several train porters in 1940 while intoxicated, embarrassing himself in front of visiting dignitaries. President Roosevelt tried to keep the incident a secret, but a rival Democratic Party faction led by Secretary of State Cordell Hull continued to circulate the story, hoping it would land in the press. After two years of mounting gossip, Roosevelt asked for Welles's resignation when he learned that the *Washington Herald* was ready to print a story about the incident. The story never appeared—newspapers explained Welles's resignation in vague political terms instead. Some newspaper columnists close to the events dropped hints, but details of Welles's embarrassing train ride did not receive full press coverage until the 1950s.

The McCarthy Era

It is now known that many influential political figures of the McCarthy era lived secret lives as gay men, including J. Edgar Hoover, Whittaker Chambers, Roy Cohn, and perhaps even Joe McCarthy himself. The most consistent target of gay rumors during the 1950s, however, was Illinois governor and two-time Democratic presidential nominee Adlai Stevenson. Stevenson's divorced status and intellectual egghead image—regarded as feminine by critics—became favorite media topics during his 1952 and 1956 presidential campaigns. Columnists jokingly

> Joe McCarthy planned to call Adlai Stevenson a "pansy" in a speech during the 1952 presidential campaign, but dropped the reference after Democrats threatened to respond by exposing an extramarital affair of Dwight D. Eisenhower.

Walter Jenkins was married with six children at the time of his scandal.

referred to him as Adelaide, and both the *Chicago Daily News* and *Confidential* magazine insinuated that Stevenson's divorce resulted from his lack of sexual interest in women. Federal Bureau of Investigation records (notoriously inaccurate) labeled Stevenson a "confirmed" homosexual. It is doubtful that these gay rumors, never well supported by evidence, influenced his presidential defeats. His divorce, however, during an era of glorification of the American nuclear family, proved a major political liability.

A scandal with more serious career implications emerged during the 1964 presidential campaign. On 7 October 1964, Walter Jenkins, longtime adviser to President Lyndon Baines Johnson, was arrested for committing "lewd acts" with another man in a Washington, D.C., Young Men's Christian Association bathroom. It was his second arrest—one years earlier had gone unnoticed by the public. In this case, the Barry Goldwater Republican campaign learned of the incident and gave the story to United Press International (UPI). The story spread across the nation over UPI's wire service, and Johnson asked for Jenkins's resignation a week later, ending a twenty-five-year professional relationship.

National security concerns figured prominently in the Jenkins scandal. Federal government policies instituted in 1953 prohibited employing homosexuals in sensitive positions because of their alleged susceptibility to blackmail by communist spies. As a top-level presidential advisor, Jenkins had access to top secret documents, and Republicans exploited the incident to portray the Johnson administration as "soft" on communism. Only two years after the Cuban Missile Crisis, anxieties over nuclear apocalypse were acutely high during the 1964 election. A Johnson television advertisement, for example, suggested that Goldwater would blow up the world if elected. The scandal had little effect on the election, with Johnson defeating Goldwater in a landslide, but Jenkins's hasty, sudden demise reflected the intermingled scapegoating of communists and homosexuals so common during the Cold War.

The Reagan Era: A Golden Age for Gay Political Scandals

A surge of well-publicized gay political scandals broke out in the 1980s. A major reorientation of American journalism had occurred during the 1970s in the wake of the Vietnam War and the Watergate crisis, as the media sought increasingly to expose the hypocrisy of public officials. Meanwhile, growing gay visibility in American society had lifted journalistic taboos on reporting homosexual issues. A resurgence in political conservatism, however, culminating in Republican Ronald Reagan's 1980 presidential election, challenged the new-found gay visibility on the streets and in the media. In this context, the gay scandal wave was an important component of the 1980s-era culture wars, which pitted conservatives against liberals on social issues including abortion, school prayer, and gun control.

Many scandal victims were conservative Republicans. In 1980 Robert Bauman, a U.S. representative from Maryland who was an outspoken "family values" proponent and the president of the American Conservative Union, was arrested after soliciting a sixteen-year-old male. Bauman blamed his homosexual behavior on alcohol, desperately denying he was gay, but his conservative financial supporters distanced themselves from him, sinking any reelection hopes. According to most interpretations, his denials and blatant political hypocrisy disturbed constituents more than did the arrest itself. Bauman had sponsored the antigay Family Protection Act and loudly supported legislation denying certain privileges to gay and lesbian veterans. By the middle 1980s, his career finished, Bauman finally accepted his sexuality and wrote a memoir, *The Gentleman from Maryland: The Conscience of a Gay Conservative* (1986).

Republican Mississippi U.S. Representative Jon Hinson's scandal was more complex. On 8 August 1980 Hinson voluntarily—and quite dramatically—announced to reporters his involvement in two homosexual incidents during the past decade, including a 1976 arrest for committing an "obscene act" with an ex-marine at the Iwo Jima Memorial. Like Robert Baumen, he apologized for his transgressions but denied that he was gay. Standing next to his wife Cynthia, Hinson described his return to heterosexuality as a "born again" experience. After checking into a psychiatric hospital, Hinson told the press he was "sick," continuing to deny his homosexual orientation. His wealthy financial backers pulled their support, ending his political career. In the 1990s Hinson came to support gay rights causes. He died of AIDS at the age of fifty-three in 1995.

Survival by Disclosure

As Bauman and Hinson suffered through their career-wrecking scandals, rumors of widespread prostitution and drug running by Capital Hill pages provoked a massive investigation in 1980. Special Counsel Joseph Califano led a multiyear investigation that scrutinized hundreds of government workers' private lives. He found scant evidence of drug running or the rumored prostitution ring, but nonetheless brought to light a few isolated cases involving congressmen that quickly grew into media sensations. One of these cases centered on the involvement of Massachusetts Democratic U.S. Representative Gerry Studds with a seventeen-year-old male page in 1973. Facing professional jeopardy, Studds came out on the floor of the House of Representatives on 14 July 1983, becoming the first openly gay member of Congress. Studds received a congressional censure after apologizing for the 1973 page incident. Massachusetts voters forgave him, reelecting him to a seventh term in 1984.

Barney Frank, also a Democratic U.S. representative from Massachusetts, survived a more complex scandal later in the decade. Elected in 1980, Frank admitted he was gay in 1987 to little fanfare or controversy. In 1989, however, reports surfaced of a male prostitution ring operating from one of Frank's apartments. A live-in housekeeper and errand boy named Stephen Gobie admitted operating an escort service from Frank's apartment. Frank quickly fired Gobie and requested that the House Ethics Committee investigate the allegation. Gobie, meanwhile, sought a book deal for his pimping escapades, telling the press that his prostitutes regularly serviced Frank. The media pursued the story, revealing Gobie as a pathological liar, and the House Ethics Committee cleared Frank of all major charges. Frank had, however, unduly used his influence to clear thirty-one parking tickets for Gobie, and the committee also discovered a misleading letter of recommendation written by Frank on Gobie's behalf. With Newt Gingrich leading the charge, many Republicans demanded Frank's expulsion from Congress, but in the end Frank received only a mild reprimand. Since the scandal, Frank has enjoyed one of the most successful careers of any openly gay or lesbian politician.

Gerry Studds. The first openly gay member of Congress, he came out in 1983—and was censured but later reelected—after an incident came to light involving a teenage male page ten years earlier. [corbis-Bettmann]

Rumors and Hearsay

Other scandals in the 1980s were sparked by rumors rather than actual transgressions. During the 1984 governor's race in Mississippi, a newspaper story claimed that three male prostitutes in Jackson's red-light district had serviced Democratic candidate Bill Allain. While investigating the charges, the media cruelly ridiculed the prostitutes—all female impersonators—in particular, a Diana Ross impersonator named Devia Ross. After inconsistencies in the story emerged, it was discovered that the female impersonators had invented the account in exchange for Republican bribes. As the scandal unfolded, Republican-hired private detectives held the trio hostage in a motel room, controlling the media's access to them. The scheme backfired on Republicans, and Allain handily won the election.

In 1989 rumors circulated about a videotape featuring a prisoner describing his sexual affair with the incoming Speaker of the House, Thomas Foley. The Democratic representative had been married for twenty-one years and had never been the object of gay rumors in the past. The tape never surfaced, and evidence suggests it was just another Republican invention. Foley became Speaker of the House but felt humiliated about having his sex life discussed in public. Political commentators have suggested that the rumors dampened Foley's political style, making him less willing to challenge Republican opposition for fear the rumor would return.

Gossip and innuendo has dominated many gay scandals of the 1990s as well. During a 1996 campaign, a Democratic rival indirectly suggested that Republican

> During the course of the Allain scandal, female impersonator Devia Ross stormed out of a hostile interview with television scandalmonger Geraldo Rivera.

> The first member of Congress to die from symptoms of AIDS was Republican U.S. representative Stewart McKinney of Connecticut in 1987. He succumbed to death shortly after spending a cold evening on Capitol Hill protesting conditions facing the homeless in Washington, D.C.

U.S. Representative John Kasich of Ohio was having an affair with his male chief of staff. Kasich's repeated denials, however, fueled more media speculation about his sexuality than the initial accusation. When Jim Kolbe, a Republican U.S. representative from Arizona, heard rumors in 1996 that *The Advocate* planned to out him in its next issue, he followed the lead of Studds and Frank by coming out first, proving that the rumors were correct in addition to saving his career.

As in Lord Cornbury's day, prevailing assumptions about gender, sexuality, and power manifest themselves in American political institutions. The rumor of Cornbury's cross-dressing is comparable to rumors over U.S. senator and former first lady Hillary Clinton's ostensible lesbianism, prevalent on Internet chat rooms, Web sites, right-wing talk radio, and the tabloid press. As Cornbury was caricatured wearing a dress, Clinton has been lampooned as overly masculine, hence a lesbian by association. As the shock of having openly gay men and women in political office diminishes, the nature of sex scandals will necessarily adjust to new circumstances. But debates over sex, gender, and sexuality will continue to be manifested in public political dramas of some form.

Bibliography

Bauman, Robert E. *The Gentleman from Maryland: The Conscience of a Gay Conservative.* New York: Arbor House, 1986.

Bonomi, Patricia U. *The Lord Cornbury Scandal: The Politics of Reputation in British America.* Chapel Hill: University of North Carolina Press, 1998.

Collins, Gail. *Scorpion Tongues: Gossip, Celebrity, and American Politics.* New York: Morrow, 1998.

Cook, Blanche Wiesen. *Eleanor Roosevelt.* 2 vols. New York: Viking, 1992, 1999.

Howard, John. *Men Like That: A Southern Queer History.* Chicago: University of Chicago Press, 1999.

King, Anthony. "Sex, Money, and Power." In *Politics in Britain and the United States: Comparative Perspectives.* Edited by Richard Hodder-Williams and James Ceaser. Durham, N.C.: Duke University Press, 1986.

———. Markovits, Andrei S., and Mark Silverstein, eds. *The Politics of Scandal: Power and Process in Liberal Democracies.* New York: Holmes and Meier, 1988.

Ross, Shelley. *Fall from Grace: Sex, Scandal, and Corruption in American Politics from 1702 to the Present.* New York: Ballantine, 1988.

Sabato, Larry J., Mark Stencel, and S. Robert Lichter. *Peepshow: Media and Politics in an Age of Scandal.* Lanham, Md.: Rowman and Littlefield, 2000.

Thompson, John B. *Political Scandal: Power and Visibility in the Media Age.* Malden, Mass.: Blackwell, 2000.

Williams, Robert. *Political Scandals in the USA.* Edinburgh: Keele University Press, 1998.

Craig M. Loftin

See also COHN, ROY; FRANK, BARNEY; GOVERNMENT AND MILITARY WITCHHUNTS; HAMMOND, JAMES HENRY; HOOVER, J. EDGAR; MISSISSIPPI; ROOSEVELT, ELEANOR, AND LORENA HICKOCK; WELLES, SUMNER.

POLITICAL SCIENCE

Broadly speaking, political science is the academic study of politics, power, government, and the activity of governments. Political scientists seek to understand the forces acting on government, the forces acting within government, and the impact of government activity on the environment in which it exists. Although the field has existed since the late nineteenth century, it has only been considered a social science, like economics and sociology, since the 1950s. The broadest subfields in the discipline include international relations, comparative politics, and American politics. Within these areas, researchers typically examine political institutions or political behavior, but the divisions between these previously distinctive areas is becoming increasingly blurred.

Early History

Political scientists began conducting research on LGBT topics in the early 1970s, but few LGBT-related works were published prior to the 1990s. The scope of this work is quite broad, covering the development of sexual identity, public opinion, voting behavior and party politics, political representation, political institutions, and public policy. Research in this area employs a range of methodological techniques, including postmodern deconstruction, qualitative historical case studies, and statistical analysis of quantitative data.

The first known presentation of political science research on LGBT issues occurred in 1972, when Keven J. Burke and Murray S. Edelman presented an ethnographic study of gay consciousness-raising groups at the annual meeting of the largest political science association, the American Political Science Association (APSA). At the 1973 annual meeting of the APSA, Kenneth Sherrill presented the first quantitative study of the LGB movement when he presented his survey research results on the opinions of LGB movement activists and leaders. Later in the 1970s and 1980s, a small number of political scientists, including Sherrill, Mark Blasius, Shane Phelan, and Robert Bailey, began conducting research on LGBT politics and sexual identity, often drawing from research in the fields of history, psychology, and sociology. Several conference presentations resulted from this early research, but few political scientists took notice because no refereed political science journals were publishing work on this topic. And although other social science organizations were grappling with LGBT issues in the 1970s, political scientists paid little attention until the 1980s.

Two of the earliest major works on LGBT politics in the United States were Toby Marotta's *The Politics of Homosexuality* (1981) and Dennis Altman's *The Homosexualization of America* (1982). Marotta's book was based on his Harvard Ph.D. dissertation examining the growth of a gay and lesbian political movement. Altman, an Australian political scientist, examined the intersection of LGBT politics and culture through a historical treatment. Another landmark study published about the same time addressed the use of homophobic language by judges in cases involving LGBT litigants. Lawrence Goldyn (1981) found that LGBT litigants were frequently exposed to homophobic comments from judges, and that the extent to which judges engaged in this behavior varied by type of case, jurisdiction, and over time, with a decrease in homophobic language over the study period. Perhaps not surprisingly, in cases where judges engaged in this type of behavior, LGBT litigants did not fare well.

In 1987, James L. Gibson tied the study of LGBT politics directly to a broader political science literature on political tolerance with the publication of survey research on attitudes toward disliked groups, including homosexuals. The connection between AIDS and homosexuality spurred research in empirical policy studies. David C. Colby and David G. Baker (1988) published their examination of the various state policy reactions to AIDS. David C. Nice (1988) conducted a landmark empirical study of the determinants of repealing state antisodomy laws and applied mainstream theories of state policymaking and statistical methods to his analysis.

By the late 1980s and early 1990s, a considerable number of researchers were developing statistical models for explaining the relationship between a variety of individual socioeconomic characteristics and attitudes on AIDS and homosexuality. In one example, Horst Stipp and Dennis Kerr (1989) explored the influence of individual attitudes toward homosexuality on attitudes about policies addressing AIDS. They found that negative attitudes toward homosexuality significantly reduced accurate knowledge about AIDS transmission and risk factors.

Perhaps the best early theoretical work on LGBT politics from a postmodern perspective was Shane Phelan's *Identity Politics: Lesbian-Feminism and the Limits of Community* (1989). Although Phelan's book was also historical, it was theoretically based in postmodern arguments concerning the individual and the social construction of identity. Phelan and others, including Mark Blasius and Craig A. Rimmerman, have continued this strain of work on LGBT politics into the 2000s.

LGBT Issues within the Profession

As these early works appeared, a movement emerged within the APSA in the 1980s to establish an LGB caucus or organized section. In 1987 the Gay, Lesbian, Bisexual Political Science Caucus was founded as the principal association of LGB people in the APSA; it maintains the stated goal of encouraging "the presentation of research on the interaction of sexual identity, theory and political behavior." By the late 1990s the caucus had over two hundred members, regularly cosponsored multiple panels at annual APSA meetings, and published the *Newsletter of the Gay, Lesbian, Bisexual Political Science Caucus.* However, the caucus has yet to achieve its goal of establishing an organized and APSA-recognized section within the association.

After concerted pressure from the caucus over the course of 1991 and 1992, the executive council of the APSA established the Committee on the Status of Lesbians, Gays, Bisexuals, and the Transgendered in the Profession (CSLGBT). Mark Blasius was selected to lead the CSLGBT, and its initial members included Cathy J. Cohen, Shane Phelan, Sarah Slavin, and Christine Di Stefano. Since its inception, its stated goal has been to assess the status of LGBT scholars in the profession, advance research on LGBT issues, develop related curriculum materials, and ensure tolerance toward LGBT political scientists.

In August 1997 the APSA Council approved changes to *A Guide to Professional Ethics in Political Science* founded on the recommendations of the Committee on Professional Ethics and the CSLGBT. These changes included the revision of existing language by adding references to sexual orientation:

> It is Association policy that educational institutions shall not discriminate on the basis of . . . sexual orientation . . . in any condition of employment except in cases in which federal laws allow religious preference in hiring. . . .

> In pursuit of the objective of ending discrimination, it is Association policy to support the principles of affirmative action and urge political science departments to pursue aggressively affirmative action programs and policies with regard to . . . minorities based on self-identified sexual orientation. (American Political Science Association 2003)

The committee conducted a survey of political scientists in September 1993 and used the results as a basis for a series of recommendations to assist in improving the status of LGBT political scientists in the profession. The survey found that a relatively hostile environment existed in some departments for LGBT political scientists, that few of those surveyed identified as LGBT, and that significant numbers of respondents suggested that academic institutional policies either discriminated against LGBT people or did not protect them against discrimination. Additionally, a fair percentage of respondents provided answers that suggested scholarship on LGBT politics should not be supported and that they did not include LGBT material in their courses. In the mid-1990s the APSA Council adopted all of the committee's recommendations as presented by Martha Ackelsberg.

The 1990s and Beyond

Coinciding with the examination of the climate for LGBT scholars and scholarly work in the 1990s was a rise in the amount of scholarship on LGBT politics. Phelan published her second work on the construction of lesbian identity, *Getting Specific,* in 1994, and Blasius published a similar but more general theoretical study, *Gay and Lesbian Politics,* that same year.

Several empirically based quantitative journal articles and book chapters on LGBT politics and AIDS also began to appear in the early 1990s. Showing their connection to the study of homosexuality and LGBT issues in psychology, some political psychologists in political science began exploring public attitudes on AIDS, homosexuality, and support for civil rights and liberties (Sniderman et al. 1991). In 1993, Robert J. Buchanan and Robert L. Ohsfeldt (1993) published a unique study on state legislator attitudes toward AIDS and homosexuality based on survey data. One interesting study of the social movement link between AIDS and LGBT activism focused on differences between LGBT activists and heterosexuals involved in the AIDS Quilt program. M. Kent Jennings and Ellen Ann Anderson (1996) used surveys of AIDS activists and found, contrary to their expectations, that heterosexuals involved in AIDS politics were more supportive of radical or confrontational tactics than were gay and lesbian activists.

But much of the most interesting work on LGBT issues and public opinion being conducted by political scientists appeared in non–political science journals in the late 1980s and early 1990s. Key examples include Richard Seltzer's 1993 empirical study of attitudes on AIDS and homosexuality over time, which appeared in the *Journal of Homosexuality,* and Ellen D. Riggle and Alan L. Ellis's 1994 study of political tolerance toward homosexuals that appeared in the same journal. Whether these studies were rejected at political science journals or simply submitted to journals outside the field is unclear.

In 1996 research began to appear on LGBT public policy, with a particular focus on antidiscrimination policy. Steven H. Haeberle (1996) published the first statistical analysis attempting to explain why some local governments adopt policies that ban discrimination based on sexual orientation. Donald P. Haider-Markel and Kenneth J. Meier (1996) followed with a broader study that included a combined analysis of local and state policies, along with an examination of the dynamics of LGBT-related policy adoption through direct democracy initiatives at the ballot box. In addition, Kenneth D. Wald, James W. Button, and Barbara A. Rienzo (1996) conducted a similar analysis at the local level based on a survey of local government officials. These three studies have provided much of the framework for all LGBT-related policy studies that have appeared since 1996, including works on local policy, the influence of LGBT political representation on local adoption of domestic partner policies, state attempts to ban recognition of same-sex marriage, and hate crime policy adoption and implementation.

The first major study of LGB voting behavior across a variety of elections was also published in 1996 with the release of Mark Hertzog's book *The Lavender Vote.* Hertzog painstakingly brought together exit poll data from a variety of sources to compare the voting patterns of LGB people with heterosexuals and to examine voting change over time. His work was extended and enhanced by Robert W. Bailey (1998, 1999, 2000), who examined LGB voting and social movement development in local politics and elections, as well as LGB voting in congressional and presidential elections. Although these studies suffer from relying on the self-identification of LGB voters, they are based on the best systematic data available concerning LGB political activity in any sphere.

Systematic empirical research on LGBT interest groups also emerged in the late 1990s and early 2000s for the first time. Working within the traditional methods for examining congressional role call voting, Haider-Markel, in two 1999 studies, examined the influence of LGBT political action committee (PAC) money and LGBT inter-

Signs of the Times. Researchers—like many politicians—have been paying increased attention to LGBT political activism, such as this demonstration in which the most prominent sign proclaims: "I am gay & I vote." [corbis]

est group lobbying on congressional voting behavior. His research suggests that LGBT groups do influence congressional voting behavior, an empirical finding that conflicts with traditional theories concerning when interest group influence is most likely to occur. Additional studies of LGBT interest groups related to policymaking at the national level included articles by Sherrill (1996), Haider-Markel (1997), and Gregory Lewis (1997), and several chapters of books by Ellen D. Riggle and Barry L. Taglock in 1999 and Craig A. Rimmerman, Kenneth D. Wald, and Clyde Wilcox (2000).

It was also in the mid-to-late 1990s that an increasing amount of research appeared using experimental designs to examine individual tolerance toward LGBT people generally and to LGBT candidates for political office specifically. Ewa A. Golebiowska (1996, 2001) used experimental studies to explore the dynamics of tolerance toward LGBT people. Golebiowska (2001, 2002), Golebiowska and Cynthia J. Thomsen (1999), and Rebekah Herrick and Sue Thomas (1999) conducted similar analyses of attitudes toward the viability of openly gay and lesbian candidates for office and the likelihood that study participants would vote for these candidates. Surprisingly, these studies concluded that little bias exists toward lesbian and gay candidates generally, but that gay male candidates who fit a stereotype of gay males, such as having effeminate mannerisms or speech, are less likely to receive support.

By the late 1990s and early 2000s, LGBT issues increasingly appeared in political science journals and books as part of broader studies on public opinion, post-materialist values in Western societies, or in combination with the systematic study of culture war issues. At the same time, Alan S. Yang (1997, 2000), Sherrill and Yang (2000), and several chapters in Rimmerman, Wald, and Wilcox (2000) and Riggle and Tadlock (1999) provided the most systematic analysis of public attitudes on homosexuality and LGBT-related policy to date, including important analysis of the change in public attitudes over time.

Historical, empirically based analysis of the LGBT movement and patterns of politics appeared around the start of the new millennium, beginning with David Rayside's *On the Fringe* (1998), a comparative analysis of LGBT politics in Western democracies; Cathy Cohen's study of race and AIDS in *The Boundaries of Blackness* (1999); Raymond A. Smith and Donald Haider-Markel's *Gay and Lesbian Americans and Political Participation* (2002); and Daniel R. Pinello's *Gay Rights and American Law* (2003), an analysis of judicial decision making in cases involving the civil rights claims of LGBT Americans. Also, theoretical research on LGBT identity-based politics and sources of power continued with the publication of several books and edited collections, including Cohen, Jones, and Tronto (1997), Blasius and Phelan (1997), Blasius (2001), and Rimmerman (2002). These studies also explored strategies for LGBT activism.

By 2003 it was quite clear that political science research on LGBT issues would continue to ask a diverse set of research questions, employ a variety of theoretical and methodological perspectives, and involve political scientists from most of the discipline's subfields. And over the years researchers have consistently increased the base of knowledge of LGBT politics and policy. Perhaps most importantly, the study of LGBT issues in political science is no longer marginalized and researchers have effectively linked theory and empirical research on LGBT issues to broader theories and literature within political science. As such, the study of LGBT politics and policy has contributed to our understanding of politics, public opinion, government, and public policy more generally.

Bibliography

Altman, Dennis. *The Homosexualization of America.* New York: St. Martin's Press, 1982.

American Political Science Association. *A Guide to Professional Ethics in Political Science.* 3d ed. Washington, D.C.: American Political Science Association, 2003. Available from http://www.apsanet.org/pubs/ethics.cfm

Bailey, Robert W. *Out and Voting: The Gay, Lesbian, and Bisexual Vote in Congressional House Elections, 1990–1996.* Washington, D.C.: Policy Institute of the National Gay and Lesbian Task Force, 1998.

———. *Gay Politics, Urban Politics: Identity and Economics in the Urban Setting.* New York: Columbia University Press, 1999.

———. *Out and Voting II: The Gay, Lesbian, and Bisexual Vote in Congressional Elections, 1990–1998.* Washington, D.C.: Policy Institute of the National Gay and Lesbian Task Force, 2000.

Blasius, Mark. *Gay and Lesbian Politics: Sexuality and the Emergence of a New Ethic.* Philadelphia: Temple University Press, 1994.

Blasius, Mark, ed. *Sexual Identities, Queer Politics.* Princeton, N.J.: Princeton University Press, 2001.

Blasius, Mark, and Shane Phelan, eds. *We Are Everywhere: An Historical Sourcebook of Lesbian and Gay Politics.* New York: Routledge, 1997.

Buchanan, Robert J., and Robert L. Ohsfeldt. "The Attitudes of State Legislators and State Medicaid Policies Related to AIDS." *Policy Studies Journal* 21 (1993): 651–671.

Burke, Keven J., and Murray S. Edelman. "Sensitivity Groups, Consciousness-Raising Groups, and the Gay Liberation Movement." Paper presented at the annual meeting of the American Political Science Association, 1972.

Cohen, Cathy J. *The Boundaries of Blackness: AIDS and the Breakdown of Black Politics.* Chicago: University of Chicago Press, 1999.

Cohen, Cathy J., Kathleen Jones, and Joan Tronto, eds. *Women Transforming Politics: An Alternative Reader.* New York: New York University Press, 1997.

Colby, David C., and David G. Baker. "State Policy Responses to the AIDS Epidemic." *Publius* 18 (1988): 113–130.

Gibson, James L. "Homosexuals and the Ku Klux Klan: A Contextual Analysis of Political Tolerance." *Western Political Quarterly* 40 (1987): 427–448.

Goldyn, Lawrence. "Gratuitous Language in Appellate Cases Involving Gay People: 'Queer Baiting' from the Bench." *Political Behavior* 3 (1981): 31–48.

Golebiowska, Ewa A. "The 'Pictures in Our Heads' and Individual-Targeted Tolerance." *Journal of Politics* 58 (1996): 1010–1034.

———. "Group Stereotypes and Political Evaluation." *American Politics Research* 29 (2001): 535–565.

———. "Individual-Targeted Tolerance and Timing of Group Membership Disclosure." *Journal of Politics* 63 (2001): 1017–1040.

———. "Political Implications of Group Stereotypes: Campaign Experiences of Openly Gay Political Candidates." *Journal of Applied Social Psychology* 32 (2002): 590–607.

Golebiowska, Ewa A., and Cynthia J. Thomsen. "Group Stereotypes and the Evaluation of Individuals: The Case of Gay and Lesbian Political Candidates." In *Gays and Lesbians in the Democratic Process: Public Policy, Public Opinion, and Political Representation.* Edited by Ellen D. B. Riggle and Barry Tadlock. New York: Columbia University Press, 1999.

Haeberle, Steven H. "Gay Men and Lesbians at City Hall." *Social Science Quarterly* 77 (1996): 190–197.

Haider-Markel, Donald P. "Interest Group Survival: Shared Interests versus Competition for Resources." *Journal of Politics* 59 (1997): 903–912.

———. "Morality Policy and Individual-Level Political Behavior: The Case of Legislative Voting on Lesbian and Gay Issues." *Policy Studies Journal* 27 (1999): 735–749.

———. "Redistributing Values in Congress: Interest Group Influence under Sub-Optimal Conditions." *Political Research Quarterly* 52 (1999): 113–144.

Haider-Markel, Donald P., and Kenneth J. Meier. "The Politics of Gay and Lesbian Rights: Expanding the Scope of the Conflict." *Journal of Politics* 58 (1996): 332–349.

Herrick, Rebekah, and Sue Thomas. "The Effects of Sexual Orientation on Citizen Perceptions of Candidate Viability." In *Gays and Lesbians in the Democratic Process: Public Policy, Public Opinion, and Political Representation.* Edited by Ellen D. B. Riggle and Barry L. Tadlock. New York: Columbia University Press, 1999.

Hertzog, Mark. *The Lavender Vote: Lesbians, Gay Men, and Bisexuals in American Electoral Politics.* New York: New York University Press, 1996.

Jennings, M. Kent, and Ellen Ann Anderson. "Support for Confrontational Tactics among AIDS Activists: A Study of Intra-Movement Divisions." *American Journal of Political Science* 40 (1996): 311–334.

Lewis, Gregory B. "Lifting the Ban on Gays in the Civil Service: Federal Policy toward Gay and Lesbian Employees since the Cold War." *Public Administration Review* 57 (1997): 387–395.

Marotta, Toby. *The Politics of Homosexuality.* Boston: Houghton Mifflin, 1981.

Nice, David C. "State Deregulation of Intimate Behavior." *Social Science Quarterly* 69 (1988): 203–211.

Phelan, Shane. *Identity Politics: Lesbian-Feminism and the Limits of Community.* Philadelphia: Temple University Press, 1989.

———. *Getting Specific: Postmodern Lesbian Politics.* Minneapolis: University of Minnesota Press, 1994.

Pinello, Daniel R. *Gay Rights and American Law.* New York: Cambridge University Press, 2003.

Rayside, David. *On the Fringe: Gays and Lesbians in Politics.* Ithaca, N.Y.: Cornell University Press, 1998.

Riggle, Ellen D., and Alan L. Ellis. "Political Tolerance of Homosexuals: The Role of Group Attitudes and Legal Principles." *Journal of Homosexuality* 26 (1994): 135–147.

Riggle, Ellen D. B., and Barry L. Tadlock, eds. *Gays and Lesbians in the Democratic Process: Public Policy, Public Opinion, and Political Representation.* New York: Columbia University Press, 1999.

Rimmerman, Craig A. *From Identity to Politics: The Lesbian and Gay Movements in the United States.* Philadelphia: Temple University Press, 2002.

Rimmerman, Craig A., Kenneth D. Wald, and Clyde Wilcox, eds. *The Politics of Gay Rights.* Chicago: University of Chicago Press, 2000.

Seltzer, Richard. "AIDS, Homosexuality, Public Opinion, and Changing Correlates over Time." *Journal of Homosexuality* 26 (1993): 85–97.

Sherrill, Kenneth. "The Political Power of Lesbians, Gays, and Bisexuals." *PS: Political Science and Politics* 29 (1996): 469–473.

———. "The Youth of the Movement: Gay Activists in 1972–1973." In *Gays and Lesbians in the Democratic Process: Public Policy, Public Opinion, and Political Representation.* Edited by Ellen D. B. Riggle and Barry L. Tadlock. New York: Columbia University Press, 1999.

Sherrill, Kenneth S., and Alan Yang. "From Outlaws to In-Laws: Anti-Gay Attitudes Thaw." *Public Perspective* 11 (2000): 20–31.

Smith, Raymond A., and Donald P. Haider-Markel. *Gay and Lesbian Americans and Political Participation: A Reference Handbook.* Santa Barbara, Calif.: ABC-CLIO, 2002.

Sniderman, Paul M., Richard A. Brody, and Philip E. Tetlock, eds. *Reasoning and Choice: Explorations in Political Psychology.* Cambridge, U.K.: Cambridge University Press, 1991.

Stipp, Horst, and Dennis Kerr. "Determinants of Public Opinion about AIDS." *Public Opinion Quarterly* 53 (1989): 98–106.

Wald, Kenneth D., James W. Button, and Barbara A. Rienzo. "The Politics of Gay Rights in American Communities: Explaining Antidiscrimination Ordinances and Policies." *American Journal of Political Science* 40 (1996): 1152–1178.

Yang, Alan S. "Trends: Attitudes toward Homosexuality." *Public Opinion Quarterly* 61 (1997): 477–507.

———. *From Wrongs to Rights: Public Opinion on Gay and Lesbian Americans' Moves toward Equality.* Washington, D.C.: National Gay and Lesbian Task Force, 1999.

Donald P. Haider-Markel

POMA, Edgar (b. 4 May 1959), playwright, poet, cultural activist.

Born in Sacramento, California, to Filipino immigrant parents, Edgar Poma is a gay Filipino author residing in the San Francisco Bay Area. Raised in a migrant camp outside Walnut Grove, California, he wrote his first literary works when he attended the University of California, Berkeley as an undergraduate. There he studied playwriting with Carlos Morton, Josephine Miles, Adrienne Kennedy, and Marvin Rosenberg. His poetry, plays, and other creative writings have explored various questions of identity, linking race and ethnicity, family, and sexuality. Poma has also written about AIDS and life in the San Francisco Bay Area and California in general. In 1983 he received the Galbraithe Prize for Poetry.

In 1981 Poma's play *Reunion* debuted in San Francisco's Latino Mission District; it had two successful runs there. *Reunion* dramatizes the struggles of a young Chicano student returning home from college with his gay lover. Originally a vignette from a student-written production entitled "El Chicano Moderno" ("The modern Chicano"), it eventually received wide recognition through Poma's collaborations with the late Bay Area Chicano gay artists Rodrigo Reyes and Hank Tavera. The reading of *Reunion* in 1981 as part of the presentation of the National Theatre of Aztlán or TENAZ (Teatro Nacional de Aztlán) at the International Latin American Theatre Festival in San Francisco signaled the first time gay issues had been addressed directly in a play in Chicano/Latino context. Though well received in the larger community, festival coordinators refused to grant the play full production space, arguing that its material might be "offensive" to Latin American participants.

Poma's literary work reflects the conflicts and struggles of his life as a gay Filipino American. Drawing from his community's historical and regional experiences, he was part of Bay Area Philipino American Writers (BAYPAW) in the early 1980s. In 1985 BAYPAW published *Without Names: A Collection of Poems,* in which Poma contributed three of his own works. The group itself, like its literary productions, emerged from an earlier cultural collective, the Kearney St. Workshop in San Francisco.

Poma's work has appeared in *Ploughshares* (Spring 1986), the *Asian Pacific American Journal* (Fall/Winter 1995), *Flippin': Filipinos on America* (1996), *Contemporary Fiction by Filipinos in America* (1997), and *Growing Up Filipino* (2003). In 1995 one of his poems was read literally by thousands of residents throughout the Bay Area when it appeared in Bay Area Rapid Transit (BART) trains as part of the city's Poetry in Transit program. Entitled "Passenger," the poem speaks poignantly about the desire to show the world to a frail companion dying of AIDS.

Poma's first full-length play about contemporary Filipino life was *Little Train,* mounted by Teatro Ng Tanaan (Theater for Everyone) at San Francisco's Mission Cultural Center. The dark two-act play was about a Filipino-American career woman dealing ineptly with her aging immigrant parents. His other plays include *Summoning* (performed at the New Conservatory Theatre), and *Studly Guy Baptized in the River* (also mounted by Teatro Ng Tanaan), *Tim the Puritan* (presented as part of HBO's first New Writers Workshop in 1994), and *Hypnotista, Warm Embrace,* and *The Fame Game* (produced for the City College of San Francisco's Festival of American Playwrights of Color, I, II, and III). In 1995 he received a California Arts Council Grant for playwriting. Commenting about his work in "The Little Boy Who Fell in the Puka," Poma remarks that the story "encompasses some of [my] favorite themes: power, migrant farm worker history, sentimentality, a nagging undercurrent of loneliness, and a terrible unmasking, all in the backdrops of Hawaii and Northern California" (Brainard, p. 160).

Bibliography

Brainard, Cecilia Manguerra, ed. *Contemporary Fiction by Filipinos in America.* Pasig City, Phillipines: Anvil Publishing, 1997.

Poma, Edgar. "The Black Kite," " Easter Light," and "In the Orchard, Behind the House." In *Without Names: A Collection of Poems.* San Francisco: Kearney Street Workshop Press, 1985.

———. "The End of Awkwardness." In *Flippin': Filipinos on America.* New York: The Asian American Writers' Workshop, 1996.

Horacio N. Roque Ramírez

See also REYES, RODRIGO; TAVERA, HANK; THEATER AND PERFORMANCE.

POOR PEOPLE'S MOVEMENTS

The impoverished and disenfranchised have long agitated for jobs and better living conditions during most major economic downturns and recessions in the United States, but until the 1960s LGBT people were not visible as such in any of these movements. Regardless of overall economic conditions, several groups within the LGBT community have struggled with poverty. LGBT people of color have been as subject as their heterosexual counterparts to institutional racism and its results: blighted neighborhoods and reservations, unsafe housing owned by absentee landlords, toxic chemical dumping in residential areas, limited access to mortgages and loans, police brutality, under-funded educational health care facilities, higher rates of drug addiction, depression, HIV infection, and incarceration, and chronic unemployment and under-employment. Lesbians have also had to contend with financial discrimination in the workplace based on their gender and perceived single status—until recently, many employers saw men as heads of families and paid lower wages to women, whom they assumed were in the workforce temporarily or part time until marrying or having children. Lesbians out on the job, particularly butch women unable or unwilling to disguise their gender presentation, have often been consigned to blue-collar work, to lower-paying service-sector work lacking benefits, or to standstills in their careers while their heterosexual co-workers are promoted. Atypical gender presentation also limits employment options for everyone, but particularly for transgender people, from middle-aged adults in high-paying professions fired when they transition from one gender to another, to young people whose parents kick them out of the home when they come out. Thousands of LGBT youth end up on the streets each year, often hustling to survive and taking drugs to survive the hustling.

The Early Homosexual Movement and the Civil Rights Movement

One of the gay movement's first organizations in the U.S. grew out of the anti-poverty organizing of the 1930s. During the Great Depression when millions of citizens were out of work, the Communist and Socialist Parties organized two types of large demonstrations: first, of the unemployed to press municipal and state governments for jobs and reformed relief systems; and second, of workers for increased wages and improved conditions. A number of these movements' organizers were homosexual—such as Harry Hay, who used his labor organizing experience and contacts to found the Mattachine Society in the 1950s—but the Communist Party asked Hay and others to keep their sexual orientation quiet.

The Poor People's Campaign

In 1968 Bayard Rustin became the first known gay man to help organize a national poor people's demonstration. Rustin had been a key strategist in the black civil rights movement before public gay-baiting led Dr. Martin Luther King, Jr., and other Southern Christian Leadership Conference (SCLC) leaders to distance themselves from him. In 1967 King and the SCLC conceived the idea of the Poor People's Campaign, a multiracial caravan of several thousand protesters who traveled to Washington, D.C., to live in a huge tent city (later called Resurrection City) and stage demonstrations at various locations. King was killed while the campaign was still in its planning stage, and Rustin, despite disagreements with SCLC leaders about strategy and tactics, agreed to step in and run the Mobilization in Support of the Poor People's Campaign, with a major demonstration planned for 19 June 1968.

The rally was successful, drawing a racially mixed crowd of about fifty thousand, but Rustin soon resigned over differences with Ralph Abernathy. The campaign itself was plagued by problems at the grassroots level, literally and figuratively—the tent camp became an ocean of mud after frequent rains that summer, and the media reported on open disagreements between groups of residents. However, lesbian peace activist Barbara Deming wrote and published a widely read essay on the self-empowerment and improved communication processes most Resurrection City residents came to experience. Deming was among the many LGBT people who were changed by participating in the Southern civil rights movement. Some of these volunteers, such as Joan Nestle, were white Northerners who had been closeted in the movement, but returned home to make political connections between the oppression in the South and their own treatment as LGBT people.

The "Negro Family" and Welfare Rights Movement

The national debate about federal subsidies for the poor heated up substantially in the mid-1960s with the release of the labor department report "The Negro Family: The Case for National Action," written by Daniel Patrick Moynihan, assistant secretary of labor for policy and research. Moynihan blamed the problems he saw in the black community—dependence upon the welfare system, an increase in out-of-wedlock births—on gender "role reversal" and the tendency of black women to dominate their families. Many civil rights leaders and white progressives denounced the report and accused Moynihan of victim blaming, but neither his critics nor his supporters questioned the assumption that the creating of a traditional nuclear family was the best way out of poverty.

Women on welfare, more concerned with their families' survival than with being perceived as "matriarchs," began organizing into grassroots groups in California in 1962; the movement quickly spread to the Northeast and Midwest. Tactics were similar to those of the 1930s unemployed movement organizations: street demonstrations against cuts in public assistance, agitation at welfare offices, and legal resolution of grievances on a case-by-case basis—advocating for women who had had their benefits illegally cut, for example. By 1967, some middle-class civil rights leaders saw the groups of mostly black welfare mothers as a field ripe for "professional" organizing, and George Wiley, former director of the Congress of Racial Equality (CORE), and several others formed the National Welfare Rights Organization (NWRO). That year the NWRO held its first national convention; by 1971 the movement had grown to nine thousand local chapters in all fifty states. But the women who had begun the movement eventually wrested control of the organization from the black and white men who ran it, and welfare activist Johnnie Tillmon became the NWRO's executive director in 1973. Tillmon formed alliances with feminist groups and attempted to educate women of other economic classes about the myths of welfare. Unfortunately, church groups and private foundations were uncomfortable dealing directly with the welfare mothers who now ran the organization and withdrew funding; by 1975 the NWRO was essentially defunct.

The organization had an impact on many women, though. When the federal government increased benefits after the War on Poverty, a program initiated in 1964 by President Lyndon B. Johnson, and welfare rights activists began to improve some conditions for recipients, the stigma of receiving welfare decreased and the number of people receiving aid increased. Many women with children used government benefits to escape abusive marriages, and others were able to continue their education. In this context, some lesbian mothers received welfare benefits and were able to raise their children while doing volunteer work for the feminist and lesbian movements.

Several grassroots urban groups concerned with poverty attempted to build coalitions with the LGBT movement after the Stonewall Riots. Although it is not often remembered as a poor people's organization (known instead for its high-profile street activism and militancy), the Black Panther Party did run successful social programs for the inner-city poor, including sickle-cell anemia testing, free breakfasts, and Afro centric home schooling for children. In a 1970 manifesto, one of the party founders, Huey Newton, advocated Panther solidarity with the emerging gay and women's liberation movements.

AIDS, Homelessness, and Trans Action

A large number of middle-class gay and bisexual men were introduced to the indignities and prejudices the poor routinely experienced in dealing with the social service system when they became sick with HIV/AIDS in the 1980s and 1990s. In response, members of the direct action group AIDS Coalition to Unleash Power (ACT UP) and other social welfare organizations began to assume a greater care-taking role as clients and friends lost their housing and were often forced to remain in the hospital, sometimes in the hall or an emergency room, because they had no homes to which they might return. ACT UP formed a housing committee to address the ensuing crisis in the gay community, but a lack of affordable housing continues to be a key problem among AIDS patients, particularly as rents skyrocket in urban areas.

Many homeless shelters refuse to serve those with HIV/AIDS, and even if the directors are welcoming, clients often find it necessary to hide their HIV-positive status or LGBT sexual orientation from other residents. Verbal, physical, or sexual assault is a distinct possibility in the shelter system, and the rape of homeless women on the street is common. Homelessness remains such a prevalent problem among LGBT youth that agencies in many cities have opened shelters for those under twenty-one. At the other end of the life span, Seattle now has a support group, Salt & Pepper, for homeless LGBT people over fifty.

The transgender community is another sector of the LGBT population forced to cope with chronic unemployment and homelessness. In 1971 Sylvia Rivera and Marsha P. Johnston founded Street Transvestite Action Revolutionaries (STAR), originally a caucus of the Gay Liberation Front, to help trans youth, many of whom could not secure employment because of their gender presentation and thus ended up on the streets selling drugs or themselves. This group initially lasted only a few years, but Rivera, a drug addict who eventually ended up homeless herself, reformed STAR in 2000 after she had gone into recovery and transwoman Amanda Milan was murdered in Times Square.

Beyond Welfare Reform and Queer Markets

When the U.S. Congress began to debate the Personal Responsibility and Work Opportunity Reconciliation Act of 1996, the law that drastically cut entitlements for the poor, individual LGBT activists and national organizations lobbied against the legislation. The National Gay and Lesbian Task Force (NGLTF) Policy Institute and the Queer Economic Justice Network held press conferences and produced publications such "Leaving Our Children Behind: Welfare Reform and The Gay, Lesbian, Bisexual and Transgender Community." They point out that the Temporary Assistance for Needy Families (TANF) program of President George W. Bush's administration, with its emphasis on marriage as a method of removing people from the public assistance rolls, discriminates against lesbian mothers and other LGBT individuals and families. It also falls in line with the Religious Right's opposition to gay and lesbian marriage and the conservative definition of family as a heterosexual marriage and children. Meanwhile, these activists and others have noted, and protested, the way marketers and slick gay and lesbian magazine publishers of the past decade have successfully sold to the public an image of the LGBT community as teeming with wealthy "double income, no kids" households. Besides increasing the invisibility of the community's poor, this message has been used by the right wing to help promote anti-LGBT legislation.

The welfare system by its very nature discourages coming out, so many of the current public LGBT welfare rights activists are former recipients. As various local and national LGBT organizations continue to focus on such middle-class concerns as corporate domestic partner benefits and gay and lesbian marriage rights, impoverished members of the community are increasingly left to fend for themselves. A few scholars have suggested that the intrusive character of government agencies assisting the poor encourages more covert coping strategies that may not be best characterized as a "movement," but is just as effective for survival. Some of these strategies—including hiding from authorities sources of cash income and relationships that might change aid recipients' household status—are similar to tactics that LGBT people have used to obscure or manage their identities. Comparisons and questions like these are especially important to examine today in light of increased government surveillance and the erosion of civil rights protection in the United States.

Bibliography

Abramovitz, Mimi. *Under Attack, Fighting Back: Women and Welfare in the United States.* New York: Monthly Review Press, 1996.

Cahill, Sean, and Kenneth T. Jones. "Leaving Our Children Behind: Welfare Reform and the Gay, Lesbian, Bisexual and Transgender Community." Washington, D.C.: National Gay and Lesbian Task Force Policy Institute, 2001. Available at http://www.ngltf.org/pi/index.cfm

Deming, Barbara. "Mud City." In *We Are All Part Of One Another.* Edited By Jane Meyerding. Philadelphia: New Society Publishers, 1984.

Gilliom, John. *Overseers of the Poor: Surveillance, Resistance, and the Limits of Privacy.* Chicago: University of Chicago Press, 2001.

Gonzalez Paz, Juana Maria. "From Battered Wife to Community Volunteer: Testimony of a Welfare Mother." In *Out of the Class Closet: Lesbians Speak.* Edited by Julia Penelope. Freedom, Calif.: Crossing Press, 1994.

Lane, Molly. "Against Fear: Salt and Pepper Group Offers Affirmation Amidst Prejudice." *Real Change News.* Available from http://www.realchangenews.org/ pastarticles/features/ articles/fea_salt_pepper.html

Moynihan, Daniel Patrick. "The Negro Family: The Case for National Action." U.S. Department of Labor, Assistant Secretary for Polity, 1965. Available from http://www.dol.gov/asp/programs/history/webid-meynihan.htm. [note: "meynihan" is correct for this URL address]

Piven, Frances Fox, and Richard A. Cloward. *Poor People's Movements: Why They Succeed, How They Fail.* New York: Pantheon, 1977.

Shepard, Benjamin, and Ronald Hayduk, eds. *From ACT UP to the WTO: Urban Protest and Community Building in the Era of Globalization.* New York: Verso, 2002.

White, Deborah Gray. *Too Heavy a Load. Black Women in Defense of Themselves.* New York: Norton, 1999.

Michele Spring-Moore

See also CAPITALISM AND INDUSTRIALIZATION; CLASS AND CLASS OPPRESSION; CROSS-CLASS SEX AND RELATIONSHIPS; HAY, HARRY; NATIONAL GAY AND LESBIAN TASK FORCE (NGTLF); RIVERA, SYLVIA; RUSTIN, BAYARD.

PORNOGRAPHY

Michel Foucault once commented that sodomy was a thoroughly confused subject. The same might be claimed for pornography. While pornography has long loomed large in a wide range of cultural discourses—legal, literary, moral, pedagogical, medical, and feminist—any definition that has been used to describe it has been, at best, provisional and open to debate. According to Walter Kendrick's book *The Secret Museum,* the word was first coined by cobbling together the Greek words for whore *(porne)* and writing *(graphein)* and was used by British Victorian archaeologists to describe the sexually explicit artifacts found in the ruins of Pompeii. Since that time the concept of pornography has been subject to significant cultural debate, but pornography is generally defined as texts or images that describe or represent sexual activity, usually with the intent of inducing sexual arousal in the viewer, reader, or audience. Applications of such a loose definition are necessarily affected by current values. Boccaccio's *Decameron* was not offensive to fourteenth-century Florentines, but it was considered obscene by British Victorians. More recently, William Burroughs's *Naked Lunch* faced a series of challenges under obscenity laws in the 1950s and 1960s. In 1964, the Supreme Court overturned a lower court's ruling that Henry Miller's *Tropic of Cancer* was obscene; the Supreme Court decision came three years after the book's U.S. publication and thirty years after it was published in Europe. Both *Naked Lunch* and *Tropic of Cancer* are now viewed as important works of twentieth-century literature.

There are two culturally similar concepts closely connected to pornography. The first is obscenity, which is loosely used to define materials (most often sexual in nature) that are offensive to commonly held standards of decency. While there have been crusades throughout history against the display and distribution of "pornography," legal codes in the United Kingdom and the United States have generally referred to obscenity, not pornography. While there is popular talk of anti-pornography laws, more accurately these are anti-obscenity laws. The second term is "erotica," which is commonly used for sexually explicit material sold in mainstream venues to a wide audience and therefore more culturally acceptable. The writer John Preston used to quip that "erotica" was a middle-class word for porn. In the past twenty years, with the production of a large amount of sexually explicit heterosexual material written by and for women, the term "erotica" has come to describe not simply a subset of pornography, but a distinct, highly lucrative category of the publishing industry.

Before the Twentieth Century

There have been, historically, a plethora of visual and written images of same-sex sexual activity. In ancient cultures these include Greek vase paintings of men, and less frequently women, engaging in sexual acts, passages in Petronius's *Satyricon,* and references to both women and men in Martial's *Epitaphs* and Catullus's poems. (Sappho's woman-centered erotic poems are more properly classified as romantic, rather than overtly sexual works.) Explicit same-sex erotic activity can also be found in works of the French Enlightenment (in Breton, Sade, and others) as well as the British Restoration (for instance, John Wilmot, Earl of Rochester's play *Sodom* [1675] and John Cleland's *Memoirs of a Woman of Pleasure* [1748]). British Victorian culture, despite very strict obscenity laws, was awash in pornographic books, no small part of which included episodes of same-sex activity. This included semi-literary writing such as *The Lustful Turk* (1838) and *Harriet Marwood, Governess* (1884) (both authored anonymously), *Under the Hill* by Aubrey Beardsley (1904), and *Teleny* (1893), allegedly written in part by Oscar Wilde. Novels such as *The Sins of the Cities of the Plains* (1881) by Jack Saul had fewer literary pretensions and were also popular. While same-sex male content in these books was usually written for a homosexual male readership, same-sex female content was aimed almost entirely at a heterosexual male readership.

In the United States literary writers who dealt with more explicitly homoerotic themes, including Walt Whitman in *Leaves of Grass* (1855), often had their works banned or suppressed. But this was not true for everyone.

Herman Melville's *Typee* (1846), *Omoo* (1847), and *Moby-Dick* (1851) all contain fairly explicit homoerotic scenes, but never elicited moral approbation. The same is true of (now) less well-known works such as Bayard Taylor's *Joseph and His Friend* (1870), Charles Warren Stoddard's *South-Sea Idyls* (1873), and Alan Dale's *A Marriage Below Zero* (1899). The difference between Whitman's reception and the reception of the others is due in part to the fact that Whitman promoted an ideology of sexual freedom, whereas Melville's and Stoddard's books were accepted as adventure stories and Taylor's and Dale's as literary novels. But the difference is also attributable to the arbitrariness of obscenity classifications.

The advent of photography in the late nineteenth century proved a boon for the production and distribution of sexually explicit images. Photographs of cross-sex and same-sex sexual activity existed, but images of the female and male nude were more widely available and popular. While female nudes were generally aimed at heterosexual men, photographs of male nudes found popularity with a homosexual male audience as well as a smaller heterosexual female one. Photography also became one of the central means of promoting the physical culture movement, which championed improving moral and psychological health through the building of strong bodies. Because photography was quickly elevated to the realm of fine art, nude photographs of either sex were often considered art rather than pornography. Indeed, the works of Baron von Gloeden (a German who primarily used Sicilian youth as his subjects), F. Holland Day (an American who specialized in eroticized religious themes), and Thomas Eakins (who also painted male nudes) defined not only the aesthetics of art photography, but a new gay male pornographic aesthetic as well. This aesthetic influenced not only the physique magazines—the manifestations of the physical culture movement that began publication in the 1950s—but, to a large degree, sexually explicit gay male photography today.

The Early Twentieth Century

Aside from the same-sex eroticism of works by Melville, Whitman, and others in the nineteenth century, there is little record of the production of overtly sexual books in the United States before the twentieth century (though books published in Great Britain were read by Americans). By the 1920s and 1930s, however, American authors were beginning to produce literary works with bolder, often more explicit, same-sex sexual themes. These works also differed from their nineteenth-century counterparts insofar as they were written with the consciousness of a homosexual identity, which had not existed in the United States before the late nineteenth century. In *Playing the Game: The Homosexual Novel in America,* the late Roger Austen chronicles a subculture of male homosexual writing in the 1920s and 1930s. Many of the unpublished works discussed by Austen were passed from person to person to avoid prosecution under federal, state, and local censorship laws. These laws regulated not only sexually explicit materials, but any materials that dealt with same-sex sexuality. While literary works that dealt explicitly with cross-sex sex were often targeted (including D. H. Lawrence's *Sons and Lovers* [1913] and *Lady Chatterley's Lover* [1928] and James Joyce's *Ulysses* [1922]), novels with overt same-sex sexual content such as Radclyffe Hall's classic lesbian novel *The Well of Loneliness* (1928) were almost always targeted. Still, courts began to restrict the scope of obscenity law during this period; most notably, in *People v. Friede* (1949) the New York Supreme Court overturned a lower court decision that had declared obscene *The Well of Loneliness.*

1950s and 1960s

Because national and state laws were so strict, even the slightest suggestion of same-sex eroticism could be enough to have a book, film, or pamphlet legally prosecuted as obscene. So could non-erotic discussions of LGB identities, communities, or politics. In 1953 the Postmaster General of Los Angeles seized the current issue of *ONE,* a respectable homophile magazine that avoided discussions or depictions of same-sex sex, based on allegations that it was "obscene, lewd, lascivious, filthy." A federal district court as well as a federal appeals court declared that *ONE* was legally obscene, using language that suggested that any writing not critical of homosexuality was ipso facto obscene. In 1958 this ruling was overturned by the U.S. Supreme Court in *ONE, Inc. v. Olesen,* thus allowing LGB material to be more easily published. In 1962, the Supreme Court ruled in *Manual Enterprises v. Day* that male physique magazines had to be treated the same as comparable heterosexual material. There were still federal, state, and local laws that prohibited the publishing and distributing of obscene materials, but a series of Supreme Court decisions from 1957 to 1966 limited enforcement of these laws, thus allowing a far greater range of homosexual and heterosexual materials to be published.

These rulings, while clearing the way for "literary" works, did not prohibit federal and state agencies from harassing, and even imprisoning, the publishers and distributors of non-literary materials, though litigation often overturned these actions. The San Diego–based

Greenleaf Press, for instance, which published both heterosexual and homosexual erotica, faced a series of obscenity charges from 1966 to 1972. Philadelphia-based *Drum* magazine also faced considerable opposition from federal, state, and local authorities in the mid-1960s. When federal and state courts were not involved, national and local pressure groups such as the Roman Catholic–based National Organization for Decent Literature (NODL) used economic boycotts to stop bookstores, card shops, and magazine stores from selling paperback novels and magazines considered offensive or immoral.

Despite the legal restraints on explicitly sexualized LGB images before and after the Supreme Court's rulings, after World War II production of LGB materials with varying degrees of sexual explicitness increased. In 1945 Robert Mizer formed the Athletic Model Guild (AMG) and in 1951 he began publishing *Physique Pictorial*, the premiere "physical culture" magazine for gay men. With candid photographs of amateur models (in many cases hustlers who used AMG as a form of advertising) taken by such noted artists as Al Urban, Dave Martin, Lon of New York, and Bruce of Los Angeles, *Physique Pictorial* set the standard for similar magazines that included *Vim*, *Grecian Quarterly*, *Adonis*, and dozens of others. These magazines provided a template later used by male nude photographers such as Roy Blakely, Kenn Duncan, and Bruce Weber.

Production of books with LGB sexual themes also increased during the 1950s. While mainstream publishing companies occasionally published books that to some degree dealt with LGB topics, those that specialized in original paperback books (nicknamed "pulps" for the wood used to produce the cheap paper) flooded newsstands, bus stations, candy stores, and card shops with a wide array of works that dealt with lesbianism. The 1950 publication of Treska Torres's *Women in Barracks*, the memoir of a French soldier, opened a floodgate of lesbian pulps that soon included Vin Packer's 1952 *Spring Fire* and Ann Bannon's 1957 *Odd Girl Out* (the first of a five-volume series that included *I Am a Woman* [1959] and *Beebo Brinker* [1962]). Hundreds of lesbian pulps were published in the 1950s and 1960s, most of them written by heterosexual men for a male heterosexual audience, but some by lesbians, including Packer (the pen name of Marijane Meaker), Bannon, Paula Christian, and Valerie Taylor. Most of these books had few sexually explicit details and while they were rarely banned or censored as obscene they did function as erotic literature for the women and men who read them. Many of these titles were so popular that they sold hundreds of thousands of copies.

Gay male novels were also published in paperback editions, although for the most part these were reprints of literary novels published by mainstream presses. By the mid-sixties, however, censorship laws had changed enough that new types of publishers came into existence. Focusing at first on mildly suggestive works and by the 1970s on explicit sexual descriptions of both heterosexual and homosexual activity, publishing companies such as Greenleaf, Brandon House, and Publisher's Export Company specialized in commercial pornography that was mass-produced and widely distributed. The lesbian titles that came from these new houses were almost entirely written by heterosexual men for a heterosexual male audience, but certainly some lesbians had access to them.

The loosening of censorship laws, the publication of these and other types of novels, and the emergence of explicitly sexual photograph books from the same publishers gave birth to the new phenomenon of the adult bookstore. Beginning in 1965 in California, the adult bookstore, selling erotic paperbacks, illustrated sex manuals, pornographic magazines and 8mm films, and sex toys, became a prominent commercial feature in almost all American cities. Along with the emergence of these bookstores came the advent of adult theaters, which were now allowed to screen sexually explicit films. This created a distribution network for a burgeoning erotic film industry that had functioned almost exclusively underground or through mail-order sales of 8mm films to be screened at home. These stores and theaters, usually operating in urban areas, were not only an outlet for new publications and films, but also became cruising spots for gay men. The adult bookstores were also in some senses the predecessors of LGBT bookstores.

An offshoot of these new developments were gay owned and operated publishers, distributors, bookstores, and theaters that not only catered to a gay audience, but saw themselves as engaging in community building and political activism as well. In Philadelphia, the homophile activist Clark Polak, who was president of the Janus Society, not only published *Drum*, an edgy, campy publication that featured fiction, personals, physique photos, and cartoons, but also owned Trojan Book Service, which published and distributed physique magazines and other pornographic materials, and several adult bookstores. A similar, even larger operation was run by H. Lynn Womack in Washington, D.C. The publisher of several physique magazines—*Manual*, *Guild Quarterly*, *Grecian Quarterly*—Womack was the person who won the groundbreaking Supreme Court case *Manual Enterprises v. Day* in 1962. Under his direction, the Guild Press, Inc. reprinted literary novels and published original pornographic work as well as physique magazines. He also ran the Guild Press Book Service, which gave subscribers access to a wide range of materials from muscle magazines and pornographic novels to best-selling books like John Rechy's *City of Night* (1963) and literary novels such as Lonnie Coleman's *Sam* (1959) and John Selby's *Madam* (1963). Polak and Womack were predecessors of the overtly gay publishers, distributors, and book clubs of today.

After the 1960s

The advent of the gay liberation movement in the 1970s brought sexually explicit gay material not just out of the closet but into the arena of politics. The earliest post-Stonewall riots newspapers such as New York's *Gay* and *Gay Today* routinely featured naked men and full frontal nudity as ways of celebrating the gay male body and gay sexuality. While these were commercial periodicals, a similar celebratory attitude toward sexuality was also seen in alternative, political publications such as *Fag Rag* (Boston), *Gay Sunshine* (San Francisco), *Gay Alternative* (Philadelphia), and *Body Politic* (Toronto). While these rejected most aspects of commercialized gay male sexuality—including commercial porn and non-gay owned bars and bathhouses—they had no problem with presenting sexually explicit images, fiction, and autobiography as political statements. Lesbian and women's liberation magazines and newspapers of the same period almost never carried images of naked or highly sexualized women, but relied more on representations of strong, non-traditionally beautiful women to convey their anti-authoritarian and anti-patriarchal messages.

Political protests against the commercialization of gay images and gay culture had little impact on mainstream gay culture. Beginning in the early 1970s, a number of glossy, sexualized gay male lifestyle magazines began publication. Taking their cue from *Playboy*, these publications, which included *Blueboy, Mandate, Honcho, Numbers, Drummer,* and *Bunkhouse,* presented full frontal male nudity, pornographic fiction, first-person narratives, cultural reviews, and often humor. This was the culmination of the social changes that had been occurring since the early 1950s. The appearance of these magazines on neighborhood newsstands also marked the emergence of a new level of public acceptance of homosexuality in everyday urban American life. This new visibility also coincided with the further commercialization of gay male pornographic films and theaters. Meanwhile filmmakers such as Arthur Bressen, Wakefield Poole, Jack Deavue, Fred Halstead, and Peter DeRome began directing sexually explicit films that they viewed as art. Their filmmaking was directly linked to the political impulses of the early gay liberation publications, which made explicit connections between gay pride, gay identity, and gay sexuality.

As the adult entertainment industry grew in the 1970s and 1980s, gay male videos proliferated. Companies such as Falcon, Catalina, All Worlds, and Vista flooded the market with an increasingly wide variety of gay male videos that catered to particular sexual interests, including sadomasochism, leather and other fetishes, role playing, athletics and working out, solo masturbation, interracial sex, and monoracial sex. As with all marketed commercial popular culture, the industry promoted its stars—Kip Noll, Richard Locke, Casey Donovan, Jack Wrangler, Joey Stefano, Ryan Idol, Jeff Stryker—who became, for their admirers, as popular as Hollywood stars. And as with Bob Mizer's AMG publications and films, much of this film and video work was a form of advertising for the sex work of its stars. Often the major video companies published film and video stills and interviews with their stars in magazines such as *Mandate* and *Drummer,* which benefited both the film companies and the publications. There are no hard financial statistics available on the adult entertainment industry. It is also difficult to separate out earnings based on homosexual material from earnings based on heterosexual materials since many production companies are owned by the same parent company. Estimates for the years 1990 to 2003, however, are that the adult entertainment video industry in the United States alone grosses $15 billion a year.

Lesbian and lesbian-feminist culture did not generally view sexually explicit imagery as a form of liberation. In fact some feminists in groups such as Woman Against Violence Against Women (WAVA) and Women Against Pornography (WAP) focused on the threats that heterosexual porn posed for women. According to theorists such as Andrea Dworkin and Catherine MacKinnon, heterosexual pornography was one of the primary causes of misogynist violence in Western culture. Other feminists disagreed strongly, arguing that sexual pleasure had to be conceptualized as central to women's liberation. At a women's and sexuality conference held at Barnard College in 1982, the "sex wars" exploded, often pitting women's liberation and lesbian activists against one another. The so-called pro-sex activists formed groups such as the Feminist Anti-Censorship Task Force (FACT) and spoke out on a wide range of issues that profoundly affected the public debate about women, feminism, and sexuality. One of the most tangible results of these debates was the emergence of a number of lesbian, and feminist, sex magazines such as *Bad Attitude* (Boston,

1983) and *On Our Backs* (Los Angeles, 1986). These magazines reclaimed lesbian and women's sexuality from what they saw as a male-dominated public discourse and placed women at the center of both production and readership. While almost all of the lesbian porn up until this point had been produced by heterosexual men for a heterosexual male audience, there had always been a lesbian audience for it and now lesbian-produced pornography aimed to reach and expand that audience. Along with publishing magazines, lesbians also began producing sex videos, although these have had none of the success of the publications.

While the feminist critique of pornography was widely regarded—among non-feminists at least—as repressive, it did have a large cultural impact by opening up public discussion about pornography. Over the last two decades various scholars and commentators have asked important questions: Are the blatantly sexualized images in mainstream advertising similar to traditional porn? What are the politics of the idealized body in gay male porn? Should porn be judged by aesthetic or political standards? Can the fantasy world of porn be criticized as racist? Does pornography lend itself to sexual liberation or is it just another manifestation of consumerism? Are there fundamental differences in how males and females experience pleasure? With the rise of the internet, pornography has perhaps never been as accessible to the U.S. public, and LGB porn has perhaps not surprisingly emerged as a central subject in controversial debates about blocking internet access in schools, public facilities, and workplaces. Mass-produced porn has been a staple of LGB cultures for just over a century and it is likely to remain a source of debate, controversy, and pleasure for the foreseeable future.

Bibliography

Austen, Roger. *Playing the Game: The Homosexual Novel in America.* Indianapolis, Ind.: Bobbs-Merrill, 1977.

Bronski, Michael. *Culture Clash: The Making of Gay Sensibility.* Boston: South End Press, 1984.

———. *The Pleasure Principle: Sex, Backlash, and the Struggle for Gay Freedom.* New York: St. Martin's Press, 1998.

De Grazia, Edward. *Girls Lean Back Everywhere.* New York: Vintage, 1993.

Duggan, Lisa, and Nan D. Hunter. *Sex Wars: Sexual Dissent and Political Culture.* New York: Routledge, 1995.

Ellenzweig, Allen. *The Homoerotic Photograph: Male Images from Durieu/Delacroix to Mapplethorpe.* New York: Columbia University Press, 1992.

Friedman, Andrea. *Prurient Interests: Gender, Democracy, and Obscenity in New York City, 1909–1945.* New York: Columbia University Press, 2000.

Hatton, Jackie. "The Pornography Empire of H. Lynn Womack." *Viewing Culture* 7 (Spring 1993): 9–32.

Hooven, F. Valentine, III. *Beefcake: The Muscle Magazines of America, 1950–1970.* Berlin, Germany: Taschen, 1995.

Kendrick, Walter. *The Secret Museum: Pornography in Modern Culture.* New York: Viking, 1987.

Meyer, Richard. *Outlaw Representation: Censorship & Homosexuality in Twentieth-Century American Art.* New York: Oxford University Press, 2002.

Morgan, Tracy. "Pages of Whiteness." In *Queer Studies.* Edited by Brett Beemyn and Mickey Eliason. New York: New York University Press, 1996.

Stein, Marc. *City of Sisterly and Brotherly Loves: Lesbian and Gay Philadelphia, 1945–1972.* Chicago: University of Chicago Press, 2000.

Stryker, Susan. *Queer Pulp: Perverted Passions from the Golden Age of the Paperback.* San Francisco: Chronicle, 2001.

Waugh, Thomas. *Hard to Imagine: Gay Male Eroticism in Photography and Film from Their Beginnings to Stonewall.* New York: Columbia University Press, 1996.

Michael Bronski

See also BOOKSTORES; CENSORSHIP, OBSCENITY, AND PORNOGRAPHY LAW AND POLICY; *DRUM*; HOMOPHILE PRESS; MAPPLETHORPE, ROBERT; MIZER, ROBERT; NEWSPAPERS AND MAGAZINES; *ONE*; PHYSIQUE MAGAZINES AND PHOTOGRAPHS; POLAK, CLARK; PUBLISHERS; SEX WARS; WOMACK, H. LYNN.

PORNOGRAPHY LAW AND POLICY. see CENSORSHIP, OBSCENITY, AND PORNOGRAPHY LAW AND POLICY.

PORTER, Cole (b. 9 June 1891; d. 15 October 1964), songwriter.

Cole Albert Porter grew up a child of wealth and privilege in Peru, Indiana. He studied piano and violin at an early age, developing a rudimentary proficiency on both instruments, and began composing pieces and songs at about age ten. His parents encouraged his artistic interests, though they hoped that their only surviving child would enter law.

He attended Worcester Academy (1905–1909) and Yale University (1909–1913), where he majored in English and minored in music and where he wrote the lyrics and music for numerous songs for college shows and football games. After one year at Harvard Law School (1913–1914), he decided on a career in musical theater, studying music at Harvard University and then in New York. In 1916, he launched his first Broadway show, *See America First.* The following year, he went abroad to aid the war effort, and he remained in Europe—mostly in

Cole Porter. Seen at his piano in 1933, this master of sophisticated and risqué lyrics—as well as memorable melodies—was one of the few Broadway greats who created both the words and the music. **[Getty Images]**

Paris and Venice—for much of the next two decades. Singing his own sophisticated and witty songs at the piano, he quickly became the toast of European society. He pursued his musical studies at the Schola Cantorum (1920–1922) and wrote a ballet with Gerald Murphy for the Swedish Ballet, *Within the Quota* (1923; orchestrated by Charles Koechlin).

From homes on both sides of the Atlantic, he became the lyricist-composer of a number of successful Broadway musical comedies, including *Fifty Million Frenchmen* (1929), *The Gay Divorce* (1932), and *Anything Goes* (1934). He also had success in Hollywood, where he kept yet another home, composing the music for *Born to Dance* (1936) and *Rosalie* (1937). With these scores, all of which yielded hit standards, Porter established himself as a master of the genre, a worthy successor to Irving Berlin and Jerome Kern. Audiences and critics especially admired the smart topical references and risqué humor of his lyrics and the sensuous harmonies and ambitious forms of his music.

In 1937, Porter broke both legs in a riding accident and for the rest of life endured numerous operations and much pain. He nonetheless continued to produce successful shows, including *Panama Hattie* (1940), *Let's Face It* (1941), and his masterpiece, *Kiss Me Kate* (1948). At the height of his fame, Hollywood released a film biography, *Night and Day* (1946), with Cary Grant playing the shorter and plainer Cole. However, in the course of the 1950s he became increasingly depressed, and after the amputation of a leg in 1958 he produced no new scores.

Porter was homosexual, and from his college days onward traveled in gay circles often in the company of such friends as Monty Woolley and Howard Sturges. In 1918, he married Linda Lee Thomas, a wealthy divorcee fifteen years his senior. Although Cole and Linda were devoted to each other, the former pursued numerous homosexual affairs throughout his married years, including those with Ballets Russes regisseur Boris Kochno, architect Eddy Tauch, and sailor Ray Kelly. During his time in Hollywood, he also held "boy parties" with attractive young men lounging poolside. Thomas accepted her husband's homosexuality, and though Porter's promiscuity sometimes placed a strain on their relationship, they remained married until her death in 1954.

Porter's complex sexual life reflected itself in his lyrics, arguably the most erotic in the history of American musical comedy. Many of his best-known songs embrace such themes as romantic abandon, casual sex, unrequited love, and prostitution. He was a virtuoso of the double entendre and of the sexual metaphor: a lover, for example, is asked "to give my ship, / A maiden trip"; a patient finds that her doctor "murmured *'molto bella,'* / When I sat on his patella"; and a girl invites "a boy, some night, / To dine on my fine finnan haddie."

Although the sexual chic and campy wit of Porter's lyrics plainly were related to his sexual orientation and experiences, he rarely referenced homosexual subjects as explicitly as in "I'm Unlucky at Gambling" from *Fifty Million Frenchmen* (1929), in which the female character who takes a croupier to the movies discovers that "he liked John Gilbert too." Otherwise, Porter used such code words as "queen," as in a 1919 song in which the singer goes to the bar of Paris's Ritz Hotel to "see the kings / And let the queens see me."

Combined with exquisite harmonies, radiant melodies, and sprightly rhythms, such clever ribaldry became irresistibly infectious, and as one of America's most popular and beloved songwriters, Porter arguably did as much to shape his country's attitudes toward love and sex as perhaps anyone else of his time.

Bibliography

Kimball, Robert, ed.. *Cole.* Woodstock, N.Y: Overlook Press, 1971, 2000. Includes a biographical essay by Brendan Gill.

McBrien, William. *Cole Porter: A Biography.* New York: Knopf, 1998.

Schwartz, Charles. *Cole Porter: A Biography.* New York: Dial Press, 1977.

Howard Pollack

See also MUSIC: BROADWAY AND MUSICAL THEATER.

PORTLAND, OREGON

Since initial settlement in 1843, Portland has been a center for Pacific import–export trade. In 1910 its population reached 207,000. Nearly a century later its metropolitan area counted 1.7 million residents.

The Scene through the 1960s

Portland's most visible early homosexual community revolved around the racially and ethnically diverse male laborers who crowded into the North End lodging district beginning in the 1880s. Same-sex sexual activities were an established part of this working-class culture and therefore the atmosphere of the North End. A separate middle-class male homosexual community had appeared in the city's white-collar central business district by 1900. In apartments, the Imperial Hotel's restroom, Lownsdale Park, and along Washington Street, men met each other for sexual affairs and more. In late 1912 a scandal involving the Young Men's Christian Association (YMCA) brought this homosexual side of Portland to public awareness and led to repressive reforms (see sidebar). Another scandal in 1928 reminded locals again of the local male homosexual underworld.

Lesbians in the pre–World War II period were less visible, but records indicate that some were incarcerated by the Women's Protective Division. Committed working- and middle-class lesbian couples also made Portland their home. Marie Equi, a physician and political activist, and her partner Harriet Speckart maintained a relationship in the city between 1906 and 1921. Equi supported a variety of radical causes such as birth control, abortion, and the Industrial Workers of the World.

One of the earliest known "transsexual" surgeries occurred in Portland when Alan Hart, born Alberta Lucille, underwent a hysterectomy and psychological treatment between 1917 and 1920. Hart then assumed the clothing of a male and married twice. Hart was a licensed physician who eventually worked in various parts of the United States. He also wrote several novels. *The Undaunted* (1936), set in a fictional northwestern city, tells the tragic story of a male homosexual lab technician.

World War II revolutionized Portland's LGB community. Thousands flocked to the city's war industries and military installations. This added to the homosexual population and it transformed formerly straight bars into cruising spots for military personnel and civilians alike. The Harbor Club, which in time served both gays and lesbians, was among the best known; the navy declared it off-limits. The corner of Park and Oak Streets in the downtown area served as a G.I. pickup spot, while Hayden Island on the Columbia River became a male nude beach.

After the war some bars became exclusively LGB while other venues, such as the Music Hall, with its drag performers, grew increasingly popular. Bathhouses, such as the Aero-Vapor, came into their own in the 1960s. A crackdown on bars, drag shows, and cruising areas in city parks occurred between 1949 and 1964; the latter year is when alarmed authorities worried that Portland was "fast becoming a small San Francisco." But during this time some homosexuals pursued other forms of private and public socializing. For example, although Portland's Imperial Sovereign Rose Court originated in 1966, a short-lived predecessor, the Court of Transylvania, appeared in 1958. Originally more for fun and socializing, in the 1960s the court system grew into a non-profit organization that sponsored drag balls and raised funds for various charities. A number of lesbians also played for The Florists, Portland's nationally known softball team, as early as the 1940s, while others flocked to their games or played in local clubs.

Institutions and Accomplishments, 1970–2002

Police harassment waned in the second half of the 1960s, which might explain why homophile organizations were slow to develop in Portland. Only after Stonewall did LGB people really organize. In 1969 a group of female impersonators founded the Portland Forum. At the same

portland's 1912 scandal

In mid-November 1912, Portland newspapers reported in outrageous tones details of a thriving male homosexual underground in the city and linked it to the local Young Men's Christian Association (YMCA). For weeks local and regional newspapers devoted ample space to coverage of the so-called YMCA scandal while authorities arrested dozens of men from as far north as Vancouver, British Columbia, and as far south as Fresno, California. Those apprehended included some high-profile individuals, including E. S. J. McAllister, a well-known lawyer and political reformer who had influenced Portland's municipal governmental system. Sensational trials followed. Several men ended up behind bars while others fled the city for good. As the sensational news spread to large dailies in cities throughout the country, many worried that a national ring of sex perverts were operating a system not unlike that of white slavers. In response, U.S. Representative A. W. Lafferty from Portland attempted to rally the federal government into action. The 1912 scandal, however, had a far greater impact at the local and regional levels, leading to legislation that would have an effect on LGB people for years to come. In 1913 the Oregon legislature expanded the definition of sodomy, hitherto rather vaguely worded in the statute, to include oral sex and "any act or practice of sexual perversity." At the same time, legislators lengthened the maximum sentence for sodomy from five to fifteen years. The scandal also broke the logjam in the legislature over eugenics, which had been debated for years. In response to the news from Portland, Oregon governor Oswald West declared the need to emasculate the "degenerates who slink, in all their infamy, through every city, contaminating the young, debauching the innocent, cursing the State" (Oregon, *General Laws, 1913.* Salem: Willis S. Duniway, 1913. Vol. 1: 18). The legislature passed the governor's sterilization bill, which specifically targeted "sexual perverts" who were "addicted to the practice of sodomy." Although Oregonians repealed (for reasons unrelated to homosexuality) the new statute in a referendum in the fall of 1913, the legislature adopted it again in 1917. Tinkered with over the years, the law remained on the books until 1965. The state's sodomy law was repealed on 1 January 1972.

time a local chapter of the Gay Liberation Front appeared. It dissolved within a year over a controversy that led lesbians to form a separate group. Between the fall and winter of 1970–1971 the LGB Second Foundation organized. It began publishing Portland's first LGB newspaper, *The Fountain*, in 1971, and opened the first Gay Community Center in May 1972. Also in 1971 the Metropolitan Community Church arrived in the city, LGB people began the *Homophile Half Hour* on a local radio station, and the first gay pride activities were held. But it was not until 1975 and 1978, respectively, when the first Gay Fair and the first LGB march took place, both in association with the commemoration of the Stonewall Riots.

While Portland's LGB scene remained centered in downtown, from the 1970s through the 1990s lesbian and LGB residential neighborhoods emerged in the northwest and the inner southeast sections of the city. During these years various organizations, restaurants, bars, and newspapers came and went, but a few had staying power. Darcelle's drag nightclub, now a Portland institution, has operated continuously since 1969. The Portland Gay Men's Chorus began in 1980 and the Lesbian Choir formed in 1986. *Just Out*, Portland's longest-running community newspaper, started in 1983. The Lesbian Community Project formed in 1985 as a grassroots, multicultural organization to promote Portland's lesbian community. The Lavender Menace, an openly lesbian softball team, competed in the Portland Parks League in the early 1970s. Racial and ethnic minority groups also appeared, including the Asian Pacific Islander Lesbians and Gays in 1990. In the early 1980s the Northwest Gender Alliance for cross-dressers and transsexuals formed. During these years AIDS also took its toll on the community. Oregon's first reported AIDS death occurred in 1981. By 1996 more than 2,400 had died. A number of groups and institutions organized in response. The Cascade AIDS Project was among the largest. AIDS Coalition to Unleash Power (ACT UP) appeared in Portland in 1988 and disbanded in 1991. Portland's first AIDS hospice, Our House, opened in 1990.

The Portland City Council in December 1974 banned discrimination against homosexuals in municipal employment. An unsuccessful attempt to repeal the ordinance occurred during the conservative times of the 1980s. That conservatism—promoted in part by the Oregon Citizens Alliance, which from the late 1980s through the 1990s launched anti-LGB campaigns throughout Oregon—only clarified the need for the legal protection of sexual minorities. The city council responded in 1991 by passing an ordinance that shielded homosexuals from discrimination in housing and employment throughout the municipality. In 2000 the city extended similar protections to transgender people. Adding emphasis to its support for the LGBT community, the city council in 2002 took steps to preserve the historic LGBT district in downtown Portland.

Bibliography

Boag, Peter. *Same-Sex Affairs: Constructing and Controlling Homosexuality in the Pacific Northwest.* Berkeley: University of California Press, 2003.

Gilbert, J. Allen. "Homosexuality and Its Treatment." *Journal of Nervous and Mental Disease* 52 (1920): 297–322.

Krieger, Nancy. "Queen of the Bolsheviks: The Hidden History of Dr. Marie Equi." *Radical America* 17, no. 5 (1983): 55–73.

Martinac, Paula. *The Queerest Places: A Guide to Gay and Lesbian Historic Sites.* New York: Henry Holt, 1997.

"Those fabulous *Florists*! Women's softball and the flowering of a lesbian community in Portland." *Northwest Gay and Lesbian Historian* 1 (1997): 1, 6.

A Walking Tour of Downtown Portland: A Century of Gay, Lesbian, and Transgender Historic Sites. Portland, Ore.: Gay and Lesbian Archives of the Pacific Northwest, 1999.

Peter Boag

See also HART, ALAN.

PRESTON, John (b. 11 December 1945; d. 28 April 1994), writer, editor, activist.

John Preston, the writer of gay male erotica and gay rights activist, was born and raised in the rural town of Medfield, Massachusetts, the oldest of five children of Jack and Nancy Preston. During the mid-1960s, he participated in a number of progressive movements, including African American civil rights and anti–Vietnam War protests. He attended Lake Forrest College, where he continued his activism and came out. He graduated in 1968 and moved briefly back with his parents. In late 1969 he moved to Minneapolis, where, in 1970, he helped to found Gay House, Inc., one of the first lesbian and gay community centers in the United States, and worked on its administration. In 1973, while taking classes in the University of Minnesota's sexual health consulting program, he began a short stint as an editor working for the newsletter of the Sex Education Council of the United States. He left this job in 1975 to be the editor of *The Advocate,* a national lesbian and gay biweekly magazine then published in San Francisco. He edited *The Advocate* for a year, and then spent two more years living in San Francisco working part-time jobs and hustling. It was when Preston moved to New York in the summer of 1978 that his writing career began. Preston worked at various writing and editing jobs, the primary one being at *Mandate,* one of the gay male lifestyle magazines that, taking their inspiration from *Playboy,* had emerged in the mid-1970s and were in the vanguard of promoting gay male issues, sexual and otherwise, to a wide audience.

In New York Preston began writing fiction and, under the name Jack Prescott, began to serialize *Mr. Benson,* a novel, in the San Francisco–based *Drummer* magazine, which catered to a homosexual sadomasochistic sensibility. The increasing popularity of *Mr. Benson*—which was aided by clever promotions as Mr. Benson tee-shirts, produced and sold by Preston himself—convinced its author to write full time. Aside from writing erotica for gay male magazines, Preston also produced a number of mass-market paperbacks of male adventure and soldier-of-fortune novels under the names Jack Hild and Mike McCray. He left New York in 1979 and moved to Portland, Maine, where he lived until his death.

In Portland Preston began to publish impressive amounts of both erotic and male action fiction. From 1984 to 1987 he wrote seven novels featuring Alex Kane, a former Marine, who spent his time righting wrongs done to gay men. (These titles were republished in 1992 and 1993 with more explicit sexual material added.) In the early 1980s he also began publishing his "Master" series—beginning with *Once I Had a Master, and Other Tales of Erotic Love* in 1984—that have, along with *Mr. Benson,* become classics of gay male sadomasochism erotica. In 1983 he published his novel *Fanny: Queen of Provincetown,* which was later dramatized by Robert Pittman. All of these titles were published by Alyson Books, a Boston-based gay publishing firm.

In 1987 Preston was diagnosed as HIV-positive, although he was to remain relatively healthy until late 1993. His response to this news was to work even harder. In 1988 Preston published his *Personal Dispatches: Writers Confront AIDS,* one of the first books from a mainstream press that dealt with the epidemic. During this time Preston moved from smaller gay publishers to mainstream publishing houses. This was also the beginning of Preston's most lasting contribution to gay and lesbian letters, editing a series of anthologies—which included *Hometowns: Gay Men Write About Where They Belong* (1991), *A Member of the Family: Gay Men Write About Their Families* (1992), *Sisters and Brothers: Lesbians and Gay Men Write About Their Lives Together* (edited with Joan Nestle, 1994), and *Friends and Lovers: Gay Men Write About the Families They Create* (1995)—that brought some of the country's best writers together to detail the emotional and psychological nuances of gay and lesbian life. Between 1992 and 1995 he also edited three volumes of the *Flesh and the Word* series that featured a variety of literary erotica, and also published a collection of autobiographical essays, including *My Life as A Pornographer, and Other Indecent Acts* (1993) and *Hustling: A Gentleman's Guide to the Fine Art of Prostitution* (1994).

During these years, Preston continued his activism, working with the Maine Lesbian and Gay Political Alliance as well as with the AIDS Project of Portland. He worked for such publications as *Lambda Book Report, OUT,* and other periodicals while maintaining a full schedule of public speaking on writing, AIDS, and activism. Richard Kasak, the publisher of the imprints Richard Kasak Books, BadBoy, and Hard Candy, published Preston's autobiographical essays and reprinted the Alex Kane and Masters series, thus giving Preston a whole new audience.

As Preston's health failed, writer and novelist Michael Lowenthal became a collaborator and editor. Under Lowenthal's supervision and guidance *Flesh and the Word 3* and *Friends and Lovers* were published. Preston's companion during this time, in a loving and nonsexual relationship, was Tom Hagerty. John Preston died on April 28, 1994. After his death a collection of essays, *Winter Light: Reflections of a Yankee Queer,* edited by Michael Lowenthal, was published.

Preston's manuscripts and correspondence were acquired in 1992 by the John Hay Library at Brown University for its Katzoff Collection.

Bibliography

Preston, John. *A Member of the Family: Gay Men Write About Their Families.* New York: Dutton, 1992.

———. *My Life as a Pornographer, and Other Indecent Acts.* New York: Masquerade Books,1993.

———. *Winter's Light: Reflections of a Yankee Queer.* Hanover, N.H.: University Presses of New England, 1995.

Michael Bronski

See also *ADVOCATE*; COMMUNITY CENTERS; LITERATURE; SADOMASOCHISM, SADISTS, AND MASOCHISTS.

PRIDE MARCHES AND PARADES

Marches and parades celebrating "pride" and protesting oppression have been a central part of LGBT culture in the United States since the gay liberation movement began in the late 1960s. Drawing on queer traditions of camp and outrageous style, these parades have been opportunities for LGBT people to make themselves visible to one another and to their surrounding communities. Most major cities and many other municipalities today host annual LGBT pride parades in late June, near the anniversary of the 1969 Stonewall Riots in New York City. In addition, LGBT people have held several major marches on Washington, D.C., demanding changes to various federal and state policies.

Because pride marches and parades constitute one of the most conspicuous forms of self-expression and display on the part of LGBT communities, they have been the focus of numerous controversies. In particular, lesbians, people of color, and transgender people have struggled to obtain prominent billing in celebrations that have often been dominated by white gay men. LGBT people have also debated whether to seek acceptability to a mainstream audience or instead to celebrate radical sexual and gender practices. Related conflicts have centered on allegations of de-politicization and excessive commercialization.

Since 1990, LGBT pride parades in major U.S. cities have become larger, more complex, and more commercial; in many cities, they are among the largest annual parades. Some LGBT activists have argued that contemporary pride parades have departed from their radical origins, while others believe that their inclusion in mainstream mass culture is a sign of progress and acceptance.

The 1960s: The Origins of Pride in Homophile Activism

Although annual LGBT pride celebrations are often associated with the memory of the 1969 Stonewall Riots, their roots can be traced to the pre-Stonewall activities of the homophile movement. Beginning in the mid-1960s, homophile organizations, influenced by the African American civil rights movement, sponsored a number of public demonstrations demanding rights for homosexuals. The first annual public demonstration was a picket organized by Mattachine Society, Daughters of Bilitis, and Janus Society activists at Philadelphia's Independence Hall each year, beginning on 4 July 1965. By picketing on the nation's birthday at the site where the Declaration of Independence was signed, demonstrators sought to illuminate the exclusion of LGB people from the nation's democratic ideals and to draw comparisons between the civil rights struggles of African Americans and those of homosexuals.

After the Stonewall Riots, which drew national attention to queer resistance to police repression, many activists felt that a dramatic shift had taken place and that the riots should be commemorated annually. In November 1969, at a regional homophile conference in Philadelphia, LGB activists decided to replace the annual Fourth of July pickets with a march honoring the anniversary of Stonewall.

That conference, and LBGT activism in the late 1960s generally, was marked by disagreements between young, radical gay liberationists and an older generation of activists who embraced a politics of what Marc Stein has called "militant respectability." The dynamic tension between these tendencies in LGBT activism has shaped the history of pride marches and parades ever since.

The 1970s: Commemorating Stonewall and Creating a Tradition

In June 1970 perhaps from two thousand to five thousand people attended the first Christopher Street Liberation Day Parade, celebrating the one-year anniversary of the Stonewall rebellion. The entourage began in Greenwich Village and marched through New York City's streets, ending in Central Park. According to historian Martin Duberman's *Stonewall* (1993), parade organizer Craig Rodwell insisted that the first parade be "a grass-roots project uncontaminated by any connection to commercial interests"; accordingly, its costs amounted to only around $1,000 (p. 271). Marchers carried placards and chanted slogans conveying radical political messages; many were connected to the Gay Liberation Front or the Gay Activists Alliance. Early pride parades were notable for the difficulty organizers had in securing permits from police; for example, in 1970 the Los Angeles police chief declared that granting a permit to homosexuals would constitute "discommoding the citizens by permitting a parade of thieves and burglars" (Duberman, p. 275).

At New York City's 1970 gay liberation parade, the march focused on the politics of "coming out," which was the watchword of the nascent gay liberation movement. Placards screamed campy and political messages like "we are the dykes your mother warned you about" and "better blatant than latent"; participants chanted slogans including "What do we want? Gay Power! When do we want it? Now!"; "Say it loud: Gay is proud!"; and famously, "Out of the closets and into the streets!" Many participants in the 1970 New York City march believed that some onlookers were closeted homosexuals, and one reason the marchers valued the parade was because it gave them a chance to publicly encourage others to come out to their friends and family. The parade concluded with the massive Gay Be-In in Central Park's Sheep's Meadow, giving birth to an annual tradition of combining highly political protests with colorful parties in city streets and parks.

Over the course of the early 1970s, LGBT marches became annual events in most major U.S. cities. They took the form of public parades through city streets and became associated with the idea of "pride." In 1970 New York City and Los Angeles were home to parades attracting several thousand people each, while fewer than one hundred participants marched in smaller events in San Francisco and Chicago. Within a few years, however, some cities were home to multiple efforts to celebrate LGBT pride each summer. In San Francisco, for example, the 1973 Gay Freedom Day Parade competed with a rival Festival of Gay Liberation; to prevent such problems in the future, a nonprofit Pride Foundation was established later in the year to coordinate the city's annual events. In Seattle the anniversary of Stonewall was celebrated with music festivals, picnics, and rallies from 1973 to 1976; in 1977 participants marched through city streets for the first time.

In October 1979 activists organized the first gay and lesbian March on Washington. The late 1970s had witnessed both progress and backlash for the LGBT movement. San Francisco's 1978 pride march was the largest to date. Protestors advocating the defeat of anti-LGBT Proposition 6, known also as the Briggs Initiative—which was in fact rejected. Marchers at the 1979 March on Washington protested other right-wing ballot measures, as well as the lenient sentence given to Dan White for killing openly gay San Francisco supervisor Harvey Milk the previous year. The 1979 march drew 100,000 participants and was accompanied by the first Third World Lesbian and Gay Conference, which led, among other things, to the formation of the National Coalition of Black Lesbians and Gays.

The Late 1970s and 1980s: Expansion, Commercialization, and the AIDS Crisis

There have been few scholarly studies of the expansion and commercialization of LGBT pride parades, although these trends have significantly reshaped the parades' character since the late 1970s, when growing numbers of LGB-owned businesses began to dominate urban LGBT public life. One recent study is Gary Atkins's *Gay Seattle* (2003), an account of the transformation of Seattle's pride parade. There a group of LGB business owners, the Greater Seattle Business Association (GSBA), sought in March 1982 to gain control over the annual march's planning and content, to change its name from a "march" to a "parade," and to move it from downtown Seattle to the growing LGB commercial district. Although the GSBA declared that it would pay for the parade's costs, it also sought to charge fees to groups seeking to join, and many member businesses expected to reap increased profits from the event's relocation.

The move was immediately protested by LGBT movement activists, who believed that relocating the event from downtown Seattle—and emphasizing celebra-

LGBT Pride Parade. One of the participants carries a sign that proclaims: "Lesbians are Beautiful." [corbis]

tion rather than protest—would dull the event's political edge. Business interests won most of their initial demands, but only after two years of conflict with activists, who wanted the march to focus on opposing the administration of President Ronald Reagan. According to Atkins, two separate events were held in 1984: a celebratory parade in the commercial district and an alternative, more political march downtown. The following year, leaders from the two factions reconciled their differences and sponsored an event together, which has since taken place each year in the LGBT commercial district. In 1990 the local Pride Foundation contracted with a bank to issue a Pride Foundation MasterCard, the first credit card to be offered by an LGBT organization, and in the early 1990s the parade was expanded to include a business fair. In some cities, business-oriented events began to be held separately from pride parades, as in the case of Chicago's Market Days and Philadelphia's Pridefest.

The trend toward commercialization was somewhat slowed by the AIDS crisis, which began to devastate the nation's urban gay communities in the early 1980s. Many pride marches and parades became highly politically charged again, with activists demanding federal support for AIDS research, treatment, and education and protesting the refusal of President Reagan even to mention the epidemic until near the end of his presidency. With tens of thousands of gay men sick and dying from the virus, radical activists formed ACT UP (AIDS Coalition to Unleash Power), which staged numerous highly disruptive public protests and formed large contingents at pride marches.

The second lesbian and gay March on Washington, held in October 1987, attracted a crowd of about half a million. It was also the scene of a massive civil disobedience action on the steps of the U.S. Supreme Court, where over eight hundred activists were arrested while protesting the Court's decision to uphold Georgia's sodomy laws in *Bowers v. Hardwick* (1986). The 1987 march also featured the first public display of the NAMES Project Foundation's Memorial AIDS Quilt on the National Mall; it later traveled to various parts of the country and became an unusually visible and accessible symbol of AIDS activism.

The 1990s: Continued Commercialization and Radicalism

The third March on Washington, in April 1993, took on an exuberant air; newly elected President Bill Clinton had recently invited LGBT leaders to a White House meeting for the first time, and he had pledged during his campaign to lift the ban on homosexuals in the U.S. military. Although he did not fulfill that pledge, many LGBT people believed that Clinton's embrace of the cause of LGB rights, his comfort with LGB people, and his appointment of openly LGB officials signaled a new relationship to national political power.

At the 1993 March on Washington, the radical Lesbian Avengers organized the first Dyke March, which quickly became an annual event in New York City, San Francisco, and Chicago. Although the motorcycle association Dykes on Bikes has been prominently featured in LGBT pride parades at least since 1972 and today conventionally heads up most cities' pride parades, lesbians frequently remain underrepresented in the planning of LGBT pride marches and parades and in the population of participants as well. Since 1993 Dyke Marches have drawn attention to sexism in the gay community and have celebrated lesbian and women's culture; sometimes open only to women and transgender people and held without a police permit, they usually take place on the same weekend as the larger LGBT pride parades. In several cities, including Chicago, New York, and Detroit,

African American pride events also began to be held in the 1990s, separate from mainstream, white-dominated pride events.

By the early 1990s LGBT pride parades were well integrated into the political life of most U.S. cities and routinely attracted millions of participants and onlookers. They had also become a vehicle for politicians, radio stations, and other businesses to reach constituents and customers, and their increasing costs were met through sponsorship by major corporations, especially liquor and beer companies. Such sponsorship was one of the key signs of the rise of targeted marketing to the LGBT population, a trend that many activists regarded as the cooptation of a radical tradition. Parade organizers, however, maintained that sponsorship and targeted marketing might encourage companies to pledge nondiscrimination toward LGBT workers and offer benefits to same-sex domestic partners; these policies were indeed adopted by a growing number of U.S. employers in the 1990s.

Other trends also signaled the depoliticization and commercialization of the parade tradition, which activists charged was increasingly focused on commodifying a narrow range of male body images. The popularity of circuit parties, attracting mostly white, middle-class gay men and sometimes scheduled in conjunction with pride events, seemed to some activists to confirm the depoliticization of the tradition of public protest. In recent years, New York City's pride parade has been altered so that it reaches an end point not in Central Park but in the West Village—a historic district and the site of the Stonewall Riots, but also a commercial area where numerous bar and nightclub owners charge hefty fees for entrance to post-parade parties.

The commercialization of the nation's LGBT pride parades, however, has coexisted with the continuing vitality of radical protest. In 1990 the militant group Queer Nation entered the New York City pride parade, distributing broadsheets declaring, "Queers Read This . . . I Hate Straights." With its conscious embrace of sex radicalism and outrageous camp style, Queer Nation sought to revitalize the tactics of ACT UP; it demanded that LGBT people voice their anger about homophobia and advocated "liberation not assimilation." In the late 1990s a group called Gay Shame was founded by New York City and San Francisco radicals who objected to the commercialization and depoliticization of LGBT "pride." Gay Shame held alternative celebrations, sometimes disrupting those cities' pride parades; in 2003 six Gay Shame activists were arrested and jailed for joining San Francisco's pride parade and protesting the inclusion of moderate heterosexual mayoral candidate Gavin Newsom.

The Politics of Transgender Visibility

The inclusion of transgender people has been, over the years, perhaps the most contentious issue surrounding the planning, content, and even the names of LGBT marches. Despite the pivotal role played by drag queens and other gender-variant people in fighting back against New York City police at the Stonewall Inn and in other forms and moments of resistance, transgender people have frequently faced opposition to their inclusion and visibility in pride marches and parades. For example, Sylvia Rivera was expelled from the rally platform at the 1973 New York City pride parade by feminists who believed that drag and transgender identity were demeaning to women, even though she had been a key participant in the riots at Stonewall.

In 1994 New York City's Heritage of Pride organization was replaced by a march called Stonewall 25, honoring the rebellion's twenty-fifth anniversary; however, the organizers of that march, which focused on international LGB rights, refused to include "transgender" in the march's name. That year, to protest both the exclusion of transgender politics and the commercialization of the event, a countermarch was held along Fifth Avenue. Focusing attention on the persistence of the AIDS crisis, this countermarch was led by Rivera. Following her death in 2002, New York City's pride march was dedicated to her memory. Rivera's shifting relationship to celebrations of Stonewall reflects the continuing difficulty of transgender people in obtaining representation in mainstream LGBT politics.

As the LGBT movement has gained a stable political foothold in Washington, tensions over the planning of marches and parades have continued to pit local grassroots radical activists against more mainstream national organizations. In 2000 the lobbying group Human Rights Campaign organized a fourth March on Washington, which was carried out over the objections of numerous longtime activists who protested the lack of grassroots input into the planning process. The march focused on the themes of family and faith. Echoing longstanding tensions in LGBT politics, these themes symbolized for some people admission to full citizenship, while for others they represented assimilation to oppressive norms.

Bibliography

Atkins, Gary L. *Gay Seattle: Stories of Exile and Belonging.* Seattle: University of Washington Press, 2003.

Duberman, Martin. *Stonewall.* New York: Dutton, 1993.

McGarry, Molly, and Fred Wasserman. *Becoming Visible: An Illustrated History of Lesbian and Gay Life in Twentieth-Century America.* New York: Penguin Studio, 1998.

Stein, Marc. *City of Sisterly and Brotherly Loves: Lesbian and Gay Philadelphia, 1945–1972.* Chicago: University of Chicago, 2000.

Stryker, Susan, and Jim Van Buskirk. *Gay by the Bay: A History of Queer Culture in the San Francisco Bay Area.* San Francisco: Chronicle Books, 1996.

Teal, Donn. *The Gay Militants.* New York: Stein and Day, 1971.

Thompson, Mark, ed. *Long Road to Freedom: The Advocate History of the Gay and Lesbian Movement.* New York: St. Martin's Press, 1994.

Vaid, Urvashi. *Virtual Equality: The Mainstreaming of Gay and Lesbian Liberation.* New York: Anchor, 1995.

Timothy Stewart-Winter

See also ATLANTA; GAY LIBERATION; HOMOPHILE MOVEMENT DEMONSTRATIONS; LESBIAN AVENGERS; MARCHES ON WASHINGTON; NEW YORK CITY; PHILADELPHIA; PUBLIC FESTIVALS, PARTIES, AND HOLIDAYS; RIVERA, SYLVIA; RODWELL, CRAIG; SEATTLE; STONEWALL RIOTS; WASHINGTON, D.C.

PRIME-STEVENSON, Edward I.

(b. 23 July 1868; d. 23 July 1942), writer.

Edward Irenaeus Prime-Stevenson, a descendent of early European settlers in New England, was born in Madison, New Jersey, to Paul E. Stevenson, a Presbyterian minister and school principal, and Cornelia Prime, who was fifty-two years old at the time of his birth. He began to write for publication while still in school, and though he was admitted to the New Jersey bar, he never practiced law. He was a music critic and book reviewer for the New York *Independent* and was on the staff of *Harper's Weekly.* His writing was broad-based and he was widely recognized as a critic of music (particularly opera), drama, and literature. While almost nothing is known about his personal life, it has generally been assumed that he was gay.

Particularly interested in European and Asian literature, Prime-Stevenson claimed to be fluent in nine languages. He wrote several novels and short stories and it was in his early novels aimed at an adolescent market that he carefully and cautiously introduced the subject of homosexuality, particularly in *The White Cockades: An Incident in the "Forty-five"* and *Left to Themselves: Being the Ordeal of Philip and Gerald.* The first, set at the time of the Jacobite Rebellion in Scotland, was later described by Prime-Stevenson as featuring a "passionate devotion from a rustic youth toward the Prince," which, with "its recognition," is "half-hinted at as homosexual in essence" (*Intersexes,* p. 367). Prime-Stevenson claimed the second novel conveyed a "sentiment of uranian [i.e., homosexual] adolescence" (*Intersexes,* pp. 367–368).

For much of his early life, Prime-Stevenson divided his time between the United States and various parts of Europe, moving to Europe permanently in 1900 because of his dislike for the homophobia of American society.

In 1908, under the pseudonym Xavier Mayne, Prime-Stevenson published *Imre: A Memorandum,* often regarded as the first homosexual novel by an American. The novel's plot centers around a love affair between Oswald, a thirty-year-old who is spending a summer of language study in Hungary, and the twenty-three-year-old Imre, a Hungarian cavalry officer. Prime-Stevenson's most important nonfiction book, *The Intersexes: A History of Similsexualism as a Problem in Social Life,* the first large-scale study of homosexuality in English, was published that same year. It is an analysis of almost everything that had been published on homosexuality up to that time in both the homophile movement press in Europe and in the psychiatric and medical literature. Since homosexuality, he believed, was inborn, it could not be cured. Although the "uranian" might suffer from social disapproval, homosexuality was neither an abnormality nor a disease, and the homosexual individual would not and could not be other than he is.

The most valuable aspect of the book (written under his pseudonym) is his first-hand observations of the LGBT subculture in the United States and Europe, ranging from the nobleman in his salon to the hustler on the street. He also recounted scandals associated with the exposure of homosexuals, the dangers of real and threatened blackmail, and the names of illustrious figures of the past whom he regarded as homosexual. In short, in modern research terms, he was an outstanding participant-observer of the LGBT scene and his observations were not matched, at least in English, until the latter part of the twentieth century.

Bibliography

"Edward Prime-Stevenson: Expatriate Opera Critic." *Opera Quarterly* 6 (fall 1988): 37–52.

Garde, Noel I. "The Mysterious Father of American Homophile Literature." *One Institute Quarterly* 1, no. 3 (fall 1958): 94–98.

———. "The First American Gay Novel." *One Institute Quarterly* 3, no.2 (spring 1960): 185–190.

Mayne, Xavier. *Imre: A Memorandum.* 1908. Critical edition, edited by James J. Gifford, Peterborough, Canada: Broadview, 2003.

———. *The Intersexes: A History of Similsexualism as a Problem in Social Life.* 1908. Reprint, New York: Arno, 1975.

"Obituary." *New York Times,* 1 August, 1942, p. 11, col. 4.

Prime-Stevenson, Edward. *Left to Themselves: Being the Ordeal of Philip and Gerald.* New York: Hunt and Eaton, 1891.

———. *The White Cockades: An Incident in the "Forty-five."* New York: Scribners, 1887.

Vern L. Bullough

PRIMUS, Rebecca (b. 1836; d. 21 February 1932), teacher, and Addie BROWN (b. 21 December 1841; d. 11 January 1870), domestic worker.

Rebecca Primus and Addie Brown were free African American women whose relationship transcended the normative boundaries of nineteenth-century female friendship. A series of 120 letters, written from Brown to Primus between 1859 and 1869, provides a rare glimpse into the private lives of two African American women engaged in an intensely emotional, and sometimes physical, relationship. Limiting our understanding of this relationship is the absence of Primus's letters to Brown. Enough evidence exists, however, to understand some elements of the relationship between these two women. One of the most important is the positioning of their committed and erotic love along a continuum of fluid sexuality that included relationships with men.

The eldest of four children, Primus was born into a well-respected and economically secure family in Hartford, Connecticut. As one of Hartford's oldest African American families, the Primuses were socially prominent and active in the small and close-knit black community. A teacher by profession, Primus used her status and education in the service of her community and race. Between 1865 and 1869, under the sponsorship of the Hartford Freedmen's Aid Society, Primus lived in Royal Oak, Maryland, where she educated newly freed Southern African Americans.

Five years Primus's junior, Brown was orphaned as a child and spent her early years with an aunt in Philadelphia. Unlike Primus, Brown lacked the privilege of high family status and received no formal education. Instead, her race, gender, and class status restricted her to a number of low-paying jobs—most of her working life was spent "in service" as a domestic worker. As these positions often required her to live in her employer's household, Brown's letters reveal work-related movement between various northeastern cities including New York, as well as Farmington, Hartford, and Waterbury, Connecticut. Brown's letters attest to the labor-intensive nature of domestic work, the toll that work took on her health, and her continued economic insecurity.

It is not known how Primus and Brown met, but when their correspondence began in 1859, Brown was already a close friend of the Primus family. Accepted by family and by community, the relationship between these two women offers an important example for exploring how close female friendships were viewed in black New England communities. Social acceptance of this friendship allows scholars to extend the findings of historians who argue that close relationships between white upper- and middle-class women were culturally acceptable. However, while white women's relationships were class-specific and emerged out of the homosocial structure of nineteenth-century white society, the relationship between Brown and Primus demonstrates the acceptance of cross-class friendships within the heterosocial black community. Female friendships were viewed as complementary to, and not competitive with, the goal of heterosexual marriage. Only when such a relationship became viewed as a hindrance to obtaining male suitors did it provoke criticism.

While Brown's letters employed the romantic language characteristic of nineteenth-century expression, they also exceeded the period's accepted definition of close female friendship. Over a nine-year period, Brown's letters reveal the changing nature of her relationship with Primus. At certain points, the letters are frankly erotic and indicate that the two women engaged in physical intimacies, although the exact nature of the sexual interplay is not known. Young and energetic, Brown described male suitors in her early letters as well as female friends, who, at least on one occasion, elicited Primus's jealous response. While the eroticism and passionate language is more marked in certain periods, the commitment and love between the two women is consistently expressed throughout the nine years.

Both women eventually married men—Brown in 1868 and Primus in 1872—but Brown's letters expressed the difficulty of such a decision. Throughout her engagement, Brown often expressed her ambivalence toward marriage and postponed the ceremony on several occasions. More importantly, perhaps, Brown lamented Primus's not being a man, for otherwise, Brown mused, she would marry her without a second thought. When expressing her love for her fiancé, Mr. Tines, Brown distinguished this sentiment from the passion she felt for Primus, suggesting an underlying and more erotically charged dimension to their relationship. After Brown finally married, her letters to Primus underscored the pragmatism of her actions, citing economic stability and love as the motivating factors. Upon Brown's move to her in-laws' home in Philadelphia, the correspondence diminished, and two years later, at the age of twenty-nine, Brown died of tuberculosis. Primus continued to teach; in 1932 she died at the age of ninety-five.

Bibliography

Baecking, Barbara. "Finding Rebecca Primus." *Northeast Magazine* (25 February, 1996): 10–22.

Griffin, Farah Jasmine, ed. *Beloved Sisters and Loving Friends: Letters from Rebecca Primus of Royal Oak, Maryland, and Addie Brown of Hartford, Connecticut, 1854–1868.* New York: Knopf, 1999.

Hansen, Karen. "'No Kisses is Like Youres': An Erotic Friendship between Two African American Women during the Mid-Nineteenth Century." *Gender and History* 7, no. 2 (August 1995): 153–182.

The Primus Papers, Connecticut Historical Society, Hartford, Connecticut.

Smith-Rosenberg, Carol. "The Female World of Love and Ritual." *Signs: Journal of Women in Culture and Society* 1 (1975): 1–30.

Laila S. Haidarali

See also ROMANTIC FRIENDSHIP AND BOSTON MARRIAGE; SAME-SEX INSTITUTIONS.

PRINCE, Virginia (b. February 1913), transgender activist, author.

Virginia Prince, a male who has lived socially as a woman since 1968, coined the term "transgender" in the 1980s. She has been a leading advocate for heterosexual cross-dressers since the early 1960s. She also played an important role in defining cross-dressing primarily as a heterosexual male activity and in distinguishing cross-dressing from transsexuality as well as from gay and lesbian styles of gender nonconformity.

Prince was born to a socially prominent family in Los Angeles, where her father was a surgeon and her mother a successful realtor. Prince's cross-dressing began around age twelve. By age eighteen, she had acquired a wardrobe of women's clothing and had begun nervously venturing out in public dressed as a woman. Although she initially cross-dressed for erotic gratification, Prince eventually developed a theory about "full personality expression" (FPE) in which the erotic pleasure of cross-dressing was not an end in itself. In Prince's view, the social process of gendering individuals was inherently limiting, reducing men and women to less than their full human potential. She saw cross-dressing as a means of tapping into that suppressed potential, nurturing neglected parts of oneself, and attaining a more complete and fulfilling sense of being.

After graduating from Pomona College, Prince married a woman and moved with her to the Bay Area to attend medical school at the University of California, San Francisco (UCSF). Prince was at this point in her life an isolated, furtive cross-dresser with no contact with a broader transgender community. That changed in 1942, when, as a postdoctoral research fellow, she attended two presentations of "transvestite cases" at UCSF's Langley Porter Psychiatric Clinic and met the individuals who had allowed their lives to be discussed: Barbara Richards, an early male-to-female transsexual, and Louise Lawrence, who did more than perhaps any other person in mid-twentieth-century America to call sympathetic scientific attention to transgender lives, and to lay the foundations for a transgender community. Lawrence was at the center of a large correspondence network of other transgender people, a network in which Prince came to play an increasingly central and influential role.

Around 1950 Prince divorced her first wife and soon thereafter remarried another woman who was more accepting of cross-dressing. By this time, Prince was president of her own medical manufacturing business and had a comfortable home in the Hollywood Hills. She was also a leading figure among Southern California members of the Lawrence correspondence network. In 1952 Prince and other network members launched a short-lived newsletter, *Transvestia.* The low-budget publication folded after only two issues, but it set the stage for a more successful and sophisticated magazine of the same name that debuted in January 1960. This second *Transvestia* was the flagship publication of Chevalier Press, which also published *Femme Mirror* (later *Sorority*), *TV Clipsheet,* and Prince's self-help books *The Transvestite and His Wife* and *How to Be a Woman Though Male.*

The fledgling cross-dressing community achieved several benchmarks in 1962. That year Prince organized the nation's first social and support organization for heterosexual cross-dressers, the Hose and Heels Club, which drew its membership from *Transvestia*'s subscription list. The group soon changed its name to Phi Pi Epsilon, a Greek-letter play on the initials FPE, and established chapters across the country. Also in 1962 the first national gathering of heterosexual cross-dressers took place in the Catskills, at a resort owned by Susanna Valenti, the *nomme de femme* of a wealthy *Transvestia* subscriber. More ominously, Prince was arrested that year on charges of mailing obscene materials—a blatant attempt to shut down Chevalier Press that coincided with a broader federal crackdown on shipping homophile publications and sexually explicit materials. Prince pleaded guilty to avoid publicity and served eighteen months of probation.

Prince's second marriage was floundering by the mid-1960s; she was also growing weary of balancing life as a businessman with her increasingly public activism on cross-dressing. She divorced and sold her company in

1966, and in June of 1968—after undergoing facial electrolysis and starting estrogen therapy—began living full time as Virginia. She did not seek sex-reassignment surgery, preferring to live as a woman with male genitalia. It was for this practice that Prince eventually coined the term "transgender," which she viewed as a middle ground between the episodic cross-dressing of the transvestite and the permanent genital transformation of the transsexual.

After retiring from business, Prince traveled extensively, both recreationally and to promote various transgender causes. As of 2003 she is still living in Los Angeles and remains active in the transgender community.

Bibliography

Prince, Virginia. "The Life and Times of Virginia." *Transvestia* 100 (1979): 5–120.

Susan Stryker

See also ERICKSON EDUCATIONAL FOUNDATION; LAWRENCE, LOUISE; TRANSGENDER ORGANIZATIONS AND PERIODICALS; TRANSSEXUALS, TRANSVESTITES, TRANSGENDER PEOPLE, AND CROSS-DRESSERS.

PRISONS, JAILS, AND REFORMATORIES: MEN'S

Sexual contact between inmates has been an inescapable feature of prison, jail, and reformatory life since the first such institution was constructed in the eighteenth century. Originally framed as a problem of moral corruption, sexual contact has since been viewed as a disciplinary, medical, treatment, sexual assault, and health problem. Yet two things have remained largely unchanged: much of what we know is gleaned from observers, not participants or victims, and regardless of their approach, most commentators frame sex as a problem and address the subject as something unique to the prison environment.

History of Sex in U.S. Prisons

Until the Jacksonian era, prisons were small-time affairs meant only as temporary holding places while inmates awaited trials. Punishment was swift. Criminals, including men charged with sodomy, were put to death, banished, whipped, put in stocks, or fined. It was not until the 1820s that incarceration emerged as a means of punishment in itself.

The first American penal institutions intended for their residents to live in complete and utter silence. Some kept inmates in cells at all times; others permitted them out only to labor. Initially, men and women, the sane and the insane, and adults as well as children were housed in the same institutions, although attempts were made to keep them apart.

Despite efforts to limit and control contact between inmates, in 1826, Louis Dwight, a prison reform advocate, released a printed broadside denouncing the conditions of most prisons. Included among his many complaints was sexual relations between inmates. "The Sin of Sodom is the Vice of Prisoners," he wrote, "and Boys are the Favorite Prostitutes. Sodomy is said to be practiced constantly among them. When a boy was sent to Prison, who was of a fair countenance, there many times seemed to be quite a strife. . . . No art was left untried, to get the boy into the same room and into the same bed. . . . Nature and humanity cry aloud for redemption from this dreadful degradation."

Although their activities were illegal according to both criminal law and prison conduct codes, inmates engaged in sexual contact, but not under conditions of their own choosing. As Dwight first described it almost two hundred years ago, sex between men and boys often occurred within the context of inmate (and sometimes staff) coercion and official complicity or indifference.

Publicly, little was said or done about the matter, but prisons across America gradually developed the practice of separating out "true" or "frank" homosexuals, men who displayed feminine characteristics and who often were "frank" and forthcoming about their preference for sex with men. This practice conformed to wider cultural views about sexuality and gender in the nineteenth and early twentieth centuries. Only those who did not conform to prevailing standards of masculine behavior were deemed "fairies," "pansies," "queens," and, later, third-sexers and homosexuals.

As medical experts entered the prison system, they offered scientific explanations that legitimized the differentiation of sexual types according to gender presentation. They also supported the practice of segregating fairies from the rest of the prison population. Segregation, it was said, prevented "homo-sexualists" from contaminating other inmates with their disease, but in practice it also served as an early form of protective custody.

Masculine men, known as wolves and jockers (and near the end of the twentieth century, booty bandits), may have been judged as immoral for seeking out sex with fairies, or younger men known as punks, but they were certainly not considered homosexual. Instead, it was widely maintained that their sexual acts were entirely "situational." According to the experts, the wolf was merely the product of a single-sex environment where men are denied a normal sexual outlet. It was a phenomenon that existed in all places where the sexes were aggregated, prison doctors argued, including the military, the navy, and concentration camps.

Emergence of Public Discussion of Sex in Prison

Not until more than one hundred years after Dwight's 1826 broadside did sex in prison become an acceptable topic for public discussion. In 1934 the newly elected mayor of New York City, Fiorello La Guardia, organized an exposé of the previous administration's running of the local prison on Welfare Island. In the extensive media coverage that followed, prison fairies and queens came to symbolize prison immorality and lax supervision. Two leading prison insiders, one a psychiatrist and the other an inspector, published book-length studies of sex in male prisons within a few years. Shortly thereafter, sex among prisoners was for the first time publicly addressed as an aspect of the prison discipline problem at the annual meeting of the national organization of corrections specialists.

The 1950s and 1960s were characterized by the twin concerns of sexual activity as both a disciplinary and a medical problem. A variety of treatments were devised, ranging from segregation to insulin coma shock therapy to drug therapy. When these efforts failed, a new generation of experts suggested that if the problem was the environment, then more heterosexual elements should be introduced to "normalize" the prison setting. Under this scheme, some states introduced measures that allowed more "heterosexual stimulants," including lifting the ban on pinup posters of movie stars, eliminating or reducing physical barriers between inmates and their female visitors, and introducing conjugal visits, a practice that had long existed in Mexico and Russia. While from outside appearances it would seem that these liberalizing measures were a positive response to the growing national and international interest in the human rights of prisoners, from an internal point of view, each initiative was adopted as part of the ongoing effort to control the inmate population.

However coercive individual negotiations may have been, sexual relationships between men often became an important source of emotional sustenance and pleasure. Sex researcher Alfred C. Kinsey was interested in sex adjustment in prison and managed to convince a number of wardens to supply him with sexually related contraband confiscated from prisoners. In addition to the smuggled and hand-made pornography were hundreds of letters exchanged between inmates. Many were filled with playful sexual overtures and promises, others with romantic and poetic promises of love and commitment. Among them were also certificates of marriage, as well as notices of divorce. Not until the 1970s, when inmates themselves were able to write about their experiences, would prison marriages become more widely known.

Emotional bonds formed between prisoners may in fact be one of the most difficult problems for those whose goal is to maintain prison order. According to an early study of inmates at an Alabama prison, it was well known that male couples forced to separate—whether by the parole or release of one or at the hands of the prison administration—often reacted violently. Researchers documented one case in which a prisoner's rage over a forced separation resulted in $400 worth of damage to the prison's wool mill. The destruction was sometimes turned inward. Social scientists in the last two decades of the twentieth century also documented cases of attempted and successful suicide. Ex-convicts sometimes committed a new offense for the express purpose of returning to a partner inside.

In a 1967 study on homosexuality in prison, the authors argued that sex was still a pariah topic in the field of criminology. Two major events changed this situation forever. First, Canadian playwright John Herbert wrote and staged a play based on his experience as an inmate in an Ontario reformatory. *Fortune and Men's Eyes* (1967) was an instant Off-Broadway hit, and MGM studios quickly bought the film rights and released it in American theaters in 1971. A now-classic drama, the story illustrates a variety of ways in which sexual consent is coerced. It also reveals how wolf-punk-fairy relationships extend well beyond sex and include the reproduction of traditional heterosexual domestic and economic roles.

One year after the play was first staged, a Philadelphia court investigated the allegations of a man who reported that he had been sexually assaulted moments after he arrived at the Philadelphia Detention Center for a pretrial evaluation. Perhaps as a reflection of the changing political values of the times, or perhaps because of a growing sensitivity to the threat of legal action, the chief assistant district attorney undertook a massive investigation into the Philadelphia prison system. Based on interviews with inmates, he described prison sexual assault as an epidemic and published his findings in a popular magazine.

Racial Dynamics of Sex in Prisons

The Philadelphia investigation interpreted sexual assault in prison as a problem of violence, not of a lack of normal sexual outlets. It also revealed that the problem had a significant racial dimension: the gradual desegregation of prisons since the 1950s added an additional element of conflict and tension to the existing sexual hierarchy. African American men, investigators claimed, were much more likely to be perpetrators of sexual violence against whites than the other way around. In a 1950s interview with a folklorist, one African American inmate in a midwestern prison suggested that this was in part the result of a lack of a cohesive group identity among whites that left white males more vulnerable. He also revealed, however, that whites benefited from this system, a point missed by the Philadelphia investigation. After a young white punk was gang-raped by African Americans, he explained, whites would move in to offer protection in exchange for regular sexual favors. Despite these complex intersections, media reports on the Philadelphia investigation tended to reinforce the long-standing image of African American men as violent rapists with insatiable sexual appetites.

These events marked the beginning of a new phase of social scientific research into sex in prison. Unlike their medical predecessors, these scholars were infused with the civil rights movement's concerns with the protection of the vulnerable and the rights of the individual. Sensational studies such as Carl Weiss and David James Friar's *Terror in the Prisons* (1974) was followed by Anthony Scacco Jr.'s 1975 edited collection *Male Rape* (which includes an essay by a prison "punk") and Daniel Lockwood's *Prison Sexual Violence* (1980). These studies provided more evidence to suggest that in addition to age, size, experience, and group or gang affiliation, race continued to function as an important category of difference that shaped the organization of prison sexual culture.

Movements to Make Prisons Safer

Few have done more to raise public and official awareness about sexual violence in America's prisons than Stephen Donaldson. An early gay activist and Quaker, Donaldson was jailed in 1973 for trespassing after he participated in a peaceful protest against the bombing of Cambodia. Once in prison he was gang-raped for two days and had to undergo reparative rectal surgery upon release. He immediately called a press conference, becoming the first victim of prison rape to speak publicly on the issue. He joined People Organized to Stop Rape of Imprisoned Persons, which later changed its name to Stop Prison Rape (SPR). In 1988, Donaldson became the organization's president and remained in that position until his death in 1996. SPR is currently a multipurpose organization. It leads public awareness and prevention campaigns, is a portal for up-to-date research on the issue, and actively lobbies federal and state officials to initiate policies that address the needs of vulnerable inmates.

In the 1980s and 1990s, much of the public focus shifted to the health crisis created by inmate sexual contact, particularly the high rates of AIDS transmission. Studies showed that inmates were infected with sexually transmitted diseases at higher rates than the general public and that rates of HIV infection were five times higher among the incarcerated than among the general public. However, subsequent campaigns to introduce condom distribution programs had little success.

Currently, male-to-female transsexuals encounter both health and safety problems. Before World War II, female-identified males would have been treated as fairies. But with the introduction of hormones and surgery, a new type of inmate, and a new type of cruelty, has emerged. Transsexuals frequently report being denied access to hormones and are placed in male institutions, often in the same cell as wolves.

Groups like the National Transgender Advocacy Coalition (NATC) actively champion the rights of trans women who have been victims of sexual violence in male prisons, including Alexandra Nicole Tucker of Newfoundland, Canada. She was raped in the Montana State Prison and launched an $18 million suit against the state and federal governments, alleging sexual harassment and assault by prisoners and guards while serving an eighteen-month sentence that began in 1999. GenderPAC, a national organization led by trans activist Riki Wilchins, also supports the landmark suit.

After decades of advocacy for better protection of inmates against sexual assault and harassment, groups such as SPR and NATC are increasingly turning to legal action. With all other avenues seemingly exhausted, it would appear that forcing federal and state legislatures to pay damages might finally result in real and meaningful efforts to address the problem of sexual assault in prison. The recent hiring of Lara Stemple as the executive director of SPR is indicative of this new direction. Stemple is a lawyer with a background of activism regarding human rights, sexual violence issues, immigrant and refugee rights, and women's rights. In 2003 the SPR was poised to oversee the successful passage of the federal Prison Rape Reduction bill under consideration by Congress.

Sexuality, Gender, and Prison Life

Compensation and protection are important elements in the struggle for justice, but the means for best understanding how sex operates as a primary way of organizing prison culture and communities is being reexamined by historians of sexuality. Scholars are paying less attention to the internal organization of prison life and are focusing more on the way sexuality and gender function as a means to organize relations of power. In "Situating Sex" (2002), historian Regina Kunzel casts a critical eye on how the concept of "situational homosexuality" obscures the way social scientists and medical experts construct the problem and argues that sexuality should be viewed not in terms of fixed identities but as fluid realities. Similarly, historian Elise Chenier in "Segregating Sexualities" (2003) examines how masculinity as a primary expression of relations of power has shaped inmate culture. Both of these scholars point to new ways of thinking about sex in prison, ways that see prison sex not simply as a prison issue, but as reflective of wider social and cultural expressions of unequal power relations.

Bibliography

Chenier, Elise. "Segregating Sexualities: The Prison 'Sex Problem' in Twentieth- Century Canada and the United States." In *Isolation: Places and Practices of Exclusion.* Edited by Carolyn Strange and Alison Bashford. New York: Routledge, 2003.

Davis, Alan J. "Sexual Assaults in the Philadelphia Prison System and Sheriff's Vans." *Trans-action* (December 1968): 8–16.

Katz, Jonathan. *Gay American History: Lesbians and Gay Men in the U.S.A.* New York: Crowell, 1976.

Kunzel, Regina. "Situating Sex: Prison Sexual Culture in the Mid-Twentieth-Century United States." *GLQ: A Journal of Lesbian and Gay Studies* 8, no. 3 (May 2002).

Lockwood, Daniel. *Prison Sexual Violence.* New York: Elsevier North Holland, 1980.

Rothman, David J. "Perfecting the Prison: United States, 1789–1865." In *Oxford History of the Prison: The Practice of Punishment in Western Society.* Edited by Norval Morris and David J. Rothman. New York: Oxford University Press, 1995.

Rotman, Edgardo. "The Failure of Reform: United States, 1865–1965." In *Oxford History of the Prison: The Practice of Punishment in Western Society.* Edited by Norval Morris and David J. Rothman .New York: Oxford University Press, 1995.

Scacco, Anthony M., Jr. *Rape in Prison.* Springfield, Ill.: Charles C. Thomas, 1975.

Sykes, Gresham M. *The Society of Captives: A Study of a Maximum Security Prison.* Princeton, N.J.: Princeton University Press, 1958.

Tewksbury Richard, and Angela West. "Research on Sex in Prison during the Late 1980s and Early 1990s." *Prison Journal* 80, no. 4 (December 2000): 368–378.

U.S. Attorney for the Eastern District of Philadelphia. *Report on Sexual Assaults in the Philadelphia Prison System and in Sheriff's Vans.* 1968.

Weiss, Carl, and David James Friar. *Terror in the Prisons: Homosexual Rape and Why Society Condones It.* Indianapolis, Ind.: Bobbs-Merrill, 1974.

Williams, Dalton Loyd. "Prison Sex at Age 16." In *Gay Roots: Twenty Years of Gay Sunshine, An Anthology of Gay History, Sex, Politics, and Culture.* Edited by Winston Leyland. San Francisco: Gay Sunshine Press, 1991.

Elise Chenier

See also ANTIWAR, PACIFIST, AND PEACE MOVEMENTS; DAVIS, KATHERINE BEMENT; KINSEY, ALFRED C.; PRISONS, JAILS, AND REFORMATORIES: WOMEN'S; SAME-SEX INSTITUTIONS; SITUATIONAL HOMOSEXUALITY; VAN WATERS, MIRIAM.

PRISONS, JAILS, AND REFORMATORIES: WOMEN'S

Since the early 1900s, researchers and outside observers have been struck by the seeming pervasiveness of homosexual relationships in women's correctional institutions. In comparison to their male counterparts, female prisoners have developed a subculture in which intimate relationships between women are widely accepted and openly expressed. Criminologist Joycelyn M. Pollock-Byrne has suggested that "to describe a woman's prison without reference to the homosexual relationships found there would be like describing the prison for men without mentioning drugs or violence" (p. 144). At the same time, however, one must also question researchers' seemingly obsessive focus on female inmate sexuality. Too often women's relationships have been studied to the virtual exclusion of many other, equally important aspects of female prison life, from discipline and social control to strategies of survival and resistance.

Unfortunately, there exists no literary tradition of female prisoners writing directly about their experiences or about their interpretation of the meaning of this inmate subculture. Descriptions of same-sex relationships in women's prisons come primarily from the writings of prison administrators and outside researchers, many of whom, until recently, have subscribed to negative or stereotypical views.

Competing Explanations

Only a small proportion of female prisoners identify as lesbian. Although some decide that they are lesbian as a result of their prison experiences, the majority return to heterosexuality upon their release. Historically, the discovery of such seemingly widespread behavioral bisexuality among otherwise heterosexual women has posed a challenge to rigid, binary conceptualizations of human sexuality. During the first half of the twentieth century, prison psychiatrists characterized prison lesbianism as a perversion engaged in by immoral and degenerate women. Since mid-century, more liberal sociologists and criminologists have portrayed prison homosexuality as a response to the "pains of imprisonment" and the deprivation of "natural" heterosexual contacts. Other scholars continue to endorse the stereotype of the predatory and masculine lesbian who "turns out" vulnerable, newly arrived, but otherwise "normal" women (the "institutional" or "situational" lesbian).

Some observers suggest that much of what has been described as female inmate homosexuality may not even include a sexual component. Instead, they emphasize the affectional aspects of women's relationships, citing human warmth, companionship, and comfort as the primary motives. While female prisoners occasionally concur with that "asexual" depiction, this interpretation also serves to normalize such relationships by downplaying their sexual and erotic elements.

1900–1945: Racialization of Prison Homosexuality

Until World War II there appears to have been little interest in, or concern with, the "problem" of female prison homosexuality. Historian Estelle B. Freedman argues that until the 1940s, "women's prison authorities concentrated on diverting inmates from *heterosexual* acts prohibited by law—especially prostitution. They rarely mentioned lesbianism as a problem, and most women's prison officials ignored evidence of homosexuality among inmates" (p. 399).

Female prison officials may have been reluctant to draw attention to same-sex relationships among inmates because many were involved in long-standing "romantic friendships" of their own. The first generation of female prison administrators consisted typically of unmarried career women who came out of the Progressive Era tradition of female reform. Some appear to have implicitly rejected the dominant psychiatric discourse that, by the 1920s, had pathologized all forms of same-sex relationships. For example, famed prison reformer Miriam Van Waters (1887–1974) was romantically involved with women throughout her life. As superintendent of the Massachusetts Reformatory for Women (1932–1957), Van Waters sought to discourage homosexual relationships among inmates; however, she consistently refused to adopt a punitive approach. Van Waters's tolerance and leniency, which led to her temporary dismissal in 1949, became increasingly rare in the post–World War II era.

The main exception to this early silence involved occasional reports about, and rabid denunciations of, cross-racial romances between white and black prisoners. For example, in a 1913 article psychologist Margaret Otis described "love-making between the white and colored girls" as a "form of perversion" purportedly "well-known among workers in reform schools and institutions for delinquent girls" (p. 113). These accounts frequently portrayed African American women prisoners as the masculine or aggressive partner. In contrast, commentators represented black women's white lovers as normal, feminine women who would return to heterosexual relations upon release from prison. Hence, during the first half of the twentieth century prison lesbianism was racialized. African American women were stigmatized as the "true" sexual deviants while white women were presented as attracted to their "masculine" qualities. These explanations fit easily with widely shared cultural stereotypes about black women's purportedly "libidinous" and "oversexed" characters.

However, a careful reading of the primary sources often reveals that white women were equally active initiators or "aggressors" in pursuing interracial relationships. As one sixteen-year-old "sex delinquent" reported in 1933 when asked how she felt after viewing romantic movies in prison, "All we can do here . . . is take some Negro girl behind the screen at the Chapel or somewhere else. Kiss them for all we are worth. That is all the thrill we get" (Dodge, p. 147). Indeed, prison officials across the country justified racial segregation in housing assignments as a means of deterring cross-racial romances, which appear to have been common.

1940s–1960s: The Construction of the Predatory Prison Lesbian

In contrast to the early decades of the twentieth century, during the 1940s and 1950s academics and outside observers became fascinated by prison lesbianism, which became a central feature of pulp novels and Hollywood B movies about women's prisons. In the postwar era, the prison lesbian was portrayed as a distinct type: a dangerous, aggressive, predatory, oversexed, and mannish sexual demon. And for the first time, the label "lesbian" was applied to white as well as black prisoners. Indeed, pulp literature and *True Confessions*–like magazines emphasized the threat that aggressive white lesbians allegedly posed to younger and more naive white inmates.

Several factors contributed to this postwar shift. These include the growing visibility of LGBT life, heightened fears of female sexuality, and Cold War paranoia. Historian Regina G. Kunzel argues that the discovery of widespread bisexuality among seemingly heterosexual female prisoners raised troubling questions about the stability of heterosexuality itself at a time when gender roles were rigidly prescribed. The concept of situational homosexuality, widely proffered by sociologists at mid-century, offered one means of containing the explosive implications of bisexuality. Instead of representing the ultimate perversity, prison homosexuality could be portrayed as a "normal" response to an abnormal environment.

1940s–1980s: The Reign of Repression and Paranoia

However, most prison authorities continued to view lesbianism as a grave moral danger. Extraordinarily repressive policies were implemented at many women's prisons. For example, at both the Federal Reformatory for Women at Alderson, West Virginia, and the Illinois State Reformatory for Women at Dwight, a no-contact rule severely punished all physical contact between prisoners, from combing another woman's hair to comforting a woman who had just learned of a death in her family. Staff vigilantly monitored inmate friendships, searching for the smallest sign of a potentially "unwholesome" relationship. The following note in a woman's prison file was typical of conditions in the 1950s: "Superintendent has observed Viola Marks and Ernestine Miller work side by side at laundry, sit together at rest periods. Advised Mrs. Scott to change station assignment of one and keep them apart as much as possible" (Dodge, p. 235). Across the nation, inmates bitterly complained that friendship was often construed as homosexuality.

High levels of official preoccupation with, and severe punishment of, suspected homosexuality continued throughout the 1960s and 1970s. At some institutions, suspected lesbians were singled out and assigned to segregated housing units. At the Los Angeles women's jail, staff decided who the "obvious homosexuals" were and assigned them to the "Daddy Tank," which consisted of solitary-confinement cells. In Illinois the segregation unit was a typical cell-block type of structure, whereas the other inmates were housed in more homelike "cottages" or dormitories. In Iowa suspected lesbians were required to wear a special yellow uniform. Some evidence also suggests that parole board members were more likely to deny parole to suspected lesbians. However, at other institutions a "homosexual orientation" was considered "so common" that no attempt was made to segregate such prisoners.

Studies of Female Inmate Homosexuality in the 1960s

Although sociologists had studied men's prisons for decades, it was not until the 1960s that the first sociological studies of female prisons appeared. Both David A. Ward and Gene G. Kassebaum's *Women's Prisons: Sex and Social Structure* (1965) and Rose Giallombardo's *Society of Women: A Study of a Woman's Prison* (1966) focused almost exclusively on homosexuality, role-playing, and pseudo-family structures. Pseudo-families, also referred to as play, make-believe, quasi, or state families, might include a range of kinship roles, including grandparents, parents, daughters, sons, cousins, and aunts. These roles, even those designated as "mother" and "father," did not necessarily involve a sexual component. Likewise, homosexual relationships often took place outside of pseudo-family structures. However, committed same-sex partnerships might be formalized as marriages, complete with a ceremony, with the partners referring to one another as husband and wife.

These researchers portrayed the inmate social world as dominated by highly stereotypical butch-femme roles. The male, or butch, role involved the adoption of male dress, hairstyle, language, and other specifically masculine behaviors. According to scholarly interpretation, butches, few in number, were in high demand and often used their position to take advantage of femmes. However, some observers warn that these depictions may represent researchers' caricatures more than reality. Karlene Faith interviewed former prisoners who had participated in Ward and Kassebaum's original study. She reports that they responded with chagrin, anger, and hilarity over how their relationships had been portrayed.

Prevalence of, and Inmates' Attitudes toward, Prison Homosexuality

In 1965 Ward and Kassebaum estimated that 19 percent of female inmates had participated in some form of homosexual relationship. However, more than half of both staff and inmates gave much larger estimates. Later studies offer equally wide-ranging estimates. Prisoners and staff continue to respond that "everybody is involved," giving estimates of 30 percent to 60 percent. However, studies that include survey responses indicate that only 25 percent of female inmates self-report involvement in a same-sex relationship. One problem is that "homosexuality" is not always carefully defined. Surveys often indicate a wide range of actual behaviors, from flirting, hand-holding, kissing, and caressing to full-fledged lovemaking. Given the reality of prison conditions, however, genital sex is always cited as the least frequent activity.

Although new inmates sometimes express concern about peer pressures to participate, reports of force and coercion are almost nonexistent. Frequently, women who initially see lesbianism as unnatural find that, over time, they become attracted to a particular woman. Previously heterosexual women are often surprised to discover new forms of eroticism and desire, as well as intimacy, in their relationships with women.

Obviously, not all prisoners accept this aspect of the inmate world. Some remain deeply repulsed. Others express tolerance but choose not to participate. Women who identified as lesbian before their incarceration may also distance themselves from "the life" in prison. Some feel that prison homosexuality and role-playing "gives real lesbians a bad name." Contrary to expectations, lesbians in prison do not have an easier time than heterosexual women. They must adjust to the same pains of imprisonment, which often includes having left a lover on the outside.

Changing Subcultures in the 1980s and 1990s

The broadening in women's roles since the 1970s, as well as the increased visibility and redefinition of lesbian life, have expanded the conceptions of same-sex relationships in both the world at large and the microcosm of the prison. The stereotypical role-playing described in 1960s studies (to the extent that it was an accurate representation) appears to have been replaced by a looser system and more flexible roles. Although some women continue to adopt a butch style, there exists much greater fluidity of identities and forms of sexual expression.

Likewise, several researchers writing in the 1980s and 1990s have also noted a decline in both the complexity of the pseudo-family system and the extent of inmate participation. This decline may mirror the decline of the extended family in the free world outside, as well as increased opportunities for prisoners to maintain contact with their own families. However, what has not changed is the fact that relationships among women prisoners, from friendships to romantic and pseudo-family relationships, continue to exhibit a high degree of racial integration.

Contemporary Issues

At the start of the twenty-first century, prison rules and regulations offer a wide range of responses to prisoners' same-sex relationships and activities. Many administrators continue to view homosexuality as a source of instability, believing that such relationships often lead to jealousy, fights, and other types of conflict. In nearly all prisons, sexual activity between prisoners is explicitly prohibited. Those caught risk severe sanctions, including loss of good time. However, some prisons tolerate a high degree of affection displayed between women. In these institutions female prisoners can be seen walking hand in hand, sitting with their arms around one another, and engaging in intimate conversations and touches. Other institutions (often minimum security) are far less tolerant of such open displays.

Regardless of institutional rules, whether or not a particular behavior is sanctioned depends on the correctional officer who witnesses it. Many officers choose to ignore minor displays of affection. Interestingly, some studies suggest that female correctional officers are more likely than male staff to perceive lesbianism as a threat and to discipline women for it. Female staff are also particularly troubled by instances, common in the folklore of women's prisons, of an otherwise heterosexual (often married with children) female officer falling "madly in love" with a female inmate.

Lesbian prisoners continue to face prejudice and discrimination, although less blatantly than in the past. It is likely that lesbian staff and correctional officers also experience a similarly mixed range of responses. However, very little research has been done on the subject of LGBT prison staff.

Bibliography

Baker, Kathryn Hinojosa. "Delinquent Desire: Race, Sex, and Ritual in Reform Schools for Girls." *Discourse* 15, no. 1 (Fall 1992): 49–68.

Dodge, L. Mara. *"Whores and Thieves of the Worst Kind": Women, Crime, and Prisons, 1835–2000.* DeKalb, Ill.: Northern Illinois University Press, 2002.

Faith, Karlene. *Unruly Women: The Politics of Confinement and Resistance.* Vancouver, Canada: Press Gang Publishers, 1993.

Freedman, Estelle B. "The Prison Lesbian: Race, Class, and the Construction of the Aggressive Female Homosexual, 1915–1965." *Feminist Studies* 22, no. 2 (Summer 1996): 397–423.

Giallombardo, Rose. *Society of Women: A Study of a Woman's Prison.* New York: Wiley, 1966.

Kunzel, Regina G. "Situating Sex: Prison Sexual Culture in the Mid-Twentieth-Century United States." *Gay and Lesbian Quarterly* 8, no. 3 (May 2002): 253–270.

Otis, Margaret A. "Perversions Not Commonly Noted." *Journal of Abnormal Psychology* 8 (1913): 113 116.

Pollock-Byrne, Joycelyn M. *Women, Prison, and Crime.* 2nd ed. Belmont, Calif.: Wadsworth Co., 1990.

Ward, David A., and Gene G. Kassebaum. *Women's Prison: Sex and Social Structure.* Chicago: Aldine, 1965.

Watterson, Kathleen. *Women in Prison: Inside the Concrete Womb.* Rev. ed. Boston: Northeastern University Press, 1996.

L. Mara Dodge

See also DAVIS, KATHARINE BEMENT; FEMMES AND BUTCHES; LOBDELL, LUCY ANN; INTERRACIAL AND INTERETHNIC SEX AND RELATIONSHIPS; PRISONS, JAILS, AND REFORMATORIES: MEN'S; ROMANTIC FRIENDSHIP AND BOSTON MARRIAGE; SAME-SEX INSTITUTIONS; SITUATIONAL HOMOSEXUALITY; VAN WATERS, MIRIAM.

PRIVACY AND PRIVACY RIGHTS

In the 1600s, English common law recognized the importance of privacy rights in cases that threatened the sanctity of the home. In the United States in 1791, this privacy principle was highlighted in the U.S. Constitution's Fourth Amendment, which prohibited unreasonable searches and seizures. In 1890, Samuel Warren and Louis Brandeis published in the *Harvard Law Review* an article entitled "The Right to Privacy," which argued for the recognition of a tort claim for the invasion of privacy. They described the core of this tort concept as "the right to be let alone."

In 1928, Brandeis, by then an associate justice of the Supreme Court, extended the private law tort concept to include recognition of a constitutional right to privacy. Dissenting in *Olmstead v. United States,* a wiretapping case in which he thought privacy principles embedded in the Fourth Amendment should apply, he claimed "the makers of our Constitution undertook to secure conditions favorable to the pursuit of happiness. They recognized the significance of man's spiritual nature, of his feelings and his intellect.... They sought to protect Americans in their beliefs, their thoughts, their emotions and their sensations. They conferred, as against government, the right to be let alone—the most comprehensive of rights and the right most valued by civilized men."

Finally, in the 1960s, the Supreme Court began recognizing a constitutional right to privacy akin to the Warren and Brandeis notion of the "right to be let alone." And, more recently, public concerns about invasions of individual rights to informational privacy have led to legislation at both the federal and state levels that seeks to protect these rights.

Tort Law and Privacy

By the 1960s, tort law had begun to recognize four distinct forms of privacy rights. Concerned about privacy invasions related to sexual identity and sexual conduct, members of the queer community were particularly interested in the tort of "intrusion upon the plaintiff's seclusion" and the tort of "public disclosure of private facts." According to the *Restatement [Second] of Torts* (1977), intrusion upon seclusion occurs whenever anyone "intentionally intrudes, physically or otherwise, upon the solitude or seclusion of another" provided the "intrusion would be highly offensive to a reasonable person" (§652B). As a general rule, people reasonably expect privacy in their bedrooms, especially when engaging in intimate acts. Tort law should protect this expectation. For example, videotaping someone during sex, without the person's permission, should in most instances qualify as a tort of intrusion. Yet, in 1999, the Mississippi Supreme Court, with four judges dissenting, held in *Plaxico v. Michael* that no invasion occurred when, in the context of a pending divorce, the husband surreptitiously took photographs of his wife and her lesbian lover engaging in sex. The husband's concern over custody of his minor child was sufficient in the court's mind to make the invasion nonoffensive to a reasonable person.

To bring a successful claim for an invasion of privacy involving the public disclosure of private facts, the claimant must show that the matter publicized "would be highly offensive to a reasonable person" (§652E). Disclosing the details of someone's intimate sexual relations usually meets this standard. The claimant must also show that the matter disclosed is "not of legitimate concern to the public" (§652D). This tort action covers only public disclosure of facts that are true. If the disclosure is false, then alternative tort actions are available, including libel and slander (which require proof of harm to reputation) and another privacy tort, public disclosure of false private facts, also known as the tort of "false light," which is actionable even without proof of harm to reputation.

"Outing"

"Outing" (making public someone's sexual orientation) became a major issue in lesbian and gay communities in the 1980s. Some activists believed outings were justified when gay or lesbian celebrities or politicians took a public antigay or antilesbian position or took a stand against support for persons with AIDS. Others believed that privacy principles trumped and that no one had the right to "out" another human being. "Outings" of public figures at least raise the possibility of a tort privacy claim. In most such cases, however, the sexual orientation of a politician or celebrity, especially if that person has taken a public stand against gay or lesbian rights, is of sufficient public interest to defeat the claim. Also, since most of these "outings" occur in the press, they are additionally protected by the First Amendment's guarantee of freedom of the press. As that guarantee is interpreted by the Supreme Court, free speech is usually the winner when the interests in a free press are balanced against the privacy claims of public figures. As a result it is practically impossible for a celebrity or politician to make a successful invasion of privacy claim when the press has revealed his or her sexual orientation.

In 1975 an ex-marine pushed a gun out of the hands of Sara Jane Moore. She had been aiming at U.S. President Gerald Ford. Thwarting an apparent assassination attack, the ex-marine became an instant hero. The *San Francisco Chronicle* identified him as an active member of San Francisco's gay community. He sued, claiming an invasion of privacy. The *Chronicle* explained that they had revealed his sexual orientation in large part to challenge the standard stereotype of gay men as effeminate. In addition, the fact of his sexual orientation was well-known in the local community. In *Sipple v. Chronicle Publishing Co.* the California court upheld the right of the press to disclose the man's sexual orientation primarily because he was not closeted and thus the facts disclosed were not private. Closeted gay men and lesbians have been more successful in bringing privacy claims when they have been outed. Disclosure of one's sexual orientation to an employer by a jilted lover seeking revenge has been found actionable. Successful cases have been brought against coworkers who have outed a colleague, hoping to use the employer's homophobia to gain a competitive edge. Disclosures about HIV status and transsexuality have also been found actionable under tort law.

Constitutional Right to Privacy

Tort law protects individuals from being harmed by other individuals. Constitutional law protects individuals from being harmed by the government. The U.S. federal Constitution does not specifically mention the right to privacy. Nonetheless in a watershed 1965 opinion, *Griswold v. Connecticut,* the court proclaimed that government could not deny married couples the right to use contraceptive devices by outlawing their use. The decision was based on the fundamental constitutional right to privacy. Justice Douglas, writing for the Court, explained that this privacy right was derived from the penumbras of several explicit rights, described in the first nine amendments to the Constitution.

In 1972, the constitutional privacy doctrine was expanded in *Eisenstadt v. Baird* to include the right of unmarried heterosexual couples to use contraception. Justice Brennan, writing for the Court, appeared to rely primarily on equal protection arguments, concluding that there was no rational reason to treat married and unmarried individuals differently with respect to access to contraception. As to the right of privacy, he wrote, "[i]f the right of privacy means anything, it is the right of the individual, married or single, to be free from unwarranted governmental intrusion into matters so fundamentally affecting a person as the decision whether to bear or beget a child." Two years later, the right was expanded in *Roe v. Wade* (1973) to include the right of a pregnant woman to decide whether or not to have a child. Another case, *Stanley v. Georgia* (1969), expanded the privacy notion further, by holding that the possession of illegal obscene material solely for personal use within the home was constitutionally protected.

Griswold, Eisenstadt, and *Roe* dealt with intimate decisions about sexual activity. *Stanley* suggested that an otherwise illegal activity could not be criminalized so long as it was confined to personal acts in the privacy of the home. Based on these decisions, gay and lesbian rights activists began to craft privacy arguments to attack the application of sodomy statutes to consenting adult sex in private. The first test case challenged the Virginia sodomy statute. In *Doe v. Commonwealth's Attorney* (1975), a three-judge court ruled two to one against the plaintiffs' challenge. The case went directly to the U.S. Supreme Court by right of appeal and the Court summarily affirmed. No reason was given for the decision.

Despite this decision, other sodomy challenges, based on privacy grounds, succeeded in the state courts of Iowa, Pennsylvania, and New York. A petition for discretionary review (known as a petition for *certiorari*) was filed by the state of New York in the New York challenge, arguing that the state's sodomy statute did not violate the privacy rights guaranteed by the U.S. Constitution. The court denied review, which in effect supported the striking down of New York's sodomy statute. Commentators claimed that the Supreme Court's action in the New York case conflicted with its earlier action in the Virginia case. The Court's message was at best ambiguous. Many activists hoped that the denial of *certiorari* in the more recent case suggested that the Court agreed with gay rights litigators on the merits—that privacy rights included protection for consensual same-sex sodomy.

In 1986, the Supreme Court spoke clearly on the matter. Michael Hardwick, who had been arrested for the crime of consensual sodomy in his own bedroom in Atlanta, challenged the Georgia statute. He claimed that his fundamental right to privacy had been invaded. Following a favorable ruling by the Court of Appeals for the Eleventh Circuit, the State of Georgia asked the Supreme Court to review the decision. On 30 June 1986, in *Bowers v. Hardwick* the Court held that the constitutional right of privacy did not include the right to engage in homosexual sodomy.

Right to Privacy in State Constitutions

Litigators then turned to state constitutions to make privacy arguments that would support striking down sodomy statutes. Ten states have specific references to privacy rights in their constitutions. Other states have a history of strong protections for privacy under their constitutions, even though privacy is not an enumerated right. Since 1986, the top courts in Montana, Kentucky, Tennessee, Arkansas, and Georgia have all struck down sodomy statutes as violating the right to privacy guaranteed under the state constitution. However, the top courts in Louisiana and Texas have upheld the sodomy statutes in their states.

Of particular interest is the Texas sodomy case, *Lawrence v. Texas.* The case began much like the *Hardwick* case. In 1997, two men were arrested for committing sodomy in the privacy of their Houston bedroom. The police had entered legally in response to an anonymous (and false) burglary report. The two men, Lawrence and Garner, were convicted and fined. They appealed their convictions, claiming that the sodomy statute violated the equal protection and privacy provisions of both the state and federal constitutions. The intermediate appellate court in Houston, in an *en banc* (full court) decision, upheld both the convictions and the constitutionality of the Texas sodomy statute. When the Texas Court of Criminal Appeals refused to review the case, the Lambda Legal Defense attorneys representing the defendants petitioned the United States Supreme Court. On 2 December 2002 the Supreme Court granted *certiorari.*

On 26 June 2003 the Supreme Court handed down its decision in *Lawrence v. Texas.* While the case does not explicitly recognize a fundamental right of privacy, the majority opinion does explicitly overrule *Bowers v. Hardwick,* saying "*Bowers* was not correct when it was decided and it is not correct today." Justice Kennedy, writing for the court, based the decision on the liberty interest in the due process clause of the Fourteenth Amendment without ever defining that liberty interest as a right of privacy. Instead he focused on the right to make personal decisions, explaining that "liberty presumes an autonomy of self that includes freedom of thought, belief, expression, and certain intimate conduct. The instant case involves liberty of the person both in its spatial and more transcendent dimensions."

Bibliography

Cain, Patricia A. *Rainbow Rights: The Role of Lawyers and Courts in the Lesbian and Gay Civil Rights Movement.* Boulder, Colo.: Westview Press, 2000.

Bowers v. Hardwick. 478 U.S. 186 (1986).

Doe v. Commonwealth's Attorney. 403 F. Supp. 1199 (E.D. Va. 1975).

Eisenstadt v. Baird. 405 U.S. 438 (1972).

Griswold v. Connecticut. 381 U.S. 479 (1965).

Lawrence v. Texas. 539 US ____, 123 S. Ct. 2472 (2003).

Olmstead v. United States. 277 U.S. 438 (1928).

Plaxico v. Michael. 735 So.2d 1036 (Miss. 1999).

Roe v. Wade. 410 U.S. 113 (1973).

Samar, Vincent J. *The Right to Privacy: Gays, Lesbians, and the Constitution.* Philadelphia: Temple University Press, 1991.

Sipple v. Chronicle Publishing Co. 201 Cal. Rptr. 665 (Cal. App. 1984).

Stanley v. Georgia. 394 U.S. 557 (1969).

Warren, Samuel D., and Brandeis, Louis D. "The Right to Privacy." *Harvard Law Review* 4 (1890): 193.

Patricia A. Cain

See also AMERICAN CIVIL LIBERTIES UNION (ACLU); COMING OUT AND OUTING; FEDERAL LAW AND POLICY; POLICING AND POLICE; RIGHTS OF ASSOCIATION AND ASSEMBLY; SODOMY, BUGGERY, CRIMES AGAINST NATURE, DISORDERLY CONDUCT, AND LEWD AND LASCIVIOUS LAW AND POLICY.

PROSTITUTION, HUSTLING, AND SEX WORK

Prostitution has often been referred to as the "world's oldest profession." However, until very recently, the assumption has been that prostitutes are women and their customers men. Although many past commercial sex exchanges have fit this model, paid sexual encounters have also involved same-sex sexual acts, either for customers' viewing pleasure or participation. Furthermore, LGBT people and sex workers of both sexes historically have been lumped into similar categories as "sexual deviants," occupying similar or overlapping ideological and geographical spaces. Thus these communities and their histories have become linked in significant ways, both as outcast groups perceived by society to be in need of detection, regulation, and, occasionally, eradication, and as allies and mutual inhabitants of the sexual underworld.

Men

Most historical evidence of male prostitution in the United States comes from court records and vice investigations. In the latter half of the 1600s, for example, Windsor, Connecticut, resident Peter Buoll made a complaint about Nicholas Sension: "He told me if I would let him have one bloo [blow] at my breech he would give me a charge of powder" (Godbeer, p. 45). In 1878, Montana Territory found a man named Mahaffey guilty of a "crime against nature" with a fourteen-year-old boy identified only as "B." whom he later identified as a "boy prostitute."

As large urban areas grew and sexual subcultures coalesced toward the end of the nineteenth century in America, male/male prostitution attained greater visibility. Concomitant to the rise of gay sexual communities was an increase in public concern with controlling the behavior of sexual deviants, including commercial sex contacts. New York City possessed perhaps the best-known gay subculture and a burgeoning population of male prostitutes. When New York City moral reformer Charles H. Parkhurst accompanied detective Charles W. Gardener to a brothel called the "Golden Rule Pleasure Club" in 1892, he was appalled to find that the young "women" residents were actually men wearing dresses and make-up and speaking in falsetto so as to appear like women. At another male brothel known as Paresis Hall in the Bowery district, dozens of male prostitutes plied their trade. Often labeled "fairies," these men solicited other men for sexual acts and received a commission for selling drinks to customers. Similar services could be found in other cities in the late nineteenth century. In Chicago, an African American girl who turned out to be a male prostitute approached German sexologist and gay advocate Magnus Hirschfeld in 1893. Male prostitutes also reportedly worked in a Turkish bath in San Francisco's Barbary Coast in the 1890s.

During the twentieth century, male prostitution became inextricably intertwined in the fabric of commercial sex in urban areas around the United States. British sex researcher Havelock Ellis reported in 1915 that male prostitutes in New York and Philadelphia wore red neckties as a symbol of their profession. Although not as visible as in larger cities, male prostitutes have also existed in smaller municipalities as well. In recent times, male prostitutes have become ubiquitous. Men sell sex to men either openly as men or dressed as women in every community in the United States. Still other men make a living as drag performers or strip-tease artists, selling sexual fantasies and occasionally sexual acts on the side. Although the rise of HIV/AIDS in the 1980s and 1990s brought with it a public health focus on all prostitutes who might transmit the disease, male sex workers, who are especially vulnerable to the virus, have come under especially intense scrutiny. Similar attention was paid to sex workers during both world wars, when men selling sex to men were scrutinized by the military, vice reformers, and other public officials. As with HIV/AIDS, the attention was due, in part, to rising concern about the spread of venereal disease from sex workers, male or female, but military and government officials were especially worried about the effects these diseases might have on soldiers' fighting capability.

Women

Historical evidence of women purchasing from or selling sex to other women is harder to find. Yet solid and anecdotal examples exist in sexological literature of the nineteenth and twentieth centuries and in other sources. For the most part, the sources portray same-sex sex acts either as a noncommercial activity, something female prostitutes engage in with other prostitutes or their girlfriends for pleasure outside of work, or as one of a repertoire of sex services that male customers might purchase. Far fewer are examples of women selling or buying sex from women. In fact, eminent sexologist Alfred Kinsey noted in 1948 that the rarest type of prostitution involved women selling homosexual sex to other women.

In the early twentieth century, American researchers frequently cited the work of French sexologist Alexander Parent-Duchâtelet, who estimated that nearly 25 percent of Parisian prostitutes engaged in homoerotic acts or had homoerotic tendencies. Furthermore, they often endorsed his explanation for same-sex behavior among prostitutes: disgust for male customers, which ostensibly drove them to have sex with women. With the advent of psychoanalytical explanations for behavior, American and European sexologists blended earlier explanations with new theories explaining how prostitutes' alleged lesbian tendencies in fact inspired their choice of profession. During this time, some argued that "latent homosexuality" drove women to sell sex to men and that many prostitutes (if not a majority) were lesbians. American sexologist James G. Kiernan, for example, noted, "tribadism is exceedingly common among harlots everywhere" (Kiernan, p.186). More likely, others argued, female prostitutes' inclination toward homosexuality was not congenital but rather directed at other prostitutes and stemmed from the legendary solidarity that leads to intense and intimate friendships among prostitutes.

Perhaps because of social perceptions that their role as head of household or entrepreneur was masculine, madams historically have been deemed to be either lesbian or engaged in sexual relationships with their "girls." Mixed-race New Orleans madam Emma Johnson, known as "The Parisian Queen of America," was reportedly a lesbian. Johnson's house became famous for its early-twentieth-century sex circuses, where women and men had sex with other women and men in any combination imaginable.

For the most part, women in the United States had neither social access to nor the financial means to purchase the services of prostitutes, even if they had the desire to do so. And, indeed, romantic friendships, at least until the early twentieth century, provided acceptable, private access to passionate emotional and physical relationships with other women. Prostitutes' writings and sexological studies of the twentieth century, however, reveal the possibility that female "johns" may have purchased sex from female prostitutes. In a study of "homosexual" men and women incarcerated on New York's Blackwell's Island in the 1920s, a gay male informant reported that his friend, a twenty-six-year-old addicted female prostitute, averaged two hundred dollars per week in a New York brothel and that there were well over two hundred such homosexual female (and one hundred male) prostitutes in New York City at the time. These numbers are likely overstated, but indicate that some same-sex trade could be had for women with means.

In the postwar period in the United States, increasing efforts to control all forms of deviant sexuality were tied to ideas of national security and the nuclear, heterosexual, patriarchal family. During this time, both lesbians and prostitutes exemplified uncontained female sexuality and became linked in the popular imagination. Although sexual attitudes regarding all forms of so-called deviancy had become increasingly liberal by the late 1960s, in the 1970s and 1980s, many feminists returned the focus to the eradication of prostitution and pornography, which they directly linked to male sexual exploitation and objectification of women. Ironically, antiprostitution feminists (many of whom identified as lesbians) worked hard to disconnect prostitutes and lesbians as a way to gain social legitimacy for the latter. In so doing, these feminists have alienated a large number of lesbians who work (and are still employed) as sex workers. At the same time, pro-sex feminists, along with prostitutes' rights groups such as COYOTE (Call Off Your Old Tired Ethics), have fought in favor of women's rights to participate in sex work without stigma. These women argue that sex work is a legitimate occupation that needs to be extracted from debates about morality, and that prostitutes deserve legal status as workers with the concomitant benefits that accompany that status, such as health care, a living wage, and attention to safety concerns while on the job. In addition, pro-sex feminists argue that any attempted control of female sexuality works at cross-purposes to all women's freedom of expression—whether lesbian, bisexual, or straight. Despite these "sex wars," connections between prostitutes and lesbians have remained strong both in fictionalized representations and on the street, and many prostitutes, strippers, and phone sex workers today claim a lesbian identity.

Shared Space and Harassment

In many cities, LGBT people and sex workers have shared and continued to share the same physical, often public, spaces. For example, following the vice crusades of the early twentieth century that closed some of the more notorious red-light districts, and later sweeps that targeted sex workers working in taverns and nightclubs, female prostitutes formed clandestine networks that provided some safety. Meanwhile, lesbians became more visible, often in these same public spaces. San Francisco's North Beach district, for instance, became the locus for these two groups of deviant women, and soon lesbians were using many of the same techniques as prostitutes to pick up sexual partners and avoid arrest. Indeed, both prostitutes and lesbians frequented the first lesbian-owned bar in San Francisco. Similarly, New York City's 42nd Street, which in the early decades of the twentieth century had possessed a reputation for female prostitution, also became known in the 1930s as one of the city's primary cruising sites for both male and transvestite prostitutes.

During the last half of the twentieth century, prostitutes and lesbians, hustlers and gay men often found themselves harassed and arrested together. Indeed, in the 1950s and 1960s, police often arrested those lesbians who were increasingly becoming visible in such public spaces as bars under antiprostitution statutes (often vagrancy or solicitation charges). While such arrests confused the two groups, police were in effect using antiprostitution laws to control the behavior of both groups of women and to regulate the spaces they frequented. Much the same held true for men cruising for sex partners in public restrooms, tearooms, and parks. Whether they were hustling or simply looking for a quick encounter with a willing partner, gay men and hustlers risked arrest for indecent exposure, crimes against nature, vagrancy, and sodomy.

Complex Sexual Identities

Same-sex prostitution has not always been directly related to an individual's stated sexual identity or preference. For example, men who considered themselves sexually "normal" in the late nineteenth century and many of the male soldiers and sailors who purchased sex from men in the first half of the twentieth century, especially those from the working class, considered themselves to be very much "heterosexual," as long as they were the penetrator or receiver of oral sex. Indeed, until the late twentieth century male consumers of sex with men have often identified as "straight," although they have considered the men with whom they had sex to be "homosexual." Today, research shows that a majority of male prostitutes are likely to identify as "heterosexual" or "bisexual" (and have either or both male or female lovers, who are often sex workers themselves), while many of their customers identify as gay. An exception to this is the large number of self-identified straight men who patronize she-male prostitutes. Somewhat the opposite holds true among female sex workers, many of who identify as lesbian (and have long-term relationships with women) despite selling sex far more frequently to men than to women.

Sex for pay has manifested in infinite combinations among people who claim any number of sexual identities (gay, lesbian, straight, bisexual, transgender)—or think little of them. Rarely do sex workers stop to wonder if the sex acts they perform make them homosexual, heterosexual, or somewhere in between. Rather, these men and women choose their profession as a means to an end and do not see it as a defining aspect of their personal identity, unless that identity is sex worker. In brothels and baths, in bars and nightclubs, and on the street, anything goes, as long as it is paid for.

Bibliography

Boyd, Nan Alamilla. *Wide-Open Town: A History of Queer San Francisco to 1965.* Berkeley: University of California Press, 2003.

Chauncey, George. *Gay New York: Gender, Urban Culture, and the Making of the Gay Male World, 1890–1940.* New York: Basic Books, 1994.

Delacoste, Frederique, and Priscilla, Alexander, eds. *Sex Work: Writings by Women in the Sex Industry.* San Francisco: Cleis Press, 1987.

Dixon, Dwight, and Joan K. Dixon. "She-Male Prostitutes: Who Are They, What Do They Do, and Why Do They Do It?" In *Prostitution: On Whores, Hustlers, and Johns.* Edited by James Elias, Vern L. Bullough, Veronica Elias, and Gwen Brewer. New York: Prometheus Books, 1999, pp. 260–266.

Ellis, Havelock. *Sexual Inversion*, Vol. 2 of *Studies in the Psychology of Sex.* 2d ed., rev. and enl. 1913. Reprint, Philadelphia: F. A. Davis Company, 1931.

Godbeer, Richard. *Sexual Revolution in Early America.* Baltimore: Johns Hopkins University Press, 2002.

Howard, John. *Men Like That: A Southern Queer History.* Chicago: University of Chicago Press, 1999.

Kahn, Samuel. *Mentality and Homosexuality.* Boston: Meador Press, 1937.

Katz, Jonathan Ned. *Gay American History: Lesbians and Gay Men in the U.S.A.* New York: Crowell, 1976.

Kennedy, Elizabeth Lapovsky, and Madeline D. Davis. *Boots of Leather, Slippers of Gold: A History of a Lesbian Community.* New York: Routledge, 1993.

Kiernan, James G. "Masturbation among Harlots." *Urologic and Cutaneous Review* 26, no. 3 (March 1922): 186.

Morse, Edward V., Patricia M. Simon, and Kendra E. Burchfiel. "Social Environment and Sex Work in the United States." In *Men Who Sell Sex: International Perspectives on Male Prostitution and HIV/AIDS.* Edited by Peter Aggleton. Philadelphia: Temple University Press, 1999, pp. 8–102.

Parent-Duchâtelet, Alexandre-Jean-Baptiste. *De la prostitution dans la ville de Paris.* Paris: Balliere, 1836, pp. 83–102.

Penn, Donna. "The Sexualized Woman: The Lesbian, the Prostitutes, and Containment of Female Sexuality in Postwar America." In *Not June Cleaver: Women and Gender in Postwar America, 1945–1960.* Edited by Joanne Meyerowitz. Philadelphia: Temple University Press, 1994, pp. 358–381.

Steward, Samuel M., and Phil Andros. *Understanding the Male Hustler.* New York: Harrington Park Press, 1991.

Heather Lee Miller

See also CRIME AND CRIMINALIZATION; CROSS-CLASS SEX AND RELATIONSHIPS; EMPLOYMENT AND OCCUPATIONS; PROSTITUTION, HUSTLING, AND SEX WORK LAW AND POLICY; PUBLIC SEX; SAME-SEX INSTITUTIONS; SODOMY, BUGGERY, CRIMES AGAINST NATURE, DISORDERLY CONDUCT, AND LEWD AND LASCIVIOUS BEHAVIOR; TOURISM.

PROSTITUTION, HUSTLING, AND SEX WORK LAW AND POLICY

Prostitution, hustling, and sex work are forms of labor, not erotic preferences or gender identities. While prostitution and hustling generally refer to the exchange of sex for money (or for nonsexual goods or services), sex work is a broader category that also includes stripping, erotic dancing, and labor in the pornography, peep show, and telephone sex industries. Self-identified LGBT, queer, and straight people work in sex industries, offering varieties of commercial sex both in line with and out of line with their own noncommercial sexual interests. LGBT people also constitute audiences and markets for commercial sex, usually but not always for the types of sex that they prefer to have in noncommercial contexts. Commercial sex (both cross-sex and same-sex) and noncommercial same-sex sex have been stigmatized and criminalized in ways that conflate and confuse these distinct but overlapping types of consensual behavior. LGBT involvement in prostitution, hustling, and sex work has been subject to particularly intense forms of legal policing and social regulation in certain contexts.

Early Policing

The first British North American colonial laws against prostitution, local ordinances criminalizing the running of "bawdy" houses (1672) and "nightwalking" (1699), failed to curtail the growth of commercial prostitution in the United States. With the rise of a market economy in the late eighteenth and early nineteenth centuries, traditional agrarian ways of life gave way to wage-labor systems in increasingly commercial and urban settings, which featured significant prostitution practices. Meanwhile, on the western frontier of the nineteenth century, predominantly male communities of entrepreneurs, laborers, miners, railroad workers, and soldiers provided large markets for prostitution. In *Gay American History* (1992), Jonathan Katz documented examples and allegations of male same-sex prostitution in prison reform literature in the 1820s, in Montana Territory court records in the 1870s, and in various other documents (that also link prostitution, lesbianism, and transgenderism) from the late nineteenth century.

The steady rise of commercial red-light districts, along with slavery's forced prostitution, betrayed a Victorian era sensibility sanctioning prostitution as a "necessary evil" providing sexual "outlets" for men outside of marriage and away from home, though such social sanction rarely extended to same-sex prostitution. Reform movements beginning in the 1830s, however, fought against prostitution. By the early twentieth century, most states had criminalized the actions of not only prostitutes (for solicitation and sale), but also those who ran houses of prostitution, promoted prostitution (including pimps), or forced or enticed people to engage in prostitution. Among those arrested were many women who had formed intimate and erotic bonds of sisterhood with other prostitutes. Male prostitution less frequently involved pimps, brothels, and physical compulsion, and so may have been less regulated than female prostitution in these respects. Somewhat less common were laws against "johns" (those who purchased the services of prostitutes). Prostitutes (male and female) and johns may well have been arrested more frequently for "disorderly conduct" than for offenses related specifically to prostitution, and this likely was the case especially for same-sex prostitution (which was not always recognized as prostitution under the law).

Social Reform

In the nineteenth and early twentieth centuries, anti-vice and social purity societies often took the lead in ensuring that antiprostitution laws were enforced. Sometimes deputized by local government, sometimes wielding political influence to secure police cooperation, antivice societies and their allies policed individuals and businesses to curb behavior and weaken institutions that were perceived to threaten the moral order valued by reformers. Campaigns against commercial sex also concerned themselves with health, hygiene, and temperance. Reform movements policing prostitution also worked to regulate nonmarital, interracial, and same-sex sexual behaviors. Given that the neighborhoods, parks, saloons, restaurants, and boardinghouses frequented by LGBT people tended to be frequented by prostitutes and their customers, the social reformers who policed prostitution had a significant impact on LGBT cultures and especially on the immigrants, workers, and poor people who participated in these cultures.

In *Gay New York* (1994), for example, George Chauncey argues that before, during, and after World War I the antiprostitution campaigns of the Society for the Prevention of Crime, the City Vigilance League, the Committee of Fourteen, and the Society for the Suppression of Vice discovered the city's extensive gay subcultures and began to target male prostitution. Especially with the mobilization of military forces during World War I and the successes of various efforts made against female prostitution, reformers shifted some of their anxieties to "male perverts," who, it was feared, would seduce young troops in the absence of an adequate supply of seductive, solicitous women. Gay men and the establishments catering to them, including restaurants, bathhouses, theaters, and other places of amusement were intensively policed. Chauncey reports that the number of men convicted for homosexual solicitation in Manhattan increased eightfold during the period from 1916 to 1920.

In *The Lost Sisterhood* (1982), Ruth Rosen argues that reformers' attention to prostitution and the anxieties surrounding "white slavery" peaked in the years from 1911 to 1915, with a coalition of antivice groups succeeding in closing red-light prostitution districts and policing commercial sex. In 1910 the federal Mann Act was passed to address racist and nativist anxieties about white women being lured away from home communities into prostitution by nonwhite and immigrant men. The Mann Act prohibited transporting women across state lines for "immoral purposes," but it left most regulation of prostitution and public sexual activity to state and local law enforcement. Red-light district abatement laws passed by states and cities across the country worked to regulate the sexual, commercial, and working-class territories of urban America.

According to William Eskridge Jr. and Nan Hunter's *Sexuality, Gender, and the Law* (1997), prostitution laws in the United States changed little in the following decades (until the 1970s). These laws were available for use by local and state authorities not only to police same-sex prostitution and LGBT people engaging in cross-sex prostitution, but also to police LGBT bars, restaurants, and other commercial establishments. Police, for example, frequently justified raids on lesbian bars in the 1950s and 1960s by claiming that cross-sex solicitation occurred on or near the premises and that prostitutes frequented these establishments. Antiprostitution laws governing the circumstances under which women could dance and serve alcohol affected lesbian culture in significant ways. Meanwhile, discourses that linked prostitution and lesbians encouraged officials to use laws against the former to harass and attack the latter.

Developments since the 1970s

According to Eskridge and Hunter, since the 1970s many states have revised their laws against prostitution. Nevada decriminalized prostitution, but other states expanded the reach of their laws to cover, for example, nonvaginal intercourse, other forms of sexual contact, same-sex and transgender prostitution, and payment for sex (in those states that had not already criminalized the actions of johns). There is no reason to believe that recent court rulings covering noncommercial private sex will soon be extended to apply to prostitution.

In her 1984 essay "Thinking Sex," Gayle Rubin places prostitution with pornography, promiscuity, and homosexual sex in the low status region of the contemporary American sex hierarchy while heterosexual, noncommercial, and monogamous sex occupy the high status regions. Financial exchange in combination with other kinds of low status sex (including same-sex sex) raises the risks of arrest and stigmatization, especially if the sexual behavior is brought to the attention of law enforcement by vigilante citizens. Transgender prostitutes appear to be subject to particularly high risks.

Law enforcement continues to conflate consensual same-sex acts with sex for money. Men cruising for anonymous, consensual, same-sex sexual encounters are often charged under antiprostitution or antisolicitation laws, even though there may not be any money exchanging hands. Given the consensual, victimless nature of sexual cruising and prostitution, which means that participants are unlikely to press charges, police frequently resort to entrapment to make arrests for both. It is often difficult to distinguish instances of consensual for-profit sex from consensual not-for-profit sex, and an accurate distinction often matters little to law enforcement officers levying the charges. Antisolicitation, antivagrancy, and disorderly conduct charges are still used to regulate the public activity of prostitutes, the poor and unemployed, and same-sex cruisers, and charges are applied at the considerable discretion of local law enforcement.

In part because of its illegal or extralegal status, the sex industry can have horrible working conditions. Without state oversight, government regulations, or legal tools to address unsafe and unfair situations, sex workers are cheated, mistreated, exploited, physically harmed, and killed. Working outside of or just within legal limits, many sex businesses spend a disproportionate amount of time and money trying to stay in business and little on the needs of their workers. Others are profitable and still exploit workers. There is little public pressure for sex businesses to share profits with illegal employees, and there are few protections for sex industry clients and consumers. Yet despite the poor working conditions and the often-illegal nature of sex work, many people of all sexual and gender orientations are employed in the sex industries by choice and by necessity. Even more people constitute the massive audiences that sustain the sex industry, with few consumer protections to screen out inferior, unsafe, and dangerous products and services. Since the 1970s, several sex positive organizations have formed to represent, promote, and empower sex workers of all gender, and sexual types, calling, for example, for the legalization of sex work. Among the more influential groups are COYOTE (Call Off Your Old Tired Ethics, 1973), USPROS (US Prostitutes, originally New York Prostitutes Collective, 1979), and the Gay Men's Health Crisis's CASH (Coalition Advocating Safer Hustling, 1993–1996).

Some recent feminists and lesbian-feminists, among them Sheila Jeffreys, Andrea Dworkin, and Catharine MacKinnon, deplore the entire enterprise of commercial sex, labeling it exploitative and dangerous to women. They seek to protect and rescue sex workers from the violence, abuse, and humiliation they find inherent and pervasive in the sexist, male-dominated sex industry. Arguing that pornographic performances and images in particular constitute a direct assault on women (and frequently sidestepping questions about male prostitution), they disagree with the idea that sex workers might find empowerment or satisfaction in their work, and they assert that theorists are mistaken in "romanticizing" sex work and pornographic products. While they succeeded in enacting some local antipornography legislation in the 1980s, they also precipitated the feminist sex wars, in which prosex feminists, including many lesbians, came to the defense of the pleasures and possibilities of sex work.

Antipornography feminists have formed alliances not only with the New Right but also with urban gentrifiers. In the 1990s local officials in New York City used zoning laws to reinvent Times Square, destroying in the process one of the world's great commercial sex districts, a lively intersection of people from all classes, races, and localities, not to mention a neighborhood with a significant amount of commercial LGBT space and public LGBT culture. While many cities, towns, and counties restrict "adult" business to certain areas, arguing that their presence will have adverse effects on the surrounding community, there is little nonanecdotal evidence to support these assumptions. Nevertheless, prostitution, hustling, and sex work remain vulnerable to local, state, and federal government action.

Within LGBT communities, there is no uniform opinion or agreement regarding sex industry law and policy. Commercial sex and noncommercial same-sex cultures share territorial and criminal histories that link their distinct yet overlapping practices. The regulation of these territories has involved combinations of citizen and state surveillance. Decriminalization of same-sex sex, public sex, and prostitution would ease the containment and policing that continue to constrain consensual sexual practices in the United States.

Bibliography

Chauncey, George. *Gay New York: Gender, Urban Culture, and the Making of the Gay Male World, 1890–1940.* New York: HarperCollins, 1994.

Eskridge, William N., Jr., and Nan D. Hunter. *Sexuality, Gender, and the Law.* Westbury, N.Y.: Foundation Press, 1997.

Jeffreys, Sheila. *The Idea of Prostitution.* North Melbourne, Australia: Spinifex, 1997.

Katz, Jonathan. *Gay American History: Lesbians and Gay Men in the U.S.A., A Documentary History.* Rev. ed. New York: Meridian, 1992.

Kennedy, Elizabeth Lapovsky, and Madeline D. Davis. *Boots of Leather, Slippers of Gold: The History of a Lesbian Community.* New York: Routledge, 1993.

Penn, Donna. "The Sexualized Woman: The Lesbian, the Prostitute, and Containment of Female Sexuality in Postwar America." In *Not June Cleaver: Women and Gender in the Postwar Period, 1945–1960.* Edited by Joanne Meyerowitz. Philadelphia: Temple University Press, 1994.

Rosen, Ruth. *The Lost Sisterhood.* Baltimore: Johns Hopkins University Press, 1982.

Rubin, Gayle. "Thinking Sex: Notes for a Radical Theory of the Politics of Sexuality." In *Pleasure and Danger: Exploring Female Sexuality.* Edited by Carole S. Vance. Boston: Routledge and Kegan Paul, 1984.

Polly J. Thistlethwaite

See also CRIME AND CRIMINALIZATION; DISCRIMINATION; EMPLOYMENT AND OCCUPATIONS; EMPLOYMENT LAW AND POLICY; FEDERAL LAW AND POLICY; PROSTITUTION, HUSTLING, AND SEX WORK; PUBLIC SEX; SEX WARS; TOURISM.

PROTESTANTS AND PROTESTANTISM

The roots of Protestant Christianity reach back to sixteenth-century reform movements in Europe. In opposition to the institutional power exercised by the medieval church, reformers such as Martin Luther argued for the Bible as the sole source of divine revelation. This reliance on biblical texts has contributed significantly to Protestant approaches to sexuality.

The insistence among early Protestants on "private judgment" in the interpretation of Scripture helps to account for the extensive variety of Protestant denominations that emerged from the Reformation, as well as the diversity of approaches to questions of sexual morality. Today, while many denominations are grouped quite loosely under the Protestant label, most of them retain an emphasis on Scripture and a high standard of personal, biblically based morality with its attendant stress on discerning appropriate—in other words, divinely sanctioned—sexual expression.

Interpretation and Application of Biblical Texts

Biblical discourse on sexuality among Protestants typically begins with the creation accounts in Genesis. These biblical texts contributed to the early reformers' rejection of mandatory clergy celibacy, because they believed marriage to be divinely instituted in the act of creation itself, yet buttressed the already well-established prohibition of same-sex sexual relations, as the gender complementarity of the Genesis account seems to demand. While several other biblical texts have played a key role in these debates (Lev. 18:22, 20:13; Rom. 1:27; I Cor. 6:9-10; and I Tim. 1:10) particularly notable is the account of God's destruction of the city of Sodom (Gen. 19). The cause of this divine act of judgement is often assigned to the supposedly homosexual male residents of that city. As Mark Jordan's research has shown, the rhetorical utility of "sodomy" as a broad category of sexual and gender deviance appeared relatively late in Christian traditions (roughly the eleventh century) but has exercised wide-ranging influence in both religious and civic affairs. Early Protestants seized on this category for theological and political confrontations with the Roman Catholic Church. Many Protestants today continue to rely on this biblical material to support, as a matter of divine decree, the dominant Euro-American cultural pattern of heterosexual marriage and family, the strictly defined gender roles of husband and wife, and the procreative purpose of sexuality.

The interpretation and application of biblical texts on sexuality remains a divisive and fiercely debated topic among Protestant Christians. This issue is made more complex by the relatively recent emergence of LGBT identities, which for some stand in contrast to LGBT behaviors, a distinction with which biblical writers were largely if not completely unfamiliar. Modern Protestants

the religious right and anti-lgbt violence

In 1979, Paul Weyrich, a political strategist, joined with Jerry Falwell, a Baptist preacher and television evangelist, to create the Moral Majority, an umbrella network for a rapidly growing number of religiously and politically conservative organizations and congregations seeking to address the "decadence" of American morality, typified by the growing acceptance of homosexuality. This movement quickly grew to four million and attracted members well beyond fundamentalist Christian circles, including Roman Catholics, conservative-minded members of mainline denominations, and Mormons. The Moral Majority even garnered endorsements from some Jewish organizations. Falwell disbanded the organization in 1986, but fellow televangelist Pat Robertson, after losing his bid for the presidential nomination in 1988, resurrected this national network in the form of the Christian Coalition.

Weyrich, Falwell, and Robertson, together with such figures as Lou Sheldon (of the Traditional Values Coalition), James Dobson (of *Focus on the Family* magazine), and Donald Wildmon (of the American Family Association), represent a broadly based movement variously called the New Right, the Evangelical Right, or simply the Religious Right. Though it no longer received as much media attention as it did in the 1980s and had dissolved much of its national institutional structure, the Religious Right nevertheless continued to exercise significant influence in matters of social policy on the local and state level, including its opposition to legislative measures guaranteeing civil rights for LGBT people, in the early twenty-first century.

Most of the national figures in this movement have stopped short of publicly advocating violence against gay men and lesbians (though Falwell, at the peak of the Moral Majority's influence, declared his intention to "stop the Gays dead in their perverted tracks"); still, many critics believed that their rhetoric, couched in traditional religious language, has fueled a violent posture. The brutal murders of an openly gay man, Matthew Shepard, on the plains of Wyoming in 1998, and of transgender teenager Eddie "Gwen" Araujo, in the San Francisco Bay area in 2002, are just two vivid examples of the kind of anti-LGBT violence in which the rhetoric of the Religious Right conceivably plays a part.

The power of religious language to fuel social action cannot be overestimated, whether in its more moderate forms ("hate the sin, love the sinner") or its extreme manifestations—as in the case of Fred Phelps, a Baptist minister who garnered media attention in the late 1980s and 1990s by organizing anti-LGBT rallies at the funerals of those who had died from AIDS-related causes, where he declared such persons worthy of divine condemnation and death because of their sexual orientation. The National Religious Leadership Roundtable, co-convened by the National Gay and Lesbian Task Force, was created in the late 1990s to counter the anti-LGBT strategies of the Religious Right and marshal the resources of various faith communities (including Protestant denominations) for proactive, religious efforts to promote social justice and bring anti-LGBT violence to an end.

tend to mirror this distinction in their ecclesial policies by condemning sexual acts between people of the same sex but encouraging the acceptance of homosexually oriented persons who remain chaste. Positions exist on either side of this view, as some Protestant churches treat both the sexual act and the person as equally sinful, while others openly embrace both the persons and their sexual expressions.

Mapping the intersections of sexually queer experience with Protestant Christianity thus presents a challenge. Common themes do appear, along with general trends, but the diversity of Protestant approaches makes a tidy map impossible to draw. Generally, incidents of publicly known same-sex relationship and sexual behavior were restricted to relatively few (usually notorious) cases from the American colonial period and into the nineteenth century. This gave way eventually to a public, politically galvanizing LGBT liberation movement of the late 1960s, during which key figures and texts emerged in the effort to mobilize a shift in religious approaches to sexual and gender diversity. This shift continues to shape the prospects for wider participation within the life of Protestant churches for LGBT people. Overall, modern and now postmodern Protestant engagements with LGBT experience will likely remain as fluid as our cultural constructs of sexuality and gender, even as religious institutions seem perpetually to lag behind the realities they seek to engage.

Mapping the Terrain of American Protestants

From the Colonial Period to 1900. The biblical predilections of Protestant Christianity arrived on the American continent with the European settlers of New England, a fact that shaped the sexual mores of American colonial life and the subsequent development of common law precedents. Drawing on such biblical passages as

Leviticus 20:13 (which prescribes death for "a man who lies with a male as with a woman"), nearly half of the original English colonies adopted capital punishment for the crime of "sodomy." While the death penalty for such acts was repealed after the Revolutionary War, this posture toward "unnatural acts" continued to influence state statutes, legal opinion, and law enforcement procedures well into the twentieth century. (When the U.S. Superme Court overturned the legal proscription of sodomy in its 2003 decision, "Lawrence v. Texas," thirteen states still retained laws prohibiting sodomy, four of which restricted the prohibition to same-sex couples.)

Prior to the nineteenth century, the discretion of same-sex-loving people and the cultural taboos associated with their behavior kept their relationships mostly hidden from public view, especially as protestant preachers continued to condemn the sin of "sodomy" from their pulpits. As Protestant missionaries began to expand their work beyond Euro-American contexts they encountered new forms of sexual diversity, usually in the form of gender nonconformity. Some Native American cultures, for example, honored the tradition of what Europeans called the *berdache*, a person who adopted either transgender or androgynous behavior within tribal life and customs and whose role in the tribe often included responsibilities the tribe understood as spiritual or otherwise sacred. Colonial and early U.S. authorities had already established a pattern of legally coercing the *berdache* to dress according to conventional gender standards, but Protestant missionaries took this further by insisting that they do so as a condition for genuine conversion to Christianity.

The nineteenth century witnessed important changes as industrialization, critical biblical scholarship, and advances in the social and physical sciences led to a liberalization of traditional forms of Protestantism. Unitarianism began to thrive, as it shifted from its reliance on biblically based Christianity to one more firmly rooted in Enlightenment rationalism and Renaissance humanism. Still, this relaxation of traditional theological tenets did not immediately alter the taboos associated with homosexuality, especially as both sexuality and gender were brought more securely into the orbit of scientific and particularly medical research where the term "homosexuality" was first coined and perceived as an illness.

The Twentieth Century. The confluence of scientific classification, Protestantism, and cultural class distinctions created new types of engagement with homosexuality in the early part of the twentieth century. George Chauncey, Jr., for example, in his research of the World War I era, suggests that a man's homosexual behavior was at this time often understood as "queer" only if he took the "woman's part" in the sexual act. This kind of gender categorization was frequently inscribed on class, especially, as Chauncey's work shows, in religious contexts. Christian ministers, for example, whose middle- or upper-class affectations were perceived as effeminate by the working class, on occasion had to defend themselves against charges of homosexual advances in pastoral relationships they argued were merely "brotherly." At the same time, liberal Protestantism continued to make singificant inroads in various denominations, seminaries and other religious instituions, paving the way for a conservative retrenchment in fundamentalist and evangelical forms of Protestant Christianity.

Evangelical and fundamentalist movements. Evangelicals encompass a wide array of traditions and communities, including the various Baptist conventions, Christian Reformed Churches, some of the regional synods of Lutheranism, the Evangelical Free Church, the Salvation Army, Assemblies of God, and Pentecostal churches. Fundamentalists appear in all of these denominations and others, tracing their origins to a late nineteenth- and early twentieth-century movement calling for a return to the "fundamentals" of Christian faith.

The reliance on pre- or anti-critical readings of the Bible, together with a general suspicion of modern cultural developments, renders these forms of Protestant Christianity the least likely to welcome openly LGBT members; indeed, many of these denominations remain some of the strongest opponents of both civil rights and ecclesial participation for LGBT people. Historically black churches (such as the African Methodist Episcopal Church, the Church of God in Christ, the Northern Baptist Convention, and a variety of "Holiness" churches), while at the forefront of racial and ethnic equality movements, tend to replicate evangelical and fundamentalist rejections of same-sex sexual practices.

The hazards of generalization. Even where these generalizations prove helpful, the temptation to map American Protestantism along neatly defined liberal and conservative lines deserves resisting. Official statements by a given denomination do not always reflect the views of its members. The Unitarians, for example, after they joined with the Universalist Church of America in 1961, were some of the first to embrace officially the ordination of lesbian and gay ministers and to permit the religious celebration of same-sex "holy unions." Yet a 1988 survey of the undeniably LGBT-positive Unitarian Universalist Association revealed a mix of opinions regarding LGBT people, and even some opposition to their ordination.

On the other hand, some evangelicals, even those who hold to literal readings of the Bible, concede the pos-

Ordination Policies in Mainline Protestant Churches

In the 1970s, most mainline Protestant denominations had spoken clearly in favor of guaranteeing civil rights for lesbian and gay people. However, this posture did not automatically translate into "ecclesial rights" with reference to ordination or marriage (the blessing of "holy unions"). The following excerpts, drawn from representative denominational statements, illustrate this split, as well as the ambiguity at work in many of these policies. This ambiguity has caused considerable confusion regarding the status of LGBT people within these churches.

The General Convention of the Episcopal Church, 1979:

> There should be no barrier to the ordination of qualified persons of either heterosexual or homosexual orientation whose behavior the Church considers wholesome. We re-affirm the traditional teaching of the Church on marriage, marital fidelity and sexual chastity as the standard of Christian sexual morality. Candidates for ordination are expected to conform to this standard. Therefore, we believe it is not appropriate for this Church to ordain a practicing homosexual, or any person who is engaged in heterosexual relations outside of marriage.

The 1991 General Convention passed further resolutions declaring heterosexuality as normative, yet calling for further study and dialogue at the diocesan level on questions regarding homosexuality.

The Presbyterian Church (U.S.A.), 1983, adopting a previous statement, in 1978, of the United Presbyterian Church in the U.S.A.:

> There is no legal, social, or moral justification for denying homosexual persons access to the basic requirements of human social existence. . . . [Yet] even where the homosexual orientation has not been consciously sought or chosen, it is neither a gift from God nor a state nor a condition like race; it is a result of our living in a fallen world. . . . Therefore our present understanding of God's will precludes the ordination of persons who do not repent of homosexual practice.

United Methodist Church, *The Book of Discipline*, 1992:

> Homosexual persons no less than heterosexual persons are individuals of sacred worth. All persons need the ministry and guidance of the Church in their struggles for human fulfillment. . . . Although we do not condone the practice of homosexuality and consider this practice incompatible with Christian teaching, we affirm that God's grace is available to all. We commit ourselves to be in ministry for and with all persons. . . . We are committed to support . . . rights and liberties for homosexual persons. . . . Moreover, we support efforts to stop violence and other forms of coercion against gays and lesbians.

sibility that biblical writers did not address the modern phenomenon of homosexual identities. Furthermore, between the obviously welcoming and the clearly hostile positions, many churches occupy a broad "mainline" space presenting ambiguous and complex positions on questions of sexual morality.

Gary David Comstock's research suggests a range of religious responses to homosexuality falling into four possible types: rejecting, semi-rejecting, semi-affirming, and affirming (see sidebar). The nuances of difference among these types infuse any attempt to generalize about Protestant Christianity with significant risk.

From the 1950s through the 1970s: Mobilization for Social Justice

Councils on Homosexuality in the Church. Post–World War II America witnessed an unprecedented surge in LGBT visibility, spurred on by the organization of "homophile associations," new sociological and psychological research, and the sexual revolution of the 1960s, all of which contributed to a re-examination of biblical texts and church practices within Protestant traditions. In 1948, with the help of a Unitarian minister, Harry Hay founded the Mattachine Society in Los Angeles, one of the first homophile associations, which later convened its first national convention, in 1953, at the First Universalist Church in Los Angeles.

The Daughters of Bilitis, an association of lesbians, was founded in 1955 in San Francisco. Two of its founding members—Phyllis Lyon and Del Martin—later worked with Cecil Williams, pastor of Glide Memorial Methodist Church (also in San Francisco), to establish the widely influential, interdenominational Council on Religion and the Homosexual. Organized in 1964 to facilitate dialogue on homosexuality in the churches, the council quickly focused its energies toward advocacy for social justice.

In 1965, the council published its *Brief on Injustices* to "expose a pattern of social, legal, and economic oppression of" homosexuals. The fact that such a report emerged from the clergy helped generate sweeping changes in the homophobic policies of San Francisco's police department. The work of the council prompted the establishment of similar organizations in Dallas, Los Angeles, Washington, D.C., Seattle, and elsewhere.

All of these organizations worked closely with clergy and lay leaders from a variety of denominations, including the United Church of Christ, the Episcopal Church, the Lutheran Church of America, and the Methodist Church. Shortly thereafter, the First National Conference on Religion and the Homosexual convened in 1971 at the Interchurch Center in New York City, with seventy participants from eleven denominations, and captured the attention of a wide range of news media.

Key Publications. The emergence of supportive clergy and advocacy groups was fostered by several key publications. A breakthrough occurred in 1955 with the appearance in Great Britain of *Homosexuality and the Western Christian Tradition* by Derrick Sherwin Bailey. This was the first scholarly work to challenge the standard interpretations of biblical passages on homosexuality and to catalogue the social and political oppression such interpretations had generated.

Two years later, the *Wolfenden Report,* published by the British Committee on Homosexual Offenses and Prostitution cited Bailey's work and contributed to the repeal of sodomy laws in Great Britain and in some parts of the United States. In 1960, Robert Wood, an ordained United Church of Christ minister, published *Christ and the Homosexual.* This was not only the first book to claim that one need not be heterosexual to be Christian, it was also the first book written by an openly gay person using his real name to make such a claim.

Even more galvanizing was *Toward a Quaker View of Sex* (1963), the first published report by an established, traditional religious organization calling for a reevaluation of Christian teaching on questions of homosexuality. Likewise, in 1967, Norman Pittenger, an Anglican theologian, published *Time for Consent: A Christian Approach to Homosexuality,* in which he argued for the full acceptance of homosexual persons within the church. This book influenced church discussions well beyond Anglicanism and the Episcopal Church. And in 1972, Ralph Blair, an evangelical minister, published *An Evangelical Look at Homosexuality,* a pamphlet in which he argued for the compatibility of same-sex sexual relations and the practice of evangelical Christian faith.

Response and reaction. These fresh ideas on sexuality urged responses in both directions, from those who were impatient for the change that such ideas promised and those who were alarmed by the momentum of that change. In 1968, Troy Perry, a former Pentecostal minister, founded the Universal Fellowship of Metropolitan Community Churches (MCC) specifically for lesbians and gay men. While he supposed that the need for a separate denomination would gradually dissipate as mainline churches grew more accepting, MCC has continued to exist and to grow (even though it was refused admission as a member of the National Council of Churches), with congregations in every major U.S. metropolitan center as well as in many suburban and rural areas.

The conservative response to such moves was typified in the late 1970s by the "Save Our Children" campaign, spearheaded by Anita Bryant in Dade County, Florida, to oppose civil rights legislation for homosexuals. Bryant's explicitly evangelical Christian rhetoric in this campaign reflected the emergence, at roughly the same time, of the Religious Right in American politics. Television evangelists such as Jerry Falwell and Pat Robertson, local pastors, and conservative political activists began mobilizing to counter the "decadence" of American morality, exemplified in their view by the increasing tolerance of the "homosexual lifestyle."

LGBT Protestants soon began creating their own caucuses and lobbying groups within their respective denominations. Some of the more prominent of these groups include Integrity (Episcopalians), American Baptists Concerned, Lutherans Concerned, Evangelicals Concerned, More Light (Presbyterians), A Common Bond (Jehovah's Witnesses), Affirmation (United Methodists), and Affirmation (Mormons). In the 1980s and 1990s, similar groups emerged for the opposite purpose: to provide a network of religious support for those wishing to change their homosexual orientation. These were broadly labeled as "ex-gay ministries," and mostly functioned apart from established denominations. They included Exodus International, Homosexuals Anonymous, Regeneration, and Desert Stream.

From the 1980s to the Present: Prospects for Spiritual Practice

Early mobilization on behalf of LGBT people in Protestant churches focused almost exclusively on securing justice in such secular spheres as housing and employment, and rarely on their full religious inclusion within the life of the church. This split between civil rights and ecclesial participation is reflected in the policy statements of some mainline Protestant denominations regarding ordination.

protestant positions on homosexuality: sample denominations

A typology based on the research of Gary David Comstock in *Unrepentant, Self-Affirming, Practicing: Lesbian/Bisexual/Gay People within Organized Religion* (1996).

Position	Denominations
REJECTING Based on select biblical texts, both homosexual activity and homosexual orientation are believed to be contrary to the divine purpose in creation, and are therefore considered sinful and condemned by God.	Southern Baptist Convention, Lutheran Church—Missouri and Wisconsin Synods, National Association of Evangelicals, Assemblies of God, Pentecostal and Holiness Churches, Jehovah's Witnesses, Church of Jesus Christ of Latter Day Saints (Mormon), Church of the Nazarene, Seventh-Day Adventists
SEMI-REJECTING Rejecting homosexual acts but not homosexual people. Either a reorientation toward heterosexual relationships, or sexual abstinence, is required.	Presbyterian Church (U.S.A.), American Baptist Churches in the U.S.A., Disciples of Christ, United Methodist Church
SEMI-ACCEPTING Relies on the primacy of female/male complementarity and the procreative purpose of sexuality to understand homosexual orientation as an acceptable but inferior way of life.	Episcopal Church (U.S.A.), Evangelical Lutheran Church of America
ACCEPTING Understands homosexuality as a God-given part of nature's diversity, and encourages full participation of LGBT people in the life of the church.	Universal Fellowship of Metropolitan Community Churches, Unitarian Universalist Association, Religious Society of Friends (Quakers), United Church of Christ

Addressing Gay Roles in the Church. In 1989, the House of Bishops of the Episcopal Church confronted a crisis in church order after one of its own ordained an openly gay man, Robert Williams, to the priesthood in defiance of the church's 1979 General Convention resolution discouraging such action. After the offending bishop faced a heresy trial (the charges were later dropped), the House of Bishops "agreed to disagree" on this matter. On 7 June 2003, the Rev. Canon V. Gene Robinson of New Hampshire was elected the denomination's first openly gay bishop. A 1986 statement from a self-study committee of the Lutheran Church of America reflects a similar inability to reach consensus: "This church can neither condemn, nor ignore, nor praise and affirm homosexuality." Likewise, the Mormon Church eventually softened its more aggressive 1970s posture of calling homosexuality "an ugly sin" and in the 1980s acknowledged its own lack of understanding in these issues by encouraging only celibacy, rather than reparative therapies, for homosexuals.

Other denominations have been far less ambiguous in their positions. In 1976, the Southern Baptist Convention urged its churches "not to afford the practice of homosexuality any degree of approval," and in 1985, it declared its opposition to identifying homosexuality "as a minority with attendant benefits or advantages" and affirmed its position that the Bible "condemns such practice as sin." At the opposite end of the spectrum, as early as 1972, the United Church of Christ (UCC) ordained William Johnson, marking the first ordination of a publicly open gay man in the history of Christianity (he later founded the gay caucus of the UCC). In 1991, the UCC passed a resolution "affirming gay, lesbian, and bisexual persons and their ministries," and calling upon their congregations "to facilitate the ordination and placement of qualified lesbian, gay, and bisexual candidates."

The urgency of the debate over ordination and on questions of marriage (the blessing of "holy unions") was fueled by a steady stream of autobiographical accounts in the 1980s and 1990s by openly LGBT clergy and those who had been denied ordination. These included Carter Heyward, who was among the first group of women ordained as priests in the Episcopal Church; Chris Glaser, who fought unsuccessfully to change the ordination policies of the Presbyterian Church; Rose Mary Denman, who lost her clergy status in an ecclesiastical trial of the United Methodist Church; Antonio Feliz, a Mormon bishop who came out as a gay man; and Mel White, a former speechwriter for Jerry Falwell and other leaders of the Religious Right, who made headlines in major media outlets when he came out as a gay man. (White went on to serve as dean at the Cathedral of Hope, an MCC congregation in Dallas.)

Toward a Wider Role. Even as the history of Protestant debates on sexuality resist generalization, the trajectory over the last century points to a much wider role for LGBT people within the life of Protestant churches than the World War II generation could have imagined. Many LGBT Christians now seek to move beyond the debates over tolerance and find ways to offer their gifts for the spiritual and intellectual well-being of their churches.

The establishment, in the late 1980s, of the Lesbian-Feminist Group and the Gay Men's Issues in Religion Group in the American Academy of Religion, the largest professional association of religious scholars in North America, has resulted in numerous publications on a wide range of topics in religion, sexuality, and gender. Conferences, retreats, and informal gatherings—such as the triennual ecumenical conference of the Welcoming Church Movement, launched in 2000 and called "Witness Our Welcome"—have likewise appeared to foster a new level of integration and contribution for LGBT Christians. Pioneering work, such as that of Virginia Ramey Mollenkott in *Omnigender: A Trans-religious Approach* (2001), has also begun to appear on the religious implications of transgender experience, a field of study largely overlooked in the history of Protestant debates on sexuality.

Giving due attention to the relation between bifurcated gender categories and the discourse on diverse sexual practices represents an important frontier for Protestant theologies, as suggested by Jordan's insights on the social and theological construction of sodomy. And while the full participation of LGBT Christians in every Protestant tradition is by no means guaranteed, American Christianity and culture has clearly undergone a significant shift when many of the twenty-first century voices advocating for LGBT justice come from openly LGBT ministers in Protestant churches.

Bibliography

Chauncey, Jr. George. "Christian Brotherhood or Sexual Perversion? Homosexual Identities And The Construction Of Sexual Boundaries In The World War I Era." In *Hidden From History: Reclaiming The Gay And Lesbian Past*, Ed. Martin Bauml Duberman, Martha Vicinus, and George Chauncey, Jr. New York: Nal Books, 1989.

Comstock, Gary David. *Gay Theology without Apology.* Cleveland, Ohio: Pilgrim Press, 1993.

———. *Unrepentant, Self-Affirming, Practicing: Lesbian/Bisexual/Gay People within Organized Religion.* New York: Continuum, 1996.

Countryman, William L., and M. R. Ritley. *Gifted by Otherness: Gay and Lesbian Christians in the Churches.* Harrisburg, Penn.: Morehouse, 2001.

Denman, Rose Mary. *Let My People In: A Lesbian Minister Tells of Her Struggles to Live Openly and Maintain Her Ministry.* New York: Harper, 1990.

Feliz, Antonio A. *Out of the Bishop's Closet: A Call to Heal Ourselves, Each Other, and Our World.* San Francisco: Aurora, 1988.

Glaser, Chris. *Uncommon Calling: A Gay Man's Struggle to Serve the Church.* New York: Harper, 1988.

Jordan, Mark D. *The Invention of Sodomy in Christian Theology.* Chicago: University of Chicago Press, 1997.

Jung, Patricia Beattie, and Ralph F. Smith. *Heterosexism: An Ethical Challenge.* Albany: State University of New York Press, 1993.

Melton, Gordon, ed. *The Churches Speak on Homosexuality: Official Statements from Religious Bodies and Ecumenical Organizations.* Detroit: Gale Research, 1991.

Mollenkott, Virginia R. *Omnigender: A Trans-religious Approach.* Cleveland, Ohio: Pilgrim Press, 2001.

Rudy, Kathy. *Sex and the Church: Gender, Homosexuality, and the Transformation of Christian Ethics.* Boston: Beacon Press, 1997.

Siker, Jeffrey S., ed. *Homosexuality in the Church: Both Sides of the Debate.* Louisville, Ky.: Westminster John Knox Press, 1994.

Tanis, Justin. *Transgendered: Theology, Ministry, and Communities of Faith.* Cleveland: Pilgrim Press, 2003.

White, Mel. *Stranger at the Gates: To Be Gay and Christian in America.* New York: Simon and Schuster, 1994.

Jay Emerson Johnson

See also AFRICAN AMERICAN RELIGION AND SPIRITUALITY; CHURCHES, TEMPLES, AND RELIGIOUS GROUPS; DALY, MARY; HETEROSEXISM AND HOMOPHOBIA; HOMOPHILE MOVEMENT; JONES, PROPHET; NEW RIGHT; PERRY, TROY; SAME-SEX INSTITUTIONS; SODOMY, BUGGERY, CRIMES AGAINST NATURE, DISORDERLY CONDUCT, AND LEWD AND LASCIVIOUS LAW AND POLICY; WIGGLESWORTH, MICHAEL.

PSYCHOLOGY, PSYCHIATRY, PSYCHOANALYSIS, AND SEXOLOGY

In the 1880s, American physicians and other scientists began investigating "sexual perversion." They were engaged in sexology, the scientific study of human sexual behavior, a field that emerged in the nineteenth century. Investigations of sexual behavior were also central to psychiatry, a medical specialty that diagnoses disorders of the mind and behavior; psychoanalysis, the school of clinical practice and theory established by Sigmund Freud; and psychology, the science of mental life and behavior.

Until the 1970s, most of the theories and practices developed by psychiatrists, psychoanalysts, psychologists, and other sexologists described homosexual and transgender behavior as pathological. There were some researchers in these fields, however, who took different positions. LGBT people occasionally produced, sometimes accepted, often ignored, periodically welcomed, and frequently confronted the conclusions of these experts. Scholars disagree on whether scientific and medical research on sexuality and gender can ever be liberating. Jennifer Terry, for instance, describes the scientific study of homosexuality as either oppressive or normalizing. Even at its more progressive, she warns, it is dangerous to subject sexual behavior to the scientific gaze. In contrast, Henry Minton asserts that gay men and lesbians successfully used emancipatory strands in American sexology to win acceptance. Joanne Meyerowitz points out that in contrast to gay men and lesbians, transsexuals initiated and funded much of the research on transsexuality and believed themselves dependent on science to meet their needs.

Inversion in the Late Nineteenth Century

In the late nineteenth century, American psychiatrists began publishing accounts of same-sex desire in medical journals. They drew upon European sexological literature, including that of Richard von Krafft-Ebing, a German psychiatrist, and Havelock Ellis, a British physician, as well as their own observations. An English version of Krafft-Ebing's *Psychopathia Sexualis* (1886) was first published in the United States in 1892, four years after his article "Perversion of the Sexual Instincts" ran in a major American psychiatric journal. Ellis's early articles on homosexuality appeared in American medical journals, and his study *Sexual Inversion* was published in the United States in 1901. Until 1920, his writings on sexuality were more widely read in the United States than were those of Freud. Until the 1890s, when the terms heterosexuality and homosexuality first appeared in the United States, sexologists labeled same-sex desire as "inversion" or "contrary sexual feeling." They asserted that an individual who expressed sexual feelings for a member of the same sex had the psyche of the opposite sex and was a sexual invert. Doctors assumed this inversion also took a physical form; inverts were effeminate men who desired masculine men or masculine women who desired feminine women. In this way, sexual desire remained heterosexual even if the bodies were not. The experts disagreed about whether inversion was caused by congenital factors or acquired through environmental influences. They also disputed whether inversion was pathological or a harmless variation.

American psychiatrists published a number of case studies of homosexuality in the late nineteenth century. They presented a harsher view of homosexuality than European sexologists. Their studies initially drew on observations of working-class Americans. Articles on female sexual inverts described women who had passed as men and were now institutionalized in mental asylums or prisons. Increasingly visible gay urban subcultures drew their attention, and they described drag balls and other places where male sexual inverts congregated. Experts feared that sexual perversion was spreading and blamed several factors, including the dangerous influences of immigration and class and race mixing. Many of them believed that sexual perversion was a sign of degeneration and advocated treatment, criminal penalties, or even sterilization.

The New Woman

Other social changes led psychiatrists and other sexologists to pathologize romantic friendships between women. By the late nineteenth century, many white middle-class American women were attending college and were working and living independent of men. Half of those attending women's colleges at the turn of the century never married, and many shared their lives with female partners. These women, many of whom became involved in the movement for female suffrage, were known as New Women. In 1895, Ellis published an article in an American medical journal, "Sexual Inversion in Women," which warned that feminism was causing increasing numbers of women to become lesbians. While Ellis believed that homosexuality in its congenital form was a benign variation deserving acceptance, he viewed "acquired" homosexuality, particularly in women, as a danger. Ellis held a much harsher view of lesbianism than he did of male homosexuality. He described congenital lesbians as masculine women who seduced heterosexual women and asserted that lesbianism was spreading rapidly. This article came on the heels of a growing American focus on lesbianism. In 1892, medical articles and national news stories analyzed the case of Alice Mitchell, a wealthy young woman from Memphis who had murdered her female lover.

American psychiatrists increasingly warned of the dangers of same-sex sexuality and, together with European sexologists, developed new medical labels: invert, pervert, and homosexual. As Michel Foucault and other scholars have noted, these terms described a type of person, in contrast to earlier notions of "sodomy" as a behavior, not an identity. Historians disagree over whether this psychiatric and sexological literature created the homosexual or codified an existing identity. Lillian Faderman believes that this literature created a lesbian identity and subculture, but at the great cost of pathologizing hitherto respected female romantic friendships. George Chauncey argues that sexologists described, but certainly did not invent, male homosexuals, who already had identities and subcultures. Lisa Duggan sees a circular process at work, whereby women in same-sex relationships became subjects of sensational media stories, which in turn became medical case studies, which in turn influenced the ways women conceptualized their identities. Siobhan Somerville argues that the new sexual taxonomies developed in the context of the classification impulses and discourses of scientific racism.

Sigmund Freud's Views on Homosexuality

In the 1910s and 1920s, the psychoanalytic theory of Freud began to enter American psychiatry and society. Freud first presented his views on sexual inversion in *Three Essays on the Theory of Sexuality* (1905). This work was translated into English by American psychoanalyst Abraham A. Brill and published in the United States in 1910, a year after Freud's only American visit, during which he gave a series of public lectures at Clark University. Freudian concepts of psychosexual development gained more of a foothold in America in the 1920s. Until World War II, however, most American psychiatrists were remarkably eclectic. They used psychoanalytic theory in combination with somatic theory, behaviorism, and other schools of thought.

Freud's views on homosexuality were complex and inconsistent, with both radical and normalizing elements. He distinguished between sexual aim (the preferred erotic activity) and sexual object (the type of partner desired). While he believed that inversion involved a deflection of sexual aim away from the ideal goal of reproductive heterosexual coitus, he did not view inverts as psychologically abnormal and did not believe that homosexuality was a mental illness. All human beings, he asserted, were constitutionally bisexual and were thus capable of sexual involvement with either sex. As a result, exclusive heterosexuality required as much of an explanation as did exclusive homosexuality. By claiming that reproductive heterosexuality was the result of a difficult developmental process that could have other outcomes, including inversion, Freud destabilized the idea of normative sexuality. While he felt that inversion was caused by arrested sexual development, he did not believe, as later psychoanalysts did, that this stunted other aspects of the personality. Inversion, he posited, was caused by both acquired and congenital factors that were outside the control of the individual. For that reason, he believed that psychoanalysts should not attempt to convert homosexuals into heterosexuals. Against the wishes of most of his colleagues, he also argued that homosexuals should not be barred from psychoanalytic training.

American psychiatrists promoted a much more normative sexuality and therefore seized upon the more conservative elements of Freudian thought. As Elizabeth Lunbeck explains, they built their discipline by studying matters of everyday life, such as marriage and sex. They needed to domesticate Freudian theory in order to make it useful. Not only were American psychoanalysts more concerned than Freud was with determining normality and abnormality, but they were also more optimistic about treatment, since they gave more emphasis to the influence of environmental factors, especially parenting.

Freud published his first full essay on lesbianism, "The Psychogenesis of a Case of Homosexuality in a Woman," in 1920. Reflecting his misogynist views, he described lesbians as masculine inverts and psychiatrically damaged. His relatively tolerant views of homosexuals primarily applied to men. Before the mid-1920s, psychiatrists generally viewed lesbians as masculine seductresses of heterosexual women rather than defining them by their choice of same-sex sexual partners. It was, as Lunbeck points out, the lesbian, not the gay man, whom psychiatrists defined as a "psychopath" in this period.

George Chauncey claims that by the 1920s most medical and scientific experts differentiated gender inversion from homosexuality, recognizing that some "inverts" were heterosexual and that some homosexuals were gender normative. Other historians have questioned whether such a distinct shift occurred. Donna Penn asserts that lesbianism remained closely associated with masculinity by many experts and lesbians well into the 1960s. Moreover some scholars of transgenderism argue that historians have falsely assumed that all "inverts" in the sexological literature were homosexual. Many of them, they point out, may have been transgendered.

Sexologists Study Lesbianism

While sexologists and psychiatrists had pathologized female romantic friendships and developed a stereotype of the lesbian as an aggressive masculine woman, alternative and more benign descriptions of lesbianism were published in the 1920s and 1930s. In *Factors in the Sex Life of Twenty-Two Hundred American Woman* (1929), sociologist Katharine Bement Davis asserted that lesbianism was widespread: 25 percent of the 1,200 college-educated white single women she surveyed had experienced an intense emotional same-sex relationship that included some form of sexual expression; 15 percent of married women had engaged in a sexual relationship with a woman. For Davis, lesbianism was a common and acceptable form of sexual expression and did not mark a woman as abnormal. Davis pointed out that her subjects were "normal individuals," unlike the institutionalized and clinical subjects upon which previous studies of sexuality had relied. Exemplifying the interdisciplinary nature of American sex research, Davis included female psychologists and psychiatrists on her research committee.

Another major study of American women was conducted by gynecologist Robert Latou Dickinson, who used sex surveys he collected between 1880 and 1920. Coauthored by Lura Beam, who had a background in applied psychology and a life-long relationship with another woman, *The Single Woman: A Medical Study in Sex Education* (1934) included a chapter on homosexuality. Although he detected lesbianism in only a few dozen cases among his two thousand female patients, Dickinson said that he had found no distinguishing features in these women and dismissed several stereotypes about lesbians. Dickinson claimed that women who had sex with other women were no more masculine than his other patients and that all who had been asked had told him that neither partner took the "male part" during sex. Almost all had married later, which only proved, Dickinson and Beam said, the theory of innate bisexuality. Most studies of homosexuality, they pointed out, had been done on men and on "psychopathic" cases of imprisoned or hospitalized individuals. An "effort to establish a type," they said, "is premature" (p. 204).

In an essay titled "The Gynecology of Homosexuality," which was included in psychiatrist George Henry's *Sex Variants* (1941), Dickinson noted that thirty-two of the forty female "sex variants" described in Henry's study had heterosexual experience. "Having tried both," he wrote, "they preferred women both as sexual partners and as loving comrades"(p. 1097). Dickinson claimed that women became lesbians because of dissatisfaction with heterosexual intercourse. He urged that lesbian sexual techniques, which provided a higher level of sexual satisfaction, be studied to improve marital sexuality. Alfred C. Kinsey later also asserted that men had much to learn from lesbian sexual practices. Unlike Kinsey, however, Dickinson felt that marital sex was preferred, and his research on, and acceptance of, homosexuality was in the service of improving heterosexual relations in marriage.

Studying Sexuality and Gender in the 1930s

In 1935, Dickinson launched a massive study of homosexual behavior, to be conducted by the Committee for the Study of Sex Variants. Dickinson established this project in order to build upon the three hundred case histories of lesbians that Jan Gay, a lesbian, had collected. Dickinson felt that this research needed to be legitimated by a committee of experts. Many of the nation's most prominent psychiatrists, psychologists, physicians, and social scientists joined the committee. They chose Henry to run the study of two hundred lesbians and gay men. He, like most other American psychiatrists engaged in sex research, used an eclectic methodology that included psychiatric interviews, psychological testing, and physical examinations.

Henry concluded that homosexuality was a form of sexual inversion caused by a combination of congenital and environmental factors. The most important etiological factor was having parents who did not follow proper gender roles. Henry, like Freud, believed that homosexual desires were universal; unlike Freud, he believed that homosexuality was a form of social maladjustment and urged that it be prevented by monitoring warning signs in effeminate boys and masculine girls.

Henry gave his subjects several psychological tests, including the Masculinity-Femininity Test (Attitude Interest Analysis Survey) developed by psychologists Lewis M. Terman and Catherine Cox Miles. In their study of sex differences, *Sex and Personality* (1936), Terman and Miles explained that since homosexuals almost always displayed inverted gender characteristics, a male homosexual would earn a score on the test much closer to the average female score. To investigate this, Terman's graduate student E. Lowell Kelly tested seventy-seven "passive male homosexuals," who took the "role of the female" in homosexual sex, and found that they had strikingly "feminine" scores (Terman and Miles, p. 240). All of the "passive male homosexuals" he interviewed, almost half of whom were prostitutes, would be considered transgendered today. They called themselves by female names, many passed as women, several worked as drag queens, and at least one had legally married his male partner. He also gave the test to forty-six male prisoners in Alcatraz who were serving sentences for sodomy. Kelly presumed that they were "active male homosexuals" and found that they had more "masculine" scores than did average men. The authors concluded that only passive males and active females were true homosexuals.

Based on a comparison of the scores of the passive male homosexuals and a group of "normal" males that consisted of ninety-eight junior high school students,

Terman and Miles developed a tentative scale to measure male sexual inversion. They thought that it could be used to detect homosexuality. Like Henry, they believed that gender behavior should be monitored to prevent homosexuality and avoid the "difficulties of adjustment as a direct result of their deviation." They urged that boys with a high feminine score be given preventive treatment to "direct their sexuality into normal channels." It is from this group of inverts, they warned, "that homosexuals are chiefly recruited." They were unsuccessful in finding enough lesbian subjects to develop a test to give to tomboys. Female inverts, they bemoaned, had "been little studied except by the psychoanalysts" (Terman and Miles, pp. 467-468).

Shifting Psychoanalytic Views of the Homosexual

While American psychiatrists and psychologists in the 1930s increasingly warned of the maladjustment suffered by homosexuals, many of their writings exhibited sympathy toward their subjects. Homosexuality, they believed, while preventable if detected early in childhood, was not curable in adults. In contrast, beginning in the 1930s psychoanalysists came to view homosexuality more as pathology. For the next thirty years, psychoanalytic descriptions of homosexuality would become increasingly negative and culturally more powerful, affecting the lives of most American LGB people.

With the rise of Nazism in Germany in the 1930s, the center of psychoanalysis moved from Vienna to New York City. Psychoanalysis gained authority in the United States with the arrival of emigré analysts, who were central figures in the field. Kenneth Lewes points out that as psychoanalysis became Americanized, it became much more rigid and judgmental about homosexuality, dropping Freud's cosmopolitan and humane views on the subject.

The most significant change was developed by Sandor Rado, an emigré analyst from Berlin, who had grown increasingly critical of Freud and wished to make psychoanalysis more acceptable to Americans. In 1940, he published "A Critical Examination of the Concept of Bisexuality," in which he dismissed Freud's belief in innate homosexuality. Rado asserted that heterosexual object choice was the inevitable result of psychosexual development unless it was blocked. Only environmental factors in early childhood could explain how homosexuality, which he labeled a perversion, could emerge. Psychoanalytic treatment could uncover the cause, and thereby cure, homosexuality with what he called "reparative adjustment," a form of therapy still in use as of the early 2000s.

Almost all psychoanalysts for the next several decades based their views of homosexuality on Rado's article. Few retained Freud's tolerance for homosexuality or his skepticism about treatment. Their view that homosexuality was a mental illness that could and should be cured underwrote not only lengthy and expensive psychoanalysis of homosexuals, but also a range of harsh somatic treatments used in association with psychotherapy by a large number of psychoanalysts, psychiatrists, and psychologists. Homosexuals were subjected to lobotomies, castration, hormonal treatment, and electrical and chemical shock therapy. Beginning in the 1950s, for example, psychologists and psychiatrists treated homosexuals with aversion conditioning therapy based on the use of nausea-inducing chemicals that were administered with images of homosexual sex. It was the presentation of a paper on aversion therapy at the 1970 American Psychiatric Association (APA) conference that led to the first LGB protest at the association's annual meetings.

Psychiatry Goes to War

The hostile view of homosexuality gained strength during and after World War II. Psychiatric screening of soldiers began in the summer of 1940, largely through the efforts of psychiatrist Harry Stack Sullivan. While Sullivan, a closeted gay man, did not believe that homosexuality was pathological and did not include it among the mental disorders that should disqualify soldiers from serving in the military, other psychiatrists added homosexuality to the list. By May 1941, psychiatrists were told to screen soldiers at induction stations for homosexuality, now considered a "psychopathic personality disorder" (Bérubé, p. 12). Previously, soldiers had been court-martialed and imprisoned if convicted of sodomy, but the new screening policies, which excluded homosexuals from entering the service if they were detected and gave them undesirable discharges if they were diagnosed while in the military, affected a larger number of people.

As Allan Bérubé points out, many psychiatrists involved in military screening efforts, including prominent psychoanalyst William C. Menninger, held relatively sympathetic views on homosexuality and tried to ameliorate military policy. In the end, they were unsuccessful. All American psychiatrists, however, gained prestige through the screening and treatment programs established during the war. The increased status psychiatry garnered, points out John D'Emilio, brought the medical view of homosexuality to the attention of the public. It also made psychiatrists culturally respected figures and widened the domain of their authority. They now saw themselves, and were seen by the public, as experts on a range of social and political issues.

By the end of the war, the leaders in American psychiatry were psychoanalysts. While they agreed that homosexuality was a developmental disorder, a number of more liberal psychoanalysts, like Menninger, viewed it as a regrettable yet widespread maladjustment. But this more tolerant view was increasingly occluded by the work of psychoanalysts who harshly condemned homosexuality.

Kinsey Challenges Psychoanalysts

Sex researcher Alfred C. Kinsey counted upon this more liberal group of psychiatrists and psychoanalysts to assist him with his challenge to the psychoanalytic orthodoxy on homosexuality. Like Freud, Kinsey believed that people were capable of responding to all types of sexual stimuli and were not defined psychologically by their sexual behavior. Going further than Freud, he asserted that there were no heterosexuals or homosexuals, only heterosexual or homosexual behaviors. Sexual behavior and desires, Kinsey believed, could only be understood as existing on a continuum, with most people falling in between the extremes of exclusive heterosexuality or homosexuality. While Freud viewed reproductive coitus as the ideal form of sexual behavior, Kinsey asserted that all consensual forms of sexuality were equally acceptable.

Kinsey's research was based on interviews, and he used sympathy and a nonjudgmental approach to win trust. He was the first sexologist to fully explore gay subcultures and gain the enthusiastic cooperation of gay men. *Sexual Behavior in the Human Male* (1948) and *Sexual Behavior in the Human Female* (1953) not only claimed that large percentages of Americans had engaged in homosexual behavior, but also presented radical arguments deconstructing notions of normality. Moreover, Kinsey repeatedly asserted that his findings disproved many central tenets of psychoanalytic theory. Chief among them was the view that homosexuality was abnormal. Behavior this widespread among humans and animals of other species, Kinsey said, could not be considered abnormal or unnatural. He confidently believed that psychoanalysts would revise their theory in light of his data.

Despite the considerable amount of ink psychoanalysts spilled criticizing Kinsey's interview methods and statistical analysis, it was his discussion of homosexuality that evoked their fury. Psychoanalysts in their reviews of *Sexual Behavior in the Human Male* repeatedly used the same analogy: just because the common cold was widespread did not mean that it was normal. They disputed Kinsey's data on the percentages of American men who had engaged in homosexual behavior and feared that homosexuals would be reassured by his findings, as many of them were, and no longer seek treatment to become heterosexual. Psychoanalytic theory on homosexuality took its most homophobic turn between 1948 and the late 1960s (in the midst of the Cold War), but the data-filled doubts cast by Kinsey opened a space for activists in the homophile movement to begin organizing for liberation.

Homosexuality on the Couch

During the 1950s, psychoanalysis helped to impose and legitimate the political repression and social conformity that marked the decade. In 1953, as the result of U.S. Senate sex perversion hearings held in 1950, President Dwight D. Eisenhower signed an executive order listing "sexual perversion" as grounds for dismissal from the civil service. Numerous sexual psychopath laws were passed by states, which led to the arrest of increasing numbers of gay men for consensual sexual behavior. Military policies toward LGB people became harsher. The language of pathology psychoanalysts used to describe homosexuality buttressed views that it was immoral and criminal.

Psychoanalysis was increasingly popularized in the 1950s. Edmund Bergler, who in the 1930s had helped run Vienna's Freud Clinic, wrote a number of books and articles, such as *Homosexuality: Disease or Way of Life?* (1956), attacking Kinsey's view of homosexuality. "There are no happy homosexuals," Bergler claimed (quoted in Lewes, p. 114). Homosexuals were "disagreeable people" who collected injustices and rabidly feared the opposite sex. But in 99.9 percent of cases, Bergler said, their dire condition was curable.

In 1962, Irving Bieber, a more highly respected psychoanalyst, published a study, *Homosexuality: A Psychoanalytic Study of Male Homosexuality*, that compared 106 male homosexuals with 100 heterosexual men, all in analytic treatment. Psychoanalysts viewed his study as a scientific validation of their theories about homosexuality. Bieber claimed that his data proved that domineering mothers and detached fathers caused male homosexuality. Drawing on Rado and reversing Freud, Bieber stated that "every homosexual is a latent heterosexual" (quoted in Bayer, p. 30). He asserted that analysts had cured 27 percent of the gay men in his study. Bieber's text remained important for the next two decades and made him the most influential analyst on homosexuality until 1973. Psychoanalyst Charles Socarides also became a leading authority on homosexuality in the 1960s. He has published numerous books in which he describes it as a severe psychopathology.

Psychoanalysts had paid far less attention to lesbians, but in the 1950s this began to change. In 1954, Frank Caprio published *Female Homosexuality,* the first medical book on lesbianism. Caprio claimed that lesbians were unstable and neurotic, but promised that they could be cured. The same year, Bergler coauthored *Kinsey's Myth of Female Sexuality* with gynecologist William S. Kroger; they described lesbians as dangerous. In 1967, a study of female patients in psychoanalysis modeled on Bieber's compared lesbians and heterosexual women and claimed that half had been cured.

Psychology in the 1950s and 1960s

American psychologists in this period presented a less unified front on homosexuality. In 1951, comparative psychologists Frank Beach and Clelland Ford published *Patterns of Sexual Behavior.* Drawing on studies of sexual behavior in nonhuman primates and cross-cultural data on seventy-six cultures, they found that forty-nine societies officially sanctioned homosexual behavior, usually in the form of a transgendered role, and that other species engaged in homosexual behavior. Just as Kinsey had done, Ford and Beach destabilized views of homosexuality as abnormal and unnatural. In contrast, clinical psychologist Albert Ellis, a leading expert on homosexuality who often lectured before chapters of the Mattachine Society (a homophile organization) and wrote numerous articles for the *Mattachine Review,* told homosexuals that their condition was pathological, a "phobic response to the opposite sex," and curable if they desired change.

But members of the emerging homophile movement in the 1950s had a more favorable psychological expert to draw on, Evelyn Hooker. In 1954, Hooker began a study of homosexual and heterosexual men who were not in clinical treatment and found that no psychological differences between the two groups appeared when they were given projective tests, including the Rorschach. Challenging psychiatric thinking on homosexuality, she asserted that homosexual men were varied and psychologically healthy except for the coping strategies they had developed to deal with an extremely homophobic society. In 1967, she chaired a National Institute of Mental Health Task Force on Homosexuality, which issued a report, completed in 1969 and published in 1972, that called for the elimination of criminal laws against consensual homosexual behavior and addressed the toll social discrimination took on homosexuals.

Shifting Diagnostic Categories

In 1952, the American Psychiatric Association (APA) included homosexuality and transvestism as sexual deviations under the category of sociopathic personality disturbance in its first *Diagnostic and Statistical Manual of Mental Disorders* (DSM), which standardized psychiatric nomenclature. A second edition published in 1968, DSM-II, described transvestism and homosexuality as sexual deviations included among the personality disorders. Significantly, the category of "transsexualism" did not appear as an official diagnosis until DSM-III was published in 1980.

Joanne Meyerowitz points out that the word "transsexual" first appeared in the United States in 1949, when psychiatrist David O. Cauldwell used the term in an article for the journal *Sexology* to describe people who desired to change sex. He, like most American psychiatrists who followed, believed that transsexuality was a form of mental illness that should be treated with psychotherapy, not surgery. Christine Jorgensen's widely publicized 1952 sex-change operation in Denmark engendered a debate among experts about transsexuality. Most psychiatrists rejected Jorgensen's view that biological sex was a continuum and that transsexuals were a blend of male and female. In contrast, endocrinologist Harry Benjamin, who publicized the term "transsexual" and became the leading scholar in the field, asserted that the sexes were overlapping and supported sex-change surgery for some.

In 1964, female-to-male transsexual Reed Erickson established a foundation to support research on transsexuality. With financial help from Erickson and backing from some colleagues, psychologist John Money established the Johns Hopkins Gender Identity Clinic in 1966. This was the first major university hospital to publicly announce that it would provide sex-change operations, which led many transsexuals to seek, although few were able to obtain, sex-change surgery. Money, a behavioral psychologist, had coined the term "gender" in 1955 to describe the way individuals socially learn how to be girls or boys. In 1964, Robert J. Stoller, a psychoanalyst, developed the concept of "gender identity." In contrast to Benjamin, Stoller believed that transsexuality was caused primarily by psychological, not biological factors. The view that transsexuality is a matter of psychological sex has dominated gender identity clinics and the practices of doctors who perform sex-change surgery. As a result, transsexuals have depended on psychiatric categories to obtain sex-change operations. In contrast, by the 1960s, homosexual men and women had begun to challenge psychiatric definitions.

Political Activism and Psychoanalysis

In the mid-1960s, Frank Kameny, the president of the Washington, D.C., chapter of the Mattachine Society,

freud on homosexuality

In October 1950, Alfred C. Kinsey sent his friend Karl M. Bowman, a psychiatrist who was an associate editor of the *American Journal of Psychiatry*, a 1935 letter written in English by Sigmund Freud to an American mother of a homosexual son, who in turn had sent it to Kinsey after the publication of *Sexual Behavior in the Human Male*. Kinsey hoped the letter would convince American psychoanalysts to change their increasingly hostile view of homosexuality. The *American Journal of Psychiatry* published the letter in April 1951 ("Historical Notes, p.786–787):

April 9, 1935

"Dear Mrs. . . .

"I gather from your letter that your son is a homosexual. I am most impressed by the fact that you do not mention the term yourself in your information about him. May I question you, why you avoid it? Homosexuality is assuredly no advantage but it is nothing to be ashamed of, no vice, no degradation, it cannot be classified as an illness; we consider it to be a variation of the sexual function produced by a certain arrest of sexual development. Many highly respectable individuals of ancient and modern times have been homosexuals, several of the greatest men among them (Plato, Michelangelo, Leonardo da Vinci, etc.). It is a great injustice to persecute homosexuality as a crime and a cruelty too. If you do not believe me, read the books of Havelock Ellis.

"By asking me if I can help, you mean, I suppose, if I can abolish homosexuality and make normal heterosexuality take its place. The answer is, in a general way, we cannot promise to achieve it. In a certain number of cases we succeed in developing the blighted germs of heterosexual tendencies, which are present in every homosexual, in the majority of cases it is no more possible. It is a question of the quality and the age of the individual. The result of treatment cannot be predicted.

"What analysis can do for your son runs in a different line. If he is unhappy, neurotic, torn by conflicts, inhibited in his social life, analysis may bring him harmony, peace of mind, full efficiency, whether he remains a homosexual or gets changed. If you make up your mind he should have analysis with me—I don't expect you will—he has to come over to Vienna. I have no intention of leaving here. However, don't neglect to give me your answer."

Sincerely yours, with kind wishes,

Freud

became the first LGB activist to call for a frontal attack on psychiatric views of homosexuality. Unlike most earlier homophile activists, Kameny told LGB people that they were the real authorities on the subject of homosexuality and urged them to take a more militant stance on this, as well as other issues. In 1970, LGB protesters disrupted several panels at the annual APA meeting in San Francisco. After the conference, a sympathetic psychiatrist met with one of the organizers of the protest and convinced the association to hold a panel presented by gay men and lesbians, including Kameny, on "Lifestyles of Non-Patient Homosexuals" (Bayer, p. 106) at the next annual meeting. Following the 1971 meetings, Kameny and another panel participant pressed for the deletion of homosexuality from DSM-II.

As a result of the political efforts of LGB activists, rather than internal developments in psychiatry, the board of the APA finally agreed to remove homosexuality as a diagnostic category in December 1973. Bieber and Socarides were outraged and organized a referendum on the decision, which was held in 1974. Fifty-eight percent of the membership supported the decision, although most psychoanalysts remained vehemently opposed and continued to view homosexuality as pathological. While the APA in December 1973 also passed a civil rights resolution calling for the end of legal discrimination against homosexuals and the elimination of laws against consensual homosexuality, it was only in 1992 that the association declared that it would allow homosexuals to be trained in psychoanalytic institutes.

Developments since 1973

When it removed homosexuality as a diagnostic category, the APA replaced it with "sexual orientation disorder," a term applying to homosexuals who wished to become heterosexual. In 1978, this diagnosis was changed to "ego dystonic homosexuality," which was finally removed in 1986. The current edition, DSM-IV, no longer includes the term "transsexualism," although the desire to physically change sex is included under "gender identity disorder" (Meyerowitz, p. 336), a category many transsexuals rely on to obtain the medical help they want. For many years before the removal of homosexuality as a diagnostic category, LGB psychiatrists socialized unofficially at the APA convention, calling themselves Gay-PA. In 1975, they organized a Committee on Lesbian and Gay Concerns, as well as a Gay, Lesbian, and Bisexual Caucus. In 1978, the APA approved an official task force on gays, lesbians, and bisexuals.

The American Psychological Association eliminated homosexuality as a category of mental illness in January 1975. At the same time, it passed a resolution calling on members to fight against any remaining stigma of mental illness attached to homosexuality. The Association of Gay Psychologists Caucus first met at the 1973 annual meeting. The *Journal of Lesbian and Gay Psychotherapy* was founded in 1989. The American Psychological Association established the Committee on Gay Concerns in 1980, and in 1984 the Society for the Psychological Study of Gay and Lesbian Issues was organized as Division 44.

Since the 1970s, LGBT psychologists and psychiatrists have run counseling centers and practices for LGBT patients and published numerous studies that have been influential in the larger psychotherapeutic community. This literature has focused on a broad range of topics, including homophobia, relationships, parenting, coming out, adolescence, and AIDS. More recent studies have examined the diversity of LGBT lives.

Yet not all developments have been positive. In the 1990s, an increasing number of groups claiming to cure homosexuals through reparative therapy appeared. Socarides and psychologist Joseph Nicolosi founded the National Association for Research and Therapy of Homosexuality in 1992. Closely allied with Christian groups, such as Exodus Institute, which was established in 1976, Socarides and Nicolosi draw on psychoanalytic theory to assert that homosexuality results from faulty gender identity and to claim to be able to cure a third of all homosexuals who seek treatment. In 1998, the APA announced its opposition to reparative therapy.

As psychiatry has increasingly focused on biochemical explanations of behavior and shifted to the use of psychotropic drugs to treat psychological disorders, psychoanalysis has to a certain extent faded as a medical specialty. Psychoanalytic theory, however, is used by many queer studies scholars in the humanities, including Leo Bersani, Judith Butler, Eve Sedgwick, and Teresa de Lauretis. They draw on the radical strands of Freudian theory and the work of French psychoanalyst Jacques Lacan to conceptualize sexualities and genders in new ways. Ironically, theoretical constructs that helped to create the homosexual and transsexual are now being used by queer scholars to deconstruct those identities.

Bibliography

Abelove, Henry. "Freud, Male Homosexuality, and the Americans." *Dissent* 33 (winter 1986): 59–69.

Alfred C. Kinsey Correspondence. The Kinsey Institute for Research in Sex, Gender, and Reproduction, Indiana University, Bloomington, Indiana.

Bayer, Ronald. *Homosexuality and American Psychiatry: The Politics of Diagnosis.* New York: Basic Books, 1981.

Bérubé, Allan. *Coming Out Under Fire: The History of Gay Men and Women in World War Two.* New York: Free Press, 1990. Reprint, 2000).

Bullough, Vern L. *Science in the Bedroom: A History of Sex Research.* New York. Basic Books, 1994.

Carlston, Erin G. "'A Finer Differentiation': Female Homosexuality and the American Medical Community, 1926–1940." In *Science and Homosexualities.* Edited by Vernon A. Rosario. New York: Routledge, 1997.

Chauncey, George Jr., "From Sexual Inversion to Homosexuality: The Changing Medical Conceptualization of Female 'Deviance.'" In *Passion and Power: Sexuality in History.* Edited by Kathy Peiss and Christina Simmons with Robert A. Padgug. Philadelphia: Temple University Press, 1989.

Davis, Katharine Bement. *Factors in the Sex Life of Twenty-Two Hundred Women.* New York: Harper and Brothers, 1929.

Dean, Tim, and Christopher Lane, "Introduction." In *Homosexuality and Psychoanalysis.* Edited by Tim Dean and Christopher Lane. Chicago: University of Chicago Press, 2001.

D'Emilio, John. *Sexual Politics, Sexual Communities: The Making of a Homosexual Minority in the United States, 1940–1970.* Chicago: University of Chicago Press, 1983.

Dickinson, Robert Latou, and Lura Beam. *The Single Woman: A Medical Study in Sex Education.* Baltimore: Williams and Wilkins, 1934.

Duggan, Lisa. *Sapphic Slashers: Sex, Violence, and American Modernity.* Durham, N.C., Duke University Press, 2000.

Ellis, Havelock. *Sexual Inversion.* Vol. 2 of *Studies in the Psychology of Sex.* 3d ed. Philadelphia: F. A. Davis, 1928. The original edition was published in 1897.

Faderman, Lillian. *Odd Girls and Twilight Lovers: A History of Lesbian Life in Twentieth-Century America.* New York: Columbia University Press, 1991.

Foucault, Michel. *The History of Sexuality. Volume I: An Introduction.* Translated from the French by Robert Hurley. New York: Vintage Books, 1990.

Freud, Sigmund. *Three Essays on the Theory of Sexuality.* Translated and revised by James Strachey. New York: Basic Books, 2000.

Hale, Nathan G., Jr. *Freud in America, Volume 1: Freud and the Americans: The Beginnings of Psychoanalysis in the United States, 1876–1917.* New York: Oxford University Press, 1971.

———. *Freud in America, Volume 2: Freud and the Americans: The Rise and Crisis of Psychoanalysis in the United States, 1917–1985.* New York: Oxford University Press, 1995.

Henry, George W. *Sex Variants: A Study of Homosexual Patterns.* New York: Paul B. Hoeber, 1948. One-volume edition; originally published in two volumes, Paul B. Hoeber, 1941.

Herman, Ellen. *Issues in Lesbian and Gay Life: Psychiatry, Psychology, and Homosexuality.* New York: Chelsea House, 1995.

"Historical Notes: A Letter from Freud." *American Journal of Psychiatry* 107 (April 1951):786–787.

Irvine, Janice M. *Disorders of Desire: Sex and Gender in Modern American Sexology.* Philadelphia: Temple University Press, 1990.

Katz, Jonathan Ned. *Gay American History: Lesbians and Gay Men in the U.S.A.* Rev ed. New York: Meridian, 1992.

———. *Gay/Lesbian Almanac: A New Documentary.* New York: Harper and Row, 1983.

Kinsey, Alfred C., Wardell B. Pomeroy, and Clyde E. Martin. *Sexual Behavior in the Human Male.* Philadelphia: W. B. Saunders, 1948.

Kinsey, Alfred C., Wardell B. Pomeroy, Clyde E. Martin, and Paul H. Gebhard. *Sexual Behavior in the Human Female.* Philadelphia: W. B. Saunders, 1953.

Lewes, Kenneth. *The Psychoanalytic Theory of Male Homosexuality.* New York: Simon and Schuster, 1988.

Lunbeck, Elizabeth. *The Psychiatric Persuasion: Knowledge, Gender, and Power in Modern America.* Princeton: Princeton University Press, 1994.

Meyerowitz, Joanne. *How Sex Changed: A History of Transsexuality in the United States.* Cambridge, Massachusetts: Harvard University Press, 2002.

Minton, Henry L. *Departing from Deviance: A History of Homosexual Rights and Emancipatory Science in America.* Chicago: University of Chicago Press, 2002.

Rado, Sandor. "A Critical Examination of the Concept of Bisexuality." *Psychosomatic Medicine* 2 (October 1940): 459–467.

Robinson, Paul. *The Modernization of Sex: Havelock Ellis, Alfred Kinsey, William Masters, and Virginia Johnson.* Ithaca, New York: Cornell University Press, 1976. Reprint, 1989.

———."Freud and Homosexuality." In *Homosexuality and Psychoanalysis.* Edited by Tim Dean and Christopher Lane. Chicago: University of Chicago Press, 2001.

Rosario, Vernon A. *Homosexuality and Science: A Guide to the Debates.* Santa Barbara: ABC-CLIO, 2002.

Silverstein, Charles. "History of Treatment." In *Textbook of Homosexuality and Mental Health.* Edited by Robert B. Cabaj and Terry S. Stein. Washington, D.C.: American Psychiatric Press, 1996.

Somerville, Siobhan. *Queering the Color Line.* Durham, N.C. Duke University Press, 2000.

Terry, Jennifer. *An American Obsession: Science, Medicine, and Homosexuality in Modern Society.* Chicago: University of Chicago Press, 1999.

Lynn Gorchov

See also BIOLOGY AND ZOOLOGY; DAVIS, KATHARINE BEMENT; HENRY, GEORGE; HOOKER, EVELYN; KINSEY, ALFRED C.; LOBDELL, LUCY ANN; MEDICINE, MEDICALIZATION, AND THE MEDICAL MODEL; MONEY, JOHN, AND ANKE EHRHARDT; PSYCHOTHERAPY, COUNSELLING, AND RECOVERY PROGRAMS; SULLIVAN, HARRY STACK.

PSYCHOTHERAPY, COUNSELLING, AND RECOVERY PROGRAMS

The declassification of homosexuality as a mental disorder by the American Psychiatric Association in 1973 marked a watershed moment in the attitude of mental health professionals toward same-sex sexual orientation. In the official eyes of one of the most influential mental health organizations in the world, sexual orientation to the same sex was no longer viewed as an "arrest of psychosexual development" to be cured with psychotherapy or analysis. Noting that a large body of empirical data gathered since the 1950s supported the conclusion that homosexuality is a normal variation of human experience and has no implication per se of pathology, the association gave its blessing for practitioners of psychotherapy to provide support for their LGB clients and to facilitate their positive adjustment to a stigmatized identity.

Since 1973, the American Psychiatric Association's position on same-sex orientation has been endorsed and expanded upon by many other mental health professional organizations. So prevalent in the early twenty-first century is the nonpathological view of homosexuality that in 1998 the American Psychoanalytic Association, traditionally considered one of the most conservative professional groups in its attitudes toward same-sex orientation, endorsed same-sex marriage. And professional publications, such as the *Journal of Gay and Lesbian Psychotherapy* (begun in 1989), regularly offer "gay-positive" articles on research, theory, and clinical practice.

Controversy and Lingering Bias

In 1973, however, the controversy was not over. A referendum showed that 37 percent of psychiatrists opposed their association's decision. In response to their disapproval, a compromise diagnosis was entered into the third edition of the American Psychiatric Association's *Diagnostic and Statistical Manual of Mental Disorders* (1980). "Ego-dystonic homosexuality" referred to those gay and lesbian patients who experienced dissatisfaction over their orientation and desired to become heterosexual. However, noting in 1987 that a period of distress and dissatisfaction with one's sexual orientation is a normal phase of identity development among gays and lesbians in the United States, the association deleted "ego-dystonic homosexuality" from its diagnostic manual.

Despite the spread of more positive attitudes, the wariness of LGB people toward mental health professions has persisted and was dramatically borne out by a 1991 study conducted by the American Psychological Association. It found that 58 percent of the 2,544 members of the association who responded to the survey reported personal knowledge of biased practice toward LGB clients. The examples cited of biased practice ranged in character from ignorance to overt repulsion and hostility. In response to this apparently high incidence of inadequate care, the American Psychological Association in 2000 approved its "Guidelines for Psychotherapy with Lesbian, Gay, and Bisexual Clients." The guidelines establish a minimum standard of care by which psychologists are urged to examine their own as well as society's prejudicial beliefs and to be aware of how such beliefs can affect the client and the therapeutic process. They are also called upon to recognize and respect the relationships and families of LGB people, to consider the special problems of diverse populations (including bisexuals) within the community, and to engage in ongoing education about LGB issues.

Although most biased and nonaffirmative treatment of LGB clients has undoubtedly been the consequence of ignorance, some mental health professionals deliberately reject an affirmative stance to their same-sex oriented clients and practice "reparative," "conversion," or "reorientation" therapies. The historical antecedents for these approaches are in psychoanalytic theory, which regarded the mature stage of psychosexual development to be heterosexuality. Due in part to the ambiguity of Sigmund Freud's writings, both proponents and opponents of conversion treatments cite Freud's writings as support for their stance on the relative health, or lack thereof, of a positive homosexual identity and life. Later psychoanalytic theorists reconstructed Freud's original thinking to portray homosexuality as due to an intrapsychic conflict, which then met the psychoanalytic definition of an illness. The descendants of these thinkers, many of whom are affiliated with the National Association for Research and Therapy of Homosexuality (founded in 1992), continue to practice conversion therapy. There is no empirical evidence that such treatments are effective. Indeed, they may be quite damaging. Both the American Psychological Association (in 1997) and the American Psychiatric Association (in 2000) have cautioned their members against practicing conversion therapy on both ethical and scientific grounds. Most other prominent medical and mental health associations have adopted similar policies.

Self-Help, Peer Support, and LGB-Affirmative Therapy

Concurrent with the debate within the mental health professions in the 1970s and 1980s, many LGB clients, recognizing that a large number of clinicians continued to consider their orientation a sickness, eschewed traditional psychotherapy for more trusted peer counselling or peer-led support groups. This tradition of reliance on peer counselling and self-help continues in the LGB community. A quick perusal through travel guides (such as *Damron's*) published for LGB people reveals the existence of community centers in most major cities in the United States, many of which offer gay-affirmative support groups, psychotherapy, and counselling. These community centers also often host meeting sites for Alcoholics Anonymous and other twelve-step programs that address various addiction issues for clients who have felt unwelcome, uncomfortable, or unsafe in groups such as these that are populated by heterosexuals. In fact, the recovery movement in the LGB community has been motivated by the unmet needs of those clients in general substance recovery programs. Substance use issues seem to be of paramount concern, whether due to the stigmatized social oppression this population faces or to the fact that one of the primary social outlets for connection to this community has been in bars and other settings in which substance use is intricately woven. Recovery programs that affirm the experience of LGB people have been a welcome addition to treatment options available.

Partly as a response to LGB distrust of the mental health professions, a post–Stonewall Riots generation of psychotherapists, many of whom identified as LGB themselves, became in the 1970s and 1980s proponents of gay-affirmative therapy. This approach, with roots in its precursor, feminist therapy, affirms same-sex orientations as equal to heterosexuality and views psychological adjustment difficulties in same-sex oriented clients as due primarily to social bias. Gay-affirmative therapists support their LGB clients in the development of positive identities and coping strategies for the oppression they encounter.

Bisexuality and Transgenderism

While their gay and lesbian compatriots made advances, bisexuals faced additional difficulties with the psychotherapy community. Often even gay-affirmative therapists have failed to view bisexuals as possessing a legitimate identity. Rather, they have assumed that bisexuals are actually exclusively same-sex oriented persons who have failed to form their gay or lesbian identities fully or that they are attempting to retain the privileges of heterosexuality by claiming partial orientation to the other sex. However, the idea that bisexuality is often a lifelong identity and no more a social or psychological construct than other sexual orientation identities appears to be taking hold among practitioners of psychotherapy.

The relationship between transgender persons' experiences and the mental health profession has also slowly evolved in a fashion similar to that followed by the history of LGB people, at least with regard to the slow process leading toward supportive therapies. It has, however, been delayed as scientists have been slower to understand the transgender phenomenon and to remove the stigma of pathology associated with it. Until the distinctions between gender identity, sexual identity, and sexual orientation became more widely understood, transgender persons were often (and still are) assumed to be homosexuals or simply cross-dressers. This misunderstanding has often resulted in rejection and oppression from LGB people as well as the larger culture.

From the late 1960s through the 1980s, the principal focus of treatment for persons who identified as transgender was the facilitation of the transition to a new sex, a process culminating in sexual reassignment surgery. Since the 1990s, however, there has been a movement away from sexual reassignment surgery as the only option for transgender persons. Many transgender advocates note that while a desire to alter one's sex may be a core characteristic of gender dysphoria for some, a perhaps more problematic experience is facing the intense and sometimes brutal oppression of a culture that remains inflexible in its tolerance of diverse gender presentations. For this reason, some mental health professionals are encouraging their transgender clients to express their gender orientations through behaviors that do not involve reassignment surgery, behaviors ranging from unobtrusive cross-dressing (such as wearing other-sex undergarments) to cosmetic surgeries and procedures. They are also helped to accept their same-sex sexual fantasies and to develop relational and vocational coping strategies to mitigate the complications resulting from the oppression associated with their identities.

As the understanding of transgenderism, its oppression, and its variety of expressions widens, the inclusion of "gender identity disorder" in the 1980 edition of the *Diagnostic and Statistical Manual* has become increasingly controversial. While some fear the removal of this diagnostic category would severely restrict access to sexual reassignment surgery for those who desire it, others argue that it pathologizes a phenomenon that, like homosexuality and bisexuality, does not per se impair psychological adjustment. Further, since studies show that a large percentage of children who identify as same-sex oriented as adults exhibit cross-gender behaviors, the diagnosis pathologizes their gender expression as well, to say nothing of heterosexual children and adults who do not conform completely to cultural gender norms.

Transgender persons continue to experience misunderstanding and nonacceptance both within and without the mental health professions. However, with the inclusion of transgender issues in the focus of activist and support organizations formerly devoted only to LGB concerns, some headway appears to be occurring.

Bibliography

Cabaj, Robert Paul, and Mickey Smith. "Overview of Treatment Approaches, Modalities, and Issues of Accessibility in the Continuum of Care." *A Provider's Introduction to Substance Abuse Treatment for Lesbian, Gay, Bisexual, and Transgender Individuals.* U.S. Department of Health and Human Services, Substance Abuse and Mental Health Services Administration, Center for Substance Abuse Treatments, 2001. Available from http://www.health.org/govpubs/BKD392/index.pdf

Committee on Lesbian, Gay, and Bisexual Concerns Joint Task Force on Guidelines for Psychotherapy with Lesbian, Gay, and Bisexual Clients. "Guidelines for Psychotherapy with Lesbian, Gay, and Bisexual Clients." *American Psychologist* 55 (2000): 1440–1451.

Denny, Dallas. "A Selective Bibliography of Transsexualism." *Journal of Gay and Lesbian Psychotherapy* 6, no. 2 (2002): 35–66.

Garnetts, Linda, et al. "Issues in Psychotherapy with Lesbians and Gay Men." *American Psychologist* 46 (1991): 964–972.

Herman, Ellen. *Psychiatry, Psychology, and Homosexuality.* New York: Chelsea House, 1995.

Isay, Richard A. "Remove Gender Identity Disorder from DSM." *Psychiatric News.* Available from http://www.psych.org/pnews/97-11-21/isay.html

Levine, Stephen B., et al. "Standards of Care for Gender Identity Disorders, 6th Version." The Harry Benjamin International Gender Dysphoria Association, 2001. Available from http://www.tgholidays.com

Marcus, Eric. *Making History: The Struggle for Gay and Lesbian Equal Rights, 1945–1990.* New York: HarperCollins, 1992.

Raj, Rupert. "Towards a Transpositive Therapeutic Model: Developing Clinical Sensitivity and Cultural Competence in the Effective Support of Transsexual and Transgendered Clients." *International Journal of Transgenderism* 6 (2002).

Shidlo, Ariel, Michael Schroeder, and Jack Drescher, eds. *Sexual Conversion Therapy: Ethical, Clinical, and Research Perspectives.* New York: Haworth Medical Press, 2001.

Wilson, Katherine K. "GIDreform.org: Challenging Psychiatric Stereotypes of Gender Diversity." Gender Identity Center of Colorado Inc., 2002. Available from http://www.transgender.org

James H. Hodnett, Karen M. Taylor

See also ALCOHOL AND DRUGS; INTERSEXUALS AND INTERSEXED PEOPLE; MEDICINE, MEDICALIZATION, AND THE MEDICAL MODEL; PSYCHOLOGY, PSYCHIATRY, PSYCHOANALYSIS, AND SEXOLOGY.

PUBLIC FESTIVALS, PARTIES, AND HOLIDAYS

In LGBT communities across the United States, festivals and holidays mark events of historical and cultural importance. At the turn of the twenty-first century, LGBT people in every state of the United States mark Pride Month in June—near the anniversary of the 1969 Stonewall Riots—with some type of celebration, and pride marches, parties, and festivities can be found in large urban centers as well as small towns and communities. Across the twentieth century, LGBT sexuality was celebrated in a variety of ways through parties, balls, pride festivals, and the adoption of holidays as LGBT events. Through these celebrations LGBT people and their allies create public space to construct, negotiate, and challenge dominant conceptions and practices of gender and sexuality.

History of Public Festivities

In the late-nineteenth and early-twentieth-century world of entertainment, LGBT and straight worlds overlapped and collided, creating social and cultural space for various festivities and balls. The earliest balls were peopled by female impersonators and cross-dressing entertainers who enjoyed celebrity status in such large urban centers as New York City and Chicago. In New York City, the Hamilton Lodge Ball was the most famous and largest drag ball, an annual event started in 1869. The event had always been a female impersonators' event and was known by the late 1920s as the Faggots' Ball. This Harlem-based spectacle attracted a diverse crowd and was a place where working- and middle-class black and white LGBT persons (including lesbian male impersonators) and straight people frolicked. During the 1920s antivice crusaders set out to do away with gay subcultures in Chicago, New York City, and other cities around the United States, working in concert with city police departments to raid LGBT establishments, arrest cross-dressed people, and censor plays and films that depicted same-sex sexuality.

With the onset of the Great Depression in 1929, LGBT culture went underground in New York City. In Harlem, for example, house parties became central to LGBT culture. In San Francisco, by contrast, the tourist industry took advantage of the city's reputation for open sexuality, and LGBT people continued to enjoy public parties and drag performances at such clubs as Mona's and Finnochio's. With the repeal of Prohibition in 1933, those states that established liquor control boards had more government control over establishments that served alcohol, which ironically gave rise to the exclusively gay bar. Boards controlled not only the serving of liquor but also attempted to control the clientele; in response, gay bar owners opened private bars to cater exclusively to gay and lesbian clients. Indeed, from the mid-1930s to the late 1960s, bars and restaurants emerged as vital social spaces for gay men and lesbians. From New York City and Philadelphia to Memphis and San Francisco, such establishments usually catered to both male and female patrons. In many cities, such as Memphis, these early bars were single-race, but Philadelphia and other locales boasted multiracial gay bars and restaurants. Women in particular also gathered publicly on softball fields, using the sport as a social venue.

After the Stonewall Riots in 1969, a new mood swept across LGBT communities, promoting liberation in place of patience and pride in place of shame. Public celebration of LGBT life became an important sign of liberation, and LGBT festivals, parades, and holidays became central places in which LGBT identities were affirmed and celebrated.

Mardi Gras

One of the oldest public festivals in the United States is Mardi Gras. The original home of Mardi Gras in the United States is Mobile, Alabama, but the grandest and most elaborate celebration is in New Orleans. Mardi Gras was traditionally the day to slaughter a fatted calf on the Tuesday before the beginning of the Lenten fast—thus, the coining of the phrase "Fat Tuesday." However, the celebration in New Orleans has developed into an epic festival and is considered by many to be an LGBT holiday. Mardi Gras krewes—local clubs that sponsor parades and events during the season—hold elaborate balls and parties where each one's king, queen, and other royalty are announced for the year. Mardi Gras royalty are elected because of their contributions and standing in the community, and among LGBT krewes, election is a testament of dedication and activism on the part of the LGBT community in New Orleans.

The roots of Gay Mardi Gras tradition go back to the 1950s. The first Gay Mardi Gras krewe was the Krewe of

Castro Street Fair. The booth of Family Link, which provides a guest house and services for families visiting people with AIDS, at this festival in San Francisco. [Dr. Michael Bettinger]

Yuga, also known as KY. It was formed in 1958 to spoof the straight, aristocratic Mardi Gras traditions. In 1962 the Krewe of Yuga held its initial ball at a private children's school, a poor choice. As the queen and maids awaited the adoration of the spectators, the ball was raided by police, and people were taken to jail. Despite this, however, Gay Mardi Gras developed in the lower French Quarter with krewes, balls, and parties. While many LGBT krewes developed later, only five remained at the turn of the twenty-first century—Amon Ra, Mwindo, Petronius, Armenius, and the Lords of Leather.

Halloween

New Orleans also boasts Gay Halloween, an event that began in 1984 and has developed into one of the largest and most celebrated weekends. Historically, Halloween was a time when police who normally enforced municipal bans on cross-dressing turned a blind eye to celebrations that were little more than gay drag balls. In more recent years, however, Halloween has become an important celebration for LGBT communities, serving as a close to National Coming Out Day on 11 October in many cities as well as an important festival in its own respect. In locations as diverse as Greenwich Village in New York City, Columbus, Ohio, and San Francisco, queer Halloween parades and parties take over the streets in late October. Revelers and observers alike have referred to Halloween as a "great gay holiday" and a holiday for cross-dressers of all persuasions.

Festivals, Circuit Parties, and Pride Events

Other LGBT festivals and celebrations abound in cities across the United States. In Key West, Florida, Fantasy Fest emerged in 1979 as a way to draw LGBT tourists to the Keys. Local businesspeople proposed an "anything goes" adult costume party similar to Mardi Gras in New Orleans, complete with private and public parties, dances, and a decadent parade down Duval Street. In late July and early August, Atlanta, Georgia, becomes Hotlanta, a four-day celebration of LGBT life, culture, and community in the city. The event began in 1978 and over the next twenty-five years developed into a long weekend of circuit parties, fund-raisers, and parades that draws over 100,000 people to downtown and midtown Atlanta. Wigstock, billed as New York City's legendary "dragstravaganza," was a yearly drag festival that took place in Tompkins Square from its beginning in 1984 until, in 1991, it became so large that the event moved to Union Square. Transgender people, drag queens, and cross-dressers converged to create a public festival celebrating drag, music, and LGBT culture in a festival that raised public consciousness about drag and transgender identity. No Wigstock was held in 2002, but the gala event was revived in 2003 as part of the East Village's HOWL festival.

Merging a party atmosphere with political activism, many events surrounding these festivals and parties serve as fund-raisers for LGBT groups and AIDS activist organizations. Circuit parties in particular serve not only as weekend-long parties and festivities but also as significant fund-raisers for AIDS awareness and activist organizations. The Red Party was the most popular circuit party. Corbett Reynolds initiated it in 1977, and gay communities across the United States (and the world) hosted Red Parties in their cities. When Reynolds died in 2002, the official Red Party was no longer a formal event, but circuit parties continue as important social events and fund-raisers. Held in cities across the globe, circuit parties in the United States include Salt Lake City's Ski Pass; Honolulu's Hurricane Party; Miami's White Party; Atlanta's Hotlanta; San Francisco's Hell Ball; Philadelphia's Blue Ball Weekend; and in Alabama, Huntsville's Moonshot. Such events are so popular and widespread that the magazine *Circuit Noize* provides details on upcoming circuit party events and describes past events. These parties often receive corporate sponsorship, engendering criticism among some that these events, and by extension the gay community, are more about commercialism and profit and less about queer cultural politics of claiming space.

Many companies have turned to hosting LGBT-only events. Since 1991, Disney World in Orlando, Florida, has been home to Gay Day at Walt Disney World, a weekend-long event that attracts over 100,000 people from around the United States and the world. In recent years such events have expanded to include Busch Gardens, Universal Studios, and Sea World. Near Cincinnati, Ohio, hundreds of LGBT people converge on King's Island amusement park for their Gay Pride celebration. Although many queer activists criticize these events as overly commercial, such festivals demonstrate the economic and cultural power of the LGBT community nationwide and illustrate growing LGBT cultural presence and influence.

Pride festivals, often held in June—Gay Pride Month—are probably the most common type of LGBT festival in cities across the United States, where LGBT community leaders organize parades and public demonstrations and celebrate LGBT sexuality. These events commemorate the 1969 Stonewall Riots, affirming the sense of gay pride and liberation that accompanied these riots and sparked a revolution. Some cities replaced former events with official "gay pride" events. For example, in Philadelphia, the 1969 Annual Reminder at Independence Hall gave way to the city's first gay pride march in 1972, but other cities, such as Memphis, organized specifically gay pride events in the mid-1970s after the concept had taken hold in the country. In some cities, communities organize additional demonstrations that recognize differences within LGBT communities. In Atlanta and Chicago, for example, there are dyke marches that attract thousands of lesbians, bisexual women, and transgender women as participants and spectators. Other cities boast marches for people of color, including New York City's Black Pride, an event that brings thousands of black LGBT people together for social and cultural celebration. Atlanta's West End is home to Black Gay Pride, a parade and social event that celebrates same-sex sexuality and confronts perceived and real homophobia in Atlanta's African American communities. In some cities, such as Columbus, Ohio, alternative proms and graduations have emerged as a way to recognize LGBT youth and provide space for young people to be recognized for their accomplishments as well as for their relationships in LGBT-identified space.

Festivals, holidays, and parties have served and continue to serve an important function in building LGBT communities. In addition to raising funds for explicitly political organizations, LGBT communities use festivals and celebrations to create a cultural space that challenges dominant discourse about gender and sexuality and sustains social life beyond formal political activism. Just as LGBT bars have been key sites in which LGBT people have created and asserted public identities, so have festivals, parties, and holidays served as the social context in which LGBT members have interacted, networked, and built a sense of solidarity.

Bibliography

McGarry, Molly, and Fred Wasserman. *Becoming Visible: An Illustrated History of Lesbian and Gay Life in Twentieth-Century America.* New York: Penguin Studio, 1998.

Rogers, Nicholas. *Halloween: From Pagan Ritual to Party Night.* Oxford, U.K.: Oxford University Press, 2002.

Rupp, Leila J. *A Desired Past: A Short History of Same-Sex Love in America.* Chicago: University of Chicago Press, 1999.

Stein, Marc. *City of Sisterly and Brotherly Loves: Lesbian and Gay Philadelphia, 1945–1972.* Chicago: University of Chicago Press, 2000.

Stephanie Gilmore, Elizabeth Kaminski

See also FILM AND VIDEO FESTIVALS; HOUSE PARTIES; MUSIC: WOMEN'S FESTIVALS.

PUBLIC SEX

Little is known about public sex between men or between women in the colonial and antebellum periods, but as U.S. cities began to increase in population and complexity in the late nineteenth century, public and semipublic spaces became important to the sexual cultures of LGBT people. Dominant bourgeois culture, however, attempts to draw strict boundaries between the public and private spheres and, at an ideological level, often relegates sex to the private sphere. In this context, public sex has been considered transgressive and has been subject to policing. This has been particularly true for LGBT public sex. In periods of intense policing especially, men and women who engage in same-sex sexual encounters in public places and transgender people who have sex in public have been vulnerable not just to physical violence but also to social harm. The appropriation of public, semipublic, and commercial spaces for sexual purposes, however, has been one way for LGBT people to claim their right to sexual pleasure and to build community within a heterosexist and sexist society.

Men typically have been more involved in same-sex public sex than have women. First, men have had greater economic freedom than women to live and work independent of family or domestic life, and men's labor has taken them out more generally into the public sphere. Second, dominant sexual ideologies have tended to cast aspersions on middle-class women's presence on public streets, classifying them as prostitutes or at least as promiscuous; consequently, men have been able to use urban public space more easily than have women. Third, women often have been more vulnerable than men to sexual violence in public. Finally, gay male cultures typically have placed a higher premium on frequent, casual sex with many partners than have lesbian cultures. Some scholars attribute these differences to underlying biological distinctions between men and women, while others believe that culture and socialization are primarily responsible. Still others caution against exaggerating these differences, suggesting that future scholarship may uncover forms and examples of lesbian public sex that have not yet been documented.

Urbanization, Public Space, and Gay Community Formation

During the period of intense urbanization and industrialization in the late nineteenth and early twentieth centuries, men and women migrated from rural areas to American cities in increasing numbers. Within the context of migrant communities that were largely same-sex or homosocial, LGBT subcultures emerged, offering their members some scope to pursue sexual pleasure. Private space for sexual intimacy was not always available to those living in cramped quarters, however. George Chauncey, for example, argues that working-class men in New York in this period, many of whom did not have private space in their apartments or tenements, were drawn to public sex.

Historians have uncovered gay men pursuing sex with men in a wide variety of urban public places in virtually every period of U.S. history for which sources are available. Men have pursued public sex in parks, under bridges, behind trees or bushes, in alleys, on beaches, and in the restrooms of public facilities, known as "tearooms" (originally "t-rooms" or "toilet rooms"). Beyond simply providing sexual release, note historians, public sex has been central to gay community formation in places ranging from large cities, such as Chicago, Atlanta, and Washington, D.C., to small cities and rural areas, such as Flint, Michigan, and Mississippi. A subculture of transsexual sex workers, sometimes soliciting or engaging in sex in public, has also developed alongside urban gay male subcultures.

In the twentieth century, some men involved in public same-sex sexual activity have identified themselves as gay, bisexual, or transgender; others have not. For some men living a "double life" in the twentieth century, furtive sex in public places offered a relatively safe way to obtain sexual pleasure with other men. For example, fully one-fourth of the men arrested for homosexual activity in New York in 1920–1921, most of whom were caught in public places, were married, and many had children. Other men who engaged in same-sex sex in public, however, identified strongly with the gay subculture and did not pursue heterosexual marriage.

Geographies and Cultures of Public Sex

By the early twentieth century, gay men had developed a complex sexual culture revolving around encounters in urban public places. Public restrooms, segregated by sex, played a central role. Many well-known tearooms were located in department stores, public libraries, or bus or train stations. Closed off from streets and businesses and reserved for bodily functions ordinarily not discussed in public, restrooms allowed men a certain scope for creating "privacy in public," as sociologist Laud Humphreys put it in his 1975 study *Tearoom Trade: Impersonal Sex in Public Places.* Following the massive highway construction of the post–World War II era, rest stops on major highways and automobiles parked in secluded places also became important sites for sexual encounters between men.

Restrooms, parks, and porn theaters offered some security from the attention of family members at home and from violent attacks by hostile bystanders; bathhouses and sex clubs provided additional safety. Men pursuing sex in all of these places often signaled their intentions to each other by hovering, loitering, and looking each other in the eye—nonverbal strategies that kept their intentions invisible to nonfriendly bystanders and passersby. In some restrooms, one man served as a guard near the entrance, so that he could alert men in compromising positions if a stranger or police officer approached. Still, these tactics did not make sex in tearooms and other public places entirely secure. Men caught having sex in public frequently were arrested and sometimes were sentenced to time in prisons or workhouses for "morals" offenses. They also were subject to violent attacks by those offended by public sex, gay sex, the sexual attentions of men, or their own sexual desires. Transsexual and transgender people, who faced the additional stigma of their gender variations becoming known or visible, have been especially subject to brutal violence in public places.

Virtually no historical scholarship has examined public sex between women specifically, though it undoubtedly occurred. One of the few exceptions is a memoir of working-class lesbian bar life in the 1950s and 1960s by Joan Nestle, who describes public flirtation and sexual activity on lesbian beaches in Brooklyn, New York, and on Fire Island. Although historians have uncovered little evidence of public sex between women before the 1970s, this may be because, in a male-dominated society, sex between women has not always registered as threatening or visible in the same ways that sex between men has.

Crackdowns and Scandals

Although gay bar culture and public sexual life were subject to policing in the early twentieth century, municipal policing became much more active in the middle decades of the twentieth century. Numerous historians have shown that arrests of and crackdowns on gay men having sex in public places were far more frequent in the mid-twentieth century than in earlier decades. In a society that was increasingly divided into people who classified themselves as homosexuals or heterosexuals, men arrested for public sex were liable to be seen not only as criminals and sinners but also as mentally ill. The risks for those arrested, then, changed just at the moment when public sex was becoming policed more intensely.

The mid-twentieth century also witnessed a major increase in the intensity of sex scandals, some of which revolved around same-sex public sex. Municipal police expanded their "vice squad" operations, with undercover officers propositioning men for sex in a technique known as *entrapment.* Many entrapped men subsequently were fired from their jobs, fined, or even jailed. John Howard documents a 1953 crackdown on a tearoom in the Atlanta Public Library, which resulted in the arrest of some twenty men; once their names were published as part of the *Atlanta Constitution*'s extensive coverage of the case, almost all these men lost their jobs or moved away. The same year, the African American activist Bayard Rustin was arrested for having sex with two young men in a parked car in Pasadena, California, an incident that permanently damaged his career in the civil rights and peace movements.

Perhaps the most famous tearoom scandal of the twentieth century broke just three weeks before the U.S. presidential election of 1964, when Lyndon B. Johnson's chief of staff, Walter Jenkins, was arrested for having sex in a public restroom in Washington, D.C. Even after Jenkins, a married man, resigned his post, the controversy continued when it was discovered that he had been arrested in the same restroom five years earlier. In line with Cold War–era associations between sexual perversion and political subversion, much of the controversy focused on Jenkins's access to classified information and the potential threat to national security that he might have posed.

Gay Liberation and the Politics of Sexual Space

In the late 1960s and early 1970s, LGBT people increasingly asserted their rights to socialize in public and commercial spaces. In this period, activists urged LGBT people to "come out" by affirming their sexual and gender identities in public. With an emphasis on making LGBT identities and behaviors acceptable in public life, the furtive quality of much sexual activity in public places came to be regarded by some as a sign of shame and oppression. The increasing size of urban sexual subcultures, if anything, probably increased the scale and visibility of public sex.

Many openly gay men and transgender people, as well as non-gay-identified men, continued to pursue casual sex in public places. According to Esther Newton, in the lesbian and gay resort on Fire Island, near New

York City, increasing numbers of gay vacationers in the 1960s expanded the area of the "Meat Rack." On this stretch of beach between the island's two towns, gay men "cruised" and pursued public sex, in couples and groups, behind bushes and in the open. Since Fire Island was a relatively isolated resort area where LGBT people predominated, many gay men relished the opportunity to pursue public sex without the threat of being arrested or assaulted. Still, public sex between men on the Meat Rack created tension between gay men and lesbians; Newton shows, for example, that gay men sometimes harassed lesbians simply for walking past the Meat Rack. A widespread joke about a "Doughnut Rack" (analogous to the gay male "Meat Rack") referenced the apparent absence of a lesbian public sex culture.

The AIDS Crisis, the Politics of Respectability, and Sex Controversies

The AIDS crisis thrust LGBT life into the media spotlight because of its association with gay men in the early 1980s. For many middle-class straight Americans, reports on the sexual transmission of the HIV virus provided their first exposure to the world of bathhouses, bars, parks, and porn theaters where many gay men sought and found sexual pleasure. The fear and uncertainty surrounding the disease led many gay men to limit the number of their sexual partners, and in several major cities, gay bathhouses were closed by municipal order. These bathhouse closures were highly controversial, especially in such cities as San Francisco and New York, with large, politically influential LGBT communities.

Beginning in the early 1970s, some LGBT activists began to advocate public sex precisely because it subverted bourgeois norms of propriety and privacy. Over the course of the next several decades, lesbian sex radicals began to sponsor "play parties"—some exclusively lesbian, others welcoming gay male and transgender participants—to dispel stereotypes of lesbian monogamy and to draw attention to female pleasure. In the 1990s, lesbian pornographers began producing such films as *Bathroom Sluts* (1991), which explicitly eroticized public sex. Also in the 1990s, some LGBT commentators, including Patrick (formerly Pat) Califia, Samuel Delany, and Tristan Taormino, embraced public sex as a positive dimension of LGBT culture, denounced the closure and marginalization of sex-related businesses, and criticized the mainstream LGBT rights movement for its advocacy of marriage, monogamy, and other norms that they considered heterosexist and assimilationist.

Public sex has continued to be controversial in LGBT communities. For some gay men, public sex is a sign of shame and disgrace, and certain community leaders have argued that public sex and other marginal sexual practices foster the spread of sexually transmitted diseases. For others, the history and practice of public sex is a symbol of sexual liberation and pride. LGBT legal advocacy organizations in the late twentieth century frequently found themselves unsure about whether to protest policing practices against the "tearoom trade," especially when the men involved were not openly affiliated with LGBT communities.

Public sex holds a critical and controversial place in debates over the shifting legal status of same-sex sexual activity. In 2003, the U.S. Supreme Court struck down state sodomy laws in *Lawrence v. Texas,* but the Court's decision upheld the right of LGBT people to pursue consensual sex only in couples and only in their private homes. Califia and other radical sex activists have argued that political action rooted in the assertion of privacy rights will only increase the dangers and risks facing people who engage in same-sex sexual or social behaviors in public and semipublic places.

Bibliography

Beemyn, Brett, ed. *Creating a Place for Ourselves: Lesbian, Gay, and Bisexual Community Histories.* New York: Routledge, 1997.

Califia, Pat. *Public Sex: The Culture of Radical Sex.* 2d ed. San Francisco: Cleis Press, 2000.

Chauncey, George. *Gay New York: Gender, Urban Culture, and the Making of the Gay Male World, 1890–1940.* New York: Basic Books, 1994.

Delany, Samuel. *Times Square Red, Times Square Blue.* New York: New York University Press, 1999.

Edelman, Lee. "Tearooms and Sympathy; or, The Epistemology of the Water Closet." In *The Lesbian and Gay Studies Reader.* Edited by Henry Abelove, Michèle Aina Barale, and David M. Halperin. New York: Routledge, 1993.

Howard, John. "The Library, the Park, and the Pervert: Public Space and Homosexual Encounter in Post–World War II Atlanta." *Radical History Review* 62 (Spring 1995): 166–187.

———. *Men Like That: A Southern Queer History.* Chicago: University of Chicago Press, 1999.

Humphreys, Laud. *Tearoom Trade: Impersonal Sex in Public Places.* Chicago: Aldine, 1975.

Leap, William L., ed. *Public Sex/Gay Space.* New York: Columbia University Press, 1999.

Nestle, Joan. *A Restricted Country.* Ithaca, N.Y.: Firebrand Books, 1987.

Newton, Esther. *Cherry Grove, Fire Island: Sixty Years in America's First Gay and Lesbian Town.* Boston: Beacon Press, 1993.

Retzloff, Tim. "Cars and Bars: Assembling Gay Men in Postwar Flint, Michigan." In *Creating a Place for Ourselves: Lesbian,*

Gay, and Bisexual Community Histories. Edited by Brett Beemyn. New York: Routledge, 1997.

Stein, Marc. *City of Sisterly and Brotherly Loves: Lesbian and Gay Philadelphia, 1945–1972.* Chicago: University of Chicago Press, 2000.

Timothy Stewart-Winter

See also BATHHOUSES; CRUISING; PROSTITUTION, HUSTLING, AND SEX WORK; PROSTITUTION, HUSTLING, AND SEX WORK LAW AND POLICY; SEX CLUBS; TEAROOMS (BATHROOMS).

PUBLISHERS

The ability to read about the individual and collective lives of people like themselves is crucial to LGBT people, most of whom grow up isolated from other LGBT people and LGBT communities. Many older LGBT people remember buying and reading pulp paperbacks of dubious quality that always had unhappy endings, simply because such works were almost the only written material widely available in the 1950s and 1960s that had anything to do with LGBT lives. That situation has changed dramatically in the United States, and the LGBT community owes much to the men and women who laid the groundwork by publishing the first books, newspapers, and magazines by and about LGBT people.

In the Beginning (1947–1969)

In 1947, Edith Eyde, a young lesbian who used the pseudonym Lisa Ben (an anagram of "lesbian"), put out a monthly magazine that was written, edited, and read by lesbians. According to Rodger Streitmatter, Ben produced twelve copies of each issue of *Vice Versa* on her typewriter at work and distributed them free, asking each person who received a copy to pass it along once she had read it. The magazine had a nine-issue run in Ben's hometown of Los Angeles before Ben's job responsibilities changed and she no longer had the time or autonomy to type copies.

The short-lived *Vice Versa* foreshadowed the hundreds of magazines, newsletters, and newspapers that followed as the LGBT press developed over the next several decades. The earliest LGBT periodicals—*ONE, Mattachine Review,* and the *Ladder*—were published by homophile organizations in the 1950s and 1960s (ONE, Inc., the Mattachine Society, and the Daughters of Bilitis, respectively), and were aimed not at making a profit but at educating LGBT readers and creating a sense of empowerment and community among them. Streitmatter reports that the *Advocate,* founded in 1967 as the *Los Angeles Advocate,* was the first gay newspaper that operated as a business, with paid staff rather than volunteer labor. Meanwhile, male physique magazines such as *Physique Pictorial,* gay pornographic publishers such as Trojan Book Service and Guild Press, and hybrid homophile/physique magazines such as *Drum* reached much larger audiences. Together, the LGBT press—journals, magazines, newsletters, and newspapers—laid the groundwork for the explosion of LGBT writing and publishing in the post–Stonewall Riots era.

The Women in Print Movement (1969–1981)

In the late 1960s and early 1970s, the second-wave feminist and lesbian feminist movements wrote the next chapter in the history of LGBT publishing. Like LGBT people, the vast majority of women had long been silenced in the public arena. The ability to speak and be heard was thus an integral part of feminist self-empowerment, and especially during the early 1970s, women put their thoughts, feelings, and visions for a feminist future into words.

The next step was to get their writing into print, and since mainstream publishers showed little interest in publishing works by unknown women writers, much less lesbians, these authors took matters into their own hands. Many produced chapbooks or self-published their poetry or fiction. Others formed their own printing presses and publishing houses. Shameless Hussy Press, the first U.S. feminist publishing house, was founded in 1969 and published the poems of its founder, Alta, as well as stories by Susan Griffin and poetry by Pat Parker. Sojourner Truth Press, a short-lived women's press collective in Atlanta (1971–1972), printed *The Furies,* a newspaper written and edited by the Washington, D.C.–based collective of the same name that included as members Rita Mae Brown and Charlotte Bunch.

Arguably the most influential feminist publisher, Daughters Press, Inc., was founded in 1972 by the novelist June Arnold and her partner, Parke Bowman. Daughters initially published Brown's *Rubyfruit Jungle* in 1973, followed by the experimental lesbian novels *Sister Gin* by Arnold (1975) and *Lover* by Bertha Harris (1976). All of these remained in print at the beginning of the twenty-first century. Persephone Press, founded in 1976, first published the groundbreaking work *This Bridge Called My Back: Writings by Radical Women of Color* (1981), edited by Cherríe Moraga and Gloria Anzaldúa, and Diana Press was both printer and publisher for some of Brown's early poetry. In the summer of 1976, Arnold reported in a *Quest* article, "Feminist Presses and Feminist Politics," that more than one hundred fifty feminist presses or journals existed across some thirty states.

All of these early feminist presses were operated by white working- and middle-class feminists. Although women of color were published, and most of the feminist presses and journals had an articulated antiracist stance, the defining presence in print was that of white feminists and lesbian feminists. To provide more writings by women of color, journals edited by white feminists typically published special issues devoted to women of color that were guest-edited by a woman of color. In 1981, one such guest editor, the lesbian feminist writer Barbara Smith, along with the lesbian feminist poet Audre Lorde, established Kitchen Table/Women of Color Press, the first press owned and operated by women of color. Kitchen Table Press published a reprint of *This Bridge Called My Back* in 1983 (it remained in print two decades later), as well as such important works by women of color as *Home Girls: A Black Feminist Anthology* (1983), edited by Smith.

The legacies of the Women in Print movement are myriad and significant. They include not only the books that remain in print three decades later and the authors, notably Brown, who established themselves as writers thanks to the movement. In addition, some longstanding institutions in feminist publishing got their starts during this period. The Feminist Press, established in 1970 to publish reprints of women's writings, and Naiad Press, founded in 1973 and dedicated to publishing popular lesbian fiction, were still in business at the beginning of the twenty-first century. Kitchen Table Press remained in business until 1999. Spinsters Ink, founded in 1978 in upstate New York, underwent changes in ownership and location over the years but was also still publishing as of 2003. And the influential *Feminist Bookstore News* (*FBN*), the *Publishers Weekly* of feminist publishing, was founded in 1976 after a hundred women involved in feminist publishing met in Omaha, Nebraska, at the first Women in Print conference. Founder Carol Seajay published *FBN* until 2000, when she ceased publication after scores of women's bookstores had gone out of business.

Early LGBT Presses (1975–1985)

For the LGBT publishing industry, the most significant aspect of the Women in Print movement was its demonstration that there was a market for books with unapologetically lesbian content. The market for gay men's books also quickly became apparent. There was some overlap in any case between the Women in Print movement and existing LGBT publications. Barbara Grier, for example, was the last editor of the *Ladder,* and after it folded in 1972, she founded Naiad Press. Lesbian feminists Del Martin, Martha Shelley, and others published in the *Advocate.* And Sasha Alyson, whose Alyson Publications, Inc., is "the leading publisher of gay and lesbian books" according to its Web site, began his career in publishing in 1977 by starting a distribution company, Carrier Pigeon, to serve feminist and other small presses (Barber, p. 8).

Alyson switched from distributing to publishing books in 1979 when he founded Alyson Publications, and with the publication of *Young, Gay, and Proud!* in 1980, Alyson became one of the pioneers in gay publishing. Other early gay presses were Gay Sunshine Press, founded in Los Angeles in 1975, and The Sea Horse Press, founded by the writer Felice Picano in New York in 1977. Like Alyson, Gay Sunshine Press was still in existence at the beginning of the twenty first century, making it the oldest continuously operating gay publisher. The Seahorse Press later merged with two other presses to form the Gay Presses of New York.

By the end of the 1970s, a sizable number of LGBT publishers existed across the United States, and mainstream publishers had begun to realize that books with LGBT content could be profitable. Works by Larry Kramer, Edmund White, and Andrew Holleran were published by mainstream houses as early as 1978. By November 1985, according to an article by John Preston in the *Advocate,* there were ten gay and lesbian publishers in existence, although it is not clear whether that count included women's presses that published books by and about lesbians.

LGBT Publishing Develops (1985–1993)

The Women in Print movement had demonstrated the value of a mutual support network for those involved in all aspects of publishing, and in the 1980s, LGBT publishers began to develop a similar infrastructure. In 1987, Lambda Rising, the LGBT bookstore in Washington, D.C., began publishing the *Lambda Rising Book Report,* later named simply the *Lambda Book Report.* The *Book Report* initiated the "Lammies," or Lambda Literary Awards, in 1988, which honored not only authors but also publishers. The list of publishers, editors, and booksellers who have won Lammies over the years is a who's who of the LGBT publishing industry. Winners include Alyson, Seajay, Larry Mitchell, Grier, Craig Rodwell, Smith, and Michael Denneny (who as an editor with St. Martin's Press had published many gay authors and created the press's Stonewall Inn Edition imprint). The *Book Report* and the Lambda Literary Awards are under the aegis of the nonprofit Lambda Literary Foundation (LLF), which also publishes the *James White Review,* a quarterly literary magazine for gay men, and sponsors an annual literary festival.

The Publishing Triangle, an organization with a mission similar to that of LLF, was founded in 1988. Its mission, according to its Web site (http://www.publishingtriangle.org), is "to further the publication of books and other materials written by lesbian and gay authors or with lesbian and gay themes [and] . . . to create support and a sense of community for lesbian and gay people in the publishing industry." The Publishing Triangle began honoring LGBT authors in 1989 with the Bill Whitehead Award for Lifetime Achievement, given in alternate years to a man and a woman writer. (As an editor at E.P. Dutton and later at Macmillan, Whitehead had worked with Edmund White, Robert Ferro, and Doris Grumbach, among others.) In later years, other awards were added: the Judy Grahn Award for lesbian nonfiction and the Randy Shilts Award for gay nonfiction; the Audre Lorde Award for lesbian poetry and the Triangle Award for gay poetry; and the Ferro-Grumley Award for literary fiction. Both the LLF and the Publishing Triangle report on and honor not only current authors, but also the foremothers and forefathers of LGBT publishing; they thus simultaneously identify and support an American LGBT literary tradition.

LGBT Publishing in Flux (1993–Present)

The LGBT publishing industry had come of age by the early 1990s, but since that time, people who follow the industry have often disagreed about the health of LGBT publishing. In the early 1990s, several writers spoke of a "boom" in LGBT publishing. By this they meant, it turns out, that mainstream publishers were publishing more LGBT books. For example, in May 1993, a *Newsweek* article carried the headline, "An 'Explosion' of Gay Writing," and remarked on the number of LGBT books being published by mainstream publishers, noting that even the Book-of-the-Month Club was publishing LGBT reprints. Another often-noted sign of a boom was the fact that several lesbian and gay authors, including Urvashi Vaid and Greg Louganis, had received six-figure advances from mainstream publishing houses.

By 1997, however, there was a general consensus that if more LGBT works were published during the early 1990s, then that situation no longer held true. Having given huge advances to LGBT authors only to have some of the books fail, some writers reasoned, major publishers had finally realized that LGBT books are not a gold mine but a "niche" market with less profit potential than had been thought. Meanwhile, some pessimistic writers contended, LGBT presses were folding, and LGBT people in general were not buying as many books as they had previously. Other writers, however, were much more optimistic, pointing to the facts that academic presses were publishing more LGBT books, that some LGBT presses reported larger profits than ever, and that even as some LGBT presses folded, others were springing up to take their place.

The focus on financial viability points to a central contradiction in the enterprise of LGBT publishing: while many LGBT presses and bookstores were founded to further larger socio-political aims, most are also for-profit businesses. Small presses (as LGBT presses are) have some advantages over larger mainstream publishers in this area. They do smaller initial printings and do not need to sell as many copies of each book, and their owners and staff are often willing to operate on a shoestring budget because they believe strongly in what they are doing. Yet the needs of authors must be factored in also, and if the overall aim is to promote LGBT authors and LGBT writing, mainstream houses with more capital may be better positioned to give their authors large advances and aggressively publicize and market their books.

In the end, both LGBT presses and mainstream publishers have something to offer LGBT authors and readers, and both are likely to keep publishing LGBT books. While large mainstream presses have the advantage of size and affluence, they are more driven by the bottom line. Less profit-driven LGBT presses typically are able to devote more time and energy to working with individual authors. They are also more likely than large publishers to take a chance on a book that may be financially risky if they think the work is important, and this is an advantage for LGBT writing as a whole.

As for the state of LGBT publishing in the early 2000s, it is certainly undergoing changes. Grier and Donna McBride have greatly reduced the number of books Naiad publishes each year as they prepared to close the press and retire in 2005. However, they planned for their succession by training Kelly Smith to run her own press, Bella Books, and have passed along many of their authors. The trend toward media mergers has also affected LGBT publishing. For example, in 2001, Joan Drury sold Spinsters Ink to Hovis Inc., which also publishes a magazine called *Colorado Women News* and promotes the press's books and authors in the magazine. Liberation Publications has taken this approach even further: it now owns Alyson Publications, the *Advocate, OUT* magazine, and the Web site Planet Out (http://www.planetout.com).

Another latter-day trend is the use of the Internet to direct-market LGBT books. The online LGBT book club InsightOut (http://www.insightoutbooks.com) offers members reprints of a wide variety of LGBT books and has reported growing profits. And mainstream publishers have not written off LGBT books. The large independent publisher Kensington Publishing, for example, issued a new catalog of LGBT books in 2003. Although its fortunes may wax and wane, LGBT publishing remains a viable if unstable enterprise, and LGBT publishers are likely to be around as long as there is a community of people who want to buy LGBT books. Despite numerous attempts to characterize it, define it, assess it, and foretell its future, the phrase most often used to describe LGBT publishing is "in flux."

Bibliography

Abbott, Charlotte. "Battering Down the Niche." *Publishers Weekly* 248, no. 17 (23 April 2001): 32–35.

Arnold, Martin. "Gay Books Are Facing the Downside of Acceptance." *New York Times* (21 October 1999).

———. "A New Phase for Gay Books." *New York Times* (27 February 2003).

Barber, Karen. "Letter from Boston." *Lambda Book Report* 4, no. 9 (March–April 1995): 8–10.

Bronski, Michael. "After the 'Boom.' " *Publishers Weekly* 246, no. 18 (3 May 1999): 38–42.

———. "The Paradox of Gay Publishing." *Publishers Weekly* 249, no. 34 (26 August 2002): 27–31.

Brownworth, Victoria. "Size Queens." *Lambda Book Report* 4, no. 12 (September–October 1995): 49.

Chesnut, Saralyn, and Amanda C. Gable. " 'Women Ran It': Charis Books and More and Atlanta's Lesbian Feminist Community, 1971–1981." In *Carryin' On in the Lesbian and Gay South.* Edited by John Howard. New York: New York University Press, 1997.

Gates, David, and Maggie Malone. "An 'Explosion' of Gay Writing." *Newsweek* 121, no. 18 (10 May 1993): 58–61.

Preston, John. "Gay Lit Goes Mainstream: The Big Business of Publishing Gay Books." *Advocate* 434 (26 November 1985): 51–54, 60.

Short, Kayann. "Publishing Feminism in the Feminist Press Movement." PhD diss., University of Colorado, 1994.

Streitmatter, Rodger. *Unspeakable: The Rise of the Gay and Lesbian Press in America.* Boston: Faber and Faber, 1995.

Syzmanski, Therese. "Legendary Lesbian Publisher Writes Her Own Happily Ever After." *Lambda Book Report* 10, no. 10 (May 2002): 10–12.

Troxell, Jane. "When Was 'Ever'—." *Lambda Book Report* 10, no. 10 (May 2002): 34.

Saralyn Chesnut

See also ANZALDÚA, GLORIA; BROWN, RITA MAE; CENSORSHIP, OBSCENITY, AND PORNOGRAPHY LAW AND POLICY; FOSTER, JEANETTE; FURIES; GRAHN, JUDY; GRIER, BARBARA; HOMOPHILE PRESS; LESBIAN FEMINISM; LORDE, AUDRE; MORAGA, CHERRÍE; NEWSPAPERS AND MAGAZINES; PARKER, PAT; PORNOGRAPHY; SMITH, BARBARA.

PUERTO RICO

As with other island countries in the Caribbean, the history of Puerto Rico is marked by the annihilation of its native inhabitants (the Taino or Arawak) after the arrival of Europeans in 1493 and the later introduction of African slaves. Indigenous sexual practices have not been widely documented, but in general are believed to have included male homosexuality and transgender behavior; the further analysis of colonial documents will hopefully shed additional light on this topic. Spanish and other European colonizers brought with them their general prejudices against sodomy, instituted through the Catholic Church and the Inquisition, but also the general ideologies and practices of Mediterranean sexualities, under which men may have sex with other men and not be stigmatized as long as they maintain a masculine image and assume the "active" role during sexual exchange. African populations, a diverse and heterogeneous group, had conflicting visions of homosexuality (more tolerated by the Yoruba and less so by the Congo), but the frequently all-male, close living quarters of slaves encouraged situational homosexual encounters. In general, pre-twentieth-century sexualities have not been widely studied, and much archival work remains to be done.

The 1898 invasion of the island by U.S. troops effectively transferred sovereignty from Spain to the United States and ushered in yet another political, cultural, and social system through the legislation and presence of a colonial government. In fact, the criminalization of male sodomy occurred for the first time in 1902, following the California law. Consensual acts between women were criminalized in 1974 along with those of men under Article 103 of the Puerto Rican penal code. Both were decriminalized on 23 June 2003 (three days before the historic U.S. Supreme Court decision on *Lawrence v. Texas* reverted the law for the entire country), thanks to the efforts of activists such as Reverend Margarita Sánchez de León, who demanded to be arrested for committing this crime in 1997. Another major victory was achieved in 2002 when Governor Sila María Calderón signed a hate crimes law that included specific protections for victims of bias crimes motivated by sexual orientation.

U.S. influence in Puerto Rico (and Puerto Rican influence in the United States) has been wide-ranging, having particular impact on women's and gay liberation. Extensive migration (in both directions) since the middle 1940s has facilitated island exposure to U.S. developments, while Puerto Rican migrants have played a central role in the U.S. LGBT movement. Drag queen Sylvia

Puerto Rico. Participants in San Juan's gay pride parade dance on a float in June 2003, shortly before male sodomy and consensual acts between women were decriminalized on the island. **[AP Photo/Tomas van Houtryve]**

Rivera's participation in the Stonewall Riots of 1969 has been documented by historian Martin Duberman and fictionalized in Nigel Finch's 1996 film *Stonewall,* where she is portrayed as La Miranda. Other important U.S.-based Puerto Rican leaders have included Antonia Pantoja, the founder of ASPIRA, a national non-profit organization devoted to the education and leadership development of Puerto Rican and Latino and Latina youths; New York City councilwoman Margarita López; and American Civil Liberties Union president Anthony Romero. Luis Aponte-Parés (in 1998 and 2001) has documented the history of queer Puerto Rican organizations in the United States, such as Hispanics United Gays and Lesbians and Boricua Gay and Lesbian Forum, both founded in 1987. Americans have been credited for establishing many commercial gay venues on the island, particularly in the Condado and San Juan.

Modern LGBT activism gained visibility in Puerto Rico with the establishment of the Comunidad de Orgullo Gay or COG (Gay Pride Community) in 1974 under the leadership of Rafael Cruet. COG also formed an Alianza de Mujeres (Women's Alliance). Early COG efforts included protests against Article 103, the appearance of Grozny Román on television and Ana Irma Rivera Lassén on the radio, as well as the first pride parade, which consisted of a caravan of cars that traveled to Luquillo Beach. COG additionally published a newspaper entitled *Pa'fuera!* (*Out!*). Other important island publications have included *Salpa'fuera* (*Come Out!*), *Puerto Rico Breeze*, and *Caribbean Heat.* The Círculo de Estudios Gay (Gay Study Group) was established in the early 1980s, while the Colectivo de Concientización Gay (Gay Awareness Collective) was formed by Mildred Braulio and other political activists in 1984; the work of both these organizations has continued under the more recent Proyecto de Derechos Humanos de Lesbianas, Gays, Bisexuales y Transgéneros (Lesbian, Gay, Bisexual, and Transgender Human Rights Project). The Coalición Puertorriqueña de Lesbianas y Homosexuales (Puerto Rican Lesbian and Homosexual Coalition) was founded in 1989, and Amigas y Amigos de los Derechos Humanos (Friends of Human Rights) in 1991. Olga Orraca, Liza Gallardo, and José Joaquin Mulinelli have played key roles in all these organizations, while Pedro Julio Serrano has become renowned for his efforts to become the first openly gay elected member of the Puerto Rico legislature.

Women's activism expanded in the 1970s through the efforts of Mujer Intégrate Ahora (Woman Integrate Now). A major turning point in lesbian island history was the establishment of the Coordinadora del Encuentro de Lesbianas Feministas (Lesbian Feminist Encounter Coordinating Group) in 1990, which successfully organized the Third Lesbian Feminist Encounter for Latin America and the Caribbean in 1992. This was the first major lesbian event held in Puerto Rico. Other lesbian organizations have included Nosotras Diez (Us Ten, 1988), Aquelarre Lésbico (Lesbian Coven, 1990), Taller Lésbico Creativo (Creative Lesbian Workshop, 1994), and Madres Lesbianas de Puerto Rico (Lesbian Mothers of Puerto Rico) led by Sandra García. The 1997 National Latino/a Lesbian and Gay Organization (LLEGO) Conference was also held in Puerto Rico to great acclaim, quite unlike the

1995 Gay Officers' Action League (GOAL) Conference, in which conference attendees were harassed by island police during a raid at a local gay bar.

AIDS has had a major impact on the island, and numerous organizations have appeared in its wake. Dr. José (Joe) Toro Alfonso's role has been central, especially in relation to the Fundación SIDA (AIDS Foundation, 1982). Other organizations include the Puerto Rico Community Network for Clinical Research on AIDS (P.R. CONCRA, 1990), Organización Coaí, Inc., and the Iniciativa Comunitaria de Investigación, or ICI (Community Research Initiative, led by Dr. José Vargas Vidot). The arrival on the island of the New York–based ACT UP Latino contingent in 1990 (including Moisés Agosto and Georgie Irrizary) was crucial in energizing island activism and also in establishing the present-day gay pride parade in San Juan. Trans-activist Cristina Hayworth secured the first permits for this parade, but infighting quickly led to the creation of the Coalición Orgullo Arcoiris, or COA (Rainbow Pride Coalition, 1992) under Herminio (Nino) Adorno. The recent San Juan AIDS Institute fraud case has been an enormous setback for island AIDS services; former director Yamil Kourí Pérez and several others were found guilty and sentenced to prison for diverting $2,200,000 in federal funds from 1989 to 1994.

Literature, scholarship, and the arts have been, along with activism, the major vehicles for the discussion and dissemination of LGBT consciousness on the island. Key writers such as René Marqués, Luis Rafael Sánchez, and Manuel Ramos Otero (among the men) and Luz María Umpierre, Nemir Matos Cintrón, and Lilliana Ramos Collado (among the women) have created moving poetic and narrative visions. Filmmakers Frances Negrón Muntaner (*Brincando el charco: Portrait of a Puerto Rican*, 1994), Aixa Ardín (*Elyíbiti*, 2001), and Jorge Oliver (*Pride in Puerto Rico*, 2000) have also helped to increase public awareness of and support for LGBT issues. The drag performer Antonio Pantojas and singers Lucecita Benítez, Sophie, and Lourdes Pérez also deserve special mention. In addition, the scholarship of individuals such as Juan Gelpí, Rubén Ríos-Avila, Agnes Lugo-Ortíz, Juanita (Ramos) Díaz-Cotto, and Arnaldo Cruz-Malavé has been crucial to the development of queer Puerto Rican studies on the island and in the United States. More recently, the Internet site Orgullo Boricua (Puerto Rican Pride, www.orgulloboricua.net) has become a very valuable resource.

Bibliography

Aponte-Parés, Luis. "Outside/In: Crossing Queer and Latino Boundaries." In *Mambo Montage: The Latinization of New York*. Edited by Agustín Laó-Montes and Arlene Dávila. New York: Columbia University Press, 2001.

Aponte-Parés, Luis, and Jorge B. Merced. "Páginas Omitidas: The Gay and Lesbian Presence." In *The Puerto Rican Movement: Voices from the Diaspora*. Edited by Andrés Torres and José E. Velázquez. Philadelphia: Temple University Press, 1998.

Braulio, Mildred. "Challenging the Sodomy Law in Puerto Rico." *NACLA Report on the Americas* 31, no. 4 (January 1998): 33–34.

La Fountain-Stokes, Lawrence. "1898 and the History of a Queer Puerto Rican Century: Gay Lives, Island Debates, and Diasporic Experience." *Centro Journal* 11, no. 1 (Fall 1999): 91–110.

Negrón-Muntaner, Frances. "Echoing Stonewall and Other Dilemmas: The Organizational Beginnings of a Gay and Lesbian Agenda in Puerto Rico, 1972–1977." *Centro Journal* 4, no. 1 (1992): 77–95; 4, no. 2 (1992): 98–115.

Ramírez, Rafael. *What It Means to Be a Man: Reflections on Puerto Rican Masculinity*. New Brunswick, N.J.: Rutgers University Press, 1999.

Rivera Lassén, Ana Irma, and Elizabeth Crespo Kebler. *Documentos del feminismo en Puerto Rico: Facsímiles de la historia*. Volume I (1970–1979). San Juan: Editorial de la Universidad de Puerto Rico, 2001.

Lawrence M. La Fountain-Stokes

See also DÍAZ-COTTO, JUANITA; LATINAS AND LATINOS; LATINA AND LATINO LGBTQ ORGANIZATIONS AND PUBLICATIONS; PIÑERO, MIGUEL; RAMOS OTERO, MANUEL; RIVERA, SYLVIA; SANCHEZ, LUIS RAFAEL; SODOMY, BUGGERY, CRIMES AGAINST NATURE, DISORDERLY CONDUCT, AND LEWD AND LASCIVIOUS LAW AND POLICY.

PULP FICTION: GAY

Though "gay pulp fiction" is a well-established literary genre in contemporary gay male culture, it is popularly linked with highly recognizable visual images associated with the cover art of paperback novels published from the 1950s to the 1970s. The bold, striking images on these covers, which range from the elegant to the crudely drawn, were almost always overtly or suggestively sexual. The resonance and popularity of these images is attested to by their pervasiveness on commercial products such as greeting cards, postcards, address books, advertisement for bars, and refrigerator magnets. They have become, in essence, a form of consumer camp, kitsch items from the past signifying an aspect of LGBT history that is, seemingly, disposable and ultimately irrelevant.

The reality of gay pulp fiction is far more complex and significant. The term "pulp fiction" is itself used in a variety of contexts. Pulp fiction is not a precise term, and it is often used loosely for books that have very different geneses and markets. The classification of publications as "pulp" began early in the century and referred to the cheap paper stock—from the least expensive wood pulp—on which they were printed. These publications were usually sensationalist men's and boys' adventure magazines. Just prior to World War II the publishing industry in the United States began printing and distributing cheaply produced—and cheaply priced—paperback books, both fiction and nonfiction, which were primarily sold on racks in train stations, drugstores, and stationery shops, and on newsstands. After the war these books reached a new level of production, and often featured in eye-catching covers—usually shocking or dramatic and always visually provocative. While such covers were created primarily for genre literature such as mysteries, crime fiction, science fiction, and romance, they were also used for popular novels and for editions of more canonical books such as *Madam Bovary, The Way of All Flesh,* and *The Scarlet Letter.*

The term "gay pulp fiction" is commonly used to describe two quite dissimilar publishing phenomena. The first, which lasted from the 1940s to the mid-1960s, was the publication by mainstream publishers of paperback editions of gay novels; the second was the emergence, after the relaxation of federal and state censorship laws, of original, mass-market paperback novels that featured increasingly explicit sexual material.

This first type of gay pulp fiction materialized in an industry context in which publishing houses marketed a large number of books in a sensationalized manner. Many of these books focused on themes concerning illegal or taboo sex—adultery, prostitution, rape, interracial relationships, lesbianism, male homosexuality—topics that were, in the words of the jacket-copy writers, "controversial," "explosive," and "shocking." The books promised to "reveal the sordid truth in a way you have never read before." Frequently, they traded on recent social obsessions and "headline news"—juvenile delinquency, motorcycle gangs, wife swapping, teen drug use, college scandals, racketeering, suburban malaise, and the erotic dangers of psychoanalysis. They were, beneath a veneer of enticing exploitation, a compendium of the not-so-hidden preoccupations and fears of the tempestuous and socially unstable postwar years. These books were both paperback originals and reprinted editions of novels and nonfiction that had been originally released in cloth (hardcover) editions. The salient and very important difference between lesbian pulps and gay pulps in this era was that almost all of the lesbian-themed books were paperback originals that were written by men for a heterosexual male readership, while the overwhelming majority of the gay-themed books were new paper editions of cloth editions of literary novels, from respected publishing houses, that were written by gay men for a wide audience of readers.

While it is generally unacknowledged in the history of LGBT publishing, there were hundreds of literary novels with gay male themes and characters published by mainstream houses between 1940 and 1969, the year of the Stonewall Riots. Because they were respected works of literary fiction, they rarely encountered problems with censorship or distribution. They were almost always reviewed in mainstream venues and treated with respect. Titles such as *The Fall of Valor* by Charles Jackson (published by Farrar, Straus, and Giroux, 1946), Stuart Engstrand's *The Sling and the Arrow* (Creative Age Press, 1947), Gore Vidal's *The City and the Pillar* (Dutton 1948), John Horne Burns's *Lucifer with a Book* (Harper Brothers, 1949), Harrison Dowd's *The Night Air* (Dial Press, 1950), Fritz Peters's *Finistère* (Farrar, Straus, and Giroux, 1951), Douglas Sanderson's *Dark Passions Subdue* (Dodd, Mead, 1952), Gerald Tesch's *Never the Same Again* (Putnam, 1956), and Lonnie Coleman's *Sam* (McKay, 1959) were first released in cloth editions and within a year were reissued in inexpensive paperback editions that sported classic pulp images and jacket copy.

To a large degree these books, many of which are not read today in spite of their literary worth, are now considered "gay pulp fiction." They display a broad range of themes, characters, and political ideologies. Because all of these novels were published just after World War II, many of their characters are veterans still dealing with the emotional and physical damage inflicted on them by the wartime years. The main characters in *The City and the Pillar, Never the Same Again,* and *The Night Air* are all attempting to readjust to civilian life. In *Lucifer with a Book* and *The Fall of Valor* the protagonists deal with bodies that were wounded in the war. Few of the novels in this period are "coming out" novels as we use the term today. These characters, even as they are discovering their sexual desires, continually see themselves as players in a broader context than just the gay world. While only a few novels deal with interracial themes—Loren Wahl's *The Invisible Glass* (Greenberg, 1950) being the most notable—many of the works make concrete connections between anti-homosexual sentiments and racism, anti-Semitism, and xenophobia. *Lucifer with a Book* makes these connections explicit, as do Ward Thomas's *Stranger in the Land* (Houghton, Mifflin, 1949), Lonnie Coleman's *The Southern Lady* (Little, Brown, 1958), and John Rae's *The Custard Boys* (Farrar, Straus, Cudahy, 1960). In contrast to contemporary gay books, many of these novels had no problem dealing with intergenerational sex and romance. *Never the Same Again, Finistère,* and James Barr's *Derricks*

(Greenberg, 1951) condone sex between adult men and teenaged boys. While most of these novels chronicle intimate relationships, they never fall into the category of the "romance novel" or even the "social problem novel," but are far more concerned with examining the evolving idea of what it means to be a "man"—in these specific cases a man who is sexually and emotionally attracted to other men—in the United States after the war.

A subset of this category of "pulped" mainstream literary fiction exists and is quite important to the emergence, in the mid-1960s, of a more sexualized paperback original pulp novel. There were a handful of paperback original novels that dealt with gay male themes. A few of these were from major, New York–based, publishers such as Fawcett Gold Medal (which published Ann Bannon's notable lesbian pulp novels). The best example of one of these original novels is *Whisper His Sin* (1954), released as by "Vin Packer," but actually written by Marijane Meaker, author of two lesbian pulps and several works of lesbian pulp nonfiction (published under the name Ann Aldrich). For the most part, however, the gay male pulp paperback originals were produced and distributed by smaller publishing houses on both the East and West Coasts. *All the Sad Young Men* by Anonymous was published in 1962 by Wisdom House. In 1964 *Lost on Twilight Road* by James Colton (the pseudonym of Joseph Hansen) was published by National Library, in Fresno, California. Similarly, paperback original presses such as Beacon and Midwood, which published "shocking" novels—mostly involving heterosexual sex—released the occasional gay-themed book such as Ben Travis's 1959 *The Strange Ones*.

By the mid-to-late 1960s, after a decade of challenges to U.S. censorship laws—mostly from book publishers and film distributors, it was possible to publish work with more explicit sexual content, and to portray homosexual and other erotic themes outside of the realm of "literary" publishing. In many ways, the history of gay publishing—and of the publishing of books with gay themes by the mainstream press—is also the history of the ongoing battle against censorship. It took a U.S. Supreme Court ruling in 1958 to reverse a 1956 ruling by a federal district court stating that the U.S. postal authorities were right in prohibiting the mailing of the homophile *ONE* magazine. The lower court had ruled that *ONE* was not protected by the First Amendment: while the contents of *ONE* might not be offensive to homosexuals, since the "social or moral standards [of homosexuals] are far below those of the general community," social standards are nonetheless "fixed by and for the great majority and not by and for a hardened or weakened minority." By the terms of this ruling, any writing that promoted homosexuality or even presented it in neutral terms was "ipso facto" pornographic. Such standards were, of course, applied selectively, and while prominent publishing companies had less to fear than small, gay-oriented magazines, the possibility of censorship was always present.

In 1959 a California judge declared that Allen Ginsberg's *Howl* was not obscene and that San Francisco's City Lights Bookstore was not in violation of the law for selling it. Later that year the U.S. Postal Service lost a suit against Grove Press in New York State federal district court; this suit had tried both to halt the publication of the first American paperback edition of D. H. Lawrence's novel *Lady Chatterley's Lover*, and to ban the use the of the mail system to transport it. The court claimed that the book, because of its literary merit, was not obscene. The case was so clear-cut that it was the last time the Post Office attempted such a suit. In 1960 the U.S. Supreme Court ruled that homosexual material (the case under consideration concerned beefcake magazines, not novels) had to be treated the same as heterosexual materials. In 1964 the Court ruled, after a series of differing state court decisions, that Henry Miller's *Tropic of Cancer*, published by Grove, was not obscene, and instituted a national standard for judging obscenity, this meant that publishers would not have to fight censorship on a state-by-state or city-by-city basis. In 1966 the Court ruled that John Cleland's 1749 novel *Fanny Hill: The Memoirs of a Woman of Pleasure*, published by George Putnam and Sons, was not obscene because it was not "utterly" without redeeming social value. The protracted Boston trial concerning Grove's 1962 publication of William Burroughs's *Naked Lunch* ended in 1966 and was the last major literary case limiting censorship in the United States.

The immediate effect of these judicial decisions was startling and allowed a new group of erotic publishers to begin operation. Well financed and connected to extensive and reliable distribution networks, these new companies published hundreds of titles every month, which became readily available in a variety of venues. The majority of these titles were for heterosexual audiences. (Books that featured lesbian content were, even more so than traditional "lesbian pulps," aimed explicitly at the heterosexual male reader.) But within this new publishing framework, there were publishers and separate lines within the larger houses—Brandon House, Greenleaf Classics, Regency Books, Pendulum Books, Frenchy's Gay Line, and Award Books, among others—whose books were aimed at a gay male audience that was eager to buy and read them. And, most importantly, most of these books were written by gay men for a gay male readership.

These new pulps—paperback originals written and distributed with an intent to sell sexualized material—functioned for gay men in much the say way that the lesbian pulps did for lesbians: they were both a visceral and visible marker of personal as well as group identity. Because they reached far more men than had read, or even been aware of, the earlier literary novels, they played a large role in expanding gay men's experience of community and in reassuring men who desired sex with other men that they were not alone. It is important to note that these books, which were easily available to most men, were being published within the context of an ever-changing political scene. Homophile groups such as Mattachine and ONE, which had started in the 1950s, had created enough of a sense of political community that large numbers of gay men were ready to see themselves as more of a public entity. Even though most of these books were decidedly nonliterary—indeed were essentially not-very-explicit soft-core porn—they were a manifestation of a sea change in the ability of the gay male community to be public. Titles such as Jack Love's *Gay Whore* (PEC; 1967), Barry Crandall's *The Muscle Swappers* (Impact Library; 1968), and Alan Atkins's *In Search of Love* (Spade Publishing; 1969) could be purchased on newsstands and in specialty bookstores. Not all of the new, more eroticized gay pulp novels were badly written. Authors such as Victor J. Banis (writing under the names V. J. Banis, Don Holliday, J. X. Williams, and Victor Jay), Richard Love (writing under the name Richard Amory), Carl Corley, Chris Davidson, and Bruce Benderson wrote highly literate fiction. Banis's *The Man from C.A.M.P.* series was a best-selling parody of cold war politics and the James Bond craze; Richard Amory's *The Song of the Loon* trilogy (1966–1968)—an overtly literary work that extolled the homoerotics of the Old West and interracial love between white men and Native Americans—sold more than 400,000 copies.

It is impossible to summarize the themes, character types, and political or social issues that run through these novels—the range of genres, styles, and ideologies is far too diverse. It is on the other hand possible to say that most of these novels reflect a new consciousness—anti-establishment, pro-personal freedom, and deeply suspicious of social and government power—that is also reflected in many mainstream works published at the same time. The Loon novels, for instance, with their rejection of civilization and embracing of a pastoral ethos are clearly reflective of the hippie and back-to-the-earth movement. Don Holliday's C.A.M.P. novels are deadly accurate political attacks on cold war politics, and Chris Davidson's use of historical settings—such as the Holocaust in *Go Down, Aaron* (Greenleaf, 1967) and the American Civil War in *A Different Drum* (Ember Library, 1967)—is emblematic of the nascent gay movement's desire to claim a history for homosexuality. Though many of these works dealt with sex, or were sexually explicit, their political ideology was forthrightly progressive.

While all gay pulp novels—both before and after the relaxation of censorship laws—provided validation of gay male sexual desires, they also performed other functions. Without denying the enjoyment—sexual or otherwise—that came from reading them, these books also functioned pedagogically. Hidden within their plots and within the details of their character's lives were maps, hints, and clues that told gay men how they might live their own lives. Because so many of the novels that dealt with homosexuality were written by gay men and drawn, to some degree, from the authors' own experiences, they are filled with insights into how gay men of the period lived. This is not to say that they were documentary in intent and effect, but rather that they provided windows into a half-hidden gay world that was not completely accessible to those who were not members. Reading through these books, it is possible to see how gay men dressed, what their homes looked like, where they lived, and how they spoke. Certainly most of this knowledge is filtered through the lens of art and storytelling—bounded also by the pressures of the marketplace—but it was present and useful to those who needed to know.

The gay pulp novel led, in a very direct way, to the formation of a post-Stonewall gay male literature. Not only did writers such as Lonnie Coleman and Harrison Dowd pioneer fiction that examined gay male lives, but also the more sexualized pulps of James Colton, Victor Banis, and Richard Amory led to major changes in how gay writers were able to write about sexuality. While many of these literary and nonliterary works are now mostly forgotten or consigned to the category of "camp," it is vital to keep in mind that they are an important chapter in gay male writing and history.

Bibliography

Bronski, Michael, ed. *Pulp Friction: Uncovering the Golden Age of Gay Male Pulps.* St Martin's, 2003.

Levin, James. *The Gay Novel: The Male Homosexual Image in America.* New York: Irvington, 1983.

Stryker, Susan. *Queer Pulp: Perverted Passions from the Golden Age of the Paperback.* Chronicle, 2001.

Michael Bronski

See also BALDWIN, JAMES; BANNON, ANN; CENSORSHIP, OBSCENITY, AND PORNOGRAPHY LAW AND POLICY; FUGATE, JAMES BARR; GINSBERG, ALLEN; HIGHSMITH, PATRICIA; LITERATURE; *ONE*; PUBLISHERS; PULP FICTION: LESBIAN; RECHY, JOHN; VIDAL, GORE.

PULP FICTION: LESBIAN

Lesbian novels published during the "Golden Age" (1950–1965) of pulp paperback production are chronicles of resistance that provided early forums for challenging fixed and conservative systems of gender and sexual identity.

Post–World War II Contexts

The novels of Claire Morgan, Ann Bannon, Valerie Taylor, March Hastings, Paula Christian, Randy Salem, Marijane Meaker (under the pen names of Vin Packer and Ann Aldrich), and Marion Zimmer Bradley were particularly influential as they debated and defined possibilities for new individual and group identities during a period in U.S. cultural history that was intensely hostile to preceived internal and external threats. These included the twin menaces of communism and homosexuality, often invoked by the medical or social "experts" who appeared in the prefaces of many pulp fiction narratives. Lesbianism, they claimed, was a sociological disease and a cause for grave national concern. It could not be "cured" but must be "understood" as a tragedy.

For many authors, however, publishers' policies and obscenity codes permitted only negative representations of lesbians. The Comstock Law passed by the U.S. Congress in 1873 had banned the circulation or sale of novels deemed obscene. In 1952 when the House Un-American Activities Commission conducted its purges of lesbians and gay men from the government and military, the House of Representatives Select Committee on Current Pornographic Materials (the so-called Gathings Committee) debated whether Tereska Torres's lesbian novel *Women's Barracks* (1950) possessed any literary merit. That these novels were published in this environment is evidence that censorship, repression, and oppression did not go unchallenged.

American Popular Fiction and Pulps

As a genre, lesbian "pulps" (so-named because of their cheap, acidic pulp paper content) did not exist as such prior to the 1950s. They did, however, emerge from two distinct strains in American publishing history. First, nineteenth-century dime novels and serial publications featured increasingly sensational adventure and romance fiction. The audiences developed by this market eagerly embraced the mass distribution of paperback fiction that was launched in 1939 by Avon Pocket Books and was followed by dozens of other publishers. World War II Armed Services Editions, distributed to soldiers, continued to develop reader tastes for sensational fiction. When, in the 1950s, Fawcett Gold Medal started to market original fiction, including lesbian fiction (long a staple of soft pornographic fiction for male audiences), these paperback books were sold in drugstores, bus stations, and other public venues, attracting both straight and LGBT audiences by their colorful covers and captions.

Second, fiction identifiable as "lesbian," somtimes arguably, existed in American fiction in the eighteenth and nineteenth centuries, and perhaps earlier, before pulp paperbacks brought that fiction to millions of readers. Some early twentieth-century lesbian texts were reprinted as pulp paperbacks. For example, Radclyffe Hall's *The Well of Loneliness* (1928) was reprinted in 1951, Lilyan Brock's *Queer Patterns* (1935) in 1951, Gale Wilhelm's modernist text *We Too Are Drifting* (1935) in 1955, and Diana Fredericks's *Diana: A Strange Autobiography* (1939) in 1955.

Sexologists and Case Histories

As negative as many pulps needed to be to conform to existing obscenity laws and publishers' mandates (lesbianism could not be represented in a positive way), lesbian readers appreciated the opportunity to read almost anything at all about other lesbians. One of the greatest strengths of the Golden Age lesbian narratives is their refusal to forfeit desire as it marks the characters' individual, gender, and sexual identities. Late nineteenth-century German sexologists had reconceptualized homosexuality from a sin to a disease by developing a byzantine system of sexual taxonomies that had become publicly codified as "inversion" before Hall's widely-read *Well of Loneliness* was published. The concept of inversion was central to the portrayal of Hall's protagonist Stephen Gordon and continued to be central to the self-images of figures in pulp romances a half-century later. Meanwhile, Sigmund Freud provided a discourse of the self that acknowledged sexual drives as universal and disrupted the clear division between "normal" and "perverse." His work was widely read at the time of the pulps' production, and his terminology, too, found its way into their narratives.

Inside the texts, however, some pulp heroines protested. Frances Ollenfield in Valerie Taylor's *Return to Lesbos* (1963), for example, contemplates leaving her husband Bill after falling in love with Erika Frohmann and visits a minister, Dr. Powell, for counsel. She fears he will "think it was a neurosis. They were always harping on that: retarded development, parental rejection, childhood trauma, inherited tendency. As if straight people didn't have all the same things to cope with" (p. 115). Making this point in her discussion with Dr. Powell, Frances tells

Queer Patterns. The cover of "a bold new novel of perversity," by Kay Addams. [Gay and Lesbian Historical Society (GLHS)]

him, "Straight people almost never realize that what seems abnormal to them might be perfectly normal for someone else" (p. 119).

After suffering a nervous breakdown, Val MacGregor in Christian's *This Side of Love* (1963) experiences a break between her "self" and how she is perceived and judged by others. She attempts to express this to her psychiatrist Dr. Rosen, "[A]t the moment there *is no me!* I'm only the projection screen many emotional yards away from the film over which I have no control" (p. 240). This same sort of distancing is experienced by Diana, the protagonist of Frederics's novel, when she reads a book on homosexuality: "I was, then, a 'pervert,' 'uranian,' 'homosexual'—no matter, all added up to the same thing. *I* was subject to arrest! *I* was grotesque, alienated, unclean!" (p. 20).

Cultural Work of the Pulps

Just as recovered nineteenth-century women's fiction demonstrates cultural and literary importance that belies dismissals of it as "domestic" and "sentimental," many post–World War II lesbian narratives provide their audiences with thoughtful, articulate characters and well-written passages. The best of these texts suggest that women can and should become physically and sexually active, noncompliant with traditional gender socialization, financially independent through work, and self-sufficient emotionally.

Several scholarly articles provide commentaries on the pulps and their historical and cultural importance. Books featuring reproductions of cover art and rhetoric, with commentaries and bibliographies, allow contemporary audiences to experience the visual impact of the pulps and to appreciate their history.

Pulp fiction disturbed and attracted mass audiences because it offered glimpses of taboo eroticism, questioned comfortable assumptions about social good and evil, sold itself through beautiful cover art, and provided moments that challenged the premises of established gender and value systems. Figures in these romances often debate the truth or falsehood of their own apparent clinical identities as "inverts," "perverts," and "narcissists," doomed to wretched lives "in the shadows" of conventional, "decent" existence. In debating whether their own lives resemble the models of abnormality and unnatural behaviors and desires that psychosocial experts ascribe to them, many figures renounce these negative images of their lives, relationships, and subjectivities. In Claire Morgan's *The Price of Salt* (1952), one of the first lesbian romances to permit the lesbian pair to remain happily together by the text's conclusion, Therese Belivet is puzzled by her love for Carol Aird but distances herself from popular negative stereotypes: "She had heard about girls falling in love, and she knew what kind of people they were and what they looked like. Neither she nor Carol looked like that" (p. 91).

In addition to challenging stereotypes, pulp authors augmented lesbian culture by inserting references to earlier pulp titles in later novels. These self-referential moments provided cultural reinscriptions that both preserved memory of the pulps as artifacts and promoted their readership. In Taylor's *A World without Men* (1963), for example, Kate Wood attempts to learn more about Erika Frohmann by exploring her books. When Kate refers to texts such as Aldrich's *We Walk Alone*, Christian's *Edge of Twilight*, and even one of Taylor's own titles, *Whisper Their Love* (p. 46), she authorizes not only the texts themselves but the lesbian existences the texts narrate, performing crucial cultural work for lesbian audiences. Sometimes characters in pulps position themselves against pulp stereotypes, affirming their ability to courageously choose love over a closeted existence (Christian, *Love Is Where You Find It,* p. 122). In addition, characters come out to each other by discussing pulp titles (Taylor, *Return to Lesbos,* pp. 45, 75) and use pulps as sexual conduct manuals (Bannon, *Beebo Brinker,* p. 78). These constitute instances of historical self-invention, when a marginalized literature establishes its substance by referring to its having been published in a prior moment in time.

The cultural work begun by the pulps continued through the work of subsequent authors of lesbian romances. The novels of Rita Mae Brown, in particular *Rubyfruit Jungle* (1973), and novels published by Naiad Press throughout the 1980s and 1990s, continued to provide lesbians a place in print. Late twentieth- and early twenty-first century circulation of zines and the public and private revolution effected by the Internet have provided additional venues for challenging dominant cultural assumptions and positions.

Pulp Authors

Many pulp best-selling authors—Bannon, Christian, Taylor—were themselves working women, writing to support children or establish economic independence. Their fiction reflects a respect for the "normalcy" that society denied them. Taylor, for example, recalls her determination to write "stories about real people—women who had jobs, families, faults, talents, friends, problems; not just erotic mannikins" (Garber, "Roundtable," p. 1). Hastings describes the joint acts of writing and reading: "Together we [author and audience] share a mutual trust in possibilities, we believe our world can materialize, we expect it to—and the novel brings forth that expectation" (Garber, "Part II," p. 8). For Bannon, the best known of pulp's lesbian authors, "I knew I was constructing a world that I was fascinated with and wanted to be part of. This is the way I could join it" (Blackwell, p. 35). Christian echoes these authors when she states, "My object was to reach out to the heterosexual readers, to make them see that one isn't a destructive pervert just because of lesbianism. The perversion was in society's attitude, forcing us all to live double lives, constantly in fear of being found out and persecuted. . . . These are not sex books. . . . They are books about feelings" (Introduction to a 1981 reprint of her 1965 novel *Amanda*).

For every high-quality Bannon or Taylor romance, however, the publishing market produced dozens of pulps whose covers, contents, and endings delivered precisely the punishing messages they promised. Hastings's publisher informed her that happy lesbian characters violated the "moral code" (Garber, "Part II," p. 8). Bradley's editor mandated that the lesbian characters must "discover men and/or come to an unhappy end, thus reaffirming heterosexuality" (Garber, "Roundtable," p. 4). Accordingly, in lesbian author Christian's *The Other Side of Desire* (1965), for example, Carrie Anderson is bored by her husband Paul, betrayed by her lover, and returns to her husband, concluding, "Even a normal gesture such as hand-holding [with him] took on a new significance for her; it was normal" (p. 156). In Fletcher Flora's *Strange Sisters* (1960), lesbian Kathy Galt commits suicide after the death of a beloved aunt, her abandonment by two lesbian lovers, her rape by a male acquaintance, and the loss of her job.

Yet few lesbians had had the opportunity, before the 1950s, to compare themselves or their lovers to accessible characters in fiction—whether stereotyped or not. Exceptions include the self-sacrificing Stephen Gordon in Hall's *Well of Loneliness* and fragmented figures in modernist American texts. The insanity of Robin Vote in Djuna Barnes's *Nightwood* (1937), the Stephen Gordon–like self-sacrifice of Jan Morale in Wilhelm's *We Too Are Drifting,* and the emotional exhaustion of Adele in Gertrude Stein's *Things as They Are* (1951) presented complex, frustrated relationships to their readers. Elisabeth Craigin's *Either Is Love* (1937) and Frederics's *Diana* both offer difficult relationships but also articulate discussions of current theories of sexuality and their relevance.

Audiences

The enormous popularity of lesbian texts among lesbians in the twentieth century demonstrated a market for fiction that would suggest answers to questions of gender and sexual identity. The depth of this hunger took the male-dominated publishing industry of the 1950s and 1960s by surprise. Dick Carroll, editor of Bannon's best-selling Fawcett Gold Medal Books, and many other publishers had not anticipated the lesbian audience that would buy them in such numbers.

For some writers and their lesbian audiences, the texts featuring depressed or angry characters became sites where, at a minimum, private truths could appear in print or even confront public censure. For many other readers, these texts simply became the only home and family they possessed, and lesbians became adept at ignoring punitive moral messages in even hostile texts and enjoying the narratives' confirmations that other lesbians existed.

Lesbian sexuality had long been a staple of pornography for male audiences, but the readers of lesbian romances—American lesbians—were often geographically and socially isolated and rarely saw themselves mirrored in the society around them or in the fiction available to them. They longed, in other words, for literary representations of ordinariness. The pulps provided this mirror by departing from the high culture of Hall, Barnes, and Stein (which until then had signified literary lesbian identity) to tell the stories, primarily, of working-class women.

Authors were deluged with letters from readers, grateful to see that their stories were not unique. Even later readers like lesbian author Dorothy Allison remarked of Bannon's *Beebo Brinker,* "Suddenly I wasn't reading porn, I was reading my own history" (Wolt, p. 22). Non-white audiences, however, did not find their histories represented by authors of diverse races and cultures. Although black lesbians are chronicled in histories, they rarely appear in the Golden Age texts. *Loving Her,* a novel concerned with an interracial lesbian relationship, was published by black author Ann Shockley in 1974 but this text falls outside the era of Golden Age pulp publication.

Survival

Ann Bannon's romances have survived through reprints by Timely Books in the 1970s, Naiad Press in the 1980s, and (as the *Beebo Brinker Chronicles*) by the Quality Paperback Book Club in the 1990s. In 2001, they were reprinted by Cleis Press. Most other pulp novels remain long out of print. Although most pulp novels were discarded or destroyed, the acid in their paper ensures the eventual self-destruction of those that survived. It is ironic that the very medium that permitted their mass circulation—cheap paper—has left most in a condition too fragile to be read. Growing numbers of archives purchase and protect pulp novels as they become increasingly valuable and rare, acknowledging their value as material artifacts of a unique cultural history and as spectacular exemplars of opportunistic marketing.

Bibliography

Adams, Kate. "Making the World Safe for the Missionary Position: Images of the Lesbian in Post–World War II America." In *Lesbian Texts and Contexts: Radical Revisions.* Edited by Karla Jay and Joanne Glasgow. New York, London: New York University Press, 1990.

Aldrich, Ann. *We Walk Alone.* New York: Fawcett Gold Medal, 1955.

Bannon, Ann. *Beebo Brinker.* Greenwich, Conn.: Fawcett Gold Medal, 1962.

Barnes, Djuna. *Nightwood* (1937). New York: New Directions, 1961.

Blackwell, Erin. "The Power of Positive Lesbian Pulp: The Secret Life of Ann Bannon." *Bay Area Reporter* 10 (February 1994): 35.

Brock, Lilyan. *Queer Patterns.* New York: Eton Books/Avon Edition, 1951.

Brown, Rita Mae. *Rubyfruit Jungle.* Plainfield, Vt.: Sisters, 1973.

Christian, Paula. *Amanda.* New Milford, Conn.: Timely Books, 1982.

———. *Love Is Where You Find It.* New York: Avon, 1961.

———. *The Other Side of Desire* (1965). New Milford, Conn.: Timely Books, 1981.

———. *This Side of Love and Edge of Twilight* (1963, 1959). New York: Belmont Books, 1966.

Craigin, Elizabeth. *Either Is Love* (1937). New York: Lion, 1952.

Faderman, Lillian. *Surpassing the Love of Men: Romantic Friendship and Love between Women from the Renaissance to the Present.* New York: Morrow, 1981.

Flora, Fletcher. *Strange Sisters.* New York: Lion Books, 1954.

Foster, Jeannette H. *Sex Variant Women in Literature* (1956). Tallahassee, Fla.: Naiad Press, 1985.

Fredericks, Diana. *Diana: A Strange Autobiography* (1939). New York: Arno Press, 1975. (Republished as *Diana: The Story of a Strange Love.* New York: Berkley, 1955.)

Garber, Eric. "Those Wonderful Lesbian Pulps: A Roundtable Discussion." *San Francisco Bay Area Gay & Lesbian Historical Society Newsletter* 4, no. 4 (Summer 1989): 1, 4–5.

Garber, Eric. "Those Wonderful Lesbian Pulps, Part II." *San Francisco Bay Area Gay & Lesbian Historical Society Newsletter* 5, no. 1 (Fall 1989): 7–8.

Grier, Barbara. *The Lesbian in Literature,* 3rd ed. Tallahassee, Fla.: Naiad Press, 1981.

Hall, Radclyffe. *The Well of Loneliness.* New York: Blue Ribbon Books, 1928.

Hamer, Diane. "'I Am a Woman': Ann Bannon and the Writing of Lesbian Identity in the 1950s." In *Lesbian and Gay Writing: An Anthology of Critical Essays.* Edited by Mark Lilly. London: Macmillan, 1990, 47–75.

Hermes, Joke. "Sexuality in Lesbian Romance Fiction." *Feminist Review* 42 (Autumn 1992): 49–66.

Kuda, Marie J. *Women Loving Women: A Select and Annotated Bibliography of Women Loving Women in Literature.* Chicago: Lavender Press, 1974.

Morgan, Claire (Patricia Highsmith). *The Price of Salt.* New York: Bantam Books, 1952.

Morse, Benjamin, M.D. *The Sexual Deviate.* New York: Lancer Books, 1963.

Shockley, Ann. *Loving Her.* Indianapolis: Bobbs-Merrill, 1974.

Stein, Gertrude. *Things As They Are: A Novel in Three Parts.* Pawlet, Vt.: Banyan Press, 1950.

Stryker, Susan. *Queer Pulp: Perverted Passions from the Golden Age of the Paperback.* San Francisco: Chronicle Books, 2001.

Taylor, Valerie. *A World without Men.* 1963. Tallahassee, Fla.: Naiad Press, 1982.

———. *Return to Lesbos.* New York: Midwood-Tower, 1963.

———. *Whisper Their Love.* New York: Fawcett Crest, 1957.

Torres, Tereska. *Women's Barracks.* New York: Fawcett Gold Medal, 1950.

Walters, Suzanna Danuta. "As Her Hand Crept Slowly Up Her Thigh: Ann Bannon and the Politics of Pulp." *Social Text* 23 (Fall–Winter 1989): 83–101.

Weir, Angela, and Elizabeth Wilson. "The Greyhound Bus Station in the Evolution of Lesbian Popular Culture." In *New Lesbian Criticism: Literary and Cultural Readings.* Edited by Sally Munt. New York: Columbia University Press, 1992.

Wilhelm, Gale. *We Too Are Drifting* (1935). New York: Berkley, 1955.

Wolt, Irene. "An Interview with Valerie Taylor." *The Lesbian Review of Books* 4, no. 3 (Spring 1998): 3–4.

Wysor, Bettie. "A Bibliography of Lesbianism in Literature." In *The Lesbian Myth.* New York: Random House, 1974.

Zimet, Jaye. *Strange Sisters: The Art of Lesbian Pulp Fiction 1949–1969.* New York: Viking Penguin, 1999.

Mary Elliott

See also BANNON, ANN; HIGHSMITH, PATRICIA; LITERATURE; PULP FICTION: GAY; RULE, JANE; SHOCKLEY, ANN ALLEN; TAYLOR, VALERIE; WILHELM, GALE.

abcdefghijklmnop**q**rstuvwxyz

Q

QÁNQON-KÁMEK-KLAÚLA (b. circa 1780s?; d. 13 June 1837), guide, healer, mediator.

Qánqon-kámek-klaúla was a Kutenai who was born female but adopted a cross-gender status, pursued mainly men's activities as an adult, and sought to be socially recognized as a man. He went to war, took a series of wives, became a renowned healer, and made prophecies that contributed to an intertribal revival movement. He was killed by Blackfoot warriors in 1837 while serving as peace negotiator.

Qánqon-kámek-klaúla was born and raised in the late eighteenth century in Lower Kutenai country, a territory comprising what are now southern British Columbia, northeastern Idaho, and northwestern Montana. As a child she was called Qúqunok Pátke, "One Standing (Lodge) Pole Woman." Lore handed down through the Kutenai people into the twentieth century recounted that she showed no sign of alternative-gender identification as a child and that she wished to marry a Kutenai man, but because of her unusually large physique none were willing when she was of age to marry. Around 1808, she became the wife of a North-West Company voyageur and left her own people for more than a year to live with him. Then the relationship ended, and Qúqunok Pátke returned to her people. At this point her desire to assume male status became apparent. Qúqunok Pátke told everyone that her white husband had used supernatural power and transformed her physically into a man. She also began to claim spiritual powers and adopted the name Kaúxuma Núpika, meaning "Gone to the Spirits." The Kutenai apparently had a recognized alternative gender role for women, called *títqattek* ("pretending to be a man"), but they did not believe her claim of physical transformation and were initially skeptical about her spiritual powers.

Nevertheless, Kaúxuma Núpika began to make a social transformation into a male role. He adopted men's shirts, leggings, and breechcloths and began to carry a gun and bow and arrows. He also began to seek a wife. After several refusals, he formed a relationship with a Kutenai widow, but the liaison did not last long. For the rest of his life, he changed wives frequently.

Kaúxuma Núpika began to go on raids and become involved in warfare. He chose his third and final name after joining an unsuccessful horse-stealing raid. On the way home from the raid, Kaúxuma Núpika was surprised when crossing a stream by his brother, who had hidden to observe his sibling and thus confirm that Kaúxuma Núpika's body remained female. That evening, Kaúxuma Núpika announced that he was renaming himself Qánqon-kámek-klaúla ("Sitting in the Water Grizzly"), in reference to his embarrassing experience when the brother observed him at the stream. But his brother scornfully declared that he would simply call him Qánqon, since he was really still a woman, and shortly afterward disclosed to the entire camp that Qánqon-kámek-klaúla remained physically female. After this other people also began to call him Qánqon (the word apparently meant "sitting" or "squatting").

In June 1811, Qánqon-kámek-klaúla traveled with his wife from his people's trading post on the Spokane River to Fort Astoria (in present-day Oregon) and made contact with fur traders there. The traders initially accepted him as male, but later a North-West Company employee, David Thompson, arrived and recognized him as the voyageur's former wife. The fur traders engaged Qánqon-kámek-klaúla and his wife as guides for a trip into the interior, up the Columbia River. En route, it became clear that Qánqon-kámek-klaúla had gained prominence among Native Americans as a prophet and dream interpreter. While traveling the four hundred miles to Fort Astoria he had prophesied a coming epidemic and widespread death. On the return trip upriver he made fresh predictions about the arrival of European traders who would distribute goods generously and create a time of abundance.

Qánqon-kámek-klaúla disappears from written records from 1811 to 1825, then reappears in fur traders' accounts as a person esteemed among his people. In those fourteen years he had won considerable respect among the Kutenai for his curing and prophetic abilities. The Kutenai of the early twentieth century remembered him as a successful healer and attributed his powers to his gender transformation. Qánqon-kámek-klaúla was clearly still an honored figure at the time he was killed in 1837, when he was trying to mediate a peace between the Blackfoot and some Flathead people whom they had surrounded. He is said to have tricked the Blackfoot in order to give the Flathead time to escape, thereby knowingly sacrificing his life. Stories that circulated in the twentieth century about the manner of his death confirmed that he had great spiritual power. Qánqon-kámek-klaúla had transformed himself from a warrior into a peacemaker by the end of his life. He left a further legacy through his prophecies, which spread widely throughout the northwest and contributed to the Prophet Dance revival movement.

Bibliography

Lang, Sabine. *Men as Women, Women as Men. Changing Gender in Native American Cultures.* Translated from the German by John L. Vantine. Austin: University of Texas Press, 1998.

Roscoe, Will. *Changing Ones: Third and Fourth Genders in Native North America.* New York: St Martin's Press, 1998.

Schaeffer, Claude E. "The Kutenai Female Berdache: Courier, Guide, Prophetess, and Warrior," *Ethnohistory* 12, no. 3 (Winter 1965): 193–236.

Thompson, David. *David Thompson's Narrative of his Explorations in Western America 1784–1812.* Edited by J. B. Tyrrell. Toronto: Champlain Society, 1916.

Vibert, Elizabeth. "'The Natives Were Strong to Live': Reinterpreting Early-Nineteenth-Century Prophetic Movements in the Columbia Plateau." *Ethnohistory* 42, no. 2 (Spring 1995): 197–229.

Robin Jarvis Brownlie

See also TRANSSEXUALS, TRANSVESTITES, TRANSGENDER PEOPLE, AND CROSS-DRESSERS; TWO-SPIRIT FEMALES.

QUEER NATION

A direct-action movement focusing on LGBT visibility and sexual freedom, Queer Nation first met in New York in April 1990. In one of the earliest articles about the group, the artist Tom Kalin claimed that the New York City Lesbian and Gay Anti-violence Project had reported a 95 percent increase in violence against LGBT people. In response, a core group from the AIDS Coalition to Unleash Power (ACT UP) declared that it was time to challenge the liberal LGBT rights movement's strategies of assimilation. At that year's gay pride march, anonymous activists distributed a confrontational manifesto titled "Queers Read This," which exhorted queers to take revolutionary action against heterosexism and included the rant "I Hate Straights." By 1991 there were sixty chapters of Queer Nation across North America. The last of these disbanded in Seattle in 1995.

Strategies, Style, Actions

In 1991, the activist Alexander S. Chee declared that Queer Nation "did not want . . . a history beyond our work in the street" (p. 15). To write the history of Queer Nation is therefore to violate its own anti-institutional spirit. Downplaying the idea of permanent and ghettoized safe spaces for LGBT people, Queer Nation encouraged parodic performance and sexual flamboyance in public, in the spaces of everyday life that had been de facto sexually segregated ever since homosexual identity had emerged. Just as many militant African Americans reclaimed the word "nigger" and sex-positive feminists reappropriated "bitch," Queer Nationals embraced the epithet "queer" and all of its connotations of eccentricity, oddness, and transgression. The name also captured a new sense of coalition among sex workers, transsexuals, practitioners of sadomasochism, nonmonogamists, and other sexual dissidents. The Boston chapter's mission statement described Queer Nation as a "loose federation of autonomous groups," but the author and activist Michael Cunningham most succinctly captured its spirit, calling it "the illegitimate child of Huey Newton and Lucy Ricardo" (p. 63).

Queer Nation's first two years saw a surge of angry and exuberant battles against sexual repression. On Mothers Day 1990, Queer Nation activists in Atlanta appeared at Cracker Barrel restaurants to celebrate the existence of LGBT families. By September 1991 the group was back for sit-ins protesting the company's firing of a lesbian employee. Later that year, Seattle and New York members trained under the Guardian Angels (the street patrol group), forming the Bigot Busters in Seattle and the Pink Panthers in New York. In May 1991, San Francisco Queer Nationals staged a "kiss in" on Gay Court street, while in Seattle, chapter members strolled through malls holding hands and kissing. California members rioted against Governor Pete Wilson's veto of Antidiscrimination Bill AB 101, organized a boycott of the Hollywood film *Basic Instinct* to protest its depiction of a bisexual killer, and took an all-gay trip to Disneyland. Seattle Queer Nationals appeared outside high schools with flyers urging heterosexual students to support their LGBT peers. New York members went on "queer nights out" to heterosexual bars, where they drank and kissed. New England chapters in Connecticut, Rhode Island, Maine, and Massachusetts gathered for "queer water sports" at an aquatic amusement park, celebrated "Red, Queer, and Blue" on the Fourth of July in Boston, and protested at L. L. Bean outlets because of the mail-order company heiress Linda Bean's opposition to Maine's comprehensive civil rights law. The Midwest was no quieter. Iowan Queer Nationals leafleted the campaign speeches of U.S. presidential candidate Tom Harkin for his support of U.S. Senator Jesse Helms, drag queen Joan Jett Blakk ran for mayor of Chicago, and the working group Coalition for Positive Sexuality distributed sex-positive pamphlets and condoms outside of the Chicago public schools.

In short, Queer Nation performed civil disobedience in a variety of supposedly straight spaces, including businesses, schools, churches, and legislatures. In this respect it followed the legacy of earlier movements for social justice. But the movement also emerged in a newer context of global capitalism and distinguished itself most dramatically from its predecessors by its focus on consumerism. The name Queer Nation itself functioned as a kind of company logo, an umbrella name under which a variety of projects could form, merge, recombine, and move on. But as Kevin Michael DeLuca notes, unlike the corporations and national lobbying groups that it imitated and parodied, Queer Nation could not purchase media time to air its messages. Instead, the group used the tactic of "culture jamming," or reappropriating mass-produced images for its own purposes.

As Lauren Berlant and Elizabeth Freeman have documented, Queer Nation's signature aesthetics and tactics emerged from ACT UP's clean black-and-white graphics and savvy use of fax and phone lines, and from the feminist, punk, and anarchist circuit of self-published magazines and wheat-pasted posters. Drawing upon the techniques of direct-action artist groups such as Gran Fury and the Guerrilla Girls, Queer Nation's actions called attention to the way advertisers erased queer eroticism even as they used it to sell their products. For instance, New York activists replaced the "P" in GAP clothing advertisements with a "Y" to point up that chain's appropriation of gay street styles. Appropriating the language and style of Absolut Vodka advertisements, they also decorated New York streets with a series of portraits of closeted actors captioned "Absolutly Queer." Seattle's and New York's mall actions featured models dressed as "go-go boys" and "diesel dykes," both parodying stereotypes and advertising queer styles. Seattle Queer Nationals sold Queer Scout Cookies, including "S & M & Ms" and "Transgender Snaps." Poking fun at ACT UP's working groups and corporate capitalism alike, working groups gave themselves extravagant acronyms, including GHOST (Grand Homosexual Outrage at Sickening Televangelists), UBIQUITOUS (Uppity Bi Queers United in Their Overtly Unconventional Sexuality), DORIS SQUASH (Defending Our Rights in the Streets, Super Queers United against Savage Heterosexism), and QUEST (Queers Undertaking Exquisite and Symbolic Transformation).

from "queers read this" (1990)

Being queer means leading a different sort of life. It's not about the mainstream, profit-margins, patriotism, patriarchy or being assimilated. It's not about executive directors, privilege and elitism. It's about being on the margins, defining ourselves; it's about gender-fuck and secrets, what's beneath the belt and deep inside the heart; it's about the night. Being queer is "grass roots" because we know that everyone of us, every body, every cunt, every heart and ass and dick is a world of pleasure waiting to be explored.

Fallout

Inevitably, of course, the contradictions inherent in Queer Nation emerged in a series of internal critiques. Directly after the formation of the San Francisco chapter, women and people of color formed focus groups such as LABIA (Lesbians and Bi Women in Action) and United Colors (a coalition of people of color). But according to Michael Cunningham, in 1991 a New York activist arrived at San Francisco meetings and outshouted women or people of color when they criticized racist or sexist remarks. Without a system to make decisions except on the basis of consensus, members were left with no way to handle tactics of majority-group intimidation, and membership declined. Writing in the influential journal *Out/Look,* several activists pointed out that Queer Nation had exactly replicated the problems of the official nation, claiming to include women and ethnic minorities but not changing its vision accordingly. Scholars such as Valerie Lehr and John Champagne have since pointed out that Queer Nation lost track of the institutional changes necessary to combat racism, sexism, and poverty, themselves interlocked with homophobia in complicated ways that the group had overlooked. Public intellectuals such as Allan Bérubé, Jefferey Escoffier, Lisa Duggan, and Michael Warner argued that even Queer Nation's brilliant parody of nationalism in the end depended upon the model of the national citizen who checked his or her differences at the voting-booth door. Notably, the Philadelphia chapter addressed this critique by calling itself "Queer Action." Other critics, including Matias Viegener and Steve La Freniere, highlighted the more liberatory possibilities articulated within independent media spheres, such as the handmade queer punk " 'zine" (a shortened form of "magazine"), distributed by mail for trade or a nominal cost, and the do-it-yourself, all-ages homocore music scene. And queer 'zines such as *Bitch Nation* published their own anti–Queer Nation manifestos.

By 1992, Queer Nation New York had few women or people of color. The Boston chapter faced allegations from within that a fundraiser was sexist. San Francisco disbanded when one member refused to agree to a written mission statement. According to the journalist Doug Sadownick, Queer Nation Los Angeles distributed a fax reading "We're here, we're queer, we're fabulous, we're finished." The Atlanta chapter sat in on a Christian Coalition meeting but did not mention abortion or homosexuality. Only the Seattle chapter continued with direct-action tactics until finally, in February 1995, Queer Nation Seattle announced that it too had closed. In 1996 a few cities saw revivals, but in general queer direct action continued under different names.

Retrenchment, Revival

Like all movements, Queer Nation was infused with the possibilities and limitations of its own moment, and Queer Nation's moment was the early 1990s. It was a product of the first Persian Gulf War era and the proliferation of global consumer markets, and its work was sometimes complicit with official nationalism and capitalism. But by the 1993 March on Washington for Lesbian, Gay, and Bisexual Rights and Liberation, it was clear that the conservative drift of LGBT politics also contributed to Queer Nation's demise. Its campy, sexy nationalism was no match for a mainstream movement that, as Alexandra Chasin and Urvashi Vaid have demonstrated, was all too willing to abandon radicalism to focus on family and military issues. Kiss-ins gave way to marry-ins; the Pink Panthers faded from visibility as LGBT people ousted from the army and navy took center stage. The group was revived in San Francisco in 2000 to protest safer-sex educators who did not themselves use condoms but seems to have been dormant since then.

Nevertheless, the influence of Queer Nation can be seen directly in such organizations as Queers against Capitalism and Queers for Peace, and indirectly in gay-straight alliances in the public schools, queer theory in the academy, and a burgeoning queer independent cinema. According to the journalist Dave Ford, in February 2003 a new activist group called Gay Shame appeared in San Francisco; their web site claims that "we are dedicated to fighting the rabid assimilationist monster of corporate gay 'culture' with a devastating mobilization of queer brilliance." Pointing the finger at repressive state institutions and sellout mainstream movements alike, renouncing the simple model of "pride," Gay Shame may revive Queer National tactics for an even meaner millennium.

Bibliography

Anonymous. 2003. *Gay Shame Mission Statement.* Available at http://www.gayshamesf.org.

Berlant, Lauren, and Elizabeth Freeman, "Queer Nationality." *boundary 2* 19, no. 1 (spring 1992): 149–180.

Berubé, Allan, and Jeffrey Escoffier, eds. *Out/Look* 11 (winter 1991): 12–23. Special section on Queer Nation.

Champagne, John. "Seven Speculations on Queers and Class." *Journal of Homosexuality* 26, no. 1 (1993): 159–174.

Chasin, Alexandra. *Selling Out: The Gay and Lesbian Movement Goes to Market.* New York: St. Martin's Press, 2000.

Chee, Alexander. "A Queer Nationalism." *Out/Look* 11 (winter 1991): 15–19.

Cunningham, Michael. "If You're Queer and You're Not Angry in 1992, You're Not Paying Attention." *Mother Jones,* May–June 1992, pp. 60–68.

DeLuca, Kevin Michael. "Unruly Arguments: The Body Rhetoric of Earth First!, ACT UP, and Queer Nation." *Argumentation and Advocacy* 36, no. 1 (summer 1999): 9–21.

Duggan, Lisa. "Making It Perfectly Queer." *Socialist Review* 22, no. 1 (1992): 11–31.

Ford, Dave. "What's That Sound? Gay Shame, Aloud." *San Francisco Chronicle,* 14 February 2003, p. 2.

Galst, Liz. "Taking It to the Streets: Nationwide Queer Street Patrols Come Out Against Antilesbian and Antigay Violence." *Advocate,* November 1991, pp. 66–67.

Kalin, Tom. "Slant: Tom Kalin on Queer Nation." *Artforum* 29 no. 3 (1990): 21–23.

Kopkind, Andrew, ed. "A Queer Nation." *Nation*, 5 July 1993. Special issue on Queer Nation.

Lehr, Valerie. "Queer Politics in the 1990s: Identity and Issues." *New Political Science*, nos. 30–31 (summer–fall 1994): 55–76.

Penn, Donna. "Queer: Theorizing Politics and History." *Radical History Review* 62 (1995): 24–42.

Rankin, L. Pauline, "Sexualities and National Identities: Re-imagining Queer Nationalism." *Journal of Canadian Studies* 35, no. 2 (summer 2000): 176–196.

Sadownick, Doug. "We're Here, We're Queer, We're Finished—Maybe." Queer Resources Directory. Available at http://www.qrd.org/qrd/orgs/QN/queer.nation.is.dead-LA.WEEKLY.

Slagle, R. Anthony. "In Defense of Queer Nation: From Identity Politics to a Politics of Difference." *Western Journal of Communication* 59, no. 2 (spring 1995): 85–102.

Smyth, Cherry. *Lesbians Talk Queer Notions*. London: Scarlet Press, 1992.

Vaid, Urvashi. *Virtual Equality: The Mainstreaming of Gay and Lesbian Liberation*. New York: Anchor Books, 1996.

Viegener, Matias. "Kinky Escapades, Bedroom Techniques, Unbridled Passion, and Secret Sex Codes." In *Camp Grounds: Style and Homosexuality*, edited by David Bergman, 234–256. Amherst: University of Massachusetts Press, 1993.

Warner, Michael, ed. *Fear of a Queer Planet: Queer Politics and Social Theory*. Minneapolis: University of Minnesota Press, 1993.

Elizabeth Freeman, with research by Kara Thompson

See also AIDS COALITION TO UNLEASH POWER (ACT UP); COMING OUT AND OUTING; NATIONALISM; QUEER THEORY AND QUEER STUDIES.

QUEER THEORY AND QUEER STUDIES

Queer theory emerged during the early 1990s as an effort to think through the politics of sexuality and gender in light of major developments in feminist theory, LGBT studies, and poststructuralism during the previous twenty years. Queer theorists began with the empirical observation that definitions of proper and improper sexual and gender identity have varied significantly over time and space, and that such definitions have played major roles in the politics—the distribution and exercise of power—of Western and non-Western cultures. They then used various heuristic tools from philosophy, literary theory, history, anthropology, and other fields to explore how current definitions came to be and how political action—broadly defined to include activities in social, cultural, and intellectual spheres—might change them. From one perspective, queer theory and queer studies can look very much like LGBT studies, and many people use these designations interchangeably. Both begin with similar empirical observations about chronological and geographic variations in gender and sexuality. But they interpret those observations using distinct conceptual frameworks that can lead to significant disagreement and conflict.

The lack of clarity in the use of the term "queer" is even greater in popular usage than it is in academic contexts. While queer theorists wish to use the term "queer" to mark some distance from "lesbian" and "gay," terms they see as connoting less radical and transgressive politics and as failing to include bisexual, transgender, and intersexed persons, many lesbians and gay men use "queer" as a synonym for the other terms. This gives the term a very broad signification that ranges from conservative, white, middle-class lesbians and gay men to sex and gender radicals and militants. Yet some conservatives and homophobes continue to use the term in its pejorative sense, leading many LGBT people and their supporters to question whether it is possible to reclaim a term that has served as a powerful weapon against LGBT people.

Defining "Queer"

For queer theorists, "queer" connotes a crossing of boundaries, the transgression of norms, and the failure to fit expected categories. Concerned about LGBT politics that reinforce boundaries, reproduce norms, and reinscribe categories, queer theorists embrace dissidence. Several queer theorists have noted that the term's value lies precisely in its resistance to definition. Thus, in a sense, to provide a definitive account of "queer" theory would entail some misunderstanding. However, we may state cautiously that many queer theorists see individual identity (including sexual and gender identity) as resulting from the interaction between cultural forms and psychological processes. Identity, rather than functioning as the starting point for political action and intellectual work, as in the prevailing account of Western liberalism, is the outcome of political—including social and cultural—processes. These processes rely heavily on substantive notions of gender, sexuality, race, class, and other categories. But the categories themselves are also the result of political context, which defenders of dominant power relations conceal by claiming that they simply reflect "nature." The categories in turn have an impact on the processes, insofar as they contribute to individuals' sense of themselves as social, cultural, and political actors or nonactors. Queer theorists face the paradox of explaining how individuals whose identities result from the operation of an oppressive system (for example, LGBT people) can resist the system's oppression. Beginning at a point when particular definitions of sexual and gender identity seem firmly entrenched, queer theorists want to unpack those definitions, examining the particular combinations of bodies, acts, and desires that they assume in order to wonder how we might combine them differently, especially without having them become disciplinary or coercive.

Several major statements of what would become queer theory appeared during the first half of the 1990s. In 1990, Eve Kosofsky Sedgwick published *Epistemology of the Closet,* which may stand as a foray in queer theory *avant la lettre.* Sedgwick did not use the term "queer" in this book but anticipated its development in her argument that the logic of concealment and disclosure around "the closet," a central image for the management of LGBT identities, was a major interpretive key for understanding modern Western culture. This was a very queer claim in its insistence that, contrary to popular belief, LGBT identities mattered for everyone, not just LGBT people, because they helped to define the entire system of cultural meanings. Attempting to move LGBT studies out of a ghetto in which its arguments seemed relevant only for understanding LGBT cultures, Sedgwick's book suggested that modern Western culture as a whole was consistently troubled by queer disruptions. Two special issues of *differences: A Journal of Feminist Cultural Studies* referred explicitly to queer theory: the first in summer 1991, under the guest editorship of the film theorist Teresa de Lauretis, "Queer Theory: Lesbian and Gay Sexualities"; the second, as a combined summer and fall issue in 1994, under the guest editorship of Judith Butler, "More Gender Trouble: Feminism Meets Queer Theory." In 1993, Michael Warner's edited collection, *Fear of a Queer Planet,* another foundational text, was published.

Also in 1993, Sedgwick published *Tendencies,* which includes the essay "Queer and Now." In this article, she argued that "queer" denotes any failure to assemble properly all of the various elements of gender identity and sexual practice that supposedly follow "naturally" and inevitably from the initial datum of one's sexual anatomy. She also argued that "queer" is necessarily a performative term that derives its force from the choice to invoke it—the most reliable indicator of queerness is simply an individual's decision to adopt the term as self-description. Here Sedgwick echoed the account of gender identity as performative that Butler had given in *Gender Trouble* (1990), a foundational queer theory text. In Sedgwick's view, "queer" is not synonymous with "lesbian/gay." It connotes, rather, a crossing of boundaries in the sense of failure to fit established categories or expectations, with respect to sexuality, but also with respect to virtually any other identity category as well. Given the increasing respectability of many white, middle-class lesbians and gay men and the increasing visibility of otherwise "heterosexual" persons who violate norms of sexuality and/or gender, Sedgwick argued that it is entirely possible to envision lesbian/gay persons who are not queer and queer persons who are not lesbian or gay. Sedgwick identified herself as queer even though she is married to a man.

The Theory and the Social Movement

In this respect, the term "queer" also had the practical effect of helping to resolve a dilemma. The "gay liberation" and "lesbian feminist" movements of the late 1960s and 1970s had given way gradually to the "lesbian/gay" movement of the late 1980s (the change in name from the National Gay Task Force to the National Gay and Lesbian Task Force in 1985 can serve as the marker event).That change, and the later shift to "queer," reflected two trends. First, white lesbians, LGBT people of color, and other groups pointed out that differences of sex, gender, race, ethnicity, and class mattered for experiencing, understanding, and organizing around issues of sexuality and gender. At best, a gay liberation movement that claimed to speak for all gay and lesbian people but in fact reflected the priorities of middle-class, white, gay men often failed to address the concerns of others. At their worst, middle-class, white, gay men could be as racist, sexist, and classist as their heterosexual counterparts. By the early 1990s, however, it had become apparent that adding "lesbian" after "gay" without making fundamental changes in gay politics was inadequate. As De Lauretis noted in her introduction to "Queer Theory: Lesbian and Gay Sexualities," "queer" had the advantage over "gay" of connoting minority sexual or gender identity in some form while avoiding the automatic association of "gay" with "white male."

Second, during the 1990s, various groups, most especially bisexuals and transgender people, announced that the categories "homosexual," "gay," or "lesbian" failed to capture their experiences of alterity and alienation along the axes of sexuality and gender. To some, "queer" seemed more promising. Members of these groups often existed in a peculiar double bind relative to the lesbian/gay movement. On the one hand, it seemed logical that bisexual and transgender people should make common cause with lesbians and gay men. Indeed, many of the earliest activists in the homophile, gay liberation, and lesbian feminist movements had been bisexual and/or transgender. On the other hand, the process of defining an identity category enables a process of inclusion and exclusion. In this case, lesbians and gay men too often excluded or ignored bisexual and transgender people, using some of the same logic that nonqueer people had long used against lesbians and gay men—accusations of promiscuity, claims that only certain identities are "natural" or "normal," and demands for conformity to predetermined standards that had more to do with access to power than with legitimate empirical or moral arguments.

Nor were "bisexual" and "transgender" the only emerging categories. Safer-sex educators began to speak of "men who have sex with men" to denote men who engaged in same-sex sexual activity but did not identify themselves as gay or bisexual. People with predominantly non-European and non–Euro-American ethnic backgrounds, noting that "homosexual" is a distinctively modern, European, and Euro-American category, returned to other cultural traditions to produce categories such as "two-spirited" to describe themselves. Those who had undergone surgery at birth to "correct" ambiguous genitalia began to organize under the rubric of "intersexed" in order to describe their suffering and oppose the practice of early surgical intervention. In 2003, the Toronto publication *Xtra* reported, "The official acronym for Pride's target groups is LGBTTIQ: lesbian, gay, bisexual, transsexual, transgender, intersex and queer. To really keep up with trends [sic], though, they need another T for two-spirited, another Q for questioning and an asterisk for those not included in the defined categories." In each of these cases, groups of people found themselves at odds with prevailing definitions and practices of gender and/or sexuality, but not because they were "gay" or "lesbian."

"Queer" as Sedgwick defined it—failing to fit existing categories—allowed for a definition of a social movement that could encompass a wide range of people, including LGBT people, but also those who were unsure of their sexual or gender identities, those who were reclaiming old or inventing new sexual and gender identities, and those who identified as "heterosexual" but wished to announce their strong support for LGBT and sexual liberation. Use of the term "queer" also directed attention to the process by which individuals come to have their identities rather than assuming that the identities are preexisting, which in turn allows for more thoughtful explanations of how individuals participate in their own oppression and how the oppressed can become oppressor in dismayingly short order.

Nevertheless, most movement leaders still prefer the acronym "LGBT" to "queer" for describing the range of persons and interests they hope to represent in mainstream electoral and legislative politics. This in part reflects beliefs about the costs and benefits of pragmatic versus radical politics. But the biggest impediment to the use of "queer" as an umbrella term for the newly expanded social movement of the mid-1990s was its continued punch as an insult to many members of LGBT communities. This problem in turn became fodder for queer theorists, who often investigate relationships among language, subjectivity, and politics; who are critical of LGBT conservatism; and who challenge the stability of all identity categories, including the category "homosexual," by demonstrating the historical weight of linguistic meaning and its impact on the development of individual identity. Psychiatrists may believe that they defined the category "homosexual" on the basis of empirical evidence, but unruly "homosexuals" routinely demonstrated the fragility of the assertion that a propensity for same-sex eroticism necessarily indicates some broader commonality of character, belief, or deportment. Intramovement conflict over the use of terms such as "queer" also reflected the generational divides that emerged as a result of very rapid change in the experiences of LGBT people, with adolescents coming out of the closet at ever-earlier ages, literally growing up queer during the late 1990s in a way that was impossible even ten years earlier. Queer theory strives to capture all of these phenomena by demonstrating the instability and fragmentation of all identity categories in the face of the apparently infinite profusion of individual experiences.

While most movement leaders continued to prefer the designation "LGBT" to "queer," some activists in the early 1990s dissented. Queer theory developed in complex dialogue with activism that labeled itself queer. In 1990, a new militant political group calling itself Queer Nation was founded in New York. Within a few years, there were dozens of Queer Nation groups across the United States. Queer Nation often aimed its protests as much at "respectable" lesbians and gay men as at "heterosexuals." The San Francisco chapter of Queer Nation, for example, included the Suburban Homosexual Outreach Program, or SHOP. Queer protest frequently involved the insistence on public representations of gender and sexual nonconformity through the creative reworking of common images, in order to demonstrate the presence of queers in unexpected places and the queerness of seemingly ordinary things. As the emphasis on dissident nonconformity suggests, academic queer theory and activist queer nationalism shared many characteristics. However, insofar as nationalism tends to assert clearly defined boundaries for identity categories and territories, queer nationalism points in the opposite direction from queer theory.

Queer Theory and LGBT Studies

Many scholars slide comfortably between "LGBT studies" and "queer studies/queer theory," but genealogies of the two fields reveal significant differences. The empirical work of LGBT studies undoubtedly underwrites queer theory, but scholars of LGBT studies typically grounded their arguments for the construction of LGBT identities more in Marxist or Marxist-feminist frameworks—John D'Emilio's "Capitalism and Gay Identity" may serve as the exemplar—or simply in the empiricism of historical research. Queer theorists, influenced by the work of the French philosopher Michel Foucault, tended to emphasize the disciplinary and productive aspects of discourses about sexuality and gender—how, for example, expert definitions of propriety became the basis for legal and medical practices that effectively imposed "homosexual," "hysterical," and other deviant identities on various populations. If the LGBT studies approach has tended toward the structural—concern for economic and other large-scale social forces that shape individual identities—the queer theory approach has tended toward the poststructural, exploring how discursive practices serve to connect large-scale structures to individualized experiences in multiple directions. The best work in each field tends to elide the distinction between them, however, showing especially how material and discursive elements usually overlap and intertwine.

Queer theorists also wonder about the model of human agency and culture that the LGBT studies approach uses. These theorists' attention to issues of meaning and agency reflect their engagement with post–World War II Continental philosophy. Although queer theorists draw broadly from those philosophical developments, the figure most widely associated with queer theory is Foucault, and the work most frequently referenced is *The History of Sexuality: Volume One, An Introduction* (1978). Whereas the LGBT studies approach rests on a broadly Enlightenment epistemology, according to which language is a transparent tool that rational individuals may use for describing the world, queer theorists typically begin with a poststructuralist suspicion of epistemology and the representational function of language, and they emphasize the fragmentation rather than the coherence of individual identity. They see language as playing a fundamental role in shaping human understanding of the world, requiring individuals to adopt recognizable although unstable identities—"male" or "female," "heterosexual" or "homosexual"—in order to communicate with others, often perpetuating oppressive meanings and practices even among those who wish to eschew them. So, for example, while an LGBT studies scholar might look at how LGBT people, in struggle with straight people, use language, a queer theorist might look at how language creates and destabilizes the very distinction between LGBT people and straight people in the first place. Again, the best work draws from both sides of the divide, rather than advocating either approach in isolation.

With their focus on discursive practices, queer theorists borrow heavily from *The History of Sexuality,* in which Foucault argued that the "deployment of sexuality" involved the use by authority figures, such as priests, parents, teachers, and psychiatrists, of perpetual self-reflection in matters of desire in order to inculcate moral subjectivity in humans. "Sexuality" in Foucault's account (and in the view of many queer theorists) does not describe an inherent set of human drives (an assumption more commonly found within LGBT studies), but reflects the administrative incitement and codification of desire as the linchpin for a historically and culturally specific system of moral and political preferences and practices. It is a discourse that provides a conceptual and practical grid for connecting and codifying everything from national populations to individual sex acts.

More than any other queer theorist, Butler has extended this exploration into the history of Western philosophy. In *Gender Trouble,* she disputed the common feminist conception of sex as the material, bodily ground onto which culture inscribes gender. Instead, she argued that the very distinction between the material and the cultural was itself a function of a gendered linguistic system, and that all gender is discursive and performative. In *Bodies That Matter,* she examined Plato's work to argue that the definition of "matter" as substance that precedes signification or linguistic definition is itself gendered, thus making the materiality of bodies a suspect ground for feminist and/or queer political and intellectual work.

Debates and Disputes

Foucault failed to incorporate gender into his account of sexuality. The title of the 1994 special issue of *differences,* "More Gender Trouble," invokes the title of Butler's book *Gender Trouble,* but it also evokes the doubts that many feminists have raised about the utility of queer theory and of queer work that derives from Foucault's work (which failed to incorporate gender into its account of sexuality). Even so, Butler and the other contributors to "More Gender Trouble" were not alone in finding Foucault's work and queer theory useful for their analysis of how power is exercised at the micro, or "capillary," level, and they thus proceeded to integrate feminist and queer insights. Sandra Lee Bartky noted in Irene Diamond and Lee Quinby's *Feminism and Foucault* (1988) that the body on which disciplinary power operates in Foucault's *Disci-*

pline and Punish looks suspiciously universal and ungendered. She then discussed empirical research indicating that women restrict their bodily comportment—how they sit, walk, and reach, and the amount of space they occupy in public places—more thoroughly than do men. According to Bartky and several other feminist scholars, disciplinary power functions to install self-regulating consciousness in individuals, as Foucault claimed, but it does so more effectively in women than in men. Foucault pointed to the exercise of disciplinary power distributed broadly through social institutions such as families, churches, schools, prisons, and factories; feminists noted the implicit claim to authority and the disciplinary effects that result when, for example, total strangers exhort fat women (a description Sedgwick applied to herself in defining herself as "queer") to diet. Gender politics, as much as the politics of sexuality, involve not only, or even primarily, actions by the state, but the quotidian discipline of social interaction at the most basic level.

The sorts of philosophical debates common among queer theorists have invited the criticism that queer theory perpetuates, rather than undermines, long-standing hierarchies in Western culture. Critics have derided queer theory as jargon-ridden and therefore accessible only to elite academics. They have taken queer theory to task for its perceived failure to account for material and structural forces, or to recognize the significance of gender and sexual identities for people who do not wish to have those identities deconstructed. They have suggested that queer theory is hopelessly utopian because of its belief that sexualities and genders labeled "queer" are necessarily oppositional and comprehensively transgressive. They have also pointed to egregious examples in which queer theorists have badly oversimplified the work of earlier scholars of LGBT studies.

While some feminist, lesbian, and antiracist critics have found "queer" a useful concept for their critical and political practices, others have raised questions about the ways in which queer theory can reenact and reproduce the power of white men. In some cases, interest in queer theory has become an occasion for gay male scholars to ignore or repudiate feminist theory. Others have argued that queer theoretical explorations distract from, and even harm, otherwise successful efforts at achieving reform through practical engagement with the political process. Ironically, despite their critique of identity, queer theorists and activists strike some critics as creating just another identity category (complete with fashion expectations and language norms). At the same time, some African American lesbian feminists have found "queer" a useful concept for their critical and political practices, even using it as a basis for critiquing barriers of identity within feminist and lesbian/gay academic and political circles.

Perhaps the most intense debates have focused on how queer theory deals with relationships among sex, gender, and sexuality. Introducing "More Gender Trouble," Butler illustrated the conceptual power of a queer theoretical approach for investigating relationships between gender and sexuality and between feminist theory and lesbian-gay studies by recovering the domain of "sexuality" for feminist scholarship from the implication in *Lesbian and Gay Studies Reader* that feminists only addressed issues of gender. The editors of the *Reader* had claimed that lesbian and gay studies would do for sexuality what feminism had done for gender, implying that the "proper objects" of study for the two fields were distinct. The title of Butler's introduction, "Against Proper Objects," conveys the suspicion that queer theorists harbor of rigid categorical (including disciplinary) boundaries. Butler insisted on reasserting the longstanding feminist concern for issues of sexuality and the often undesirable effects—from a queer perspective, but presumably also from lesbian/gay and feminist perspectives—of insisting on clean-cut categorizations.

Arguments about gender and sexuality as axes for the exercise of power and about the historical weight of language and discourse led Foucault and queer theorists to reject standard accounts of identity in favor of conceptions of "subjectivity" that explore how individuals become bound to a seemingly fixed sense of identity through the exercise of disciplinary power. This is a major point of dispute for critics of queer theory. They argue that an account of individual identity that overemphasizes social, cultural, and political determinants leaves no room for resistance to domination, which derives in the standard version of twentieth-century liberalism from an individual's capacity to apply universal moral standards to oppressive situations and to use those moral universals as the basis for demanding an end to oppression. Foucault's and queer theorists' accounts of subjectivity challenge the liberal account in two ways, first by suggesting that human identity results from, rather than originating, politics, and second by arguing for the historical variability of moral standards.

Yet this queering of subjectivity at least has the virtue, compared to the liberal account of humans as rational actors enforcing universal moral norms, of explaining how individuals participate in their own oppression without blaming them: it accounts for the ambiguity inherent in the perspectives of individual queers who may demand equal opportunity and equal treatment publicly even as they remain closeted about their sexual or gender identity within their families of origin. Further, some observers have suggested that the critics of queer theory only prove queer theorists right by engaging in denunciations of queer intellectual work that seem to rest more on the emotional responses of threatened identities and the desire to discipline unruly queers than on the rational, dispassionate scholarship the critics claim to defend.

Transgender theorists and activists have played important roles in these debates. Illustrating the influence of queer theory and queer politics, for example, the organization Gender PAC, originally a transgender civil rights group, now eschews claims on behalf of transgender persons in favor of an opposition to all gender classifications as oppressive and discriminatory. Its leaders base this position expressly on Butler's queer critique of identity politics. Other transgender activists respond, however, that Gender PAC fails to recognize the class- and race-specificity of Butler's position, and that a philosophical refusal of identity is useless in the face of overt harassment by passersby and disciplinary practices that occur daily during otherwise routine interactions on city streets. In other words, Gender PAC may want to do away with gender classifications, but in the real world, gender classifications matter. This dispute illustrates both the influence of queer theory in the political sphere and the contentious character of queer theoretical claims.

Queer Theory in the Disciplines

Even so, queer theory has influenced scholars in a wide range of disciplinary and interdisciplinary fields, as the array of books that invoke "queer" in their titles or contents indicates. Literary criticism, Sedgwick's discipline, is the best example, with such volumes as Jonathan Goldberg, *Queering the Renaissance* (1994), and Glenn Burger, *Chaucer's Queer Nation* (2003). De Lauretis introduced queer theory to her home discipline of film studies with *The Practice of Love: Lesbian Sexuality and Perverse Desire* (1994). Scott Bravman, *Queer Fictions of the Past: History, Culture, and Difference* (1997), is queer scholarship by a historian. The philosopher John Corvino queered his discipline (which is also Butler's) as editor of *Same Sex: Debating the Ethics, Science, and Culture of Homosexuality* (1997) by combining contributors from multiple disciplines in a single volume. The collection edited by Gordon Brent Ingram and others, *Queers in Space: Communities, Public Places, Sites of Resistance* (1997), offers scholarship from geography and architecture while making a queer claim for the public visibility of gender and sexual minorities. Robert McRuer and Abby Wilkerson, *Desiring Disability: Queer Theory Meets Disability Studies* (2003), is only one example from the emerging field of disability studies. *Standards and Schooling in the US: An Encyclopedia* (2001) includes a section titled "queer sexuality." The *Handbook of Postmodern Biblical Interpretation* (2000) contains a chapter on "sexuality," but also one on "queer theory."

To some extent, such uses of the concept represent a normalization that may seem to violate the spirit of the origin of queer theory. However, as Foucault argued in "Nietzsche, Genealogy, History," the search for a pure, unsullied origin is a hallmark of Western practices of control. The origin and effects of queer theory are multiple. As Butler has argued with respect to gender, the most useful strategy of queer resistance would appear to involve not efforts to dismantle the system, but the incessant profusion of meanings within it.

Bibliography

Abelove, Henry. "The Queering of Lesbian/Gay History." In *Radical History Review* 62 (Spring 1995): 44–57.

Abelove, Henry, David M. Halperin, and Michele A. Barale, eds. *Lesbian and Gay Studies Reader.* New York: Routledge, 1993.

Butler, Judith. *Gender Trouble: Feminism and the Subversion of Identity.* New York: Routledge, 1990.

———. *Bodies that Matter: On the Discursive Limits of "Sex."* New York: Routledge, 1993.

———. *More Gender Trouble: Feminism Meets Queer Theory.* Bloomington: Indiana University Press, 1994. Reprint of "More Gender Trouble: Feminism Meets Queer Theory," *differences: A Journal of Feminist Cultural Studies* 6, nos. 2–3 (summer–fall 1994): 1–27.

Cruz-Malave, Arnaldo, and Martin F. Manalansan IV, eds. *Queer Globalizations: Citizenship and the Afterlife of Colonialism.* New York: New York University Press, 2002.

De Lauretis, Teresa. *Queer Theory: Lesbian and Gay Sexualities.* Bloomington: Indiana University Press, 1991. Reprint of "Queer Theory: Lesbian and Gay Sexualities," *differences: A Journal of Feminist Cultural Studies* 3, no. 2 (Summer 1991).

———. *The Practice of Love: Lesbian Sexuality and Perverse Desire.* Bloomington: Indiana University Press, 1994.

D'Emilio, John. "Capitalism and Gay Identity." In *Lesbian and Gay Studies Reader.* Edited by Henry Abelove et al. New York: Routledge, 1993.

Diamond, Irene, and Lee Quinby, eds. *Feminism and Foucault.* Boston: Northeastern University Press, 1988.

Duggan, Lisa. "Making It Perfectly Queer." In *Sex Wars: Sexual Dissent and Political Culture.* Edited by Lisa Duggan and Nan Hunter. New York: Routledge, 1995.

Foucault, Michel. *The History of Sexuality: Volume One, An Introduction.* Translated by Robert Hurley. New York: Pantheon, 1978.

———. "Nietzsche, Genealogy, History." In *Language, Counter-memory, Practice: Selected Essays and Interviews by*

Michel Foucault. Edited by Donald F. Bouchard. Ithaca, NY: Cornell University Press, 1977.

———. *Discipline and Punish: The Birth of the Prison.* Translated by Alan Sheridan. New York: Vintage Books, 1995.

Garber, Linda. *Identity Poetics: Race, Class, and the Lesbian-Feminist Roots of Queer Theory.* New York: Columbia University Press, 2001.

Hawley, John C., ed. *Postcolonial and Queer Theories: Intersections and Essays.* Westport, Conn.: Greenwood Press, 2001.

Jagose, Annamarie. *Queer Theory: An Introduction.* New York: New York University Press, 1996.

Sedgwick, Eve Kosofsky. *Epistemology of the Closet.* Berkeley: University of California Press, 1990.

———. *Tendencies.* Durham, N.C.: Duke University Press, 1993.

Spargo, Tamsin. *Foucault and Queer Theory.* New York: Totem Books, 1999.

Thomas, Calvin, ed. *Straight with a Twist: Queer Theory and the Subject of Heterosexuality.* Urbana: University of Illinois Press, 2000.

Turner, William B. *A Genealogy of Queer Theory.* Philadelphia: Temple University Press, 2000.

Warner, Michael, ed. *Fear of a Queer Planet: Queer Politics and Social Theory.* Minneapolis: University of Minnesota Press, 1993.

William B. Turner

See also CULTURAL STUDIES AND CULTURAL THEORY; LGBTQ STUDIES; PHILOSOPHY; QUEER NATION; WOMEN'S STUDIES AND FEMINIST STUDIES.